331.7   The Encyclopedia of
ENC   careers and
            vocational guidance

$129.95   50546A00814128

DATE			

The Encyclopedia of
Careers and Vocational Guidance

NINTH EDITION

The Encyclopedia of Careers and Vocational Guidance

WILLIAM E. HOPKE

Editor-in-Chief

VOLUME 2

A–Fir

J.G. FERGUSON PUBLISHING COMPANY
Chicago, Illinois

Library of Congress Cataloging-in-Publication Data

The Encyclopedia of careers and vocational guidance / William E. Hopke, editor-in-chief. — 9th ed.
    p. cm.
  Includes indexes.
  ISBN 0-89434-149-9 (set). $129.95
  1. Vocational guidance—Handbooks, manuals, etc.   2. Occupations—Handbooks, manuals, etc.   I. Hopke, William E.
HF5381.E52 1993
331.7′02—dc20

90-22141
CIP

ISBN 0-89434-149-9 (set)

Printed in the United States of America
Q-8

Editorial Staff

Editorial Director: C. J. Summerfield

Assistant Editor: Holli Cosgrove

Contributing Editors: Susan Ashby, Jim Garner, Liz Kaufmann, Beth Racine, Noelle Watson

Writers: Kathryn Cairns, Pamela Dell, Lillian Flowers, Jim Garner, Bob Green, Sally Jaskold, Amy Kennedy, Marvin Martin, Phyllis Miller, Pat Oleck, Marjorie Pannell, Jeanne Rattenbury, Tom Riggs, Fran Sherman, M. Uri Toch, Carol Yehling, Liz Yokas, Lee Yost

Photo Editor: Carol Parden

Indexer: Schroeder Indexing Services

Cover Design: Susan Kortendick, Creative Impulse

Contents

Volume 2: A to Fir

KEY TO OCCUPATIONAL CATEGORIES

 Industry Profiles. This represents the articles that outline descriptions of industries in Volume 1.

 Professional, Administrative, and Managerial Occupations. Covering careers that involve extensive academic training or practical training, these occupations include many of the jobs that require undergraduate or graduate school education.

 Clerical Occupations. Clerical occupations are those involved with handling the records, communications, and general office duties required in every business.

 Sales Occupations. This section includes sales careers for goods, services, and property, and careers for sales-related business.

 Service Occupations. Careers in service comprise occupations that assist people in various aspects of life, from protection by law enforcement to physical care.

 Agriculture, Forestry, and Conservation Occupations. Encompassing the occupations that work with various elements of nature, this category includes skilled and technicians' work related to farm production, mining, animal care, and wildlife services.

Processing Occupations. These are occupations that involve the mixing, treating, and recomposition of materials, chemicals, and products, normally through the use of machinery or tools.

Machine Trades Occupations. Careers in machine trades are those that work with machine assembly, maintenance, and repair. They work with metals, plastics, wood, paper, and stone in construction and repair.

 Bench Work Occupations. With an emphasis on hand tools and dexterity skills, bench workers make and repair products that require manual deftness, such as jewelry or optical equipment.

Structural Work Occupations. This category details the occupations involved in construction and repair of all large structures from bridges to homes.

Emerging Technician Occupations. Falling mainly into the fields of science and technology, these technicians occupations are either not yet catalogued into one of the sections following or will not be catalogued into an existing field.

Engineering and Science Technician Occupations. These technicians work with scientists and engineers as part of a team trained in the technical aspects of the work performed.

Broadcast, Media, and Arts Technicians Occupations. The technicians who operate, maintain, and repair the equipment involved in broadcasting and the arts are trained to run electronic, electrical, and mechanical equipment.

Medical and Health Technician Occupations. Responsible for the technical equipment used in medical fields, these technicians run the sophisticated machinery used by medical specialists.

Miscellaneous Occupations. In this section are the occupations that require skilled or semi-skilled levels of training. This includes a diverse range of job categories, including graphics arts, transportation, and technicians in information services as well as other fields.

Accountants and auditors

Definition

Accountants compile, analyze, verify, and prepare such business and financial records as profit and loss statements, balance sheets, cost studies, and tax reports. Within this broad sphere, accountants may specialize in areas such as auditing, tax work, cost accounting, budgeting and control, or systems and procedures. Accountants also may specialize in a particular business or field; for example, *agricultural accountants* specialize in drawing up and analyzing financial statements for farmers and for farm equipment companies.

History

Accounting records and bookkeeping methods have been used from early periods of history to the present time. Records found in Babylonia date back to 3600 B.C., and accounts were kept by the Greeks and the Romans.

Modern accounting began with the technique of double-entry bookkeeping, which was developed in the 15th and 16th centuries. Luca Pacioli, an Italian mathematician, is generally credited with developing double-entry bookkeeping. He printed his treatise on accounting and bookkeeping in 1494.

After the Industrial Revolution, business became more complex, and the need for more sophisticated accounting methods grew. With the development of government and industrial institutions in the 19th and 20th centuries, accurate information and records to aid in making decisions on economic and management policies and procedures, as well as periodic reports for both public and private use, became necessary.

The accounting profession in the United States dates back only to 1880, when English and Scottish investors began buying stock in American companies. To keep an eye on their investments, they sent over British accountants, many of whom realized the great potential that existed in the accounting field and stayed to establish their own businesses.

Federal legislation, such as the income tax in 1913 and the excess profits tax in 1917, helped bring about an accounting boom that has made the profession one of the largest in business today.

Nature of the work

Accountants' duties depend upon the size and nature of the firm or institution in which they are employed. The major fields of employment are public, private, and government accounting.

Public accountants work independently on a fee basis or as a member of an accounting firm, and they perform a variety of tasks for any business or individual wishing to make use of their services. Among the services performed are auditing bookkeeping accounts and records, preparing and certifying financial statements, conducting financial investigations and furnishing testimony in legal matters, and assisting in formulating certain budget policies and procedures.

Private accountants, sometimes called *industrial* or *management accountants*, handle financial records of the firm at which they are salaried employees.

Government accountants work on the financial records of government agencies or, when necessary, audit the records of private companies. In the federal government, many accountants are employed as *bank examiners*, *Internal Revenue agents*, and *investigators*, as well as in regular accounting positions.

Each of these areas employs accountants specializing in a particular aspect of accounting.

General accountants supervise, install, and devise general accounting, budget, and cost systems. They are responsible for maintaining records, balancing the books, and preparing and analyzing statements on all financial aspects of business for administrative officers, who can then make sound business decisions.

Budget accountants review expenditures of departments within a firm to make sure expenses allotted are not exceeded. They also aid in drafting new budgets and may devise and install budget control systems.

Cost accountants are responsible for determining unit costs of products or services by analyzing records and depreciation data. They classify and record all operating costs, including manufacture and distribution, for use by management in controlling expenditures.

Property accountants keep records of equipment, buildings, and other property either owned or leased by a company. They prepare amortization schedules and statements that show appreciation or depreciation in value, which are used for income tax purposes.

1

ACCOUNTANTS AND AUDITORS

The accountant reviews on-line data before posting it to the general ledger.

Systems accountants design and set up special accounting systems for organizations whose needs cannot be handled by a standardized system. This may involve installation of machine accounting processes and includes instructing relevant personnel in the new methods.

Tax accountants prepare federal, state, or local tax returns of an individual, business, or corporation according to prescribed rates, laws, and regulations. They also may conduct research on the effects of taxes on firm operations and recommend changes to reduce taxes. This is one of the most involved of all fields of accounting, and thus many specialize in one particular phase of tax accounting such as individual income, property, or corporation.

Auditors examine and vouch for the accuracy and completeness of accounting records of an establishment by inspecting items in books of original entry, such as daybooks or journals, to ensure proper transaction records. They may also prepare financial statements for clients. *Internal auditors* conduct the same kind of examination and evaluation for one particular company. Because they are salaried employees of that company, their financial audits then must be certified by a qualified independent auditor. Internal auditors also review procedures and controls, appraise the efficiency and effectiveness of operations, and make sure their companies are complying with corporate policies and government regulations.

Tax auditors review financial records and other information provided by taxpayers to determine the appropriate tax liability. State and federal tax auditors usually work in government offices, but they may perform a field audit in a taxpayer's home or office.

Revenue agents are employed by the federal government to examine selected income tax returns, and, where it seems necessary, to conduct field audits and investigations to verify the information reported and adjust the tax liability accordingly.

Chief bank examiners enforce good banking practices throughout a state. They schedule bank examinations to ensure that the financial institutions comply with state laws, and, in certain cases, take steps to protect a bank's solvency and the interests of its depositors and shareholders.

Requirements

Accountants must work well on their own and with others, as they often may supervise and instruct people with whom they are associated. High ethical standards and a pleasing personality are essential for success in the field in general. These qualities are almost indispensable in public accounting, because clients must be found and retained to remain in business. Other necessary skills include: facility in working with figures; ability to think logically; good oral and written expression; neat, accurate, and orderly work habits; and sound judgment.

High school students preparing for an accounting career should be proficient in arithmetic and numerical concepts. Familiarity with computers also is important because the accounting field depends upon these tools. Proficiency in high school subjects such as general business training, bookkeeping, and mathematics is an advantage.

Post-high school training in accounting may be obtained in a wide variety of institutions such as private business schools, junior colleges, universities, and correspondence schools. A bachelor's degree with a major in accounting is generally recommended by professional associations for those entering the field. It is possible, however, to become a successful accountant by completing the program of any of the above-mentioned institutions. A four-year college curriculum usually includes about two years of liberal arts courses, a year of general business subjects, and a year of specific accounting work.

Better positions, particularly in public accounting, often require a bachelor's degree with a major in accounting. Often, large public accounting firms prefer people with a master's degree in accounting. For beginning positions in accounting, the federal government requires four years of college (including 24 semester hours in accounting or auditing) or an equivalent combination of education and experience.

Special requirements

Certified public accountants (CPAs) must pass a special qualifying examination and hold a certificate issued by the state in which they wish to practice. In most states, a college degree is required for admission to the CPA examinations. Most states require certification or registration to practice as a public accountant, and requirements vary considerably. Only a few states have no regulations concerning practice in accountancy except for the CPA. Interested students may obtain information about regulations from the board of accountancy in the state in which they plan to practice.

The Uniform CPA examination of the American Institute of Certified Public Accountants is used by all states. Nearly all states require at least two years of public accounting experience or its equivalent before a CPA certificate can be earned. More than 9 out of 10 successful CPA candidates in recent years have been graduates of four-year college or university programs.

A few states already require CPA candidates to have a graduate degree and other states may soon follow suit.

To become a Certified Internal Auditor (CIA), college graduates with two years of experience in internal auditing must pass a four-part examination given by the Institute of Internal Auditors.

Accountants who meet the required educational and professional standards set by the National Association of Accountants may earn a Certificate in Management Accounting by passing a series of exams.

Opportunities for experience and exploration

To explore the accounting field, interested high school students should visit offices to observe the practice of accounting. Part-time employment during the school year or summer also provides an opportunity to gain some knowledge about the type of work involved. It also may be possible to gain some experience in school and community organizations and through service in the Armed Forces. The work-study and internship programs found in the curricula of some colleges offer an opportunity to obtain experience in public accounting or in business firms. Previous work experience is very helpful in qualifying for positions upon completion of training.

Methods of entering

Junior public accountants usually start in jobs involving fairly routine duties such as counting cash, verifying additions, and other detailed work. In private accounting, beginners are likely to start in clerical positions such as cost clerk, ledger clerk, and timekeeper. They may also enter as junior internal auditors, and as trainees in technical or junior executive positions. In the federal government, most beginners are hired as trainees.

Advancement

Junior public accountants usually advance to semi-senior positions within two or three years and to senior positions within another several years. Those successful in dealing with top-level management may eventually become supervisors, managers, and partners in larger firms or go into independent practice. Private accountants in firms may become chief plant accountant, senior internal auditor, or manager of internal auditing, depending on their specialty. Some become controllers, treasurers, or corporation presidents. Federal government trainees are usually promoted within a year or so.

Although advancement may be rapid for able accountants, especially in public accounting, those with inadequate academic preparation are often assigned to routine jobs and find it difficult to obtain promotions. Accountants who want to get to the top of their profession usually find it necessary to continue their study of accounting and related areas in their spare time. Even those who have already obtained college degrees, gained experience, and earned a CPA certificate may spend many hours in study and research to keep up with business and legal developments in their work. Thousands of practicing accountants have enrolled in formal courses offered by universities and professional associations to specialize in certain areas of accounting, broaden or update their

ACCOUNTANTS AND AUDITORS

professional skills, and become eligible for advancement and promotion.

Employment outlook

Accountants are employed wherever business, industrial, or government organizations are located. Most of them, however, work in large urban areas.

In the 1990s, almost one million people are employed as accountants, making the field one of the largest professional employment fields in business. By far the largest number of accountants are found in private business and industry, but some work in federal, state, and local government agencies. About one-third are certified public accountants (CPAs). A number of accountants are self-employed.

It is expected that employment opportunities for accountants will grow much faster than the average for all occupations through the 1990s because of the complex and changing systems of taxation, growth in both the size and the number of business corporations that have to make financial reports to stockholders, a more general use of accounting in the management of business, and more use of accounting services by small business firms. The increased use of new types of record-keeping systems and of computers will create a demand for well-trained accountants to serve as consultants to managers of various business and industrial organizations. The increasing complexity of accounting should create a greater demand for college-trained accountants. Applicants who gained actual experience in part-time jobs while still in school will have an advantage when applying even for entry-level positions. For certified accountants, such as CPAs, the range of job opportunities should be greater than for other accountants.

Major industrial centers will continue to be the best source of jobs; however, there will also be many openings in small industrial communities. Accountants without college degrees may find more opportunities among small businesses and in accounting and tax preparation firms, especially in less populated areas.

Accounting jobs are more secure than most during economic downswings. Despite fluctuations in the national economy, there is a continuing need for financial data and tax reports.

Earnings

Beginning salaries of accountants with a bachelor's degree averages $26,600 a year; those with a master's degree average $31,100 a year. Experienced accountants earn between $37,000 and $80,000, depending on the demands of their work. Accountants who are in charge of all accounting for large firms have annual salaries ranging from $43,000 to more than $74,000. Auditors' salaries average $28,000 for beginners and range from $36,800 to more than $53,000 for experienced professionals. Government salaries for accountants and auditors range from about $21,000 for starting junior accountants and auditors to an average of about $40,000 for those with experience.

In public accounting firms, beginning accountants average $25,300 a year. Junior public accountants average $31,100, with some of them earning more than $45,600 annually. Experienced accountants, particularly those who were owners and partners, often earn considerably more.

Conditions of work

Accountants ordinarily work between 35 and 40 hours a week and, in general, work under the same conditions as most office workers. Public accountants are subject to considerable pressure during the busy tax period, which runs from November to April. During this time, and often at other times as well, they may find it necessary to work long hours and more than five days a week. Most of the public accountant's work is performed in the client's office, and sometimes a considerable amount of traveling is necessary to serve clients whose offices are not located nearby. Private and governmental accountants are also sometimes involved in travel. Most, however, work in the same place daily and have more regular working hours.

GOE: 11.06.01; SIC: Any industry; SOC: 1412

◇ **SOURCES OF ADDITIONAL INFORMATION**

American Institute of Certified Public Accountants
1211 Avenue of the Americas
New York, NY 10036

American Woman's Society of Certified Public Accountants
401 North Michigan
Chicago, IL 60611

EDP Auditors Association
455 East Kehoe Boulevard
Suite 106
Carol Stream, IL 60188

Foundation for Accounting Education
200 Park Avenue, 10th floor
New York, NY 10166

Institute of Management Accountants
10 Paragon Drive
Montvale, NJ 07645

National Society of Public Accountants
1010 North Fairfax Street
Alexandria, VA 22314

For information on accreditation and testing, please contact:

Accreditation Council for Accountancy
National Society of Public Accountants
and Taxation
1010 North Fairfax Street
Alexandria, VA 22314

Institute of Internal Auditors
249 Maitland Avenue
Altamonte Springs, FL 32701

◇ **RELATED ARTICLES**

Volume 1: Accounting; Banking and Financial Services; Business Management
Volumes 2–4: Actuaries; Bookkeeping and accounting clerks; Cashiers; Financial institution clerks and related workers; Financial institution officers and managers; Financial institution tellers; Risk managers; Statisticians; Tax preparers

Actors

Definition

Actors play parts or roles in dramatic productions on the stage, in motion pictures, or on television or radio. They impersonate, or portray, characters by speech, gesture, song, and dance.

History

Drama was refined as an art form by the ancient Greeks, who used the stage as a forum for topical themes and stories. The role of actors became more important than in the past, and settings became more realistic with the use of scenery. Playgoing was often a great celebration, a tradition carried on by the Romans.

Drama became more religious in focus during the Middles Ages, but this changed with the rediscovery of Greek and Roman plays in the Renaissance. Through different periods of history, the role and responsibilities of actors changed and grew as theater developed various forms, including musical comedy, vaudeville, opera, and Japanese Kabuki.

In the United States, New York gradually became the center of theater and remains so, although community theater companies abound throughout the country. Hollywood is the recognized center of the motion picture industry and television. Other major production centers are Miami, Chicago, San Francisco, Dallas, and Houston. Today, paid employment in motion pictures greatly exceeds paid employment in the theater. The greatest source of employment for actors is television commercials, which account for about 50 percent of all actors' earnings.

Nature of the work

The imitation or basic development of a character for presentation to an audience often seems like a glamorous and fairly easy job. In reality, it is demanding, tiring work requiring a special talent.

The actor must first find a part available in some upcoming production. This may be in a comedy, drama, musical, or opera. Then, having read and studied the part, the actor must audition before the director and other people having control of the production. This requirement is often waived for established artists.

If selected for the part, the actor must spend hundreds of hours in rehearsal and must memorize many lines and cues. In addition to such mechanical duties, the actor must determine the essence of the character being portrayed and the relation of that character in the overall scheme of the play. Radio actors must be especially skilled in expressing character and emotion through voice alone.

While studying and perfecting their craft, many actors work as *extras,* the nonspeaking characters that people the background on screen or stage.

Some actors eventually go into other, related occupations and become *dramatic coaches, drama teachers, producers, stage directors, motion picture directors, television directors, radio directors, stage managers, casting directors,* or *artist and repertoire managers.*

Requirements

As acting becomes more and more involved with the various facets of our society, a college degree will become more important to those who hope to have an acting career. It is assumed that the actor who has completed a liberal arts program is more capable of understanding the wide variety of roles that are available. In addition, graduate degrees in the fine arts or in drama are nearly always required should the individual decide to teach dramatic arts.

College can also serve to provide acting experience for the hopeful actor. More than 500 colleges and universities throughout the country offer dramatic arts programs and present theatrical performances. Actors and directors recommend that those interested in acting gain as much experience as possible through acting in plays in high school and college or in those offered by community groups.

Prospective actors will be required not only to have a great talent for acting but also a great determination to succeed in the theater and motion pictures. They must be able to memorize hundreds of lines and should have a good speaking voice. The ability to sing and dance is important for increasing the opportunities for the young actor.

Special requirements

Performers on the Broadway stages must be members of the Actors' Equity Association before being cast. While union membership may not always be a requirement, many actors find it advantageous to belong to a union that covers their particular field of performing arts. These organizations include the Actors' Equity Association (stage), Screen Actors Guild or Screen Extras Guild (motion pictures and television films), or American Federation of Television and Radio Artists (TV, recording, and radio). In addition, some actors may benefit from membership in the American Guild of Variety Artists (nightclubs, and so on), American Guild of Musical Artists (opera and ballet), or organizations such as the Hebrew Actors Union or Italian Actors Union for productions in those languages.

Opportunities for experience and exploration

The best way to explore this career is to participate in school or local theater productions. Even working on the props or lighting will provide insight into the field.

Also, attend as many dramatic productions as possible and try to talk with people who either are currently in the theater or have been at one time. They can offer much advice to individuals interested in a career in the theater.

Many books, such as *Beginnings,* by Kenneth Branagh, have been written about acting, not only concerning how to perform but also about the nature of the work, its offerings, advantages, and disadvantages.

Methods of entering

Probably the best way to enter acting is to start with the local or college productions and to gain as much experience as possible on that level. Very rarely is an inexperienced actor given an opportunity to perform on stage or in film in New York or Hollywood. The field is extremely difficult to enter; the more experience and ability beginners have, however, the greater the possibilities for entrance.

Those venturing to New York or Hollywood are encouraged first to have enough money to support themselves during the long waiting and searching period normally required before a job is found. Most will list themselves with a casting agency that will help them find a part as an extra or a bit player, either in theater or film. These agencies keep names on file along with a description of the individual's features and experience, and if a part comes along that may be suitable, they contact that person. Very often, however, names are added to their lists only when the number of people in a particular physical category is low. For instance, the agency may not have enough athletic young women on their roster, and if the applicant happens to fit this description, her name is added.

These actors and actresses are performing a scene from William Shakespeare's play *Henry IV, Part 1.*

Advancement

New actors will normally start in bit parts and will have only a few lines to speak, if any. The normal procession of advancement would then lead to larger supporting roles and then, in the case of theater, possibly to a role as understudy for one of the main actors. The understudy usually has an opportunity to fill in should the main actor be unable to give a performance. Playing leading roles, either on the stage or in television or film, is the next step, and perhaps stardom, but only a very small number of actors ever reach that pinnacle.

Employment outlook

Motion pictures, television, and the stage are the largest fields of employment for actors, and most of the opportunities for employment in these fields are either in Hollywood or in New York. On stage, even the road shows often have their beginning in New York, with the selection of actors conducted there along with rehearsals.

Slower than average growth opportunities are expected through the 1990s because of the decrease in theatrical and motion picture productions. Also, nonprofit theaters are losing their funding. However, opportunities may open up with the expansion of public television broadcasting, the video industry, and cable television.

The field is overcrowded now and is expected to be so for years to come. This is true in all areas of the arts, including radio, television, motion pictures, and theater, and even those who are employed are normally employed during only a small portion of the year. Many actors must supplement their income by working in other areas, as secretaries, waiters, or taxi drivers, for example. Almost all performers are members of more than one union to take advantage of various opportunities as they become available.

It should be recognized that of the 100,000 or so actors in the United States today, an average of only about 20,000 are employed at any one time. Of these, very few have ever achieved stardom. A somewhat larger number are well known, experienced performers who are frequently cast in supporting roles. The great majority are still looking for the right break. There are many more applicants in all areas than there are positions.

Earnings

The wage scale for actors is largely controlled through bargaining agreements reached by various unions in negotiations with producers. These agreements normally control the minimum salaries, hours of work permitted per week, and other conditions of employment. The Actors' Equity Association represents actors who work in the theater; the Screen Actors Guild and the Screen Extras Guild represent those who work in motion pictures or film, television and TV commercials; and the American Federation of Television and Radio Artists represents those who work in television or radio. In addition, each artist enters into a separate contract that may provide for higher salaries.

ACTORS

In the 1990s, actors in Broadway productions earn a minimum weekly salary of about $900. Those in smaller productions "off-Broadway" receive minimums that ranged from $295 to $520 a week depending on the size of the theater. The rate for touring shows is an additional $80 a day.

Motion picture and television minimum rates are $448 daily or $1558 for a five-day week. Extras earn a minimum of $91 a day. Motion picture actors also receive additional payments known as residuals as part of their guaranteed salary. Many motion picture actors receive residuals whenever films, TV shows, and TV commercials in which they appear are rerun, sold for TV exhibition, or put on videocassette. Residuals often exceed the actors' original salary and account for about one-third of all actors' income.

The annual earnings of persons in television and movies are affected by frequent periods of unemployment. The Actors' Equity Association and the Screen Actors Guild reported that in the 1990s more than 80 percent of their members earned $5,000 or less annually and less than 5 percent earned more than $35,000 from acting.

In all fields, well known actors have salary rates above the minimums, and the salaries of the few top stars are many times higher. The average annual earnings, however, are usually low (only $12,000 for screen actors in the 1990s) for all but the best-known performers because of the periods of unemployment.

Conditions of work

Actors work under varying conditions. Those employed in motion pictures may work in air-conditioned studios one week and be on location in a hot desert the next.

Those in stage productions perform under all types of conditions. The number of hours employed per day or week vary, as do the number of weeks employed per year. Stage actors normally perform eight shows per week with any additional performances paid for as overtime. The basic work week after the show opens is about 36 hours unless major changes in the play are needed. The number of hours worked per week is considerably more before the opening, because of rehearsals. Evening work is a natural part of a stage actor's life. Rehearsals often are held at night and over holidays and weekends. If the play goes on the road, much traveling will be involved.

A number of actors cannot receive unemployment compensation when they are waiting for their next part, primarily because they have not worked enough to meet the minimum eligibility requirements for compensation. Sick leaves and paid vacations are not usually available to the actor. However, union actors who earn the minimum qualifications now receive full medical and health insurance under all the actors' unions. Those who earn health plan benefits for 10 years become eligible for a pension upon retirement.

The acting field is very uncertain. Aspirants never know whether they will be able to get into the profession and, once in, there are uncertainties as to whether the show will be well received and, if not, whether the actors' talent can survive a bad show.

GOE: 01.03.02; SIC: 7929; SOC: 324

◇ SOURCES OF ADDITIONAL INFORMATION

Actors' Equity Association
165 West 46th Street
New York, NY 10036

American Federation of Television and Radio Artists
260 Madison Avenue
New York, NY 10016

American Guild of Musical Artists
1727 Broadway
New York, NY 10019

American Guild of Variety Artists
184 Fifth Avenue
New York, NY 10019

Associated Actors and Artistes of America (AFL-CIO)
165 West 46th Street
New York, NY 10036

National Association of Schools of Theatre
11250 Roger Bacon Drive, Suite 21
Reston, VA 22090

Screen Actors Guild
7065 Hollywood Boulevard
Hollywood, CA 90028

◇ **RELATED ARTICLES**

Volume 1:   Broadcasting; Motion Pictures; Performing Arts
Volumes 2–4:   Adult and vocational education teachers; Clowns; Comedians; Dancers and choreographers; Literary agents and artists' managers; Magicians; Models; Musicians; Radio and television newscasters and announcers; Radio and television program directors; Singers; Stage production workers; Stunt performers

Actuaries

Definition

Actuaries use formulas and statistics to calculate the probability of such unfortunate events as death, disability, sickness, and unemployment that insurance companies and pension plans insure against. They determine the proper basis and methods for valuing these and other liabilities so that insurance and pension organizations can pay claims and still stay in business.

Actuaries set formulas that try to predict the number of policies that will incur losses and how much money the company will pay in claims. This determines the overall cost of insuring a group, company, or individual. Increase in risk raises potential cost to the company and the company raises their rates to cover this.

Casualty actuaries specialize in property and liability insurance, life actuaries in health and life insurance. In recent years, an increasing number of actuaries deal only with pension plans.

Although almost half of all actuaries in the United States today are employed in insurance companies, the federal and state governments, as well as private business and industry, make up a portion of employers for actuaries. Private consulting practices are also important areas in which actuarial work may be found.

History

The term *actuary* was used for the first time in 1762 in the charter for the Equitable Society of London, which was the first life insurance company to use scientific data in figuring premiums. The basis of actuarial work was laid in the early 18th century when Frenchmen Blaise Pascal and Pierre de Fermat derived an important method of calculating actuarial probabilities, resulting in what is now termed the science of probability.

The first mortality table was produced in the late 17th century when Edmund Halley noticed the regularity of various social phenomena, including the excess of male over female births. Halley, an English astronomer, for which Halley's Comet is named, is known as the father of life insurance. As more complex forms of insurance were developed in the 19th century, the need for actuaries grew.

In 1889, a small group of qualified actuaries formed the Actuarial Society of America. Two classes of members, fellows and associates, were created seven years later, and special examinations were developed for use in determining eligibility for membership. Forms of these examinations are still in use today. By 1909, another group, the American Institute of Actuaries, was created, and these two groups consolidated in 1949 into the present Society of Actuaries.

In 1911, the Casualty Actuary Society was formed as a result of the development of workers' compensation laws. The compensation laws opened many new fields of insurance, and the Casualty Actuarial Society has since moved into all the many aspects of property and liability insurance.

The first actuaries were concerned primarily with statistical, mathematical, and financial calculations needed in the rapidly growing field. Today they deal with problems of investment, selection of risk factors for insurance, agents' compensation, social insurance, taxation, development of policy forms, and many other aspects of insurance.

ACTUARIES

Nature of the work

Actuaries are basically mathematicians who design and maintain insurance and pension programs on a sound financial basis. They may be employed by a number of different types of insurance companies, including life, health, accident, automobile, fire, or workers' compensation organizations. They may deal in pension programs sponsored and administered by various levels of government, private business, or fraternal or benevolent associations. Whatever the nature of the employer's product, actuaries are key to the sound financial management of the various insurance plans involved.

Using a knowledge of mathematics, probability, statistics, and principles of finance and business, actuaries determine premium rates and the various benefits of insurance plans. To do this, they must first assemble and analyze statistics and other pertinent information. Based on this information, they are able to develop mathematical models of rates of death, accident, sickness, disability, or retirement and construct tables regarding the probability of such things as unemployment or property loss from fire, theft, accident, or natural disaster. After calculating all probabilities and the resulting costs to the company, the actuaries can determine the premium rates for insurance to cover the expected losses from such circumstances.

For example, based on analyses, actuaries are able to determine how many of each 1,000 people 21 years old today are expected to survive to age 65. They can calculate how many of them are expected to die this year or how many are expected to live until age 85. The probability that such an insured person may die during the period before reaching 65 is a risk to the company. The actuaries must figure a price for the premium that will cover all claims and expenses as they occur and still be profitable for the company assuming the risk. At the same time, the price must be competitive with what other insurance companies are charging. In the same way, actuaries calculate premium rates and determine policy provisions for each type of insurance coverage. Most actuaries specialize either as casualty actuaries, dealing with property and liability insurance, or as life actuaries, working with life and health insurance. In addition, those who concentrate on pension plans form a third, and growing, group of specialists.

Actuaries work in many departments in insurance companies, including underwriting, group insurance, investment, pension, sales, and service. In addition to their own company's business, they analyze characteristics of the insurance business as a whole. They study general economic and social trends, as well as legislative, health, and other developments, all of which may affect insurance practices. With this broad knowledge, some actuaries reach executive positions where they can influence and help determine company policy. Actuary executives may communicate with government officials, company executives, policyholders, or the public to explain complex technical matters. They may testify before public agencies regarding proposed legislation that has a bearing on the insurance business, for example, or explain proposed changes in premium rates or contract provisions.

Actuaries employed by the federal government may work with a particular type of governmental insurance or pension program, such as veterans' insurance or social security. Those who work for state governments are concerned with the supervision and regulation of insurance companies, the operations of state retirement or pension systems, and problems related to unemployment insurance and workers' compensation. Others may be employed as consulting actuaries, working on a fee basis, to set up pension and welfare plans for various unions or governmental agencies or private enterprise. They calculate the amount of future benefits to be paid to the workers and determine how much the employer will contribute to the plans. These pension plans are evaluated by actuaries enrolled under the provisions of the Employee Retirement Income Security Act of 1974 (ERISA), who prepare reports on their financial soundness.

Requirements

A bachelor's degree with a major in mathematics or statistics is usually required for entry into actuarial work. A degree in actuarial science is even more advantageous. Potential employers are interested both in ability and achievement in mathematics as well as in an applicant's personal characteristics. Actuaries must be able to work either by themselves or with others and be able to express themselves clearly both in speech and in writing. It is absolutely necessary that they maintain high ethical standards if they expect to make progress within the field and if they expect to represent their company as the company wishes to be represented. In fact, standards of practice are set by the Actuarial Standards Board.

Prospective actuaries should also have a talent for detail work and be able to concentrate for long periods of time; the stress level among actuaries is relatively high. Also, a broad outlook and the ability to think along far-reaching outlines of policy planning is necessary if they are to understand overall business and economic problems and trends.

High school students interested in being actuaries should take as much mathematics as possible. They should continue this training on through the bachelor's degree, taking courses in elementary and advanced algebra, differential and integral calculus, descriptive and analytical statistics, principles of mathematical statistics, probability, and numerical analysis. Because mathematics and statistics are essential requirements for actuaries, some companies may hire applicants with degrees in engineering, economics, or business administration, provided their background in the essentials is strong enough. Computer science is vital to actuarial training. Courses in accounting and insurance also are useful. Although only about 30 colleges and universities offer a degree in actuarial science, degrees in mathematics and statistics are available at several hundred schools.

Special requirements

Full professional status in an actuarial specialty is based not only on previous training, both formal and on-the-job, but also on the successful completion of a series of examinations. The actuary may become an "associate" in the Society of Actuaries after the successful completion of 5 examinations out of a total of 10 for the life and health insurance and pension fields, and in the Casualty Actuarial Society after successfully completing 7 out of 10 in the property and liability field. Persons who successfully complete the entire series of exams for either organization are granted full membership and the title "fellow." The American Society of Pension Actuaries gives seven examinations in the pension field. It awards membership after the successful completion of two actuarial examinations and confers fellowship status on those who pass three actuarial and two advanced consulting exams.

Because the first parts of the examination series of each society cover similar materials, students need not commit themselves to a specialty until they have taken three examinations. These three test competence in subjects such as linear algebra, numerical methods, operations research, probability, calculus, and statistics. Completion of the entire series may take from 5 to 10 years.

Preference in employment is usually given to those people who have completed at least

Two actuaries are discussing data from a computer printout.

the first two examinations and to those with experience. Students proposing to become actuaries should complete at least two of the preliminary examinations while still in college, as these examinations cover subjects usually taught in colleges and universities, whereas the more advanced examinations cover aspects of the profession itself. These preliminary examinations may also help students in determining prior to graduation whether or not they will enter the actuarial profession.

Consulting pension actuaries who service private pension plans and certify their solvency must be enrolled by the Joint Board for the Enrollment of Actuaries, a U.S. government agency. To be accepted, applicants must meet certain experience and educational requirements as stipulated by the Joint Board.

Opportunities for experience and exploration

Exploration of the work of the actuary may be initiated in a number of different ways. Inquiries sent to the organizations listed at the end of this article will result in basic information. Visits to insurance companies for talks with actuaries or insurance employees in general are another possibility. Summer employment is offered by a number of insurance companies that are willing to hire and train college undergraduates during summer months. Beginning actuaries often rotate among jobs to learn various actuarial operations and different phases of insurance work. At first they may prepare tabulations for actuarial tables or perform other simple tasks. With experience, they may prepare correspondence, reports, and research. Because of the need for additional trained actuaries, insurance companies are encouraging young people to talk with their employees and representatives regarding the possibility of careers in actuarial science.

Methods of entering

The best way to enter this occupation is by taking the necessary beginning examinations already mentioned while still in college. Once students have graduated and passed these exams successfully, they are in a very good position to apply for beginning jobs in the field and can command higher starting salaries. After a position is secured and some time has been spent in on-the-job training, newcomers in the field will be ready to take the more advanced examinations that will qualify them as a fellow in a particular society. These examinations are usually taken by those in junior actuarial positions because they require extensive home study and experience in insurance work.

Advancement

Advancement within the profession to assistant, associate, or chief actuary is dependent to a great degree upon the individual's on-the-job performance, competence on the actuarial examinations, and the display of leadership capabilities.

Some actuaries qualify for administrative positions in underwriting, accounting, or investment because of their broad general knowledge and knowledge of the insurance field. Many advance to administrative or executive positions, such as head of a department, vice-president or president of a company, manager of an insurance rating bureau, partner in a consulting firm, or, possibly, state insurance commissioner. Advancement is open to actuaries in many areas.

Employment outlook

The prospects for entry into the field are excellent and are expected to remain so through the 1990s, especially for applicants who have passed at least two professional exams while at college and who have a good background in statistics and mathematics. Currently a shortage of fully qualified actuaries exists, and even more will be needed as the number and type of insurance and pension programs grow.

Actuaries will be in particular demand in the insurance field to establish rates in the several new areas of coverage that are growing, such as prepaid legal, dental, and kidnap insurance. As more people are living longer, the insurance industry must meet the need for improved and extended health care and retirement benefits, and actuaries must determine rates based on probabilities of such factors as retirement, sickness, and death. In many cases, actuarial data that have been supplied by rating bureaus are now being developed in new actuarial departments created in companies affected by new competitive rating laws that are being passed in many states. Other new areas of insurance coverage that will involve actuaries include product and pollution liability insurance, as well as greater workers' compensation and medical malpractice coverage. Increasingly in the future, actuaries will be employed by non-insurance businesses or will work in business- and investment-related fields.

About 13,000 actuaries are employed in the United States in the 1990s. Nearly half of these work for private insurance companies, the majority in life insurance, the rest in property and casualty insurance. More than 40 percent of all actuaries are employed by independent consulting firms. Some actuaries work for rating bureaus (associations that supply actuarial data to member companies), and others are in business for themselves or are employed by private organizations to administer independent pension and welfare plans. Still others are employed by federal or state government agencies or teach in colleges and universities. Many actuaries work in five cities that are major insurance company head-quarters: New York, Hartford, Chicago, Philadelphia, and Boston.

Because of new state and federal legislation in areas relating to pension reform, no-fault automobile insurance, competitive rating, and other new proposals, a real need will exist in the field of actuarial studies. This trend will continue throughout the 1990s. In addition, the need for actuaries is not likely to be affected by economic recession, especially in the field of insurance, which is considered a priority by most individuals and businesses.

Earnings

The average starting salary in the life insurance field for workers with a bachelor's degree is $28,300 a year in the 1990s. New college graduates who have not passed any actuarial examinations earn slightly less. Some companies offer merit increases or bonuses to those who pass examinations. Salary ranges depend on the part of the country in which an actuary wishes to work.

Although data are not available for casualty companies and consulting firms, actuaries in those fields earn similar salaries to those in the insurance field. Most companies give merit increases to actuaries as they gain experience and pass examinations. In the insurance field, actuaries who became associates in the 1990s earn average salaries of $43,100; those who become fellows are paid $61,900 a year. Top executive salaries for actuaries in the life insurance field earn much more.

Conditions of work

Actuaries can normally expect to work in quiet, pleasant, and well lighted facilities. They usually spend most of the day working at a desk or table. Many, however, find it necessary to travel to various units of the organization or to other businesses. This is especially true of the consulting actuary.

Actuaries usually work 35 to 40 hours per week, receive vacation with pay, and are covered by sickness, accident, hospitalization insurance, and pension plans.

GOE: 11.01.02; SIC: 63; SOC: 1732

◇ **SOURCES OF ADDITIONAL INFORMATION**

American Academy of Actuaries
1720 I Street, NW, 7th Floor
Washington, DC 20006

American Society of Pension Actuaries
2029 K Street, NW, 4th Floor
Washington, DC 20006

Actuarial Standards Board
1720 I Street NW, 7th floor
Washington, DC 20006

Society of Actuaries
475 North Martingale Road, Suite 800
Schaumburg, IL 60173

◇ **RELATED ARTICLES**

Volume 1: Accounting; Insurance
Volumes 2–4: Accountants and auditors; Economists; Insurance agents and brokers, life; Insurance agents and brokers, property and casualty; Mathematicians; Risk managers; Statisticians

Adult and vocational education teachers

Definition

Adult and vocational education teachers teach courses that help prepare post–high school students and other adults for specific occupations or that provide personal enrichment. *Adult education teachers* offer basic education courses, such as reading and writing, or continuing education courses, such as literature and music. *Vocational education teachers* offer courses designed to prepare adults for specific occupations, such as computer programmer or automobile mechanic.

History

Organized education for adults has existed in America since early colonial times, when courses were started to help people make up for schooling they might have missed as children or to help them prepare for jobs. Apprenticeships were an early form of vocational education in the American colonies as individuals were taught a craft by working with a skilled person in a particular field. For example, a young boy might agree to work for a printer for 5 to 10 years and at the end of that time would be able to open up his own printing business. Training programs continued to develop as carpenters, bricklayers, and other craftspeople learned their skills through vocational training courses.

Peak periods in adult education typically occurred during times of large waves of immigration. Evening schools filled with foreign-born persons eager to learn the language and culture of their new home and to prepare for the tests necessary for citizenship.

In the aftermath of the Industrial Revolution, the impact of science and technology on patterns of living has become so great that people need continuing education to adapt their lifestyles. Also, the rise in educational levels with each generation has spawned a new appreciation for education: the more people learn, the more they want to learn.

In 1911, Wisconsin established the first State Board of Vocational and Adult Education in the country, and in 1917 the federal government threw its support behind the continuing education movement by funding vocational training in public schools for individuals over the age of 14. Immediately after World War II, the federal government took another large stride in financial support of adult and vocational education by creating the G.I. Bill of Rights, which provided money for veterans to pursue further job training.

Today colleges and universities, vocational high schools, private trade schools, private businesses, and other organizations offer adults the opportunity to prepare for a specific occupation or pursue personal enrichment. More than 20 million people in the United States take advantage of this opportunity each year, creating many jobs for teachers in this field.

Nature of the work

Adult and vocational education courses take place in a variety of settings, such as high schools, universities, religious institutions, and businesses. Job responsibilities entail many of the same skills as that of a full-time teacher, including planning and conducting lectures, supervising the use of equipment, grading homework, evaluating students, writing and preparing reports, and counseling students.

Adult education teachers are concerned with either basic education or continuing education. Basic education includes reading, writing, and mathematics courses, and is designed for students who have not finished high school and who are too old to attend regular high school courses. Many of these student return to school to earn the equivalent of a high school diploma (GED).

Basic education teachers should be able to deal with students at different skill levels, including some who might not have learned proper study habits. These teachers should be able to explain clearly information that is often complex and unfamiliar. Patience and good communication skills are important.

Adult education teachers who focus on continuing education ordinarily instruct students who have finished high school or college and are taking courses for personal enrichment. Class topics might include history, art appreciation, photography, and a host of other subjects. Teachers should be well versed in their field and be able to communicate knowledge and enthusiasm. Adult education teachers also must be able to teach students who are at different levels of ability and be able to demonstrate techniques if a particular skill, such as painting, is being taught.

Vocational education teachers generally prepare students for specific careers that do not require a college degree, such as cosmetologist, chef, or automobile repair worker. Teaching methods usually include demonstrating techniques with the students observing and then attempting these techniques. A vocational education teacher also will need to present effectively appropriate material in lectures and discussion groups.

Requirements

Most adult and vocational education teachers have professional experience in their area of teaching. Requirements vary according to the subject and level being taught, and the state in which the instruction takes place. Many states now require a teacher to have a bachelor's or graduate degree in the subject being taught. To teach vocational education courses, an instructor usually needs several years experience in a particular field as well as any professional certification that that field requires. Teacher certification and coursework covering techniques in teaching vocational subjects also may be required to teach in high schools and technical and community colleges.

Many adult education teachers must also have prior experience in their chosen field as well as teacher certification. Specific skills, however, are often enough to secure a continuing education teaching position. For example, a person well trained in painting may be able to teach a course on painting even without a college degree or teaching certificate.

An adult or vocational teacher should feel comfortable teaching a wide variety of students. Some of these students may have had behavioral patterns that kept them from completing a comprehensive high school. Patience, energy, and good communications skills are vital. A teacher should be able to explain sometimes complex information in a variety of ways and with patience and compassion. Many hours of out-of-class preparation may be required, especially when a teacher is just beginning.

Leadership skills are important as a teacher directs and influences a large number of students and also may work with a teacher's assistant. A teacher should be comfortable talking in front of a group and also be able to counsel students one-on-one. A teacher must be able to work effectively with students in the classroom and also work with administrative officials, such as a principal, in the development of course material.

Special requirements

Many states require teacher certification for both adult and vocational education teachers. For information on certification requirements contact the department of education of the individual states.

Opportunities for experience and exploration

High school students have many opportunities to see adult or vocational education teachers at work. Often high schools will be the site of an adult or vocational education class and students may discuss career questions with teachers before or after an actual class. Some high school instructors may teach adult or vocational education courses part time, and these instructors may be another good source for career information. Registering for a continuing education or vocational education course is another way of discovering the skills and disciplines needed to succeed in this field.

Students who think they may be interested in becoming adult education instructors might consider volunteering to tutor their peers in high school and college. Also, those with special skills or hobbies might offer to share their knowledge at local community centers or retirement homes.

Methods of entering

Most people entering the field have several years of professional experience in a particular area, a desire to share that knowledge with other adults, and often, a teaching certificate or academic degree. People with these qualifications should contact colleges, private trade schools, vocational high schools, or other appropriate institutions to receive additional information about employment opportunities.

Advancement

A skilled adult or vocational education teacher may become a full-time teacher, a school administrator, or a director of a vocational guidance program. To be an administrator, a master's degree or a doctorate may be required. Advancement also may take the form of higher pay and additional teaching assignments. For example, a person may get a reputation as a skilled ceramics teacher and be employed by other adult education organizations as an instructor.

Employment outlook

Employment opportunities are expected to grow about as fast as the average for all occupations during the 1990s. The biggest growth areas are projected to be in computer technology, automotive mechanics, and medical technology. As demand for adult and vocational education teachers continues to grow, major employers will be vocational high schools, private trade schools, community colleges, and private adult education enterprises. The federal government will also offer opportunities such as the Department of Agriculture's programs to teach farming skills. Labor unions also will have a need for teachers, as they offer continuing education opportunities to their members.

About half of all employment opportunities are part-time, so many adult and vocational ed-

A teacher is teaching new American citizens the English language.

Conditions of work

Working conditions vary according to the type of class being taught and the number of students participating. Courses are usually taught in a classroom setting, but also in a technical shop, laboratory, art studio, music room, or other location, depending on the subject matter. Average class size is usually between 10 and 30 students, but may vary, ranging from one-on-one instruction to large lectures attended by 60 to 70 students.

Like many other types of teachers, adult and vocational education teachers may only work 9 or 10 months a year, with summers off. About half of the adult and vocational education teachers work part time, averaging anywhere from 2 to 20 hours of work per week. For those employed full-time, the average work week is between 35 and 40 hours. Much of the work is in the evening or on weekends, as many adult students work on weekdays.

GOE: 11.02.01, 11.02.02; SIC: 82; SOC: 239

ucation teachers also have other jobs, often in unrelated areas.

Earnings

Full-time adult and vocational education teachers can expect to earn an average of $26,100 a year. In general, instructors average between $18,300 and $37,200 a year, with some highly skilled teachers earning even more. Earnings vary widely, according to the subject, the teacher's experience, and the geographic region of the institution.

Because many adult and vocational education teachers are employed part-time, they are often paid by the hour, with no health insurance or other benefits. Hourly rates range from $6 to $50 an hour and depend on the subject being taught, the training and education of the instructor, and the geographic region of the institution.

◇ **SOURCES OF ADDITIONAL INFORMATION**

American Vocational Association
1410 King Street
Alexandria, VA 22314

American Association for Adult and Continuing Education
1112 16th Street, NW, Suite 420
Washington, DC 20036

National Community Education Association
801 North Fairfax Street, Suite 209
Alexandria, VA 22314

◇ **RELATED ARTICLES**

Volume 1: Education
Volumes 2–4: College and university faculty; Education directors; Museum teachers; School administrators; Teachers, kindergarten and elementary school; Teachers, preschool; Teachers, secondary school

Advertising Directors

Definition

A company will choose the best advertising method by which to reach their audience, and it is the *advertising director* who puts the whole advertising package together. It can be done through newspapers, magazines, television, radio, posters, billboards, circulars, mailings, catalogs, exhibits, newspapers or magazine inserts, and in-store displays. The advertising director oversees the staff that is required to produce all the different types of ads needed for a client.

History

Advertising as a business enterprise began in the 1900s. When advertising through newspapers and radios was first done, it was usually someone from within the company who designed and produced the ads.

As industries realized how important advertising was, they relied on specialists who knew how to create effective advertisements. With the increase in the number of newspapers and magazines, the increased ability to advertise improved the type of advertisements seen. Ad directors worked for individual companies to produce the company's ad campaigns.

Advertising agencies were commonly used by companies by the 1920s. Specialists worked for agencies who could develop the needed package for an ad; this included slogans, jingles, images, and campaign strategy. An advertising director would oversee the elements that went into a campaign, and worked hand-in-hand with the creative team to increase sales for the client company. They did the research needed to determine who was buying a product and what was needed to increase the number of customers. With these specialists, the modern advertising era was born.

Nature of the work

Advertisements are created to bring specific attention to a specific product, an event or sale, a particular service, or in general to encourage consumer loyalty to a product and increase the public awareness of that product or service. Political candidates may use advertising to encourage votes and explain issues. A hospital may use advertising to create awareness of a new line of health care services. Real estate agents will use advertising to sell homes, office buildings, and property.

Many people will work together in creating an advertising campaign. These positions include *advertising directors*, who supervise the day-to-day activities of producing ads. The ad director has a staff that may work together on only one particular project or may work together on every project that director has. To make sure that every piece of the advertising production is moving well, an *account executive* is assigned to oversee each client. It may be necessary too for additional employees to report on the various steps within the process of producing an advertisement and in most situations, having meeting after meeting and decision after decision regarding an effective advertising campaign. Account executives maintain direct contact with clients and solicit new business. *Creative directors* oversee the image a client wants to inspire. *Research and development (R & D) directors* may be needed to research consumer buying trends, the market for a specific product or service, and opinions on what effect this product or service may have. *Media planners* are used to decide which avenue can best sell the product, and the timing involved to introduce it. For a certain event or specific promotion, buyers are needed to determine the costs involved in producing an advertisement, determining printing and production costs and buying advertising space. *Copywriters* are used to develop a catchy phrase or jingle as well as explain the product or service in a print or oral format.

When a business decides they want to promote something, they approach an advertising agency in hope of increasing and attracting sales by enticing potential customers. They need to know the audience to which they are appealing; whether it be businesses, government, the general public, or even other retailers. The market may also be broken down to other factors, such as region, age, income, or lifestyle.

A business may bid out a project, which means that various advertising agencies propose how they would serve the client, how much their advertising campaign would cost, and what the returns should be on the company's investment. Each agency usually makes numerous presentations, showing their ideas

Through the use of account executives and creative teams, advertising directors and creative directors work together to produce a client's total advertising campaign.

on storyboards. They also explain previous projects they have worked on, demonstrating how they sold the product and why. In essence, they show a potential client their portfolio, which may include television advertisements, print advertisements, and radio spots they have designed.

For a company to make a decision, it could take weeks, even months, and consideration for budget allowances must be made as well. Once a decision is made on a particular advertising agency, a representative from the client company will meet with the creative director and advertising director of the agency. The team evaluates the client's needs and assigns an account executive who will deal with the business aspects of the client/agency relationship. Next the creative team, with the art director and copywriter, will produce different advertisements, developing ideas to present to the client. The creative director will then decide which ideas are best to present to the client, and he or she will meet with the client to go over the ideas. During this time, the account executive is working with the media buyers to develop a schedule for the project and make sure the costs involved are within the client's budget.

When the ad campaign is approved by the client, production can begin. This process may take some time. If it is a simple brochure, it may only take a few days to produce, but if it is a national promotion of a new product, it may take months to do the research and to develop the proper method of introduction and

advertising. Many revisions will be made before a final approval is granted. If the ad is to be printed, typesetting and illustration are required. Color may play an important role, as well as design and use of text and images. In developing a radio or television commercial, a studio, technicians, and actors may be needed. All of these processes and steps are supervised by the advertising director and he or she is required to meet frequently with other staff within the various departments to check on progress.

Requirements

Maturity and creativity are key qualities for an advertising director. Motivation, creative flexibility, and patience are also important. Advertising directors should possess tact, good judgment, and an excellent ability to establish and maintain personal and professional relationships. This is important because the director will make and maintain many, many contacts with clients, freelancers, and business people. Any person within the advertising industry must be able to communicate effectively, both verbally and in writing. The advertising director should understand visual communication involving illustrations, art, and photography. He or she should possess an ability to solve problems quickly, as problems evolve regularly during the preparation of a major ad campaign. It is important that the ad director be curious and pay attention to trends and images and what society finds important to buy, as well as the concerns and the psychology behind specific buying patterns.

The majority of advertising agencies hire college graduates. These degrees can vary widely and include English, journalism, business administration, marketing or fine arts. Most colleges offer degrees in advertising or some form of a communications degree. Courses in psychology, sociology, economics, and any art mediums are also helpful. Advertising directors may have graduate degrees in advertising, art, or marketing.

Many employers prefer a broad liberal arts background with a college curriculum including courses in marketing, market research, sales, consumer behavior, communication methods, and technology. Courses in management and the completion of an internship is highly recommended. It is important to have a familiarity with the various computer programs used in design and management. The latest technology provides amazing capabilities for designers for everything from type and color to prepress and animation.

Opportunities for experience and exploration

There are various ways of gaining advertising experience. Volunteering for a non-profit organization in the public relations department can provide valuable education in dealing effectively with the public and targeting various organizations for fund raising. Volunteering at a local radio station to promote more listeners or perhaps raise money is another way of gaining experience. Organizing an event at your school and handling the advertising campaign to promote that event will also prove invaluable in gaining insight into advertising and promotion in general.

Learning about printing and photography is also helpful. By working on a school publication, you can learn the different steps involved in getting something professionally printed. Photography clubs and classes help develop the skills needed to recognize good technical skills in a photographer. The same thing is true for art classes. Learn as much as you can about the creative side of advertising.

Methods of entering

The advertising arena is immense with various specialized areas. When looking for employ-

ment, one could look at a large company that might have its own in-house services within their public relations and advertising department. Many of the largest companies will have some staff dedicated to working with advertising and promotion. The other alternative is to go directly to an advertising agency, where competition may be higher.

Most agencies offer special training programs for those just starting with a company. The agency's daily operations are explained, as well as the specific departments and variety of positions needed to produce an ad campaign.

Internships are popular with students, where they are able to work within an agency while in school. They provide experience working with an agency and give the student a good sense of the rhythm of the job and the type of work that will be performed by an entry level staff member. It also helps a student or recent graduate improve his or her resume.

Advancement

In smaller advertising agencies where a position may not have a precise job description within the limited staff, advancement may occur slowly, since the ad director will be doing most of the work available anyway. Emphasis is placed on experience, ability, and leadership in the promotion to advertising director. In larger firms, management training programs will precede advancement. Continuing education is occasionally provided in larger companies, either at a local college or through special seminars provided by professional societies. In larger firms, advancement occurs more quickly, due to a larger number or positions, and more defined roles for each of the staff.

Depending on the company, the rank above advertising director may be vice-president of the company, executive director over several advertising directors, or president of the company.

Employment outlook

Most opportunities for employment will be in larger cities with a high concentration of business, such as Chicago, New York, and Los Angeles. Employment is expected to remain somewhat flat in the 1990s as businesses are being required to cut back on their advertising budgets because of economic recession.

The successful candidate will be a college graduate with a great deal of creativity, strong communication skills and extensive experience within the advertising industry. Those able to speak another language will benefit, due to the increased competition in products and services offered in foreign markets. Some service industries, such as computer and data processing firms and environmental clean-up companies, are growing rapidly, so background knowledge in those fields may help.

Job competition is high for the position of advertising director. However, job competition depends on the specific industry served, location, and employer size.

Earnings

An experienced advertising director can expect to earn about $60,000 or more per year. In smaller agencies the salary may be lower, and in larger agencies it will be higher. Salary bonuses of up to 10 percent or higher are common for advertising directors. Fringe benefits typically include vacation and sick leave, health and life insurance, and retirement benefits.

Conditions of work

It is not uncommon for people in advertising to work long hours, including evenings and weekends. Promotion work can require meetings after normal business hours. Some travel may be involved to meet with clients or attend conferences within the industry.

Usually the work environment is an advertising agency is highly charged with energy and is both visually and psychologically exciting. It is a creative environment where lots of ideas are exchanged between fellow employees.

As deadlines are critical in advertising, it is important that one possess the ability to handle deadline pressure and stress effectively. Pa-

tience is essential, as decisions can go through many revisions, in response to the viewpoints of the client and staff. Flexibility is important as well. The creative director cannot remain fixed on one campaign when the client wants another.

In advertising one must really enjoy working with lots of different people and be very creative with ideas and concepts. Working under pressure is unavoidable.

GOE:11.09.01; SIC: any industry; SOC: 164

◇ SOURCES OF ADDITIONAL INFORMATION

American Advertising Federation
14400 K Street, NW, Suite 1000
Washington, DC 20005

American Association of Advertising Agencies
666 Third Avenue, 13th floor
New York, NY 10017

Association of National Advertisers
155 East 44th Street
New York, NY 10017

◇ RELATED ARTICLES

Volume 1: Advertising; Marketing
Volumes 2–4: Advertising workers; Art directors; Cartoonists and animators; Commercial artists; Marketing research personnel; Media planners and buyers; Writers

Advertising workers

Definition

The purpose of advertising is to attract buyers for products and services. *Advertising workers* include a wide variety of people whose jobs include planning, researching, creating, produc-

ing, and placing ads for clients who make or have products or services to sell. Advertising workers appeal to the public through newspaper and magazine ads, radio and television commercials, and outdoor displays such as billboards and murals.

History

Advertising has been around as long as people have been buying and selling goods and services. Probably the oldest form of advertising, word-of-mouth, still exists today as happy customers pass along product information to their friends and acquaintances. Following the invention of the printing press, merchants advertised their services by posting handbills anywhere that crowds might gather. In the 18th century, when newspapers gained popularity, they became an important venue for advertisements. One of the problems confronting merchants in those days was where to place their advertisements to generate the most business, and consequently some people began to specialize in accepting advertisements and posting them conspicuously. These agents were the first advertising workers. As competition grew, many of these agents offered to compose as well as post the advertisements for their clients.

In more recent times, advertising has become very important to businesses. With increased competition among new businesses, advertising has become vital. The advertising worker's job also has grown more complex as the means of advertising become more numerous—newspapers, magazines, posters, billboards, radio, and television. Today, advertising is a necessity in the marketing of mass-produced goods. Advertising informs many people of what is for sale, where, at what price, and why they should buy it.

Nature of the work

There are a number of major categories of advertising workers. Job descriptions may differ for each worker, although they do have a correlation in their work. Large advertising agencies may employ hundreds of people to work in a dozen different departments, while small agencies may have a handful of employees whose responsibilities cover more than one aspect of the work. Most agencies, however, have at least five departments: contact, planning, and marketing; research and development; media; creative; and production.

Advertising agency managers are concerned with the overall activities of the agency. They formulate plans to generate more business by soliciting new accounts or additional business from established accounts. They meet with department heads to coordinate their operations and to set up policies and procedures.

Account executives are responsible for maintaining good relations between the agency and specific clients assigned to the executives. After studying a client's advertising problems, account executives develop an advertising campaign or strategy, including a budget. With the client's approval, then, they work with all the departments of the agency (research, media, creative, production) to complete the campaign. As a necessary part of the job, account executives must be able to sell ideas and have some knowledge of overall marketing strategies.

In some agencies, an account supervisor directs the work of several account executives and may be directly responsible to the head of the agency.

Research and development directors gather and analyze information needed to make a client's advertising campaign successful. They try to find out who the buyers will be and what theme will have the most impact, what kind of packaging and price will have the most appeal, and which media will be most effective.

Research and development directors conduct local, regional, or national surveys to determine potential sales for the product or service offered and gather information about competitors' products, prices, sales, and methods of advertising. They use this information to study the client's product and to determine how it may be used to best advantage. To find the advantages and disadvantages of a client's product in relation to competing products, samples are often distributed to a segment of the public. Later, the users of these samples are asked their opinion of the product. This information may be used immediately to find the most convincing selling theme or later as testimonials for the product. With the available information on purchasing power, buying habits, and preferences of people, research directors can help determine how, when, and where the client's product might be introduced to the public.

Media planners are specialists employed by agencies because of their ability to determine which print or broadcast media will be most effective. They choose the medium that will reach the greatest number of potential buyers with minimal cost to the client. Media planners must know and be able to judge what kinds and how many people in what parts of the nation can be reached through various publications, radio and television broadcasts, and other media.

Media buyers, often referred to as *space buyers* or *time buyers* (space referring to newspapers and magazines, and time referring to radio and television), do the actual purchasing of time and space, under a general plan laid down by the media director, who supervises the work of

This artist is using a blade to carefully cut and paste artwork for a new advertisement that he is designing.

planners and buyers. Buyers maintain heavy telephone contact and keep up extensive correspondence with people from the media.

Media assistants are responsible for the detail work involved in planning and buying space and time. They keep detailed records of when an ad appeared, for which client, and at what cost. They also help planners research and analyze the numbers and percentages of consumers using media.

Creative directors develop the creative concept for advertising materials and direct the activities of artists and writers involved in carrying out the plans. They confer with the client and with agency department heads to determine the approach to be taken and to set up budgets and schedules. When layouts are completed, the creative director presents them to the client for approval.

Art directors plan the visual presentation of the client's message. Just as copywriters create a message with words, art directors create a message with pictures and designs that reinforces the advertising strategy and copy. Art directors who work on filmed commercials combine film techniques, music and sound, and actors to influence the viewers.

Art directors need to have a basic knowledge of graphics and design, printing, photography, and film making. With the help of layout artists, they decide on placement of pictures and text, choose typefaces for the printed matter, and make sketches of the ads. Generally several layouts are submitted to the client, who chooses one. The art director then selects an illustrator or photographer, or a TV producer, and the project goes to the production department of the agency.

Copywriters take the ideas submitted by account executives and creative directors and write descriptive copy in the form of headlines, jingles, slogans, and other techniques designed to attract the attention of potential buyers. Some products appeal to special groups of people, such as business executives or sports enthusiasts; the media these people read or watch would be used to sell products to them. In addition to being able to write, copywriters must know something about people and what makes them buy; they also must know the product and be familiar with the various advertising media.

Copywriters work closely with art directors to make sure that type and artwork together form a unified, eye-catching arrangement. In large agencies, copywriters may work under the supervision of a copy chief.

Production departments in large ad agencies may be divided into print production and radio and TV production departments, each with its own managers and staff.

Production managers and their assistants convert and reproduce written copy and artwork into printed, filmed, or tape-recorded form so it can be presented to the public. They work closely with printing, engraving, and other firms concerned with the reproduction of advertisements and must be familiar with various printing processes, papers, inks, typography, still and motion picture photography, and other processes and materials.

Many advertising workers are not necessarily found in an advertising agency. In the advertising field, talent can be used in positions such as artists and writers, researchers and statisticians, media specialists and administrators, accountants, secretaries, clerks, photographers, and printers. Advertising workers are employed in many kinds of business organizations. However, the greater number are employed by advertising agencies that plan and prepare advertising material for their clients on a commission or service fee basis.

Some large companies and nearly all department stores prefer to handle their own advertising. Advertising workers in such organizations prepare ads especially for their employers. They may also be involved in the planning, preparation, and publication of special promotional materials such as sales brochures or articles describing the activities of the organization.

Some advertising workers are employed by owners of advertising media such as newspapers, magazines, radio and television networks, and outdoor advertisers. Workers employed in these media are mainly *sales representatives* who sell advertising space or broadcast time to advertising agencies or companies that maintain their own advertising departments.

Advertising services and supply houses employ photographers, photoengravers, typographers, printers, marketing research specialists, product and package designers, producers of display materials, and others who assist in the preparation of various advertising materials.

Requirements

So many different kinds of work are done by advertising workers that it would be impossible to write a single set of qualifications for all of them. As far as educational requirements are concerned, no one pattern of education or background preparation for success as an advertising worker can be found. The American Association of Advertising Agencies notes that most agencies employing beginners prefer college graduates. While art directors, TV producers, and production department workers are less likely to need a college degree, for copywriters and for media and research workers, it is almost mandatory. Copywriters should have at least a bachelor's degree. Media directors and research directors with a master's degree have a distinct advantage over those with only an undergraduate degree. And some research department heads have doctorates. Most account executives have a degree in business administration.

While the requirements of agencies may vary somewhat, graduates of liberal arts colleges or graduates with majors in such fields as journalism, business administration, or marketing research are preferred. A good knowledge of English is a necessity for advertising workers, but their education should also include a variety of literature courses and social studies courses such as sociology, psychology, and economics. Other courses useful to advertising workers include writing, math and statistics,

advertising and marketing, art, philosophy, and languages. Some 900 degree-granting institutions throughout the United States offer specialized majors in advertising as a part of their curriculum.

In addition to the variety of educational and work experiences necessary for those interested in advertising, personal characteristics are also important. Advertising workers must like and be able to get along well with people. Workers must be able to function independently but also must be able to cooperate with others in the joint effort needed to plan and carry off an advertising program. Advertising workers also are involved with numerous clients whose products or services differ. Advertising is not, therefore, a job that involves routine, and workers must be able to meet and adjust to the challenge presented by each new product or service advertised. The ability to think clearly and logically is important, because commonsense approaches rather than gimmicks convince people that something is worth buying. Imagination is also necessary, not only to create effective advertising, but also to keep up with consumer demand and, if possible, to anticipate it. In general, advertising workers should be imaginative, flexible, creative, and be interested in people. They should have the ability to sell ideas, products, and services of their clients.

Opportunities for experience and exploration

Some experience can be gained by taking writing and art courses in school. Summer vacation jobs in advertising or sales provide good background. Part-time or full-time work in a local department store or newspaper office also is helpful. Some advertising or research organizations employ students to interview people or do other types of work connected with marketing research. In some cases it may be possible to obtain work in an advertising agency as a clerk or messenger who picks up or distributes to various departments within an agency or to service houses associated with an agency.

Internships in an advertising agency or department store that does its own advertising are a way of exploring and determining where an individual's personal characteristics and qualifications can best be used in advertising work. Work in marketing departments of large companies that do a lot of advertising is also valuable experience.

ADVERTISING WORKERS

Methods of entering

Some of the larger advertising agencies recruit college graduates and place them in training programs designed to acquaint the beginner with all aspects of advertising work, but these opportunities are limited and highly competitive. Many graduates, however, enter by applying to businesses that have a need for beginners in advertising work. Newspapers, radio and television stations, printers, photographers, as well as advertising agencies, are but a few examples of businesses employing advertising workers. People who have had work experience in sales positions often enter the advertising field. High school graduates employed in advertising may find it necessary to begin as clerks or assistants to research and production staff members or to copywriters. The *Standard Directory of Advertising Agencies* lists the names and addresses of ad agencies. Persons interested in applying for employment with any of these companies can find the directory in almost any public library.

Advancement

The path of advancement in an advertising agency generally leads from trainee to skilled worker to division head and then to department head. It may also lead from department to department as an employee gains responsibility with each move. Opportunities are limitless for those with talent, leadership capability, and ambition. Many of the top advertising executives reached that position before the age of 40.

Management positions require experience in all aspects of advertising, including work experience in an agency, with advertisers, and in various advertising media. If copywriters, account executives, and other workers employed by advertising agencies demonstrate outstanding ability to deal with clients and supervise co-workers, they usually have a good opportunity to advance to management positions. Other workers, however, prefer to acquire specialized skills, and for them advancement may mean more responsible work and increased pay.

Advertising workers in department stores, mail order houses, and other large firms that have their own advertising departments also can earn promotion. Advancement in any phase of advertising work is usually dependent on experience, training, and past work effectiveness. Some qualified copywriters and account executives set up their own agencies.

Employment outlook

In the 1990s more than 250,000 persons work in jobs that require knowledge of advertising skills and techniques. Advertising agency workers are concentrated in Chicago, New York, and Los Angeles, but retail and small advertising firms are located throughout the country.

Employment opportunities in the advertising field are expected to increase through the 1990s. A demand should arise for additional workers to create and carry out advertising plans so that advertisers can effectively compete in a market overflowing with domestic and foreign products and services being offered to consumers.

It is projected that advertising agencies will enjoy faster than average employment growth, as will industries that service the agencies and other businesses in the advertising field, such as those that offer commercial photography, art, graphics services, and direct mail. Opportunities for advertising workers look favorable in the radio and television industry as well, as this medium is increasingly used for commercial messages.

Openings will become available to replace workers who change positions, retire, or leave the field for other reasons. Competition for these jobs will be keen, however, because of the large number of qualified professionals in this traditionally desirable field. Opportunities will be best for the well qualified and well trained applicant. Employers favor those who are college graduates and who have experience and can demonstrate a high level of creativity and strong communications skills. Persons who are not well qualified or prepared for agency work will find the advertising field increasingly difficult to enter. This also will be true for those who seek work outside of agencies.

Earnings

Salaries of advertising workers vary depending on the type of work, the size of the agency, its geographical location, the kind of accounts handled, and the agency's gross earnings. Salaries also are affected by amount of education, aptitude, and experience.

The wide range of jobs in advertising makes it difficult to estimate average salaries for all of them. Entry-level jobs, of course, may pay considerably less than the figures given in the following paragraphs. A young person interested in advertising should realize that salaries are dependent on such factors as experience, the quality of work produced, size and location of the advertising agency, and its accounts.

In the 1990s, earnings for experienced workers in advertising agencies average $71,200 a year for the chief executives, $59,700 for account supervisors, and $31,400 for account executives. Research directors make $61,000 a year. In the creative departments, the directors earn $59,000, the copywriters $35,900, and the art directors $34,000. Salaries for media workers average $46,000 for media directors, $25,600 for media planners, and $23,500 for media buyers. Production managers are paid about $31,000 a year.

In other businesses and industries, heads of advertising departments annually earn about $57,000, and advertising managers make $38,000. Media managers are paid $45,000, whereas media planners and media buyers average $26,400 a year. Salaries of advertising workers are generally higher in consumer product firms than in industrial product firms because of the competition in consumer product sales.

Conditions of work

Persons interested in advertising work will find that the best opportunities for employment are found in large cities, especially in New York, Chicago, Detroit, and Los Angeles. The same is true for those interested in entering the field through advertising service and media. Some major agencies, however, do operate branches in various smaller cities throughout the nation, and a number of independent agencies also exist in and around large metropolitan areas. Conditions in most agencies are similar to those found in other offices throughout the country, except that workers must frequently work under great pressure to meet deadlines. A normal 40-hour week can be expected, but often there is evening and weekend work when necessary. Bonus checks and time off during slack periods

sometimes are means of compensation for unusual workload and hours. Usually advertising workers find their jobs a constant challenge to their initiative, imagination, and creative abilities.

GOE: 01.02.03, 01.06.01, 11.09.01; SIC: 7311, 8999; SOC: 125, 322, 3313, 4153, 71

◇ **SOURCES OF ADDITIONAL INFORMATION**

American Advertising Federation
Education Services Department
1400 K Street, NW, Suite 1000
Washington, DC 20005

American Association of Advertising Agencies
666 Third Avenue, 13th Floor
New York, NY 10017

Association of National Advertisers
155 East 44th Street
New York, NY 10017

Association of Canadian Advertisers
#803, 180 Bloor Street, West
Toronto ON M5S 2V6

◇ **RELATED ARTICLES**

Volume 1: Advertising; Marketing; Packaging; Public Relations
Volumes 2–4: Advertising directors; Commercial artists; Display workers; Marketing research personnel; Media specialists; Packaging and paper products technicians; Photographers; Public relations specialists; Writers

Aerobics Instructors and fitness trainers

Definition

Aerobics instructors and *fitness trainers* teach proper exercise techniques to people interested in physical fitness.

Aerobics instructors choreograph and teach aerobics classes of varying types. Classes are geared toward people with general good health as well as to specialized populations, including the elderly or those with health problems, such as heart disease, that affect their ability to exercise. Men as well as women enjoy the lively exercise routines set to music.

Depending on where they are employed, fitness trainers help devise conditioning programs for individual clients, who may be weight trainers or athletes, both amateur and professional. Fitness trainers motivate their clients to follow their exercise programs and monitor their progress. When injuries occur, either during training or sporting events, fitness trainers determine the extent of injury and administer first aid for such things as blisters, bruises, and scrapes; following more serious injury, they help the athlete perform rehabilitative exercises.

History

Only recently has physical fitness become an organized industry. For many years, only professional athletes were trained by athletic or fitness trainers. Now, their services are usually available to anyone who joins a health club. With the popularization of weight training equipment, knowledgeable instructors were needed to teach beginners how to safely and effectively use the equipment.

Aerobics is also regarded much differently now than when it first became popular in the late 1970s and early 1980s. The flashy leotards and shrieking class members have been replaced by serious athletes seeking to shape and tone specific muscle groups; their instructors are no longer just people who "did well in class"—they are highly trained, certified professionals. Aerobics itself has diversified; it includes many options, only one of which is dance. In fact, to underscore this fact, the IDEA Foundation has changed its slogan from the International Dance and Exercise Association to "The Association for Exercise Professionals." This past decade has seen the introduction of several new branches of aerobics, including aqua-aerobics, step-aerobics, interval training, and interval-circuit training.

Aqua-aerobics is a very popular form of low-impact aerobics. Impact refers to the stress placed on joints and bones during exercise. Since the water supports the body and creates resistance, it is the ideal exercise medium. Participants do not even need to know how to swim, since all the movements are done standing upright, or holding onto the side of the pool.

The latest development is step-aerobics. In 1986, an aerobics instructor and body builder named Gin Miller developed a formal step-training program after using the technique to recover from a knee injury. Basically, step aerobics involves the use of a specially designed stool or bench that sits from 4 to 12 inches off the ground. Participants step up and down in different patterns, which provides an excellent cardiovascular workout.

In the late 1980s, Arlette Perry, an exercise physiologist with the University of Miami's Human Performance Laboratory, determined that interval training (alternating intense exercise movements with slower-paced movements) was better for aerobic fitness than a steady level of exercise, since it achieves higher heart rates.

Today, aerobics classes are used in cross-training, where athletes combine several different fitness activities to train for a certain sport. A popular workout is circuit training or interval circuit training (ICT), which combines aerobic exercise with muscle-strengthening weight lifting for a full-body workout. In circuit training, the workout equipment is arranged to work one group of muscles at a time, alternating so that one set of muscles can rest while the next group is worked. As the athlete moves through each piece of equipment in the circuit, the heart rate remains elevated, without the participants tiring as quickly as they would if repeating the same exercise.

New trends in fitness include aerobics classes for the whole family, as well as the use of *personal fitness trainers*. In fact, the demand for qualified personal trainers has become so great that the IDEA Foundation started offering personal-training certification in 1990.

Nature of the work

There are three general levels of aerobics classes: low-impact, moderate, and high-intensity. A typical class starts with warm-up exercises—slow stretching movements to aid flexibility; followed by 35 minutes of non-stop activity to raise the heart rate; then ends with a cool-down period of stretching and slower movements. Instructors teach class members to monitor their heart rates and to listen to their bodies for information on personal progress.

Aerobics instructors prepare their classes beforehand. They choose exercises to work different muscles, and music to motivate students during each phase of the program; upbeat music for the all-out exercise portion, and more soothing music for the cool-down phase. Instructors stand in front of their class to demonstrate each step of the routine until the class can follow along. They then incorporate the routines into a sequence that is set to music.

This is usually an ongoing process, with new routines added as the class progresses. Some classes are the drop-in type, with new students starting all the time. The instructor either faces the class or a mirror in order to observe the students' progress and to insure that they do the exercises correctly.

In a health club, fitness trainers evaluate their client's fitness level with physical examinations and fitness tests. Using various pieces of testing equipment, they can determine such things as percentage of body fat and optimal heart and pulse rate. Clients fill out a questionnaire about their medical background, general fitness level, and fitness goals. The fitness trainer uses all this information to design a customized workout plan utilizing weights and other exercise options including swimming, running, and so on to help clients meet these goals. Trainers also advise clients on weight control, diet, and general health.

To start clients' exercise programs, the trainer often demonstrates the proper use of weight lifting equipment to reduce the chance of injury, especially for beginners. The trainer observes clients as they use the equipment; this enables him or her to correct any problems before injury occurs.

Fitness trainers who work for professional, college, or high school athletic teams are known as *athletic trainers*. Basically, athletic trainers perform the same types of activities as fitness trainers, but on a more specialized level. They work with athletes to strengthen certain muscles to improve their performance in their sport.

Fitness and athletic trainers also tape weak or injured hands, feet, knees, or other parts of the body at risk for injury. This helps strengthen them and keep them in the correct position to prevent further injury or strain. Many fitness trainers help athletes with therapy or rehabilitation, using special braces or other equipment to support or protect the injured part until it heals. Trainers ensure that the athlete does not overdo the exercise, risking further damage.

Requirements

Aerobics instructors need a high school diploma; many also have a college degree in dance exercise or related field such as exercise physiology. For high school students, courses in physical education, biology, and anatomy are particularly helpful.

Because it is virtually impossible to be hired unless certified, potential aerobics instructors

An aerobics instructor leads a class through arm and leg exercises.

must first become certified by an organization such as the IDEA Foundation, which is recognized world-wide. Those interested should request a copy of the dance exercise instructor manual, study it, and then pass a three-and-a-half hour test. The information needed to pass the test covers such topics as: how medications affect the body; the role of nutrition in performance; how to teach special populations; and how to handle injuries in class. Aerobics instructors also must be certified in CPR (cardiopulmonary resuscitation).

Other organizations that offer certification include the Aerobics and Fitness Association of America (AFAA) and the American College of Sports Medicine (ACSM).

Students interested in becoming fitness trainers need a bachelor's degree from an accredited athletic training program, or in a related field such as physical education or health. This, however, will require an additional 1,800 hours in an internship with a certified fitness or athletic trainer. To prepare, high school students should take general science, chemistry, biology, physiology, mathematics, and physics.

College-level courses include anatomy, biomechanics, chemistry, first aid, health, kinesiology, nutrition, physics, physiology, physiology of exercise, practicum in athletic training, psychology, and safety.

For those interested in working as a trainer for a college or professional team, a master's degree is generally required; many go on to receive doctoral degrees.

Some states require fitness trainers to be state licensed; others will soon follow suit. In addition, The National Athletic Trainers' Association and the American Athletic Trainers Association certify fitness trainers who have graduated from accredited college programs or have completed the necessary internship following a degree in a related field. Candidates for certification generally need Red Cross certification in CPR or as an EMT (emergency medical technician).

Whichever career path they follow, aerobics instructors and fitness trainers are expected to remain updated in their fields, becoming thoroughly familiar with the most recent knowledge and safety practices. They must take continuing education courses and seminars to keep their certification current.

Special requirements

Aerobics instructors and fitness trainers are expected to be physically fit, but not necessarily specimens of human perfection. For example, members of an aerobics class geared to overweight people might feel more comfortable with a heavier instructor; a class geared towards the elderly may benefit from an older instructor.

Opportunities for experience and exploration

A visit to a health club or YMCA aerobics class is a good way to observe the work of fitness trainers and aerobics instructors. Part-time or summer jobs are sometimes available for high school students in these facilities, and it may be possible to volunteer in a senior citizen center where aerobics classes are offered.

If possible, enroll in an aerobics class or train with a fitness trainer to experience first-

hand what their jobs entail, and to see what makes a good instructor.

Aerobics instructor workshops are taught to help prospective instructors gain experience. These are usually offered in adult education courses at such places as the YMCA. Unpaid apprenticeships are also a good way for future instructors to obtain supervised experience before teaching classes on their own. The facility may allow prospective aerobics instructors to take their training class for free if there is a possibility that they will work there later on.

Opportunities for student fitness trainers are available in schools with fitness trainers on staff. This is an excellent way for students to observe and assist a professional fitness trainer on an ongoing basis, to decide if the job is for them.

Methods of entering

Students should utilize their school's placement office for information on available jobs. Often the facility that provided their training or internship will hire them or can provide information on available job openings in the area. Students can also find jobs through classified ads and by applying to health and fitness clubs, YM/YWCAs, JCCs (Jewish community centers), local schools and colleges, park and recreation districts, church groups and organizations, major employers, and any other likely sponsor of aerobics classes or fitness facilities.

Advancement

Experienced aerobics instructors can go on to become instructor trainers, providing tips and insight on how to present a class and what routines work well.

A bachelor's degree in either sports physiology or exercise physiology is especially beneficial for those who wish to advance to *health club director* or to teach corporate wellness programs.

Fitness trainers working at schools can advance from assistant positions to *head athletic director*; sometimes this requires changing to another school. Fitness trainers may go on to instruct new fitness trainers on the college level. Some work in sports medicine facilities, usually in rehabilitation work. In health clubs, fitness trainers can advance to become health club director or work in administration. Often, fitness trainers who build up a reputation and a following go into business for themselves as personal trainers.

Employment outlook

Because of the country's ever-expanding interest in physical well-being and fitness, the job outlook for aerobics instructors should remain strong through the year 2000.

Fitness trainers are also in strong demand, especially at the high school level. Some states now require that high schools have a fitness trainer on staff. The glamour jobs in professional sports are very competitive.

Earnings

Aerobics instructors are usually paid by the class, and generally start out at about $10 per class. Experienced aerobics instructors can earn up to $50 or $60 per class. Health club directors usually earn about $30,000 per year.

Fitness trainers earn between $15,000 and $35,000 per year, depending on geographic location, and number of years experience. High school athletic trainers who are also high school teachers will earn a teacher's salary plus an extra payment to serve as trainer, from $2,500 to $3,900 per year. Those who serve as trainers for professional athletic teams will earn between $22,800 to $54,000 per year or more. Although a sports season will last only about six months, the athletes train year-round to remain in shape, and require the trainers to guide them.

Conditions of work

Most weight training and aerobics classes are done indoors. Athletic trainers must work outdoors during sporting events such as baseball and football, and in cold skating rinks for hockey games. The position often calls for quite a bit of travel, especially when the team plays away games, or, in the case of professional athletes, when they head to training camp prior to the season's opening.

Both aerobics instructors and fitness trainers need a positive, outgoing personality in order to motivate people to exercise. The aerobics instructor helps class members, who may be at different fitness levels, become physically fit. This includes making the class enjoyable yet challenging so that its members will return class after class. The instructor also needs to be unaffected by complaints of class members, some of whom may find the routines too hard or too easy, or who may not like the music selections. Instructors need to realize that these complaints are not personal attacks.

Fitness trainers need to be able to work on a one-to-one basis with both amateur and professional athletes. They often must work with athletes who are in pain after an injury, and must be able to coax them to use muscles they would probably rather not. They must possess patience, especially for beginners or those who are not athletically inclined, and offer encouragement to help them along. It is rewarding to help others achieve their fitness goals.

GOE: 10.02.02; SIC: 7991; SOC: 34

◇ **SOURCES OF ADDITIONAL INFORMATION**

American College of Sports Medicine
PO Box 1140
Indianapolis, IN 46206

American Council on Exercise
PO Box 910449
San Diego, CA 92191-0449

The IDEA Foundation
The Association for Exercise Professionals
6190 Cornerstone Ct. East
Suite 202
San Diego, CA 92121-4729

National Athletic Trainers' Association
2952 Stemmons Freeway
Suite 200
Dallas, TX 75247

◇ **RELATED ARTICLES**

Volume 1: Sports
Volumes 2–4: Dancers and choreographers; Emergency medical technicians; Occupational therapists; Physical therapist assistants; Physical therapists; Respiratory therapists; Sports instructors; Sports occupations

Aeronautical and aerospace technicians

Definition

Aeronautical and aerospace technicians work with aircraft and spacecraft. Using their skills, they work with engineers and scientists to design, construct, test, operate, and maintain the basic structures of aircraft and spacecraft, as well as propulsion and control systems. Many aeronautical technicians assist engineers in preparing equipment drawings, diagrams, blueprints, and scale models. They collect information, make computations, and perform laboratory tests. Their work may include: estimating weight factors and centers of gravity, evaluating stress factors, and working on various projects involving aerodynamics, structural design, flight-test evaluation, or propulsion problems. Other aeronautical technicians estimate the cost of materials and labor required to manufacture the product, serve as manufacturers' field service technicians, and engage in technical writing.

There are no clear cut definitions of "aeronautical technology" and "aerospace technology," in fact, many employers use the terms interchangeably. This lack of a clear distinction also occurs in education, where many schools and institutes offer similar courses under a variety of titles: aeronautical, aviation, or aerospace technology. In general, however, the term "aerospace industry" refers to manufacturers of all kinds of flying vehicles: from piston and jet-powered aircraft that fly inside the earth's atmosphere, to rockets, missiles, satellites, probes, and all kinds of manned and unmanned spacecraft that operate outside the earth's atmosphere. The term "aeronautics" is often used within the aerospace industry to refer specifically to mechanical flight inside the earth's atmosphere, especially to the design and manufacture of commercial passenger and freight aircraft, private planes, and helicopters.

On the other hand, many publications refer to jobs in the engineering and development of all kinds of flying vehicles as "aeronautical technology," and to those employed in this area as "aeronautical technicians" or "aircraft technicians." In general, and despite its title, this article refers to aeronautical technicians; however, the term "aeronautical and aerospace technicians" is used periodically to remind readers that both terms are current and accurate.

History

Both aeronautical engineering and the aerospace industry had their births in the early 20th century. The very earliest machine-powered and heavier-than-air aircraft, such as the first one flown by Wilbur and Orville Wright in 1903, were crudely constructed and often the result of costly and dangerous trial-and-error experimentation.

As government and industry took an interest in the possible applications of this new invention, however, our knowledge of aircraft and the entire industry became more sophisticated. By 1908, for instance, the Wright brothers had received their first government military contract, and by 1909, the industry had expanded to include additional airplane producers, such as Glenn Curtiss in the United States and several others in France.

Aeronautical engineering and the aerospace industry have been radically transformed since those early days, mostly because of the demands of two world wars and the tremendous increases in scientific knowledge that have taken place during this century. The past three or four decades especially have brought dramatic developments: the jet engine, rocket propulsion, supersonic flight, and manned voyages outside the earth's atmosphere.

During this same time frame, aeronautical engineers found themselves taking on increasingly larger projects and were more in need of trained and knowledgeable assistants to help them. Over the years, these assistants have been known variously as engineering aides, engineering associates, and, most recently, as aeronautical technicians. Their task today is to take on assignments that require technical skills but do not necessarily require the scientist's or engineer's special training and education.

To meet this assignment (and unlike the aides and associates of some decades ago who usually trained on the job, often using only one type or piece of equipment), today's technicians are educated in technical institutes and junior colleges where they are taught the fundamentals of science, technology, and mathematics and how to apply these to scientific problems.

In light of the continuing shortage of professionally trained engineers and scientists, the work of aeronautical technicians has become especially crucial; their work frees the engineers and scientists to concentrate their efforts on problems and projects that only they can handle.

Nature of the work

Aeronautical and aerospace technicians are principally employed by government agencies, commercial airlines, educational institutions, and aerospace manufacturing companies. Most of those employed by manufacturing companies engage in research, development, and design; the remainder work in production, sales engineering, installation and maintenance, technical writing and illustrating, and other related fields. Those employed by government and educational institutions are normally assigned to do research and specific problem-solving tasks. Airlines employ technicians to supervise maintenance operations and the development of procedures for new equipment.

In all of these settings, aeronautical technicians work side by side with engineers and scientists in all major phases of the design, production, and operation of aircraft and spacecraft technology. The aeronautical technician position includes: collecting and recording data; operating test equipment such as wind tunnels and flight simulators devising tests to ensure quality control; modifying mathematical procedures to fit specific problems; laying out experimental circuits to test scientific theories; and evaluating experimental data for practical applications.

The following paragraphs describe specific jobs held by aeronautical technicians, and some may be used in other industries as well. Fuller descriptions of the work associated with some of these titles are provided in separate entries.

Aerospace physiological technicians operate devices used to train pilots and astronauts. These devices include pressure suits, pressure chambers, and ejection seats that simulate flying conditions. These technicians also operate other kinds of flight training equipment such as tow reels, radio equipment, and meteorological devices. They interview trainees about their medical histories, which helps detect evidence of conditions that would disqualify pilots or astronauts from further training.

Aircraft launch and recovery technicians work on aircraft carriers, to operate, adjust, and repair launching and recovery equipment such as catapults, barricades, and arresting nets. They disassemble the launch and recovery equipment, replace defective parts, and keep track of all maintenance activities.

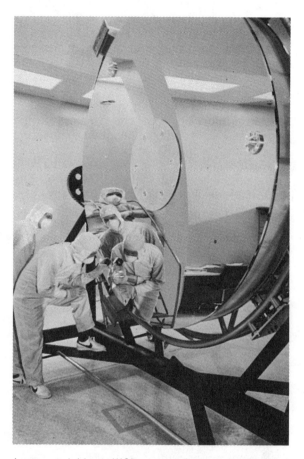

Aerospace technicians at NASA prepare a reflective device before sending it into space. They must maintain a sterile environment by covering nearly all exposed parts of their bodies.

Electronics technicians assist engineers in the design, development, and modification of electronic and electromechanical systems. They assist in the calibration and operation of radar and photographic equipment, and also operate, install, troubleshoot, and repair electronic testing equipment.

Engineering technicians assist with review and analysis of post-flight data, structural failure, and other factors that cause failure in flight vehicles.

Industrial engineering technicians assist engineers in preparing layouts of machinery and equipment, work-flow plans, time-and-motion studies, and statistical studies and analyses of production costs to produce the most efficient use of personnel, materials, and machines.

Instrumentation technicians test, install, and maintain electronic, hydraulic, pneumatic, and optical instruments. These are used in aircraft systems and components in manufacturing as well as research and development. One important responsibility is to maintain their assigned research instruments. As a part of this maintenance, they test the instruments, take readings and calibration curves, and calculate correction factors for the instruments.

Liaison technicians check on the production of aircraft and spacecraft as they are being built for conformance to specifications, keeping engineers informed as the manufacturing progresses, and investigate any engineering production problems that arise.

Mathematical technicians assist mathematicians, engineers, and scientists by performing computations involving the use of advanced mathematics.

Mechanical technicians use metalworking machines to assist in the manufacture of one-of-a-kind parts. They also assist in rocket-fin alignment, payload mating, weight and center-of-gravity measurements, and launch-tower erection.

Metallurgical technicians work with metallurgists in processing and converting metals into finished products. They test metals and alloys to determine their physical properties and develop new ways of treating and using metals and alloys.

Target aircraft technicians repair and maintain pilotless target aircraft. They assemble, repair, or replace aircraft parts such as cowlings, wings, and propeller assemblies, and test aircraft engine operation.

Technical illustrators draw accurate and clear illustrations for operating manuals used by aviation mechanics, electronics technicians, flight crews, flight instructors, and to assist in aircraft, spacecraft, and avionics maintenance.

Technical sales or field representatives serve as the link between the manufacturer and the customer, advising customers on correct installation procedures, and assisting with maintenance problems.

Technical writers write about technical or scientific matter in technical manuals, instruction manuals, bulletins, catalogs, and publicity releases. They also arrange for the preparation of tables, charts, illustrations, and other artwork for publication.

Tool designers develop new tools and devices, or redesign those already in use for efficient mass production.

make, maintain, or assemble items, large or small.

Post–high school education is required to become an aeronautical technician; therefore, students should determine the precise admissions requirements of the institutions they plan to attend as early as possible in their high school years. A strong science and mathematics background is essential. Useful high school courses include: algebra through quadratics, plane and solid geometry, trigonometry, physics, chemistry, social studies, economics, history, laboratory procedures, blueprint reading, drafting, and industrial and machine shop practice. English, speech, and courses in the preparation of test reports and technical writing are extremely helpful to develop communication ability.

Although many students will not recognize an interest in this field early enough to obtain all these courses, this should not keep them from entering the field. Many two-year post–high school programs offer a pretechnical curriculum to fill in the missing subjects.

Specialized preparation for aeronautical technicians may be obtained in two or three years from colleges or universities, junior or community colleges, technical institutes, vocational-technical schools, through industry on-the-job training, or in work-study programs in the U.S. Armed Forces. High school graduation is normally a prerequisite for enrollment in any of these programs. Graduates from a junior or community college may earn an associate degree in engineering or science. When selecting a school to attend, check the listings of such agencies as the Accreditation Board for Engineering Technology, the National Council of Technical Schools, and the regional accrediting associations for engineering colleges.

In general, post–high school programs strengthen the student's background in science and mathematics. Beyond that, an interdisciplinary curriculum is more helpful than one that specializes in a narrow field. Other courses, which are basic to the work of the aeronautical scientist and engineer, should be part of a balanced program. These include: basic physics, nuclear theory, chemistry, mechanics, and computers, including data-processing equipment and procedures.

Requirements

Aeronautical and aerospace technicians must be able to learn basic engineering skills. They should like and be proficient in mathematics and the physical sciences, able to visualize size, form, and function. Technicians must be able to

Special requirements

Only a few aeronautical technician positions require licensing or certification; however, certificates issued by professional organizations do enhance the status of qualified engineering technicians.

Those working with nuclear powered engines or testing radioactive sources usually need certification. Licensing may be required for those working on aircraft in some test programs, and some safety-related positions require certification.

Security clearances are required in agencies which carry on work related to national defense.

Aeronautical technicians may become affiliated with professional groups, and may or may not belong to unions. If they do, union membership requirements are usually determined by existing agreements between employers and unions.

Opportunities for experience and exploration

Visiting an aerospace research or manufacturing facility is one of the best ways to learn more about this field. Because there are so many such facilities connected with the aerospace industry throughout the United States, there is sure to be one in nearly every area. Local newspaper, radio, or television news reports often present special features about these facilities, especially at times such as the launching of an important spacecraft, the development of new or redesigned artificial satellites, or the introduction of a new aircraft. The local library's reference department can also help students locate the nearest facility.

Finding part-time or summer employment at such a facility is, of course, one of the best ways to gain experience or learn more about the field.

Students should not overlook the educational benefits of visiting local museums of science and technology, or aircraft museums or displays, if available. Some Air Force bases or Naval Air Stations also offer tours to groups of interested students. The tours may be arranged by teachers or career guidance counselors.

In addition, shop and science courses with lab sections train students in the proper use of equipment and give them a feel for the work they may do in the future.

Methods of entering

The best way for students to obtain an aeronautical or aerospace technician's job is through their school's placement service. Jobs may also be obtained through state employment offices, newspaper advertisements, by application for government employment, and through industry work-study programs offered by many aircraft companies.

Advancement

Aeronautical and aerospace technicians learn on the job. As they gain experience in the specialized areas, employers turn to them as experts who can solve problems, create new techniques, devise new designs, or develop practice from theory.

Most advancement involves taking on additional responsibilities. For example, with experience, a technician may take on supervisory responsibilities, overseeing several trainees, assistant technicians, or others. Such a technician may also be assigned independent responsibility—especially on some tasks usually assigned to an engineer. Technicians with a good working knowledge of the company's equipment and who have good personalities may become company sales or technical representatives. With additional formal education, a technician may become an aeronautical or aerospace engineer.

Employment outlook

Employment levels in the aerospace industry are influenced by a number of factors: levels of defense spending, appropriations for space programs; the health of commercial airlines; and the country's general level of economic activity. Although it is unlikely that all of these factors will be constantly favorable through the coming decade, there is reason to expect at least some growth in each of these areas through the 1990s.

The aerospace industry's diversity of products and markets contribute to its economic stability. The same company that makes components for airlines may also make parts for jet fighters or communications satellites. Although the government cutbacks in defense spending will reduce the demand for those in defense-related activities, the well trained technician who is ready and willing to learn new skills should continue to find employment opportunities in this field.

Earnings

The actual salary a person receives will depend on his or her technical specialty, educational preparation, work experience, ability, and geographical location. Starting salaries average between $15,000 to $20,000 per year, and, with experience, can go as high as $48,000 for avionic technicians; $54,000 for electronics, radar or navigation technicians; and $66,000 for drafters.

Benefits depend on employers, but usually include paid vacations and holidays, sick pay, insurance, and a retirement plan.

Nearly all companies offer some form of tuition reimbursement for further education. Some offer cooperative programs with local schools, combining classroom training with practical paid experience.

Conditions of work

The aerospace industry, with its strong emphasis on quality and safety, is a very safe place to work. Special procedures and equipment make otherwise hazardous jobs extremely safe. The range of work covered means that the technicians can work in small teams in specialized research laboratories or in test areas that are large and hospital-clean. Aerospace technicians are at the launch pad, involved in fueling and checkout procedures, and back in the blockhouse sitting at an electronic console. They may work in large test facilities or in specialized shops, designing and fabricating equipment. They travel to test sites or tracking stations to construct facilities or troubleshoot systems. Working conditions vary with the assignment, but the work climate is always challenging, and co-workers are well trained, competent people.

Aeronautical technicians may perform inside activities involving confined detail work, they may work outside, or a combination of both.

Aeronautical and aerospace technicians work in many situations: alone, in small teams, or in large groups. Commonly, technicians participate in team projects—coordinated efforts of scientists, engineers, and technicians working on specific assignments. They concentrate on the practical aspects of the project and must get along well with and interact cooperatively with the scientists responsible for the theoretical aspects of the project.

Aeronautical technicians must able to perform under deadline pressure, meet strict requirements and rigid specifications, and deal with potentially hazardous situations. They must be willing and flexible enough to acquire new knowledge and techniques to adjust to the rapidly changing technology. In addition, technicians need persistence and tenacity, especially when engaged in experimental and research tasks. They must be responsible, reliable, and willing to accept greater responsibility.

Aeronautical technology is never far from the public's attention, and aeronautical technicians have the satisfaction of knowing that they are viewed as being engaged in vital and fascinating work.

GOE: 05.01.01; SIC: 372, 376; SOC: 3719

◇ **SOURCES OF ADDITIONAL INFORMATION**

Aerospace Education Association
1810 Michael Faraday Drive, Suite 101
Reston, VA 22090

Students for the Exploration and Development of Space
MIT Building, W20-445
77 Massachusetts Avenue
Cambridge, MA 02139

American Institute of Aeronautics and Astronautics
370 L'Enfant Promenade, SW
Washington, DC 20024

Aerospace Industries Association of America
1250 I Street, NW
Washington, DC 20005

General Aviation Manufacturers Association
1400 K Street, NW, Suite 801
Washington, DC 20005

National Aeronautics and Space Administration
600 Independence Avenue, SW
Washington, DC 20546

Aerospace Industries Association of Canada
#1200, 60 Queen Street
Ottawa ON K1P 5Y7

◇ **RELATED ARTICLES**

Volume 1: Aviation and Aerospace

Aerospace engineers

Definition

Aerospace engineering encompasses the fields of aeronautical (aircraft) and astronautical (spacecraft) engineering. *Aerospace engineers* work in teams to design, build, and test machines that fly within the earth's atmosphere and beyond. Although aerospace science is a very specialized discipline, it is also considered one of the most diverse. This field of engineering draws from such subjects as physics, mathematics, earth science, aerodynamics, and biology. Some aerospace engineers specialize in designing one complete machine, perhaps a commercial aircraft, whereas others focus on separate components such as for missile guidance systems.

History

The roots of aerospace engineering can be traced as far back as to when people first dreamed of being able to fly. Thousands of years ago, the Chinese developed kites and later experimented with gun powder as a source of propulsion. In the 15th century, Renaissance artist Leonardo da Vinci created drawings of two devices that were designed to fly. One, the ornithopter, was supposed to fly the way birds do, by flapping its wings; the other was designed as a rotating screw, closer in form to today's helicopter.

In 1783, the Montgolfier brothers of France designed the first hot-air balloon that could be used for manned flight. In 1799 an English baron, Sir George Cayley, designed an aircraft that was one of the first not to be considered "lighter than air," as balloons were. He developed a fixed-wing structure that led to his creation of the first glider, in 1849. Much experimentation was performed in gliders and the science of aerodynamics through the late 1800s. In 1903 the first mechanically powered and controlled flight was completed in a craft designed by Orville and Wilbur Wright.

The big boost in airplane development occurred during World War I. In the early years of the war, aeronautical engineering comprised a variety of engineering skills applied toward the development of flying machines. Civil engineering principles were used in structural design, while early airplane engines were devised by automobile engineers. Aerodynamic design itself was primarily empirical, with many answers coming from liquid-flow concepts established in marine engineering.

The evolution of the airplane continued during both world wars, with steady technological developments in materials science, propulsion, avionics, and stability and control. Airplanes became larger and faster. Today we pretty much take airplanes for granted, even though commercial vehicles became common only as recently as the 1960s and 1970s. The first U.S. jetliner, the Boeing 707, began service in the late 1950s; later came airliners constructed for the various worldwide and national routes we have today.

Robert Goddard developed and flew the first liquid-propelled rocket in 1926. The technology behind liquid propulsion continued to evolve, and in 1938 the first U.S. liquid rocket engine was tested. More sophisticated rockets were eventually created to enable aircraft to be launched into space. The world's first artificial satellite, Sputnik I, was launched by the Soviets in 1957. In 1961 President John F. Kennedy urged the United States to be the first country to put a man on the moon; on July 20, 1969, astronauts Neil Armstrong and Edwin Aldrin, Jr., accomplished that goal.

Today, aerospace engineers design spacecraft that explore beyond the earth's atmosphere, such as space shuttles and rockets. They create missiles and military craft of many types, such as fighters, bombers, observers, and transports. Today's engineers go way beyond the dreams of merely learning to fly.

Aerospace engineers work on a full-scale model of a newly designed Air Force missile.

Nature of the work

Although the creation of aircraft and spacecraft involve professionals from many branches of engineering (e.g., materials, electrical, and mechanical), aerospace engineers in particular are responsible for the total design of the craft, including its shape, performance, propulsion, and guidance control system. In the field of aerospace engineering, professional responsibilities vary widely depending on the specific job description. *Aeronautical engineers* work specifically with aircraft systems, and *astronautical engineers* specialize in spacecraft systems.

Throughout their education and training, aerospace engineers thoroughly learn the complexities involved in how materials and structures perform under tremendous stress. In general, they are called upon to apply their knowledge of the following subjects: propulsion, aerodynamics, thermodynamics, fluid mechanics, flight mechanics, and structural

analysis. Less technically scientific issues must also often be dealt with, such as cost analysis, reliability studies, maintainability, operations research, marketing, and management.

There are many professional titles given to certain aerospace engineers. *Analytical engineers* use basic engineering and mathematical theory to solve questions that arise during the design phase. *Stress analysts* determine how the weight and loads of structures behave under a variety of conditions. This analysis is often performed with computers and complex formulas.

Computational fluid dynamic (CFD) engineers use sophisticated high-speed computers to develop models used in the study of fluid dynamics. Using simulated systems, they determine how elements flow around objects; simulation saves time and money and eliminates risks involved with actual testing. As computers become more complex, so will the tasks of the CFD engineer.

Design aerospace engineers draw from the expertise of many other specialists. They devise the overall structure of components and entire crafts, meeting the specifications developed by those more specialized in aerodynamics, astrodynamics, and structural engineering. Design engineers use computer-aided design (CAD) programs for many of their tasks. *Manufacturing aerospace engineers* develop the plans for producing the complex components that make up aircraft and spacecraft. They work with the designers to ensure that the plans are economically feasible and will produce efficient, effective components.

Materials aerospace engineers determine the suitability of the various materials that are used to produce aerospace vehicles. Aircraft and spacecraft require the appropriate tensile strength, density, and rigidity for the particular environments they are subjected to. Determining how materials such as steel, glass, and even chemical compounds react to temperature and stress is an important part of the materials engineer's responsibilities.

Quality control is a task that aerospace engineers perform throughout the development, design, and manufacturing processes. The finished product must be evaluated for its reliability, vulnerability, and how it is to be maintained and supported.

Marketing and sales aerospace engineers work with customers, usually industrial corporations and the government, informing them of product performance. They act as a liaison between the technical engineers and the clients to help ensure that the products delivered are performing as planned. Sales engineers also need to anticipate the needs of the customer, as far ahead as possible, to inform their companies of potential marketing opportunities. They also keep abreast of their competitors and need to understand how to structure contracts effectively.

Requirements

High school students interested in aerospace careers should follow a program designed for potential entrance into a college engineering major. Main focus should be put on mathematics, science, computers, and English. Important electives include mechanical drawing and industrial arts.

A bachelor's degree with a major in aerospace engineering is usually required for entry into the field, but other majors are sometimes acceptable. For example, the National Aeronautics and Space Administration (NASA) recommends a degree in any of a variety of disciplines, including biomedical engineering, ceramics engineering, chemistry, industrial engineering, materials science, metallurgy, optical engineering, and oceanography.

In the first two years of an aerospace degree program, the student typically does extensive course work in the physical sciences, mathematics, computer science, and basic engineering. Students are also expected to complete course work in the traditional liberal arts, including English, history, and social science. It is in the later years of undergraduate study that the focus is more on specialized subjects.

Students continuing on to graduate school are concerned more with research and further specialization, with a thesis required for a master's degree and a dissertation required for a doctorate. About one-third of all aerospace engineers go on to graduate school to get a master's degree. Generally, a year or two beyond undergraduate school is required for a master's; a doctoral degree could take up to five years.

Opportunities for experience and exploration

Students who like to work on model airplanes and rockets may be good candidates for an aerospace engineering career. Working on special research assignments supervised by science and math teachers supervise is good, as is working on cars and boats, which provides a good opportunity to discover more about aerodynamics.

Exciting opportunities are often available at summer camps and academic programs throughout the country. For instance, the International Aerospace Camp (see address listed at the end of this article) presents a 10-day session focusing on aerospace study and career exploration. Instruction in model rocketry and flight are also offered. In addition, the camp provides jobs for qualified college students.

It is also a good idea to join a science club. For example, the Junior Engineering Technical Society provides member students with an opportunity to enter academic competitions, explore career opportunities, and design model structures. The *JETS Report* is one type of journal that students should read; it offers articles on industry and student news and club activities.

Methods of entering

As in most engineering fields, in the various divisions of aerospace engineering there tends to be a hierarchy of workers. This is true in research, design and development, production, and teaching. In an entry-level job, one is considered simply an engineer, perhaps a junior engineer. After a certain amount of experience is gained, depending on the position, one moves on to work as a project engineer, supervising others. Then, as a managing engineer, one has further responsibilities over a number of project engineers and their teams. At the top of the hierarchy is the position of chief engineer, which involves authority over managing engineers and additional decision-making responsibilities.

As engineers move up the career ladder, the type of responsibilities they have tend to change. As juniors, engineers are highly involved in technical matters and scientific problem solving. As managers and chiefs, engineers have the responsibilities of supervising, cost analyzing, and relating with clients.

Advancement

All engineers must continue to learn and study technological progress throughout their careers. It is important to keep abreast of engineering advancements and trends by reading industry journals and taking courses. In aerospace engineering especially, changes occur rapidly, and those who eye promotions must be prepared. Those who are employed by colleges and universities must continue teaching and conducting research if they want to have tenured (more guaranteed) faculty positions.

Employment outlook

The employment outlook for aerospace engineers is expected to be stable through the year 2005. Most openings will be for those positions left by engineers retiring and transferring. Although the defense industry is expected to spend less for military aircraft, missiles, and other aerospace systems in the late 1990s, there is anticipation of further spending in the private sector. The present fleet of commercial aircraft is aging and will need to be replaced with newer, more technologically advanced (faster, quieter, and more fuel-efficient) vehicles. A continued demand for business aircraft, helicopters, and spacecraft is also expected.

Aerospace engineers also have opportunities in non-aerospace industries, such as ground and water transportation, communications, construction, and energy. For example, these engineers have historically been part of design teams that develop automobiles and boats. They also are called upon to design many types of structures that must withstand severe winds, like high- rise buildings.

Earnings

Starting salaries for aerospace engineers with a bachelor's degree are generally much higher than those for most other occupations. In the early 1990s, entry-level aerospace engineers earn a yearly average of $30,509; after a number of years' experience, they earn about $32,000 to $41,500. Those with graduate degrees earn usually between $35,000 and $50,000 in their first post-graduate jobs. Engineers with many years of experience can earn up to $70,000 and more per year.

Workers in government jobs do not earn as much as those in private industry (anywhere from $14,000 to $8,000 less than comparable civilian jobs). However, both sectors tend to award the basic benefits such as paid vacations, health insurance, and pension plans.

Conditions of work

Aerospace engineers work in various settings depending on their job description. Many aircraft-related engineering jobs are found in Texas, Washington, and California. Those involved in research and design usually work at desks in well-lit air-conditioned offices. They spend much time at computers and drawing boards. Engineers involved with the testing of components and structures often work outside at test sites or at locations where controlled testing conditions can be created; these places can be considered large laboratories.

In the manufacturing area of the aerospace industry, engineers often work on the factory floor itself, assembling components and making sure that they conform to design specifications. This job requires much walking around large production facilities, like aircraft factories or spacecraft assembly plants.

Engineers are sometimes required to travel to other locations to consult with companies that make materials and other needed components. Many also go to remote test sites to observe and participate in flight testing.

Aerospace engineers are also employed with the Federal Aviation Administration (FAA) and commercial airline companies. Here they may perform a variety of duties, including performance analysis and crash investigations. Companies that are involved with satellite communications need the expertise of aerospace engineers to better interpret the many aspects of the space environment and the problems involved with getting a satellite launched into space.

GOE: 05.01.07; SIC: 8711; SOC: 1622

◇ SOURCES OF ADDITIONAL INFORMATION

Aerospace Education Foundation
1501 Lee Highway
Arlington, VA 22209

American Institute of Aeronautics and Astronautics
370 L'Enfant Plaza
Washington, DC 20024

University of North Dakota
International Aerospace Camp
Box 8216 University Station
Grand Forks, ND 58202

Junior Engineering Technical Society
1420 King Street, Suite 405
Alexandria, VA 22314

Agribusiness technicians

Definition

Agribusiness technicians use their business, economics, and agriculture background to organize, operate, and manage farms and agricultural businesses. Agribusiness technicians, also called *agricultural business technicians*, work in businesses which propagate plants and animals; produce agricultural supplies and services; and process and market agricultural products.

Agribusiness technicians also help provide farmers with financial credit, power, fuel, transportation services, and other farm supplies and services. They may help arrange contracts for the marketing, delivery, and processing of farmers' products.

History

Agribusiness technology, a relatively new field, stems from the application of science, technology, and business management techniques to the field of agriculture. As late as the early 19th century, there were virtually no agricultural businesses to provide farms with goods and services, or to market their products. Instead, the typical family farm raised its own horses and oxen, grew its own seed, made its own implements, and built its own buildings, usually from materials at hand. In addition, most of the produce was consumed by the family itself.

Agricultural businesses began appearing in the middle of the 19th century, with the introduction of the reaper and moldboard. It was not until the self-propelled gasoline tractor was introduced in the late 19th and early 20th centuries that it became profitable to supply farmers with machinery and equipment.

The systematic application of scientific knowledge to the problems of agriculture began to reach significant levels by the late 19th century. By 1910, the value of commercial fertilizer had been demonstrated, but farmers still resisted using it because of its high price. Further research found ways to lower the cost and improve application methods—all of which lead to its popular and widespread use today.

Similarly, developments in seed and feed started out slowly in the early part of this century. It was not until after World War II that the scientific feeding of livestock became a successful commercial industry. Genetic developments improved many varieties of seeds, especially corn, and so caught on quickly. Today the seed industry produces seeds for a wide variety of crops.

On the business side, agribusiness has profited because farmers started selling those products they once consumed. This shift, which created needs for transportation, processing, storing, selling, and marketing, was already well on its way during the 19th century. However, new technology and business strategies have expanded possibilities, creating new opportunities and markets for those who process, distribute, and sell farm products.

Thus, because of this century's developments in science, technology, and business techniques, the industry has grown from supplying farmers with a narrow range of manufactured items (such as tools and harnesses) to a thriving enterprise supplying a wide variety of goods and services needed on the farm. This entire field has grown so rapidly that it is virtually a new area of endeavor for each generation. In fact, the development of agribusiness has been so rapid that the profession of agribusiness technician is still relatively unknown outside of the agricultural community.

A cotton researcher from a southern university brings many agribusiness technicians together to discuss the latest development in cotton production.

Nature of the work

Agribusiness technicians perform in several very different capacities. The three main areas of employment are: management of an agricultural business or one closely related to agriculture; sales, services, and distribution; and record keeping.

Technicians can find employment in the area of business management with large farms or farm-service businesses. For instance, they may work as part of a personnel-management office for a large corporate farm or dairy. In such a position, they may hire and fire employees, coordinate work plans with farm managers, and oversee the entire structure of salaries for farm or other production workers.

Agribusiness technicians may also work for credit institutions to: solicit the business of farmers and agricultural business people, make appraisals of real estate and personal property, organize and present loan requests, close loans, and service those loans with periodic reviews of the borrower's management performance and financial status.

Another option is to work in a field capacity for a food company or other business that buys farm products. Two kinds of technician careers are the *dairy production field-contact technician* and the *poultry field-service technician.*

Dairy production field-contact technicians serve as contact people between dairy companies and the farms which produce the milk. They negotiate long- or short-term contracts to purchase milk and milk products according to agreed specifications; meet with farmers to test milk for butterfat content, sediment, and bacteria; and to discuss ways to solve milk-production problems and improve production. They may, for instance, suggest methods of feeding, housing, and milking to improve production or comply with sanitary regulations. They may set up truck routes to haul milk to the dairy; solicit membership in cooperative associations; or even sell items such as dairy-farm equipment, chemicals, and feed to the farmers they contact.

Poultry field-service technicians represent food-processing companies or cooperative associations. They inspect farms to insure compliance with agreements involving facilities, equipment, sanitation, and efficiency; they also advise farmers on how to improve the quality of their products. Technicians may examine chickens for evidence of disease and growth rate to determine the effectiveness of medication and feeding programs. They may then recommend changes in equipment or procedures to improve production. They inform farmers of new techniques, government regulations, and company or association production standards so they can upgrade their farms to meet requirements. They may recommend laboratory testing of feeds, diseased chickens, and diet supplements. In these cases, they often gather samples and take them to a laboratory for analysis. They report their findings on farm conditions, laboratory tests, their own recommendations, and farmers' reactions to the company or association employing them.

Agribusiness technicians are also employed in sales and services. One example of such service is aerial crop spraying. Technicians contact farmers to offer cost estimates based on acreage involved, crops grown, insecticide needed, and other factors, including physical hazards involved. Other services include the distribution of farm produce on both a national and international level, advisory and support services from food-processing companies, and insurance coverage against fire or liability.

Another employment option for agribusiness technicians is in record keeping. The records that farmers and other agricultural business people must keep are becoming more detailed and varied every year. Agribusiness technicians may set up complete record-keeping systems. They analyze records and help farmers make management decisions based on the facts accumulated. Computerized record keeping is common now, so there is a tremendous need for agricultural records technicians who can easily use this equipment and help farmers get maximum benefit from the output. Technicians are needed to gather information for specific enterprises, sometimes deciding what data is necessary and how the problem can best be presented to the computer. Further, they analyze the output and make practical applications of the information.

The following paragraphs describe some specific jobs held by agribusiness technicians; each position is appropriate for entry-level agribusiness technicians.

Beginning technicians often work as *sales representatives* for agricultural products or services, including grease and oils, farm record systems, or farm machinery.

Agribusiness technicians may work as *farm sales representatives,* finding the best markets for the produce of farms on a local, state, or national level. They travel quite a bit and work closely with records technicians or other personnel of the farm or farms they represent.

Farm representatives work for banks, cooperatives, or federal lending institutions. They sell their organizations' services to farmers or agricultural business people, make appraisals, and do the paperwork involved in lending money.

Purchasing agents do all the buying for a large farm or farm-service business, purchasing large quantities at lower per-unit costs.

Food-processing field-service technicians, sometimes called *field-contact technicians,* furnish advice to farmers and sell the services of the food-processing company to the farms.

Requirements

Three qualities are necessary for successful agribusiness technicians. First, they must be able to work well with other people, which includes being able to delegate responsibility and to establish friendly relations with farmers, laborers, and other contact people. Second, agribusiness technicians must analyze management problems and make sound decisions based on existing data. And, third, they must be able to communicate well with others. They should be able to present written and oral reports; offer comments and advice clearly; and, when necessary, train other workers for a particular job.

A high school diploma is an absolute necessity for anyone interested in becoming an agribusiness technician. While in high school, interested students should take the broadest possible selection of courses, specifically, social studies; laboratory science (biology, chemistry, or physics); mathematics; and, if possible, agriculture and business. English literature and composition will be particularly helpful, since oral and written communications are central to the work of the agribusiness technician.

After completion of high school, it is necessary to train in a two-year agricultural or technical college. The program will provide basic economic theory; training in analyzing and solving practical problems; and intensive communications training, such as public speaking and report writing.

Typical first-year courses in an agricultural or technical college include English, biology, health and physical education, introductory animal husbandry, principles of accounting, agricultural economics, microbiology, botany, introductory data processing, soil science, and principles of business.

Typical second-year courses include marketing agricultural commodities, farm management, social science, agricultural finance, agricultural marketing institutions, forage and seed crops, personnel management, and agricultural records and taxation.

Opportunities for experience and exploration

High school students interested in this field should seek summer or part-time employment in their desired specialty area—for example, a clerical job in a farm insurance agency, or a laborer in a feed and grain company. Because many technical colleges offer evening courses, it might be possible to obtain permission during senior year to audit a course or even to take it for future college credit.

Once enrolled in junior college, supervised occupational experience is an integral part of the educational program, further helping the student to decide upon a specialty area.

Methods of entering

Summer employment often leads to an offer of a permanent job with the same employer if the person has made a favorable impression. College faculty members are often another good source of job leads; they have personal contacts outside the campus, and many employers get in touch with them directly.

In addition, employers carry on recruitment programs, post flyers on college bulletin boards, or use college enrollment lists to reach prospective employees through direct mail.

Agribusiness technicians need only be interested in their vocation and have the initiative to look around them. Employers usually seek out their services.

Advancement

The ultimate aim of many technicians is to own a business. Technicians can start their own companies in any agricultural business area, or act as independent agents under contract to perform specific services for a group of firms. For example, an experienced agribusiness technician may purchase data-processing equipment time, set up necessary programs, collect data, and return an analysis of data to firms contracting for the service.

Other technicians develop careers as consultants or market researchers. In farm insurance, they may advance from writing insurance policies to become claims adjuster or underwriter for their company.

Some other positions that experienced agribusiness technicians might hold include:

Farm managers oversee all operations of a farm, work closely with owners and other management, customers, and all farm departments on larger farms.

Regional farm credit managers supervise several of a bank's farm representatives. They may suggest needed training for these farm representatives, recommend changes in lending procedures, and conduct personal audits of randomly selected farm accounts.

Sales managers act as liaisons between company sales representatives and individual dealers, distributors, or farmers.

Employment outlook

The employment outlook for this profession is moderately good. As small farms continue to give way to large corporate farms, the technician's services will be in increasing demand. The large corporate farm, as never before, requires highly trained specialists to handle its vast and diversified management operations. Since the demand for such people exceeds the supply, numerous employment opportunities will most likely be available into the 21st century.

Earnings

Annual starting salaries for agribusiness technicians with a two-year college degree range approximately from $14,000 to $18,000, with reasonable advances to be expected with growing experience, especially in the sales area. Senior technicians may earn $25,000 a year or more.

Fringe benefits vary widely, depending upon the employer. Some amount to as much as one-third of the base salary. More employers are providing such benefits as pension plans, paid vacations, company insurance, and tuition refunds for further education. For those working in relatively remote or isolated areas, recreational facilities and programs are often provided.

Conditions of work

Because the field is so large, working conditions vary greatly. Those who work in sales are likely to travel a good deal, with a few nights spent on the road or even a few weeks spent out of the country. Technicians employed by banks or data-processing services usually work in clean, pleasant surroundings. The technician who goes into farm management or who owns a farm needs to work outdoors in all kinds of weather.

Technicians must be able to delegate responsibility and authority and follow up on these assignments until a project is completed satisfactorily. They should be able to demonstrate a particular job physically as well as theoretically (i.e., be willing to get their hands dirty when necessary); be able to establish rapport with both their superiors and their subordinates; be well informed on their specialties, and willing to keep this information current.

Agribusiness technicians are often confronted with problems requiring careful thought and decision. They must be able to remain calm when things get hectic, to make sound decisions, and then to stand by their decisions in the face of possible disagreement. It is a profession that requires initiative, self-reliance, and the ability to accept responsibilities which may bring blame at times of failure as well as substantial rewards for successful performance. For those technicians who possess the qualities of leadership and a strong interest in the agricultural business, it can be a challenging, exciting, and highly satisfying profession.

GOE: 03.01.01, 08.01.03; SIC: 8748; SOC: 1449, 5627

Canadian Agricultural Economic Society
#907, 151 Slater Street
Ottawa ON K1P 5H4

U.S. Department of Agriculture
Department of Public Information
Washington, DC 20250

◇ SOURCES OF ADDITIONAL INFORMATION

National FFA Organization
National FFA Center
PO Box 15160
Alexandria, VA 22309

Agribusiness Council
2550 M Street, NW
Suite 300
Washington, DC 20037

Agriculture Council of America
1250 I Street, NW
Suite 601
Washington, DC 20005

Agricultural and Industrial Manufacturers Representatives Association
5818 Reeds Road
Mission, KS 66202

◇ RELATED ARTICLES

Volume 1: Agriculture; Business Management; Food Processing; Sales
Volumes 2–4: Agricultural-equipment technicians; Agricultural extension service workers; Animal production technicians; Bookkeeping and accounting clerks; Buyers, wholesale and retail; Credit analysts, banking; Dairy products manufacturing workers; Data-processing technicians; Farm crop production technicians; Farmers; Farm equipment mechanics; Food technologists; Grain merchants; Management analysts and consultants; Manufacturers' sales workers; Meat packing production workers

Agricultural equipment technicians

Definition

Agricultural equipment technicians work with an array of modern farm machinery; they assemble, adjust, operate, maintain, modify, test, and even help design it. Such machinery includes automatic animal feeding systems; milking machine systems; and tilling, planting, harvesting, irrigating, drying, and handling equipment. They also often supervise skilled mechanics and other workers who keep machines and systems operating at maximum efficiency.

History

When primitive people ceased to be nomadic hunters and started to plant grains and fiber-producing crops, they slowly developed tools for planting, tilling, harvesting, and processing farm products. First, these primitive farmers developed hand tools; then, over the centuries, came tools powered by oxen and horses, which greatly increased the farmer's productivity.

The Industrial Revolution, which brought great advances in the design and use of specialized machinery for strenuous and repetitive work, quickly spread to agricultural production. In 1831 Cyrus McCormick's reaper was the forerunner of modern agricultural equipment.

The combined efforts of governmental experiment stations, which developed high-yielding, standardized varieties of farm crops, and the agricultural equipment-producing companies brought rapid development in farm machinery during the first half of the twentieth century.

In the late 1930s, the abundance of inexpensive petroleum fuels made gasoline and diesel engines economical for farm machinery. During the early 1940s, the resulting explosion in complex and powerful farm machinery multiplied production and replaced most of the horses and mules used on farms in the United States.

In part because of advances in mechanization, today's farmer in the United States can produce on average enough agricultural output to feed and clothe more than fifty people, whereas the average production of farmers in other countries serves the needs of fewer than ten people. Agricultural products are now among the most important export commodities for our nation.

Modern farming is heavily dependent upon very complex and expensive machinery. It therefore requires highly trained and skilled technicians and farm mechanics to install, operate, maintain, and modify the machinery that ensures the nation's farm productivity.

Recent developments in agricultural mechanization and automation make the career of agricultural equipment technicians both challenging and rewarding. Sophisticated machines are being used to plant, cultivate, harvest, and process food; to contour, drain, and renovate land; and to clear land and harvest forest products in the process. Qualified agricultural equipment technicians are needed not only to service and sell this equipment, but also to manage it on the farm.

Farming is big business and is becoming increasingly competitive. The successful farmer may have very large amounts of money invested in land and machinery, perhaps hundreds of thousands or millions of dollars. For this investment to pay off, it is vital that the machinery be kept in good operating condition and that it be ready to go when needed. Thus prompt, reliable service from the farm equipment manufacturer and dealer is necessary for the success of both farmer and dealer. Interruptions or delays because of poor service are costly for everyone involved. To provide proper service, manufacturers and dealers need technicians and specialists who possess agricultural and engineering knowledge, in addition to technical skills.

Nature of the work

Agricultural equipment technicians work in a wide variety of jobs both on and off the farm. In general, most agricultural equipment technicians find employment in one of three areas: equipment manufacturing, equipment sales and services, and on-farm equipment management.

Technicians employed by equipment manufacturing firms are involved principally with design and testing of agricultural equipment such as farm machinery; irrigation, power, and electrification systems; soil and water conservation equipment; and agricultural harvesting and processing equipment. There are two kinds of technicians working in this field: the *agricultural engineering technician* and the *agricultural equipment test technician.*

Agricultural engineering technicians usually work directly under the supervision of design engineers. They prepare original layouts and complete detailed drawings of agricultural equipment. They also review plans, diagrams, and blueprints to ensure that new products comply with company standards and design specifications; to do this they must use their knowledge of biological, engineering, and design principles. They also maintain a working knowledge of all equipment and materials used in the industry to assure appropriate utilization.

Agricultural equipment test technicians check experimental and production agricultural machinery and equipment, testing motors, tractors, and accessories to evaluate their performance. In particular, they make sure the equipment conforms with operating requirements, such as horsepower, resistance to vibration, and strength and hardness of parts. They test under actual field conditions on company-operated research farms and under more controlled conditions, using test equipment and recording instruments such as bend-fatigue machines, dynamometers, strength testers, hardness meters, analytical balances, and electronic recorders.

Test technicians also record the data gathered during these tests; compute values such as horsepower and tensile strength using algebraic formulas; and subsequently report their findings using graphs, tables, sketches, and descriptions of test procedures and results in test data logs.

Some test technicians evaluate depth of tillage or harvesting capabilities for different types of crops using agricultural equipment attachments.

After the design and testing phases are complete, other agricultural equipment technicians work with engineers to perform any necessary adjustments in the equipment design. By performing these functions under the general supervision of the design engineer, technicians do the engineers' "detective work" allowing them to devote more time to research and development.

Three agricultural equipment technicians inspect a new tractor. Given the expense of such large tractors, it is important that the tractors remain in excellent condition. Thus, the technicians service them on a regular basis.

Large agricultural machinery companies may employ agricultural equipment technicians to supervise production, assembly, and plant operations.

Most manufacturers market their products through regional sales organizations to individual dealers. Technicians may serve as sales representatives of regional sales offices, where they are assigned a number of dealers in a given territory and sell agricultural equipment directly to them. They may also conduct sales-training programs for those dealers to help them demonstrate and sell equipment to farmers.

These technicians are also qualified for sales work within dealerships, either as equipment sales workers or parts clerks. These technicians should be able to demonstrate to customers various features of the equipment and to appraise the value of used equipment for trade-in allowances. Technicians in these positions may advance to sales or parts manager positions.

Some technicians involved in sales become *systems specialists*. They work for equipment dealerships assisting farmers to plan for and install various kinds of mechanized systems, such as irrigation or materials-handling systems, grain bins or drying systems.

In the service area, technicians may work as *field service representatives* forming a liaison between the companies they represent and the dealers. They assist the dealers in product warranty work, diagnose service problems, and update dealer service personnel on new service information and techniques. Some technicians in this area specialize in public relations work or they may hold dealer service training sessions.

These service technicians may begin their careers as specialists in certain kinds of repairs. *Hydraulic specialists*, for instance, maintain and repair the component parts of hydraulic systems in tractors and other agricultural machines. *Diesel specialists* rebuild, calibrate, and test diesel pumps, injectors, and other diesel engine components.

Many service technicians aim for the position of *service manager* or *parts department manager*. Service managers assign duties to the repair workers, diagnose tractor and machinery problems, estimate repair costs for customers, and efficiently manage the repair shop.

Parts department managers in equipment dealerships maintain proper inventories of all the parts that may be requested either by customers or by the service departments of the dealership. They deal directly with customers, parts suppliers, and dealership managers, and so must be good at both sales and purchasing, as well as being effective business managers.

AGRICULTURAL EQUIPMENT TECHNICIANS

Technicians working on the farm have varied activities—the most important is to keep machinery in as nearly perfect working condition as possible during the growing season. During off-season periods they may overhaul or modify equipment, or simply keep the machinery in good working order for the next season.

Some technicians find employment as *on-farm machinery managers*. These technicians usually work on large farms servicing or supervising the servicing of all automated equipment. They also monitor the field operation of all machines and keep complete records of costs, utilization, and repair procedures relating to the maintenance of each piece of mechanical equipment.

Requirements

Agricultural equipment technicians must often function as engineering-type technicians. They must have a knowledge of physical science and engineering principles, along with the mathematical techniques that support these principles. They must have a working knowledge of farm crops, machinery, and the related products used with them.

A high school diploma is a necessity for anyone planning further education in the field of agricultural equipment technology. The high school curriculum should include: as much mathematics as is available, four years of English and language skills, social sciences, natural sciences (especially those with laboratory sections), mechanical drawing, shop work, and any other pre-engineering or practical mechanics courses that the school offers.

Vocational agriculture courses, while not absolutely necessary, are extremely useful to help future technicians understand the needs and problems of the farmers with whom they will be working. Many people, educated in urban areas without access to such programs at the high school level, have graduated from two-year agricultural technician programs in community or technical colleges, technical institutes, or four-year colleges and have found highly successful careers in this field.

Because agricultural equipment technicians may work in either sales or engineering positions, their curriculum at both the high school and the post-secondary level should be oriented toward both fields.

The post-secondary curriculum for the agricultural equipment technician should include courses in general agriculture, agricultural power and equipment, practical engineering, hydraulics, agricultural-equipment business methods, electrical equipment, engineering, social science, economics, and sales techniques. On-the-job experience during the summer is invaluable, and is frequently included as part of the regular curriculum. Students are placed on a farm, functioning as technicians-in-training. They may also work in an approved farm equipment dealership where their time is divided between the sales, parts, and service departments. Occupational experience, one of the most important phases of the post-secondary training program, gives students an opportunity to discover which field best suits them and which phase of the business they prefer. Upon completion of this program, most technical and community colleges award an associate degree.

Typical agricultural equipment technology courses offered during the first year of a two-year program include communication skills; drawing, sketching, and diagramming; agricultural machinery; technical physics and mathematics; diesel and gasoline engines; hydraulics; technical reporting; and business organization.

Second-year courses may include equipment selling, distributing, and servicing; hydraulic equipment and air conditioning; principles of farm mechanization, computers, and automatic controls; materials handling; power unit testing and diagnosis; advanced agricultural equipment; and agricultural business management and accounting.

It is still possible to enter this career by starting as an inexperienced worker in a machinery manufacturer's plant or on a farm with considerable mechanized equipment. This approach is becoming increasingly difficult because of the machinery's complexity. Because of this, some formal classroom training is necessary, and many people find it difficult to complete even part-time study of the field's theory and science while also working a full-time job.

Opportunities for exploration

Possibilities for exploring the career of agricultural equipment technician are more plentiful for persons who live in farming areas. However, even those who live in towns or cities away from farm work can explore and become acquainted with this career.

Vocational agriculture education programs in high schools may be found in most rural settings and many suburban settings and even in some urban schools. The teaching staff and counselors in these schools can provide considerable information about the career.

Light industrial machinery is used for so many purposes in both the country and the city that it is always possible to watch it being used and to talk with people who own, operate, and repair it.

Summer and part-time work on a farm, in an agricultural equipment manufacturing plant, or in an equipment sales and service business offers opportunities to work on or near agricultural and light industrial machinery. Such a job may provide a clearer idea about the various activities, challenges, rewards, and possible limitations of this career.

Methods of entering

The demand for qualified agricultural equipment technicians exceeds the supply. Operators and managers of large, well-equipped farms and farm equipment companies in need of employees keep in touch with colleges offering agricultural equipment programs. Students who do well during their occupational experience period usually have an excellent chance of going to work for the same employer after graduation. Many colleges have an interview day on which personnel representatives of manufacturers, distributors, farm owners or managers, and dealers are invited to recruit students completing technician programs. In general, any student who does well in a training program can expect employment immediately upon graduation.

A moderate percentage of students in agricultural technician programs are sons, daughters, or other close relatives of farm owners and operators. They are often assured immediate employment by returning full-time to the farm in which they may have an ownership interest. These enterprising students have prepared themselves to be future owners and operators of farms in the best way possible to assure success.

Advancement

Opportunities for advancement and self-employment are excellent for those with the initiative to keep abreast of continuing developments in the farm equipment field. Technicians often attend company schools in sales and service or take advanced evening courses in colleges.

Employment outlook

Agricultural equipment businesses now demand more know-how than ever before. A variety of complex specialized machines and mechanical devices are steadily being produced and modified to help farmers improve the quality and productivity of their labor. These machines require trained technical workers to design, produce, test, sell, and service them. Trained workers are also needed to instruct the final users in their proper repair, operation, and maintenance.

The demand for agricultural equipment technicians is great and should increase as our growing population catches up with our ability to produce food, fiber, and shelter. Additionally, the need will grow as we increase our export of agricultural products to foreign markets in exchange for raw materials, oil, and other goods.

As agriculture becomes more technical, the agricultural equipment technician assumes an increasingly vital role in helping farmers solve problems that interfere with efficient production. These opportunities exist not only in the United States but also worldwide, as agricultural economies everywhere become mechanized. Inventive technicians with training in modern business principles will find expanding employment opportunities abroad.

Technological advances in power and equipment offer many new employment opportunities. Automated forest products machines, light industrial equipment, and automated lawn and garden equipment are only a few allied fields that are undergoing change and growth.

Earnings

Starting salaries for agricultural equipment technicians range from approximately $13,700 to more than $18,000 per year for those who have graduated from a two-year technical or community college. After more training and experience, technicians may earn a much larger salary (often ranging from $20,000 to $35,000). Those working on farms often receive room and board as a supplement to and incentive above their annual salary. The salary that technicians eventually receive depends, as do most salaries, on individual ability, initiative, and the supply of skilled technicians in the field of work or locality.

In addition to their salaries, most technicians receive fringe benefits such as health and retirement packages, paid vacations, and other benefits usually received by engineering technicians.

Technicians employed in sales usually are paid on an incentive basis. They may receive a bonus from farm equipment sales in addition to their basic salary.

Conditions of work

Working conditions vary according to the type of field chosen: farm machinery applications, care, and management; research, development, and manufacturing; customer equipment servicing and maintenance; or sales.

The technician who is a part of a large farming operation might work either indoors or outdoors depending on the season and the tasks that need to be done. Planning schedules of machine overhaul and the directing of such work usually are done in enclosed spaces equipped for such work. As the name implies, field servicing and repair are done outside in the field.

Some agricultural equipment sales representatives work in their own or in nearby communities; others must travel widely. Work hours vary according to the distances between customers and their accessibility.

In agricultural equipment research, development, and production, technicians usually work under typical factory conditions: some in an office or laboratory; others in a manufacturing area; or, in some cases, field testing and demonstration must be performed where the machinery is to be used.

For technicians who assemble, adjust, modify, or test equipment, and for those who provide customer service, application studies, and maintenance services, the surroundings may be similar to large automobile service centers.

In all cases, safety precautions must be a constant concern. Appropriate clothing, cleaning up oil spills and other dirt in workplaces, and careful lifting or hoisting of heavy machinery must be a way of life. While safety practices have improved greatly over the years, certain risks do exist. Heavy lifting may cause injury, and burns and cuts are always possible. The surroundings may be noisy and grimy. Some of the work is performed in cramped or awkward positions. Gasoline fumes and odors from oil products are a constant factor. The technician ordinarily works a forty-hour week, but emergency repairs may require working overtime.

Successful agricultural equipment technicians must have a good scientific and engineering background combined with technical skills. They must be reliable and willing to work outdoors. A farm background is desirable, but not essential.

The challenge of constant change in agricultural equipment and in farming methods is a part of this career. The technician can expect new types of farming procedures, new hybrids and strains of crops and livestock, and new techniques for soil conservation and use. In the next several decades, new methods must be found to turn marginally productive land into economically efficient acreage. This becomes increasingly important as millions of acres of prime crop-production land are covered by buildings, cities, and roads or are eroded away and lost to productive farm use.

Skilled agricultural equipment technicians can find work suited to their personalities: they can work independently or with others, indoors or outdoors, and can either travel or work in one place. They are important to the community's and nation's well-being because they help to produce needed food and fiber commodities.

GOE: 05.01.07, 05.03.07; SIC: 7699; SOC: 3719, 389

◇ **SOURCES OF ADDITIONAL INFORMATION**

U.S. Department of Agriculture
Washington, DC 20250

Accreditation Board for Engineering and Technology
345 East 47th Street
New York, NY 10017

National FFA Organization
PO Box 15160
Alexandria, VA 22309

Agricultural and Industrial Manufacturers Representatives Association
5818 Reeds Road
Mission, KS 66202

Farm and Industrial Equipment Institute
410 North Michigan Avenue
Chicago, IL 60611

◇ **RELATED ARTICLES**

Volume 1: Agriculture; Engineering; Machining and Machinery

Volumes 2–4: Agribusiness technicians; Farm equipment mechanics; Farmers; Industrial machinery mechanics; Manufacturers' sales workers

Agricultural extension service workers

Definition

Agricultural extension service workers distribute information and instructions concerning improved methods of agriculture and home economics to the country's rural population. They advise farmers regarding farm management, crops and their rotation, varieties of seeds, fertilization, soil conservation, livestock breeding and feeding, use of new machinery, and marketing. They also supervise the work of home demonstration agents and counsel young people's clubs.

History

In the late eighteenth century, President George Washington decided to establish an educational agency of the federal government dedicated to assisting the nation's farmers. Washington's proposal eventually developed into what is now known as the Department of Agriculture.

President Thomas Jefferson furthered the plan when he developed the concept of schools for the farmers. This responsibility was eventually delegated to the state agricultural or land–grant colleges established under the Morrill Act of 1862 and promoted by President Abraham Lincoln.

Once established, the state agricultural colleges were not at all certain what agricultural information was factual enough to teach. Through the Hatch Act of 1887, experimental stations were created through which information regarding soils, crops, livestock, fruits, and machinery could be gathered. They became sources of information to both the agricultural colleges and the farmers.

While the method for gathering data was established, one major difficulty still needed to be solved—there was no effective way of getting the information to the farmers without bringing them to the college. The solution was to send people into the field who were familiar with the farmers' work and who were educated in the agricultural sciences. These workers would carry the latest information to the farmers personally so that they could apply it to their farm operations.

Thus, the concept of today's agricultural extension service was developed and placed in operation in 1914 on a federal basis by the passage of the Smith–Lever Act. The service was opened to any state that wished to join the educational project on a cooperative basis, and most states accepted the opportunity. Because of this, every state agricultural college in the nation today has an extension service as one of its major departmental classifications.

Nature of the work

Agricultural extension service workers normally are engaged in teaching agricultural subjects at places other than college campuses. They conduct these educational programs to help people analyze and solve agricultural problems. They cover such areas as soil and crop improvement, livestock, farm machinery, fertilizers, new methods of planting, and any other information that may be of assistance to the farmer. Much of the information is offered on an informal basis, possibly while the farmer is engaged in planting or harvesting or in small evening meetings of five or six farmers. Other information is offered at more formally scheduled meetings and sessions when the extension service worker speaks before larger groups and makes presentations.

County-agricultural agents work closely with federal extension service workers in gathering

AGRICULTURAL EXTENSION SERVICE WORKERS

This agricultural extension service worker explains to a farmer how stubble mulching can protect farmland from soil deterioration.

information to be presented to the farmers. Information on agronomy (theory and practice of soil management and crop production), livestock, marketing, agricultural economics, home economics, horticulture (growing of fruits), and entomology (study of insects) may come either from the state agricultural college or from the federal government's Agricultural Extension Service. The county agricultural worker's job is to review the new information, decide what is most pertinent to local operations, and then present it as effectively as possible to the farmers in that particular area. The county or federal extension service agent's work is primarily educational in nature and is aimed at increasing the efficiency of agricultural production and marketing and the development of new and different markets for agricultural products.

County agricultural agents also work closely with *county home-demonstration agents,* who assist and instruct the homemakers in the county in improving home life. This may include advice on preserving fruits and vegetables, improving nutrition, balancing family budgets, and handling family stress. The home demonstration agent is responsible for keeping up to date in any area relating to the rural home and for sharing this information with the people in a particular county or group of counties.

Four-H Club agents organize and direct the educational projects and activities of the 4-H Club, including analyzing the needs of individuals and the community, developing teaching materials, training volunteers, and organizing exhibits at state and county fairs. Four-H clubs introduce children and adolescents to techniques in raising animals and plants, including breeding, husbandry, and nutrition.

Both the county home-demonstration agents and the county agricultural agents rely on mass communication for spreading information. Newspapers, radio and television broadcasts, and other types of information sources available within the area are used to reach the people who have the greatest need for this information.

There is a degree of specialization involved, especially at the federal level. Federal agricultural extension service workers often become program leaders who are responsible for developing and maintaining relationships with various land–grant colleges, universities, government agencies, and private agencies involved in agriculture. In some cases, they also become educational research and training specialists responsible for developing research programs in all phases of extension work. The results of these programs are shared with the various state agencies. Subject-matter specialists develop programs through which new information can be presented to the farmers effectively, while educational media specialists condense information and distribute it as it becomes available to the states for use in their local extension programs. These extension service workers may be designated as *extension service specialists.* Those at higher supervisory levels, who direct and coordinate the work of other extension service workers, are called *extension service specialists-in-charge.* An extension service worker who is in charge of programs for a group of counties is a *district extension service agent.*

Federal agricultural extension service workers are employed by the U.S. Department of Agriculture to assist county extension officers and supervisors in planning, developing, and coordinating national, regional, and state extension programs. They have their headquarters in Washington, D.C. County agricultural agents are normally employed jointly by the Department of Agriculture and the agricultural college in each state. The work of the federal extension service agent and the county agent is meant to complement and supplement one another.

County agents may also specialize, especially in those counties employing more than two or three agents. Many counties in which different forms of agriculture are conducted will often have five or more agents. The nature of the demands on these workers makes their specialization a necessity. A single county may employ specialists in fruit and grain production, dairying, poultry production, farm machinery, pest control, soils, nursery management, environmental impacts, and livestock.

Requirements

The work of the agricultural extension service worker normally requires a background of practical farming experience and a thorough knowledge of the types of problems confronting farmers. Farmers may naturally prefer to work with people whom they feel have a complete understanding of their work.

Extension service workers are required to have a bachelor's degree, usually with a major in either agriculture or home economics. Those who hope to join the on-campus staff at the state agricultural college are usually expected to have at least a master's degree. The college program will normally include courses in English, history, chemistry, biology, economics, education, sociology, and speech, as well as animal science, crop production, agricultural geology, horticulture, soils, and farm management. A number of colleges have developed regular agricultural extension curriculums to be followed by those hoping to enter the field.

After graduation from college, county agents are kept up to date on the latest programs, policies, and teaching techniques through in-service training programs run by the state agricultural college and the Department of Agriculture. Attendance at such programs may be optional or mandatory.

The high-school student looking forward to a career as an extension service agent should take courses in English literature and composition, algebra, geometry, biology, physics, and the social sciences, including history and political science or government.

Extension agents must enjoy working with people, be assertive without being antagonistic, have a particular affinity for farmers and their problems, and have the ability to teach. They must also be patient and willing to learn from farmers. They should have the ability to organize group projects, meetings, and broad educational programs that both adults and young people involved in agriculture will find stimulating and useful. Agents should have the professional interest and enthusiasm that will enable them to keep up with the huge amount of new agricultural information constantly being released. They must be willing to learn and use the latest teaching techniques to get their information out to the residents of the area.

Opportunities for experience and exploration

Students may explore the work of agricultural extension service agents while in high school by reading the pamphlets and occupational information brochures published about this field, or by visiting with an agricultural extension service agent. Any of the state agricultural colleges will send materials or give interested students the names of extension service agents in a particular area so that the student can write for information. Students may find it possible to visit the agent in the office or in the field.

Another way to learn more is to join groups such as 4-H, the National FFA Organization, Future Homemakers of America, and scouting. Students may volunteer to work at an extension office. It may also be possible to visit with farmers or others engaged in agriculture, thus gaining their impressions of the work carried on by the agricultural extension service agents in their particular county. High school counselors can also assist the young people hoping to gather additional information regarding this field.

Methods of entering

The person entering extension service work will normally need a college diploma. While the college's placement service may be of some help in finding a job, most applicants will need to apply to the director of the extension service at the agricultural college in the state in which they hope to work. If a job vacancy is available, the director of the extension service will screen the qualifications of the various applicants and submit the names to a board or council that will be responsible for making the final selection.

Advancement

Competent agricultural extension agents as a rule are promoted fairly rapidly and early in their careers. The promotions may be in the form of assignments to more responsible positions within the same county, reassignment to a different county within the state, or a raise in salary. Many agents, after moving through a succession of more responsible extension jobs, may join the staff at the state agricultural college. Many directors of existing extension services began their careers in this way.

It is also possible to branch out into other areas. Agricultural extension service agents may often go into related jobs, especially those in industries which specialize in agricultural products. Former extension service agents can sell fertilizer, seed, feed, or farm machinery. The training they have received and their background in agriculture provides for flexibility in employment possibilities.

AGRICULTURAL EXTENSION SERVICE WORKERS

Employment outlook

Agricultural extension service agents are employed in nearly every agricultural county in the nation. In those counties where farmers are producing a number of crops, there may be as many as ten or more agents employed. Approximately 19,775 extension service agricultural agents are currently working in the United States, and the number of jobs is expected to increase at about the rate that is average for all jobs. In the future, their work will branch out and extend to new and additional segments of the population, including the many rural non-farming families and various suburban residents who are coming to recognize the value of the assistance rendered by agricultural extension service workers. In addition, the farming industry is becoming more complex, and a greater degree of specialization will be needed on the part of extension service workers. In the coming years, farm people will become even more aware of the need for their county agents. New farming technologies will need to be explained and applied to individual farms. Extension service agents will be needed in depressed rural areas where their services may help the residents earn better livings for their families.

In addition to this, the idea of agricultural extension service programs is spreading to many foreign countries. There should be an increasing demand for our county and federal agents to assist their counterparts in other countries in setting up and operating agricultural extension service programs.

Earnings

The earnings of agricultural extension service agents vary from state to state and from county to county. The average annual salary of extension agents, however, was $25,000 a year in the 1990s. Salaries for experienced home demonstration agents averaged about $23,000 a year.

Conditions of work

The work itself is often taxing both mentally and physically. Extension service agents with a heavy workload may find themselves faced with problem after problem requiring them to work in the field for long periods of time. They may be in their office handling routine matters every day for a month and then not work in the office for the next six weeks. (Agents usually have a private office where they can speak in confidence with those who seek assistance.) As a rule, agricultural extension service agents spend about half of their time in the field working with farmers on specific problems, scheduling or conducting group meetings, or simply distributing new updated information. They usually drive from 500 to 1,500 miles per month while on the job.

The work may be hard on the agent's family, since evening meetings will be required and the agent will be invited to many weekend activities as well. For example, agents may conduct small informal meetings on Monday and Tuesday nights to discuss particular problems being faced by a small group of farmers in the county. They may be home on Wednesday, work with a student's 4-H club on Thursday, conduct another meeting on Friday, and then judge a livestock show at the county fair on Saturday.

The hours are not regular and the pay is not particularly high for the number of hours put into the job. Agents may often have demands from people who do not understand their function and responsibilities. The job can be rewarding, however. In addition to the opportunity to work out-of-doors, there is the satisfaction of working with people who genuinely appreciate the time, advice, and assistance the agent brings.

In many states the jobs of agricultural agents are under civil service retirement plans, with a minimum retirement age of 62 and an average retirement age of 65. In some states, the agents come under the teachers' retirement program. Both types of plans are usually satisfactory in providing a good pension.

GOE: 11.07.03; SIC: 076; SOC: 239

◇ SOURCES FOR ADDITIONAL INFORMATION

Federal Extension Service
U.S. Department of Agriculture
Washington, DC 20250

Food and Agriculture Careers for Tomorrow
Purdue University
127 Agricultural Administration Building
West Lafayette, IN 47907

You may also want to consult your local county extension office.

Agricultural scientists

Definition

Agricultural scientists study all aspects of living organisms and the relationships of plants and animals to their environment. They may conduct basic research in laboratories or in the field to increase knowledge; then, they may apply this knowledge to such things as increasing crop yields and improving the environment. Some agricultural scientists plan and administer programs for testing foods, drugs, and other products. Others direct activities at public exhibits, like a zoo or botanical garden. Some teach in colleges and universities, or work as consultants to business firms or the government. And some work in technical sales and service jobs for manufacturers of agricultural products.

History

Before 1840, agricultural developments relied on the collected experiences of farmers handed down over generations. In that year, however, Justius von Liebig of Germany published *Organic Chemistry in Its Applications to Agriculture and Physiology,* and launched the systematic development of the agricultural sciences. A formal system of agricultural education soon followed in both Europe and the United States. The history of the various components of agricultural science overlaps that of many disciplines, including biology, botany, genetics, nutrition, breeding, and engineering. Discoveries and improvements in these fields contributed to advances in agriculture. Some milestones include: In the 17th and 18th centuries, the practice of crop rotation and the application of manure as fertilizer greatly increased yields. Farm mechanization became important with the invention of the mechanical reaper in 1831 and the gasoline tractor in 1892. Chemical fertilizers were first used in the 19th century; pesticides and herbicides soon followed. In 1900 the research of a 19th-century Austrian monk, Gregor Johann Mendel, was rediscovered. He used generations of garden peas to test his theories that provided the foundation for the science of genetics.

Nature of the work

Agricultural scientists who apply their knowledge of biology to agricultural matters such as food, fiber, and horticulture have many different titles and duties, some of which are described below.

AGRICULTURAL SCIENTISTS

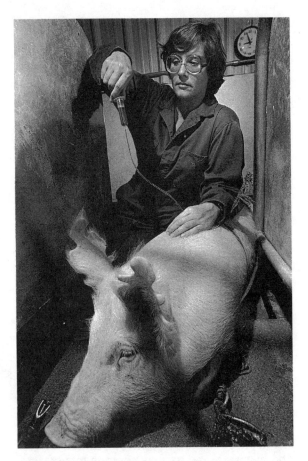

An agricultural scientist takes a blood sampling from a swine for an animal stress study. The study will determine what effects, if any, modern methods of raising livestock have on farm animals.

Agronomists investigate large-scale food-crop problems, conduct experiments, and develop new methods of growing crops to ensure more efficient production, higher yields, and improved quality. They are concerned with the control of plant diseases, pests, and weeds. They also may analyze soils to find ways to increase production and reduce soil erosion.

Animal scientists conduct research in and develop improved methods for housing, breeding, feeding, and controlling diseases of domestic farm animals.

Apiculturists study and do research with bees. They investigate causes of and ways of controlling disease in bees, study the phases and effects of pollination, and experiment in breeding improved bee strains.

Botanists are concerned with plants and their environment, structure, heredity, and economic value in such fields as agronomy, horticulture, and medicine.

Horticulturists study fruit and nut orchards as well as garden plants such as vegetables and flowers. They conduct experiments to develop new and improved varieties to increase crop quality and yields, and to improve plant culture methods for the landscaping and beautification of communities, parks, and homes.

Dairy scientists study the selection, breeding, feeding, and management of dairy cattle. For example, they research how various types of food and environmental conditions affect milk production and quality. They also develop new breeding programs to improve dairy herds.

Poultry scientists similarly study the breeding, feeding, and management of poultry to improve the quantity and quality of eggs and other poultry products.

Animal breeders specialize in improving the quality of farm animals. They may work for a state agricultural department, agricultural extension station, or university. Some of their work is done in a laboratory, but much of it is done outdoors working directly on animals. Using their knowledge of genetics, animal breeders develop systems for breeding economically important animals to achieve desired characteristics such as strength, fast maturation, resistance to disease, and quality of meat.

Plant breeders apply genetics to improve plants' yield, quality, and resistance to harsh weather, disease, and insects. They might work on developing strains of wild or cultivated plants that may prove of economic value.

Plant pathologists research plant diseases and the decay of plant products to identify symptoms, determine causes, and develop control measures. They attempt to predict outbreaks by studying how different soils, climates, and geography affect the spread and intensity of plant disease.

Much of the research conducted by agricultural scientists is done in laboratories and requires a familiarity with research techniques and the use of laboratory equipment and computers. Some research, however, is carried out wherever necessary; thus, a botanist may have occasion to examine the plants that grow in the volcanic valleys of Alaska, or an animal breeder to study the behavior of animals on the plains of Africa.

A worker similar to the agricultural scientist is the *agricultural engineer*, who applies engineering principles to problems in the food and agriculture industries. These engineers design or develop agricultural equipment and machines, supervise their production, and conduct tests on new designs and machine parts. They develop plans and specifications for agricultural buildings and utilities and for drainage and irrigation systems. They work on flood control, soil erosion, and land reclamation projects. They design food processing systems and equipment to convert farm products to consumer foods. Agricultural engineers contribute to making farming easier and more profitable through the introduction of new farm machinery and through advancements in soil and water conservation.

Agricultural engineers in industry may be engaged in *research* or in the *design, testing,* or *sales* of equipment.

Requirements

The educational requirements are exceptionally high for agricultural scientists, and a doctorate is usually mandatory for those who teach in colleges or universities, who are involved in independent research, or who hold administrative or management positions in this field. People with a relevant master's degree may be employed in applied research, that is, the practical application of the findings of basic researchers to specific agricultural problems.

A bachelor's degree may be acceptable for some beginning jobs, and new graduates may be hired as testing or inspecting technicians, or as technical sales or service representatives. Promotions, however, are very limited for these employees unless they earn advanced degrees.

The type of degrees earned must relate directly to agricultural and biological science. Undergraduates should have a firm foundation in biology, with courses in chemistry, physics, and mathematics. Most colleges and universities have agricultural science curriculums, although liberal arts colleges may emphasize the biological sciences. State universities usually offer agricultural science programs, too.

Candidates for advanced degrees in agricultural science usually are required to do fieldwork and laboratory research along with their classroom studies and preparation of a thesis.

Agricultural scientists are expected to be familiar with research techniques and know how to use laboratory equipment and computers. Research in this field may be conducted independently or as part of a group; researchers should be self-motivated enough to work effectively alone, yet able to function cooperatively as a team member when necessary. They also need the ability to communicate their findings both verbally and in writing.

Personal characteristics generally shared by agricultural scientists are an abiding curiosity about the nature of living things and their environment, systematic work habits in their approach to investigation and experimentation, and the persistence to continue or start over

when experiments are not immediately successful.

The work done in offices and laboratories does not require unusual strength, but physical stamina is necessary for those scientists who do field research in remote areas of the world.

People in this field who teach in public schools will have to satisfy the state's requirements for education and experience. Skill in communicating is also of primary importance to those who teach.

Opportunities for experience and exploration

People who are considering careers as agricultural scientists have a number of ways to test their interest in and acquire familiarity with the field.

Students may begin in high school to study courses such as biology, chemistry, physics, and mathematics, and to learn how to operate a computer. It may be possible for some students to act as laboratory assistants to their science teachers. Field trips to research laboratories may be arranged, along with lectures by or interviews with agricultural scientists.

Part-time and summer jobs may provide experience related to the students' goals. Students who have had college courses in biology may find work as laboratory assistants or aides. Graduate students often have the opportunity to work on research projects at their universities. Depending on their age and educational level, other students may consider possible work in such places as hospitals and veterinarian's offices, florist shops, landscape nurseries, orchards, farms, zoos, aquariums, botanical gardens, and museums. Volunteer work is often available in hospitals and animal shelters.

Methods of entering

Agricultural scientists often are recruited prior to graduation. The college or university placement offices are a source of information about jobs, and students may arrange interviews with the recruiters who visit the campus.

Direct application may be made to the personnel departments of colleges and universities, private industries, or nonprofit research foundations. People interested in positions with the federal government may contact the local offices of state employment services and the U.S. Office of Personnel Management, or the Federal Job Information Centers, which are located in various large cities throughout the country. Private employment agencies are another method that might be considered. Large companies sometimes conduct job fairs in major cities and will advertise them in the business sections of the local newspapers.

A less direct way but one that is frequently used by more experienced scientists is to become active in professional associations and to use the personal contacts made there for job referrals and introductions.

Advancement

Advancement in this field depends on education, experience, and quality of job performance. Agricultural scientists with advanced degrees generally start in teaching or research and advance to administrative and management positions, such as supervisor of a research program. The number of such jobs is limited, however, and often the route to advancement is through specialization. The narrower specialties are often the most valuable. The ability of certain programs to obtain financial grants and other funding help the workers involved to advance.

People who enter this field with only a bachelor's degree are much more restricted. After starting in testing and inspecting jobs or as technical sales and service representatives, they may progress to advanced technicians, particularly in medical research, or become high school biology teachers. In the latter case, they must have had courses in education and meet the state requirements for teachers.

Employment outlook

In the 1990s, about 25,000 people work as agricultural scientists in the United States. In addition, several thousand are employed in colleges and universities in both teaching and research. Some also work for the federal, state, or local government. Others work in private industry, mostly for agricultural services, fertilizer, and seed companies. About 3,000 are self-employed.

The employment of agricultural scientists is expected to be good through the late 1990s as private industry gets more involved in such areas as applying biotechnology, including recombinant-DNA research, to agriculture. However, because of decreased funding, there will not be many new positions in federal agencies. Some openings will occur as older, experienced employees retire or leave the field for other reasons.

The outlook is good for persons with advanced degrees; others will face stiff competition. Some holders of agricultural and biological degrees will enter related occupations as agricultural and biological technicians, medical laboratory technologists, or health care professionals.

The field of agricultural science is not much affected by economic fluctuations. Employees involved in teaching, long-term research projects, and agricultural activities rarely lose their jobs during a recession.

Earnings

In the 1990s beginning agricultural scientists with a bachelor's degree earn between $19,700 and $21,200 a year. Average salaries in the federal government vary depending on areas of specialty. For example, employees with a degree in animal science earn about $48,800 a year; those with degrees in horticulture average $40,500.

Conditions of work

Agricultural scientists work regular hours, although researchers may choose to work longer when their experiments have reached a critical point.

They generally work in offices, laboratories, or classrooms where conditions are clean, healthy, and safe. Some agricultural scientists such as botanists periodically take field trips, which require strenuous physical activity and where living facilities are primitive.

GOE: 02.02.02; SIC: 07; SOC: 1853

◇ SOURCES FOR ADDITIONAL INFORMATION

American Dairy Science Association
309 West Clark Street
Champaign, IL 61820

American Society of Agronomy
Crop Science Society of America
Soil Science Society of America
677 South Segoe Road
Madison, WI 53711

National Association of Animal Breeders
Box 1033
Columbia, MO 65205

Office of Higher Education Programs
U.S. Department of Agriculture
Room 350A, Administration Building
14th Street and Independence Avenue SW
Washington, DC 20013

◇ **RELATED ARTICLES**

Air traffic controllers

Definition

Air traffic controllers organize and direct the movement of aircraft into and out of the airport. They issue control instructions and advisories by radio to the pilots to provide for the safe, orderly, and expeditious flow of air traffic both in the air and on the ground.

History

The history of air traffic controllers follows very closely the development of air travel in general. It is difficult to determine when air traffic controllers began their work, but as daily flights increased, some method of control became necessary. Added to these passenger-carrying flights were thousands of cargo or air-freight flights, all of which placed a tremendous traffic burden on the existing airport facilities.

Also, it was necessary that pilots receive in-flight information on weather, other air traffic in their area, and flight conditions in general. Thus, air traffic controllers were employed to assist in carrying out these control functions. The use of *Instrument Landing System* (ILS) allowed the number of planes being tracked to increase dramatically. *Airport Surveillance Radar* allows controllers to survey air activity in a 50-mile radius.

Nature of the work

Almost all air traffic controllers are employees of the Federal Aviation Administration (FAA), which is responsible for ensuring the safe, orderly, and expeditious flow of air traffic. Controllers work in one of three different areas: airport traffic control towers, en route air traffic control centers, or flight service stations.

Tower air traffic control specialists supervise flight operations within a specific area surrounding an airport. These employees are stationed in about 440 airport control towers to issue clearances or authorization to the pilots of planes ready for takeoff, those preparing to land, and those flying within the area. They coordinate the altitudes at which planes within the area will fly and advise the pilots regarding weather, wind direction, and the relative position of other aircraft. Their advice is based on their own observations, information received from the National Weather Service, en route air traffic control centers, flight service stations, aircraft pilots, and other sources.

Controllers maintain separation between landing and departing aircraft, transfer control of planes on instrument flights leaving their airspace to the en route controllers, and receive control of planes on instrument flights coming into their airspace from controllers at adjacent facilities.

Air traffic control specialists control the movements of a number of aircraft within the

AIR TRAFFIC CONTROLLERS

The air traffic controller monitors the flow of airplanes in and out of an airport. Such a task involves intense concentration.

area, and these vehicles usually appear as tiny bars, or "blips," on a radar screen. Because of this, they must be able to recall quickly the registration number of each plane under their control, its type and speed, and its position in the air and must take these facts into consideration as they give instructions and information to other aircraft. They also must remain in contact with the air traffic control centers, to more efficiently control traffic and prevent congestion in the area.

En route air traffic control specialists work at one of 24 regional centers in the United States. They coordinate the movements of en route aircraft between airports but out of range of the airport traffic controllers. Through radar and electronic equipment, they maintain contact with planes within their area, giving instructions, air traffic clearances, and advice about flight conditions. They keep track of all flights within the center's airspace and transfer control of the aircraft to controllers in the adjacent center or to the approach control or terminal when the craft enters that facility's airspace. En route controllers work in teams of two or three, depending on how heavy the traffic is in their area.

Flight service station air traffic control specialists make up the third group of controllers. They provide pre-flight or in-flight assistance to pilots from more than 275 flight service stations linked by a broad communications system. These controllers give pilots information about the station's particular area, including terrain, weather, and anything else necessary to guarantee a safe flight. They may suggest alternate routes or different altitudes, alert pilots to military operations taking place along certain routes, inform them about landing at airports that have no towers, assist pilots in emergency situations, and participate in searches for missing or overdue aircraft.

Requirements

Trainees for air traffic control positions are selected from applicants who receive a high score on a federal civil service examination. The written test measures aptitudes for arithmetic, abstract reasoning, three-dimensional spatial visualization, and other indicators of an ability to learn the controller's duties.

Applicants for airport tower or en route traffic control jobs must be less than 31 years of age, pass physical and psychological examinations, and have vision that is or can be corrected to 20/20.

They must also have completed a four-year degree program in a recognized college or have three years of responsible experience in administrative, professional, investigative, technical, or other types of work that would prepare the applicant to take on a position of great responsibility. Equivalent combinations of the previously mentioned requirements are also considered.

All applicants are interviewed in an effort to determine if the candidates have the required alertness, decisiveness, motivation, the necessary poise, and the ability to work under extreme pressure.

Those accepted into the training program receive 11 to 17 weeks of intensive instruction at the FAA Academy in Oklahoma City. There they receive training in the fundamentals of the airway systems, civil air regulations, radar, and aircraft performance characteristics. They practice on machines designed to simulate emergency situations to determine their emotional stability under pressure. The standards for those who successfully complete this program are very high; about 50 percent of the trainees are dropped during this period.

After completing the program, it takes several years of experience, rigorous on-the-job training, and further study to become a fully qualified controller.

New controllers at airport towers usually begin as ground controllers. As they become progressively more competent, they move up to local controllers, departure controllers, and finally arrival controllers. New en route controllers begin by delivering printed flight plans to teams, before advancing to radar associate controllers and then radar controllers.

Persons hoping to enter the field must be articulate, have a good memory, and self-control. It is imperative that they be able to express themselves clearly, remember rapidly changing data that affects their decisions, and be able to operate calmly under very difficult situations involving a great deal of strain. They must also be able to make good, sound, and quickly derived decisions. A poor decision may mean the loss of a large number of lives.

Special requirements

Air traffic controllers are required to take a physical examination every year and a performance exam twice a year.

The only license they hold is the air traffic control certificate. Failure to become certified within a specific time is cause for dismissal.

Opportunities for experience and exploration

High school students interested in this occupation should arrange a visit for on-site observations of the type of work involved. Talks with those employed in the field also would be helpful.

A number of opportunities exist in the military service for people to gain experience in these and related jobs, which provide an excellent opportunity for exploration while the individual is gaining necessary experience.

Other possibilities include talking with pilots, who see air traffic controllers from a different viewpoint.

Most airlines will supply those interested with all the information available in these two areas, and many will be helpful in arranging interviews either with those employed as traffic controllers or with pilots.

Methods of entering

As might be expected, experience in related fields, including those of pilots, air dispatch operators, navigators, or other positions in the military service, or in actual air control work is a necessity for the person who does not have a college degree, and it is desirable even for those with the degree. Thus, one of the better methods of entering would be to start in one of the related fields, either with a civilian airline or in the military service.

The first step in becoming an air traffic controller starts with the federal civil service system, which requires beginners to pass the written examination, the physical examination, and the interview. Placement is on a competitive basis.

Advancement

After becoming a controller, those who do particularly well may reach the level of supervisor or manager. Many others advance to even more responsible positions in air control, and some might move into the top administrative jobs with the FAA. Competitive civil service status can be earned at the end of one year on the job, and career status after the satisfactory completion of three years of work in the area.

In the case of both airport control specialists and en route control specialists, the responsibilities become more complex with each successive promotion.

Employees in the higher grades may be responsible for a number of different areas, including the coordination of the traffic control activities within the control area; the supervision and training of en route traffic controllers or airport traffic controllers in lower positions, and management in various aeronautical agencies.

Employment outlook

The demand for people in this field is expected to grow slowly through the late 1990s because of the expected production of new, automated control equipment. There will be some increase in opportunities because of greater demand for air travel, but most of the job openings will occur when older, more experienced controllers change employment, retire, or otherwise leave the field. Competition for these jobs will be stiff, however, because the relatively high pay and liberal retirement program of this occupation attract many more qualified applicants than are needed to fill the openings.

The vast majority of all air traffic controllers work for the Federal Aviation Administration, although some work for the Department of Defense. Most air traffic controllers work in control towers at key airfields. Some are employed at air route traffic control centers and flight service stations throughout the United States, Guam, and Puerto Rico. Others are employed by private air traffic control companies to provide service to non-FAA towers.

In this relatively small field, employment opportunities will be best for college graduates and individuals with civil or military experience as controllers, pilots, or navigators. Those who are hired will enjoy more job security than workers in most other occupations. Air traffic controllers may face a decline in their workload during recessions, when there is less demand for air travel, but they are seldom laid off.

Earnings

In the 1990s, trainees start at about $21,400 a year. The average salary for all controllers is about $47,200 a year. Some workers with a great deal of seniority earn much more. Because of the complexity of their job duties and the tension involved in their work, air traffic controllers are offered special dispensation or compensation, including a more liberal retirement program, than other federal employees.

Conditions of work

Depending on length of service, air traffic controllers receive 13 to 26 days of paid vacation and 13 days of paid sick leave per year, plus life insurance and health benefits. In addition, they are permitted to retire earlier and with fewer years of service than other federal employees.

Controllers are employed on a basic 40-hour week, If they work additional hours, they receive overtime pay or equivalent time off. They may be required to work nights and weekends on a rotation basis, because most control towers and centers must be operated 24 hours a day, seven days per week. Usually a higher salary is paid those who work between 6:00 P.M. and 6:00 A.M. This may amount to about 10 percent above the regular base pay.

The working facilities are usually clean, well lighted, and ventilated.

GOE: 05.03.03; SIC: 4581, 9621; SOC: 392

◇ **SOURCES OF ADDITIONAL INFORMATION**

Air Traffic Control Association
2300 Clarendon Boulevard, Suite 711
Arlington, VA 22201

Federal Aviation Administration
Office of Personnel and Training
800 Independence Avenue, SW
Washington, DC 20591

National Association of Air Traffic Specialists
4740 Corridor Place, #C
Beltsville, MD 20705

Canadian Air Traffic Control Association
#1100, 400 Cumberland Street
Ottawa ON K1N 8X3

◇ **RELATED ARTICLES**

Volume 1: Aviation and Aerospace; Military Services; Transportation
Volumes 2–4: Aeronautical and aerospace technicians; Airplane dispatchers; Avionics technicians; Flight engineers; Pilots; Radio and telegraph operators

Air-conditioning, refrigeration, and heating mechanics

Definition

Air-conditioning, refrigeration, and heating mechanics install, repair, and service the machinery used to cool and heat interior environments. Some mechanics specialize in installing new equipment for customers, while other mechanics specialize in service (maintenance and repair) activities. Mechanics may work on just one type of equipment, such as gas furnaces or commercial refrigerators, or they may work with a variety of cooling, refrigeration, and heating systems.

History

Since ancient times, people have come up with many different ways of heating, cooling, and ventilating indoor spaces. In the 20th century, there have been major advances in the methods and equipment used to regulate temperature and air quality inside buildings and in smaller enclosed areas. One of the most important of these advances was the development of synthetic refrigerant gases, such as the various Freon gases. By the 1930s, relatively inexpensive, effective refrigeration systems using such gases were becoming common, replacing stored ice as the usual means of keeping food chilled. By about 1950, similar systems for cooling air were increasingly in use in home air-conditioning units.

In both refrigerators and in simple air conditioners, a refrigerant circulates in a closed cycle through sets of evaporator and condenser coils, first absorbing heat from the place that needs cooling and then discharging the heat outside. The central air-conditioning and heating systems in today's buildings frequently involve equipment based on the same principle, together with a furnace and ducts to carry conditioned air to all parts of the building. Often referred to as environmental control systems, these systems control the temperature, cleanliness, humidity, and even the motion of the air in homes, offices, stores, factories, schools, and other buildings.

Modern heating and cooling equipment greatly improves the comfort and convenience of many aspects of our lives. Refrigerators and freezers allow foods, drugs, and other perishable items to be transported long distances and stored safely for long periods of time. Some manufacturing processes and equipment now rely on precise control of air temperature and quality. Just as the use of climate control equipment and refrigeration has continued to expand in recent decades, the need for skilled mechanics in this field has also grown. The field now provides many different job opportunities. In the 1990s, there are approximately 185,000 air-conditioning, heating, and refrigeration mechanics employed in the United States.

Nature of the work

Air-conditioning, refrigeration, and heating systems often involve many components. Central air-conditioning, for example, uses fans, compressors, condensers, and evaporators to cool and adjust the humidity of air. Then the treated air is distributed throughout a building in a network of metal ducts. To do their job well, mechanics may need to work with a wide variety of mechanical, electrical, and electronic devices, as well as pipes, vents, and duct work.

Some mechanics work on only one type of cooling, heating, or refrigeration equipment. *Window air-conditioning unit installer-servicers,*

An air-conditioning refrigeration mechanic inspects the safety features of an air-conditioning system in an industrial plant.

work on window units only. Some mechanics specialize in either installation or service (maintenance and repair) tasks, but many mechanics handle both kinds of jobs. *Air-conditioning and refrigeration mechanics* install and also service central air-conditioning systems and a variety of refrigeration equipment. The air-conditioning installations may range from small wall units, either water- or air-cooled, to large central plant systems. The commercial refrigeration equipment may include display cases, walk-in coolers, and frozen-food units such as those in supermarkets, restaurants, and food processing plants.

To install new equipment, air-conditioning and refrigeration mechanics travel to private homes, office buildings, stores, factories, hotels, restaurants, and new construction sites. In the course of installing equipment, mechanics follow blueprints, design specifications, and manufacturers' recommended procedures. They must be good welders, solderers, and pipe fitters to be able to connect together the duct work, refrigerant lines, and electric power source. After completing the installation, the mechanics must check their work, using various testing devices.

In maintenance work, these mechanics inspect and examine the various parts of the system to detect leaks and other faults. They must adjust compressors and motors, as well as thermostatic controls to keep temperatures at specified levels.

When mechanics are called on to repair equipment, they often must first diagnose the cause of a breakdown. To do this, they may disassemble brushes, valves, springs, and connections to inspect their condition. After the trouble is located, they may need to install new piping, packing, valves, pipe couplings, or other parts, or they may completely overhaul a pump or a compressor to put the equipment back into working order.

In carrying out repairs, mechanics are careful not to let the refrigerant gases escape, because they often contain chemicals called chlorofluorocarbons (CFCs). If CFCs are released into the earth's atmosphere, they contribute to the breakdown of the planet's protective ozone layer, endangering plant and animal life everywhere. By trapping the gases in special containers and recycling CFCs, mechanics can help keep the earth's ozone layer from being depleted.

Other mechanics are *furnace installers*, also called *heating-equipment installers*. Following blueprints and other specifications, they install oil, gas, electric, solid-fuel (such as coal), and multi-fuel heating systems. They move the new furnace into place and attach fuel supply lines, air ducts, pumps, and other components. Then they connect the electrical wiring and thermostatic controls, and, finally, they check the unit for proper operation.

Maintenance and repair of the oil- and gas-burning equipment may be handled by other specialized mechanics. *Oil-burner mechanics* maintain and repair oil-fueled heating systems to keep them in good operating condition. If a system is not working properly during cold weather, oil-burner mechanics may clean burner nozzles, check and adjust the thermostat and other furnace controls, and replace broken parts to correct the problem. More extensive maintenance work is routinely done in the warm weather, when the heating system can be shut down. Usually during the summer, mechanics replace oil and air filters; vacuum vents, ducts, and other parts that accumulate soot and ash; and adjust the burner so that it achieves maximum efficiency in operation.

Gas-burner mechanics, also called *gas-appliance servicers*, have duties similar to those of oil burner mechanics, except that they maintain and repair gas-fueled heating systems. Their work also changes with the season. During the winter they mostly make repairs and adjustments to correct malfunctions. In the summer they inspect and clean systems to get them ready for the heating season. Gas-burner mechanics may also repair other gas appliances such as cooking stoves, clothes dryers, water heaters, outdoor lights, and grills.

Other air-conditioning, refrigeration, and heating mechanics who specialize in a limited range of equipment include *evaporative cooler installers, hot-air furnace installer-and-repairers, solar-energy system installers and helpers,* and *air and hydronic balancing technicians.*

In their work on refrigerant lines and air ducts, air-conditioning, refrigeration, and heating mechanics use a variety of hand and power tools, including hammers, wrenches, metal snips, electric drills, pipe cutters and benders, and acetylene torches. To check electrical circuits, burners, and other components, mechanics work with volt-ohmmeters, manometers, and other testing devices.

Sometimes part of the installation and repair work on cooling and heating systems is done by other craft workers, especially on large jobs, where workers are covered by union contracts. For example, the duct work on a large air-conditioning system might be done by sheet-metal workers, the electrical work by electricians, and the installation of piping, condensers, and other components by pipe fitters. Room air conditioners and home refrigerators are sometimes serviced by appliance repairers.

Most air-conditioning and refrigeration mechanics and furnace installers are employed by cooling and heating contractors. Most oil-burner mechanics work for fuel oil dealers, and most gas-burner mechanics for gas utility companies. Supermarket chains, school systems, manufacturers, and other organizations with large air-conditioning, refrigeration, or heating systems employ some mechanics. About one-fifth of the total number of mechanics are self-employed.

Requirements

Many air-conditioning, refrigeration, and heating mechanics acquire their skills through on-the-job training that consists of working several years under the guidance of experienced mechanics. Trainees usually begin as helpers doing simple jobs such as carrying materials, insulating refrigerant lines, and cleaning furnaces. As they acquire more skills and knowledge, they are given more difficult tasks, such as cutting and soldering pipes and sheet metal and checking electrical circuits. After four or five years on the job, mechanics are able to do all types of repairs and installations.

Mechanics who have completed training programs, either in apprenticeships or at vocational schools, can receive preference in hiring or advancement. A high school diploma or its equivalent is usually required for entry into training programs in this field. High school courses in mathematics, physics, mechanical drawing, electricity, and blueprint reading are especially good preparation for students who are considering this kind of work. Some high schools offer courses specifically related to air-conditioning, refrigeration, and heating.

Many private trade and technical schools, two-year colleges, and the Armed Forces offer programs in air-conditioning, refrigeration, and heating. The course work in these programs covers such subjects as air-conditioning, refrigeration, and heating theory; design and construction of equipment; and the basics of installation, maintenance, and repair.

Many mechanics learn their job by completing an apprenticeship program. Apprenticeships are run by unions in cooperation with air-conditioning, refrigeration, and heating contractors. To be considered for such a program, an individual must be a high school graduate and pass a mechanical aptitude test. Apprenticeships typically last four years and combine varied work experience under qualified supervision with classroom study in related subjects, such as the use and care of tools, safety practices, blueprint reading, and air-conditioning theory.

Experienced mechanics can keep up with changes in technology and expand their skills by taking courses offered by associations such as the Refrigeration Service Engineers Society, the Petroleum Marketing Education Foundation, and the Air-Conditioning Contractors of America.

Many mechanics are members of the United Association of Journeymen and Apprentices of the Plumbing and Pipefitting Industry or the Sheet Metal Workers International Association. Union membership is not required in all job situations.

Opportunities for experience and exploration

High school students may gauge their interest in the kinds of work done in this field by taking shop classes, mechanical drawing, mathematics, applied physics, and electronics. Actual work experience is difficult for high school stu-

dents to obtain, because without training they generally do not have the necessary skills for the job. Field trips to construction sites, service shops, and technical schools, however, can help students get an overall view of the occupation.

Methods of entering

People seeking to enter the air-conditioning, refrigeration, and heating field as apprentices should contact air-conditioning, refrigeration, and heating contractors in their area, or the local chapters of the unions that frequently operate training programs jointly with contractors. These include the United Association of Journeymen and Apprentices of the Plumbing and Pipefitting Industry or the Sheet Metal Workers International Association. Applicants for these apprenticeships must be approved by the local joint union-management apprenticeship committee.

If local apprenticeship programs are filled, applicants may wish to enter the field as on-the-job trainees. In this case they usually contact either potential employers directly or the state employment service.

Advancement

Several opportunities for advancement are open to mechanics with some experience. If they are able to get along well with people and show good judgment and planning skills, they may be able to advance to supervisory positions. Another possibility is becoming an *estimator*. Estimators figure the costs of installing equipment. They must have a thorough knowledge of the systems to be installed and the work involved in installation. In addition to this, they must also be personable and have good judgment, as well as a knack for performing many calculations.

In some regions of the country, air-conditioning, refrigeration, and heating mechanics may become city or county inspectors, inspecting the work done by contractors. Other experienced mechanics work for the manufacturers of heating and cooling equipment as *manufacturer's service specialists*. Some mechanics may eventually even go into business for themselves, operating a repair shop or a contracting business.

Employment outlook

The job prospects for air-conditioning, refrigeration, and heating mechanics are expected to increase about as fast as the average for all occupations throughout the next decade. Even if rates of new construction of residential, commercial, and industrial buildings are limited because of economic downturns, the need to keep up and replace old systems should provide continuing job opportunities. Interest in new energy-saving heating and cooling systems will also spur some replacement of existing systems.

Beginning mechanics, however, may find the competition heavy for jobs as helpers or apprentices because these trades have attracted so many people. Employers generally give preference to graduates of training programs that emphasize hands-on experience.

Earnings

The earnings of air-conditioning, refrigeration, and heating mechanics vary according to the type of equipment they install or service. Mechanics who install large commercial units usually make more than those working with small home systems. The median annual pay for qualified mechanics working under union contracts in the 1990s is about $23,000, although some experienced workers make $37,400 and more. Mechanic apprentices earn about 40 percent of the regular mechanic's wage at the beginning of their training, with increases to about 85 percent during the last year of apprenticeship. Mechanics who work on both air-conditioning and heating equipment generally earn more than those who limit their work to only one or the other.

Mechanics often work extra hours during busy seasons, for which they receive overtime pay. Employment in businesses that service both air-conditioning and heating equipment is fairly steady year-round, but some employers may temporarily reduce hours or lay off some mechanics when peak periods end. Mechanics usually receive fringe benefits such as health insurance, retirement pay, and paid vacations.

Conditions of work

Most air-conditioning, refrigeration, and heating mechanics have a 40-hour workweek. Some may have to work overtime or irregular hours during seasonal peaks, and they may have reduced hours or temporary layoffs at other times. Independent mechanics are also affected by the seasonal aspect of the work and have to budget their business finances and schedules accordingly.

Mechanics work in a variety of places and situations. They may work in a well ventilated repair shop one day, on customers' premises the next, and the following week at a new office building. Some days they must cooperate with other skilled craft workers, such as electricians and plumbers, when making installations. When they make service calls to private homes, they usually work independently. They may have to instruct customers in the use and care of equipment. On these calls, mechanics need to be tactful, courteous, and neat, and they should try to answer all the customer's questions.

Air-conditioning, refrigeration, and heating mechanics often have to lift heavy objects as well as stoop, crawl, or crouch when making repairs and installations. Possible hazards of the trade include burns, electric shocks, falls, and exposure to refrigerants. However, good safety practices can eliminate nearly all the these dangers.

GOE: 05.05.09, 05.10.04; SIC: 1711; SOC: 616

◇ **SOURCES OF ADDITIONAL INFORMATION**

Air-Conditioning and Refrigeration Institute
1501 Wilson Boulevard, 6th Floor
Arlington, VA 22209

Mechanical Contractors Association of America
1385 Piccard Drive
Rockville, MD 20850-4329

National Association of Plumbing-Heating-Cooling Contractors
PO Box 6808
Falls Church, VA 22040

Petroleum Marketing Education Foundation
5600 Roswell Road, NE, N-318
Atlanta, GA 30342

United Association of Journeymen and Apprentices of the Plumbing and Pipefitting Industry of the U.S. and Canada
PO Box 37800
Washington, DC 20013

Canadian Refrigeration and Air Conditioning Contractors Association
#308, 5468 Dundar Street, West
Islington ON M9B 6E3

◇ **RELATED ARTICLES**

Volume 1: Construction; Engineering
Volumes 2–4: Air-conditioning, refrigeration, and heating technicians; Boilermaking occupations; Construction inspectors, government; Construction laborers; Cost estimators; Electrical repairers; Electrical technicians; Electricians; Electromechanical technicians; Mechanical technicians; Pipe fitters and steam fitters; Sheetmetal workers; Welders; Welding technicians

Air-conditioning, refrigeration, and heating technicians

Definition

Air-conditioning, refrigeration, and heating technicians work on systems that control the temperature, humidity, and air quality of enclosed environments. They help design, manufacture, install, and maintain climate-control equipment. They usually assist engineering personnel, specializing in one phase such as refrigeration. Some technicians, however, specialize in balancing the heating, cooling, and ventilating systems to meet total performance standards in building designs.

The tasks that air-conditioning, refrigeration, and heating, technicians may perform include planning the requirements for the various stages of fabricating, installing, and servicing climate-control and refrigeration systems; recommending appropriate equipment to meet specified needs, based on their familiarity with supplier catalogs and technical data; and calculating heating and cooling capacities of proposed equipment units. These technicians may also work with estimating cost factors, preparing layouts and drawings for fabricating parts and assembling systems, and fabricating customized parts. Air-conditioning, refrigeration, and heating technicians also install test apparatus on the customer's premises, then analyze and report the results to fine-tune the planned system; install systems for customers; test for compliance with codes and contract specifications; and diagnose problems in systems under service contract so that they may be repaired by service personnel.

History

Many years ago, mechanical refrigerators and central heating systems were considered luxuries in the home. It was rare for a business to provide air-conditioning for its employees and customers. Now, because our expectations for comfort and convenience have changed vastly, such things are now considered necessities.

Until the early twentieth century, naturally occurring ice, which was cut and stored for later use, provided refrigeration. Although the first experiments with artificial refrigeration began nearly 200 years before, it was not until the mid-1800s that the operating principles of mechanical refrigerators were understood. In 1842, Dr. John Gorrie invented a cold-air machine to relieve the suffering of yellow fever patients in an Apalachicola, Florida, hospital. After the Civil War a number of companies using ammonia-absorption machines established artificial ice-making plants in the southern states.

During the early 1900s, progress consisted of advances in refrigerants, which are the working fluids of refrigeration and air-conditioning systems. As these substances are cycled through refrigeration equipment, they change back and forth from a liquid to a gas and from

This air-conditioning and heating technician is inspecting a system that he recently installed. The system is designed for an large apartment complex.

quality led to the introduction of piped hot water heating, which does not rely on such high temperatures. Ventilation for comfort and health became a greater problem as buildings were designed to hold more people, and various arrangements were devised to combine heating with the circulation of fresh air.

The scientific study of air-conditioning, including the regulation of the moisture content of the air, received a big boost in 1911 when Willis Carrier, an American inventor, published the results of his extensive research. Air-conditioning was developed initially for industrial applications, particularly in textile mills, but by 1930 or so, it was becoming common in stores, theaters, and other large buildings.

Initially, the equipment for the limited capacity air-conditioning, heating, and refrigeration systems was simple, and the skills needed to maintain them were comparatively easy to learn. Most technicians and mechanics for this early equipment were trained by manufacturers and distributors. But as the field has expanded over the years and the equipment has become much more sophisticated, workers need specialized knowledge and skills. Broad instruction is now frequently provided at public and private schools and by trade associations. The activities of today's technicians are diverse, reflecting the differences between various branches of the industry.

a gas to a liquid, alternately absorbing and releasing heat. This enables them to transfer heat from an area to be cooled and release it elsewhere. Although commercial electric refrigerators first appeared in the 1920s, it was not until the discovery of Freon 12, a safe refrigerant, that refrigerators became common. Today, modern equipment utilizes a wide variety of synthetic refrigerants, depending on the cooling job to be done and the types of evaporators, condensers, and compressors in the system.

Since the 1960s, thermoelectric refrigeration has been developed for some industrial uses. This technique relies on semiconductor materials and their unusual properties, rather than heat exchange with refrigerants or very cold substances such as dry ice or liquid nitrogen.

The ancient Greeks and Romans constructed buildings with central heating and ventilation systems, but this knowledge was lost during the Middle Ages in Europe. During the Industrial Revolution, piped steam heating began to appear in factories, churches, assembly halls, and other large buildings. Around 1830, its uncomfortable drying effect on air

Nature of the work

Today, many industries depend on carefully controlled temperature and humidity conditions while manufacturing, transporting, or storing their products. Many common foods are readily available only because of extensive refrigeration. Less obviously, numerous chemicals, drugs, explosives, oil, and other products our society needs must be produced using refrigeration processes. For example, some computers need to be kept in a certain temperature and humidity; spacecraft must be able to withstand great heat while exposed to the rays of the sun and great cold when the moon or earth block the sun, while maintaining a steady internal environment; the air in tractor trailer cabs must be regulated so that truck drivers can spend long hours behind the wheel in maximum comfort and safety. Each of these applications represents a different segment of a large and very diverse industry.

Most air-conditioning, refrigeration, and heating technicians are employed by manufacturers of environmental control equipment; distributors, dealers, or contractors who market, install, and service equipment; or firms concerned with air-conditioning, refrigeration, and heating among various other allied fields (for example, a consulting engineering firm, a gas or electric utility, or a building contractor).

Technicians employed by a manufacturer generally work in the research or engineering departments. In a research laboratory, they may conduct operational tests on experimental models and efficiency tests on new units coming off the production lines. They might also investigate the cause of a breakdown reported by customers, then determine the reason and possible solutions.

Engineering-oriented technicians employed by manufacturers often work with design engineers. They may perform tests needed for final adjustments in designs of new equipment, or they may assist engineers in fundamental research and development, technical report writing, and application engineering. Other engineering technicians serve as liaison representatives, coordinating the design and production engineering for the development and manufacture of new products.

Manufacturers may also employ technicians as sales representatives to call on distributors and dealers. These technicians must have a thorough knowledge of their products. They may explain newly developed equipment, ideas, and principles, or assist dealers and distributors in the layout and installation of the unfamiliar components.

Dealers and distributors, the second largest type of employer, also offer opportunities for technicians to become sales workers. In general, such technicians contact prospective buyers and help them plan air-conditioning, refrigeration, and heating systems. They help the client select appropriate equipment and estimate costs. Employed by a distributor, the technician will usually provide information and assistance to dealers, contractors, and other quantity purchasers; employed by a dealer, a technician would work with or for individual customers. Dealers sometimes assign technicians to prepare estimates and designs for customers, although the technician is not directly involved in selling.

Technicians may also become service representatives for dealers and distributors. For a dealer, they might install new equipment; maintain customers' existing units; and troubleshoot problems. Working in a distributor's service department, a technician assists dealers and contractors with their more difficult service problems. Finally, some technicians may work for contractors who only do installation and service work.

An air-conditioning, heating, and refrigeration technician repairs a cooling unit. Such work requires manual skill.

Firms in allied or associated fields, the third category of employer, furnish excellent opportunities, particularly for those with specialized training. A consulting engineering firm, for example, may need a technician who can determine heating and cooling load requirements, select equipment, design distribution systems, draw necessary plans, and help prepare specifications for various projects. Certain types of building contractors, such as mechanical contractors, may utilize technicians to estimate costs of climate-control installations, select fittings and equipment, coordinate and help supervise workers in various building trades, and check out the completed system.

Firms that manufacture the instruments and systems that monitor and regulate heating and cooling equipment may hire technicians to work in development and design, production, application engineering, and testing of the control equipment for strength and accuracy.

A final example of an allied (related field) employer is a gas or electric utility company that uses technicians as promotion representatives, working with dealers who sell air-conditioning and heating equipment to the public.

Since the beginnings of the industry, an attraction of air-conditioning, refrigeration, and heating technology is the possibility of opening an independent business. Many technicians draw on their skills and experience, plus other qualities and resources, to successfully establish themselves as entrepreneurs. Sometimes a new enterprise for selling air-conditioning, heating, and refrigeration equipment forms as an outgrowth of a general appliance store. The service and maintenance end of the industry also provides good opportunities for a knowledgeable technician seeking independence. Frequently such businesses combine marketing with services provided directly to consumers.

Requirements

The requirements for becoming an air-conditioning, refrigeration, and heating technician vary with the area of the industry. In general, the successful technician fills the gap between the skilled worker and the engineer, with some of the abilities of each. Manipulative skill and dexterity in handling equipment is needed, particularly for individuals who specialize in installation and servicing. The ability to diagnose problems by assessing indicators that the equipment presents is another requirement. Although this skill may come naturally to some people, it can be fostered and developed through practice.

Other necessary skills include: an acquaintance with the theory and principles of engineering, especially for technicians who must explain the functioning of equipment or assist engineers in research and design activities; some mathematical background and a tolerance for working with numbers; and the ability to read blueprints, building drawings, and electrical diagrams. In many specialty areas within the industry, the rapidly changing pace means that technicians must be able to read, comprehend, and make use of current periodicals and publications in the field. They also must be able to write reports, both formal and informal, that are concise and complete descriptions of tests, experiments, and research. Technicians increasingly need good computer skills, as more air-conditioning, refrigeration, and heating systems and components are being installed with microcomputer controls.

In high school, a student considering air-conditioning, refrigeration, and heating technology as a career should take at least one year of physics and two years of mathematics, including two years of algebra or one year each of algebra and geometry. If possible, students should also include courses in engineering drawing, blueprint reading, and metal shop. Courses in computers and English composition are particularly important to the prospective technician.

A high school diploma is always a prerequisite for admission to college-level programs and technical institutes. It is nearly always required for entrance into the various educational programs that manufacturers operate to train employees.

Employers generally prefer graduates of two-year applications-oriented training programs. This kind of training includes a strong background in mathematical and engineering theory. However, the emphasis is on the practical uses of such theories, not on explorations of their origins and development, such as one finds in engineering programs.

In addition to technical courses, the subjects a student can expect to cover in a two-year technical program include advanced algebra, trigonometry, physics, English and technical writing, and perhaps industrial orientation.

Special requirements

For the most part, no special licensing or certification is required for air-conditioning, refrigeration, and heating technicians. In some areas of the field—for example, those who work with design and research engineers—certification is increasingly the norm and viewed as a basic indicator of competence. Even where there are no firm requirements, it is generally better to be qualified for whatever license or certification is available.

Some parts of the United States have local requirements for certification. It is possible that future state or federal requirements will be instituted for technicians working in certain phases of the environmental control industry.

In some jobs, technicians may be required to join a union.

Opportunities for experience and exploration

A student trying to decide on a career in air-conditioning, refrigeration, and heating technology may have to base the choice on a variety of indirect evidence. Part-time or summer work is usually not available to students because of their lack of the necessary skills and knowledge. It may be possible, however, to arrange field trips to service shops, companies that develop and produce heating and cooling equipment, or other firms concerned with the environmental control field. Such visits can give the student a firsthand overview of the day-to-day work. A visit with a local contractor or to a school that conducts an air-conditioning, refrigeration, and heating technology training program can also be very helpful. Some individuals have been exposed to the field while serving in the Armed Forces and have pursued further training on returning to civilian life. Prospective technicians may also contact heating and refrigeration associations, such as those listed at the end of this article, for information about how to get started in this field.

An important way to test interest in the occupation is through relevant courses such as physics, mathematics, mechanical drawing, and shop work. The student who dislikes the theoretical aspects of science is likely to be at a disadvantage, because technical training programs, and most jobs in the field, generally require understanding of air-conditioning, refrigeration, and heating theory.

Methods of entering

Many students in two-year programs work during the summer between the first and second years at a job related to their area of training. Their employers may hire them on a part-time basis during the second year and make offers of full-time employment after graduation. Even if such a job offer cannot be made, the employer may be aware of other companies that are hiring and help the student with suggestions and recommendations, provided the student's work record is good.

Some schools make on-the-job training part of the curriculum, particularly during the latter part of their program. This is a valuable way for students to gain practical experience in conjunction with classroom work.

It is not unusual for graduates of two-year programs to receive several offers of employment, either from contacts they have made themselves or from companies that routinely recruit new graduates. Oftentimes, regular interview periods are scheduled at some schools by representatives of larger companies. Other, usually smaller, prospective employers may contact specific faculty advisors who in turn make students aware of opportunities that arise.

In addition to using their school's job-placement services, resourceful students can independently explore other leads by responding to want ads in local papers and contacting manufacturers and contractors or the state employment service.

Finally, student membership in the local chapter of a trade association, such as one of those listed at the end of this article, will often result in good employment contacts.

Advancement

On-the-job experience is one route to increased reward and responsibility, but additional formal education, particularly in night school or trade-association training courses, helps to open up opportunities more rapidly. Technicians increase their value to employers and themselves with continued training. For example, a technician employed by a manufacturer may progress to the position of sales manager, who acts as liaison with distributors and dealers, promoting and selling the manufacturer's products, or to field service representative, who solves unusual service problems of dealers and distributors in the area. Or the technician may specialize in research and development, designing some components of new systems; solve complicated problems in the design or testing of existing systems; and select replacements for obsolete equipment.

Similar career growth and development is possible in most technical careers, depending on the individual's inclination and the type of employer. Working for a dealer or distributor, advancement could mean promotion to a service manager position, overseeing the personnel who install and service equipment. Another possible specialization is mechanical design, which involves designing piping, duct work, controls, and the overall distribution systems for consulting engineers, mechanical contractors, distributors, or even manufacturers. And, as mentioned earlier, advancement may mean setting up a separate business to sell some combination of skills and parts directly to the consumer.

Employment outlook

Employment in the air-conditioning, refrigeration, and heating field is expected to increase about as fast as or faster than the average for all occupations through the 1990s. Some openings will occur because experienced workers retire or transfer to other work. Other openings will be generated as more climate-control systems are installed in new and existing buildings and as old applications for the technology are expanded and new ones developed.

Comfort is only one of the major reasons for environmental control. Conditioned atmosphere is a necessity in any precision industry where temperature and humidity can affect fine tolerances. As products and processes become more complex and more highly automated, the need for closely controlled conditions becomes increasingly important. For example, electronics manufacturers must keep the air bone-dry for many parts of their production processes to prevent damage to parts and to maintain nonconductivity. Pharmaceutical and food manufacturers rely on pure, dirt-free air. High-speed multicolor printing requires temperature control of rollers and moisture control for the paper racing through the presses. There is every reason to expect that these and other sophisticated industries will rely more in the coming years on precision control of room conditions. The actual amount of industry growth (and thus demand for technicians) will hinge on the overall health of the nation's economy.

Employment levels for technicians involved with service and repair of climate-control equipment is generally less sensitive to economic downturns, because the need to service and repair equipment already in place is not tied to economic conditions.

Despite recent moderation in the cost of some energy sources, a general interest in energy conservation does appear to persist in this country. Because of this, installation of more energy-efficient air-conditioning and heating systems in existing buildings should be a spur to future growth in the industry.

Earnings

The earnings of air-conditioning, refrigeration, and heating technicians vary widely according to the level of training and experience, the nature of their work, type of employer, region of the country, and other factors. In private industry the average beginning salary for air-conditioning, refrigeration, and heating technicians who have completed a two-year post-secondary–school program is around $14,000. Salaries for all air-conditioning, refrigeration, and heating technicians, including those with several years' experience, usually fall between $20,000 and $40,000 and average around $25,000 a year.

Conditions of work

The working conditions for air-conditioning, refrigeration, and heating technicians vary considerably depending on the area of the industry in which they work. For the most part, the hours are regular, although certain jobs in production may involve shift work, and service technicians may have to be on call some evenings and weekends to handle emergency re-

pairs. In laboratories or industrial plants and at construction sites, safety training minimizes any dangers associated with the mechanical and electrical equipment on the job. Those technicians employed by distributors, dealers, and consulting engineers usually work in an office or similar surroundings and are subject to the same benefits and conditions as other office workers. Some technicians—for example, sales representatives or service managers—usually go out periodically to visit customers or installation and service sites.

Technicians performing maintenance and repair work in the field may encounter extremes of temperature when servicing outdoor or rooftop equipment, and cramped quarters when servicing indoor commercial or industrial equipment.

GOE: 05.03.07, 05.05.09; SIC: 1711; SOC: 3713, 616

◇ **SOURCES OF ADDITIONAL INFORMATION**

Air-Conditioning and Refrigeration Institute
1501 Wilson Boulevard
Arlington, VA 22209

Air Conditioning Contractors of America
1513 16th Street, NW
Washington, DC 20036

Refrigerating Engineers and Technicians Association
111 East Wacker Drive, Suite 600
Chicago, IL 60601

American Society of Heating Refrigeration and Air-conditioning Engineers
1791 Tullie Circle, NE
Atlanta, GA 30329

Refrigeration Service Engineers Society
1666 Rand Road
Des Plaines, IL 60016-3552

◇ **RELATED ARTICLES**

Architectural and building construction technicians; Construction laborers; Energy-conservation technicians; Mechanical technicians; Service sales representatives; Solar collector technicians

Aircraft mechanics and engine specialists

Definition

Aircraft mechanics and engine specialists examine, service, repair, and overhaul aircraft and aircraft engines. They also repair, replace, and assemble parts of the airframe (the structural parts of the plane other than the power plant or engine).

History

On December 17, 1903, an airplane designed and built by Wilbur and Orville Wright made history's first successful powered flight. Since that day, advances in aircraft design and in the air-transportation industry have been enormous, with changes still continuing at a rapid pace. The complexity of aircraft design has made the job of aircraft mechanics a very important one. With the growth of both commercial airlines and military aviation, the work of skilled aircraft mechanics has become vital to the safety of millions of people and to our national economy and defense.

Nature of the work

The work of aircraft mechanics and engine specialists employed by scheduled airlines varies according to whether they are employed as *line maintenance mechanics* or *overhaul mechanics*.

Line maintenance mechanics are all-around craft workers who make repairs on all parts of the plane. Working at the airport, they make emergency and other necessary repairs in the time between when aircraft land and when they take off again. They may be told by the pilot, flight engineer, or head mechanic what repairs need to be made, or they may thoroughly inspect the plane themselves for oil leaks, cuts or dents in the surface and tires, or any malfunction in the radio, radar, and light

equipment. In addition, their duties include changing oil, cleaning spark plugs, and replenishing the hydraulic and oxygen systems. They work as fast as safety permits so the aircraft can be put back into service quickly.

Overhaul mechanics keep the aircraft in top operating condition by performing scheduled maintenance, making repairs, and conducting inspections required by the Federal Aviation Administration (FAA). Scheduled maintenance programs are based on the number of hours flown, calendar days, or a combination of these factors.

Overhaul mechanics work at the airline's main overhaul base on either or both of the two major parts of the aircraft: the airframe, which includes wings, fuselage, tail assembly, landing gear, control cables, propeller assembly, and fuel and oil tanks; or the power plant, which may be a radial (internal combustion), turbo jet, turbo prop, or rocket engine.

Working on parts of the aircraft other than the engine, the airframe mechanics inspect the various components of the airframe for worn or defective parts. They may check the sheet-metal surfaces, measure the tension of control cables, or check for rust, distortion, and cracks in the fuselage and wings. They consult manufacturers' manuals and the airline's maintenance manual for specifications and to determine whether repair or replacement is needed to correct defects or malfunctions. Airframe mechanics repair, replace, and assemble parts using a variety of tools, including power shears, sheet-metal breakers, arc and acetylene welding equipment, rivet guns, and air or electric drills.

Aircraft power-plant mechanics inspect, service, repair, and overhaul the engine of the aircraft. Looking through specially designed openings while working from ladders or scaffolds, they examine the external appearance of an engine for such problems as cracked cylinders, oil leaks, or cracks or breaks in the turbine blades. They also listen to the engine in operation to detect sounds of malfunctioning, such

Aircraft mechanics must be knowledgeable in many aspects of airplane maintenance. On a given day, they may be asked to repair anything from serious engine problems to simple door jams.

essary repair and maintenance work. The planes, however, are generally small and the work less complex than in repair shops.

In small, independent repair shops, mechanics must inspect and repair many different types of aircraft. The airplanes may include small commuter planes run by an aviation company, private company planes and jets, private individually owned aircraft, and planes used for flying instruction.

Requirements

The first requirement for prospective aircraft mechanics is a high school diploma. Courses in mathematics, physics, chemistry, and mechanical drawing are particularly helpful because they teach the principles involved in the operation of an aircraft, and this knowledge is often necessary to making the repairs. Machine shop, auto mechanics, or electrical shop courses may be desirable to test the student's mechanical aptitudes.

Certification by the FAA may also be a requirement for aircraft mechanics. Most of the mechanics who work on civilian aircraft have FAA authorization as *airframe mechanics, power-plant mechanics,* or *aircraft inspectors.* Airframe mechanics are qualified to work on the fuselage, wings, landing gear, and other structural parts of the aircraft; power-plant mechanics are qualified for work on the engine. Mechanics may qualify for both airframe and power-plant licensing, allowing them to work on any part of the plane. Combination airframe and power-plant mechanics with an inspector's certificate are permitted to certify inspection work done by other mechanics. Mechanics without certification must be supervised by those who are certificated.

FAA certification is granted only to aircraft mechanics with previous work experience: a minimum of 18 months for an airframe or power-plant certificate, and at least 30 months working with both engines and airframes for a combination certificate. To qualify for an inspector's certificate, mechanics must have held a combined airframe and power-plant certificate for at least three years. In addition, all applicants for certification must pass written and oral tests and demonstrate their ability to do the work authorized by the certificate.

At one time, mechanics were able to acquire their skills through on-the-job training. This is rare today. Now most mechanics learn the job either in the Armed Forces or in trade schools approved by the FAA. The trade schools provide training with the necessary

as sticking or burned valves. The test equipment used to check the operation of an engine includes ignition analyzers, compression checkers, distributor timers, and ammeters.

If necessary, the mechanics remove the engine from the aircraft, using a hoist or a forklift truck, and take the engine apart. They use sensitive instruments to measure parts for wear and use X-ray and magnetic inspection equipment to check for invisible cracks. Worn or damaged parts such as carburetors, superchargers, and magnetos are replaced or repaired; then the mechanics reassemble and reinstall the engine.

Aircraft mechanics adjust and repair electrical wiring systems and aircraft accessories and instruments; inspect, service, and repair pneumatic and hydraulic systems; and handle various servicing tasks, such as flushing crankcases, cleaning screens, greasing moving parts, and checking brakes.

Mechanics may work on only one type of aircraft or on many different types, such as jets, propeller-driven planes, and helicopters. For greater efficiency, some specialize in one section, such as the electrical system, of a particular type of aircraft. Among the specialists, there are *airplane electricians; pneumatic testers* and *pressure sealer-and-testers; aircraft body repairers* and *bonded structures repairers,* such as *burnishers* and *bumpers;* and *air conditioning mechanics, aircraft rigging and controls mechanics, plumbing and hydraulics mechanics,* and *experimental-aircraft testing mechanics.*

Mechanics who work for businesses that own their own aircraft usually handle all nec-

tools and equipment in programs that range in length from 2 years to 30 months. In considering applicants for certification, the FAA sometimes accepts successful completion of such schooling in place of work experience, but the schools do not guarantee an FAA certificate, or jobs for that matter.

The experience acquired by aircraft mechanics in the Armed Forces sometimes satisfies the work requirements for FAA certification, and veterans may be able to pass the exam with a limited amount of additional study. But jobs in the military service are usually too specialized to satisfy the FAA requirement for broad work experience. In that case, applicants for FAA approval will have to complete a training program at a trade school. Schools occasionally give some credit for material learned in the service. Nevertheless, aircraft mechanics with military experience usually find it an asset when seeking employment, because employers consider trade school graduates with this experience to be the most desirable applicants.

Aircraft mechanics must be able to work with precision and meet rigid standards. Their physical condition is also important. They need more than average strength for lifting heavy parts and tools, as well as agility for reaching and climbing. And they should not be afraid of heights, since they may work on top of the wings and fuselages of large jet planes.

In addition to education and certification, union membership may be a requirement for some jobs, particularly for mechanics employed by major airlines. The principal unions organizing aircraft mechanics are the International Association of Machinists and Aerospace Workers and the Transport Workers Union of America. In addition, some mechanics are represented by the International Brotherhood of Teamsters, Chauffeurs, Warehousemen and Helpers of America.

Opportunities for experience and exploration

To test their interest in the work of aircraft mechanics, students should take such courses as shop, mathematics, and applied physics. Working with electronic kits, tinkering with automobile engines, and assembling model airplanes are also good ways of gauging their ability to do the kinds of work performed by aircraft mechanics.

A guided tour of an airfield can give a brief overall view of this industry. Even better would be a part-time or summer job with an airline in

An airplane mechanic presents problems in the hydraulic system of the landing gear to the captain.

an area like the baggage department. Small airports may also offer job opportunities for part-time, summer, or replacement workers.

In addition, experience with aircraft in the Armed Forces or the Civil Air Patrol is an excellent way of acquiring some technical knowledge plus a feel for the occupation.

Methods of entering

High school graduates who wish to become aircraft mechanics may enter this field by enrolling in an FAA-approved trade school. These schools generally have placement services available for their graduates.

Another method is to make direct application to the employment offices of individual airlines or the local offices of the state employment service. The field may also be entered through enlistment in the Armed Forces.

Advancement

Promotions depend in part on the size of the organization for which an aircraft mechanic works. The first promotion after beginning employment is usually based on merit and comes in the form of a salary increase. To advance further, many companies require the mechanic to have a combined airframe and power-plant certificate, or perhaps an aircraft inspector's certificate.

AIRCRAFT MECHANICS AND ENGINE SPECIALISTS

Advancement could take the following route: journeyman mechanic, head mechanic or crew chief, inspector, head inspector, and shop supervisor. With additional training, a mechanic may advance to engineering, administrative, or executive positions. With business training, some mechanics open their own repair shops.

Employment outlook

Overall, the outlook for aircraft mechanics is good for the next decade. A moderate increase in the number of jobs is expected as a result of growth in the industry. In addition, many openings will occur because of an expected large number of retirements. However, employment growth will be restricted by a greater use of automated equipment that speeds repairs and maintenance.

Qualified mechanics, particularly if they are willing to relocate, should find plenty of opportunities in general aviation, where most employment opportunities are with small companies. Because the wages paid by small companies are usually low, there will not be as much competition for these jobs as for jobs with airlines and large private companies. In fact, it is likely that many of the openings that occur will be the result of experienced mechanics' leaving for better-paying jobs in the larger companies.

The airline jobs will be more difficult to obtain because the high wages they pay attract a larger number of qualified applicants than there are jobs available. Also, during a recession, when people have less money for travel, airlines could cut the number of flights they operate. As a result, fewer mechanics would be needed for maintenance. This means that mechanics may face layoffs when economic conditions are poor.

The number of mechanics employed by the federal government may go up or down. These jobs are affected by changes in defense spending, and the number of openings will decrease if there is a reduction in the nation's defense budget.

Earnings

Aircraft mechanics in the 1990s earn an average of about $30,000 per year. Some skilled, experienced mechanics make about $45,000. Beginning mechanics can expect to earn from $20,000 to $30,000 a year. Mechanics working for the

federal government receive an average of $32,400 a year.

Most major airlines are covered by union agreements. Their mechanics generally earn more than those working for other employers. An attractive fringe benefit for airline mechanics and their immediate families is reduced fares on their own and most other airlines.

Conditions of work

Of the roughly 122,000 aircraft mechanics currently employed in the United States, well over half work for scheduled airlines. Each airline usually has one main overhaul base, where most of its mechanics are employed. These bases are found along the main airline routes or near large cities, including New York, Chicago, Los Angeles, Atlanta, San Francisco, and Miami.

About one-sixth of aircraft mechanics work for the federal government. Many of these mechanics are civilians employed at military aviation installations, while others work for the FAA, mainly in their headquarters in Oklahoma City. About one-fifth of all mechanics work for aircraft assembly firms. Most of the rest are general aviation mechanics employed by independent repair shops at airports around the country, by businesses that use their own planes for transporting employees or cargo, certificated supplemental airlines, or by crop-dusting and air-taxi firms.

Most aircraft mechanics work a five-day, 40-hour week. Their working hours, however, may be irregular and often include nights, weekends, and holidays, because airline schedules call for three eight-hour shifts around the clock, with extra work needed around major holidays.

When doing overhauling and major inspection work, aircraft mechanics generally work in hangars with adequate heat, ventilation, and light. If the hangars are full, however, or if repairs must be made quickly, they may work outdoors, sometimes in unpleasant weather. Outdoor work is frequent for line maintenance mechanics, who work at airports, because they must make minor repairs and preflight checks at the terminal to save time. To maintain flight schedules, or to keep from inconveniencing customers in general aviation, the mechanics often have to work under time pressure.

The work is physically strenuous and demanding. Mechanics often have to lift or pull as much as 50 pounds of weight. They may stand, lie, or kneel in awkward positions, sometimes in precarious places like on a scaffold or ladder.

Noise and vibration are common when testing engines. Regardless of the stresses and strains, aircraft mechanics are expected to work quickly and with great precision.

Although the power tools and test equipment are provided by the employer, mechanics may be expected to furnish their own hand tools.

GOE: 05.05.09, 06.01.04; SIC: 4581; SOC: 6113, 6116

Future Aviation Professionals of America
4959 Massachusetts Boulevard
Atlanta, GA 30337

Professional Aviation Maintenance Association
500 Northwest Plaza, Suite 809
St. Ann, MO 63074

◇ **SOURCES OF ADDITIONAL INFORMATION**

Air Transport Association of America
1709 New York Avenue, NW
Washington, DC 20006

Aviation Maintenance Foundation International
PO Box 2826
Redmond, WA 98073

◇ **RELATED ARTICLES**

Volume 1: Aviation and Aerospace; Transportation
Volumes 2–4: Aeronautical and aerospace technicians; Aerospace engineers; Automobile mechanics; Automobile technicians; Avionics technicians; Electrical technicians; Flight engineers; Fluid power technicians; Instrumentation technicians

Airplane dispatchers

Definition

Airplane dispatchers plan and direct commercial air flights according to government and airline company regulations. They read radio reports from airplane pilots during flights and study weather reports to determine any necessary change in flight direction or altitude. They send instructions by radio to the pilots in the case of heavy storms, fog, mechanical difficulties, or other emergencies. Airline dispatchers are sometimes called flight superintendents.

History

Although airplanes were used for military transportation purposes by the United States as early as 1909, they were mostly a novelty until 1914, when the first passenger service was organized. This operation provided air transpor-

tation from Tampa to St. Petersburg, Florida, a distance of 23 miles. Although the service lasted only three months, it was a history-making venture.

In March of 1917, the U.S. Post Office Department received a grant of $100,000 to experiment with airmail service. By 1920, the service was in operation from coast to coast, and in 1924 it was expanded to include both day and night flights. This development became the backbone of the commercial airlines that soon grew up in the United States. However, it was not until Charles Lindbergh made his historic flight across the Atlantic in 1927 that the public became enthusiastic about air travel possibilities.

Aviation developed rapidly during World War II, mainly because of the need for new and different types of airplanes to be used in the war effort. Since the war, growth has continued both in terms of aircraft design and the volume of business handled by the air-transportation

Prior to flight, pilots check the dispatchers' reports regarding weather, routes, and flight specifications.

industry. Today air travel is an essential component of the U.S. transportation system, with over 460 million passenger miles per year.

During the early days of aviation, the airplane dispatcher served in a number of capacities, including that of station manager, meteorologist, radio operator, and even mechanic. Often pilots were pressed into service as dispatchers because of their knowledge of weather and of the needs of flight crews.

Although dispatchers were used prior to 1938, it was not until then that the federal government began licensing them. Since that time, the work of dispatchers has become more involved and complicated, and the airline industry has relied on them extensively to make a major contribution to the safety of commercial air travel.

Nature of the work

Airplane dispatchers are employed by commercial airlines, and they maintain a constant watch on factors affecting the movement of planes during flights. Dispatchers are responsible for the safety of flights and for making certain that they are operated on an efficient, profit-making basis. The work of dispatchers, however, is not the same as that of air traffic controllers, who are employees of the federal government.

Airplane dispatchers are responsible for giving the company's clearance for each flight that takes off during their shift. Their judgments are based on data received from a num-

ber of different sources. In their efforts to make certain that each flight will end successfully, they must take into consideration current weather conditions, weather forecasts, wind speed and direction, and other information. Before flights, they must decide whether the airplane crew should report to the field or whether the airline should begin notifying passengers that their flight has been delayed or canceled. Dispatchers may also have to determine whether an alternate route should be used, either to include another stop for passengers or to avoid certain weather conditions.

Upon reporting to the field before a flight, the pilot confers with the dispatcher and determines the best route to use, the amount of fuel to be placed aboard the aircraft, the altitude at which the flight will be flown, and the approximate flying time. The pilot and the dispatcher must agree on the conditions of the flight, and both have the option of delaying or canceling it should conditions became too hazardous to ensure a safe trip.

Dispatchers may also be responsible for maintaining records and for determining the weight and balance of the aircraft after loading. They must be certain that all intended cargo is loaded aboard each of the appropriate flights. They must also be certain that all their decisions, such as those about the cargo, are in keeping with the safety regulations of the Federal Aviation Agency (FAA), as well as with the rules established by their own airline.

Once the planes are in the air, dispatchers keep in constant contact with the flight crews. A dispatcher may be responsible for communications with as many as 10 or 12 flights at any one time. Contact is maintained through a company-owned radio network that enables each company to keep track of all of its planes. Dispatchers keep the crews informed about the weather that they will encounter, and they record the positions and other information reported by the planes while they are en route. If an emergency occurs, dispatchers coordinate the actions taken in response to the emergency.

Following each flight, the pilot checks with the dispatcher for a debriefing. In the debriefing, the pilot brings the dispatcher up to date about the weather encountered in the air and about various other conditions related to the flight, so that the dispatcher will have this information available in scheduling subsequent flights.

Good judgment is an important tool of airplane dispatchers, for they must be able to make fast, workable, realistic decisions. Because of this, dispatchers often experience strains and tensions on the job, especially when many flights are in the air or when an emergency occurs.

In larger airlines, there is a certain degree of specialization among dispatchers. An assistant dispatcher may work with the chief dispatcher and have the major responsibility for just one phase of the dispatching activities, such as analyzing current weather information, while a senior dispatcher may be designated to take care of another phase, such as monitoring the operating costs of each flight.

Requirements

Airplane dispatchers must be licensed by the Federal Aviation Administration. They may prepare for the FAA licensing examination in several different ways. They may work at least one year in a dispatching office under a licensed dispatcher, complete an FAA-approved airline dispatcher's course at a specialized school or training center, or show that they have spent two of the previous three years in air traffic control work or a related job.

Candidates who meet the preliminary requirements must also pass an examination covering such subjects as Civil Air regulations, radio procedures, airport and airway traffic procedures, weather analysis, and air-navigation facilities. In addition to a written test, they must also pass an oral examination covering the interpretation of weather information, landing and cruising speeds of various aircraft, airline routes, navigation facilities, and operational characteristics of different types of aircraft. They must not only demonstrate a knowledge of these areas to become a licensed dispatcher; they are also expected to maintain these skills once licensed. Various training programs, some of which may be conducted by their employers, will assist them in staying current with new developments, which are frequent in this job.

Airplane dispatchers are also required to "fly the line" at least once each year. This involves flying as cockpit observers over the portion of the system that they service. This requirement enables dispatchers to maintain a hands-on familiarity with airline routes and flight operations.

Assistant dispatchers are not always required to be licensed. Thus, it may be possible to begin work in a dispatcher's office prior to licensure. Most airlines prefer, however, that applicants for dispatchers' jobs have at least two years of college, with preference given to college graduates. Training in meteorology, mathematics, and physics is helpful.

Airline dispatchers need to be able to work well either by themselves or with others and to assume responsibility for their decisions. Their job requires them to think and act quickly and sensibly under the most trying conditions. Hundreds of lives may be under their guiding hand at any one time, and a poor decision could result in tragedy.

Special requirements

Airline dispatchers must be at least 21 years old and in good health. Their vision must be good, although corrective eyeglasses may be used.

Opportunities for experience and exploration

Aside from pursuing the course of study mentioned previously, there is little opportunity for an individual to explore the field of airplane dispatching directly. Part-time or summer jobs with airlines may provide interested students with a chance to observe some of the activities related to dispatching work. Military service can also offer excellent experience if is associated with flight operations, meteorology, or other related work.

Methods of entering

The occupation is not easy to enter because of its relatively small size and the special skills required. The nature of the training is such that it is not easily put to use outside of this specific area. Few people leave this career once they are in it, so only a few positions other than those caused by death or retirement become available.

People who are able to break into the field are often promoted to assistant dispatchers jobs from related fields. They may come from among the airline's dispatch clerks, meteorologists, radio operators, or retired pilots. Obviously, airlines prefer those people who have had a long experience in ground-flight operations work. Thus, it is probably wise to plan on starting out in one of these related fields and eventually working into a position as airline dispatcher.

Advancement

The usual path of advancement is from dispatch clerk to assistant dispatcher to dispatcher and then, possibly, to chief flight dispatcher or flight dispatch manager or assistant manager. It is also possible to become a chief flight supervisor or superintendent of flight control.

The line of advancement varies depending upon the airline, the size of the facility where the dispatcher is located, and the positions available. At smaller facilities, there may be only two or three different promotional levels available.

Employment outlook

In the 1990s, there are only about 1,000 dispatchers employed by the scheduled airlines. A smaller number are employed by certificated supplemental airlines and private firms. An expected increase in air traffic in coming years may mean a slight increase in the number of airplane dispatchers needed. However, because of the relatively small size of this occupational field, its employment outlook is not particularly good.

Most of the increase in numbers of flights will be offset by the use of more automatic communications equipment. With improved communications equipment, a single dispatcher will be able to cover a larger area than is currently possible. The development of more foreign-flag airlines may provide other job opportunities, but the people for these jobs will probably be found among the employees of those airlines.

Earnings

In the 1990s, assistant airline dispatchers are earning an average of between $30,000 and $36,000 annually. Licensed dispatchers earn about $47,000 per year. Flight superintendents make up to about $52,800, and shift chiefs, $64,800.

Conditions of work

Airplane dispatchers are normally stationed at airports near a terminal or hangar, but in facilities away from the public. Some airlines use several dispatch installations, while others use a single office. Because dispatchers make decisions involving not only thousands of people but also a great deal of money, their offices are often located close to those of management, so that the managers can remain in close contact with the dispatchers.

Frequently the offices where airplane dispatchers work are full of noise and activity, with telephones ringing, computer printers chattering, and many people talking and moving about to consult charts and other sources of information. The offices usually operate 24 hours per day, with each dispatcher working 8-hour shifts, plus an additional half-hour used in briefing the relief person.

Dispatchers generally have at least two weeks of vacation with pay each year. In many cases, this increases to three weeks after 10 years and to four weeks after 15 or 20 years. Dispatchers are normally covered by group hospitalization and pension plans.

Many lives depend on airplane dispatchers every day. This means that there is often considerable stress in their jobs. Dispatchers must constantly make rapid decisions based on their evaluation of a great deal of information. Adding to the tension is the fact that they may work in noisy, hectic surroundings. However, dispatchers can feel deep satisfaction in knowing that their job is vital to the safety and success of airline operations.

GOE: 05.03.03; SIC: 4581; SOC: 392

◇ **SOURCES OF ADDITIONAL INFORMATION**

Air Transport Association of America
1709 New York Avenue, NW
Washington, DC 20006-5206

Future Aviation Professionals of America
4959 Massachusetts Boulevard
Atlanta, GA 30337

◇ **RELATED ARTICLES**

Volume 1: Aviation and Aerospace; Transportation
Volumes 2–4: Air traffic controllers; Flight engineers; Meteorological technicians; Meteorologists; Radio and telegraph operators

Animal production technicians

Definition

Animal production technicians help breed, raise, and market a variety of farm animals: cattle, sheep, pigs, horses, mules, chickens, turkeys, geese, and ducks; and other more exotic animals, such as ostriches, alligators, and minks. Technicians, when principally involved with the breeding and feeding of animals, are sometimes referred to as *animal husbandry technicians.*

In general, animal production technicians are concerned with the propagation, feeding, housing, health, and economics (production and marketing) of animals. These technicians work in many different settings and capacities: they may supervise unskilled farm workers, serve as field representatives assisting in the sales of animals or animal products to customers, serve as sales representatives for farm-product or farm-services vendors, or act as purchasing agents for food-processing and packaging firms. The diversity of employment available for well-trained and well-qualified animal production technicians makes this career extremely flexible. As science progresses, opportunities for these technicians will become even broader.

History

Raising cattle, hogs, sheep, and poultry is one of the oldest occupations on earth. When humans learned to domesticate livestock, it gave them the ability to feed themselves without relying on hunting skills or the presence of wild animals. When people shifted from hunting-and-gathering to crop and animal production, the entire structure of civilization shifted. Mankind moved from a nomadic existence that followed migrating herds of wild animals to a settled life that allowed the building of cities and houses.

Different livestock thrived in different climates and land types. Mountainous and rugged land was suitable for sheep and goats, flat land was good for large cattle to graze. Farms could raise one type of animal or many. It depended on the skills, the needs, and the land of the farmer. As transportation improved with the building of railroads, the ability of the farmer to sell stock improved as well.

Production of beef cattle and sheep became a large-scale operation in the United States dur-ing the nineteenth century as city populations increased, and the grazing areas of the Great Plains regions opened. The famous Texas Longhorn cattle descended from cattle brought to the West Indies by Columbus. Cattle ranching requires large areas of grassland, and until the 1880s, the open range of government-owned land in the West served as "free" pasture for cattle and sheep. A hundred years later, cattle and sheep ranches in the Southwest now average tens of thousands of acres in size, are privately owned, with hundreds or thousands of animals on each ranch, representing huge investments for their owners. Cattle may still graze on government land, but there are more restrictions on grazing rights.

Animal production farming is the leading agricultural enterprise in the nation. Food supplies must keep pace with population growth. The demand for animal products continually increases as new products are developed and old products are improved.

The methods, techniques, and business management principles needed for profitable production today are far different and more complex than even a few decades ago. The application of science and technology to animal production has caused a marked change in the type of resources used by the farm owner. As the reliance on human labor has dropped, capital investments in feed, machinery, and fertilizers has increased.

As farm owners increasingly rely on technological advancement to sustain and build production, the demand for a higher level of technical competence increases. Each year better educated men and women are needed to supply the materials of production and to raise, distribute, and market the products of animal production.

Nature of the work

Most animal production technicians are employed either as *livestock production technicians,* working with cattle, sheep, swine, or horses; or as *poultry production technicians,* working with chickens, turkeys, geese, or ducks.

Most livestock production technicians find employment either on livestock farms or ranches or with the businesses that service these farms and ranches. On a farm or ranch, they might be involved in animal feed prepa-

ANIMAL PRODUCTION TECHNICIANS

This animal production technician is supervising a group of calves. Theses calves were part of a reproduction program that enhances the number of calves born in a year. Embryos from registered cows with high production records were transplanted into surrogate mothers who then produced small herds of genetically uniform animals.

ration. A typical entry-level job is the *scale and bin tender* who weighs and records all feed grain entering, leaving, or being used in the feeding yards. This person also arranges for proper grain storage and keeps an accurate inventory of all animals and types of feed on hand.

Another entry-level position is the *feed-mixing technician* who weighs, mixes, and blends animal feed according to recommendations made by the ration technician.

The *ration technician* is an experienced livestock production technician who selects the most desirable feed and supplements to keep animals healthy and growing rapidly, and to produce the best return for the dollar invested. The ration technician must know the nutritional needs of each type of livestock which he or she works with. Nutritional requirements will change with factors such as age, pregnancy, season, and health, and the ration technician must know how to adjust the feed.

Experienced livestock production technicians interested in animal feeding may also be employed as *feed buyers* or *feed lot managers*. Feed buyers supply the feed needed for all of a farm's operations, and buy the kinds most suitable and economical for each operation.

Feed lot managers supervise the entire feed lot operation. They must be familiar with shipping, receiving, mixing of feeds, buying and selling of livestock, and the work of each employee.

Another farm position for livestock production technicians is the *disease prevention technician*. This technician protects animals from disease and parasites, administers disease prevention treatments such as dipping and vaccination, conducts frequent examinations, and treats livestock for cuts, wounds, and minor diseases.

Off-farm livestock production technicians work in a variety of different capacities. Once again, they may be involved with feed preparation. Since small producers of cattle, sheep, and hogs often do not have facilities to store, mix, or grind feed, they must rely on feed companies, which hire technicians to perform the various feed-related activities already described.

Livestock production technicians also sell, service, and sometimes install the mechanical equipment used in livestock production. These include trucks and tractors, mechanized feed mixers and feed carriers, and manure-turning machines.

Another off-farm occupation is judge and purchaser of livestock. Technicians working in this area are usually employed by slaughterhouses or meat-packing companies, for which they inspect, grade, and weigh livestock to determine value and yield. They may also arrange for the transportation and sale of the livestock.

Some off-farm livestock production technicians are employed as *veterinarians' assistants.* They assist in the care of animals under treatment, sterilize equipment, and administer medication under the direction of the veterinarian.

In the work of bird production, technicians can be divided into seven areas. In breeding-flock production, technicians may work as *farm managers,* directing the operation of one or several farms. They may be *flock supervisors* with five or six assistants working directly with farmers under contract to produce hatching eggs. On pedigree breeding farms, technicians may oversee all the people who transport, feed, and care for the poultry. Technicians in breeding-flock production look for ways to improve efficiency in the use of time, materials, and labor; and they also seek to make effective use of data-processing equipment.

In hatchery management, technicians operate and maintain the incubators and hatchers, where eggs develop as embryos. Technicians in this area must be trained in incubation, sexing, grading, scheduling, and effectively using available technology.

The production and marketing of table eggs requires poultry technicians to handle birds on pullet-growing farms and egg farms. Experienced poultry technicians often work as supervisors of flocks and manage those who provide the actual care of the flocks. Poultry technicians may also work in or supervise smaller, specialized production units, which may clean, grade, or package eggs for wholesale or retail trade.

The egg processing phase begins when the eggs leave the farm. *Egg processing technicians* handle egg pickup, trucking, delivery, and quality control. With experience, technicians in this area work as *supervisors* and *plant managers.* These technicians need training in egg processing machinery and refrigeration equipment.

Technicians in poultry meat production supervise the production, management, and inspection of birds bred specifically for consumption as meat. Technicians may work directly with flocks or in supervisory positions.

Poultry meat processing and sales technicians supervise or carry out the task of picking up meat birds at the farms on schedule to keep processing plants operating efficiently. Technicians working as plant supervisors handle all phases of processing, including inspection for quality, grading, packaging, and marketing. They also operate machinery, as well as maintain and manage plant personnel.

Finally, poultry technicians are employed in the sales and service of poultry equipment, feed, and supplies.

Within these seven broad areas, a number of specific kinds of jobs are commonly performed by poultry technicians. The following short paragraphs describe some of these jobs, each appropriate for entry-level technicians.

Poultry graders certify the grade of dressed or ready-to-cook poultry in processing plants according to government standards.

Poultry husbandry technicians conduct research in breeding, feeding, and management of poultry. They examine selection and breeding practices in order to increase efficiency of production and to improve the quality of poultry products.

Poultry inspectors certify wholesomeness and acceptability of live, dressed, and ready-to-cook poultry in processing plants.

Egg candlers inspect eggs to determine quality and fitness for consumption or incubation, according to prescribed standards. They check to see if eggs have been fertilized and if they are developing correctly.

Egg graders inspect, sort, and grade eggs according to size, shape, color, and weight.

Some poultry technicians also work as *field-contact technicians,* inspecting poultry farms for food processing companies. They ensure that growers maintain contract standards for feeding and housing birds and controlling disease. They tour barns, incubation units, and related facilities to observe sanitation and weather protection procedures. Field-contact technicians make sure that specific grains are administered according to schedules, inspect birds for evidence of disease, and weigh them to determine growth rates. This occupation is described in more detail in the article titled "Agribusiness technicians."

One area of animal production technology that merits special mention is that of artificial breeding. Three kinds of technicians working in this specialized area of animal production are the *artificial-breeding technician,* the *artificial-breeding laboratory technician,* and the *poultry inseminator,* sometimes called an *artificial insemination technician.*

Artificial-breeding technicians collect and package semen for artificial insemination. They examine the semen under a microscope to determine density and motility of sperm cells, and they dilute the semen according to standard formulas. They transfer the semen to shipping and storage containers with identifying data such as the source, the date taken, and the quality. They also keep records related to all of their activities. In some cases they may also be responsible for inseminating the females.

Artificial-breeding laboratory technicians handle the artificial breeding of all kinds of animals, but most often these technicians special-

ANIMAL PRODUCTION TECHNICIANS

ize in the laboratory aspects of the activity. They measure purity, potency, and density of animal semen, and add extenders and antibiotics to it. They keep records, clean and sterilize laboratory equipment, and perform experimental tests to develop improved methods of processing and preserving semen.

Poultry inseminators collect semen from roosters and fertilize hens' eggs. They examine the roosters' semen for quality and density; measure specified amounts of semen for loading into inseminating guns; inject semen into hens; and keep accurate records of all aspects of the operation. This area of animal production should have a good future as poultry production expands.

All of these jobs have some application in areas beyond cattle and poultry production. Animals raised for fur or skin also require extensive technological assistance. Mink farms, ostrich farms, and alligator farms are all animal production industries that need husbandry, feeding, and health technicians. As the popularity of one species rise or falls, others replace it, and new animal specialists are needed.

Requirements

Much of the work done by animal production technicians involves physical labor, often outdoors, in all kinds of weather conditions.

High school students seeking to enter this field will find that the more agricultural background they acquire in high school, the better prepared they will be. In addition, courses in mathematics, business, communications, chemistry, and mechanics will be valuable. A high school diploma is nearly always necessary to enter any technical education program beyond the high school level.

Many colleges offer two-year programs in animal science or animal husbandry where additional knowledge, skills, and specialized training may be acquired. Animal production technicians also need the ability to speak well to conduct meetings, and to work cooperatively with individuals as well as groups of people.

Opportunities for experience and exploration

Children of farm families have the greatest opportunity to decide whether this career appeals to them. For those who have not grown up on a farm, however, there are summer jobs available on livestock farms that will help them decide if this type of work is what they want. In addition, organizations such as 4-H Clubs and National FFA Organization (Future Farmers of America) offer good opportunities for hearing about, visiting, and participating in farm activities.

For at-home experience, raising pets is a good introduction to the skills needed in basic animal maintenance. Learning how to care for, feed, and house a pet provides some basic knowledge of working with animals. There are many books on animal care that can help someone interested in learning about animals.

Other opportunities that provide animal maintenance experience include volunteering to work at anti-cruelty society centers, animal shelters, veterinary offices, and pet breeders' businesses.

Methods of entering

Most available programs in animal production technology are relatively new, and many job placement procedures have not been developed to the fullest degree. However, many avenues are open and employers recognize the importance of education at the technical level. Many junior colleges participate in a "learn-and-earn" program, in which the college and prospective employer jointly provide the student's training, both in the classroom and actual on-the-job work with livestock and other animals. Most technical programs offer placement services for graduates, and the demand for qualified people often exceeds the supply.

Advancement

Even when a good training or technical program is completed, the graduate often must begin work at a lower level before advancing to positions with more responsibility. But the technical program graduate will advance much more rapidly to positions of major responsibility and greater financial reward than the untrained worker.

Those graduates willing to work hard and keep informed of changes in their field may advance to livestock breeder, feedlot manager, supervisor, or artificial breeding distributor. If they can raise the money, they can own their own livestock ranches.

Employment outlook

Continuing changes are expected in the next few years, in both the production and the marketing phases of the animal production industry. Because of the costs involved, it is almost impossible for a one-person operation to stay in business. As a result, cooperatives and corporations will become more prevalent with greater emphasis placed on specialization. This, in turn, will increase the demand for technical program graduates. Other factors, such as small profit margins, the demand for more uniform products, and an increasing foreign market, will result in a need for more specifically trained personnel. This is a new era of specialization in the animal production industry; graduates of animal production technology programs have an interesting and rewarding future ahead of them.

Earnings

Salaries vary widely depending on the kind of employer, the technicians' educational and agricultural background, the kind of animal the technicians work with, and the geographical areas in which they work. In general, the salaries of all agricultural technicians tend to be lower in the northeast part of the nation and higher in California and some parts of the Midwest, such as Minnesota and Iowa. Currently, starting salaries for animal production technicians range from approximately $12,000 a year, or sometimes less, to $16,000 a year or more. In addition, many technicians receive food and housing benefits that can be equal to an additional several thousand dollars a year. Other fringe benefits vary according to type of employer but can include paid vacation time, health insurance, and pension benefits.

Conditions of work

Working conditions vary from operation to operation, but certain factors always exist in varying degrees. Much of the work is done outside in all types of weather, and often requires long, irregular hours and work on Sundays and holidays. Salaries are usually commensurate with the hours worked, and there are usually slack seasons when time off is given to repay any extra hours worked. But the most important feature is the desire to work with animals. If one is not comfortable around animals, or is not really interested in them, this is not a wise career choice.

Animal production technicians are often their own bosses and make their own decisions. While this can be considered an asset to those who value independence, prospective animal production technicians must realize that self-discipline is the most valuable trait to possess for success.

GOE: 02.04.02, 03.02.04, 03.04.05; SIC: 021; SOC: 382

◇ **SOURCES OF ADDITIONAL INFORMATION**

National Cattlemen's Association
PO Box 3469
Englewood, CO 80155

National Grain and Feed Association
725 15th Street, NW
Suite 500
Washington, DC 20005

U.S. Department of Agriculture
Washington, DC 20250

Canadian Cattlemen's Association
#216, 6715 8th Street, North East
Calgary AB T2E 7H7

◇ **RELATED ARTICLES**

Volume 1: Agriculture; Wildlife Management
Volumes 2–4: Agricultural extension service workers; Agricultural scientists; Agribusiness technicians; Biological scientists; Biological technicians; Buyers, wholesale and retail; Dairy products manufacturing workers; Farmers; Medical technologists; Purchasing agents; Veterinarians

Animal trainers

Definition

Animal trainers teach animals to obey commands, to compete in shows or races, or to perform tricks to entertain audiences. They also may teach dogs to protect property or to act as guides for the visually impaired. Animal trainers may specialize with one type of animal or with several types.

History

The training of animals actually began thousands of years ago for very practical purposes. Evidence found in archaeological digs indicates that dogs, for example, were trained to help hunt down wild game for food, to herd other domesticated animals, such as goats and sheep, and to stand guard at campsites and outside of dwellings.

People quickly saw the advantages of training larger animals to do much of the heavy labor involved in farming and building. Horses, water buffalo, elephants, and camels are some animals used by various cultures to pull wagons and plows and to carry heavy loads.

Animal training today is still an important activity. Some animals are trained simply to be well behaved pets, others for sports or entertainment. Some are taught to do useful work. Dogs, for example, can be trained to assist in police work, guide the blind, guard valuable property, and work with farm animals.

Nature of the work

Many animals are capable of being trained, including horses, elephants, cockatoos and seals. The techniques used to train them, however, are basically the same, regardless of the type of animal.

Animal trainers conduct a program consisting primarily of repetition and reward to teach animals to behave in a particular manner and to do it consistently. First, trainers evaluate an animal's temperament, ability, and aptitude to determine whether it is trainable and which methods would be most effective. Then, by painstakingly repeating routines many times, rewarding the animal whenever it does what is expected, they train it to obey or perform on command. In addition, animal trainers generally are responsible for the feeding, exercising, grooming, and general care of the animals, either handling the duties themselves or supervising other workers.

Trainers usually specialize and are identified by the animal they work with. Some of them organize or direct animal shows and sometimes take part in an act. They also may rehearse animals for specific motion pictures, stage productions, or circus programs, and sometimes cue the animals during a performance.

Not all trainers prepare animals for the entertainment field, however. *Dog trainers,* for example, may work with dogs to be used in police work, training them to search for drugs or missing people. Some train guard dogs to protect private property; others train guide dogs for the blind and may also help dog and master function as a team.

Horse trainers specialize in training horses for riding or for harness. They talk to and handle the horse gently to accustom it to human contact, then gradually get it to accept a harness, bridle, saddle, and other riding gear. Trainers teach horses to respond to commands that are either spoken or given by use of the reins and legs. Draft horses are conditioned to draw equipment either alone or as part of a team. Show horses are given special training to qualify them to perform in competitions. Horse trainers sometimes have to retrain animals that have developed bad habits, such as bucking or biting. Besides feeding, exercising, and grooming, these trainers sometimes make arrangements for breeding the horses and may help mares deliver their foals.

A highly specialized occupation in the horse-training field is that of *racehorse trainers,* who must create a training plan for each horse individually. By studying the animal's performance record and becoming familiar with its behavior during workouts, trainers can adapt their training methods to take advantage of each animal's peculiarities. Like other animal trainers, racehorse trainers oversee the exercising, grooming, and feeding of their charges. They also clock the running time during workouts to determine when a horse is ready for competitive racing. Racehorse trainers coach jockeys on how best to handle a particular horse during a race and may give owners advice on purchasing horses.

Requirements

People wanting to be animal trainers should like animals and have a genuine interest in working with them.

Establishments that hire trainers often require previous experience as an animal keeper or aquarist, because proper care and feeding of the animals is an essential part of a trainer's responsibilities. Racehorse trainers often begin as jockeys or grooms in training stables.

Although there are no formal education requirements to enter this field, animal trainers in zoos, circuses, and the entertainment field are sometimes required to have some education in animal psychology in addition to their caretaking experience. Trainers of guide dogs for the blind prepare for their work in a three-year course of study at a school that trains the dogs and instructs their blind owners.

Most trainers begin their careers as keepers and gain on-the-job experience in evaluating the disposition, intelligence, and trainability of the animals they look after. At the same time, they learn to make friends with their charges, develop a rapport with them, and gain their confidence. The caretaking experience is an important building block in the education and success of an animal trainer. Although previous training experience may give job applicants an advantage in being hired, they still will be expected to spend time caring for the animals before advancing to the position of trainer.

Special requirements

Racehorse trainers must be licensed by the state in which they work. Otherwise, there are no special requirements for this occupation.

Opportunities for experience and exploration

Students wishing to enter this field would do well to learn as much as they can about animals, especially animal psychology, either through course work or library study. Interviews with animal trainers and tours of their workplaces might be arranged to learn first-hand about the practical aspects of the occupation.

Part-time or volunteer work in animal shelters, pet shops, or veterinary offices offers would-be trainers a chance to become accustomed to working with animals and to discover whether they have the aptitude for it. Experience can be acquired, too, in summer jobs as animal caretakers at zoos, aquariums, museums that feature live animal shows, amusement parks, and for those with a special interest in horse racing, stables or riding stables.

Methods of entering

People who want to become animal trainers generally start out as animal keepers or caretakers and rise to the position of trainer only after acquiring experience within the ranks of an organization. They enter the field by applying directly for a job as animal keeper, letting the employer or their supervisor know of their ambition so they will eventually be considered for promotion.

Students with some background in animal psychology and previous experience caring for a specific animal may find summer jobs as trainers at large amusement or theme parks, but these jobs are not plentiful, and application should be made early in the year.

Advancement

Most establishments have very small staffs of animal trainers, which means that the opportunities for advancement are limited. The progression is from animal keeper to animal trainer. A trainer who directs or supervises others may be designated head animal trainer or senior animal trainer.

Some animal trainers go into business for themselves and, if successful, hire other trainers to work for them. Others become agents for animal acts.

Employment outlook

The demand for animal trainers is not great, because most employers have no need for a large staff and tend to promote from within. Applicants must be well qualified to overcome the heavy competition for the jobs that are available. The field is expected to remain limited through the 1990s even though some openings may be created as zoos and aquariums expand or provide more animal shows in an effort to increase revenue.

Earnings

Salaries of animal trainers can vary widely depending on specialty and place of employment.

Because of this diversity, formal salary ranges are not available for most of these occupations. In the field of racehorse training, however, trainers are paid an average fee of from $35 to $50 a day for each horse, plus 10 percent of any money their horses win in races. Show horse trainers may earn as much as $30,000 to $35,000 a year. Trainers in business for themselves set their own fees for teaching both horses and owners.

Conditions of work

The working hours for animal trainers vary considerably, depending on type of animal, performance schedule, and whether travel is involved. For some trainers, such as those who work with show horses, the hours can be long and quite irregular.

Except in warm climates, animal shows are seasonal, running from April or May through mid-autumn. During this time, much of the work is conducted outdoors. In winter, trainers work indoors, preparing for the warm-weather shows. Trainers of aquatic mammals, such as dolphins and seals, must feel at ease working around, in, and under water.

The physical strength required depends on the animal involved. Pushing or pulling an elephant into position, for example, is quite different from manipulating a dog.

Trainers who work with wild animals need to exercise particular caution, as there is always the danger of a previously docile animal becoming temperamental.

This occupation calls for an infinite amount of patience. Trainers must spend long hours repeating routines, rewarding their pupils for performing well, while never getting angry with them or punishing them when they fail to do what is expected. Trainers must be able to exhib-

it the authority to keep the animals under control without raising their voices or using physical force. Calmness under stress is particularly important when dealing with wild animals.

GOE: 03.03.01; SIC: 0752, 7948; SOC: 328, 5617

◇ **SOURCES OF ADDITIONAL INFORMATION**

American Association of Zoological Parks and Aquariums
Route 88, Oglebay Park
Wheeling, WV 26003

Animal Caretakers Information
Humane Society of the U.S. Companion Animals Division
5430 Grosvenor Lane, Suite 100
Bethesda, MD 20814

Canadian Association of Zoological Parks and Aquariums
℅ Calgary Zoo
PO Box 3036
Calgary AB T2M 4R8

◇ **RELATED ARTICLES**

Volume 1: Biological Sciences; Wildlife Management
Volumes 2–4: Agricultural scientists; Animal production technicians; Dog groomers; Equestrian management workers; Fishers, commercial; Fish-production technicians; Veterinarians; Veterinary technicians; Zookeepers

---

Anthropologists and archaeologists

Definition

Anthropologists and *archaeologists* study the origin and evolution of humans from a scientific point of view. The main difference between the two is that anthropologists focus on studying people, like tracing their physical development

through history, and archaeologists are concerned with people's cultures and societies. In a sense, the work of anthropologists is dependent upon that of archaeologists; since archaeologists are directly involved in excavation, part of what they uncover is important to the work of anthropologists.

History

Although anthropology dates back to Aristotle, it became an established science during the era of colonial exploration and expansion, because of increased contact with different peoples of the world. Anthropology developed during the Industrial Revolution, along with the study of geology, and Darwin's theory of evolution. Archaeology is a newer social science, beginning with the discovery of Roman ruins in the 18th century.

With developments in technology and fieldwork and increased support of governments, these fields have expanded to cover a broad range of social sciences.

Nature of the work

Anthropology and archaeology are concerned with the study and comparison of people in all parts of the world, their physical characteristics, customs, languages, traditions, material possessions, and social and religious beliefs and practices. Anthropologists and archaeologists constitute the smallest group of social scientists, yet they cover the widest range of subject matter.

Anthropological data, including that acquired by archaeological techniques, may be applied to solving problems in human relations in fields such as industrial relations, race and ethnic relations, social work, political administration, education, public health, and programs involving transcultural or foreign relations.

Cultural anthropology, the area in which the greatest number of anthropologists specialize, deals with human behavior and studies aspects of both extinct and current societies, including religion, language, politics, social structure and traditions, mythology, art, and intellectual life. *Cultural anthropologists,* also called *ethnologists,* classify and compare cultures according to general laws of historical, cultural, and social development. To do this effectively, they often work with smaller, less complex, and perhaps more easily understood societies, like the tribal societies of Asia.

Archaeologists have a particularly important role in the areas of cultural anthropology. They apply specialized techniques to reconstruct a record of past cultures by studying, classifying, and interpreting artifacts such as pottery, clothing, tools, weapons, and ornaments, to determine cultural identity. They obtain these artifacts through excavation of sites including buildings and cities, and establish the chronological sequence of the development of

Two anthropologists study stone tools from Zaire that are believed to be among the oldest known utensils fashioned by prehistoric humans.

each culture from simpler to more advanced levels. *Prehistoric archaeologists* study cultures that existed prior to the period of recorded history, while historical archaeologists study more recent societies. The historic period spans several thousand years in some parts of the world and sometimes only a few hundred years in parts of the Western hemisphere. *Classical archaeologists* concentrate on ancient Mediterranean and Middle Eastern cultures. An *artifacts conservator* or preservationist restores and preserves artifacts found at archaeological sites. Through the study of the history of specific groups of peoples, whose society may be extinct, cultural anthropologists and archaeologists are able to reconstruct their cultures, including the pattern of daily life and the areas in which the members of that society expressed the greatest interest.

Anthropologists also may be involved in the application of anthropological concepts to current problems, using their research to find solutions. *Anthropological linguists* study the ways in which people use language and how this affects and is affected by their behavior. *Anthropological psychologists* study the effect of culture on the individual's personality. One of

An urban archaeology team examines artifacts that will provide clues to the living patterns of early 19th-century city dwellers in Philadelphia.

the most relevant specializations to modern life is urban anthropology in which the effect of current social and cultural trends is projected and necessary changes proposed. *Urban anthropologists* work with architects, designers, and city planners on housing projects. Some assist social services to provide better health care and education to immigrant groups.

Physical anthropologists are concerned primarily with the biology of human groups. They study the differences between the members of past and present human societies and are particularly interested in the geographical distribution of human physical characteristics. Some physical anthropologists concentrate on the human and primate skeletal remains from various areas of the world and, through the study of these remains, learn more about the people and their society. They apply their intensive training in human anatomy to the study of human evolution and to establish differences between races and groups of people. Their work on the effect of heredity and environment on cultural attitudes towards health and nutrition enables medical anthropologists to help develop urban health programs. *Anthropometrists* research growth and development by measuring the human body and skeleton.

Some anthropologists use archaeological data to study the daily life, routine, and interests of peoples who lived many years ago. Those studying ethnology are interested in living people, usually simple societies, and their customs and beliefs. Linguistics is the scientific study of languages, which leads to a more thorough understanding of the people who spoke those languages. Other anthropologists specialize in cultural theory, or the study of contacts between various cultures, including the characteristics of cultural change.

Archaeologists often must travel extensively to perform field work on the site where a culture once flourished. Site work is often slow and laborious. Conducting digs to uncover artifacts may take years to produce valuable information.

Another important aspect of archaeology is the cleaning, restoration, and preservation of artifacts. This work may take place on the site of discovery to minimize deterioration of textiles and mummified remains. Careful recording of the exact location and condition of artifacts is essential for further study.

Many anthropologists work for the federal and state governments, teach in colleges and universities, and work in museums. Those employed by the government serve as consultants to save or restore valuable cultural resources. They may survey a site and assess its value before the start of a construction project such as a hydroelectric power plant or highway.

Teachers may lecture to groups on various subjects related to anthropology including sociology or geography. In addition to teaching, they may research and write papers or articles for public presentation or publication in professional journals.

Those employed in museums often will find themselves combining both their management and administrative duties with their training in anthropology in carrying out various field work projects, including excavations and research on various anthropological collections already gathered.

An important part of museum work performed by artifact conservators is the cleaning, repairing, and reinforcing of specimens such as weapons, tools, and pottery, using chemical and skilled mechanical techniques. Artifacts may be restored by polishing, joining together broken fragments, or other procedures.

Requirements

High school students planning to enter anthropology should study English composition and literature, mathematics (preferably beyond algebra), history, geography, natural science, computer science, and foreign languages. Typing, sketching, simple surveying, and photography also may be helpful.

The high school graduate should be prepared for a long training period beyond high school. Most of the better positions in anthropology and archaeology will require a doctorate, which entails about four to six years of work beyond the bachelor's degree. Before starting graduate work, however, the undergraduate will probably study such basic courses as psychology, sociology, history, geography, mathematics, logic, English composition, and literature, as well as modern and ancient languages.

The final two years of the undergraduate program will provide an opportunity for specialization not only in anthropology but in some specific phase of the discipline.

Students planning to become physical anthropologists should concentrate on the biological sciences. The physical sciences and oral history/folklore studies are an important supplement to archaeological studies, as is field training arranged through the university. A wide range of interdisciplinary study in languages, history, and the social sciences, as well as the humanities, is particularly important in cultural anthropology, including the areas of linguistics and ethnology. Independent field study also is done in these areas.

In starting graduate training, students should select an institution that has a good program in the area in which they hope to specialize. This is important, not only because the training should be of a high quality, but because most graduates in anthropology and archaeology will receive their first jobs through their graduate universities. Employers often look first to the graduates of the institutions offering the strongest programs in anthropology and archaeology.

Assistantships and temporary positions may be available to holders of bachelor's or master's degrees but are usually available only to those working toward a doctorate.

Opportunities for experience and exploration

Anthropology and archaeology may be explored in a number of ways. For example, Boy Scout and Girl Scout troops participate in camping expeditions for exploration purposes. Local amateur anthropological or archaeological societies may have weekly or monthly meetings and guest speakers, carry on study of developments in the field, and engage in exploration on the local level.

Trips to museums also will introduce students to the world of anthropology and archaeology. Both high school and college students may work in museums on a part-time basis during the school year or during summer vacations. Voluntary archaeological work also is available. This experience can be of great value to those considering the field.

Methods of entering

The most popular way of entering these occupations is through graduate schools. Graduates in anthropology or archaeology might be approached prior to graduation by prospective employers. Often, professors will provide the student with introductions as well as recommendations.

Students often have an opportunity to work as a research assistant or a teaching fellow while in graduate school, and frequently this experience is of tremendous help in qualifying for a job in another institution. Also, graduates may be able to remain at the institution from which they received their degrees to teach or engage in research.

Advancement

Because of the relatively small size of this field, advancement is not likely to be fast and the opportunities for advancement may be somewhat limited. Most people beginning their teaching careers in colleges or universities will start as instructors and eventually advance to assistant professor, associate professor, and possibly full professor. Researchers on the college level have an opportunity to head research areas and to gain recognition among colleagues as an expert in many areas of study.

Anthropologists and archaeologists employed in museums also have an opportunity to advance within the institution.

Employment outlook

About 7,000 anthropologists and archaeologists are employed in the United States in the early 1990s. It is anticipated that most new jobs arising through the rest of the 1990s will be nonteaching positions in consulting firms, research institutes, corporations, and federal, state, and local government agencies. Among the factors contributing to this growth is increased environmental, historic, and cultural preservation legislation. There is a particular demand for people with the ability to write environmental impact statements.

Archaeologists with a master's degree may be supervisors in charge of digging or collecting specimens. These people may be hired on a full-time or on a temporary contract basis for consulting firms, government agencies, academic institutions, and museums. The fields of environmental protection and historic preservation are growing, and interest in ethnic studies may spur demand for anthropological research in that area as well.

Although college and university teaching has been the largest area of employment for anthropologists, the demand is expected to decline in this area through the 1990s as a result of the steady decrease in student enrollment. Overall, the number of job applicants will be greater than the number of openings available. Competition will be great even for those with doctorates who are seeking faculty positions, and many will find only temporary or nontenured jobs. Junior college and high school teaching jobs will be very limited, and those holding a bachelor's or master's degree will have few opportunities. Other areas of potential employment include foreign jobs. Museums and local governments conduct archeological studies and may require outside expertise. Strong language skills and extensive work in the field are normal prerequisites.

Earnings

Salaries for faculty in colleges and universities vary depending on the institution, with the lower range in those schools that grant only undergraduate degrees in anthropology or archaeology. In the 1990s, instructors earn about $26,800 annually. Salaries for associate professors average about $44,800 annually, and full professors earn $62,900 or more a year.

Entry-level positions with the federal government for those with bachelor's degrees range from $14,800 to $18,400 a year. Anthropologists and archaeologists with master's degrees receive a starting salary of about $22,500, and those with doctorates generally start at around $27,200. The average annual salary for all anthropologists and archaeologists in the federal government is around $38,800.

Many anthropologists and archaeologists earn additional income through writing for publication or through summer jobs.

Conditions of work

The majority of anthropologists and archaeologists are employed by colleges and universities and, as such, have good working conditions, although field work may require extensive travel and difficult living conditions. They are normally under regular academic vacation and sick leave plans, and most colleges and univer-

sities having programs in anthropology and archaeology will have good retirement plans. The physical facilities are normally clean, well lighted, and ventilated.

Anthropologists and archaeologists work about 40 hours a week, and the hours may be irregular. Physical strength and stamina is necessary for field work of all types. Those working on excavations, for instance, may work during most of the daylight hours and spend the evening planning the next day's activities. Those engaged in teaching may spend many hours in laboratory research or in preparing lessons to be taught. The work is interesting, however, and those employed in the field are usually highly motivated and unconcerned about long, irregular hours or primitive living conditions.

GOE: 11.03.03; SIC: 822; SOC: 1919

◇ SOURCES OF ADDITIONAL INFORMATION

American Anthropological Association
1703 New Hampshire Avenue, NW
Washington, DC 20009

Archaeological Institute of America
675 Commonwealth Avenue
Boston, MA 02215

Society for American Archaeology
808 17th Street, NW, Suite 200
Washington, DC 20006

U.S. Department of the Interior
Washington, DC 20240

Wenner-Gren Foundation for Anthropological Research
220 Fifth Avenue, 16th floor
New York, NY 10001

◇ RELATED ARTICLES

Appliance repairers

Definition

Appliance repairers install and service many kinds of electrical and gas appliances, such as washing machines, dryers, refrigerators, ovens, and vacuum cleaners. Some repairers specialize in one type of appliance, such as microwave ovens, while others work with a variety of appliances used in homes and business establishments.

History

Although some small home appliances, including irons and coffee percolators, were patented before the twentieth century began, only a few types of appliances were in general use before the end of World War I. Around that time more efficient and inexpensive electric motors were developed, and electric and gas utility companies began extending their services into all parts of the nation. Many new labor-saving appliances began to appear on the market. At home and at work, people relied increasingly on a wide variety of machines to make everyday tasks easier and more pleasant. Soon many kinds of equipment like washers and kitchen ranges were considered an essential part of a middle-class life.

Especially since the end of World War II, there has been a tremendous growth in the use and production of home appliances. The country's growing population, together with the general expectation of a rising standard of living, accounts for much of the growth in this field. In addition to improved versions of old products, the public has wanted to buy numerous new kinds of appliances, such as electric can openers, room air conditioners, and in-sink food waste disposers.

As the overall use of appliances has grown in recent decades, the need for qualified people to install, repair, and service them has also grown. But today's repairers need a different mix of knowledge and skills than was needed by the appliance repairers of years ago. This is because today's appliances often involve complex electronic parts. To consumers, a big advantage of electronic components is their superior reliability. However, the fact that modern electronic appliances need fewer repairs means that the demand for appliance repairers is no longer growing as fast as the use of new appliances.

Nature of the work

Appliance repairers use a variety of methods and tools to figure out exactly why appliances need repair. They may inspect machines for frayed electrical cords, cracked hoses, and broken connections; listen for loud vibrations or grinding noises; sniff for fumes or burning materials; look for fluid leaks; watch as gears turn; and feel other moving parts to determine if they are jammed or too tight. They may find the cause of trouble by using special tools made for particular appliances or testing devices such as voltmeters and ammeters. They must be able to combine all their observations into a diagnosis of the problem before they can repair the appliance.

Repairers often need to take apart and examine the inside of an appliance. To do this, they often use ordinary hand tools like screwdrivers, wrenches, and pliers. They may follow instructions in service manuals and troubleshooting guides. They may consult wiring diagrams to understand electrical circuits. They look for problems like electrical shorts, worn or defective belts, switches, circuit boards, and other items, and they clean, lubricate, and adjust parts so that they function as well as possible.

Repairers who service gas appliances may replace pipes, valves, thermostats, and indicator devices. In installing gas appliances, they may need to measure, cut, and thread pipes, connect the pipes to gas feeder lines, and do simple carpentry work like cutting holes in floors to allow pipes to pass through.

Appliance repairers who make service calls to homes and businesses often must answer customers' questions and complaints. They may advise customers about the care and use of their appliances. In addition, these repairers must be able to order parts from catalogs and record the time they have spent, the parts they have used, and whether a warranty applies to the repair job. They may need to estimate the cost of repairs, collect payment for their work, and sometimes sell new or used appliances. Many repairers who make service calls drive light trucks or automobiles equipped with two-way radios so that as soon as they finish one job, they can be dispatched to another.

Although many appliance repairers service many kinds of appliances, there are also repairers who specialize in one kind or one brand of appliances. *Window air-conditioning unit installer-*

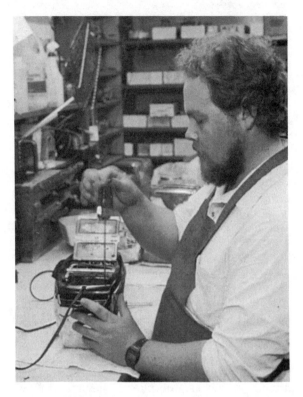

An appliance repairer disassembles the bottom of a toaster to replace some damaged parts.

servicers, for example, work only with portable window units, while *domestic air-conditioning installers* handle both window and central systems in homes.

Household appliance installers specialize in installing refrigerators, freezers, washing machines, clothes dryers, kitchen ranges, and ovens; *household appliance servicers* maintain and repair these units.

Small electrical appliance repairers handle portable household electrical appliances such as toasters, coffee makers, lamps, hair dryers, fans, food processors, dehumidifiers, and irons. Customers with appliances like these that need servicing usually bring them to repairers who work in repair shops.

Gas appliance repairers install, repair, and clean gas appliances such as ranges or stoves, heaters, and furnaces, and they advise customers on safe, efficient, and economical use of gas.

Requirements

Applicants for jobs as appliance repairers usually must be high school graduates with some knowledge of electricity (especially wiring diagrams) and if possible, electronics. Applicants

may be hired as helpers who acquire most of their skills through on-the-job experience. Some employers assign such helpers to accompany experienced repairers when they are sent to do repairs in customers' homes and businesses. The trainees observe and assist the experienced repairers in diagnosing and correcting problems with appliances. Other employers assign helpers to work in the company's shop where they begin by learning how to rebuild used appliances and to make simple repairs. At the end of 6 to 12 months, they usually know enough to make most repairs on their own, and they may be sent on service calls alone.

An additional year or two of experience is often required for trainees to become fully qualified. During this period, they may round out their knowledge of certain aspects of their work by attending service schools sponsored by appliance manufacturers or local distributors, often on company time. Trainees can also expect to study service manuals to familiarize themselves with some appliances, especially new models. Reading manuals and attending courses is a continuing part of any repairer's job.

Many repairers learn their job skills through public and private technical and vocational schools that provide formal classroom training and laboratory experience in the service and repair of appliances. The length of these programs varies, with many lasting from one to two years. Correspondence courses that teach basic appliance repairing are also available. Although formal training in the skills needed for appliance repairing can be a great advantage for job applicants, beginning repairers should still expect to need some additional on-the-job training to acquaint them with the work done in their new employer's shop.

Special requirements

In some states, appliance repairers may need to be licensed or registered. Licenses are granted to applicants who meet certain standards of education, training, and experience, and who pass an examination.

Opportunities for experience and exploration

People who are interested in appliance servicing work can begin exploring the field by talking to employees of local appliance repair shops and appliance dealerships. These employees may know about part-time or summer jobs that allow students to observe and perhaps help out with repairing. Gas and electric utility companies and appliance manufacturers may also be a source of useful job experience. Other ways students can judge their interest and aptitude for this work include taking shop courses, especially electrical shop, and assembling electronics equipment from kits.

Methods of entering

A typical way of starting out in this occupation is to become a helper in a repair shop where the employer trains qualified beginners as their work at their job. Another way is to take courses in appliance repairing at a vocational or technical school. Newly hired beginners who have completed such programs usually need much less on-the-job training and may be able to take on greater responsibilities fairly soon.

Advancement

The kinds of advancement that are possible for repairers depend mainly on their place of employment. In a small repair shop of three to five people, advancement is likely to be slow, because the owner is probably doing most of the supervisory and administrative tasks. In working for a large retailer, a factory service center, or a gas or electric utility company, however, a repairer could progress to supervisor, assistant service manager, and service manager.

Another route of advancement leads to teaching at a factory service training school. A repairer who knows the product, does the work with proficiency, and can speak effectively to groups can conduct classes to train other repairers. Technical and vocational schools that offer courses in appliance repair work may also hire experienced repairers to teach classes.

For some appliance repairers, the goal is opening an independent repair business. This step usually requires a knowledge of business management and a significant investment in tools, parts, vehicles, and other equipment.

Some repairers who work for appliance manufacturers can move into positions where they write service manuals, sell appliances, or act as manufacturers' representatives to appliance distributors.

Employment outlook

In the 1990s, there are around 70,000 appliance repairers employed throughout the country in repair shops and by appliance manufacturers and retail dealers, utility companies, and various firms that service specific kinds of equipment such as coin-operated washers, dryers, and dry-cleaning machines. Over the next 10 or 15 years, the total number of repairers is not expected to change much. Although Americans will certainly continue buying and using more appliances, today's machines are often made with electronic components, which require fewer repairs than their non-electronic counterparts. Thus the dependability of the technology built into these new appliances will tend to restrain growth in the repair field. Most of the openings that arise will be because workers are leaving their jobs and must be replaced.

Earnings

The earnings of appliance repairers vary widely according to the workers' geographical location, skills, experience, the kind of equipment serviced, and other factors. One study of repairers in unionized shops indicates that in the 1990s their earnings range from less than $11,400 to over $34,800 annually, with the median at $21,840. Apprentices are usually paid less than repairers who have completed their training period. Employees of gas utility companies and other large companies generally have a relatively high hourly wage. Opportunities for overtime pay are most favorable for repairers of major appliances, such as refrigerators, stoves, and washing machines. In addition to regular pay, many workers receive paid vacations and sick leave, health insurance, and other benefits such as employer contributions to retirement pension plans.

Conditions of work

Appliance repairers generally work a 40-hour week, although some work evenings and weekends. The working conditions they encounter vary with the kind of appliances they install or repair. Repairers who fix small appliances work indoors at a bench and seldom have to handle heavy objects. Repair shops are generally well lighted, properly ventilated, and equipped with the necessary tools.

Repairers who work on major appliances must deal with a variety of situations. They

93

normally work in various customers' homes and businesses, so they may spend several hours each day driving from one job to the next. To do repairs, they may have to work in small or dirty spaces or in other uncomfortable conditions. They may have to crawl, bend, stoop, crouch, or lie down to carry out some repairs, and they may have to move heavy weights.

In any appliance repair work, repairers have to be sure to follow good safety practices. They sometimes handle potentially dangerous tools, gas, and electric current. Beginners are always instructed in the procedures and precautions necessary to prevent accidents.

There is little seasonal fluctuation of employment in this occupation since repairs on appliances are needed at all times of the year and the work is done indoors. Repairers who work on cooling equipment, such as refrigerators and air conditioners, may need to put in extra hours during hot weather.

A feature of this work that appeals to many people is that repairers often work alone or with a minimum of supervision.

GOE: 05.10.03; SIC: 762; SOC: 6156

◇ **SOURCES OF ADDITIONAL INFORMATION**

National Association of Retail Dealers of America
10 East 22nd Street
Lombard, IL 60148

◇ **RELATED ARTICLES**

Volume 1: Electronics; Public Utilities
Volumes 2–4: Air-conditioning, refrigeration, and heating mechanics; Communications equipment mechanics; Electric-sign repairers; Electricians; Line installers and cable splicers; Office machine servicers; Signal mechanics; Telephone and PBX installers and repairers

▉ Architects

Definition

Architects are responsible for the planning, design, and supervision of construction of all types of facilities. They consult with clients, plan layouts of structures, prepare sketches of proposed buildings, write specifications, and prepare scale and full-sized drawings.

Architects also may help clients to obtain bids, select a contractor, and negotiate the construction contract, and they also visit construction sites to ensure that the work is going according to specification.

History

The history of architecture follows that of human civilization since the first architects designed buildings for people to use. Thus, the architecture of any period reflects the culture of its people. Outstanding works of architecture have been found in many ancient cultures; the Greeks, for example, are considered the first to have beautified architectural harmony. The most famous of their structures, the Parthenon designed by Ictinus, was the apex of simplicity and subtle beauty.

Architecture of early periods has influenced that of later centuries, including the work of contemporary architects. The field continues to develop as new techniques and materials are discovered, as architects blend creativity with function.

Nature of the work

The architect normally has one goal: to design a building that will satisfy the client. To obtain this goal, the architect must wear many hats. The job begins with learning what the client wants. The architect takes into consideration local and state building and design regulations, climate, soil on which the building is to be constructed, water tables, zoning laws, fire regulations, the client's financial limitations, and numerous other requirements and regulations. The architect then prepares a set of plans that, upon the client's approval, will be developed into final design and working drawings.

The final design will show the exact dimensions of every portion of the building, including the location of electrical outlets and fixtures, plumbing, heating and air-conditioning facilities, windows, doors, and all other features of the building.

The architect works closely with engineers to determine the type of materials to be used in the construction and usually works with a consulting engineer on the plumbing, heating, and electrical work to be done.

The architect then will assist the client in getting bids from general contractors, one of which will be selected to construct the building to the specifications. The architect will assist the client through the completion of the job, making certain the correct materials are used and that the specifications are faithfully followed.

Throughout the process the architect works closely with the crew. The crew might well consist of an architectural designer, who specializes in design drawings; a structural designer, who designs the frame of the building in accordance with the work of the architectural designer; the project manager or job superintendent, who sees that the full detail drawings are completed to the satisfaction of the architect; and the specification writer and estimator, who will convert the drawings into terminology and instructions that can be understood by the contractor and all the subcontractors.

The architect's job is very complex. He or she is expected to know construction methods, engineering principles and practices, and materials. Architects also must be up-to-date on new design and construction techniques and procedures. Although architects once spent most of their time designing buildings for the wealthy, they are now more often involved in the design of small or large housing developments, individual dwellings, supermarkets, industrial plants, office buildings, shopping centers, air terminals, schools, banks, and dozens of other types of buildings. They may specialize in any one of a number of fields including building appraisal, city planning, teaching, architectural journalism, furniture design, lighting, design, or government service.

Architects work in large, spacious offices so that drafters have the room and light needed to design structures. These particular architects are using a computer system to calculate design specifications.

Regardless of the area of specialization, the architect's major task is that of understanding the client's needs and then reconciling them into a meaningful whole.

Requirements

People interested in architecture should be well prepared academically and be intelligent, observant, responsible, and self-disciplined. They should have a concern for detail and accuracy, be able to communicate effectively both orally and in writing, and be able to accept criticism constructively. Although great artistic ability is not necessary, architectural aspirants should be able to visualize spatial relationships and have the capacity to solve technical problems. Mathematical ability is also important. In addition, architects should possess organizational skills and leadership qualities, and be able to work well with others.

High school students hoping to enter the profession should take a college preparatory program that includes courses in English, mathematics, physics, art (especially free-hand drawing), social studies, history, and foreign languages. Courses in business and computer science also will be useful.

Because most state architecture registration boards require a professional degree, high school students are advised, early in their senior year, to apply for admission to one of the 93 schools of architecture that are accredited by the National Architectural Accrediting Board (NAAB). Competition to enter these schools is high. Grades, class rank, and aptitude and achievement scores count heavily in determining who will be accepted.

Most schools of architecture offer a five-year program leading to a bachelor of architecture degree or a six-year master of architecture program. In the six-year program, a pre-professional degree is awarded after four years, and the graduate degree after a two-year program to satisfy licensing requirements. Many students prepare for an architecture career by first earning a liberal arts degree, then completing a three- to four-year master of architecture program.

A typical college architecture program includes courses in architectural history and theory, building design, including its technical and legal aspects, science, and liberal arts.

Special requirements

All states and the District of Columbia require that individuals be licensed before calling themselves architects or contracting to provide architectural services in that particular state. The requirements for licensure generally include graduation from an accredited school of architecture and three years of practical experience, or internship, in a licensed architect's office before the individual is eligible to take the rigorous four-day Architect Registration Examination.

Opportunities for experience and exploration

Most architects will welcome the opportunity to talk with young people interested in entering architecture and may be willing to have them visit their offices where they can gain a first-hand knowledge of the type of work done by architects.

Other opportunities may include visiting the design studios of a school of architecture or working for an architect or building contractor during summer vacations. Also, many architecture schools offer summer programs for high school students. Books and magazines on architecture provide a broad understanding of the nature of the work and the values of the profession.

Methods of entering

Those entering architecture following graduation start as interns in an architectural office where they assist in preparing architectural plans. They also may handle related details, such as administering contracts, researching building codes and construction materials, and writing specifications. Some architecture graduates go into allied fields such as construction, engineering, landscape architecture, or real estate development. Others may develop graphic, interior design, or product specialties. Still others put their training to work in the theater, film, or television fields or in museums, display firms, and architectural product and materials manufacturing companies.

Advancement

Architects in large firms are given progressively more complex jobs and may advance to supervisory or managerial positions. Some become partners in established firms, but the eventual goal of many architects is to establish their own practice.

Employment outlook

Over 100,000 licensed architects are employed in the United States in the 1990s. Most of them work in architectural firms. About one-quarter are self-employed. Others work for builders, real estate developers, or other businesses with large construction programs. A smaller but growing number are employed in government agencies such as the Departments of Defense, Interior, Housing and Urban Development, and the General Services Administration.

Job prospects are good since growth in the field is expected to be as fast as average through the rest of the decade. The number of architects needed will depend on the volume of construction. The construction industry is extremely sensitive to fluctuations in the overall economy, and a recession could result in lay-offs. On the positive side, employment of architects is not likely to be affected by the growing use of computer technologies. Rather than replacing architects, computers are being used to make more and better designs.

Competition for employment will continue to be strong, particularly in prestigious architectural firms that offer potential for advancement. Most job openings will not be newly created positions but will become available as architects transfer to other occupations or leave the field.

Earnings

Recent graduates of a school or college of architecture start between $18,000 and $22,000 a year in the 1990s. Newly licensed architects earn an average of $36,100, and those with several years of experience earn $66,300 or more.

Well established architects who are partners in an architectural firm or who have their own businesses generally earn much more than do the salaried employees. Those who are partners in very large firms can earn more than $100,000 a year.

The average salary for architects working in the federal government in the 1990s is about $36,500.

Conditions of work

Architects normally work a 40-hour week with their working hours falling between 8:00 A.M. and 6:00 P.M. There may be a number of times when they will have to work overtime, especially when under pressure to complete an assignment. Self-employed architects may be required to work more irregular hours and often will meet with clients in their homes or offices during the evening.

Architects usually work in comfortable offices. They may, however, spend a considerable amount of time outside of the office visiting clients or viewing the progress of a particular job in the field. There is usually considerable variation in the routine.

GOE: 05.01.07; SIC: 8712; SOC: 161

◇ **SOURCES OF ADDITIONAL INFORMATION**

American Institute of Architects
1735 New York Avenue, NW
Washington, DC 20006

American Institute of Architecture Students
1735 New York Avenue, NW
Washington, DC 20006

National Council of Architectural Registration Boards
1735 New York Avenue, NW, Suite 700
Washington, DC 20006

National Institute for Architectural Education
30 West 22nd Street
New York, NY 10010

Institut de Recherches En Architecture du Canada
1825, boul Rene-Lévesque, Ouest
Montreal PQ H3H 1R4

◇ **RELATED ARTICLES**

Volume 1: Construction; Engineering
Volumes 2–4: Architectural and building construction technicians; Civil engineers; Drafters; Landscape architects; Miscellaneous engineers; Urban and regional planners

Architectural and building construction technicians

Definition

Architectural and building construction technicians help architects and engineers plan and design structures. They also test materials, build and inspect structures, and construct models. They transport, store, inspect, and use all types of construction materials.

History

Historians often judge societies of the past by the beauty, usefulness, and permanence of their buildings. A civilization's architecture and construction reflect its goals and ideals. The architectural forms and buildings of the past have influenced builders through the centuries.

People working in architecture and construction begin with the most basic human needs for housing and shelter. They provide homes, churches, schools, theaters, public buildings, industrial plants, and any other needed buildings.

Modern building methods use hundreds of materials and many special construction procedures. They require highly trained technicians to assist the architects and construction engineers. These technicians attend to many details and help ensure that no mistakes are made in the complex activities and processes involved in building safe, beautiful, and useful buildings.

Nature of the work

Architectural and building construction technicians help turn the architect's designs into reality. *Architectural technicians* help architects design buildings. *Building construction technicians* help plan and control the details of building the structure. They inspect job sites and supervise construction crews by checking every step of construction against the blueprints and specifications. The technicians make sure the materials are right, the dimensions correct, and that structural features are located correctly. To do this, they use equipment such as surveying transits and laser beam devices to ensure floors and walls are level or at the correct height. Technicians are hired to inspect construction progress and help appraise buildings, and they may even investigate for casualty insurance companies.

In general, architectural technology applies engineering principles to the design and planning of structures. Construction technology involves construction work itself. Thus, architectural technicians may perform more of their work inside the office at a desk or a drawing board, while construction technicians may expect to spend more of their time at the construction site.

Architectural and building construction technicians—like most skilled technicians—are members of a team working towards a particular objective. Their activities vary greatly, and there is plenty of variety for an individual technician's talents. The buildings range from single-family homes to factories, high-rise apartments, and tall office buildings with more than forty acres under a single roof. Architecture and construction also involve a challenging variety of materials, from conventional hardwood lumber and concrete to plastics, fiberboard, ceramics, glass, cloth, and metals.

In very broad terms, architectural and building construction technicians work in five kinds of situations: 1) architectural and engineering offices; 2) construction companies and government agencies related to construction; 3) building supply companies; 4) plant engineering and operations departments; and 5) government agencies engaged in building inspection, appraisal, and planning.

In architectural and engineering offices the technician assists professional staff members. For instance, in an architect's office the technician may help complete presentation drawings, calculate excavation cuts and fills, complete the architect's sketches, transform these sketches into working prints, and help prepare specifications.

Because the architect represents the owner of the building, an architectural technician helps the architect inspect the construction, estimate percentages of completion, and make sure the construction is on schedule. Near the end of the work, the technician may assist in inspecting the structure for "sign-off" (acceptance by the owner), making certain that required corrections have been made, and, for certain types of contracts, helping check the costs. In general, architectural technicians perform whatever tasks the architect can pass on to them.

The building construction technician who is employed by a construction company may work both in the office and at the job site, depending on what needs to be done. Large construction companies accept jobs within a radius of several hundred miles of their home office. A few very large construction companies contract for work overseas. The construction technician in such a company may expect to move from one job site to another as each job is completed.

The technician's duties in a construction company may range from entry-level jobs, such as materials checker or timekeeper, to construction supervisor for the entire job. The construction technician, acting as an inspector or supervisor, carries heavy responsibilities which require experience beyond schooling. The pay for such positions reflects these responsibilities.

Some architectural and building construction technicians work in sales for building supply companies. As construction materials and methods become more complex and varied, only trained personnel can effectively sell them. The construction supply salesperson should know product uses and limitations, building codes, deliveries, and methods of fitting deliveries into construction schedules. The salesperson should know permissible substitutions of materials and must understand construction methods.

Large manufacturing plant engineering and operations departments also hire technicians. Many large plants cannot afford to depend on outside companies for maintenance. These plants employ their own maintenance, renovation, and even new construction personnel in a department most often called plant engineering. Maintaining the wiring, plumbing, heating, and ventilating systems, as well as the building itself, calls for trained construction technicians to plan, supervise, and inspect. These technicians hold well-paid, responsible jobs.

Various levels of government also engage in architectural and construction work. Government agencies often regulate construction, usually by developing and enforcing zoning and building codes. Cities and counties often employ either architectural or construction technicians as building inspectors and appraisers.

Architectural and building construction technicians may work in businesses quite different from those described earlier. For instance, some may work as inspectors and adjustors for fire insurance companies. Some work for savings institutions and insurance companies that lend money to builders. Others work with real estate developers and still others become purchasing agents.

Architect's assistants or *junior engineers* help architects or engineers write specifications and make calculations for quantity estimates or to complete drawings.

Architectural drafters draw, sketch, and make models. A position like this is the most common starting position for architectural or building construction technicians.

Structural drafters or *detail checkers* perform the same duties as architectural drafters, except with more emphasis on concrete, steel, glass, or precast parts of buildings. They check architectural prints for dimensions, section views, and mechanical equipment lines. This position is best suited for an architectural technician.

Assistant plant engineers or *building supervisors* oversee personnel in plant maintenance, renovation, and minor new construction.

Architectural sales representatives, building supplies salespeople, or *manufacturer's representatives* call on architects and engineers to explain the use of materials and products. They may furnish specifications and shop drawings, materials take-offs (estimates of kinds and quantities of materials needed), and prices of materials.

Estimators or *assistant estimators* make or help make materials estimates.

An architectural and building construction technician confers with the supervisor of a construction site. The technician must make sure that the specified materials are being used and that the building is being constructed as planned.

Requirements

The well-prepared technician should have a background broad enough for any of the five general areas listed in the preceding section. In order to obtain this background, technicians need to train in a formal post–high school program in architectural or building construction technology. Vocational schools and technical institutes offer the best programs. Typically, such programs last two years of full-time classes, and upon graduation, students receive a certificate, diploma, or associate degree. A few technical colleges offer four-year degrees in architectural engineering technology. These graduates receive bachelor's degrees, and are sometimes called technologists to distinguish them from the two-year graduates.

Prospective technicians may wonder which of the two fields—architecture or construction—they should enter. In general, a person who enjoys mathematical calculations, drawing, and sketching buildings should prepare for architectural technology. The person who enjoys working in the open and watching structures take shape should consider building construction technology. Architecture deals more with computation, calculation, and abstract creation. Construction deals more with actual building and operation.

For indoor work in architectural technology, technicians do not need to meet any physical requirements. But on many construction projects, technicians must be able to visit the job site, ride construction hoists, and walk on scaffolding that might be several stories above the ground.

Like almost anyone planning a technical career, prospective architectural and building construction technicians should plan for the future while in high school. Skill in arithmetic and basic algebra is essential for architecture and construction. Some skill in geometry and trigonometry is almost as essential. Courses in drawing will be useful even though the student must later take more drawing courses. Writing courses are also important, because technicians must make written and oral reports.

Almost all schools that train architectural and building construction technicians require applicants to have two years of high school algebra, a year of trigonometry or geometry, and one or two years of physical science, preferably physics with laboratory work. Schools may require applicants to have four years of high school English and language skills courses.

During the last year of high school, students should take the standard college entrance examinations and aptitude tests required to enter the school of their choice.

If students wait too long to prepare to enter a technical school program, they may not meet the entrance requirements. These students must then find a school that offers noncredit remedial courses.

Programs in architectural and construction technology vary between schools; all, however, share one basic approach—a blend of theory presented in classroom lectures and outside reading, along with applied studies in labs and at field sites. These programs all have a clear purpose: to train students in the practical application of theoretical concepts. Architectural technology programs usually include courses in architectural design, as well as mathematics through calculus. Construction technology programs usually focus on building practices and construction methods.

Typical first-year courses include introductory architectural drawing, technical mathematics, applied physics, building materials and construction methods, communication skills,

construction planning and control, and architectural history.

Second-year courses include architectural drawing and model building, elementary surveying, advanced architectural drawing, technical reporting, building service systems, contracts, specifications and office practices, computer applications, general and industrial economics, and construction cost estimating.

Theoretical courses are especially important to help students understand the underlying scientific and mathematics principles, which enables them to understand changes and stay updated on the job.

Special requirements

Architectural and building construction technicians do not usually need any type of license. These technicians, however, often work and consult with licensed craft workers, such as plumbers and electricians. Construction technicians often must supervise skilled, licensed craft workers.

Even though licenses are not required, some technicians work towards them. For instance, some technicians take additional training, acquire specified work experience, and pass the examination for licensed architects or land surveyors. Other technicians become certified engineering technicians. Such certification, even if not required on a job, represents professional achievement.

After completing a certain number of years on the job, architectural and building construction technicians may also take an examination to become a licensed land surveyor. Successful completion of this examination enables technicians to operate their own surveying business.

Opportunities for experience and exploration

High school students interested in architectural and building construction should talk to their counselors and teachers. Whenever possible, students should visit construction sites, where technicians can explain their jobs. Sometimes high school students can get summer work on construction jobs. This is one of the very best ways to gain first-hand knowledge of the field.

Some post–high school technical schools feature cooperative programs where students study for a few months and then work for pay with an architectural firm or construction company. This helps them learn the job and see why the theory taught in school is important. Often these programs lead to jobs with employers upon graduation.

Methods of entering

Some people work their way into architectural or building construction technology by starting with no special education or training. They go from high school to an hourly routine architectural or construction job, such as a carpenter's helper. Eventually, they either work their way up in a skilled trade or become technicians. This is the long hard way to become a technician, however, and often the study needed to learn the relevant science and theory never gets done.

The ideal way to find a job in architectural or building construction technology is to graduate from a recognized technical school, community college, or vocational program. These can be public or private. Employment managers and other recruiters regularly visit schools that offer programs in architectural or building technology. Graduates can usually choose from several job offers, with many students accepting jobs weeks before they graduate.

Every good technical school offers placement help and counseling, and some even help alumni who wish to change jobs. In addition to those jobs offered through their school's placement office, graduating students may also seek their own openings, applying directly to the employment offices of desirable companies. Other students who worked in cooperative education programs will often continue working with the same company after graduation. Such programs help the students pay their school expenses and gain practical experience.

Completion of a formal program in architectural or building construction technology qualifies a person for many beginning technician jobs. Those trained in architectural technology find work in construction. Conversely, some persons originally trained in construction technology work in architectural offices. Students should not limit their job searches to architectural firms and construction companies; as mentioned earlier in this article, building supply companies, industrial plant engineering departments, and some federal government agencies need well-trained technical personnel.

Advancement

As architectural and building construction technicians gain practical experience, new career possibilities open up. Some technicians eventually own their own contracting businesses; the very successful contractor or developer can become wealthy. Technicians who prefer to work for someone else can advance with experience.

A few jobs held by experienced architectural and, particularly, building construction technicians are described in the following paragraphs:

Chief drafters or *job captains* supervise and plan the work of architectural or structural drafters. They also draft the more important projects.

Contractors operate their own construction businesses and may eventually become developers of houses, larger buildings, or other types of construction. This position requires financial resources as well as skill, ingenuity, and experience. *Field inspectors* represent contractors, clients, architects, or owners in checking construction work at various stages. They ensure compliance with the contract, working prints, specifications, and approved construction practices.

Building inspectors ensure that construction complies with local codes. They inspect buildings, proposed sites, property line placements, set-backs, and construction progress for a county or municipality.

Plant engineers maintain, repair, rehabilitate, or construct new plant utility services. They may also oversee large heating systems or boilers used in industrial processing. They supervise plant personnel to carry out duties within their responsibility.

Surveyors determine property lines, set up corner stakes, batter boards, utility line stakes, and other markers for construction crews. This is sometimes an entry-level job; large construction projects, however, require very well-trained and experienced surveyors.

Employment outlook

The future is bright for architectural and building construction technicians. The population continues to increase and most people want to own their own homes; they must have buildings in which to work, and schools for their children to attend; there is a constant need to renovate and modernize homes, offices and commercial buildings; older buildings must be replaced. Many cities, aided by state, federal, or private funds, are rebuilding or rehabbing entire sections.

Architectural and building construction technicians should become increasingly impor-

ARCHITECTURAL AND BUILDING CONSTRUCTION TECHNICIANS

tant employees for several reasons: the architectural and construction industry is adapting existing products, finding new products to use in building projects, and developing new ways to increase efficiency. Much of this work calls for computers and new approaches that require technicians' skills. While untrained or even semiskilled labor cannot contribute much to new techniques, a trained technician can. Also, many buildings must be made more energy-efficient and fireproof; a number will be rebuilt entirely in years to come. This effort will also require the skills of trained technicians. In addition, the development of new industries and the movement of companies from old plants in one part of the country to new plants in another is causing whole new communities to be built. This trend obviously increases the need for all kinds of architectural and building construction personnel, including technicians.

Earnings

Architectural and building construction technicians earn salaries comparable to those of most engineering technicians. They are usually salaried workers, not hourly wage earners. Beginning salaries for graduates of two-year technical programs range from approximately $14,000 to $18,000 a year and average around $17,000 a year. Graduates with more experience usually earn $20,000 to $30,000 a year and average around $25,000 a year. Some senior technicians earn as much as $37,000 a year or more. Those technicians who start their own businesses or who take overseas jobs can expect even higher pay.

Job benefits other than salary vary with the individual company. In general, large companies offer more benefits but less opportunity. Typical benefits for the construction industry include sick leave, paid vacations and holidays, and insurance. Some companies pay part or all of a technician's cost of additional schooling. In higher job levels, technicians may qualify for bonuses. Technicians do not usually receive extra pay for overtime; however, they often receive compensatory time off to make up for overtime.

Employment in construction fluctuates with the season, the availability of mortgage money, labor problems, and other factors. Work fluctuation, however, affects hourly laborers much more than it affects technicians. Generally, a technician can expect steady career-type work, with less fear of layoffs than an hourly worker.

Conditions of work

Working conditions vary for these technicians. The architectural technician working inside an architectural or engineering office can expect safe, comfortable working conditions. Architectural offices are almost always clean, comfortable, and well lighted. An architectural technician can do much of the work seated at a desk or on a drawing stool.

Technicians' jobs on construction sites are generally as safe as the technicians make them. If safety precautions are followed, care is exercised on job sites, and a hard hat is worn on the job, the technician should be safer at work than at home. On the other hand, construction work is dangerous for the careless person. Probably the three greatest dangers are: being struck by falling objects; working at heights; and failing to step carefully. Minor hazards also exist from snagging oneself on nails or other projections. Certain construction equipment is dangerous if improperly used. Technicians ordinarily will not actually operate these pieces of equipment, but they must pay attention when working near them. The careful technician should work a lifetime without injury. Working in a construction office away from the job site is of course as comfortable and safe as working in an architectural office.

On the job site, the architectural or building construction technician must dress for the weather. Until all walls are up, the work may go on in hot or cold weather, rain or shine. Generally, the materials being used will determine whether a crew works during certain weather conditions. For example, construction crews try to avoid pouring concrete in freezing weather or finishing roofing in rainy weather. But unless the work is in a warm climate, technicians on site must accept unpleasant weather. They must also wear work clothing for all weather conditions and often potentially dirty conditions.

Construction sites are usually cluttered in the early stages of the job. Construction technicians must cope with mud, dust, and trash. As the structure nears completion and cleanup, the site itself will be cleaner. Because of these job site conditions, architectural and building construction technicians usually dress less formally than do many other technicians. In fact, on many job sites, engineers, architects, technicians, and job supervisors may all be wearing khaki or blue work clothes. Technicians who always work inside will normally wear standard office attire.

Responsible companies furnish safety clothing or equipment such as hard hats. Sometimes companies furnish rubber boots, prescription-ground safety glasses, steel-toed shoes, and gloves. Technicians will almost always furnish their own regular clothing.

Technicians are not usually considered hourly laborers, but rather as members of a support team. They will ordinarily not be affiliated with a craft union.

Architectural or building construction technicians must uphold craftsmanship in their work and that of other supervised employees.

The architectural and the building construction technician also needs patience. An architectural technician may spend hours on a detailed estimate or days helping an architect prepare working drawings. Such tasks demand a willingness to pay attention to details, verify dimensions, or to check such apparently minor matters as window schedules and wiring plans. At the construction site, construction technicians must patiently make sure that every bit of work is done according to specifications. They must watch for errors that would later be hard to correct—errors such as a course of brick off-level or a joist with too much sag.

Both architectural and building construction technicians must have the ability to organize work. Most construction jobs require a planned or even computerized sequence. Technicians must visualize how the various stages fit with one another. Computers and planning will help in scheduling many large jobs. The architect, the contractor, and their technicians, however, must organize the work sequence and must constantly check it as the plan is carried out.

This technician career and jobs to which it leads bring the challenge of change. New methods, new materials, and new projects all bring an interesting variety of activities. Constant study to keep up with these changes is a necessary part of the career.

GOE: 05.01.07, 05.01.08; SIC: 8712; SOC: 3719, 6479

◇ SOURCES OF ADDITIONAL INFORMATION

Alliance of Women in Architecture
PO Box 5136
FDR Station
New York, NY 10022

American Institute of Building Design
1412 19th Street
Sacramento, CA 95814

American Society of Certified Engineering Technicians
PO Box 371474
El Paso, TX 79937

Associated General Contractors of America
1957 E Street, NW
Washington, DC 20006

National Architectural Accrediting Board
1735 New York Avenue, NW
Washington, DC 20006

National Institute for Architectural Education
30 West 22nd Street
New York, NY 10010

◇ RELATED ARTICLES

Volume 1: Construction; Engineering
Volume 2–4: Air-conditioning, refrigeration, and heating technicians; Architects; Assessors and appraisers; Boilermaking occupations; Bricklayers and stonemasons; CAD/CAM technicians; Carpenters; Cement masons; Civil engineering technicians; Construction inspectors, government; Construction laborers; Drafters; Drafting and design technicians; Drywall installers and finishers; Electrical repairers; Electricians; Elevator installers and repairers; Glaziers; Health and regulatory inspectors; Industrial designers; Industrial engineering technicians; Labor union business agents; Lathers; Layout workers; Marble setters, tile setters, and terrazzo workers; Painters and paperhangers; Plasterers; Plumbers; Roofers; Sheet-metal workers; Structural-steel workers; Welders; Welding technicians

Archivists

Definition

Archivists contribute to the study of the arts and sciences by analyzing objects, like historical documents, artifacts, and living plants and animals, to determine which are significant enough to be preserved for posterity. Archivists keep track of records such as letters, contracts, photographs, and blueprints.

History

Archivists have established themselves as professionals only in the last hundred years or so. In the past museums accumulated objects rapidly and sometimes indiscriminately, accepting items regardless of their actual merit. By the 18th century, museums were holding so many items that they had to formulate acquisition policies to keep from becoming community attics full of possibly useless articles. The idea of arranging collections in a systematic order was pioneered by the renowned Louvre museum in France when it opened in 1793.

Each year, as new scientific discoveries are made and new works are published, the need for sifting through and classifying items increases. Archivists, because of their education, can best determine the value of collections and best help the general public understand and appreciate them. Like librarians, they know exactly where items are kept, whether within their own collections or in those of others. And like historians, they can explain the significance of such items in the development of civilization.

Nature of the work

Archivists analyze documents, such as government records, minutes of corporate board meetings, letters from famous people, and charters of nonprofit foundations. To determine which ones should be saved, they consider such factors as when each was written, who wrote it, and for whom it was written. Then, archivists appraise documents based on their knowledge of political, economic, military, and social history. Archives are kept by various organizations, including government agencies, corporations, universities, and museums, and the value of documents is dictated by whoever owns them. For example, the U.S. Army may not be interested in General Motors' corporate charter, and General Motors may not be interested in a Civil War battle plan. Archivists understand and serve the needs of their employers.

After selecting appropriate documents, archivists help make them accessible to others by preparing reference aids such as indexes, guides, bibliographies, descriptions, and microfilmed copies of documents. For easy retrieval, they file and cross-index selected documents in alphabetical and chronological order. Archivists may also preserve and repair historical documents.

Many archivists conduct research using the archival materials at their disposal, and they may publish articles detailing their findings. They may advise government agencies, scholars, journalists, and others conducting research by supplying available materials and information.

Depending on the size of their employing organization, archivists may perform many or few administrative duties. Such duties may include preparing budgets, representing their institutions at scientific or association conferences, soliciting support for institutions, and interviewing and hiring personnel. Some help formulate and interpret institutional policy. They may plan or participate in special research projects and write articles for scientific journals.

Requirements

Archivists usually must have at least a master's degree in history or a related field. For some positions, a second master's degree in library science or a doctorate degree is prerequisite. Candidates with bachelor's degrees may serve as assistants while they complete their formal training.

Archivists often need to be knowledgeable in a number of fields because so many sciences overlap. More than 70 colleges offer undergraduate courses in archival science or museum science.

Archivists must be "detail-oriented" people who enjoy long hours of research and like working alone, unsupervised.

Opportunities for experience and exploration

Students interested in archival work should study history and literature and might try to get part-time jobs in libraries. A fun extra-credit project could be to construct a "family archive," consisting of letters, birth and marriage certificates, special awards, and any other documents that would help someone understand a family's history. Many museums and cultural organizations train volunteer guides called "docents" to give tours of their institutions; college students can work as docents over the summer or even part-time during the school year.

Methods of entering

Candidates for positions as archivists should apply to institutions for entry-level positions only after completing their undergraduate degrees. Many would-be archivists choose to work part-time, or even without pay, as research assistants, interns, volunteers, to gain the experience that will help them secure permanent positions.

Advancement

Archivists usually work in small sections, units, or departments, so internal promotion opportunities are limited. Promising archivists advance by transferring to larger units with supervisory positions.

Because the best jobs as archivists are contingent upon education, the surest path to the top is to pursue one or more doctorates. Ambitious archivists should also attend conferences and workshops to stay current with developments in their fields. Archivists can enhance their status by conducting independent research and publishing their findings.

Employment outlook

Job opportunities for archivists are expected to increase about as fast as the average for all occupations through the year 2000. There will be fewer positions available in federal government archives. Competition for jobs as archivists is keen. Candidates with related work or volunteer experience will be in a better position to find full-time employment.

An archivist organizes the stock of medieval artifacts for a museum.

Earnings

Salaries for archivists vary considerably from institution to institution and may depend upon education and experience. People employed by the federal government or by prestigious museums generally earn far more than those working for small organizations. In the 1990s, starting salaries for archivists with bachelor's degrees average between $17,000 and $18,000 a year. Professionals with master's degrees start at $25,700; those with doctorates, $31,100 and up. Archivists employed by the federal government earn about $42,800 a year.

Conditions of work

Many archives are small, one-person offices. Archivists have little opportunity for physical activity.

Archivists tend to work either alone or with very few co-workers. But because they are usually passionate about their work, most do not mind the solitude of their environments. Also, they do not operate under as much stress as many other professionals do.

GOE: 11.03.03, 11.07.04; SIC: 8231, 8412; SOC: 2520

◇ **SOURCES OF ADDITIONAL INFORMATION**

Society of American Archivists
600 South Federal Street, Suite 504
Chicago, IL 60605

Association of Canadian Archivists
PO Box 2596, Station D
Ottawa ON K1P 5W6

◇ **RELATED ARTICLES**

Art Directors

Definition

Art directors formulate the concepts and supervise the production of any type of visual material that appears in print or on-screen, that is, in books, magazines, advertisements, newspapers, television commercials, posters, and packaging. Art directors work in advertising agencies, publishing houses, film studios, and animation studios.

Art directors working for publishing houses are responsible for evaluating existing illustrations, formulating presentation styles and techniques, researching illustrations and photos, hiring artists and photographers, working with the layout, and preparing a budget. They work closely with text editors. In magazine work and in television commercials, the art director sets the general look of the visual elements and approves the props, costumes, and models. In television commercials, the art director is involved in casting, editing, and selecting the music. Art directors usually oversee a staff who perform the detail work.

History

The first books were illustrated by hand in a technique called "illumination" whereby artists used egg-white tempera on vellum to paint their subjects. Each copy of each book had to be printed and illustrated individually, often by the same person.

The first book to use printed illustrations appeared in 1461. Prints were made through lithography, woodblock, and other means of creating duplicate images. Although many copies of the same illustration could now be made, publishers were heavily dependent upon individual artists to create the original works. Given the cost of producing such works, illustrations up until the 1800s were used primarily for educational purposes only, and examples include medical books, maps, nature studies, and historical works. Artists commonly were used to supervise the production of art work, and text editors usually assigned the illustration work: what was to be illustrated and how.

The development of children's books in the mid-1800s changed this. Whimsical drawings and creative illustrations were used to enhance stories such as *Alice in Wonderland*. About the same time mass-market magazines were developing, and these publications have always been heavily dependent upon illustrations. Some magazines like *The Saturday Evening Post* developed such a specific style of illustration that it established the reputations of illustrators like Norman Rockwell. As publishing grew more complex and new technologies developed (photography, film, computers), publishers and advertisers began to need specialists in acquiring and using illustrations. The first art directors were probably staff artists whose positions evolved into ones with more supervisory duties.

Art direction became a full-time job as the use of color illustration and photos became a regular part of publishing. Eventually magazines developed that were entirely dependent on photos and illustration. Women's magazines, like *Vogue* and *Harper's Bazaar*, and photo magazines like *National Geographic* and *Life* relied so much on illustration, that the photo editor and art director carried as much power as the text editor.

Animation brought in a whole new arena for art directors. Animated short films, such as the early Mickey Mouse cartoons, were usually supervised by an art director. Walt Disney was the art director on many of his early pictures. As full length films moved into animation, the sheer number of illustrations required more than one art director to oversee the project.

Art directors now supervise almost every type of visual project produced today. From television to film, and from comic books to coffee-table photo books, art directors select and supervise every element of the way those projects look.

Because art directors often have several projects going at once, all in different stages of development, they must be well organized and able to switch gears in an instant.

Nature of the work

All projects must begin with a concept: the message to be conveyed. In advertising, art directors may begin with the client's concept or, working with the copywriter, be required to come up with one. An art director in a publishing house may work with the writer and the editor in developing a concept. Once the concept is known, the next step is deciding the most effective way to communicate it. If there is text, should the art director choose illustrations based on specific text references or should the illustrations fill in the gaps in the copy? If the piece is being revised, existing illustrations must be reevaluated. Once it is decided what is to be illustrated, sources must be found. The art director and his or her staff may use photo agencies and freelancers as suppliers. These are places where photo and art libraries are kept, and photos and illustrations from files on thousands of different subjects can be found. If the desired illustration does not exist, it may have to be commissioned or designed by one of the staff designers. Commissioning a photo or illustration means the art director contacts a photographer or illustrator and explains what is needed. A price is settled on and the artist creates the image specifically for the art director.

Once the illustrations are secured, they must be presented in an appealing manner. The art director supervises (and may help in the production of) the layout of the piece and presents the final piece to the client or supervisor. Laying out is the process of figuring out where every image will be placed on the page or film. The size, the style, and the method of reproduction must all be specifically indicated so the image is recreated as the director intended it.

Art directors normally work on more than one project at a time and so must have the ability to keep straight numerous unrelated details. They often work under pressure of a deadline, and yet must remain calm and cheerful when dealing with clients and staff. Because they are supervisors, they are often called upon to resolve problems, not only with projects but with employees as well.

Art directors usually have years of experience working at lower level jobs in the field before gaining the knowledge needed to supervise a project. The art director has to understand completely how printing presses, film reproduction, and other manufacturing techniques are done. They have to know the wide range of ways images can be manipulated to fill the particular need of the project.

Requirements

A college degree is usually a requirement for those interested in becoming art directors; however, in some instances it is not absolutely necessary. A fine arts degree is usually the most appropriate to move into this field, with courses in graphic design, art history, photography, writing, business administration, communication, psychology, and a foreign language. Courses in advertising, photography, filmmaking, business, set direction, and fashion are important for those intending to go into advertising, while courses in art history, creative writing, and photography are important for those targeting general publishing.

The ability to work well with various people and organizations is important for an art director. While it is not necessary to have artistic talent, a creative outlook is important. An art director must always be aware of new techniques, trends, and attitudes. And because deadlines are a constant part of the work, an ability to handle stress and pressure well is a key quality.

Because of the rapidly increasing use of computers in design work, it is essential to have a thorough understanding of how computer art and layout programs work. In smaller companies, the art director may be responsible for operating this equipment; in larger companies, there may be a staff person who does this under the direction of the art director. In either case, the director must know what can be done with this equipment.

Math skills are important for art directors. Most of the elements of sizing an image involve calculating percentage reduction or enlargement of the original picture. This must be done with a great degree of accuracy if the overall design is going to work. Figuring out type size and other dimensions of the project has to be done within 1/32 of an inch, or 1/24 of a second for film. Errors can be extremely costly and may make the project look sloppy.

Accuracy and attention to detail are enormous parts of the job. When the art is done correctly, the public normally pays no notice. But when a project is done badly or sloppily, many people will notice, even if they have no design training.

Opportunities for experience and exploration

High school students can get an idea of what an art director does by working on the staff of the school newspaper, magazine, or yearbook. It may also be possible to secure a part-time job assisting the advertising director of the local newspaper, or working in an advertising agency.

Methods of entering

Because an art director's job involves a good deal of experience, it is not normally considered an entry-level position. Typically, a beginner is hired as an assistant to an established director. Recent graduates wishing to enter advertising should have a portfolio of their work containing 7 to 10 sample ads to show an understanding of the business and media in which they want to work.

Serving as an intern is a good way to gain experience and make contacts in the business. Graduates should also consider taking an entry-level job in a publisher's art department to gain initial experience. Either way, an aspiring art director must be willing to acquire his or her credentials by working on various projects. This may mean working in a variety of areas such as advertising, marketing, editing, and design.

College publications offer a chance to gain experience and a portfolio. Part-time work on small outside publications may also be available.

Advancement

While some may be content upon reaching the position of art director to remain there, many art directors go on to take on more responsibility within their organizations or become illustrators or television directors. Those in advertising may start agencies of their own, while those in publishing may launch their own magazines.

Many people who get to the position of art director do not advance beyond the title, but move on to more prestigious places to work. Competition for positions in companies that have national reputations, such as *Time* or *Rolling Stone*, will be keen because of the sheer number of people interested. At smaller publications, or local companies, the competition may be less intense since one is competing mainly against the local market.

Employment outlook

Producers of products will always need advertisers to inform their potential customers; publishers will always want some type of illustrations to enhance their books and magazines. The extent to which these positions are in demand are, like many other positions, dependent upon the economy in general; when times are tough, people, and businesses, spend less, and cutbacks are made. Instead of hiring full-time art directors, many companies are hiring freelance art directors to whom they do not have to pay insurance benefits. On the whole, job openings for art directors in both publishing and advertising should increase at an average rate into the year 2000.

Earnings

The job title "art director" can mean many different things depending on the company. In general, however, art directors in advertising agencies earn about 10 percent more than their counterparts in general publishing. A beginning art director can expect to make somewhere around $30,000 dollars per year, with some positions in larger companies going as high as $100,000. Earnings are usually dependent upon the size of the company and the reputation of the art director. The majority of companies offer insurance benefits and retirement plans, and some offer incentives and bonuses.

Conditions of work

A survey conducted by *Folio* in 1989 found art directors get more reward out of their work, over and above the money they make.

The work of an art director requires creativity, imagination, curiosity, and a sense of adventure. The work is varied: art directors must be able to work with specialized material such as graphics and make a presentation to a board of directors on the ideas behind their work. There must be a strong desire to communicate information to the public in an eye-catching way. A good sense of humor is important as well, due to the timetable involved with many projects.

To be competitive, art directors must stay abreast of the latest technologies within whatever media they work. With the increased dependence on computer aided design in everything from business cards to television commercials, an art director must be a jack-of-all-trades.

GOE: 141.031-010; SIC: 2711, 2721, 2731; SOC: 322

◇ **SOURCES OF ADDITIONAL INFORMATION**

Joel Garrick
c/o School of Visual Arts
209 East 23rd Street
New York, NY 10010

Art Directors Club
250 Park Avenue South
New York, NY 10003

Society of Motion Picture and Television Art Directors
11365 Ventura Boulevard, Suite 315
Studio City, CA 91604

◇ **RELATED ARTICLES**

Volume 1: Advertising; Book Publishing; Broadcasting; Magazine Publishing; Motion Pictures; Newspaper Publishing
Volumes 2–4: Advertising directors; Advertising workers; Cartoonists and animators; Commercial artists; Magazine editors

---

Assemblers

Definition

Assemblers put together the parts of products that are being manufactured. Assemblers work in many industries and on a wide variety of products, usually in factory settings. The training and skills of assemblers vary according to the products they fabricate. Some assemblers, called *precision assemblers*, are highly trained workers who make products that conform to exact specifications. Other assemblers need to master only a few procedures, and their work is comparatively simple and repetitive.

History

Modern systems of manufacturing products had their beginnings in the Industrial Revolu-

Aided by computers, these assemblers put together electronic parts at a Honeywell plant.

tion of the 18th and 19th centuries. It was during this period that many products made to be sold were first assembled in factories, rather than in homes or in small shops as they had been before.

Bringing together materials, tools, and workers in factories was a much cheaper and more efficient way to produce large quantities of goods. Mass production in factories was associated with important changes in manufacturing methods, including the use of powered machines and the standardization of parts in many products. As manufacturing came to depend on parts being uniform and predictable, it was increasingly important for manufacturing processes to be well organized and carefully supervised.

By about the beginning of the 20th century, nearly all large-scale manufacturing was done in factories. The work became mechanized and routine and was broken down into the simplest steps. In most industries today, manufacturing is elaborately organized, with various categories of workers performing different specific functions. Assemblers are one category of workers in many factories. Their activities vary greatly from factory to factory, but in general they are responsible for fitting together parts that have already been made in an earlier industrial process.

Nature of the work

All assemblers put together parts of products. They work with all kinds of materials and on all kinds of products large and small. Some assemblers are called *floor assemblers,* because they work with large, heavy machines and equipment on shop floors. In contrast, other assemblers may be referred to as *bench assemblers,* because they put together small items while working at a bench.

Many assemblers are employed in the aircraft, automobile, and electronics industries. Other assemblers put together everything from faucets to bicycles, sandals to billiard tables, jewelry, boats, musical instruments, and mining machinery. In some kinds of assembly work, such as building cars, one finished product is assembled by a large number of workers on an assembly line, with each worker doing a limited set of assembly tasks. Other products, for example fishing lures, are assembled mostly by one person.

Semiskilled assemblers usually follow well established instructions to carry out largely repetitive tasks. They may use hand tools such as pliers, screwdrivers, soldering irons, power drills, and wrenches. Among the many kinds of assemblers in this group are *electrical accessories assemblers,* who put together mechanical parts of electrical equipment like light sockets, switches, and plugs. They fit together, by hand, small parts such as plastic socket bases, shafts, contacts, springs, washers, and terminals, in a prearranged sequence. Then they may test the operation of the product they have assembled and remove any faulty parts. *Hand assemblers* in a paper goods factory fit together and secure fabricated parts of paper containers, such as spout-type salt containers or powder-puff boxes. *Hypodermic needle assemblers* use special tools and gauges to insert needles into needle hubs and inspect finished assemblies for defects.

Precision assemblers may work only on assembling certain sections of a product, such as the landing gear of an airplane, or on aligning and fitting together the sections into a finished whole, like the airplane that rolls out of a hangar ready to fly. Some precision assemblers work on making prototypes of products under development, such as missile guidance systems.

The work of all precision assemblers is characterized by the high degree of accuracy it requires. These workers must be able to understand detailed specifications and to exercise independent judgment in applying instructions. They may need to accurately interpret blueprints and drawings, written text, computerized drafting systems, and verbal instructions. Precision assemblers often use specialized tools and measuring equipment, and many do their work in awkward, hard-to-reach locations, such as inside a gear box. On the job they may deal with various kinds of engineers and technicians.

Precision assemblers include *precision electrical and electronic assemblers*, who put together equipment such as aircraft guidance systems, computers, and appliance controls. *Precision electromechanical equipment assemblers* are involved in making devices like pilot ejection seats and tape drives. *Precision machine builders* construct various kinds of equipment, such as engines, turbines, and the big machines used in manufacturing plants in many industries. *Precision aircraft assemblers* assemble the parts of airplanes.

Requirements

For many semiskilled assembler jobs, there are no particular educational requirements. A high school education may be required, especially for advancement to supervisory or skilled positions. High school courses in mechanical and industrial arts, including work in blueprint reading and electronics, are helpful preparation for many assembler jobs.

Many precision assemblers are hired because of the abilities they demonstrate while working at other less-skilled jobs, either with the same company or at an outside firm. Sometimes knowledge in a specialized subject area is also required for precision assembly work. Appropriate training may be gotten at technical schools and colleges or through service in the armed forces.

In general, assemblers, both skilled and semiskilled, need good hand-eye coordination and the ability to tolerate working on routine tasks at a steady, rapid pace. Assemblers who work with small parts must have good eyesight, either with or without corrective eyeglasses.

Special requirements

Applicants for some assembler jobs may be tested for color blindness. This is because many electrical and electronic devices are made with wires of different colors that assemblers must be able to distinguish.

Opportunities for experience and exploration

A part-time or summer job in a factory that employs assemblers, or even just a visit to a factory, can provide a useful idea of what some assemblers do. High school courses in subjects like shop and electronics can also introduce students to the tasks and tools that are part of assembly work. Some people have their first experience of assembling while serving in the military, and they develop high-level skills that they can later use to land a civilian job.

Methods of entering

The most common way of starting out in this field is to apply directly to a factory that employs assemblers. The classified ads section of local newspapers is a good place to look for leads to jobs of this kind. Inexperienced people are often hired and trained on the job in semiskilled assembling work. The training period may last only a few hours or at most a few weeks. Because factories usually have training programs based on their own assembly methods, employers may actually prefer beginners with no previous experience in assembly work.

Advancement

Unless they seek out additional job training, many assemblers have few advancement possibilities. Some can eventually become quality inspectors or supervisors in their factories. In some industries, assemblers who develop the right combination of skills can move into precision assembler positions. Experienced precision assemblers may be qualified to work as product repairers, fixing factory products that inspectors have determined are defective. Some experienced assemblers decide to enter training programs in a skilled trade related to their assembly work. Others with enough technical background may advance to work as computer operators or programmers involved in controlling the computer-assisted automated production equipment used in some factories.

ASSEMBLERS

Employment outlook

The future demand for assemblers will vary somewhat by industry, but the general trend across the nation will be toward a declining need for assembly workers. Just as goods are made differently today than they were in the past, so the methods used in manufacturing will keep on changing in years to come. In an effort to increase output and better control product uniformity, many factories are changing their assembly operations to rely wherever possible on robots, computers, and automated equipment. In these factories, existing assembler jobs may be changed into new, higher-skilled positions or eliminated altogether. Factories that are the most likely to see assemblers replaced by automated equipment include those that manufacture computer, communications, electrical, and electronics devices and equipment. Highly skilled precision assemblers are less likely to be affected by the trend toward automation than are semiskilled assemblers, because their work often requires the kind of knowledge and judgment that robots and computers cannot yet match.

Another factor contributing to the expected decrease in assembler jobs is the move many U.S. companies are making to relocate their factories to other countries where labor costs are lower. This trend may turn out to have as big an effect on the employment prospects for assemblers as the shift to automation, especially in selected industries. Many precision assemblers will be affected by assembly operations being moved out of the United States. According to one estimate, between 1990 and 2005, about one precision assembly job in three in the United States will disappear, either because of moves overseas or automation.

Switching to automated manufacturing processes or moving plants overseas will not make economic sense for many factories, however. Many assemblers, both semiskilled and skilled, will continue to be needed, and some new openings will become available as a result of normal job turnover.

Earnings

The earnings of assemblers vary widely, depending on the kind of skills needed, the type of product assembled, the size and geographical location of the plant, whether they are covered by union agreements, and how they are paid. Some assemblers are paid a straight wage, while others are paid according to the number of items they assemble. Assemblers who are paid by the piece and can work quickly may be able to make more money than those who receive a fixed wage.

In the 1990s, the average annual earnings for precision assemblers is roughly $16,000, with most making between $12,000 and $20,000. If they work for companies where workers are unionized, such as automobile or airplane manufacturers, precision assemblers may make $20,000 to $32,000 or more. Assemblers who do not do skilled precision tasks usually make significantly less money than precision assemblers, sometimes not much above minimum wage levels. In some industries assemblers enjoy a number of good fringe benefits, such as holiday and vacation pay, health and life insurance, and retirement pensions.

Conditions of work

Working conditions for assemblers vary a great deal. For example, some assemblers work in clean, rather quiet, well lighted rooms, while others work in the midst of oil, grease, and noisy machines. Some assemblers must move large or heavy objects; others work with such small parts and tools that they use magnification to see their work better. Those who work on assembly lines may be under pressure to complete each assembly in the time that it takes for the items to move past them on a conveyor belt. Many assemblers must stand to perform their work.

Doing assembly work often takes patience and a mature attitude, because the job is very routine and repetitive, yet it must be done at a quick and steady pace. Many assemblers spend their entire workday right next to their fellow workers, so they need to be able to get along well with others, day after day.

In some industries, assemblers belong to labor unions. The unions include the International Association of Machinists and Aerospace Workers; the International Union of Electrical, Radio, and Machine Workers; the International Brotherhood of Electrical Workers; and the United Automobile, Aerospace and Agricultural Implement Workers of America.

GOE: 06.02, 06.04; SIC: Any industry; SOC: 6812, 6867, 772

◇ **SOURCES OF ADDITIONAL INFORMATION**

**Motor Vehicle Manufacturers Association
of the United States**
7430 Second Avenue, Suite 300
Detroit, MI 48202

National Association of Manufacturers
1331 Pennsylvania Avenue, NW, Suite 1500N
Washington, DC 20004

Motor Vehicle Manufacturers Association
#1602, 25 Adelaide Street, East
Toronto ON M5C 1Y7

Assessors and appraisers

Definition

Assessors and *appraisers* collect and interpret data to make judgments about the value, quality, and use of property. Assessors are government officials who evaluate property for the express purpose of determining how much the real estate owner should pay the city or county government in property taxes. Appraisers evaluate property to help people make decisions about purchases, sales, investments, mortgages, or loans.

Assessors are public servants who are either elected or appointed to office, while appraisers are employed by private businesses such as accounting firms, real estate companies, and savings institutions, and by larger assessors' offices.

History

Until the 1930s most assessors were lay people, and unscientific methods were used to estimate the value of property. With the advent of computers, assessing has become much more scientific. Today, assessments are based on a combination of economic and statistical analysis and common sense.

Appraising, too, was informal until the early part of the 20th century. In 1922 the National Association of Real Estate Boards (NAREB) defined specializations of its real estate functions to encourage professionalism in the industry. An independent appraisal division was not organized, however, because appraisers were few and the importance of sound appraisals was not then widely appreciated.

At that time, appraisal work was largely performed as a part-time adjunct to a general real estate business, by people who were not specifically trained in the field. As a result, the "boom" period of the 1920s saw many abuses of appraisals, such as making of loans in excess of the real value of the property based on inaccurate estimates. The events of the Great Depression in the 1930s further highlighted the need for professionalism in appraising. Real estate owners defaulted on their mortgages, real estate bond issues stopped paying interest, and real estate corporations went into receivership. The NAREB eventually recognized appraising as a significant branch of specialization in 1928, but clearly defined appraisal standards and appraisal treatises were not formulated until the 1930s.

Since then, appraising has emerged as a complex profession offering many responsibilities and opportunities. Reliable appraisals are required when real estate is sold, mortgaged, taxed, insured, or developed. Buyers and sellers of property want to know the property's market value as a guide in their negotiations, and may need economic feasibility studies or advice about other investment considerations for a proposed or existing development. Mortgage lenders also require appraisals before issuing loans, and insurance companies often need an estimate of value before underwriting a property.

Nature of the work

Property is divided into two distinct types: real property and personal property. Real property is land and the structures built upon the land, while personal property includes all other types of possessions. Appraisers answer questions about the value, quality, and use of real property and personal property based on selective research into market areas, the application of analytical techniques, and professional judgment derived from experience. In evaluating real property they try to analyze the supply and demand for different types of property, such as residential dwellings, office buildings, shopping centers, industrial sites, and farms, to estimate their values. Appraisers analyze construction, condition, and functional design. They review public records of sales, leases, previous assessments, and other transactions pertaining to land and buildings, to determine the market values, rents, and construction costs of similar properties. Appraisers collect information about neighborhoods such as availability of gas, electricity, power lines, and transportation. They also may interview people familiar with the property, and they take into account the amount of money needed to make improvements on the property.

Appraisers also must consider such factors as location and changes that could influence the future value of the property. A residence worth $200,000 in the suburbs may be worth only a fraction of that in the inner city or in a remote rural area. But that same suburban residence may depreciate in value if an airport is scheduled to be built nearby. After conducting a thorough investigation, appraisers usually prepare a written report that documents their findings and conclusions.

Assessors, also called *valuer-generals* and *assessment commissioners*, perform all these appraising duties, and then go one step further to compute the amount of tax to be levied on property, using applicable tax tables. The primary responsibility of the assessor is to prepare an annual assessment roll, which lists all properties in a district and their assessed values. To prepare the assessment roll, assessors and their staffs must first locate and identify all taxable property in the district. To do so, they prepare and maintain complete and accurate maps, which show the size, shape, location, and legal description of each parcel of land. Next, they collect information about other features of parcels, such as zoning, soil characteristics, and

availability of water, electricity, sewers, gas, and telephones. They describe any building and how land and buildings are used. This information is put in a parcel record. They analyze relationships between property characteristics and sales prices, rents, and construction costs to produce valuation "models" or formulas that are used to estimate the value of every property as of the legally required assessment date. For example, assessors try to estimate how much an additional bedroom adds to the value of a residence, how much an additional acre of land adds to the value of a farm, or how much competition from a new shopping center detracts from a downtown department store. Finally, assessors prepare and certify an assessment roll listing all properties, owners, and assessed values and notify owners of the assessed value of their properties. Because taxpayers have the right to contest their assessments, assessors must be prepared to defend their estimates and methods.

Most appraisers deal with land and buildings, but some evaluate other items of value. *Personal property assessors* help the government levy taxes on owners of taxable personal property by preparing lists of personal property owned by businesses and, in a few areas, householders. In addition to listing the number of items, these assessors also estimate the value of taxable items.

Art appraisers determine the authenticity and value of works of art, including paintings, sculptures, and antiques. They examine works for color values, style of brushstroke, and other characteristics to establish their age or to identify the artist. Art appraisers are well versed in art history, art materials, techniques of individual artists, and contemporary art markets, and they use that knowledge to assign values. Art appraisers may use complex methods such as X rays and chemical tests to detect frauds.

Requirements

Good appraisers are good investigators. They must be familiar with sources of information on such diverse topics as public records, construction materials, building trends, economic trends, and governmental regulations affecting use of property. They should know how to read survey drawings and blueprints, and be able to identify features of building construction.

Appraisers must understand equity and mortgage finance, architectural function, demographic statistics, and business trends. Many of these skills are learned on the job, but because appraising is a complex profession, candidates should have some college education, and, preferably, a college degree.

High school students who are interested in this field should take courses in mathematics, civics, English, and, if available, accounting and computer science. College students should enroll in mathematics, engineering, economics, business administration, architecture, and urban studies classes. A degree in finance, economics, statistics, mathematics, urban studies, computer science, public administration, business administration, or real estate and urban land economics is desirable. Art appraisers should hold at least a bachelor's degree in art history.

Basic training in assessment and appraisal is offered by professional associations such as the International Association of Assessing Officers, the American Institute of Real Estate Appraisers, and the Society of Real Estate Appraisers.

Special requirements

Some states have certification standards for appraisers; interested students may contact the local real estate board to learn more about these. Also, some states may require assessors who are government employees to pass civil service or other examinations before they can start work.

Opportunities for experience and exploration

To learn the particulars of building construction that appraisers need to know, students might consider applying to construction companies for summer jobs. To practice the methods used by appraisers, students may want to write detailed analyses of assets and shortcomings when choosing a college or buying a car.

Methods of entering

After acquiring mathematical and technical knowledge in the classroom, people interested in appraising should apply to local assessors, real estate brokers, or large accounting firms. Because assessing jobs are often civil service jobs, they may be listed with government employment agencies.

Advancement

Appraising is a dynamic field, affected yearly by new legislation and technology. To distinguish themselves in the business, top appraisers continue their education and pursue certification through the various national appraising organizations, such as the American Institute of Real Estate Appraisers, the Society of Real Estate Appraisers, the American Society of Appraisers, and the International Association of Assessing Officers. Certified appraisers are entrusted with the most prestigious projects and can command the highest fees.

Employment outlook

In the 1990s, employment for this area will grow at the average rate for all occupations. In general, appraisers and assessors work in a very secure field. As long as governments levy property taxes and as long as people buy and sell property, they will need appraisers to help them make decisions. The real estate industry, however, is influenced dramatically by the overall health of the economy, and so appraisers in real estate can expect to benefit more than average during periods of growth, and suffer more than average during recessions and depressions.

Earnings

Many variables affect the earnings of assessors and appraisers, but generally speaking, salaries range from $20,000 for beginners to $60,000 and above for professionals with 30 years' experience and additional credentials. Appraisers employed in the private sector tend to earn higher incomes than those in the public sector. Assessors' salaries generally increase as the population of the jurisdiction increases. Earnings at any level are enhanced by higher education and professional designations.

Conditions of work

Appraisers and assessors have a variety of working conditions, from the comfortable offices where they do their paperwork to outdoor construction sites, which they visit in both the heat of summer and the bitter cold of winter. Many appraisers spend mornings at their desks and afternoons in the field. Experienced appraisers may frequently have the opportunity to travel out of state.

Assessors' offices might employ administrators, property appraisers, mappers, systems analysts, computer technicians, public relations specialists, typists, and clerical workers. In small offices, one or two people might handle most tasks; in large offices, some with hundreds of employees, specialists are more common.

Appraising is a very people-oriented occupation. Appraisers must be unfailingly cordial, and they have to deal calmly and tactfully with people who challenge. Appraising can be a high-stress occupation. Appraisers feel great pressure to appraise accurately because a lot of money rides on their calculations.

GOE: 11.06.03; SIC: 9311; SOC: 1135

◇ SOURCES OF ADDITIONAL INFORMATION

Appraisal Institute
875 North Michigan Avenue, Suite 2400
Chicago, IL 60611

American Society of Appraisers
PO Box 17265
Washington, DC 20041

International Association of Assessing Officers
1313 East 60th Street
Chicago, IL 60637

◇ RELATED ARTICLES

Volume 1: Construction; Real Estate
Volumes 2–4: Architects; Architectural and building construction technicians; Construction inspectors, government; Property and real estate managers; Real estate agents and brokers

Astronauts

Definition

Astronauts conduct experiments and gather information while in space flight. They also conduct experiments with the spacecraft itself to develop new concepts in design, engineering, and the navigation of a vehicle outside the earth's atmosphere.

History

Robert H. Goddard of the United States and Hermann Oberth of Germany are recognized as the fathers of space flight. It was Goddard who designed and built a number of rocket motors and ground tested the liquid fuel rocket. Oberth published *The Rocket into Interplanetary*

Space in 1923, which discussed technical problems of space and described what a spaceship would be like.

Although there were few significant advances beyond this initial firing until after World War II, the Soviets and Germans did carry on experiments in the 1930s, and it was quite evident in the 1940s that space flights were to become a reality. The U.S. government began a number of experiments concerned with weightlessness, investigations of isolation in space flight, the amount of oxygen needed in flight, and the types of food, clothing, and temperature controls to be used.

The actual space age began, however, in October 1957, when Sputnik I was launched by the U.S.S.R. In response, the United States created in 1958 an independent government agency, the National Aeronautics and Space

Administration (NASA) to develop a U.S. space program. Its first goal, to put a man on the moon by the end of the 1960s, was accomplished in 1969 when Neil Armstrong landed. In the mid-1970s, astronauts carried out the first repair work in space and proved people could live and work for months in a state of weightlessness.

In April 1981, the United States launched the first orbiting space shuttle, designed for repeated flights into space. Today, space shuttles are used almost routinely for scientific missions and to launch satellites farther into space.

Nature of the work

Although the nature of the work carried on by astronauts varies from flight to flight and is expected to change radically from year to year, their major concern today is one of carrying out experiments and research. Satellites released from a shuttle can be propelled into much higher orbits than the spacecraft itself is capable of reaching, thus permitting a much wider range of observation.

While on their missions, astronauts may deploy and retrieve satellites or service them. They also may operate laboratories related to astronomy, earth sciences, materials processing, or manufacturing and engage in other activities. One of the goals for the near future is the development of a permanent U.S. space station. Astronauts will be involved in setting up and servicing such projects.

The basic crew of a space shuttle is made up of at least five people: the commander, the pilot, and three mission specialists, all of whom are NASA astronauts. Some flights also call for a payload specialist, who becomes the sixth member of the crew. From time to time, other experts will be on board. Depending on the purpose of the mission, they may be engineers, technicians, physicians, or scientists such as astronomers, meteorologists, or biologists.

The commander and the pilot of a space shuttle are both *pilot astronauts* who know how to fly aircraft and spacecraft. Commanders are in charge of the overall mission. They maneuver the orbiter, supervise the crew and the operation of the vehicle, and are responsible for the success and safety of the flight. Pilots help the commanders control and operate the orbiter and may help manipulate satellites by using a remote control system. Like other crew members, they sometimes do work outside the craft or look after the payload.

The mission specialists are also trained astronauts. They work along with the com-

One of the first roles of astronauts was lunar exploration; one of the future expeditions may be voyages to Mars.

mander and the pilot. Mission specialists work on specific experiments, perform tasks outside the orbiter, use remote manipulator systems to deploy payloads, and handle the many details necessary to carry out the mission. One or more payload specialists may be included on flights. A payload specialist may not be a NASA astronaut but is an expert about the cargo being carried into space.

Although their actual work is conducted in space, astronauts are involved in extensive groundwork before and during launchings. Just prior to lift-off, they take their positions quickly and go through checklists to be sure nothing has been forgotten. Computers on board the space shuttle perform the countdown automatically and send the vehicle into space. When the rocket boosters are used up and the external fuel tank becomes empty, they separate from the orbiter. Once in orbit, the astronauts take control of the craft and are able to change its position or course or to maneuver into position with other vehicles.

Astronauts are part of a complex system. Throughout the flight, they remain in nearly constant contact with Mission Control and various tracking stations around the globe. Space technology experts on the ground monitor each flight closely, even checking the crew members' health via electrodes fitted to their bodies. Flight directors provide important information to the astronauts and help them solve any problems that may arise.

Astronauts perform many kinds of experiments in space. They test themselves, animals, plants, and minerals to see how they are affected by an environment in which there is no gravitational pull.

An important part of their work is the deployment of satellites. Communications satellites transmit telephone calls, television programs, educational and medical information, and emergency instructions. Other satellites are used to observe and predict weather, to chart ocean currents and tides, and to measure the earth's various surfaces and check its natural resources. Space telescopes taken above the earth's atmosphere allow astronomers to study the solar and other star systems more thoroughly than is possible from the ground.

In conducting tests, astronauts use or operate a number of special cameras, sensors, meters, and other highly technical equipment.

Between flights, as part of their general duties, astronauts may travel to companies that manufacture and test spacecraft components, where they talk about the spacecraft and its mission.

Requirements

There are actually three major requirements for selection as a pilot astronaut candidate. Candidates must be jet pilots with many hours of experience in the flying of high-performance, jet-propelled aircraft; candidates must be college graduates with a minimum of a bachelor's degree in engineering, the physical or biological sciences, or mathematics; and they must be between five feet four inches and six feet four inches tall. Mission specialists may be as little as five feet tall.

Pilot candidates must have acquired 1,000 hours jet pilot time. Graduation from an armed forces test pilot school is desirable. Pilot candidates are normally selected on the basis of superior academic achievement, extensive flying skills, physical condition, and an insatiable intellectual curiosity. As individuals they must be able to respond intelligently to strange and different conditions and circumstances.

Actual training as astronauts includes instruction in all aspects of space flight and consists of classroom instruction in astronomy, astrophysics, meteorology, star navigation, communications, computer theory, rocket engines and fuels, orbital mechanics, heat transfer, and space medicine. Much of their training involves field work and practical application of the classroom theory. Their laboratory work, for instance, will include work in space flight simulators during which many of the actual characteristics of space flight will be simulated

along with some of the emergencies that may occur in flight.

To insure their safety while in flight, astronauts also learn to adjust to changes in air pressure and extreme heat and observe their physical and psychological reactions to these changes. They need to be prepared to respond to various possible circumstances.

Their training includes trips to the factories in which the various vehicles, including the spacecraft and rocket boosters, are built. The astronauts must gain a complete understanding of their craft and such trips assist them in gaining this understanding. They also develop new breathing habits to maintain calm in stressful situations and provide control over physical responses.

Those who are accepted into the training program are not promised space flight at the time of acceptance. Their suitability for the job is continuously measured during one year of training at the Johnson Space Center in Houston, Texas. Those not qualifying for space flights work in the various ground procedures involved in the preparation and execution of space flights.

High school students interested in a career as an astronaut should follow a regular college-preparatory curriculum in high school but should endeavor to take as much work as possible in mathematics and science.

Astronauts must be highly trained, skilled pilots with a tremendous desire to learn about outer space and to participate in the highly dangerous exploration of it. They must have a deep curiosity with extremely fine and quick reactions. They may have to react in emergency conditions that may never before have been experienced, and to do so they must be able to remain calm and to think quickly and logically.

Special requirements

Astronauts must pass specific tests devised by the space program, including physical exams with exceptionally high standards for vision, hearing, and blood pressure. The test for pilot astronauts is even stricter than that for mission specialists.

Opportunities for experience and exploration

Students who wish to become astronauts may find it helpful to write to various organizations concerned with space flights. It may also help to speak with individuals in colleges and universities who are involved in various aspects of space investigation including astronomers, meteorologists, or others engaged in the sciences.

Methods of entering

Entrance into the profession involves much experience as a pilot or extensive scientific experience. Those hoping to qualify as pilot astronauts are encouraged to gain experience in all kinds of flying, perhaps through the military service, as well as experience as a test pilot. People interested in becoming mission specialist astronauts should earn at least one advanced degree and gain experience in one or more fields. Applications may be made when vacancies for astronauts and openings of new programs are announced.

Advancement

Advancement is not a formal procedure. Those who gain experience as astronauts will likely work into positions of management as they retire from actual flight status. Some astronauts may direct future space programs, or head space laboratories or factories.

Employment outlook

Because of the nature of the program at the current time, including the great expense involved in each flight and the consequential limited number of flights, there is no need for a large number of astronauts.

Much of the demand will depend upon the success of the programs and the relative rapidity with which the programs develop. Plans for future expansion include a space station where private firms will manufacture substances and items that can be made more perfectly in space, like vaccines, enzymes, crystals, metal alloys, and ball bearings. The satellite communications business is expected to grow as private industry becomes more involved in producing satellites for commercial use. But these projects are not likely to change significantly the employment picture for astronauts before the year 2000.

Earnings

Salaries for astronauts who are members of the armed forces consist of base pay, an allowance for housing and subsistence, and flight pay. In the 1990s, the total is over $44,000 a year for a major and $54,000 for a full colonel.

The rate of pay for civilians is different. A civil service rating of GS–15 earns between $52,000 and $66,000 a year. Astronauts who are neither military nor civil service employees receive similar compensation.

In addition, astronauts get the usual benefits, including vacations, sick leave, health insurance, retirement pensions, and bonuses for superior performance. They work a normal 40-hour week when preparing and testing for a spaceflight, but, as countdown approaches and activity is stepped up, they may work long hours, seven days a week. While on a mission, of course, they work as many hours as necessary to accomplish their objectives.

Conditions of work

Astronauts do work that is difficult, challenging, and potentially dangerous. They work closely as a team because their safety depends on their being able to rely on one another.

The training period is rigorous, and conditions in the simulators and trainers can be restrictive and uncomfortable. Exercises to produce the effect of weightlessness may cause air sickness in new trainees.

Astronauts on a spaceflight have to become accustomed to floating around in cramped quarters. Because of the absence of gravity, they must eat and drink either through a straw or very carefully with fork and spoon. Bathing is accomplished with a washcloth, as there are no showers in the spacecraft. Astronauts buckle and zip themselves into sleep bunks to keep from drifting around the cabin. Sleeping is generally done in shifts, which means that lights, noises, and activity are a constant factor.

During the launch and when working outside the spacecraft, astronauts wear specially designed spacesuits to protect them against various facets of the new environment.

GOE: none; SIC: 9661; SOC: none

American Institute of Aeronautics and Astronautics
The Aerospace Center
370 L'Enfant Promenade, SW
Washington, DC 20024

Astronaut Candidate Program
Mail Code AHX
NASA-Johnson Space Center
Houston, TX 77058

National Aeronautics and Space Administration
Office of Educational Programs and Services
Code XEP
Washington, DC 20546

Canadian Aeronautics and Space Institute
#601, 222 Somerset Street, West
Ottawa ON K2P 2G3

◇ RELATED ARTICLES

Volume 1: Military Services; Physical Sciences; Transportation
Volumes 2–4: Aeronautical and aerospace technicians; Aerospace technicians; Air traffic controllers; Astronomers; Aircraft mechanics and engine specialists; Avionics technicians; Engineers; Flight engineers; Pilots

Astronomers

Definition

Astronomers study the universe and its celestial bodies by collecting and analyzing data. They also compute positions of stars and planets, and calculate orbits of comets, asteroids, and artificial satellites. They make statistical studies of stars and galaxies, and prepare mathematical tables giving positions of the sun, moon, planets, and stars at a given time. Astronomers also study the size and shape of the earth and the properties of its upper atmosphere through observation and through information obtained by means of spacecraft and earth satellites.

History

The term *astronomy* is derived from two Greek words, *astron,* meaning star, and *nemein,* meaning to arrange or distribute. It is one of the earliest of the sciences. Many ancient civilizations established calendars based on the study of stars, including the Babylonians, Chinese, Mayans, and Egyptians.

Modern astronomy was born with the theory of the sun-centered universe, proposed by Nicolaus Copernicus in 1543. The 17th century saw major developments by Kepler, Galileo, and Newton. Spectroscopy and photography became important research aids in the 19th century, and in the 20th century the use of balloons and satellites equipped with various types of observational equipment have aided in the gathering of pertinent information.

Nature of the work

Astronomers study the universe and all of its celestial bodies. They collect, select, and analyze information about the moon, planets, sun, and stars, which they use to predict their shapes, sizes, brightness, and motions.

They are interested in the orbits of comets, asteroids, and even artificial satellites. Information on the size and shape, the luminosity and position, the composition, characteristics, and structure as well as temperature, distance, motion, and orbit of all celestial bodies is of great relevancy to their work.

The launching of space vehicles and satellites has increased the importance of factual material concerning the makeup of heavenly bodies and their particular environments. This information has a direct relationship to the maintenance of astronauts in space.

Although the telescope is the major instrument used in observation, many other complex devices are also used by astronomers in carrying out these studies, including spectrometers for the measurement of wavelengths of radiant energy, photometers for the measurement of light intensity, balloons for carrying various measuring devices, and electronic computers for processing and analyzing all the information gathered.

Astronomers use ground-based telescopes for night observation of the skies. They have also launched orbiting telescopes that will magnify the stars at a much greater percentage than land based capability allows.

Astronomers are usually expected to specialize in some particular branch of astronomy.

The *astrophysicist* is concerned with applying the concepts of physics to stellar atmospheres and interiors.

Specialists in celestial mechanics are concerned in part with the motions and positions of objects in the solar system. They would thus have a particular interest in the calculation of orbits of earth-launched objects.

Radio astronomers study the source and nature of celestial radio waves, with extremely sensitive radio telescopes.

Many fields are available for specialization and, as more information becomes available through research and study, even greater specialization is expected to develop.

The great majority of astronomers either teach or do research or a combination of both. Astronomers in many colleges and universities are expected to teach such subjects as physics and mathematics in addition to astronomy. Other astronomers are engaged in such activities as the development and design of astronomical instruments, administration, technical writing, and consulting.

Requirements

The very nature of the work of astronomers calls for individuals with a strong but controlled imagination. They must be able to see relationships between what may appear to be, on the surface, unrelated facts, and they must be able to form various hypotheses regarding these relationships. They must be able to concentrate over long periods of time. They should also express themselves well both in writing and speaking.

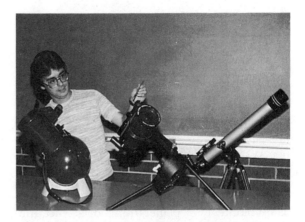

This astronomer is demonstrating how to use three different types of telescopes. The telescopes vary in capacity and complexity.

Formal training should begin in high school, where prospective astronomers should take mathematics (including analytical geometry and trigonometry), science courses (including chemistry and physics), English, foreign languages, and courses in the humanities and social sciences.

Students should then select a college program with wide offerings in physics, mathematics, and astronomy. They should take as many of these courses as feasible. Those hoping to attain a high level of professional achievement will find a doctorate a necessity. Although it is possible to begin work in the field with a lesser degree of preparation, advancement is much more probable for those with such training. This formal training will normally take about three years beyond the bachelor's degree.

Graduate school entrance requirements include an undergraduate major in physics or astronomy and physics, a B average or better, and satisfactory performance on the Graduate Record Exam (GRE). Bachelor's degrees in astronomy are offered by more than 60 institutions in the United States in the 1990s, and more than 65 institutions offer doctorates in the field. A sampling of the astronomy courses typically offered in graduate school are celestial mechanics, galactic structure, radio astronomy, stellar atmospheres and interiors, theoretical astrophysics, and binary and variable stars.

Some graduate schools require that an applicant for a doctorate spend several months in residence at an observatory. In most institutions the graduate student is allowed the flexibility to take courses that will be of the most value in the chosen astronomical specialty or particular field of interest.

ASTRONOMERS

Opportunities for experience and exploration

A number of summer or part-time jobs are usually available in observatories. The latter may be either on a summer or year-round basis. These jobs not only offer experience in astronomy but often act as stepping stones to good jobs upon graduation. Students employed in observatories might work as guides or as assistants to astronomers.

Students can test their interest in this field by working part time, either as an employee or as a volunteer, in planetariums or science museums.

Methods of entering

A chief method of entry for astronomers with a doctorate is to register with the college's placement bureau and to wait to be contacted by one of the agencies looking for astronomers.

Graduates with bachelor's or master's degrees could normally obtain semiprofessional positions in observatories, planetariums, or in some of the larger colleges and universities offering training in astronomy. Their work assignment might be as research assistants, optical workers, observers, or technical assistants. Those employed by colleges or universities might well begin as instructors. Federal government positions in astronomy are usually earned on the basis of competitive examinations given periodically by the Board of U.S. Civil Service Examiners for Scientific and Technical Personnel. Jobs with some municipal organizations employing astronomers are often based on competitive examinations. The examinations are usually open to those with bachelor's degrees.

Advancement

Because of the relatively small size of the field, advancement may be somewhat limited. A professional position in a large university or governmental agency is often considered the most desirable post available to an astronomer because of the opportunities it offers for additional study and research. Those employed in a college may well advance from instructor to assistant professor to associate professor and then to professor. There is also the possibility of eventually becoming a department head.

Opportunities also exist for advancement in observatories or industries employing people in astronomy. In these situations, as in those in colleges and universities, advancement depends to a great extent on the astronomer's ability, education, and experience.

Employment outlook

Astronomy is one of the smallest science fields, employing only about 3,500 people in the 1990s. Currently, there are about 150 openings each year for professional astronomers. These result from the normal turnover when workers retire or leave the field for other reasons. Competition for these jobs, particularly among new people entering the profession, will continue to be strong. It is anticipated, however, that the employment outlook for astronomers will become more favorable by the late 1990s.

Approximately 60 percent of professional astronomers are faculty members at colleges and universities or are affiliated with those institutions through observatories and laboratories. About 30 percent are employed by the federal government directly or by federally supported national observatories and laboratories. Fewer than 10 percent work in business and private industry, although the number of these jobs available is growing rapidly. The rest work in planetariums, science museums, or other public service positions involved in presenting astronomy to the general public; teach physics or earth sciences in secondary schools; or are science journalists and writers.

The greatest growth in employment of astronomers is expected to occur in business and industry. Companies in the aerospace field will need more astronomers to do research that can affect their competitive position. Astronomers will be hired by consulting firms that supply astronomical talent to the government for specific tasks. In addition, a number of companies will hire astronomers to work in related areas where they can use their background and talents in instrumentation, remote sensing, spectral observations, and computer applications.

The federal government is also expected to provide a greater number of employment possibilities for astronomers. Several agencies, including the National Aeronautics and Space Administration (NASA), the U.S Naval Observatory, the Army Map Service, and the Naval Research Laboratory employ trained astronomers.

Few new observatories will be constructed, and those currently in existence are not expected to greatly increase the size of their staffs.

Earnings

In educational institutions salaries are normally regulated by the salary schedule prevailing in that particular institution. Starting salaries for assistant professors in the 1990s average about $30,000 for nine months. As the astronomer advances to higher-level teaching positions, the salary increases significantly. Full professors and department heads can make $62,900 or more in an academic year.

Average salaries for astronomers employed in government are comparable to those in the larger universities, but the freedom to pursue independent research is not available to government and industry astronomers.

Well trained and experienced astronomers will often find their services in demand as consultants. Fees for this type of work may run as high as $200 per day in some of the more specialized fields of astronomy.

Conditions of work

Astronomers' activities may center around the optical telescope. Most telescopes are located high on a hill or mountain and normally in a fairly remote area where the air is clean and the view is not affected by lights from unrelated sources. There are some 300 of these observatories in the United States.

Astronomers working in these observatories usually are assigned to observation from three to six nights per month and spend the remainder of their time in an office or laboratory where they study and analyze their data. They also must prepare reports. They may well work with others on one segment of their research or writing and then work entirely alone on the next. Their work is normally carried on in clean, quiet, well ventilated, and well lighted facilities.

Those astronomers in administrative positions, such as director of an observatory or

planetarium, will maintain fairly steady office hours but may also work during the evening and night. They usually are more involved in administrative details, however, and not so much in observation and research.

Those employed as teachers will usually have good facilities available to them, and their hours will vary according to class hours assigned. Work for those employed by colleges and universities may often be more than 40 hours per week.

GOE: 02.01.01; SIC: 8412; SOC: 1842

◇ **SOURCES OF ADDITIONAL INFORMATION**

Amateur Astronomers Association
1010 Park Avenue
New York, NY 10028

American Astronomical Society
Astronomy Department
University of Texas
Austin, TX 78712

American Institute of Physics
335 East 45th Street
New York, NY 10017

International Planetarium Society
Creighton University Physics Department
2500 California Street
Omaha, NE 68178

◇ **RELATED ARTICLES**

Volume 1: Biological Sciences; Chemistry; Education; Museums and Cultural Centers; Nuclear Sciences; Physical Sciences
Volumes 2–4: Astronauts; College and university faculty; Geologists; Geophysicists; Meteorologists; Museum curators; Physicists; Planetarium technicians

Auctioneers

Definition

Auctioneers appraise, assemble, advertise, and sell articles to the highest bidder during an auction. They act as salespeople for the family, company, or agency selling the items to be auctioned. Depending on their area of expertise, they may auction off anything from a rare book to an entire office building.

History

Prior to the development of department stores, rural families had their own methods for dispensing and acquiring the items and machinery they needed. For small or individual items a barter or trade might be made to exchange a needed tool or other possession. When many different items were being sold, however, a family would hold an auction. An auctioneer would be hired to assist the family in dispensing their property if they needed to raise cash or if they were moving and could not bring along all of their possessions.

Since that time, auctions have become a popular way to buy farm equipment, real estate, artwork, livestock, or personal property from estates. An auction dispenses of many varied items in a fairly quick manner by selling one item to the highest bidder and moving through the collection of goods from start to finish. Auctions have also a become popular way to raise money for charities and other groups. They are fun as well as functional and have become increasingly common in both rural areas and cities.

Nature of the work

An auctioneer's work has two main facets: the selling itself and the preliminary preparation and evaluation. The latter takes more time and skill and is less familiar to most people. Prior to the auction itself, the auctioneer will meet with the sellers and determine the property to be sold. An auctioneer will make note of the lowest bid, called the "reserved bid," that the sellers will accept for each item. The auctioneer will also advise clients when an item should be sold "absolute," or without a minimum bid. If

there are legal aspects to be discussed, an auctioneer will confer with the sellers.

The most time-consuming activity is often the appraisal of the goods. The auctioneer determines the value of each and compares it to the reserve bid established by the sellers. The auctioneer will make notes on the type of item being sold, its history, and any unique qualities the item might have. This background information can encourage higher bids and increase buyer interest.

Once the appraisal has taken place, an auctioneer must organize the items out in the area where the auction will be held. Sometimes the auctioneer puts out a catalogue or booklet describing the items for sale for that particular day. It may also list the sequence in which the items will be sold so that buyers will know when the items they want will be up for sale. In addition to the catalogue, auctioneers organize any advertising needed to promote the sale. Newspaper and magazine ads, flyers, signs, and broadcast announcements can reach people from many different areas and bring in a good crowd. Some rural areas hold auctions as special attractions for tourists around summer holidays or to commemorate town events and local celebrations.

Usually the auctioneer will organize and set up the auction far enough in advance for people to come early, peruse the area, and gain an idea of what is of interest to them. Antique furniture and clothing, farm equipment, and artwork are some of the things sold by auctions. Other auctions concentrate on large industrial machinery or cars, as well as livestock, stamps, coins, and books.

The auctioneer works to help the buyer as well as the seller. An auctioneer is familiar enough with the potential value of the items to encourage prices or begin bids at a certain price. The encouragement and stimulation an auctioneer provides, however, is often matched by the excitement and competition among the buyers. Auctioneers must be quick-thinking and comfortable addressing crowds, not only offering them information about the items for sale but acting at times as an entertainer to keep the crowd interested.

Auctioneers coordinate the pace of the auction and judge which items should be sold first. Sometimes to boost people's interest, an auctioneer may save the most popular items for last. At other times, the best articles are sold first so that those who weren't able to purchase their first choice will feel free to bid on other items.

Auctioneers commonly enlist the help of assistants who bring the items to the auctioneer and keep a steady flow of goods being passed on. In addition, another assistant may be in charge of collecting money, issuing receipts, and keeping track of the purchaser of each item.

Most auctions follow a typical pattern. The items for sale are made available to the buyers' inspection in a catalog or a display. In the case of real estate auctions, however, photographs may be circulated. In some instances, land that is miles away can be sold, though the auctioneer will describe some history and features of the area. Often these types of auctions take less time, but the preparation is more detailed. Auctioneers must know the dimensions of the buildings they are selling, boundary lines for lots and farms, and whether any money is owed or any environmental hazard exists on the property, as well as information on terms of payment and zoning laws.

While standing on the bed of a pickup truck, an auctioneer sells farm equipment that is displayed in the background.

Requirements

Auctioneers must be effective speakers. Their job is to command attention and interest in the items through the power of their voice and their personal manner and good humor. Auctioneers should have a great deal of stamina, since auctions often take place outdoors in warmer weather and can last for many hours at a stretch. Auctioneers must also be alert so they can keep track of the crowd activity and the progress of the assistants as well as the selling of the goods.

Due to all the deliberation that goes into preparing an auction, they should also like working with people. A keen sense of evaluation and an absolutely honest nature will make for a successful auctioneer.

Special requirements

Training for auctioneers is available at many schools located around the country. Basic instruction is available at the Missouri Auction School in Kansas City, while more advanced training for established auctioneers takes place at the National Auctioneers Association in Kansas and the Certified Auctioneers Institute at Indiana University in Bloomington. Information about these and other training providers

can be found in the *American Trade Schools Directory*.

Auctioneer training can involve appraising, item presentation and, of course, speech classes so that auctioneers do not strain their voices while working long hours. Auctioneers who intend to concentrate on specific areas may take classes to supplement their training. Livestock and real estate auctions require specialized knowledge. In addition, some auctioneers have backgrounds in art or antiques.

Though most auctioneers are bonded because they handle large sums of money, licensing for auctioneers varies from state to state. Some auctioneers are required to pass examinations and pay licensing fees. Auctioneers who work in specialized areas, such as real estate or livestock, have other requirements. Auctioneers who sell land must be licensed real estate sales agents or brokers. For selling livestock for human consumption, auctioneers will find that many states require additional licensing. Auctioneers should be familiar with laws and regulations in the states in which they practice.

Opportunities for experience and exploration

Students wishing to explore the field of auctioneering would do well to attend some auctions and see firsthand the responsibilities that are involved. Also, classes in speech, drama, and communication are helpful because auctioneers rely heavily on their voices, not only for speaking and presentation, but also to get the buyer's attention through style and performance.

AUCTIONEERS

Charities and other social organizations occasionally use nonprofessionals for fund-raising auctions. Also, auctioneers often hire part-time assistants so they can get experience "working ring."

Related occupations

Other occupations that require some of the same interests and aptitudes as those of auctioneers include assessors and appraisers, retail sales workers, real estate managers and brokers, wholesale and retail buyers, and purchasing agents.

Methods of entering

Beginning auctioneers may work as assistants, handling money and receipts or bringing over the sale items to the experienced auctioneer. They may also begin by working local and county fairs or smaller auctions.

Sometimes professional trade schools offer placement services or internships that link beginners with established practitioners. Beginners may have to work part time until they gain more experience and become better known. Auctioneers who work for large auction houses may receive more assignments as they get more experience and complete any training offered by their firm.

Advancement

Experienced auctioneers can make a good reputation for themselves. Since most auctioneers get paid by commission, they may decide to specialize in selling real estate, farm equipment, or artwork, items that are likely to bring in more revenue for less preparation and shorter presentations.

Auctioneers who work with auction houses may move up in the ranks and get the more prestigious assignments. Auctioneers also may advance as they develop their individual knowledge in areas such as art and antiques, real estate, or farm equipment.

Working as an auctioneer may also become more of a hobby or side job for people who branch off into different lines of work but still enjoy conducting auctions.

Employment outlook

Conducting auctions can be either a full-time occupation or part-time work. The areas of interest and expertise an auctioneer follows may also have an influence on employment possibilities. Livestock, farm equipment, and farm land is most often sold in rural areas. Because many auctioneers get jobs based on their reputation and notoriety within an area, they may need to live in or near there or travel through frequently enough to make their names familiar to people.

Art auctions are usually held in urban areas and may require a more specialized background. Auctioneers with good skills and personality as well as a strong delivery, however, often have little trouble finding work. For an ambitious auctioneer who is willing to travel to various jobs and invest time gaining experience, regular employment is possible, either as an independent or as a staff member of an auction firm.

Earnings

Auctioneers have the potential to earn above-average wages. Part-time auctioneers in the 1990s earn close to $10,000 and full-time auctioneers may earn more than $20,000. On a daily basis, pay ranges between $100 and $2,000.

Auctioneers usually get paid on commission. This may occur once an auctioneer has gained suitable experience or has specialized in a particular area. Part-time auctioneers may supplement their income by assisting more experienced workers, acting as cashiers or helping with publicity or organization of the items.

Conditions of work

Because auctioneers often travel to where their assignment is, they can encounter a wide range of working conditions. Auctions are held year round. They take place in cities as well as small towns and occur in all types of weather. Auctioneers may work outside during a state fair or inside in a large hall. The type of goods being sold may also dictate their working conditions; for instance, farm equipment is commonly sold outdoors on the site of the owner's farm.

Auctioneers are often set up with a podium and microphone, since certain auctions may draw more than two thousand people. This allows the auctioneer to keep the crowds' attention when the noise and activity level become distracting or stressful.

Social and psychological factors

Auctioneers have the opportunity to work independently, travel to different areas and earn considerable wages without the restriction of traditional working hours. They should enjoy meeting and working with different people and working unpredictable hours. They should also be self-starters, because they have to keep their name in front of people even when an auction isn't being held.

Motivated auctioneers can learn about many different subjects and gain experience while they earn a good income. Some auctioneers are good performers as well, and gain satisfaction from working a crowd and matching buyers with sellers.

GOE: 08.02.03; SIC: 7389; SOC: 447

◇ **SOURCES OF ADDITIONAL INFORMATION**

Missouri Auction School
1600 Genesee
Kansas City, MO 64102

National Auctioneers Association
8880 Ballentine
Overland Park, KS 66214

◇ **RELATED ARTICLES**

Volume 1: Advertising; Marketing; Public Relations; Real Estate; Sales
Volumes 2–4: Assessors and appraisers; Buyers, wholesale and retail; Purchasing agents; Real estate managers and brokers; Retail sales workers

Audio control technicians

Definition

Audio control technicians set up, operate, and maintain the equipment which regulates volume and sound quality during radio and television broadcasts. Technicians set up microphones where they will pick up the best sound and adjust acoustical curtains or blinds within the studio to control reverberation (echo). During broadcasts they switch on appropriate microphones; balance the sound from different microphones using volume, fader, and mixer controls; and monitor audio signals by listening through headphones and watching control-panel dials. In addition to this, technicians play recorded music and sound effects as part of programs, blending sound levels and coordinating sounds with televised pictures where necessary.

In smaller stations, audio control technicians will also be called on to maintain sound transmission equipment and controls, and function as field technicians during remote transmissions.

History

When recordings were first made in the late 1800s and early 1900s, they were recorded directly onto tin, glass, or wax surfaces. Usually recorded with one microphone, the recorder had little opportunity to adjust sound. The farther away from the microphone an instrument was, the softer the sound on the recording. Radio programs also used one microphone for shows. The stories told on radio used specific techniques to give an effect that helped tell the story. For example, if the character was supposed to be leaving the scene, he could just speak while walking away a few steps. The actor's distance from the microphone would reduce the power of his voice in the broadcast and he would sound like he was far away.

With the advent of magnetic tape recording in the 1940s, sound quality improved dramatically. Stereo taping introduced two or more channels. Each channel represented a different voice, or segment of the performance. So, the singer can be one channel, the piano another,

An audio control technician in a television studio maintains the sound quality and enhances the program by adding recorded music in the background.

and the drums another channel. The audio control technician can adjust the force, the loudness, and the intensity of each of those channels to keep one from overpowering the other. The art of audio blending was born. The effects of using more than one microphone changed the methods used to combine and blend sounds.

Computers, starting in the late 1960s and through the 1990s improved the audio control technicians' ability to control sound. Computers allowed for more specific control of all the different sound elements. Unwanted sound could be reduced or removed from a broadcast. Recorded sound, electronically produced sound, and naturally produced sound that was electronically shifted, all added to the range of things the technician could use for a broadcast or recording. If you can hear it, you can record it, and with some things, even if you can't hear it, you can record it and then make it audible to the human ear.

Nature of the work

Audio control technicians work with microphones and sound transmitting and recording equipment. In the studio, they operate equipment that regulates the quality of the sound being transmitted or recorded; operate controls that switch broadcasts from one microphone to another, or from one studio to another; switch transmission from live broadcasting to interviews, tapes, compact discs (CDs), or other recorded material; or switch from the studio to remote broadcasting locations.

For both radio and television programs, audio operations are very complex and so must be precisely timed. Broadcasts of concerts, for example, may involve dozens of microphones, placed so that individual instruments or singers can be highlighted.

Audio control technicians also give instructions to studio personnel about sound quality and other technical matters. At remote locations, they set up, adjust, and operate equipment used to broadcast or record on-the-spot interviews, sports events, or news reports.

In smaller radio and television stations, audio control technicians may also perform a wide variety of related duties. For disk-jockey programs, for instance, they might operate the compact disc player. With more experience, they might assume some of the duties of the technical director. In larger stations, duties are more specialized.

Audio control technicians work in support of technical engineering and supervisory personnel who specify, install, and maintain the sound recording and transmitting equipment of the station. Engineering and supervisory personnel are responsible for the most demanding technical work of broadcasting. They usually have bachelor's or master's degrees in electrical or electronics engineering.

Requirements

Persons interested in a career as an audio control technician should study high school mathematics at least through solid geometry, as well as physics and any other available physical science courses. They should be prepared to take at least two years of technical training beyond high school at a community college or technical institute. Those persons who hope to rise to an administrative technical level, such as chief engineer, should aim toward a bachelor's degree in electrical or electronics engineering. Courses in a two-year technical program are likely to include basic and advanced electronics, communication theory, high-frequency receiver theory, as well as engineering mathematics, drawing, and technical writing.

On-the-job training, once the accepted road to a career as a broadcast technician, is no longer an available option. Stations prefer applicants with advanced technical training and have no trouble finding them. All new technicians receive training in station procedures, but they are expected to be thoroughly grounded in the fundamentals of broadcast technology.

Persons interested in careers in this field should have a strong interest in working with electronic equipment. They should have good hearing. They must be able to make decisions quickly and reliably in sometimes distracting surroundings.

Opportunities for experience and exploration

There are numerous ways for students interested in a career as an audio control technician to gain some experience and learn more about the work. Many high schools, community colleges, and technical institutes have radio and television stations of their own where students can experience the actual production of a broadcast program. Many schools also have clubs for persons interested in broadcasting that sponsor trips to broadcasting facilities, schedule lectures, and provide a place where students can meet others with similar interests.

Local radio and television station technicians are usually willing to share their experience with interested young people. They can be a helpful source of informal career guidance. Visits or tours can be arranged by school officials, which allow students to see technicians involved in their work and perhaps the chance to speak with them about their activities.

Students should also consider finding part-time or summer employment at a local television or radio station. Even the simplest tasks can offer opportunities to learn more about the field and will demonstrate interest to future employers.

Methods of entering

Audio control technicians looking for their first job should apply directly to the chief engineer or the personnel manager of the station where they wish to work. Help in arranging interviews or career counseling in general can be obtained from the placement office of the applicant's school.

New technicians at a station, even those with formal training and experience, normally begin employment with a period of instruction from the chief engineer or a senior engineer. Each station has its own procedures that technicians must learn and follow carefully.

Most technicians begin their careers in small stations where their responsibilities are varied. As they gain experience and skill they work into more responsible positions and may move to larger stations. Those who exhibit above-average abilities may move into supervisory positions. A college engineering degree, however, is becoming increasingly necessary for advancement to higher technical positions.

The number of noncommercial, educational radio and television stations is increasing. They offer another opportunity for entry into the field.

Another option for students is to find employment through the school where they were trained. Most of these institutions have student placement services and are in contact with employers in need of technicians.

Work-study programs offer another excellent method of getting started in a career field. These programs are run by schools in cooperation with local employers and offer students the opportunity to have part-time or summer employment in jobs related to the student's studies. Very often, the part-time or summer employer becomes the student's full-time employer after graduation.

Advancement

Advancement throughout the broadcast industry is usually from a trainee position to one of independent responsibility and then to a supervisory position. The path of the successful technician often leads from a small station, where the opportunity to perform a wide variety of duties provides excellent experience, to larger stations, where there are more supervisory positions to aim for and where the financial rewards are potentially greater.

Higher technical positions, such as chief engineer, are increasingly open only to graduate electrical or electronics engineers.

Broadcast engineering is a competitive field. Some technicians turn to teaching (in technical schools or in high schools that have radio stations) as a means of advancement. High school teaching requires a college degree and certification.

Employment outlook

The employment outlook for audio control technicians is influenced by the fact that competition is always extremely keen for positions in large metropolitan stations. Those technicians who are best prepared in electronics will have an advantage. However, there are usually good prospects for entry-level positions in smaller stations and in smaller cities.

Overall, the need for audio control technicians is expected to grow about as fast as the average for all other occupations through the year 2000. New openings will appear as new stations open and as currently employed technicians retire or advance to higher positions. The growth of cable television systems is expected to create openings in various related fields. This increased need may be offset by the increasing use of computerized automatic switching devices and other new labor-saving technology. These new kinds of equipment, however, do require maintenance work, which is often performed by qualified audio control technicians.

Earnings

Audio control technicians entering this field can expect a starting salary of about $17,000 a year if they begin work with a radio station. Television technicians can expect somewhat higher salaries, about $18,000 to $19,000 a year. These averages are based on a standard forty-hour work week; overtime is fairly common, especially in smaller stations, and is usually paid at time-and-a-half.

In radio, audio control technicians average about $22,000 a year (this includes those with considerable experience). The average for television technicians is approximately $24,000 a year. Highly accomplished senior broadcast technicians may earn between $33,000 and $50,000 a year or more. Salaries also vary according to the person's education, experience, and the geographical location of the job.

Conditions of work

Audio control technicians in studios work in air-conditioned, soundproofed surroundings. They wear headphones much of the time, and they work with numerous dials and switches that they must adjust as necessary. Timing is critical in the broadcasting industry. Technicians must make many split-second decisions and adjustments for which they alone are responsible.

When working in remote setups, technicians are required to work in all kinds of weather and sometimes in uncomfortable loca-

tions. They must be able to set up and adjust their equipment on the spot to carry out their part of a broadcast.

Most radio and television stations operate twenty-four hours a day, seven days a week. Shift work may be necessary, especially for new employees. The work of broadcast technicians is not physically strenuous, although it may involve standing for long periods while adjusting or repairing equipment.

On the positive side, technicians can take pride in their ability to master the complex, and sometimes hectic, operations necessary to maintain a radio or television station on the air. Their work also offers constantly varying subject matter and opportunities to meet new challenges.

Broadcast technicians usually work behind the scenes with little public contact. They work closely with their equipment and as members of a small crew of experts whose closely coordinated efforts produce smooth-running programs. Constant close attention to detail and to making split-second decisions can cause tension. In emergency situations, especially in small stations, long hours and high pressures may result. When equipment fails, pressure to return it to service is great. Persons who enjoy meeting challenges will find satisfaction in coping with these emergencies.

GOE: 05.10.05; SIC: 483; SOC: 393

◇ SOURCES OF ADDITIONAL INFORMATION

Society of Broadcast Engineers
7002 Graham Road, Suite 118
Indianapolis, IN 46220

Canadian Association of Broadcasters
P.O. Box 627, Stu. B
Ottawa ON K1P 5S2

◇ RELATED ARTICLES

Volume 1: Broadcasting; Electronics; Recording
Volumes 2–4: Electronics technicians; Field technicians; Sound mixers; Sound technicians; Sound-effects technicians; Sound-recording technicians; Studio technicians; Transmitter technicians; Video technicians

Audiovisual technicians

Definition

Audiovisual technicians, also called *educational media technicians*, produce educational audiovisual materials, and operate and repair the equipment used to show the materials to their intended audience. Some technicians make films in a school or other organization's audiovisual department. Others operate, adjust, repair, and diagnose major difficulties in systems that include equipment such as loudspeakers, video monitors, slides, movie film, overhead projection equipment, and tape recorders. Audiovisual technicians may also acquire materials and equipment, and store or package them for shipment.

History

Audiovisual technicians' equipment developed from a series of 19th century inventions, including the carbon-arc-lighted projector for slides or photographs, motion picture photography, and the phonograph. Developments in 20th century electronics led to radio, television, videotape, and modern microphone systems that amplify and modify sounds.

As a result of these advances, a lot of complex equipment is available today to facilitate presentations in classrooms, business meetings, and anywhere else needing microphone systems to amplify speakers' voices. Audiences can watch graphic representations along with hearing the speaker. Large screens project videos, charts, graphs, slide illustrations, films, and overhead images to audiences. Even small conferences and discussion groups in schools, government, industry, and churches use up-to-date media technologies.

Traditionally, the lecture has been the time-honored means of relaying information, with little or no response from the listeners. Unfortunately, studies have shown that listeners have a hard time understanding and remembering what the lecturer tries to teach them. However, if students can also see, feel, or even interact with the subject being taught, they learn faster, understand better, and retain the material much longer. Because our society is so visually oriented and complex, the need to present material so that it is easily grasped and retained is more important than ever.

Nature of the work

Audiovisual materials present ideas in films, videos, programmed learning materials, photos, tape recordings, television programs, or a combination of various media. They are most often used in education, advertising, and anywhere people wish to convey information.

In the field of education, many different people prepare audiovisual materials for student use. Behavioral psychologists work both with teachers and curriculum groups to decide which knowledge and skills should be taught. Teachers and curriculum groups then work with media specialists who translate the learning objectives into plans for audiovisual materials. Other specialists evaluate the materials' effectiveness, measuring how well they work as teaching tools.

Those technicians who produce audiovisual materials begin their work once the script or storyboard has been established. Working from their understanding of overall project goals and the specific information to be presented, they select the scenes and locations for shooting motion pictures and still photographs; acquire any necessary props; set up equipment such as cameras, microphones, and lights; shoot the tape or film; and later edit and splice it into the finished product to meet original specifications. Before releasing the finished item, they operate projectors, tape players, and other equipment to show it to the people who requested that it be made. In some projects, technicians may be involved in ordering or preparing simpler materials, such as transparencies for overhead projection, charts, posters, or displays.

Many technicians are employed mainly to operate the audiovisual or sound-reproduction equipment. They may work for museums, zoos, or libraries that offer educational or public service shows to entertain or inform their visitors. Technicians may operate motion picture projectors in auditoriums or lecture halls. In a more complicated program, the presentation is aided by audiovisual materials to illustrate, clarify, or enhance the impact of the talk. Technicians operate various equipment for slides, video, audio tape, and discs to produce pictures, background music, oral commentary, and sound effects. They may have to coordinate their part of the presentation with the speaker by following instructions, such as notations on a script, or by cues.

131

Many audiovisual technicians are employed by educational institutions to maintain the equipment and provide services such as recording important lectures and symposiums.

These technicians also maintain the equipment and materials in good working condition. They make minor adjustments and routine repairs, and notify the appropriate personnel when a major repair is needed. Before a presentation, technicians must position, install, and connect all the necessary equipment such as microphones, amplifiers, and lights. They test the setup to make sure that it functions correctly and is ready to operate. After the presentation, they may have to put equipment back into storage, prepare for the next presentation, or pack up rented or borrowed program materials so that they can be sent somewhere else.

Some audiovisual technicians who operate equipment travel to different locations to help present programs. For example, technicians who work for large companies may set up and operate equipment at conventions, trade shows, and employee training sessions held in various plants. In some school districts, or regional networks of school districts, technicians transport shared equipment and materials between different locations where they are to be used.

Audiovisual technicians are responsible for record keeping related to program materials, whether these are part of a permanent media library in their department, or rented or borrowed from outside sources. These technicians must catalogue, duplicate, label, and repair materials, and make a record of each usage. Materials from outside sources require another form of record-keeping: they must be requested in advance, orders must be confirmed, and materials need to be checked in and returned on time.

Some audiovisual technicians specialize in the installation and repair of audiovisual equipment. Using their knowledge of electronics, they inspect the equipment for defects, then repair or replace parts using hand tools, soldering irons, and electronic testing devices. Some audiovisual equipment is quite sophisticated and expensive, so technicians must know when it is better to return equipment to the manufacturer or a specialty repair shop instead of attempting the repairs themselves.

Audiovisual technicians are employed by school systems, college and university media centers, industrial training centers, marketing education centers, advertising agencies, government agencies, and the Armed Forces. Some work in businesses that provides audiovisual equipment and services to hotels or convention centers. Other technicians work for regional boards of cooperative education services. These are organizations formed by several school districts to provide specialized services to all the districts. Usually such a board has regional film and video libraries and traveling library, television, and media services.

Requirements

Audiovisual technicians need about two years of post-secondary school technical training. Technicians who install, operate, adjust, and service audiovisual equipment need to learn some electronics and mechanical skills; those who transform ideas and concepts into tangible media forms must develop their artistic abilities while learning about materials and equipment. In addition, certain personal qualities are helpful, such as creativity and the ability to communicate easily with others.

In high school, prospective audiovisual technicians should take courses that teach language skills (reading, writing, speaking), two years of mathematics, one year of physics or chemistry with laboratory, drawing, and, if available, elementary drafting and courses that introduce electronics.

Many public and private technical institutes, community colleges, and some divisions of four-year colleges offer programs to prepare audiovisual technicians. These programs are usually the quickest and best way to prepare for the career. They may have various names, such as audiovisual technology, media technology, or audiovisual library technology.

Audiovisual technicians need a general preparation in the media and media equipment field. Typical first-year courses in technical training programs include graphic design, audiovisual history, basic learning theory, equipment operation and maintenance, duplicating processes, basic photography, basic electronics, English, mathematics, and science.

Second-year courses may include audio materials production, television production, technical aspects of television, advanced graphics, advanced photography, internship in audiovisual technology, audiovisual office management, psychology, sales techniques, and technical writing.

There are other ways to prepare for the career. Sometimes people already working in related areas like public relations, industrial training, electronics or mechanical technicians with a special interest in the visual arts or audiovisual materials and equipment can get on-the-job training or study part-time to move into the field.

Technical training programs in the military can provide some of the skills necessary for this field. Such training, however, does not always provide a thorough understanding of the processes and equipment that technicians will encounter, so some additional study may be required.

Most employers provide an organized orientation period for new employees, during which they must learn the products or services of the employer's organization.

Although not a requirement, audiovisual technicians may find it useful to become certified by the Institute for the Certification of Engineering Technicians. Affiliations with photographic, electronics, technical communications, or technical media associations keep technicians in touch with new developments and give them access to a wider range of people working in the same field.

Special requirements

Some employers have special requirements, such as security clearances in the military or in some industrial training situations. To work for some government agencies, technicians must pass Civil Service examinations.

Opportunities for experience and exploration

Students may be able to get valuable career insight and information in a vocational program taught in their school, or from teachers of drafting and electrical shop courses. Hobbies such as ham radio or photography can provide experience similar to that of audiovisual technicians.

Interested students may be able to find opportunities for involvement as amateur audiovisual technicians. School programs may need to be recorded or may utilize visual aids. Public address systems may be used to amplify speeches, plays, or concerts. Working as an audiovisual aide or volunteer can help the prospective technician become familiar with the equipment, methods, and tasks involved in audiovisual work. There are opportunities for the same type of involvement at a community college, technical institute, or four-year college.

Getting to know some of the people at local companies that supply audiovisual equipment and services is another way to learn firsthand about the career. Such contacts may lead to part-time work.

Methods of entering

Audiovisual program graduates often find employment through the placement office at their school. In addition, many school districts, colleges, universities, businesses, and industries advertise in newspapers for audiovisual technicians.

In some states, technicians who wish to work for public schools and universities or government agencies are required to take competitive civil service exams. There is usually a new employee probationary period ranging from three months to a year. During this period, newly employed technicians may receive training or orientation on the job. After this, they usually assume full responsibility for all duties.

Advancement

Technicians may advance to positions as supervisors or senior technicians within the department or area where they work.

Attending a four year bachelor's degree program in audiovisual technology can open up more supervisory and administrative job possibilities for ambitious technicians. These programs emphasize expertise in both conventional and rapidly changing technologies, as well as in management and supervisory techniques and skills.

Experienced audiovisual technicians have increasing opportunities to move into sales, demonstration, and service jobs for distributors of audiovisual equipment. Experienced technicians also may start their own business or join a company that provides audiovisual equipment and service to hotels, conference centers, large corporations, and government agencies.

Employment outlook

The increasing use of films, records, video and audio tapes, overhead transparencies, and related teaching tools in today's schools, libraries, and workplaces suggests that trained audiovisual technicians will continue to be needed. In general, audiovisual technicians appear to have a good future because the number of job openings exceeds the number of well-qualified applicants. In business and industry, corporate educational centers need media support staff to train personnel. The increasing complexity of industrial jobs forces employers to provide organized educational and training programs for their employees; for the best results, they use audiovisual methods at these training programs.

Because of a continuing general emphasis on cost-cutting in government, the outlook for jobs in the public sector may not be as good. At some point technicians who work for public schools or government agencies may find that funds are reduced for audiovisual programs and personnel.

Earnings

Starting salaries for audiovisual technicians vary depending on the requirements of the job, the technician's training, the type of employer, and other factors. Beginners may receive $13,000 to $16,500 a year, although some technicians make more and a few make less. Experienced technicians may move up to advanced positions that pay salaries of $20,000 to $72,800 or more per year, with the average being $34,000. Benefits may include sick leave, paid holidays and vacation time, health insurance, and a pension plan. Technicians who succeed with their own company have the highest potential earnings.

Conditions of work

Working conditions for audiovisual technicians are usually pleasant, attractive, clean, and safe. Technicians are almost always provided with all the tools and materials they need.

Audiovisual technicians usually work 35 to 40 hours a week. Some employers operate on Saturday mornings in addition to regular business hours. Some technicians in larger institutions may work either a split or an evening shift. Technicians who provide the equipment and audiovisual services for hotels, conference centers, or major corporate training centers often must work long hours and during weekends. Some programs might start almost as soon as the previous ones are finished. To provide the equipment and service for a conference with more than one hundred separate sessions can be a collective task for several technicians, requiring many hours of exacting work. The financial rewards for this work are naturally greater than for other, less demanding, jobs.

Audiovisual technicians must keep up-to-date with the rapid changes that occur in the materials, methods, and equipment in this field. They will find that basic scientific principles do not change rapidly, but that the specific details of equipment and processes do.

Audiovisual technicians should know how to work well under pressure, coordinate simultaneous requests, and maintain the discipline necessary for teamwork. They must be able to accept constructive criticism. A sense of humor and a pleasant disposition are valuable personal qualities. The ever-changing challenge of providing information to people can be one of the major satisfactions of this career.

GOE: 01.03.01, 05.05.10, 05.10.05; SIC: 8231; SOC: 399, 6151, 7479

◇ **SOURCES OF ADDITIONAL INFORMATION**

Association of Audio-Visual Technicians
2378 South Broadway
Denver, CO 80210

Association for Informational Media and Equipment
PO Box 865
Elkader, IA 52043

Electronics Industries Association
20001 Pennsylvania Avenue NW, Suite 1000
Washington, DC 20006

Institute of Electrical and Electronics Engineers
345 East 47th Street
New York, NY 10017

National Electronic Sales and Service Dealers Association
2708 West Berry Street
Fort Worth, TX 76109

Automobile mechanics

Definition

Automobile mechanics repair malfunctions and provide routine maintenance services for the mechanical and electrical parts of passenger cars, vans, and small trucks with gasoline engines. Some automobile mechanics are generalists who work on any part of a car; others specialize in one kind of system within vehicles, such as transmissions or brakes.

History

In the late 19th century, there were many people working on developing a self-propelled passenger vehicle that could run on roads. Most of the vehicles they experimented with were never very important. Powered by steam or electricity, they were expensive to build and operate and often required drivers to have engineering skills. Then about 1885, two German engineers, Gottlieb Daimler and Carl Benz, both developed successful single-cylindered, gasoline-powered, internal-combustion engines. The machines they built are considered the earliest direct ancestors of modern automobiles.

The development of the automobile began to accelerate. In the United States in the 1890s, various vehicles of the horseless carriage type appeared, made by such pioneers as the Duryea brothers, Charles Edgar and J. Frank; Henry Ford; and Ransom Eli Olds, who de-signed and sold the first commercially successful American car, the Oldsmobile, in 1901.

Yet these automobiles were still produced in small numbers, because of limited manufacturing facilities and small consumer demand. Cars were considered mostly a curiosity for the rich. For a long time there were very few shops where mechanics provided maintenance and repair services; owners had to rely on themselves or take the car back to its builder.

Several developments in the first two decades of the 20th century helped make automobiles more popular. New designs for cars put the engine under a hood instead of beneath the driver. Cars became faster and enclosed, with the riders protected from the weather. Gasoline became more available and its price went down, making it a cost-effective fuel. Perhaps most important change was the introduction of assembly-line production by Henry Ford. By 1913, Ford's Model T was manufactured using methods that made the cost of automobiles so reasonable that for the first time Americans began to regard cars as a necessity of life. With more people on the roads, government bodies from local to federal became involved in road-improvement projects. America entered the automotive age.

As automobiles became more numerous and as more complex models were introduced, the need for skilled mechanics became obvious. Car owners could no longer do their own repairs. At first, mechanics were usually people who had learned general skills by trial and error, perhaps on their own. Today formal train-

An automobile mechanic gives a car its annual inspection.

ing is usually considered a necessity for automobile mechanics. In addition, more and more mechanics now are specialists. Automobiles have become so sophisticated that it is very difficult for one person to know how to maintain and repair all the different systems in different cars. The field of automobile mechanics has become a large one, with over 750,000 mechanics employed across the nation.

Nature of the work

Many mechanics feel the most interesting part of their work is figuring out the source of problems in the functioning of vehicles. Diagnosing mechanical and electrical troubles requires a broad knowledge of how cars work, the ability to make accurate observations of the problem, and the ability to reason through to a conclusion about what went wrong. Quickly diagnosing problems is, for many mechanics, the most challenging part of their job.

When a car is not operating properly, the owner usually brings it to the mechanic and describes its mechanical or electrical difficulties. At a dealership or larger shop, the customer may talk with a *repair-service-estimator*, who writes down the description and relays it to the mechanic. The mechanic may test-drive the car or use testing devices, such as motor analyzers, spark-plug testers, or compression gauges, to determine the problem. A customer might say, for example, that the car's automatic transmission isn't shifting gears at the right times. The mechanic must know how the functioning of the transmission depends on the engine vacuum, the throttle pressure, and sometimes the on-board computer. Each of these factors needs to be checked, well as the transmission. In each check there will be clues that enable the me-

chanic to correctly diagnose the trouble. After finding the cause of a problem, the mechanic makes adjustments or repairs. If a part is too badly damaged or worn to be repaired, or if it cannot be repaired at a reasonable cost, the mechanic replaces it.

Mechanics also do many routine tasks that keep a car in good operating condition and prevent breakdowns before they occur. Prior to the sale of an automobile, the dealer's mechanics check and adjust various parts of the car. After the car is sold, periodic checkups are necessary, because normal use and the passage of time inevitably cause wear and deterioration of parts of the automobile. In doing preventive maintenance, mechanics may follow a checklist to be sure they do not overlook anything important. They lubricate parts and they adjust or replace as needed components of any of the car's systems that might cause trouble, including belts, hoses, spark plugs, brakes, filters, transmission and coolant fluids, and many other items.

Because automobiles are increasingly complex machines, many mechanics specialize in the repair or service of specific parts. These specialists usually work in larger shops with different departments, in car diagnostic centers, or in small shops that concentrate on a particular type of repair work.

Tune-up mechanics evaluate and correct engine performance and fuel economy. They may use computerized diagnostic equipment and other sophisticated devices to locate malfunctions in fuel, ignition, and emissions-control systems. They adjust ignition timing and valves and may replace spark plugs, points, triggering assemblies in electronic ignitions, and other parts to bring engine performance up to maximum efficiency.

Brake repairers work on drum and disk braking systems, parking brakes, and hydraulic systems. They inspect, adjust, remove, repair, and reinstall such items as brake shoes, disk pads, drums, rotors, wheel and master cylinders, and hydraulic fluid lines. Some mechanics specialize in both brake and front-end work.

Front-end mechanics are concerned with suspension and steering systems. They assess wear to front-end parts like springs and shock absorbers and linkage parts like tie rods and ball joints, replacing the parts that are too worn. They align and balance wheels, often using special alignment equipment and wheel-balancing machines.

Transmission mechanics adjust, repair, and maintain gear trains, couplings, hydraulic pumps, valve bodies, clutch assemblies, and other parts of automatic transmission systems. Because transmissions are delicate and complex mechanisms, transmission mechanics need numerous special tools and a good deal of experience and training, including a knowledge of hydraulics.

Automotive air-conditioning mechanics install, maintain, and service air conditioners. They regularly recharge air-conditioning systems and sometimes service or replace components such as compressors, condensers, lines, and evaporators.

Automobile-radiator mechanics clean radiators, using caustic solutions. They locate and solder leaks and install new radiator cores. In addition, some radiator mechanics also repair car heaters and air conditioners and solder leaks in gas tanks.

Other specialist mechanics in the automotive field include *muffler installers, automobile-accessories installers, motor dynamometer testers, motorcycle mechanics, vehicle-fuel-systems converters, brake adjusters, clutch rebuilders, hand spring repairers, heavy repairers, motorcycle subassembly repairers, automotive-generator-and-starter repairers,* and *automatic-window-seat-and-top-lift repairers.*

As more automobiles rely on a variety of electronic components, it is increasingly important for mechanics to be well acquainted with the basics of electronics. Electronic controls and instruments can be found in nearly all the systems of today's cars. Diagnosing and correcting problems with electronic parts often involves the use of special tools and computers and is part of the job for specialists in any of these systems and for generalist mechanics.

Many different tools are used by automobile mechanics, ranging from simple and inexpensive hand tools to complicated and expensive equipment. Mechanics usually must furnish their own hand tools. Beginners are expected to accumulate tools as they gain experience. After a number of years, mechanics may have thousands of dollars invested in tools. It is usually the employer's responsibility to furnish the power tools, engine analyzers, and other test equipment.

To maintain and increase their skills and to keep up with new technology, automobile mechanics must regularly read service and repair manuals, shop bulletins, and other publications. Sometimes they take part in training programs sponsored by manufacturers that update them on new and advanced techniques for servicing and repairing vehicles.

Mechanics who work in small shops may prepare the estimates of the cost of repairs, including materials and labor, before starting the job. In larger repair shops, a service manager or repair-service-estimator generally prepares the estimates.

Requirements

Most employers today prefer to hire high school graduates who have completed some kind of formal training program in automobile mechanics. A wide variety of such programs are offered today in high schools, community and junior colleges, and vocational and technical schools. There are also training programs sponsored by automobile manufacturing companies and apprenticeships. Usually the programs that students attend after completing high school provide a better foundation for a career as an automobile mechanic than high school automotive courses alone.

Post-secondary training programs prepare students through a blend of classroom instruction and hands-on, practical experience. They range in length from six months to two years or more, depending on the type of program. Shorter programs usually involve intensive study. The longer programs typically alternate classroom courses with periods of work experience. Some programs at two-year colleges include courses in subjects such as applied mathematics, reading and writing skills, and business practices, and lead to an associate degree. At over 100 community colleges around the country, there are programs conducted in association with automobile manufacturers that allow students to combine significant work experience with hands-on classroom study of up-to-date equipment and new cars provided by car manufacturers. Students alternate periods of several weeks or months in the classroom with periods when they are employed in dealership service departments. These mechanics may take up to four years to finish their training, but they become familiar with the latest technology and also earn as they learn.

One indicator of quality in a training program for mechanics is certification by the National Automotive Technicians Education Foundation (NATEF), which is affiliated with the National Institute for Automotive Service Excellence. NATEF certifies many kinds of programs. To date, over 2,000 programs have been certified or are in the process of being certified. Although NATEF certification is voluntary, it is desirable because it assures students that the program meets certain standards established by automobile manufacturers and leaders in the field of automotive technology training.

Although formal post-secondary training programs are considered a better way to learn, some mechanics learn the trade on the job. Their training consists of working for several years under the guidance of experienced mechanics. Usually trainees begin as helpers, lubrication workers, or service station attendants who gradually acquire the skills and knowledge necessary for almost any service or repair task they encounter.

Employers who hire trainees are generally interested in people who have mechanical aptitude and demonstrate some knowledge of how automobiles work. In high school, prospective trainees should take any courses related to automobile repair that are available. Basic mathematics and English courses that sharpen reading skills are also important, because mechanics need to read and work with technical manuals and equipment specifications. Other useful subjects include electronics, blueprint reading, and applied physics and chemistry.

While beginners may be able to make simple repairs after only a few months' experience, it usually takes a year or two for trainees to be able to do most of the routine service and repairs that come into the shop. Another year or two of experience may be needed for trainee mechanics to be able to handle all types of repairs. Mechanics who specialize in complex areas, such as transmission repairs, can expect to need still another additional year or two before they are fully qualified. On the other hand, mechanics in less difficult fields, such as radiator or brake specialists, may be able to learn their jobs in a much shorter time.

Mechanics sometimes get special or additional training that is made available through the cooperation of employers and automobile manufacturers. Automobile dealers may send promising beginners to factory-sponsored mechanic training programs; factory representatives may come to repair shops to conduct short training sessions; and experienced mechanics may be sent to factory training centers to learn to repair new models or to receive special training in particular areas like automatic transmissions or air-conditioning repair.

Some people qualify as automobile mechanics by completing formal apprenticeships offered through automobile dealers and independent repair shops in cooperation with labor unions. However, apprenticeships have become less common than they once were, as post-secondary programs in vocational and technical schools and community colleges have become the accepted standard training in this field. Sometimes apprenticeships involve correspondence courses, but more often courses are conducted at local schools and colleges.

Apprenticeship programs typically involve three or four years of training. A four-year program might require about 8,000 hours of practical shop experience, working on brakes, chassis, transmissions, engines, electrical systems, exhaust emission controls, and other components, and at least 576 hours of formal classroom instruction on these subjects, as well as additional topics such as motor theory, reading blueprints and shop manuals, and job safety practices.

Like training programs, individual mechanics may be certified by the National Institute for Automotive Service Excellence. While certification is voluntary, it is a widely recognized standard of achievement for automobile mechanics. Mechanics may apply to be certified in one or more of eight different service areas, such as tune-ups, brakes, suspension, or electrical system repair. Master mechanics are certified in all eight areas. To qualify for certification in each area, mechanics must have at least two years' experience and pass a written examination. Completion of an auto mechanics program in high school, vocational or trade school, or community or junior college may be substituted for one year of experience. To maintain their certification, mechanics must retake the examination every five years.

Special requirements

Membership in a labor union may be a requirement for some automobile mechanics. The unions organizing automobile mechanics include the International Association of Machinists and Aerospace Workers; the International Union, United Automobile, Aerospace and Agricultural Implement Workers of America; the Sheet Metal Workers International Association; and the International Brotherhood of Teamsters, Chauffeurs, Warehousemen and Helpers of America.

Opportunities for experience and exploration

Automobile mechanics is a field that offers good opportunities for experience and exploration. In high school shop courses, individuals can appraise their mechanical ability and interest in this work. Tinkering with cars as a hobby provides valuable firsthand experience in the work of a mechanic. In addition, part-time work in a service station can give a feel for the kind of problems that mechanics face on the job. Experience with vehicle repair work in the Armed Forces is another way many people learn about their interest in this field.

Methods of entering

Often the best way to start out in this field is to attend one of the many post-secondary training programs available throughout the country. Trade and technical schools usually provide job placement assistance for students in this field, and some promise a job for qualified graduates. Schools often have contacts with local employers who need to hire well-trained people. Some schools also teach students good interviewing and resume-writing skills should they want to change jobs in the future.

People seeking to enter apprenticeships should contact local employers in the field or the local offices of labor unions that organize their workers. The state employment service can also supply information about apprenticeships.

People who want to start out as mechanic's helpers or trainees and learn all their skills on the job usually contact potential employers directly or follow leads from local employment agencies.

Advancement

As automobile mechanics who are generalists gain experience, some find that they can move into specialist areas that pay better. If they have certain personal characteristics, such as the ability to deal with people, good judgment, and planning skills, mechanics may advance to positions such as shop supervisor, service manager, or repair-service estimator. Among other possibilities are becoming a car or truck sales worker or a parts department manager for a dealer.

Some mechanics eventually go into business for themselves, opening an independent repair shop or a service station. About one automobile mechanic in five is self-employed in this way.

Employment outlook

The prospects for well-trained automobile mechanics are good. During the next decade, employment opportunities for automobile mechanics are expected to increase about as rapidly as the average for other occupations. The number of vehicles on the road is also expected to increase as the number of drivers in the population increases. If the trend toward keeping older cars in operation continues, drivers will tend to buy more repairs and mainte-

nance services. As new cars continue the trend toward greater technological complexity, they will require more highly skilled mechanics to work on them. For this reason, the outlook is best for mechanics with good formal training. On the other hand, many new cars are being built to be more reliable than cars have been in the past, and they will presumably need fewer routine services.

Most new jobs for mechanics are expected to be in independent repair shops, specialty car care chains, and dealerships. Fewer gasoline service stations will provide repair services for cars, reducing the number of mechanics as employees.

In addition to a greater demand for automobile mechanics because of broad growth in the industry, thousands of new job openings will occur when experienced mechanics must be replaced because they retire, die, or change positions.

Fluctuations in economic conditions have little effect on employment in this field; mechanics generally enjoy the security of steady work. Beginners may find it more difficult getting a job during an economic slump, however, when employers may be more reluctant to take on inexperienced workers.

Earnings

The earnings of automobile mechanics vary according to the type of work they do, their employer, and geographical location. In the 1990s, highly skilled mechanics employed on a full-time basis by automobile dealers in cities can earn salaries in the range of $39,000 annually. Many mechanics with more average skills have earnings around $27,000. Depending on their duties, semiskilled mechanics may make about $19,000 or less.

In many automobile dealership repair departments and independent repair shops, experienced mechanics are paid a percentage of the labor costs charged to the customer. This commission is usually paid in addition to a guaranteed minimum salary. Total earnings thus depend on the amount of work the mechanics are able to complete. Mechanics who can finish repairs in less than average time have the best incomes.

During their training period, apprentices and students who are alternating work with classroom study may start at rates close to minimum wage, but their pay level increases as they become more skilled.

Conditions of work

Automobile mechanics are employed by a wide range of businesses and organizations, including the service departments of manufacturers' dealerships, independent repair shops, gasoline service stations, and automotive supply stores and department stores with automotive service facilities. Other mechanics work for federal, state, and local governments, taxicab and automobile leasing companies, and other organizations that maintain their own vehicles. Mechanics are also employed in automobile manufacturing plants to adjust and repair cars that come off the assembly lines. Most automobile mechanics work in small settings where there are no more than five mechanics, but some work in larger shops with more than 100 employees.

Most automobile mechanics have a standard workweek of about forty hours, although some may work longer hours. For the most part, their work is performed indoors. Some older repair shops may be cold and drafty in the winter and hot in the summer. Most shops, however, are well ventilated and kept at comfortable temperatures. Repair shops can be noisy, especially when there are power tools and engines running. In most shops work areas are kept clean and clear of debris, and there are strict safety procedures that help mechanics avoid accidents with potentially hazardous equipment and materials.

In the course of performing their duties, mechanics must stoop, bend, crouch, and lift heavy objects. They frequently handle automobile parts that are covered with grime and grease. Minor accidents are common, such as tripping over crawlers or jack handles, cuts from broken tools, burns, and allergic reactions to solvents or oils.

GOE: 05.05.09; SIC: 7538; SOC: 6111

◇ **SOURCES OF ADDITIONAL INFORMATION**

Automotive Service Association, Inc.
1901 Airport Freeway, Suite 100
PO Box 929
Bedford, TX 76095-0929

Automotive Service Industry Association
444 North Michigan Avenue
Chicago, IL 60611-3975

Motor Vehicle Manufacturers Association of the U.S., Inc.
7430 Second Avenue, Suite 300
Detroit, MI 48202

For information about becoming a certified automobile mechanic, write to:

National Institute for Automotive Service Excellence
13505 Dulles Technology Drive
Herndon, VA 22071-3800

Automotive Service Repair Association
#2, 10171–107th Street
Edmonton AB T5J 1J5

◇ **RELATED ARTICLES**

Volume 1: Automotives
Volumes 2–4: Aircraft mechanics and engine specialists; Automobile repairers; Automobile-repair-service estimators; Diesel mechanics; Farm-equipment mechanics; Gasoline service station attendants

Automobile repairers

Definition

Automobile repairers repair and refinish damaged parts of bodies of vehicles such as automobiles, buses, and light trucks. Using hand tools and power tools, they straighten bent frames and body sections, replace badly damaged parts, smooth out minor dents and creases, remove rust, fill small holes, and renew painted surfaces so that vehicle finishes look nearly new.

In small shops, automobile repairers may perform all of these tasks and also replace safety glass; however, in most shops, repairers specialize in either body repairs or automotive painting. In large shops, body repairers may specialize in one type of repair, such as frame straightening, fender repairing, or glass installation.

History

The earliest true automobile, built in 1769, was a huge, clumsy, three-wheeled, steam-powered open carriage for moving artillery. It was capable of carrying four passengers at just over two miles per hour. It was the first success in a long series of attempts to build a self-propelled passenger vehicle to run on regular roads. Although various steam vehicles were developed and put into use during the next century and a half, it was not until the internal combustion engine was developed in the late 19th century that automobiles began to be sufficiently fast, safe, and trouble-free to capture the imagination of the American public.

Around the turn of the 20th century, many people were experimenting with ways of improving automobiles, and numerous automobile manufacturing firms were established in response to the growing interest in cars. Among the new firms was the Ford Motor Company. In 1908 Henry Ford revolutionized automobile manufacturing by beginning assembly-line production of his Model T, thus bringing the price of cars for the first time to levels that many people could afford. Instead of being a rare luxury, cars soon became commonplace, crowding the roads and transforming the lives of millions of ordinary Americans within a few decades.

After a few years of use and perhaps damage from accidents, many cars and other vehicles needed some body work or refinishing. As vehicle bodies and finishes became more varied and elaborate, shops that provided these services were established. Today, body shops, vehicle dealers, independent repair garages, organizations that maintain their own fleets of vehicles, and businesses that specialize in painting employ around 250,000 workers with various repairing skills.

Nature of the work

When a motor vehicle has been damaged in a traffic accident, it is the job of body repairers to restore the body and body parts to as near as

Automobile-body repairers prepare a damaged car for body work. Parts of the car are removed so that the frame can be realigned.

possible their original condition. Most body repairers work only on cars and small trucks. A few work mainly on large trucks, buses, or tractor trailers. Among body repairers, some specialists include *used-car renovators; truck-body builders and apprentices; automobile-bumper straighteners; squeak, rattle and leak repairers,* and *automobile-body customizers.*

The first person to examine a damaged vehicle brought into a shop is generally a shop supervisor or estimator, who determines the extent of the damage and estimates how long the repairs will take and how much they will cost. The estimate is submitted to the owner of the vehicle for approval before any work is done. Then the vehicle is turned over to the body repairers with instructions concerning what needs to be done and how much time repairs should take. Body repairers generally work by themselves with minimal supervision beyond the original directions. In large, busy shops, repairers may be assisted by helpers or apprentices.

Vehicle bodies today may include steel, aluminum, various metal alloys, fiberglass, and plastic. Different techniques are used in repairing the different materials. Most repairers do work on all of them, although some specialize in fiberglass bodies.

Body repairers may need to remove items like upholstery, accessories, electrical and hydraulic window- and seat-operating equipment, and trim in order to get to the parts that need repair. If the frame or a body section of the vehicle has been bent or twisted, *frame repairers and straighteners* can sometimes restore it to its original alignment and shape by chaining or clamping it to an alignment machine that uses hydraulic pressure to pull the damaged metal into position.

After the frame is straight, dents in the metal body can be corrected in several different ways, depending on how deep they are. If a fender, section of a body panel, or grill is too badly damaged to repair, the body repairers remove it with hand tools, a pneumatic metal-cutting gun, or acetylene torch, then weld on a replacement part. Some dents can be pushed back out with hydraulic jacks, pneumatic hammers, prying bars, and other hand tools. To smooth small dents and creases, repairers may position small anvils called dolly blocks against one side of the dented metal and hit the opposite side with various specially designed hammers. Tiny pits and dimples are removed with pick hammers and punches. Dents that cannot be corrected with this treatment may be filled with solder or a putty-like material that becomes hard like metal after it cures. When the filler has hardened, the repairers file, grind, and sand the surface smooth in the correct contour and prepare it for painting. In many shops the final sanding and painting are done by other specialists, who may be called *automotive painters*.

Some vehicles have fiberglass or plastic bodies or body parts, which are more difficult to repair and often require complete replacement of parts. Body repairers remove the damaged panels and, if the dents look like they can be repaired, they determine the exact type of plastic material. Depending on the material, repairers may be able to use a hot-air welding gun or immerse a plastic part in hot water to soften it so it can be pressed back into its original shape by hand. Dents that cannot be worked out in such ways may be filled with new plastic material.

To complete the job of restoring everything to its proper position, body repairers may aim headlights, align wheels, and do similar tasks. Once the body work is complete, vehicles are ready for painting.

Automotive painting is a highly skilled, labor-intensive job that requires a fine eye and attention to detail for the result to be pleasing to the customer. Some paint jobs require that less than the whole vehicle be painted, so the painter must mix pigments to match the original color. This can be difficult if the original paint is faded.

The first step in painting is to be sure the surface is sanded completely smooth and is free of rust, original paint, and dirt. Areas that are not to be painted, such as chrome trim, windows, headlights, and mirrors, are removed or masked. Then several coats of primer coating, paint, and sealer are applied by hand with a sprayer. Lacquer is used for metal bodies, and acrylic for plastic. The painter must adjust the spray nozzle for the kind of primer or paint, and apply it carefully so that it goes in the proper thickness, without any runs.

Between coats, the car is dried, often with special infrared equipment or under heat lamps. Then it is lightly sanded to remove any irregularities and to help the next coat adhere better. After the last coat of paint, the painter may polish the vehicle.

Requirements

A high school diploma is not a requirement for becoming an automobile repairer, but employers often prefer to hire high school graduates. Courses that are useful preparation for this work include shop, applied mathematics, and if possible, automobile body repair, auto painting and refinishing, and auto mechanics, which are offered by many high schools, vocational schools, and private trade schools. Good reading skills are important because repairers must sometimes follow exact instructions and diagrams in technical manuals.

Many automobile repairers acquire their skills through several years of on-the-job training. They start as helpers, working alongside more experienced repairers, observing and learning, starting with the simplest tasks first. Usually three or four years are needed for helpers to become skilled in body repair work, while two to three years may be needed to acquire expert painting skills.

A few apprenticeships are available in both the body repair and automotive painting fields. In an apprenticeship program, practical on-the-job experience is combined with classroom study in related subjects such as job safety procedures, mathematics, and business management. Apprenticeships are an excellent way to learn occupational skills.

Technical schools and two-year colleges also offer programs in automobile repair. As automotive technology changes, the materials and methods involved in repair work change. Formal training programs can provide a good up-to-date grounding in the techniques needed for repairing various kinds of new vehicles.

A recognized standard of achievement in this field is certification by the National Institute for Automotive Service Excellence. Certification is voluntary, but it is an indicator that the worker is well qualified. To become certified, repairers must pass a written examination and have at least two years of work experience. Completion of a high school, vocational school, or trade school program in automobile repair may be substituted for one year of experience. To remain certified, repairers must take the examination again at least every five years.

Automobile body repairers are expected to furnish their own tools, although employers may provide power tools. Good hand tools are an investment, and repairers usually accumulate them as they gain experience. After years in the business, experienced workers may have a collection of tools worth thousands of dollars.

While union membership is not a requirement for all body repairers, many belong to the International Association of Machinists and Aerospace Workers; the International Union, United Automobile, Aerospace and Agricultural Implement Workers of America; the Sheet Metal Workers International Association; or the International Brotherhood of Teamsters, Chauffeurs, Warehousemen and Helpers of America. Most of the body repairers who are union members work for large automobile dealers, trucking companies, and bus lines.

Opportunities for experience and exploration

High school students can learn about this kind of work and begin to prepare for it by taking various industrial arts courses. Many high schools, along with vocational schools and private trade schools, offer instruction in automobile body repairing and painting. Automobile mechanics courses are also part of a solid foundation for anyone who plans to work in the automobile repair field.

For a practical viewpoint, students should first seek permission to visit local repair shops to observe and talk to the automobile repairers employed there. A part-time or summer job in a service station, garage, or automotive supply store could give students an opportunity to become familiar with some of the problems and equipment they would encounter on the job. Buying an old car to repair and refinish is also a very good way to find out first-hand what the work involves.

Methods of entering

People who want to become automobile repairers most often begin as trainees, either in apprenticeships or in positions where they assist experienced repairers while learning on the job. Information about apprenticeships and other training programs, as well as details about work opportunities, may be obtained from locals of the unions mentioned previously or from local offices of the state employment service. Prospective automobile repairers often apply directly to possible employers, such as car dealers and body-repair shops. Job leads may be found in newspaper want ads or through school placement offices or private employment agencies.

Advancement

Advancement in this occupation often takes the form of salary increases. With experience and managerial ability, however, automobile repairers may advance to positions such as shop supervisors, estimators, or service managers. Once they know the job, many workers decide to go into business for themselves, setting up their own repair shop or perhaps a custom paint shop. A few become automobile damage appraisers for insurance companies.

Employment outlook

During the next decade, employment of automobile repairers is expected to increase at about the same rate as the average for other occupations. The overall demand for vehicle body and paint work is expected to increase, but this will not mean that many new jobs are created. Most job openings will probably occur when experienced repairers stop working to retire or move into other jobs.

The need for both body and paint work will remain strong because the number of motor vehicles, and thus the number of accidents, will grow. Many new vehicles will be fairly small, light in weight, and easily damaged in collisions. Many vehicles will be made with plastics, new alloys, and aluminum parts that are difficult to work with after they are damaged. Increased opportunities for automotive painters will also come from the trend toward repainting and refurbishing older vehicles instead of buying expensive new ones.

The automobile repair business is not greatly affected by changes in economic conditions. Major body damage must be repaired to keep a vehicle in safe operating condition. During an economic downturn, however, people tend to postpone minor repairs until their budgets can accommodate the expense. Nevertheless, body repairers are seldom laid off. Instead, when business is bad, employers hire fewer new workers. During a recession, inexperienced workers face strong competition for entry-level jobs. People with formal training in repair work and automobile mechanics are likely to have the best job prospects in such times.

Earnings

Experienced automobile body repairers in large cities in the 1990s make about $36,000 to $45,000 a year. Experienced painters average roughly $21,000, with earnings ranging from about $15,000 to $35,000. Helpers and trainees are generally paid 30 to 60 percent of the wages earned by skilled workers. Geographical location also affects earnings. Repairers in the South tend to make more money than those in other regions, while repairers in the Northeast tend to make less.

In many automobile dealerships and repair shops, automobile repairers work on commission. That is, they receive a percentage—usually 40 to 50 percent—of the labor costs charged to customers. The total amount they earn varies, then, depending on how many repair jobs need to be done and how fast the repairers can work. Employers often guarantee a minimum level of pay in addition to the commission. Helpers and trainees are paid a flat rate until they become skilled enough to work on commission. Repairers who work for trucking companies, bus lines, and other businesses that maintain their own vehicles receive a straight wage and do not work on commission.

In addition to regular earnings, shops may provide fringe benefits such as paid vacations and sick leave, health insurance, pension plans, clean work clothing, and discounts on work done on the employee's own cars.

Conditions of work

In an effort to reduce dust and dangerous fumes, most automobile repair shops are well ventilated. Body repair work can be very noisy and dusty, with hammering, sanding, and power tools whining much of the time. Because repairers must do welding and handle hot or jagged pieces of metal and broken glass, they often use special equipment like safety glasses, masks, and protective gloves. Body repairers routinely need to lift heavy objects weighing up to 75 pounds. Their work often requires them to stretch, bend, kneel, and crouch in awkward and cramped positions.

Automotive painters have to wear respirators and other protective gear, and they work in specially ventilated rooms to keep from being exposed to paint fumes and other hazardous chemicals. Painters may need to stand for hours at a time as they work.

Automobile repairers usually work 40 to 48 hours a week. The practices at each shop and the amount of work on hand determine the hours worked. Self-employed repairers often work the longest hours.

Automobile repairing appeals to people who enjoy working with their hands, don't mind getting dirty, and are self-reliant and resourceful in working out solutions to a variety of problems. Like a jigsaw puzzle, each damaged vehicle presents a unique challenge. Repairers depend on a thorough knowledge of automobile construction and repair techniques to help them develop appropriate methods for each job. Being able to turn a wrecked or rusted old car into one that looks like new provides a real sense of accomplishment.

GOE: 05.05.06, 05.10.07; SIC: 7532; SOC: 6115, 7669

◇ **SOURCES OF ADDITIONAL INFORMATION**

Automotive Service Association, Inc.
1901 Airport Freeway, Suite 100
PO Box 929
Bedford, TX 76095-0929

Automotive Service Industry Association
444 North Michigan Avenue
Chicago, IL 60611-3975

Motor Vehicle Manufacturers Association of America, Inc.
7430 Second Avenue, Suite 300
Detroit, MI 48202

National Institute for Automotive Service Excellence
13505 Dulles Technology Drive
Herndon, VA 22071-3415

◇ **RELATED ARTICLES**

Volume 1: Automotives

Volumes 2–4: Automobile mechanics; Automobile-repair-service estimators; Automobile technicians; Farm-equipment mechanics; Forge shop occupations; Machinists; Painters and paperhangers; Welders

Automobile sales workers

Definition

Automobile sales workers help customers in selecting a new or used car. They are familiar with the type and model of the car they are selling. They know the features of the car and can provide a valuable service to the customer by assisting in this important decision. Automobile sales workers also perform a service to the dealer who employs them by making sure the dealer's customers are happy with their purchases.

History

Automobile sales workers have been around since the first line of automobiles was produced for commercial sale. In the 1870s, when the first steamer vehicles were designed, the cars were usually designed by and belonged to the owner. When larger scale production began, however, the designer had to supervise the manufacturing process and had no time left to sell his product. Thus, it became necessary to hire sales people who knew how the vehicle operated, and the occupation of the automobile sales worker was created.

Nature of the work

An automobile sales worker may sell either new cars, used cars, or both. The sales worker is employed by an automobile dealer. The dealer may specialize in only one or a small handful of automobile makes.

Usually the first contact the sales worker has with the customer occurs when the customer walks into the showroom. In slow seasons, however, it may be necessary for the sales worker to go looking for customers. This can be done through newspaper or television advertising, business cards or fliers placed on automobiles mentioning a trade-in price, telephone soliciting, or various other methods of marketing.

The automobile sales worker will strike up a conversation with the potential customer in the showroom, mentioning the various features and benefits of each make of car and answering questions. The automobile sales worker must use some psychology to understand customers and make a sale. Some customers may be interested only in the appearance of the car and its ease of handling. Other customers may be more concerned with the car's performance and engine specifications. The sales worker must be able to figure out specifically what it is the customers want and point out these features of the automobile to aid the customers in their purchasing decision. The sales worker will also describe features such as warranty and repair programs. The sales worker should be accurate in all this information and not mislead the customer in any way.

An automobile represents a large investment and customers may hesitate before taking the final step. The sales worker must be able to convince the customer that he or she is doing the right thing and getting a good automobile. The sales worker must also be convinced that the product is good and priced reasonably, or else the sales pitch will ring hollow.

Once the customer has decided on a particular automobile, the sales worker places the order and draws up the necessary papers. This may include financing and insurance. The sales worker explains the conditions of the warranty and gives the automobile a final inspection before handing the car keys to the customer. If customers are pleased with the service of the sales worker, they will come back to that dealer with future business and will also recommend the sales worker to any friends who are shopping for a car.

One of the elements of car sales that differs from other types of retailing is that some bartering takes place between the customer and the salesperson. The price of the car is deter-

AUTOMOBILE SALES WORKERS

An automobile sales worker must know the varieties of cars on the market, including the competition's cars.

mined through negotiations, as the customer tries to pay the least amount while the sales worker tries to get the highest fair market price. Usually the sales worker has an absolute price for each car, below which the dealer will not make any money on the sale. The sales worker must balance the need for setting a high price with the possibility that the customer will decide not to buy.

Requirements

A pleasant personality is necessary for successful sales workers. Automobile sales workers must be able to influence people and must be able to overcome sales resistance. They must also have a thorough knowledge of the product they are selling. Good personal appearance and manners are important requirements. Automobile sales workers must also be familiar with finance and insurance rates and be able to explain these to customers.

Special requirements

The National Automobile Dealers Association is in the process of launching a national program to certify, on a voluntary basis, all sales workers in the industry. This voluntary organization is called the Society of Automotive Sales Professionals (SASP). However, automobile sales workers are not required to be licensed or certified or satisfy any other formal requirements.

Opportunities for experience and exploration

For those students interested in this occupation, it is important to know how an automobile runs. Books are available in the library that explain the principle of automobile mechanization. Any type of sales experience can help young people decide if they have the aptitude and personality for sales work. New and used car dealers frequently hire students to wash cars after school. Other small jobs such as changing tires, batteries, and lights are also available to students.

Methods of entering

There are several ways to become an automobile sales worker, but the best way is to have some experience in selling to customers. Naturally, the greater the amount of experience, the sooner a person will be able to enter auto sales. A high school graduate who has some experience and has shown initiative can be made into an aggressive sales worker with additional on-the-job training. At the weekly sales meeting, the worker's progress will be evaluated. Some large auto dealers provide special classes on sales training. In addition, some automobile manufacturers provide training manuals and other educational materials.

Certain courses and education beyond high school will benefit sales workers in many ways. Auto dealers prefer their sales force to have had such courses as psychology, business law, public speaking, math, and English, as these all come in handy on the job.

Advancement

A successful automobile sales worker who can manage other people in addition to selling automobiles may advance to assistant sales manager, sales manager, or general manager. With enough business sense and hard work, the sales worker may one day open his or her own auto dealership.

Employment outlook

The U.S. automobile industry experienced a severe decline in sales in the 1970s and again in the early 1990s, partly because of competition from foreign cars and partly because of a general recession that prompted many prospective buyers to postpone their purchases. Employment opportunities in the auto sales industry at that time were extremely limited. The availability of auto sales jobs is tied very closely to swings in the overall economy. About 182,500 people are currently employed as new and used automobile sales workers.

Earnings

Earnings depend on the area of the country in which the sales worker is employed. A generally small number of car sales occur in rural areas, while a greater turnover in the car market occurs in urban and suburban areas. A downturn in the regional economy will have an effect on car sales as well. Some automobile agencies pay on a straight salary basis, while others pay a commission.

Automobile sales workers made an average salary of more than $26,000 a year in the 1990s. Those working for dealers who sold fewer than 200 autos annually averaged less, while those who worked for dealers selling more than 1,000 cars a year averaged more. Most dealers provide paid vacations, and many provide life insurance, hospitalization, and medical plans.

Conditions of work

The work of an auto sales worker is neither strenuous nor messy. Automobile showrooms are usually clean and light. New cars are always clean. While used cars are normally kept outside on a lot, most are cleaned thoroughly before being put out for sale.

Families and other customers frequently shop for cars after regular working hours in the evening and on Saturdays. Some automobile dealers are open on Sunday. An automobile sales worker generally must work some evening and weekend hours, although those with more seniority may get to set their own schedules.

Competition between auto dealerships can be very fierce. Because automobile sales workers are constantly in competition, they can feel the resulting strain. Their income is directly tied to their performance and the performance of the dealership. In spite of these pressures, it is important that the sales worker be pleasant and get along well with people.

There may be discouraging days when sales workers make no sales, so they must be able to maintain their sense of self-confidence and determination to overcome these slack periods. This is particularly true during periods of a slow general economy and slumping auto sales.

GOE: 08.02.02; SIC: 5511; SOC: 4342

◇ **SOURCES OF ADDITIONAL INFORMATION**

National Automobile Dealers Association
8400 Westpark Drive
McLean, VA 22102

◇ **RELATED ARTICLES**

Volume 1: Automotives; Business Management; Sales
Volumes 2–4: Door-to-door sales workers; Electronic sales and service technicians; Financial services brokers; Insurance agents and brokers; Manufacturers' sales workers; Real estate agents and brokers; Retail managers; Retail sales workers; Route drivers; Service sales representatives; Travel agents; Wholesale trade sales workers

Automobile technicians

Definition

Automobile technicians work on mechanical automotive parts, usually specializing in one area. *Automotive cooling system technicians* inspect and test cooling systems, analyze system malfunctions, and estimate repair or replacement costs.

Automotive, diesel, and gas turbine technicians help automotive engineers design, develop, maintain, and repair automotive equipment and all kinds of vehicles and equipment powered by gasoline, diesel, or turbine engines.

Automotive exhaust technicians conduct tests on automotive vehicles to check exhaust emissions.

History

Combustion engines, used in cars today, came about slowly, starting with the discovery of mechanical devices that made work easier or faster (such as moving objects and people). Wheels and axles were used for vehicles such as carts, wagons, and carriages for thousands of years before the 1st century B.C., when the Romans discovered ball bearings, and how to hitch a front axle to a wagon to provide flexible steering.

The next milestone occurred when Hero of Alexandria developed the first crude steam engine in the 1st century A.D. However, it was only about 400 years ago that Leonardo da Vinci and other European machine designers discovered how to modify wheels into gears. Da Vinci envisioned an automobile powered by an engine and foresaw the principles of transmissions with gear ratios that would control power speeds. He also saw the need to use bearings to overcome friction.

In 1769, James Watt and Nicolas-Joseph Cugnot both built usable steam engines that, with refinements, were used for transportation, manufacturing, and other industrial uses. In England, France, and Germany, steam buses for transporting people became fairly common. One of the first buses, built in England by Sir Goldsworthy Gurney in 1829, could carry eighteen people on a regular schedule from London to Bath, a distance of 170 kilometers. In time, the steam automobile evolved from such buses.

By the 1880s the basic principles of electricity were discovered and electrically motored automobiles were developed and on the market. They were quiet and comfortable, but not noteworthy because their batteries were too heavy and had to be recharged too often to be widely accepted.

By the early 1880s, engineers in Europe and the United States had learned enough about wheels, shafts, gears, steam cylinders, hydraulic pumps, and elementary electrical sparking devices to attempt to combine them into an automobile. Gasoline, kerosene, alcohol, and benzene were available as cheap fuels for internal combustion engines.

The first successful high-compression engines grew out of the research of Daimler and Benz in Germany, and Peugeot and Renault in France; all of whom produced engines and built automobiles between 1885 and 1889. Meanwhile, in the United States, Henry Ford, Eli Olds, and Frank Duryea were working on gasoline engines, and automobile development. At the same time, wagons with engines became the precursors of modern trucks, the hauling vehicles of the 20th century.

By the 1890s, the western world needed better land transportation. The thousands of people living on farms and in small cities needed a cheap way to travel from home to town or to larger cities, as well as trucks for hauling farm and forest products to market. The newly created automobiles promised unprecedented personal mobility if only they could be made more powerful, less noisy, more comfortable, more dependable, and safer to operate.

The jobs of automotive engineers and automobile technicians both came into being in the period between 1880 and 1910. In Europe and the United States, the fierce competition to develop faster, fancier, and cheaper automobiles caused many small companies to develop and produce successful automobiles.

The challenge to build automobiles pleasing to the public at a price many people could afford brought to light the special genius of Henry Ford. He, along with engineers and technicians, designed, built, and marketed thousands of his first "Model A" Fords beginning in 1903. From 1903 until 1908, they designed and built 18 different models ("B" through "S") and finally the famous Model T, which was enormously successful. It was the first mass market car: simple, roomy, dependable, and very affordable. More than 15 million were built during the next two decades.

Worldwide automobile racing began in 1898, only a few years after the first autos were built. The competition to set records for the fastest automobile became a way for auto makers to prove the quality of their machines. Henry Ford personally drove his Model 999 to win the 1903 fastest car record at a speed of 147 kilometers per hour.

Their success in races popularized Ford cars, which helped sell them to a growing market. It also helped Ford designers and technicians develop important new technology, such as use of alcohol fuel for racing cars.

The most important development Henry Ford brought to the auto industry was an efficient assembly-line production method for making his automobiles. His engineers and production technicians designed a carefully timed system for bringing parts together at assembly stations. These stations divided the work of assembling the car into separate simple steps. The system reduced the cost of the Model T Ford from $850 in 1908 to $380 in 1926. On October 31, 1925, more than 9,000 Model Ts were completely assembled—a production record that stood for many years.

European and U.S. manufacturers continued to build more refined and technologically complicated automobiles in the 1920s and 1930s. They developed better and more powerful engines, more sophisticated muffling designs, automatic gear-shifting transmissions, self-starters, electrical ignition, automatic speed controllers, supercharged engines, large luxury autos, and small sports cars. All were produced by increasingly higher precision manufacturing and assembling technology.

In recent years, important changes have greatly affected the work of automobile technicians as well as the engineers and managers they support. In 1973, the Arab oil-producing nations stopped exporting petroleum to the West, then raised oil prices. The resulting fuel shortage and the consequences (long lines at the gas stations, extremely high prices) forced the U.S. auto industry to completely redesign its cars for greater fuel efficiency.

Meanwhile, the Japanese and western European automobiles had already been designed to be smaller, more fuel-efficient, and less air-polluting; large numbers of them were imported into the United States, causing serious unemployment among U.S. automobile workers. Both Japan and West Germany improved their automobile manufacturing and assembly operations by using modern robots and computer-aided manufacturing processes, making them more efficient than U.S. automobile manufacturers.

After completing an annual check up, an automobile technician tightens the bolts on a vehicle's engine.

The changes that forced U.S. automotive engineers, managers, and their technicians to redesign their automobiles and to develop computer-aided manufacturing processes have made important changes in the skills and knowledge automobile technicians must acquire. They have also sharply increased the demand for well-prepared technicians in the field.

Nature of the work

Automotive cooling system technicians work with vacuum and pressure testing equipment to check hoses and radiators, and with electrical testing equipment such as voltmeters and ammeters to check electrical components. On the basis of their examination, they prepare estimates of repair costs for customers and may make recommendations about repair versus replacement on the basis of their experience and their examination of the system. Occasionally, especially in smaller repair facilities, they may also help perform the repairs using appropriate hand tools. They compile charges and, when the work has been completed and approved, send them to the billing department.

Automotive, diesel, and gas turbine technicians work in a great variety of industries and positions. They may be broadly grouped into five general categories, as described in the following paragraphs.

Research and development technicians prepare engines or related equipment for testing. This often involves calibration and installation of various electronic, mechanical, and hydraulic instrumentation devices. The technician then conducts the test, records data, and reports the results.

AUTOMOBILE TECHNICIANS

Service representatives try to ensure that the customer receives the maximum performance from an engine. They may diagnose poor performance, correct the problem, test the engine to insure proper performance, and report the problem to the manufacturer's research and development division.

Sales representatives advise customers, matching the best kind of unit to their needs. They need a thorough understanding of the company's products plus the ability to apply mathematics and science principles to analyze customer requirements.

Some related technical positions may include *drafting and design technicians* in transportation and power companies, *safety engineers, service* and *sales engineers* for oil companies, and *insurance claims adjusters* with transportation insurance companies. In these positions the technician's practical understanding of automotive, diesel, or gas turbine engines provides the necessary background for the related type of technical work.

Technicians who work in service or operator capacities are mainly found in dealerships or wholesale distributors. They may be *service managers* for automotive, tractor, or engine dealers.

In the manufacturing plant, numerous jobs are available to technicians. They can work as *machine maintenance employees, machine operators, quality control personnel,* and *production supervisors.* Many firms will hire these technicians and start them in such positions, advancing them when they become more experienced or when openings become available.

Within these broad areas, many automotive, diesel, and gas turbine technicians work principally at one specialized activity or with one specific kind of product. Following is a list of some of the jobs open to entry-level technicians.

Utility technicians compare fuels by testing and rating them on laboratory test engines.

Engineering testers record data obtained from diesel engines running with different lubricating oils to determine performance and wear characteristics.

Safety and maintenance supervisors inspect trucks and tractor-trailers for safety equipment.

Automotive field-test technicians work in manufacturing research and development, preparing vehicles for road tests in field proving grounds.

Associate research technicians prepare test engines and related instruments in the laboratory section of a petroleum company.

Engine test cell technicians prepare gas turbine and jet engines for operation in a test cell.

Lubrication sales technicians prepare lubricant and maintenance schedules and procedures for truck fleet operators, heavy construction equipment, road-building concerns, and manufacturing companies.

High-performance-engine technicians who work at dealerships analyze, test, and maintain new high-performance engines that are available to the public. Those who work in car-racing design test, analyze, and maintain high-performance engines in the various auto racing fields. They also redesign and make special parts for better design and performance.

Requirements

The best way to prepare for an automotive technician career is to complete a formal post-secondary program. Most such programs take two years, although there are several four-year programs. Training is offered by many community colleges and technical schools and by some automotive manufacturers. The programs should include training in mathematics through algebra and geometry, and language training that allows technicians to read technical manuals and write reports with correct spelling, grammar, and punctuation.

It is possible to start as an unskilled worker with a high school or equivalent education, but it is very difficult to get the necessary science background without a formal program. Certain branches of the U.S. Army, Navy, and Marines offer this type of training. In addition, a few apprenticeship programs are available, but most will not provide thorough preparation by themselves.

High school students entering a technician training program should have completed at least two years of mathematics, preferably one year of algebra and one year of plane geometry. Completion of third year mathematics is advisable. The student should have taken at least one year of a laboratory science, preferably physics or chemistry. Basic drafting, automotive, electrical, and metals courses are also very helpful. It is also necessary that the student develop the ability to work as a productive member of a team. Those students interested in working as automotive, diesel, and gas turbine technicians should prepare themselves for rigorous college-level programs.

First year courses in a post-secondary program often include mathematics, English composition, engineering drawing, hydraulic and power brakes, basics of internal combustion engines, physics, instruments, measurement, basic electricity and electronics, alignment, balance and control, and gears and transmissions.

Second year courses may include physics, sociology, circuit analysis and instrumentation, generators, alternators and regulators, internal combustion engines, economics, political science, engine technology, fuel systems, and digital or other computer controls. Some schools offer cooperative programs where students work for pay at an employer's place of business. These are excellent programs that provide valuable realistic experience.

People who eventually plan on going into business for themselves should also take courses in business management and accounting.

Certification is required for some kinds of work, especially that involving public vehicles. In addition, dealerships often give preference to personnel who have certificates of special training from industry educational centers. Although employers do not require employees to hold college degrees, these are recognized as valuable records of educational preparation, which may give the job applicant an advantage over other less qualified applicants.

Opportunities for experience and exploration

High school libraries and guidance offices, technical institutes, community colleges, and vocational schools can be good sources of information about this career. It is helpful to visit schools that offer technician training and to talk with students enrolled in the program. Visiting workplaces where these technicians are employed also helps students form an opinion about how suitable their own talents are for the work involved in this career.

Methods of entering

Many graduates of technical programs secure jobs during the last semester of school. Recruiters from automotive and diesel factories and automotive equipment dealers usually visit schools where these programs are offered. Although the more varied types of industries do not regularly recruit, students can still learn about job openings from their department heads, teachers, or placement officers. Graduating students may also apply directly to the personnel office of any auto, truck, or tractor dealership or to the many related industries.

Advancement

As automobile technicians gain experience, they become more valuable to their employers. Some advance from associate or junior laboratory technicians to senior engineering technicians. Others are promoted from district representatives to supervisory positions at the regional or manufacturing level. Some examples of advanced technical positions are described in the following paragraphs.

Service managers in a dealership plan the automotive service department, select equipment, organize and manage the shop, select and train personnel, assist in diagnosing customer problems, and develop an effective service department.

Design engineering technicians design specific engine parts for automotive and diesel trucks. Working under the direction of a design engineer, they calculate sizes, determine locations, select materials, and determine tolerances.

District sales engineering technicians promote new sales, conduct analyses of fuel and lubricant information for use in the field, and develop customer relations. They organize and teach short-term lubrication and maintenance schools for manufacturing and heavy equipment service and maintenance personnel.

Senior product development technicians supervise diesel engine testing that is being conducted in engine dynamometer test cells. They gather and check the accuracy of all data collected, make sure proper procedures are used in running the tests, and write reports on their findings.

Present trends indicate that the *high-performance-engine technician* may become the most important staff member of the automotive service department. This specialist may advance into one of the many auto racing fields. The high-performance-engine technician is responsible for the reliable operation of the most sophisticated power plants in the automotive business. Critical analysis, dynamometer and balance testing, design, and retrofitting are the main responsibilities of this specialist. Generally, this technician guides the major operations of the racing team.

Employment outlook

Modern industry, agriculture, and the military have all come to depend on flexible, efficient, and mobile-powered equipment. This equipment is used to help build highways, extract minerals from the earth, irrigate farms, propel tanks and weapons, and so forth. This continuing demand has created a need for technicians who can maintain, operate, and repair such equipment.

The worldwide competition for the automobile, truck, and light industrial automotive product markets is creating many opportunities for highly qualified technicians in the design of better, more fuel-efficient automotive machinery and for more cost-efficient production of the machines themselves.

Despite these favorable factors, students interested in a career in automotive, diesel, and gas turbine technology should keep in mind that most jobs in this field are in manufacturing, and the outlook for many manufacturing industries in this country is somewhat uncertain. The employment figures in the automobile industry, for instance, have fallen from the levels reached during the 1970s and are not expected to return. On the other hand, one of the factors driving down employment in manufacturing is the movement toward more automation and greater productivity per employee. Technicians involved with this aspect of the industry should find a continuing demand for their skills.

Earnings

Graduates of automotive, diesel, and gas turbine programs in technical schools enter employment at salaries ranging around $16,000 to $21,000 per year; the average beginner's salary is often about $18,000. With three to five years of work and study on the job, the technician's earnings may increase to a range of $26,200 to over $31,240 per year. Further advancements often allow technicians with seven to ten years' experience to earn from $30,000 to more than $40,000 per year. This is especially true of technicians entering sales engineering positions who have increased their knowledge through additional specialized courses or have passed special certifying examinations.

Technicians who are graduates of a two-year high-performance-engine curriculum, which is available in some new vocational and technical programs, have an earning potential of $26,000 to $31,000 per year to start. Top-rated technicians in the speedway racing circuit earn approximately $40,000 per year. Chief technicians on winning teams may earn $60,000 per year.

Benefits often include paid vacations and health and life insurance. Some employers will pay for additional education.

Conditions of work

The workplaces in the automotive field are so varied that technicians usually can find working conditions to suit their preferences. Design, test, and research and development technicians often work in engineering design departments or in laboratories. These working conditions are usually clean, comfortable, and well lighted, with regular working hours. Sometimes testing may require senior technicians who are supervising or managing the tests to put in longer hours, for which they may be paid extra or given time off.

The research and development laboratories of transportation and power industries normally maintain very high standards for cleanliness and safety. Equipment is usually well guarded to prevent accidents, and safety engineering staff are continually working to improve safety practices.

Service-oriented technicians usually work indoors in garage facilities and they usually work alone. They should be able to talk comfortably with strangers, however, because they may need to gather information from customers about their cars and explain test results and required repairs to them. Field work in servicing or testing various kinds of equipment may be outdoors in all kinds of weather, for which special clothes may be needed. Field repair may involve physical labor when technicians must rig their own lifts. Resourcefulness and careful judgment must be exercised to make the work safe.

Successful technicians must be disciplined, systematic, and analytical, and have careful work habits. They must understand every detail of every part, how all the parts work together, and what happens if parts are not assembled or working correctly.

Technicians must be able to perform as team members. As they sometimes work alone, they also must be capable of working without supervision. Often their work includes supervising others, so they must be able to understand and work with people. Above all, technicians must understand the science and mathematics that support their work. Although principles remain the same, materials and designs change. Technicians cannot keep up with changes in their field if they do not understand the underlying science and mathematics.

GOE: 05.05.09; SIC: 7538; SOC: 6881

◇ SOURCES OF ADDITIONAL INFORMATION

Automotive Service Association
PO Box 929
Bedford, TX 76095

**Motor Vehicle Manufacturers Association
of the United States**
7430 Second Avenue
Suite 300
Detroit, MI 48202

◇ RELATED ARTICLES

Volume 1: Automotives
Volumes 2–4: Agricultural equipment technicians; Air-conditioning, refrigeration, and heating mechanics; Automobile mechanics; Automobile-repair-service estimators; Diesel mechanics; Farm-equipment mechanics

Automobile-repair-service estimators

Definition

Automobile-repair-service estimators act as the link between car owners seeking repair or maintenance on their vehicles and the mechanics who perform the work. They are employed in automobile dealerships and larger repair shops. They inspect and test vehicles brought in for repairs to determine what work needs to be done. They estimate the costs of the work and prepare a detailed work order. They may perform minor adjustments and repairs on cars, and they may act as supervisors of the mechanics who carry out repair work.

History

Since the beginning of the 20th century, gasoline-powered passenger vehicles have evolved from a rare curiosity into an integral part of American life. In the year 1900, there were fewer than 8,000 cars on the road. By 1990, there were over 190 million motor vehicles, including cars, trucks, and buses, registered in the United States. The diverse cars now on American roads come from many countries around the world, as well as the United States. Technologically complex, aerodynamically designed, and full of accessories, they are radically different from the vehicles that a few generations ago competed with horse-drawn carriages.

Since they were first built, one aspect of automobiles has remained the same: from time to time they need repair and maintenance. As cars have become more numerous, the need for car repair facilities and qualified personnel has grown. In the larger repair shops today (generally those with more than 20 employees), it is efficient to have one or more people whose duties are to assess the work to be done and figure out for customers what the cost of the work will be.

Nature of the work

Being a repair-service estimator involves more than just filling out an itemized list of the costs of parts and labor and then arranging for mechanics to do the work. The job requires solving problems, considerable technological know-how, and public relations and sales skills. Above all, a successful estimator must be a good communicator.

There are two general types of repair estimating. The first involves a fairly simple process. Manufacturers establish guidelines for when routine maintenance tasks should be done on cars. When cars are brought in for this kind of scheduled maintenance, the repair-service estimator simply fills out a repair order containing basic necessary information—the owner's name and address, the make and year of car, mileage, and description of the work to be done.

AUTOMOBILE-REPAIR-SERVICE ESTIMATORS

A service estimator must consult several manuals before quoting a price for repairs.

It is when a car is brought in for repairs beyond normal maintenance that the estimator's job is more complicated. If the owner gives a vague description of a malfunction, the estimator must correctly question the customer to discover as much as possible about the problem. It may be necessary to visually inspect the vehicle and perhaps road test it to make a tentative diagnosis of the problem.

The estimator also figures out the costs and estimates how long it will take to do the work, explaining to the customer just what is wrong and why the repairs are needed, even if they seem expensive. Often service estimators must impress upon wary customers that the work will improve the vehicle's performance, make it safer, and prevent more serious—and more expensive—problems. In these situations the estimator is using sales, public relations, and education skills.

In large dealerships, a shop dispatcher may route the work to the various mechanics; in smaller shops, it is often the responsibility of the repair-service estimator. In either case, the estimator continues to act as the link between the customer and the mechanic, answering customer questions and relaying any information from the mechanic to the car owner about the car's condition. After the repairs are completed, the estimator often road tests the car to make sure it is running properly. When the customer comes to pick up the vehicle, the estimator answers all questions about the work that has been done and settles any complaints about the quality of workmanship and the repair costs. If any errors have been made on the bill or if any grievance regarding workmanship is found to be justifiable, the estimator may adjust the charges accordingly, after obtaining the approval of the service manager.

Requirements

Automobile-repair-service estimators should be interested in automobile technology, and they should like to work with people. They should understand how cars operate, and they should be able to provide clear, accurate, but uncomplicated explanations to people who are not very familiar with the technical aspects of how motor vehicles function.

Most repair-service estimators receive on-the-job training from experienced estimators and service managers in the shop where they are employed. Sometimes they also assist the shop dispatcher, helping to route work to mechanics. The length of the training period varies, depending on the trainee's background, and may be one to two years. Some repair-service estimators enroll in automobile manufacturer-sponsored training programs.

To be accepted into such a training program, an applicant should be a high school graduate, at least 21 years old, and should have some junior college or trade or vocational school training in automotive technology and motor vehicle repair. Other beneficial subjects for prospective estimators to have studied include speech, English, applied mathematics, and sales techniques. Sometimes mechanic trainees, parts-counter trainees, or experienced mechanics are trained for estimator positions.

The fact that the repair-service estimator may be the customer's only contact with the shop means that employers want to hire estimators who have a pleasing, courteous, even-tempered personality and a neat appearance. Estimators need to listen well and communicate effectively so that they build confidence in customers. After all, they are trying to encourage customers to bring their business back to the same shop the next time they need repair services.

Opportunities for experience and exploration

The best way to find out about what repair-service estimators do is to get job in a repair shop or automobile dealership. Even a part-time job might provide an opportunity to observe how experienced workers evaluate service and repair problems that customers bring in to the shop. If this is not possible, it may be helpful simply to talk to estimators, a shop service manager, or mechanics about the work they do.

Methods of entering

Repair-service estimators are frequently employees of a repair shop who are promoted into estimator positions. Other estimators secure their jobs by applying directly to repair facilities or by answering job advertisements in local newspapers. State employment service offices also can be a good source of information on job openings.

Advancement

Repair-service estimators who demonstrate leadership abilities may be promoted to supervisory or service manager positions. With the right combination of skills, they may be able to start their own business, such as a service station or auto repair shop. With additional training, another possibility for some estimators is to go to work for a car insurance company as a damage appraiser, estimating the costs of repairs for insurance claim settlements.

Employment outlook

This is a small occupational field with good potential for the future. In the 1990s, there are about 18,000 people working as repair-service estimators, primarily in metropolitan areas. During the next decade the growth rate for this occupation will probably be about the same as the national average for all occupations. In addition to the newly created jobs, openings will develop when people currently employed as estimators retire, die, or leave to take other jobs. Most jobs will probably continue to be in metropolitan areas where the demand for auto repairs is highest and there are more large repair shops.

Because of the nature of the automobile repair business, repair-service estimators can expect that their employment will not be significantly affected by ups and downs in the economy. Even in tight times, most auto repairs cannot be put off. The risk of a breakdown or of incurring greater repair expenses makes most motorists pay attention to maintenance schedules. In addition, the tendency during bad economic times is to fix up old cars rather than to purchase new ones.

Earnings

In the 1990s, automobile-repair-service estimators earn, on the average, about 25 percent more than other non-supervisory workers in industry, excluding those in farming. Statistics gathered from 24 large cities indicate that average annual earnings are roughly $24,000.

Some service estimators are paid on a combined salary and commission basis, receiving a basic minimum amount plus a percentage of the total cost of repairs and parts purchased by their customers. Other estimators work on a straight commission basis.

Conditions of work

For the most part, estimators work indoors in clean, well-lighted, well-heated shops and offices. While the work that they do is seldom physically strenuous, it is sometimes stressful. Estimators usually work 40 to 48 hours a week, and they spend much of that time on their feet. Repair shops are extremely busy at times, especially in the morning when customers bring their cars in for repairs and in the evenings when they come to pick them up. Interacting with the public sometimes requires dealing with irate, dissatisfied customers.

Some estimators belong to unions, including the International Brotherhood of Teamsters, Chauffeurs, Warehousemen and Helpers of America; the Sheet Metal Workers International Association; and the International Association of Machinists and Aerospace Workers.

GOE: 05.07.02; SIC: 7538; SOC: 6881

◇ **SOURCES OF ADDITIONAL INFORMATION**

Automotive Service Industry Association
444 North Michigan Avenue
Chicago, IL 60611-3975

National Institute for Automotive Service Excellence
13505 Dulles Technology Drive
Herndon, VA 22071-3415

National Automobile Dealers Association
8400 Westpark Drive
McLean, VA 22102

Canadian Automobile Association
1775 Courtwood Crescent
Ottawa ON K2C 3J2

Avionics technicians

Definition

Avionics (a term formed by combining the words "aviation" and "electronics") is the application of electronics to the operation of aircraft, spacecraft, and missiles. *Avionics technicians* work with the electronic devices that are components of aircraft communication, navigation, and flight-control systems. They inspect, test, adjust, and repair these systems, and also complete maintenance-and-overhaul documentation for the equipment they work on. They calibrate and adjust the frequencies of communications apparatus when it is installed, and perform periodic checks on those frequency settings.

History

The field of avionics grew out of World War II, when military aircraft were operated for the first time using electronic equipment. As aircraft rapidly grew more complicated, the amount of electronic apparatus needed for navigation and monitoring equipment performance greatly increased. The World War II B-29 bomber carried several thousand avionic components; the B-52 of the Vietnam era carried 50,000; and the B-58 supersonic bomber required more than 95,000.

The development of large ballistic missiles during and after World War II and the rapid growth of the U.S. space program after 1958 increased development of avionics technology. Large missiles and spacecraft require many more electronic components than even the largest and most sophisticated aircraft. Computerized guidance systems became especially important with the advent of manned space flights.

Avionics continues to be an important branch of aeronautical and astronautical engineering. The aerospace industry places great emphasis on research and development, assigning a much higher percentage of its trained technical personnel to this effort than is usual in industry. In addition, stringent safety regulations require constant surveillance of in-service equipment. For these reasons there is high demand for trained and experienced avionics technicians and engineers to help in the development of new satellites, spacecraft, aircraft, and their component electronic systems, and to maintain those in service.

Nature of the work

Avionics technicians assist avionics engineers in developing new electronic systems and components for aerospace use. They also adapt existing systems and components for application in new equipment. For the most part, however, they install, test, repair, and maintain navigation, communication, and control apparatus in existing aircraft and spacecraft.

Technicians use apparatus such as circuit analyzers and oscilloscopes to test and replace such sophisticated equipment as transceivers and Doppler radar systems, as well as microphones, headsets, and other standard electronic communication apparatus.

New equipment, once installed, must be tested and calibrated to prescribed specifications. Technicians also adjust the frequencies of radio sets and other communication equipment by signaling ground stations and then adjusting setscrews until the desired frequency has been achieved. Periodic maintenance checks and readjustments enable avionics technicians to keep equipment operating on proper frequencies. The technicians also complete and sign maintenance-and-overhaul documents recording the history of various equipment.

Avionics technicians involved in the design and testing of new apparatus must take into account all operating conditions, determining its weight limitations, resistance to physical shock, atmospheric conditions it will have to withstand, and other factors. For some sophisticated projects, technicians will have to design and make their tools first, and then use them to construct and test new avionic components.

The range of equipment in the avionics field is so broad that technicians usually specialize in one area, such as radio equipment, radar, computerized guidance, or flight-control systems. New specialty areas are constantly opening up as innovations occur in avionics. The development of these new specialty areas requires technicians to keep informed by reading technical articles and books, and attending seminars and courses about the new developments, which are often sponsored and offered by manufacturers.

Avionics technicians usually work as part of a team, especially if involved in research, testing, and development of new products. They are often required to keep notes and records of their work and to write detailed reports.

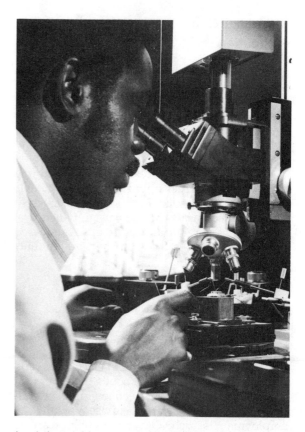

An avionics technician uses a microcircuit television microscope that enables him to make minute adjustments on miniaturized electronic circuits.

Requirements

Avionics technicians must have completed a course of training at a post-high school technical institute or community college that includes at least one year of electronics technician training. If not trained specifically in avionics, they should obtain a solid background in electronics theory and practice. Further specialized training will be done on the job, where technicians work with engineers and senior technicians until they are competent to work without direct supervision.

Larger corporations in the aerospace industry operate their own schools and training institutes. Such training rarely includes theoretical or general studies but concentrates on areas important to the company's functions. The U.S. Armed Forces also conduct excellent electronics and avionics training schools; their graduates are in high demand in industry after they leave the service.

Persons interested in pursuing a career in avionics should take high school mathematics courses at least through solid geometry and preferably through calculus. They should develop language skills in order to read complex and detailed technical articles, books, and reports; to write technical reports; and to present those reports to groups of people when required.

Students who are thinking about this kind of work should also have an aptitude for science and mathematics. In addition, they will need to have good manual dexterity and mechanical aptitude and the temperament for exacting work.

Federal Communications Commission (FCC) regulations require that anyone who works with radio transmitting equipment have a restricted radiotelephone operator's license. Such a license is issued upon application to the FCC and is issued for life.

AVIONICS TECHNICIANS

Opportunities for experience and exploration

It is possible to visit factories and test facilities where avionics technicians work as part of teams designing and testing new equipment. It is also possible to visit a large airfield's repair facilities where avionics technicians inspect, maintain, and calibrate communications and control apparatus.

Useful information about avionics training programs and career opportunities is available from the U.S. Armed Forces as well as from trade and technical schools that offer such programs. These organizations are always pleased to answer inquiries from prospective students or service personnel.

Methods of entering

Those entering the field of avionics must first obtain the necessary training in electronics. Following that training, the school's placement officer can help locate prospective employers, arrange interviews, and advise about an employment search. Other possibilities are to contact an employment agency (many specialize in technical placement) or to approach a prospective employer directly.

Advancement

Avionics technicians usually begin their careers in trainee positions, until they are thoroughly familiar with the requirements and routines of their work. Having completed their apprenticeships, they are usually assigned to work independently, with only minimal supervision, doing testing and repair work. The most experienced and able technicians go on to install new equipment and to work in research and development operations. Many senior technicians move into training, supervisory, sales, and customer relations positions.

Employment outlook

The aerospace industry as a whole is closely tied to government spending and to political change, as well as to downturns in the economy. The economy also affects the aircraft and airline industries strongly. The cancellation of one spacecraft program or a fall in airline travel that leads to employee cutbacks may throw a large number of avionics technicians out of work, making competition for the remaining jobs very keen.

On the positive side, avionics is an important and developing field for which there will be need through the foreseeable future, and for which more and more trained technicians will be required.

Earnings

Beginning avionics technicians earn about $18,000 to $20,000 a year. The median salary is about $24,400. Experienced senior avionics technicians earn salaries around $30,400 a year, and sometimes go as high as $48,000 a year. Federal government employees (not including Armed Forces personnel) on the average earn slightly less than avionics technicians employed by private aerospace firms. Their jobs, on the other hand, have greater security.

Conditions of work

Avionics technicians work under pleasant indoor conditions. Because this work is very precise, the successful avionics technician has a personality suited to meeting exact standards and working within small tolerances. Technicians sometimes work in closely cooperating teams, and so, need the ability to work with a team spirit of coordinated effort.

GOE: 05.05.10; SIC: 4581; SOC: 6151

◇ **SOURCES OF ADDITIONAL INFORMATION**

General Aviation Manufacturers Association
1400 K Street, NW, Suite 801
Washington, DC 20005

Aerospace Industries Association of Canada
#1200, 60 Queen Street
Ottawa ON K1P 5Y7

◇ **RELATED ARTICLES**

Volume 1: Aviation and Aerospace; Engineering

Volumes 2–4: Aeronautical and aerospace technicians; Aerospace engineers; Aircraft mechanics and engine specialists; Astronauts; Flight engineers; Pilots

Bakery products workers

Definition

Bakery products workers produce bread, cakes, biscuits, pies, pastries, crackers, and other baked goods in commercial and manufacturing bakeries.

History

Baking, the process of cooking food using dry heat, is perhaps the oldest method of cooking. The ancient Egyptians are credited with building the first known ovens, which were cylindrical and made of clay from the banks of the Nile. Later cultures introduced various technological improvements. By the middle of the second century B.C., there were professional bakers in Rome, and ordinary people could buy bread instead of having to make it themselves. The first mechanical dough mixer—powered by a horse or donkey walking in circles—was built by Romans. In European cities in the Middle Ages, bakers formed associations called guilds, which carefully regulated how bread was made and how bakers were trained. Outside of cities, however, most baking was done at home or in a single village oven.

Most early American settlers also lived in small communities and relied on their own wood-burning fireplaces to bake their own bread at home. Buying bread, cake, or pie from someone else was practically unheard of. But the beginnings of an industrial society changed the American idea of self-sufficiency. Urban workers and apartment dwellers did not always have the time or facilities to make their own baked goods. In addition, technology made possible huge ovens, mixers, and ways of controlling heat and measurements that enabled manufacturers to make mass quantities of good baked food at reasonable prices.

Today, most Americans buy bread at the grocery store and seldom bake their own. Manufactured cookies and crackers are found on the shelves of nearly every American kitchen. The freshness, taste, and consistency of these products are the responsibility of bakery products workers.

Nature of the work

Most bakery workers participate in only some of the stages involved in creating a baked item. All-round bakers, who develop recipes and mix, shape, bake, and finish baked goods, usually work in small businesses, hotels, or restaurants. They may, however, supervise workers in a manufacturing bakery, along with the *bakery supervisor*. Other workers are usually designated by the type of machine they operate or the stage of baking they are involved with.

In preparing the dough or batter for goods baked in a large bakery, different workers make the different components. *Blenders* tend machines that blend flour. Skilled technicians known as *broth mixers* control flour sifters and various vats to measure and mix liquid solutions for fermenting, oxidizing, and shortening. These solutions consist of such ingredients as yeast, sugar, shortening, and enriching ingredients mixed with water or milk. The broth mixer must carefully control the temperature of the broth—if it is just a few degrees too hot or cool, the dough or batter will not rise properly. The broth mixer runs these solutions through a heat regulator and into dough-mixing machines.

Dough mixers operate equipment to mix ingredients for bread using a set formula. They measure ingredients and put them into a huge mixing machine. In old two-story bakeries, ingredients were measured on the second floor and then dumped into the mixer on the first

159

A bakery products worker packages coconut cakes topped with pineapple slices for retailers throughout the community.

floor. Newer bakeries are all on one floor. After the flour, water, and yeast or broth are in the mixer, the worker starts the machine, setting instruments to control time, speed, and temperature. Dough mixers then push the dough into heat- and humidity-controlled ferment rooms, where the dough begins to rise into what is known as sponge. After the sponge has risen, mixers bring the batch of dough back to the mixer and mix it again. Batches can weigh as much as a ton.

Dough-mixer operators use their judgment and experience in mixing dough using semiautomatic equipment. During mixing they check the temperature of the broth, the viscosity of dough, and the speed of mixing. They feel the dough to make sure it is the right consistency and may regulate a machine that divides the dough into loaves, recording the temperature, feed rate, and viscosity of the dough.

Other workers who are involved with dividing dough into loaves are *dividing-machine operators*, who control machines that automatically divide and shape dough into units of specified size, weight, and shape before baking. *Dough-brake-machine operators* tend machines that knead bread dough before it is divided.

After it is in loaf pans, dough is usually allowed to rise again, a stage called proofing. It is then sent to the ovens.

Batter mixers tend machines that mix ingredients for batters for cakes and other products. These workers must select and install mixing utensils in huge mixers, depending on the kind of batter to be mixed. They regulate the speed and time of mixing and check the consistency of the batter.

Other kinds of mixers and shapers include *unleavened-dough mixers,* who use a five-position mixer to make matzo, *sweet-goods-machine operators*, who roll and cut sweet dough to make rolls and other sweets products, and *pretzel twisters*, who form pretzel shapes out of dough by hand or machine. *Cracker-and-cookie-machine operators* roll dough into sheets and form crackers or cookies before baking. They check the machine's work and remove any malformed items before baking. *Wafer-machine operators* perform similar tasks with wafer batter. *Batter scalers* operate machines that deposit measured amounts of batter on conveyors. *Doughnut makers* and *doughnut-machine operators* mix batter for, shape, and fry doughnuts. Some workers operate machines that grease baking pans or that place pie crusts and fillings into pie plates for baking.

Bench hands perform a variety of tasks by hand. They form dough into loaves or buns by rolling it to a specified thickness with a rolling pin or machine, sprinkling flour as necessary to keep the dough from sticking. They knead the dough and cut it into loaves, weigh them, and place them in baking pans. They may use dividing machines to form buns.

When the products are ready for baking, they are sent to the ovens. *Oven tenders* tend stationary or rotary hearth ovens. They place pans of dough or batter on long wooden paddles, slide them into the oven, and regulate the heat and humidity in the oven during baking. They note the color of the goods as they bake, remove them, and place them on racks or conveyors to cool. An automatic depanner lifts loaves out of pans.

Many other workers perform jobs that finish goods after they are baked. *Slicing-machine operators* slice bread, cakes, and other items and place them on conveyors to be packaged. *Chocolate temperers* ready chocolate for *enrobing-machine operators* to use in coating or spraying of baked products such as cookies, snack cakes, and crackers. *Cake decorators, decorators,* and *icers* put glazes, icings, and decorations on baked goods by hand, while *machine icers* use machines to coat baked products with premixed icing. *Depositing-machine operators* put filling on cookies or crackers, and *filling-machine tenders* insert cream filling into snack cakes.

Bakery helpers and *bakery workers* have more general duties. Helpers grease pans, move supplies, measure dump materials, and clean equipment. Bakery workers sit at benches or conveyor belts, where they may fill, enrobe, slice, package, seal, stack, or count baked goods.

When baked goods are ready for delivery and sale, *checkers* prorate and distribute baked goods to *route-sales drivers*, who deliver products to stores or other customers and try to drum up new or increased business along their routes. Bakeries also employ *bakery maintenance engineers*, also called *bakery-machine mechanics* or *plant mechanics*, to keep the many mixers, ovens, and other machines in good order.

Requirements

Most bakers begin as bakery helpers, who usually need to be high school graduates. Other bakery workers are hired after they have acquired useful skills through education in technical schools or in the U.S. Armed Forces. However, they usually need to finish learning on the job.

The skills that bakery helpers need to become bakers in wholesale baking plants can be learned in several ways. In some companies, bakery helpers can learn through formal apprenticeships. Apprenticeships consist of a blend of classroom and on-the-job instruction and take several years to complete.

After they have some experience, bakery workers who have proven they are good employees but want to upgrade their skills may attend training courses offered by the American Institute of Baking, perhaps with the employer or a scholarship paying their expenses. Other workers take correspondence courses and seminars offered by the American Baking Institute at various locations. Bakers who successfully complete this training receive specialty certification in bread, cake, or cracker production.

Some chef training schools have bakery programs for students interested in learning diverse baking skills from basic bread to gourmet pastries.

Some companies provide apprenticeships for employees who are training to be bakery maintenance engineers. Other workers seeking to qualify as bakery maintenance engineers take classes, correspondence courses, and seminars offered by the American Baking Institute in this field.

Special requirements

Many bakery workers must pass physical examinations and receive certificates stating they are free from contagious diseases. They must remain in good health.

In many bakeries the workers belong to unions. A major union is the Bakery, Confectionery, and Tobacco Workers International. Route drivers often belong to the International Brotherhood of Teamsters, Chauffeurs, Warehousemen, and Helpers of America.

Opportunities for experience and exploration

Attending a baking school is a very good way to get hands-on experience of the various work activities in bakeries. High school students may be able to obtain part-time or summer employment as bakery helpers. They may also be able to arrange to tour a local bakery and talk with a worker or two to find out more about the field.

Methods of entering

Aspiring bakers should apply directly to bakeries for jobs as helpers or apprentices, from which they may move into machine-operator positions. Placement offices at baking schools can usually help students find jobs or apprenticeships. State employment offices and newspapers may also provide leads.

Advancement

Helpers who learn machine-operator skills may move into these skilled positions, but usually only after years of experience. Because bakeries use many different kinds of machines and processes, versatile workers are the most likely to be promoted. Apprentices are taught as many skills as possible.

Skilled machine operators can move into supervisory slots or become all-round bakers. These bakers may also move into work in hotels, restaurants, or retail bakeries. They may even open their own bakeries and bake their goods by hand.

Some experienced bakery workers can be promoted into management positions. The trend, however, is to fill management slots in bakeries with people who have college degrees in management or other business fields. Route-sales drivers may work into sales manager positions or become route supervisors.

Employment outlook

Approximately 48,000 people are employed in production bakeries. The U.S. Department of Labor predicts that bakery employment will change little in the next few years, although other experts predict a slow decline in employment because of increased automation in baking plants. Many current positions will become available every year as workers retire or change jobs. Jobs for route drivers and maintenance workers should continue to be in good supply.

Earnings

In the 1990s, bakery workers are earning an average of about $20,000 a year. They are often paid time and a half for overtime and premium pay for Sunday work. Route drivers often work on commission, receiving base pay plus a percentage of their sales. Workers in apprentice positions are normally paid less than the full wages of experienced employees. As they approach the end of their training, their wages are increased toward the level of fully qualified workers.

In addition to regular pay, employees often receive benefits like paid vacations and holidays, health insurance, and pension plans. Union-shop bakeries offer union-company pension plans, paid for by the bakers.

Conditions of work

Bakery workers usually work 40 hours a week, and some work night and evening shifts. Because baked goods can be frozen until they are needed, the number of plants operating around the clock is less than it used to be.

Bakery plants vary in terms of comfort. Some are air-conditioned. All are clean, since bakeries must meet state and federal standards. Workers are protected by local, state, and federal safety laws.

Bakery employees wear uniforms and caps or hairnets for sanitary reasons. Machines can be noisy, and working near ovens can be hot. Some jobs are strenuous, requiring heavy lifting.

GOE: 06.02.15; SIC: 205; SOC: 8619; 8725

◇ **SOURCES FOR ADDITIONAL INFORMATION**

American Bakers Association
1111 14th Street, NW, Suite 300
Washington, DC 20005

American Institute of Baking
1213 Bakers Way
Manhattan, KS 66502

For information on employers and employment opportunities, contact:

American Society of Bakery Engineers
2 North Riverside Plaza, Room 1733
Chicago, IL 60606

Bakery, Confectionery, and Tobacco Workers International Union
10401 Connecticut Avenue
Kensington, MD 20895

◇ **RELATED ARTICLES**

Volume 1: Baking; Food Service
Volumes 2–4: Canning and preserving industry workers; Confectionery industry workers; Cooks, chefs, and bakers; Dietetic technicians; Food technologists; Macaroni and related products industry workers; Route drivers

Barbers

Definition

A *barber* performs the personal services of cutting, trimming, shampooing, coloring, and bleaching hair and of trimming and shaping beards and mustaches. The barber may fit and groom artificial hair pieces, such as wigs.

History

The history of barbering may be traced far beyond the turn of the century when Barber Shop Quartets became so popular. One of the most ancient trades, barbering is described by writers of ancient Greece. Relics of rudimentary razors have been found dating to the Bronze Age, and drawings of people in early Chinese and Egyptian cultures show men with shaven heads, indicating the existence of a barbering profession.

Barbers often did more than just haircuts. Treatment of illnesses by bloodletting, originally done by monks, was appointed as a task for barbers in 1163 by the papacy, after the work was deemed inappropriate for the clergy. While trained physicians were already an established group at this time, they supported and encouraged the use of barbers for routine medical tasks such as the treatment of wounds and abscesses. From the 12th century to the 18th century, barbers were known as barber-surgeons. They performed medical and surgical services such as extracting teeth, treating disease, and cauterizing wounds.

Barbers began to organize and form guilds in the 14th century. In France, a barber's guild was formed in 1361. In 1383, the barber of the king of France was decreed to be the head of that guild. The Barbers of London was established as a trade guild in 1462.

Barbers distinguished themselves from surgeons and physicians by their title—they were referred to as "doctors of the short robe" and the university-trained doctors were "doctors of the long robe." In England during the first part of the 16th century, laws were established that began to limit the medical activities of barbers. They were allowed to let blood and to perform tooth extractions only, while surgeons were banned from performing activities relegated to barbers, such as shaving.

Surgeons separated from the barbers' guild in England in 1745, and in 1800 established their own guild, the Royal College of Surgeons. Laws were passed that restricted the activities of the barbers to nonmedical practices. Barbers continued to be trained through apprenticeships until the establishment of barber training schools at the beginning of the 20th century.

The barber remains a respected tradesperson. Today, the red-and-white-striped barber pole still stands, not only as a symbol of the barber shop but of the barber-surgeon, the white depicting bandages that were used and the red symbolizing the patient's blood.

Women did not patronize barbershops until the 1920s. The bob cut, in which women had their hair cut above the shoulders or neck, was the first modern women's hairstyle that used a razor for cutting. Women regularly used barbers for hair styling and cutting after the bob became widespread and accepted in mainstream society. This opened the door for women to join the profession, trained to work with women's hair styles.

Nature of the work

In general, the duties of the barber are well defined. Barbers cut, trim, shape, style, tint or bleach, and shampoo hair. They give shaves, facials, scalp treatments, and massages. They advise customers on grooming habits and cosmetic aids. They also trim and style beards and mustaches, fit and style wigs, and perform other personal services for customers incidental to good grooming.

Barbers use, with trained skill, certain tools in their services, such as scissors, clippers, razors, combs, brushes, vibrators, hot towels, tweezers, and razor sharpeners. The barber's tools and working surroundings must be kept in aseptic and sterile condition.

In their training, barbers learn some aspects of human physiology and anatomy, including the bone structure of the head and elementary facts about the nervous system. Barbers either cut hair as the customers request, or they decide how to cut it by studying the head contour, the quality and texture of the hair, and the personal features of the customer. Each customer is an individual and no two possess the same types of personal and physical characteristics.

Barbers may be employed in shops that have as few as one or two operators, or as

163

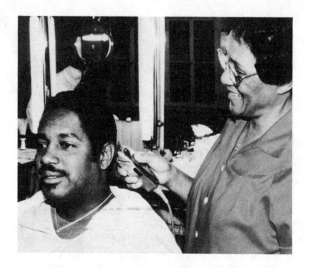

Good communication and people skills are part of the barber's job.

In most states barbers must first be licensed as barber apprentices. After a specified period of employment (usually one to two years), the apprentice may take another written and practical examination to qualify for a license as a journeyman barber. When barbers move from one state into another, they must satisfy the license requirements of the state into which they are moving. Some states will recognize the license from another state, in which case the barber does not need to be retested.

Training opportunities are available in about 400 private barber colleges and public vocational training schools. Training periods are generally nine months to one year. Most training institutions require approximately 1,000 to 1,800 hours of formal instruction, including courses in hygiene, anatomy, skin and scalp diseases, and sanitation. Other course work includes lectures, demonstrations, and practice in the art of barbering, and the use and care of tools and equipment. Some schools instruct their students in business management and practices, the psychology of sales and advertising, professional ethics, and unionism. Some states have schools that offer advanced course work for barbers who wish to specialize in such techniques as hair coloring or styling. Students should be careful to select barber schools that have training programs that meet at least the minimum requirements of their state. Some schools require students to purchase their basic barbering instruments at a cost of about $430.

A barber needs certain aptitudes to be successful. Finger dexterity is important because it is needed in all aspects of a barber's work. Hand-eye coordination is equally necessary.

Pleasant personal qualities are very important to the successful barber. Customers look for a tactful, pleasant, courteous, friendly barber who likes people and is skilled. A barber needs to present a neat, clean and well-groomed appearance. At all times barbers must be in control of their tempers and try to give the best service possible.

Special requirements

Barbers in most states must pass written and practical examinations to be licensed as apprentice barbers and more advanced examinations to be licensed as journeymen barbers. The cost of licenses, examinations, and annual renewals varies from state to state. Usually, fees for these examinations range from $15 to $85. Health certificates are required in most states. Information on special requirements may be obtained from individual state boards of barber examiners.

many as ten or more employees. Some barbers work in combination barber-and-beauty shops, while others are employed in shops in hotels, hospitals, and resort areas. Those who operate their own shops must also take care of the details of business operations. Bills must be paid, orders placed, invoices and supplies checked, equipment serviced, and records and books kept. The selection, hiring, and termination of other workers are also the owner's responsibilities. Barber shop employees may include manicurists, shoe shine attendants, assistant barbers, and custodial help. Like other responsible businesspeople, barber shop owners are likely to be asked to participate in civic and community projects and activities.

Requirements

The educational and training requirements for barbers vary among the states. Some states require potential barbers to have the minimum of an eighth-grade education; others require a high school education. Nearly all states now require barbers to be licensed or certified by a state board of examiners. To obtain a license or certification in almost any state, the individual must pass a practical examination demonstrating his or her skills and ability and a written test reflecting his or her knowledge of the trade. The great majority of states will not examine anyone younger than 16 or 18 who applies for a license. Applicants must also be able to obtain health certificates, and in almost every state they must be graduates of a barber school that is state-approved.

Opportunities for experience and exploration

Those who are interested in becoming barbers may explore this occupation in a number of different ways. Students may visit barber colleges and talk to members of the administration, teachers, and students and request permission to visit a class in barbering instruction. Potential students may observe and talk with licensed barbers who are practicing the trade. They may wish to seek summer employment in barber shops as clean-up and errand workers so that they can observe firsthand the work of the barber.

Methods of entering

Barbering jobs are most frequently obtained by either applying in person or by enlisting the aid of barbering unions. The largest union for barbers is the United Food and Commercial Workers International Union. Nearly all barber colleges assist their graduates in locating employment opportunities. Applicants also use the placement services of state or private employment agencies. Newspaper advertisements and personal references are good sources for job opportunities. Some salons have their own training programs from which they hire new employees.

Advancement

Barbers usually begin as licensed barber apprentices. Through experience and study, apprentices advance to journeymen barbers. Within small barber shops there is very little opportunity for advancement except by seniority and skill to the assignment of the "first chair," which is most often the chair nearest the shop entrance. Barbers can change their place of employment and move to bigger, more attractive, and better-equipped shops.

Many barbers aspire to be self-employed and own their own shop. There are many things to consider when contemplating going into business. Usually it is essential to obtain experience and financial capital before seeking to own a shop. The cost of equipping a one-chair shop can be very high. Some barbers with greater ambition aspire to owning a large shop or even a chain of barber shops.

Employment outlook

Approximately 94,000 persons were employed as barbers in the United States in the 1990s. About three out of four own their own shops, while one of every three works part time.

Future employment opportunities for barbers are not as predictable as the opportunities that might be available in other occupations. Most openings that present themselves will be to replace those who leave the trade for other work, retire, or die.

Employment may rise slightly in the coming years, as new shopping centers and suburban areas continue to open and grow with the expanding population. Barbers who specialize in hairstyling will increase their business opportunities greatly, since men as well as women patronize full-service salons in greater numbers. The competent and well-trained barber should find employment without too much difficulty, but it may not always be in the geographic locality or in the shop desired.

Earnings

Tips from customers must be considered an important factor in determining a barber's salary. The amount to be earned in tips is unpredictable and depends on the locale of employment, the personality and skill of the barber, individual shop policies, and the income levels of the customers.

In the 1990s, barbers with some experience earn about $16,500 to $21,500 a year. Hairstylists and some barbers who own their own shops have incomes of $24,000 a year or more. Most barbers work on a commission basis, receiving from 50 to 70 percent of what they are paid by customers. Others work for set salaries plus a percentage commission. Only a small number of barbers work for a salary without commission.

Paid vacations, medical insurance, and death benefits are available to some employees, especially those who belong to a union.

Conditions of work

Barbers usually work a five- or six-day week, which averages approximately forty to fifty hours. Weekends and days preceding holiday seasons may be unusually busy workdays. Some employers allow barbers to have extra days off when business is down and slack periods occur.

Barbers work in shops that must, by law, meet and maintain strict state sanitation codes. Shops are usually comfortably heated, ventilated, and well lighted. Barbers are usually assigned a chair position and their own work area in a shop. They are required to be on their feet most of their working hours but little walking is involved. In general, they work in a small space.

Hazards of the trade include nicks and cuts from scissors and razors, minor burns when care is not used in handling hot towels, and occasional skin irritations arising from the constant use of grooming aids that contain chemicals. Some of the chemicals used in hair dyes can be quite abrasive and plastic gloves are usually required for handling and contact. Pregnant women are advised to avoid contact with many of those chemicals present in hair products. The nature of the work requires the barber to repeat the same activities and services over and over. A barber must like the work and be interested in people in order to find the job satisfying.

GOE: 09.02.02; SIC: 7241; SOC: 5252

◇ SOURCES OF ADDITIONAL INFORMATION

Hair International/Associated Master Barbers and Beauticians of America
1318 Starbrook Drive
Charlotte, NC 28210

National Association of Barber Styling Schools
304 South 11th Street
Lincoln, NE 68508

National Barber Career Center
3839 White Plains Road
Bronx, NY 10467

Barber's Association of British Columbia
#411, 207 West Hastings Street
Vancouver BC V6B 1H7

◇ RELATED ARTICLES

Volume 1: Personal and consulting services
Volumes 2–4: Cosmetologists; Electrologists

Bartenders

Definition

Bartenders mix and dispense alcoholic and nonalcoholic drinks in hotels, restaurants, cocktail lounges, and taverns. Besides mixing ingredients to prepare cocktails and other drinks, they serve wine and beer, collect payment from customers, order supplies, and arrange displays of bar stock and glassware. Bartenders or their assistants may also prepare fruit for garnishes, serve simple appetizers, wash glasses, and clean the bar area.

History

Tending bar was only one of the duties of the innkeeper of yesteryear. When inns and small hotels were a family affair, and the drinks dispensed were no more complicated than a tankard of ale or a mug of mulled wine, bartending specialists were not required. Today's large hotels and restaurants call for a variety of experts, not the least of which are the bartenders. Even in the average neighborhood cocktail lounge or tavern, they may have to cope with requests for such exotic concoctions as Screaming Zombies, Harvey Wallbangers, Golden Cadillacs, Singapore Slings, and hundreds of new "shooter" recipes.

Nature of the work

Bartenders take orders from waiters and waitresses for customers seated in the restaurant or lounge; they also take orders from customers seated at the bar. They mix drinks by combining exactly the right proportion of liquor, wines, mixers, and other ingredients. Bartenders must know dozens of drink recipes off the top of their heads. They should also be able to measure accurately by sight so they can prepare drinks quickly without wasting anything, even during the busiest periods. They may be asked to mix drinks to suit a customer's taste, and they also serve beer, wine, and nonalcoholic beverages.

A well stocked bar has dozens of types and brands of liquors and wines, as well as beer, soft drinks, soda and tonic water, fruits and fruit juices, and cream. Bartenders are responsible for maintaining this inventory and ordering supplies before they run out. They arrange bottles and glassware in attractive displays and often wash the glassware. In some of these duties they may be assisted by *bartender helpers,* also known as "bar backs."

Bartenders are responsible for collecting payment on all drinks that are not served by the waiters or waitresses of the establishment. This is done by either keeping a tab as the customer orders drinks and then totaling the bill before the customer leaves, the same way the wait staff does for food bills, or by charging every time a drink is served. In either case, the bartender must be able to calculate the bill quickly and accurately. Although many cash registers add the bill, the bartender must have a mental sum figured out to make sure the bill from the cash register is correct.

Bartenders who own their businesses must also keep records and hire, train, and direct the people who work for them.

Today special machines can automatically mix and dispense drinks. They are generally found in larger operations. But even if they became more widespread, they could not replace bartenders. Bartenders still have the knowledge and expertise needed to fill unusual orders or to dispense drinks manually in case the automatic equipment breaks down or does not function properly.

In combination taverns and packaged-goods stores, *bar attendants* also sell unopened bottles of alcoholic and nonalcoholic beverages to be taken from the premises. *Taproom attendants* prepare and serve glasses or pitchers of draft beer.

One of the more important aspects of a bartender's job is making sure a customer does not drive a car after consuming too much alcohol. The bar and the bartender who sold a customer drinks can be held responsible if the customer is arrested or has an accident while driving under the influence of alcohol. It is no longer just an act of kindness to limit the number of drinks or to keep someone from driving under the influence, it's the law. The bartender has to keep a constant evaluation of the customers that are

At peak business times such as happy hours and weekend evenings, bartenders must be able to take orders and serve drinks quickly.

being served in the bar. It is the responsibility of the bartender to say when a customer has had too much alcohol.

Requirements

Bartenders must know how to mix a variety of cocktails, how to stock a bar, and how to dress and conduct themselves properly. They must be familiar with state and local laws concerning the sale of alcoholic beverages. Many vocational and technical schools offer complete courses in bartending, but many bartenders learn their trade on the job. They may have had previous experience as bartender helpers, waiters' assistants, or waiters or waitresses.

Bartenders must be in good physical condition to stand long hours while working and to lift heavy cases of beverages or kegs of beer. Because they deal with the public, they must have a pleasant personality and a clean, neat appearance.

Special requirements

Generally, bartenders must be at least 21 years of age, although some employers prefer those who are older than 25. In some states, bartenders must have health certificates assuring that they are free of contagious diseases. Because of the large sums of money collected in some bars, bartenders must sometimes be bonded.

The principal union for bartenders is the Hotel Employees and Restaurant Employees International Union (AFL-CIO), but membership is not a requirement. The union's influence is generally confined to large cities.

BARTENDERS

Opportunities for experience and exploration

Because of the age requirement, students under the age of 21 will find it difficult to get actual bartending experience. Part-time or summer jobs as waiters' assistants or waiters or waitresses, however, will put them in a position where they can watch a bartender at work and in that way learn how to mix drinks and do other bartending tasks. Preparing drinks at home is good experience, although in itself it does not qualify a person to become a bartender. Any part-time or summer job that involves serving food and beverages to the public will give students the opportunity to see if they have the right temperament for this occupation.

Further career exploration may include talking with school counselors, visiting vocational schools that offer bartending courses, interviewing bartenders, and reading bar guides and manuals.

Methods of entering

Persons who are interested in becoming bartenders often begin by working as bartender helpers, waiters' assistants, or waiters or waitresses. Small restaurants, neighborhood bars, and vacation resorts usually offer a beginner the best opportunity. Many people tend bar part-time while working at other jobs or attending college, often serving at banquets and private parties at restaurants, hotels, or in private homes. Vocational schools that offer bartending courses sometimes help their graduates find jobs.

Application may be made directly to hotels, restaurants, cocktail lounges, and other businesses that serve alcoholic beverages. Some employment agencies specialize in hotel and restaurant personnel. Information about job opportunities may also be obtained from the local offices of the state employment service.

Advancement

With experience, a bartender may find employment in a large restaurant or cocktail lounge where the pay is higher. Opportunities for advancement in this field, however, are limited. A few persons may earn promotions to head bartender, wine steward, or beverage manager.

Some bartenders go on to open their own taverns or restaurants.

Employment outlook

Approximately 400,000 bartenders are employed in the 1990s, about 70 percent of them in restaurants and bars. Most others work in hotels and private clubs, while less than 10 percent are self-employed.

Employment of food service workers in general is expected to increase faster than the occupational average through the late 1990s. New restaurants, hotels, and bars will open as the population grows and as spending for food and beverage outside the home increases. People with higher incomes and more leisure time will go out for dinner more frequently and take more vacations. As large numbers of women join the work force, families will dine out more often. Little change is expected in the employment of bartenders, however, as consumption of alcoholic beverages—particularly cocktails—continues to decline.

Openings regularly occur as older bartenders retire, die, or leave the occupation. There is a high turnover rate, too, because many bartenders are students or others who do not plan to make bartending a career.

Earnings

Earnings for this occupation cover a broad range. With tips, full-time bartenders in the 1990s earn an average of about $12,720 a year. Bartenders may earn more than half their money as tips. About 20 percent earn more than $21,700. Besides wages and tips, bartenders usually get free meals at work and may be furnished bar jackets or complete uniforms.

Conditions of work

Many bartenders work more than 40 hours a week. They work nights, weekends, and holidays, and split shifts are common. They have to work quickly and under pressure during busy periods. Also, they need more strength than average to lift heavy cases of liquor and mixers.

Many bartenders feel the difficulties of the job are more than offset by the opportunity to talk to friendly customers, by the possibility of one day managing or owning a bar or restaurant, or by the need for good part-time work.

It is important that individuals entering this field like people, since they will be in constant contact with the public. Even when the work is hardest and the most hectic, bartenders are expected to be friendly and attentive to their customers. Patrons of a bar will often use the bartender as a sounding board, a psychiatrist, and a confessor. All they really want is a sympathetic ear. Good bartenders will appear interested without getting personally involved in other people's problems.

The success of a restaurant or cocktail lounge depends on satisfied customers. For this reason, teamwork among the serving staff is crucial. Often working in cramped quarters, bartenders must cooperate quickly and willingly with other food and beverage service workers, and make their place of work friendly and inviting to customers.

GOE: 09.04.01; SIC: 5813; SOC: 5212

◇ **SOURCES OF ADDITIONAL INFORMATION**

A directory of colleges and other schools that offer programs and courses in hospitality education is available from:

Council on Hotel, Restaurant, and Institutional Education
1200 17th Street, NW
Washington, DC 20036

General information, training materials, and a monthly newsletter for bartenders are available from:

American Bartenders Association
PO Box 15527
Sarasota, FL 34277

Educational Foundation of the National Restaurant Association
250 South Wacker Drive
Chicago, IL 60606

Canadian Association of Provincial Liquor Commissioners
Saskatchewan Liquor Control Board
PO Box 5054
Regina SK S4P 3M3

◇ **RELATED ARTICLES**

Volume 1: Food Service; Hospitality
Volumes 2–4: Caterers; Cooks, chefs and bakers; Fast food workers; Food service workers; Restaurant and food service managers

Bicycle mechanics

Definition

Bicycle mechanics repair and service all types of bicycles using hand tools and power tools. They may also be called upon to assemble new bikes that come into the shop from the manufacturer to be sold. They may do routine maintenance and tune-ups or completely rebuild damaged or old bicycles.

History

Bicycles have been said to be the most efficient means ever devised to turn human energy into propulsion. The first successful bicycle was built in Scotland around 1839. It, like the bicycles built for many years afterward, had a large front wheel that was pedaled and steered and a smaller wheel in back for balance. In time, advances in design and technology improved the

Bicycle mechanics are busiest in the spring and summer months when bicyclers do the most damage to their bikes.

ease with which riders could balance, steer, brake, and get on and off bicycles. The first modern-looking bicycle, with equal-sized front and rear wheels and a loop of chain on a sprocket drive, was built in 1874. By the early 1890s, pneumatic tires and the basic diamond-pattern frame had made bicycles stable, efficient, fairly cheap machines. Bicycle riding became a popular recreation and, in some countries around the world, a major form of transportation. In the 20th century, bicycle performance was further improved by lightweight frames in new designs and improved gear mechanisms, tires, and other components. Especially after automobiles became the dominant vehicles on American roads, bicycles were usually considered children's toys in the United States. However, the 1960s saw a resurgence in their popularity among adults that has continued to this day.

Nature of the work

Repairing bicycles takes mechanical skill and careful attention to detail. Many repairs, such as replacing brake cables, are relatively simple, while others can be very complicated. Mechanics use a variety of tools to repair and maintain bikes, including wrenches, screwdrivers, drills, vises, and specialized tools. There are many different brands of bikes, both domestic and

foreign, and each has its own unique qualities and mechanical problems.

Bike mechanics work on both new and used bicycles. Cyclists bring in bikes for emergency repairs and for routine tune-ups. Mechanics repair and recondition used bikes that their shop buys from the public or takes in trade from customers who buy new bikes. After the mechanics return the used bikes to good operating condition, the shop sells them. Many new bikes come from the manufacturer in need of assembly. Mechanics working at the bike dealership must put them together and adjust them so that they operate properly. Many department stores and discount houses that sell bikes contract out this type of assembly work to bike shops, and it can be very profitable.

Some of the basic repairs that bikes need can easily be done by the owner, but many cyclists lack the tools, the time, or the inclination to learn how to service their bikes. They prefer to take most problems to professional bike mechanics. One example is fixing a flat tire. Leaks in clincher tires (those with a separate inner tube) can be fixed at home or given to a bicycle mechanic. On the other hand, repairing sew-up tires (which have no inner tubes) is a more complicated process that generally requires a mechanic. Mechanics can also build wheels, replace and tighten spokes, and true, or align, the wheels. When a wheel is built, the spokes are laced between the rim and the hub of the wheel, then tightened individually with a special wrench until the wheel spins without wobbling. Mechanics use a truing machine to test the balance of the wheel as it spins.

The gear mechanism on multiple-speed bikes is another common concern for bicycle mechanics. On some bikes, gears are shifted by means of a derailleur, which is located on the back wheel hub or at the bottom bracket assembly where the pedals and chain meet. The derailleur needs adjustment often. The mechanic aligns the front and rear gears of the derailleur to reduce wear on both the chain and the gear teeth and adjusts the mechanism to keep the pressure on the chain constant. Gear mechanisms differ greatly among different makes of bicycle, and mechanics have to keep up with current models and trends.

Bicycle mechanics have to be able to spot trouble in a bike and correct problems before they become serious. They may have to straighten a bent bike frame using a special vise and a heavy steel rod. They may adjust or replace the braking mechanism so that the force on the brakes is spread evenly. They may need to take apart, clean, grease, and reassemble the headset, or front hub, and the bottom bracket that houses the axle of the pedal crank.

Mechanics who work in a bike shop sometimes work as salespeople, advising customers on their bike purchases and handling sales of a wide range of accessories, including helmets, clothing, racks and bags for carrying items, mirrors, locks, and much more. In some shops, especially those located in resort areas, bike mechanics may also work as *bicycle-rental clerks*. Where winters are cold and biking is seasonal, bike mechanics may work part of the year on other recreational equipment such as camping gear, snowmobiles, or small engines.

Requirements

Completion of high school or other formal education is not necessarily required for a job as a bicycle mechanic, although employers may prefer applicants who are high school graduates. Students who are considering this kind of work would benefit by taking shop classes and courses that introduce business practices.

Bicycle maintenance courses are offered at some technical schools, and there are at least three privately operated training schools for bicycle mechanics. Bicycle manufacturers may also offer factory instruction to mechanics employed by the company's authorized dealers.

For the most part, however, bike mechanics learn informally on the job. At least two years of hands-on training and experience is required to become a thoroughly skilled mechanic, but because new makes and models of bikes are constantly being introduced, there are always new things to learn. Many times, when a new model of bike is introduced, bike mechanics have to prove that they can service it before they are authorized by the bike's manufacturer or distributor to do repairs. Only after the bike distributor has visited the bike mechanics on the job and is satisfied that their work is competent is the shop officially permitted to sell and service the new kind of bike.

Some people work as mechanics with the dream of one day opening their own bike shop. These people would find it very helpful to take high school and college courses in accounting, finance, and small business management.

Opportunities for experience and exploration

Bike shops sometimes hire inexperienced students as assistants to work on a part-time basis or during the summer, when their business is most brisk. Such a job is probably the best way to find out about this work. Many people get interested in bicycle mechanics because they repair and maintain their own bikes. Various magazines devoted to recreational cycling and serious bicycle racing, including technical aspects of how bicycles are constructed and operated, are for sale at larger newsstands or available at libraries.

Methods of entering

If a bike shop has enough business, a part-time or temporary assistant who has demonstrated the ability to do good work may be hired for a full-time job. Beginners who have no such experience should try contacting local bike shops to find one that is willing to hire trainees. People who have learned something about bike repair and have accumulated the tools they need may be able to start doing repair work independently, perhaps using ads and referrals to gradually build a small business.

Advancement

There are few opportunities for advancement for bicycle mechanics unless they combine their interest in bikes with another activity. After a few years on the job, they may be able to take over managing the bike shop where they work. Some mechanics move on to jobs with the bicycle department of a large department or sporting goods store, and from there move up to department manager or regional sales manager. Another possibility is to become a sales representative for a bicycle manufacturer or distributor.

Some bicycle mechanics want to own and operate their own bike store. If they gain enough experience, and save or borrow enough money to cover start-up costs, they may be able to establish a successful new business. To prepare for this it is very advisable to take college courses in business, management, and accounting.

Employment outlook

This is a small occupational field, employing about 15,000 people nationwide. Its small size means that the total number of future job openings will be limited. The U.S. Department of Labor suggests that the rate of employment growth in this field will be slower than the average for other occupations over the next decade or so. Nonetheless, cycling is a popular activity, and there will continue to be some opportunities for bicycle mechanics. People are bicycling for fun, for fitness, for transportation, and some for the thrill of racing. Bikes don't burn gas and pollute the atmosphere, and they are relatively cheap and versatile. The reasons why bikes are popular are not likely to change soon. And as long as bikes are popular, bicycle mechanics will be needed to keep them in good operating order.

Bicycle repair work is relatively immune to fluctuations in the economy. In times of economic boom, people buy more new bikes and mechanics are kept busy by assembling, selling, and servicing them. During economic recessions, people bring their old bikes to mechanics for repair.

Earnings

Many bicycle mechanics work a standard 40-hour week. They may work more hours in the spring when people bring their old bikes out of storage, and perhaps fewer hours in the winter, depending on the nature of their employer's business. Trainee mechanics without experience may start at about the minimum wage, but as they gain skill and experience, they can earn $10.00 per hour or more. Earnings also vary de-

pending on geographical location and the size of the city or town. There are few opportunities for high pay for the person who stays a bicycle mechanic.

Conditions of work

Bicycle mechanics do much of their work indoors at a work bench. Though they sometimes get grease and dirt on their hands and clothing, the work in general is not very strenuous. Most heavy work such as painting, brazing, and frame straightening is done in larger bike shops and specialty shops.

Mechanics work by themselves or with a few co-workers as they service bikes, but in many shops they also deal with the public. The atmosphere around a bike shop can be hectic, especially during peak seasons in shops where mechanics must double as clerks.

GOE: 05.10.02; SIC: 7699; SOC: 6179

◇ **RELATED ARTICLES**

Volume 1: Machining and Machinery; Sales
Volumes 2–4: Counter and retail clerks; General maintenance mechanics

Billing clerks

Definition

Billing clerks produce the bills and other documents that companies use to settle customers' accounts. They make entries in business ledgers, write and send invoices, and verify purchase orders. They are responsible for posting items in accounts payable or receivable, calculating customer charges, and verifying the company's rates for certain products and services. They must make sure that all entries are accurate and up-to-date. At the end of the tax year billing clerks may have to work with auditors and answer any questions they may have about billing procedures and specific accounts.

History

As long as people have engaged in trade and commerce, there has been the need to record business transactions. Wealthy traders during the early Egyptian and Babylonian civilizations often used slaves to make markings on clay tablets to keep track of purchases and sales.

With the rise of monarchies in Europe, billing clerks were needed to record the business transactions of kings, queens, and other wealthy individuals, and also to monitor the status of the royal treasury. Monks were often in charge of this activity. The Industrial Revolution, with its increase in the level of commercial transactions, heightened the need for billing clerks in all areas of business.

Today, although modern technology has changed the way they record transactions, billing clerks continue to occupy a central role in the business world. Without billing clerks, a company would not know how much money it expects to receive, how much it has been paid already for its goods and services, and how much it owes other companies.

Nature of the work

Billing clerks are responsible for keeping records and up-to-date accounts of all business transactions. This entails a wide variety of duties. They type and mail bills for services or products provided and update files to reflect payments when they arrive. They also check invoices that come from other companies to ensure that the products or services specified on them have in fact been delivered and there are no overcharges or other errors. Billing clerks check that invoices are paid in a timely manner.

The billing clerk is responsible for entering all transaction information onto the firm's account ledger. This ledger lists all the items bought or sold in the company's transactions, as well as the credit terms and the dates. For example, if a billing clerk works for an insurance company, the transaction sheet will reflect when and how much customers must pay on their insurance bills. As payments come in, the billing clerk applies credit to customer accounts and applies any discounts that are available. All correspondence is carefully filed for future reference. Calculators are a billing clerk's primary tool, and computers increasingly are being used to process and store information.

Billing clerks are also often responsible for preparing summary statements of financial status, profit and loss statements, and payroll lists and deductions. These reports are submitted periodically to company management, who can then gauge the company's financial performance. Clerks also write company checks, compute federal tax reports, and tabulate personnel profit shares.

Billing clerks set up shipping and receiving dates. They check customer orders before shipping to make sure that all the items ordered are there and that all costs, shipping charges, taxes, and credits are included. Billing clerks are also troubleshooters. They contact suppliers or customers when payments are past due or incorrect and help solve the minor problems that invariably occur when companies interact.

These billing clerks are verifying invoices and completing purchase orders. Large companies require several billing clerks to process their invoices.

Billing clerks may have a specific role within a company. These areas of specialization include:

Invoice-control clerks post items in accounts payable or receivable ledgers and verify the accuracy of billing data.

Passenger rate clerks compute fare information for business trips and then provide this information to business personnel.

C.O.D. (cash-on-delivery) clerks calculate and record the amount of money collected on C.O.D. delivery routes.

Interline clerks compute and pay freight charges for airlines or other transportation agencies that carry freight or passengers as part of a business transaction.

Settlement clerks compute and pay shippers for materials forwarded to a company.

Billing-control clerks compute and pay utility companies for services provided.

Rate reviewers compile data relating to utility costs for management officials.

Services clerks compute and pay tariff charges for boats or ships used to transport materials.

Foreign clerks compute duties, tariffs, and price conversions of products exported to or imported from foreign countries.

Billing-machine operators prepare bills and statements through the use of billing machines.

Deposit-refund clerks prepare bills for utility customers.

Raters calculate premiums to be paid by customers of insurance companies.

Telegraph-service raters compute costs for sending telegrams.

Billing clerks may work in one specific area or they may be responsible for two or more of the aforementioned jobs.

BILLING CLERKS

Requirements

A high school diploma is usually sufficient for a beginning billing clerk, although business courses in the operation of office machinery and bookkeeping are also helpful. Prospective billing clerks should have excellent organization skills, some mechanical ability (for operating business machines), the ability to concentrate for long periods of time on repetitious tasks, and good mathematical skills. Legible handwriting is also a necessity.

High school students should take courses in English, mathematics, and as many business-related courses such as typing and bookkeeping as possible. Community colleges and vocational schools often offer business education courses that will provide training for file clerks.

Opportunities for experience and exploration

Students can get experience in this field by taking on clerical or bookkeeping responsibilities with a school club or other organization. In addition, some school work–study programs may have opportunities with businesses for part-time, practical on-the-job training. Individuals may have the opportunity to get training in the operation of business machinery (calculators, word processors, and so on) through evening courses offered by business schools. Another way of gaining insight into the responsibilities of a billing clerk is to talk to someone already working in the field.

Methods of entering

Those interested in securing an entry-level position should contact an appropriate company directly. Major employers of billing clerks include hospitals, insurance companies, and any other large company. Jobs may also be located through classified advertisements in the newspaper.

High schools sometimes have job placement services to help qualified graduates find employment. Most companies provide entry-level billing clerks with about one month of on-the-job training, during which time company policy and procedures are explained. Billing clerks work with experienced personnel during this period.

Advancement

Billing clerks usually begin their employment in the more routine tasks such as the simple recording of transactions by hand or machine. With experience, they may advance to more complicated assignments and assume a greater responsibility for the total work to be completed. With additional training, billing clerks may be promoted to the position of bookkeeper or accountant. Billing clerks with strong leadership skills may become group managers or supervisors.

The high turnover rate in the billing clerk position increases the chances for promotion and advancement. The number and kind of opportunities, however, may depend on the place of employment and the ability, training, and experience of the employee.

Employment outlook

Approximately 413,000 billing clerks are employed in the 1990s. Although the increased use of data-processing equipment and other types of office machines may reduce the number of billing clerks needed at any one location, the growing volume of business transactions should lead to growth in employment opportunities for billing clerks through the year 2005. The federal government should continue to be a good source of job opportunities, and private companies should also have numerous openings. Banks and other financial institutions employ about 40 percent of the country's billing clerks. Employment opportunities should be especially good for those trained to operate modern office machinery. In the future, more individualized and complex billing applications will require workers with greater technical expertise.

Earnings

Beginning billing clerks earn an average of between $10,500 and $14,000 a year, depending on the size and geographic location of the company and the skills of the worker. Experienced clerks average between $15,000 and $23,000 per year; the higher wages are paid to those with the greatest number of job responsibilities. Full-time workers also receive paid vacation, health insurance, and other benefits.

Conditions of work

As is the case with most office workers, billing clerks work an average 37 to 40 hours a week, with most of their time spent seated at a desk. The working environment is usually well ventilated and well lighted, but the job itself can be fairly routine and repetitive. Clerks spend the majority of their time entering business transactions on ledgers and then handling billing and related correspondence. Billing clerks often interact with accountants and other office personnel and may work under close supervision. Billing clerks should have an even temperament and the ability to work well with others. They should find systematic and orderly work appealing and they should like to work on detailed tasks.

GOE: 07.02.04; SIC: Any industry; SOC: 4715, 4718

◇ SOURCES OF ADDITIONAL INFORMATION

Career information is available from local business schools and from:

Office and Professional Employees International Union
265 West 14th Street, Suite 610
New York, NY 10011

Canadian Society of Business Practitioners
#206, 3852 Finch Avenue, East
Scarborough ON M1T 3T4

◇ RELATED ARTICLES

Volume 1: Accounting; Banking and Financial Services; Business Management; Insurance
Volumes 2–4: Accountants and auditors; Bookkeeping and accounting clerks; Cashiers; Collection workers; Counter and retail clerks; Financial institution clerks and related workers; Financial institution tellers; General office clerks; Insurance policy processing occupations; Reservation and transportation ticket agents; Shipping and receiving clerks; Stock clerks

Bindery workers

Definition

Binding is the final step in the production of books and magazines. *Bindery workers* take the printed pages that go into books, pamphlets, catalogs, and magazines, and fold, cut, sew, staple, stitch, or glue them together to produce finished reading materials. Some bindery workers perform highly specialized tasks which require a certain amount of training; other bindery workers perform simple, repetitive tasks which are easily mastered.

History

Bookbinding is an ancient and honored craft. As early as the third century A.D., when books were still written on papyrus and animal skins, pages of parchment manuscripts were kept stored between two boards. During the Middle Ages, bookbinding was developed into a fine art by monks in monasteries who decorated the board covers of sacred books with costly bindings made of elaborately worked metal, jewels, ivory, and enamel.

Around the year 900, the English introduced the use of leather to cover the boards and soon became leaders in this field. English kings employed official binders responsible for decorating the books in the royal library. Nobles and other powerful figures followed their monarchs' lead and also established libraries of luxuriously bound volumes. The fine bindings made for royal or noble patrons were usually decorated with coats of arms or family crests. In this way, the bookbinder became highly regarded as an artist.

With the invention of the printing press in the 15th century, the way was opened for an ever-increasing number of books. Because of the growing demand for books among ordinary citizens, the making and binding of books was transferred from the monasteries and palaces to the shops of printers and binders. Soon the names, initials, or emblems of printers and binders were stamped onto the book covers they made.

Today, most bookbinding is done in a routine manner by automated machines, but it is still possible to secure richly bound books, handcrafted by highly skilled workers, at prices from several hundred to several thousand dollars. These are frequently special limited editions of contemporary books or restorations of damaged but important old books. The average modern book, however, is simply bound in paper, cloth, or a composite material that can be purchased inexpensively. The art of fine bookbinding, together with the skills of the hand bookbinder, is increasingly rare.

Nature of the work

Although originally a handicraft, modern bookbinding operations are practically all mechanized. The average bookbinder today is a highly skilled machine operator who knows little or nothing about hand bookbinding. This bookbinder sets up and operates folding, gathering, sewing, stitching, trimming, case-making, and covering machines.

The average bookbinder may work at one of several different kinds of binderies: edition binderies, which specialize in making large numbers (or "runs") of books and magazines; pamphlet binderies, which make pamphlets; trade or job binderies, which produce smaller quantities on a contract basis for printers and publishers; and manifold or loose-leaf binderies, which bind blank pages and forms into ledgers, notebooks, checkbooks, diaries, and notepads. In addition, some bookbinders are employed in large libraries where they concentrate on repairing old, worn, or damaged bindings.

Bindery work can consist of one or more steps. Some binding jobs, such as preparing leaflets or newspaper inserts, require only a single step, in this case folding. The most complicated binding work is edition binding, or the production of books from large printed sheets of paper. Book pages are usually not produced individually, but are printed on a large sheet of paper six or eight at a time. These large sheets are folded by machine into units called "signatures," and the signatures are joined together in the proper order to make a complete book. Full-page illustrations are usually printed separately on different paper stock and inserted into the signature either by hand or by machine. The signatures are then assembled into the proper order by a gathering machine and sewed or glued together to make what is called a "book block." After gathering, the book blocks are compressed in a machine to ensure compactness and uniform thickness, trimmed to the proper size, and reinforced with fabric strips glued along the spine. The covers for the book are created separately and are pasted or glued to the book block by machine. Books may undergo a variety of finishing operations, such as gilding the edges of pages and wrapping with paper dust jackets before they are finally inspected and packed for shipment.

These same operations, or operations that are very similar, are also used in the binding of magazines, catalogs, and directories. In large binderies, the operations are usually done in an assembly-line fashion by bindery workers who are trained in just one or two procedures. Some workers specialize in operating equipment such as folding or gathering machines, while others specialize in setting up and adjusting equipment to make it ready for a particular job. In many shops, much of the work is done by semi-skilled bindery workers who perform tasks assigned by an experienced worker or bookbinder. For example, semi-skilled bindery workers may punch holes in sheets of paper, stamp numbers on sheets, fasten sheets or signatures together with a machine stapler, or feed covers and signatures into various machines for stitching, folding, gluing or other processes.

Bindery workers are often referred to by the name of the particular machine they operate: for example, *folding, saddle-stitching, automatic gluing, book-sewing, covering, rounding and backing,* and *case-making machine operators.* Other specialists include *book trimmers, forwarders, inkers, casers, book repairers,* and *pressers.*

In spite of machines and technology, a small number of *bookbinders* still work in hand binderies. These highly skilled workers design original or special bindings for limited editions or restore and rebind rare or damaged books for private collections and museums. This hand work requires creative ability, knowledge of materials, and a thorough background in the history of binding. Hand bookbinding is perhaps the only kind of binding work that gives the individual the opportunity to work at a variety of bindery jobs.

Approximately 78,000 people are bindery workers. Of these, about 7,000 are bookbinders and about 71,000 are bindery machine operators, setters, and setup operators. Most jobs are in commercial printing plants or in bindery shops that serve businesses that print material but are not equipped to bind it into finished products. A few workers are employed by large libraries or by book publishers, which normally contract out the printing and binding work that is necessary in making books.

While many of the binding processes are mechanized, bindery workers must ensure that the machines are running smoothly.

Requirements

Most bindery workers learn their craft through on-the-job training. Inexperienced workers usually start by doing simple tasks such as moving paper from cutting machines to folding machines. As workers gain experience, they advance to more difficult tasks and learn how to operate one or more pieces of equipment. A one- to three-month training period is generally required to learn how to operate a new piece of equipment.

People with some knowledge of binding operations are likely to have an advantage when they apply for employer-provided training. High school students interested in bindery careers can gain some exposure to bindery work by taking shop courses or attending a vocational-technical high school. Occupational skill centers, often operated by unions, can also provide an introduction to the industry. Postsecondary training programs in graphic arts, offered at vocational and technical schools and community and junior colleges, can also be the first step toward a career in the bindery field.

A few formal apprenticeships are available for workers interested in learning certain highly specialized skills. A four-year apprenticeship usually is necessary to teach bookbinders how to restore rare books and to produce valuable collectors' editions. The restoration of rare and old books includes the costly and delicate procedure of reducing the acid content of the paper. Several techniques are available and all require special equipment and training. The acid-laden paper crumbles easily and requires careful handling.

A two-year apprenticeship program is usually appropriate for bindery workers whose occupations are less complicated. Most union shops require an apprenticeship program to combine on-the-job training with some formal classroom instruction. Four-year college programs are recommended for people who want to work in bindery shop management.

Accuracy, neatness, patience, and good eyesight are among the qualities needed for these occupations. Finger dexterity is essential for workers who count, insert, paste, and fold, while mechanical aptitude is required of those who operate some kinds of automated equipment. Artistic ability and imagination are required for hand bookbinding. In general, employers look for individuals with good skills in language and applied mathematics.

Opportunities for experience and exploration

There are several ways to explore the occupations of bookbinders and bindery workers. Students may be able to find out firsthand about bindery work through a summer job in a local bindery. By observing actual work situations and talking with experienced employees, they can both learn and earn.

In addition, many trade and vocational schools offer courses that teach the basics of the trade. Some schools even have work–study arrangements with trade or job binderies that enable students to broaden their experience in the field. Contacts made during this training period may be useful in securing full-time employment after graduation. Often, too, experience gained in a trade school can be used to shorten the length of an apprenticeship period.

Methods of entering

The best way for people who plan to become skilled bookbinders to start out in the field is to apply for a place in an apprenticeship program. Information on apprenticeships is available through the state employment service, binderies, or the area offices of unions such as the Graphic Communications International Union. People seeking bindery worker jobs may enter a two-year apprenticeship program in the same way.

People who want to start working first and learn all their skills on the job should contact potential employers directly, especially if they want to work in a small nonunion bindery. Openings for trainee positions may be listed in newspaper want ads and with the state employment service. Trade school graduates may find jobs through their school's placement office.

Advancement

Some skilled workers can advance to supervisory positions, but opportunities for this type of advancement are limited to larger binderies. Advancement is likely to be faster for workers who have completed an apprenticeship program than for those who have learned skills solely through on-the-job training. People who have the necessary business knowledge and can invest a substantial amount of money may want to open up their own bindery shops.

Employment outlook

Over the next decade, employment in the bindery field is not expected to keep up with the average rate of growth for other occupations. This is because the binding process is becoming increasingly mechanized. New automated equipment in binderies can perform a number of operations in sequence, beginning with raw stock at one end of the process and finishing with the final product. These machines shorten production time, increase plant productivity, and reduce overall labor requirements. As a result, the jobs of many semi-skilled workers are being eliminated. The greatest number of job

openings in the next decade will occur when experienced workers must be replaced because they are changing jobs or leaving the labor force. Workers with experience will have the best chance of getting the jobs that become available.

On the other hand, the printing industries will probably grow in coming years, as more materials of many kinds are printed. Commercial printers will probably be hiring more bindery workers than they have in the past as the total volume of new catalogs, newspaper inserts, direct mail advertising, magazines, and books grows.

There will continue to be relatively few openings for hand bookbinders. The most highly skilled and specialized hand bookbinders will have the best employment opportunities.

Earnings

Bindery workers' earnings vary according to the type of work they do and the region of the country where they live. Skilled bookbinders usually have earnings that are below the average pay for other printing craft workers. In the 1990s, the wages of bindery workers who are labor union members are in the range of $21,800 to $30,000 per year. Wages are generally higher in unionized plants than in nonunion shops. Most union contracts provide for time-and-a-half pay for overtime and double time for Sunday and holiday work.

Bindery workers with no experience or training begin at about minimum wage. Apprenticeship pay starts at about half of the rate paid to skilled bookbinders and grows to about 85 percent of the rate toward the end of the training period.

Conditions of work

The average workweek for bookbinders and bindery workers is between 35 and 40 hours. Modern binderies are usually well lighted and well ventilated, but they are often noisy. Although bindery workers are subject to few dangers, they must be careful to avoid injury while operating stitching and stapling machines and power cutters. Certain jobs can be very tiring, because they require standing for long periods of time and repeatedly reaching and stretching while feeding materials into machines. Some workers must stoop, kneel, and lift and carry heavy items. Because many tasks are done in an assembly-line manner, bindery workers need to be able to tolerate doing repetitious, monotonous tasks.

GOE: 05.05.15, 06.04.04; SIC: 2789; SOC: 6844, 7649

◇ **SOURCES OF ADDITIONAL INFORMATION**

Binding Industries of America
70 East Lake Street
Chicago, IL 60601

Graphic Communications International Union
1900 L Street, NW
Washington, DC 20036

Graphic Arts Technical Foundation
4615 Forbes Avenue
Pittsburgh, PA 15213

Printing Industries of America
100 Dangerfield Road
Alexandria, VA 22314

◇ **RELATED ARTICLES**

Volume 1: Book Publishing; Magazine Publishing; Printing
Volumes 2–4: Archivists; Compositors and typesetters; Electrotypers and stereotypers; Lithographic occupations; Machine tool operators; Photoengravers; Printing press operators and assistants

Biochemists

Definition

A *biochemist* studies the chemical composition of living organisms. This scientist identifies and analyzes the chemical processes related to biological functions such as reproduction and metabolism. The biochemist also studies the effect of environment on living tissue.

History

Biochemistry is a fairly new science. By the early 19th century, pioneer biochemists had begun to identify the materials found in living cells. A tremendous impetus to biochemistry was the mechanics of the fermentation process that had been practiced for some 2,000 years. Biochemists have widened their searches in recent years to include the composition of protein molecules and chromosomes that make up human life itself. They are on the threshold of synthesizing these elemental substances. It is a field that crosses over into other sciences; for example, there have been many recent discoveries in genetics and molecular structures.

Nature of the work

Most biochemists employed in the United States work in the fields of medicine, biomedicine, nutrition, and agriculture. In medicine, they investigate the causes and cures of disease and methods of diagnosis. In biomedicine, they delve into genetics, brain function, and physiological adaption. In nutrition, they examine the effects of food deficiencies on human performance, including the ability to learn. In agriculture, they undertake studies to discover more efficient methods of crop cultivation and storage and ways to control pests.

Biochemists' principal tool in recent years has been the electron microscope, which permits them to examine molecular structures, but they also devise new instruments and analytical techniques as needed.

About seven out of ten biochemists are engaged in pure research, often for a university medical school or nonprofit organization such as a foundation or research institute. The remaining 30 percent do applied research, using the discoveries of basic research to solve practical problems or develop products. For example, the discovery of how a living organism

BIOCHEMISTS

This biochemist conducts research on the effects of radiation and other pollutants on living matter. These experiments require concentration and precision.

chemistry is intensive. To earn a master's degree requires about two years of course work and seminars, as well as an original laboratory research project. Candidates for a doctorate must engage in original research leading to new scientific findings and must write a formal thesis. Study for a doctorate generally takes about four years.

Biochemists who wish to work in a hospital may need certification by a national certifying board such as the American Board of Clinical Chemistry.

Opportunities for experience and exploration

The analytical, specialized nature of most biochemistry makes it unlikely that a student interested in the profession will gain much exposure to it before college. Many high school chemistry and biology courses, however, allow students to work with laboratory tools and techniques.

Methods of entering

Biochemists fresh from a college undergraduate program usually begin work in industry or government as research assistants doing testing and analysis. In the drug industry, for example, they may analyze the ingredients of a product to verify and maintain its quality. Biochemists with a master's degree may enter the field in positions in management, marketing, or sales, whereas those with a doctorate often go into basic or applied research.

forms hormones led to hormone synthesis in the laboratory and production on a mass scale. The distinction between basic and applied research is one of degree, however; biochemists often engage in both types of work.

Requirements

At the very least, beginning biochemists require a bachelor's degree in biochemistry or in chemistry, genetics, microbiology, or biology to qualify for jobs as research aides or technicians. Graduate training in biochemistry is a necessity, however, for positions in research and teaching and for advancement in all types of work.

Some schools award a bachelor's degree in biochemistry, and all colleges and universities offer a major in biology or chemistry. Undergraduate courses include chemistry, biology, biochemistry, mathematics, physics, statistics, and computer science. Graduate study in bio-

Advancement

Biochemists with a graduate degree have more opportunities for advancement than do those with only an undergraduate degree. Some graduate students become research or teaching assistants in colleges and universities, qualifying for professorships when they receive their advanced degrees. Experienced biochemists who have doctorates can move up to high-level administrative positions and supervise research programs. Other highly qualified biochemists, who prefer to devote themselves to research, often become leaders in a particular aspect of their profession.

Employment outlook

The prospects for biochemists through the 1990s are excellent. Employment will increase in health-related fields, where the emphasis is on finding cures for such diseases as cancer, muscular dystrophy, AIDS, and mental illness. Additional jobs will be created to produce genetically engineered drugs and other products in the new and rapidly expanding field of genetic engineering. In this area, the outlook is best for biochemists with advanced degrees who can conduct genetic and cellular research.

Biochemists with bachelor's degrees who have difficulty entering their chosen career also may find openings as technicians or technologists, or may choose to transfer their skills to work in the other biological sciences.

Earnings

Starting salaries for biochemists employed by colleges and universities are comparable to those for other professional faculty members. In the 1990s, assistant professors earn an average of $37,800 per year; associate professors, about $44,800; and full professors, about $62,900. In industry, the average income for all biochemists with a bachelor's degree is $21,000 per year; for those with a master's, $27,000; and for those with a doctorate, $36,200. Starting salaries for biochemists in the federal government in the 1990s range from about $14,800 to $18,400 a year for those with a bachelor's degree, from about $18,400 to $22,500 for people with a master's degree, and from about $27,200 to $33,600 for biochemists with a doctorate.

Conditions of work

Biochemists work generally in clean, quiet, and well lighted laboratories where physical labor is at a minimum. They must, however, take the proper precautions in handling chemicals and organic substances that could be damaging.

Biochemists in industry generally work a 40-hour week, although they, like their counterparts in research, often put in many extra hours. Much personal time must be devoted to keeping up with the literature in their field. Many biochemists travel occasionally to attend meetings or conferences. Those in research write papers for presentation at meetings or for publication in scientific journals.

Individuals interested in biochemistry must have the patience to work for long periods of time on a project without positive results. Biochemistry is often a team affair, and the individual should be able to work well with others. Successful biochemists are continually learning and increasing their skills.

GOE: 02.02.03; SIC: 2836, 8071, 8221; SOC: 1854

◇ **SOURCES OF ADDITIONAL INFORMATION**

American Association for Clinical Chemistry
2029 K Street, NW, 7th Floor
Washington, DC 20006

American Association of Pathologists
9650 Rockville Pike
Bethesda, MD 20814

American Chemical Society
1155 16th Street, NW
Washington, DC 20036

American Institute of Biological Sciences
730 11th Street
Washington, DC 20001

American Society for Biochemistry and Molecular Biology
Education Information
9650 Rockville Pike
Bethesda, MD 20814

◇ **RELATED ARTICLES**

Volume 1: Biological Sciences; Chemicals and Drugs; Chemistry
Volumes 2–4: Biological scientists; Biological technicians; Biomedical engineers; Biomedical technicians; Chemical technicians; Chemists; Laboratory technicians; Medical laboratory technicians

Biological scientists

Definition

Biological scientists study the origin, development, anatomy, function, distribution, and other basic principles of living organisms. They are concerned with the nature of life itself; with humans, microorganisms, plants, and animals; and with the relationship of each organism to its environment. Biological scientists do research in many specialties that advance the fields of medicine, agriculture, and industry.

History

Biology can be divided generally into two fields of study—plants and animals. However, as this science developed, other areas branched off these two, so that the history of biology is the history of its branches.

Nature of the work

Biology can be divided into many specialties. The *zoologist* studies all types of animals to learn their origin, interrelationships, classification, life histories, habits, diseases, relation to environment, growth, genetics, and distribution. Another major division is that of microbiology. The *microbiologist* studies bacteria, viruses, molds, algae, yeasts, and other organisms of microscopic or submicroscopic size.

The interests of the biologist differ from those of the chemist, physicist, and geologist, who are concerned with nonliving matter.

Biological scientists, or *life scientists*, may be identified by their specialties. For example, *anatomists* study animal bodies from basic cell structure to complex tissues and organs. They determine the ability of body parts to regenerate and investigate the possibility of transplanting organs and skin. Their research is applied to human medicine. *Physiologists* are biological scientists who specialize in studying all the life stages of plants or animals. Some specialize in a particular body system or a particular function such as respiration. *Entomologists* study insects and their relation to other life forms. *Histopathologists* investigate diseased tissue in humans and animals. *Parasitologists* study animal parasites and their effects on humans and other animals.

A *pharmacologist* may be employed as a researcher by a pharmaceutical company and spend most of the time working in the laboratory. This may be experimenting on the effects of various drugs and medical compounds on mice or rabbits. Working within a controlled environment, pharmacologists precisely note the type, quantity, and timing of medicines administered as a part of their experiments. Periodically, they make blood smears or perform autopsies to study different reactions. They usually work with a team of researchers, headed by one with a doctorate and consisting of several biological scientists with master's and bachelor's degrees and some laboratory technicians.

Biological scientists may also work for government agencies concerned with public health. *Staff toxicologists*, for example, study the effects of toxic substances on humans, animals, and plants. The data they gather are used in consumer protection and industrial safety programs to reduce the hazards of accidental exposure or ingestion. *Public-health microbiologists* conduct experiments on water, foods, and the general environment of a community to detect the presence of harmful bacteria so that pollution and contagious diseases can be controlled or eliminated.

Other specialists in the field of biology include the following:

Aquatic biologists study animals and plants that live in water and how they are affected by their environmental conditions, such as the salt, acid, and oxygen content of the water, temperature, light, and other factors. *Marine biologists* specialize in the study of salt water organisms.

Biophysicists apply physical principles to biological problems. They study the mechanics, heat, light, radiation, sound, electricity, and energetics of living cells and organisms and do research in the areas of vision, hearing, brain function, nerve conduction, muscle reflex, and damaged cells and tissues.

Cytologists, sometimes called *cell biologists*, examine the cells of plants and animals, including those cells involved in reproduction. They use microscopes and other instruments to observe the growth and division of cells and to study the influences of physical and chemical factors on both normal and malignant cells.

Ecologists study the distribution and abundance of organisms and their relation to their environment.

Gently helping a giant tortoise swim, the zoologist is careful not to touch the healing neck sore.

Geneticists study heredity in various forms of life. They are concerned with how biological traits such as color, size, and resistance to disease originate and are transmitted from one generation to another. They also try to develop ways to alter or produce new traits, using chemicals, heat, light, or other means.

Mycologists study edible, poisonous, and parasitic fungi, such as mushrooms, molds, yeasts, and mildews, to find those useful to medicine, agriculture, and industry. Their research results in benefits such as the development of antibiotics, the propagation of mushrooms, and methods of retarding fabric deterioration.

Nematologists study nematodes (roundworms) that are parasitic to plants, transmit diseases, attack insects, or attack other nematodes that exist in soil or water. They investigate and develop methods of controling these organisms.

Requirements

Biological scientists must be systematic in their approach to solving the problems that they face. They should have a probing, inquisitive mind, and an aptitude for biology, chemistry,

and mathematics. Patience and imagination also are required.

Useful high school courses include English, biology, physics, chemistry, Latin, geometry, and algebra. Prospective biological scientists also should obtain a broad undergraduate college training. In addition to courses in all phases of biology, useful related courses include organic and inorganic chemistry, physics, and mathematics. Modern languages, English, biometrics (the use of mathematics in biological measurements), and statistics are also useful. In view of the growing use of computers to help solve the problems of science, course work or computer experience would be valuable. Undergraduate programs include laboratory practice and may involve field or collecting work.

Nearly all institutions offer undergraduate training in one or more biological sciences. These vary from liberal arts schools offering basic majors in botany and zoology to large universities that permit specialization, in areas such as entomology, bacteriology, and physiology, at the undergraduate level.

For the highest professional status, a doctorate is required. This is particularly true of top research positions and most higher level college teaching openings. A large number of colleges and universities offer courses leading to a master's degree and a doctorate. A study made by the National Science Foundation showed that among a group of biological scientists listed on the National Scientific Manpower Register, 10 percent held a bachelor's degree, 33 percent held a master's or professional medical degree, and the remaining 57 percent had earned a doctorate.

Candidates for a doctorate specialize in one of the subdivisions of biology. A number of sources of financial assistance are available to finance graduate work. Most major universities have a highly developed fellowship (scholarship) or assistantship (part-time teaching or research) program.

Outside organizations, such as the U.S. Public Health Service and the National Science Foundation, make awards to support graduate students. In a recent year, for example, the Public Health Service made 8,000 fellowship and training grants. In addition, major universities often hold research contracts or have their own projects that provide part-time and summer employment for undergraduate and graduate students.

Special requirements

A state license may be required for biological scientists who are employed as technicians in general service health organizations such as hospitals or clinics. To qualify for this license, proof of suitable educational background is necessary.

Opportunities for experience and exploration

Students may measure their aptitude and interest in the work of the biologist by taking courses in this area. Laboratory assignments, for example, provide actual information on techniques used by the working biologist. Many schools hire students as laboratory assistants to work directly under a teacher and help administer the laboratory sections of courses.

School assemblies, field trips to federal and private laboratories and research centers, and career conferences provide additional insight into career opportunities. Advanced students often are able to attend professional meetings and seminars.

Part-time and summer positions in biology or related areas are particularly helpful. Students with some college courses in biology may find summer positions as laboratory assistants.

Graduate students may find work on research projects being conducted by their institution. Beginning college and advanced high school students may find employment as laboratory aides or hospital orderlies or attendants. Despite the menial nature of these positions, they afford a useful insight into careers in biology. High school students often have the opportunity to join volunteer service groups at local hospitals. Student science training programs (SSTPs) allow qualified high school students to spend a summer doing research under the supervision of a scientist.

Methods of entering

Biological scientists seeking employment as teachers usually will find their college placement office the best source of assistance. Public and private high schools and an increasing number of colleges hire teachers through the college at which they studied. Private employment agencies also place a significant number of teachers. Some teaching positions are filled through direct application.

Biological scientists interested in private industry and nonprofit organizations also may apply directly for employment. College seniors often participate in campus interviews conducted by representatives of employing organizations. Private and public employment offices frequently have listings from these employers. Experienced biological scientists often change positions on the basis of meeting people at professional seminars and national conventions.

Special application procedures are required for positions with governmental agencies. Civil service applications for federal, state, and municipal positions may be obtained by writing to the agency involved and from high school and college guidance and placement bureaus, public employment agencies, and at post offices.

Advancement

In a field as broad as biology, numerous opportunities for advancement exist. To a great extent, however, advancement depends on the individual's level of education. A doctorate is generally required for college teaching, independent research, and top-level administrative and management jobs. A master's degree is sufficient for some jobs in applied research, and a bachelor's degree may qualify for entry-level jobs.

With the right qualifications, the biologist may advance to the position of project chief and direct a team of other biological scientists. Many use their knowledge and experience as background for administrative and management positions. Often, as they develop professional knowledge, biological scientists move increasingly from strictly technical assignments into positions in which they interpret biological knowledge.

The usual path of advancement in biology, as in other sciences, comes from specialization and the development of the status of an expert in a given field. Biological science may also be coupled with other major fields to explore problems that require an interdisciplinary approach: biochemistry, biophysics, biostatistics (or biometrics). Biochemistry, for example, uses the methods of chemistry to study the composition of biological materials and the molecular mechanisms of biological processes.

Employment outlook

A faster than average increase in employment of biological scientists is predicted through the 1990s, although competition will be stiff for the high-paying jobs, and government jobs will be less plentiful.

Advances in genetic research leading to new drugs, improved plants, and medical discoveries should open up some opportunities. Private industry also should need more biological scientists to keep up with the advances in biotechnology. Efforts to preserve the environment also may result in an increased number of jobs.

Biological scientists with advanced degrees will have the advantage in finding positions, although this varies by specialty, with genetic, cellular, and biochemical research showing the most promise. Scientists with only a bachelor's degree may find openings as science or engineering technicians, or health technologists and technicians. Many colleges and universities are cutting back on their faculties, but high schools and two-year colleges may have teaching positions available. High school biology teachers are not considered to be biological scientists, however.

Because biological scientists are usually employed on long-term research projects or in agriculture, which are not greatly affected by economic fluctuations, they rarely lose their jobs during recessions. In the 1990s, over 62,000 biological scientists are employed in the United States. Another 30,000 work on the faculties of colleges and universities. Many work in research and development laboratories for private industry, mainly in pharmaceutical, chemical, and food companies. About 40 percent are employed by the federal government and by state and local governments. Some hold nonteaching positions at colleges or universities; others work for nonprofit research organizations or hospitals, or are self-employed.

Earnings

In the 1990s, biological scientists with bachelor's degrees who work for the federal government earn salaries of $41,700 to $50,900 a year, depending on their area of specialty.

Beginning salaries in private industry average $21,800 a year for people with bachelor's degrees. Most earn an average from $20,700 to $45,200 a year. In general, the highest salaries are earned by biological scientists in business and industry, followed in turn by those who are self-employed, working for nonprofit organizations, in military service, and working for the U.S. Public Health Service or other positions in the federal government. The lowest salaries are earned by teachers and by those working for various state and local governments.

Conditions of work

The actual work environment of the biologist varies greatly depending upon the position and type of employer. One biologist may work outdoors or travel much of the time. Another wears a white smock and spends years working in a laboratory.

Biological scientists frequently work under some pressure. For example, those employed by pharmaceutical houses work in an atmosphere of keen competition for sales that encourages the development of new drug products and, as they are identified, the rapid testing and early marketing of these products. The work is very exacting, however, and the pharmaceutical biologists must exercise great care to ensure that adequate testing of products has been properly conducted.

GOE: 02.02.03; SIC: 2836, 8071, 8221, 8731, 8733; SOC: 1854

◇ **SOURCES OF ADDITIONAL INFORMATION**

American Association of Pathologists
9650 Rockville Pike
Bethesda, MD 20814

American Institute of Biological Sciences
730 11th Street, NW
Washington, DC 20001

American Institute of Nutrition
9650 Rockville Pike
Bethesda, MD 20814

American Physiological Society
9650 Rockville Pike
Bethesda, MD 20814

American Society for Cell Biology
9650 Rockville Pike
Bethesda, MD 20814

American Society for Microbiology
1325 Massachusetts Avenue, NW
Washington, DC 20005

American Society for Biochemistry and Molecular Biology
9650 Rockville Pike
Bethesda, MD 20814

American Society of Zoologists
104 Sirius Circle
Thousand Oaks, CA 91360

Entomological Society of America
9301 Annapolis Road
Lanham, MD 20706

Federation of American Societies for Experimental Biology
9650 Rockville Pike
Bethesda, MD 20814

Genetics Society of America
9650 Rockville Pike
Bethesda, MD 20814

National Institutes of Health
Bethesda, MD 20014

U.S. Department of Health and Human Services
Washington, DC 20201

Canadian Biochemical Society
Department of Biochemistry
University of Western Ontario
London ON N6A 5C1

◇ **RELATED ARTICLES**

Volume 1: Biological Sciences; Chemicals and Drugs; Chemistry; Environmental Sciences; Health Care
Volumes 2–4: Agricultural scientists; Biochemists; Biological technicians; Chemical technicians; Chemists; Ecologists; Food technologists; Medical laboratory technicians; Naturalists

Biological technicians

Definition

Biological technicians assist biologists in the study of living organisms. Their work may include: pharmaceutical and medical research, where they may help to find a cure for such things as AIDS or cancer; biotechnology research and development, where they help develop new products utilizing the latest genetic advances such as gene splicing and recombinant DNA; or, they may work in police crime laboratories, analyzing criminal evidence.

In the course of their work, technicians may perform laboratory experiments to analyze substances such as blood, body tissue, and food. They also do experiments with living organisms such as molds, fungi, and microscopic organisms as well. They then gather and record the data obtained during these experiments. This work enables biologists to draw conclusions about the functioning of organisms and to develop new products such as medications, food additives, insecticides, and fertilizers for use in business and industry.

History

Assistants to experimenters have been used for centuries. As experiments developed that were complex, involved, or long-term, the head researcher could not accomplish all of the work. Trained assistants that were able to comprehend the complexities of the project and manage the tasks involved were needed to maintain scientific study.

As the complexity of science increased in the 20th century, the skills needed to assist research biologists also increased. Training beyond high school was important, as was a concentration of classes in the specific field where the research was to be done.

Nature of the work

Biological technicians may work with laboratory animals, insects, or microscopic organisms. They utilize a variety of laboratory techniques and equipment such as microscopes, chemical scales, and centrifuges. To ensure the integrity of experiments, they carefully control the conditions under which they are performed. They then record instrument readings and often analyze their data to indicate overall trends.

Some biological technicians are involved in the exciting new area of biotechnology research. Biotechnology involves modifying organisms to meet some need, particularly in medicine, agriculture, or energy management. Genetic engineering is one such field. Biological technicians in this field help research scientists to transfer genetic material from one kind of animal, plant, or microorganism to another in order to create a slightly different organism. For example, by transplanting specific genes, scientists can produce a breed of crop plant with better yields or improved resistance to insect infestations or to freezing temperatures.

Another field of biotechnology that involves technicians is monoclonal antibody research. Technicians in this field work in laboratories where new kinds of antibodies are being created by cloning them from a single hybrid cell. Some biological technicians may also help set up the procedures necessary to manufacture these new products for market.

Requirements

People interested in careers as biological technicians should take as many high school sci-

This biological technician is a member of an immunology research team. She is studying the effect of certain antibodies on various types of cancerous tumors in mice.

ence courses as possible, including biology, chemistry, and physiology. They should also have mathematics training through at least solid geometry and be well versed in the elements of statistics. They should have at least an additional year of post-high school training in biology, laboratory procedures, microbiology, and organic chemistry. They should have sufficient language skills to read technical literature and to write detailed reports on their laboratory experiments and the resulting data.

In addition to biological training, technicians who work with animals should feel comfortable handling common laboratory animals, such as mice, rats, and guinea pigs.

Opportunities for experience and exploration

For students interested in learning more about this field, visits to research laboratories can provide perhaps one of the most vivid means of exploration. Through such visits, students can witness technicians actually involved in their work, and may be able to speak with several of them, or with their employers about opportunities for technicians in that industry or company.

Students should also consider finding part-time or summer employment in a company or other organization that employs biological technicians. Even the most menial of tasks will offer opportunities to learn more about the field and will demonstrate interest to potential future employers.

Methods of entering

Most schools have student placement services and are in constant touch with those industries and agencies in need of technicians.

Another method of entering is through on-the-job training programs offered by various companies. Those people who successfully complete such training programs are usually assured of a position with the company giving them training.

One particularly successful variation of the on-the-job training program is the work–study program. Such programs are run by schools in cooperation with local agencies and businesses and offer students the opportunity to find part-time or summer employment in jobs related to the students' studies. Very often the part-time or summer employer will become the student's full-time employer following graduation.

Advancement

Technicians usually begin work under the direct and constant supervision of an experienced technician or scientist. Then, as they gain experience, they are given more responsible assignments, often carrying out particular work programs under only very general supervision.

From there, technicians may move into supervisory positions, and those with exceptional ability can sometimes qualify for professional positions after receiving additional training. In general, technicians can advance by going to a higher-level technician's job, earning a supervisory post, or advancing to the professional ranks.

Promotion will usually depend upon the acquisition of additional training, as well as on-the-job performance. Those technicians who fail to obtain additional training may be limited in advancement possibilities.

Employment outlook

Because of the growth of biotechnology, the employment outlook for biological technicians is quite good through the year 2005. Many companies are developing or expanding their research and development departments, and will need technicians to assist the biologists in these departments.

Employment of science technicians in general is dependent to some degree on the general level of economic activity. During a recession, for instance, fewer technicians are hired and some are even laid off, as there is a slackening in research and development activity, in new product design, and in other engineering and scientific activities. All industries will need to hire new technicians to replace those who are retiring or leaving their jobs for other reasons. Well trained science technicians—especially those who are flexible about geographical location and certain other job conditions—will usually have no trouble finding employment.

Earnings

Salaries for biological technicians vary considerably, depending upon education, experience, type of employer, and the geographical location. Most biological technicians who graduate from two-year technical training programs earn salaries between $16,000 and $30,000 a year and average approximately $24,700 a year.

Starting salaries range between $13,000 to $15,000 a year. Top salaries for senior biological technicians can sometimes reach as high as $37,000 to $50,000 a year or more.

Conditions of work

Biological technicians work primarily under pleasant laboratory conditions of controlled temperature and humidity. If a project includes working with larger animals, technicians may spend time in barns or other housing facilities. Some biological technicians conduct experiments on live animals, a practice which has caused some controversy in recent years, and may continue to be argued about for some time to come. Technicians need to reconcile the two conflicting arguments involved: the gains in medical knowledge based on the animal experiments, versus the protection of animals from harm.

The work of biological technicians is not very strenuous but does require lifting and bending. It often also requires long hours at the microscope, which can lead to eyestrain.

GOE: 02.04.02; SIC: 8071; SOC: 382

◇ SOURCES OF ADDITIONAL INFORMATION

American Institute of Biological Sciences
Office of Career Service
730 11th Street NW
Washington, DC 20001-4521

◇ RELATED ARTICLES

Volume 1: Biological Sciences
Volumes 2–4: Agricultural scientists; Animal production technicians; Biochemists; Biological scientists; Biomedical engineers; Biomedical equipment technicians; Chemical technicians; Clinical chemists; Farm crop production technicians; Medical laboratory technicians; Medical technologists; Pharmaceutical industry workers; Pharmacy technicians

Biomedical engineers

Definition

Biomedical engineers are highly trained scientists who employ engineering and life science principles in research conducted on the biological aspects of animal and human life. They develop new theories, and they modify, test, and prove existing theories on life systems. They design health care instruments and devices or apply engineering principles to the study of human systems.

History

Biomedical engineering is one of many new professions created by advancements in technology. It is an interdisciplinary field that brings together two time-honored professions—biology and engineering.

Biology is the study of life, and engineering uses sources of energy in nature and the properties of matter in a manner that is useful to humans, particularly in machines, products, and structures. A combination of the two fields, biomedical engineering developed primarily after 1945, as new technology allowed for the application of engineering principles to biology. The artificial heart is just one in a long list of products of biomedical engineering. Other products include artificial organs, prosthetics, use of lasers in surgery, cryosurgery and ultrasonics, and use of computers and thermography in diagnosis.

Nature of the work

Biomedical engineers are employed in industry, in hospitals, in research facilities of educational and medical institutions, in teaching, and in government regulatory agencies.

In using engineering principles to solve medical and health-related problems, the biomedical engineer works closely with life scientists, members of the medical profession, and chemists. Most of the work revolves around the laboratory. There are three interrelated work areas: research, design, and teaching.

Biomedical research is multifaceted and broad in scope. It calls upon engineers to apply their knowledge of mechanical, chemical, and electrical engineering as well as anatomy and physiology in the study of living systems. Using computers, they employ their knowledge of graphic and related technologies to develop mathematical models that simulate physiological systems.

In biomedical engineering design, medical instruments and devices are developed. Engineers work on artificial organs, ultrasonic imagery devices, cardiac pacemakers, and surgical lasers. They also may design and build systems that will update hospital, laboratory, and clinical procedures. A final design implication is the assisting of health care personnel in observing and treating physical disabilities and ailments.

The teaching aspect of biomedical engineering is on the university level. Teachers may conduct classes, advise students, serve on academic committees, and supervise or conduct research.

BIOMEDICAL ENGINEERS

This biomedical engineer examines the contents of a test tube, comparing his observations with a computer readout.

Within the field of biomedical engineering, an individual may concentrate on a particular specialty area. Some of the well established ones are bioinstrumentation, biomechanics, biomaterials, systems physiology, clinical engineering, and rehabilitation engineering. These specialty areas frequently depend on one another.

Bioinstrumentation is the application of electronics and measurement principles and techniques to develop devices used in diagnosis and treatment of disease. Computers are becoming increasingly important in this specialty.

Biomechanics is mechanics applied to biological or medical problems. Efforts in this area have developed, among other things, the artificial heart, the artificial kidney, and the artificial hip.

Biomaterials are both living tissue and materials used for implantation. The selection of an appropriate material to place in the human body may be one of the most difficult tasks faced by the biomedical engineer.

Systems physiology involves using engineering strategies, techniques, and tools to gain a comprehensive and integrated understanding of living organisms ranging from bacteria to humans. Biomedical engineers in this specialty examine such things as the biochemistry of metabolism and the control of limb movements.

Clinical engineering is the application of technology for health care in hospitals. The clinical engineer is a member of the health care team along with physicians, nurses, and other hospital staff.

Rehabilitation engineering is a new and growing specialty area of biomedical engineering. Its goal is to expand the capabilities and improve the quality of life for individuals with physical impairments. Rehabilitation engineers often work directly with the disabled individual.

Requirements

Biomedical engineers should have a strong willingness to learn. They should be scientifically inclined and be able to apply their knowledge in problem solving. This is a far-ranging, interdisciplinary profession that requires long years of schooling so that a broad background in both engineering and biology can be gained. In particular, biomedical engineers have to be familiar with chemical, material, and electrical engineering as well as physiology and computers.

Most engineers possess an undergraduate degree in biomedical engineering or a related field of engineering and an advanced degree (preferably a Ph.D.) in some facet of biomedical engineering.

Opportunities for experience and exploration

Several ways exist to explore the opportunities available in this occupation. Undergraduate and graduate courses offer a great deal of exposure. Securing employment in a hospital or other facility where biomedical engineers are employed can also provide insight into the field, as can interviews with qualified personnel.

Methods of entering

A variety of routes may be taken to gain employment as a biomedical engineer. Recent graduates may use college placement services. They may apply directly to employers, often to personnel offices in hospitals and industry. A job may be secured by answering an advertisement in the employment want-ad section of a newspaper. Information on job openings also is available at the local office of the U.S. Employment Service.

Advancement

Advancement opportunities are tied directly to one's educational and research background. In a nonteaching capacity, a biomedical engineer with an advanced degree can rise to a supervisory position.

In teaching, a doctorate in biomedical engineering follows the usual academic career ladder. By demonstrating excellence in research, teaching, and departmental committee involvement, one can move from instructor, to assistant professor, then to full professor, department chair, or dean.

The ability to receive research grant funding also can be a means of advancing in both nonteaching and teaching sectors.

Employment outlook

In the 1990s, there are more than 4,000 biomedical engineers in the United States. They are employed in all parts of the country in hospitals, colleges and universities, medical and engineering schools, federal and state agencies, and private industry.

It is expected that there will be a greater need for skilled biomedical engineers through the 1990s. Prospects look particularly good in the large health care industry, which will continue to grow rapidly, primarily because people are living longer. New jobs will become available in biomedical research in prosthetics, artificial internal organs, computer applications, and instrumentation and other medical systems. In addition, a demand will exist for teachers to train the biomedical engineers needed to fill these positions.

Earnings

How much a biomedical engineer earns is dependent upon the amount of education and experience. In the 1990s, the federal government pay scale for holders of a bachelor's degree ranges from approximately $19,000 to $24,000 a year. Biomedical engineers with a master's degree could start at about $26,000; and those with a doctorate, at around $28,000. The average salary for all engineers in the federal government is $38,000 a year.

In colleges and universities in the 1990s, salaries for full-time faculty members on nine-month contracts range from about $26,800 for instructors to $62,900 for professors. In addition, university professors can supplement their income significantly by writing and consulting.

Earnings in the private sector generally run higher than those in government or education.

Conditions of work

This is a highly demanding job intellectually. Relatively little physical labor is required but long hours are frequently spent in the laboratory. The work involves much use of sophisticated machinery and cooperation with other qualified personnel.

Those engaged in university teaching will have much student contact in the classroom, the laboratory, and the office. They also will be expected to serve on relevant committees while carrying their teaching, research, and writing loads. As competition for teaching positions increases, the requirement of professors to publish papers will increase. Professors usually are responsible for obtaining government or private research grants to support their work.

GOE: 02.02.01; SIC: 8711; SOC: 1639

◇ **SOURCES OF ADDITIONAL INFORMATION**

American Society for Engineering Education
11 Dupont Circle, NW, Suite 200
Washington, DC 20036

Biomedical Engineering Society
PO Box 2399
Culver City, CA 90231

Canadian Medical and Biological Engineering Society
Room 164, M-50, National Research Council of Canada
Ottawa ON K1A 0R8

◇ **RELATED ARTICLES**

Volume 1: Biological Sciences; Engineering
Volumes 2–4: Biomedical engineers; Biomedical equipment technicians; Biologists; Ergonomists; Instrumentation technicians; Miscellaneous engineers; Orthotic and prosthetic technicians; Prosthetists and orthotists

Biomedical equipment technicians

Definition

Biomedical equipment technicians handle the complex medical equipment and instruments found in hospitals, clinics and research facilities. This equipment is used in medical therapy and diagnosis, and includes: heart–lung machines, artificial-kidney machines, patient monitors, chemical analyzers, and other electrical, electronic, mechanical, or pneumatic devices.

The technician's main duties are to inspect, maintain, repair, and install this equipment. They disassemble equipment to locate malfunctioning components; repair or replace defective parts; and reassemble the equipment, adjusting and calibrating it to ensure that it operates according to manufacturers' specifications. Other duties of biomedical equipment technicians include: modifying equipment according to the directions of medical or supervisory personnel; arranging with equipment manufacturers for equipment repair when necessary; and safety-testing equipment to ensure that patients, equipment operators, and other staff members are safe from electrical or mechanical hazards. Biomedical equipment technicians work with hand tools, power tools, measuring devices, and manufacturers' manuals.

Technicians may work for equipment manufacturers as salespeople or as service technicians, or for a health care facility specializing in the repair or maintenance of specific equipment such as that used in radiology, nuclear medicine, or patient monitoring.

History

Today's complex biomedical equipment is the result of advances in three different areas of engineering and scientific research. The first, of course, is our ever-increasing knowledge of the human body and of the disease processes that afflict it. Although the accumulation of medical knowledge has been going on for thousands of years, most of the discoveries leading to the development of medical technology have occurred during the last 300 years. Plus, during the past 100 years especially, we have learned a great deal about the chemical and electrical nature of the human body.

The second contribution to biomedical technology's development is the field of instrumentation—the design and building of precision measuring devices. Throughout the history of medicine, physicians and medical researchers have tried to learn about and to monitor the workings of the human body with whatever instruments were available to them. However, it was not until the Industrial Revolution of the 18th and 19th centuries that the field of instrumentation began to develop the kind of instruments needed to detect the human body's many subtle and rapid processes.

The third area is mechanization and automation. Biomedical equipment often relies on mechanisms such as pumps, motors, bellows, control arms, etc. These kinds of equipment were initially developed and improved during the Industrial Revolution; however, it was not until the 1950s that the field of medical technology began incorporating the use of automation. During the 1950s, researchers developed machines for analyzing the various components of blood and for preparing tissue specimens for microscopic examination. Probably the most dramatic development of this period was the introduction of the heart–lung machine by John Haysham Gibbon of Philadelphia in 1953, a project he had been working on since 1937.

Since the 1950s, the growth of biomedical technology has been especially dramatic. Thirty years ago, even the most advanced hospitals had only a few pieces of electronic medical equipment; today such hospitals have thousands. And, to service this equipment, the biomedical equipment technician has become an important member of the health care delivery team.

In a sense, biomedical equipment technicians represent the newest stage in the history of technicians. The first generation of technicians were skilled assistants who had learned a trade and gone to work for an engineer or scientist. The second generation learned a technology, such as electronics. The most recent generation of technicians needs integrated instruction and competence in at least two fields of science and technology. For the biomedical equipment technician, the fields may vary but they will most often be electronics and human physiology.

Nature of the work

Biomedical equipment technicians act as an important link between technology and medicine.

They repair, calibrate, maintain, and operate the biomedical equipment working under the supervision of researchers, biomedical engineers, physicians, surgeons, and other professional health care providers.

Biomedical equipment technicians may work with thousands of different kinds of equipment. Some of the most frequently encountered are the following: patient monitors; heart–lung machines; kidney machines; blood–gas analyzers; spectro-photometers; X-ray units; radiation monitors; defibrillators; anesthesia apparatus; pacemakers; bloodpressure transducers; spirometers; sterilizers; diathermy equipment; patient-care computers; ultrasound machines; and diagnostic scanning machines including the CT (computed tomography) scan machine, PETT (positive emission transaxial tomography) scanner, and MRI (magnetic resonance imagery) machines.

Repairing faulty instruments is one of the chief functions of biomedical equipment technicians. They investigate equipment problems, determine the extent of malfunctions, make repairs on instruments that have had minor breakdowns, and expedite the repair of instruments with major breakdowns, for instance, by writing an analysis of the problem for the factory. In doing this work, technicians rely on manufacturers' diagrams, maintenance manuals, and standard and specialized test instruments, such as oscilloscopes and pressure gauges.

Installing equipment is another important function of biomedical equipment technicians. They inspect and test new equipment to make sure it complies with performance and safety standards as described in the manufacturer's manuals and diagrams, and as noted on the purchase order. Technicians may also check on proper installation of the equipment or, in some cases, install it themselves. To ensure safe operations, technicians need a thorough knowledge of the regulations related to the proper grounding of equipment, and they need to actively carry out all of the details to insure safety.

Maintenance is the third major area of responsibility for biomedical equipment technicians. In doing this work, technicians try to catch problems before they become more serious. To this end, they take apart and reassemble devices, test circuits, clean and oil moving parts, and replace worn parts. They also keep complete records of all machine repairs, maintenance checks, and expenses.

In all three of these areas, a large part of the technicians' work consists of consulting with physicians, administrators, engineers, and other related professionals. For instance, they

A biomedical equipment technician repairs a malfunctioning electronic monitor. In this case, he has had to expose the entire piece of equipment to replace a wire.

may be called upon to aid hospital administrators' decisions about the repair, replacement, or purchase of new equipment. As part of their maintenance and repair responsibilities, they consult with medical and research staffs to determine that equipment is functioning properly and safely. They also consult with medical and engineering staffs when called upon to modify or develop equipment. In all of these activities, they use their knowledge of electronics, medical terminology, human anatomy and physiology, chemistry, and physics.

In addition, biomedical equipment technicians are also involved in a range of other related duties. Some biomedical equipment technicians maintain inventories of all instruments in the hospital, their condition and location, and operator. They reorder parts and components, assist in providing people with emergency instruments, restore unsafe or defective instruments to working order, and check for safety regulation compliance.

Other biomedical equipment technicians may help physicians, surgeons, nurses, and researchers conduct procedures and experiments. In addition, they must be able to explain to staff members how to operate these machines, the conditions under which certain apparatus may or may not be used, how to solve small operating problems, and how to monitor and maintain equipment.

In many hospitals, technicians are assigned to a particular service, such as pediatrics, surgery, or renal medicine. These technicians become specialists in certain types of equipment. However, unlike electrocardiograph technicians or dialysis technicians, who specialize in one kind of equipment, for the most part biomedical equipment technicians must be thoroughly familiar with a large variety of instruments. They might be called upon to prepare an artificial kidney or to work with a blood–gas analyzer, which is a millivolt meter with water circulating to keep blood at body temperature during analyses, and which requires the use of calibration gases. Biomedical equipment technicians also maintain pulmonary function machines. These machines examine and measure the patient's breathing, analyze the gases moving in and out of the lungs and the way in which they distribute themselves throughout the lung system, and measure breathing efficiency. Pulmonary function machines are used in clinics for ambulatory patients, in hospital laboratories, in departments of medicine for diagnosis and treatment, and for the rehabilitation of cardiopulmonary patients.

While most biomedical equipment technicians are trained in electronics technology, there is also a need for technicians trained in plastics to work on the development of artificial organs, and for people trained in glassblowing to help make the precision parts for specialized equipment.

Many biomedical equipment technicians work for medical instrument manufacturers. These technicians consult and assist in the construction of new machinery, helping to make decisions concerning materials and construction methods used in the manufacture of the equipment.

Requirements

Biomedical equipment technicians need mechanical ability, and should enjoy working with tools. Because this job demands quick decision-making and prompt repairs, technicians should work well under pressure. They should also be extremely precise and accurate in their work, and have good communication skills.

Biomedical equipment technicians require post-high school education, usually a two-year program leading to an associate degree. While still in high school, prospective technicians should take courses in chemistry, biology, and physics; these courses will provide a helpful background for further study. Courses in English, mathematics, electronics, shop, and drafting will also help prepare students for further education and for work as technicians.

Biomedical equipment technology is a relatively new program in two-year colleges. Some schools refer to these programs as "medical electronics technology" or "biomedical engineering technology." During the course of

these programs, students receive instruction in anatomy, physiology, electrical and electronic fundamentals, chemistry, physics, biomedical equipment construction and design, safety in health care facilities, medical equipment troubleshooting, and communications skills. In addition to the classroom work, programs often provide students with practical experience in repairing and servicing equipment in a clinical or laboratory setting under the supervision of an experienced equipment technician. In this way, students learn in some detail about electrical components and circuits, the design and construction of common pieces of machinery, and computer technology as it applies to biomedical equipment.

By studying various pieces of equipment, technicians learn a problem-solving technique that applies not only to the equipment studied, but also to equipment they have not yet seen and even to equipment that has not yet been invented. Part of this problem-solving technique includes learning how and where to locate sources of information.

Some biomedical equipment technicians receive their training in the U.S. military. During the course of an enlistment period of four years or less, military personnel can receive training that prepares them for entry-level or sometimes advanced-level positions later in the civilian work force.

The Association for the Advancement of Medical Instrumentation, affiliated with the International Certification Commission for Clinical Engineering and Biomedical Technology, issues a certificate for biomedical equipment technicians based on a written examination and educational preparation. This program provides an opportunity for technicians to demonstrate that they have attained an overall knowledge of the field, and many employers prefer to hire technicians with this certificate. In some cases, the educational requirements for certification may be waived for technicians with appropriate employment experience.

Opportunities for experience and exploration

It is difficult for interested students to gain any direct experience on a part-time basis in biomedical equipment technology. The first opportunities for students to gain experience generally come in the clinical and laboratory phases of their training programs. Interested students, however, can explore some aspects of this career in a number of different ways. They can visit their school or community library to seek out some of the many books written about careers in medical technology, or, they can join a hobby club devoted to chemistry, biology, radio equipment, or electronics.

Perhaps the best way to learn more about this job is to set up, with the help of teachers or guidance counselors, a visit to a local health care facility, and arrange for a biomedical technician to speak to interested students, either on site, or at a career exploration seminar hosted by the school. It would also be highly desirable for interested students to visit a school offering a program in biomedical equipment technology to discuss career plans with an admissions counselor.

Methods of entering

Most schools offering programs in biomedical equipment technology work closely with local hospitals and industries, and school placement officers are usually informed about appropriate openings when they are available. In some cases, recruiters may visit a school during a student's final semester to conduct interviews. Also, many schools place students in part-time hospital jobs to help them gain practical experience. Students are often able to return to these hospitals for full-time employment after graduation.

Another effective method of finding employment is to write directly to hospitals, research institutes, or biomedical equipment manufacturers. Other good sources of leads for job openings include state employment offices and newspaper want ads.

Advancement

With increased experience, biomedical equipment technicians can expect to work with less and less supervision, and in some cases they may find themselves supervising other, less experienced technicians. They may advance to positions in which they serve as instructors, assist in research, or have administrative duties. Although many supervisory positions are open to biomedical equipment technicians, some positions are not available without additional education. In large metropolitan hospitals, for instance, the minimum educational requirement for biomedical engineers, who do much of the supervising of biomedical equipment technicians, is a bachelor's degree—many engineers have a master's degree as well.

Employment outlook

Because of the increasing use of medical electronic devices and other sophisticated biomedical equipment, the demand for skilled and trained biomedical equipment technicians is growing much faster than the average, and should continue through the year 2005.

In hospitals, the need for more biomedical equipment technicians exists not only because of the increasing use of biomedical equipment but also because hospital administrators realize that these technicians can help hold down costs. Biomedical equipment technicians do this through their prevention and maintenance activities and by taking over some routine activities of engineers and administrators, thus releasing those professionals for activities that only they can perform. Through the coming decades, cost containment will remain a high priority for hospital administrators, and as long as biomedical equipment technicians can contribute to that effort, the demand for them should remain strong.

For the many biomedical equipment technicians who work for the companies that build, sell, lease, or service biomedical equipment, job opportunities should continue to grow also.

The federal government also employs biomedical equipment technicians in its hospitals, research institutes, and the military. Employment in these areas will depend largely on levels of government spending. In the research area, spending levels may vary; however, in the health care delivery area, spending should remain high for the foreseeable future.

Earnings

Salaries for biomedical equipment technicians vary in different institutions and localities and according to the experience, training, certification, and type of work done by the technician. In general, entry-level salaries range from $16,288 to $20,360 for technicians working in hospitals and from $20,000 to $23,414 for technicians working for manufacturers or governmental agencies. Experienced technicians earn about $19,000 to $25,450 when working in a hospital and about $25,000 to $35,630 when working for a manufacturer. Senior technicians earn about $25,000 to $35,000 in hospitals and about $35,000 to $45,800 working for a manufacturer. Experienced and senior technicians working for government agencies earn from $25,000 to $35,500 a year.

Conditions of work

Working conditions for biomedical equipment technicians vary according to employer and type of work done. Hospital employees generally work a 40 hour week; however, their schedule may sometimes include weekends, holidays, or being on-call for emergencies. Technicians working for equipment manufacturers may have to do extensive traveling to install or service equipment.

The physical surroundings in which biomedical equipment technicians work may vary from day to day. On some days, technicians may work in a lab or treatment room with patients and staff; on others, they may consult with engineers, administrators, or other staff members, and still others may be spent at a work bench repairing equipment.

Because a good portion of their job involves working with people, successful biomedical equipment technicians must possess a number of interpersonal skills. First, they must know how to give instruction to people about how to operate equipment. Some of the people these technicians may instruct include physicians, nurses, physical therapists, medical and radiological technologists. Some may have some experience with similar kinds of equipment, but many may not have. More importantly, some people may take instruction better than others. A biomedical equipment technician involved in instruction needs to be patient, diplomatic, and sensitive to others' needs.

Many biomedical equipment technicians will also come in contact with patients. They cannot allow themselves to become upset at the sight of blood or critically ill patients. Just as do other health care professionals, biomedical equipment technicians need a good bedside manner.

Biomedical equipment technicians should also be able to handle stress well. When called upon to operate or repair equipment in emergency situations, they should be able to do so calmly and competently. In such situations, tempers sometimes flare, and technicians should remember that the angry outbursts of others are often the response to stress and are not meant personally.

Finally, biomedical equipment technicians should be prepared for a lifetime of continuing education. They need to keep informed about all of the latest developments in their field. This means reading professional journals and manufacturers' literature, attending seminars, and taking classes. By continuing their education in this way, biomedical equipment technicians are best able to give good advice when it is needed, to handle their own responsibilities well, and to ensure themselves increasing responsibility and professional recognition.

GOE: 02.04.02; SIC: 384; SOC: 389, 6179

◇ **SOURCES OF ADDITIONAL INFORMATION**

National Society of Biomedical Equipment Technicians
3330 Washington Boulevard
Suite 400
Arlington, VA 22201-4598

◇ **RELATED ARTICLES**

Volume 1: Biological Sciences; Electronics; Health Care
Volumes 2–4: Biomedical engineers; Clinical chemists; Dialysis technicians; Electrocardiograph technicians; Electroencephalographic technicians; Electronics technicians; Instrumentation technicians

---

Bodyguards

Definition

Bodyguards protect their clients from injury, kidnapping, harassment, or other types of harm.

They may guard a politician during a political campaign, a business executive on a worldwide trip, a movie star going to the Academy Awards, or anyone else who wants personal protection. Bodyguards may be employed by a government agency, a private security firm, or directly by an individual who wants protection.

Bodyguards work in potentially dangerous situations, and therefore must be trained to anticipate and respond to emergencies. They may carry weapons. Bodyguards combine the ability to act in a tense situation with the understanding of how to avoid many of these situations.

History

People, especially rich and powerful people, have always needed protection. Be it a king or queen who mingled with his or her subjects or a Roman Senator who met with various plaintiffs in a legal case, people who made important decisions or controlled large sums of money always had a number of guards they could trust by their side.

As security demands became more complex, the role of bodyguard evolved and expanded. No longer was it enough to simply know how to use a gun or to be particularly adept at fist fighting. Bodyguards were expected to help devise strategies to avoid problem situations. They used new surveillance techniques, planning strategies, and other tactics to anticipate possible dangerous situations.

In recent times, bodyguards have become involved in many different types of situations. Rock stars or movie stars hire bodyguards to protect them against getting mobbed by overzealous fans. Executives from large corporations are also likely to enlist the aid of a bodyguard to protect against possible kidnapping or other types of harm. Bodyguards often accompany their clients overseas because police in other countries may not be able to provide the type of security these people have come to expect. Bodyguards often drive their clients from place to place while on assignment.

Nature of the work

Although a bodyguard's ultimate responsibility is relatively straightforward—that is to protect a client from danger—there are a wide variety of tasks involved in this assignment. Bodyguards are part personal aide and part police officer: as a personnel aide they help plan and implement a schedule and as a police officer they protect the client at a public or private event.

Bodyguards face possible danger whenever they are on duty. When there was an attempted assassination of President Ronald

Accompanying Madonna, two bodyguards look out for potential trouble as people flock behind.

Reagan in March 1981, for example, bodyguards quickly shielded the president as gunshots were fired. Bodyguards may have to sacrifice their own security in defense of those they are hired to protect. Of course, bodyguards are not just sitting targets. They are highly trained in how to react in any situation, life-threatening or not. Skilled bodyguards do all they can to minimize danger for those they are protecting, as well as themselves. Most assignments are carried out in a relatively uneventful fashion.

By keeping a watchful eye on their clients, bodyguards are able to avoid many possible problems. In many cases, people are not actually out to harm a client, but are simply interested in meeting an important person. Bodyguards should not overreact to these encounters, and in most cases a polite warning eliminates any possible problem.

Bodyguards often work in tandem with other security people as part of a large security operation. For example, bodyguards may help develop a plan to safeguard a major politician who is giving a speech, while security guards will develop a plan to safeguard the building where the speech will take place. All security personnel will meet to discuss overall arrangements to ensure that specific details are worked out. Typically, one person will coordinate the security operations.

Bodyguards are hired to protect their clients, and activities that infringe on this job must be avoided. At a presidential dinner, for example, a bodyguard must keep an eye on his or her client, and not become engaged in idle chatter with guests. Bodyguards should not confuse the power and excitement of an assignment with self-importance. Indeed, it is the type of person who can remain calm in the midst of an exciting event and can sense possible danger when all eyes are elsewhere that can make a skilled bodyguard.

Requirements

Bodyguards often begin their careers as police officers, where they learn the necessary skills of crowd control, use of weapons, and emergency response. Some people may also receive training in the armed services, and in this way develop the skills necessary to protect themselves and others.

Generally, bodyguards will receive some higher education (including a college degree), although this is not always necessary. A well educated person can often be the most responsive to rapidly changing situations, and course work in crowd psychology, law, and criminal justice can help a bodyguard better understand the demands of the job. On-the-job experience with different types of people in stressful situations (such as that experienced by police officers) is an integral part of the training.

Since many bodyguards are former police officers, bodyguards generally must be above the minimum age for police officers. This minimum age varies from 18 to 21, depending on the city or state. If a bodyguard comes from the police ranks, that person must also have passed a thorough physical exam.

Although bodyguards must be physically fit, they do not necessarily need to be big and tough. A bodyguard must combine intelligence and sensitivity with an ability to act quickly if danger strikes.

Many bodyguards receive training in martial arts, and increasingly they are incorporating a study of counter intelligence operations, electronic security devices, and surveillance techniques. Often, bodyguards will have training in first aid.

Bodyguards who travel overseas must be well versed in the language and culture of the host country. Good verbal skills are vital and a bodyguard must be able to communicate directions to people at all times. A bodyguard must also be aware of what to expect in any situation. That is why an understanding of the customs of a certain area can help the bodyguard perceive unusual events and be alert for possible problems.

Since bodyguards often work with important people and around sensitive information, they may be required to take a lie detector test before they begin work. They may also have background checks conducted of their work and personal histories.

Bodyguards should obviously have a keen eye for detail and be able to spot trouble long before it happens. This ability to anticipate problems is crucial. A good bodyguard should rarely actually have to stop a kidnapping attempt as it occurs, for example, but rather prevent the attempt from happening through a combination of careful planning and skilled observation. If action is needed, however, the response must be swift and effective. Bodyguards are often trained with weapons and in the martial arts; those who carry weapons need to be properly licensed.

Opportunities for experience and exploration

Because bodyguards must be mature and highly skilled, it is difficult to obtain real opportunities to explore this career while still in high school. Nevertheless, there are chances to take classes and talk to people to get a feel for the demands of the profession. Classes in criminal justice should give an indication of the challenges involved with protecting people. Talking to a police officer who works part-time as a bodyguard is another good way of learning about opportunities in this field.

Without the requisite skills and experience, it is difficult to get summer work as a bodyguard. It may be possible, however, to work in some other capacity at a security firm that hires bodyguards and in this way interact with bodyguards and learn more about the day-to-day rewards and challenges of the profession.

Methods of entering

Many people begin a career as a bodyguard on a part-time basis, often taking on assignments while off-duty as a police officer. The reason most people start part-time is that the police training they receive is ideal preparation for work as a bodyguard. In addition to the excellent training a police officer receives, the officer is also often in a good spot to receive job offers. Someone looking for a bodyguard may call the local police station and ask if there are officers willing to take on an assignment. Then, as a person acquires greater experience in being a bodyguard and more and more community members know of the person's skills and availability, additional work becomes available. That person may then work full-time as a bodyguard or continue on a part-time basis.

Advancement

Those who enter the field as part-time bodyguards may soon find full-time work. As bodyguards develop their skills and reputation, they may be hired by a private security firm or a governmental agency. They may be given additional training in intelligence operations, surveillance techniques, and the use of sophisticated firearms.

Some bodyguards find opportunities as personal protection and security consultants. These consultants work for private companies, evaluating personal security operations and recommending changes. Bodyguards may also find their niche in another aspect of the security industry, such as a working as a security guard.

Employment outlook

Career opportunities are likely to grow throughout the 1990s, as more and more people look to bodyguards for protection. The threat of kidnapping and terrorism are growing (especially for politicians, celebrities, business leaders, and others that enjoy wide recognition), and these individuals will take steps to safeguard themselves and their families by hiring bodyguards.

Governmental agencies will continue to hire bodyguards, but much of the growth in employment will take place in the private sector. Many bodyguards will find work with private security companies.

As is the case in other fields, those with the most skill and experience will enjoy the best employment prospects. There are some women who work as bodyguards, but the vast majority of bodyguards are men.

Earnings

Many bodyguards begin their careers on a part-time basis and earn between $25-$50 per hour for routine assignments. These assignments might last several hours. Full-time bodyguards can expect to earn between $21,500 and $135,000 per year, depending on their experience, the importance of their client, and the type of assignment. If an assignment is highly dangerous or classified, for example, the earnings generally are higher. If special skills are needed (such as electronic surveillance), wages also tend to be higher. Full-time bodyguards average around $41,000 per year.

Conditions of work

A bodyguard goes wherever his or her client goes. This means that the job can be very physically demanding. If a politician decides to walk briskly along a parade route to greet supporters, for example, the bodyguard must have the stamina to keep up. The bodyguard must be able to do more then simply keep up with a client, however. Bodyguards must also have the strength and coordination to take actions to protect their client, if the situation warrants it. A bodyguard must be able to act swiftly and decisively to thwart any attempt to harm a client.

Bodyguards must be able to risk their own safety to protect their clients. They should be comfortable handling firearms and using physical means of restraining people.

The job of bodyguard is not only physically demanding, but also can be very stressful emotionally. A bodyguard must be constantly on the watch for possible problems and must realize that a dangerous situation could be only minutes or seconds away. A bodyguard must maintain a high degree of alertness at all times.

While the possibility of danger is ever present, a bodyguard cannot overreact to situations. Each encounter must be evaluated differently. A person asking a movie star for an autograph must be handled differently, for example, than an angry citizen demanding to know why a politician voted in a certain way. A bodyguard should work to minimize possible conflict whenever possible.

Since bodyguards must accompany their clients at all times, there is no set work schedule. Bodyguards often work highly irregular hours, such as late evenings followed by morning assignments. It is also not unusual to work weekends, since this is when many high-profile clients make public appearances. Travel is also a frequent component of the job.

Working with high-profile clients (such as movie stars and politicians) can be very exciting and many people will enjoy rubbing elbows with the rich and famous. It is not unusual for a bodyguard to come into contact with a wide array of performers and business leaders in the course of an assignment. Many might also enjoy the glamour and excitement of world travel (should the assignment call for this), although others may find the stress and pace of travel to be undesirable.

Bodyguards should have good communications skills. They must be able to work closely with different types of people, creating a climate of trust with their clients.

GOE: 04.02.02; SIC: 7381; SOC: 5144

American Society for Industrial Security
1655 North Fort Myer Drive
Arlington, VA 22209

◇ **RELATED ARTICLES**

Volume 1: Law
Volumes 2–4: Deputy U.S. marshals; Detectives; FBI agents; Forensic experts; Intelligence officers; Police officers; Security consultants; Security guards; Security technicians

◇ **SOURCES OF ADDITIONAL INFORMATION**

International Bodyguard Association
9842 Hibert Street, Suite 161
San Diego, CA 92131

Boilermaking occupations

Definition

Boilermakers and *boilermaker mechanics* are concerned with constructing, assembling, and repairing boilers, vats, tanks, and other large metal vessels that are designed to hold liquids and gases. Boilermakers lay out, cut, fit, bolt, weld, and rivet heavy metal plates, boiler tubes, and castings. Boilermaker mechanics maintain and repair boilers and other vessels made by boilermakers.

History

Boilers first became important during the Industrial Revolution, when steam power emerged as a practical way to drive various kinds of machinery. A boiler is an apparatus that heats a liquid, usually water, and converts it to vapor. Boilers were made and used in England by the beginning of the 18th century. Manufacturers first used iron, then changed to steel in boilers, because steel could withstand more heat and pressure in use. During the 19th and 20th centuries, a series of design changes and improved alloys have made boilers useful in a wide variety of industrial applications.

The number of workers who made boilers, tanks, vats, and similar storage apparatus increased as such equipment became more specialized and the range of applications for it grew broader. In this century, the industries contributing to the demand for the skills of boilermakers have included naval shipyards and other federal installations, the construction industry, steel manufacturing, petroleum refineries, railroads, the chemical industry, and gas and electric utility companies.

Because boilers are often operated at extremely high pressures, faulty construction, bad repairs, or improper operation can be very dangerous. During the late 19th century, regulations were put in place in a few local areas in an effort to prevent accidents caused by careless construction. It was not until 1908, however, that rules and regulations were developed to apply to any sizeable area. Massachusetts created a Board of Boiler Rules in that year, and Ohio followed with its own set of rules in 1911. By 1934, 19 states and 15 cities had such codes. Today, as a result of the combined efforts of industry, labor unions, and government, safety codes are practically universal. The American Society of Mechanical Engineers has been a leader in the promotion and enforcement of the codes of safe manufacture and maintenance.

Nature of the work

Boilermakers, including boilermaker mechanics, usually work at or close to the site where the boiler, tank, or vat is installed. Such sites include petroleum refineries, schools and other institutions with large heating plants, factories where boilers are used to generate power to run machines, factories that make and store products like chemicals or beer in large tanks, and atomic energy plants.

Some boilermakers, called *layout workers*, work in shops or factories where boilers and other large vessels are made. Following drawings, blueprints, and patterns, layout workers mark pieces of metal plate and tubing to indicate how the metal will be cut and shaped by other workers into the sections of vessels. Once the sections are fabricated, other workers at the shop, called *fitters*, temporarily put together the plates and the framework of the vessels. They check the drawings and other specifications and bolt or tack-weld pieces together to be sure that the parts fit properly.

In doing the final assembly at the site, boilermakers first refer to blueprints and mark off dimensions on the base that has been prepared for the finished vessel. They use measuring devices, straight edges, and transits. They attach rigging equipment, like hoists, jacks, and rollers, to any prefabricated sections of the vessel that are so large that they must be lifted into place with cranes. After crane operators move the sections close to the correct position, the boilermakers fine-tune the alignment of the parts. They use levels and check plumb lines, and then secure the sections in place with wedges and turnbuckles. With cutting torches, files, and grinders, they remove irregularities and precisely adjust the fit, and finally weld and rivet the sections together. They may also attach other tubing, valves, gauges, or other parts to the vessel, and then test the container for leaks and defects.

Boilermakers are also extensively involved in shipbuilding and in repairing the hulls, bulkheads, and decks of ships. In a typical repair, boilermakers first remove damaged metal plates by drilling out rivets and cutting off rivet heads with a chipping hammer. Then they take measurements of the damaged plates or make wooden patterns of them so that new plates can be made. They install the new plates, reaming and aligning rivet holes, then fastening on the plates by driving in rivets. Sometimes similar work is done on ships' boilers, condensers, evaporators, loaders, gratings, and stacks.

Boilermaker mechanics maintain and repair boilers and other vessels. They do routine cleaning and inspections of boilers, fittings,

A fitter at a boilermaking plant welds metal sections together.

valves, tubes, controls, and other parts. When necessary, they check the vessels to identify specific weaknesses or sources of trouble. They may dismantle the units to replace worn or defective parts, using hand and power tools, gas torches, and welding equipment. Sometimes repairs require that they use metalworking machinery such as power shears and presses to cut and shape parts to specification. They strengthen joints and supports, and they put patches on weak areas of metal plates. Like fabrication and installation work, all repairs must be done in compliance with state and local safety codes.

Requirements

A high school diploma is usually required for applicants to the boilermaking trade, and it is almost always essential for advancement to supervisory positions. Although in the past many people have become boilermakers simply by working in this trade, apprenticeships are now strongly recommended.

Formal apprenticeships usually last four years. They are run by joint union-management committees. An apprentice receives on-the-job practical training while working as a helper under the supervision of an experienced boilermaker. In addition to working, trainees attend classes in the technical aspects of the trade. The subjects that apprentices study include some that are introduced in high school shop courses, such as blueprint reading, welding techniques, mechanical drawing, the physics and chemistry of various metals, and applied mathematics. While on the job, apprentices practice the knowledge they have acquired in the classroom. They develop such skills as using rigging and hoisting equipment, welding, riveting, and installing auxiliary devices and tubes onto vessels.

Mechanical aptitude and manual dexterity are important characteristics that prospective boilermakers should have. The work can be very strenuous, and stamina is needed for jobs that require continuous exertion. Before they begin work, boilermakers may need to pass a physical examination showing that they are in good enough health to do the work safely. On the job, they have to be able to work well despite noisy surroundings, odors, working at heights or in small enclosed spaces, and other discomforts and dangers.

Opportunities for experience and exploration

It may be possible to observe boilermakers or other workers who use similar skills as they work on construction projects or on other repair and maintenance jobs. For example, equipment operators lifting heavy objects with elaborate rigging or welders may sometimes be seen working at sites where large buildings are being erected. High school courses about related subjects, such as blueprint reading and metal working, can give students an idea of some of the activities of boilermakers. Perhaps with the help of shop teachers or guidance counselors, students may be able to arrange to talk with people working in the trade. More information may be obtained by contacting the local union-management committee in charge of apprenticeships for boilermakers.

Methods of entering

Public employment offices, local union offices, and employers of boilermakers are potential sources of information on apprenticeships. The number of apprenticeships is limited by unions to levels such that new workers can reasonably expect to find employment in the trade. Because of the limitation, only the best applicants are accepted, and there may be a waiting period before the apprenticeship starts.

Sometimes workers begin as helpers in repair shops and enter formal apprenticeships later. Various helper jobs are advertised in newspapers. Vocational and technical schools and sometimes high schools with metal shop courses can help their graduates locate positions. Other good approaches are to apply directly to employers and to contact the local office of the state employment service.

Advancement

Upon completing their training program, apprentices qualify as journeyman boilermakers. With experience and the right kind of leadership abilities, boilermakers may be able to advance to positions such as supervisor, gang leader, or superintendent.

In fabrication shops, layout workers and fitters who start as helpers can learn the skills they need in about two years. In time they may move up to become shop supervisors, or they may decide to become boilermakers who work on-site to assemble vessels.

Employment outlook

In the next 10 to 15 years, the number of boilermakers is expected to change very little. The trend now is to repair rather than replace boilers, so boilermaker mechanics can expect slightly better opportunities during this period.

Fewer new boilers and similar vessels built by boilermakers will be needed because relatively few new power plants and factories will be built. Furthermore, many new boilers will be smaller than they have been in the past, and thus will require less assembly work on-site. Design changes in the railroad industry and in shipbuilding will also contribute to the slow rate of growth in the boilermaker trade.

During economic downturns, boilermakers, including layout workers and fitters, may be laid off, because many industries stop expanding their operations and install very few new boilers. On the other hand, boilermaker mechanics are less affected by downturns, because they work more on maintaining and repairing existing equipment, which requires their services regardless of economic conditions.

Nonetheless, there will continue to be many job openings every year as experienced boilermakers leave their jobs for other occupations, retire, or die. Workers who have completed apprenticeships will have the best opportunities for good jobs.

Earnings

Boilermakers who work full time in the 1990s can expect earnings that average in the range of $29,000 to $35,000 per year. Earnings can vary according to the part of the country where they work, the industry that employs them, and their skill and experience. Pay rates are usually highest for boilermakers doing installation work in the construction industry and lower for those employed in manufacturing industries, although workers in construction may not be employed as steadily.

Workers who install boilers and other vessels tend to make more money than those who repair and maintain vessels. Among employees in boiler fabrication shops, layout workers generally earn more and fitters earn less. Both layout workers and fitters normally work indoors, and as a result their earnings are not limited by seasonal variations in weather.

Apprentices usually start at at least 60 percent of the experienced worker's rate, and the percentage rises during the period of the apprenticeship.

Most boilermakers are members of unions, and union contracts set their wages and benefits. The largest union is the International Brotherhood of Boilermakers, Iron Ship Builders, Blacksmiths, Forgers, and Helpers. Other boilermakers are members of the Industrial Union of Marine and Shipbuilding Workers of America; the Oil, Chemical, and Atomic Workers International Union; the United Steelworkers of America; the International Association of Machinists and Aerospace Workers; and the United Automobile, Aerospace, and Agricultural Implement Workers of America. Among the fringe benefits established under union contracts are health insurance, pension plans, and paid vacation time.

Conditions of work

The boilermaker trades tend to be more hazardous than many other occupations. Boilermakers often work with potentially dangerous tools and equipment; they must manage heavy materials; and they may climb to heights to do installation or repair work. Despite great progress in recent years in preventing accidents, the rate for boilermakers of on-the-job injuries remains higher than the average for all manufacturing industries. Employer and union safety programs and standards set by the federal government's Occupational Safety and Health Administration are helping to control dangerous conditions and reduce accidents.

The work boilermakers do often requires physical exertion and may be carried on in extremely hot, poorly ventilated, noisy, and damp places. At times it is necessary to work in cramped quarters inside boilers, vats, or tanks. At other times, the workers must handle materials and equipment several stories above ground level. Sometimes installation workers work on jobs that require them to remain away from home for considerable periods of time.

To protect against injury, boilermakers use a variety of special clothing and equipment. They may wear hardhats, safety glasses and shoes, harnesses, and respirators. Usually they work a 40-hour week, but in some jobs, deadlines mean they must work overtime.

GOE: 05.05.06; SIC: 34; SOC: 6814

◇ **SOURCES OF ADDITIONAL INFORMATION**

Industrial Union of Marine and Shipbuilding Workers of America
5101 River Road, Suite 110
Bethesda, MD 20816

International Brotherhood of Boilermakers, Iron Ship Builders, Blacksmiths, Forgers and Helpers
753 State Avenue, Suite 570
Kansas City, KS 66101

Canadian Boiler Society
3266 Douglas Street
Burlington ON L7N 1G9

◇ **RELATED ARTICLES**

Volume 1: Construction; Energy; Machining and Machinery
Volumes 2–4: Forge shop occupations; Industrial machinery mechanics; Iron and steel industry workers; Layout workers; Pipe fitters and steam fitters; Sheet-metal workers; Structural-steel workers; Welders; Welding technicians

Book editors

Definition

Book Editors acquire and prepare written material for publication in book form. Such formats include text books, reference books, and books of fiction and nonfiction (trade books). Book editors are similar to but to be distinguished from newspaper and magazine editors, not only in the types of materials they edit, but also in the time-frames in which they operate. Magazine and newspaper editors work against daily, weekly, or monthly deadlines, while book editors' deadlines are usually in terms of months or years.

Book editors operate under a variety of titles ranging from *editorial assistant* to *editor-in-chief*. Publishing houses generally agree on their use of these titles, but variations in meaning and order of importance are not uncommon.

A book editor's duties include evaluating a manuscript, accepting or rejecting it, rewriting, correcting spelling and grammar, researching and fact checking, and if necessary, returning the manuscript to the author for rework. Book editors may work directly with printers in arranging for proofs and with artists and designers in arranging for illustration matter and determining the physical specifications of the book.

History

The history of book editing is tied closely to that of the history of the book and bookmaking and the history of the printing process. The first "books" were scribed on clay tablets by Mesopotamians or written on papyrus rolls by Egyptians. The revolutionary development of the book form as it is known today began with something called the codex. Instead of a long strip of vellum or parchment (both derived from animal skins) the codex was constructed of a folded strip, which formed individual pages, that was then bound on one side. The codex enjoyed a distinct advantage over the roll in that its pages could carry writing on both sides, and it could be opened to any section of the work without the awkwardness of rolling and unrolling. It was not until about A.D. 400,

however, that the codex became dominant over the roll.

The codex remained the common book form during the Middle Ages, experiencing little change until the introduction of papermaking in the West in the 8th century. By the 15th century, paper leaves had commonly replaced those of vellum and parchment. After the fall of Rome in the 5th century A.D., monasteries became the chief places where books were produced in the West. Monks painstakingly wrote books out by hand in elaborate script. Through this period, book content was largely religious in nature.

The 15th century invention of the printing press by German goldsmith Johannes Gutenberg and of movable type in the West revolutionized the craft of bookmaking. Books could now be mass produced. What is more, it became more feasible to make changes to copy before a book was put into production. Printing had been invented hundreds of years earlier in Asia, but books did not proliferate as quickly as they did in the West, which saw millions of copies in print by 1500.

In the beginning of publishing, authors worked directly with the printer, and the printer was often the publisher and seller of the authors' work. Eventually, however, booksellers began working directly with the authors and eventually took over the role of publisher. The publisher then became the middleman between author and printer.

The publisher worked closely with the author, and sometimes acted as the editor; the word editor, in fact, derives from the Latin word *editus*, which also means publisher. Eventually specialists were hired to perform the editing function. These editors, who were also called *advisors* or *literary advisors* in the 19th century, became an integral and indispensable part of the publishing business. The editor, or sponsor as he is called in some houses, sought out the best authors, worked with them and became their advocate in the publishing house. So important did some editors become that their very presence in a publishing house could determine the quality of author that might be published there. Some author–editor collaborations have become legendary. The field has grown through the 20th century, with computers greatly speeding up the process by which editors move copy to the printer.

Nature of the work

The editorial department is generally the main core of any publishing house. (Specialized separate firms have developed that only do editorial work; their clients may be publishers that have a very limited or no editorial staff.) Procedures and terminology may vary from one type of publishing house to another, but there is some general agreement among the essentials. Publishers of trade books (books which are usually sold in book stores), text books, and reference books all have somewhat different needs for which they have developed different editorial practices. All of the different types of book editors work toward a single purpose, however: preparing the author's manuscript for publication.

The *editor* has the principal responsibility in evaluating the manuscript, which may have been commissioned by the editor or submitted without solicitation to the publisher. The editor responsible for seeing a book through to publication may hold any of several titles. The highest level editorial executive in a publishing house is usually the editor-in-chief or *editorial director*. The person holding either of these titles directs the overall operation of the editorial department, and in some cases he works directly with the firm's most important authors. An *executive editor* can also occupy the highest position in an editorial department, although he can work under the top positions, as well. The next level of editor is sometimes the *managing editor*, who keeps track of schedules and deadlines and must know where all manuscripts are at any given time. Other editors who handle copy include the *associate editors, senior editors, assistant editors, editorial assistants,* and *copy editors*. Also contributing to the final book product are the *index editors*, who are especially important in the text and reference book field.

In a trade book house, the editor, usually at the senior or associate position, works with a manuscript that he has solicited from an author or has been submitted by a known author or his agent. Editors who seek out authors to write manuscripts are also known as *acquisitions editors*. Usually the editor and the author or his agent enter into a contractual agreement that specifies what the author must produce and what he will receive in the way of compensation. After the editor receives the manuscript he must read and evaluate it to be sure that it meets the agreed upon specifications. If he finds the work acceptable he will usually write a report on it and send it on to a second editor, possibly one of the executive editors, for ap-

A book editor checks pages for any mistakes before a book is printed.

proval. Sometimes the editor has to present his report verbally to a committee, which makes the final decision on publication. If the manuscript is not acceptable as is, the editor returns it to the author with his recommendations for changes. If a work is too long or too short, the editor suggests where the author should cut or add. In a work of nonfiction, say a biography, the manuscript might also include unverifiable or unacceptable information that might have to be cut or modified.

Unsolicited manuscripts also come into the house. These arrive in huge numbers—perhaps as many as 5,000 a year in a medium-sized house. An editor may read some of these manuscripts, but more often they are read by assistant editors. A few may be sent through for approval, but most are returned to the authors with a rejection notice.

In text book and reference book houses editors commonly do more researching, revising, and rewriting than trade book editors do. The authors they solicit are often scholars, who may be brilliant but lack good writing skills. These editors are often required to be skilled in certain subjects, particularly the sciences. Editors must be sure that the subject is comprehensively covered and organized according to a pre-agreed upon outline; if there is missing information in the copy (sometimes referred to as a hole) the editor may ask the author to fill it in. Editors contract for virtually all of the material that comes into text and reference book houses. Editors who edit heavily or ask an author to revise extensively must learn to be highly diplomatic; the art of author-editor relations is a critical aspect of the editor's job.

In the course of his editing duties the book editor may need to consult with various other departments or outside sources to complete work on the book. He could be involved with the art or production people in making the final decision on design of the book and the most appropriate typefaces to use. He might also have to deal with indexers, bibliographers, and marketing people.

When the editor is satisfied with the manuscript, it goes to the copy editor, either directly or through the managing editor. The copy editor usually does the final editing of the manuscript before it goes to the typesetter. This can involve few or many processes depending on the type of manuscript. On almost any type of manuscript the copy editor is responsible for correcting errors of spelling, punctuation, grammar, and usage. Almost all publishing houses develop their own style, that is, their preferred way of spelling, punctuating, and usage. House style determines such items as which words are to be capitalized, when to italicize, how to use quotes, and when to abbreviate. Some publishers even produce extensive style manuals, although they will generally also refer to such standard publications as *A Manual of Style* published by The University of Chicago Press.

The copy editor marks up the manuscript to indicate where different kinds of typefaces are used and where charts, maps, graphs, and photos may be inserted. The copy editor may go beyond these fundamentals and also become involved in fact checking and research, especially when working on nonfiction, text, and reference books. It is important for the copy editor to discover any inconsistencies in the text; for instance, a character might have blond hair in the first chapter and auburn hair in the third chapter. When the copy editor discovers an error in fact or an inconsistency, he may query the author. Such queries are usually placed in the margin of the manuscript, but if there are many they might be typed out on a separate sheet and keyed to the manuscript.

When the copy editor is through with his work he sends it to the typesetter who sets the type and pulls galley proofs, which are returned to the copy editor. Very often the type has been set by computer and the copy editor can make changes to the proofs by computer. Queries to the author are transferred to the proofs, which are then sent back to the author for approval. In some cases the proofs first go to the editor, who checks them, modifies the copy editor's work where necessary, and then sends the proofs on. When the work is returned, the copy editor checks the author's changes, irons out any disputes, and inputs the changes. Another set of proofs are pulled, and the copy editor makes final adjustments and okays the proofs for printing. The copy editor may also check the index, as well as captions and the placement of illustrations.

The editor of a book might, as he reviews the manuscript, make some of the kinds of changes usually left to the copy editor, and he might add his own queries, as well. Sometimes there is little editing to do, as in a book of poetry; once it has been approved for publication, it usually needs only to be marked up for the printer. In a large publishing house the job of marking up copy is sometimes separated from the copy editor's duties and given to a *production editor*, who then sees the manuscript through the production process. In a very small house one editor might do the work of all of the editors described here. There can also be separate *style editors* (also called *line editors*), *fact checkers*, and *proofreaders*. An assistant editor could be assigned to do many of the kinds of jobs handled by the senior or associate editors, although their work is more closely supervised. Editorial assistants provide support for the other editors and may be required to edit less important works, proofread, type inserts, keep records, and handle some administrative duties.

Requirements

A college degree is almost certainly a requirement for entry into the field of book editing. For general editing, a degree in English or journalism is particularly valuable, although most degrees in the liberal arts are acceptable. Degrees in other fields, such as the biological and physical sciences, psychology, mathematics, or applied arts can be useful in publishing houses that produce books related to those fields. Text book and reference book houses in particular seek out editors with strengths in certain subject areas. Whatever the type of degree, the aspiring book editor needs to place considerable emphasis on writing and communications courses in his educational program. Editors should be intimately familiar with the English language and English usage.

The beginning book editor, and especially the copy editor, should have a sharp eye for detail and a compulsion for accuracy. Intellectual curiosity, self-motivation, and a respect for deadlines are important characteristics for editors to have. Book editors should develop sharp research skills, especially for their early careers. Good, clear handwriting and neat work are important assets to an applicant. Typing skills have long been essential for editors, and today computer skills are equally important since much editing is done today on-line. Since a book editing career could begin with a job typing manuscripts or reading proof, a familiarity with proofreader's marks can be helpful in finding a first job.

It goes without saying that a person seeking a career in book editing is someone who not only loves to read, but loves books for their own sake, as well. People who are not avid readers are probably not going to go far as book editors. The craft and history of bookmaking itself is also something in which a young book editor should be interested. A keen interest in any subject, be it a sport, a hobby, or an avocation can lead one into special areas of book publishing.

Opportunities for experience and exploration

There are a number of ways that a high school student can go about preparing for a career in book editing. Book publishers do look for extracurricular experiences in the background of entry-level applicants. Working on the school newspaper, the yearbook, the literary magazine, or any other of the school's publications can be very helpful. Any experience gained this way, whether actually writing or editing or in some other capacity will be of value, even if done for no pay. Many publishers now offer unpaid internship programs, which allow students to work for a specified length of time in the editorial department just to gain experience. Any writing or editing experience will be helpful, however. Even jobs in an advertising agency or the communications department of a large firm can provide useful experience.

Another way of obtaining insight into book publishing is through interviews. Book editors are often happy to provide interviews to eager students, provided you are respectful of their busy schedules. Newspaper and magazine editors can also provide useful information. Schools often hold career workshops in which professionals describe their jobs; students who aspire to book editing should request that a book editor be invited to be one of the speakers.

Students should also read all they can about the craft of editing. The school and local

public library are good places to begin checking for such reading materials. Some books that cover editing practices or are otherwise useful to editors include *Opportunities in Book Publishing* by John Tebbel and three books sometimes sold as a set: *Elements of Style* by William Strunk, Jr. and E.B. White, *Elements of Editing* by Arthur Plotnik, and *Elements of Grammar* by Margaret Schertzer.

Methods of entering

Any writing or editing background will provide valuable experience for entering into book editing. The publisher will expect the applicant to have at least a bachelor's degree, a carefully crafted resume detailing educational and work background, and samples of the prospective editor's work. The samples can consist of clippings from the school newspaper, copies of tear sheets from a yearbook or from work done during an internship, and exceptional papers from editing or journalism courses. Bylined (signed) articles are, of course, more impressive. In many cases the applicant will have to take a copyediting test to get a book editing job.

Entry-level positions in book editing are quite various, depending on the publisher, his policies, and the needs of the moment. The prospective editor may begin his career as an editorial assistant, a copy editor, a production editor, a proofreader, a fact checker, or a researcher. Competition for editorial jobs is keen, however, and an applicant may be well advised to accept a job as a typist or a clerk in the editorial department just to get a foothold in the industry.

To find openings in book editing, the college placement office is a good place to start. The classified section of the newspaper should also be checked. Young graduates can compile a list of book publishers by checking the most recent edition of *Literary Market Place* and send out resumes with cover letters to the heads of editorial departments. Applicants who have had internships or part-time jobs with publishers will have a definite advantage in applying to those same publishers. Most book publishers are located in or near large cities, so persons in rural areas would most likely have to relocate to get into book editing.

In a large publishing house beginners usually work at a single job, such as proofreading or researching, which they learn very well before advancing to another position. In a small firm, the beginner is likely to handle a variety of duties as an editorial assistant, and would probably break into editing sooner than his counterpart in a large firm. Some of the larger publishers have formal training programs, but in most cases the neophyte will learn through on-the-job training.

Advancement

The positions of editorial assistant or copy editor are the most likely entry-level jumping off points for promotion in the editorial department. The next step up is usually to assistant editor, which would entail more full scale editing duties. Assistant editors are generally promoted to associate or, possibly, senior editor. In some houses associates are higher than seniors and in others it is the reverse. At the associate or senior level, editors become responsible for taking a book or major article from the commissioning stage through production. Progression to this stage of editing usually takes several years or longer depending on the ability of the editor and the size and policies of the publishing house. Above the associate and senior levels are the executive editorial positions, including the managing editor, executive editor, general editor, editor-in-chief, and editorial director. Except for managing editor, any of the executive positions can also carry the title of vice president. Occasionally, an editor-in-chief or editorial director becomes president of the company.

Promotions in editorial departments can be slow, and many editors get impatient and frustrated waiting for their opportunity to advance. Editors often find they can move ahead more quickly by changing companies and taking a more advanced position. Others, after acquiring the necessary experience, become freelance editors.

Employment outlook

The book publishing industry has been expanding steadily, but the downturn in the economy in the early 1990s caused many companies to restructure and trim personnel. As a result competition for editorial jobs, which has always been great, will be even greater during the 1990s. The long-range outlook, however, is good, with the industry expected to continue to expand and the number of editorial jobs increase to the end of the century, although at a slower rate than in the 1980s. Competition will continue to be great, nevertheless, because of the large numbers of people who are attracted to the book publishing field. The best opportu-

nities will probably lie with technical book publishers, and editors with technical and scientific specialties will have a definite advantage.

Earnings

Book editing, like much of the editorial field, is rather low paying, especially at the beginning positions. Entry-level jobs, such as editorial assistant, range from $16,400 to $21,000 in the early 1990s. Editors in more advanced positions earn from $22,000 to $39,000 annually. The annual salary for supervisory editors ranges from $25,300 to $42,500. The average annual salary for book editors employed by the federal government is $35,000. It is quite common for book editors to supplement their salaries by doing freelance work.

Conditions of work

Working conditions vary with the type of publishing house, but suffice it to say that there is one common element in book editing, as there is in all types of editing, and that is pressure. Although deadlines for book editors are much farther apart than for newspaper or magazine editors, the pressures of the job are nevertheless great. Publishers invest huge amounts of money in books, and the editorial and mechanical work must be done on time or the publisher loses money. Anyone entering the book editing profession must be able to work under pressure and produce work on deadline.

Regular office hours for publishing companies range from 35 to 40 hours a week. For most editors, however, those hours have little significance, especially when deadlines near and work has fallen behind. Dedicated editors will work as long as necessary to get the job done, and it is not uncommon for them to work on weekends. Editors, especially beginning editors, must be able to take criticism; a managing or senior editor may tear a younger editor's work apart, but that is how the business is learned.

The general environment of a publishing house also varies with the size and type of publisher. Generally speaking the offices of a book publisher will not be as crowded and noisy as those of a newspaper. The offices of text or reference book editors, in fact may be exceptionally quiet. Most editors, even beginning ones, will have an office or cubicle to work in. In today's modern publishing house editors are as likely to have a computer at their disposal as a typewriter. Publishers usually offer employee benefits that are about average for U.S. industries. There are other benefits, however. Most editors enjoy working with people who like books and have backgrounds similar to their own; editors work with ideas and the milieu of an editorial department is generally intellectual and stimulating. Book editors sometimes have the opportunity to work with noted authors and they sometimes interview celebrities. Some book editors have the opportunity to travel—to attend meetings and conferences, to meet with authors, or to do research.

GOE: 01.01.01; SIC: 2731; SOC: 3312

Book Publishers Professional Association
c/o Little Brown and Company
146 Davenport Road
Toronto, Ontario, Canada M5R 1J2

Association of American Publishers
220 East 23rd Street
New York, NY 10010

National Association of Independent Publishers
2299 Riverside Drive, Box 850
Moore Haven, FL 33471

◇ **SOURCES OF ADDITIONAL INFORMATION**

Literary Market Place, published annually by R. R. Bowker, lists the names of publishing companies in the United States and Canada as well as their specialties and the names of their key personnel. The periodical *Publishers Weekly* includes news about editors and writers and has a classified section that lists openings for editors and writers.

American Book Producers Association
160 Fifth Avenue
New York, NY 10010

◇ **RELATED ARTICLES**

Volume 1: Book Publishing
Volumes 2–4: Film editors; Indexers; Magazine editors; Newspaper editors; Screenwriters; Writers

---

Bookkeeping and accounting clerks

Definition

Bookkeeping and accounting clerks are the financial record keepers of government, businesses, and other organizations. They compute, classify, record, and verify numerical data in order to develop and maintain accurate financial records.

History

The history of bookkeeping has developed along with the growth of business and indus-

trial enterprise. The first known records of bookkeeping date back to about 3000 B.C., from the people of the Middle East and the Egyptians. These people employed a system of numbers to keep a record of merchants' transactions and of the grain and farm products that were distributed from storage warehouses. The growth of selling and trading activities brought about the necessity of bookkeeping systems.

Sometime after the start of the 13th century the decimal numeration system came into use throughout Europe, simplifying bookkeeping record systems. The merchants of Venice—one of the busiest trading centers in the world at that time—are credited with the invention of

BOOKKEEPING AND ACCOUNTING CLERKS

A bookkeeper shows a questionable entry on a computer-generated ledger to her supervisor. Bookkeepers must be able to locate any errors and correct them.

the double entry bookkeeping method that is so widely used today.

An industrial United States, which has been expanding in size and growing in its complexity throughout most of its history, has continued to seek simplified modifications and quicker methods in bookkeeping procedures. Through technological developments, such as bookkeeping machines, computers, and electronic data-processing equipment, many improvements have been introduced to the field since World War II.

Nature of the work

Bookkeeping workers are employed in keeping systematic records and up-to-date accounts of financial transactions for businesses, institutions, industries, charities, and other organizations. The bookkeeping records of a firm or business are a vital part of its operational procedures. These records reflect the assets and the liabilities, as well as the profits and losses, in a business's operation.

Bookkeeping clerks may record these business transactions daily on computer databases, so clerks often work on computers inputting information. (Accounting records are decreasingly posted directly onto ledger sheets, in journals, or on other types of written accounting forms.) Periodically, accountants may prepare summary statements of the financial transactions of funds received and those paid out. Management relies heavily on these bookkeeping records for information because it bases many important decisions on what these records show about the organization's overall performance. The records are also necessary in

making income tax reports and quarterly reports for stockholders.

Many bookkeeping workers are either employed in general bookkeeping jobs or as *accounting clerks* or as *account information clerks*. Places of employment may be in retail and wholesale businesses, manufacturing firms of all sizes, hospitals, schools, charities, and other types of institutional agencies. Many clerks are classified as *financial institution bookkeeping and accounting clerks, insurance firm bookkeeping and accounting clerks, hotel bookkeeping and accounting clerks*, and *railroad bookkeeping and accounting clerks*.

General bookkeepers and *general-ledger bookkeepers* are usually employed in smaller business operations. This type of worker may perform all the analysis, maintain the financial records, and complete any other tasks that are involved in keeping a full set of bookkeeping records. A general bookkeeper usually performs most of the work by hand with the aid of such office equipment as typewriters, adding machines, and calculators. These employees may have other general duties in an office such as mailing statements, answering telephone calls, and filing materials. *Audit clerks* verify figures and sometimes are responsible for sending them on to an *audit clerk supervisor*.

In large business operations, an accountant may supervise a department of bookkeeping workers and bookkeeping machine operators. In these situations employees usually perform specialized tasks. *Billing and rate clerks* and *fixed capital clerks* may be responsible for posting items in accounts payable or receivable ledgers, making out bills and invoices, or verifying the company's rates for certain products and services. *Account information clerks* are responsible for preparing reports, compiling payroll lists and deductions, writing company checks, and computing federal tax reports or personnel profit shares. Large companies may employ workers to systematize, record, and compute many other types of information as well.

Accounting clerks usually perform many of their work functions by hand; however, they generally use adding machines or calculators for computational work. Accountants may be responsible for setting up the bookkeeping system to be used in a business organization and for interpreting facts disclosed in bookkeeping. These workers often perform both accounting and bookkeeping tasks.

In large business organizations, bookkeepers and accountants may be classified by grades, such as Bookkeeper I or II. The job classification determines the duties the worker will perform.

Requirements

Education is an important asset to the individual seeking a position as a bookkeeping worker. Employers require a high school diploma and give preference to those who have included in their schooling business subjects such as business math, business machine operations, typing, computer training, and bookkeeping. Some employers seek those persons who have completed a junior college curriculum or those who have attended a post–high school business training program. In many instances, employers offer on-the-job training in machine operations and for various types of entry-level positions. In some areas, school work-study programs are available in which schools, in cooperation with business, are able to offer part-time, practical on-the-job training in combination with academic study. These programs often help students obtain more immediate employment in similar types of work after graduation. Individuals may often have the opportunity to receive training through evening courses offered by business schools.

A major criticism made by business executives in recent years has been the lack of employee skills and training with regard to using correct grammar, spelling, and punctuation on the job. Individuals interested in bookkeeping and accounting work should pay particular attention to their academic course work in high school, placing a heavy emphasis on all aspects of English and business mathematics.

Aptitudes necessary to successful job performance in this profession include a degree of mechanical ability (for operating business machines), strong powers of concentration, and mathematical ability.

Bookkeeping workers need to have an even temperament, congenial disposition, and the ability to work well with others. These individuals should find systematic, neat, and orderly work appealing and they should enjoy working on detailed tasks. Accuracy and legible handwriting are necessities.

In general, relatively little walking or physical movement is required other than the use of the hands, so people with some types of physical disabilities can be employed in these positions.

Special requirements

There are no special requirements for these positions in the way of mandatory certification or licensing. Many of these workers belong to unions. Larger unions include the Office and Professional Employees International Union; the International Union of Electronic, Electrical, Salaried Machine, and Furniture Workers; and the American Federation of State, County, and Municipal Employees. Depending on their place of business, the clerk may also be represented by the same union as the other manufacturing employees there.

Opportunities for experience and exploration

Individuals who are interested in bookkeeping work may gain experience through participating in high school work-study programs or by obtaining part-time or summer work in beginning bookkeeping jobs or in related office work.

Students can also volunteer to be bookkeepers for student groups and clubs. Most clubs have some type of income or cash flow, so a bookkeeper is required to maintain the financial records. This is an excellent way to get experience while still in school.

To find out what bookkeeping workers generally do, students can talk with individuals employed in this type of work or with high school guidance counselors. They might also visit schools that offer business training courses.

Methods of entering

Interested applicants may locate job opportunities by applying directly to firms they know have openings, or to those for whom they would like to work when positions open in the future. Jobs may also be located through reading newspaper classified advertisements.

Some high schools have job placement services or contacts with business firms that are interested in interviewing their graduates, especially those applicants who have followed a business curriculum. Business schools and junior colleges will generally assist their graduates in locating employment. Other sources of aid can be found through state employment agencies or through private employment bureaus.

Advancement

Industrious and well trained bookkeeping workers may find many promotional opportunities in this field. Bookkeeping workers generally begin their employment in more routine tasks such as the simple recording of transactions by hand or machine. With experience, they may advance to more complex assignments for example, training on the use of the computer, and assume a greater responsibility for the total work to be completed.

Beginning workers may start as bookkeeping clerks, typists, machine operators, cashiers, or sometimes as office assistants performing general office duties. Advancement may be to positions as office or division manager, department head, accountant, or auditor, or from Bookkeeper II to Bookkeeper I, when job positions are graded.

The extremely high turnover rate in these occupations increases the chances for promotion. As in other occupations, however, the number and kinds of opportunities will also depend on the place of employment and the ability, training, experience, and initiative of the employee.

Employment outlook

In the 1990s, more than 2.2 million people worked in bookkeeping jobs. However, a decline is expected in the employment of bookkeeping and accounting clerks through the year 2005. While the economy will grow and the demand for accounting services will increase, automation of office functions will also grow and improve overall productivity. Virtually all new positions for bookkeeping and accounting clerks will be created in small, rapidly growing organizations. Excellent computer skills will be important for the candidate looking for work. Large organizations are likely to continue to consolidate departments to eliminate duplicate work functions, reducing demand for workers. Despite lack of growth, job openings will be numerous because of the number of people already working in the field. The turnover rate in these occupations is high, and it is expected that many persons will leave the field when they retire or move on to other fields.

Job opportunities in the future will likely be good for bookkeepers who are trained and capable of keeping complete sets of books for a business, but the bulk of the jobs are apt to be for bookkeeping and accounting clerks and others who will perform routine work assignments. With more and more companies paring back their work force, opportunities for temporary work should continue to grow.

Earnings

In the 1990s beginning accounting clerks in private business make an average of $14,000 a year. Experienced bookkeepers average $20,700. The average starting salary for accounting clerks in government jobs is $15,160; experienced workers earn an average of $19,496 a year. Most full-time bookkeepers and accounting clerks earn between $13,440 and $21,240 a year.

Conditions of work

The majority of office workers, including bookkeeping workers, usually work a 40-hour week, although some employees in the Northeast may work a 35- to 37-hour week. These employees usually receive six to eight paid holidays yearly and in most places of employment one week paid vacation after six to twelve months of service. Paid vacations may increase to four weeks or more, depending on length of service and place of employment. Fringe benefits may include hospitalization and life insurance, sick leave, and retirement plans.

Bookkeeping and accounting clerks usually work in pleasant surroundings that are well ventilated, lighted, and provided with comfortable furnishings. While the work pace is usually steady, it can also be repetitive, especially in large companies where the employee is often assigned only one or two specialized job duties.

Physically, the work can produce eyestrain and nervousness. Bookkeepers usually work with other people and sometimes under close supervision. Bookkeeping and accounting positions can seem confining to some people who need more variety and stimulation in their work. In addition, the constant attention to detail and the accuracy that these jobs require can place considerable responsibility on the worker.

GOE: 07.02.01; SIC: Any industry; SOC: 4712

◇ **SOURCES OF ADDITIONAL INFORMATION**

American Institute of Certified Public Accountants
1211 Avenue of the Americas
New York, NY 10036

National Society of Public Accountants
1010 North Fairfax Street
Alexandria, VA 22314

National Association of Accountants
10 Parson Drive
Montvale, NJ 07645

Canadian Institute of Accredited Public Accountants
670 Avenue Hyde Park
Dorval PQ H9P 1Z6

◇ **RELATED ARTICLES**

Volume 1: Accounting; Banking and Financial Services; Insurance
Volumes 2–4: Accountants and auditors; Actuaries; Billing clerks; Collection workers; Cost estimators; Filing clerks; Financial institution clerks and related workers; Financial institution tellers; General office clerks; Insurance claims representatives; Insurance policy processing occupations; Mathematicians; Shipping and receiving clerks; Statistical clerks; Statisticians; Tax preparers

Border patrol officers

Definition

Border patrol officers patrol more than 6,000 miles of border between the United States and Canada and between the United States and Mexico, as well as the coastal areas of the Gulf of Mexico and Florida. It is their duty to enforce laws regulating the entry of aliens and products into the United States They are employed by the Immigration and Naturalization Service (INS) of the U.S. Justice Department.

History

As long as civilizations have created borders for their countries, people have guarded those borders and fought over them. All over the world societies have created rules and regulations for entry into their communities. Some welcomed strangers from other lands, but other societies only allowed foreigners to live among them briefly before requiring them to leave. The borders between the United States and its northern and southern neighbors have been peacefully maintained almost continuously since the founding of the countries.

However, federal immigration laws make it necessary for border patrol officers to protect the citizens of the United States by patrolling the borders. Their job is to prevent illegal entry at all of the borders, and to arrest or deport those who attempt to enter illegally. In recent years an increase in narcotics trafficking has made the job of the border patrol officer even more challenging. In addition to preventing the entry of aliens, border patrol officers also prevent the entry of illegal substances.

Nature of the work

Border patrol officers are federal law enforcement officers. The laws that they are hired to enforce deal with immigration and customs. United States immigration law states that people wishing to enter the United States must apply to the government for permission to do so. Those who want to work, study, or vacation in the United States must have appropriate visas. Those who want to move here and stay must apply for citizenship. Customs laws regulate materials, crops, and goods entering the United States To ensure that foreigners follow these rules, border patrol officers are stationed at every border entry point of the United States.

Members of the border patrol cover the border on foot, on horseback, in cars or jeeps, in motor boats, and in airplanes. They track people near the borders to detect those who attempt to enter the country illegally. They may question people who live or work near the border to help identify illegal aliens. When border patrol officers find violators of United States

BORDER PATROL OFFICERS

Undocumented aliens working as field hands are arrested and deported by border patrol officers.

law they are authorized to apprehend and detain the violators. They may deport illegal aliens or arrest anyone seen to be assisting foreigners to enter the country illegally.

Officers work with local and state law enforcement agencies in discharging their duties. Although the uniformed patrol is directed from Washington, D.C., the patrol must have a good working relationship with officials in all of the border states. These local and state agencies can be very helpful to border patrol officers. They are aware of peculiarities of the terrain as well as of the operating procedures of potential aliens or drug smugglers.

Border patrol officers work 24 hours a day along the borders with Mexico and Canada. During the night they may use night vision goggles to spot trespassers. In rugged areas that are difficult to patrol on foot or on horseback, helicopters are used for greater coverage. At regular border crossing points, officers check all incoming vehicles for people or materials hidden in car trunks or truck compartments.

The prevention of drug smuggling has become a major part of the border patrol officer's work. The increase in drug traffic from Central and South America has led to increased efforts by the INS to control the border with Mexico. Drug-sniffing dogs have been added to the patrol's arsenal. Work for these officers has become more dangerous in recent years, and all border patrol officers are specially trained in the use of firearms.

Some employees of the INS may specialize in areas of immigration or customs. *Immigration inspectors* enforce laws pertaining to border crossing. They work at airports, seaports, and border crossing points, and may question people arriving in the United States by boarding boats, trains, or airplanes. They arrest violators of entry or immigration laws.

Deportation officers are responsible for the deportation of aliens found to have violated U.S. immigration law.

Customs officers work to prevent the import of illegal merchandise. Most of their work is involved with illegal narcotics. Customs officers search cargo of ships and airplanes; baggage in cars, trucks, trains, or buses; and mail. They work with travelers as well as with the crews of ships or airplanes. If they discover evidence of drug smuggling or other customs violations, they are responsible for apprehending the offenders.

Occasionally border patrol officers may also be called upon to help local law enforcement groups in their work. This may involve searching for lost hikers or travelers in rugged wilderness areas of the northern or southern United States.

Requirements

A high school diploma is required for anyone wishing to train as a border patrol officer. Knowledge of Spanish is also helpful, and it is taught as part of the 16-week training course. Like other federal law enforcement officers, border patrol officers are trained at the Federal Law Enforcement Training Center in Glynn County, Georgia. The course teaches the basics of the immigration laws they will uphold. They undergo physical training and instruction in law enforcement and the safe use of firearms. The Spanish studies are unique to this branch of law enforcement. After graduation from training, all border patrol officers are initially stationed along the border with Mexico.

Test scores on an entrance exam admit potential patrol officers to the training program. Post–high school education is helpful, and college majors in criminal justice, criminology, law enforcement, or police science are recommended. Good character references are important, and civil service tests are also sometimes required.

Opportunities for experience and exploration

Because of the nature of border patrol work, experience is not possible for students before entering the field. Courses in immigration law, Spanish, and criminal justice are helpful. Also, since the job can be very demanding physically, stamina and strength may be built up through a program of exercise.

School and local libraries may have books with information on criminal justice and law enforcement. Two sources are *Border Patrol Agent* by Eve P. Steinberg, and *Conflict at the Border: True Tales of a U.S. Customs Border Officer* by Charles S. Park. The National Border Patrol Council, which is an association of INS employees, publishes a monthly newsletter called *The Educator*. Copies may be obtained by contacting the council, whose address is listed at the end of this article.

Methods of entering

As discussed above, border patrol officers begin their careers with a 16-week training course. They can only be accepted into the course with a high school diploma or its equivalent and after passing an entrance exam.

Once they complete the course, they will be stationed along the Mexican border. Border patrol officers take orders from their sector chiefs. With experience and training, border patrol officers can advance to other positions. They may become immigration inspectors or examiners, deportation officers, or special agents.

Advancement

Some border patrol officers may concentrate on the prevention of drug smuggling. They may advance to become plain-clothes investigators who spend months or even years cracking a smuggling ring. They may lead criminal investigations into an alien's background, especially if there is suspicion of drug involvement. Others may prefer the immigration area, and work checking passports and visas at border crossings.

With experience, some border patrol officers leave the front lines and work in the service areas of the INS. They may interview people who wish to become naturalized citizens, or administer examinations or interviews. Many of the higher echelon jobs for border patrol officers require fluency in Spanish. Advancement within the border patrol comes with satisfactory work. To rise to the supervisory positions, however, border patrol officers must be able to work competitively. These positions are earned based on the agency's needs as well as on merit.

Employment outlook

Employment for border patrol officers is expected to increase faster than average through the year 2005. There has been growing public support of drug prevention activities, including the prevention of drug smuggling. The public support of the war on drugs has enabled the INS to continue to increase its surveillance of U.S. borders. This means that even though many government workers are being cut, border patrol officers are less likely to lose their jobs. Economic problems in Latin America have led some people to participate in drug-smuggling activities, and have led others to try to cross the U.S. border illegally. Border patrol officers will continue to prevent these activities.

Earnings

A beginning border patrol officer earns around $17,000 per year. With more experience and good job performance, the salary increases to between $22,000 and $28,000 per year. Border patrol officers earn extra money for working overtime. The top 10 percent of all inspectors and compliance officers earn more than $44,000 annually.

The federal government is a good employer, and benefits packages include insurance and retirement plans, as well as paid vacations and holidays.

Conditions of work

The work of a border patrol officer can be tiring and stressful. The hours are irregular, since officers must cover the borders continuously. Most border patrol officers spend more time outdoors in jeeps, cars, helicopters, or on horseback, than they do in offices. The work is dangerous, and many decisions must be made quickly.

Despite the difficulty of the job, it can be very rewarding. Border patrol officers perform a necessary function, and know they are contributing to the health of their society.

GOE: 04.02.03; SIC: 9221; SOC: 5132

◇ **SOURCES OF ADDITIONAL INFORMATION**

Immigration and Naturalization Service
425 I Street, NW
Washington, DC 20536

National Border Patrol Council
PO Box 2102
Laredo, TX 78041

◇ **Related Articles**

Volume 1: Civil Service; Foreign Service; Military Services
Volumes 2–4: Correction officers; Customs officials; Deputy U.S. marshals; Detectives; FBI agents; Foreign service officers; Intelligence officers; Police officers; Security consultants; Security guards

Brake operators, brakers

Definition

Brake operators are a group of railroad workers who do much more than operate brakes. Working at the direction of train conductors, they do the physical work involved in adding cars onto trains and removing them from trains at stations and in rail yards. They perform various other tasks, both in rail yards and on trains on the road. Depending on their activities, they may be designated *brakers, brake couplers, yard couplers,* or *switch tenders.*

History

There have been brake operators working on railroads since the second quarter of the 19th century. Before the invention of air brakes by George Westinghouse in the 1860s, brakes had to be set by hand on each car of trains. Workers who operated brakes also served as flaggers, and they sometimes had to walk ahead of trains that were behind schedule to see that no other trains came upon them unexpectedly.

In the latter part of the 19th century, various inventions made the job of the brake operator much easier and less dangerous. In the

20th century, however, new technology has so altered the brake operator's work that automation and mechanization now threaten the existence of many jobs in this field.

Nature of the work

Brake operators perform a variety of important tasks, many of them related to adding and removing cars at train stations and in railroad yards.

At stations and in yards, they may function as flaggers, operating flags and lights to tell train engineers to start and stop and signaling other warnings that ensure the safety of the train. As switch tenders, they throw the track switches in yards that turn trains from one track to another. Brake operators may also serve on train crews as road freight brake couplers, checking couplings and airhoses and setting and releasing brakes.

At other times brake operators act as inspectors. They may check, for example, to see that air brake equipment is working as it should and that tools and other items are stored in their proper places. They may inspect trains while they are in motion or while they are stopped, looking for any indication of trouble, from sticking brakes to overheated bearings. They make minor adjustments when necessary and report any need for major repairs.

As passenger-train brakers, brake operators help passengers on and off trains and open and close outside doors. They assist conductors in collecting tickets and looking after the general comfort of passengers. Other responsibilities in this job can include inspecting and operating the air-conditioning, heating, and lighting equipment.

As yard switch tenders, or yard couplers, brake operators work in rail yards performing such jobs as switching, stopping, and distributing cars on proper tracks for the purpose of loading or unloading. They also help assemble and disassemble trains before and after runs.

Requirements

Most railroad companies prefer to hire applicants who have completed high school. In addition, brake operators need to have good hearing and eyesight. They cannot be color blind because they need to distinguish the different colors of signals. Brake operators need to have physical stamina, manual dexterity, and good hand-eye coordination. Employers often require applicants to pass a physical examination and tests that screen for drug use.

Opportunities for experience and exploration

High school students may learn more about this kind of work by talking to experienced brake operators and by visiting a railroad yard. Because most brake operators are members of the United Transportation Union, a good first step may be to contact the local office of this union. Some high schools and vocational schools offer general courses in railroad shop crafts and maintenance work.

Methods of entering

Prospective brake operators may apply for work at local railroad company offices or at the local branch of the United Transportation Union. Once accepted, new employees are trained on the job by experienced workers. Before going on the road, beginning brake oper-

This switch tender works inside the railroad yard, signaling traffic toward the assigned tracks.

ators often must pass a written examination on the rules of railroad operation and on the specific procedures that apply to their particular job. After meeting their employer's examination requirements and demonstrating practical ability on trial trips, the names of newly qualified workers are placed on a list called the "extra board." The people whose names have been on the extra board the longest are subject to being called for work assignments when regular workers are absent for vacations, illness, or other reasons. Sometimes brake operators remain on the extra board for several years before they have enough seniority to obtain their first permanent assignment.

Advancement

When a brake operator advances, it is usually to the position of conductor. Two important factors, however, enter into any advancement in this field. First is the matter of seniority: sometimes railroad workers must spend ten years as brake operators before they have the opportunity to advance. Second, railroad workers seeking to become conductors must take oral and written examinations covering such topics as timetables, signals, brake systems, and general operating procedures. While they are waiting for openings as conductors to become available, brake operators in freight service often try to transfer to passenger service. This work is considered more desirable because it is less strenuous and often involves shorter hours. Some brakers may become baggage handlers rather than conductors.

Employment outlook

Employment throughout the railroad transportation field is declining, and brake operators are among the rail workers most affected by this trend. The decline in employment of all rail workers is related to a general decrease in demand for rail services, as other kinds of freight and passenger transportation become cheaper in comparison. Contributing specifically to the decline in the number of brake operators is the increased use of computers to keep track of and direct cars in rail yards. In addition, computer-assisted devices on trains now can take over some of the jobs formerly done by brake operators, such as checking for certain malfunctions. As a consequence, the traditional rules about the number of crew members who must be on trains have been changed, and the number has been reduced from five to two or three crew members per train. These changes mean that employment opportunities for brake operators will continue to be quite limited in future years.

As the number of brake operators declines because of automation, it is expected that many workers already in the field will be gradually shifted to other railroad jobs that may require further training and possibly qualifying examinations.

Earnings

Earnings of brake operators are determined by contracts between company management and the union. Working full-time, they make on average at least $46,000 per year in freight service and $36,000 in yard service. However, the pay varies widely according to the particular job the brake operators perform, the miles traveled or hours worked, and other factors. For example,

pay differentials are given for work on long-haul trains and for work in mountainous country. Extra pay is also earned for runs of more than 118 miles on freight trains and more than 150 miles on passenger trains. Time-and-a-half pay is customary for overtime hours.

Conditions of work

Brake operators with seniority usually have a 40-hour workweek and work the most regular hours. The less desirable hours—at night, on weekends, and on holidays—are usually worked by people with less seniority. Because freight trains are usually not run on a schedule, brake operators who work on freight runs may be called on short notice and at odd hours. They may need to be away from home several nights a week.

Brake operators must be outside in all kinds of weather. The job can be physically demanding, especially for workers on trains that stop frequently to add on and drop off cars. Workers are constantly climbing up and down and getting off moving cars. The danger of accidents is always present, particularly for brake operators who work on freights and in busy rail yards where activity is concentrated.

GOE: 05.12.05, 09.01.04; SIC: 4011; SOC: 8233

◇ **SOURCE OF ADDITIONAL INFORMATION**

United Transportation Union
14600 Detroit Avenue
Lakewood, OH 44107-4250

◇ **RELATED ARTICLES**

Volume 1: Transportation
Volume 2–4: Locomotive engineers; Public transportation operators; Signal mechanics

Bricklayers and stonemasons

Definition

Bricklayers are skilled workers who construct and repair walls, partitions, floors, arches, fireplaces, chimneys, and other structures from brick, concrete block, gypsum block, and precast panels made of terra-cotta, structural tile, and other masonry materials. *Stonemasons* build stone walls, floors, piers, and other structures, and they set the decorative stone exteriors of structures such as churches, hotels, and public buildings.

History

Sun-baked clay bricks were used in constructing buildings more than 6,000 years ago in Mesopotamia. Along with brick, stone was used in ancient Egypt in many structures. The Romans introduced masonry construction to the rest of Europe and made innovations in bricklaying, including the use of mortar and different types of bonds, or patterns. As the Roman Empire declined, so did the art of bricklaying. During the period of cathedral building in Europe, from about the 10th century to the 17th century, stonemasons formed guilds in various cities and towns. These guilds functioned much as today's unions do. They had the same categories of workers: apprentices, journeymen, and masters. Not until the great fire of London in 1666 did the English start to use brick again in building. The Chinese also were expert in bricklaying and stonemasonry, the best example of their work being the Great Wall of China. High in the Andes of South America, Incan stoneworkers had perfected their art by the 12th century.

Although some brick houses made with imported bricks were built in Florida by the Spaniards, the first bricks made by Europeans in North America were manufactured in Virginia in 1612. These were handmade from clay, just as in ancient times. Machines were not used in the manufacturing of bricks until the mid-18th century. Changes in the content of bricks came shortly afterwards. Concrete and cinder blocks were developed, as was structural clay tile. The patent for a sand brick, a combination of sand and hydrated lime, was granted about this time too.

Today, attractive kinds of brick called face brick can be used where appearance is impor-tant, helping to popularize brick in modern construction. Various colors of brick can be made by using iron oxides, iron sulfides, and other materials. By varying the bond and the hue of brick, many interesting artistic effects can be achieved.

Stone is a very durable, adaptable material for building purposes, although it may be much more difficult to cut and transport than alternative materials. Today it remains popular, particularly as a way to enhance the appearance of important structures such as hotels, public buildings, and churches. In modern construction, a thin covering of stone veneer about two inches thick is applied in various patterns to exterior surfaces of buildings. The veneer is anchored and supported on a steel frame.

Nature of the work

When bricklayers or stonemasons begin work on a job, they usually start by examining a blueprint or drawing to determine the designer's specifications. Then they measure the work area to fix reference points and guidelines in accordance with the blueprint.

If they are building a wall, bricklayers traditionally start with the corners or leads, which must be precisely established if the finished structure is to be sound and straight. The corners may be established by more experienced bricklayers, with the task of filling in between the corners left to less experienced workers. Corner posts, or masonry guides, may be used to define the line of the wall, speeding the building process. A first dry course may be put down without mortar so that the alignment and positioning of the brick can be checked.

In laying brick, bricklayers use a metal trowel to spread a bed or layer of soft mortar on a prepared base. Then they set the brick into the mortar, tapping and working each brick into the correct position. Excess mortar is cut off, and the mortar joints are smoothed with special tools that give a neat, uniform look to the wall. In walls, each layer of brick, or course, is set so the that vertical joints do not line up one on top of another, but instead form a pleasing, regular pattern. The work must be continually checked for horizontal and vertical straightness with mason's levels, gauge strips, plumb lines, and other equipment. Sometimes it is necessary to cut and fit brick to size using

219

While the work of a bricklayer may look easy, it takes considerable skill to place bricks evenly on mortar.

a power saw or hammer and chisel. Around doors and windows, bricklayers generally use extra steel supports in the wall.

Bricklayers must know how to mix mortar, which is made of cement, sand, and water, and to spread it so that the joints throughout the structure will be evenly spaced, with a neat appearance. They may have helpers who mix the mortar, as well as move materials and scaffolding around the work site as needed.

Some bricklayers specialize in working with one type of masonry material only, such as gypsum block, concrete block, hollow tile used in partitions, or terra-cotta products. Other bricklayers called *refractory masons* work in the steel and glass manufacturing industries and specialize in installing firebrick and refractory tile linings of furnaces, kilns, boilers, cupolas, and other high-temperature equipment. Still others are employed to construct manholes and catch basins in sewers.

Stonemasons work with two types of stone: natural cut stone, such as marble, granite, limestone, or sandstone; and artificial stone, which is made to order from concrete, marble chips, or other masonry materials. They set the stone in many kinds of structures, including piers, walls, walks, arches, floors, and curbstones. On some projects, the drawings that stonemasons work from specify where to set certain stones that have been previously identified by number. In such cases, helpers may locate the stones and bring them to the masons. Large stones may have to be hoisted into place with derricks.

In building stone walls, masons begin by setting a first course of stones in a bed of mortar, then build upward by alternating layers of mortar and stone courses. At every stage, they may use leveling devices and plumb lines, correcting the alignment of each stone. They often insert wedges and tap the stones into place with rubber mallets. Once a stone is in a good position, they remove the wedges, fill the gaps with mortar, and smooth the area using a metal tool called a tuck pointer. Large stones may need to be anchored in place with metal brackets that are welded or bolted to the wall.

Similarly, when masons construct stone floors, they begin by spreading mortar. They place stones, adjusting their positions using mallets and crowbars, and periodically checking the levelness of the surface. They may cut some stones into smaller pieces to fit, using hammer and chisel or a power saw with a diamond blade. After all the stones are placed, the masons fill the joints between the stones with mortar and wash off the surface.

Some stonemasons specialize in setting marble. Others work exclusively on setting alberene, which is an acid-resistant soapstone used in industrial settings on floors and for lining vats and tanks. Other specialized stone workers include *composition stone applicators*, *monument setters*, *patchers*, and *chimney repairers*. *Stone repairers* mend broken slabs made of marble and similar stone.

Bricklayers and stonemasons sometimes use power tools, such as saws and drills, but for the most part they use hand tools, including trowels, jointers, hammers, rulers, chisels, squares, gauge lines, mallets, brushes, and mason's levels.

Requirements

The best way to become a bricklayer or stonemason is to complete an apprenticeship. Vocational schools also provide training in these fields. However, many people learn their skills informally on the job simply by observing and helping experienced workers over a period of years. The disadvantage of this approach is that informal training is likely to be less thorough, and it may take workers much longer to learn the full range of necessary skills for the trade.

Apprenticeship programs are sponsored by contractors or jointly by contractors and unions. Applicants for apprenticeships need to be at least 17 years old and in good physical condition. High school graduates are usually preferred. A good background for applicants would include any available high school courses in shop, basic mathematics, blueprint reading, and mechanical drawing.

Apprentices spend three years learning as they work under the supervision of experienced bricklayers or stonemasons. In addition, they receive at least 144 hours of classroom instruction in related subjects such as blueprint reading, applied mathematics, and layout work. In the work portion of their apprenticeship, they begin with the simple jobs, like carrying materials and building scaffolds. After they become familiar with one task, they change to another, eventually experiencing a broad range of activities. In the course of an apprenticeship, a worker can become qualified to work with more than one kind of masonry material.

Inexperienced beginners who plan to learn the trade informally and on the job usually begin as helpers or laborers doing simple tasks. They learn more complex jobs whenever the opportunity presents itself. As they gradually become more useful employees, they may find more ways to increase their skills.

Opportunities for experience and exploration

Opportunities are limited for most high school students to experience directly the work in this field. Occasionally it is possible for students to secure summer employment on construction projects and observe bricklayers or stonemasons. Students who are already enrolled in vocational bricklaying programs can gain some practical experience as part of their instruction. Otherwise, a field trip to a construction site can give an overall view of the type of work done by bricklayers and stonemasons.

Methods of entering

The two main ways that people start out in these fields are in formal apprenticeship programs and as helpers or laborers who gradually learn on the job. Helper jobs can be found through newspaper want ads, at the local office of the state employment service, or by contacting appropriate contractors.

People seeking to apply for apprenticeships can obtain more information from local contractors who hire bricklayers or stonemasons, the state employment service, or the local office of the International Union of Bricklayers and Allied Craftsmen.

Another option may be to enter a bricklaying program at a vocational school. Such a program combines classroom instruction with work experience. Vocational school placement offices may be able to help qualified graduates to secure jobs that utilize their skills.

Advancement

Bricklayers and stonemasons with enough skill and experience may advance to supervisory positions. Some union contracts require a supervisor if three or more workers are employed on a job.

Supervisors sometimes become superintendents at large construction sites. With additional technical training, bricklayers and stonemasons may become *estimators*. Estimators look at building plans, obtain quotations on masonry material, and prepare and submit bids on the costs of doing the proposed job. Another possible advancement is to become a city or county inspector who checks to see if the work done by contractors meets local building code regulations. A few bricklayers and stonemasons go into business for themselves as contractors.

Employment outlook

There are about 152,000 bricklayers and stonemasons employed in the United States. Over the next 10 to 15 years, employment opportunities in both fields are expected to rise at rates about the same as the average for all other occupations. There will probably be increased construction of many kinds of buildings, and the popularity of brick and stone is growing, especially ornamental brickwork and stonework on building fronts and in lobbies. Technological developments in construction techniques, however, will affect the job outlook. For example, bricklayers will probably be installing more precast panels made of various types of masonry material instead of individual bricks, a trend that may tend to restrain the demand for bricklayers. Bricklayers who specialize in refractory repair will also find their job opportunities declining.

During economic downturns, bricklayers and stonemasons, like other workers in construction-related jobs, can expect to have fewer job opportunities and perhaps be laid off.

Earnings

The median annual earnings of bricklayers and stonemasons are over $26,000, with a range between about $13,600 and $43,600. Most make between $17,400 and $35,600. Earnings for those who work outside can be affected by bad weather, and earnings are lower for workers in areas where the local economy is in a slump. The pay also varies according to geographical region, with rates highest in the West.

The beginning hourly rate for apprentices is about half of the rate for experienced workers. In addition to regular pay, various fringe benefits such as health and life insurance, pensions, and paid vacations are available to many workers in this field.

Conditions of work

Most bricklayers and stonemasons have a 40-hour workweek. They are usually paid time-and-a-half for overtime and double-time for work on Saturdays, Sundays, and holidays.

Most of the work is done outdoors, where conditions may be dusty, hot, cold, or damp. Often workers must stand on scaffolds that are high off the ground. They may need to bend or stoop constantly to pick up materials. They may be on their feet most of the working day, or they may kneel for long periods.

Some of the hazards in this work are falling off a scaffold, being hit by falling material, and other injuries common to lifting and handling heavy material. In much of the country, construction work is seasonal, with time lost because of bad weather conditions.

Apprentices and experienced workers must furnish their own hand tools and measuring devices. Contractors supply the materials for making mortar, scaffolding, lifts, ladders, and other large equipment used in the construction process.

Well-qualified bricklayers and stonemasons can often find work at wages higher than those of most other construction workers. But be-cause the work is seasonal, bricklayers and stonemasons must plan carefully to make it through any periods of unemployment.

GOE: 05.05.01; SIC: 1741; SOC: 6412, 6413

◇ **SOURCES OF ADDITIONAL INFORMATION**

Associated General Contractors of America
1957 E Street, NW
Washington, DC 20006

Brick Institute of America
11490 Commerce Park Drive
Reston, VA 22091

International Union of Bricklayers and Allied Craftsmen
815 15th Street, NW
Washington, DC 20005

National Association of Home Builders
Home Builders Institute
15th and M Streets, NW
Washington, DC 20005

Clay Brick Association of Canada
#GZ, 1 Sparks Avenue
Willowdale ON M2H 2W1

◇ **RELATED ARTICLES**

Volume 1: Construction
Volumes 2–4: Architectural and building construction technicians; Cement masons; Construction laborers; Floor covering installers; Marble setters, tile setters, and terrazzo workers; Plasterers

---

Broadcast technicians

Definition

Broadcast technicians, also referred to as *broadcast engineers*, or *broadcast operators*, operate and maintain the electronic equipment used to record and transmit the audio for radio signals and the audio and visual images for television signals to the public. They may work in a broadcasting station or assist in broadcasting directly from an outside site as a *field technician*.

History

At the end of the 19th century Guglielmo Marconi, an Italian experimenter, successfully sent radio waves across a room in his home, and helped launch the 20th century into the age of mass communication. Marconi quickly realized the potential for his experiments with radio waves. By 1901 he had established the Marconi Wireless Company in England and the United States and soon after successfully transmitted radio signals across the Atlantic ocean for the first time.

At first radio signals were used to transmit information and for communication between two points, but eventually the idea that the radio could be used for entertainment was developed, and in 1919, the Radio Corporation of America, or RCA, was founded. Families everywhere gathered around their radios to listen to music, drama, comedy, and news programs. Radio became a commercial success, and radio technology advanced, creating the need for many skilled technicians to operate the complicated electronic equipment.

In 1933 frequency modulation, or FM, was introduced. (Originally there had been only amplitude modulation, or AM.) This vastly improved the quality of radio broadcasting. At the same time experimentation was occurring with higher frequency radio waves, and in 1936 at the World's Fair in New York City, RCA demonstrated television.

The effect television had on changing mass communication was as dramatic as the advent of the radio. Technology continued to advance with the introduction of color imaging, which became widely available in 1953. The number of VHF and UHF channels continued to increase, and in the 1970s cable television and subscription television became available, increasing the amount and variety of programming. The continuing advances in broadcast technology ensure the need for trained broadcast technicians who understand and can maintain the highly technical equipment used in television and radio stations.

Nature of the work

Broadcast technicians are responsible for the transmission of radio and television programming, including live and recorded broadcasts. Broadcasts are usually transmitted directly from the station; however, technicians are capable of transmitting signals on location from specially designed, mobile equipment. The specific tasks of the broadcast technician depend on the size

A broadcast technician monitors the quality of the image and sound that the cameraman is recording at a broadcast done away from the television station.

of the television or radio station. In small stations technicians have a wide variety of responsibilities. Larger stations are able to hire a greater number of technicians specifically delegating responsibilities to each technician. In both small and large stations, however, technicians are responsible for the operation, installation, repair, and thorough knowledge of the equipment.

The *chief engineer* in both radio and television is the head of the entire technical operation, and must orchestrate the activities of all the technicians to ensure smooth programming. The chief engineer is also responsible for the budget, and must keep abreast of new broadcast communication technology, which may be implemented.

Larger stations also have an *assistant chief engineer* who manages the daily activities of the technical crew, controls the maintenance of the electronic equipment, and ensures the high performance standards of the station.

Transmitter operators beam the signals from the broadcasting station to the public. A combination of live and recorded material is often used. The transmitter operator must determine, regulate, and log the strength of the signal being sent.

Maintenance technicians are directly responsible for the electronic equipment. The installation, adjustment, and repair of the equipment are all responsibilities of the maintenance technician.

Audio control engineers regulate the quality and strength of the sound being recorded through the use of microphones, amplifiers, and a variety of audio equipment.

Video control engineers ensure the quality, brightness, and content of the visual images being recorded and broadcast. The pictures recorded by the cameraman are selected one frame at a time before being transmitted to the public.

Field technicians using mobile equipment operate away from the broadcasting station on location to obtain live and recorded footage that is directly transmitted to the public, or is transmitted back to the broadcasting station for processing.

Requirements

Broadcast technicians must have both an aptitude for working with highly technical electronic and computer equipment and minute attention to detail to be successful in the field. Preparation for a career in broadcast technology should include a strong background in math, science, and electronics, and possibly include courses in microwave technology, computer engineering, and physics.

To obtain an entry-level position, a high school diploma and technical school training are required. Positions that are more advanced require a bachelor's degree in broadcast communications, or a related field. Seeking education beyond a bachelor's degree will further the possibilities for advancement, although it is not required.

Special requirements

FCC certification is required of all broadcast technicians, as is a general operator's license. Although a first-class operator's license is not required by governmental standards, it is necessary for employment advancement in the field of broadcasting.

Opportunities for experience and exploration

In most towns and cities there are public-access cable television stations and public radio stations where high school students interested in broadcasting and broadcast technology can obtain an internship. Experience is necessary to begin a career as a broadcast technician, and volunteering at a local broadcasting station is an excellent way of gaining experience. Most colleges and universities also have radio and television stations where students can gain experience with broadcasting equipment.

Exposure to broadcasting technology also may be obtained through building and operating an amateur, or ham, radio and experimenting with electronic kits. Ensuring interest, dexterity, and understanding of home operated broadcasting equipment will aid in promoting success in education and work experience within the field of broadcasting.

Methods of entering

Most technicians begin their careers in small stations and eventually advance to larger broadcasting stations after gaining experience. Career advancement may happen more quickly if a technician has volunteer or internship experience, or an advanced degree.

Advancement

Broadcast technicians usually move from smaller to larger stations once experience has been obtained. Entry-level technicians deal exclusively with the operation and maintenance of their assigned equipment. As experience is gained, a broadcast technician directs the activities of entry-level technicians and makes judgements on the quality, strength, and subject of the material being broadcast.

After several years of experience, a broadcast technician may advance to assistant chief engineer who directs the daily activities of all of the broadcasting technicians in the station and the field technicians broadcasting on location. Advancement to chief engineer usually requires at least a college degree and many years of experience. A firm grasp of management skills, budget planning, and a thorough knowledge of all aspects of broadcast technology are the requirements to become the chief engineer of a radio or television station.

Employment outlook

Broadcasting technology is rapidly advancing, especially in radio broadcasting where manual broadcasting equipment is being replaced with automated equipment, thus reducing the number of broadcasting technicians needed to operate the equipment. As technological advances are made, most broadcasting equipment will shift to automated, computer-controlled equipment. The need for maintenance of the equipment will remain, as will the need for coordination of programming; however, the job market is expected to remain stagnate for broadcast technicians throughout the next decade. The competition will be high for broadcast technician positions, favoring the more experienced and better-educated applicants.

Earnings

Larger stations usually pay higher wages than smaller stations, and television stations tend to pay more than radio stations. For radio stations the salary for a technician averages $22,000 a year, and chief engineers average $26,000 a year. In television stations a technician's salary averages $21,000 a year and a chief engineer's $44,000 a year.

Conditions of work

Most technicians work in a broadcasting station that is modern and comfortable. The hours and days worked usually are standard; however, because most broadcasting stations operate 24 hours a day, seven days a week, there are technicians who must work at night, on weekends, and on holidays. Broadcasts also occur outside of the broadcasting station on location sites, which can be anywhere and in all kinds of weather.

GOE: 01.02.03; SIC: 483, 484, 489; SOC: 393

◇ **SOURCES OF ADDITIONAL INFORMATION**

Federal Communications Commission
1919 M Street, NW
Washington, DC 20554

National Association of Broadcasters Employment Clearinghouse
1771 N Street, NW
Washington, DC 20036

Broadcast Education Association
National Association of Broadcasters
1771 N Street, NW
Washington, DC 20036

◇ **RELATED ARTICLES**

Volume 1: Broadcasting; Electronics
Volumes 2–4: Audio control technicians; Audiovisual technicians; Cable television technicians; Field technicians; Sound technicians; Sound-effect technicians; Sound-recording technicians; Studio technicians; Transmitter technicians

---

Business managers

Definition

Business managers plan, organize, direct, and coordinate the operations of firms in business and industry.

History

Management plays an important part in any enterprise in which one directs another person or group of people. In fact, civilization could not have grown to its present level of complexity without the planning and organizing involved in effective management. Some of the earliest examples of written documents had to do with the management of business and commerce. Accumulation of vast amounts of wealth necessitated effective record-keeping of taxes, trade agreements, laws, and rights of ownership.

The technological advances of the Industrial Revolution brought about the need for a distinct class of managers. Skilled, trained managers were needed to organize and operate complex factory systems. Also, the divided efforts of specialized workers in factories had to be managed and coordinated.

As businesses began to diversify their production, industries became so complex that the administration of production had to be decentralized. The authoritarian type of manager faded with the expanded scope of managers and the transition to the professional manager took place. In the 1920s large corporations began organizing their growth around decentralized administration with centralized policy control.

Managers provided a forum for the exchange and evaluation of creative management ideas and technical innovations. Eventually these management concepts spread from manufacturing and production to office, personnel, marketing, and financial functions. Today management is more oriented toward results than toward activities, a philosophy that recognizes individual differences in styles of working.

Nature of the work

Management is found in every industry, including the larger industries of food, clothing, banking, education, health care, and business services. All types of business have managers to formulate policies and administer the firm's operations. They may oversee other employees or be responsible for a specific department such as sales and marketing.

Business managers direct their department's daily activities within the context of the organization's overall plan. They implement organizational policies and goals. This may involve developing sales or promotional materials, or analyzing the department's budgetary requirements. Business managers are responsible for hiring, training, and supervising staff. They may coordinate their department's activities with other departments.

If the business is privately owned, the owner may be the manager. In a large corporation, there will be an entire management structure above the business manager.

The hierarchy of managers includes top executives such as the *president*, who establishes an organization's goals and policies along with others, like the *chief executive officer, executive vice presidents,* and the *board of directors.* Top executives plan business objectives and develop policies to coordinate operations between divisions and departments and establish procedures for attaining objectives. Activity reports and financial statements are reviewed to determine progress and revise operations as needed. The president also directs and formulates funding for new and existing programs within the organization. Public relations plays a big part in the lives of executives as they deal with executives and leaders from other countries or organizations, and with customers, employees, and various special interest groups. Although the president or chief executive officer retains ultimate authority and responsibility, the chief operating officer may be the one to oversee the day-to-day operations of the company. Other duties may include serving as chairman of committees, such as management, executive, engineering, or sales.

The *executive vice president* directs and coordinates the activities of one or more departments, depending on the size of the organization. In very large organizations, the duties of executive vice presidents may be highly specialized; for example, they may oversee the activities of business managers of marketing, sales promotion, purchasing, finance, personnel training, industrial relations, administrative services, data processing, property management, transportation, or legal services. In smaller organizations, an executive vice president might be responsible for a number of these departments. Executive vice presidents also assist the chief executive officer in formulating and administering the organization's policies and developing its long-range goals. Executive vice presidents may serve as members of management committees on special studies.

Requirements

The educational background of business managers varies as widely as the nature of their diverse responsibilities. Most have a bachelor's degree in liberal arts or business administration. In college, their major is often related to the department they direct or the organization they administer; for example, accounting for a business manager of finance, computer science for a business manager of data processing, engineering or science for director of research and development.

During a meeting, the business manager and two employees discuss ideas to streamline operations.

Graduate and professional degrees are common. Many managers in administrative, marketing, financial, and manufacturing activities have a master's degree in business administration (MBA) or management science. Managers in highly technical manufacturing and research activities often have a master's degree or doctorate in a technical or scientific discipline. A law degree is mandatory for business managers of corporate legal departments, and hospital managers generally have a master's degree in health services administration or business administration. In some industries, such as retail trade or the food and beverage industry, competent individuals without a college degree may become business managers.

Opportunities for experience and exploration

To get experience as a manager, start with your own interests. Whether you're involved in drama, sports, school publications, or a part-time job, there are various managerial duties associated with any organized activity. These can involve planning, scheduling, managing other workers or volunteers, fund-raising, or budgeting. Local businesses also have job opportunities through which you can get first-hand knowledge and experience of management structure.

Methods of entering

Generally, those interested in management will need a college degree, although many retail stores, grocery stores, and eating and drinking establishments hire promising employees who have a high school diploma. In some industries, managers need at least a bachelor's degree in a field related to the industry or in business administration; often they also need a graduate degree. Degrees in computer science are an advantage.

Many organizations have management trainee programs that college graduates can enter. Such programs are advertised at college career fairs or through college job placement services. Often, however, these management trainee positions in business and government are filled by employees who are already working for the organization and who demonstrate management potential.

Advancement

Most business management and top executive positions are filled by experienced lower-level managers and executives who display valuable mangerial traits such as leadership, self-confidence, creativity, motivation, decisiveness, and flexibility. In small firms, where the number of jobs is limited, advancement to a higher management position may come slowly. In large firms, promotions may occur more quickly.

Advancement may be accelerated by participating in different kinds of educational programs available for managers. These are often paid for by the organization. Company training programs broaden knowledge of company policy and operations. Training programs sponsored by numerous industry and trade associations and continuing education courses in colleges and universities can familiarize managers with the latest developments in management techniques. Participation in interdisciplinary conferences and seminars can expand knowledge of national and international issues influencing the manager's firm. Because of the large number of people employed as middle managers, competition for jobs is keen and a proven commitment to improving one's knowledge of the field may be important in setting one apart from the competition.

Other more personal factors may influence one's ability to advance to higher management positions. Top managers must have well developed personal relations skills and be able to communicate effectively, both orally and in writing. Other traits considered important for top executives are intelligence, decisiveness, intuition, creativity, honesty, loyalty, a sense of responsibility, and planning, and organizing abilities.

Business managers may advance to higher positions, such as executive or administrative vice president, in their own firm or they may move to a corresponding position in a larger firm. Similarly, vice presidents may advance to peak corporate positions—president or chief executive officer. Presidents and chief executive officers, upon retirement, may become members of the board of directors of one or more firms. Sometimes business managers establish their own firms.

Employment outlook

In the 1990s business managers hold more than three million jobs, and employment is expected to increase as fast as the average for all occu-pations. The large number of competent lower-level managers seeking top management positions, however, should result in substantial job competition. Individuals whose accomplishments reflect strong leadership qualities and improved productivity will have the best job opportunities.

Projected employment growth does vary by industry. Employment of management in the computer and data processing fields is expected to double. Firms supplying management, consulting, public relations, and other business services will probably experience very rapid growth. Management needs in engineering, architectural, and surveying services firms are expected to grow rapidly, and the demand for management is also expected to increase in some health care industries, such as out patient clinics and social services facilities. Much faster than average employment growth is projected for management in the hotel, restaurant, and travel industries, but it will be slower in education. Some manufacturing industries are expected to have very little change in their management needs.

Earnings

Salary levels for business managers vary substantially, depending upon the level of responsibility, length of service, and type, size, and location of the organization. Top-level managers in large firms can earn much more than their counterparts in small firms. Also, salaries in large metropolitan areas such as New York City are higher than those in smaller cities. Generally, too, salaries in manufacturing and finance are higher than salaries in state and local governments.

In the 1990s, the average annual salary for business managers is around $50,000. Top executives of large corporations are the most highly paid management personnel. Their base salary can exceed $1 million, and additional compensation, in the form of stocks and other fringe benefits, may equal their salary.

Although it is very difficult to find work at an equivalent level, top executives are often provided with a good compensation package if they are laid-off or dismissed by the board of directors.

Business managers in the private sector receive additional compensation in the form of bonuses, stock awards, company-paid insurance premiums, use of company cars, paid country club memberships, expense accounts, and generous retirement benefits.

Conditions of work

Business managers are provided with comfortable offices near the departments they direct. Top executives may have spacious, lavish offices, and may enjoy such privileges as executive dining rooms, company cars, country club memberships, and liberal expense accounts.

Managers often travel between national, regional, and local offices. Top executives may travel to meet with executives in other corporations, both here and abroad. Meetings and conferences sponsored by industries and associations occur regularly and provide invaluable opportunities to meet with peers and keep up with the latest developments. In large corporations, job transfers between the parent company and its local offices or subsidiaries are common.

Business managers often work long hours under intense pressure to attain, for example, production and marketing goals. The long hours—an 80-hour work week is not uncommon—limit time available for family and leisure activities.

Considerable skill in managing people is required. The executive or manager needs to delegate authority and assign responsibility, motivate employees, and handle complaints and problems.

GOE: 11; SIC: Any industry; SOC: Any industry

◇ SOURCES OF ADDITIONAL INFORMATION

American Management Association
Information Resource Center
135 West 50th Street
New York, NY 10020

National Management Association
2210 Arbor Boulevard
Dayton, OH 45439

Women in Management
2 North Riverside Plaza, Suite 2400
Chicago, IL 60606

Information about business managers in specific industries may be obtained from organizations listed in encyclopedias or directories of associations.

◇ RELATED ARTICLES

Volume 1: Business Management
Volumes 2–4: City managers; Clerical supervisors and managers; College administrators; Data base managers; Financial institution officers and managers; Health services administrators; Hotel and motel managers; Industrial traffic managers; Landscapers and grounds managers; Literary agents and artists' managers; Management analysts and consultants; Miscellaneous engineers; Property and real estate managers; Radio and television program directors; Range managers; Restaurant and food service managers; Retail business owners; Retail managers; Risk managers; School administrators

Buyers, wholesale and retail

Definition

The *buyer* purchases merchandise from manufacturers and wholesalers at an appropriate price, in sufficient quantity, and with sufficient customer appeal to warrant its rapid and profitable resale to the public by the department store or chain store for which the retail buyer works or, in the case of the wholesale buyer, resale to retail firms, commercial establishments, and other institutions. Sometimes a buyer is referred to by the type of goods purchased, for example, jewelry buyer or toy buyer.

History

As the early American retail stores became more specialized and grew in size, a functional division occurred in store operations. Owner-operators, who performed almost all of the store's tasks, were replaced by sales clerks, receiving and shipping clerks, advertising managers, personnel officers, and buyers.

A wider range of available merchandise called for more astute selection and purchasing techniques. The development, in turn, of railroads, automobiles, and airplanes permitted buyers to travel to metropolitan areas where goods were available for firsthand examination.

The buyer is now a key part of the retail and wholesale industry, which has annual sales in the billions of dollars and employs millions of workers.

Nature of the work

Wholesale and retail buyers are part of a complex system of production, distribution, and merchandising. They both are concerned with recognizing and satisfying the huge variety of consumer needs and desires. Both wholesale and retail buyers usually specialize in acquiring one or two lines of merchandise.

Wholesale buyers purchase goods from manufacturers or from other wholesalers and sell it to retailers. They must be familiar with products and manufacturers, and be able to anticipate their customers' requirements. Wholesale buyers service retail outlets of all sizes throughout the country and must be able to satisfy their diverse needs in a timely and cost-effective manner. They consult catalogs and computerized directories to learn about the products that are available, and they often consult with retail buyers to keep abreast of consumer preferences.

Retail buyers work under one of two organizational patterns. In the first, working directly under a merchandise manager, the buyer combines purchasing activities with direct supervision of salespeople in the department involved. Thus, one person purchases the goods and then takes responsibility for their success-

ful marketing. In the second pattern, merchandising and buying are separated. Buyers serve as specialists and have no supervisory responsibilities. In this case, however, buyers cooperate with the sales staff to promote maximum sales.

Assistant buyers work directly with experienced buyers. They also spend much of their time maintaining sales and inventory records. In addition, they may accompany buyers on purchasing trips or act for buyers who are away.

Regardless of the method of organization, all retail buyers perform many functions in common. The size of the store that employs them, the types of goods that they purchase, and their own personal philosophy of the role of the buyer directly affect the nature of their work. All buyers must know three things: their employer, their goods, and their customers.

Retail buyers must understand the basic merchandising policies of their store. The amount of purchases will be affected by the size of the buyer's annual budget, the timing in each buying season, and trends in the market. Success in buying is directly related to the clearly labeled profit or loss shown by particular departments.

All buyers are experts in the merchandise with which they deal. They order goods months ahead of their expected sale. They must be able to predetermine salability based upon cost, style, and competitive items. Buyers must be able to ascertain directly such product elements as purpose, construction, durability, quality, and style. Additionally, buyers must be well acquainted with the best sources of supply for each type of goods they purchase.

Depending upon the location, size, and type of store, a retail buyer may deal directly with traveling salespeople (ordering from samples or catalogs); may order by mail or by telephone directly from the manufacturer or wholesaler (based largely upon past selling experience); or may travel to key cities to visit merchandise showrooms and manufacturing establishments. Most use a combination of these approaches.

Buying trips to such cities as New York, Chicago, and San Francisco are an important part of the work of the buyer for a larger store. Buyers of such specialized products as glassware, china, liquors, and gloves may make yearly trips to major European production centers. Sometimes manufacturers of similar items organize trade shows to attract a number of buyers. Buying trips are difficult; six to eight suppliers may be visited in a single day. The buyer must be able to estimate quickly the opportunity for profitable sale of the merchandise while examining it. The important element is not how much the buyer personally likes the merchandise, but how much the customers will buy. Most buyers operate under an annual purchasing budget for the departments that they represent.

As new merchandise appears on the shelves of their stores, buyers often work with salespeople to point out its distinctive features and elements of style.

Mergers between stores and expansion of single department stores into chains of stores have created central buying positions. These buyers order in unusually large quantities. As a result, they may develop a set of specifications for goods desired and ask manufacturers to bid on the right to provide these goods, rather than merely selecting products from those that are already available. Goods purchased by central buyers may be marketed under either the manufacturer's label (as is normally done) or ordered with the store's label or a chain brand.

To meet this competition, independent stores often retain the services of resident buyers who operate in major manufacturing or wholesaling areas. Often these resident buyers are not employed exclusively by one store, but they may buy for many stores located in different cities. The resident buying operation permits group-buying of salable goods at the most advantageous price.

Requirements

A college degree is not required for the job of the buyer, but is becoming increasingly more significant. Retailing experience is also a distinct advantage.

High school courses that are helpful include business mathematics, English, speech, economics, home economics, and merchandising.

Prospective buyers may take collegiate training in one of the specialized retailing institutions. They also may attend a general college or university. Useful courses include business administration, marketing, retailing, buying, and economics. The wide variety of college backgrounds among successful buyers suggests that employers are flexible in terms of preferred major. Newly hired graduates may have a major in merchandising, marketing, fashion, fashion design, or advertising.

Personal qualifications are particularly important. The buyer must be intelligent, enthusiastic, energetic, analytical, and venturesome. Buyers also must be able to work well with all kinds of people.

The buyer often meets with sales representatives to examine and discuss merchandise. If the buyer is impressed with the product, she will consider purchasing quantities of it.

Opportunities for experience and exploration

The best method of exploring interest and aptitude in retailing and buying is through part-time or summer employment in a store. One of the best times to look for such work is during the Christmas holiday season.

Some high schools and clubs offer distributive education work that provides actual experience in a retail store. Door-to-door selling experience also provides a measure of aptitude for retailing.

Methods of entering

Most prospective buyers secure their first position by direct application to the personnel office of a particular retail establishment.

Because of the knowledge of retailing required, preliminary work experience in a store often is necessary before promotion to the level of buyer. In fact, most buyers begin their careers as retail salesclerks. The next step up the ladder is usually the job of head of stock. The head of stock maintains stock inventory records and keeps the merchandise itself in a neat and well organized fashion to both protect its value and permit easy accessibility. The head of stock usually supervises the work of several employees. This person also works in an intermediate position between the salespeople on the floor and the buyer who provides the merchandise.

The next step to becoming a full-fledged buyer may be that of assistant buyer. For many department stores, promotion to full buyer requires this experience.

Large department stores or chains operate executive training programs for college graduates seeking buying and other retail executive positions. A typical program consists of sixteen weeks of successive work experience in a variety of departments. This on-the-job experience is supplemented by formal classroom work that is most often conducted by senior executives and training department personnel. Following this orientation, trainees are placed in junior management positions for an additional period of supervised experience and training.

Advancement

The position of buyer offers an opportunity for a substantial career in itself. Buyers are key employees of the stores or companies that employ them. As they serve on their jobs, buyers are given increased responsibility that takes the form of greater independence in activity, more authority to make commitments for merchandise, and transfer to the most difficult buying assignments.

Buyers may be promoted to merchandise manager and supervise other buyers, help develop the store's merchandising policies, and coordinate buying and selling activities with related departments.

If buyers find no opportunity for top buying positions with their employer or seek advancement beyond the buyer level, they may secure a more promising position with one of the many other retail stores in the United States. Experience in one store is highly applicable to the work of other establishments in the same line.

Because of their grasp of retailing fundamentals and the fact that the quality of their performance is clearly demonstrated, many top executive positions in the retail industry are filled by persons from the ranks of buyers. Some buyers become merchandise managers, vice-presidents in charge of merchandising, or even store presidents.

Many buyers use their knowledge of the retail business and the contacts they have developed with potential suppliers to provide background to help themselves in setting up their own business.

Employment outlook

Of the 360,000 wholesale and retail buyers employed throughout the country in the 1990s, most work for department stores, clothing stores, grocery stores, machinery wholesalers, electrical goods distributors, and grocery wholesalers. About three-fifths of these jobs are in retail establishments.

Prospects for buyers are expected to increase through the 1990s at a slower than average rate. The growth of branch stores is expected to create a demand for buyers, but this will be offset by other factors. Centralization of buying, as stores consolidate or participate in joint purchasing activities, may reduce the number of buyers needed, as will the increased use of the tools of automation.

Competition will be keen because the field of merchandising is attractive to many college graduates, and job seekers can be expected to outnumber the opportunities available. Qualified applicants will be given preference over newcomers to the field.

Earnings

How much a buyer earns depends on the quantity and type of product purchased, as well as on the employer's sales volume. Mass merchandisers such as discount or chain department stores pay among the highest salaries.

In the 1990s, most buyers earn between $17,600 and $34,600 a year. Buyers who prove that they can operate in the competitive conditions that mark their field may earn more than $46,700 a year.

In addition to basic salary, buyers often receive cash bonuses based on their performance and may be offered incentive plans such as profit sharing and stock options. Benefits usually include an employee's discount of 10 to 20 percent on merchandise purchased for personal use.

Conditions of work

Buyers work in a dynamic atmosphere. They must make important decisions on an hourly basis. The results of their work, both successes and failures, show up quickly on the profit and loss statement. As stores must hire buyers who can produce the greatest margin of profit, buyers work under conditions of constant pressure.

Buyers frequently work long or irregular hours. Prior to purchasing expeditions, extra hours may be required to bring records up-to-date, review stocks, know the store's overall marketing design for the coming season, and plan most effectively for the time spent on travel.

If they combine buying with sales supervision, buyers work long hours. Most stores are open evenings and weekends. Buyers must be prepared to handle cases of customer complaints.

An important advantage of buying is the varied nature of the work and the fact that no two days are ever alike. As they note the results of one season's activities, buyers plan how to improve upon past results.

GOE: 08.01.03; SIC: Any industry; SOC: 1442

◇ **SOURCES OF ADDITIONAL INFORMATION**

National Retail Merchants Association
100 West 31st Street
New York, NY 10001

Retail Council of Canada
#600, 210 Dundas Street, West
Toronto ON M5G 2E8

◇ **RELATED ARTICLES**

Volume 1: Marketing; Sales
Volumes 2–4: Counter and retail clerks; Export-import specialists; Purchasing agents; Retail business owners; Retail managers; Retail sales workers; Manufacturers' sales workers; Wholesale trade sales workers

Cable television technicians

Definition

Cable television technicians inspect, maintain, and repair antennas, cables, and amplifying equipment used in cable television transmission.

History

In 1927 the first workable cathode-ray-tube camera was invented by a 16-year-old boy named Philo T. Farnsworth, and improvements by Vladimir Zworykin made the system practical. It was demonstrated in 1929, and regular television programming began at the World's Fair of 1939, although it was later interrupted by World War II.

In 1946 the interest and energy that had been diverted from television returned. The first commercial broadcasts were beamed along the East Coast (all early broadcasts originated in New York City) and gradually made their way to cities farther west, until by 1951 broadcasts were reaching coast-to-coast. In 1950 there were 6 million television sets in the United States; by 1960 there were 60 million.

The growth of cable television transmission systems greatly affected the broadcast industry.

The birth of cable television can be traced to the development of coaxial cable (copper wire inside a copper tube, both with the same axis), which was invented in the 1930s in the Bell Telephone Laboratories, primarily to improve telephone transmission. It was soon found that a coaxial cable could also carry television transmissions very efficiently. One coaxial cable can carry sixty television signals, enabling a cable system to offer a wide variety of programming and still reserve channels for public-service use.

At first cable television transmission was used to carry television signals to areas where conventional transmission could not reach: valleys, extremely hilly regions, and large cities where buildings interfered with radio waves. By the late 1970s, however, cable television systems in the United States numbered about 3,500, and they were competing with conventional networks in areas that both could serve. In the 1990s, more than half of the households in the United States are served by cable.

Nature of the work

Cable television technicians perform a wide range of duties in a variety of settings. Televi-

233

A cable television technician adjusts a transmission line. Thousands of people rely on his expertise to ensure quality cable reception.

sion cables usually follow the routes of telephone cables, running along poles in rural and suburban areas, and through tunnels in cities. Working in tunnels and underground cable passageways, technicians inspect cables for evidence of damage and corrosion. Using diagrams and blueprints, they trace cables to locate sites of signal breakdown. They may also work at pole-mounted amplifiers, where they analyze the strength of incoming television signals, using field-strength meters and miniature television receivers to evaluate reception. At customers' homes, they install the terminal boxes, explain the workings of the cable system, answer questions, or respond to complaints that may indicate cable or equipment problems. When major problems arise, they repair or replace damaged or faulty cable systems.

Cable television technicians use various electrical measuring instruments (VOMs, Field Strength Meters) to diagnose causes of trans-

mission problems. They also use electricians' hand tools (including screwdrivers, pliers, etc.) to dismantle, repair, or replace faulty sections of cable or disabled equipment, such as amplifying equipment used to boost the signal at intervals along the cable system.

An important aspect of the work of cable television technicians involves implementing regular programs of preventive maintenance on the cable system. Technicians inspect connections, insulation, and the performance of amplifying equipment, using measuring instruments and viewing the transmitted signals on television monitors.

Requirements

Persons interested in careers as cable television technicians should take high school mathematics courses at least through plane geometry and have a solid knowledge of shop math. They should have sufficient language skills in order to read technical manuals and instructions and to follow detailed maintenance procedures. They should also be prepared to follow a one- or two-year technical training program such as those offered at a community college or technical institute. Courses should include the basics of electrical wiring and electronics, broadcasting theory and practice, blueprint and schematic diagram reading, and physics.

Acute vision, with no color-perception deficiency, is essential for analyzing cable reception. Technicians must be able to climb utility poles, work at heights comfortably, and to work in confined spaces easily. They should also feel at ease with electrical equipment and electricians' tools.

Cable television technicians must be able to deal with people, analyze clients' descriptions of reception problems, and explain cable system costs and operations when necessary. Because of the extensive public service that this work requires, strong interpersonal skills are a plus.

Opportunities for experience and exploration

Because of the special training required, rarely are any part-time or summer technician jobs available for high school students. However, educational seminars are offered by local cable T.V. stations across the country; these are available to interested student groups and can be arranged through a school guidance counselor or teacher. These presentations provide valuable career information and an opportunity to speak with cable technicians and their employers about the field. For more information about these seminars, contact the Society of Cable Television Engineers, Inc. (listed at the end of this article), for the name and address of the nearest local chapter.

Methods of entering

Two ways to enter this field are: to enter as an unskilled installer, and move up after receiving on-the-job training; or to complete two years of an electronics program in a technical school, and seek assistance in the school's job placement office, which will have job information for cable television technicians.

Advancement

Cable workers may advance from entry-level position to *line technician*, and then on to supervisory and administrative positions such as *lead technician*, *chief technician*, and *plant manager*.

Employment outlook

Compared to the rapid growth in cable jobs in the 1980s, growth in the 1990s appears somewhat flat. Since most of the country is now wired for cable, the emphasis is no longer on installing the systems, but rather on maintaining and upgrading them. There is still some growth in the industry, and there will always be jobs for those with necessary skills and training, especially as technicians retire or leave the field.

Earnings

Most cable television technicians are paid an hourly wage, which varies greatly depending on geographic location. Generally, starting wages range between $7.00 per hour in the south and southeast, to $9.00 in the northeast and California. Maximum salaries range up to $9.50 per hour in the south/southeast; and to $14.00 per hour in the northeast and California. The median salary is $11.50 per hour.

Conditions of work

The work is moderately heavy, involving occasional lifting of up to fifty pounds. A large part of the cable television technician's time is spent on poles or in confined spaces; these activities require care and precision. As with all maintenance work around conductors, there is some danger of electrical shock. The coaxial cables used to transmit television signals are from one-half to over one inch in diameter. Cables have to be manipulated into position for splicing, which involves medium to heavy physical work.

GOE: 05.05.05; SIC: 483; SOC: 6151

◇ SOURCES OF ADDITIONAL INFORMATION

Society of Cable Television Engineers
669 Exton Commons
Exton, PA 19341

Ontario Society for Cable Television Engineers
45060 Fieldgate Drive
Mississauga ON L4W 3W6

◇ RELATED ARTICLES

Volume 1: Broadcasting; Telecommunications
Volumes 2–4: Communications equipment mechanics; Electrical repairers; Electrical technicians; Electricians; Electronics technicians; Line installers and cable splicers; Telephone and PBX installers and repairers; Telecommunications technicians; Transmission and distribution occupations

CAD/CAM technicians

Definition

CAD/CAM technicians assist industrial designers and engineers by using computer-controlled systems to design products and carry out automated industrial processes. CAD is an abbreviation for Computer-aided Design, or Computer-aided Drafting. CAM stands for Computer-aided Manufacturing.

Computer-aided design normally uses computers to establish the structures and materials needed in a new product, and then to create the required diagrams, drawings, and specification lists needed to manufacture the product. Computer-aided manufacturing uses computers to determine which manufacturing processes and equipment are needed to make the product, and to monitor and control the automated manufacturing of the product. In some fields, such as architecture, CAD activities are separate from manufacturing activities; in many areas, however, CAD and CAM are linked parts of an automated industrial design and manufacturing process.

History

CAD/CAM technology came about in the 1970s with the development of microprocessors (computer processors in the form of miniaturized integrated circuits contained on tiny silicon chips). Microprocessors opened up many new uses for computers by greatly reducing the size of computers while also increasing their power and speed.

Amazingly enough, the drafters and designers working to develop these microprocessors were also the first to benefit from this technology. Until that point, designing and drafting were done the old fashioned way, with pen and paper on a drafting board. As the circuits on the chips became too complex to diagram in this way, the designers began to use the chips themselves to help store information, create models, and produce diagrams for the design of new chip circuits. This was just the beginning of computer-assisted design and drafting technology. Today, there are tens of thousands of CAD work stations in industrial settings. Makers of CAD equipment expect their products to continue to sell very well in the years to come, so that by about the year 2000 nearly all drafting tasks will be done with such equipment.

The field of computer-aided manufacturing has grown just as quickly and dramatically. Before the 1970s, manufacturing processes were assisted by only a few relatively simple automated mechanisms. And until just a few years ago, CAM technology was associated almost exclusively with the use of some simple robotic devices in automobile and aircraft assembly lines. Developments in the computer field, especially in microprocessors, have created many new uses in manufacturing. Japan led the world in introducing computers into factories on a widespread basis. More recently, a wide variety of industries in the United States has expanded the use of automated manufacturing processes.

By fine-tuning microprocessor applications, small companies as well as large ones benefit from the increased efficiency and versatility in design and manufacturing that computers allow. CAD/CAM technology leads many manufacturers to enhanced productivity and more competitive positions in their product markets. In some industries, CAD/CAM has made it possible to develop and produce new products ten to twenty times faster than before. This success leads some experts to predict an increase in the nation's overall productivity by perhaps as much as ten times its present level in the next few decades.

Nature of the work

CAD/CAM technicians use computers to help design, improve, modify, or produce manufactured items and manufacturing systems. CAD/CAM technicians may be involved in any aspect of the manufacturing process from start to finish; however, they usually specialize in one aspect of CAD/CAM technology, either in CAD technology or CAM technology.

Technicians specializing in CAD technology work in the design and drafting activities associated with new product research and development. These technicians must combine drafting and computer skills. They work in any field where detailed drawings, diagrams, and layouts are important aspects of developing new product designs—for example, in architecture, electronics, and in the manufacturing of automobiles, aircraft, computers, and missiles and other defense systems.

CAD/CAM technicians work under the direction and supervision of CAD/CAM engineers and designers, experts highly trained in applying computer technology to industrial design and manufacturing. These designers and engineers plan how to relate the CAD technology and equipment to the design process. They are also the ones who give assignments to the CAD technicians.

These technicians work at specially designed and equipped interactive computer graphics work stations. They call up computer files that hold data (information) about a new product; they then run the programs to convert that information into diagrams and drawings of the product. These are displayed on a video display screen, which then acts as an electronic drawing board. Following the directions of a CAD engineer or designer, the CAD technician enters changes to the product's design into the computer. The technician then merges these changes into the data file, then displays the corrected diagrams and drawings.

The software in CAD systems is very helpful to the user—it offers suggestions and advice and even points out errors. The most important advantage of working with a CAD system is that it saves the technician from the lengthy process of having to produce, by hand, the original and then the revised product drawings and diagrams.

The CAD work station is equipped to allow technicians to perform calculations, develop simulations, and manipulate and modify the displayed material. Using typed commands at a keyboard, a stylus or light pen for touching the screen display, a mouse, joystick, or other electronic methods of interacting with the display, technicians can move, rotate, zoom in on any aspect of the drawing on the screen, and project three-dimensional images from two-dimensional sketches. They can make experimental changes to the design and then run tests on the modified design to determine its qualities, such as weight, strength, flexibility, and the cost of materials that would be required. Compared to traditional drafting and design techniques, CAD offers virtually unlimited freedom to explore alternatives, and in far less time.

When the product design is completed and the necessary information is assembled in the computer files, technicians may store the newly developed data, output it on a printer, transfer it to another computer, or send it directly to another step of the automated testing or manufacturing process.

A CAD/CAM technician uses a sophisticated computer to translate his drawings onto the screen.

Once the design is approved for production, CAD technicians may use their computers to assist in making detailed drawings of certain parts of the design. They may also prepare designs and drawings of the tools or equipment, such as molds, cutting tools, and jigs, that must be specially made in order to manufacture the product.

Technicians specializing in CAM technology usually work in one of two aspects of manufacturing: they either set up the manufacturing processes to operate with maximum efficiency and organization; or they run, maintain, and repair computer-controlled manufacturing apparatus, from simple automated devices to sophisticated robots.

Technicians who set up manufacturing processes use computers to aid their work. They gather data from various sources on the availability and location of parts and materials, conditions on the factory floor, and other similar variables in manufacturing. These pieces of data are combined in a central computer with management personnel's instructions and requirements about the manufacturing process. The technicians use the output information to help keep automated manufacturing equipment producing smoothly.

In some factory settings, the specially programmed computer determines the best way to make the needed products, then initiates, controls, and changes the automated production processes from start to finish. This can be very productive and highly cost effective: it allows the company to easily make changes if they need to adjust the number of items made, or if they must modify the product's design. They may do so right on the factory floor, and will not waste resources or lose time by manually making the changes.

An even more comprehensive type of computer-controlled system is known as computer-integrated manufacturing (CIM). CIM links all the manufacturing functions in one master system: the design, drafting, and manufacturing specifications along with such business-related activities as accounting, purchasing, and forecasting. Because of its complexity, CIM is being used in only a few manufacturing industries; because of its potential benefits, however, CIM promises to become much more important in the future. As more of these complex systems come into use, more CAD/CAM technicians will undoubtedly be needed to install, maintain, and repair them.

CAM technicians involved with automated and computer-controlled manufacturing equipment perform tasks that may be similar to those performed by robotics technicians, whose work is described in a separate article (see *Robotics Technicians*). CAM technicians may assist in all phases of engineering related to robots and other computer-controlled manufacturing equipment, from design and development to installation, repair, and maintenance.

Many kinds of machine tools—lathes, punch presses, milling machines, and others—can be computer controlled. These machines can be made so they operate alone on the factory floor, or they can be linked in clusters. This makes such equipment relatively easy to introduce into a manufacturing process. Today, computer-controlled machine tools are used in many industries, particularly those that produce metalworking machinery, automobiles, aircraft, spacecraft and artificial satellites and construction equipment.

Technicians working with the design and development of new robotic devices or automated equipment (such as machine tools) are part of a design team. Working closely with engineers, they carry out tests on systems and materials that are proposed for new machines. After the initial testing is complete, they may help build prototype models and produce the blueprints and manufacturing specifications used in building the machine.

Some CAM technicians assist with assembly or testing of finished machines or components to be sure they meet the design team's specifications.

CAM technicians often control, monitor, and modify the operations of the robotic devices and other computer-controlled manufacturing equipment. As they monitor these operations, the collected data, which is often in an electronic form, can be fed back into a computer to quickly and thoroughly analyze the manufacturing process. This helps determine anticipated output, materials consumption, and production efficiency. This data may then be used to further modify the operations of the automated equipment.

CAM technicians may also work as robot operators, especially in some kinds of specialized settings where the robot operation is apt to be complicated or even somewhat unpredictable. CAM technicians may also work as robotics technician trainers, teaching other employees how to install, use, and maintain the robots.

Finally, CAM technicians may work as maintenance technicians. These technicians make service calls to repair and maintain robots and other automated equipment. They may also install computer-controlled machines and help the client establish in-house maintenance and repair programs.

No matter what their specialty, CAD/CAM technicians keep records of all their test procedures and results. They may need to present written reports, tables, or charts to document their test results or other findings. If a particular system, subsystem, or material has not met a testing or production requirement, technicians may be asked to suggest a way to rearrange the system's components or substitute alternate materials.

Requirements

CAD/CAM technicians need to think logically, have good analytical skills, and be methodical, accurate, and detail-oriented in all their work. They should be able to work as part of a team, as well as independently, since they will spend long periods of time in front of video-display screens.

CAD/CAM technicians must be able to read and understand complex engineering diagrams and drawings. The minimum educational requirement for CAD/CAM technicians is a high school diploma. Interested high school students should take courses that provide them with a solid background in algebra, geometry, trigonometry, physics, machine-shop skills, drafting, and electronics, and they should take whatever computer courses are available to them. They should also take courses in English, especially those that improve their communications skills.

Some companies will accept technicians who have actual work experience with CAD/CAM technology instead of formal training in the field; however, acquiring that experience without training is very difficult. Therefore, most prospective CAD/CAM technicians undertake formal training beyond the high school level, usually in a two-year associate degree program taught at a technical school or community college.

Such a program should include courses in drafting and basic engineering topics, such as hydraulics, pneumatics, and electronics. It should include courses in: data processing; computer programming, systems, and equipment, especially video-display equipment; computer graphics; product design; industrial and architectural drafting; and computer peripheral equipment and data storage. Some two-year programs may also require the student to complete courses in technical writing, communications, social sciences, and the humanities.

In addition, some companies have their own training programs, which can last as long as two years. Requirements for entry into these company-run training programs vary from company to company.

Students considering a career in CAD/CAM technology should realize that such a career will require taking continuing-education courses even after they have found jobs. This continuing education is necessary because technicians need to know about recent advances in technology that may affect procedures, equipment, terminology, or programming concepts.

Although CAD/CAM technicians do not need to be licensed or become union members to get a job, membership in a professional organization will help them keep current with developments in the field.

Opportunities for experience and exploration

There are a number of ways to gain first-hand knowledge about the field of CAD/CAM technology. Unfortunately, part-time or summer jobs involved directly with CAD/CAM technology are very hard to find; however, drafting-related jobs can sometimes be found, and many future employers will look favorably on applicants with this kind of experience. In addition, jobs relating to other engineering fields, such as electronics or mechanics, may be available, and they offer the student an opportunity to become familiar with the kind of workplace in which technicians may later be employed.

In addition, high school courses in computers, geometry, physics, mechanical drawing, and shop work will give a student a feel for the mental and physical activities associated with CAD/CAM technology. Other relevant activi-

ties include membership in high school science clubs (especially computer and electronics clubs); participating in science fairs; pursuing hobbies that involve computers, electronics, drafting, mechanical equipment, and model building; and reading books and articles about technical topics.

Methods of entering

Probably the most reliable method for entering this field is through the school's placement office. This is especially true for students who graduate from a two-year college or technical institute: recruiters from companies employing CAD/CAM technicians sometimes visit such schools, and placement-office personnel can help students meet with these recruiters.

Graduates of post-high school programs who conduct their own job search might begin with architects, building firms, manufacturers, high-technology companies, and government agencies. They can contact prospective employers by phone or with a letter stating their interest in employment, accompanied by a resume that provides details about their education and job experience. State or private employment agencies may also be helpful, and classified ads in newspapers and professional journals may provide additional leads.

Advancement

CAD/CAM technicians who demonstrate their ability to handle more responsibility can expect to receive promotions after just a few years on the job. They may be assigned to designing or manufacturing work that requires their special skills or experience, such as troubleshooting problems with systems they have worked with; or they may be promoted to supervisory or training positions. As trainers, they may teach courses at their workplace or at a local school or community college.

In general, as CAD/CAM technicians advance, their assignments become less and less routine, until they may actually have a hand in designing and building equipment. Technicians who continue their education and earn a bachelor's degree may become data-processing managers, engineers, or systems or manufacturing analysts.

Other routes for advancement include becoming a sales representative for a design firm or for a company selling computer-assisted manufacturing services or equipment. It may also be possible to become an independent contractor for companies using or manufacturing CAD/CAM equipment.

Employment outlook

The employment outlook for CAD/CAM technicians is excellent. Many companies in the near future will feel pressures to increase productivity in design and manufacturing activities, and CAD/CAM technology provides some of the best opportunities to improve that productivity. By some estimates, there will be as many as a million jobs available for technically trained personnel in the field of CAD/CAM technology by the start of the next century.

In the field of CAM technology, the number of industrial robots in use will increase substantially during the 1990s. Companies already using robots will probably increase their reliance on these devices, and, more importantly, companies not presently using robots will find ways to make use of them. For prospective CAM technicians, this expansion means more trained technicians will be needed to design, build, install, monitor, maintain, and repair the robots.

Earnings

Starting salaries for CAD/CAM technicians who are graduates of two-year technical programs typically fall in the range of $18,325 to $22,396 a year; however, actual salaries will vary widely depending on geographic location, exact job requirements, and the training needed to obtain those jobs. With increased training and experience, technicians can earn salaries of approximately $30,500 a year, and some technicians with special skills, extensive experience, or added responsibilities may earn more.

Benefits usually include insurance, paid vacations and holidays, pension plans, and sometimes stock-purchase plans.

Conditions of work

The work conditions for CAD/CAM technicians vary, depending on the technology involved. CAD technicians almost always work in clean, quiet, well-lighted, air-conditioned rooms. Most CAD technicians spend most of their days at a work station. While the work does not require great physical effort, it does require patience and the ability to maintain concentration and attention for extended periods of time. Some technicians may find they suffer from eyestrain from working long periods in front of a video-display screen.

CAM technicians are more likely to work in a factory setting where noise levels will probably be higher, although those involved with the development and testing of CAM equipment and systems often work in fairly quiet settings. CAM technicians are also apt to be fairly active, moving about, bending, lifting, or carrying equipment. Some technicians involved with CAM technology will confront potentially hazardous conditions, such as the use of laser beams, arc-welding equipment, or hazardous chemicals. Although plant safety procedures will protect the attentive and cautious workers, carelessness in such settings can be particularly dangerous.

CAD/CAM technicians, because of their training and experience, are valuable employees. They are called upon to exercise independent judgment and to be responsible for valuable equipment. Out of necessity, they also sometimes find themselves carrying out routine, uncomplicated tasks. CAD/CAM technicians must be able to respond well to both kinds of demands. Most CAD/CAM technicians work as part of a team. They are required to follow orders, and may encounter situations in which their individual contributions are not fully recognized. Successful CAD/CAM technicians are those who work well as team members and who can derive satisfaction from the accomplishments of the team as a whole.

Increasing productivity in the industrial design and manufacturing fields will ensure the long-term economic vitality of the country; CAD/CAM technology is one of the most promising developments in this search for increased productivity. Knowing that they are in the forefront of this important and challenging undertaking can provide CAD/CAM technicians with a good deal of pride and satisfaction.

GOE: 05.03.02, 05.05.11; SIC: 871; SOC: 3719, 372

◇ **SOURCES OF ADDITIONAL INFORMATION**

American Design and Drafting Association
966 Hungerford Road, Suite 10-B
Rockville, MD 20854

Association for Integrated Manufacturing Technology
5411 East State Street
Rockford, IL 61108

Institute of Electrical and Electronics Engineers
345 East 47th Street
New York, NY 10017

Computer-Aided Manufacturing, International
1250 East Copeland Road, Suite 500
Arlington, TX 76011

Robotic Industries Association
PO Box 3724
900 Victors Way
Ann Arbor, MI 48106

Society of Manufacturing Engineers
Education Department
PO Box 930
One SME Drive
Dearborn, MI 48121

◇ **RELATED ARTICLES**

Volume 1: Computer Hardware; Computer Software; Engineering
Volumes 2–4: Computer programmers; Data-processing technicians; Drafting and design technicians; Electrical and electronics engineers; Graphics programmers; Industrial designers; Industrial engineering technicians; Robotics technicians

Calibration technicians

Definition

Calibration technicians, also known as *standards laboratory technicians,* work in the electronics industry and in aircraft and aerospace manufacturing. They test, calibrate, and repair electrical, mechanical, and electronic instruments used to measure and record voltage, heat, magnetic resonance, and other factors.

Nature of the work

Calibration technicians set up standardized laboratory equipment to test and measure the accuracy of instruments, and they plan the sequence of procedures to test and calibrate them using blueprints, schematic drawings, and other data. As part of their inspection of recording systems and measuring instruments, they measure parts for conformity to specifications using micrometers, calipers, and other precision instruments; and they repair or replace parts, using jeweler's lathes, files, soldering irons, and other tools. They also help engineering personnel to develop calibration standards, devise formulas to solve problems in measurement and calibration, and to write pro-

cedures and practical guides for other calibration technicians. Calibration tools are now so refined that surfaces can be measured to one-thousandth of an inch.

Requirements

Calibration technicians should be high school graduates and should have attended a two-year post–high school training program. During the course of their training, they should: receive instruction in algebra, calculus, and statistics; develop their language skills to the point that they can read newspapers, manuals, and encyclopedias; write letters and reports with proper spelling and punctuation; and express themselves clearly in informal conversation and in formal discussions.

Opportunities for experience and exploration

Students interested in testing their abilities at, and learning more about, calibration work can

A calibration technician measures the strength of elastomer rubber by stretching it to its breaking point. He is testing the rubber to determine its practical use.

Methods of entering

Most two-year training schools have some form of placement program for graduates. Placement offices and guidance counselors at school should be able to provide assistance. Classified advertisements may list entry-level jobs.

Conditions of work

Calibration technicians work both indoors and outdoors and the physical demands connected with their work are generally light. Depending on the type of equipment they are working on, the calibration may be extremely precise and the work very exacting. This type of work requires patience, attention to detail, and strong organizational skills. Forgetting to do something, or doing something carelessly may endanger the lives of those operating the equipment being calibrated.

GOE: 02.04.01; SIC: 36; SOC: 3711

build small electronic equipment and adapt or adjust it. Kits are available in some electronic shops for building radios and other small appliances. This gives some basic understanding of electronic components and applications.

Some communities and schools also have clubs for people interested in electronics. They may provide some classes or projects that help people learn basic skills in construction, repair, and adjustment of electrical and electronic products.

Model building, particularly in hard plastic and steel, gives the student a good understanding of how pieces fit together and how to adjust parts to fit exactly as needed. It may also help build hand skills for those who want to work with precision instruments.

◇ **RELATED ARTICLES**

Volume 1: Aviation and Aerospace; Electronics; Engineering
Volumes 2–4: Aeronautical and aerospace technicians; Avionics technicians; Electronics technicians; Electronics test technicians; Instrumentation technicians; Miscellaneous engineers

Canning and preserving industry workers

Definition

Canning and preserving industry workers do a wide variety of routine tasks in food processing plants that can, preserve, and quick-freeze such foods as vegetables, fruits, frozen dinners, jams, jellies, preserves, pickles, and soups. They also process and preserve seafood, including shrimp, oysters, crab, clams, and fish.

History

As soon as people learned to grow and harvest food, they faced a problem—keeping that food from spoiling so that it could last until the next harvest. Centuries ago, people discovered that salting, drying, and pickling could preserve many meats, fruits, and vegetables. In colonial times in America, most of this preserving was done in the home. Families grew their own fruits and vegetables and canned them to make them last through the winter months. Since then, advances in refrigeration and sanitation and new applications of many industrial processes to food preparation have almost completely transferred the business of preserving food to large factories. Very few Americans today grow and preserve large quantities of their own food. But factory-preserved fruits, fish, soup, and vegetables are found in almost every refrigerator and kitchen cupboard in the nation.

Canning workers weigh cans of tuna and add extra chunks to those that are under the required weight.

Nature of the work

In order to operate successfully, a food-processing plant must have a good supply of the foodstuff it processes. Therefore, many workers in the canning and preserving industry work outside processing plants arranging this supply of raw materials. *Field contractors* negotiate with farmers to grow certain kinds of food crops for processing. They work with farmers to decide what to plant, how to grow the crop, and when to harvest it. They reach agreements concerning price, the quantity that will be delivered, and the quality standards that the crop must meet. *Purchasing agents* purchase raw materials and other goods for processing.

When unprocessed food arrives at the factory, *graders,* including *fruit-buying graders,* examine produce and record its quality, or grade, and mark it for separation by class, size, color, and condition.

Wharf laborers unload catches of fish for processing from the wharf and transport the fish to the processing plant's storage area. *Fish-bin tenders* sort fish according to species and size.

At the plant, the *plant superintendent* coordinates processing activities to coincide with crop harvesting. The *plant manager* hires workers, contacts buyers, and coordinates maintenance and operation of plant machinery.

Most processing of food is done with automatic machines. *Dumping-machine operators* run machines that grip, tilt, and dump boxes of produce onto conveyor belts leading to washing vats. Workers then wash food and inspect

the produce, removing damaged or spoiled items before they can be processed. *Sieve-grader tenders* and *sorting-machine operators* tend machines that sort vegetables, shrimp, and pickles according to size.

Many foods are bathed in brine, a concentrated solution of salt in water that acts as a preservative. *Brine makers* measure ingredients for the solution and boil it in a steam cooker for a specified amount of time. They test the solution's salinity with a hydrometer and pump it to a processing vat. They may also operate the vats and empty and clean them when necessary.

Plants that process fish and shellfish may kill, shell, and clean the fish before processing. *Crab butchers* butcher live crabs before canning. *Fish cleaners* and *fish-cleaning-machine operators* scale, slice open, and eviscerate fish. Using a shucking knife, *shellfish shuckers* pry open oyster, clam, and scallop shells and remove the meat. Shrimp are often shelled by machines that are operated by workers who must make adjustments according to the size of the shrimp. Later *separator operators* remove any sand or remaining shell particles from shellfish meats using water or air agitating machines. Alternatively, *bone pickers* look for shell particles by placing shellfish meats under ultraviolet light and picking shell bits out by hand. Other workers operate machines that wash, steam, brine, and peel shellfish.

Often only one part of a fruit or vegetable is wanted for processing. Many workers operate machines that peel or extract the desired parts from produce. *Finisher operators* run machines that remove the skin and seeds from tomatoes, leaving pulp that is used in sauces and catsup. *Lye-peel operators* run machines that use lye and water to remove skins of fruits and vegetables. *Fruit-press operators* run power presses to extract juice from fruit for flavorings and syrup, and *extractor-machine operators* extract juice from citrus fruits.

Food must often be cut into pieces of the proper size and shape for preserving. *Meat blenders* grind meat for use in baby food. Many workers operate machines that cut or chop produce, and *fish butchers* and *fish choppers* cut fish into pieces and lengths for freezing or canning.

Next, many foods are cooked. Some are cooked before and others after they are sealed in packages. Many vegetables are blanched (scalded with hot water or steam) before packaging, by *blanching-machine operators. Kettle cooks* and their *helpers* cook other fish, fruits, and vegetables in large kettles before packaging. These workers must measure and load water and uncooked food into the kettles; stir, monitor, and test foods as they cook; and remove cooked food from the kettles. Other workers cook fish, meat, and vegetables by deep-frying before freezing. *Vacuum-kettle cooks* vacuum-cook fruits and berries for jam and jelly.

Other foods, including many vegetables, are processed after they have been sealed in cans. *Packers* fill cans or jars with food to specified volume and weight. Other workers operate closing machines to put an airtight seal on the containers. Containers are then taken to retort chambers. Retorts are like huge steam pressure cookers, and they can heat food containers to temperatures between 240°F and 260°F. *Retort operators* load, start, and stop these machines according to specifications. Food must then be quickly cooled to stop cooking. *Pasteurizers* kill bacteria in bottles, canned foods, and beverages using a hot water spray or steam.

Some food is preserved using brine. *Picklers* mix ingredients for pickling vegetables, fruits, fish, and meat and soak these foods for a specified period of time. *Briners* immerse fresh fish fillets in brine to condition them for freezing. *Brineyard supervisors* coordinate activities of brining workers.

Some cooked food is prepared for canning by removing extra moisture, and some fish is smoked to preserve it. *Fish smokers* put salt-cured fish on racks in a smoke chamber and turn a valve to admit smoke into the chamber.

Many foods are frozen fresh or after blanching. *Freezing-room workers* move racks of packaged food in and out of freezing rooms. They keep track of the amount of time food has been in the freezing room and remove the food when it is sufficiently frozen to transport to a warehouse or onto delivery trucks. *Freezer-tunnel operators* quick-freeze foods.

Other foods, especially fruits, are preserved by drying. *Dehydrator tenders* bleach and dehydrate fruit, while other workers dry eggs, milk, and potatoes for processing into powders and flour.

Once food has been canned, it is labeled, tested, and inspected. *Vacuum testers* tap can lids with sticks to make sure they are vacuum sealed. *Can inspectors* check seams of closed food and beverage cans by cutting and taking measurements of seams of sample cans. *X-ray inspectors* X ray jars of baby food to ensure they contain no foreign materials.

Other workers are employed to clean cooking kettles and other equipment. *Production helpers* perform a variety of unskilled tasks in canning and preserving plants. Workers may also be designated according to the food they prepare—*steak sauce makers, mincemeat makers, relish blenders,* and *horseradish makers,* for example.

Cook room supervisors and *preparation supervisors* monitor and coordinate the activities of workers in preparing and canning foods. *Fish-processing supervisors* train new workers and inspect fish.

In large plants, each worker may perform one specific task. In smaller plants, one worker may perform many of the tasks necessary to preserve the food.

Requirements

In hiring applicants for food-processing jobs, most employers prefer high school graduates. Beginning workers seldom need any previous special experience or training, and usually they can learn their jobs quickly. Many plants provide orientation sessions for new workers and programs on safety and sanitation.

Manual dexterity is a useful characteristic for many workers in the canning and preserving industry, as are reliability and willingness to learn.

Special requirements

Workers who perform routine tasks in food-processing plants do not need to have special qualifications, but some skilled and technical staff in plants in some states must by licensed. In addition, retort room supervisors are required by the Food and Drug Administration to attend an instructional program in retort operation.

Opportunities for experience and exploration

It may be possible to arrange to tour a food-processing plant. Such a visit can be a good way to get a general overview of the jobs that various workers do in the plant. Talking to people employed in different jobs in canning or preserving plants is another good way to learn something about the field. Because some food-processing work is seasonal, part-time job opportunities for students may be limited. However, temporary employment, such as during summer harvest season, may be possible for some people.

Methods of entering

Applying to canneries, freezing plants, and other food-processing plants is the most direct method of finding work in this area. Employers may advertise openings in newspaper want ads or with the state employment service.

Advancement

Most canning and preserving industry workers with a high school education start out as sorters or helpers or in similar unskilled positions. Advancement opportunities from these positions are limited. In time, some workers can become machine tenders, machine operators, inspectors, or work crew leaders. Some experienced workers move into field contractor positions.

Employment outlook

Fewer than 80,000 people work in the canning industry in the 1990s, and this number is expected to decline into the year 2000. The outlook for employment in some other sectors of the food-processing industry, such as frozen foods, is a little better, but the jobs of all processing workers are threatened to some degree by automation. Wherever it is efficient and economical, machines may take over some of the tasks that people have been doing, with the result that fewer processing workers will be needed. As the food-processing industry grows, researchers and technical workers with specialized expertise and college-level training will have the best employment opportunities.

Still, many jobs in the canning and preserving industry cannot be done by machines. Every year many new openings will develop as workers in these jobs leave them for other occupations, retire, or die.

In some kinds of food processing, such as the fish canneries in Alaska, employment levels are related to weather and other natural factors that vary from year to year.

Earnings

Although some products can be processed at any time during the year, the level of activity in many food-processing plants varies with the season, and earnings of workers vary accordingly. Limited information about the earnings for these workers indicates that in the 1990s the average worker working 40 hours a week in the canning and preserving industry makes about $12,000 per year. Inspectors and other staff with some technical training earn closer to $14,500 per year. Wages depend greatly on geographic location, the size of the plant, and other factors.

Conditions of work

Canning and preserving plants are located in many parts of the country. Most plants are located close to the supply source and are staffed by local people who sometimes hold other jobs as well. During harvest season, plants may operate 24 hours a day, with three work shifts.

In plants where food is frozen, some workers spend considerable time in temperatures that are well below freezing. These workers wear special clothing and take periodic warm-up breaks during the day. Canneries, on the other hand, may be damp, noisy, and odorous. In some jobs, workers need to be on their feet for long periods of time, and often the tasks are very repetitive.

GOE: 06.04.15; SIC: 203, 2091; SOC: 7759

◇ **SOURCES OF ADDITIONAL INFORMATION**

American Farm Bureau Federation
225 Touhy Avenue
Park Ridge, IL 60068

Food Processors Institute
1401 New York Avenue, NW, Suite 400
Washington, DC 20005

American Frozen Food Institute
1764 Old Meadow Lane, Suite 350
McLean, VA 22102

Institute of Food Technologists
221 North LaSalle Street, Suite 2120
Chicago, IL 60601

The Ford Institute of Canada
#1409, 130 Albert Street
Ottawa ON K1P 5G4

◇ **RELATED ARTICLES**

Volume 1: Baking; Food Processing
Volumes 2–4: Bakery products workers; Food technologists; Macaroni and related products industry workers; Meat packing production workers

Career counselors

Definition

Career counselors, or *career/vocational counselors*, provide advice to individuals or groups about occupations, careers, career decision making, career planning, and other career development related questions or conflicts.

History

The history of career counseling in the United States dates back to the turn of the century and the founding of the National Career Development Association (formerly NVGA) in 1913. In 1980 the National Career Development Association established a committee for the pre-service and in-service training of vocational guidance personnel. Based on several professional studies, the training committee developed a list of competencies necessary for people who planned to perform career and vocational counseling. In 1984 the NCDA established its national credentialing process. The National Board for Certified Counselors now certifies professional career counselors to work in both public agencies and in the private sector.

Nature of the work

A certified career counselor helps people make decisions and plan life and career directions. Strategies and techniques are tailored to the specific need of the person seeking help. Counselors conduct individual and group personal counseling sessions to help qualify life and career goals. They administer and interpret tests and inventories to assess abilities and interests and identify career options. They may use career planning and occupational information to help individuals better understand the work world. They assist in developing individualized career plans, teach job hunting strategies and skills, and help develop resumes. Sometimes this involves resolving personal conflicts on the job. They also provide support for people experiencing job stress, job loss, and career transition.

To work as a professional, one must demonstrate minimum competencies in six designated areas. These six areas are general counseling, information, individual and group assessment, management and administration, implementation, and consultation. Professional career counselors work in both private and public settings and are verified by the National Board for Certified Counselors (NBCC).

Requirements

Career counselors must be competent in general counseling. They must have skills in building good relationships and the ability to use counseling techniques in assisting individuals with career choice and life career plans. Career counselors must have a good background in education, training, employment trends, labor market, and career resources. They should be able to provide information about job tasks, functions, salaries, requirements, and future outlooks related to broad occupational fields.

In addition, counselors must understand the changing roles of men and women and the linkage of work, family, and leisure. Knowledge of testing techniques and measures of aptitude, achievement, interests, values, and personality is required. The ability to evaluate job performance and individual effectiveness is helpful. The career counselor must also have management and administrative skills.

The minimum educational program in career and vocational counseling is a graduate degree in counseling or a related field from a regionally accredited higher education institution, and a completed supervised counseling experience, which includes career counseling. A growing number of institutions offer post-master's degrees with training in career development and career counseling. Such programs are highly recommended for people who wish to specialize in vocational and career counseling. These programs are frequently called "Advanced Graduate Specialist Programs" or "Certificates of Advanced Study Program."

Opportunities for experience and exploration

People interested in becoming career counselors should seek out professional career counselors and discuss the field with them. They also might contact the National Board for Certified Counselors (NBCC) for certification information. They may consult the National Career Development Association for competency statements and consumer guidelines. Undergraduate students interested in career counseling should take courses in counseling, psychology, sociology, and business management and administration.

Methods of entering

Journals specializing in information for career counselors frequently have job listings or information on job hotlines and services. School placement centers also are a good source of information, both because of their standard practice of listing job openings from participating firms and because schools are a likely source of jobs for career counselors. Placement officers

A career counselor leads a seminar to discuss the prospects of self-employment.

should be aware of which schools are looking for applicants.

Advancement

New employees in agencies are frequently considered trainees for the first six months to a year of their employment. During the training period, they acquire the specific skills that will be required of them during their tenure with the agency. Frequently, the first year of employment is probationary. After several years' experience on the job, counselors may reach supervisory or administrative positions.

In private practice counseling, one may advance by expanding one's practice and hiring other career counselors as employees or by expanding one's knowledge base and venturing out into related fields, such as consultation with business and industry. The opportunities for advancing in private practice are excellent. However, in both the private and public sector, a master's degree is generally recommended.

Employment outlook

Employment opportunities for career counselors are expected to show a faster than average increase through the end of the 1990s. As a result of technological, social, and economic factors, many employees presently in the labor force will be displaced. These workers will have to be counseled and trained for other occupations, creating a demand for career counselors. There are also career counseling specialties developing in markets such as placement of the disabled or the learning impaired. Private practice counseling, and career counseling in particular, is on the increase throughout the United States.

Earnings

Salaries vary greatly within the career and vocational counseling field. Average salaries range from $24,200 to $40,000 a year. Direct providers of service average from $27,000 to $32,000 per year. Directors of career counseling centers earn over $49,300 a year. Those in business or industry earn somewhat higher salaries.

In private practice, the range is yet wider. Some practitioners earn as little as $17,700 per year and others earn in excess of $100,000 per year.

Often, people who work in agencies have part-time practices of career counseling. This is frequently the way that people start out in private practice, where average earnings, depending on the section of the country in which one lives, range from $28,000 to $45,000 per year. To succeed in private practice, the practitioner should have entrepreneurial skills, as well as counseling skills.

Conditions of work

Most career counselors work in pleasant offices. All career counseling positions require contact with people and many require contact with clients of diverse ages and backgrounds. Regular hours are typical for people working in agencies.

Private practice may require extremely long hours. Flexible schedules to provide services in the evenings and on weekends are sometimes required.

Depending on the type of counseling done, group lectures may be part of the counselor's job. Addressing classes, or groups of clients, or establishing target jobs, developing resumes, or handling interviews, may be part of the counselor's role.

GOE: 10.01.02; SIC: 8211; SOC: 24

◇ **SOURCES OF ADDITIONAL INFORMATION**

American Association for Counseling and Development
5999 Stevenson Avenue
Alexandria, VA 22304

Career Planning and Adult Development Network
4965 Sierra Road
San Jose, CA 95132

Career Information Advisory Group
44 Appian Drive
North York ON M2J 2P9

◇ **RELATED ARTICLES**

Volume 1: Human Resources; Social Services
Volumes 2–4: Career guidance technicians; College career planning and placement counselors; Employment counselors; Guidance counselors; Personnel and labor relations specialists

---

Career guidance technicians

Definition

Career guidance technicians assist guidance counselors by collecting and organizing information about careers and occupations for school career information centers. They usually work under the direction of a librarian or career guidance counselor.

Nature of the work

The principal duty of career guidance technicians is to help order, catalog, and file materials relating to job opportunities, careers, technical schools, scholarships, careers in the Armed Forces, and other programs. Guidance technicians also help students and teachers find materials relating to a student's interests and aptitudes. These various materials may be in the form of books, pamphlets, magazine articles, microfiche, videos, computer software, or other media.

Often career guidance technicians help students take and score self-administered tests that determine their aptitude and interest in different careers or job-related activities. If the career guidance center has audiovisual equipment, such as VCRs or film or slide projectors, career guidance technicians are usually the ones who are responsible for the equipment, to keep it in good condition, and to help people to operate it.

To assist the counseling and guidance staff, career guidance technicians may sometimes schedule students' appointments with the school guidance counselors, and they may give talks to parents, to students, or to other groups about the activities and services of the career guidance center. They may also help keep records of students enrolled in work-study or other vocational programs. If guidance technicians are aware of a student's interest, they make contact with the student when a job is posted.

Requirements

Career guidance technicians need to be high school graduates. In addition, most employers look for applicants who have completed two years of training beyond high school, usually at a junior, community, or technical college. These two-year programs, which usually lead to an associate degree, may combine classroom instruction with practical or sometimes even on-the-job experience.

Career guidance technicians need good reading and writing skills. They should be able to read and understand newspapers, magazine articles, dictionaries, instruction manuals, and encyclopedias. They should be able to write letters and reports with proper spelling, punctuation, and grammar, and be able to speak clearly and easily in front of a group of people. In addition, they also need to have had some training in mathematics, including algebra and geometry.

In addition to meeting these educational requirements, career guidance technicians should enjoy helping and working with other people, especially students. They also need to be well organized and to feel comfortable using organized systems for finding and storing information.

A career guidance technician at a college operates a computer software program that lists all of the events of the day including the scheduled interviews for recruiting companies.

Opportunities for experience and exploration

Working part-time or as a volunteer in a library will provide students with some of the basic skills for learning about information resources, cataloguing, and filing. Assisting schools or clubs with any media presentation, such as video or slide shows, will help familiarize a student with the equipment and room arrangement that best suits a room.

Since some public speaking may be involved in the work of a career guidance technician, speech and forensics clubs at school will help the interested student develop good public presentation skills.

Methods of entering

Training schools should have some form of career placement for graduates. Newspapers may list entry level jobs. But one of the best methods is by contacting libraries and education centers to inquire about their needs for assistance in developing or staffing their career guidance center.

Employment outlook

Libraries and schools have had increasingly limited budgets for staff and resources. Competition for jobs in the educational market is increasingly stiff. The needs of outplacement centers, employment agencies, and Armed Forces offices are remaining somewhat stagnant. If there is an increased focus on retraining workers or educating students about career options, there may be an increase in the future demand for career guidance technicians.

Earnings

Salaries vary according to the technician's education, experience, and the geographical location of the job. In general, however, career guidance technicians who are graduates of two-year post-high school training programs can expect to receive starting salaries averaging around $15,000 to $20,000 a year. With increased experience they will earn more, usually up to $30,000 a year and sometimes more.

Conditions of work

Career guidance technicians work in very pleasant surroundings, usually in the career guidance office of a college or vocational school. They will interact with a great number of students, some of whom are eagerly looking for work, others who are more tense and anxious. The technician must remain unruffled in order to ease any tension and provide a quiet atmosphere.

GOE: 11.02.04; SIC: 8211; SOC: 4632

◇ **SOURCES OF ADDITIONAL INFORMATION**

Career Planning and Adult Development Network
4965 Sierra Road
San Jose, CA 95132

The National Career Development Association
5999 Stevenson Avenue
Alexandria, VA 22304

◇ **RELATED ARTICLES**

Volume 1: Education; Human Resources; Library and Information Science
Volumes 2–4: Career counselors; College career planning and placement counselors; Employment counselors; File clerks; General office clerks; Guidance counselors; Librarians; Library technicians; Teacher aides

Carpenters

Definition

Carpenters cut, shape, level, and fasten together pieces of wood and other construction materials, such as wallboard, plywood, and insulation. Many carpenters work on constructing, remodeling, or repairing houses and other kinds of buildings. Other carpenters work at other construction sites, such as those where roads, bridges, docks, boats, mining tunnels, wooden vats, and a wide variety of other structures are built. A carpenter may specialize in building the rough framing of a structure, and thus be considered a *rough carpenter* or he may specialize in the finishing details of a structure, such as the trim around doors and widows, and thus be considered a *finish carpenter*.

History

Wood has been used as a building material since the dawn of civilization. Stone axes, saw-like tools, and borers were, in fact, among the earliest tools developed by humans. After ancient craft workers learned to fashion items from metal, the use of metal tools spread throughout much of the world. Specialized tools began to be made for particular tasks, including working with wood. Tools that resembled modern hand tools first began to be made around 1500 B.C. By the Middle Ages, many of the basic techniques and the essential tools of carpentry were perfected, and they have changed little since that time.

The role of carpenters, however, has changed. In the past, buildings were mostly built with braced-frame construction, which made use of large, heavy timbers held together with mortised joints and diagonal bracing. In this kind of construction, carpenters were often the principal workers on a house or other building. Since the mid-19th century, balloon-frame construction, which makes use of smaller and lighter pieces of wood, has simplified the construction process, and concrete and steel have replaced wood for many purposes, especially in floors and roofs. But as some carpentry tasks in building construction have become easier, other new jobs, such as making forms for poured concrete, have added to the importance of carpenters at construction sites.

Nature of the work

Carpenters are the largest group of workers in the building trades. There are over a million carpenters in the United States today. About 80 percent work for contractors involved in building, repairing, and remodeling buildings and other structures. Manufacturing firms, schools, stores, and government bodies employ most other carpenters.

Carpenters do two basic kinds of work: rough carpentry and finish carpentry. Rough carpentry involves constructing and installing temporary structures and supports, wooden structures used in industrial settings, as well as parts of buildings that are usually covered up when the rooms are finished. Among the structures built by such carpenters are scaffolds for other workers to stand on, chutes used as channels for wet concrete, forms for concrete foundations, and timber structures that support machinery. In buildings, they may put up the frame, install rafters, joists, subflooring, wall sheathing, prefabricated wall panels and windows, and many other components.

Finish carpentry involves installing hardwood flooring, staircases, shelves, cabinets, trim on windows and doors, and other woodwork and hardware that makes the building look complete, inside and outside. Finish carpentry requires especially careful, precise workmanship, because the result must have a good appearance, in addition to being sturdy. Many carpenters who are employed by building contractors do both rough and finish work on buildings.

Although they do many different tasks in different settings, carpenters generally follow approximately the same basic steps. First they look over blueprints or plans for information (or get instructions from a supervisor) about the dimensions of the structure to be built and the

Working in a metropolitan area, a carpenter builds a barricade to keep pedestrians away from the construction. Such barricades are not removed until the construction is complete.

type of materials to be used. Sometimes local building codes determine how a structure should be built, so carpenters need to know about such regulations. Using rulers, framing squares, chalk lines, and other measuring and marking equipment, they lay out how the work will be done. Using hand and power tools, they cut and shape the wood, plywood, fiberglass, plastic, or other materials. Then they nail, screw, glue, or staple the pieces together. Lastly, they use levels, plumb bobs, rulers, and squares to check their work, and they make any necessary adjustments. Sometimes carpenters work with prefabricated units for components such as wall panels or stairs. Installing these is a much less complicated task, because much less layout, cutting, and assembly work is needed.

Carpenters who work outside of the building construction field may do a variety of installation and maintenance jobs, such as repairing furniture, changing locks, and installing ceiling tiles or exterior siding on buildings. Other carpenters specialize in building, repairing, or modifying ships, wooden boats, wooden railroad trestles, timber framing in mine shafts, woodwork inside railcars, storage tanks and vats, or stage sets in theaters.

Requirements

Carpenters can acquire the skills of their trade in various ways, through formal training programs and through informal on-the-job training. Of the different ways to learn, an apprenticeship is considered the best, because it provides a more thorough and complete foundation for a career than other kinds of training. However, the limited number of available apprenticeships means that not all carpenters can learn their trade in this way.

Many carpenters pick up skills informally on the job while they work as carpenter's helpers. Usually employers prefer applicants who have completed high school. They begin with little or no training and gradually learn as they work under the supervision of experienced carpenters. The skills that helpers develop depend on the jobs that their employers contract to do. Working for a small contracting company, a beginner may learn about relatively few kinds of carpentry tasks. On the other hand, a large contracting company may offer a wider variety of opportunities to learn. Becoming a skilled carpenter by this method can take much longer than an apprenticeship, and the completeness of the training varies. Some people who are waiting for an apprenticeship to become available work as helpers to gain experience in the field.

Other carpenters learn skills in vocational educational programs offered in trade schools and in correspondence courses. Vocational programs can be very good, especially as a supplement to other practical training. But without additional hands-on instruction, vocational school graduates may not be well enough prepared to get many jobs in the field, because some programs do not provide sufficient opportunity for students to practice and perfect their carpentry skills.

The best way to become a carpenter is to complete an apprenticeship, a training program usually lasting three to four years. Apprenticeships are administered by employer groups and local chapters of various labor unions that organize carpenters. Applicants for apprenticeships must meet the requirements of local apprenticeship committees. Typically, applicants must be at least 17 years old and must show that they have some aptitude for carpentry and enough education to complete the training.

Apprenticeships combine on-the-job work experience with classroom instruction in a planned, systematic program. Initially, apprentices work at such simple tasks as building concrete forms, rough framing, and nailing subflooring. Toward the end of the training they may work on finishing trimwork, fitting hardware, hanging doors, and building stairs. In the course of this experience, they become familiar with the tools, materials, techniques, and equipment of the trade, and they learn how to do layout, framing, finishing, and other basic carpentry jobs.

The work experience is supplemented by about 144 hours of classroom instruction per year. Some of this instruction concerns the correct use and maintenance of tools, safety practices, first aid, building code requirements, and the properties of different construction materials. Among other subjects that apprentices study are the principles of layout, blueprint reading, shop mathematics, and sketching. Both on the job and in the classroom, carpenters learn how to work effectively with members of other skilled building trades.

A good high school background for prospective carpenters would include carpentry and woodworking courses, as well as other shop classes, applied mathematics, mechanical drawing, and blueprint reading. Carpenters need to have manual dexterity, good eye-hand coordination, and a good sense of balance. They need to be in good physical condition, because the work involves a great deal of activity. Stamina is much more important than physical strength. On the job, carpenters may have to climb, stoop, kneel, crouch, and reach.

Opportunities for experience and exploration

High school students may begin finding out about the work that carpenters do by taking courses such as wood shop, applied mathematics, drafting, and other industrial arts. Simple projects such as building birdhouses or shelving at home can also help people gauge their ability and interest in the field. Summer employment at a construction site can provide a useful overview of the work performed in the construction industry and perhaps the opportunity to talk with carpenters on the job. Some people first learn about carpentry while serving in the U.S. Armed Forces.

Methods of entering

Two important ways of starting out in carpentry are by completing an apprenticeship program and by gradually gaining experience and skills on the job. Information about apprenticeships can be obtained by contacting the local office of the state employment service, area contractors that hire carpenters, or the local offices of the United Brotherhood of Carpenters and Joiners of America, a union that cooperates in sponsoring apprenticeships. Helper jobs that can be filled by beginners without special training in carpentry may be advertised in newspaper classified ads or with the state employment service. Another possibility is contacting potential employers directly.

Advancement

After they have gained enough experience, carpenters may be promoted to positions where they are responsible for supervising the work of other carpenters. If their background includes exposure to a broad range of construction activities, they may eventually advance to positions as general construction supervisors. Carpenters who are skillful at mathematical computations and have a good knowledge of the construction business may become estimators. Some carpenters go into business for themselves, doing repair or construction work as independent contractors.

Employment outlook

Overall, the outlook for carpenters over the next 10 to 15 years is about the same as the average for other occupational fields. Total employment of carpenters is expected to increase moderately, as new construction and renovations of existing structures continue. But at any one time, building activity and thus job opportunities will be better in some geographic areas than in others, reflecting regional and local variations in economic conditions.

Even if construction activity is strong in coming years, several factors will contribute to a slower rate of employment growth than at times in the past. One factor is the trend toward increasing use of prefabricated building components, which are more quickly and easily installed than parts made by traditional construction methods. The use of prefabricated materials is likely to mean that fewer skilled carpenters will be needed. Also, many new lightweight, cordless tools like nailers and drills are making the work of carpenters easier and faster, thus tending to reduce the total number of workers needed.

Job turnover is relatively high in the carpentry field. Many people prefer to switch to another occupation after working for a while because they find their skills are too limited to get the best jobs or they don't like the work. As a result, every year thousands of job openings will become available. Carpenters with good all-around skills, such as those who have completed apprenticeships, will have the best chances of being hired for the most desirable positions.

Nonetheless, carpenters can expect that they may go through periods of unemployment. The number of available jobs is always related to various economic factors, and during an economic downturn fewer building projects are started. Carpenters need to plan for the possibility of major ups and downs in their income.

Earnings

In the 1990s, the majority of carpenters who do not own their own businesses have earnings that range between $15,800 and $29,700 per year. Some make as little as about $12,400, while a few have earnings of at least $38,400. Starting pay for apprentices is about 50 percent of the experienced worker's pay scale. It is increased periodically so that by the last phase of training, the pay of apprentices is 85 to 90 percent of the carpenter's rate. Fringe benefits such as health insurance, pension funds, and paid vacations are available to most workers in this field.

Conditions of work

Carpenters may work either indoors or outdoors. If they are engaged in rough carpentry, they probably do most of their work outdoors. They may have to work on high scaffolding or in a basement making cement forms. A construction site can be noisy, dusty, hot, cold, or muddy. Often carpenters must be physically active throughout the day, constantly standing, stooping, climbing, and reaching. Some of the possible hazards of the job include being hit by falling objects, falling off a ladder, muscle strains, and cuts and scrapes on fingers and hands. Carpenters who use proper safety practices and procedures can minimize these hazards.

Work in the construction industry involves changing from one job location to another and from time to time being laid off because of poor weather or shortages of materials. Workers in this field must be able to arrange their finances so that they can make it through periods of unemployment. Most carpenters belong to the United Brotherhood of Carpenters and Joiners of America.

GOE: 05.05.02; SIC: 1751; SOC: 6422

National Association of Home Builders
Home Builders Institute
15th and M Streets, NW
Washington, DC 20005

United Brotherhood of Carpenters and Joiners of America
101 Constitution Avenue, NW
Washington, DC 20001

Ontario Carpentry Contractors Association
#305, 1 Greensboro Drive
Rexdale ON M9W 1C8

◇ SOURCES OF ADDITIONAL INFORMATION

ABC/Merit Shop Foundation
729 15th Street, NW
Washington, DC 20005

Associated General Contractors of America
1957 E Street, NW
Washington, DC 20006

◇ RELATED ARTICLES

Volume 1: Construction
Volumes 2–4: Architectural and building construction technicians; Construction laborers; Drywall installers and finishers; Furniture manufacturing occupations; Lathers; Plasterers

Cartographers

Definition

Cartographers prepare maps, charts, and drawings from aerial photographs and survey data. They also conduct map research, investigating topics such as how people use maps.

History

Explorers, warriors, and traders have all used maps as a way of navigating around the world or establishing property rights. Early civilizations, such as the Egyptians and the Greeks, used maps drawn on papyrus to show a specific trade route or to trace the conquests of an army. Advances such as the establishment of a system of measuring longitude and latitude

helped create more uniform and accurate mapping procedures.

In the 14th and 15th centuries, mapmaking began to change because of the impact of world travel. Explorers such as Christopher Columbus began to observe and collect geographic information from around the world and use this information to make maps.

Mapmaking continued to develop as surveying and other means of mathematical measurements evolved. Today, the most sophisticated technology is used in compiling geographic information and planning and drafting maps. Such advances have significantly changed the cartographer's job. In the last few years, computer and satellite technology has been applied to mapmaking with great success. For example, video signals from a satellite detector are digitized and transmitted to earth where a computer process is used to read the data and create a map with enhanced geographic patterns, such as vegetation and soils. With the addition of computer mapping software and data merging software, mapping exercises can be done in a fraction of the time that it once took. It also permits far larger amounts of data to be collected with just the flip of a switch. Clearly computer-driven display devices will be the primary mapmaking tools of the future.

Nature of the work

Cartographers use manual and computerized drafting instruments, standard mathematical formulas, photogrammetric techniques, and precision stereoplotting apparatus. They work along with other mapping scientists to plan and draft maps and charts. For example, a cartographer may work with a land surveyor to interpret geographic information and transfer that information into a series of symbols that are plotted onto a map. Cartographers must therefore be skilled in reading and understanding detailed photographs or drawings, and must be able to use drafting tools to create an accurate representation of these data. They must also be able to plot the names of places onto overlays from which a final map is made. Cartographers often work with old maps, using updated information to keep these maps current. Research also may be a part of the job. Cartographers must be trained in computer science.

Several areas of specialization within the field of cartography exist. *Cartography supervisors* design maps and coordinate and oversee the activities of all those involved in the mapmaking process. Supervisors often are employed in larger mapmaking operations.

Cartographic drafters prepare the maps by detailing natural and constructed features, political boundaries, and other features. Most drafters now prepare maps through a hand technique called "scribing," a process by which a sharp tool is used to scratch line impressions on a coated plastic sheet. This process has replaced the traditional ink drawings that were used for generations.

Mosaicists lay out photographic prints on tables according to the sequence in which photographs were taken to form a photographic mosaic of the geographic area. These mosaics are subsequently used in photogrammetric activities such as topographic mapping. Mosaicists also examine aerial photographs to verify the location of established landmarks.

A cartographer uses a special computer tool to update the features of a map.

Photogrammetrists prepare original maps or charts from aerial photographs and survey data and apply mathematical formulas to identify the scale of cartographic features.

Stereo-plotter operators prepare maps from aerial photographs, using instruments that produce simultaneous projections of two photographs taken of the same area.

Topographical drafters prepare and correct maps from original sources, such as other maps, survey notes, and aerial photographs.

Requirements

High school students should take courses in geography, mathematics (including algebra and trigonometry), mechanical drawing, and computer science. A bachelor's degree in engineering or a physical science, such as geography or geodesy, is highly recommended. A college program should include courses in technical mathematics, surveying and measurements, drafting, and photogrammetry and mapping. Field work also may be required.

Opportunities for experience and exploration

One of the best opportunities for experience is a summer job or internship with a construction firm or other company that prepares maps. The federal government also may have some summer or part-time opportunities for cartographic assistants.

Methods of entering

Most cartographers are hired upon completion of a bachelor's degree in engineering or geography. People who are interested in becoming a technician may be able to secure an entry-level position after completing a specialized training program, which takes about two years. A portfolio of completed maps may be required by employers during the interviewing process.

Advancement

As is the case in most professions, advancement is linked to the quality of work performed, training, and experience. A cartographer who proves adept at drafting and designing maps and understands the other steps in the mapmaking process stands a good chance of becoming a supervisor. A cartographer, however, should expect to work directly on maps throughout a career.

Employment outlook

In the 1990s, some growth in employment of cartographers and other mapping scientists may occur in the private sector. The increasing demand for sophisticated land and sea maps will require specialized mapping skills. Little or no growth is expected in employment by departments and agencies of the federal government. The greatest growth in employment will be in Geographic Information Systems (GIS), which involves sophisticated mapping systems.

Earnings

Most of the approximately 5,000 cartographers in the federal government earn between $16,900 and $61,600 annually, with the average wage about $33,800 per year. Those in the private sector also have a wide salary range. An entry-level cartographer may earn $18,000 per year, while a highly trained cartographer could easily earn $42,000 or more annually. Cartographers with specialized skills earn the highest salaries.

Conditions of work

Cartographers mainly work in a typical office setting with easy access to drafting tables and computer mapping systems. Most cartographers never actually visit the locations that they are mapping. The average work week is between 35 to 40 hours, although occasionally longer hours are required if a mapping project is on a deadline.

Cartographers may choose to work on a freelance basis. Project hires allow companies to bring in cartographers for a short-term basis to accomplish mapping needs, without hiring a permanent staff. For large map-producing companies, project cartographers may be brought in to help during heavy deadline work. Because of the cost of mapping, most small companies buy rights to maps produced by large firms.

Cartographers must pay close attention to detail and be patient, systematic, and accurate in their work. They should be able to work cooperatively and take direction from a supervisor.

Cartography supervisors should have leadership abilities. At times, the ability to work long hours under pressure may be needed.

GOE: 05.03.02; SIC: 7399; SOC: 3734

◇ **SOURCES OF ADDITIONAL INFORMATION**

General information about career opportunities in cartography and two free pamphlets ("Cartography: A Career Guide" and "Careers in Cartography, Geodesy, and Surveying") are available from:

American Congress on Surveying and Mapping
5410 Grosvenor Lane, Suite 210
Bethesda, MD 20814

General information on careers in photogrammetry and a pamphlet titled "Careers in Photogrammetry" are available from:

American Society of Photogrammetry and Remote Sensing
5410 Grosvenor Lane, Suite 210
Bethesda, MD 20814

North American Cartographic Information Society
6010 Executive Boulevard
Suite 100
Rockville, MD 20852

◇ **RELATED ARTICLES**

Volume 1: Book Publishing; Engineering; Magazine Publishing
Volumes 2–4: Geographers; Graphics programmers; Miscellaneous engineers; Surveying and mapping technicians; Surveyors

Cartoonists and animators

Definition

Cartoonists and animators are illustrators who draw pictures and cartoons to amuse, educate, and persuade people.

History

Cartoons have become an everyday phenomenon in the 20th century. We see cartoons in the editorial and funny pages of daily newspapers, in comic books, textbooks, and magazines, in movie theaters, children's television, and commercials. Many cartoon characters have become household words, such as *Little Orphan Annie*, *Superman*, and *Charlie Brown*. Some comic strips create fantasy worlds for their readers to escape to; others, such as Walt Kelly's *Pogo* and Garry Trudeau's *Doonesbury*, are so relevant to the real world that their readers may often refer to them rather than the evening news to learn about current events.

Animation, a specialization of cartooning, has come to the forefront over its parent art, due largely to Walt Disney. A current trend in animated movies is live-action features in which human actors interact with cartoon characters to stunning effect. Because of the many applications of their work, cartoonists and animators have become busy and popular artists.

Nature of the work

Cartoonists draw illustrations for newspapers, books, magazines, greeting cards, movies, television shows, civic organizations, and private businesses. Cartoons most often are associated with newspaper comics or with children's television, but they are also used to highlight and interpret information in publications as well as in advertising.

Whatever their individual specialty, cartoonists and animators translate ideas onto paper or film in order to communicate these ideas to an audience. Sometimes the ideas are original; other times they are directly related to the news of the day, to the content of a magazine article, or to a new product. After cartoonists come up with ideas, they discuss them with their employers, which include editors, producers, and creative directors at advertising agencies. Next, they sketch drawings and submit these for approval. Employers may suggest changes, which cartoonists then make. Cartoonists use a variety of art materials including pens, pencils, markers, crayons, paints, transparent washes, and shading sheets. They may draw on paper, acetate, or bristol board.

Comic-strip artists tell jokes or short stories with a series of pictures. Each picture is called a frame, or a panel, and each frame usually includes words as well as drawings. *Comic book artists* also tell stories with their drawings, but their stories are longer, and they are not necessarily meant to be funny.

Motion-cartoonists, or *animators*, draw a great number of pictures, each of which varies only a little from the ones before and after it in a series. When these drawings are photographed in sequence and then projected at high speeds, they appear to be moving. One can achieve a similar effect by drawing stick figures on the pages of a note pad, and then flipping through the pages very quickly.

Editorial cartoonists comment on society by drawing pictures with messages that are usu-

CARTOONISTS AND ANIMATORS

Cartoonists have an ability to emphasize distinctive features of nearly all types people, animals, and even objects.

ally funny, but which often have a satirical edge. Their drawings often depict famous politicians. *Portraitists* are cartoonists who specialize in drawing caricatures. Caricatures are pictures that highlight someone's prominent features, such as a large nose, to make them recognizable to the public. Most editorial cartoonists are also talented portraitists.

Storyboard artists at advertising agencies may draw cartoons that give a client an idea of what a television commercial will look like before it is produced. If the client likes the idea, the actions represented by cartoons in the storyboard will be reproduced by actors on film.

Requirements

Cartoonists and animators must be creative. In addition to having artistic talent, they must generate ideas, although it is not unusual for cartoonists to collaborate with writers on ideas as well. Whether they create cartoon strips or advertising campaigns, they must be able to come up with concepts and images that the public will respond to. They must have a good sense of humor and an observant eye to detect people's distinguishing characteristics and society's incongruities.

Cartoonists and animators need not have a college degree, but some art training is usually expected by employers. To comment insightfully on contemporary life, it is also useful to study political science, history, and social studies. Animators must attend art school to learn specific technical skills.

Cartoonists and animators need to be flexible people. Because their art is much more commercial than painting and sculpting, they must be willing to accommodate their employers' desires if they are to build a broad clientele and earn a decent living. They must be able to take suggestions and rejections gracefully.

Opportunities for experience and exploration

High school students who are interested in becoming cartoonists or animators should submit their drawings to their school paper. They also might want to draw posters to publicize activities, such as sporting events, dances, and meetings.

Methods of entering

Formal entry-level positions for cartoonists and animators are rare, but there are several ways for artists to enter the cartooning field. Most cartoonists and animators begin piecemeal, selling cartoons to small publications, like community newspapers, that buy freelance cartoons. Others assemble a portfolio of their best work and apply to publishers or the art departments of advertising agencies. Cartoonists and animators should be willing to work for what equals less than minimum wage to get established.

Advancement

Like that of all artists, cartoonists' success depends upon how much the public likes their work. Cartoonists and animators have succeeded when they work for the most prestigious clients at the best wages.

Employment outlook

Job opportunities for cartoonists and animators are expected to grow faster than average through the year 2000, but competition for both salaried and freelance cartooning jobs is keen. Almost two-thirds of all visual artists are self-employed, but freelance work can be hard to come by and many freelancers earn little until they acquire experience and establish a good reputation.

Earnings

Freelance cartoonists may earn anywhere from $100 to $1,200 or more per drawing, but top dollar generally goes only for big, full-color projects such as magazine cover illustrations. Most cartoonists and animators average from $200 to $1,500 a week, although syndicated cartoonists on commission can earn much more. Comic strip cartoonists are usually paid according to the number of publications that carry their strip. Self-employed artists do not receive fringe benefits such as paid vacations, sick leave, health insurance, or pension benefits.

Conditions of work

Most cartoonists and animators work in big cities where employers such as television studios, magazine publishers, and advertising agencies are located. They generally work in comfortable environments, at drafting tables or drawing boards with good light. Staff cartoonists work a regular 40-hour work week, but may occasionally be expected to work evenings and weekends to meet deadlines. Freelance cartoonists have erratic schedules, and the number of hours they work may depend simply on how much money they want to earn. They may often work evenings and weekends, but are not required to be at work from nine to five, Monday through Friday.

Cartoonists and animators often follow instructions that are contrary to what they would most like to do, which can be frustrating. Many freelance cartoonists spend a lot of time working alone at home, but cartoonists have more opportunities to interact with other people than most working artists.

GOE: 01.02.03; SIC: 27, 7351; SOC: 324

◇ **SOURCES OF ADDITIONAL INFORMATION**

National Cartoonists Society
157 West 57th Street, Suite 904
New York, NY 10019

Society of Illustrators
128 East 63rd Street
New York, NY 10021

◇ **RELATED ARTICLES**

Volume 1: Book Publishing; Broadcasting; Design; Magazine Publishing; Motion Pictures; Newspaper Publishing
Volumes 2–4: Advertising workers; Commercial artists; Graphics designers; Graphics programmers; Painters and sculptors

---

Cashiers

Definition

Cashiers are employed in many different businesses and perform a variety of duties depending on their job titles and places of employment. In general, cashiers are responsible for handling money received from customers for products sold or services rendered.

One of the principal tasks of a cashier is operating a cash register. The cash register records all the monetary transactions going into or out of a particular work station. These transactions can include credit card charges, personal checks, refunds, and exchanges. To assist in inventory control, the machine often tallies the specific products that are sold.

History

The history of the employment of cashiers has developed along with the growth and expansion of business and industry. In earlier times, when most businesses were small and independently owned, merchants were usually able to

A pleasant personality and the ability to work quickly and efficiently are important qualities in a good cashier.

take care of most of the aspects of their own businesses, including receiving money from customers. When the retailing sector evolved, large department stores, supermarkets, and self-service stores became more common. As they grew, more and more businesses began to employ cashiers to receive customers' money, make change, provide customer receipts, and wrap the merchandise purchased.

Nature of the work

Cashiers are employed in many different types of businesses and establishments, and their specific job duties are usually dictated by the type of business that employs them. However, all cashiers perform certain types of similar tasks. In any field the cashier usually receives the money paid by customers, makes change, and provides customers with payment receipts either automatically or upon request. In some drug or department stores, depending on the number of people on staff, they may package or bag any merchandise purchased.

Cashiers must usually keep very accurate records of the amount of money that changes hands during their work shifts so that they can compute their final balances. In some establishments cashiers prepare the bank deposits for the management. In large businesses, where cashiers are often employed in very responsible positions, they may receive and record cash payments made to the firm and handle payment of the firm's bills by cash or by check. In some instances, cashiers prepare sales tax reports, compute income tax deductions for employees' pay rates, and prepare paychecks and payroll envelopes. In certain businesses such as currency exchanges, cashiers cash checks, re-

ceive utility bill payments, and sell various licenses and permits.

Cashiers usually operate some type of cash register or other business machine in their work. These machines may be very simple in their operation: they print out the amount of the purchase, automatically add the total amount, provide a paper receipt stub for the customer, and open the cash drawer for the cashier. Other machines, such as those used in hotels and very large department stores and supermarkets, may record other types of transactions, as well as compute the amount of change the customer should receive. Frequently these more complex machines will print out itemized bills of a customer's purchases or the services rendered. Other machines used by cashiers may include adding machines, change-dispensing machines, and others that help them do their work.

The job titles of different cashiers usually depend on where they are employed. In supermarkets they may be called *check-out clerks* or *grocery checkers*; in utility companies they may be called *bill clerks* or *tellers*; and in theaters they may be called *ticket sellers* or *box office cashiers*. Cafeterias may call the position *cashier-checker*, *food checker*, or *food tabulator*. Special job titles may be given to those employed as cashiers in large business firms, such as *disbursement clerks*, *credit cashiers*, or *cash accounting clerks*.

In addition to handling money *theater box office cashiers* and *information clerk-cashiers* may also answer telephone inquiries and operate machines that dispense tickets and change. *Restaurant cashiers* may receive telephone calls for meal reservations and for special parties, keep the reservation book current, type the menu, stock the sales counter with candies and smoking supplies, and seat customers.

Department store or *supermarket cashiers* may bag or wrap purchases. During slack periods they may price the merchandise, restock shelves, make out order forms, and perform other duties similar to those of *food and beverage order clerks*. Those employed as hotel cashiers usually keep accurate records of telephone charges and room-service bills to go on the customer's account. They may also be in charge of customers' safe deposit boxes, receiving money or customers' bills, handling credit card billing, and notifying room clerks of customer checkouts.

Cashier supervisors, money-room supervisors, and *money counters* may act as cashiers for other cashiers—receiving and recording cash and sales slips from them and making sure their cash registers contain enough cash to make change for customers. Other cashier positions include *gambling cashiers*, who may buy and sell chips for cash; *parimutuel ticket cashiers and sellers,* who buy and sell betting tickets at race tracks; *paymasters of purses,* who are responsible for collecting money for and paying money to racehorse owners; and *auction clerks,* who are responsible for collecting money from winning bidders at auctions.

Requirements

Students who are interested in becoming cashiers should recognize that some employers will require that potential employees be a minimum of 18 years of age and a high school graduate. Some employers seek applicants with previous job experience, sometimes favoring those who possess special skills in typing, elementary accounting, or sales. High school students may find that courses in bookkeeping, typing, business machine operations, business arithmetic, and related areas are assets in developing specific job skills. Students may frequently be able to gain both the needed academic training and practical job experience through diversified cooperative training programs, sometimes called "distributive education," in their high schools. These programs are also offered at two-year community colleges.

Business schools in many cities offer special training programs for cashiers. Many times private business organizations will operate brief training courses. Some businesses and firms require all new cashiers to take special training programs because of the nature of their work. In many instances, in both large and small firms, cashiers are given on-the-job training with experienced cashiers who work with and supervise the trainee. Firms will often fill cashier positions by promoting employees from within their own staff, for example, clerk-typists, baggers, ushers, and others.

The majority of cashiers are employed in positions in which they are in constant personal contact with the public. Personal appearance and attitude are thus very important in a cashier's work. A pleasant disposition and a desire to serve the public are important. Tact and diplomacy, accompanied by a smile, are real personal assets.

Cashiers should possess an aptitude for accuracy in mathematical computations, as well as good hand-eye coordination, and finger dexterity in order to be able to work at the rapid pace the job often requires. Among the duties of the cashier, accuracy is of the greatest importance.

Special requirements

The nature of the work of some cashiers demands that they handle large sums of money. Therefore, some cashiers must be able to meet the standards set up by bonding companies. Bonding companies evaluate applicants for risks, and frequently fingerprint applicants for registration and background checks. Not all cashiers are required to be bonded, however.

In some areas cashiers may be required to join a union, but fewer than 20 percent of cashiers are union members.

Opportunities for experience and exploration

Students are frequently able to find part-time employment in cashiering positions that will enable them to explore their interest and aptitude for this type of work. While in high school related job experience can sometimes be obtained by working in the school bookstore or cafeteria, or by participating in community activities such as raffles and sales drives that require the handling of money.

Other methods of job exploration may include visiting business schools that have programs for training cashiers and talking with persons already employed in cashier positions.

Methods of entering

Individuals may enter this field by applying directly to the personnel directors of large business firms or to the managers or owners of small businesses. Applicants may learn of job openings through newspaper "help wanted" columns, through friends and business associates, or through business school placement agencies. Private or state employment agencies can also help.

For cashier jobs, employers may require that applicants furnish personal references from schools they have attended or from former employers, attesting to their character and personal qualifications.

Advancement

Individuals employed as cashiers usually have some opportunities for advancement, depending on the size and type of business, personal initiative, experience, and special training and skills.

Cashier positions often provide people with the business skills to move into other types of clerical jobs or managerial positions. Opportunities for promotion are greater within larger firms than in small businesses or stores. Cashiers sometimes advance to cashier supervisors, shift leaders, division managers, or store managers. In hotels, they may be able to advance to room clerks or related positions.

Employment outlook

In the 1990s, cashiers in the United States number nearly 2.6 million, most employed in supermarkets and grocery stores. Large numbers of cashiers also work in department, drug, shoe, and other retail stores, and many are employed in restaurants, hotels, theaters, and hospitals.

Through the late 1990s job openings for cashiers will be more plentiful than for any other occupation. The Bureau of Labor projects a 26 percent increase in the number of cashiers employed through the year 2005.

The country's economic growth will account for some of this demand. However, most job openings will result from the need to replace workers leaving the field. A high job turnover rate exists in this occupational group; almost one-third of those employed leave their jobs annually, to assume family responsibilities, retire, return to school, or take different jobs.

Job openings for cashiers increased greatly during the 1970s and 1980s as businesses turned more and more to self-service operations, supermarket buying, and other modern merchandising methods. However, most businesses likely to turn to self-service have already done so, and the growth in opportunities resulting from this change is expected to be minor.

Factors that may somewhat limit the number of positions open in the future will be the increased installation of automatic change-making machines, vending machines, and other types of automatic and electronic equipment that will decrease the number of cashiers needed in some business operations.

Future job opportunities will probably be more readily available to those people who have obtained specialized training in bookkeeping, typing, business machine operations, and general office skills. Many part-time job opportunities should also be available.

Earnings

The minimum salary established by state and federal laws is often the starting salary for inexperienced cashiers. The current federal minimum wage is $4.25 per hour. However, employers can pay those workers younger than 20 years of age a lower training wage for up to six months. In some states, the minimum wage is governed by state law, and where state minimum wages are higher, the establishment must pay at least that amount.

In the 1990s, the median weekly salary for cashiers is about $11,200 a year. Most cashiers earn between $8,800 and $15,100 a year. Wages are generally higher for union workers, however. Experienced, full-time cashiers belonging to the United Food and Commercial Workers International Union average about $27,900 a year. Beginners make much less, averaging about $5.90 per hour. Cashiers employed in restaurants generally earn less than those employed in other types of cashiering work.

In general, the fringe benefits available to these employees are somewhat limited. Depending on the size and type of business, they may participate in group plans for life and hospitalization insurance, and receive one- to two-week paid vacations or longer, depending on the length of employment. They sometimes have the benefit of employee retirement programs. The majority of these benefits are available to employees who are paid on a weekly salary basis, usually those working in large businesses or in department stores. Many employers find it cheaper to hire part-time workers and avoid paying for benefits.

Conditions of work

Cashiers usually work a five-day, 40-hour work week in the majority of large retail businesses and supermarkets. In some cases, cashiers are expected to work on Saturdays because of heavy business volume. Their hours may differ considerably from those of other clerical workers, since many cashiers must work split shifts to cover rush-hour periods and weekends when many people shop and go out for entertainment.

The work of the cashier is usually not too strenuous, but employees often need to stand during most of their working hours. The amount of physical movement required depends upon the type of cashiering job and the place of employment. Cashiers must be able to work rapidly and sometimes under pressure during rush hours.

Work places are usually pleasant and attractively decorated. Many business firms today are air-conditioned and most of them are well ventilated and lighted; the work area itself, however, may be rather small and confining because many cashiers work behind counters, in cages or booths, or in other small spaces. Work spaces for cashiers are frequently located near the entrances and exits in business firms, so cashiers may be exposed to drafts.

GOE: 07.03.01; SIC: Any industry; SOC: 4364

◇ **SOURCES OF ADDITIONAL INFORMATION**

For information about job opportunities in this field, contact the local office of your state employment service.

◇ **RELATED ARTICLES**

Volume 1: Food Service; Sales
Volumes 2–4: Bookkeeping and accounting clerks; Buyers, wholesale and retail; Financial institution clerks and related workers; Financial institution tellers; Hotel and motel managers; Restaurant and food service managers; Retail managers; Retail sales workers

Caterers

Definition

Caterers plan, coordinate, and supervise food service at parties and other social functions. Working along with their clients, they purchase appropriate supplies, plan menus, supervise food preparation, direct serving food and refreshments, and ensure the overall smooth functioning of the event. As entrepreneurs, they are also responsible for budgeting, bookkeeping, and other administrative tasks.

History

Catering is part of the food servicing industry and as such has been around for as long as there have been restaurants. Once viewed as a service available only to the very wealthy, who used caterers to supplement their own hired staff for grand occasions, catering today is used by many people for many different types of gatherings.

Nature of the work

A caterer is a chef, a purchasing agent, a personnel director, and an accountant. Often a caterer will also play the role of host, allowing clients to enjoy their own party. A caterer's responsibilities will vary according to the size of the catering firm and the specific needs of individual clients. While preparing quality food is a concern no matter what the size of the party, larger events require far more planning and coordination. For example, a large catering firm may organize and plan a formal event for a thousand people, including planning and preparing a seven-course meal, decorating the hall with flowers and wall-hangings, employing 20 or more wait staff to serve food, and arranging the entertainment. The catering firm will also set up the tables and chairs and provide the necessary linen, silverware, and dishes. A catering company may organize 50 or so such events a month or only several a year. A smaller catering organization may concentrate on simpler events, such as preparing food for an informal buffet for 15 people.

These caterers are setting up a buffet table at a large banquet.

Caterers not only service individual clients, but also industrial clients. A caterer may supervise a company cafeteria or plan food service for an airline or a cruise ship. Often these caterers may take over full-time supervision of these food operations, including ordering the food and other supplies, supervision of personnel and food preparation, and overseeing the maintenance of equipment.

A caterer needs to be flexible in food-preparation approaches, that is, able to prepare food on- or off-premises depending on logistical considerations and the wishes of the client. If the caterer is handling a large banquet in a hotel or other location, for example the caterer will usually prepare the food on-premises, using kitchen and storage facilities as needed. The caterer might also work in a client's kitchen for an affair in a private home. In both cases, the caterer must visit the site of the function well before the actual event to determine how and where the food will be prepared. Caterers may also prepare the food off-premises, working either in their own kitchens or in a mobile kitchen.

Working with the client is obviously a very important aspect of the caterer's job. Clients always want their affairs to be extra special, and the caterer's ability to present such items as a uniquely shaped wedding cake or to provide

beautiful decorations will enhance the atmosphere and contribute to customer satisfaction. The caterer and the client work together within a budget to develop a menu and atmosphere the client can enjoy. Many caterers have their own special recipes, and they are always on the lookout for quality fruits, vegetables, and meats. The caterer should have an eye for detail and be able to make fancy hors d'oeuvres and eye-catching fruit and vegetable displays.

Although caterers can usually prepare a variety of dishes, they may have a specialty, like Cajun or Italian cuisine. The caterer may also have a special serving style, such as serving food in Renaissance period dress, that sets him or her apart from other caterers. Developing a reputation by specializing in a certain area is an especially effective marketing technique.

The caterer is a coordinator, working with suppliers, food servers, and the client to ensure an event comes off as planned. The caterer must be in frequent contact with all those involved in the affair, making sure, for example, that the food is delivered on time, the flowers are fresh, and the entertainment performs as promised.

Good management skills are extremely important. The caterer must know how much food and other supplies to order, what equipment will be needed, how many staff to hire, and be able to coordinate the various activities so as to ensure a smooth-running event. Purchasing the proper supplies entails knowledge of a variety of food products, their suppliers, and the contacts needed to get the right product at the best possible price.

Caterers with a large operation may appoint a manager to oversee an event. The manager will take care of the ordering, planning, and supervising responsibilities, and may even work with the client.

As entrepreneurs, caterers have many important day-to-day administrative responsibilities, such as overseeing the budgeting and bookkeeping of the operation. The caterer must make sure that the business continues to make a profit while keeping its prices competitive. Caterers must know how to figure costs and other budget considerations, plan inventories, buy food, and ensure compliance with health regulations.

Caterer helpers may prepare and serve hors d'oeuvres and other food and refreshments at social functions, under the supervision of the head caterer. They also help arrange tables and decorations, and then assist in the clean-up.

Requirements

Although there are no specific educational or professional requirements, a caterer should combine the ability to understand proper food preparation with the ability to manage a food service operation. Many people develop these skills through on-the-job training, beginning as a caterer's helper or as a worker in a restaurant.

As the catering business has grown more competitive, many successful caterers are choosing to get a college degree in business administration, home economics, nutrition, or a related field. Others get their training through the various vocational schools and community colleges that have begun to offer apprenticeships and other forms of professional training.

Interested high school students should take courses in mathematics, business administration, and home economics. They also should take courses in English and other communications courses. A college program should include course work in nutrition, health, and business management.

Special requirements

Most states require caterers to be licensed, and inspectors may make periodic visits to ensure that local health and safety regulations are being maintained in the food preparation process.

As a measure of professional status, many caterers become certified through the National Association of Catering Executives (NACE). To qualify for certification, caterers must meet educational and professional requirements and pass a written examination. Further information on the certification process is available from the NACE at the address given at the end of this article.

Opportunities for experience and exploration

An aspiring caterer can get part-time work in a restaurant or as an assistant banquet manager at a hotel. With some experience and training, it might even be possible to work as a manager with a large catering company. High school students may work in the school cafeteria or might even consider setting up their own small catering service by working at parties for friends and relatives.

Methods of entering

Some caterers get into the profession as a matter of chance after helping a friend or relative prepare a large banquet or volunteering to coordinate a group function. Most caterers, however, begin their careers after graduating from college with a degree in a program such as home economics, or finishing a culinary training program at a vocational school or community college.

Qualified people may begin work as a manager for a large catering firm or as a manager for a hotel banquet service. An individual will most likely start a catering business only with a large amount of experience, and plenty of money to cover the purchase of equipment and other start-up costs.

Advancement

As with most service oriented businesses, the success of a caterer depends on the quality of work and a good reputation. Well known caterers can expand their business, often growing from a small business to a larger operation. This may mean hiring assistants and buying more equipment to be able to serve a larger variety of clientele. Caterers who initially worked out of their own home kitchen may get an office or even relocate to another area in order to take better opportunity of catering opportunities. Sometimes successful caterers will use their skill and reputation to secure a full-time position in a large hotel or restaurant planning and coordinating banquets. They also may work full-time for an industrial client, such as a company cafeteria or airline.

Employment outlook

Because of the strong food service industry in the United States, employment opportunities in catering should continue to grow through the 1990s. Opportunities will be good for firms that can handle weddings, bar and bat mitzvahs, business functions, and other celebrations.

Competition is keen because many hotels and restaurants are branching out to offer catering services. Like all service industries, catering is sensitive to the economy, and a downturn in the economy may limit catering opportunities. Despite the competition and possible economic considerations, highly skilled and motivated caterers should be in demand throughout the country, especially in and around large metropolitan areas.

Earnings

Earnings vary widely depending on the size and location of the catering operation and the skill and motivation of the individual entrepreneur. Many caterers charge according to the number of guests attending a function. In many cases, the larger the event, the larger the profit. Earnings are also influenced by whether a caterer works full- or part-time. Even very successful caterers often remain at it part-time, either because they enjoy their other job or to protect themselves against a downturn in the economy.

The general salary range for a full-time caterer might be anywhere between $15,000 and $60,000 per year, depending on skill, reputation, and experience. An extremely successful caterer can easily earn more than $75,000 annually. A part-time caterer may earn $5,000 to $11,000 per year, subject to the same variables as the full-time caterer. Because a caterer is an independent business person, vacation and other benefits are usually not part of the salary structure.

A caterer who works as a manager for a company cafeteria or other industrial client may earn between $18,000 and $30,000 per year, with vacation, health insurance, and other benefits usually included.

Conditions of work

A caterer often works long hours planning and preparing for an event, and the day of the event might easily be a 14-hour workday from setup to cleanup.

There is a lot of variety in the type of work a caterer does. The caterer must always work closely with all types of clients and be able to adapt to last minute changes.

Caterers often spend long hours on their feet, and although the work can be physically and mentally demanding, caterers usually have a great deal of work flexibility. As entrepreneurs, they can usually take time off when necessary. Caterers often work more than 60 hours a week when busy, with most of the work on weekends and evenings, when events tend to be scheduled.

Caterers must be able to plan ahead, work gracefully under pressure, and have an ability to adapt to last minute mishaps. Attention to detail is critical, as is the ability to work long hours under demanding situations. A caterer must be able to direct a large staff of workers in the kitchen and be able to interact with clients and guests.

GOE: 11.11.04; SIC: 5812; SOC: 1351

◇ SOURCES OF ADDITIONAL INFORMATION

Information on certification and other career information is available from:

National Association of Catering Executives
1019 Los Angeles Avenue
Atlanta, GA 30306

Career information is available from:

Mobile Industrial Caterers Association
7300 Artesia Boulevard
Buena Park, CA 90621

◇ RELATED ARTICLES

Volume 1: Baking; Food Processing; Food Service
Volumes 2–4: Cooks, chefs, and bakers; Dietetic technicians; Dietitians; Fast food workers; Food service workers; Food technologists; Health and regulatory inspectors; Home economists; Restaurant and food service managers

Cement masons

Definition

Cement masons are skilled workers who place and finish the concrete surfaces in many different kinds of construction projects ranging from small patios and sidewalks to highways, dams, and airport runways.

History

Cement is a building material that hardens when mixed with water. Various kinds of cement have been used for thousands of years. The ancient Egyptians and the Greeks both made cements, but the most effective cements were made by the Romans. They developed a kind of cement made from slaked lime and volcanic ash and used it throughout Europe in building of roads, aqueducts, bridges, and other structures. After the collapse of the Roman Empire, the art of making cement mostly disappeared.

In the 18th century, through the experiments of an English engineer, John Smeaton, a cement was developed that set up even under water. Smeaton successfully used this cement in building the famous Eddystone Lighthouse, in Devon, England. Later it was used in some parts of the Erie Canal, the waterway built to connect the Great Lakes and New York City.

In 1824, an English stonemason, Joseph Aspdin, developed the first portland cement mixture. To make it, he burned and ground together limestone and clay. He called his product "portland" cement because it resembled the limestone quarried on the Isle of Portland. Portland cement was very strong and water-resistant, and it soon became the most widely used cement. The first American portland cement plant was built in 1871. Cement manufactured today is essentially the same material as Aspdin's portland cement.

Cement is seldom used by itself in large quantities. More often, it is mixed with another material. Cement mixed with sand forms mortar that is used, for example, in brick walls and buildings. Cement mixed with gravel or crushed rock forms concrete, which is a cheap, versatile, strong, and durable structural material. Today concrete is one of the most widely used building materials in the world. With the development of ways to reinforce concrete with metal and the appropriate machinery for handling it, concrete has become useful for many purposes, including bridges, roofs, highways, dams, swimming pools, sculpture, fence posts, helicopter pads, and missile launching sites.

Nature of the work

The principal work of cement masons, also known as *concrete masons*, is to put into place and then smooth and finish concrete surfaces in a variety of different construction projects. Sometimes they add colors to the concrete to change its appearance or chemicals to speed up or slow down the time that the concrete takes to harden. They use various tools to create specified surface textures on fresh concrete before it sets. They may also fabricate beams, columns, or panels of concrete. Most cement masons are employed by concrete contractors or general contractors to help build roads, shopping malls, factories, and many other structures. A small number of masons are employed by manufacturers of concrete products.

Cement masons must know their materials well. They must be able to judge how long different concrete mixtures will take to set up and how factors like heat, cold, and wind will affect the curing, or hardening, of the cement. They need to be able to recognize these effects by examining and touching the concrete. They need to know about the strengths of different kinds of concrete and how different surface appearances are produced.

In addition to understanding the materials they work with, cement masons must also be familiar with blueprint reading, applied mathematics, building code regulations, and the procedures involved in estimating costs and quantities of materials.

On a construction job, the preparation of the site where the concrete will be poured is very important. Cement masons begin by setting up the forms that will hold the wet concrete until it hardens into the desired shape. The forms must be properly aligned and must allow for concrete of the correct dimensions, as specified in the original design. In some structures, reinforcing steel rods or mesh are set into place after the forms are put in position. The cement masons then pour or direct the pouring of the concrete into the forms so that it flows smoothly rather than drops unevenly. The cement masons or their helpers spread and tamp

Cement masons smooth the concrete foundation of a house that is part of a low-cost residential development.

the fresh concrete into place. Then the masons level the surface by moving a straightedge back and forth across the top of the forms.

Using a bull float, which is a large wooden trowel, cement masons begin the smoothing operation. This process covers up the larger particles in the wet concrete and brings to the surface the fine cement paste in the mixture. On projects where curved edges are desired, cement masons may use an edger or a radius tool, guiding it around the edge between the form and the concrete. They may make grooves or joints at intervals in the surface to help control cracking.

The process continues with more finishing work, either done by hand with a small metal trowel or with a power trowel. This smoothing gets out most remaining irregularities on the surface. On driveways, sidewalks, and similar projects, cement masons may use a brush or broom on the concrete to attain a nonslip surface texture. Or they may embed pebbles in the surface. Afterward, the concrete must cure to reach its proper strength, a process that can take about a week.

On structures like walls or columns that expose surfaces when the forms are removed, cement masons must leave a smooth and uniform finish. To achieve this, they may rub down high spots with an abrasive material, chip out rough or defective spots with a chisel and hammer, and fill low areas with cement paste. They may finish off the exposed surface with a coating of a cement mixture to create an even, pleasing appearance.

Cement masons use a variety of hand and power tools, ranging from simple chisels, hammers, trowels, edgers, and leveling devices to pneumatic chisels, concrete mixers, and troweling machines. Smaller projects like sidewalks and patios may be done by hand. But on large-scale projects like highways, power-operated floats and finishing equipment are necessary. Although power equipment can speed many tasks, on most projects there are still corners or other inaccessible areas that require hand work.

There are various specialists whose jobs involve covering, leveling, and smoothing cement and concrete surfaces. Among them are *concrete-stone finishers,* who work with ornamental stone and concrete surfaces; *concrete rubbers,* who polish concrete surfaces; and *nozzle cement sprayers,* who use spray equipment to apply cement mixtures to surfaces.

Poured concrete wall technicians are another occupational group whose activities are related to those of cement masons. These workers use surveying instruments to mark construction sites for excavation and to set up and true (align correctly) concrete forms. They direct the pouring of concrete to form walls of buildings, and after removing the forms, they may waterproof lower walls and lay drainage tile to promote drainage away from the building. Unlike cement masons, poured concrete technicians generally have at least two years of technical training in such subjects as surveying and construction methods.

Requirements

Cement masons can learn their skills either on the job or in apprenticeship programs. Many people with no special skills or experience begin work in helper positions and gradually learn the trade informally over an uncertain number of years by working with experienced masons. However, apprenticeships are the recommended way to acquire the necessary skills, because they provide more balanced, in-depth training through programs that last two to three years.

Many cement masons who pick up skills on the job begin as construction laborers or cement mason helpers. In considering applicants for helper jobs, most employers prefer to hire people who are at least 18, who are in good physical condition, and who possess a driver's license. The ability to get along with co-workers is important, because cement masons often work in teams. Although a high school diploma may not be required, applicants who have taken high school shop courses, blueprint reading, and mechanical drawing may have an advantage. Trainees usually begin with easy tasks such as edging and jointing, then progress to more difficult work such as final finishing of surfaces.

Apprenticeships are usually jointly sponsored by local contractors and unions. To enter apprenticeship programs in most parts of the country, applicants must be approved by the local joint labor–management apprenticeship committee. They may have to take a written test and pass a physical examination. The training consists of a combination of planned work experience and classroom instruction. On the job, apprentices learn about handling the tools and materials of the trade, about layout work and finishing techniques, and about job safety. The classroom instruction involves at least 144 hours each year in such related subjects as mathematics, blueprint reading, architectural drawing, procedures for estimating materials and costs, and local building regulations.

Opportunities for experience and exploration

High school students can learn more about their own aptitude for this kind of work by taking courses such as general mathematics, drafting, and various shop classes. In addition, summer employment as part of a construction crew can provide valuable firsthand experience. Some people are introduced to the building construction trades, including the work of cement masons, while they are serving in the military, especially with the Army Engineering Corps.

Methods of entering

People who want to become cement masons can enter this field either through formal apprenticeship programs or by obtaining a job that offers the opportunity for on-the-job training. For information about becoming an apprentice, it is possible to contact local cement contractors, the offices of the state employment service, or the area headquarters of one of the unions that organize cement masons. Many cement masons are members of either the Operative Plasterers and Cement Masons International Association or the International Union of Bricklayers and Allied Craftsmen.

People who wish to become on-the-job trainees can contact directly contractors in the area who may be hiring helpers. They may also want to follow up on job leads from the state

employment service or newspaper classified ads.

Advancement

After they have gained some skills and become efficient workers in their trade, cement masons may specialize in one phase of the work. They may become, for example, *lip-curb finishers, expansion joint finishers,* or *concrete paving-finishing machine operators.*

Experienced masons with good judgment, planning skills, and the ability to deal with people may advance to supervisory positions. Supervisors with a broad understanding of the other construction trades may eventually become job superintendents, in charge of the whole range of activities at the job site. Cement masons may also become estimators for concrete contractors, calculating materials requirements and labor costs. Only a few cement masons decide to open their own contracting businesses, usually doing small projects like sidewalks and patios.

Employment outlook

Employment opportunities for cement masons are expected to increase more slowly than the average for all occupations over the next 10 to 15 years. Construction activity is expected to expand during this period, and concrete will be a very important building material. Cement masons will be in demand to help build roads, bridges, buildings, and many other structures. Yet the productivity of cement masons will be improved considerably by the introduction of better equipment, tools, and materials. That is, fewer cement masons will be needed to do the same amount of work. The net effect will be that employment in this occupation will not keep up with the increasing use of concrete in construction.

Nonetheless, many new openings will arise every year as experienced workers move into other occupations or leave the labor force. In areas where the local economy is thriving and there are plenty of building projects, there may sometimes be a shortage of cement masons. At other times, even skilled masons may experience periods of unemployment because the economy is in a downturn and the level of construction activity has fallen.

Earnings

The earnings of cement masons vary widely according to factors such as geographical location, whether they do much overtime work, how much bad weather or local economic conditions reduce the hours they work, and whether they are union members. Working overtime, usually at time-and-a-half rates, is frequently possible, because once concrete has been poured, the finishing operations must be completed quickly. Nonunion workers generally have lower wage rates than union workers.

In the 1990s, most cement masons have earnings somewhere between $15,900 and $31,200 per year. A few earn over $40,000, while some make as little as about $13,100. Apprentices start at wages that are about 50 to 60 percent of a fully qualified mason's wage. They receive periodic raises, so that in the last phase of training, their wage is between 90 and 95 percent of the experienced worker's pay.

Conditions of work

Cement masons do strenuous work, and they need to have good stamina. They stay active much of the time, especially when concrete has been poured and needs to be finished immediately. Many cement masons work outdoors. In general, concrete cannot be poured in cold or rainy weather, but temporary heated shelters are sometimes used to extend the time when work can be done. Masons work in a variety of locations, sometimes on the ground, sometimes on ladders and scaffolds. They may need to lift or push weights, and they often kneel, bend, and stoop. To protect their knees, many masons routinely wear kneepads. They may also wear water-repellent boots and protective clothing.

Common hazards on the job include falling off ladders, being hit by falling objects, muscle strains, and rough hands from contact with wet concrete. By exercising caution and following established job safety practices, cement masons can minimize their exposure to hazardous conditions.

GOE: 05.05.01; SIC: 1771; SOC: 6463

◇ **SOURCES OF ADDITIONAL INFORMATION**

Associated General Contractors of America
1957 E Street, NW
Washington, DC 20006

International Union of Bricklayers and Allied Craftsmen
815 15th Street, NW
Washington, DC 20005

Operative Plasterers and Cement Masons International Association of the United States and Canada
1125 17th Street, NW
Washington, DC 20036

Portland Cement Association
5420 Old Orchard Road
Skokie, IL 60077

Canadian Masonry Contractors Association
#201, 1013 Wilson Avenue
Downsview ON M3K 1G1

◇ **RELATED ARTICLES**

Volume 1: Construction
Volumes 2–4: Architectural and building construction technicians; Bricklayers and stonemasons; Construction laborers; Drywall installers and finishers; Marble setters, tile setters, and terrazzo workers; Plasterers

Ceramics and materials engineers

Definition

Although seemingly obscure fields of interest, materials engineering, and ceramics engineering in particular, bear fruits that are seen all around us at all times. The materials that make up nearly every item we use in our daily lives—tools, clothing, toys, vehicles, furniture, cookware—undoubtedly have been researched, tested, and developed by materials engineers.

Materials engineers evaluate items such as metals, ceramics, and polymers in order to recommend the best materials for the manufacture of products. *Ceramics engineers* could be considered specialized materials engineers, for they work with one particular type of material, ceramics, which are nonmetallic minerals and rocks. They perform research, design machinery and processing techniques, and oversee the technical aspects of the production of ceramic products.

History

The items we utilize today are different from those used thousands of years ago, but our basic needs—for food, shelter, and clothing—have not changed from those of early societies. As far back as the Stone Age, people have been creating tools for hunting and gathering food—these people could be considered the first materials engineers.

The use of shells and hollow bones as food containers and cookware had developed into the making of bricks and pottery from clay. Originally, clay was probably merely dried in the sun to harden before use, but by 7,000 years ago it was being fired to make it more durable. People who worked with clay can be thought of as the first ceramics engineers, and we can consider tool makers of the later Copper and Bronze Ages as among the earliest materials engineers. By about 3000 B.C., copper was being fired and mixed with tin, a process that hardened the copper and created bronze. Although more rare than copper at the time, iron was also being used. The production of iron by smelting its ores has now been practiced throughout many centuries.

One can get an idea of the historical development of materials engineering by considering the evolution of various manufacturing procedures: the hammering of copper into tools thousands of years ago; the melting of copper ore by campfire; the gold-plating of American Indian face masks; the building of the wrought-iron Eiffel Tower; and finally the production of semiconductors in this century.

When we refer to ceramics we often think mainly of objects made of clay—such as ornamental jars, figurines, and cups and saucers. Thousands of years ago, ceramics makers may have been limited by a dependence on this one raw material, but today ceramics include a wide variety of other materials as well. Now ceramics are made for much more than household or artistic uses. In the 19th century, engineers became concerned with what are called industrial ceramics—products made from inorganic, nonmetallic constituents having industrial or technical applications. The earliest industrial ceramics were porcelains for high-voltage electrical insulation. Today they are currently used mainly in mechanical engineering and electrical/electronics engineering applications. Ceramics engineers are working with much more advanced materials as well (many produced by chemical processes), including high-strength silicon carbides, nitrides, and fracture-resistant zirconias for replacing metal parts in gas turbines and diesel engines.

Nature of the work

Think of an item as simple as a dinner plate, then consider one as complex as an airplane. In order to have been produced, both types of items must have been evaluated by materials engineers to determine the best components that would create the finished product. Such engineers have decided that glass or clay would be best for plates, and that an organized array of metals, ceramics, plastics, and wiring is best for building planes.

In general, materials engineers are given some type of blueprint for products that are to be made (or they conceive the product themselves) and they review technical factors to determine the ideal combination of materials that will compose the products. Metals, ceramics, polymers (which are giant molecules, such as protein, built of units of smaller molecules, such as glucose), fibers, plastics, and paper are examples of materials that might be considered. The engineers base their conclusions on evaluation of a number of factors, such as the

An engineer studies the computer reading of one phase of ceramic production.

Materials process engineers work to develop methods of finding, obtaining, processing, and refining the actual materials that make up products. For instance, the ceramics process engineer would be involved in finding natural deposits of clay, refining the clay to wash away unwanted minerals, and processing it in water to dissolve any other impure particles. *Materials research engineers* are concerned with forming general principles of materials. They use their scientific knowledge and curiosity to examine such factors as heat resistance and compression. Their studies are often published in scientific journals. *Materials technicians* are those who assist engineers and researchers in such tasks as running equipment and taking measurements.

When referring to ceramics, many people think merely of simple items such as coffee cups and knickknacks. But ceramics engineering involves much more than these household products. Clay is not the only material used in this specialty—a ceramic is any nonmetallic, inorganic material that is processed with high-temperature technology. Glass, cement, and porcelain enamel are just a few ceramic materials.

Like other materials engineers, ceramics engineers work toward the development of new products. They use their scientific knowledge to also anticipate new applications for existing products that can be improved upon. *Ceramics research engineers* conduct experiments and perform other research. They study the chemical properties—such as sodium content—and physical properties—such as heat resistance—of materials as they develop the ideal mix of elements for each product's application. Many research engineers are fascinated by the chemical and thermal interactions of the oxides that make up many ceramic materials. *Ceramics design engineers* take the information culled by the researchers and further develop actual products to be tested. They also design equipment used in ceramics manufacturing, such as grinders, milling machines, sieves, presses, and drying machines.

Ceramics test engineers test materials that have been chosen by the researchers to be used as sample products, or they might be involved in ordering raw materials and making sure the quality meets the ceramics industry standards. Other ceramics engineers are involved in more hands-on work, such as grinding raw materials and firing products. Maintaining proper color, surface finish, texture, strength, and uniformity are further tasks that are the responsibility of the ceramics engineer.

Beyond research, design, testing, and manufacturing, there are the *ceramics products sales*

strength of the material, its weight, its cost, and its applications, meaning the uses to which the finished product will be put.

Consider cars being driven across a bridge. Bridges must be made of the right combination of materials in order to withstand the weight of traffic. Materials engineers who design bridges must know how to judge the strength of such materials as steel, concrete, and rubber. They must know the answers to questions like "What makes steel hard?" "What makes concrete crackable?" and "What makes rubber stretchy?" Two main factors that materials engineers examine and measure are stress, which is the weight or load on a material, and strain, which is the amount of changed shape of a material under stress. They also measure stretching force, or tension, and squeezing force, or compression.

The materials that engineers work with are often found in nature, such as ores, oils, resins, compounds, and sand. Before a product is considered "finished," its materials have to be put through a number of stages, including refining, processing, fabricating, assembling, cleaning, painting, and packaging. Materials engineers will either recommend existing materials, improve current ones, or develop new ones for use in the product being considered. They also test failed products to correct problems or recommend repairs.

engineers. The industry depends on these people to anticipate customers' needs and report back to researchers and test engineers on new applications.

Ceramics engineers often specialize in one or a few areas, including the following (which are associated with selected products in each niche): glass (windows, light bulbs, tableware, electronic equipment parts); structural clay (sewer pipe, roofing tile); ceramic coatings (bath tubs, enameled cookware, jewelry); cement (for building materials); and whitewares (pottery, china, wall tile, plumbing fixtures, electrical insulators, spark plugs).

Requirements

In preparation for college engineering programs, students should take the following courses: four years of English; two years of algebra and history (or algebra and a foreign language); one year of geometry, physics, and chemistry; and half a year of trigonometry. In addition, taking functions, analytical geometry, and calculus classes gives students a better chance of being accepted at selective colleges.

Materials engineers are generally expected to have a bachelor's degree in engineering before being considered for employment in the field. Alternatively, some engineers are hired in materials positions if they have passed either a two- or a four-year program in engineering technology, which involves preparation for more practical, technical work rather than theoretical applications. College graduates with degrees in one of the natural sciences or mathematics may also be qualified for various entry-level materials engineering positions.

College courses are initially geared toward getting the student to think logically and analytically. Thus the first two years of engineering programs typically center around mathematics, physics, chemistry, and computer courses. Students should be inspired and challenged to approach problems first theoretically and then practically. For instance, after students are presented with a problem, they will first contemplate how it would be solved, then formulate a step-by-step method by which to solve it, and then actually tackle the problem according to that method. This thinking process should be nurtured throughout all the core college courses geared toward materials engineering, for engineers are expected to have such an aptitude for problem solving.

In the junior and senior years of college, students focus particularly on their area of specialization. For materials engineers who decide

that ceramics will be their main discipline, classes and problems will be concentrated around issues in the industrial ceramics engineering discipline. During the last two years of undergraduate education, it is wise to consider and evaluate one's goals in the field and determine whether one prefers research, production, design, sales, or management. Focusing on this objective makes it less difficult to plan a job search.

Entry-level jobs can be applied for after students have received the bachelor's degree. However, many students go on for master's degrees because it provides further qualification; continuing in a graduate program allows students to keep abreast of new technology and adds to their chances of being considered for promotions and higher-paying, more challenging positions. For those who wish to become teachers or do further research in ceramics engineering, a graduate degree is required.

Opportunities for experience and exploration

For high school students interested in materials engineering and ceramics engineering in particular, it is a good idea to take on special research assignments from teachers who can provide guidance on topics and methods. There are also summer academic programs where students with similar interests spend a week or more in a special environment. The Worcester Polytechnic Institute, for example, offers a 12-day program focusing on science, math, and engineering. Sports such as swimming and softball are also offered. It's also a good idea to join a science club, like the Junior Engineering Technical Society. Member students compete in academic events, take career exploration tests, and enter design contests where they build models of such things as spacecraft and other structures based on their own designs. (For further information on camps and special programs, write to the addresses listed at the end of this article.)

For hands-on experience with materials, taking pottery or sculpture classes is suggested. These classes allow students to literally feel their way with such materials as clay and glass. Students can learn how the materials are obtained and how they can be shaped and fired. This gives an opportunity to learn first-hand about stress and strain, tension and compression, heat resistance, and ideal production equipment. In pottery classes students can also learn about glazes and how various chemicals affect different materials.

Those interested in ceramics engineering careers should also inquire with established manufacturing companies about internships and summer employment opportunities. College placement centers can also help find employers who participate in cooperative education programs, whereby students work at a materials engineering job in exchange for course credits.

Methods of entering

As mentioned earlier, entry-level jobs in materials and ceramics engineering require at least a bachelor's degree. First jobs often involve working with a team supervised by experienced engineers. Or, new employees might find themselves assisting researchers in the lab. Continuing research experience can lead to higher-level jobs in production and marketing. After becoming familiar with the materials and products being developed, engineers may be assigned to on-the-job training in production areas. Engineers may go on to work as supervisors. Some decide to transfer to teaching positions at universities after working a number of years in the industry.

Advancement

Opportunities for advancement are available especially for those who continue their education throughout their work years. Technology is always advancing and new products and applications are developed, so engineers who keep abreast of issues in materials science are more likely to succeed. Some materials engineers leave the field after many years to take top-level management positions in other industries. Those who are employed by universities must continue teaching if they want to gain tenured (that is, further guaranteed) positions.

Employment outlook

A diversified range of companies hire people with education in materials engineering, including manufacturing companies, development and design companies, research organizations, and government and educational institutions.

Employment opportunities in materials engineering are expected to grow through the first years of the 21st century. In the late 1980s, the number of bachelor's degrees in engineering was declining, which means that in the late 1990s companies may be looking for more applicants in engineering specialties. Manufacturers will most likely be continuing to enhance productivity, and industry competition will force companies to improve products.

Also, materials engineers will be needed to help build and repair bridges, roads, pollution control systems, and other infrastructures. Many materials engineers continue to be employed in such long-term projects even during recessions (although cutbacks in certain industries, such as defense, may end in less work and even layoffs).

Earnings

In the 1990s, the beginning annual salary for ceramics engineers with a bachelor's degree is about $32,000 in private industry; for those with a master's degree, about $35,000; and for those with a doctorate, about $50,000. Engineers with many years' experience can earn more than $90,000 a year. Salaries for government employees begin at about $23,000 and average about $49,000.

Conditions of work

Working conditions in materials engineering positions vary depending on the specific industry and department one works in. Hands-on engineers work in plants and factories. Researchers work mainly in laboratories, research institutes, and universities. Those in management positions work mostly in offices, and teachers of course work in school environments.

Most ceramics engineers work in ceramics and glass manufacturing plants. Those who are responsible for quality control are in the production areas; those who do the actual grinding and firing of clay may be found in hot, noisy parts of the plant. Sales engineers, on the other hand, are often on the road, traveling between their customers' offices and their own office headquarters.

GOE: 05.01.01, 05.01.04, 05.01.05, 05.01.07; SIC: 8711; SOC: 1623

SOURCES OF ADDITIONAL INFORMATION

American Ceramic Society
735 Ceramic Place
Westerville, OH 43081

Junior Engineering Technical Society
1420 King Street, Suite 405
Alexandria, VA 22314

National Institute of Ceramic Engineers
735 Ceramic Place
Westerville, OH 43081

Worcester Polytechnic Institute
Frontiers in Science, Mathematics and
Engineering
100 Institute Road
Worcester, MA 01609

Canadian Ceramic Society
#110, 2175 Shippard Avenue East
Willowdale ON M2J 1W8

RELATED ARTICLES

Volume 1: Ceramics; Engineering
Volumes 2–4: Cement masons; Forge shop
occupations; Glass manufacturing workers; Glaziers; Industrial designers; Industrial engineers;
Iron and steel industry workers; Metallurgical
engineers; Plastics technicians; Research assistants; Textile technicians; Tool makers and die
makers; Welders

Chemical engineers

Definition

Chemical engineers develop methods of manufacturing large quantities of chemicals and other products requiring chemical processing. They also design and operate processing equipment and plants. Trained in chemistry, physics, and mathematics, chemical engineers work on a wide variety of products, such as plastics, synthetic rubbers, detergents, antibiotics, synthetic fuels, pulp and paper, pharmaceuticals, and foodstuffs.

History

Chemical engineering, defined in its most general sense as applied chemistry, existed even in early civilizations. Ancient Greeks, for example, distilled alcoholic beverages, as did the Chinese, who by 800 B.C. had learned to distill alcohol from rice. Aristotle, the Greek philosopher of the 4th century B.C., wrote about a process to obtain fresh water by evaporating water from the sea.

The foundations of the modern field of chemical engineering were laid out during the Renaissance, when experimentation and the questioning of accepted scientific theories became widespread. This period saw the development of many new chemical processes, such as those for sulfuric acid (for fertilizers and textile treatment) and alkali (for soap). The atomic theories of John Dalton and Amedeo Avogadro, developed in the early 1800s, became an important theoretical underpinning for both chemistry and chemical engineering.

With the birth of large-scale manufacturing in the mid-19th century, modern chemical engineering began to take shape. Chemical manufacturers were soon required to seek out chemists who also had knowledge of manufacturing processes. These early chemical engineers were called chemical technicians or industrial chemists. The first course in chemical engineering was taught in 1888 at the Massachusetts Institute of Technology, and by 1900 "chemical engineer" had become a widely used job title.

In the 20th century chemical engineers were employed in increasing numbers to design new and more efficient ways to process

Chemical engineers must spend time making on-site inspections of plants in order to anticipate potential problems or correct existing ones.

chemicals and chemical products. In the United States chemical engineers were especially important in the development of petroleum-based fuels for the automotive industry. The achievements of chemical engineers—from the large-scale production of plastics, antibiotics (including penicillin), and synthetic rubbers to the development of high-octane gasoline—have greatly affected our daily lives.

Nature of the work

Chemical engineering is the smallest of the four major engineering disciplines (the others, in order of size, are electrical, mechanical, and civil). Because chemical engineers are rigorously trained in not only chemistry but also physics and mathematics, they are among the most versatile of all engineers. Their main concern, however, is transforming raw materials into desired products.

The work of chemical engineering generally begins with an idea for a product—for example, plastic wrap for food packaging or a fat substitute for low-calorie, low-cholesterol ice cream. Product ideas may originate with the company's marketing department; with a chemist,

chemical engineer, or other specialist; or with a customer. The basic chemical process is then developed in a laboratory, usually by a chemist or chemical engineer.

Once the basic process has been established, the goal of the chemical engineer is to determine how the product can most efficiently be produced on a large scale—that is, at a manufacturing plant—while still guaranteeing a consistently high-quality result. The chemical engineer must not only develop the large-scale process but also be involved in designing the required manufacturing equipment and physical plant. Chemical engineers are often assisted in plant and equipment design by mechanical and electrical engineers. Among the factors that must be taken into account are capital investment in a new plant, the possibility of converting an existing plant to the new process, utility costs, the number of people needed to run the plant, the cost of raw materials, and transportation costs of bringing the materials to the plant. Part of the chemical engineer's job is, in fact, to be an industrial economist.

Within the field of chemical engineering, all manufacturing processes can be broken down into a number of steps called unit operations—for example, filtration, absorption, evaporation, distillation, fluid flow, the moving of solids, heat transfer, drying, mixing, and extraction. These are, in short, ways to transport, bring together, separate, or otherwise alter the physical or chemical properties of raw materials. For example, fermentation, a chemical reaction used in the production of wine, can be brought about by the unit operations of heat transfer and distillation. Other chemical reactions commonly employed in chemical engineering processes are nitration, used, for example, in the manufacture of toluene, a raw material in many dyes; polymerization, a reaction important in making synthetic fibers, rubbers, and plastics, in which very large molecules, or polymers, are created usually by joining smaller molecules end to end; and hydrogenation, commonly used in the manufacture of cooking oils, requiring the addition of hydrogen to an unsaturated organic molecule.

A given product might be able to be produced by a number of different processes, each using a different set of unit operations. Chemical engineers spend a great deal of time determining which of these will produce a consistently high-quality result and, among these, which can be put into operation for the least amount of money.

Once a manufacturing process has been chosen, chemical engineers usually test the process at an experimental factory. This factory, called a pilot plant, is built at a scale much larger than a laboratory but still quite smaller than the expected size of the final manufacturing plant. It is at the pilot plant that chemical engineers are able to make any necessary modifications. Many processes fail to perform as hoped, and despite attempts at correction, some must be abandoned at this stage.

If a process is successfully run at a pilot plant, additional testing may be done at an even larger experimental factory or the process may begin operation at a manufacturing plant. Chemical engineers must be present at the manufacturing plant as well, at first to work out any additional problems in the process and then to maintain and operate the equipment at the plant.

At some large companies, a chemical engineer will not be directly involved in all of the above responsibilities. Some may work only in the research and development stage, while others devote all their time to operating existing processes at a manufacturing plant. Still others may work in supervisory or managerial positions, and thus their involvement in day-to-day operations might be limited.

At smaller companies, a chemical engineer often is involved in all stages of a project, as well as in areas traditionally handled by other specialists, such as mechanical engineers. Consultants also commonly work in a wide range of chemical engineering areas.

Requirements

A bachelor's degree in chemical engineering is generally considered the minimum educational requirement for entering the field. For some jobs, however, a master's or even a Ph.D. may be necessary, especially for positions in research, teaching, and administration.

There are about 145 accredited undergraduate programs in chemical engineering in the United States. Admissions requirements vary considerably from program to program, but most require a strong background in mathematics and sciences. High school students interested in chemical engineering should thus take rigorous math and science classes, including algebra, geometry, chemistry, and physics. Calculus, earth science, and biology are also recommended.

Students are advised to find a chemical engineering program approved by the Accreditation Board for Engineering and Technology. Accreditation should guarantee that instruction will be of good quality, and any student wishing to apply to a graduate program in chemical

engineering will need a bachelor's degree from an accredited college or university.

In a typical four-year chemical engineering curriculum, the first two years are spent studying mathematics, chemistry, and physics, as well as taking various classes in the social sciences and humanities, including English. The last two years emphasize engineering and the advanced study of mathematics and science. Among the required engineering subjects are fluid dynamics, chemical kinetics, thermodynamics, mass transfer operations, and unit operations.

Some undergraduate engineering curricula require more than four years to complete. A number of schools offer a five- or six-year cooperative program coordinating classroom study with practical experience working for an engineering firm. Through this type of program, students are also provided the opportunity to finance part of their education.

There are some five-year programs that allow a student to receive two bachelor's degrees, one in engineering and the other in a liberal arts field. In such programs, a student may spend the first three years in liberal arts course work and the last two in the engineering school. Five-year programs leading to a master's degree in chemical engineering also exist.

There are about 140 accredited chemical engineering graduate programs in the United States. In graduate school, students specialize in one aspect of chemical engineering, such as polymerization, chemical kinetics, or biotechnology. A graduate degree is essential for those who want to teach or conduct research at a university or college. Graduate education is also helpful in obtaining promotions within an engineering firm. Some companies offer tuition-reimbursement programs to encourage employees to take graduate courses. Chemical engineers should be prepared to continue their education throughout their careers to keep up with the rapid advances in technology.

A master's degree generally takes one to two years of full-time study beyond undergraduate school, while a Ph.D. program in chemical engineering usually lasts between four and six years. For engineers who want to become managers, a master's degree in business administration may be helpful.

In general, chemical engineers must be competent in mathematics, comfortable in working with abstract concepts, and capable of visualizing structures or mechanical operations in three dimensions. They must also be able to make clear sketches (not finished art work) of complex objects or operations and to explain ideas and devices to others in precise and understandable language. Because computers are playing an increasingly large role in chemical engineering, computer literacy is essential. Other important qualities for the chemical engineer are a concern for accuracy, honesty, perseverance, and the ability to work with others.

Special requirements

Chemical engineers need to be licensed if they want to work for the public sector. All 50 states and the District of Columbia have licensing requirements, which include graduation from an accredited engineering program, a written exam, and at least four years of engineering experience. About one-third of all chemical engineers are licensed. Those who are licensed are called registered engineers.

Opportunities for experience and exploration

There are a number of ways a high school student can explore the field of chemical engineering. Students should look for high school clubs or organizations, as well as extracurricular activities, such as the Junior Engineering Technical Society (JETS). Some construction projects, research laboratories, and manufacturing plants have summer or part-time work for students.

Methods of entering

Most chemical engineers obtain their first position through contacts made at their college or university placement office or through a recommendation by one of their professors. Others may find employment with companies where they had summer or work-study jobs. Professional journals and newspapers often list job openings. For a small fee, the American Institute of Chemical Engineers offers employment services to students who are within eight months of graduation.

Advancement

Students completing an undergraduate degree in chemical engineering generally enter the field as an assistant to an already established engineer. Some chemical engineers are placed in special training programs designed to orient the engineer to company processes, procedures, policy, and products. Advancement and greater responsibility usually occur as a result of more experience and education.

Higher-level jobs include technical service and development officers, team leaders, and managers and executives. For promotion to a managerial position, a master's degree in business administration may be helpful. Chemical engineers sometimes apply their technical experience in other areas of a company, such as sales and marketing, while others may start their own consulting firm.

Employment outlook

According to the U.S. Bureau of Labor Statistics, there are some 50,000 chemical engineers employed in the United States in the early 1990s. Other organizations, such as the American Institute of Chemical Engineers, define the profession more broadly and thus place the figure around 120,000. More than two-thirds of chemical engineers work in manufacturing companies, primarily in the chemical, petroleum, and related industries. About one-fifth are employed by engineering services or consulting firms, designing chemical plants and doing other work on a contractual basis. A small number work for institutions of higher education and agencies of the federal government or are independent consultants.

Employment opportunities are expected to increase at a rate no better than average throughout the 1990s and into the 21st century. Since the mid-1980s, however, the number of graduates in chemical engineering has dropped considerably, thus improving the employment prospects of those who do receive degrees.

Although the chemical industry is expected to expand rapidly, the number of jobs in that industry will likely not keep pace because of anticipated productivity improvements and because more work will be contracted to consulting firms. Chemical engineers may find better opportunities in the field of pharmaceuticals, as well as in biotechnology, food processing, waste disposal, electronics, and other nontraditional industries.

Earnings

Chemical engineers are generally well paid. In private industry, the starting salary for a chemical engineer with a bachelor's degree averages around $39,000 in the early 1990s. Compensation increases substantially with greater experience or education. The average salary for all chemical engineers is about $67,000, and senior engineers with administrative responsibilities earn as much as $65,000 to $90,000 or even more.

Salaries in the federal government are usually lower. In the early 1990s the average starting salary for a chemical engineer with an undergraduate degree is as much as 30 percent lower in the federal government than in the private sector. The average salary for all chemical engineers in the federal government is about $53,000.

Chemical engineers who work for a large company or the federal government receive a good benefits package, including vacation time, sick leave, health and life insurance, and a pension and savings plan. Self-employed consultants must provide their own benefits.

Conditions of work

Most chemical engineers work in clean, well maintained offices, laboratories, or plants. Travel to new or existing plants may be required. Some chemical engineers work with dangerous chemicals, but the adoption of safe working practices greatly reduces their potential health hazards.

The workweek for a chemical engineer is generally 40 hours, although overtime is often expected. Irregular hours also may be necessary from time to time, especially by those who maintain and operate equipment at manufacturing plants.

GOE: 05.01.07; SIC: 8731; SOC: 1626

◇ SOURCES OF ADDITIONAL INFORMATION

American Institute of Chemical Engineers
345 East 47th Street
New York, NY 10017

American Chemical Society
1155 16th Street, NW
Washington, DC 20036

Accreditation Board for Engineering and Technology
345 East 47th Street
New York, NY 10017

Junior Engineering Technical Society (JETS)
1420 King Street
Suite 405
Alexandria, VA 22314

Canadian Chemical Producers Association
#805, 350 Sparks Street
Ottawa ON K1R 7S8

◇ RELATED ARTICLES

Volume 1: Energy; Engineering; Plastics
Volumes 2–4: Chemical technicians; Chemists; Petroleum technicians; Plastics technicians

Chemical technicians

Definition

Chemical technicians assist chemists and chemical engineers in the development, testing, and manufacture of chemical products. Most chemical technicians are designated as *chemical-laboratory technicians* or *chemical-engineering technicians*. In general, the distinction between these two careers is that the chemical-laboratory technician is more concerned with the laboratory testing that goes on during both the development and the manufacturing of chemical products. The chemical-engineering technician is more concerned with the actual manufacturing aspects of the product.

More specifically, chemical-laboratory technicians conduct tests to determine the chemical content, strength, stability, purity, and other characteristics of a wide range of materials, including ores, minerals, pollutants, and con-

This chemical technician is performing routine laboratory tasks so that scientists may turn their full attention to research.

sumer products such as foods, drugs, plastics, dyes, paints, detergents, paper, and petroleum. Often this testing is done as part of a research and development program for new products and materials. The testing, however, may also be involved with a variety of other fields: establishing processing and production methods; quality control; maintenance of health and safety standards; environmental testing; and fields involving experimental, theoretical, or practical applications of chemistry and related sciences.

Chemical-engineering technicians work closely with chemical engineers to develop and improve the processes and equipment used in chemical plants. They test equipment and instruments used to manufacture chemicals and chemical products. In order to establish standard operating procedures and recommend changes or modifications, they observe and record equipment performance, operating characteristics, and the processes involved. To communicate their findings, they prepare tables, charts, sketches, diagrams, and flow charts that record and summarize the collected engineering data.

Chemical-engineering technicians also build, install, modify, and maintain chemical-processing equipment. Some technicians observe, instruct, confer with, and direct the activities of equipment operators and other technical personnel.

Although the chemical-laboratory technician is chiefly concerned with the product's characteristics and the chemical-engineering technician is chiefly concerned with the manufacture of the product, there are areas where their activities overlap. For instance, both types of technicians are concerned with new product

development and must be aware of the goals and constraints of the other. In addition, they often perform similar tasks, such as setting up testing apparatus and preparing chemical solutions for use in manufacturing or processing materials. Both chemical-laboratory and chemical-engineering technicians may also become involved in technical writing or selling chemicals or chemical products.

History

Modern chemistry has roots going back thousands of years to the earliest human efforts to extract medicinal juices from plants and to shape metals into tools and utensils for daily life. As late as the Middle Ages in Europe, chemistry was concerned chiefly with the study of metals and the search for cures for diseases. Alchemy, where the focus was on turning metals into gold and finding a single cure for everything, was a mixture of science and superstition and was a colorful chapter in the history of chemistry.

In the late 18th century, chemistry became established as a scientific discipline through the great discoveries of scientists such as Antoine Lavoisier, Henry Cavendish, and Amedeo Avogadro. Also during that century, the range of products attributed to chemistry and chemical processes began to expand, chiefly because of the demands and discoveries created by the Industrial Revolution.

During the 20th century, and especially following World War I, the application of chemical principles to human needs and problems rapidly increased to include the entire range of manufactured goods and consumer products such as gasoline, antifreeze, weed killers, adhesives, water repellents, furniture polishes, and meat tenderizers.

This rapid expansion increased the need for professionally trained chemists as well as assistant chemists who, with their combination of basic knowledge and manual skills, were able to handle many of the tasks and problems that did not require the special training of the professional chemist or chemical engineer. By handling these simpler tasks and problems, the assistant chemists increased the productivity of the chemist and chemical engineer, allowing them to concentrate their efforts on those problems requiring their special skills.

In time, these assistants became known as technicians, and today the growing complexity of industrial processes and the increase in industrial research and development have led to a growing dependence upon them in the chemical and other related industries.

Nature of the work

Most chemical technicians work in the chemical industry, one of the largest in the United States. Many others work in the petroleum, aerospace, metals, electronics, automotive, and construction industries. Other chemical technicians are employed by educational institutions and government agencies.

The majority of chemical technicians perform work connected with one of four areas: research and development, design and production, quality control, and customer service. The first of these areas mainly requires the services of chemical-laboratory technicians; the second, chemical-engineering technicians; the last two offer opportunities for both kinds of chemical technicians.

In research and development, chemical technicians help create new chemical products and find new ways to make chemicals from different starting materials. They set up and conduct tests on chemical processes and products being developed or improved. Those helping with experiments take measurements, make computations, then tabulate and analyze the results. They may have to vary certain experimental conditions—for instance, a chemical solution's concentration, the temperature, or the pressure—until a satisfactory result is obtained. They may then analyze the results, using both simple and quite complex equipment and procedures to determine the quantities of each component.

In the design and production area, mainly chemical-engineering technicians are employed to plan the processes, then design and operate the manufacturing equipment used to make the product developed in the research laboratories. They work with pipelines, valves, pumps, and metal and glass tanks; assist chemical engineers in answering manufacturing questions, such as how to transfer materials or heat from one point to another; help install equipment; and train and supervise operators on the production line. The work may require them to work at drawing boards, to operate small-scale equipment for designing or evaluating manufacturing processes or equipment, or to use computers to design new plants or to maintain operations of a production facility.

Chemical technicians working in quality-control test raw materials received by the company to determine if they are good enough to use. They keep a close watch on every step in the chemical process and test the final product to assure that the product meets all required specifications. An error by the chemical technician in this area can result in the loss of huge amounts of money and material. Many technicians in this area work with computers to obtain the fast and accurate information they need. Technicians trained in quality control are often called upon to help establish quality-control standards and to design quality-assurance techniques.

Chemical technicians in the customer-service field work to keep their company's established customers and gain new ones. Changes in customer needs and in business competition create new demands for chemicals and give chemical technicians many opportunities to handle customer problems. As many companies sell their products to other manufacturing companies, chemical technicians in this area need to understand the nature of their customers' products and manufacturing processes as well as their own products and processes.

Within these four broad areas, many chemical technicians work principally at one specialized activity or with one specific kind of product. The following short paragraphs describe some of these jobs, all of them open to entry-level chemical technicians.

Food-product technicians enforce quality-control standards for food by analyzing sugar and vitamin content, shelf life, and microorganism counts.

Fuel technicians determine viscosity (thickness) of oils and fuels, measure flash points (the temperature at which the fuels spark or catch fire) and pour points (the coldest temperature at which the fuel still behaves as a liquid), and evaluate the heat productivity of fuels.

Pilot-plant operators make erosion and corrosion tests on new construction materials in small-scale or pilot plants. They evaluate new pumps, make new chemicals for field testing, and report on the effectiveness of new design concepts.

Chemical-design technicians work with data from operating plants and pilot plants. They prepare drawings of chemical processing units and make cost estimates for products, processes, and equipment.

Applied-research technicians work as part of an applied research team and use their knowledge of basic chemical concepts to help design new manufacturing or research equipment. Applied research refers to work that takes information or a product obtained in experiments and uses it in practical applications.

Nuclear-laboratory technicians determine rates of nuclear disintegration, prepare complex chemical compounds, evaluate shielding materials, and calibrate measuring equipment.

Chemical technicians in most of these areas share certain routine activities. They must often maintain and repair the equipment they use, as well as install new equipment or supervise those doing the installation. Chemical technicians in all of these areas may also move into related activities: technical writing, technical sales, and employee supervision.

Requirements

Successful chemical technicians must have both the ability and the desire to use both mental and manual skills. They should also have a good supply of patience because experiments must frequently be repeated several times. They should feel at ease doing close detail work and be able to follow directions closely when dealing with unfamiliar equipment or processes. Chemical technicians also need good communications skills and the ability to keep clear, accurate, and complete records.

Most employers of chemical technicians prefer to hire graduates of two-year college programs specifically designed to train technicians. To meet the entrance requirements of these programs, prospective chemical technicians should begin their educational preparations while in high school and plan on earning a high school diploma. They need at least one year of algebra, and one year of a science, preferably chemistry, that includes laboratory experience. Several colleges that offer programs to prepare chemical technicians require as much as three years of mathematics, including algebra, geometry, and trigonometry; two years of physical sciences, including chemistry; and four years of English and language skills.

Students are advised to take one or more of the standard college entrance examinations, such as the ACT or SAT.

Realizing that many students become aware of technical career possibilities too late to satisfy college requirements, many community and technical colleges that offer a program to prepare chemical technicians have also developed a schedule of noncredit courses that allow students to meet the requirements.

Once enrolled in a two-year college program designed for chemical technicians, students should expect to take a number of chemistry courses with strong emphasis on laboratory work and the presentation of data. These courses will include basic concepts of modern chemistry, such as atomic structure, descriptive chemistry of both organic and inorganic substances, analytical methods including instrumental analysis, and physical properties of substances.

Students should also expect to take courses in mathematics, physics, psychology, industrial safety, and management techniques. Courses that improve the student's ability to write technical reports and to communicate orally are especially important.

It may be possible for a student to take courses for a specific area of employment, including biology, chemical engineering, metallurgy, or electronics.

Special requirements

Only a small number of chemical technicians need to be licensed or certified. Those who work with food products, especially milk or dairy products, may be required to have state or local licenses. Chemical technicians working with radioactive isotopes may need a license or certification for certain types of work.

Opportunities for experience and exploration

Part-time and summer employment is sometimes available as production workers in certain manufacturing plants which produce chemicals or consumer products. Although these positions do not provide direct chemical technician experience, production workers are often supervised by a chemical technician, thus providing a valuable opportunity to learn about the field.

If relevant employment is difficult to secure, students can test their interest and abilities in different ways. For example, the junior high school student who has enjoyed science as a hobby through the use of a chemistry set at home or who has performed simple experiments in school science courses has had experience with chemistry and an opportunity to test his or her interest in the field. High school students can determine the strength of their interests in science by assessing the quality of their experiences in high school science classes.

In addition, chemistry teachers or high school guidance counselors may be able to arrange field trips to industrial laboratories or manufacturing companies. Through such visits students are able to observe technicians involved in the field, and it may be possible to speak with several of these people regarding their work or with their employers about possibilities for technicians in that industry or company.

Methods of entering

Most graduates of chemical technology programs find jobs during the last term of their two-year programs. Company recruiters regularly visit most colleges where chemical technology programs are offered. The placement staff and the teachers at the school are frequently able to give useful advice about employment opportunities.

If students do not find a job while still in school or wish to work for a particular employer, they may apply directly to personnel offices at companies of interest. In addition, many opportunities are listed in the classified ads of newspapers or through private and public employment offices.

Some schools have a cooperative education program that permits regularly enrolled students to work as chemical technicians while still in school. Students in such programs develop a good knowledge of the employment possibilities and frequently stay with the cooperative employers.

Advancement

Chemical technicians become more valuable to their employers as they gain experience. Those who take additional courses or show that they can accept responsibilities are often given promotions. Many technicians prefer promotions that allow them to continue working in the laboratory, plant, or office where they started their careers. Others prefer to use their experience as background for a different type of work. The following paragraphs describe some of the different types of work available to chemical technicians who have gained the required experience.

Chemical-process analysts work to prevent failure of chemical-processing equipment. They compare new equipment with older equipment and try to find the least expensive ways to do a given job.

Chemical-process supervisors maintain schedules, prevent downtime, point out problems to design and engineering staffs, and supervise small groups of workers.

Quality-control specialists train inexperienced chemical technicians, test new procedures, and supervise routine quality-control operations.

Chemical-research associates suggest and evaluate procedures to make new compounds, modify instruments, prepare patent reports, and make literature searches.

Customer-service specialists work with customers' processing units, suggest design changes, locate spare components, and correspond with customers.

Chemical-design specialists supervise drafters, incorporate new instruments into existing processing units, determine construction materials, and evaluate bids.

Air and water pollution technologists use precision measurement equipment, survey geographical areas, design sampling systems, and identify pollution sources.

Chemical-instrumentation technicians determine instrument accuracy, troubleshoot erratic equipment, modify equipment, and design new auxiliary apparatus.

Product-evaluation technicians design and construct test apparatus, make commercial compounds, and suggest changes and improvements in chemical products.

Employment outlook

The employment outlook for chemical technicians varies according to the industry in which they are employed. The pharmaceutical industry offers the best opportunities. A variety of factors, including the growing number of older people in our society with their need for more medical services, has created an increased demand for pharmaceutical products. This increased demand has led to a need for more chemical technicians both in the research and development area and in production operations.

Employment levels for chemical technicians involved in either research or manufacture of consumer and industrial chemical products are more dependent on general economic conditions. Regardless of these conditions, however, the chemical and chemical-related industries will continue to become increasingly sophisticated in both their products and their manufacturing techniques. There will always be a demand for technicians who can contribute to the development of successful new products and to finding more efficient and economical ways to produce these products. Because of this, employment levels for chemical technicians in general are expected to rise faster than the average of all occupations through the mid-1990s.

Earnings

Chemical technicians on their first job who have completed a two-year post-high school training program earn approximately $24,000 a year in private industry. Experienced technicians with similar post-high school training earn salaries averaging approximately $30,000 a year. Some senior technicians earn as much as $42,000 a year or more. Salaries for technicians in the federal government will be somewhat lower.

Benefits depend on the employer, but they usually include paid vacations and holidays, insurance, and tuition refund plans. If the technician belongs to a union, wages and benefits depend on the union agreement.

Conditions of work

The chemical industry is noted as one of the safest industries in which to work. Laboratories and plants normally have safety committees and safety engineers who closely observe equipment and practices to prevent hazards. Chemical technicians usually receive safety training both in school and at work, so that potential hazards are recognized and appropriate measures are taken.

Most chemical laboratories are maintained in a clean and well-lighted condition. Most companies avoid crowding so that chemical technicians usually have a very few people working in the immediate area. Chemical plants are usually as clean as other types of manufacturing operations. The number of operating personnel is usually very low for the space involved. Processing equipment may be either inside a building or out in the open, depending upon the characteristics of the manufacturing unit.

Chemical technicians are involved in work that may range from uncomplicated, routine tasks to those that are highly complex and challenging. Although prospective technicians should have a tolerance for both kinds of work, it is possible to find jobs that focus on one or the other of these kinds of work.

Many chemical technicians act as intermediaries between professionally trained scientists or engineers and skilled laboratory or production workers. Some technicians may feel awkward in this position. Technicians who do best in this role enjoy the challenge of being able both to carry out carefully and to issue clearly the instructions and directions required in chemical laboratory or production technology.

GOE: 02.04.01; 05.01.08; SIC: 8731; SOC: 3719; 3831

◇ SOURCES OF ADDITIONAL INFORMATION

American Chemical Society, Chemical Technician Division
Educational Activities Department
1155 16th Street, NW
Washington, DC 20036

American Institute of Chemical Engineers
345 East 47th Street
New York, NY 10017

Chemical Industry for Minorities in Engineering
PO Box 1310
Wilmington, DE 19899-1310

Chemical Manufacturers Association
Educational Department
2501 M Street, NW
Washington, DC 20037

Canadian Chemical Producers Association
#805, 350 Sparks Street
Ottawa ON K1R 7S8

Junior Engineering Technical Society (JETS)
1428 King Street, Suite 405
Alexandria, VA 22314

(Note to students: include a stamped, self-addressed envelope with your request.)

◇ RELATED ARTICLES

Volume 1: Chemicals and Drugs; Chemistry; Engineering
Volumes 2–4: Chemists; Industrial chemicals workers; Industrial engineering technicians; Medical laboratory technicians; Paint and coatings industry workers; Petroleum refining workers; Petroleum technicians; Pharmaceutical industry workers; Pharmaceutical technicians; Pharmacologists; Plastics products manufacturing workers; Plastics technicians

Chemists

Definition

The *chemist* performs analytical and research work in the field of chemistry, and may make quantitative and qualitative analyses to determine chemical and physical properties of many substances. Chemists also are trained to make a variety of chemicals and perform tests on manufactured goods, such as foods, drugs, plastics, dyes, paints, and petroleum products. They may supervise research activities in industry and prepare reports about research projects.

History

Chemistry was first studied and applied more than 5,000 years ago. Originally chemistry was the art of extracting medicinal materials from plants. In the Middle Ages chemistry, or alchemy as it was then called, was concerned with the study of metals and the search for a universal cure for disease. Today, with the increasing speed of scientific and material progress, chemistry involves a great deal more than medicines and precious metals. Chemists contribute to advances in medicine, space science, and other similar frontier areas, as well as a wide range of manufactured goods and consumer products.

Nature of the work

About half of today's chemists are engaged in research and development. The majority of these chemists work on applied research projects to improve and create new products. Drugs for use in medicine, synthetic materials to replace the demand on dwindling natural material supplies, and fuels that can meet the demand of space travel are only a few examples of the products that chemists have helped develop.

Other research chemists work on basic research projects. The main purpose of basic research is to extend scientific knowledge rather than to solve immediate practical problems. Many important practical applications, however, have resulted from basic research. Chemists also work in analysis and testing because various tests must be made at practically every stage in the manufacture of a product.

Some chemists are employed in college teaching and administrative work, while others are employed in production, patent work, technical sales, technical writing, technical library work, materials purchasing, and market research.

Within the various branches of chemistry there are many fields from which to choose. Agricultural chemists, adhesives chemists, paint chemists, nutritional chemists, petroleum chemists, leather chemists, and pharmaceutical chemists are examples of specialized chemists. The following are several other specializations.

Water-purification chemists analyze the filtered water in purification plants and test samples from various points along the distribution system to make sure it meets prescribed standards. They determine and monitor the kinds and amounts of chemicals needed to purify and soften the water to make it suitable for drinking.

Wastewater-treatment plant chemists investigate the efficiency of wastewater treatment processes to ensure that water pollution control requirements are met. They test samples of streams, raw and treated wastewater, sludge, and other by-products for various solids, acids, alkalinity, and other substances and devise ways to improve the treatment processes.

Instrumentation chemists examine the wastewater discharged by industries using a municipal wastewater treatment plant to see if it meets pollution control requirements. Any variation that shows up in the analysis is used to determine surcharge assessments to be levied against the company that is at fault.

Each field is further divided into subfields and more specialized occupations. *Chemical laboratory chiefs* head up chemical labs and are responsible for planning and carrying out programs for research, product development, improvement of manufacturing processes, and analysis and testing of substances, compounds, liquids, and gases. As chief chemists, they direct the laboratory staff, review and interpret reports, and keep management advised of activities under their control.

Laboratory supervisors train, assign, and oversee workers who perform chemical and physical tests to ensure the quality of products. They help develop tests, solve testing problems, and compile test information related to the operating efficiency of the equipment or processes.

The preparation of a substance through extraction involves complex and delicate laboratory procedures.

Food chemists develop and improve foods and beverages. They analyze methods of cooking, canning, freezing, and packaging, and study their effects on the appearance, taste, aroma, freshness, and vitamin content of various products. They test samples of cereal, dairy products, meats, vegetables, beer, and other goods to make sure they comply with food laws. They experiment with new foods, additives, and preservatives.

Colorists develop color formulas to match customer specifications for printing textile and plastic materials. They also coordinate color shop activities with the production schedule of the printing department.

Perfumers devise formulas for perfumes and other aromatic products and set production standards for the compounding and distillation departments. They test fragrances by smelling samples in an air-filtered room. Characteristics they check include odor, body, harmony, strength, and permanence.

Assayers determine the value and properties of ores and minerals. They separate metals from the impurities and conduct tests involving spectrographic analysis, chemical solutions, and a variety of chemical and laboratory equipment.

While completing their training in college or in graduate work, chemists usually concentrate their work in one of the five main branches of chemistry: organic, inorganic, physical, analytical, or biochemistry.

The organic chemist specializes in the chemistry of carbon and its compounds, most of which are substances originally derived from animal and vegetable matter. The main job is to determine structure, composition, and other physical and chemical properties.

The inorganic chemist is concerned with compounds of noncarbon structure, including most of the metals and minerals.

The physical chemist is interested in the study of the quantitative relationships between the chemical and physical properties of organic and inorganic substances—for example, how a substance designed for use in a space capsule is affected by heat of reentry.

The analytical chemist, as the term implies, analyzes the exact chemical composition of substances and tests them to determine quality, purity, and other characteristics.

The biochemist is concerned with chemical reactions of living organisms and the effect of chemicals on life processes.

Requirements

A bachelor's degree in chemistry is usually regarded as the minimum educational requirement for the beginning chemist. People hoping to obtain better, more responsible jobs should plan on extensive graduate work. Chemists employed in supervisory positions in industry, in teaching, or in research positions in industry or universities usually have their doctorates.

Interested students should have an aptitude for mathematics and the natural sciences, combined with an ability to express themselves easily in the company of others. They should take three to four years of English; four years of mathematics, including algebra, geometry, and trigonometry; three to four years of science, including biology, chemistry, and physics; two years of social studies; and at least two years of a foreign language (preferably German, French, or Russian) prior to entering college. Computer experience is also helpful. The college training leading to a bachelor of science degree in chemistry includes required courses in analytical, inorganic, organic, and physical chemistry supplemented by courses in mathematics, physics, biology, and liberal arts. College students should also try to take additional courses in German, French, and/or Russian, because many technical papers valuable for research are written in these languages, and a reading knowledge of at least one of them may be required to earn an advanced degree. College students are also urged to study a programming language.

Because graduate training is essential for most responsible positions, particularly in research and teaching, many students obtain either a master's degree or a doctorate in chemistry after completing their undergraduate work. In graduate school a chemistry student is required to have courses in a specialty or field of interest, plus a great deal of laboratory research.

Opportunities for experience and exploration

High school students have many opportunities to get involved in different aspects of science through hobbies, school projects, clubs, and science fairs. Some students may obtain part-time jobs in chemical labs as assistants and thereby observe the chemical field firsthand.

Methods of entering

Professors who have worked closely with chemistry students throughout their college careers are often able to guide students into branches of chemistry best suited to their individual interests and abilities.

Some schools offer cooperative education programs wherein a student can work for a bachelor's degree in chemistry and at the same time gain related work experience. Upon graduation such students are usually selected for more responsible jobs. Beginning chemists with a bachelor's degree usually start out as trainees in laboratory research and development or in analysis and testing, quality control, technical service, production, or sales.

Advancement

Most graduates with a bachelor's degree in chemistry begin work in company-sponsored training programs. Most recent graduates are likely to find employment in manufacturing industries, particularly industrial chemicals. Some advance into high-level research and management positions. With experience and the benefit of additional industrial training, many chemists advance to more responsible positions.

Chemists with a master's degree can usually qualify for applied research positions in government and private industry, and for teaching positions in colleges and universities. A doctorate offers the chemist the best possibility for advancement, however, because it is required for basic research work, higher-level college or university teaching, and for many top-level positions in various other areas of employment.

Employment outlook

About 83,000 chemists are employed in the 1990s. Of the almost 60 percent who worked for manufacturing companies, most are with chemical manufacturers. Chemists also are employed by federal agencies (primarily the departments of Defense, the Interior, Health and Human Services, and Agriculture); state and local governments (mostly in health and agriculture); nonprofit research organizations; and colleges and universities.

The employment outlook in all these areas through the 1990s is expected to grow at an average rate. The output of the chemical industry, where most of the jobs are, is expected to increase. However, the number of people graduating with degrees in chemistry is higher than the number of positions available.

The most promising areas should be in pharmaceuticals and biotechnology. Career fields are dependent on new development in research and technology, and the petroleum refining and most other manufacturing industries that use chemists are expected to show very little growth, if any.

Some chemistry graduates may choose to teach high school chemistry; others may qualify as engineers, particularly if they have taken engineering courses. Those with a doctorate may be employed as college or university faculty.

Earnings

A chemist's earning power is determined by a combination of several factors: ability, education, experience, and initiative. In the 1990s, the average starting salaries per year in private industry for well qualified, inexperienced chemists with these various college degrees are as follows: bachelor's, $23,000; master's, $30,000; and doctorate, $44,000. Earnings increase markedly with experience. Experienced chemists in private industry have median salaries of $39,000 with a bachelor's degree, $45,000 with a master's, and $55,000 with a doctorate.

Federal government salaries in the 1990s average $46,800 a year.

In addition to salary, the industry offers a number of fringe benefits. The industrial chemist is usually qualified to obtain group insurance plans, retirement programs, bonuses, hospitalization plans, and others. University teachers often have the advantage of similar fringe benefits, as do chemists employed in the federal government.

Conditions of work

The chemist usually works a 35- to 40-hour week. Laboratories are well equipped and well lighted. The work is typically indoors and characterized by a close working relationship with other chemists. They often have the opportunity to publish the results of this work in technical journals and to present talks on the research to local and national groups of chemists.

GOE: 02.02.01, 02.02.02. 02.02.03; SIC: 2819, 2833, 3559, 8221, 8731; SOC: 1845

◇ SOURCES OF ADDITIONAL INFORMATION

American Association for Clinical Chemistry
2029 K Street, NW, 7th Floor
Washington, DC 20006

American Chemical Society
1155 16th Street, NW
Washington, DC 20036

International Chemical Workers Union
1655 West Market Street
Akron, OH 44313

Chemical Institute of Canada
#550, 130 Slater Street
Ottawa ON K1P 6E2

◇ RELATED ARTICLES

Volume 1: Biological Sciences; Chemicals and Drugs; Chemistry; Plastics
Volumes 2–4: Biochemists; Chemical engineers; Chemical technicians; Food technologists; Industrial chemicals workers; Laboratory technicians; Medical laboratory technicians; Miscellaneous engineers; Pharmaceutical industry workers; Pharmacists; Pharmacologists; Soil scientists; Toxicologists

Child care workers

Definition

Child care workers care for groups of children housed in various kinds of institutions funded by private organizations or city, county, or state governments. They also work with children who attend day care centers because the parents work. Children may be institutionalized because of abuse, neglect, or disability. The relationship between child care workers and the children in their charge often focuses on providing personal guidance and encouraging suitable life skills so that the children may lead active and productive lives on their own. The position of child care worker offers a person the challenges of working with groups of children who have different backgrounds and needs, supervising groups and other employees, and establishing one-on-one relationships with each child in the work environment. While the work can be physically demanding and emotionally draining, one of the biggest benefits is the feeling of achievement and of having a positive influence on someone's life.

History

Care for children without families, the traditional orphans, was begun in the 4th century by the Roman Catholic Church. By the 1600s monasteries also managed orphanages and homes for abandoned babies. Children, if not orphaned, may have been abandoned because of physical disabilities or emotional disorders. The parents may also have abandoned a child because of poverty.

Institutions for the mentally and physically disabled were, for the most part, mere warehouses for those living there. Little effort was made to improve the skills, education, or comfort of the residents. Orphanages, at their worst, sold children as indentured workers after a child reached the age of seven.

As human understanding of child welfare improved through the 19th and early 20th centuries, many remedies were established to the state of orphanages and institutional care. By the middle of the 20th century, child welfare was a focus of training for those who worked in the field. The needs of a child were much better understood and better met by the facilities charged with their care.

Nature of the work

The responsibilities of the child care worker include many of the tasks found in a traditional home environment. Child care workers have such duties as waking the children up in the morning and making sure they have a nutritious breakfast. The child care worker must also see that the children are properly dressed and ready for their daily routine, which may include school (or other type of instruction), therapy, or planned daily activities. A child care worker may be counted on to assist children with their homework and studies, as well as help them develop skills for daily living such as proper hygiene or manners. A child care worker may also be responsible for formal instruction, whether it be a class or a part of a child's therapy program. Certain household tasks—cooking, laundry, or other chores—may be delegated to some of the older, more capable children to encourage their participation and independence. Such assignments can benefit the group as a whole and establish a healthy sense of cooperation and community.

A child care worker's responsibility to the children does not end with the roles of teacher and disciplinarian, however. In the evenings and on weekends the child care worker may be expected to engage in recreational activities with the children. Planning outings, holiday activities (such as baking and making crafts), and sports and games allows the children and child care worker to develop a more open and friendly relationship.

Child care workers often educate children through entertaining means. In this case, a worker engages them with playful songs.

Continual, caring interaction with all of the children is a significant part of the day-to-day routine. The amount of time that a child care worker invests in the children is the aspect of this job that makes it closely related to parenthood. In addition, it is in the diversity of these duties that child care workers find their greatest challenges and rewards.

The child care worker may find a significant number of children in institutions who are victims of abuse, mentally or emotionally disturbed, delinquent, or disabled. In addition to being resourceful and patient, the child care worker must be quick-thinking to handle the small crises and disagreements that are inevitable in a group setting. The person must also be firm to reinforce house rules and impart discipline. It is important for the child care worker to be strong-willed yet adaptable to a variety of needs, whether physical or emotional, and to understand the inherent challenges that the children face due to their particular circumstances.

Requirements

One advantage for prospective child care workers is that no special training or education is required for entry-level positions. Personal maturity, reliability, and a humane spirit are all vital qualities, and people lacking these will not enjoy or succeed at the work, no matter what their educational achievements.

The majority of institutions list only a high school degree as an essential educational requirement for this position. Child care workers often receive training on the job to become familiar with the rules and regulations specific to that institution or center.

CHILD CARE WORKERS

All this having been said, there are many possibilities for education and development for people in this field. Most two-year college programs offer courses that a child care worker would find beneficial, such as classes in child or behavioral psychology and sociology. In addition, arts and crafts, cooking, sewing, metal work and woodcraft, and other skill-oriented courses can be useful, since children can learn from any number of activities and projects.

Those interested in pursuing a four-year college degree may want to consider studying psychology, early childhood or special education, or course work in physical or occupational therapy. The degree that a person earns may direct him or her to particular institutions in search of employment.

Beyond any formal education, the child care worker must have certain personal qualifications for this particular line of work. Patience, compassion, resourcefulness, and a sense of fairness are characteristics that the child care worker will find necessary in handling small groups of children. Since this is an area where service to others and attention to their needs are at the root of all activities, an even temper and personal strength are imperative.

Special requirements

Depending on the level of education that a child care worker pursues, certain special requirements may be necessary. For instance, therapists and teachers are required to have state and professional certification. Also, the child care worker may choose to attend workshops and seminars to develop a specific area of interest or specialization. One example of special training is teachers who learn sign language to work with deaf children.

Opportunities for experience and exploration

For people interested in becoming child care workers, ample opportunities for exposure to this field exist. Presently, part-time employment positions comprise more than 40 percent of the total number of jobs, and many institutions welcome volunteer assistance as well. In this way, a student may be able to work in a variety of departments and receive a reasonable introduction to a particular institution and the field of child care work in general.

In addition, most neighborhoods offer opportunities for exploration at places such as community centers, day care institutions, and local agencies for the disabled. Contacting or volunteering at any of these community resources can help interested people focus on their further career and education.

Methods of entering

As mentioned previously, formal training is not always a requirement in this field. Many people employed as child care workers have already gained informal experience in child care from their personal family experiences.

As with any social service work, it is highly recommended that you spend some time doing the work as a volunteer before making your career choice to study in this field. Because of the continual energy level and emotional involvement in social work, it takes a dedicated and committed individual to do well in this field. It is best to make sure you have the energy and temperament suited to a career in child care by exploring the job through volunteer or part-time employment.

People with educational experience in child care or child development should check with their school placement offices for information on job openings in their area. Contacting institutions directly is also recommended for people trying to enter this field.

Advancement

As in many professions, personal advancement depends heavily on continued service and training. Child care workers may receive promotions and additional responsibilities after some months on the job and after demonstrating good performance. Once the child care worker has become acquainted with the field in general, he or she may choose to pursue additional education to support an area of specialization. There is also significant turnover in this line of work, which can help workers advance more readily, either within their current institution or at another one.

Employment outlook

The number of child care workers in the 1990s is estimated to be more than 600,000. By the year 2000 government projections estimate the number of people in this field will rise to more than 700,000. Religious organizations and special interest groups for the needy are providing more services for children, thereby increasing the size and number of institutions. This growth, combined with the high employee turnover rate, means that most child care workers should be able to find suitable employment.

Earnings

Beginning child care workers with no prior experience can expect to earn the minimum hourly wage at most institutions. Salaries for full-time child care workers range from $11,000 to $15,000 a year. At institutions where the child care worker lives on the premises with the children, employees' room and board is often figured into their salary.

Fringe benefits are usually offered to child care workers as a part of their employment package. Though the benefits vary, they may include health and life insurance benefits, paid holidays, and vacation time. In addition, some of the larger institutions may offer some kind of pension or retirement benefits.

Conditions of work

Because different institutions vary with regard to their purpose and available facilities, the living conditions of the child care worker and the children are also diverse. Most institutions offer clean but simple apartments or cottages for their on-campus staff. If the child care workers live in group housing with the children, they are usually assigned to separate areas of the dormitories. For supervision and direction, child care workers may be required to report to more experienced employees or to couples who reside at the institution and function as dorm parents.

Child care workers frequently put in long hours, because caring for the needs of children can be very unpredictable. There are always a few hours set aside each day, however, for the child care worker to have some individual time to relax, accomplish personal tasks, attend seminars or workshops, and meet with co-workers.

GOE: 10.03.03; SIC: 835; SOC: 5264

◇ **RELATED ARTICLES**

Volume 1: Education; Health Care; Social Services
Volumes 2–4: Adult and vocational education teachers; Child life specialists; Human services workers; Kinesiotherapists; Nannies; Nursing and psychiatric aides; Psychologists; Recreation workers; Recreational therapists; Rehabilitation counselors; Teacher aides; Teachers, kindergarten and elementary school; Teachers, preschool; Teachers, secondary school

Child life specialists

Definition

Child life specialists work in health care settings to help children, adolescents, and their families through illness or injury. They are members of the complete health care team in hospitals or ambulatory care facilities.

One of the primary roles of the child life specialist is to ease the anxiety and stress that often accompany hospitalization or injury. They help children, adolescents, and their families maintain living patterns that are as close to normal as possible, and they try to minimize the potential trauma of hospitalization. Child life specialists do this by providing opportunities for play and relaxation, interaction with other children, and personalized attention. They also encourage family involvement, as such involvement can play a major role in helping children and adolescents cope with difficult situations.

Some hospitals refer to their child life specialists as *play therapists, activity therapists, patient activity specialists,* or *therapeutic recreation specialists.*

Enjoying a game with this child life specialist, these children get a chance to forget for a while that they are in a hospital.

History

Physicians and nurses used to be the only adults responsible for the care of children in hospitals. Many parents felt that the particular needs of their children were not being met. Social workers joining the health team were sometimes not specially trained to work with children.

In the 1970s the Association for the Care of Children's Health (ACCH) formed a committee for child life and activity specialists. Their goal was to encourage the growing number of child life professionals. They recognized that the interruption that a hospitalization or even an ambulatory procedure created in a child's life could have negative consequences for the child's growth and development. Infants, children, and adolescents alike may suffer from the effects of hospitalization. This can make it more difficult for them to respond to medical treatment. Child life specialists have therefore become an integral part of a child's health care team.

Nature of the work

When children are hospitalized, many of their new experiences are frightening. For young children, separation from their familiar homes and families can be traumatic. For older children, repeated blood tests, needles, or painful procedures can cause fears or nightmares. Emotional damage can be a danger even for adolescents. Child life specialists try to ease the potential trauma of hospitalization. They play an important role in comforting both the patients and their families.

The child life specialist uses recreational activities, art projects, cooking, music, and outdoor play. The program is tailored to meet the needs of individual patients. Some children are unable to express their fears and concerns, and may need the child life specialist to draw them out. Some children use the child life specialist to help them understand what is happening to them. Still others need the child life specialist to explain emotional outbursts or withdrawal to their families.

In most hospitals the child life specialist works in a special playroom. Sometimes the specialist may go to the child's hospital room. In outpatient facilities, the specialist may work in a waiting room or designated playroom. Child life specialists may use dolls and medical instruments to show a child where the doctor will be working. They may help the children act out their concerns by having the children give a doll a shot like the one they have just received. They also may observe the child comforting a doll, or explaining procedures that they have experienced.

The emotional effects and anxiety a child may feel may not be dependent on the length of a hospital stay or even on the severity of the illness or injury. Child life specialists must be tuned in to the child's or adolescent's own concerns and approach them with care.

Child life specialists become familiar and trusted adults to their patients in hospital settings. Often they are the only professionals who do not perform tests on the children, poke them, or probe them. When a child is hospitalized for an extended period of time, the child life specialist may be the one to plan a birthday party in the hospital, or celebrate successful completion of one particular treatment or phase of treatment.

Child life specialists may provide such services as preadmission orientation visits, hospital tours once a patient is admitted, and basic explanations of the procedures to be performed. They also serve as advocates for children's issues by promoting rooming-in or unrestricted parental or sibling visits. The ideal ratio of child life specialists to children should be about one to fifteen. Most child life programs in hospitals are autonomous and report to hospital administrations like other hospital departments and programs.

Child life programs often work with school programs within hospitals. Specialists may work with teachers to coordinate curriculum with recreational activities. They also may encourage hospital administrations to provide adequate classroom facilities and the best-qualified teachers.

Child life assistants work under the direct supervision of child life specialists. They help the specialist in many ways, often performing the same functions as the specialist.

Child life administrators supervise the staffs of child life personnel. In larger hospitals, the administrators work with other hospital administrators to run the child life programs smoothly within the hospital setting.

Child life specialists have the potential to turn their patients' hospitalizations into growth experiences. Children are very resilient, and with proper care by their entire health team, they can emerge from hospital stays with a sense of accomplishment and heightened self-esteem.

Requirements

A bachelor's degree is required for child life specialists. Majors in education, child development, and psychology are the best preparation for the field. Internships in child life prepare child life specialists for their work. Any supervised experience in a health care setting is beneficial. Those responsible for hiring child life specialists look for an understanding of family dynamics, interpersonal communication, child development, educational play, and basic medical terminology.

Child life assistants usually have a degree from a two-year college. They also benefit from internship experience. Certification as a child life specialist is available through the Child Life Certifying Commission.

A child life administrator is usually required to have a master's degree in child development, behavioral psychology, education, or a related field. Child life administrators must also have experience supervising staff members, managing budgets, and preparing educational materials.

Some colleges and universities have specific child life programs that include courses in liberal arts as well as courses related to child or adolescent health. The *Directory of Child Life Programs in North America,* published by ACCH, is a good source for finding information on these programs.

Opportunities for experience and exploration

High school students interested in the child life area should take courses in psychology or child development. Volunteer opportunities often exist for students in local hospitals. Outpatient facilities also sometimes use students as volunteers or interns. Local child life programs at both hospitals and pediatric ambulatory care facilities occasionally have student interns who are in college preparing for a career in child life.

The Child Life Council offers an associate membership to students who are interested in the field. With membership comes a subscription to the council's newsletter, which can give a student a better understanding of the work of a child life specialist.

Many summer camps for children with health problems or disabilities hire high school or college students to be counselors or aides. This is excellent preparation for a child life career.

Methods of entering

Hospitals often let child life programs hire their own staff. Interested students should ask for information at the hospital's placement office. Sometimes career or placement offices in schools have job listings from local hospitals and outpatient facilities.

The Child Life Council keeps a job bank with listings from hospitals and clinics for members. Also, the colleges and universities with child life programs are well equipped to help students find jobs in the field.

Advancement

After receiving a diploma or degree from a two year college, someone interested in child life may get a job as a child life assistant. After a few years working and becoming comfortable with patients and their families, an assistant may be promoted to child life specialist. Usually, however, a child life specialist must have a bachelor's degree.

To be promoted to child life administrator, assistant director, or director, advanced degrees are usually required. Also, the specialist needs to show expertise in the field as well as the ability to supervise others. The child life director must keep abreast of the latest research in the psychosocial development of hospitalized or ill children.

Employment outlook

The outlook for child life specialist jobs is steady through the year 2000. More hospitals (especially larger teaching hospitals) are opening child life centers. Also, there has been an increase in the kinds of health care services provided by pediatric ambulatory or outpatient facilities. These usually employ fewer child life specialists, but as they continue to offer more services, more positions will become available.

Earnings

Those entering the child life field have starting salaries ranging from $17,000 to $21,000 per year. In larger metropolitan teaching hospitals the salaries tend to be higher than in smaller community hospitals. Some outpatient facilities pay very well, but they hire fewer child life specialists. Typical salaries for physician's assistants and art therapists, which are related jobs, are about $20,000 to $28,000 annually. Child life administrators or directors can earn more than $30,000 per year.

Conditions of work

Child life specialists must be comfortable in hospital settings. They must adjust easily to being around children who are sick. Since the children and their families need so much support, child life specialists must be emotionally stable. Their own support network of family and friends should be strong, so that the specialist can get through difficult times at work. Child life specialists may have patients who die, and this can be devastating.

Most child life personnel work during regular business hours, although specialists are occasionally needed on evenings, holidays, or weekends to work with the children. It is important for child life personnel to have hobbies or outside interests to avoid becoming too emotionally drained from the work. The rewards of a child life career are great. Many child life specialists see the direct effects of their work on their patients and their patients' families. They see anxiety and fear being eased, and they see their patients come through treatments and hospitalizations with a renewed pride.

GOE: 11.07.04; SIC: 806; SOC: 3039

◇ **SOURCES OF ADDITIONAL INFORMATION**

Association for the Care of Children's Health
Child Life Council
7910 Woodmont Avenue
Suite 300
Bethesda, MD 20814

◇ **RELATED ARTICLES**

Volume 1: Education; Health Care; Social Services
Volumes 2–4: Health services administrators; Homemaker-home health aides; Medical assistants; Nurses; Nursing and psychiatric aides; Physical therapists; Physician assistants; Protestant ministers; Psychiatric technicians; Psychologists; Social workers; Teachers, kindergarten and elementary school; Teachers, preschool; Teachers, secondary school; Therapists, miscellaneous

Chiropractors

Definition

Chiropractors are health practitioners who treat patients primarily by manual manipulation, also called adjustments, of parts of the body, especially the spinal column. This approach to health care is based upon the principle that interference with the nervous system impairs normal functions and lowers resistance to disease. Chiropractic manipulation, particularly of the spinal column, is intended to assist the nervous system to function properly.

History

Chiropractic is a system of treatment founded by Daniel D. Palmer of Iowa in 1855. It is based on the principle that a person's health is determined largely by the nervous system, the network of the body by which the sensation of pain and pleasure, heat and cold, touch, and all the senses are transmitted to the brain. The core of the central nervous system is the spinal cord, which is protected by the bones of the vertebrae that make up the backbone or spinal column. Many believe that moving the bones of the back by gentle manipulation can relieve pressure on the nerves that emerge between the vertebrae and thus ease any pain or discomfort caused by such pinching. The relief of interference in the nervous system by chiropractic is intended to restore normal functions of the body and increase resistance to disease. This health practice includes such adjustments, massage, and nutrition principles. It has its greatest popularity in the United States, and chiropractic is practiced widely here and in Canada.

Nature of the work

Chiropractors do not use prescription drugs or surgery. Most chiropractors use X rays to help locate the source of patients' difficulties in the spine and other joints. In addition to manipulation or adjustment, chiropractors may use light, water, electric, massage, heat, and ultrasound therapy, as well as biofeedback to aid the relief of symptoms. They also prescribe diet, rest, exercise, and support of the afflicted part of the body.

Chiropractors are not medical doctors, although general hospitals began accepting chiropractors as staff members in 1983. Most chiropractors, however, maintain offices in a professional building with other specialists or at their clinics. In addition, they may serve on the staff of a hospital that specializes in chiropractic treatment or in alternative health care centers and clinics.

Many people consult a chiropractor because they know another person who has been successfully treated or because they do not wish to use drugs or to have surgery if they can avoid it. Chiropractic treatment involves practitioners' using their hands to move and manipulate the spine and other joints while the patient is relaxed. Knowledge of anatomy, skillful positioning, firm movement, and sometimes great control of strength are needed to achieve the desired effect.

Often the treatment must be repeated through a series of visits by the patient, and the chiropractor may prescribe things for the patient to do at home to maintain and improve the results of the manipulation. Most chiropractors will take a general history of the patient's health that can help in both diagnosis and treatment. Chiropractors do not merely relieve symptoms but practice with an overall intention to promote good health and well-being in their patients.

Requirements

The most important requirement in any health care profession is the desire to help people in need and to promote wholeness and good health. High school students interested in the field of chiropractic should take as many courses in biology, zoology, and chemistry as possible. Math and physics are important to the understanding of movement and stress. Chiropractic requires a scientific aptitude, a good business sense, and the ability to put patients at ease.

All chiropractic colleges require a minimum of two years of undergraduate study, including courses in the social sciences, biology, chemistry (general and organic), physics, psychology, and communications. The course work in a chiropractic college is generally an additional four years and emphasizes classes in manipulation and spinal adjustments. Most offer a

CHIROPRACTORS

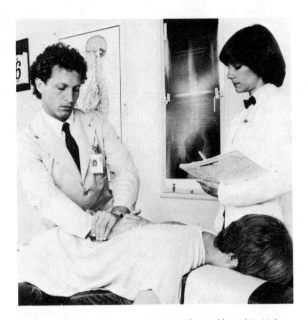

A chiropractor administers treatment to a patient as his assistant takes notes.

Opportunities for experience and exploration

Students may obtain a part-time or summer job in a clinic area specializing in chiropractic. Other health care work in nursing homes or hospitals is also of value.

Methods of entering

A newly licensed chiropractor might begin working in a clinic or in an established practice with another chiropractor. Most chiropractors work in cities with a population of 50,000 or more.

Advancement

A chiropractor may start as a salaried employee in a large practice. Most chiropractors set up a new practice or purchase an established one. A successful practitioner may establish a group practice or set up a clinic with associated health care practitioners.

broad curriculum, including subjects such as physiotherapy and nutrition. In most chiropractic colleges the first two years consist of classroom and laboratory work in subjects such as anatomy, physiology, and biochemistry, while the last two years stress clinical work with patients. The degree awarded upon completion of chiropractic training is Doctor of Chiropractic (D.C.).

Special requirements

All 50 states and the District of Columbia regulate the practice of chiropractic by certain educational requirements. In addition, chiropractors must pass a state board examination to obtain a license to practice. The educational requirements, as well as the type of practice for which a chiropractor may be licensed, varies from state to state. In general, a four-year course following two years of undergraduate work is needed and most state boards recognize only academic training in chiropractic colleges accredited by the Council on Chiropractic Education.

Several states require that chiropractors pass a basic science examination, and most state boards accept the National Board of Chiropractic Examiners' test given to fourth-year chiropractic students in place of a state examination. All states require an examination for licensure.

Employment outlook

Of the nearly 42,000 chiropractors in the 1990s, about 70 percent are in private practice, and the great majority practice alone, without partners. Some chiropractors work in clinics or are employed as assistants to other practitioners, and a few have faculty or research positions at chiropractic colleges.

Demand for chiropractic will increase through the 1990s with the growth of public acceptance of the profession as well as the broader coverage of chiropractic services by public and private health insurance. Employment of chiropractors is expected to grow faster than the rate for all professions. College enrollments are also increasing, however, and new chiropractors may find it increasingly difficult to establish a practice in those areas where other practitioners already are located. Also, the cost of equipment such as X ray and other diagnostic tools is very high for a private practitioner, and group practices with other chiropractors or related health care professionals are likely to provide more opportunity for employment or for purchasing a share of a practice.

Earnings

Chiropractors in well established practices in the 1990s earn an average of $74,000 a year after expenses. Beginning chiropractors earn around $20,000, or if working with an established practitioner as an associate, about $25,000 a year. However, annual salaries vary a great deal, from $24,000 to over $180,000.

Conditions of work

Chiropractors may take an office in a professional building or in their home. They can usually set their own hours, but the workweek is generally 35 to 40 hours.

Chiropractic requires a keen sense of observation to diagnose a condition and determine the appropriate treatment. Considerable hand dexterity is needed but exceptional strength is not necessary. More important is sureness of movement and a genuine desire to help patients. Chiropractors should be able to work independently and handle responsibility and be painstaking with detail. Sympathy and understanding are desirable for dealing effectively with patients.

GOE: 02.03.04; SIC: 8041; SOC: 289

◇ **SOURCES OF ADDITIONAL INFORMATION**

American Chiropractic Association
1701 Clarendon Boulevard
Arlington, VA 22209

Council on Chiropractic Education
4401 Westown Parkway, Suite 120
West Des Moines, IA 50265

International Chiropractors Association
1110 North Glebe Road, Suite 1000
Arlington, VA 22201

Canadian Chiropratic Association
1396 Eglinton Ave. West
Toronto ON M6C 2E4

◇ **RELATED ARTICLES**

Volume 1: Biological Sciences; Health Care
Volumes 2–4: Ergonomists; Kinesiotherapists; Medical assistants; Nurses; Nursing and psychiatric aides; Physical therapist assistants; Physical therapists; Physicians

Circus performers

Definition

Circus performers entertain with a wide variety of unusual acts that terrify, amuse, and amaze their audiences. Circus artists seem to defy death as they swing from a trapeze or walk a tightrope high above the ground. Some perform gymnastic feats on the ground, and clowns entertain with their absurd antics. Because their live performances are so dramatic and spontaneous, circus performers are seldom seen in films or on television.

Among the common types of circus performers are trapeze artists, tightrope walkers, jugglers, animal trainers, band musicians, clowns, and acrobats. Most learn their skills by working as an apprentice to an already established circus performer.

History

Circus stunts have always been a part of social and religious ritual cultures all over the world. Alaskan Eskimo shamans could swallow 18 inches of a smooth stick. Native American shamans performed acrobatics, magic, clowning and escape acts. In India, stunts included sitting on swings of sharp stakes, contortions, and snake charming. An 800-year-old temple carving in Cambodia shows jugglers, a trained monkey act on a perch pole, musicians, and a high-wire act with flaming torches performing before a large crowd.

The first circus was started in London, England, by Philip Astley in 1768. His show centered around the horsemanship and trick-riding skills he learned in the cavalry. One of his stunt

Carefully balancing two women below them, the trapeze artists put on an exciting and dangerous show.

growth of the large circuses and gradually caused many of the smaller ones to fold.

Nature of the work

Circus historian George Chindahl has identified as many as 200 different circus acts, and new ones are being created every day. *Aerialists* perform vaulting, leaping and flying acts, such as trapeze, rings and cloud swings. Balancing acts include *wire walkers* and *acrobats*. *Jugglers* handle a variety of objects, such as clubs, balls, or hoops and perform on the ground or on a high wire. *Aquatic performers* perform water stunts, usually only in very large circuses. *Animal trainers* work with lions, tigers, bears, elephants, or horses. *Circus musicians* play in bands which provide dramatic and comedic accompaniment for all acts.

Other common circus entertainers are magicians, contortionists, ventriloquists, puppeteers, sword-swallowers, fire-eaters, daredevil performers, and trick bicyclers. Many circus performers combine several skills. All circus acts are physically demanding, requiring strength, endurance, and flexibility.

Circus work is seasonal. Performers work during the summer, perhaps in two or three shows a day on weekends and holidays. During the winter months, they train, improve their acts, and sometimes take jobs in television, videos, or on stage.

Circus performers can spend up to ten years to train for their specialty. Once they have developed their act, they may join one particular circus for one or several seasons, or they may travel from circus to circus as independent acts. In either case, there is a great deal of travel involved.

Requirements

There are no educational requirements for circus performers. Those who have a high school or college education, however, will have an advantage because they will be better able to manage their business affairs.

There is no formal training school in the United States for circus performers. Most circus performers learn their skills as apprentices to well-established acts. There are a few skills that can be learned on your own in a few weeks or months, such as juggling, unicycling, and puppetry.

Athletic training that develops coordination, strength, and balance is necessary for al-

riders, Billie Button, combined agility and skill with awkward clumsiness, which gave him the distinction of being the first circus clown. Button's popularity with audiences inspired Astley to enlarge his show to include additional animals, tightrope walkers, acrobats, and clowns.

The word "circus" was first used when Charles Hughes, a former member of Astley's troupe, formed his own show, called the Royal Circus, in 1782. By the 1820s, small traveling circuses set up canvas tents throughout Europe and America.

In the 1830s, P.T. Barnum traveled with the comical midget, Tom Thumb. His show expanded to include animals, clowns, acrobats, and human curiosities. In 1881, he combined his circus with competitor James A. Bailey's circus. It became the largest attraction of its type in America and was called Barnum and Bailey's Greatest Show on Earth.

A Wisconsin family named Rungeling opened up a circus in 1884 called Ringling Bros. Circus, with animal acts, a band, and clowns. The one ring circus gave way to three rings, which allowed three separate acts to perform simultaneously.

In 1907, the Ringlings purchased their competitors' circus, which became the Ringling Bros. and Barnum and Bailey Circus. It was in its prime in the early 1900s—by the late 1920s it had 5,000 employees and used 240 railroad cars for transportation. Economic depression and competition with television, movie theaters, and other forms of entertainment slowed the

most all circus performers. Other beneficial training would include acting, music, dance, and for those interested in animals, veterinary care.

Special requirements

Circus performers must be physically fit. You must be able to withstand the rigors of your act, as well as the hardships of constant travel. Some acts require unusual strength, flexibility, or balance.

Opportunities for experience and exploration

If circus performance interests you, see a circus. Go to every circus that comes to your area. Talk to the performers about their work. Ask outright if there are jobs available, or write to circuses to express your interest in finding circus work.

Gymnastics teams, drama clubs, and dance troupes give performance experience and may help you decide if you have talent for this type of work. Those interested in animal training should volunteer at nearby zoos or stables.

You may wish to join an association of jugglers, unicyclists, or another specialty. They often hold festivals, events, and seminars where you can train, get to know other circus performers, and perhaps find a mentor who can help you get into the field.

Methods of entering

Circus performers usually enter the field through one of three methods. First, they join a circus nearby as an apprentice and work their way up through the ranks. They may start as part of a set-up or clean-up crew, or they may care for animals. Then, as they get to know performers, they become an apprentice. After learning the necessary skills, they gradually work their way into the act.

The second way to start a career as a circus performer is to purchase an existing act. Beginners do not usually start with this method. The buyer often receives training, costumes, and equipment as a condition of purchase.

The third method is to enter a pre-professional program that offers a placement service once training is completed. There are very few of these programs in the United States.

Today, most circus performers develop their acts and then hire an agent who finds work for them. There are only a few agents in the United States who specialize in circus acts. Performers have to audition for potential employers the agent finds.

Circus performers say it's wise to get as much work in as many different places as you can, and don't limit your skills. Develop a specialty or gimmick, but learn several skills.

The journal *The Circus Report* prints classified ads for job opportunities.

Advancement

It helps if you're born into a circus family and you can begin training as soon as you are able to walk. But many successful circus performers started at the bottom as laborers and learned their skills by watching. Once performers know of your interest, they are happy to train and coach you.

Employment outlook

P.T. Barnum once said, "As long as there are children, there will always be circuses." Circuses will continue, though their formats change with the times.

Traditional circuses are changing for several reasons. Tents are seldom used because they are costly and impractical. It's often more convenient to perform in an arena. Also, many animal acts are being eliminated because of concerns for animal rights. There is less emphasis on props and equipment, to make travel easier and cheaper. Circus acts are more flexible: they are able to perform in either a three-ring format or on a proscenium stage. Circuses are becoming more theatrical, using professional designers, lighting, and musicians. They often have a special theme. Specialty circuses are expanding, such as Cirque du Soleil, Big Apple Circus and Pickle Family Circus.

Those who work in a resident company of a circus become well known, and have greater job security. Unfortunately, that means fewer openings are available. Now, however, there are more and more opportunities for circus performers outside the circus. And there are always good opportunities for new, unusual, never-been-seen acts. The private party business is growing, and circus performers may be used in television and music videos. Even with the changes, the popularity of circuses has remained steady and should remain so in the next 10 years.

Earnings

Most circus performers are not motivated by the money. Although many can earn a decent living, it is rare that circus performers earn high salaries. Gunther Gebel-Williams, whose popularity as an animal trainer made him a headliner and eventually helped him become part owner of a circus, is an exception to the rule. Earnings vary depending on skill, experience, and popularity.

Aquatic performers and jugglers can earn $15,000 to $20,000 per year. Stunt performers can make up to $20,000 to $28,000 per year. A family of aerialists can earn $1,800 to $3,000 per week, and since families who travel with circuses usually get room and board free, they can save a large portion of their paychecks. Individual performers with less star appeal earn $125 to $300 per week.

Circus artists who are able to book other engagements outside the circus earn single-performance fees that vary widely.

Conditions of work

Circus performers work long hours performing, and even longer hours preparing their acts. The learning and relearning periods are intense and physically demanding. There is heavy travel involved and most acts require expensive equipment, props, and costumes. Circus performers often pay for their own transportation, and manage their own business affairs. Rarely do they get a paid vacation.

Circus performers enjoy being able to choose their engagements and be their own bosses. They have the freedom to create their own art form that showcases their particular talent. They face the continual challenge of creating new routines never done before.

GOE: 12.02.01; SIC: 7929; SOC: 328

◇ **SOURCES OF ADDITIONAL INFORMATION**

American Guild of Variety Artists
184 Fifth Avenue
New York, NY 10019

International Circus Hall of Fame
20 North Broadway
Peru, IN 46970

Circus World Museum
426 Water Street
Baraboo, WI 53913–2597

◇ **RELATED ARTICLES**

Volume 1: Performing Arts
Volumes 2–4: Actors; Animal trainers; Clowns; Comedians; Dancers and choreographers; Magicians; Musicians; Stunt performers

---

City managers

Definition

A *city manager* is an administrator who coordinates the day-to-day running of a local government. Usually an appointed position, the manager directs the administration of city or county government in accordance with the policies determined by the city council or other elected authority.

History

For centuries the administration of government has been carried out by people appointed to perform specific services such as collecting taxes, planning streets and water supply, and law enforcement. These civil servants have been assigned their responsibilities in democratic societies by elected officials, mayors, or local councils. Because the term of office to which officials are elected may be only a few years, it has always been necessary to have people with special skills to maintain the continuity of running a government.

It is no longer possible for towns and cities to develop at random. Long-term plans and people to carry them out are needed in every town or city of any size. Many aspects of city life such as building public works, including health and sanitation provision, and collecting the revenues needed to construct and maintain them must go on irrespective of the government or party in power.

Population growth and industrial expansion place increasing pressure on housing, transportation, recreation, and other facilities of cities. Problems associated with the growth of modern cities and towns, such as air and water pollution and rising crime rates, must be dealt with. To effectively deal with problems, as well as with the overall running of the town or city, many communities are hiring these specialists in urban management techniques.

Nature of the work

A city manager, also called a *town manager*, is usually appointed by the community's elected officials and is responsible to them, directing and coordinating the administration of local government policy. The city manager may in turn appoint department heads and staff needed under state or local ordinances. An important part of the city manager's work is supervising the activities of departments that collect and disburse taxes, enforce law, maintain public health, construct public works, and purchase supplies and equipment. The city manager must prepare annual budgets of the costs of these services and submit estimates to the elected officials for approval. In addition the city manager must provide reports of ongoing and completed work to the representatives of the people that live in the city.

The city manager must also plan for future growth and expansion of population and the need for public services. This may require preparing and writing proposals and recommending zoning regulations controlling the location and development of residential and commercial areas. It may be necessary to present these proposals at meetings of the elected authority as well as at public meetings of citizens.

Most city managers work in a council-manager form of government, where an elected council appoints the city manager as the chief administrative officer. Many other city manag-

The responsibilities of a city manager involve attending civic hearings and participating in discussions with elected officials.

ers work for municipalities that have a mayor-council form of government and the mayor appoints the city manager. A few city managers work for county governments, metropolitan or regional planning organizations, councils of governments, and even large corporations that must maintain a large work force overseas.

City managers work closely with *urban planners* to coordinate new and existing programs. In smaller cities that have no planning staff, that work may be done entirely by the manager. Additional staff may be provided for the city manager, including an *assistant city manager, department head assistants, administrative assistants*, and *management analysts*.

The staff of a city manager have a variety of titles and responsibilities. Changes in administration are studied and recommended by management analysts. Administrative and staff work such as compiling statistics and planning work procedures is done by *administrative assistants*, also called *assistants to the city manager* or *executive assistants*. Department head assistants may work in several areas, such as law enforcement, finance, or law, but are generally responsible for just one area. Assistant city managers are responsible for specific projects such as developing the annual budget, as well as organizing and coordinating programs. They may supervise city employees and perform other administrative tasks, answering correspondence, receiving visitors, preparing reports, and monitoring programs.

Requirements

A college education and preferably a graduate degree in public or business administration are the minimum requirements for those seeking a career in city management. In some cases a graduate degree in a field related to public administration, such as urban planning, political science, or law, may be accepted.

Interested high school students should pursue a broad college preparatory program that includes mathematics, statistics, and social studies. Computer science is an important tool in any administrative preparation. About 350 colleges and universities offer bachelor's and master's degrees in public administration. Degree requirements in some schools include completion of an internship program in a city manager's office that may last from six months to a year, during which time the degree candidate observes local government operations and does research under the direct supervision of the city manager.

People planning to enter city management positions frequently must pass civil service examinations. This is one way to become eligible for appointments to local government. Other requirements will vary from place to place. Most positions require knowledge of computerized tax and utility billing, electronic traffic control, and applications of systems analysis to urban problems.

Opportunities for experience and exploration

One way for high school and college students to learn about public administration is to become involved in student government. In addition, summer jobs in their local government offices can provide experience and some understanding of areas in city management in which they may be interested.

Methods of entering

Nearly all city managers begin as management assistants. Most new graduates work as management analysts or administrative assistants to city managers for several years to gain experience in solving urban problems, coordinating public services, and applying management techniques. Others work in a specific department such as finance, public works, or planning. They may acquire supervisory skills and also work as an assistant city manager or department head assistant.

Advancement

Advancement takes place as the beginning assistant moves to more inclusive and responsible jobs within local government. At least five years of experience are generally necessary to compete for the position of city manager. City managers are often employed in small cities at first and during their careers may seek and obtain appointments in growing cities.

Employment outlook

In the 1990s more than 11,000 city managers are employed. Although city management is a growing profession, the field is still relatively small. Few job openings are predicted through the 1990s, and applicants with only a bachelor's degree will have difficulty finding employment. Even an entry-level job often requires an advanced degree. In greatest demand are those people who can use the more sophisticated management techniques.

There is keen competition for job openings since the number of applicants exceeds demands for city managers, as well as for administrative assistants and assistant city managers.

Earnings

The average salary for all city managers in the 1990s is more than $57,000 a year. Individual earnings, of course, vary depending on the person's education and experience, as well as on the size of the city. In a very large city, an experienced city manager may earn more than $125,000 a year. In smaller towns, salaries average $33,000 a year.

Salaries are set by the city council, and good city managers are sometimes given higher than average pay as an incentive to keep them from seeking more lucrative opportunities. Benefits for city managers include paid vacations, health insurance, sick leave, and retirement plans. Cities may also pay travel and moving expenses and provide a city car or a car allowance.

Conditions of work

City managers generally work in offices. They often work overtime at night and on weekends reading and writing reports or finishing paperwork. To provide information to citizens of current government operations or to advocate certain programs, city managers frequently appear at public meetings and other civic functions. When a problem arises or a crisis occurs, they may be called to work at any hour.

GOE: 11.05.03; SIC: 9111; SOC: 112

◇ **SOURCES OF ADDITIONAL INFORMATION**

The personnel offices of the local governments in your area can provide information about positions. Information on county governments can be obtained by writing to:

National Association of Counties
440 First Street, NW
Washington, DC 20001

◇ **RELATED ARTICLES**

Volume 1: Politics and Public Service
Volumes 2–4: Business managers; Management analysts and consultants; Political scientists; Urban and regional planners

Civil engineering technicians

Definition

Civil engineering technicians help civil engineers design, plan, and build public as well as private works to meet the community's needs. They are employed in a wide range of projects, such as highways, drainage systems, water and sewage facilities, railroads, subways, airports, dams, bridges, and tunnels.

Civil engineering technicians who work in the planning stages of a construction project estimate costs; prepare specifications for materials; or carry out surveying, drafting, or designing assignments. Other civil engineering technicians, working in the actual construction phases, help the contractor or superintendent schedule construction activities or inspect work to assure that it conforms to blueprints and specifications.

Technicians are frequently involved in community planning, urban renewal, or other kinds of development projects. They may also work in allied fields, such as building-materials manufacturing.

History

Engineering, both military and civil, is one of the oldest of professions. The pyramids of ancient Egypt, and the bridges, roads, and aqueducts of the Roman Empire (some of which are still in use), are examples of ancient engineering feats.

Although, from earliest times, engineers have been at work building locks and dams, public buildings, cathedrals, and highways, until the 19th century most of the highly trained and knowledgeable engineers were military engineers. It was not until the 18th century in France and England that civil engineers began to organize themselves into professional societies to exchange information or plan projects. At that time, most civil engineers were still self-taught, skilled craft workers. Thomas Telford, for instance, Britain's leading road builder and first president of the Institution of Civil Engineers, started his career as a stonemason. And John Rennie, the builder of the new London Bridge, began as a millwright's apprentice.

Three civil engineering technicians refer to blueprints before they approve of the installation of pipelines.

The first major educational programs intended for civil engineers were offered by the Ecole Polytechnique, founded in Paris in 1794. It was followed by courses at the *Bauakadamie*, founded in Berlin in 1799, and at University College, London, founded in 1826. In the United States, the first courses in civil engineering were taught at Rensselaer Polytechnic Institute, founded in 1824.

From the beginning, civil engineers have required the help of skilled assistants to handle the many details that are part of all phases of civil engineering. Traditionally, these assistants have possessed a combination of basic knowledge and good manual skills. As construction techniques have become more sophisticated, however, there is an increased need for assistants to be technically trained in specialized fields relevant to civil engineering.

These technically trained assistants are known today as civil engineering technicians. Just as separate educational programs and professional identity developed for the civil engineer in the 18th and 19th centuries, so it is for civil engineering technicians in this century. Today, the civil engineering technician is a respected member of the civil engineering team comprising scientists, engineers, technicians, and craft workers.

Nature of the work

Civil engineering technicians engage in varied activities. State highway departments utilize their services to collect data, to design and draw plans, and to supervise the construction and maintenance of roadways. Railroad and airport facilities require similar services. Cities and counties need to have transportation systems, drainage systems, and water and sewage facilities planned, built, and maintained with the assistance of civil engineering technicians.

Civil engineering technicians participate in all stages of the construction process. During the planning stages, they help engineers prepare lists of materials needed and help estimate project costs. One of the most important technician positions held at this stage is that of the *structural engineering technician*. Structural engineering technicians calculate the size, number, and composition of beams and columns, and investigate allowable soil pressures which develop from the weight of these structures. If the pressure will cause excessive settling or some other failure, they design special piers, rafts, pilings, or footings to prevent structural problems.

During the planning stages, civil engineering technicians help engineers with drafting and prepare drawings, maps, and charts; during the actual construction phase, construction technicians assist building contractors and site supervisors in preparing work schedules and cost estimates and in performing work inspections. One of their most important duties is to ensure that each step of construction is completed before workers arrive to begin the next stage.

Some technicians specialize in certain types of construction projects. *Highway technicians*, for example, perform surveys and cost estimates as well as plan and supervise highway construction and maintenance. *Rail and waterway technicians* survey, make specifications and cost estimates, and help plan and construct railway and waterway facilities. *Assistant city engineers* coordinate the planning and construction of city streets, sewers, drainage systems, refuse facilities, and other major civil projects.

Other technicians specialize in certain phases of the construction process. For example, *materials technicians* sample and run tests on rock, soil, cement, asphalt, wood, steel, concrete, and other materials. *Photogrammetric technicians* use aerial photographs to prepare maps, plans, and profiles. *Party chiefs* work for licensed land surveyors, survey land for boundary-line locations, and plan subdivisions and other large-area land developments.

There are other specialized positions for civil engineering technicians: *research engineering technicians* test and develop new products and equipment; *sales engineering technicians* sell building materials, construction equipment, and engineering services; and *water resources technicians* gather data, make computations and drawings for water projects, and prepare economic studies.

Requirements

A student contemplating a career in civil engineering technology needs a desire to be a builder or planner, an understanding of mathematics and sciences, an ability to get along with others, an aptitude for learning, and the ability to think and plan ahead.

Prospective technicians should take all the mathematics, sciences, and communications subjects available to them in high school. In general, they should follow the course for admission to a four-year engineering college.

The courses that are especially helpful include mathematics (with at least two years of algebra, plane and solid geometry, and trigonometry); physics (with laboratory experience); chemistry; biology; and any other general science courses.

Because the ability to read and interpret the material is very important, four years of English and language skills courses are basic requirements. Reports and letters are an essential part of the technician's work, so a firm grasp of English grammar is important.

Other useful courses include mechanical drawing and any available shop courses. Civil engineering technicians often make use of mechanical drawings to convey their ideas to others, and neat, well-executed drawings are important to convey a sense of accuracy and competence.

Prospective civil engineering technology students should be careful to choose a technical institute that offers an accredited program in civil engineering technology. In such programs, more mathematics and science subjects, including physics, will be studied to prepare the student for later specialty courses, such as surveying, materials, hydraulics, highway and bridge construction and design, structures, railway and water systems, heavy construction, soils, steel and concrete construction, cost and estimates, and management and construction technology. Students can also take courses in computer programming and photogrammetry.

A great deal of the student's time will be spent in laboratory and field study in these specialties. This hands-on experience prepares technicians for their special role in the civil engineering team.

In addition, drafting procedures and techniques will be developed and polished in intermediate and advanced-level courses. Courses in law, human relations, economics, and professional ethics are available and recommended. English is the most important of the nontechnical subjects, as technicians need to convey their thoughts to others. Courses in public speaking and report writing are also a good idea.

To advance in professional standing, civil engineering technicians should try to become a Certified Engineering Technician. Civil engineering technicians may also, upon completion of the required years of service, take an examination for licensing as a Licensed Land Surveyor. Successful completion of this examination enables technicians to operate their own surveying businesses.

Opportunities for experience and exploration

One of the best ways to acquire first-hand experience in this field is through part-time or summer work with a construction company. Even if the job is menial, young people can still observe surveying teams, site supervisors, building inspectors, skilled craft workers, and civil engineering technicians at work at their jobs. If such employment is not possible, students can organize field trips to various construction sites or to facilities where building materials are manufactured.

Courses in shop and drafting will also provide future technicians with excellent opportunities to sample some of the work they may be doing later.

Methods of entering

Most students receive assistance from their school to find jobs upon graduation. Most schools maintain placement offices, which many prospective employers will contact when they have job openings. The placement offices, in turn, help the student or graduate prepare a resume of relevant school and work experiences, and usually arrange personal interviews with prospective employers.

Many schools also have cooperative work-study programs with particular companies and government agencies. Under such a program, the company or government agency often becomes the new technician's place of full-time employment after graduation.

Some students make use of state and private employment services with job listings in this field. Others consult want ads or write directly to possible future employers. Students should also take every opportunity to meet and get to know people in the field. Such people often know about present and future job openings and can pass the word along to interested newcomers.

Advancement

Civil engineering technicians must study and learn throughout their careers. They must learn new techniques, master the operation of new equipment, and study to give themselves greater depth in their chosen fields and to keep themselves abreast of the latest developments. Some technicians move on to supervisory positions, while others get additional education and become civil engineers. A few of the opportunities for technicians with advanced skills and experience follow.

Associate municipal designers direct workers to prepare design drawings and feasibility studies for dams and municipal water and sewage plants.

Associate structures designers direct workers to prepare design drawings and cost estimates of structural features, such as foundations, columns, piers, and beams.

City or county building inspectors review and then approve or reject plans for construction of large buildings.

City and county engineers operate, plan, and direct engineering or public works departments.

Licensed land surveyors operate land surveying businesses as owners or partners.

Photogrammetrists direct the preparation of maps and charts from aerial photography.

Project engineers or *resident engineers* supervise numbers of projects and field parties for city, county, or state highway departments.

Finally, some technicians go on to become *construction superintendents* or even owners of their own construction company, supply company, or laboratory testing company.

Employment outlook

The employment outlook for civil engineering technicians is good. Although the total amount of civil construction may be affected by general economic conditions and levels of government spending, there will remain a need for more technicians to assist civil engineers and to relieve them of any duties that may be delegated. Despite short-term or even protracted periods of economic dislocation, there will remain pressing needs for construction projects that address the problems of urban redevelopment, water shortages, transportation systems, indus-

trial waste pollution, and traffic congestion. All of this points to a continuing and expanding demand for civil engineering technicians.

Earnings

Civil engineering technicians usually begin their first jobs at a salary range of about $16,500 to $29,000 a year, with the higher paying jobs going to those with advanced education. Most experienced technicians earn between $33,000 to $49,390 or more per year. Some senior technicians earn as much as $71,500 a year or more.

The incomes of many civil engineering technicians who operate their own construction, surveying, or equipment businesses are quite attractive. Some of these companies can earn millions of dollars each year.

As in all industries, paid vacations, pension plans, and insurance are normal parts of the benefits paid to civil engineering technicians. Many companies pay the superintendent a bonus if a job is completed ahead of schedule or if the job is completed for less than the estimated cost. These bonuses sometimes amount to more than the employee's regular annual salary.

Conditions of work

Technicians usually work 40 hours a week with extra pay for overtime work. Working conditions vary from job to job: technicians who enjoy being outdoors may choose a job in construction or surveying; those who prefer working indoors may choose to work in a consulting engineer's office on computations, drafting, or design, or they may work inside on map plotting, materials testing, or making various calculations from field notes and tests. In either site, the work done by civil engineering technicians is usually cleaner than the work done by most other construction trades workers.

The work of civil engineering technicians may vary from the uncomplicated and routine to the highly complex and personally challenging. A successful civil engineering technician needs a high tolerance for both kinds of activities.

Civil engineering technicians feel the pride that comes from being a member of a team that constructs major buildings, bridges, or dams. In a way, such projects become monuments to the efforts of each member of the team. And there is the accompanying satisfaction that the project has improved, if only in a modest way, the quality of life in a community.

GOE: 05.01.07; SIC: 8711; SOC: 3719

◇ **SOURCES OF ADDITIONAL INFORMATION**

American Congress on Surveying and Mapping
5410 Grosvenor Lane
Bethesda, MD 20814-2122

American Society for Engineering Education
11 Dupont Circle, Suite 200
Washington, DC 20036

American Society of Certified Engineering Technicians
PO Box 371474
El Paso, TX 79937

American Society of Civil Engineers
345 East 47th Street
New York, NY 10017

Canadian Council of Land Surveyors
PO Box 5378, Station 7
Ottawa ON K2C 3J1

◇ **RELATED ARTICLES**

Volume 1: Construction; Engineering
Volumes 2–4: Architectural and building construction technicians; Cartographers; Drafting and design technicians; Geographers; Laboratory technicians; Surveyors; Traffic technicians; Urban and regional planners

---

Civil engineers

Definition

Civil engineers are involved in the design and construction of the physical structures that make up our surroundings, such as roads, bridges, buildings, and harbors. The profession of civil engineering involves theoretical knowledge applied to the practical planning of the layout of our cities, towns, and other communities. It is concerned with modifying the natural environment and building new environments to better the life-styles of the general public. Civil engineers are highly trained problem solvers, devising ways to unclog airports, fix decaying roadways, and purify polluted land, water, and air.

History

In today's society we often take for granted our dependence on the infrastructure of our cities and towns—such as the highways, waterways, airports, tunnels, and buildings that benefit our daily activities. We may never stop to consider a time when these structures were not yet established, not realizing that living in solid buildings and traveling on land, in the air, and over water were never more common than now.

People who cleared out caves, slashed out trails in the forest, and laid rocks across streams might be considered the first civil engineers, but civil engineering didn't begin to be established as a science until around the 18th century. Then for many years it was considered part of military engineering, which involved creating such things as fortresses, roads, and bridges to aid troops in warfare and defense. People who were skilled in the mechanics of materials, machines, and hydraulics were often employed for military matters. Eventually, craftspeople such as stonemasons, carpenters, and tool makers became known as civil engineers.

A civil engineer verifies that the building under construction conforms to the blueprints designed by the architect.

Throughout the 18th and 19th centuries, more and more people formed engineering societies to learn from each other. They promoted ideas about building lighthouses, canals, and other large public works. These organizations were born in Britain and France, and other groups later began forming throughout Europe and the United States.

One might trace the evolution of civil engineering methods by considering the building and many reconstructions of England's London Bridge. In Roman and medieval times, several bridges made of timber were built over the Thames River. Around the end of the 12th century, these were rebuilt into 19 narrow arches mounted on piers. A chapel was built on one of the piers, and two towers were built for defense. A fire damaged the bridge around 1212, yet the surrounding area was considered a preferred place to live and work, probably because it was the only bridge over which one could cross the river. The structure was rebuilt many times during later centuries using different materials and designs. By 1830 it had only five arches. More than a century later, the center span of the bridge was remodeled, and part of it was actually transported to the United States to be set up as a tourist attraction.

Working materials for civil engineers have changed during many centuries. For instance, bridges, once made with timber, then with iron and steel, are today made mainly with concrete that is reinforced with steel. The high strength of the material is necessary because of the abundance of cars and other vehicles that travel over the bridges.

As the population continues to grow and communities become more complex, structures that civil engineers must pay attention to have to be remodeled and repaired. New highways, buildings, airstrips, and so forth must be designed to accommodate public needs. Today, more and more civil engineers are involved with water treatment plants, water purification plants, and toxic waste sites. Increasing concern about the natural environment is also evident in the growing number of engineers working on such projects as preservation of wetlands, maintenance of national forests, and restoration of sites around land mines, oil wells, and industrial factories.

Nature of the work

Civil engineers use their knowledge of materials science, engineering theory, economics, and demographics to devise, construct, and keep up our physical surroundings. They apply their understanding of other branches of science—such as hydraulics, geology, and physics—to design the optimal blueprint for the project. Civil engineers are also known as *structural engineers*.

Feasibility studies are conducted by *surveying and mapping engineers* to determine the best sites and approaches for construction. They extensively investigate the chosen sites to verify that the ground and other surroundings are amenable to the proposed project. These engineers use sophisticated equipment, such as satellites and other electronic instruments, to measure the area and conduct underground probes for bedrock and groundwater. They determine the optimal places where explosives should be blasted in order to cut through rock. If a highway is being planned, for instance, they have to measure and investigate miles of land.

Many civil engineers work together strictly as consultants on projects, advising their clients. These consultants usually specialize in one area of the industry, such as water systems, transportation systems, and housing structures. Clients include individuals, corporations, and the government. Consultants will devise an overall design for the proposed project, perhaps a nuclear power plant commissioned by an electric company. They will estimate the cost of constructing the plant, supervise the feasibility studies and site investigations, and advise the client on whom to hire for the actual labor involved. Consultants are also responsible for such details as accuracy of drawings and quantities of materials to order.

Other civil engineers work mainly as contractors and are responsible for the actual building of the structure; they are known as *construction engineers*. They interpret the consultants' designs and follow through with the best methods for getting the work done, usually working directly at the construction site. Contractors are responsible for scheduling the work, buying the materials, maintaining surveys of the progress of the work, and choosing the machines and other equipment used for construction. During construction, these civil engineers must supervise the labor and make sure the work is completed correctly and efficiently. After the project is finished, they must set up a maintenance schedule and periodically check the structure for a certain length of time. Later, the task of ongoing maintenance and repair is often transferred to local engineers.

There are several other positions that civil engineers specialize in. *Transportation engineers* are concerned mainly with the construction of highways and mass transit systems, such as subways and commuter rail lines. When devising plans for subways, engineers are responsible for considering the tunneling that is involved. *Pipeline engineers* are specialized transportation engineers who are involved with the movement of water, oil, and gas through miles of pipeline.

Hydraulic and irrigation engineers are often employed by utility companies (for example, those that supply electricity) that need access to steady sources of water. These engineers design dams, operate flood control, and maintain such sites as wells and reservoirs. *Geotechnical engineers* are those who work with underground rock and soil to determine the safety of sites. They are called upon to plan earthquake forecasts and design plans for how to deal with such natural disasters.

The fastest-growing area in civil engineering involves environmental issues such as toxic waste and nuclear power. *Environmental engineers* work on water-purification systems, wastewater projects, and garbage disposal and recycling plants. They are also involved with control and prevention of air pollution, often advising clients on how to appropriately dispose of gas, oil, grease, and other chemical compounds. *Sanitary engineers* are also considered environmental engineers, specializing in public works such as national parks and public sanitation systems.

Requirements

Considering the complexities involved in civil engineering, one should not be surprised that engineers must have a broad, lengthy educational background. The discipline is based on applied sciences yet requires an understanding of practical methods. Attainment of full professional status takes an average of 8 to 10 years of serious study and training.

A bachelor's degree is considered essential in the field, and about 30 percent of civil engineering students continue school to receive a master's degree. To prepare for college, students should focus on mathematics (algebra, trigonometry, geometry, and calculus), the sciences (physics and chemistry), computer science, and English and the humanities (history, economics, and sociology). Students should also aim for honors-level courses.

In college, it is wise for students to think about what specialty or department they might especially want to work in. In addition to the core engineering curriculum (including mathematics, science, drafting, and computer applications), students will probably choose from the following types of courses: structural analysis; materials design and specification; geology; hydraulics; surveying and design graphics; soil mechanics; and oceanography. Bachelor's degrees can be achieved through a number of programs: a four- or five-year accredited college or university; two years in a community college engineering program plus two or three years in a college or university; five or six years in a co-op program (attending classes for part of the year and working in an engineering-related job for the rest of the year); or eight to ten years of part-time evening engineering courses.

Basic personal characteristics that are often found in potential civil engineers are an avid curiosity; a passion for mathematics and science; an aptitude for problem solving, both alone and with a team; and an ability to visualize multidimensional, spatial relationships.

Special requirements

More than a third of civil engineers go on to study and qualify for a professional engineer (P.E.) license. It is often required before one can work on public projects, and because many of the jobs are found in such government specialties, many engineers take the necessary steps to obtain the license. Registration guidelines are different for each state—they involve educational, practical, and teaching experience. Applicants must take an examination on a specified date.

Opportunities for experience and exploration

In high school, it is a good idea to join such organizations as the Junior Engineering Technical Society (see address listed at the end of this article). Students can compete in academic challenges, join engineering design contests, and read guidance and informational publications such as the JETS Report. Those interested in the field should try creating their own structural designs and build small-scale models of them.

One exceptional way to become involved in civil engineering is to attend a summer camp or study program where many other students who have similar interests gather for academics as well as recreational activities. For example, the Worcester Polytechnic Institute in Massachusetts has a 12-day summer program for students in junior and senior high school. Studies and events focus on science and math and include specialties for those interested in civil engineering. A number of sports, such as swimming, basketball, and track and field, are also offered (see address listed at the end of this article).

After high school, another way to learn about civil engineering duties is to work on a construction crew that is involved in the actual building of a project designed and supervised by engineers. Such hands-on experience would provide an opportunity to work near many types of civil workers. Try to work on highway crews or even in housing construction.

Methods of entering

To establish a career as a civil engineer, one must first receive a bachelor's degree in engineering or another appropriate scientific field. Entry-level jobs usually involve routine work often as a member of a supervised team. After a year or more (depending on job performance and qualifications), one becomes a junior engineer, then an assistant to perhaps one or more

supervising engineers. Establishment as a professional engineer comes after passing the P.E. exam.

Research engineers start out conducting lab tests and basic research projects; with time and experience, they are promoted to assignments as designers. They can work their way up to more responsible tasks such as planning, supervising, and cost analyzing. Positions in management are at the top of the ladder in most civil-engineering jobs.

Advancement

Professional engineers with many years' experience often join with partners to establish their own firms, in either design, consulting, or contracting. Some leave long-held positions to be assigned as top executives in industries such as manufacturing and business consulting. Also, there are those who return to academia to teach high school or college students. For all of these potential opportunities, it is necessary to keep abreast of engineering advancements and trends by reading industry journals and taking courses.

Employment outlook

In the late 1990s, civil engineers are expected to continue to be needed for the maintenance and repair of public works such as highways and water systems. It is anticipated that the field will grow at least until the turn of the century. The need for civil engineers will also depend on the government's decisions to spend further on renewing and adding to the country's basic infrastructure. As public awareness of environmental issues continues to increase, civil engineers will also find expanding employment opportunities at wastewater sites, recycling establishments, and toxic dump sites created by industrial and municipal waste.

Earnings

Civil engineers are among the lowest paid in the engineering field. However, starting salaries are usually higher than for other occupations. Entry-level civil engineers with a bachelor's degree earn approximately $28,000 per year in private industry; those with a master's degree, about $35,000; and those with a doctorate, about $47,000. Those working in government jobs earn less than those in private companies.

As with all occupations, salaries are higher for those with more experience. The average salary for those in mid-level positions is $46,000 in private industry and $42,000 in government jobs. Others earn as much as $88,000 a year.

Conditions of work

Many civil engineers work regular 40-hour weeks, often in or near major industrial and commercial areas. Sometimes they are assigned to work in remote areas and foreign countries. Because of the diversity of civil engineering positions, working conditions vary widely. Offices, labs, factories, and actual sites are typical environments for engineers. About 40 percent of all civil engineers can be found working for various levels of government, usually involving large public-works projects such as highways and bridges. Consultants probably spend more time in offices than do the other civil engineers. However, all employees in civil engineering work in an office environment at least some of the time, working on designs, orders, and contracts and discussing plans with other workers and clients over the phone.

A typical work cycle involving various types of civil engineers involves three stages: planning, constructing, and maintaining. Those involved with development of a campus compound, for example, would first need to work in their offices developing plans for a survey. Surveying and mapping engineers would have to visit the proposed site to take measurements and perhaps shoot aerial photographs. Some of the consultants would also be supervising at the site. The measurements and photos would have to be converted into drawings and blueprints. Geotechnical engineers would dig wells at the site and take core samples from the ground. If anything fishy was found at the site, such as toxic waste or unexpected water, the consultant would inform the client and the contractor to determine what should be done.

Actual construction would be the next step after all problems were resolved. The contractors would most often be out at the site, checking on the schedule and progress and supervising the laborers and machinery. Very often, a field trailer on the site becomes the engineers' makeshift offices. The campus might take several years to build—it is not uncommon for en-

gineers to be involved in very long-term projects. If contractors anticipate that deadlines will not be met, they often put in weeks of 10- to 15-hour days on the job.

After construction is complete, engineers spend less and less time at the site. Some may be assigned to stay on-site to keep daily surveys of how the structure is holding up and to solve problems when they arise. Eventually, the project engineers finish the job and move on to another long-term assignment.

GOE: 05.01.07; SIC: 8711; SOC: 1628

◇ **SOURCES OF ADDITIONAL INFORMATION**

American Society of Civil Engineers
345 East 47th Street
New York, NY 10017

Institute of Transportation Engineers
525 School Street, SW, Suite 410
Washington, DC 20024

Junior Engineering Technical Society
1420 King Street, Suite 405
Alexandria, VA 22314

Worcester Polytechnic Institute
Frontiers in Science, Mathematics and Engineering
100 Institute Road
Worcester, MA 01609

◇ **RELATED ARTICLES**

Volume 1: Civil Service; Construction; Engineering; Waste Management
Volumes 2–4: Architectural and building construction technicians; Bricklayers and stonemasons; Cement masons; Ceramics and materials engineers; Civil engineering technicians; Construction inspectors, government; Construction laborers; Environmental engineers; Groundwater professionals; Landscape architects; Millwrights; Operating engineers; Structural-steel workers; Surveyors; Urban and regional planners; Wastewater treatment plant operators

Clerical supervisors and managers

Definition

Clerical supervisors and managers direct and coordinate the work activities of clerks within an office. They supervise office workers in their tasks and confer with other supervisory personnel in planning department activities. Clerical supervisors and managers often define job duties and develop training programs for new workers. They evaluate the progress of their clerks and work with upper management officials to ensure that the office staff meets productivity and quality goals. Clerical supervisors and managers often meet with office personnel to discuss job-related issues or problems, and they are responsible for maintaining a positive office environment.

History

The growth of business that has occurred since the Industrial Revolution has been accompanied by a corresponding growth in the amount of work done in offices. Records, bills, receipts, contracts, and other paperwork have proliferated. Phone calls and other communications have multiplied. Accounting and bookkeeping practices have become more complicated.

The role of the clerical supervisor and manager has also grown over time. In the past, such supervisors were responsible mainly for ensuring productivity and good work from their clerks and reporting information to management. Today, clerical supervisors and managers play a more active part in the operations of busy offices. They are responsible for coordinating the activities of many departments, informing management of departmental performance, and making sure the highly specialized sectors of an office run smoothly and efficiently every day.

Nature of the work

As modern technology and an increased volume of business communications become a normal part of daily business, offices are becoming more and more complicated places in which to work. By directing and coordinating the activities of clerks and other office workers, clerical supervisors and managers are an integral part of an effective organization.

The day-to-day work of clerical supervisors and managers involves organizing and overseeing many different activities. Although specific duties vary with the type and size of the particular office, all supervisors and managers have several basic job responsibilities.

Supervisors and managers are usually responsible for interviewing prospective employees and making recommendations on hiring. They train new workers, explain office policies, and spell out performance criteria. Supervisors are also responsible for delegating work responsibilities. This requires a keen understanding of the strengths and weaknesses of each individual worker, as well as the ability to determine what needs to get done and when it must be completed. For example, if a supervisor knows that one worker is especially good at filing business correspondence, that person will probably be assigned to any important filing tasks. Supervisors often know how to do many of the tasks done by their subordinates and assist or relieve them whenever necessary.

Supervisors not only train clerical workers and assign them job duties but also recommend increases in salaries, promote workers when approved, and occasionally fire them. Therefore, supervisors must carefully observe clerical workers performing their jobs (whether answering the telephones, opening and sorting mail, or inputting computer data) and make positive suggestions for any necessary improvements. Managers who can communicate sensitively and effectively both verbally and in writing will be better able to carry out this kind of leadership. Motivating employees to do their best work is another important component of a clerical manager's responsibilities.

Clerical supervisors and managers must be very good at human relations. Differences of opinion and personality clashes among employees are inevitable in almost any office, and the manager or supervisor must be able to deal with grievances and restore good feelings among the staff. Supervisors and managers meet regularly with their staff, alone and in groups, to discuss and solve any problems that might affect people's job performance.

Planning is a vital and time-consuming portion of the job responsibilities of clerical supervisors. Not only do supervisors plan the work of subordinates, they also assist in planning current and future office space needs, work schedules, and the types of office equipment and supplies that need to be purchased.

Supervisors and managers must always keep their superiors informed as to the overall situation in the clerical area. If there is a delay on an important project, for example, upper management must know the cause and the steps being taken to expedite the matter.

Offices can be hectic places. Deadlines on major projects can create tension, especially if some workers are sick or overburdened. Clerical supervisors and managers must constantly juggle the demands of their superiors with the capabilities of their subordinates. Thus, clerical supervisors need an even temperament and the ability to work well with others. Additional attributes that are important include organizational ability, attention to detail, dependability, and trustworthiness.

Requirements

A high school diploma is essential for this position, and a college degree is highly recommended. Since many offices promote supervisors and managers from clerical workers within their organization, relevant work experience is also helpful. Prospective clerical managers and supervisors must have good leadership and communications skills, including the ability to set priorities, organize work schedules, and motivate others. As more offices are taking care of their office needs through electronic methods, experience with computers is becoming increasingly important.

High school students should take courses in English, speech and communications, mathematics, sociology, history, and as many business-related courses such as typing and bookkeeping as possible.

In college a student should pursue a degree in business administration or at least take several courses in business management and operations. In some cases, an associate's degree is considered sufficient for a supervisory position. Many community colleges and vocational schools offer business education courses that help train clerical supervisors and managers.

Opportunities for experience and exploration

Before worrying about supervisory duties, students should try to get experience in fulfilling clerical responsibilities. Interested students may get this type of experience by taking on clerical or bookkeeping responsibilities with a school club or other organization. This type of volunteer work allows people to practice office skills such as opening and sorting mail, answering telephones, and filing business documents.

Individuals may have the opportunity to get training in the operation of business machinery (calculators, word processors, and so on) through evening courses offered by business schools. In addition, some school work-study programs may have opportunities for part-time, on-the-job training with local businesses.

Methods of entering

Qualified persons should contact the personnel offices of individual firms directly. This is especially appropriate if the candidate already has previous clerical experience. College placement offices or other job placement offices may also know of openings. Jobs may also be located through "help wanted" advertisements.

Often, a firm will recruit clerical supervisors from its own clerical staff. A clerk with potential supervisory abilities may be given periodic supervisory responsibilities. Later, when an opening occurs for a manager or supervisor, that person may be promoted to a full-time position.

Advancement

With experience, skilled supervisory personnel may be promoted to a group manager position. Promotions, however, often depend on the supervisor getting a college degree or other appropriate training. Firms usually encourage their employees to pursue more education and may even pay for some tuition costs.

Employment outlook

Although the increased use of data-processing machines and other types of automated equipment may reduce the number of supervisory personnel needed at any one location, the growing economy should increase the number of clerical workers needed throughout the country. Therefore, employment of clerical supervisors and managers is expected to grow at an average pace through the next decade or so.

With slower employment growth in some clerical occupations, clerical supervisors and managers may have smaller staffs and be asked to perform more professional tasks.

An estimated 1,218,000 individuals were employed as clerical supervisors in 1990. The Department of Labor projects an increase of 263,000 jobs in this field through the year 2005.

The federal government should continue to be a good source for job opportunities. Private companies, particularly those with large clerical staffs such as hospitals, banks, and telecommunications companies, should also have numerous openings. Employment opportunities will be especially good for those trained to operate computers, word processors, and other types of modern office machinery.

Earnings

In the 1990s beginning clerical supervisors and managers earn an average salary of between $15,000 and $20,000 a year, depending on the size and geographic location of the company and the person's individual skills. Experienced supervisory personnel average between $20,000 and $34,000 per year. Higher wages will be paid to those who work for larger private companies located in and around major metropolitan areas. Full-time workers should also receive paid vacations, health insurance, and other benefits.

Conditions of work

As is the case with most office workers, clerical supervisors and managers work an average 35- to 40-hour week, although overtime is not unusual. Although many clerical supervisors and managers work a standard nine-to-five shift,

the fact that many workplaces operate around the clock means that some supervisory personnel may have to work evenings as well as weekends and holidays.

Most offices are pleasant places to work. The environment is usually well ventilated and well lighted, and the work is not physically strenuous. The manager's job can be stressful, however, as it entails supervising a variety of employees with a variety of personalities, temperaments, and work habits.

GOE: 07.01.02; SIC: Any industry; SOC: 71

◇ **SOURCES OF ADDITIONAL INFORMATION**

American Management Association
Management Information Services
135 West 50th Street
New York, NY 10020

National Management Association
2210 Arbor Boulevard
Dayton, OH 45439

Canadian Management Centre of AMA Intl.
#300, 100 University Avenue
Toronto ON M5J 1V6

◇ **RELATED ARTICLES**

Volume 1: Business Management
Volumes 2–4: Business managers; Data base managers; General office clerks; Hotel and motel managers; Postal clerks; Receptionists; Retail managers; Secretaries

Clinical Chemists

Definition

Clinical chemists are specialized lab technologists who prepare lab specimens and analyze the chemicals and hormones found in body fluids (blood, urine, spinal fluid, and gastric juices). These laboratory tests help physicians detect,

diagnose, and treat disease. For example, such tests can determine the level of medication in the blood to see whether a patient is taking the proper dosage and whether the body is responding to the treatment.

Because of their advanced education and training, clinical chemists handle more sophisticated equipment and testing than laboratory technologists. They may order, purchase, maintain, and repair the specialized equipment and instruments required for the laboratory tests. They design new laboratory procedures and establish or continue training and supervision of other employees.

Clinical chemists work most often in hospital, clinic, and commercial laboratories. They also work in medical schools or teaching hospitals and in industry.

History

Probably the first clinical chemistry report was that of Sasruta, a Hindu physician, who in 600 B.C. noted the sweet taste of diabetic urine. Hippocrates, though, was the first to apply techniques such as those used in clinical chemistry. He taught his students to base diagnoses on urine's color, consistency, and cloudiness and the appearance of fatty substances.

Not so long ago, physicians personally performed all diagnostic tests for their patients. Because there were only a limited number of tests, and a limited number of patients, this was easily accomplished. However, advances in medical knowledge and testing procedures coupled with the specialized technology and equipment needed to perform the tests made it impossible for individual physicians to remain up-to-date in all testing areas and still continue to treat patients. As a result, specialists were needed to handle the testing and analyses for the physicians. The specialists who analyze and evaluate test specimens are known as clinical chemists.

Nature of the work

Clinical chemists working in the laboratory may measure and analyze the components of a drop of blood or a piece of body tissue. They use equipment ranging from basic test tubes, beakers, and flasks, to complicated gas chromatograph/mass spectrometers (GC/MS) and work with reagents (chemical solutions) as simple as an alkali solution or as complex as an monoclonal antibody chemically linked to an enzyme.

Laboratory duties depend on the test being performed. If the test is automated, the chemist is responsible for calibrating (setting), loading specimens, and monitoring the instruments to make sure all goes correctly. After the results are ready, the chemist verifies their accuracy

and sends them out or reports them to the attending physician. A test that is more involved, such as in identifying cell types in leukemia, requires very different procedures, including special stains and chromosome studies.

New procedures are continuously making old ones obsolete, while others have withstood the test of time. Whether conducting the actual tests, or developing tests for others to perform, all clinical chemists are concerned with four qualities of an analysis: *Sensitivity:* detecting early changes in tissue, before a disease is far advanced; *Specificity:* measuring or determining a component without interference from other components; *Simplicity:* replacing time-consuming labor-intensive tests with quick one- or two-step procedures, which may help physicians make faster diagnoses, and perhaps save lives; and *Economy:* making once-expensive tests affordable and more easily accessible to those who need them. Automation has played a big part in making once exotic tests more commonplace.

Job responsibilities vary depending on the level of education achieved. In general, those entering the field with a bachelor's degree become *clinical chemistry technologists*. They perform routine tests for service and/or research; develop new test methods under the supervision of doctorate-level staff; perform quality-control tests; and participate in continuing education.

With a master's degree a clinical chemist may become *section or shift supervisor,* or *chief technologist;* be responsible for daily quality control; handle project management in industry; manage a clinical laboratory; and teach medical technology students.

Those with a doctorate may become *director of clinical chemistry* in a hospital or laboratory; take overall responsibility for research and new test development; direct an academic clinical chemistry program; have overall responsibility for laboratory performance and management; teach medical students, staff, pathology residents, and laboratory personnel; and consult with attending physicians about interpretation of test results.

Although clinical chemistry is basically a service-oriented field, responsibilities are wide-ranging. All clinical chemists also conduct research, provide education, and handle administration on various levels, depending on the level of education and place of employment.

In a medical school or teaching hospital, the clinical chemist's main tasks are to perform basic research; make test-patient correlations; train new physicians, medical technology students, and clinical chemistry trainees; and man-

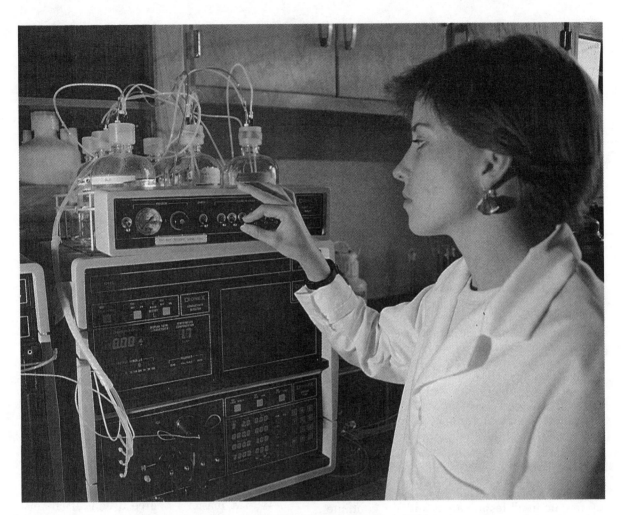

Maintaining and monitoring complex laboratory equipment is part of the daily routine for a clinical chemist.

age clinical laboratory activities, training programs, and research projects.

In a private community hospital, the clinical chemist provides information to assist physicians in diagnosis of disease and patient management; develops research methods; makes test-patient correlations; provides in-service training of laboratory and house staff; manages clinical laboratory activities; and develops in-service training methods.

In industry, the clinical chemist performs applied research, developing test reagents (solutions) and instrumentation for use in patient care; provides information to clinical laboratories by supplying and supporting test reagents and instrumentation; trains salespeople and laboratory professionals in the company's products; and manages development, manufacturing, education, and sales.

In commercial or reference laboratories, clinical chemists perform special testing to provide information to hospital laboratories, clinics, and physicians' offices; develop testing methods; conduct service-related training of laboratory staff and clinical chemistry professionals; and manage the clinical laboratory and customer service activities.

In addition, many clinical chemists publish their research findings in trade journals or other publications. Some clinical chemists may even be asked to testify as expert witnesses at court hearings.

Requirements

Since entry-level jobs in the field of clinical chemistry require a bachelor's degree, interested high school students should plan on attending a minimum of four years of post-high school education at a college or university, preferably one accredited by the American Chemical Society.

While in high school, students should take as many chemistry, biology, and physics classes as possible, especially those that provide laboratory experience. In addition, classes in mathematics and computers will be of great help.

In college, the course of study will consist of 32 semester hours of chemistry, including classes in analytical, biochemical, organic, inorganic, and physical chemistry. In addition, courses in medical technology, mathematics, and physics will prove helpful. A bachelor's degree plus one year of post-graduate practical experience will make candidates eligible for certification as a clinical chemistry technologist by the National Registry in Clinical Chemistry.

After completing the requirements for a bachelor's degree, most students go on to earn their master's degree. Advanced courses plus a thesis project in a specialized field, and additional courses in instrumentation, statistics, and quality control are needed to reach this objective. Students may also perform tests, develop new methods, and act as a supervisor. Following four years of practical experience, candidates are eligible to become certified clinical chemists with the National Registry in Clinical Chemistry.

A great number of clinical chemists go on to receive their doctorate degree. To achieve this, students need 48 hours of chemistry courses, as well as practical laboratory experience, and must complete a research thesis. Training includes working as a consultant to physicians; providing laboratory data and assisting in its interpretation; learning the theory, operation, and maintenance of all instruments and procedures that are used; conducting original research, either analytical or metabolic in nature, related to disease; learning administration, including the application of ethics in medicine and science; and teaching, in preparation for directing a laboratory. Clinical chemists with advanced degrees (Ph.D.'s or M.D.'s) become eligible for certification by the American Board of Clinical Chemistry.

Special requirements

Most states require clinical chemists to be licensed or registered, as do most employers. In order to gain certification, applicants must meet the eligibility requirements, as well as pass an examination. In addition to the National Registry in Clinical Chemistry, other agencies offer certification; these are noted at the end of this article.

Opportunities for experience and exploration

Any opportunity to work with laboratory equipment is helpful for exploring the field of clinical chemistry. If they are available, high school students should consider joining their school's chemistry or biology clubs. They may do volunteer work in hospitals or other medical facilities where laboratories are located. Students can visit a medical laboratory to watch and learn about the work; while there, it may be possible to talk with clinical chemists about their career. A high school science teacher or guidance counselor may be able to arrange such a visit.

Methods of entering

College career guidance offices usually receive notices of job openings. Often, companies and laboratories will conduct on-campus employment interviews to recruit the top graduates of a college or university. Local hospitals and laboratories frequently post job openings, and almost always advertise locally or nationally in newspaper help wanted advertisements. Students may benefit by calling or writing to hospitals or companies they would like to work for, and leaving a copy of their resume on file. They may be called in for interviews when job openings occur.

Advancement

As in many professions, advancement in the field of clinical chemistry is generally the result of greater experience and education. Although career advancement can be achieved by becoming a sales representative or consultant, for the best advancement and highest earning potential, clinical chemists usually need a Ph.D. in clinical chemistry, or in one of the biological sciences (chemistry, biochemistry, or even pathology).

Clinical chemists with advanced degrees handle administrative tasks, including the design of laboratory space, the selection of equipment, the hiring of new employees, the evaluation of personnel, and the setting up and running of a full-scale quality control program. Some may run a university's clinical chemistry department, or coordinate a teaching program and manage the faculty.

Employment outlook

Because of the increased volume of medical testing, the outlook for clinical chemistry jobs is good through the year 2000.

Earnings

Those entering the career earn between $21,000 and $28,000 a year. Experienced clinical chemists will earn more. Clinical chemists with Ph.D.'s in administrative positions earn between $40,000 and $70,000 or more.

Conditions of work

Generally, laboratory conditions are always comfortable, climate-controlled environments, with modern up-to-date furnishings and equipment.

The daily tasks of clinical chemists range from tedious time-consuming procedures that require many complex steps, to automated tests where hundreds of determinations are made per hour, with test results generated on a computer printout.

Clinical chemists must be patient and extremely detail-oriented, with the ability to observe and note small differences and inconsistencies in their findings. They must be able to communicate well with the many people they deal with: physicians, nurses, and other lab personnel. In supervisory positions, they must be able to delegate responsibility and motivate employees to do their best work.

They must be able to handle problems such as instrument malfunctions, bad reagents, or patients who require special laboratory studies.

As with any medically oriented career, there is always a health risk involved when handling blood and body fluids. Established safety procedures and precautions greatly minimize or alleviate the chances of infection or illness: these include wearing protective gear such as safety goggles and rubber gloves.

Because the technology is ever-changing, clinical chemists are always learning. They can expect to attend courses, seminars, and workshops on the latest techniques and developments.

Clinical chemists can feel a sense of accomplishment knowing that their work may help save someone's life, or alleviate physical pain.

GOE: 02.02.03; SIC: any industry; SOC: 362

◇ SOURCES OF ADDITIONAL INFORMATION

American Association for Clinical Chemistry
Education Department
2029 K Street NW, 7th Floor
Washington, DC 20006

American Board of Clinical Chemistry
Applications Officer
2029 K Street NW, 7th Floor
Washington, DC 20006

American Medical Association
Allied Health and Accreditation
535 North Dearborn Street
Chicago, IL 60610

American Medical Technologists
710 Higgins Road
Park Ridge, IL 60068

American Society for Medical Technology
7910 Woodmont Avenue, Suite 1301
Bethesda, MD 20814

American Society of Clinical Pathologists
2100 West Harrison Street
Chicago, IL 60612

National Registration in Clinical Chemistry
1155 16th Street, NW
Washington, DC 20036

◇ RELATED ARTICLES

Volume 1: Chemicals and Drugs; Chemistry; Health Care
Volumes 2–4: Biochemists; Biological technicians; Biomedical engineers; Chemical technicians; Chemists; Health services administrators; Laboratory technicians; Medical laboratory technicians; Pharmacologists

Clowns

Definition

Clowns dress in outlandish costumes, paint their faces, and use a variety of performance skills to entertain audiences. They work in circuses, amusement parks, schools, malls, rodeos, and hospitals, as well as on stage, in films, and even on the street. Clowns are actors and comedians whose job is to make people laugh.

History

The earliest record of a clown dates from about 2270 B.C., when an Egyptian Pharaoh referred to "A divine spirit . . . to rejoice and delight the heart." Clowns have been called pranksters, mirthmakers, jesters, comics, jokers, buffoons, harlequins, fools, merry-andrews, mimes, and joeys. Though the names and styles change, clowning appears in almost every culture throughout history.

Kings and rulers in early Egyptian, Greek, and Roman empires kept fools for their own personal entertainment. During the Middle Ages and Renaissance, court jesters were hired for their musical and juggling skills, as well as for their verbal wit. Art from this time period shows jesters in colorful and bizarre clothing: exaggerated collars, bells, pointed caps, and unusual shoes. Although these clowns were often employed by kings and nobles, most of them were traveling minstrels, or street performers, who were skilled in storytelling, juggling, singing, magic, tightrope walking, and acrobatics.

After the Renaissance, clowns became stage characters in roles such as country bumpkins or dim-witted servants. Harlequins, known for their black and white patchwork clothes, and Pierrots, whose trademark was the whiteface makeup, emerged during this time.

The word "clown" was first used in 16th-century England to describe a clumsy, country oaf. Small traveling street theaters used them to attract audiences to their plays.

Threatened by the competition from these traveling troupes, large city theaters tried to maintain a more dignified position. In the 1700s, laws were passed to restrict street performances, but the laws said nothing about silent acting. As a result, the art of pantomime flourished, and it is still a major tool of clowns today.

The "King of Clowns" was Joseph Grimaldi, an Englishman whose career lasted from 1781 until 1828. Clowns around the world still celebrate memorial services and birthday parties to honor the profound influence he had on their art.

When Philip Astley created the first circus in 1768, Billie Button became the first circus clown. Since then, such famous clowns as Yankee Dan, Tom Belling, Lou Jacobs, and Emmett Kelly have been major attractions at circuses.

Nature of the work

A clown's job is first and foremost to make people laugh, although he may also attract attention, sell goods or services, or communicate ideas. Amateur clowns perform as a hobby, often working as volunteers in hospitals and nursing homes. Professional clowns are highly trained and usually have several skills. Their performance may include balloon sculpture, magic, puppetry and ventriloquism, juggling, acrobatics, balancing acts, music, stilt walking, or unicycling. Most professional clowns are proficient at word play and must have a quick wit to interact with their audiences.

Mimes are silent clowns. They communicate with exaggerated movements and facial expressions. Marcel Marceau is probably the most famous mime. *Auguste clowns* use slapstick humor. They are the ones who trip and fall, get into trouble, and act the silliest. The word "auguste" was a slang term used in Berlin in the 1860s for a stupid, bumbling fool. *Whitefaces* are characterized more by sadness than by their mischievousness. They are named for their white makeup, and they usually wear caps that make them look bald. *Character clowns* have unique routines and usually work alone rather than with a partner or in a large group. A popular type of character clown is the *hobo* or *tramp clown* who wears ragged clothes and is naive and somewhat sad. Charlie Chaplin and Emmett Kelly were famous tramp clowns.

Clowns still work in large circus arenas, usually together with a team of other clowns. More and more clowns, however, are finding work outside the circus. They may work in amusement parks, theater, shopping malls, and television and video, as well as for birthday parties and business promotions.

Clowns must travel to find work. They must be able to adapt to a variety of conditions,

Clowns entertain with unusual makeup and costumes combined with silly pantomimes.

clowns; they come in all shapes, sizes, and ages. Clowns do need training in various skills, such as magic or juggling.

Ringling Bros. and Barnum & Bailey Circus, the largest circus in America, has its own Clown College. Tuition, room, and board are free, but enrollment is limited and applicants must be under age 25. Ringling hires all its clowns from Clown College graduates, though they do not guarantee all graduates a job.

Clowning is physically demanding, so training in athletics, such as tumbling, is important. Acting classes are also helpful. Clowns who want to develop a verbal comedy routine would benefit from classes in writing, drama, and public speaking.

Opportunities for experience and exploration

Those who want to become clowns should find opportunities to meet other clowns. There are associations for amateurs and professionals which offer seminars and events where you can meet clowns and learn from them.

Theaters and acting schools sometimes offer classes in clowning and mime. There are classes, seminars, and camps scattered throughout the United States which offer training in clowning skills, including movement, acrobatics, mime, dance, makeup, costume, and ensemble work.

Another way to learn about clowning is to watch the masters. Some classic performances are available on film, such as those of Charlie Chaplin, Marcel Marceau, Red Skelton, and Emmett Kelly.

When you have achieved some clowning skills, you may wish to volunteer at local hospitals or nursing homes. Some clowns start by performing their routines on the street for tourists and workers on their lunch hours.

Methods of entering

Making friends with experienced clowns is the best way to become a clown yourself. They can recommend potential employers and help you perfect your routines. Clowning clubs may list job opportunities for its members. Such clubs hold regular meetings, known as "clown alleys," as well as special events which offer good opportunities for networking.

Beginning clowns need to make themselves known and develop a following. Many clowns

from a large arena to a small hospital room. They often perform outdoors. Clowning tends to be seasonal work—more jobs are available during the summer and on weekends and holidays. Every audience is different, so clowns must be flexible in their routines and like to interact with people.

Requirements

Clowns need no advanced degrees or certification, although a high school education is preferable. There are no physical requirements for

start by working at birthday parties, picnics, and church events. Later they may audition for work in carnivals, business promotions, television commercials, and circuses. Some clowns hire an agent to find jobs for them.

Advancement

Very few clowns achieve world recognition. A clown can become the major attraction at a circus, but it is rare. A few clowns become local celebrities and are in great demand in their own cities.

Employment outlook

In 1980 there were about 10,000 clowns; in 1992 it is estimated there are 50,000 to 100,000 clowns worldwide. Most of them are amateur clowns.

About 95 percent of clowns work part time and supplement their incomes with other jobs. Since there are a limited number of circuses, clowns are finding more opportunities outside the circus, especially in the party and festival business.

In the next decade, the ranks will continue to swell, while the number of jobs will remain fairly constant.

Earnings

Most clowns do not work for money. They are clowns because they enjoy performing and are satisfied with the reward of seeing smiles on people's faces. Because the job market for clowns is unpredictable, and because of the freelance nature of clowning, there are no set salaries.

Ringling circus clowns earn less than $200 per week to start, including room and board. Circus clowns can earn $400–$500 per week.

For engagements outside the circus, a clown can earn $50 for a single show up to $400 if highly skilled, but there is no upper limit. Clowns who work festivals, street fairs, and rodeos can earn $100 to $200 per engagement. A clown's weekly income can vary widely—they may earn $300 one week, $1,000 the next, and nothing the next.

For a child's birthday party, $50 to $150 for a 30- to 90-minute show is typical. Price varies with length of show, degree of skill, and reputation of the entertainer. A popular party clown with a following can earn $400 to $500 for a two-hour party.

Clowns usually have to pay their own expenses, insurance, and taxes, and have no paid vacations or retirement benefits. Most hold other full-time or part-time jobs.

Conditions of work

Clowns work irregular hours in varied conditions. They may be on their feet for hours at a time, in full costume and makeup. Costumes are expensive—a pair of shoes alone can cost $200. Some clowns have equipment that needs to be transported and kept in good repair.

To find the best jobs, clowns must travel often, staying in hotels and spending long hours on the road. They face stiff competition and often receive no recognition for their work. They are anonymous, especially if they work as part of a team.

Clowns work mostly weekends, summers, and holidays, although party clowns and those who find television jobs work year round. Professional clowns enjoy a great freedom in their schedules, the ability to choose employers, and the opportunity to travel. Most of all, clowns thrive on the laughter of their audiences.

GOE: 01.03.02; SIC: 7929; SOC: 328

◇ **SOURCES OF ADDITIONAL INFORMATION**

American Guild of Variety Artists
184 Fifth Avenue
New York, NY 10019

Clown Hall of Fame and Research Center
114 North Third Street
Delavan, WI 53115

Clowns of America International
PO Box 570
Lake Jackson, TX 77566–0570

◇ **RELATED ARTICLES**

Volume 1: Performing Arts
Volumes 2–4: Actors; Circus performers; Comedians; Magicians; Stunt performers

Coal mining operatives

Definition

Coal mining operatives extract coal from surface mines and underground mines. To do this, they operate complex and expensive machinery that drills, cuts, scrapes, or shovels earth and coal so that the fuel can be collected. Since coal is hard to reach, large portions of earth must be removed from the surface or dug out of mines so the coal mining operatives can get to it. Some coal mining operatives are explosives experts who use dynamite and other substances to remove earth and make the coal accessible.

History

Even before the development of agriculture or weaving, Stone Age people were mining for minerals buried in the earth: flints to make weapons, mineral pigments for painting pictures and bodies, and precious metals and stones for ornamentation. At first they dug open pits to reach the more easily accessible materials. Then they built primitive tunnels underground, where early miners used sticks and bones to dig out soft or broken rocks. As time went on, early miners learned to break hard rocks by driving metal or wooden wedges into cracks in the surface. An early method for dealing with particularly large, stubborn rocks was to build fires alongside them until they became thoroughly heated and then to dash cold water against them. The sudden contraction would cause the rocks to fracture.

Breaking through rock barriers became less tedious when, in the 17th century, Europeans began to use gunpowder introduced from China to explode them. It was not until the invention of dynamite in 1866, however, that modern mining techniques were born.

The coal industry played a vital role in the rapid industrial development of the United States. Its importance increased dramatically during the 1870s with the expansion of the railroads and the development of the steel industry, and during the 1880s when steam was first used to generate electric power. The production of bituminous coal doubled each decade from 1880 to 1910, and by 1919 production was more than 500 million tons.

Coal was the country's primary source of energy until after 1920, when it was almost replaced by hydroelectric power and oil fuel. Its use further declined after World War II, when natural gas became the fuel of choice. Oil and natural gas are generally preferred because they are cheaper, cleaner, and easier to handle, but today the rising price of oil and its uncertain supply are making coal a major energy source again. Coal production in the United States reached one billion tons for the first time in 1990. Today more than half of the nation's electricity is generated by burning coal.

Nature of the work

Coal mining operatives work in two kinds of coal mines: surface and underground. The mining method used is determined by the depth and location of the coal seam and the geological formations around it. In surface or strip mining, the overburden—the earth above the coal seam—has to be removed before the coal can be dug out. Then, after the mining has been completed, the overburden is replaced so the land can be reclaimed. For underground mining, entries and tunnels are constructed so that workers and equipment can reach the coal.

The machinery used in coal mining is extremely complex and expensive. There are power shovels that can move 3,500 tons of earth in an hour and continuous mining machines that can rip 12 tons of coal from an underground seam in a minute. Longwall shearers can extract the coal at an even faster rate. The job of coal mining operatives is to operate these machines safely and efficiently. Their specific duties depend on the type of mine that employs them and the machinery they operate.

Bulldozer operators use a tractor equipped with a concave blade across the front to remove trees, rocks, soil, and other obstructions from the mining area. They push rocks and dirt within reach of the shovels and scoops that remove the overburden. They also help replace the overburden when mining has been completed.

Machine drillers operate drilling machines to bore holes in the overburden at points selected by the blasters. They must be careful that the drill doesn't bind or stop while in operation. They may replace worn or broken drill parts using hand tools, change drill bits, and lubricate the equipment.

Blasters study the rock formation of the overburden to determine where explosives should be placed, what type to use, and how much. They instruct the machine drillers about where to bore the necessary holes, then set the explosive charges in the holes and detonate them to fracture the overburden.

Stripping shovel operators and *dragline operators* control the shovels and draglines that scoop up and move the broken overburden, which is pushed within their reach by the bulldozers. With the overburden removed, the coal is exposed so that machines with smaller shovels can remove it from the seam and load it into trucks.

Underground mining uses three methods to extract the coal that lies deep beneath the surface. These methods are continuous, longwall, and conventional mining.

Continuous mining is the most widely used method of mining underground coal. It is a system that uses a hydraulically operated machine that mines and loads coal in one step. Cutting wheels attached to hydraulic lifts rip coal from the seam. Then mechanical arms gather the coal from the tunnel floor and dump it onto a conveyor, which moves the coal to a shuttle car or another conveyor belt to be carried out of the mine. *Continuous-mining machine operators* sit or lie in the cab of the machine, drive it into the mining area, and manipulate levers to position the cutting wheels against the coal. They and their helpers may adjust, repair, and lubricate the machine and change cutting teeth.

In longwall mining, coal is also cut and loaded in one operation. With steel canopies supporting the roof above the work area, the mining machinery moves along a wall while its plow blade or cutting wheel shears the coal from the seam and automatically loads it onto a conveyor belt for transportation out of the mine. *Longwall-mining machine operators* advance the cutting device either manually or by remote control. They monitor lights and gauges on the control panel and listen for unusual sounds that would signal or indicate a malfunction in the equipment. Their assistants, called *tailers*, help advance the plow blade, adjust the depth of the cutting tool, signal when it is properly positioned, and adjust and make minor repairs to the machinery. As the wall in front of the longwall mining machine is cut away, the operator and the tailer move the roof supports forward, allowing the roof behind the supports to cave in.

Conventional mining, unlike continuous or longwall mining, is done in separate steps: first the coal is blasted from the seam, then it is picked up and loaded. Of the three underground methods, conventional mining requires the largest number of workers. *Cutter operators* work a self-propelled machine equipped with a

These coal miners operate a mining machine that performs a roof-bolting operation.

circular, toothed chain that travels around a blade 6 to 15 feet long. They drive the machine into the working area and saw a channel along the bottom and sides of the coal face, a procedure that makes the blasting more effective because it relieves some of the pressure caused by the explosion. Cutter operators may also adjust and repair the machine, replace dull teeth, and shovel debris from the channel. Using mobile machines, *drilling-machine operators* bore blast holes in the coal face after first determining the depth of the undercut and where to place the holes. Then *blasters* place explosive charges in the holes and detonate them to shatter the coal. After the blast, *loading-machine operators* drive electric loading machines to the area and manipulate the levers that control the mechanical arms to gather up the loose coal and load it onto shuttle cars or conveyors to be carried out of the mine.

Mining work is hard, dirty, and often dangerous. Mine workers are often characterized by the concern they have for their fellow miners. There is no room for carelessness in this occupation. The safety of all workers depends on teamwork, with everyone alert and careful to avoid accidents.

Requirements

A high school diploma is not necessary, but coal miners must be at least 18 years of age and in good physical condition to withstand the rigors of the work.

Federal laws require that all mine workers be given safety and health training before starting work and be retrained annually thereafter. Union contracts and some state laws also require preservice training and annual retraining in subjects such as health and safety regulations and first aid.

The union to which most coal miners belong is the United Mine Workers of America, although some are covered by the Southern Labor Union, the Progressive Mine Workers, or the International Union of Operating Engineers. Some independent unions also operate within single firms.

Opportunities for experience and exploration

Because of the age limitation for coal mining operatives, opportunities do not exist for most high school students to gain actual experience. Students over the age of 18 may be able to find summer work as laborers in a coal mine, performing routine tasks that require no previous experience. Older students may also investigate the possibility of summer or part-time employment in metal mines, quarries, oil drilling operations, heavy construction, road building, or truck driving. While this work may not be directly related to their career goals, the aptitudes required for the jobs are similar to those needed in mining, and the experience may prove useful.

Methods of entering

The usual method of entering this field is by direct application to the employment offices of the individual coal mining companies. However, mining machine operators must "come up through the ranks," acquiring the necessary skills on the job.

New employees start as trainees, or "red hats." After the initial training period, they work at routine tasks that do not require much skill, such as shoveling coal onto conveyors. As they gain more experience and become familiar with the mining operations, they are put to work as helpers to experienced machine operators. In this way, they eventually learn how to operate the machines themselves.

In union mines, when a vacancy occurs and a machine operator job is available, an announcement is posted so that any qualified employee may apply for the position. In most cases the job is given to the person with the most seniority.

Advancement

The opportunities for advancement for coal mining operatives are limited. The usual progression is from trainee to general laborer to machine operator's helper. After acquiring the skills needed to operate the machinery, the helpers may apply for machine operator jobs as they become available. All qualified workers, however, will be competing for those positions, and vacancies are almost always filled by the workers with the most seniority. A few coal mining operatives become supervisors, but additional training is required for supervisory or management jobs.

Employment outlook

In 1990 the U.S. coal industry employed approximately 24,000 mining machine operatives. More than half of these were heavy-equipment operators. The rest included blasters and those classified by the machines they operate: continuous mining, drilling, loading, cutting, hoisting, and longwall mining machine operators.

The employment of coal mining operatives is expected to decline compared with the national occupational average through the 1990s. Openings for coal mining operatives will occur as older, experienced workers retire, die, or leave the occupation.

Coal is mined in 26 states. Employment is concentrated mostly in the Appalachian area, including West Virginia, Kentucky, Pennsylvania, and Virginia, although large numbers of workers are also found in Ohio, Illinois, Alabama, and Wyoming. Because coal is a major resource for the production of such products as steel and cement, it is strongly affected by changes in overall economic activity. In a recession the demand for coal drops, and many miners may be laid off.

Earnings

Production workers in coal mining are paid better than those in the mining industry as a whole, and much better than the average for all production workers in private industry. In the 1990s coal miners average $12.97 per hour, compared to $11.00 for all miners and $7.98 for workers in private industry (except farming).

Among the coal mining operatives, the average hourly rates vary. Highest paid are the power-shovel operators at $12.80 an hour. Longwall miner operators are close behind with

$12.75. Continuous-mining machine operators earn $12.69, while their helpers receive $12.49. Loading-machine operators average $12.20 an hour. Cutting-machine operators are paid $12.18 and their helpers $12.13. Bulldozer operators earn $12.01, blasters $11.90, and machine drillers $11.81. These hourly figures do not include overtime or incentive pay. Operatives who work the evening shift receive an additional $.24 an hour; those on the night shift an additional $.36 an hour.

Conditions of work

Coal mining is hard work involving harsh and sometimes hazardous conditions. Workers in surface mines are outdoors in all kinds of weather, while those underground work in tunnels that are cramped, dark, dusty, wet, and cold. They are all subjected to loud noise from the machinery and work that is physically demanding and dirty.

Since passage of the Coal Mine Health and Safety Act in 1969, mine operators have improved the ventilation and lighting in underground mines and have taken steps to eliminate safety hazards for all workers. Nevertheless, operators of the heavy machinery both on the surface and below ground run the risk of injury or death from accidents. Other possible hazards for underground miners include roof falls or cave-ins, poisonous or explosive gases, and long exposure to coal dust. After a number of years, workers may develop pneumoconiosis, or "black lung," which is a disabling and sometimes fatal disease.

Most coal miners also receive health and life insurance, as well as pension benefits. The insurance generally includes hospitalization, surgery, convalescent care, rehabilitation services, and maternity for the workers and their dependents. The size of the pension depends on the worker's age at retirement and the number of years of service.

Most mine workers are given 10 holidays a year. Those who work in mines covered by a contract between the Bituminous Coal Operators Association and the United Mine Workers receive 14 days of paid vacation a year. After working six years, they get one extra day a year up to a maximum of 13 additional vacation days. There are generally three regular vacation periods during the year, and the miners must take their vacations during one of them. After one year, mine workers also are entitled to five personal/sick days and four floating vacation days that may be taken anytime. Miners not covered by a BCOA-UMW contract usually get two weeks of vacation after one year.

GOE: 05.11; SIC: 12; SOC: 8319

◇ SOURCES OF ADDITIONAL INFORMATION

American Mining Congress
1920 N Street, NW
Suite 300
Washington, DC 20036

International Union, United Mine Workers of America
900 15th Street, NW
Washington, DC 20005

American Coal Foundation
1130 17th Street, NW
Washington, DC 20036

Career Information Department
Society of Mining Engineers
PO Box 625002
Littleton, CO 80162-5002

The Coal Association of Canada
#502, 205–9 Avenue South East
Calgary AB T2G 0R3

◇ RELATED ARTICLES

Volume 1: Energy; Metals; Mining; Physical Sciences
Volumes 2–4: Coal mining technicians; Construction laborers; Geological technicians; Geologists; Geophysicists; Groundwater professionals; Industrial-truck operators; Logging industry workers; Mining engineers; Petroleum drilling workers; Petrologists; Roustabouts; Surveyors

Coal mining technicians

Definition

Coal mining technicians take part in a wide variety of coal mining activities where they help to extract, prepare, and transport coal. Their training enables them to not only assist coal mining engineers and managers but also assume independent responsibilities where they survey, map, and plan the mining of a coal field or direct the drilling of test holes and analyzing of test samples. Training covers the methods, equipment, techniques, and procedures used in underground coal mining, surface mining, and coal beneficiation (the cleaning, purification, and conditioning of coal for market).

In their work they also manage safe mining operations and train other workers in mine safety practices; help manage the disposal of mine waste and the reclamation (recovery) of strip-mine areas after coal has been removed; and prepare required environmental-impact reports on the mining operation. As the coal is mined, they test and analyze its quality, and measure and test the levels of air impurities in mines. They assemble, operate, and maintain specialized machinery and equipment, and plan how to get the most salable product from each deposit of coal by the least expensive method.

History

No one knows when coal was first discovered and used for fuel; even ancient peoples in several areas of the globe seem to have known about it. There is evidence that coal was burned in Wales during the Bronze Age about 3,000 to 4,000 years ago, and by the early Romans in Britain. The first industrial use of coal was in the Middle Ages in England. Consequently, the English were far more advanced in mining methods than other nations for many years.

The first Americans to use coal were the Hopi Indians around the 11th century. In the 17th century a Jesuit missionary found the Algonquin Indians "making fire with coal from the earth," and later in that century the French explorers Jacques Marquette and Louis Joliet reported coal use in what is now Illinois.

Commercial mining started in the United States around 1750, near Richmond, Virginia, with the first recorded commercial shipment of American coal—thirty-two tons from Virginia

to New York. Most of the coal produced was used to manufacture shells and shot for the Revolutionary War.

At first, the use of coal as a fuel source in the United States lagged far behind that in England because of the readily available supply of timber from the vast and plentiful North American woodlands. It was easier to fell a tree than to dig for coal. Wood was the major source of fuel for industry; for home heating; and, through charcoal, which is made from charred wood, for metallurgical production, from early colonial times until 1885.

Around 1760, the soldiers of Fort Pitt, Pennsylvania, were using bituminous (soft) coal mined nearby for fuel. This mine was located in one of the most valuable coal deposits in the United States, which today is known as the Great Appalachian Field. It extends nearly 900 miles from Pennsylvania to Alabama.

Coal fired the furnaces and fed the steam engines that began the Industrial Revolution in this country. Coal superseded wood as the nation's main fuel around 1885 and continued as the chief source of commercial energy until replaced by petroleum in the 1950s.

The earliest method of coal production was strip mining, which involves gathering deposits near the earth's surface. Early strip mining did not produce large amounts of coal, because methods of removing soil that lay over the coal were crude and slow. Beginning in 1910, this type of mining became more practical as powered machinery came into use.

Early underground mining was also crude and very difficult at best, based on hand use of the pick, shovel, and crowbar. The coal, once broken from the ground, was removed from the mine in wheelbarrows. People provided all of the power in both the mining and removal of coal. Eventually, horses or mules were used to haul the coal out of the mine. Blasting powder was also used to break coal loose, but the rest of the work was still done by hand.

Beginning about 1830, many new machines for coal mining were invented. Most of them used steam power fueled by wood or coal. This made underground coal mining more profitable.

During the last 150 years, the advances in mechanical devices to make underground coal production easier and more efficient have been staggering. Early important inventions included punching and cutting machines, chain cutters for undermining coal, compressed air and steam drills, locomotives for hauling waste rock and coal out of mines, and hoisting machines.

Modern technology and improved management have revolutionized coal mining in the last half century. Specialized machinery has been developed that replaces human effort with electric, pneumatic, hydraulic, and mechanical power—remotely controlled in some applications by computers. This means that highly skilled technicians and workers are needed to direct, operate, maintain, modify, and control the work performed by very expensive machinery. For the past two decades, about twenty schools have been providing successful two-year post-secondary programs for coal mining technicians. Using this education, coal mining technicians have become an essential part of the support staff to the skilled workers, engineers, and managers of mining operations.

A coal mining technician measures the viscosity of a coal-oil mixture fuel sample.

Nature of the work

Coal mining is an extractive industry that removes from the earth a nonrenewable natural resource that fills a need at the time it is mined.

The depth where coal can be found varies from a few feet below the earth's surface in the West to approximately 800 feet in the Midwest and much deeper in some of Appalachia. It is located and mined in approximately twenty-seven of the fifty states. Mining methods include strip mining and underground mining. The coal mining technician performs a wide variety of duties throughout the industry.

Those who work in surface mines work outdoors in all kinds of weather to expose the seam of coal. By the time the mining actually starts, coal mining technicians have already helped the managers, engineers, and scientists to survey, test drill, and analyze the coal deposit for depth and quality. They have also mapped the surface and helped plan the drilling and blasting to break up the rock and soil that cover the coal. The technicians have also helped prepare permits that must be filed with federal and state governments before mining may begin. Information must be provided on how the land will be mined and reclaimed; its soil, water conditions, and vegetation; wildlife conservation; and how archaeological resources will be protected.

The coal mining technicians also assist the mining engineers and superintendents to select the machinery used in mining. Such a plan must include selecting machines of a correct size and capacity to match other machinery, and planning the sequences for efficient use of machines. The plan also includes mapping roads out of the mine pit, planning machine and road maintenance, and above all, using safety methods for the whole operation.

Various methods may be used to remove the coal from an underground coal mine, and each requires the professional use of complex specialized equipment. The same kind of surveying, drilling, testing, mapping, and planning needed in surface mining is also used in underground mining. In some ways, however, the planning, machinery, and selection of mining methods are more complex in underground mining.

Underground mining is done in areas where it is too expensive to remove the soil and extract the coal as done in surface mining. Usually, underground mines are 100 to 1,000 feet below the surface.

Underground mines are found in most of the coal-producing states. They are classified as shaft, slope, or drift mines, depending on the angle at which the tunnel between the surface opening and the coal seam is cut. A shaft mine is entered through a vertical tunnel known as a shaft. Usually shaft mines are used to mine a coal bed that is 100 feet or more below the surface, but some of the deepest go to 2,000 feet and below.

When the coal seam is nearer to the surface, a sloping tunnel is cut from the surface on a downward slant to the coal seam. Drift mines are simple mining tunnels that cut directly from the surface opening to the seam on a horizontal path. They are used in hilly areas where un-

COAL MINING TECHNICIANS

A coal mining technician at a research center monitors an experimental installation that produces gas from coal.

derground mining is necessary, but where the coal is easily approached on a relatively level tunnel pathway.

In the underground mines, there are a variety of jobs performed by many specialized workers. Workers use mining machinery to cut the coal from the face and load it onto shuttle cars. The shuttle cars transport the coal onto a conveyor belt or mine car for removal from the mine. As coal is removed, pillars of coal, wooden or steel supports, and steel roof bolts and roof plates are used to hold up the mine roof to prevent it from collapsing.

In addition, large quantities of air—at least 3,000 cubic feet of air per minute—must be supplied to each underground working face. This air is circulated through the active working areas of the mine. It removes the poisonous or explosive gases and dust produced during mining. Rock dust is sprayed on the side walls and roof to prevent the formation of explosive dust mixtures.

Some specific entry-level jobs for coal mining technicians are described in the paragraphs that follow.

Survey helpers, surveyors, or *survey drafters* operate surveying instruments to gather numerical data. They calculate tonnage broken and incentive pay, map mine development, and provide precise directions and locations to the work force. They also conduct studies on operations and equipment to improve methods and reduce costs.

Ventilation technicians operate dust counting, gas quantity, and air volume measuring in-

struments. They record or plot this data, and plan or assist in planning the direction of air flow through mine workings. Ventilation technicians also help prescribe the fan installations required to accomplish the desired air flow.

Industrial engineering assistants observe work practices and obtain related time and process measurements; they also help plan more efficient materials handling and work methods.

Geology assistants gather geological data as mining activities progress. They identify rocks and minerals; record and map structural changes; locate drill holes; and identify rocks, coal, and minerals in drill cores. They also map geological information from drill core data, gather samples, and map results on mine plans.

Mill technicians in coal cleaning and beneficiation regularly determine and control mill feed density. They also analyze mill solutions for correct chemistry, and routinely check the quality of the final product. In the laboratory, these technicians conduct ore beneficiation tests, using flotation, gravity, or magnetic concentration methods.

Chemical analysts analyze mine, mill, and coal exploration samples, using volumetric or instrumental methods of analysis. They also write reports on the findings.

Requirements

The coal mining industry requires educated, ambitious employees who want to make a lasting career for themselves. To keep their skills sharp and knowledge up to date, coal mining technicians should expect to study throughout their careers by enrolling in courses offered through professional associations, junior colleges, and technical colleges. Continuing education credits may also be available.

Preparation for a career as a mining technician is best begun in high school. Students should take mathematics and science courses that provide an educational base for a two-year training program at one of the schools with mining technology programs. High school students who plan to be technicians should complete at least two years of mathematics, including algebra and geometry; and four years of English and language skills courses, with emphasis on reading, writing, and communication training.

Students should also complete a strong course in physics, and, if possible, chemistry with laboratory study. These courses, combined with mathematics, provide the necessary foundation for the study of electronics, advanced physics, and other engineering-type technical courses in the post-secondary school program. They also prepare students for assignments in surveying and mapping, preparation of coal, equipment maintenance, blasting, crushing, coal cleaning, and other specialized course work.

High school students who are considering this career should learn to use computers—particularly computer-aided drafting and design software programs. A high school course in mechanical drawing or drafting gives useful experience for the surveying and mapping tasks the technician may perform.

It is possible to start a coal mining career as an unskilled worker with a high school diploma. But it is difficult to advance within the coal mining industry without the foundation skills. In general, companies prefer employees who bring formally acquired technical knowledge and skills to the job.

The real value of technicians to the coal mining industry is their ability to apply an integrated scientific and mathematical background, specialized skills, and technical knowledge to a practical situation in the field. A technical college education will prepare coal mining technicians to function this way.

The first year of study in a typical two-year coal mining technician program in a technical or community college includes courses in the basics of coal mining, applied mathematics, mining law, coal mining ventilation and atmospheric control, communications skills, technical reporting, fundamentals of electricity, mining machinery, physical geology, surveying and graphics, mine safety and accident prevention, roof and rib control, and industrial economics and financing.

A typical second year in a program continues to build a solid technical base with courses in mine instrumentation and electrical systems, mine electrical maintenance, mine hydraulic machinery, machine transmissions and drive trains, basic welding, coal mine environmental impacts and control, coal and coal mine atmosphere sampling and analysis, mine machinery and systems automation and control, application of computers to coal mining operations, first aid and mine rescue, and institutions and organizations.

In some programs, students spend the summer working as interns at coal mining companies. Internships are especially advantageous—they provide a clear picture of the field and help students choose the work area that best fits their abilities. Students gain experience using charts, graphs, blueprints, maps, and machinery. They also develop job confidence

through an approach to the real operation of the industry.

Certain personal qualifications are also needed for success in this career. The ability to work with others and to accept supervision is most important. Technicians must also learn to work independently and accept responsibility. Coal mining technicians must be accurate and careful workers. Mistakes can prove expensive or hazardous to the technician and to other workers.

Laws governing the coal industry vary from state to state, and so do the requirements for certification of mine workers. Typically, a state may require that any person engaged at the face of the mine, as a *coal loader, loading machine operator, cutting machine operator, driller, shooter, timberman,* or *roof bolter,* first obtain a certificate of competency as a miner. This certificate is often obtained from the state's miner's examining board. In some cases, a miner may obtain a certificate of competency after completing one year of underground work. A miner who has an associate degree in coal mine technology, however, may be able to obtain the certificate after completing six months of underground experience.

For those seeking a certificate of competency as a mine examiner or manager, a state may also require at least four years of underground experience; graduates with associate degrees in coal mining technology, however, may be able to qualify after only three years of experience.

Coal mining technician students can usually meet the state's criteria for employment while still in their technician preparatory program. It is important to be familiar with these criteria if technicians plan to work in a state other than the one where they begin their education and work experience.

Opportunities for experience and exploration

Local high schools, community colleges, and technical institutes can provide considerable information on coal mining technician careers. If it can be arranged, a visit to a producing coal mine makes it possible to observe the machinery and the work. Workers on the job can also supply information about the career. One of the best opportunities for experience is a summer job with a coal mining company, preferably in an activity closely related to the mining operation.

COAL MINING TECHNICIANS

Methods of entering

Coal mining technicians are usually hired by recruiters from major employers before completing their last year of technical school. Industry recruiters regularly visit the campuses of schools with coal mining technician programs and work with the school's placement officers.

Many two-year graduates take jobs emphasizing basic operational functions. Technicians are then in a position to compete for higher positions, in most cases through the system of job bidding, which considers such factors as formal education, experience, and seniority.

In some cases, graduates already have jobs; their employers may have sent them to school to obtain the needed preparation. Graduates usually have special interests that qualify them for technical positions in one or more of the following areas: production, planning and control, maintenance, repair, electrical, welding, support services, surveying and mapping, or environmental control and management.

Most companies provide orientation sessions to familiarize the newcomer with company operations. This may include a review of state and federal laws that concern coal mining and health and safety training. After that, continuous study, careful work, and on-the-job learning are a way of life for the technician.

Advancement

For the coal mining technician who works steadily and keeps up to date on new technological developments, opportunities for advancement are excellent. Some technicians may advance to management positions such as section supervisors, production superintendents, or mine managers. The possibilities are attractive for knowledgeable, dependable individuals.

After a period of on-the-job experience, coal mining technicians may become supervisors, sales representatives, or possibly even private consultants or special service contractors. The following are a few examples of such advancement patterns and jobs.

Shift bosses are responsible for the efficient operation of a certain mine area. They train new workers and enforce strict safety practices. *Mine superintendents* or *captains* are responsible for the total mining area. They supervise the work of all shift bosses.

Technical sales representatives work for a manufacturer of mining equipment and supplies and sell such products as explosives, flotation chemicals, rock drills, hoists, crushers, grinding mills, classifiers, materials handling equipment, and safety equipment.

Special services consultants provide consulting services, either independently or as a partner in a consulting business. This work is also a route to advancement for the experienced technician with an excellent record of scientific and field success.

Employment outlook

Employment levels for all mining occupations are expected to remain about the same or to decline through the year 2000, because of low growth in the demand for coal. In the long run, demand for coal may well increase; this, however, will depend largely on the availability and price of other energy sources such as oil, natural gas, and nuclear energy, as well as coal from other countries.

Even if national employment levels do not improve, there will continue to be some need for well-trained coal technicians. New technicians will be required to replace those retiring or leaving their jobs for other reasons. Also, more efficient and technologically sophisticated coal mining systems and further enforcement of health, safety, and environmental regulations may increase the need for coal mining technicians.

Earnings

Establishing a scale of earnings for coal mining technicians is difficult because of the many different work situations involved and the great variation in their working conditions. Normally, the Bituminous Coal Operators' Association and the labor unions that represent the workers contract for a set scale of pay for the industry.

According to the best information available at this time, earnings are broken down according to the type of mining done. Underground coal miners average a low of $14.97 per hour, and a high of $16.61, with the median wage of $15.84. Strip miners earn between $15.99 and $17.37 per hour, with the median wage at $16.36. Those who prepare plants and facilities earn between $15.95 and $16.54 per hour.

Benefits for workers within the coal mining industry are progressive and competitive with those of most energy industries today, and they may include education benefits, health and life insurance, work schedules, paid holidays, and health benefits.

Many coal companies now provide tuition payment plans so that their employees can take college courses related to their jobs. This is an incentive to continue the education process and thus ensure a better employee. The arrangement is especially beneficial for technicians who need to keep up with new technology and learn new skills.

Within five years, coal mining technicians whose pay started near $20,000 may be earning $32,000 to $40,000 if they are effective, competent workers who demonstrate the ability and desire to assume greater responsibilities. Those who become highly successful technical sales directors, managers, or specialized consultants after several years may earn considerably more than $40,000 per year.

Conditions of work

Coal mining takes place in a hazardous environment. There is a danger of mine explosions, roof falls, and a wide variety of other mine-related accidents. In the past, working conditions have varied from mine to mine and state to state. State and federal regulations, however, have been established over the years, greatly improving working conditions, although coal mining is still considered dangerous.

Coal mining machine operators, supervisors, engineers, and their supporting technicians work under unusual and often harsh conditions. At surface mines, operators work outside and may be exposed to bad weather. In underground mines, operators work in tunnels that may be cramped, dark, dusty, wet, and cold. At times, several inches of water may be on the tunnel floor. In both surface and underground mines, operators and other crew members are exposed to loud noise from the continuous operation of large machinery. And, although much of the work is done by machines, most mining jobs are physically demanding and almost always involve getting dirty from dust, the coal processing procedure, waste, mud, and atmospheric contamination.

Because there are so many activities going on at the same time, coal mining technicians must always be alert to avoid accidents and hazards as they work. Employers offer safety instruction, and supply certain items of safety equipment and health care services. In the end, however, coal mining technicians' safety and health depend on their own intelligence, alertness, and judgment in potentially dangerous work conditions.

Since the passage of the Coal Mine Health and Safety Act in 1969, the coal mining industry has taken many steps to improve ventilation and lighting in underground mines and to eliminate the many inherent safety hazards. Nevertheless, mining machine operators and other coal mining workers, including supervisors and technicians, must constantly be alert. They must recognize and correct safety hazards, acting quickly and correctly to get the crew to safety in dangerous situations.

In both surface and underground mines, workers may be injured or killed in accidents involving mining machinery. In underground mines, all workers face the additional hazards of roof cave-ins, accumulation of poisonous and explosive gases, and exposure to coal dust. Coal mining workers exposed to coal dust over a period of many years may develop pneumoconiosis (black lung), a disabling and sometimes fatal disease.

Much of the personal satisfaction and reward in this career depends on becoming accustomed to doing difficult work in dark, potentially dangerous places. Underground mining requires workers to wear battery-operated hat lights. Usually no other lights are used except those on the machines and at the entrance and face of the mine. Under such conditions, teamwork is essential, as is a tolerance for being enclosed and underground. The ability of coal mining workers to get along well and communicate with co-workers is essential, because fellow workers' safety is dependent upon their concern for one another.

Coal mining technicians must be patient, systematic, accurate, and objective in their work. They must have the urge and the ability to keep learning. They must be able to work cooperatively, especially in a subordinate role under experienced managers, professional engineers, and scientists. They must be able to plan ahead. These qualities, along with integrity, will determine the success of the technician in this field.

GOE: 05.01.08, 05.02.05, 05.11.02; SIC: 124; SOC: 3719

◇ **SOURCES OF ADDITIONAL INFORMATION**

American Institute of Mining, Metallurgical and Petroleum Engineers
345 East 47th Street
New York, NY 10017

American Mining Congress
1920 N Street, NW
Suite 300
Washington, DC 20036

Bituminous Coal Operators' Association
303 World Center Building
918 16th Street, NW
Washington, DC 20006

International Union United Mine Workers of America
900 15th Street, NW
Washington, DC 20005

National Coal Association
1130 17th Street, NW
Washington, DC 20036

Society of Mining Engineers, Inc.
900 15th Street, NW
Washington, DC 20005

◇ **RELATED ARTICLES**

Volume 1: Engineering; Mining
Volumes 2–4: Civil engineering technicians; Coal mining operatives; Geological technicians; Geologists; Health and regulatory inspectors; Industrial safety-and-health technicians; Miscellaneous engineers; Occupational-safety-and-health workers; Surveying and mapping technicians

---

 # Collection workers

Definition

Collection workers, often known as *bill collectors* or *collection agents*, are employed to persuade people to pay their overdue bills, thereby maintaining the financial well-being of a department store, hospital, bank, public utility, or other business. Collection workers may also work for collection companies that are hired by the business to which the money is owed. These workers contact delinquent debtors, inform them of the delinquency, and either secure some amount of money or arrange a new payment schedule. If all else fails, they may be forced to repossess property or hand over the account to an attorney for legal proceedings.

History

Debt collection is one of the world's oldest vocations. In literature, the most famous—and unsuccessful—attempt to retrieve an overdue debt occurred in Shakespeare's *Merchant of Venice*, featuring the character Shylock as the collector. Debt collection also figures prominently in the works of Charles Dickens.

In the past, people who were unable to pay their debts were sent to prison, indentured as servants or slaves until the amount owed was paid off, or recruited by force to colonize new territories. Today, debtors face less harsh consequences, but the proliferation of credit opportunities has expanded the field of debt collection. Charge accounts are now offered by department stores, banks, credit unions, gasoline stations, and other businesses. Many people buy furniture or other expensive items "on time," meaning they place a small sum down and pay off the balance plus interest over a certain period of time. People take out mortgages from financial institutions to finance home purchases. The result of all these credit opportunities is that some people will take on too much debt and either fail to meet these obligations or refuse to pay them. When creditors do not receive their payments on time, they call in the collection worker.

Nature of the work

A collection worker's main job is to persuade people to pay bills that are past due. The procedure is generally the same in both collection firms and businesses that employ collection workers. However, the duties of the various workers may overlap, depending on the size and nature of the company.

When routine billing methods—monthly statements and notice letters—fail to secure payment, the collection worker receives a bad-debt file. This file contains information about the debtor, the nature and the amount of the unpaid bill, the last charge incurred, and the date of the last payment. The collection worker then contacts the debtor by phone or mail to request full or partial payment or, if necessary, to arrange a new payment schedule.

If the bill has not been paid because the customer believes it is incorrect, the merchandise purchased was faulty, or the service billed for was not performed, the collector takes appropriate steps to settle the matter. If after investigation the debt is still valid, the collector again tries to secure payment.

In cases where the customer has not paid due to a financial emergency or poor money management, a new payment schedule can be arranged. In instances where the customer goes to great or fraudulent lengths to avoid payment, the collector may recommend that the file be turned over to an attorney.

When all efforts to obtain payment fail, collection workers known as *repossessors* are assigned to locate the merchandise on which the debtor still owes money and return it to the seller. Goods such as furniture or appliances can be picked up in a truck. To reclaim automobiles and other motor vehicles, the repossessor may be forced to enter and start the vehicle with special tools if the buyer does not surrender the key.

In large agencies, some collection workers specialize as *skip tracers*. Skip tracers are assigned to locate debtors who skip out on their debts—that is, who move without notifying their creditors to evade payment of their bills. Skip tracers act like detectives, searching telephone directories and street listings and making inquiries at the post office in an effort to locate the missing debtor. They try to elicit information about that person's whereabouts by interviewing, phoning, or writing to former neighbors and employers, local merchants, friends, relatives, and references listed on the original credit application. Skip tracers follow up every lead and prepare a report of the entire investigation.

Collection workers also perform clerical duties, such as reading and answering correspondence, filing, or posting amounts paid to people's accounts. In some small companies, they may offer financial advice to customers or contact them to inquire about their satisfaction with the handling of the account. In larger companies, *credit and loan collection supervisors* may oversee the activities of several other collection workers.

While speaking with a debtor on the telephone, a collection worker refers to computer files for verification of unpaid bills.

Collection work is emotionally taxing. It involves listening to the bill payers' problems and sometimes to verbal attacks directed at both the collector and the company. Some people physically threaten repossessors and other collection workers. Because debtors can be very emotional about money and credit problems, the job is potentially stressful.

Requirements

This is a people-oriented job that requires someone who can get along with others. It involves a great deal of phone communication on a delicate subject. Collection workers need a pleasant manner and voice. They must be sympathetic and tactful, yet assertive and persuasive enough to overcome any reluctance on the part of the debtor to pay the overdue account. In addition, collectors must be alert, quick-witted, and imaginative to handle the unpredictable and potentially awkward situations that are encountered in this type of work.

A high school education is usually sufficient for this occupation. Courses in psychology and speech are particularly helpful. Collection procedures and telephone techniques are learned on the job in a training period spent under the guidance of a supervisor or an experienced collector. The legal restrictions on collection activities, such as when and how calls can be made, are also covered. The American Collectors Association conducts special seminars for its members to assist collectors in improving their collection and skip-tracing skills. A basic knowledge of legal proceedings is helpful for supervisors.

Opportunities for experience and exploration

The best way to explore collection work is to secure part-time or summer employment in a collection or credit office. Students may wish to interview a collection worker to obtain first-hand information about the practical aspects of this occupation.

Methods of entering

The usual way of entering the collection field is to apply directly to an employer. The "help wanted" section of the newspaper may provide information on job openings, as will a visit to the local office of the state employment service.

Advancement

Advancement opportunities are good, though limited. Workers with above-average ability can become supervisors or collection managers. A few progress to other credit positions, such as credit authorizer, credit manager, or bank loan officer. Some may branch out to open their own collection agency.

Employment outlook

The development of a credit-based economy has created a larger number of bad debts, necessitating expanded collection services. In the 1990s, approximately 185,000 collection workers are employed by commercial banks, finance companies, credit unions, and collection agencies, as well as in public utilities and retail and wholesale businesses.

Jobs in this field are expected to grow faster than the national average for all occupations. The Department of Labor projects a 62 percent growth in the number of people in this occupation through the year 2005.

The continued growth of retail stores, coupled with the extension of credit cards to greater numbers of people, will result in an increased demand for collection workers. A system that relies more and more on credit for the purchase of goods and services must expect an increasing number of delinquent accounts, which means additional collectors will be required to service the accounts on an individual basis. Automation has had some impact on the field, however, eliminating the need for people to perform several functions that were previously handled by collectors.

Periods of recession in the economy increase the amount of personal debt that goes unpaid. Therefore, unlike many occupations, collection workers usually find that their employment and workloads increase during economic slumps.

Of more significance than the creation of new jobs are the openings that will occur as collectors move to other occupations. Some will leave because of the stress involved in persuading people to pay their bills, others because they do not collect enough debts to earn an adequate salary. For these same reasons, employers have difficulty recruiting applicants for collection work. On the plus side, however, this creates a promising employment situation for people with the proper aptitudes and temperament.

Job opportunities exist throughout the United States, especially in heavily populated urban areas. Companies that have branch offices in rural communities often locate their collection departments in nearby cities. Competition for positions will be strongest in large metropolitan banks, which generally offer higher salaries and better advancement opportunities.

Earnings

Collection workers may receive a salary plus a bonus or commission on the debt amounts they collect. Others work for a flat salary with no commissions. Since the pay system varies among different companies, incomes vary substantially. While the available information is limited, it appears that in the 1990s beginning collectors earn between $14,500 and $24,000 a year. Those with experience can earn as much as $36,000, depending on how much they are able to collect from debtors. The median income for all bill collectors is about $19,000.

Conditions of work

Most of the time, collectors work in pleasant offices, seated at a desk and spending a great deal of time on the telephone. Because of the large quantity of work done over the phone, many companies use phone headsets and program-operated dialing systems such as speed-dial or automatic redial. Companies with complicated phone programs usually train their employees on how to operate the system.

Rarely does a collector have to make a personal visit to a customer. Repossession proceedings are undertaken only in extreme cases. The legal aspects must be understood when repossession is required.

These workers put in 40 hours a week but often stagger their schedules. They may start late in the morning and work into the evening, or they may take a weekday off and work on Saturday. The ability to find debtors at home has an effect on their schedule.

GOE: 07.02.02, 07.04.02; SIC: 6021, 6141; SOC: 4712, 4786

◇ **SOURCES OF ADDITIONAL INFORMATION**

American Collectors Association
PO Box 39106
Minneapolis, MN 55439-0106

Canadian Payments Association
#1212, 50 O'Connor Street
Ottawa ON K1P 6L2

◇ **RELATED ARTICLES**

Volume 1: Banking and Financial Services
Volumes 2–4: Accountants and auditors; Bookkeeping and accounting clerks; Credit analysts, banking; Financial institution clerks and related workers; Financial institution officers and managers; Fund-raisers; Tax preparers; Telemarketers

---

College administrators

Definition

College administrators coordinate and oversee the programs such as admissions and financial aid in public and private colleges and universities. They frequently work with a team of people to develop and manage student services.

History

Before the Civil War, most U.S. colleges and universities managed their administration with a president, a treasurer, and a part-time librarian. Members of the faculty often were responsible for the administrative tasks of the day, and there was no uniformity in college admissions requirements.

By 1860 the average number of administrative officers in U.S. colleges was still only four, but as the job of running an institution ex-

panded in scope and function—in response to ever-increasing student enrollment—the responsibilities of administration began to splinter. After creating positions for *registrar, secretary of faculty, chief business officer,* and a number of departmental deans, most schools next hired a director of admissions to oversee the application and acceptance of students. In addition, several eastern schools and a few prominent college presidents, President Eliot of Harvard and President Butler of Columbia among them, saw the need to establish organizations whose purpose would be to put an end to the chaos. The College Entrance Examination Board was formed to create standardizing college entrance requirements. By 1910 there were 25 leading eastern colleges using the Board's standard exams.

After World War II, returning veterans entered America's colleges and universities by the thousands. With this great influx of students, college administrators were needed to better or-

COLLEGE ADMINISTRATORS

College financial aid administrators must analyze each applicant's monetary situation before granting tuition aid.

ganize the university system. During this time, financial aid administration also became a major program. Today, as the costs of a college education continue to rise dramatically, college financial aid administrators are needed to help students find student loans, grants, scholarships, and work-study programs.

Nature of the work

The job of college administrator is demanding and diverse. Administrators are responsible for a wide range of tasks in areas such as counseling services, admissions, alumni affairs, financial aid, and business. The following are some of the different types of college administrators.

College admissions directors review cases of general and special admission and coordinate recruitment activities. They are responsible for planning and producing application and admissions materials, reviewing students applications, and developing the school's recruiting program. They are in charge of maintaining student files and often oversee computerized record keeping. Such directors are closely involved in the recruiting of new students and are responsible for carrying out administrative policies of the college or university.

College financial aid administrators direct the scholarship, grant-in-aid, and loan programs that provide financial assistance to students. Most colleges and universities have such programs to help students meet the costs of tuition, fees, books, and other living expenses. The administrator keeps students informed of the financial assistance available to them. At smaller colleges, this work might be done by a single person, the *financial aid officer*. At larger

colleges and universities, the staff might be much larger, and the financial aid officer will head a department and direct the activities of *financial aid counselors,* who handle most of the personal contact with students.

Other college administrators include *college admissions counselors* who review records, interview prospective students, and process applications for admission. The *dean of students* is responsible for the student-affairs program, including such areas as student housing. *Registrars* prepare class schedules, make classroom and student assignments, and maintain grade records.

Requirements

Those who wish to become college administrators must usually obtain at least a master's degree in a field such as student counseling and personnel services or in higher education administration. It will be an asset to have training in computer science and data processing.

This job requires that a person show an aptitude for organizing and coordinating work in an efficient manner. As a manager, the college administrator must be decisive and have a sound understanding of managerial principles and practices, which may be achieved both on the job and by taking college courses.

High school and college students interested in this field would do well to have courses in English, foreign languages, social sciences, and mathematics. A bachelor's degree in any field is usually acceptable, but most students major in student personnel, administration, or subjects such as economics, psychology, or sociology. Other important studies may include education, counseling, information processing, business, and finance.

Opportunities for experience and exploration

To learn something about what the job of administrator entails, high school and college students may talk to the admissions personnel in their own school or in nearby schools. Another possibility would be to talk to college recruiters on high school campuses.

College admissions offices frequently hire college students for part-time jobs or internships in their department, and this is an excellent opportunity to gain firsthand experience. Students are often hired as residence hall directors and advisors, student union officers, student housing aides, activities advisors, and assistants to various faculty and staff members.

Methods of entering

There are several different types of entry-level positions available in the typical admissions office. College students who are able to get part-time work or an internship at the admissions office where they attend school will find that this is a great advantage when seeking work in this field after graduation. Any other experience working with people or with computerized data also is helpful.

Advancement

Entry-level positions, which usually require only a bachelor's degree, include admissions counselors, who advise students regarding admissions requirements and decisions; evaluators, who check high school transcripts and college transfer records to determine whether applying students may be admitted; and recruiters, who visit high school campuses to provide information about their school and to interest students in applying for admission.

Advancement from any of these positions will depend on the way in which an office is organized as well as how large it is. One may move up to assistant director or associate director, or, in a larger office, into any specialized divisions such as freshman or graduate admissions, minority admissions, transfer admissions, or foreign student admissions. Advancement also may come through transferring to larger schools or systems.

Workshops and seminars are available through professional directors associations for those interested in staying informed and becoming more knowledgeable in their field, but it is highly unlikely that an office employee may gain the top administrative level without a graduate degree.

Employment outlook

The number of administrators employed at any time is determined by college and university enrollment and by state and local expenditures for education.

Employment in the field of education administration is expected to grow at the average rate for all occupations through the 1990s. However, declining college enrollments and leaner budgets will most likely make the job market very competitive through the 1990s. Administration offices, however, are expected to remain relatively unaffected by this trend.

Earnings

Salaries for college administrators vary widely among two-year and four-year colleges and among public and private institutions, but are generally comparable to those of college faculty. In the 1990s the median yearly pay is $45,900 for a director of admissions. Financial aid directors earn an average of $38,300 a year. Earnings may range from an annual $21,000 for those just beginning in the field and go up to approximately $70,000 or more for an admissions department head.

Conditions of work

The college or university environment is usually a pleasant place in which to be employed. Offices are often spacious and comfortable and the campus may be a scenic, relaxing work setting.

Employment as a director of admissions is usually on a 12-month basis. The position requires much direct contact with students and so working hours may vary according to student needs. It is not unusual to work long hours during peak enrollment periods, such as the beginning of each quarter or semester. Directors are sometimes required to work evenings and weekends to provide wider student access to the admissions services.

College administrators may frequently travel to other colleges and to career fairs, high schools, and professional conferences to interview and provide information about the school for which they work.

College administrators must be very organized and have great skill in leading and dealing with others, both staff and students. It is important that they have the patience and tact to handle a wide range of personalities as well as an emotional steadiness when confronted with unusual and unexpected situations.

GOE: 11.07.03; SIC: 8221; SOC: 1281

College and university faculty

Definition

College or university faculty members instruct students in specific subjects. They are responsible for oral lectures and the giving and grading of examinations. They also may carry on research, write for publication, and aid in administration. Some college and university faculty members serve as consultants to various educational or scientific organizations.

History

The idea of a college or university goes back many centuries. They evolved slowly from monastery schools, which trained a select few for the professions, notably the profession of theology. The terms college and university are today virtually interchangeable in the United States, although originally they designated very different kinds of institutions.

Two of the most notable of the early European universities were the University of Bologna in Italy, thought to have been established in the 12th century, and the University of Paris, which was chartered in 1201. These universities were considered to be models after which other European universities were patterned.

Oxford University in England was probably established during the 12th century. Oxford University served as a model for early American colleges and universities, and today is still considered one of the world's leading institutions.

Harvard, the first U.S. college, was established in 1636. Its stated purpose was to train men for the ministry. The early colleges all were established for religious training. With the growth of state-supported institutions in the early 18th century, the process of freeing the curriculum from ties with the church began. The first liberal arts curriculum was introduced with the establishment of the University of Virginia in 1825. The innovations made in higher education by this college were to be adopted later by other colleges and universities.

Although the original colleges in the United States were patterned after Oxford University, they later came under the influence of German universities. During the 19th century, more than 9,000 Americans went to Germany to study. The emphasis in German universities was on scientific method. Most of the people who had studied in Germany returned to the

United States to teach in universities, bringing with them this objective, factual approach to education and to other fields of learning.

Colleges for women developed more slowly than those for men. The first, Wesleyan Female College in Macon, Georgia, was established exactly 200 years after the founding of Harvard College.

The junior college movement in the United States has been one of the most rapidly growing educational developments. Junior colleges first came into being just after the turn of the 20th century.

Nature of the work

College and university faculty members have three main functions to perform. Their first and most important job is the teaching responsibility. Most college and university teachers are in class approximately 9 to 12 hours each week. However, they may put in two hours of preparation for every hour spent in class so the actual time devoted to teaching responsibilities may be approximately 36 hours each week. Associate professors and full professors may spend only six to eight hours a week in actual classroom work.

The standard teaching technique for college and university faculty members is the lecture method. Many other methods are also used, however. In some courses, teachers rely heavily on laboratories to transmit course material. Some faculty members employ the discussion method as a teaching device. Others use visual aids to instruct students. Many combine all methods or go from one to the other.

Another important responsibility of the college and university faculty member is the advising of students. Not all serve as faculty advisers, but those who do must set aside a large block of time to see the students for whose program they are responsible. Faculty advisers may have any number of students assigned to them, from fewer than ten to more than one hundred, depending on the amount of responsibility that the adviser is expected to assume and the administrative policies of the college in which they work. Their responsibility for the student may involve looking over a planned program of studies to make sure that students meet requirements for graduation, or it may involve working intensively with each student on many aspects of college life.

A third responsibility of college and university faculty members is that of research and publication. Faculty members who are heavily involved in research programs sometimes are

University faculty spend much of their time conducting research with the assistance of graduate students.

assigned a smaller teaching load than those who are not so involved. Most faculty members who do research publish their findings in various scholarly journals. They also write books based on research findings or on their own knowledge and experience in their field. Most textbooks are written by college and university teachers.

Some faculty members eventually rise to the position of *department head* and have charge of the affairs of an entire department, such as English, mathematics, or biological sciences.

Department heads, faculty, and other professional staff members are aided in their myriad duties by *graduate assistants*, who may help develop teaching materials, conduct research, give examinations, teach lower-level courses, or carry out a variety of other activities.

Some college and university faculty members are *extension work instructors*. This means that they conduct classes at times and places other than the normal ones for the benefit of people who otherwise would not be able to take advantage of the institution's resources. They may teach courses in the evenings or on weekends. They may travel away from the campus and meet with a group of students at another location. The teacher may work in the extension division entirely and meet all classes off campus, or may divide the time between on-campus and off-campus teaching.

An extension work instructor may give instruction by correspondence to certain students who are not able to come to the campus at that time. Correspondence courses usually are available only to undergraduate students. There may be a standard course of study for the subject, and the teacher's responsibility may be primarily to grade the papers that the student sends in at periodic intervals and to advise the student of progress. The teacher may perform this service in addition to other duties or may be assigned to correspondence work as a major teaching responsibility.

The teacher in the junior college has many of the same kinds of responsibilities as does the teacher in the four-year college or university. Because junior colleges offer only a two-year program, the faculty member will teach only undergraduates and will not be concerned with tutorial methods that must be employed when working with advanced graduate students.

Requirements

At least one advanced degree is required to be employed as a teacher in a college or university. The master's degree is considered the minimum standard, and graduate work beyond the master's is usually desirable. A doctorate is required to advance in academic rank above instructor in most institutions.

The faculty member in a junior college may be employed with only a master's degree. Advancement in responsibility and in salary, however, are more likely to come to those who have earned a doctorate. A number of states that maintain public junior colleges require state certification for teaching in these schools. A faculty member must have completed the master's degree and certain courses in education to qualify.

The high school student who is interested in college teaching should enroll in a college-preparatory course. The student will want to take subjects that will give a wide background of information upon which to base a later specialty.

Opportunities for experience and exploration

One way for high school students to gain exposure to the field is to visit the campuses of colleges and universities. They should first make an appointment, however, and then seek permission to visit classes or to talk with some of the college faculty members. Another good means for exploration is to attend college fairs, often held in large cities, where representatives from colleges and universities are available to describe their institutions and teaching programs.

Methods of entering

The placement office in the college or university from which the prospective teacher receives a degree will have a list of teaching vacancies in the student's field. The student may choose from among the positions available and apply to one or to several colleges.

The graduate student's major professor will often know of vacancies on the faculties of other colleges and universities. Many graduate students find positions because of the professional relationships of the faculty members under whom they have studied.

Some professional associations maintain lists of teaching opportunities in their areas. They may also keep lists of applicants for positions to put college administrators in touch with people who might like to apply.

Advancement

The usual advancement pattern for the college teacher is from instructor, to assistant professor, to associate professor, to full professor. All four academic ranks are concerned primarily with teaching and research. College faculty members who have an interest in and a talent for administration may be advanced to head of department, or to dean of their college. A few become college or university presidents.

The instructor is usually an inexperienced college teacher. He or she may hold a doctorate or may have completed all the requirements for one except for the dissertation. Most colleges look upon the rank of instructor as the period during which the college is trying the teacher out. Instructors usually are advanced to the position of assistant professors within three to four years.

Most colleges have clearly understood promotion policies from rank to rank for faculty members and many have written statements about the number of years in which instructors and assistant professors may remain in grade. Administrators in many colleges hope to encourage younger faculty members to increase their skills and competencies and thus to qualify for the more responsible positions of associate professor and full professor.

Employment outlook

There are approximately 712,000 faculty members employed in American colleges and universities in the early 1990s. About 70 percent of them teach in public institutions. Approximately 30 percent of the full-time faculty members teach in universities, almost 50 percent in four-year colleges, and more than 20 percent in two-year colleges.

The employment outlook for college and university faculty members should increase at the average rate throughout the 1990s. The demand for faculty members in universities and colleges will depend in part on the size of the college-age population and the proportion who attend college.

There will continue to be keen competition for the openings that become available. Many applicants may have to accept part-time or short-term positions, or nonacademic jobs in government or industry.

The best employment opportunities for college and university faculty members are in the departments of engineering, computer science, the health sciences, the physical sciences, and mathematics. These college departments are experiencing some faculty shortages because many teachers have left for more attractive jobs in nonacademic fields.

Earnings

The average college or university faculty member is employed for a period of 9 or 10 months a year, and the stated salary is for that period. One may earn additional salary by teaching in summer school or by spending the summer writing for publications, working as a consultant, conducting research projects, or performing other income-producing work.

The salaries vary widely according to faculty rank and type of institution. Faculty members in public colleges and universities generally have higher salaries than those in private schools. In general, faculty members in four-year schools average higher salaries than those in two-year institutions. In the 1990s, full professors average about $62,400; associate professors, $44,800; assistant professors, $37,800; and instructors, $26,800.

Most colleges and universities offer other benefits in addition to salary. Benefits often include retirement plans, insurance plans, and leave policies. Some colleges also offer faculty housing. Occasionally, this housing is without cost, but usually there is a modest rental fee.

Conditions of work

A college or university is usually a pleasant place in which to work. There is an atmosphere of purposefulness and of alertness that usually provides a stimulating environment in which to work.

The college or university faculty member will often have to share an office with one or more colleagues. One seldom will have a private secretary, but will share secretarial service with one or several fellow faculty members.

Except for their time in class, the announced office hours when they meet with students, and the time needed for their academic meetings, college faculty members' time may be arranged as they see fit. They may spend time in study, in research, or in the laboratory. College faculty members establish their own patterns of work, according to their own special needs and interests. Most college teachers work more than 40 hours each week. Although the time spent in class may require only a fraction of the normal working week, the college teacher's many additional duties and interests will keep one on the job a great many hours beyond what is generally considered to be an average working period.

GOE: 11.02.01; SIC: 8221; SOC: 22

◇ SOURCES OF ADDITIONAL INFORMATION

American Association of University Professors
1012 14th Street, NW, Suite 500
Washington, DC 20005

American Federation of Teachers
555 New Jersey Avenue, NW
Washington, DC 20001

National Education Association
1201 16th Street, NW
Washington, DC 20036

Canadian Education Association
#8–200, 252 Bloor Street West
Toronto ON M5V 1V5

College career planning and placement counselors

Definition

Career planning and placement counselors are college personnel workers who help students choose a career, seek out prospective employers in that field, and prepare for interviewing and other job search techniques.

History

In the United States, the first funded employment office was established in San Francisco in 1886. There, employers would gather with men seeking jobs, and agreements were reached on the basis of capability and demand. Today the system is a highly evolved one, and public and private placement services perform the essential task of matching skills and jobs in our complex society.

Nature of the work

College career planning and placement counselors may specialize in some specific area appropriate to the students and graduates of the school, such as law and education, part-time and summer work, internships, and field placements. In a liberal arts college, the students may need more assistance in identifying an appropriate career. To do this, the counselor administers interest and aptitude tests and interviews the student to determine career goals.

The counselor may work with currently enrolled students who are seeking internships and other work programs while still at school. Alumni who wish to make a career change also seek the services of the career counseling and placement office at their former school.

College placement counselors also gather complete job information from prospective employers, and make the information available to interested students and alumni. Just as counselors try to find an applicant for a particular job listing, they also must seek out jobs for specific applicants. To do this, they will call potential employers to encourage them to hire a qualified individual.

College placement and career planning counselors are responsible for the arrangements and details of on-campus interviews by large corporations and maintain an up-to-date library of vocational guidance material and recruitment literature.

Counselors also give assistance in preparing the actual job search by helping the applicant to write resumes and letters of application, as well as by practicing interview skills through role-playing and other techniques. They also provide information on business procedures and personnel requirements in the applicant's chosen field.

Some career and placement counselors work with secondary school authorities, advising them on the needs of local industry and specific preparation requirements both for employment and for further education. In two-year colleges the counselor may participate in the planning of course content, and in some smaller schools the counselor may be required to teach as well.

Requirements

A master's degree in guidance and counseling, education, college student personnel work, a behavioral science, or related fields is commonly the minimum educational requirement for becoming a college career planning and placement counselor. Graduate work includes courses in vocational and aptitude testing, counseling techniques, personnel management and occupational research, industrial relations, and group dynamics and organizational behavior.

Opportunities for experience and exploration

Students interested in this career should seek out professional placement people and discuss the field with them. In addition they should take courses in psychology, sociology, counseling, personnel administration, and business subjects.

Methods of entering

Sometimes alumni interested in working for their alma mater find employment as an assistant in the college or university placement office. Other occupational areas that provide an excellent background for college placement work include teaching, business, public relations, previous placement training, positions in employment agencies, and experience in psychological counseling.

Advancement

Opportunity for advancement to assistant and associate placement director, director of student personnel services, or similar administrative positions depends largely upon the type of college or university and the size of the staff. In general, a doctorate is preferred and may be necessary for advancement.

Employment outlook

In the United States more than 5,000 people work as college career and placement counselors in the 1990s. There will be few job opportunities in college placement through the late 1990s because of an anticipated leveling off in the enrollment of students. Therefore, competition in this field will be stiff. Graduates that have a master's degree in counseling or a related field, in addition to a business or industry background, will have the advantage in finding employment.

Earnings

Annual earnings of career planning and placement counselors in the 1990s vary greatly among educational institutions. The average salary is about $31,200. Earnings are lowest in the Southeast and highest in the Far West. Larger institutions generally offer the highest salaries. Benefits include holidays and vacations, pension and retirement plans, and in some institutions, reduced tuition.

Conditions of work

Although college placement and career planning counselors normally work a 40-hour week,

A college career planning and placement counselor goes over a student's aptitude test with him, discussing possible colleges he may apply to.

irregular hours and overtime are frequently required during the peak recruiting period. Counselors receive the same employment benefits as other professional personnel employed by colleges and universities, and generally work on a 12-month basis.

GOE: 10.01.02; SIC: 8221; SOC: 24

◇ **SOURCES OF ADDITIONAL INFORMATION**

American Association for Counseling and Development
5999 Stevenson Avenue
Alexandria, VA 22304

College Placement Council
62 Highland Avenue
Bethlehem, PA 18017

Canadian Guidance and Councilling Foundation
#202, 411 Roosevelt Avenue
Ottawa ON K2A 3X9

For information on colleges and universities that offer training in guidance and counseling as well as on state certification and licensure requirements, contact your state department of education.

For information about job opportunities and entrance requirements, contact your state employment service office.

◇ **RELATED ARTICLES**

Volume 1: Education; Social Services
Volumes 2–4: Career counselors; Career guidance technicians; College administrators; Employment counselors; Employment firm workers; Guidance counselors; Personnel and labor relations specialists; Psychologists

Comedians

Definition

Comedians are entertainers who make people laugh. They use a variety of techniques to amuse their audiences, including telling jokes, composing and singing humorous songs, wearing funny costumes, and doing impersonations. Comedians perform in nightclubs, comedy clubs, coffee houses, theaters, television shows, films, and even business functions, such as trade shows and sales meetings. Comedians often travel around the country, performing in front of thousands of people or relatively small crowds, depending on their popularity and skill.

History

Throughout history, people have enjoyed humorous interpretations of the events that make up their daily lives. Comedy began as a type of drama that presented events in a comic way and thereby sought to amuse its audience. These dramas were not always funny, yet they were usually lighthearted and had happy endings (as opposed to tragedies that had sad endings).

The Greeks and Romans had playwrights such as Aristophanes and Plautus who successfully used humor as a type of mirror on the social and political customs of the time. They wrote plays that highlighted some of the particularities of the rich and powerful as well as common people. In later years, the English playwright William Shakespeare and the French playwright Moliere used wit and humor

to point out some of the shortcomings of society. In more recent times, the Austrian-born playwright Fritz Hochwalder sometimes used satire to accent the darker side of human nature.

Comedy is, of course, not simply confined to the theater. In the early part of the 20th century there were the slapstick movies of the Keystone Cops and Buster Keaton. Some of Charlie Chaplin's films also used the technique of farce and wild chase scenes to create comedic situations. The Marx Brothers were masters of the use of insults and sight gags to create a sense of anarchy and in that way to poke fun at the rich and powerful.

Stand-up comedians have also played a role in the development of comedy. Stand-up comedians, such as Milton Berle and Bob Hope, performed in nightclubs and other venues, and often used current events in their routines. These comedians were performers who had started their careers in vaudeville as stage entertainers.

As with other types of comedy, stand-up comedians did more than simply make people laugh—they attempted to make people think. The stand-up comedian was a social critic who used humor as the medium for the message. For example, in the early 1960s Lenny Bruce caused a great deal of controversy in the United States by using his nightclub routines to question the role of organized religion in society and argue for less censorship.

Currently, comedy enjoys wide popularity as a performing art. There are hundreds of comedy clubs across the country, and audiences are flocking to see stand-up comedians, comedy improvisational groups, and film and television comedies.

Nature of the work

Although making people laugh may sound like a pretty simple assignment, comedians work very hard at this task. It is a fine line between being funny and being silly, and a good comedian is able to make people laugh without resorting to gimmicks or immature pranks.

Comedians may use colorful costumes, music, or other techniques to create a festive atmosphere, or they may appear in regular attire. In any case, it is the writing and timing that makes a comedian unique. Each comedian will attempt to develop a style that presents events in a humorous and memorable way.

Perhaps the most common form of comedic performance is the stand-up comic. Stand-up comedians usually perform in nightclubs or comedy clubs, entertaining audiences with jokes, stories, and impressions.

Stand-up comedians often travel around the country, performing in a variety of settings. They may have to adapt their performances somewhat, depending on the makeup of the audience. The length of the performance is determined by whether the comedian is the main act or an opening act. A main act will last from 30 minutes to an hour, while an opening act may be just a few minutes.

Another popular type of comedy show is the comedy improvisational group. Improvisation is a form of acting in which no set script is used and actors make up their own dialogue as they go along. The improvisational form allows for a kind of spontaneity that traditional performances do not. These groups perform comedic skits and dances, sing humorous songs, and otherwise amuse their audiences. Many comedy groups will perform a number of scripted skits and then improvise a number of skits based on audience suggestions.

Comedians are story tellers. No matter where they perform, they engage their audiences and make the audiences care about their characters. Many comedians use their own life stories as material, weaving a picture of people and places designed not only to evoke laughter but also understanding.

Comedians may perform their work live or on tape. Usually a taping is done in front of an audience, as comedians need the laughter and other feedback of an audience to be most effective.

Comedians who perform on film or television have the same restrictions as other actors and actresses. They must adhere to strict schedules and perform routines repeatedly before the director decides a scene is finished.

As with other performance artists, comedians often find themselves looking for employ-

Comedian Eddie Murphy jokes with talk-show host Arsenio Hall, while taping *The Late Show* program.

ment. Comedians may work for a number of weeks in a row and then face a period of unemployment. To find work, many comedians hire booking agents to locate club owners willing to hire them. Other comedians attempt to find work on their own. A person's success in finding work will be largely influenced by skill and style, but also to an extent by personal contacts and a bit of good fortune.

For comedians who are uncomfortable in front of an audience, there is the opportunity to write material for other performers. Not all people who write comedic material are former comedians, but all understand elements of humor and ways of using words and images to make people laugh.

Requirements

The overriding requirement for a comedian is to be funny. There are no set educational standards, and few colleges and universities offer specific courses on how to become a comedian. Nevertheless, becoming a comedian is not a secret. It takes a lot of hard work and, as with

COMEDIANS

other performance skills, practice, practice, practice. Many communities have improvisational groups that provide a training ground for aspiring actors and comedians. Some comedy clubs may also offer classes.

Making people laugh is not a skill that is easily taught. Most good comedians have an inborn talent and have made jokes or performed humorous skits since childhood. This means more than simply being the class clown; it is the ability to see events in a humorous light and share this perspective with others. Above all else, a comedian must have a keen sense of timing. A funny line, delivered improperly, often sounds rather ordinary.

Comedians come in all shapes and sizes. Indeed, it is often the person who looks and feels somewhat different who is able to see the foibles of human nature and develop material that pokes fun at society without being nasty. A comedian should be able to take material from his or her own background (be it growing up in a small town, having overbearing parents, or other situation) and interpret this material in such a way that it has an appeal to others.

A comedian should obviously have good communications skills and be able to write in a succinct and humorous manner. It is also necessary to have a strong stage presence. Often, budding comedians will take English and composition classes, as well as speech and acting courses, to help develop skills in these areas. Accounting and bookkeeping skills are also helpful, as comedians usually have to prepare their own financial records.

Comedians should be keen observers of daily life and be perceptive enough to recognize the humor in day-to-day events. But comedians should not be overly sensitive and become unduly disappointed if audiences do not respond to their jokes at every performance.

Opportunities for experience and exploration

The field of comedy offers a number of good opportunities for career exploration. For example, many improvisational groups have classes in acting and performance techniques. These groups are a good place to learn skills, make contacts, and have fun. Of course, there is no substitute for hands-on experience and most comedy clubs and coffee houses have "open mike" nights where aspiring comedians can get on stage and try out their material in front of a real audience. For those who are uncomfortable

performing in front of strangers, it might be possible to stage a performance for family and friends.

It is also possible to learn by watching. Going to a comedy club or coffee house to observe comedians is a very good way to learn about the performance aspects of this career. It is also possible to talk informally with a comedian and in this way learn more about the profession. There are also a number of books that describe exercises and techniques for comedians.

Methods of entering

Getting started as a comedian is often very difficult. There are thousands of people who want to make people laugh, but relatively few venues for aspiring comedians to get exposure.

To find an opportunity to perform, a comedian may have to repeatedly call local nightclubs, bars, or coffee houses. Generally, these clubs will already have a number of comedians they use.

A very common way for a comedian to get his or her first break is to audition at a local club. These auditions are not private showings for club owners, but rather actual performances in front of audiences. Usually, comedians are not paid at these auditions, but those who show the most promise are often invited back to put on paid performances.

Many comedians also begin their careers as part of a comedy improvisational group. These groups offer novice comedians a chance to refine their skills, developing techniques and contacts before starting out on their own. On the national level, comedians such as Eddie Murphy, Chevy Chase, and Gilda Radner received wide exposure as part of the Saturday Night Live improvisational group before beginning lucrative individual careers. Of course, many comedians choose to remain in improvisational groups throughout their careers.

Advancement

Many comedians begin work as stand-up comedians at local clubs while others begin as part of an improvisation group. Those who find success and satisfaction at this level may go on to perform at larger clubs and theaters. Some may also find work in the corporate world, entertaining at trade shows and other meetings. Extremely successful comedians may go on to tape comedy routines for broadcast or even have their own television shows.

Comedians may also branch out somewhat in their career goals. Some may choose to write material for other comedians or review comedic performances for the local media. There are also some who choose to become comedy club owners or talent agents, creating employment opportunities for other comedians.

Comedy writers may go on to work for advertising agencies, using humor as a means of creating commercials or other promotional materials. Others may develop television or movie scripts.

Employment outlook

As with the other performance arts, there will always be more people who want to be comedians than there are job opportunities. Comedians, however, enjoy more solid employment prospects than actors or actresses. There are hundreds of comedy clubs across the country (usually in larger cities) and each club needs performers to get their audiences laughing. Of course, the most lucrative jobs will go to those with the best reputation, but thousands of comedians will continue to find work throughout the 1990s.

There is also a growing trend for private companies to hire comedians to perform at sales meetings and trade shows. The comedians are used to increase interest in products and create an enjoyable sales environment. Talent agencies now increasingly book comedians to work at these events.

For those who choose to work as comedy writers or entertainment critics, the competition for jobs should be keen, yet there are good career opportunities. There are a large number of comedy shows on the national networks and on cable television, and these should provide a good market for skilled comedy writers.

Earnings

People who only look at the incomes of well known comedians will get a mistaken notion of how much comedians earn. Eddie Murphy or Andrew Dice Clay might earn $200,000 for one performance, but the vast majority of comedians earn far more average wages. In fact, many comedians practice their craft part-time (evenings and weekends) and have other full- or part-time jobs.

In large comedy clubs, a headline comedian can expect to earn between $1,000 and $20,000 per week, depending on his or her drawing power. Those who perform as an opening act might earn between $125 and $350 per week. Headline comedians at smaller clubs will earn between $300 and $800 per week. Of course, those just starting out will earn very little (remember, most club owners do not pay comedians who are auditioning); yet beginners will be in a good position to learn the craft and make valuable contacts.

Comedians who entertain at trade shows and sales meetings can earn several hundred dollars per show, yet these assignments tend to be infrequent.

Comedy writers have a very wide pay scale. Those who write for well known comedians are paid about $50 for every joke used. (Of course, many jokes are rejected by the performer.) Full-time comedy writers for the *Tonight Show* and other television shows can expect to earn between $50,000 and $150,000 per year, depending on their skill, experience, and the budget of the show.

Conditions of work

Full-time comedians usually spend a lot of time traveling between shows. A comedian may have a strong following in the Midwest, for example, and in the course of a week have two shows in Detroit, two shows in Chicago, and a show in St. Louis. Some people may find this life-style exciting, but for many it is exhausting and somewhat lonely. Those who perform as part of an improvisational troupe may also travel a lot.

Once a comedian has developed a good following, the traveling may subside somewhat. Often, a comedian will perform at one or two clubs in the same city on a fairly regular basis.

Performing in front of an audience can be very demanding. Not all audiences are receptive (especially to new material) and a comedian may encounter unresponsive crowds. It is also not uncommon for comedians to perform for small audiences in bars and nightclubs. Many of these nightclubs may be small, dark, and filled with smoke.

Despite these challenges, comedians can have fascinating careers. They experience the thrill of performing in front of audiences, and having an impact on people's lives. Comedians may go on to achieve a good deal of fame, especially those who perform on television or in the movies.

As creative artists, comedians may find it very satisfying to express their views and get positive feedback from others. There can be a lot of pleasure in making people laugh and seeing others enjoy themselves.

Comedians usually work late into the night, often not starting performances until 9 P.M. or 10 P.M. They also generally work on weekends, when people have more time to go to nightclubs and comedy clubs. For those who work as part-time comedians, it is not uncommon to have a day job and then perform at night.

Comedy writers may also have to work at other jobs to make ends meet financially. They might prepare material in their homes or in small offices with other writers.

Full-time writers for movies and television shows may have a more traditional 9–5 work schedule, although it is also not uncommon to work a great deal of overtime when preparing for a show.

GOE: 01.03.02; SIC: 7929; SOC: 328

Commercial artists

Definition

Commercial artists create artwork that is designed to attract the attention of readers or viewers and to stimulate their interest in particular products or ideas found in publications, packaging, television, or advertising. Commercial artists specialize in various types of art or in one communications media.

Commercial art differs from fine art in that it is normally done to enhance or promote a product. Some commercial art, however, may cross over as fine art if it is executed well. Fine art is art admired on its own merit.

Commercial artists work for a variety of employers, including advertising agencies, publishing houses, retail stores, public relations firms, and government agencies. A majority are self-employed.

History

Art has long been used as a means of communication. Although language developed to communicate knowledge and ideas more effectively and productively, art has developed as a means for communicating some of the more intense emotional aspects of life. Historically, art and literature have been considered the chief sources of knowledge about other people and other cultures. Commercial art might be considered that pictorial part of a civilization devoted to communicating the various ways in which the products of its businesses and industries can be useful.

Commercial art is a relatively new field. With the growth of American business and industry and increased competition for markets, the work of the commercial artist has assumed considerable importance. Producers of similar products are competing for customers. Producers of different products, although not in direct competition, must attract the potential buyer by indicating the significance of their own product. The necessity to advertise has long been recognized, but the emphasis on the communicative aspects of art, as a result of newspapers, magazines, and television, has grown rapidly.

Nature of the work

Commercial artists prepare illustrations and designs for advertisements and displays such as those in newspapers, magazines, and television commercials; food store displays; packaging for various merchandise; wallpaper and gift wrapping designs; greeting card illustrations; and roadside billboards. They may also illustrate magazine articles or books, or deal with the production of spot illustrations or cartoons.

The work involves drawing; sketching; painting; lettering; retouching photographs; making charts, maps, and cartoons; or designing to communicate an idea.

Most commercial artists begin their careers as paste-up and mechanical artists, letterers, or assistant package designers. They may advance to various positions depending upon their qualifications and interests.

Graphic designers, or *layout artists,* plan the style and arrangement of photographs, artwork, and type for communications media such as books, magazines, newspapers, television, and print or TV advertising. They prepare sample layouts and supervise the work of others who execute the ideas. Book designers are graphic artists who specialize in books, including the design of book jackets, selection of type, and illustrations for the text.

Illustrators prepare drawings and illustrations for consumer advertisements and illustrations for magazine articles and books. *Medical and scientific illustrators* have training in biology and the physical sciences so they can draw accurate illustrations of parts of the human body, animals, or plants. Their work is in demand for use in textbooks, medical journals, lecture presentations, and medical advertising. *Fashion illustrators* specialize in distinctive illustrations of the latest women's and men's fashions.

Two other specialties among commercial artists are *cartoonists* and *animators*. Cartoonists draw newspaper comic strips, political cartoons, or comic books. They must have the creative ability to generate ideas or work with a partner who thinks up the ideas. Animators draw a series of many pictures that are put onto film to make an animated cartoon. Most animators are employed in the motion picture industry.

The commercial artist gets a starting idea from the producers of goods, who describe the message they want to convey and the various media and materials that might be used. Preliminary sketches or designs are prepared to show the general arrangement of the illustration and the amount of space to be used. Layout work, beyond the preliminary or draft

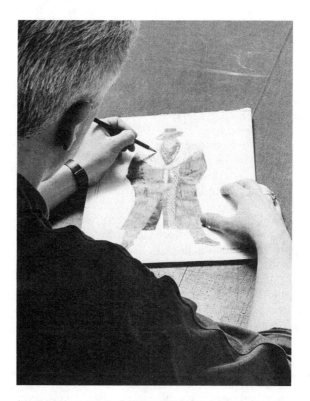

A textile designer puts the finishing touches on a sketch of menswear.

stage, focuses on the size, color, and arrangement of pictured and lettered material.

Requirements

An artistic ability is the most important requirement for this career. The ability to draw, to sketch, or to letter is basic. One also needs to know how to deal with color and composition. Most important in an artist is an ability to come up with original ideas, to be imaginative and creative, and to think of new ways to express both old and new ideas.

Persistence is also essential. Commercial artists must be able to stick with a project not only until they are satisfied but also until they satisfy others. Thus, they must be able to take correction and be able to work with others on special group assignments.

Although natural ability and certain personal qualifications are a basic consideration, training in the techniques of applied art is an essential part of the preparation of the commercial artist. High school art courses offer an opportunity to study the fundamentals of design and color, and the basic lettering and drawing techniques. Because the commercial artist is required to work on projects dealing with all phases of society and life, a general academic education and extensive educational training in the fine arts of painting, sculpture, and architecture are important parts of the preparation. Preparation beyond high school can be secured at four-year colleges or universities, junior colleges, or specialized art schools.

A growing number of art schools, particularly those connected with a university, require four or more years of study and offer a bachelor of fine arts degree. In this course of study, the student gets a liberal arts education, plus work in perspective, design, color harmony, composition, use of pencil, pen, and other art media. Subsequent study includes drawing from real life, advertising layout, lettering, typography, and illustration.

Experience in photography is sometimes useful, as is some background in business practices. Freelance commercial artists must have the ability to sell themselves and their work. Students interested in medical or scientific illustrating should obtain education in the area of interest. College courses in science, as well as in the arts, are essential.

Commercial artists usually maintain a portfolio containing examples of their best work. The portfolio is essential in seeking employment, particularly initial employment, and in obtaining freelance assignments.

Opportunities for experience and exploration

Most elementary, junior high, and senior high school programs provide opportunities for students to explore their interest in art and to identify their strengths and weaknesses. In many schools, students have formal art courses in which they are exposed to a variety of art media. Special projects as part of other courses or as part of in-school or out-of-school activities (posters for various events, holiday and extracurricular organization decorations, or school bulletin boards) also can be used to explore one's interest and ability in activities similar in nature to the duties of a commercial artist.

At the senior high school or higher education level, part-time and summer work possibilities offer a chance to observe actual working conditions. Many talented individuals will find their services in demand in connection with local fund-raising drives or community events. Some students, to gain experience, have offered their services to local merchants.

Methods of entering

Graduates of commercial art schools and college or university art programs will find the placement services of their institutions helpful in locating positions. Each year a number of openings become available in the advertising departments of business and industrial firms, advertising agencies, and commercial art studios. Many firms and business organizations, such as greeting card companies, television studios, motion picture studios, department stores, sign shops, publishing firms, and printing houses, employ a number of staff artists.

Many initial jobs in commercial art are routine, and beginning commercial artists are apt to assist the more experienced artists. They may perform routine color or layout jobs, make corrections, or paste and assemble model advertisements. On-the-job training is a vital part of one's program of preparation and serves as a means of getting started in the field. Some apprenticeship opportunities, for those who are unable to finance training in art beyond high school, are available in printing, display, and outdoor advertising.

Advancement

Young artists who show ability in beginning jobs can look forward to advancement as layout artists, illustrators, and letterers or to other specialized functions within the field. Some become art directors and assume major executive positions; others move to freelance work after having established a good reputation. From on-the-job apprentice or helper levels of employment, one becomes more involved with the creative and challenging aspects of technical and managerial problems.

Employment outlook

Employment in this field is expected to grow rapidly through the 1990s. Increased emphasis on visual appeal in communications, products, and services will result in the creation of new jobs in television marketing, advertising agencies, and graphic arts studios. Many are attracted to what they consider a glamorous field, however, making the competition heavy for salaried and freelance jobs. Nevertheless, artists with exceptional talent are always in great demand; those with outstanding portfolios will be shown preference by employers.

Commercial artists and graphic designers hold about 230,000 jobs in the 1990s. Almost 60 percent of these workers are self-employed. The majority of commercial artists work in large cities such as New York, Boston, Chicago, Los Angeles, and San Francisco, where the largest users of commercial art are located. Employers of commercial artists include advertising agencies and graphic arts studios; publishers of books, magazines, newspapers, catalogs, and calendars; companies that publish house journals; and organizations that handle their own advertising, such as retail stores, motion picture and television companies, government agencies, and firms that manufacture appliances, home furnishings, and other durable goods. In addition, commercial artists work for public relations and publicity firms, commercial printers, display companies, and mail order houses.

Earnings

Earnings depend upon the experience and background of the artist. In the 1990s, beginners with a degree in design or graphic design earn an average salary of $20,400. The median income for all full-time salaried commercial artists is $21,400 a year; average annual salaries range from $15,700 to $29,600. An experienced specialist can earn as much as $100,000 a year.

It is most difficult to establish the earnings of the freelance commercial artist for a number of reasons: the income is dependent upon the amount of artwork sold; the fee for various artists is related in part to their reputation and the demand for their work; and costs for different types of work vary. Because of the many variables, the income of freelance commercial artists ranges from as little as $12,500 a year to over $100,000.

Conditions of work

The commercial artist generally works 35 to 40 hours weekly. Occasionally, the production or seasonal demands of the employer necessitate work under pressure with strict deadlines and, sometimes, budget limitations. The tensions of rush work, particularly if the project involves a considerable amount of creativity, are further complicated when the job requires the cooperation of a number of individuals. The commercial artist works in well lighted, ventilated studios or offices. The freelance artist usually works irregular hours.

GOE: 01.02.03; SIC: 7336; SOC: 322

◇ **SOURCES OF ADDITIONAL INFORMATION**

American Institute of Graphic Arts
1059 Third Avenue
New York, NY 10021

Association of Medical Illustrators
1819 Peachtree Street NE
Atlanta, GA 30309

National Association of Schools of Art and Design
11250 Roger Bacon Drive, Suite 21
Reston, VA 22090

National Cartoonists Society
157 West 57th Street, Suite 904
New York, NY 10019

Society of Illustrators
128 East 63rd Street
New York, NY 10021

Society of Publication Designers
60 East 42nd Street, Suite 1416
New York, NY 10165

Canadian Graphics Arts Institute
19 Duncan Street
Toronto ON M5H 3H1

◇ **RELATED ARTICLES**

Volume 1: Advertising; Book Publishing; Design; Magazine Publishing; Newspaper Publishing; Packaging; Textiles
Volumes 2–4: Advertising workers; Art directors; Cartoonists and animators; Drafting and design technicians; Fashion designers; Graphics designers; Industrial designers; Interior designers and decorators; Lithographic occupations; Painters and sculptors; Photoengravers

Communications equipment mechanics

Definition

Communications equipment mechanics install, repair, and maintain electronic communications equipment, especially equipment used in telephone switching and transmission systems. Most communications equipment mechanics work in telephone company offices or on customers' premises.

History

Alexander Graham Bell patented the first practical telephone in 1876. By 1878, a commercial telephone company that switched calls between its local customers was operating in New Haven, Connecticut. For many years, telephone connections were made by operators who worked at central offices of telephone companies. A company customer who wanted to speak with another customer had to call the operator at a central office, and the operator would connect the two customer lines together by inserting a metal plug into a socket.

Today, automatic switching equipment has replaced operators for routine connections like this, and telephones are carrying much more than voice messages between local customers. Vast quantities of information are sent across phone lines in the form of visual images, computer data, and telegraph and teletypewriter signals. Furthermore, telephone systems today are part of larger interconnected telecommunications systems. These systems link together telephones with other equipment that sends information via microwave and television transmissions, fiber optics cables, undersea cables, and signals bounced off satellites in space. High-speed computerized switching and routing equipment makes it possible for telecommunications systems to handle millions of calls and other data signals at the same time.

As telecommunications equipment has evolved from simple switchboards to complicated modern systems, telephone companies have established increasingly complex installations, housed in many branch offices. A variety of occupations have also evolved to meet the need to install and maintain the equipment. Today's communications equipment mechanics include specialists who work on many different components of the global telecommunications network.

Nature of the work

In general, communications equipment mechanics are concerned with making sure that telecommunications systems stay in good working order. Most workers in this group are employed by telephone companies or by equipment manufacturers, and many work at telephone company installations. Depending on their particular specialty, they may install, test, and calibrate different kinds of equipment, check it for malfunctions, and clean and repair it.

Central office equipment installers, also called *equipment installation technicians*, are specialists in setting up and taking down the switching and dialing equipment located in telephone company central offices. They install equipment in newly established offices, update existing equipment, add on to facilities that are being expanded, and remove old, outdated apparatus. To do this work, they follow diagrams and blueprints and use a variety of hand and power tools. Their job may take them to different central offices, perhaps located throughout an assigned territory that includes several states. On small jobs, installers may work with only one or two other installers, but on large projects they may be part of a crew that includes several hundred other workers.

Central office repairers, also called *switching equipment technicians* or *central office technicians*, work on the switching equipment that automatically connects lines when customers dial calls. They analyze defects and malfunctions in equipment, make fine adjustments, and test and repair switches and relays. Some switching equipment contains moving parts that need to be kept cleaned and greased. These workers use various special tools, gauges, meters, and ordinary hand tools.

Frame wirers work at the distributing frames or panels where customers' lines come into the central office. Following printed diagrams, they connect and disconnect wires and cables, inspect and repair wires, and remake connections to change circuit layouts. They use soldering irons and other hand tools.

Trouble locators, or *transmission testers*, test customers' lines within the central office to find causes and locations of malfunctions reported by customers. They report the nature of the trouble to maintenance crews and coordinate their activities to clear up the trouble. They may contact customers to arrange service calls. Trouble locators work at special switchboards equipped with devices that help them find the sources of problems in the system. They also use electrical testing devices such as voltmeters. Some trouble locators work in cable television company offices, diagnosing subscribers' problems with cable television signals and dispatching repairers if necessary.

Many telephone companies are replacing trouble locators with *maintenance administrators,* who perform essentially the same kind of task but who use much more highly automated testboards and other equipment to analyze circuits. Maintenance administrators enter data into computer files and interpret computer output about trouble areas in the system.

Other workers in this field are concerned with PBXs, or private branch exchanges, which are direct telephone lines that businesses install to bypass regular phone company lines. PBX equipment can handle both voice and data communications and can provide specialized services like electronic mail and automatic routing of calls at the lowest possible cost. *PBX installers* install these systems. They may assemble customized switchboards for customers. *PBX repairers* maintain and repair PBX systems and associated equipment. In addition, they may work on mobile radiophones and microwave transmission devices.

Many workers in this group are concerned with other kinds of communications equipment that are not part of telephone systems. Among these are *radio repairers and mechanics,* who install and repair radio transmitters and receivers. Sometimes they work on other electronics equipment at microwave and fiber optics installations. *Submarine cable equipment technicians* work on the machines and equipment used to send messages through underwater cables. Working in cable offices and stations, they check and adjust transmitters and printers and repair or replace faulty parts. *Office electricians* maintain submarine cable circuits and rearrange connections to ensure that cable service is not interrupted. *Avionics technicians* work on the electronic components in aircraft communication, navigation, and flight control systems. *Signal maintainers* or *track switch maintainers* work on railroads. They install, inspect, and maintain the signals, track switches, gate crossings, and communications systems throughout rail networks. *Instrument repairers* work in repair shops, where they repair, test, and modify a variety of communications equipment.

A communications equipment mechanic repairs a large switchboard panel. Such work requires a steady hand.

Requirements

Employers of communications equipment mechanics generally prefer applicants who have prior training in electronics, acquired informally at another job or in formal training programs, such as those offered by vocational schools, technical institutes, junior and community colleges, correspondence courses, some high schools, and the armed forces. Even entry-level positions in this field may require previous training in electronics. The programs that provide suitable training for the different kinds of communications equipment mechanics vary somewhat in content and length. They may take one to two years to complete.

Applicants for entry-level positions may have to pass tests of their knowledge and tests that determine their general mechanical aptitude and manual dexterity. Once hired, employees often go through company training programs. They may study practical and theoretical aspects of electricity, electronics, and mathematics that they will need to know for

353

their work. Experienced workers also may attend training sessions from time to time. They need to keep their knowledge up to date as new technology in the rapidly changing telecommunications field affects the way they do their jobs.

Special requirements

Some communications equipment mechanics must be able to identify the different color-coded wires in telephone equipment, so they cannot be color-blind.

Some workers in this field must obtain a license. Federal Communications Commission (FCC) regulations require that anyone who works with radio transmitting equipment must have a restricted radiotelephone operator's license. Such a license is issued upon application to the FCC and is granted for life.

Opportunities for experience and exploration

In high school, students can begin to find out about the work of communications equipment mechanics by taking whatever electronics, computer, and electrical shop courses are available, and also other shop courses that help them become familiar with using various tools. Teachers or guidance counselors may be able to help interested students to arrange a visit to a telephone company central office where they can see telephone equipment and observe workers on the job. It may be possible to obtain a part-time or summer helper job at a business that sells and repairs electronics equipment. Such a job could provide the opportunity to talk to workers whose skills are like those needed by many communications equipment mechanics. Serving in the armed forces in a communications section can be an excellent way to learn about this field and gain some useful experience.

Methods of entering

People who are interested in becoming communications equipment mechanics can apply directly to the employment office of the local telephone company. New employees often start out as frame wirers. The mechanics and technicians who work in central offices are fre-

quently workers who have transferred from other positions within the same company or another company in the industry. Outside applicants who do not already have good training and skills are likely to face especially stiff competition.

Manufacturers of telephone and other electronic communications equipment also employ these workers, and job seekers can apply directly to such companies. Information on job openings in this field may be available through the offices of the state employment service. Because many communications equipment mechanics are members of unions such as the Communications Workers of America and the International Brotherhood of Electrical Workers, job seekers can try contacting their local offices for job leads and assistance.

Advancement

The advancement possibilities for communications equipment mechanics depend on the area of the telecommunications industry in which they work. The key to advancement for many of these workers will be additional training and new skills.

Technical workers in telephone central offices are usually given regular promotions after they have gained work experience. Frame wirers may move into positions as central office repairers and trouble locators. Becoming a central office equipment installer requires completing a special training program. Some workers can become supervisors or administrative staff workers. With further training, perhaps at an engineering college or technical institute, they may become engineering assistants.

For many of these workers, however, advancement will be complicated by the changes that the telephone industry is presently undergoing. New electronic equipment is being installed that will reduce the need for many kinds of workers, and those who stay in the field will have to compete for fewer positions. Workers with the best qualifications will stand the best chance of advancing to the most desirable jobs.

Employment outlook

Employment of communications equipment mechanics is expected to decline significantly during the next 10 to 15 years. This is because some areas of the telecommunications industry, and the telephone industry in particular, is in the process of being completely transformed by new technology. Maintenance and repair work on the new equipment will require fewer workers than the industry has employed in the past.

The old equipment that relies partly on electromechanical devices is being replaced with new electronic equipment that is much more trouble-free. Telephone systems are coming to depend entirely on computers and software to switch calls, not mechanical devices that break, wear out, and need to be periodically cleaned and lubricated. The new systems are compact and reliable and have features that let them diagnose their own malfunctions. When problems occur, it is usually possible simply to replace parts rather than repair them. By the time the industry has completed its changeover, many communications equipment mechanics will be laid off.

Nonetheless, every year some new workers will be hired to replace workers who change to other occupations or leave the labor force.

Earnings

Earnings of communications equipment mechanics vary, with some employers paying more than others. Most workers in this group who are employed by telephone companies are union members, and their earnings are set by contracts between the union and the company. According to information on one large group of union workers in the telephone industry, central office installers, central office technicians, and PBX installers together average at least $36,000 a year; frame wirers average over $31,000; and telephone installers and repairers average $36,000 or more. Starting pay for some workers is in the range of $16,000.

Most workers in this field receive extra pay for hours worked at night or on weekends. In addition, they usually receive fringe benefits that include paid vacations, sick leave, group insurance plans, and retirement pensions.

Conditions of work

Communications equipment mechanics usually work 40 hours a week. Some work shifts at night, on weekends, or on holidays, because telecommunications systems must give uninterrupted service and trouble can occur at any time.

Central telephone offices are clean, well lighted, and well ventilated. The telephone industry's safety record is among the best.

GOE: 05.05.05, 05.10.03; SIC: 1731; SOC: 615

◇ **SOURCES OF ADDITIONAL INFORMATION**

Communications Workers of America
501 Third Street, NW
Washington, DC 20001

International Brotherhood of Electrical Workers
1125 15th Street, NW
Washington, DC 20005

United States Telephone Association
900 19th Street, NW, Suite 800
Washington, DC 20006

◇ **RELATED ARTICLES**

Volume 1: Electronics; Telecommunications
Volumes 2–4: Avionics technicians; Electromechanical technicians; Electronics technicians; Instrument repairers; Office-machine servicers; Telephone and PBX installers and repairers

Compositors and typesetters

Definition

Compositors and *typesetters* set type, design and lay out pages, and make photographic images of text and pictures. Traditionally, compositors and typesetters worked on large, complicated machines that produced metal type from molten lead. Today, most compositors and typesetters work with computers and with various photographic or video devices. The two terms, "compositors" and "typesetters," have essentially the same meaning and are used interchangeably in the industry.

History

The history of modern printing begins with the invention of movable type in the 15th century. The first complete book known to have been printed from movable type was a Bible produced in Germany by Johannes Gutenberg around 1455. For several centuries before that, some books had been printed from carved wooden blocks. But most of the books of ancient and medieval times were laboriously copied by hand. They were so expensive that they were chained so they could not be stolen.

Gutenberg's movable type made it possible to use the same letters over and over. This reduced the cost and difficulty of making the books, and books rapidly became more plentiful.

Benjamin Franklin, the famous American inventor, diplomat, and political leader of the 1700s, was also a printer. He began as an apprentice printer and later held several exalted positions in government. Yet in the beginning of his will, written when he was 86, he identified himself as a printer. Peter Zenger, the 18th century printer who ardently fought for freedom of the press, is another example of a printer who realized the power and privilege of his craft.

Ottmar Mergenthaler, a German immigrant to the United States, invented the Linotype machine in 1886. Linotype allowed the typesetter to set type from a keyboard which used a mechanical device to set letters in place. Before this invention, printers were setting type by hand, one letter at a time, picking up each letter individually from their typecases as they had been doing for more than 400 years. At about the same time, Tolbert Lanston invented the Monotype machine, which also had a keyboard but set the type as individual letters. These inventions allowed compositors to set type much faster and more efficiently. Using these machines, newspapers advanced from the small two-page weekly of Franklin's time to the huge editions of today's metropolitan daily press. The volume of other periodicals, advertisements, books, and other printed matter has also greatly increased.

In the 1950s, a new system called photocomposition began to be introduced into commercial typesetting operations. In this system, typesetting machines used photographic images of letters, which were projected onto a photosensitive surface to compose pages. Instructions to the typesetting machine about which letters to project and where to project them were fed in through a punched-paper or magnetic tape, which was in turn created by an operator at a keyboard. In time, videocomposition mostly replaced photocomposition. In this newer system, letters exist only in digital form, as a series of bits or bytes in a computer, which are projected as a video image on a photosensitive surface.

Most recently, typesetting has come into the home and office in the form of V publishing programs that can run on a small personal computer. These systems resemble videocomposition systems in that they store letters in digitized form, but they usually rely on laser printers to create an image of a page.

Modern developments in computerized typesetting technology for both commercial applications and for home and office use are changing the face of the typesetting industry. No one can predict what the future of this industry will be. Most likely, successful typesetting companies will be those which take full advantage of the latest developments in technology and find new ways to provide innovative services to their customers.

Nature of the work

Typesetting operations involve a wide range of activities. Some of the most common are design and markup, keyboarding, proofreading, computer operations, paste-up, and camera operation.

Typically, typesetting work on a book or other printed product begins when a manuscript or other kind of prepared copy comes into the typesetting plant. The copy may be from a publishing house or some other source, such as a corporate customer needing to typeset a brochure, catalog, report, or promotional mailing.

Design and markup workers inspect and analyze the manuscript or other copy that is to be typeset. They determine the customer's wishes or make recommendations regarding the size and style of the type to use, how to arrange the type on the page, and how to position illustrations, headings, page numbers, and other printed elements. When they have determined all of the specifications, they mark up the manuscript with all necessary markings so that the keyboard operator will have enough information to keyboard the text.

Keyboard operators create computer files that include the text that will be typeset, as well as all of the necessary computer codes and tags that indicate size and style of type and other information needed by the typesetting equipment to compose pages. Today, many keyboard operators working for typesetting companies are home workers. Home workers come to the office of the typesetting company periodically to pick up or deliver work or to receive instructions or training, but they do most of their work at home, usually on small portable personal computers. Some keyboard operators work in the typesetting plant, usually to handle small jobs that must be done quickly, such as entering proofreading corrections into previously keyboarded material. Many publishers today provide the text of books to typesetters already keyboarded onto floppy disks or diskettes. To some extent, this is reducing the role of keyboard operators within typesetting companies; however, most companies still need well-trained, conscientious workers to handle keyboard operations both inside and outside the office.

Because no keyboard operator can type with perfect accuracy, typesetting companies employ *proofreaders*. Proofreaders carefully read the keyboarded text (usually in the form of a printout or laser printer proof) and compare it to the manuscript or other materials that the keyboard operator worked from. The proofreader marks all necessary corrections onto the printout or proof, using a special set of symbols to indicate changes, insertions, and deletions. Like keyboard operators, many proofreaders are home workers, although some proofreading is also done by in-house personnel.

The heart of all commercial typesetting operations today is the computer. Computers move text files from one workstation or department to another, from markup to input, input

Typesetters use computers to compose text and set it into type. With the aid of software, much of this work can be done in-house.

to proofing, and so on. Computers also reformat text files as they go from a keyboard operator's diskette to a laser printer or to the company's main computer or from the main computer to a page makeup terminal, where details of the final appearance of the page are worked out. Computers also create the final set of instructions that are fed into the composing machine that makes the final page. *Computer operators* in typesetting companies are responsible for all of these activities, as well as the ongoing upkeep and improvements to their machinery—installing new software, new typefaces, and new interfaces to new equipment.

As powerful as computers and computer-driven equipment can be, many typesetting companies still rely on human beings for some aspects of creating a final page. People who do this work are usually called *paste-up workers,* and their activities include positioning illustrations, laying out columns of type, and adding in last-minute changes. Paste-up workers usually work on light tables and do their work with small sharp knives and various kinds of wax, paste, or adhesive tape. The work requires a steady hand and a good eye.

After the final version of the page has been assembled, a photographic negative of the page is made. This negative is used to make the printing plate that goes onto the printing press. Sometimes this work is done by a camera operator in the typesetting plant, and sometimes it is done as part of a prepress operation in the printing plant. In either case, *camera operators* photograph the page to be printed. Operators adjust light and expose the film and then sweep negatives or positives through a series of chemical baths.

As technological and economic forces change the typesetting industry, new jobs may emerge or become more important. Publishing companies may come to rely on typesetting

COMPOSITORS AND TYPESETTERS

companies to assist in designing their publications. If so, *graphics designers* who can select appropriate type faces and arrange text elements on the page in an attractive way may play a more important role within typesetting companies. With the growing importance of computerization, publishing companies may also look to typesetters to be computer service vendors, who reprocess or reformat electronic text files in new ways. As this trend continues, programmers and data analysts will also play an important role in typesetting companies.

Requirements

Educational requirements for compositors and typesetters vary according to the type of work they are doing. Design and makeup workers usually have at least finished high school and often have completed some college as well. They usually have had training in computers, especially in the use of personal computers and word processing software, and some introduction to graphic arts and design.

Most typesetting companies prefer keyboard operators and proofreaders to have a high school diploma. Many operators and proofreaders have education beyond that level. However, the chief requirement for a keyboard operator or proofreader is carefulness and accuracy. Patience and stamina are also important qualities, as both of these jobs can seem boring and it can be difficult to maintain concentration over long periods of time.

Most computer operators in typesetting companies have graduated from either a two-year or four-year college. Typically, they have majored in computer science but also have acquired some training or experience in graphic arts.

Most paste-up artists and camera operators are also high school graduates, and they may have had some college training as well. Paste-up artists especially need training in the graphic arts. Camera operators need to have experience or training in a wide range of photographic equipment and techniques.

Most compositors and typesetters are involved, in one way or another, with the written language. Because of this, typesetting companies look for employees with good language skills—good spelling, a solid understanding of basic grammar and punctuation rules, and a familiarity with the format and appearance of well-printed books. Students can acquire these skills through high school and college English courses, especially those that put emphasis on writing.

Graphic arts courses are taught in many high schools, and some community and technical colleges offer formal graphics arts programs.

Many workers in this field are members of unions.

Opportunities for experience and exploration

Opportunities for exploring this field are plentiful. There are typesetting businesses in many communities. They may admit visitors with appointments, and many will welcome interested young people who are considering typesetting as an occupation.

Part-time employment also offers good opportunities to learn about the requirements, duties, and benefits of this work. Printing and graphic arts classes at many high schools can provide valuable experience and insights. School publications, particularly at the college level, may do their own typesetting.

Methods of entering

Many people enter the typesetting field through jobs as helpers. In small towns, direct application to the local typesetting or printing shop or newspaper is a good way to start out. Students who take graphic arts courses at community and junior colleges may be able to find help in locating entry-level jobs at their school's placement office. It is also possible to find openings through newspaper classified ads and the offices of the state employment service.

Advancement

As workers gain experience, they may be promoted to positions with greater responsibility. Some move into supervisory positions. Those who continue their training in a specialized field such as computer programming can advance to higher paying positions.

A common ambition of many people in typesetting is to have shops of their own. While a great majority of people in this business are employed by others, many of the typesetting establishments in this country are small shops operated by their owners.

Employment outlook

Employment in the typesetting field is expected to grow about as fast as the average for other occupations during the next 10 to 15 years. The demand for printed materials is expected to rise, but the increasing use of computers by publishers and authors will reduce the need for some kinds of typesetting employees.

Experienced individuals and graduates of post-secondary programs in computer graphics technology will have the best chances of finding satisfactory employment.

Earnings

Earnings of typesetting workers vary widely according to the job, their level of experience and training, and location and size of the company that they work for. Experienced equipment operators in typesetting plants can have earnings in the range of $28,000 a year. Computer professionals in typesetting firms earn higher salaries. Keyboard operators and proofreaders who are home workers are often paid on a piecework basis, and their earnings vary according to their own productivity.

Conditions of work

In small shops, the usual workweek is 40 hours. Most in-house typesetting workers receive fringe benefits that include paid vacations and holidays, sick leave, insurance plans, and pension programs. Home workers may not receive any of these benefits.

Most typesetting plants are clean, quiet, and air-conditioned. The work is safe and not physically demanding. Workers involved with developing film negatives and making proofs of negatives may be exposed to unpleasant-smelling chemicals.

GOE: 05.05.13; SIC: 2791; SOC: 6841

◇ SOURCES OF ADDITIONAL INFORMATION

Graphic Arts Technical Foundation
4615 Forbes Avenue
Pittsburgh, PA 15213

Printing, Publishing, and Media Workers Sector of the CWA
Communications Workers of America
501 Third Street, NW
Washington, DC 20001

National Composition and Prepress Association of the Printing Industries of America
100 Daingerfield Road
Alexandria, VA 22314

Canadian Graphic Art Institute
19 Duncan Street
Toronto ON M5H 3H1

◇ RELATED ARTICLES

Volume 1: Book Publishing; Printing
Volumes 2–4: Book editors; Electrotypers and stereotypers; Graphics designers; Lithographic occupations; Photoengravers; Printing press operators and assistants; Typists and word processors

Computer programmers

Definition

Computer programmers work in the field of electronic data processing. It is their job to write and to code the instructions that control the work of a computer, which can only follow carefully prepared instructions about what to do on each assignment. Systems programmers specialize in maintaining the general instructions that control an entire computer system; this includes giving instructions to the system on how to allocate time to the jobs fed into it.

History

Data processing systems and their support personnel are a product of World War II. The amount of information that had to be compiled and organized for war efforts became so numerous that it was not possible for people to collect it and put it in order in time for the necessary decisions to be made. It was obvious that a quicker way had to be devised to gather and organize information if decisions based on logic and not on guesses were to be made.

The first computer to be put to use on civilian problems was installed by the Bureau of the Census in 1951 to help compile data from the 1950 census. This machine was large and complicated, and seemed impractical to design, install, and use for problems of less scope than analysis of the entire population. However, three years later the first computer was installed by a business firm. Since 1954, many thousands of data processing systems have been installed in government agencies, industrial firms, banks, insurance agencies, educational systems, publishing houses, colleges and universities, and scientific laboratories.

Nature of the work

Broadly speaking, there are two types of computer programmers: systems programmers and applications programmers. Systems programmers maintain the instructions, called programs or software, that control the entire computer system, including both the central processing unit and the equipment with which it communicates, such as terminals, printers, and disk drives. Applications programmers write the

software to handle specific jobs and may specialize as *engineering and scientific programmers*, or as *business programmers*. Some of the latter specialists may be designated *chief business programmers*, who supervise the work of other business programmers.

Programmers often work from descriptions prepared by systems analysts, listing in detail the steps the computer must follow to complete a task. In smaller companies, analysis and programming may be handled by the same person, called a programmer-analyst.

A programmer analyzes the request that is being made of the instrument, finds out the problem and type of results wanted, discovers the kinds of data that will be needed to attack the problem, and plans the way in which the machine will have to respond to produce the information required. Programmers prepare a flow chart to show the steps in sequence that the machine must make. They must pay attention to minute detail and instruct the machine in each step of the process. These instructions are then coded in a programming language, such as BASIC, COBOL, FORTRAN, PASCAL, or RPG. When the program is completed, the programmer tests its working practicality by having it perform on simulated data. If the machine responds according to expectations, actual data will be fed into it and the program will be activated. If the computer does not respond as anticipated, the program will have to be "debugged," or examined for errors that must be eliminated. Finally, the programmer prepares an instruction sheet for the computer operator who will run the program.

The programmer's job concerns both an overall picture and minute details. Programmers work from two points of view: from that of the people who want certain information produced and from that of technological problem-solving. The work is equally divided between meeting the needs of other people and comprehending the capabilities of the machines.

Electronic data systems do not involve just one machine. Depending upon the kind of system being used, the operation may require other machines such as printers. The introduction of newer computers often requires the rewriting of entire programs.

The visible results of the work of the programmer may be in one of several forms, such as magnetic tape or disks, that can be stored easily and fed back into the machine at any future time for further study. The computer will print the results of the program at a high rate of speed in a way that is comprehensible to the specific machine language being used.

Programmers may specialize in certain types of work depending on the kind of problem to be solved and the place of work. Making a program for a payroll is, for example, very different from programming the study of structures of chemical compounds. *Information system programmers* specialize in programs for storing and retrieving physical science, engineering, or medical information; text analysis; and language, law, military, or library science data. *Process control programmers* develop programs for systems that control automatic operations for commercial and industrial enterprises, such as steel making, sanitation plants, combustion systems, computerized production testing, or automatic truck loading. *Numerical control tool programmers* program the tape that controls the machining of automatic machine tools.

Requirements

Most employers of programmers prefer college graduates. Employers, however, have been known to take people as programmers who have attended college but who have not graduated. Personal qualifications such as a high degree of reasoning ability, patience, and persistence, as well as an aptitude for mathematics, are often as influential as formal training in obtaining entry-level positions with data systems. Many personnel officers administer aptitude tests to determine potential for the work of a programmer. Employers usually send new employees to computer schools before they will be qualified to assume programming responsibilities. They are usually sent to school at company expense; the training period may last as long as five weeks. It generally takes a year or more before a programmer can master all aspects of the job.

A few high schools in large urban areas have courses to train students in using data processing equipment. Many junior and community colleges have also begun two-year programs in data processing, which create opportunities for graduates to seek employment in technical jobs with computer systems. Many colleges and universities now offer courses and degree programs in computer sciences.

Some employers whose work is highly technical require that programmers be qualified in the area in which the firm or agency operates to be considered for a position. Engineering

Computer programmers must understand exactly how a computer works. Only then can they design and install a program that runs smoothly.

firms, for example, prefer to employ young people with an engineering background and then provide them with training in the acquisition of data processing skills.

Those employers who require a college degree do not always state the major field in which the degree is to be obtained, although mathematics is highly favored. Other majors may be business administration, accounting, engineering, or physics. Entrance requirements for jobs with the federal government are much the same as those in private industry.

Opportunities for experience and exploration

Interested high school students might visit a large bank or insurance company in the community and seek an appointment to talk with one of the programmers on the staff. Future programmers may be able to visit the data processing center and see the machines in operation. They might talk with a sales representative from one of the large manufacturers of data processing equipment and request whatever brochures or pamphlets the company publishes.

It is a good idea to start early and get some hands-on experience operating a computer. Joining a computer club and reading professional magazines are other ways to become more familiar with this career field.

High school and college students who can operate a computer may be able to obtain part-time jobs in business computer centers or in some larger companies.

Methods of entering

There is no standard way to secure an entry-level position as a programmer. Someone with the necessary qualifications should apply for a position with the particular industry or agency desired. In some instances, an applicant for a job may express an interest in data processing to the personnel officer. There may be an opportunity for direct placement in the data system department of the firm. Some accept placement in another department of the firm, and transfer when there is a vacancy in data processing.

Application for a job may also be made to the manufacturers of data processing equipment, to learn a great deal about all aspects of computer operations.

Advancement

The programmer who is more interested in the analysis aspect of the job than in the actual charting and coding of the program may want to consider acquiring additional training and experience to become a systems programmer or systems analyst. One may be interested in administration and may wish to become head of the programming department. One may wish to take on additional responsibility for the total computer operation and be placed in charge of the data systems center.

As programmers acquire experience, their salaries are increased. This may represent adequate advancement for programmers who enjoy the kind of work they do and have no wish to change jobs.

Employment outlook

There are about 565,000 computer programmers employed in the 1990s. They work for manufacturing companies, data processing service firms (including those that write and sell software), banks, insurance companies, government agencies, and colleges and universities throughout the country.

Employment opportunities for computer programmers should be excellent through the 1990s as the use of computers increases. Businesses, scientific organizations, government agencies, and schools continue to look for new applications for computers and to make improvements in software already in use. Also, there is a need to develop complex operating programs that can use higher-level computer languages and can network with other computer equipment and systems.

Job applicants with the best chances of employment will be college graduates with a knowledge of several programming languages, especially the new ones that apply to computer networking and data-base management, and those who have participated in work-study programs or have had training in an applied field such as accounting, science, engineering, or management. Competition for jobs will be heavier among graduates of two-year data processing programs and among people with equivalent experience or with less training.

Earnings

Most full-time programmers in the 1990s earn between $25,700 and $42,300 per year, with a median of about $34,000. The federal government offers programmers with a college degree a beginning salary from $17,000 to $21,000, depending on the academic record.

Programmers in the West and the North are generally paid more than those in the South. Also, the pay for programmers is higher in public utilities and data processing service firms than in banks and schools.

Conditions of work

Most programmers work under pleasant conditions. The machines require an atmosphere that is dust free and in which the temperature is constant both in summer and in winter. Because machine operations are often fairly new in most agencies and firms, the offices in which they are housed are usually newly designed and decorated.

The average programmer works between 35 to 40 hours weekly. In some job situations, the programmer may have to work nights or weekends on short notice when the program is going through its trial runs, or when there are many demands for additional services.

Most programmers receive the customary vacation and sick leave, and are included in such company benefits as group insurance and retirement benefit plans.

Because the occupation is relatively new, many programmers are also young. They are engaged in an exploratory operation to determine the best ways in which to accomplish a job for which large organizations feel a great need.

GOE: 11.01.01; SIC: Any industry; SOC: 3971, 3972, 3974

◇ **SOURCES OF ADDITIONAL INFORMATION**

Association for Computing Machinery
1515 Broadway
New York, NY 10036

Data Processing Management Association
505 Busse Highway
Park Ridge, IL 60068

Institute for the Certification of Computer Professionals
2200 East Devon Avenue, Suite 268
Des Plaines, IL 60018

Data Processing Management Association of Canada
4267 Moorpark Place
Victoria BC V8Z 6P1

◇ **RELATED ARTICLES**

Volume 1: Computer Hardware; Computer Software; Electronics
Volumes 2–4: Computer-service technicians; Data base managers; Data entry clerks; Graphics designers; Graphics programmers; Numerical control tool programmers; Systems analysts

Computer-service technicians

Definition

Computer-service technicians install, program, operate, maintain, and service computer systems. They diagnose problems caused by mechanical or electrical malfunctions in individual computer units and in complex systems, such as local area networks (LANs).

The installation, construction, operation, and maintenance of mainframe computers, minicomputers, and microprocessors require a strong background in basic mathematics and the physical sciences. An understanding of electronic circuits and mechanical devices used to construct and install computers is also necessary. Computer-service technicians are experts in the use of instruments to detect weaknesses or failures in computer systems. In addition to a thorough knowledge of computer hardware, the computer-service technician must remain current on the many software applications. Because of the increasing use of computers by businesses, the employment outlook is excellent.

History

The computer-service technician career began to develop in the mid-1960s, during the time when computers were becoming commonly used in business, research, and government.

The first experimental versions of modern computers were built during the 1940s. Compared to present-day computers, these computers were expensive and inefficient. Some early computers used as many as 50,000 vacuum tubes, were very large, and used great amounts of electric power. Moreover, they had to be kept in air-conditioned rooms to work correctly.

Technical improvements made during the 1950s led to the first commercial computers. Their manufacturers leased them to users instead of selling them. This made the manufacturer responsible for servicing the customer's computer system. Computer-service engineers were trained by the company to keep the customer's data processing system and computers

363

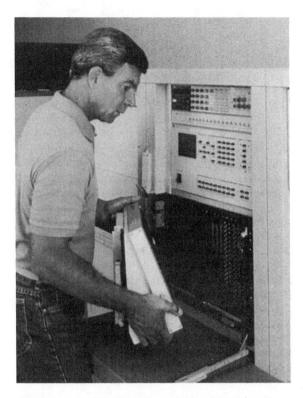

A computer-service technician replaces a broken element of a main-frame computer system. After the installation, he will check that the new device is running smoothly.

in good working order. By the late 1950s and early 1960s the transistor was developed. It gradually took the place of vacuum tubes and helped make computers much smaller, more reliable, and less expensive.

In the late 1960s, the introduction of integrated circuitry made possible the development of minicomputers, which were smaller and cheaper than earlier computers but just as powerful. This was the first phase of the computer revolution. As new uses for minicomputers became evident in manufacturing, hospitals, airline ticket scheduling, and business offices, the number of computers greatly increased. New companies that produced minicomputers sprang up. These changes led to a great demand for highly skilled technicians who could keep these computers operating.

Many technical institutes, community colleges, and specialized schools started programs to prepare computer-service technicians. Some minicomputer manufacturers cooperated with schools to start such programs, and some companies opened private schools in various parts of the country.

The second phase of the computer revolution began in the early 1970s when the microprocessor became the heart of the modern computer. The discovery of how to store information on a tiny silicon chip (approximately .03 by .03 inches in size) rapidly caused new developments. The silicon chip opened up many new uses for computers. In addition, its development greatly reduced the computers' cost and increased the number of computer applications. This, in turn, increased the need for computer-service technicians, a need that is still growing.

Nature of the work

Computer-service technicians may work for either a computer manufacturer or a computer owner who wants to apply computer technology. Technicians who work for a manufacturer may help the circuit designer develop new and improved circuits for computer systems already in production. Here the technician may build new circuits for testing purposes, or for the finished version which will be used as a model in the final production process.

The manufacturer often controls the research and development along with the manufacturing of new electronic devices, such as integrated circuits and other solid-state devices. This allows technicians to work alongside physicists, chemists, metallurgists, or other specialists responsible for the final computer product.

Technicians working for the computer manufacturer may also work at the customer's or user's facilities. There they must make sure that the computer system's regular preventive maintenance is performed, including overall checking for processing errors, instrument analysis of system or unit performance, and general troubleshooting.

At the customer's office or plant, technicians assist in site planning and system installation. The site planning helps ensure that the customer has the most trouble-free performance from the computer system after it is installed.

System installation is usually the manufacturer's responsibility, particularly if the equipment is new. The technician who installs the system can quickly communicate any problems to the manufacturer. Usually with the help of the purchaser's technicians, the manufacturer's computer-service technician uncrates new computer hardware at the work site and carefully documents the items. Next, the equipment is inspected for shipping damages, and major components are placed into the unit or system according to the engineering drawings. The check-out phase is next, in which the technician runs special computer programs that certify the proper memory components, cathode-ray-tube terminals, printers, and other input and output devices. The computer-service technician usually has the resources of the manufacturer only a telephone call away if problems occur that cannot be solved at the work place.

An increasing number of computer users also employ computer-service technicians to fully integrate the computer into the user's special application or task. These technicians provide valuable assistance to the owner, making sure that the newly acquired systems are properly used by the other employees at the site, and may be called on to provide special training sessions as newly installed devices are added. When the company does not purchase a service contract to maintain the system, the computer-service technician may become an operations assistant to supervise or manage the care of the system.

Computer users may choose to purchase their computer maintenance services from a specialized contracting company which provides such services under an agreement or contract. These specialists provide the maintenance services as required and serve as the maintenance resource in some cases where manufacturer-supplied maintenance costs are considered too high by the customer. The computer-service engineering technicians working in such an environment provide the same expertise and repair service as that otherwise supplied by the manufacturer. Technicians who work for computer-service contracting companies often provide service for more than one user, and thus gain experience and expertise in several different customer's systems and uses of computers.

Some examples of entry-level jobs in the field are described in the following short paragraphs.

Electronics technicians in manufacturing assist engineers in the design and installation of computer-based systems for process and machine control. They may be required to develop the routine portions of a design and often do much of the initial installation and testing of new equipment.

Field-service technicians provide corrective and preventive maintenance for computer-based systems. Technicians may work for a computer supplier and provide special services to customers as needed. Technicians also may be assigned to the customer's site on a full-time basis.

Quality-test technicians inspect and test digital measurement systems. These technicians are often required to use sophisticated analyzers to carry out the testing procedures.

Traffic-signal technicians are responsible for the inspection, fabrication, and acceptance of new equipment. They provide remedial maintenance to vehicle detection equipment, safety equipment, computer peripheral equipment, and communications equipment.

Terminal technicians specialize in the maintenance of computer terminals such as video-display units, keyboard data entry systems, and printers.

Laboratory technicians perform technical tasks connected with construction, installation, adjustment, maintenance, and operation of computer-controlled devices.

Requirements

Computer-service technicians must be able to function as highly skilled engineering technicians in a highly technical field. Computers and their related equipment are largely electrical and electronic devices, but they are also mechanical structures. The technicians who service and maintain them must therefore understand mechanical devices and the basic principles of mechanics as well as electronics.

Technicians who install, service, and maintain computers or computer systems must have a working knowledge of basic mathematics through algebra and trigonometry. A knowledge of computer programming and microprocessors is essential. They must also be able to follow instructions, both written and spoken, and be able to communicate effectively. A high degree of manual dexterity is helpful, since technicians must also be able to assemble and disassemble parts of a computer.

The best way to prepare for this career is to attend an accredited two-year post-secondary program in a public or private technical institute, community college, or specialized technical school. These programs are designed to provide students with the basic knowledge and skills needed for computer-service and usually require about two academic years or its equivalent.

Some people with extensive electronics training and experience in the military services can, with additional study, enter the field and gradually learn the job.

Those who plan to enter post-secondary programs should take two years of high school mathematics, including algebra; at least three years of language and communication courses; and at least one year of physics or chemistry with laboratory experience. A basic knowledge of computer programming is very desirable.

COMPUTER-SERVICE TECHNICIANS

A typical college-level curriculum for these technicians in the first year might include courses in computer programming, electrical/electronic circuits, algebra and trigonometry, electronic and electrical drawing, physics of mechanics, physics of heat and light, written and spoken communication, and economic and cultural patterns. The second year might include courses in computer systems and central processors, microcomputers, computer languages and operating systems, calculus, physics of electricity, process control systems, communications, technical report writing, and political and community patterns.

Graduates may receive an associate degree or a certificate of completion, to verify educational accomplishment.

The need for good eyesight, color vision, hand-eye coordination, and physical dexterity is also important. All who enter this exacting career must be systematic, scientific, analytical, accurate, patient, and persistent in their working methods.

Special Requirements

There are no licensing requirements in most computer-service jobs. Technicians who work in areas that come under the Federal Communications Commission's (FCC) jurisdiction may find an FCC license to be useful. If employed by companies that do a substantial amount of government work, technicians may be required to undergo a security clearance investigation before they can be hired.

Opportunities for experience and exploration

Prospective technicians should investigate the schools in their own communities to see if any offer an accredited program in computer-service. By visiting such schools in the area, prospective technicians can learn more about the programs offered and get a feel for what it might be like to be enrolled in such a program.

Students in high school or post-secondary school should talk to their guidance counselors or teachers, who may also be able to provide more information about this career.

Another good way of exploring the career is through membership in a computer club or users' group. These clubs, which have developed as the use of personal and home computers has grown, have been organized in many areas by the microcomputer or personal computer users and suppliers.

Methods of entering

Graduates of computer-service engineering programs usually find their first job through their school's placement center. Employers regularly work with placement officers to hire new technicians. Many employers make regular visits to schools to interview graduating students. Placement offices keep listings of companies that have expressed interest in students.

Graduating students can also write to or visit potential employers. The classified sections of newspapers constantly advertise job openings in computer-service technology.

The well-prepared technician may enter a variety of entry-level positions where the employer provides on-the-job training to help the technician become familiar with the job. Some employers also provide further specialized training for highly technical jobs if needed.

Advancement

The computer servicing field offers a variety of advancement opportunities because of the tremendous growth in the field. Technicians may advance to positions of increased responsibility as service technicians for an equipment user or system supplier. They may supervise technicians in large companies with extensive computer-controlled automation applications. If they work for a computer manufacturing and sales company, they may supervise crews of customer-service technicians. Some technicians go on to own or manage a private company that provides contract engineering service to users of computers, computer systems, and computer-controlled systems.

Computer sales managers help customers design computer systems and then supervise the delivery, installation, servicing, and monitoring of the customer's equipment.

Senior research and development technicians might design and test components of a new system, solve technical problems that may arise in the design or testing of completed systems, and supervise the design of factory or field adaptations to existing systems.

Employment outlook

Opportunities for employment in the computer field are excellent. In the coming years, business, government, and other organizations are expected to acquire increasing amounts of computer equipment to manage information, assist in manufacturing processes, and use in an ever-widening variety of other applications.

Employment growth for computer-service technicians will be slower than in recent years, and probably slower than the growth of computer equipment manufacturing. The reason is that the newer equipment is more reliable and easier to repair. However, employment of computer-service technicians is still expected to grow faster than the average of all other occupations through the year 2005. In addition to job openings for computer-service technicians created by growth in the field, even more job openings will be created as employers need to replace computer-service technicians who transfer, get promoted, or retire. All of these factors taken together suggest that there will probably be thousands of job openings for computer-service technicians every year through the year 2005.

Earnings

In highly industrialized areas of the country, computer-service technicians will be in greater demand and can command a higher wage and more attractive benefits. Typical starting salaries for graduates of two-year engineering technology programs range between $16,000 and $24,544 per year, plus benefits that often include educational reimbursement.

Fully trained service technicians are paid average yearly salaries of approximately $30,420. Senior technicians with several years of experience earn from $30,420 to $41,000 per year. Those who advance to high supervisory or management positions, operate their own businesses, or enter major sales and service positions may earn upward of $50,000 per year or more.

Conditions of work

Working conditions are generally good for the computer-service technician. Computers are usually housed in air-conditioned, well-lighted, attractive environments. The most strenuous work is probably installation, because of the necessity of uncrating and positioning equipment.

Under some conditions, technicians are required to work around dangerously high voltages and will need to be aware of appropriate safety measures.

The computer-service technician who works for a computer company or contractor usually will be required to drive a car from one assignment to another. In such cases, the technician is expected to see that the vehicle is cared for properly.

Very often the computer-service technician will find it necessary to work overtime to get a customer's system back into operation. How this extra time is to be accounted for may vary, ranging from compensatory time off to overtime pay.

With the rapid increase in the use of computers and computer-controlled robots, computer-service technicians may find themselves working in factory environments. There they will need to wear protective clothing and be especially aware of the hazards associated with factory work.

Computer-service technicians deal not only with complex high-technology hardware but also with operating and management personnel. They must be able to work at peak levels of activity for extended periods of time with customers who are under pressure from top management to have their computer hardware operating. These situations require a large amount of patience and tact.

The work of computer-service technicians is vital to the well-being of those whom they serve and to the nation's economic future. They keep the nation's most expensive and advanced machinery operating.

The career is a demanding one. It requires constant study to keep up with changes and new systems. The rewards are great, however, in job satisfaction and financial reward.

GOE: 05.05.05; SIC: Any industry; SOC: 3711

◇ **SOURCES OF ADDITIONAL INFORMATION**

Institute of Electrical and Electronics Engineers
Computer Society
345 East 47th Street
New York, NY 10017

Canadian Computer Dealer Association
P.O. Box 724, Stn. B
Willowdale ON M2K 2R1

Association for Computing Machinery
11 West 42nd Street
3rd Floor
New York, NY 10036

Institute for Certification of Computer Professionals
2200 East Devon Avenue
Suite 268
Des Plaines, IL 60018

Confectionery industry workers

Definition

Confectionery industry workers manufacture and package sweets, including bonbons, hard and soft candy, stuffed dates, popcorn balls, and many other types of confections.

History

People all over the world love sweets. Confections have been made since ancient times. The word "sugar" comes from Sanskrit, the ancient language of India. The cacao bean, from which chocolate is made, has been cultivated in Central America for thousands of years. Spanish explorers imported the bean to West Africa, where most of the world's supply of cacao bean is now produced.

European confectioners have the reputation for creating the world's best confections, but most candies Americans consume today are mass-produced in American factories. A significant number of such factories are small, employing fewer than 20 workers.

Nature of the work

Confectionery workers operate machines to mix and cook candy ingredients, to form candy mixtures into shapes, and to package them for sale. Many different machines are used to make the molded, filled, pulled, whipped, and coated candies that Americans eat. Some candy-making jobs are done by hand.

Pantry workers assemble, weigh, and measure candy ingredients such as sugar, egg whites, and butter, following a fixed formula. To each batch of ingredients they attach a card denoting the formula used, so the next workers will know which candy is to be made from that batch.

Confectionery cookers cook candy mixtures according to a formula, using open-fire or steam-jacketed kettles or pressure cookers. They load ingredients into the machine and start the machine's agitator to mix them. They then set controls regulating the temperature and pressure at which the candy will be cooked and turn valves to admit steam or other heat. They may be responsible for checking the consistency of the batch and adjusting the sugar content if necessary. When the cooking is done they empty the batch onto slabs or cooling belts or into beaters.

Chocolate temperers melt chocolate using water-jacketed tempering kettles that alternately heat and cool the chocolate until it is the proper consistency. The workers who operate these machines regulate the temperature, mix and agitate the chocolate in the tank, and test the chocolate's viscosity, adding cocoa butter or lecithin as needed. This chocolate is used in molded candies or as a coating.

After the candy mixture is cooked, it is formed. Some candy is kneaded on slabs and cut into pieces. *Rollers* knead soft candy into rolls, which are cut into slices and shaped to form bonbon centers. *Rolling-machine operators* do a similar operation with machines, rolling slabs of candy to specified thicknesses before cutting. *Candy spreaders* pour and spread batches of cooked candy, such as fudge, caramel, and toffee, onto slabs or into trays before cutting and decorating. The cutting is sometimes done by a machine. *Cutting machine operators* select and install cutting disks according to the size and shape of candy pieces required. *Hand candy-cutters* cut pieces manually.

Other kinds of candy must be spun or pulled into rope-like strands before cutting. *Spinners* and *candy pullers* perform these tasks. A *center-machine operator* runs a machine that makes soft-candy centers for bonbons and chocolates. Other machines make different shapes. *Ball-machine operators* operate rolling machines that form candy balls and disks, and *lozenge makers* run machines that roll dough into sheets and then emboss and cut it into candy lozenges. *Lollipop machine operators* make lollipops.

Many kinds of candy are made using molds. *Starch-makers* operate machines that make starch molds in which gum or jelly candy is formed. *Molding-machine operators* mold these candies using a mold-printing board. *Molding-machine-operator helpers* feed the candy-filled starch molds onto conveyors or racks of machines that empty the molds, remove any remaining starch from the candies, and deposit candies in trays. *Hand candy-molders* pour liquid candy into chilled molds to form solid figures such as animals, people, and Christmas trees. Another kind of hand molder is a *kiss setter,* who forms candy kisses using a spatula. *Deposit-machine operators* operate machines that deposit metered amounts of fluid candy into molds or directly onto conveyors. They must check the temperature and flow of the fluid and weigh formed candy samples to assure they meet specifications. *Fruit-bar makers* grind dried fruit and shape it into bars.

After candy centers are made, they must be coated, or enrobed. *Enrobing-machine feeders* arrange candy centers in a specified pattern on a conveyor, removing any malformed items. *Enrobing-machine operators* run machines that coat candy with melted chocolate or other coatings. They adjust the flow of coating mixture and allow coated candies to cool before further processing. In some plants, candy is dipped by *hand workers,* who scoop coating materials onto slabs and swirl centers, fruits, or nuts through the coating and then remove them. Sometimes workers called *enrobing-machine corders* mark tops of machine-coated candies to simulate a hand-dipped appearance. They dip out a little

A plant supervisor inspects the size of Hershey chocolates as they come out of an assembly line. Measurement inspection is an important part of quality control.

semi-liquid chocolate out of a supply container and use it to draw a line or bead on the top of a newly enrobed piece of candy.

Other workers do similar tasks. *Sanding-machine operators* sugar-coat gumdrops and orange slices. *Coating-machine operators* coat candy and nuts with syrup, coloring, or other materials to glaze or polish them.

Popcorn balls and flavored popcorn are also considered confections. *Corn poppers* operate gas ovens that pop corn. They measure corn, oil, and salt into the popper and remove the corn when it has popped. *Popcorn-candy makers* measure ingredients and cook flavored syrup, then coat popcorn with the syrup. *Cheese sprayers* spray a mixture of cheese and coconut oil onto popcorn, salt it, and take it to the packing room.

Some workers, including *decorators* and *garnishers,* use icing or nuts to decorate candy. Other workers make candy that is used to decorate other edibles. *Marzipan mixers* mix almond paste for marzipan cake decorations, which are formed by *marzipan molders. Casting-machine operators* form sugar decorations for cakes by forcing a sugar paste through a die, a device for molding shapes, and depositing the decorations on a paper sheet.

CONFECTIONERY INDUSTRY WORKERS

Many plants employ *inspectors* who check and weigh products to make sure they meet company standards.

In some plants, *candy makers* are responsible for many of the steps in production, including formulating recipes and mixing, cooking, and forming candy. *Candy-maker helpers* help candy makers by tending machines, mixing ingredients, washing equipment, and performing other tasks. In large plants these various jobs are often performed by different workers, under the direction of *candy supervisors*. Candy-making plants also employ *factor helpers*, who move trays from machine to machine and help confectionery workers in other ways.

After candy is formed, it is packaged, usually by machine, and delivered to distributors and eventually to retail stores.

Requirements

A high school diploma is usually a requirement for applicants for jobs as confectionery industry workers. After they are hired, employees learn production skills on the job. High school courses in chemistry, biology, and shop are useful as background for some jobs, but skills are gained only through experience. For some advanced positions, such as candy maker, workers may need technical expertise in food chemistry or other fields, as well as a solid knowledge of the industry. Confectionery workers should have good manual dexterity and should be in good health.

Special requirements

Confectionery workers, like workers in many food industries, may have to pass physical examinations to show that they are in good health before they can begin work at a plant.

Opportunities for experience and exploration

High school students may be able to obtain part-time or summer employment at a large candy-making factory to learn more about this work. Some plants offer tours of their operation to the public.

Methods of entering

Job seekers should apply directly to local plants for employment. Newspaper want ads and the offices of the state employment service are good sources for leads. In addition, the Bakery, Confectionery and Tobacco Workers International Union, to which many workers belong, may provide information about local openings.

Advancement

Workers who are willing to learn about all aspects of confectionery-making can advance to positions as candy makers or supervisors. The greater the range of specialized knowledge and skills a worker has, the greater the chance for advancement. The size of the plant and the rate of turnover among employees also affect promotion opportunities.

Employment outlook

Candy sales in the United States are expected to hold about steady or perhaps increase slightly in coming years, suggesting that there will continue to be many employment opportunities for confectionery workers. Many new openings will arise every year as workers already in the field change to other occupations or leave the labor force. Most opportunities will be in large wholesale confectionery companies.

Workers should realize that in some plants production processes may be redesigned to become increasingly automated. Therefore, fewer workers may be needed for those jobs where it is economical for machines to do the work formerly done by people.

Earnings

Confectionery workers' wages vary widely depending on such factors as the workers' skills and the size and location of the plant. In general, workers on the Pacific Coast earn more than those in other regions. The average annual earnings for experienced production workers in the 1990s is about $23,400. Candy makers can earn more, with salaries starting around $18,720.

Most confectionery workers earn time-and-a-half pay for overtime work and receive such fringe benefits as paid vacations, holidays, sick days, and insurance and pension plans.

Conditions of work

Most confectionery industry workers are employed in large candy-making factories, although about a third of the nation's roughly 700 confectionery plants employ fewer than 20 workers. Plants are located all over the country—in Illinois, California, New York, Ohio, and Pennsylvania, especially. Most plants are modern, clean, and well lighted. Workers who tend machines must exercise caution, but working conditions are generally very safe. The work is usually not physically demanding. Like many kinds of production work, some jobs in this field involve a great deal of repetition and routine, since each worker performs only a few tasks. Confectionery workers usually work 38 to 40 hours a week. They are often provided with clean uniforms to wear on the job.

GOE: 06.02.15, 06.04.15; SIC: 2064; SOC: 7664, 7755, 8769

◇ **SOURCES OF ADDITIONAL INFORMATION**

National Confectioners Association of the United States
7900 Westpark Drive, Suite A-320
McLean, VA 22102

Bakery, Confectionery and Tobacco Workers International Union
10401 Connecticut Avenue
Kensington, MD 20895

Confectionery Manufacturers Asso. of Canada
#101, 1185 Eglenton Avenue, East
Don Mills ON M3C 3C6

◇ **RELATED ARTICLES**

Volume 1: Baking; Food Processing
Volumes 2–4: Bakery products workers; Canning and preserving industry workers; Cooks, chefs, and bakers; Dairy products manufacturing workers; Food technologists; Macaroni and related products industry workers

Congressional aides

Definition

Congressional aides are the men and women who staff the offices of the senators and representatives of the United States Congress. They fulfill a vast host of duties and bear considerable influence on the operation of government and the legislation it produces. Members of Congress typically include among their staff members an *administrative assistant (AA), legislative assistants (LAs),* a *press secretary, an office manager, a personal secretary, a legislative correspondent,* and a *computer operator.* Aides are generally divided into two groupings: personal staff and committee staff. They may work in an office in Washington, D.C., or in a local district and state office.

History

During the early years of Congress, senators and representatives were resistant to the idea of aides because they thought it might reflect upon their own competency. It was not until about 1840 that, upon the urging of some chairmen, a few part-time clerks were allowed to be hired on a per diem basis. In 1856 the first funding for full-time aides was appropriated. The first aides were mostly clerical workers, such as stenographers and receptionists, and the account from which aides are paid to this day is named "clerk-hire." By the early 1890s, both senators and representatives were allowed to hire personal aides, but there were still only about 100 workers by that period. It wasn't until 1924 that a comprehensive pay bill appropriating funds for all legislative employees was enacted.

By the end of World War II, the improvements in communications and transportation in the country allowed voters to make increasingly greater demands on their elected officials. Also, issues and casework had become increasingly complex, and congressional staffs lacked

Congressional aides can work long hours in unusual conditions during a campaign.

personnel with technical expertise and skills. Demands for the reform of staffing procedures resulted in the Legislative Reorganization Act of 1946. The act allowed each House and Senate standing committee to employ a staff made up of four professional and six clerical workers. A provision of the act recommended that each member of Congress hire an administrative assistant. By that same year the personal staffs of representatives were allowed five employees and that of senators, six. The 1946 act had also better defined the distinction between personal aides and committee aides, stipulating that the professional committee workers be confined to committee work only. That rule has not been strictly enforced, however.

Congressional staffing continued to expand after 1946. In 1965 a committee was formed to further analyze staffing needs. It focused on increasing the number of personal and committee staff, expanding the number of scientific and technical hires, and increasing the pay scale to attract more qualified persons to government work. Another Legislative Reorganization Act, passed in 1970, increased the number of professional staff on standing committees from four to six. By 1974 the number of permanent professional aides on House committees was brought to 18 and the number of clerical help to

12; the total of 30 aides continued to be the staff size in the early 1990s. Senate committee staffs vary in size. In 1977 the Senate directed that committee staffs should be allocated in proportion to the number of minority and majority party members on a standing committee. Senate committees commonly have 40 or more aides, with more working on the subcommittees. In 1991 representatives could have up to 18 full-time and four temporary aides on their personal staffs, whose salaries were paid out of a $475,000 clerk-hire budget allowance. Senators can hire as many aides as they choose within their budget allocation. The allocation in 1991 ranged from $814,000 for states with a population of less than a million to $1,760,000 for states with populations of more than 28 million; the larger the staff the smaller the individual salaries. Staff sizes usually ranged from about 30 to more than 40 aides.

From modest beginnings in the 19th century, staff sizes have grown enormously, causing Congress to allocate more funds to construct new housing and office accommodations. From 399 committee aides in 1947, the number grew to 2,999 by 1989—an increase of more than 650 percent. Similarly, total personal aides went from 2,030 in 1947 to 11,406 in 1989—an increase of more than 400 percent.

Nature of the work

Congressional aides work at a variety of jobs, either on the personal or committee staffs of the members of Congress. A basic difference between the two types of staff is that the committee staffs are more strictly concerned with work that involves the construction and passage of legislation, while the personal staffs also deal with matters concerning the home state. The personal staffs of senators and representatives are similar except that the representative's staff is structured on a smaller scale. Personal aides are generally loyal supporters of the congressman for whom they work and are usually disciples of his political philosophy. Generally, personal staffs are divided into four main branches: administrative, legislative, press, and state offices. Committee staff are structured somewhat differently, being divided more generally between professional and clerical branches; nonetheless, the tasks and job titles are similar to those of the personal staffs. The following job descriptions are typical of a senatorial personal staff, and many would apply to a representatives staff as well.

Administrative Staff: *Administrative assistants* are the chief of staff and the top management officials overseeing all office functions. The AA is the congressman's right hand man and often performs as his alter ego and surrogate. AAs are often in charge of developing operating plans, goals, and objectives. Their duties may include such other responsibilities as preparing the office budget; monitoring office expenditures; hiring, appraising, and terminating staff, and representing the congressman at meetings, events, functions, and so on.

Administrative assistant secretaries provide clerical and administrative support to the administrative assistants. They maintain the AAs' daily schedule, make travel arrangements, screen incoming correspondence and phone calls, draft correspondence, type documents and memoranda, and maintain files. *Personal secretaries* are the congressmen's executive, administrative, and confidential assistants. They attend to congressmen's daily administrative and clerical needs and coordinate the daily schedule of senatorial appointments; they handle expense accounts, review and deal with the congressmen's personal correspondence, maintain personal files, greet scheduled visitors, and (for historical purposes) maintain a log of how congressmen's time is spent.

Schedulers are responsible for scheduling congressmen's calendars, coordinating with the personal secretaries on a daily basis the scheduled appointments, meetings, events, and general demands for the congressmen's time; they

also make travel arrangements as necessary. *Office managers* oversee administration of the personal staff offices; their responsibilities may include monitoring mail flow, office accounts, personnel administration, equipment, furniture supplies, and the filing system; they must insure that Senate and House procedures are followed at all times. *Mailroom managers* are responsible for devising plans for handling the enormous crush of mail that arrives in congressional offices each day; they maintain mass mailing records for filing with the Senate and prepare reports on mail volume and contents for the congressman and appropriate staff. *Receptionists* maintain the reception room: greeting visitors, taking telephone calls, stocking handout literature, dealing with incoming deliveries to the office, responding to special requests, and also assisting with typing, computer entry, and filing. *Computer terminal operators* have primary responsibility for managing the computerized correspondence system.

Legislative staff: *Legislative directors* are responsible for all legislative activities in the office. They manage and direct the legislative assistants; establish a legislative agenda and program; set the staff's priorities and goals; recommend co-sponsorship of legislation and review status of current legislation; and accompany congressmen to congressional sessions as required.

Legislative assistants are each responsible for all aspects of the coverage of issue areas in which they have developed some expertise. They brief congressmen on the status of legislation for which they are responsible and prepare floor statements and amendments for them; they may also write speeches for the congressmen on certain issues. *Legislative correspondents* are responsible for researching and drafting responses to correspondence received in the congressmen's offices; they must be aggressive researchers, and they may be called upon to assist with speech writing and attend meetings as background for responding to inquiries. *Legislative secretaries* perform administrative and clerical support for the legislative director and legislative assistants; they establish and maintain legislative files in which they include Congressional Record reprints, speeches, resource materials, voting records, and bill histories, as well as maintaining telephone support and utilizing the computer system.

Press secretaries are the primary spokespersons for congressmen in their dealings with the media and the public. They screen and respond to daily inquiries from the press; plan and coordinate media coverage; coordinate press conferences and requests for appearances and interviews; prepare press releases, columns, and newsletters; prepare formal speeches; and supervise the review of daily newspapers, routing clippings to the appropriate persons. *Press assistants* aid the press secretaries in their range of duties.

State directors are responsible for state office operations. They represent their congressman in all areas of the state, while maintaining close communication with the Washington, D.C., office and with district community business leaders and constituent groups; state directors also maintain liaisons with the state's political leaders and coordinate the congressman's visits to the state, sometimes accompanying him on his state tour. *State office managers* administer state operations and coordinate and manage constituent services; they supervise casework (related to constituent problems) and ensure that it is performed in a timely manner. State office managers assist the state directors in the performance of their duties and are also involved with the selection of candidates for U.S. military academies and the supervision of intern programs.

Caseworkers serve as a Congressman's ombudsman for constituents, working directly with persons having difficulties with the federal government in such areas as veteran's claims, social security, and tax returns; they log cases, contact appropriate agencies, check relevant government regulations, handle correspondence, and represent the Congressman at hearings and other meetings involving casework.

Committee aides, usually hired by the committee chairman, do much the same kind of work as the personal staff aides, with the exception of the state staff. The clerical staff provides support services for the committee members and the professional staff. Its routine duties include updating the committee calendar, distributing committee publications, referring bills to the appropriate departments and officials for comment, handling files, providing stenographic work, and opening and sorting mail. The professional staff deals with committee policy and legislative matters generally; it handles legal and other types of research, public relations, statistical and other technical work, and the drafting of amendments. Professional staff are also likely to deal with lobbyists on specific issues that come before the committee. The staff helps committee chairmen plan the committee agendas, and they are heavily involved in the preparation of reports that are sent to the full chamber. Principal committee aides, especially those most familiar with a particular bill, often accompany the chairman or the bill's sponsor when the bill is debated on the floor.

Requirements

Congressional aides are employed in a wide variety of jobs, many of which are similar to jobs in the regular workplace and require the same types of skills and training. Most people who want to become aides, however, should have a high interest in government and politics; in school they should take courses in relevant subjects, and they should get involved in school government and school committees. Working in local political offices or volunteering to work in the election campaigns of local candidates also provides good background for a congressional aide career. Through such work, individuals can make the personal contacts that are often influential in being considered for a position on a congressional staff. A limited number of internships are available on the various staffs; these are low-paying or volunteer positions, but they provide excellent training for the aspiring aide candidate.

Generally speaking, aides should have a good understanding of the U.S. government system, especially its legislative process; they should develop the ability to get along with people of widely varying backgrounds and points of view; and they should be effective communicators with good writing and communication skills. Most aides are young and well educated and come from a variety of backgrounds. The following are some of the average educational backgrounds and statistical information for some common Senate aide positions as reported by the Congressional Management Foundation.

Administrative assistant: almost all AAs have at least a bachelor's degree and some 40 percent hold a graduate degree; almost 20 percent have a law degree. More than 70 percent are male and about 98 percent are white. They tend to be somewhat older than other staff.

Legislative director: all legislative directors have a college degree and more than 60 percent have an advanced degree, including almost 30 percent in law. More than half are male and some 90 percent are white. They tend to have spent about half of their careers in Congress.

Press secretary: almost 70 percent of the press secretaries hold a bachelor's degree and some 28 percent have an advanced degree. About 70 percent are male and almost 95 percent are white.

Office manager: more than 60 percent of the office managers have a bachelor's degree and about 15 percent have a master's degree; almost 19 percent have had some college and about 4 percent have had high school educations or less. More than 75 percent are female and almost 92 percent are white.

Personal secretary: about 65 percent of the personal secretaries have a bachelor's degree, almost 24 percent have had some college, and almost 8 percent have had a high school education or less. Some 96 percent are female and over 90 percent are white. They have the highest average age and the longest tenure.

Legislative assistant: more than 90 percent of the LAs have a bachelor's degree and over 40 percent have an advanced degree. A little more than half of the LAs are male, and more than 90 percent are white.

Scheduler: Some 75 percent of the schedulers have a bachelor's degree and about 20 percent have had some college. A small percentage have an advanced degree. About 95 percent of schedulers are women and about 95 percent are white.

Legislative correspondent: more than 90 percent of the legislative correspondents have bachelor's degrees and a small percentage have master's degrees. They are split evenly between male and female and almost 96 percent are white.

State director: about 85 percent of the state directors have at least a bachelor's degree and 25 percent have a graduate degree. About 74 percent are male and just over 90 percent are white.

State office manager: almost 70 percent of state office managers have a bachelor's degree or better and almost 27 percent have had some college; less than 4 percent have had a high school education or less. About 75 percent are female and some 86 percent are white; about 7 percent are hispanic and about 5 percent are black.

Caseworker: about 62 percent of caseworkers have a bachelor's degree and a small percentage have an advanced degree; almost 22 percent have had some college and about 11 percent have a high school education or less. About 80 percent are white, 10 percent black, and 8 percent Hispanic.

Opportunities for experience and exploration

Students interested in pursuing a career as a congressional aide should work on school committees, take active part in clubs, and become involved in school government, preferably taking leadership roles wherever possible. They should take as many courses in civics, political science, U.S. history, and other social studies subjects as possible. Students should also follow current events through newspapers and other media. Volunteering to work for candidates in local elections or for political organizations also provides a good background for aspiring students, as does serving as a congressional page. Internships available in local and Washington, D.C., offices can provide actual on-the-job experience as an aide. The Congressional Management Foundation can be contacted for information on internships.

Methods of entering

Most of the better-paying congressional aide jobs require a college degree. Many of the people entering the field and wishing to advance have an advanced degree, and a degree in law is especially useful. Political science majors are often interested in applying for aide jobs. An internship in the office of a senator or representative or even in some other area of government provides a natural entry for aide applicants. There is no question that congressional aide jobs, like other political jobs, are often obtained as the result of personal contacts. Working on the political campaigns of candidates can provide the contacts necessary for being considered for a job on a congressman's staff. Of course there is risk involved—one's candidate could lose; but the experience is still of value.

Advancement

Advancement in any of the congressional aide jobs is directly related to one's ability, experience on Capitol Hill, and willingness to make personal sacrifices to complete work efficiently and on time. The highest office on congressional staffs is that of administrative assistant. It is possible for anyone on staff to rise up through the ranks to become an AA, and, in fact, there are indications that AAs are frequently promoted into their positions from within the office ranks. Obviously everyone cannot reach the top position, but advancement to higher staff positions is available to those who show they have the ability to take on greater responsibility. Legislative directors and state directors are probably the most directly in line for the AA's job. Legislative assistants and state office managers (also called *regional directors*) are in the best position to move into their respective directors' jobs. The legislative correspondent can move up to assistant, and state caseworkers can move up to the state manager's or director's job. Assistant press secretaries are in an obvious position to move into the press secretary's spot, although hiring from outside is not uncommon. The top secretarial position is that of personal secretary, and any of the other secretaries can aspire to that position or that of scheduler. Any of the administrative staff, such as the receptionist or the mail room manager, can move toward the office manager's position.

Employment outlook

The number of congressional aide jobs is determined by appropriations from Congress. The size of committee and personal staffs, for the most part, grew steadily from the end of the 19th century until about the mid-1980s, after which they leveled off. An exception is the Senate committee staffs, which actually reached its peak in 1976, was reduced the next year, and remained fairly stable after that. In 1989 there were 14,405 congressional aides working on the committee and personal staffs in Washington and in the state offices. It is not likely that this number will greatly increase or decrease in the 1990s. There is legislation that controls the amount that can be budgeted by Congress and there is great pressure on the government to control spending because of the budget deficit. A certain number of job openings occur through attrition, but appointments occur in greater numbers when administrations change after an election. At that time persons who have worked within a congressman's campaign are likely to have the inside track on available positions.

Earnings

There are few regulations that affect the pay scales for personal staffs. Both the House and Senate draw salaries for staff from appropriations allotted to the clerk-hire account. The highest salaries allowable on Senate staffs in 1991 was $120,000, and in the House, $101,331. The minimum pay was $1,530 in the Senate and $1,200 in the House, although these were normally for interns. The House abides by the minimum wage laws. Wages are in almost all cases higher per position in the Senate than they are in the House.

Raises average 5.5 percent in the Senate and 4.4 percent in the House. Most Senate and House employees qualify for cost of living adjustments. The following are average salaries for similar positions in the Senate and House: administrative assistant, Senate, $81,349,

House, $65,557; legislative director, Senate, $65,801, House, $43,037; state director, Senate, $60,847, House, $43,853; press secretary, Senate, $53,429, House, $35,868; office manager, Senate, $46,538, House, $31,178; legislative assistant, Senate, $40,861, House, $28,147; state caseworker, Senate, $23,513, House, $22,395. Some of the Senate positions are combined in the House; for instance, the Senate's personal secretary, at an average salary of $45,881, and the scheduler, at an average salary of $34,339, are combined as the personal secretary in the House, at an average salary of $33,749.

The highest paid committee aides in 1991 received $99,215 in the Senate and $115,092 in the House. Committee staff are entitled to the same cost-of-living increases as other employees in Congress.

Conditions of work

Oddly enough, while Congress makes laws to protect workers and to ensure civil rights among the general populace, it has, in many cases exempted itself from those same laws. Due to this lack of protection for congressional workers, Capitol Hill has been dubbed "The Last Plantation." Members of Congress contend that they should not be regulated like firms in the private sector because of the political nature of their institution and the necessity for choosing staff on the basis of loyalty; they also feel that it would breech the principle of the separation of powers if the executive branch had the power to enforce labor regulations in Congress.

Congressional jobs carry a certain amount of glamour, but for many employees this wears thin when faced with long hours, cramped quarters, constant pressure, and the sometimes whimsical demands of the congressmen at whose pleasure they serve. Studies show that women and nonwhites on the Hill seem to be particularly taken advantage of, being concentrated in the lower-paying jobs. Aides have complained that they have little recourse when they have suffered unjustly in their jobs, although regulations have been set up to allow them to file complaints. The House has been somewhat more active in allowing formal legislation to apply to its aides. An Office of Fair Employment Practices has been set up in the House, and that body has also accepted the provisions of the Fair Labor Standards Act to apply to its staff members. Both the House and Senate have passed resolutions that bar discrimination in hiring on the basis of ethnicity, religion, sex, handicap, or age. Congressmen, however, can consider political affiliation in hiring and may consider applicants solely from their home state.

Although there are regulations governing the use of personnel in political campaigns, aides are frequently called upon to give extra time during election years, sometimes using vacation days and holidays to do so. Aides are also restricted by the ethics rules that apply to the members of Congress. They cover such areas as honoraria, other outside income, gifts, travel, financial disclosure, and postemployment lobbying.

GOE: 07.04.04; SIC: none; SOC: 149

◇ **SOURCES OF ADDITIONAL INFORMATION**

The Congressional Management Foundation
513 Capitol Court, NE, Suite 100
Washington, DC 20002

Senate Placement Office
Hart Senate Office Building
Room SH 142B
Washington, DC 20510

House Placement Office
House Annex #2
Room 219
Washington, DC 20510

The Democratic National Committee
430 South Capitol Street, SE
Washington, DC 20003

The Republican National Committee
310 First Street, SE
Washington, DC 20003

◇ **RELATED ARTICLES**

Volume 1: Politics and Public Service; Foreign Service
Volumes 2–4: Lawyers and judges; Lobbyists; Political scientists

Construction inspectors, government

Definition

Construction inspectors work for federal, state, and local governments. Their job is to examine the construction, alteration, or repair of highways, streets, sewer and water systems, dams, bridges, buildings, and other structures to ensure that they comply with the building codes and ordinances, zoning regulations, and contract specifications.

History

Construction is one of the major industries of the modern world. Public construction includes such structures as public housing projects, schools, hospitals, administrative and service buildings, industrial and military facilities, highways, and sewer and water systems.

Because public construction is paid for out of tax money, bonds, or other public funds, the government has an obligation to the people to see that work is carried out legally, properly, safely, and economically. To ensure this, the government employs construction inspectors.

Nature of the work

This occupation is made up of four broad categories of specialization: building, electrical, mechanical, and public works.

This construction inspector is examining the width and evenness of a vertical steel beam. Uniformity is essential in the construction of skyscrapers.

Building inspectors examine the structural quality of buildings. They check the plans before construction, visit the work site a number of times during construction, and make a final inspection when the project is completed. Some building inspectors specialize in areas such as structural steel or reinforced concrete buildings.

Electrical inspectors visit work sites to inspect the installation of electrical systems and equipment. They check wiring, lighting, generators, and sound and security systems. They may also inspect the wiring for elevators, heating and air-conditioning systems, kitchen appliances, and other electrical installations.

Mechanical inspectors inspect plumbing systems and the mechanical components of heating and air-conditioning equipment and kitchen appliances. They also examine gas tanks, piping, and gas-fired appliances. Some mechanical inspectors specialize in elevators, plumbing, or boilers.

Elevator inspectors inspect both the mechanical and the electrical features of lifting and conveying devices, such as elevators, escalators, and moving sidewalks. They also test their speed, load allowances, brakes, and safety devices.

Plumbing inspectors inspect plumbing installations, water supply systems, drainage and sewer systems, water heater installations, fire sprinkler systems, and air and gas piping systems; they also examine building sites for soil type to determine water table level, seepage rate, and other conditions.

Heating and refrigeration inspectors examine heating, ventilating, air-conditioning, and refrigeration installations in new buildings and approve alteration plans for those elements in existing buildings.

Public works inspectors make sure that government construction of water and sewer systems, highways, streets, bridges, and dams conforms to contract specifications. They visit work sites to inspect such things as excavations, mixing and pouring concrete, and asphalt paving. They also keep records of the amount of work performed and the materials used so that proper payment can be made. These inspectors may specialize in highways, reinforced concrete, or ditches.

Construction inspectors often use measuring devices and other test equipment, take photographs, keep a daily log of their work, and write reports. If any detail of a project does not comply with the various codes, ordinances, or contract specifications, or if construction is being done without proper permits, the inspectors have the authority to issue a stop-work order.

Requirements

People interested in becoming government construction inspectors must be high school graduates who have taken courses in drafting, algebra, geometry, and English. Employers prefer graduates of an apprentice program, people with at least two years toward an engineering or architectural degree, or graduates of a community or junior college. Required courses include construction technology, blueprint reading, technical math, English, and building inspection.

Most construction inspectors have several years' experience either as a construction contractor or supervisor, or as a craft or trade worker such as carpenter, electrician, plumber, or pipefitter. This experience demonstrates a thorough knowledge of construction materials and practices, which is necessary in inspections.

Construction inspectors receive most of their training on the job. The first two weeks or so are spent under the supervision of an experienced inspector, learning about inspection techniques; codes, ordinances, and regulations; contract specifications; and how to keep records and prepare reports. Then the new inspector is put to work on a simple project, such as a residence, and is gradually advanced to more complex types of construction.

Special requirements

Some states require certification for employment. Inspectors can earn a certificate by passing examinations on construction techniques, materials, and code requirements. The exams are offered by three model code organizations: the International Conference of Building Officials; Building Officials and Code Administrators International, Inc.; and Southern Building Code Congress International, Inc.

Government construction inspectors are expected to have a valid driver's license because they must be able to travel to and from the construction sites. They must also pass a civil service exam.

Opportunities for experience and exploration

Students who are thinking of a career in construction can take manual training and shop courses. Vocational high schools offer a variety of such courses.

Field trips to construction sites and interviews with contractors or building trade union officials are a good way to gain practical information about what it is like to work in the industry and how best to prepare for it.

Summer jobs at a construction site provide an overview of the work involved in a building project. Students may also seek part-time jobs with a general contracting company, with a specialized contractor (such as a plumbing or electrical contractor), or as a carpenter's helper. Jobs in certain supply houses will help students become familiar with the materials used in construction.

Methods of entering

People right out of high school usually enter the construction industry as a trainee or apprentice. Information about these programs may be obtained from local contractors, building trade unions, or school vocational counselors. Graduates of technical schools or colleges of construction and engineering may expect to start work as an engineering aide, drafter, estimator, or assistant engineer.

Those who wish to become construction inspectors for the government may have to gain their initial experience in private industry. Jobs may be found through school placement offices, employment agencies, and unions or by applying directly to contracting company personnel offices. Application may also be made directly to the employment offices of the federal, state, or local government.

Advancement

An engineering degree is usually required to become a supervisory inspector.

The federal, state, and large city governments provide formal training programs for their construction inspectors to keep them abreast of new building code developments and to broaden their knowledge of construction materials, practices, and inspection techniques. Inspectors for small agencies can upgrade their skills by attending state-conducted training programs or taking college or correspondence courses.

Employment outlook

In the 1990s, federal, state, and local governments employ about 60,000 construction and building inspectors in the United States; more than half of these inspectors work in municipal and county building departments. Large inspection staffs are employed by cities and suburbs that are experiencing rapid growth. Federal inspectors may work for such agencies as the Department of Defense, the Tennessee Valley Authority, or the Departments of Housing and Urban Development, Agriculture, and Interior.

The demand for government construction inspectors through the 1990s is expected to grow as fast as the average rate for all occupations. There will likely be increased construction activity, as well as a rising concern for public safety and improved quality of construction. However, some responsibilities currently handled by inspectors will be assumed by engineers, construction managers, and maintenance supervisors.

The level of new construction fluctuates with the economy, but maintenance and renovation continue during the downswings, so inspectors are rarely laid off.

CONSTRUCTION INSPECTORS, GOVERNMENT

Earnings

In the 1990s, construction inspectors are paid a median salary of about $31,100 a year. Building inspectors earn slightly more than other types of inspectors. In general, salaries are slightly higher in the North and West than in the South and are considerably higher in large metropolitan areas.

Construction inspectors who work for the federal government in the 1990s earn an average annual salary of approximately $26,100.

Conditions of work

Construction inspectors work both indoors and outdoors, dividing their time between their offices and the work sites. They generally travel to and from the sites in a government car.

Inspection sites are dirty and cluttered with tools, machinery, and debris. Although the work is not considered hazardous, inspectors must climb ladders and stairs and crawl under buildings. The work calls for an ability to coordinate data, diagnose problems, and communicate with people at different levels.

The hours are usually regular, but when there is an accident at a site, the inspector has to remain on the job until reports have been completed. The work is steady year-round, not seasonal as are some other construction occupations. In slow construction periods, the inspectors are kept busy examining the renovation of older buildings.

GOE: 05.03.06; SIC: Any industry; SOC: 1472

SOURCES OF ADDITIONAL INFORMATION

Building Officials and Code Administrators International
4051 West Flossmoor Road
Country Club Hills, IL 60478

International Conference of Building Officials
5360 South Workman Mill Road
Whittier, CA 90601

Southern Building Code Congress International
900 Montclair Road
Birmingham, AL 35213

Information about employment in this field by the federal government may be obtained from:

U.S. Office of Personnel Management
1900 E Street, NW
Washington, DC 20415

Department of Housing and Urban Development
Administrative Officer
451 7th Street, SW
Washington, DC 20410

Additional information on a career as a state or local government construction inspector may be obtained from the state or local employment service.

Canadian Construction Association
85 Albert Street, 10th Floor
Ottawa ON K1P 6A4

RELATED ARTICLES

Volume 1: Construction
Volumes 2–4: Architectural and building construction technicians; Civil engineering technicians; Miscellaneous engineers

Construction laborers

Definition

Construction laborers do a wide variety of routine physical tasks at construction sites of buildings, highways, bridges, and other public and private building projects. Depending on the type of project, the activities of construction laborers may include tasks like carrying materials used by craft workers, cleaning up debris, operating cement mixers, or laying and sealing together lengths of sewer pipe. Laborers may be closely supervised, and their work is usually intended to make the work of more skilled workers flow more smoothly.

History

Construction is an ancient human activity. The first structures built in the distant past were probably simple temporary shelters made of perishable materials. As people sought to extend their control over their environment, some built more durable and more elaborate structures for many different purposes. Many remarkable examples of enormous, well-coordinated building projects survive from long ago at sites around the world. Among these are the Egyptian pyramids, Roman roads and aqueducts, Mayan temples, and the Great Wall of China.

In the past, when people wanted simple structures built, they may well have done the work themselves. But inevitably the larger, more complex structures required the efforts of many workers. These workers included both skilled specialists in certain activities and others who assisted the specialists or did numerous other less complicated but necessary physical tasks. Today the people who provide this kind of aid may be called construction laborers or *helpers*. Their work usually does not require great skill, but it is essential to getting the job done.

Nature of the work

Construction laborers are employed on all kinds of construction jobs, such as building bridges, viaducts, piers, office and apartment buildings, highways, streets, pipelines, railroads, river and harbor projects, sewers, tunnels, and waterworks. Many laborers are employed by private firms that contract to do these construction jobs. Others work for state or local governments on public works or for utility companies in such activities as road repair. Construction laborers are also involved in building remodeling, demolition, and repair work.

At the direction of supervisors or other skilled workers, construction laborers perform a wide variety of duties, such as loading and unloading materials, erecting and dismantling scaffolding, digging and leveling dirt and gravel, wrecking old buildings, removing rubble, pouring and spreading concrete and asphalt, removing forms from set concrete, and carrying supplies to building craft workers. They may use equipment ranging from ordinary picks and shovels to various kinds of machines used in construction, such air hammers or pile-driving equipment.

Construction laborers are generally considered unskilled workers, because they are not regularly required to exercise significant independent judgment based on their training or experience. Laborers do not ordinarily get the chance to develop specialized skills on the job. On some jobs, laborers are consistently assigned to one type of routine task; on other jobs, they are rotated through different tasks as the job progresses. Some laborers tend to work in one branch of the construction industry, such as laying pipelines or building roads. Others transfer from one area of construction to another depending mainly on the availability of work.

To do their job well, some construction laborers may need to be familiar with the duties of skilled craft workers, as well as a variety of tools, machines, materials, and methods used at the job site. Some laborers do work that requires a considerable amount of know-how, such as those who work with the explosives used to break up bedrock before excavation work can begin on some construction projects. These workers must know how different kinds of explosives can be used safely, avoiding both injury and property damage. Another example of laborers who need specialized knowledge are those who work in pressurized areas while constructing dam and bridge foundations. Laborers in these kinds of special situations are usually given training on the job by their supervisors.

CONSTRUCTION LABORERS

A construction worker steadies and guides a section of flooring as a crane places it on top of a construction site.

Requirements

Construction work can be quite strenuous, so employers seek workers who are physically fit enough to do the job for which they are hiring. Laborers must usually be at least 18 years old and reliable, hard-working, and able to follow oral or written instructions.

Some employers prefer high school graduates. In general, though, no particular training is necessary for most entry-level construction laborer jobs. Beginners learn whatever job skills they need informally as they work under the supervision of more experienced workers. Those who must work with potentially dangerous equipment or materials normally receive special instruction in safety procedures that minimize the chance of accidents.

Opportunities for experience and exploration

People who are interested in this work can often get summer jobs as laborers on building or construction projects. This is the best kind of experience students can have to help them evaluate their interest and potential in this field. They may also benefit by talking to local contractors or to local officials of the Laborers' International Union of North America, a union to which many laborers belong.

Methods of entering

The usual first step in getting a job in this field is applying directly to a construction contractor or to the local office of the Laborers' International Union. Good leads for jobs may be found through the state employment service and the classified advertising sections of local newspapers. When they are first employed, laborers are assigned to the most straightforward, simple tasks, but after they have some experience they may be given more varied or more difficult work.

Advancement

Without additional training, construction laborers usually have limited opportunities for advancement. Some laborers move into jobs as mechanics or skilled operators of construction equipment. Workers who show responsibility and good judgment may be promoted to supervisory positions. Some are admitted to training programs such as apprenticeships in the building trades and eventually become skilled craft workers. High school graduates are more likely than other laborers to be able to take advantage of training opportunities that can lead to skilled, higher-paying jobs.

Employment outlook

A moderate increase is predicted for the next 10 to 15 years in the total volume of construction activity nationwide. However, job opportunities for laborers will probably change at about the same rate as jobs in other occupations. Certain technological developments, such as more efficient grading machinery and mechanical lifting devices, may mean that the rate of increase in employment of construction laborers will not be as great as the expected increase in construction activity. Furthermore, the level of construction activity is always affected by local economic conditions. Regions that are prosperous will offer better job possibilities for construction laborers than areas where the economy is not expanding.

Nonetheless, this is a large employment field and turnover is high among laborers. For these reasons, every year there will be many new job openings, mainly in connection with large projects, because employers need to replace those workers who have changed jobs or left the labor force.

Earnings

Construction workers often receive substantial hourly wages, but the hourly rates are often poor indicators of annual earnings. The seasonal nature of construction work and time lost because of other factors can significantly reduce the total income of construction workers. There is also a great difference in the wages paid to construction laborers in different parts of the country. Pay is higher for laborers with certain kinds of special experience or doing certain kinds of tasks. Overall, in the 1990s, laborers who are employed on a full-time basis have earnings roughly in the range of $16,000 to $29,000 or more per year.

Conditions of work

Construction laborers do heavy physical work. They may need to lift heavy weights, kneel, crouch, stoop, crawl, or work in awkward positions. Much of the job is outdoors, sometimes in hot or cold weather, in wind or rain, in dust, mud, noise, or other uncomfortable conditions. Laborers may be exposed to fumes, odors, or irritating chemicals.

Construction laborers need to be constantly aware that the work can be dangerous. When using tools and machines, climbing ladders and scaffolding, walking where unfinished structures may collapse, or where objects may fall from above, they must always be careful to observe good safety practices. They often need to wear gloves, hats, and eye, mouth, or hearing protection to help avoid injury.

Although construction laborers can have rather good earnings during some periods, the industry is subject to ups and downs, and workers need to plan for periods of low earnings. People who are able to go where the jobs are, sometimes to construction sites that are inconveniently located, can be more steadily employed. In general, most jobs are located in more densely populated and industrialized sections of the country.

At times, work schedules, weather conditions, or other factors require that laborers work night or weekend shifts, and sometimes extra hours beyond the standard 40-hour week.

GOE: 05.12.03; SIC: 15, 16; SOC: 871

◇ **SOURCES OF ADDITIONAL INFORMATION**

Associated General Contractors of America
1957 E Street, NW
Washington, DC 20006

Laborers' International Union of North America
905 16th Street, NW
Washington, DC 20006

Canadian Construction Association
85 Albert Street, 10th Floor
Ottawa ON K1P 6A4

◇ **RELATED ARTICLES**

Volume 1: Construction
Volumes 2–4: Architectural and building construction technicians; Bricklayers and stonemasons; Carpenters; Cement masons; Civil engineering technicians; Construction inspectors, government; Drywall installers and finishers; Lathers; Plasterers; Stevedoring occupations

Cooks, chefs, and bakers

Definition

Cooks, chefs, and *bakers* are employed in the preparation and cooking of food, usually in large quantities, in hotels, restaurants, cafeterias, and other establishments and institutions. Cooks plan menus, determine the ingredients needed, and order food from suppliers. They measure and mix ingredients, season food, test food while it is being cooked, and apportion and arrange it on serving plates. They may wash and prepare vegetables and fruits. Cooks may be specialists in one particular type of food preparation, such as bakers, sauce cooks, or vegetable cooks. Others work in specialized places, such as *railroad train cooks, passenger and cargo ship cooks,* or *psychiatric hospital cooks.*

The primary responsibility of chefs is to supervise and coordinate the activities of the specialists engaged in preparing and cooking foods. In addition to many of the same duties assigned to cooks, chefs select and develop recipes; hire, train, and dismiss workers; and keep time and payroll records. Some chefs specialize by type of cuisine, such as French, German, or Italian.

The duties of bakers are in many ways similar to those of cooks and chefs, but they specialize in the preparation of breads, rolls, biscuits, and other baked goods.

History

The art of cookery is as ancient as the history of humankind. The early Greeks, Egyptians, and Romans valued cooks as highly respected members of society.

France has offered the world some of the finest cooks and chefs. Historical records reflect the rabid interest the French people have in the art of cookery. Even today, cooks and chefs who know the art of French cuisine are highly valued and work in some of the world's most luxurious hotels and restaurants.

The hostelries of early American days provided food and rest for weary travelers. Although these inns and taverns sometimes employed cooks who weren't family members, the food was often marginal in quality. It was not until hotels were built in the large cities that the occupation of cook was really developed.

The pleasure of dining out has become big business in the United States. The public has a range of choices—from the simplest, most inexpensive meal to the most expensive and elaborate. Whether a restaurant prides itself on "home cooking" or on exotic foreign cuisine, its cooks and chefs are largely responsible for the reputation it acquires.

Nature of the work

Cooks and chefs are primarily responsible for the preparation and cooking of foods. Chefs usually supervise the work of cooks; however, the skills required and the job duties performed by each may vary depending upon the size and type of establishment.

Cooks and chefs begin by planning menus in advance. They estimate the amount of food that will be required for a specified period of time, order it from various suppliers, and check it for quantity and quality when it arrives. Following recipes or their own instincts, they measure and mix ingredients for soups, salads, gravies, sauces, casseroles, and desserts. They prepare meats, poultry, fish, vegetables, and other foods for baking, roasting, broiling, and steaming. They may use blenders, mixers, grinders, slicers, or tenderizers to prepare the food; and ovens, broilers, grills, roasters, or steam kettles to cook it. During the mixing and cooking, cooks and chefs rely on their personal judgment and experience to add seasonings; they constantly taste and smell food being cooked and pierce it with a fork to test it for doneness. To fill orders, they carve meats, arrange food portions on serving plates, and add appropriate gravies, sauces, or garnishes.

Some larger establishments employ specialized cooks, such as *pie makers, pastry cooks,* and *pastry cook helpers.* The *Chef de Froid* designs and prepares buffets, and *larder cooks* prepare cold dishes for lunch and dinner. Other specialists are *raw shellfish preparers, carvers,* and the *garde manger* who specializes in preparing cold meats and dishes made from leftovers.

In smaller establishments that do not employ specialized cooks or kitchen helpers, the general cooks may have to do some of the preliminary work themselves, such as washing, peeling, cutting, and shredding vegetables and fruits; cutting, trimming, and boning meat; cleaning and preparing poultry, fish, and shellfish; and baking bread, rolls, cakes, and pastries.

Commercial cookery is usually done in large quantities, and many cooks, including *school cafeteria cooks* and *mess cooks*, are trained in "quantity cookery" methods. Numerous establishments today are noted for their specialties in foods, and some cooks work exclusively in the preparation and cooking of exotic dishes, very elaborate meals, or some particular creation of their own for which they have become famous. Restaurants that feature national cuisines may employ *foreign food specialty cooks*.

In the larger commercial kitchens, chefs may be responsible for the work of a number of cooks, each preparing and cooking food in specialized areas. They may, for example, employ expert cooks who specialize in frying, baking, roasting, broiling, or sauce cookery. Cooks are often titled by the kinds of specialized cooking they do, such as fry, vegetable, or pastry. Chefs have the major responsibility for supervising the overall preparation and cooking of the food.

Additional duties of chefs may include training cooks on the job, planning menus, pricing food for menus, and purchasing food. Chefs may be responsible for determining portion weights to be prepared and served. Among their other duties they may supervise the work of all members of the kitchen staff. The kitchen staff may assist by washing, cleaning, and preparing foods for cooking; cleaning utensils, dishes, and silverware; and assisting in many ways with the overall order and cleanliness of the kitchen. Most chefs spend part of their time striving to create new recipes that will win the praises of customers and build their reputations as experts. Many, like *pastry chefs* and *ice-cream chefs* focus their attention on particular kinds of food.

Expert chefs who have a number of years of experience behind them may be employed as *executive chefs*. These chefs do little cooking or food preparation. Their main responsibilities are management and supervision. Executive chefs interview, hire, and dismiss all kitchen personnel, and they are sometimes responsible for the dining room waiters, waitresses, and other employees as well. These chefs consult with the restaurant manager regarding the profit and loss of the food service and ways to increase business and cut costs. A part of their time is spent inspecting equipment. Executive chefs are in charge of all food services for special functions such as banquets and parties, and many hours are spent in the coordination of the work for these activities. They may supervise the special chefs and assist them in planning elaborate arrangements and creations in food preparation. Executive chefs may be assisted by *sous chefs*.

Years of training and experience go into preparing food that both tastes and looks delicious.

Smaller restaurants may employ only one or two cooks and kitchen helpers to assist them. In these jobs, cooks and helpers work together to prepare all the food for cooking and keep the kitchen in a sanitary condition. Because smaller restaurants and public eating places usually offer standard menus with little variation, the cook's job becomes rather standardized and does not involve the preparation of a wide variety of dishes. Such establishments may employ *specialty cooks, barbecue cooks, pizza bakers, automat-car attendants, food order expediters, kitchen food assemblers,* or *counter supply workers.* In some restaurants food is cooked as it is ordered; cooks preparing food in this manner are known as *short-order cooks.*

Regardless of the duties performed, cooks and chefs are largely responsible for the reputation and monetary profit or loss of the eating establishment in which they are employed.

Bakers perform work similar to that of cooks and chefs as they prepare breads, rolls, muffins, biscuits, pies, cakes, cookies, and pastries. Bakers may be supervised by a *head baker*. In large establishments, *second bakers* may supervise other bakers who work with a particular type of baked goods. Bakers are often assisted by *baker helpers*.

Requirements

The occupation of chef, cook, or baker has specific training requirements. Many cooks start

COOKS, CHEFS, AND BAKERS

Chefs are known for their specialties. Often the success of a restaurant depends on the quality and the uniqueness of the cuisine.

sity programs often emphasize training in supervisory and management skills.

A successful chef or cook should demonstrate a keen interest in food preparation and cooking and have a desire to experiment in developing new recipes and new food combinations. With these traits and the necessary technical knowledge, skills, and training, chefs and cooks can find genuine satisfaction in the trade.

Cooks, chefs, and bakers should be able to work as part of a team and to work under pressure during rush hours, in close quarters and with a certain amount of noise and confusion. These employees need a mild temperament and patience to contend with the public daily and also to work closely with many other kinds of employees.

Immaculate personal cleanliness and good health are necessities in this trade. Applicants should possess physical stamina and be without serious physical impairments because of the mobility and activity the work requires. These employees spend many working hours standing, walking, and moving about.

Chefs, cooks, and bakers must possess a keen sense of taste and smell. Hand and finger agility, hand-eye coordination, and a good memory are helpful. An artistic flair and creative talents in working with food are definitely strengths in this trade.

The principal union for cooks and chefs is the Hotel Employees and Restaurant Employees International Union (AFL-CIO).

out as kitchen helpers and acquire their skills on the job, but the trend today is to obtain training through high schools, vocational schools, or community colleges. Professional associations and trade unions sometimes offer apprenticeship programs; one example is the three-year apprenticeship program administered by the local offices of the American Culinary Federation in cooperation with local employers and junior colleges or vocational schools. Some large hotels and restaurants have their own training programs for new employees. The armed forces also offer good training and experience.

The amount of training required varies with the position. It takes only a short time to become an assistant or a fry cook, for example, but it requires many years of training and experience to acquire the skills necessary to become an executive chef or cook in a fine restaurant.

Although a high school diploma is not required, it is an asset to job applicants. For those planning a career as a chef or head cook, courses in business arithmetic and business administration are useful.

Culinary students spend most of their time learning to prepare food through hands-on practice. At the same time, they learn how to use and care for kitchen equipment. Training programs often include courses in menu planning, determining portion size, food cost control, purchasing food supplies in quantity, selecting and storing food, and using leftovers. Students also learn hotel and restaurant sanitation and public health rules for handling food. Courses offered by private vocational schools, professional associations, and univer-

Special requirements

To protect the public's health, chefs, cooks, and bakers are required by law in most states to possess a health certificate and to be examined periodically. These examinations, usually given by the state board of health, make certain that the individual is free from communicable diseases and skin infections.

Opportunities for experience and exploration

Students may explore their interest in this occupation by obtaining part-time and summer jobs in food-service establishments. Employment may be available in fast food or other restaurants, or in institutional kitchens as a sandwich or salad maker, soda-fountain attendant, or kitchen helper. Jobs as waiters or waiters' assistants may be available in larger hotels or summer resorts, which provide the opportunity to observe firsthand the work of chefs and cooks.

Practicing and experimenting with cooking at home and in high school home economics courses is another way of testing one's interest in becoming a cook, chef, or baker.

Methods of entering

Apprenticeship programs are one method of entering the trade. These programs usually offer the beginner sound basic training and a regular salary. Upon completion of the apprenticeship, cooks may be hired full time in their place of training or assisted in finding employment with another establishment. Cooks are hired as chefs only after they have acquired a number of years of experience. Cooks who have been formally trained through public or private trade or vocational schools or in culinary institutes may be able to take advantage of school placement services.

In many cases, a cook begins as a *kitchen helper* or *cook's helper* and, through experience gained in on-the-job training, is able to move into the job of cook. To do this, the person sometimes starts out in a small restaurant, perhaps as a short-order cook, grill cook, or sandwich or salad maker, and transfers to larger establishments as he or she gains experience.

School cafeteria workers who want to become cooks may have an opportunity to receive food-services training. Many school districts, with the cooperation of school food-services divisions of the state departments of education, provide on-the-job training and sometimes summer workshops for interested cafeteria employees. Similar programs are offered by some junior colleges, state departments of education, and school associations. Cafeteria workers who have completed these training programs are often selected to fill positions as cooks.

Job opportunities may be located through employment bureaus, trade associations, unions, contacts with friends, newspaper want ads, or local offices of the state employment service. Another suggested method is to apply directly to restaurants or establishments where the individual would like to work. Small restaurants, school cafeterias, and other eating places with simple food preparation will provide the greatest number of starting jobs for cooks. Job applicants who have had courses in commercial food preparation will have an advantage in large restaurants and hotels, where hiring standards are often high.

Advancement

Advancement in this trade depends on the personal qualifications, skill, training, experience, originality, and ambition of the individual. It also depends somewhat on the general business climate and employment trends.

Cooks with experience can advance by moving to other places of employment for higher wages or to establishments looking for someone with a specialized skill in preparing a particular kind of food. Cooks who have a number of years of successful job experience may find chef positions open to them; however, in some cases it may take 15 or 20 years to obtain such a position, depending on personal qualifications and other employment factors.

Expert cooks who have obtained supervisory responsibilities as head cooks or chefs may advance to positions as executive chefs or to other types of managerial work. Some go into business for themselves as caterers or restaurant owners; others may become instructors in vocational programs in high schools, colleges, or other academic institutions.

Employment outlook

In the 1990s, approximately 1,680,000 cooks, chefs, and bakers work in the United States. Most work in hotels and restaurants, but many work in schools, colleges, airports, and hospitals. Still others are employed by government agencies, factories, private clubs, and other organizations.

The employment of chefs, cooks, and bakers will experience faster-than-average growth through the 1990s, compared with all other occupations. The Department of Labor projects 246,000 new jobs (a 33 percent increase) for fast food cooks through the year 2005, and 257,000 new jobs (a 47 percent increase) for restaurant cooks. The demand will grow with the population. As people earn higher incomes and have more leisure time, they dine out more often and take more vacations. The families of working women will dine out frequently as a convenience. Many job openings occur annually as older, experienced workers retire, die, or transfer to other occupations.

Earnings

The salaries earned by chefs and cooks are widely divergent and depend on many factors, such as the size, type, and location of the establishment, and the skill, experience, training, and specialization of the worker. Salaries are usually pretty standard among the same type of establishment. For example, restaurants and diners serving inexpensive meals and a sandwich-type menu generally pay cooks less than establishments with medium-priced or expensive menus. The highest wages are earned in the West and in large, well-known restaurants and hotels.

In the 1990s, the median salary for short-order cooks is about $12,000, with most earning between $10,400 and $13,520. The median salary for bread and pastry bakers is $13,000, with most earning between $11,960 and $14,560. Fast food workers generally earn the minimum wage of $4.25 an hour. Cooks and chefs in famous restaurants, of course, earn much more; many executive chefs may be paid $50,000 a year or more.

Chefs and cooks usually receive their meals free during working hours and are furnished with any necessary job uniforms.

Conditions of work

Working conditions vary with the place of employment. Many kitchens are modern, well lighted, well equipped, and air-conditioned, but some older, smaller eating places may be only marginally equipped. The work of cooks can be strenuous, with long hours of standing, lifting heavy pots, and working near hot ovens and ranges. Possible hazards include falls, cuts, and burns, although serious injury is uncommon. Even in the most modern kitchens, cooks, chefs, and bakers usually work amid considerable noise from the operation of equipment and machinery.

Experienced cooks may work with little or no supervision, depending on the size of the food service and the place of employment. Less experienced cooks may work under much more direct supervision from expert cooks or chefs.

Chefs, cooks, and bakers may work a 40- or 48-hour week, depending on the type of food service offered and certain union agreements. Some food establishments are open 24 hours a day, while others may be open from the very early morning until late in the evening. Establishments open long hours may have two or three work shifts, with some chefs and cooks working day schedules while others work evenings.

All food-service workers may have to work overtime hours, depending on the amount of business and rush-hour trade. These employees work many weekends and holidays, al-

though they may have a day off every week or rotate with other employees to have alternate weekends free. Many cooks are required to work early morning or late evening shifts. For example, doughnuts, breads, and muffins for breakfast service must be baked by 6 or 7 a.m., which requires bakers to begin work at 2 or 3 a.m. Some people find it very difficult to adjust to working such late and irregular hours.

GOE: 05.05.17; SIC: 5812; SOC: 5214

◇ SOURCES OF ADDITIONAL INFORMATION

American Culinary Federation
10 San Bartola Road
PO Box 3466
St. Augustine, FL 32084

American Institute of Baking
1213 Bakers Way
Manhattan, KS 66502

Chefs de Cuisine Association of America
830 8th Avenue
New York, NY 10019

Educational Foundation of the National Restaurant Association
250 South Wacker Drive
Chicago, IL 60606

Educational Institute of the American Hotel and Motel Association
PO Box 1240
East Lansing, MI 48826

British Columbia Chefs Association
Main Post Office, P.O. Box 2007
Vancouver BC V6B 3P8

Bakery Council of Canada
#101, 1185 Eglinton Avenue East
Don Mills ON M3C 3C6

◇ RELATED ARTICLES

Volume 1: Baking; Food Processing; Food Service
Volumes 2–4: Bartenders; Dietetic technicians; Dietitians; Enologists; Fast food workers; Food service workers; Food technologists; Meatcutters; Restaurant and food service managers

Coremakers

Definition

Coremakers and related workers in the foundry industry prepare cores that are used in making metal castings. In the founding process, molten metal is poured into a mold that contains a solid central core, usually made of sand or a sand mixture. The metal cools and solidifies. When the core is removed, the desired cavity or shape remains in the metal in place of the core. Coremakers make cores in many different sizes and shapes depending upon the size and shape desired in the final casting.

History

Coremaking has been a part of foundry work since techniques were first developed to make molded metal articles. The earliest cores were made by hand from wood or metal. By today's standards, they would be considered very crude.

During the 1800s, the use of metals in industrial applications expanded greatly. The years following the Civil War saw the full flowering of the Industrial Revolution in the United States. Many new types of machines were invented, and coremaking, along with other foundry work, was an important activity in producing these machines.

The 20th century has also been a time of increasing production of metal articles and machinery, and more and more of these items are made of cast metals. Today, automobiles, airplanes, farm machinery, mining machinery, furnaces, stoves, refrigerators, air-conditioners, armaments, and many other items that are essential to our lives are made with the help of coremakers.

Nature of the work

Cores are used in manufacturing metal castings that have hollow centers. The core establishes the open area in the object, such as the hole running through a pipe or tube. Cores for almost any metal casting are made according to approximately the same basic procedures. Cores may be large or small, and made by hand or by machine. *Bench coremakers* work at benches making smaller cores, usually by hand. In contrast, *floor coremakers* make large cores on the floor of a foundry.

In general, coremakers begin their work by cleaning a core box with blasts of compressed air. A core box is often a block of wood or metal hollowed out to the shape of the desired core. After it is cleaned, they dust fine sand over the interior of the core box so that the finished core will not stick to the box, but instead will slip out easily. Then they partially fill the box with sand or a sand mixture. They may do this either by hand or with the help of machines. They tightly pack the sand into the box, using hand or power tamping tools. Periodically, when the core sand reaches certain levels in the box, they may insert wires that have been bent to the proper shape to add strength to the core. Special care is taken to ram the sand solidly and compactly into the core box so there will be no air pockets or other weaknesses in the finished core. The box is then inverted on a flat surface and lifted off of the core. Any cracks or chips on the core are repaired or smoothed out. Cores may be baked to harden them before they are used in making metal castings.

Machine coremakers tend machines that make sand cores for use in casting metals. First they fasten a prepared core box to the machine and operate the machine to partly fill the box with sand from an overhead chute. Then they turn on a compressed-air valve that causes the box to move up and down in a series of sharp jolts so as to pack the sand tightly in the box. They position reinforcing wires in the sand as the core takes shape in the box. When the core box is completely filled and compressed, they cover the box, and by using a lever, turn the box over and remove the core from it onto a table. The raw core is then ready for baking and finishing. Machine coremakers usually work in large factories where a great many identical parts must be made.

Some machine coremakers, called *core-blower operators*, operate blower-type machines that blow sand into a core box to make a core. Other machine coremakers, called *pipe coremakers*, operate machines that form cores around which metal pipes are cast. These bench workers mix sand and other materials and put the mixture into a machine that forces it through a tube, making a core. After removal from the tube, the core may be baked to dry it out, and perhaps coated and baked again to make the core exactly the desired diameter.

COREMAKERS

A coremaker assembles small, intricate cores that will be used in castings for aerospace equipment.

After cores are formed, *core checkers* use various gauges and measuring tools to make sure that the cores are of the correct size and shape.

Core-oven tenders put newly made, raw cores into ovens and raise the heat to the proper temperature to harden and strengthen the cores. These workers must know how to regulate the fire so that the oven will be maintained at the exact temperature required. The tenders remove the baked cores, allow them to cool, and deliver them to the finishers.

Core setters are workers who position the finished cores in molds before the molten metal is poured in to make castings.

Coreroom foundry laborers assist coremakers in various ways, such as hauling sand, fastening sections of cores together, applying a graphite solution to give cores a smooth finish, transporting cores to and from the ovens, and so on.

Requirements

Employers who hire workers for entry-level laborer or helper jobs in coremaking operations sometimes accept applicants with only an eighth-grade education. Several months of on-the-job training and experience may be enough for these beginners to learn how to make simple cores and operate ovens. In time, people who start out as helpers may be able to pick up sufficient skills on the job to become full-fledged coremakers.

However, it is usually considered necessary to complete an apprenticeship to become an all-around, fully qualified coremaker. Apprentices receive on-the-job training from skilled coremakers in a planned program that teaches them all phases of coremaking. They learn bench coremaking, floor work, oven tending, machine coremaking, core finishing, core assembling, and other skills necessary for intricate multiple-part coremaking. Apprenticeships, which typically last four years, also include classroom instruction in related subjects, such as applied mathematics and the study of the different qualities of various metals. Applicants for apprenticeships usually need to be high school graduates.

Because the work that coremakers do can be quite strenuous, coremakers should be in good health. Floor coremakers engage in heavy work, usually requiring more physical strength than bench coremakers, who make small cores. Some types of hand coremaking require a high degree of manual dexterity.

Opportunities for experience and exploration

People who are interested in this kind of work may be able to obtain a job as a helper in a coremaking operation. Teachers or school counselors may be able to arrange for interested individuals or groups of students to visit a foundry to observe the work in progress and to ask questions about it.

Methods of entering

The usual way of getting a job in coremaking is by direct application to the company. New employees usually work as helpers to learn the basics of coremaking. Information on openings at area companies may be located through the local offices of the state employment service or through the classified advertising sections of newspapers. Because a large number of the workers in foundries are members of unions, it may be a good idea to contact the local offices of the unions that organize these workers.

Advancement

People who start in helper positions may advance to become coremakers if they can prove that they know how to do the work. Experienced coremakers who show responsibility and leadership qualities may become shop supervisors. Sometimes advancement means transferring from foundry work dealing with one kind of metal to work dealing with a different metal.

Employment outlook

In the coming years, more and more of the work involved in coremaking and mold-making is likely to be done by machines. As activities in foundries become increasingly automated, the average productivity of each worker is greater. Thus while the production of many kinds of cast metal items may rise in the future, an increased demand for cores for metal casting will probably not mean an increased demand for coremakers. For this reason, employment in the field is not expected to grow and may in fact decline over the next 10 to 15 years. In the 1990s, there are about 22,000 coremakers and mold makers.

Nonetheless, new workers will be needed to replace those who transfer to other jobs or leave the labor force altogether. Opportunities for jobs will vary from place to place, as some regions have a much greater concentration of foundries. The availability of jobs will also vary with business conditions, with fewer job openings arising during economic downturns. Well-qualified coremakers, who are among the most highly skilled foundry workers, will be in more demand than unskilled or semiskilled workers.

Earnings

Coremakers working in foundries have higher average earnings than production workers in manufacturing as a whole. Production workers in iron and steel foundries have earnings that average in the range of $18,000 a year, while the same workers in nonferrous foundries average closer to $16,500.

Most coremakers belong to unions, so their hours of work, overtime pay, health insurance plans, and other fringe benefits are established by contract between the unions and the companies. Among the unions that represent coremakers are the Glass, Molders, Pottery, Plastics and Allied Workers International Union; the United Steelworkers of America; and the International Union, United Automobile, Aerospace and Agricultural Implement Workers of America.

Conditions of work

Foundry workers, including coremakers, sometimes face unpleasant or potentially dangerous conditions on the job. Newer foundries have improved working conditions, but traditionally foundries are very noisy, hot, and smoky. Many foundry operations produce irritating fumes. Concrete floors may make the coremaker's job hard on the feet. Coremakers have the lowest injury rates among foundry workers, but the rate is somewhat higher than the average for all manufacturing workers.

GOE: 06.04.08; SIC: 3543; SOC: 7542

◇ **SOURCES OF ADDITIONAL INFORMATION**

Glass, Molders, Pottery, Plastics and Allied Workers International Union
608 East Baltimore Pike
PO Box 607
Media, PA 19063

American Foundrymen's Society
505 State Street
Des Plaines, IL 60016-8399

Canadian Tooling Manufacturers Association
P.O. Box 1931, Stn. A
Cambridge ON N6A 6J9

◇ **RELATED ARTICLES**

Volume 1: Metals
Volumes 2–4: Forge shop occupations; Iron and steel industry workers; Machinists; Molders; Tool makers and die makers

Correction officers

Definition

Correction officers guard people who have been arrested and are awaiting trial, or who have been tried, convicted, and sentenced to serve time in a penal institution. They search prisoners and their cells for weapons, drugs, and other contraband; inspect windows, doors, locks, and gates for signs of tampering; observe the conduct and behavior of inmates to prevent disturbances or escapes; and make verbal or written reports to superior officers. Correction officers assign work to inmates and supervise their activities. They guard prisoners who are being transported between jails, courthouses, mental institutions, or other destinations. When necessary, these workers may have to use weapons or force to maintain discipline and order.

History

At one time the punishment for criminal behavior was left in the hands of the injured individual or, in a murder case, his or her blood relatives. This resulted in blood feuds, which could carry on for years and which eventually were resolved by the payment of money to the victim or the victim's family. When kingdoms emerged as the standard form of government, certain actions came to be regarded as an affront to the king or the peace of his domain, and the king assumed the responsibility for punishing the wrongs committed by a subject or his clan. In this way, crime became a public offense.

Early criminals were treated inhumanely—often put to death for minor offenses, exiled, forced into hard labor, mutilated, turned into slaves, or left to rot in dungeons. Eventually the belief that punishment alone deters crime began to weaken, and the practice of imprisonment became more and more common. Houses of correction were designed in the hope of rehabilitating prisoners through austere living and hard work. The earliest of the penitentiaries was Bridewell, established in London in 1553. Out of these institutions came the prison reform movement, which gained impetus in the 18th century and continues today.

Nature of the work

This occupation is concerned with the safekeeping of persons who have been arrested and are awaiting trial, or who have been tried, found guilty, and are serving time in a correctional institution. Correction officers maintain order in accordance with an institution's policies, regulations, and procedures.

To prevent disturbances or escapes, correction officers carefully observe the conduct and behavior of the inmates at all times. They watch for forbidden activities and infractions of the rules, as well as for poor attitudes or unsatisfactory adjustment to prison life on the part of the inmates. They try to settle disputes before violence can erupt. They may search the prisoners or their living quarters for weapons or drugs and inspect locks, bars on windows and doors, and gates for any evidence of tampering. The inmates are under guard constantly—while eating, sleeping, exercising, bathing, and working. They are counted periodically to be sure all are present. Some officers are stationed on towers and at gates to prevent escapes. All rule violations and anything out of the ordinary are reported to a superior officer such as a *chief jailer*. In case of a major disturbance, correction officers may use weapons or force to return order.

Correction officers give work assignments to prisoners, supervise them as they carry out their duties, and instruct them in unfamiliar tasks. Correction officers are responsible for the physical needs of the prisoners, such as providing or obtaining meals and medical aid. They assure the health and safety of the inmates by checking the cells for unsanitary conditions and fire hazards.

These workers may escort inmates from their cells to the prison's visiting room, medical office, or chapel. Certain officers called *patrol conductors* guard prisoners who are being transported between courthouses, prisons, mental institutions, or other destinations, either by van, car, or public transportation. Officers at a penal institution may also screen visitors at the entrance and accompany them to other areas within the facility. From time to time, they may inspect mail addressed to the prisoners, checking for contraband; help investigate crimes committed within the prison; or aid in the search for escapees.

Some *police officers* specialize in guarding juvenile offenders being held at a police station house or detention room pending a hearing, a transfer to a correctional institution, or a return to their parents. These workers often investigate the background of first offenders to check for a criminal history or to make a recommendation to the magistrate regarding disposition of the case. Lost or runaway children are also placed in the care of these officers until their parents or guardians can be located.

Immigration guards guard aliens held by the immigration service awaiting investigation, deportation, or release. *Gate tenders* check the identification of all persons entering and leaving the penal institution.

In most correctional institutions, psychologists and social workers are employed to counsel inmates with mental and emotional problems. It is an important part of a correction officer's job, however, to supplement this with informal counseling. Officers may help inmates adjust to prison life, prepare for return to civilian life, and avoid committing crimes in the future. On a more immediate level, they may arrange for an inmate to visit the library, help inmates get in touch with their families, suggest where to look for a job after release from prison, or discuss personal problems. In some institutions, correction officers may lead more formal group counseling sessions.

Correction officers usually keep a daily record of their activities and make regular reports, either verbal or written, to their supervisors. These reports concern the behavior of the inmates and the quality and quantity of work they do, as well as any disturbances, rule violations, and unusual occurrences that may have taken place.

Head correction officers supervise and coordinate the activities of correction officers during an assigned watch or in an assigned area. They perform roll call and assign duties to the officers; direct the activities of groups of inmates; arrange the release and transfer of prisoners in accordance with the instructions on a court order; maintain security and investigate disturbances among the inmates; maintain prison records and prepare reports; and review and evaluate the performance of their subordinates.

In small communities, correction officers (who are sometimes called *jailers*) may also act as deputy sheriffs or police officers when they are not occupied with guard duties.

Requirements

Candidates for the occupation of correction officer generally must be 21 years of age and have a high school diploma or its equivalent. Indi-

A prison guard observes the actions of inmates while they venture out of their cells for a brief period.

viduals with less than a high school education may be considered for employment if they have qualifying work experience. Other requirements include good health, physical strength, sound judgment, and the ability to think and act quickly.

The training for correction officers ranges from the special academy instruction provided by the federal government and some states to the informal, on-the-job training furnished by most states and local governments. The training academies have programs that last from four to eight weeks and instruct trainees on institutional policies, regulations, and procedures; the behavior and custody of inmates; security measures; and report writing. On the other hand, on-the-job trainees spend two to six months under the supervision of an experienced officer. During that time, they receive similar training while gaining actual experience. Correction officers may be given additional training periodically as new ideas and procedures in criminal justice are developed.

CORRECTION OFFICERS

Some states require applicants for this job to have one or two years of previous experience in corrections or related police work, and a few have a mandatory written examination. Correction officers who work for the federal government and most state governments are covered by civil service systems or merit boards and may be required to pass a competitive exam for employment.

Special requirements

In many states, applicants may be asked to pass a physical exam in which their physical fitness, eyesight, and hearing are checked against specific standards. In addition, some states may require random or comprehensive drug testing of their officers, either during hiring procedures or while employed at the facility.

Opportunities for experience and exploration

Because of the age requirement and the nature of the work, there are no opportunities for young people to gain actual experience while still in school. Between the ages of 18 and 21, however, individuals may prepare for employment by taking college courses in criminal justice or police science. They may also look into obtaining a civilian job as clerk or other worker for the police department or other protective service organization.

Methods of entering

To apply for a job as correction officer, individuals should contact federal or state civil service commissions, state departments of correction, or local correctional institutions and facilities and ask for information about entrance requirements, training, and job opportunities.

Advancement

With additional education and training, experienced officers may qualify for promotion to head correction officer or advancement to some other supervisory or administrative position. Some officers transfer to related areas, such as probation and parole.

Employment outlook

As the general population has increased, so has the jail and prison population—and the necessity for correction officers to guard the inmates. In 1990, there were approximately 230,000 correction officers employed in the United States. Almost half of these worked in state-run correctional facilities such as prisons, prison camps, and reformatories. Most of the rest were employed at city and county jails or other institutions, while a few thousand worked for the federal government.

Employment in this field is expected to increase much faster than the average for all jobs. It is estimated that another 142,000 jobs will be created within the next 15 years, an increase in employment of 61 percent. The extremely crowded conditions in today's correctional institutions have created a need for more correction officers to guard the inmates more closely and relieve the tensions. A greater number of officers will also be required as a result of the expansion or new construction of facilities. As prison sentences become longer through mandatory minimum sentences set by state law, the number of prisons needed will increase. In addition, many job openings will occur from a characteristically high turnover rate, as well as from the normal need to fill vacancies caused by the death or retirement of older workers.

Because security must be maintained at correctional facilities at all times, correction officers can depend on steady employment. They are not usually affected by poor economic conditions or changes in government spending. Correction officers are rarely laid off, even when budgets need to be trimmed. Instead, because of the high turnover, staffs can be cut quickly simply by not replacing those officers who leave.

Most jobs will be found in relatively large institutions located near metropolitan areas, although opportunities for correction officers exist in jails and other smaller facilities throughout the country.

Earnings

There is a wide variation in wages for correction officers, depending on the level of government that employs them. Local governments pay an average starting salary of around $18,700 a year, and top earnings average $24,300. Median earnings are about $20,600.

State governments pay correction officers an average starting salary of $18,400 per year, while salaries range from $12,400 in Kentucky to $29,400 in California. The average salary range for experienced officers is $14,700 to $37,400. The average salary for all state correctional officers is $22,900.

The federal government pays a starting salary of $18,900 a year, with maximum salaries in excess of $41,000 for sergeants and other supervisors. The average for all federal correction officers and sergeants is $23,800 per year. Supervisory corrections officers start at $25,700 a year.

Benefits for correction officers may include uniforms or a cash allowance to buy their own; hospitalization and major medical insurance, either wholly or partially paid for; and disability and life insurance. Officers who work for the federal government and for most state governments are covered by civil service systems or merit boards.

Conditions of work

Work schedules for correction officers may include nights, weekends, and holidays, because prison security must be maintained around the clock. The workweek, however, generally consists of five eight-hour days, except during emergencies, when many officers work overtime.

Correction officers may work indoors or outdoors, depending on their duties. Conditions can vary even within an institution: some areas are well lighted, ventilated, and temperature-controlled, while others are overcrowded, hot, and noisy. Officers who work outdoors, of course, are subject to all kinds of weather. Correctional institutions occasionally present unpredictable or even hazardous situations. If violence erupts among the inmates, correction officers may be in danger of injury or death. Although this risk is higher than for most other occupations, correction work is usually routine.

Correction officers need physical and emotional strength to cope with the stress inherent in dealing with criminals, many of whom may be dangerous or incapable of change. A correc-

tional officer has to remain alert and aware of the surroundings, the prisoners' movements and attitudes, and any potential for danger or violence. This continual heightened level of alertness may create psychological stress for some workers.

GOE: 04.01.01; SIC: 9223; SOC: 5133

◇ **SOURCES OF ADDITIONAL INFORMATION**

For information on a career in the correction field and about schools that offer programs in criminal justice, financial aid, and job listings, write to:

CEGA Services, Inc.
Correctional Careers Dept.
PO Box 81826
Lincoln, NE 68501

Additional information on correction careers is available from:

The American Correctional Association
8025 Laurel Lakes Court
Laurel, MD 20707

Canadian Correctional Association
P.O. Box 2590, Main P.O.
Edmonton AB T5J 2G3

◇ **RELATED ARTICLES**

Volume 1: Civil Service; Politics and Public Service
Volumes 2–4: Border patrol officers; Deputy U.S. marshals; FBI agents; Parole officers; Police officers; Recreation workers; Recreational therapists; Security consultants; Security guards; Social workers

Cosmetologists

Definition

Cosmetologists, often called *beauty operators, beauticians,* or *hairdressers,* perform professional personal services for customers to aid them in improving their personal appearance. They cut, style, and dye hair; perform facials; apply makeup; and do manicures.

History

The desire to improve one's personal appearance is not a recent vogue in our culture. Neolithic cave drawings, writers of antiquity, and historical excavations all depict ancient people's interest in hairstyles and in oils, perfumes, and other articles that would help them look and feel better. Egyptian women of 8,000 years ago, especially those of wealth and nobility, took elaborate care of their hair and used cosmetics such as eye makeup and lip color. Royalty in the Middle Ages had servants who styled, cut, and cared for their hair. Portraits and paintings from colonial days show that the high-fashion hair designs and powdered wigs of the day were worn by men and women alike.

Until about 70 years ago beauticians performed their services in customers' homes. The beauty salons now known to the U.S. public have emerged as public establishments only in recent years. Today, beauty shops are prevalent almost everywhere and the services of cosmetologists are available to everyone. The public now regards the services of cosmetologists as more than a luxury; an attractive appearance can bolster personal morale and feelings of confidence, and also aid a person's success professionally. In the United States, beauty shops are among the largest of the personal service industries.

Nature of the work

Cosmetologists perform personal grooming services for customers that may include styling, cutting, trimming, straightening, permanent waving, coloring, tinting, bleaching, and shampooing hair. Cosmetologists may also give facials, massages, manicures, pedicures, and scalp treatments, and may shape and tint eyelashes and eyebrows. They sometimes do makeup analyses, suggest cosmetic aids, and advise customers on what products to use and how to use them for the best results. Many specialize as *hairstylists.* Today, many cosmetologists called *wig dressers* are trained in the styling and care of wigs. Through advanced training, cosmetologists may specialize in some aspect of their work, such as permanent waving, cutting hair, or setting only the more difficult, high-fashion hairstyles. In small shops the cosmetologist's job duties may also include making appointments for customers, cleaning equipment, and sterilizing instruments.

Cosmetologists use certain tools and equipment in their work, such as scissors, razors, brushes, clippers, cosmetic aids, massage and manicure equipment, hair dryers, towels, and reclining chairs. Most of the equipment and tools are provided by the shop owners.

In some shops, *manicurists* tend to customers' nails, filing and polishing them, and trimming the cuticles. Cosmetologists work in close personal contact with the public. They may have customers at any age level. Some even specialize in children's haircuts.

The work of barbers and that of cosmetologists are closely related, and both barbers and cosmetologists perform their services in the same type of surroundings. Although some beauty shops may be decorated to appeal more to a female clientele, many men now prefer to have their hair cut and styled by cosmetologists. Cosmetologists are employed in privately owned shops throughout the country, many of them small businesses. They may also be employed in beauty shops in large department stores, drugstores, hospitals, nursing homes, and hotels. Cosmetologists may be employed to demonstrate hairstyles and cosmetic products in various retail stores, fashion centers, photographic centers, and television studios. With advanced training, some cosmetologists may qualify to teach in beauty culture colleges and vocational training schools.

Cosmetologists serving the public must have pleasant, friendly, yet professional attitudes, as well as skill, ability, and an interest in their craft, if they want to build a following of steady customers. The nature of the work demands that cosmetologists be aware of the psychological aspects of dealing with all types of customers.

Although many of the services performed by cosmetologists are repetitive in nature, the individual personalities of the public add to the interest, satisfaction, and challenge of the occupation. Cosmetologists have a continual challenge for creativity and artistic flair in their jobs through hair styling, fashion creation, and makeup work for customers.

Requirements

Almost all cosmetologists learn their craft at an accredited vocational school. The National Association of Cosmetology Schools estimates that more than 3,900 public vocational and private training schools for cosmetologists operate across the country.

Although a high school education strengthens any applicant's chances of success—both personally and professionally—the minimum educational requirement for entrance to most training schools is successful completion of the eighth grade. Depending on the state, some schools require applicants to have a high school diploma. Applicants who think that they might like to teach beauty culture at some time in their careers will need a high school education and, very likely, two to four years of college training.

The majority of private schools offer training programs lasting six to nine months; in some states, however, courses require from 12 to 15 months for completion. Public vocational school programs may cover a span of two or three years equal to the last three years of high school, because academic subjects are also a part of the curriculum.

Courses at cosmetology schools may include lectures, demonstrations, and practical work. Classroom training can include such subjects as anatomy, elementary physiology, hygiene, sanitation, applied chemistry, shop planning, applied electricity, and business basics. In practical training, students usually practice their techniques on mannequins and on each other. As students gain experience, they may work on customers who come to the training clinics for their lower prices.

The cost of beauty culture training programs varies among schools. It is determined by such factors as the adequacy of the school's physical plant, training facilities, staff, location, and length of formal training. Tuition may also be affected by the requirements of the state board of examiners.

Cosmetologists in all states must obtain a license. In some states applicants must first pass an examination to qualify as a junior cosmetologist. After passing this exam and practicing for one year, they are eligible to take a second exam for senior cosmetologist. Fees for

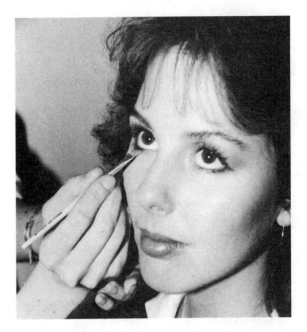

Cosmetologists often give their customers makeovers. Such work requires a steady hand and a delicate touch.

license examinations and yearly renewals are different in every state.

The number of hours of formal course training that students must have before they can apply for cosmetologist's licenses with a state board of examiners varies among the states. States may require from 1,000 hours (six months) to 2,500 hours (15 months) of combined practical and classroom training. Some states allow applicants to complete this requirement in apprenticeship programs. These programs, however, are gradually decreasing in number as state boards of examiners realize that applicants need more formal and technical training.

Applicants must meet other criteria to be eligible to take the state board examinations for licenses. In the majority of states, the minimum age requirement is 16. Because standards and requirements vary from state to state, students are urged to contact the licensing board of the state in which they plan to be employed.

Opportunities for experience and exploration

The occupation of cosmetologist may be explored by visiting the various training institutions, such as public vocational high schools and private beauty colleges. Some schools may permit potential students to visit and observe training classes. Watching and talking with licensed cosmetologists may provide additional information. There is little opportunity to explore this occupation through part-time work experience; however, some individuals may obtain summer or weekend jobs as general shop helpers.

Methods of entering

Cosmetologists secure their first jobs in various ways. The majority of beauty colleges and private and public vocational training schools aid their graduates in locating job opportunities. Many schools have formal placement services.

Applicants may also apply directly to beauty shops in which they would like to work. Applicants may hear about openings through newspaper want ads or city or state employment services.

Advancement

Most cosmetologists begin their careers as general beauticians performing a variety of services. In some states a person must begin as a junior operator; after a year of experience at this level, the individual is eligible to take an examination to become licensed as a senior cosmetologist. Some pursue advanced educational training to become specialized in one aspect of beauty culture, such as hairstyling or coloring.

Through skill, training, and seniority, a hairdresser may advance to a position as shop manager. After they have built a loyal clientele, some people may aspire to open their own shop. Cosmetologists may also advance by moving to beauty shops that are located in more affluent areas.

After some years of practical experience and, in many cases, additional academic training, some cosmetologists may become teachers in schools of beauty culture. These opportunities, however, are usually open only to those who possess exceptional skills and abilities.

Cosmetologists may find that their background in beauty culture can help them move into different fields. They may move into jobs such as representatives of cosmetic companies or equipment firms, beauty editors for magazines, makeup artists in motion picture and television studios, or inspectors on state licensing examination boards. Other related job opportunities include *body makeup artists,* who work with photographers and models; *mortuary beauticians;* and *scalp treatment operators.*

Employment outlook

Thousands of job opportunities are expected to be available for cosmetologists through the 1990s. The market for cosmetologists is expanding as the general population increases, more shops are opened in suburban shopping centers, and working women seek out cosmetic services more frequently. Good employment opportunities are becoming increasingly available to the part-time cosmetologist.

An estimated 650,000 people were employed as cosmetologists in the 1990s. The number of male workers in this field is increasing steadily. Currently, the demand for cosmetologists far outnumbers the supply.

Earnings

Salaries of cosmetologists depend on a number of factors, such as experience, ability, speed of performance, income level of the shop's clientele, shop location (suburban or urban), and the salary arrangement between the worker and the salon. Most cosmetologists are employed on a commission basis, while others receive a base salary plus 40 percent to 50 percent commission. Tips are also an important factor in the cosmetologist's earnings.

Considering all of these factors, it is difficult to quote exact salary figures for the entire profession. Estimates are that the salaries for experienced operators in the 1990s range from $15,600 to $25,000. Beginning cosmetologists with average skill earn from $12,000 to $13,000. In exclusive city salons, expert operators, specialists, and top hair stylists earn much more.

Fringe benefits in this occupation may include group health and life insurance and one-to two-week paid vacations. The availability of fringe benefits varies widely, depending on the employer. Furthermore, these benefits, except for paid vacations, are usually available only to those employed by beauty salon chains and large establishments such as department stores and nursing homes.

Conditions of work

Most cosmetologists work a 40-hour week, although some may work 44 to 48 hours weekly. Working hours usually include Saturdays and, very frequently, evening appointments. They may sometimes work according to a shift schedule. Holiday seasons and special community events may result in increased business, which would involve overtime work.

The nature of the cosmetologist's job requires standing for most of the work day. The continual use of water, shampoos, lotions, and other solutions with chemical contents may cause skin irritations.

Cosmetologists usually work in attractive, well lighted and comfortably ventilated shops. Surroundings and place of employment, the attitude of the employer, and the skill and experience of the operator will determine the degree of supervision under which the cosmetologist must work.

The cosmetologist may find it trying to work constantly in such close, personal contact with the public at large, especially when they strive to satisfy customers who are difficult to please or disagreeable. The work demands an even temperament, pleasant disposition, and patience. For some individuals these constant demands may create nervous strain and tension.

GOE: 09.02.01; SIC: 7231; SOC: 5253

Cost estimators

Definition

Cost estimators compile and analyze economic data to prepare estimates of the cost of construction or manufacturing projects. They conduct studies and use data, such as labor and material costs, to help contractors or other project planners determine how much a project will cost and if a project should be done.

History

People in business need to be able to predict how much a future project will cost to determine what they can charge the customer in return. No effective business project can be undertaken without a thorough assessment of the potential costs. This information has become more important as mass production techniques have made business decisions much more expensive and long-term commitment vital to economic success.

As production techniques become more specialized, it has become necessary to have specialists responsible for collecting and analyzing cost information on the many facets of production. Costs of labor, materials, transportation, equipment, and many other factors all must be collected and interpreted before a construction or manufacturing decision can be made. The cost estimator fulfills this function and is the vital link between a product idea and its implementation.

As long as there are buildings to be constructed or new products to be manufactured, there will be a continuing need for experts who can establish how much a project will cost so that the people paying for the project will be

A group of administrators attend a presentation given by a cost estimator. The cost estimator must be prepared to answer the challenging questions of his clients.

surance costs of that same project. It is then the responsibility of a chief estimator to combine the reports and submit one development proposal.

The cost estimator's role is to bring together complex data in assessing costs. In the manufacturing process, for example, an estimator may work with engineers to develop charts showing that labor costs should go down as the project progresses because the workers will learn the manufacturing process, become more efficient, and thereby increase productivity. Charts may also be used to measure how prices for a particular part compare with prices paid in the past and what can be expected to be paid in the future.

To be effective, an estimator must know current prices for labor, materials, and other factors that influence costs. An estimator should also be able to compute and understand accounting and mathematical formulas and be able to make sound decisions based on these computations. Increasingly, computers are being used to do the routine calculations, leaving the estimator more time to analyze data and evaluate effective production techniques.

Particular areas of specialization within the field of cost estimating include the following.

Paperboard box estimators estimate the cost of manufacturing paperboard boxes based on material costs and quality, quantity, and packaging considerations. They work with production personnel to develop procedures to minimize waste and thereby reduce costs.

Printing estimators estimate the labor and material costs of printing and binding books, pamphlets, and other printed matter. They work with customers to analyze production costs, using such factors as size and number of pages, paper stock requirements, and binding operations.

able to make wise business decisions and plan accordingly.

Nature of the work

Cost estimators collect and analyze information on various factors influencing costs, like the labor, materials, and machinery needed for a particular project. The scope of work is largely determined by the type and size of the project being estimated. On a large building project, for example, the estimator reviews architectural drawings and other bidding documents before any construction begins. Then the estimator visits the potential construction site to collect site development costs such as for electricity and other services.

After compiling a thorough understanding of the construction process and the people and machinery involved, the estimator writes a quantity survey, or "takeoff," by completing standard estimating forms that include information on dimensions of the project.

Sometimes more than one estimator is used on a project, and estimators may specialize in one area. For example, one estimator may assess the electrical costs of a project while another concentrates on the transportation or in-

Requirements

Construction and manufacturing firms usually prefer estimators to have experience with their procedures and a thorough knowledge of the costs involved in production. To prepare for this on-the-job training, a high school student should take courses in accounting and mathematics. English courses and courses in writing are recommended. Post-secondary two-year training programs, such as those offered at community colleges or technical schools, are also helpful. Course work should include physics and technical drawing, as well as specific courses covering manufacturing and construction processes.

Some employers request that an entry-level estimator have a bachelor's degree in civil engineering or mathematics. The federal government, for example, will only accept entry-level applicants with a college degree.

Although there are no licensing requirements, many cost estimators find it helpful to become certified. To become certified, an estimator must have between three and seven years of experience in the field and pass a written and oral test. Information on certification procedures and other professional training is available from organizations such as the American Society of Professional Estimators and the National Estimating Society.

Opportunities for experience and exploration

Experience is especially important in a field such as this, with so much emphasis on on-the-job training. Part-time work with a construction crew or manufacturing firm, especially during the busy summer months, is a good way to gain experience. Talking with those in the field is another way of finding out about career opportunities.

Methods of entering

Many cost estimators are trades people who display a particular aptitude or interest for cost analysis. For example, an experienced plumber may become an estimator on the contracting projects done by the company. Other people complete a two-year training program or bachelor's degree and then enter the work force.

Advancement

As in many professions, promotions for cost estimators are dependent on skill and experience. Advancement usually comes in the way of more responsibility and higher wages. A skilled cost estimator at a large construction company may become a chief estimator. Some experienced cost estimators also go into consulting work.

Employment outlook

Employment for cost estimators is expected to increase about as fast as the average through the 1990s. Many cost estimators work in the construction field, where employment depends on the amount of construction that takes place. Residential construction is expected to slow over the next decade, but commercial and industrial buildings should pick up the slack.

Experienced cost estimators and highly trained college graduates have the best job prospects.

Earnings

Salaries vary according to the size of the construction or manufacturing firm, and the experience and education of the worker. Average starting salaries range between $16,000 and $20,000 a year. Those with college degrees can earn up to $30,000 in their beginning years. Very experienced cost estimators earn as much as $75,000 annually. Those with certification should earn between $30,000 and $50,000 per year, and some specialists make even more.

Conditions of work

Much of the work takes place in a typical office setting, with accounting records and other information close by. However, estimators visit construction sites or manufacturing facilities to inspect production procedures. Often the work entails consulting with engineers, work supervisors, and other professionals involved in the production or manufacturing process. Estimators usually work a 40-hour week, although longer hours may be required if a project is on deadline. Overtime hours almost always occur in the summer when construction projects are in full force.

Estimators should be able to work long hours collecting and analyzing complex economic data. They should be well organized and be able to work under deadline pressure.

GOE: 05.03.02; SIC: Any industry; SOC: 149

◇ **SOURCES OF ADDITIONAL INFORMATION**

Information about career opportunities and professional training is available from:

American Association of Cost Engineers
PO Box 1557
Morgantown, WV 26507

American Society of Professional Estimators
6911 Richmond Highway
Suite 230
Alexandria, VA 22306

National Estimating Society
101 South Whiting Street, Suite 313
Alexandria, VA 22304

◇ **RELATED ARTICLES**

Volume 1: Construction; Design; Engineering; See also specific industries
Volumes 2–4: Accountants and auditors; Actuaries; Assessors and appraisers; Mathematicians; Miscellaneous engineers

Costume designers

Definition

Costume designers plan and create clothing and accessories for all characters in a theatrical production. They study the play and work closely with directors to design costumes that evoke a particular time, place, and personality. They may design for stage, film, television, dance, or opera productions.

History

Costume design has been an important part of the theater since the early Greek tragedies, when actors wore masks and long robes with sleeves, unlike the dress of the day. By the time of the Roman Caesars, stage costumes had become very elaborate and colorful.

After the fall of Rome, the theater disappeared for some time, but it returned in the form of Easter and Nativity plays. Priests and choirboys wore their usual robes with some simple additions, such as veils and crowns. Plays then moved from the church to the marketplace, and costumes again became important.

During the Renaissance, fantastic mythological costumes were designed for the Italian intermezzi, triumphs, and pageants, the French ballets de cour, and the English masques by such famous designers as Torelli, Jean Berain and Burnacini. From 1760 to 1782, Louis-Rene Boquet designed costumes using wide paniers, forming a kind of ballet skirt covered with rococo detail. But by the end of the 18th century, there was a movement toward more classical costumes on the stage.

During the early 19th century, historical costumes became popular, which meant that Elizabethan, Stuart, and other details were added to contemporary dress. Toward the end of the 19th century, realism became important, and actors wore the dress of the day, often their own clothes. Since this trend meant fewer jobs for costume designers, they turned to lighter musical productions and opera to express their creativity.

In the early 20th century, Diaghilev's Russian Ballet introduced a non-naturalism in costumes, most notably in the designs of Leon Bakst. This trend gave way to European avant-garde theater, in which costumes became abstract and symbolic.

Since the 1960s, new materials, such as plastics and adhesives, have greatly increased

A costume designer works on a detailed and colorful outfit. Many of these elaborate costumes will reflect the personalities of the characters wearing them.

the costume designer's range. Costume design is less likely to conform to trends.

Nature of the work

Costume designers first read the play to find out its theme, geographical location, and time period, who the characters are, their relationships and functions, the kind of dialogue, and action. They meet with the director to learn his or her interpretation of the play. They discuss the characters, period and style, the time frame for the production, and the budget.

Designers then plan a rough costume plot, which is a list of costume changes by scene for each character. They research the history thoroughly. They plan a preliminary color scheme and sketch the costumes, including gloves, footwear, hose, purses, jewelry, umbrellas, canes, fans, bouquets, and masks. The costume designer or an assistant collects swatches of fabrics and samples of various accessories.

After completing the research, final color sketches are painted or drawn and mounted for presentation. Once the director approves the designs, the costume designer solicits bids from contractors; finds, pulls or rents costumes; and shops for fabrics, notions, trim, and accessories. Measurements of all actors are taken. Designers work closely with drapers and sewers in costume shops, hairstylists and make-up artists. They supervise fittings and attend all dress rehearsals to make final adjustments and repairs.

Requirements

Costume designers need at least a high school education. A college degree is not a requirement, but in this highly competitive field, it gives a sizable advantage, and most costume designers today have a bachelor's degree. Many art schools, especially in New York and Los Angeles, have BFA and MFA programs in

403

costume design. A liberal arts school that has a strong theater program is also a good choice.

Costume designers need sewing, draping and flat patterning skills, as well as training in basic design techniques and figure drawing. English, literature, and history classes help students learn how to analyze a play and research the clothing and manner of various historical periods. Costume designers must prepare a portfolio of their work, including three or four dozen photographs and sketches from two or three shows.

Some theatrical organizations require membership in United Scenic Artists, a union that protects the interests of designers on the job and sets minimum fees. Beginning designers become members by passing an exam. More experienced designers must submit a portfolio for review.

Opportunities for experience and exploration

Those interested in a costume design career should join a theater organization, such as a school drama club or a community theater. School dance troupes or film classes also may offer opportunities to explore costume design.

The Costumer's Handbook and *The Costume Designer's Handbook*, both by Rosemary Ingham and Elizabeth Covey, are invaluable resources for beginning or experienced costume designers. Both books explain in detail the various steps in the costume design process.

Methods of entering

Most high schools and colleges have drama clubs and dance groups that need costumes designed and made. Community theaters, too, may offer opportunities for design students to assist in costume production. Regional theaters hire several hundred costume technicians each year for seasons that vary from 28 to 50 weeks.

Many beginning designers enter the field by becoming an assistant to a successful designer. Established designers welcome newcomers and are generous mentors.

Some start working at costume shops, which require membership in the International Ladies Garment Workers Union, but they may hire non-union workers for specific time periods. Some begin as shoppers, who swatch fabrics, compare prices, buy yardage, trim, and accessories. This is a great way to learn where to

find materials, how much they cost, and also helps a prospective designer make valuable contacts in the field. Other positions good for beginners are: *milliner's assistant, craft assistant,* or *assistant to the draper.*

Schools with BFA or MFA programs in costume design may offer internships that can lead to jobs after graduation. Another method of entering costume design, though less successful, is to write to regional theaters and send your resume to the theater's managing director.

Before you become a costume designer, you may find it advisable to work as a freelance design assistant for a few years until you have acquired experience, reputation, contacts, and an impressive portfolio.

Advancement

Beginning designers must show they are willing to do a variety of tasks. The theater community is small and intricately interconnected, so if you work hard and are flexible, you will gain a good reputation quickly. Smaller regional theaters tend to hire designers for a full season to work with the same people on one or more productions, so the opportunities for movement are few.

Employment outlook

The poor economy of recent years has had an effect on theaters. Many are cutting their budgets or doing smaller shows. The cable television business, however, is growing rapidly and will continue to grow in the next decade.

New York City is the main proving ground for theater designers, as Hollywood is for film designers. Costume design, however, is becoming more decentralized because of the number of regional theaters throughout the United States and because cable television companies operate at locations across the country. As a result, designers must be willing to travel.

Competition is stiff and will remain so throughout the next decade, depending on the economy. The number of qualified costume designers far exceeds the number of jobs available.

Earnings

Costume designers who work on Broadway or for dance companies in New York City must be members of United Scenic Artists union, which sets minimum fees, requires producers to pay into pension and welfare funds, protects the designer's rights, establishes rules for billing, and offers group health and life insurance.

An assistant on a Broadway show earns about $775. A costume designer for a Broadway musical with a minimum of 36 actors earns around $17,500. For opera and dance companies, salary is usually by costume count.

For feature films and television, costume designers earn daily rates for an eight-hour day or a weekly rate for an unlimited number of hours. Designers sometimes earn royalties on their designs.

Regional theaters usually set individual standard fees which vary widely, beginning around $200 per week for an assistant. Most of them do not require membership in the union.

Conditions of work

Costume designers put in long hours at painstaking detail work. It is a demanding profession that requires you to be brave, tough, flexible, artistic, and practical. The work can be erratic—a busy period followed by weeks with no work. In spite of the importance of costumes to a production's success, the designer usually gets little recognition compared to the actors and director.

Designers meet a variety of interesting and gifted people. Every play, film, or concert is different and every production situation is

unique, so for costume designers, there is no steady routine. Costumer designers must play many roles: artist, sewer, researcher, buyer, manager and negotiator.

GOE: 01.02.03; SIC: none; SOC: 6859

SOURCES OF ADDITIONAL INFORMATION

Costume Designers Guild
14724 Ventura Boulevard
Sherman Oaks, CA 91403

The Costume Society of America
55 Edgewater Drive
PO Box 73
Earlesville, MD 21919-0073

RELATED ARTICLES

Volume 1: Apparel; Motion Pictures; Performing Arts; Textiles
Volumes 2–4: Actors; Fashion designers; Jewelers and jewelry repairers; Shoe and leather workers and repairers; Stage production workers; Tailors and dressmakers; Textile manufacturing occupations; Textile technicians

Counter and retail clerks

Definition

Counter and retail clerks work as intermediaries between the general public and businesses that provide goods and services. They take orders and receive payments for services such as videotape rentals, automobile rentals, and laundry and dry cleaning services. They often assist customers with their purchasing or rental decisions, especially when sales personnel are not available. They may also prepare billing statements, keep records of receipts and sales, and balance money in their cash register.

History

The first retail outlets in the United States sold food staples, farm necessities, and clothing. Many times these general stores also served as the post office and became the social and economic center of the community.

A number of changes occurred in retailing during the mid- and late-19th century. The growth of retail stores selling specific products such as clothing, hardware items, and groceries reflected the growing diversity of available products and customer tastes.

Counter clerks must have knowledge of the items they sell. In this case, the clerk must be familiar with the several different types of cheese.

This growth of retail outlets has continued at a steady pace. The variety of retail stores today is staggering—everything from bicycle shops, watch repair shops, and computer shops, to video stores, electronics stores, and athletic footwear boutiques. All these outlets need qualified counter and retail clerks to assist customers and receive payment for the services or products that customers buy.

Nature of the work

The specific nature of the work depends on the type of business that employs the counter clerk. In a service establishment such as a shoe repair shop, for example, the clerk receives the shoes to be repaired or cleaned from the customer, examines the shoes, gives a price quote and a receipt to the customer, and then sends the shoes to the work department for necessary repairs or cleaning. The shoes are marked with a tag specifying what work needs to be done and to whom the shoes belong. After the work is completed, the clerk returns the shoes to the customer and collects payment.

In a rental establishment such as a bicycle store, *bicycle-rental clerks* prepare rental forms and quote rates to customers. The clerks answer customer questions regarding operation of the bikes. They often take a deposit to cover any accidents or possible damage. Clerks also check the bicycles to be certain they are in good working order and make minor adjustments, if necessary. With long-term rentals, such as storage-facility rentals, clerks notify the customers when the rental period is about to expire and when the rent is overdue. *Film-rental clerks* greet customers, check out tapes, and accept payment. Upon return of the tapes, the

clerks check the condition of the tapes and then put them back on the shelves.

In smaller shops with no sales personnel or in situations where the sales personnel are unavailable, counter and retail clerks assist customers with purchases or rentals by demonstrating the merchandise, answering the customers' questions, accepting payment, recording sales, and wrapping their purchase or arranging for its delivery.

In addition to these duties, clerks may also prepare billing statements to be sent to customers. They may keep records of receipts and sales throughout the day and balance the money in their registers when their work shift ends. They sometimes are responsible for the display and presentation of products. In supermarkets and grocery stores, clerks stock shelves and bag food purchases for the customers.

Service-establishment attendants, such as those in a laundry, take clothes to be cleaned or repaired, and write down the customer's name and address. *Watch-and-clock-repair clerks* receive clocks and watches for repair and examine the timepieces to estimate repair costs. They may make minor repairs, such as replacing a watch band; otherwise the timepiece is forwarded to the repair shop with a description of needed repairs.

Many clerks have job titles that describe what they do and where they work. These include: *laundry-pricing clerks; telegraph-counter clerks; photo-finishing counter clerks; tool-and-equipment-rental clerks; airplane-charter clerks; baby-stroller and wheelchair-rental clerks; storage-facility-rental clerks; boat-rental clerks; hospital-television-rental clerks; trailer-rental clerks; automobile-rental clerks; fur-storage clerks;* and *self-service-laundry-and-dry-cleaning attendants*.

Counter and retail clerks must be able to adjust to alternating periods of heavy and light activity. No two days—or even customers—are alike. Because some customers can be rude or even hostile, clerks must exercise tact and patience at all times. Clerks must also be prepared to work many evening and weekend shifts.

Requirements

Although there are no specific educational requirements, most employers prefer workers to have a high school diploma. High school students should take courses in English, speech, and mathematics. Any business-related courses such as typing and those covering principles in retailing would also be helpful. Legible handwriting and the ability to add and subtract numbers quickly are a necessity.

Counter and retail clerks should have a pleasant personality and an ability to interact with a variety of people. They should also be neat and well groomed, and have a high degree of personal responsibility.

Opportunities for experience and exploration

There are numerous opportunities for part-time or temporary work as a clerk, especially during the holiday season. Many high schools have developed work-study programs that combine courses in retailing with part-time work in the field. Store owners cooperating in these programs often hire these students as full-time workers after they complete the course.

Methods of entering

Those interested in securing an entry-level position should contact stores directly. Workers with some experience, such as those who have completed a work-study program in high school, should have the greatest success, but most entry level positions do not require any previous experience. Jobs are often listed in help wanted advertisements.

Most stores provide new workers with on-the-job training in which experienced clerks explain company policies and procedures and teach new employees how to operate the cash register and other necessary equipment. This training usually continues for several weeks until the new employee feels comfortable on the job.

Advancement

Counter and retail clerks usually begin their employment doing the more routine tasks such as checking stock and operating the cash register. With experience, they may advance to more complicated assignments and assume some sales responsibilities. Those with the skill and aptitude may become sales people or store managers, although further education is normally required for management positions.

The high turnover rate in the clerk position increases the opportunities for being promoted. The number and kind of opportunities, however, may depend on the place of employment

and the ability, training, and experience of the employee.

Employment outlook

Approximately 4.75 million people work as retail clerks in the United States. Because of the proliferation of retail outlets, job opportunities for counter and retail clerks are expected to grow faster than average through the 1990s. The Department of Labor predicts that more than 1.3 million additional people will be hired in this field.

As is currently the case, major employers will be laundry or dry cleaning establishments, automobile rental firms, and supermarkets and grocery stores. The continued growth in video rental stores and other rental services will also increase the need for skilled clerks. There should also be an increase in the number of opportunities for temporary or part-time work, especially during busy business periods.

Earnings

Beginning counter and retail clerks in the 1990s generally earn around the minimum wage of $4.25 an hour. Experienced clerks should average between $3.75 an hour and $9.00 an hour; the higher wages will be paid to those with the greatest number of job responsibilities. Full-time clerks should average between $150 and $220 a week, with some clerks earning somewhat more. Those workers who have union affiliation (usually those who work for supermarkets) may earn considerably more than their nonunion counterparts.

Full-time workers, especially those who are union members, may also receive benefits such as a paid vacation and health insurance, but this is not the industry norm.

Conditions of work

Although a 40-hour workweek is common, many stores operate on a 44- to 48-hour workweek. Most stores are open on Saturday and many on Sunday. Most stores are also open one or more weekday evenings, so working hours may vary from week to week and will inevitably include evening and weekend hours. Most counter and retail clerks work overtime during Christmas and other rush seasons. Part-time clerks generally work during peak business periods.

Most clerks work indoors in well-ventilated and well-lighted environments. The job itself can be fairly routine and repetitive. Clerks often spend much of their time on their feet. The advantages of this type of work include no major physical or occupational hazards.

GOE: 07.03.01, 08.02.02, 08.02.03; SIC: Any industry; SOC: 4363

◇ **SOURCES OF ADDITIONAL INFORMATION**

National Retail Federation
100 West 31st Street
New York, NY 10001

◇ **RELATED ARTICLES**

Volume 1: Sales
Volumes 2—4: Cashiers; File clerks; Financial institution tellers; General office clerks; Postal clerks; Retail sales workers

---

Court reporters

Definition

Court reporters record the testimony given at hearings, trials, and other legal proceedings. They use stenotype machines to take shorthand notes of public testimony, judicial opinions, sentences of the court, and other courtroom matters. Most court reporters transcribe the notes of the proceedings by using computer-aided transcription systems that print out regular, legible copies of the proceedings. The court reporter's job is vital to the integrity of our country's judicial system.

History

To record legal proceedings, court reporters use shorthand, a system of abbreviated writing that has its beginnings in script forms developed more than 2,000 years ago. Ancient Greeks and Romans used symbols and letters to record poems, speeches, and political meetings.

Europeans, such as the Englishman Timothy Bright, began to develop systems of shorthand in the 15th and 16th centuries. These systems were refined throughout the 17th and 18th centuries. Shorthand was used primarily in personal correspondence and for copying or creating literary works.

Shorthand began to be applied to business communications after the invention of the typewriter. The stenotype, the first shorthand machine, was invented by an American court reporter in 1910. Before the introduction of dictaphones, tape recorders, and other electronic recording devices, shorthand was the fastest and most accurate way for a secretary or reporter to copy down what was being said at a business meeting or other event.

Nature of the work

Court reporters are responsible for accurately recording all testimony by witnesses, lawyers, judges, and other participants at legal proceedings. They use symbols or shorthand forms of complete words to record what is said as quickly as it is spoken. People in court may speak at a rate of between 250 and 300 words a minute, and court reporters must record this testimony word for word.

The tool used by court reporters to record these proceedings is called a stenotype machine. The stenotype machine has 24 keys on its keyboard, each of which will print a single symbol. Unlike a typewriter, the operator can press more than one key at a time to print different combinations of symbols. Each symbol or combination represents a different sound, word, or phrase. As testimony is given, the reporter strikes one or more keys to create a phonetic representation of the testimony on a strip of paper. The court reporter later uses these strips of paper to transcribe the speech into legible, full-page documents or stores them for reference purposes.

Accurate recording of a trial is vital because the court reporter's record becomes the official transcript for the entire proceeding. In our legal system, court transcripts can be used after the trial for many important purposes. If a legal case is appealed, for example, the court reporter's transcript will become the foundation for any further legal action. The appellate judge will refer to the court reporter's transcript to see what happened in the trial and how the evidence was presented.

Because of the importance of accuracy, a court reporter who misses a word or phrase must interrupt the proceedings to have the words repeated. By the same token, the court reporter may be asked by the judge to read aloud a portion of recorded testimony during the trial to refresh everyone's memory. Court reporters must pay close attention to all the proceedings and be able to hear and understand everything. Sometimes it may be difficult to understand a particular witness or attorney due to poor diction, a strong accent, or a soft speaking voice. Nevertheless, the court reporter cannot be shy about stopping the trial and asking for clarification.

Court reporters must be adept at recording testimony on a wide range of legal issues, from medical malpractice to income tax evasion. In some cases, court reporters may record testimony at a murder trial or a child-custody case. Witnessing tense situations and following complicated arguments are unavoidable parts of the job. The court reporter must be able to remain detached from the human drama that unfolds in court while faithfully recording all that is said.

Computers play a large role in helping court reporters fulfill their job responsibilities. Computer programs help convert the symbols and words of a stenotype machine into standard English. This process requires the use of a specially constructed stenotype machine to record the symbols so that they can be fed into the computer. The computer-based system is not only very efficient and accurate. It also saves time because the computer can print out a transcript of the trial more quickly than the court reporter can type a transcript on a typewriter or word processor. These transcripts may then be used promptly by a judge or jury before rendering a decision or after a trial for review purposes.

Court reporters must listen attentively to each word spoken during trials and simultaneously record them on a machine.

Many court reporters are employed by city, county, state, or federal courts. Others work for themselves or as employees of freelance reporting agencies. These freelance reporters are hired by attorneys to record the pretrial statements, or depositions, of experts and other witnesses. When people want transcripts of other important discussions, freelance reporters may be called on to record what is said at business meetings, large conventions, or similar events.

A new application of court-reporting skills and technology is in the field of television captioning. Using specialized computer-aided transcription systems, reporters can produce captions for live television events, including sports events and national and local news, for the benefit of hearing-impaired viewers.

Requirements

Court reporters must have a high school diploma or its equivalent. Those interested in this profession should take English, typing, and other related business courses in high school. Aspiring court reporters should have comprehensive training in grammar and spelling. Training in Latin can also be a great benefit because it increases a court reporter's understanding of the many medical and legal terms that can arise during court proceedings. Knowledge of other foreign languages can also helpful.

Court reporters are required to complete a specialized training program in shorthand reporting. These programs usually last two years and include instruction on how to write at least 225 words a minute on a stenotype machine. Other topics covered include typing, transcription methods, English grammar, and the principles of law. For court cases involving medical issues, students must also take courses to become familiar with human anatomy and physiology. Basic medical and legal terms are also explained.

Degree programs in shorthand reporting are offered at various community colleges and business and vocational schools. Although some university programs exist, they are rare.

Some states require court reporters to be certified as proficient by the National Court Reporters Association (NCRA) or to be licensed by state officials. It may also be necessary for court reporters employed by the federal government to pass a civil service examination. When working in a legal proceeding, court reporters are considered officials of the court.

Opportunities for experience and exploration

High school students or others interested in pursuing a career as a court reporter are encouraged to talk with professionals already working in the field to learn more about its rewards and responsibilities. Attending actual court sessions is also informative. Because only those with the appropriate credentials are allowed to work as court reporters, it is impossible to get any hands-on experience before completing the required training. Part-time work as a secretary or stenographer may also help interested persons learn more about the job responsibilities of a court reporter.

Methods of entering

After completing the required training, court reporters usually work for a freelance reporting company that provides court reporters for business meetings and courtroom proceedings on a temporary basis. Job placement counselors at schools offering training programs often are helpful in locating employment opportunities. Qualified reporters can also contact these freelance reporting companies on their own. Occasionally a court reporter will be hired directly out of school as a courtroom official, but ordinarily only those with several years of experience are hired for full-time judiciary work.

Advancement

Skilled court reporters may be promoted to a larger court system or to an otherwise more de-

manding position, with an accompanying increase in pay and prestige. Those working for a freelance company may be hired permanently by a city, county, state, or federal court. Those with experience working in a government position may choose to become a freelance court reporter and thereby have greater job flexibility and perhaps earn more money. Those with the necessary training, experience, and business skills may decide to open their own freelance reporting company.

Employment outlook

Employment opportunities for skilled court reporters should continue to grow through the 1990s. The rising number of criminal court cases and civil lawsuits will cause both state and federal court systems to expand. Job openings will also arise due to retirement or attrition. Job opportunities should be greatest in and around large metropolitan areas, but qualified court reporters should be able to find work in most parts of the country.

As always, job prospects will be best for those with the most training and experience. Because of the reliance on computers in many aspects of this job, this type of experience and training is very important.

Earnings

Earnings vary according to the skill and experience of the court reporter, as well as his or her geographic location. Those just out of school may earn between $21,000 and $30,000 a year. Those employed by large court systems generally earn more than their counterparts in smaller communities. Experienced court reporters can expect to earn between $25,000 and $60,000 a year or more.

Court reporters that work in small communities or as freelancers may not be able to work full-time. Freelancers are usually not paid a yearly salary but rather earn their wages based on the number of transcript pages they provide. Successful court reporters with jobs in business environments may earn more than those in courtroom settings, but such positions carry less job security.

Those working for the government or full-time for private companies usually receive health insurance and other benefits, such as paid vacations and retirement pensions. Freelancers may or may not receive health insurance or other benefits, depending on the policies of their agencies.

Conditions of work

Offices and courtrooms are usually pleasant places to work. Under normal conditions, a court reporter can expect to work a standard 37- to 40-hour week. During lengthy trials or other complicated proceedings, court reporters often work much longer hours. They must be on hand before and after the court is actually in session and must wait while a jury is deliberating. Although weekend work is uncommon, a court reporter must be willing to work irregular hours, including some evenings. Court reporters must be able to spend long hours transcribing testimony with complete accuracy. There may be some travel involved, especially for freelance reporters.

Court reporters must be familiar with a wide range of medical and legal terms and must be assertive enough to ask for clarification if a term or phrase goes by without the reporter understanding it. Court reporters must be as unbiased as possible and accurately record what is said, not what they believe to be true.

Patience and perfectionism are vital characteristics, as is the ability to work closely with the judge and other court officials.

GOE: 07.05.03; SIC: 7339, 9211; SOC: 4623

◇ **SOURCES OF ADDITIONAL INFORMATION**

Career and certification information is available from:

National Court Reporters Association
8224 Old Courthouse Road
Vienna, VA 22182

◇ **RELATED ARTICLES**

Volume 1: Law
Volumes 2–4: Data entry clerks; Interpreters; Lawyers and judges; Paralegals; Secretaries; Stenographers; Typists and word processors

---

Credit analysts, banking

Definition

Credit analysts in banking analyze financial information to determine the amount of risk involved in lending money to businesses or individuals. They contact banks, credit associations, and others to obtain credit information and then prepare a written report of findings in which customer credit limits are suggested.

History

Only 50 or 75 years ago, lending money was based mainly on a person's reputation. Money was lent after a potential borrower talked with friends and business acquaintances. Now, of course, much more financial background information is demanded and only accepted forms of accounting are used to determine if a loan applicant is a good risk. For example, the use of credit cards and other forms of borrowing has skyrocketed in the last several years. As business and financial institutions have grown more complex, credit analysis has become a large industry, creating the need for a group of professional experts in the field.

Nature of the work

Credit analysts normally concentrate on one of two different areas. Commercial and business analysts evaluate risks in business loans; consumer credit analysts evaluate personal loan risks. In both cases an analyst studies financial documents, like a statement of assets and lia-

CREDIT ANALYSTS, BANKING

Credit analysts rely heavily on computers to calculate complex formulas and organize data. They must be proficient in spreadsheet software, word processing, and often statistical software as well.

bilities, submitted by the person or company seeking the loan, and consults with banks and other financial institutions who have previously loaned money to the applicant.

The scope of work used in a credit check depends in large part on the size and type of loan being requested. A background check on a $3,000 car loan, for example, is much less detailed than a $400,000 commercial improvement loan for an expanding business. In both cases financial statements and references will be checked by the credit analyst, but the larger loan will entail a much closer look at economic trends to determine if there is a market for the product being produced and the likelihood of the business failing. Because of these responsibilities, many credit analysts work solely with commercial loans.

In studying a commercial loan application, a credit analyst is interested in determining if the business or corporation is well managed and financially secure and if the existing economic climate is favorable for the success of such an operation. To do this, a credit analyst examines balance sheets and operating statements to determine the assets and liabilities of a company, its net sales, and its profits or losses. An analyst must be familiar with accounting and bookkeeping methods to ensure that the applicant company is operating under accepted principles. A background check of the leading officials of the applicant company is also done to determine if they personally have any loans outstanding. An on-site visit to the company by the analyst may also be necessary

to compare how its operations stack up against similar companies.

Analyzing economic trends to determine market conditions is another responsibility of the credit analyst. To do this, the analyst computes dozens of ratios to show how successful the company is in relationship to other similar businesses. Profit-and-loss statements, collection procedures, and a host of other factors are all analyzed. This ratio analysis can also be used to measure how successful a particular industry is likely to be given existing market considerations. Economic indicators are collected and mathematical formulas are applied. As in many other professions, the use of computers is revolutionizing the collection and analysis of information. Now, many computer programs are available to highlight economic trends and interpret other important data.

The credit analyst always provides a report on findings to bank executives. This report will include a complete financial history of the applicant, and usually conclude with a recommendation on the amount of loan, if any, that should be advanced. Bank executives use this report extensively in making final loan decisions.

Requirements

Credit analysts should have an aptitude for mathematics and be able to make sound decisions after analyzing detailed financial information. They should be able to work with both customers and coworkers and be able to communicate effectively, in written and verbal form.

Interested high school students should take courses in mathematics, accounting, and bookkeeping. English writing courses also are beneficial. Most credit analysts have a bachelor's degree in accounting, finance, or business administration. Course work should include business management, economics, statistics, and accounting. Some credit analysts go on to receive a master's in business administration (MBA) or a master's in some other related field.

Opportunities for experience and exploration

A part-time job as a bank clerk or teller will help familiarize a person with banking procedures. This is a good way of making contact with banking officials. Various clubs and organizations may have opportunities for volunteers to develop experience working with budgets and other financial statements.

Methods of entering

Most entry-level positions go to college graduates with degrees in fields such as accounting, economics, and business administration.

Advancement

There are many good advancement possibilities for a skilled credit analyst. Promotions may include a job with more responsibility, such as a middle management position at a bank, with a corresponding increase in salary. Those in a smaller bank may be promoted within or may chose to move to a larger financial institution.

Employment outlook

As the field of cash management grows, banks and other financial institutions need more credit analysts. Therefore, job prospects are expected to grow faster than average through the 1990s. There may be some competition for highly desired positions. Banks hire about half of the credit analysts, so opportunities should be best in areas with a great number of banks.

Earnings

Wages depend on experience and education. The size of the financial institution is also a determining factor; large banks tend to pay more than smaller facilities. Starting salaries for those with a bachelor's degree range between $14,000 and $20,000 per year. Those entering with an MBA or other master's degree can expect to earn $20,000 to $32,000 a year, perhaps more.

Conditions of work

Most credit analysts work in typical modern office settings. A commercial credit analyst may visit a business or corporation seeking a loan. An analyst can expect to work a 40-hour week, but overtime may be necessary if a project is on deadline.

A credit analyst should be able to spend long hours reading and analyzing financial reports. Attention to detail is critical. The analyst should be able to understand the economic and other factors that determine why some businesses succeed and others do not. Credit analysts should be able to work in pressurized situations, with loans of millions of dollars possibly dependent on their analysis.

GOE: 11.06.03; SIC: 61; SOC: 1419

◇ SOURCES OF ADDITIONAL INFORMATION

For general information about careers in banking contact:

American Bankers Association
1120 Connecticut Avenue, NW
Washington, DC 20036

General information about the area of consumer credit is available from:

National Foundation for Consumer Credit
8611 Second Avenue
Suite 100
Silver Spring, MD 20910

◇ RELATED ARTICLES

Volume 1: Banking and Financial Services; Insurance
Volumes 2–4: Accountants and auditors; Bookkeeping and accounting clerks; Collection workers; Economists; Financial institution clerks and related workers; Financial institution officers and managers; Financial institution tellers; Insurance claims representatives

Cryptographic technicians

Definition

Cryptographic technicians operate cryptographic equipment used for coding, decoding, and sending secret messages. They are mainly employed by the government, for positions in all branches of the military, and in government agencies such as the National Security Agency, the Department of State, and any other intelligence operations. Cryptographic technicians are also employed by industries that transact confidential business via computer, such as the banking industry.

Nature of the work

In the U.S. Armed Forces, cryptographic technicians, (called "CTs" or "Crypto Clerks") play an important role in our military success. When military personnel are far from home on a training mission or at war, they rely on messages sent from headquarters to update them on world events and give them orders. In the Air Force, for example, to send information to a flight crew on a 20-hour training mission, secret signals must be transmitted via radio waves, using either HF (high frequency), UHF (ultra high frequency), or SATCOM (satellite communications). Because other nations have access to these same frequencies, the messages must be in code to protect national military secrets. In the plane, the cryptographic technician decodes the message, which might alter a set of targets to hit, or instruct the pilot to land at a different Air Force base.

The banking industry, or any other industry requiring computer security, must prevent unauthorized access in order to protect the accounts or data in the files. For instance, when transferring funds from one bank to another, the message is usually sent by computer. To prevent unauthorized transfers, the banks send the message in code with some means to authenticate the transaction.

In order to code and send secret messages, cryptographic technicians first select the particular code that they should use for the message. Then they set up their machine to translate the message into that code, and they type the message into the machine. The machine converts the message into code form in a process known as encryption. After the message is encrypted, the technicians send the message to a receiver via telephone lines, satellites, or other kinds of communication links.

When receiving a coded message, cryptographic technicians feed the incoming transmission into a decoding machine and take the resulting message to its intended receiver. If a message appears to have been improperly coded, technicians may try to straighten out the message using special decoding procedures and equipment, or they may request that the message be sent again.

In sending and receiving coded messages, cryptographic technicians may operate teletype machines or radio transmitters and receivers.

Requirements

Cryptographic technicians need to be high school graduates. In addition, they need to receive special training that lasts from six months to a year. This kind of training is offered by branches of the U.S. Armed Forces and government agencies that employ cryptographic technicians, and occasionally by other organizations.

While in high school, students interested in becoming cryptographic technicians should take courses in mathematics and English. They should be able to add, subtract, multiply, and divide with ease and be able to compute ratios and percentages. They should be able to read equipment and instruction manuals and be able to write reports with proper grammar, spelling, and punctuation. Students should also look for courses that train them in typing and in the operation of computers and business machines. These courses can be taken in high school, but training after high school in a business school will also be helpful.

Due to the secret nature of their work, cryptographic technicians often need government clearance, which involves a thorough investigation of the applicant's character and records for the past 10 years. Employers seek those who can be trusted to maintain confidentiality.

Earnings

Salaries vary according to an individual's education, experience, and the geographical location of the job. In general, however, technicians who are graduates of two-year post-high school training programs can expect to receive starting salaries averaging around $15,000 to $20,000 a year. With increased experience they will earn more, usually up to $35,000 a year and sometimes more.

Technicians working in the federal government's civilian work force or for the armed forces will find their salaries determined by their rank or grade level. Technicians who work for local and state government agencies will also find their salaries determined by government rules. Their salaries will also vary from town to town and from state to state.

GOE: 07.06.02; SIC: 9711; SOC: 4793

A cryptographic technician uses a computer to help him decipher a coded message.

◇ **SOURCES OF ADDITIONAL INFORMATION**

International Association for Cryptologic Research
PO Box 303
Palo Alto, CA 94302

New York Cipher Society
17 Alfred Road W
Merrick, NY 11566

American Cryptogram Association
18789 West Hickory Street
Mundelein, IL 60060

◇ **RELATED ARTICLES**

Volume 1: Civil Service; Military Services
Volumes 2–4: Data entry clerks; FBI agents; Security consultants; Transmitter technicians

Customs officials

Definition

Customs officials are federal workers who are employed by the U.S. Customs Service, which is an arm of the Treasury Department, to enforce laws governing imports and exports and to combat smuggling and revenue fraud. The U.S. Customs Service generates revenue for the government by assessing and collecting duties and excise taxes on imported merchandise. Amid a whirl of international travel and commercial activity, customs officials process travelers, baggage, cargo, and mail, as well as administer certain navigation laws. Stationed in the United States and overseas at airports, seaports, and all crossing as well as points along the Canadian and Mexican borders, customs officials examine, count, weigh, gauge, measure, and sample commercial and non-commercial cargoes entering and leaving the United States. It is their job to determine whether or not goods are admissible and, if so, how much tax or "duty" should be assessed on them. To prevent smuggling, fraud, and cargo theft, customs officials also check the individual baggage declarations of international travelers and oversee the unloading of all types of commercial shipments.

CUSTOMS OFFICIALS

History

Countries collect taxes on imports and sometimes on exports as a means of producing revenue for the government. Export duties were first introduced in England in the year 1275 by a statute that levied taxes on animal hides and on wool. American colonists in the 1700s objected to the import duties (levied under the Townshend Acts) England forced them to pay, charging "taxation without representation." Although the British government rescinded the Townshend Acts, it retained the tax on tea, which led to the Boston Tea Party on December 16, 1773.

After the American Revolution, delegates at the Constitutional Convention decided that "no tax or duty shall be laid on articles exported from any state" but approved taxing imports from abroad. Until 1816 these customs assessments were used primarily for revenue. Although the Tariff Act of 1816 declared that the main function of customs laws was to protect American industry from foreign companies, the U.S. Customs Service generates more government money than any other federal agency besides the Internal Revenue Service.

Nature of the work

Like shrewd detectives, customs officials enforce U.S. Customs Service laws by controlling imports and exports and by combatting smuggling and revenue frauds. They make sure that people, ships, planes, and trains—anything used to import or export cargo—comply with all entrance and clearance requirements at borders and ports. Inspectors carefully and thoroughly examine cargo to make sure that it matches the description on a ship's or aircraft's manifest. They inspect baggage and personal items worn or carried by travelers entering or leaving the United States by ship, plane, or automobile. They are authorized to go aboard a ship or plane to determine the exact nature of the cargo being transported. They review cargo manifests, inspect cargo containers, and supervise unloading activities to prevent smuggling, fraud, or cargo thefts. They may have to weigh and measure imports to see that commerce laws are being followed to protect American distributors in cases where restricted trademarked merchandise is being brought into the country. In this way they can protect the interests of American companies.

Customs inspectors examine crew and passenger lists, sometimes in cooperation with the police who may be searching for criminals.

They are authorized to search suspicious individuals and to arrest them if necessary. They are also allowed to conduct body searches of suspected individuals to check for contraband. They check health clearances and ship's documents in an effort to prevent the spread of disease that may require quarantine.

Individual baggage declarations of international travelers come under their scrutiny. Inspectors who have baggage examination duty at points of entry into the United States classify purchases made abroad and, if necessary, assess and collect duties. All international travelers are allowed to bring home certain amounts of foreign purchases, such as perfume, clothing, tobacco, and liquor without paying taxes. However, they must declare the amount and value of their purchases on a customs form. If they have made purchases above the duty-free limits, then they must pay taxes. Customs inspectors are prepared to advise tourists about U.S. Customs regulations and allow them to change their customs declarations if necessary and pay the duty before baggage inspection. Inspectors must be alert and observant to detect undeclared items. If any are discovered, it is up to the inspector to decide whether an oversight or deliberate fraud has occurred. Sometimes the contraband is held and a U.S. Customs hearing is scheduled to decide the case. A person who is caught trying to avoid paying duty is fined. When customs violations occur, inspectors must file detailed reports and often later appear as witnesses in court.

Customs officials often work with other government agents and are sometimes required to be armed. They cooperate with special agents for the Federal Bureau of Investigation, the Drug Enforcement Administration, the U.S. Immigration and Naturalization Service, the Food and Drug Administration, and with public health officials and agricultural quarantine inspectors.

Business magnates, ships captains, and importers are inspectors' daily contacts as they review manifests, examine cargo, and control shipments transferred under bond to ports throughout the United States.

Some of the specialized fields for customs officials are as follows:

Customs patrol officers conduct surveillance at points of entry into the United States to prohibit smuggling and detect customs violations. They try to catch people illegally transporting smuggled merchandise and contraband such as narcotics, watches, jewelry, weapons, fruits, plants, and meat that may be infested with pests and diseases. Armed and equipped with two-way communication devices, they function much like police officers. On the waterfront they monitor piers, suspect ships, and crew members. They are alert for items being thrown from the ship to small boats nearby. They provide security at entrance and exit facilities of piers and airports, make sure all baggage is checked, maintain security at loading, exit, and entrance areas of customs buildings and during transfer of legal drug shipments to prevent highjackings or theft.

Using informers and other sources, they gather intelligence information about illegal activities. When probable cause exists, they are authorized to take possible violators into custody, using physical force or weapons if necessary. They assist other customs personnel in developing or testing new enforcement techniques and equipment.

Customs pilots, who must have a current FAA commercial pilot's license, conduct air surveillance of illegal traffic crossing U.S. borders by air, land, or sea. They apprehend, arrest, and search violators and prepare reports used to prosecute the criminals. They are stationed along the Canadian and Mexican borders as well as along coastal areas, flying single- and multi-engine planes or helicopters.

Canine enforcement officers train and use dogs to prevent smuggling of all controlled substances as defined by customs laws. These include marijuana, narcotics, and dangerous drugs. After a 12-week basic training course in the Detector Dog Training Center, they are assigned to posts, generally working with one dog that has been paired with them. They work in cooperation with customs inspectors, customs patrol officers, and special agents to find and seize contraband and arrest smugglers. Currently, most of these officers are used at entry points along the Mexican border.

Import specialists become technical experts in a particular line of merchandise, such as wine or electronic equipment. They keep up-to-date on their area of specialization by going to trade shows and importers' places of business. Merchandise for delivery to commercial importers is examined, classified, and appraised by these specialists, who must enforce import quotas and trademark laws. They use import quotas and current market values to determine the unit value of the merchandise in order to calculate the amount of money due the government in tariffs. Import specialists question importers, check their lists, and make sure the merchandise matches the description and the list. If they find a violation, they call for a formal inquiry by customs special agents. Problems include fraud and violation of copyright and trademark laws. If the importer meets federal requirements, the import specialist then issues a permit that authorizes the release of

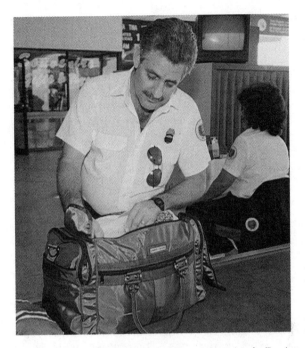

A customs inspector in San Juan, Puerto Rico, checks a bag for illegal merchandise through airport security.

merchandise for delivery. If not, the goods might be seized and then sold at public auction. These specialists encourage international trade by authorizing the lowest allowable duties on merchandise.

Customs chemists form a subgroup of import specialists who protect the health and safety of Americans. They analyze imported merchandise such as textile fibers, lead content, and narcotics. In many cases, the duty collected on imported products depends on the chemist's analysis and subsequent report. Customs chemists often serve as expert witnesses in court. The customs laboratories in Boston, New York, Baltimore, Savannah, New Orleans, Los Angeles, San Francisco, Chicago, Washington, D.C., and San Juan, Puerto Rico have specialized instruments that can analyze materials for their chemical components. These machines can determine the amount of sucrose in a beverage, the fiber content of textiles, the lead oxide content of fine crystal, toxic chemicals, or prohibited additives.

Special agents are plainclothes investigators who make sure that the government obtains revenue on imports and that contraband and controlled substances don't enter or leave the country illegally. They investigate smuggling, criminal fraud, and major cargo thefts. Their targets include professional criminals as well as tourists who give false information on baggage declarations. Often working undercover, they cooperate with customs inspectors and the Federal Bureau of Investigation. Allowed special powers of entry, search, seizure, and arrest, these agents have the broadest powers of search of any law enforcement personnel in America. For instance, they do not need probable cause to justify search or seizure near a border or port of entry. However, probable cause, but not a warrant, is necessary to conduct a search in the interior of the United States.

Requirements

Applicants must be U.S. citizens and at least 21 years of age. They must have earned at least a high school diploma, but a college degree is preferred. They are required to have three years of general work experience involving contact with the public. However, four years of college is considered the equivalent of three years of work experience. They must be in good physical condition and possess emotional and mental stability. They must demonstrate the ability to apply correctly regulations or instructional material and to make clear, concise oral or written reports.

Like all federal employees, they must pass a physical examination and undergo a security check. They must also pass a federally administered standardized test, called the Professional and Administrative Career Examination (PACE). Entrance-level appointments are at grades GS–5 and GS–7.

Special agents must establish an eligible rating on the Treasury Enforcement Examination (TEA), a test that measures investigative aptitude; successfully complete an oral interview and personal background investigation; and be in excellent physical condition. Although they receive extensive training, they need to have two years of specialized criminal investigative or comparable experience. Applicants with sufficient specialized law-enforcement experience or education should establish eligibility on the Mid-Level Register for appointment grades GS–9, 11, and 12.

Opportunities for experience and exploration

High school students can select several ways to learn about the various positions available at the U.S. Customs Service. They can talk with people employed as customs inspectors, consult their high school counselors, or contact local labor union organizations and offices for additional information. Information on federal government jobs is available from offices of the state employment service, area offices of the U.S. Office of Personnel Management, and Federal Job Information Centers throughout the country.

Methods of entering

Applicants may enter the various occupations of the U.S. Customs Service by applying to take the appropriate civil service examinations. Interested applicants should note the age, citizenship, and experience requirements described above and realize that they will undergo a background check and a drug test. If hired, applicants will receive exacting on-the-job training.

Advancement

All customs agents have the opportunity to advance through a special system of promotion from within. Although they enter at the GS–5 or GS–7 level, after one year they may compete for promotion to supervisory positions or simply to positions at a higher grade level in the agency. The journeyman level is grade GS–9. Supervisory positions at GS–11 and above are available on a competitive basis. After attaining permanent status (i.e., serving for one year on probation), customs patrol officers may compete to become special agents. Entry-level appointments for customs chemists are made at GS–5. However, applicants with an advanced degree and/or professional experience in the sciences should qualify for higher-graded positions. Advancement potential exists for journeyman level at GS–11 and to specialist, supervisory, and management positions at grades GS–12 and above.

Employment outlook

Employment as a customs official is steady work that is not affected by changes in the economy. With the increased emphasis on law enforcement and detection of the illegal importation of drugs and pornography and the prevention of the export of sensitive high technology items, the outlook for steady employment in the U.S. Customs Service is likely to grow and remain high.

Earnings

The federal government employs approximately 75,000 customs workers, whose average GS ranking is 9.3. The salary range for customs workers in 1990 is from $26,100 to $38,500, with the average salary reported as $31,537.

Conditions of work

The customs territory of the United States is divided into nine regions that include the 50 states, the District of Columbia, Puerto Rico, and the U.S. Virgin Islands. In these regions are nearly 300 ports of entry along land and sea borders. Customs inspectors may be assigned to any of these ports or to overseas work at airports, seaports, waterfronts, border stations, customs houses, or the U.S. Customs Service Headquarters in Washington, D.C. They usually get their first choice, if possible.

A typical work schedule is eight hours a day, five days a week, but customs employees often work overtime or long into the night. United States entry and exit points must be supervised 24 hours a day, which means that workers rotate night shifts and weekend duty. Customs inspectors and patrol officers are sometimes assigned to one-person border points at remote locations where they often perform immigration and agricultural inspections in addition to regular duties. They often risk physical injury from criminals violating customs regulations.

Fringe benefits include overtime pay, paid vacations, sick leave, military leave, low-cost group hospitalization, life insurance, and retirement annuities.

GOE: 11.10.04; SIC: none; SOC: 1473

◇ **SOURCES OF ADDITIONAL INFORMATION**

National Treasury's Union
901 E Street, NW
Suite 600
Washington, DC 20004

U.S. Customs Service
Office of Human Resources
1301 Constitution Ave. NW
Washington, DC 20229

U.S. Customs Service Regional Office
55 East Monroe
Chicago, IL 60603

◇ **RELATED ARTICLES**

Volume 1: Chemicals and Drugs; Civil Service
Volumes 2–4: Border patrol officers; Export-import specialists; Health and regulatory inspectors

Dairy products manufacturing workers

Definition

Dairy products manufacturing workers set up, operate, and tend continuous-flow or vat-type equipment to process milk, cream, butter, cheese, ice cream, and other dairy products following specified methods and formulas.

History

Dairy products are a common and important part of our diet. A good source of many nutrients, dairy products include various kinds of milk, cheese, butter, cream, ice cream, and yogurt. About 90 percent of the dairy products in

A dairy products worker distributes fresh cottage cheese into containers covered with cheese cloth. The containers collect whey as the cottage cheese is drained.

ple moved away from farm sources of dairy products and into cities.

Another important development was the introduction of pasteurization, named for the noted French chemist Louis Pasteur. Many harmful bacteria can live in fresh milk. In the 1860s, Pasteur developed the process of pasteurization, which involves heating a foodstuff to a certain temperature for a specified period of time to kill the bacteria, then cooling the food again. In modern dairy pasteurization, the milk is heated to 145°F for 30 minutes, then cooled rapidly. Sanitation is extremely important in dairy production, and today it is monitored carefully by government health inspectors.

Dairy farms are located in many parts of the county, especially in the Northeast, Great Lakes, Corn Belt, Appalachian, and Southern Plains regions, and in California and Washington. Dairy processing plants are usually located near dairy farms to keep transportation costs down and to ensure the quality of dairy products.

America's dairy farms are so productive that by law the federal government intervenes in the dairy industry to support the farm price of milk. With no mandated ceiling on milk output, the federal government must buy, at a given price, the industry's surplus production. Because fresh milk is highly perishable, the government acquires manufactured products such as butter, cheese, and nonfat dry milk.

Nature of the work

Dairy products manufacturing workers handle a wide variety of machines that process milk, manufacture dairy products, and prepare the products for shipping. Workers are usually classified by the type of machine they operate. Workers at some plants handle more than one type of machine.

Whole milk is delivered to a dairy processing plant from farms in large containers or in special tank trucks. The milk is stored in large vats until *dairy-processing-equipment operators* are ready to use it. First, the operator connects the vats to processing equipment with pipes, assembling whatever valves, bowls, plates, disks, impeller shafts, and other parts are needed to prepare the equipment for operation. Then the operator turns valves to pump a sterilizing solution and rinse water throughout the pipes and equipment. While keeping an eye on temperature and pressure gauges, the operator opens other valves to pump the whole milk into a centrifuge, where it is spun at high speed to separate the cream from the skim milk. The

the world, and almost all the dairy products in this country, come from cow's milk; the rest are made from the milk of goats, sheep, reindeer, yaks, and other animals. About a half of the milk consumed in many countries is in fluid form; the remainder is made into products that are more stable and readily preserved.

Since herd animals were first domesticated, mankind has kept cattle for meat and milk. From its ancient beginnings in Asia, the practice of keeping cattle spread across much of the world. Often farmers kept a few cows to supply their family's dairy needs. Because fresh milk spoils easily, milk that was not consumed as a beverage had to be made into a product like cheese. Before the invention of refrigeration, cheese was the only dairy product that could be easily transported across long distances. Over the centuries, many distinctive types of hard cheeses have became associated with various regions of the world, such as Cheddar from England, Edam and Gouda from Holland, Gruyere from Switzerland, and Parmesan and Provolone from Italy.

A real dairy products industry has developed only in the last century or so, with the development of refrigeration and various kinds of specialized processing machinery, the scientific study of cattle breeding, and improved road and rail transportation systems for distributing manufactured products. The rise in urban populations also gave an extra impetus to the growth of the industry, as more and more peo-

milk is also pumped through a homogenizer to produce a specified emulsion (consistency that results from the distribution of fat through the milk) and, last, through a filter to remove any sediment. All this is done through continuous-flow machines.

The next step for the equipment operator is pasteurization, or the killing of bacteria that exist in the milk. The milk is heated by pumping steam or hot water through pipes in the pasteurization equipment. When it has been at the specified temperature for the correct time, a refrigerant is pumped through refrigerator coils in the equipment, which quickly brings the milk temperature down. Once the milk has been pasteurized, it is either bottled in glass, paper, or plastic containers, or it is pumped to other storage tanks for further processing. The dairy-processing-equipment operator may also add to the milk specified amounts of liquid or powdered ingredients, such as vitamins, lactic culture, stabilizer, or neutralizer, to make products such as buttermilk, chocolate milk, or ice cream mix. The batch of milk is tested for acidity at various stages of this process, and each time the operator records the time, temperature, pressure, and volume readings for the milk. The operator may clean the equipment before processing the next batch of whole milk.

Processed milk includes a lot of nonfat dry milk, which is far easier to ship and store than fresh milk. Dry milk is made in a gas-fired drier tended by a *drier operator*. The drier operator first turns on the equipment's drier mechanism, vacuum pump, and circulating fan, and adjusts the flow controls. Once the proper drier temperature is reached, a pump sprays liquid milk into the heated vacuum chamber where milk droplets dry to powder and fall to the bottom of the chamber. The drier operator tests the dried powder for the proper moisture content and the chamber walls for burnt scale, which indicates excessive temperatures and appears as undesirable sediment when the milk is reconstituted. *Milk-powder grinders* operate equipment that mills and sifts the milk powder, ensuring a uniform texture.

For centuries, butter was made by hand in butter churns, in which cream was agitated with a plunger until pieces of butter congealed and separated from the milk. Modern butter-making machines perform the same basic operation on a much larger scale. After sterilizing the machine, the *butter maker* starts a pump that admits a measured amount of pasteurized cream into the churn. The butter maker activates the churn and, as the cream is agitated by paddles, monitors the gradual separation of the butter from the milk. Once the process is complete, the milk is pumped out and stored, and the butter is sprayed with chlorinated water to remove excess remaining milk. With testing apparatus, the butter maker determines the butter's moisture and salt content and adjusts the consistency by adding or removing water. Finally, the butter maker examines the color and smells and tastes the butter to grade it according to predetermined standards.

In addition to the churn method, butter can also be produced by the butter-chilling method. In this process, the butter maker pasteurizes and separates cream to obtain butter oil. The butter oil is tested in a standardizing vat for its levels of butter fat, moisture, salt content, and acidity. The butter maker adds appropriate amounts of water, alkali, and coloring to the butter oil and starts an agitator to mix the ingredients. The resulting mix is chilled in a vat at a specified temperature until it congeals into butter.

Cheesemakers cook milk and other ingredients according to formulas to make cheese. The cheesemaker first fills a cooking vat with milk of a prescribed butterfat content, heats the milk to a specified temperature, and dumps in measured amounts of dye and starter culture. The mixture is agitated and tested for acidity, because the level of acidity affects the rate at which enzymes coagulate milk proteins and make cheese. When a certain level of acidity has been reached, the cheesemaker adds a measured amount of rennet, a substance containing milk-curdling enzymes. The milk is left alone to coagulate into curd, the thick, protein-rich part of the milk used to make cheese. The cheesemaker later releases the whey, the watery portion of the milk, by pulling curd knives through the curd or using a hand scoop. Then the curd is agitated in the vat and cooked for a period of time, with the cheesemaker squeezing and stretching samples of curd with the fingers and adjusting the cooking time to achieve the desired firmness or texture. Once this is done, the cheesemaker or a *cheesemaker helper* drains the whey from the curd, adds ingredients such as seasonings, and then molds, packs, cuts, piles, mills, and presses the curd into specified shapes. To make certain types of cheese, the curd may be immersed in brine, rolled in dry salt, pierced or smeared with a culture solution to develop mold growth, or placed on shelves to be cured. Later, the cheesemaker samples the cheese for its taste, smell, look, and feel. Sampling and grading is also done by *cheese graders*, experts in cheeses who are required to have a state or federal license.

The distinctive qualities of various kinds of cheeses depend on a number of factors, including the kind and condition of the milk, the cheese making process, and the method and duration of curing. For example, cottage cheese is made by approximately the method described above. However, the *cottage cheese maker* at the last cooking stage starts the temperature low and slowly increases it. When the curd reaches the proper consistency, the cottage cheese maker stops the cooking process and drains off the whey. This method accounts for cottage cheese's loose consistency. Cottage cheese and other soft cheeses are not cured like hard cheeses and are meant for immediate consumption.

Process cheese products are made by blending and cooking different cheeses, cheese curd, or other ingredients such as cream, vegetable shortening, sodium citrate, and disodium phosphate. The *process cheese cooker* dumps the various ingredients into a vat and cooks them at a prescribed temperature. When the mixture reaches a certain consistency, the cooker pulls a lever to drain the cheese into a hopper or bucket. The process cheese may be pumped through a machine that makes its texture finer. Unheated cheese or curd may be mixed with other ingredients to make cold pack cheese or cream cheese. Other cheese workers include *casting-machine operators,* who tend the machines that form, cool, and cut the process cheese into slices of a specified size and weight, and *grated-cheese makers,* who handle the grinding, drying, and cooling equipment that makes grated cheese.

Ice cream is usually made from milk fat, nonfat milk solids, sweeteners, stabilizer (usually gelatin), and flavorings such as syrup, nuts, and fruit. Ice cream can be made in individual batches by *batch freezers* or in continuous-mix equipment by *freezer operators.* In the second method, the operator measures the dry and liquid ingredients, such as the milk, coloring, flavoring, or fruit puree, and dumps them into the flavor vat. The mix is blended, pumped into freezer barrels, and injected with air. In the freezer barrel, the mix is agitated and scraped from the freezer walls while it slowly hardens. The operator then releases the ice cream through a valve outlet which may inject flavored syrup for rippled ice cream. The ice cream is transferred to a filling machine that pumps it into cartons, cones, cups, or molds for pies, rolls, and tarts. Other workers may process the ice cream into its various types, such as cones, vari-colored packs, and special shapes. These workers include *decorators, novelty makers, flavor room workers,* and *sandwich-machine operators.*

Newly hired inexperienced workers in a dairy processing plant may start out as *dairy helpers, cheese maker helpers,* or *cheese making laborers.* Beginning workers may do any of a wide variety of support tasks, such as scrubbing and sterilizing bottles and equipment, attaching pipes and fittings to machines, packing cartons, weighing containers, and moving stock. If they prove to be reliable, workers may be given more responsibility and assigned tasks such as filling tanks with milk or ingredients, examining canned milk for dirt or odor, monitoring machinery, cutting and wrapping butter and cheese, or filling cartons or bags with powdered milk. In time, workers may be trained to operate and repair any of the specialized processing machines found in the factory.

Requirements

Most dairy products manufacturing workers learn their skills from company training sessions and on-the-job experience. Employers prefer to hire workers with at least a high school education. Courses that can provide helpful background for work in this field include mathematics, biology, and chemistry. Machine shop classes can also be useful for the experience gained in handling and repairing heavy machinery.

Special requirements

To assure that consumers are receiving safe, healthful dairy foods, many dairy products manufacturing workers must be licensed by a state board of health or other local government unit. Licensing is intended to guarantee workers' knowledge of health laws, their skills in handling equipment, and their ability to grade the quality of various goods according to established standards. Some workers, such as cheese graders, may need to be licensed by the federal government as well.

Opportunities for experience and exploration

People who think they may be interested in working in the dairy products manufacturing industry may be able to find summer jobs as helpers in dairy processing plants. Assisting or at least observing equipment operators, cheese makers, butter makers, and other workers as they work is a good way to learn about this field.

Methods of entering

The best place to find information about job openings may be at the personnel offices of local dairy processing plants. Other good sources of information include newspaper classified ads and the offices of the state employment service.

Advancement

After gaining some experience, dairy products manufacturing workers may advance to become shift supervisors or production supervisors. Formal training in related fields is necessary in order to move up to such positions as laboratory technician, plant engineer, or plant manager.

Workers who wish to change industries may find that many of their skills can be transferred to other types of food processing. With further training and education, they may eventually become dairy plant inspectors or technicians employed by local or state health departments.

Employment outlook

The demand for American dairy products will probably remain high in the foreseeable future. Among the products that have grown in popularity in recent years are cheeses, ice cream, and lowfat milk. Despite this demand, employment in the dairy products manufacturing industry is expected to decline over the next 10 to 15 years. Improvements in technology and increased automation are two important factors contributing to this trend. The demand for laboratory technicians, plant engineers, and other technical staff is expected to remain strong.

Earnings

Earnings of dairy products manufacturing workers vary widely according to the responsibilities of the worker, geographical location, and other factors. In the 1990s, the overall average earnings for dairy production workers is estimated to be in the range of $15,000 to $20,000 per year. Overtime pay is common for those who work more than a 40-hour week. Production supervisors, plant engineers, and plant managers can earn $30,000 per year or more.

Conditions of work

Because of the strict health codes and sanitary standards to which they must adhere, dairy plants are generally clean, well ventilated workplaces, equipped with modern, well maintained machines. When workplace safety rules are followed, dairy processing plants are not hazardous places to work.

Many dairy products manufacturing workers stand during most of their workday. In some positions the work is very repetitive. Although the milk itself is generally transported from tank to tank via pipelines, some workers have to lift and carry other heavy items, such as cartons of flavoring, emulsifier, chemical additives, and finished products like cheese. To clean vats and other equipment, some workers have to get inside storage tanks and spray the walls with hot water, chemicals, or live steam.

GOE: 06.02.15; SIC: 202; SOC: 7476

◇ SOURCES OF ADDITIONAL INFORMATION

American Dairy Science Association
309 West Clark Street
Champaign, IL 61820

International Dairy-Deli-Bakery Association
PO Box 5528
313 Price Place, Suite 202
Madison, WI 53705

Milk Industry Foundation
888 16th Street, NW
Washington, DC 20006

Dairy Producers Co-operative Ltd.
P.O. Box 560
Regina SK S4P 3A5

◇ RELATED ARTICLES

Volume 1: Food Processing
Volumes 2–4: Bakery products workers; Canning and preserving industry workers; Confectionery industry workers; Food technologists; Laboratory technicians; Macaroni and related products industry workers; Meat packing production workers

Dancers and choreographers

Definition

Dancers perform dances alone or with others. Through dancing, they attempt to tell a story, interpret an idea, or simply express rhythm and sound by supplying preconceived physical movements to music. *Choreographers* create or develop dance patterns and teach them to performers. They sometimes direct and stage presentations of their work.

History

Dancing is one of the oldest of the arts. The first formal dances were the ritualistic, symbolic dances of early tribal societies: the dance designed to excite the emotions, such as the war dance; the dance purporting to communicate with the gods, such as the rain dance. Dances are an important part of any culture. In the United States, for example, the square dance became a part of our folkways. Dancing has become a popular leisure-time activity, a popular form of entertainment, and, for those who provide the entertainment, a career.

Nature of the work

Dancers usually dance together as a chorus. As they advance in their profession, dancers may do special numbers with other selected dancers and, when a reputation is attained, the dancer may do solo work. There are four basic types of dancing, and, although some dancers become proficient in all four, most dancers attempt to specialize in one specific area.

The *acrobatic dancer* performs a style of dancing characterized by difficult gymnastic feats.

The *ballet dancer* performs artistic dances suggesting a theme or story. Ballet is perhaps one of the most exacting and demanding forms of dance. Most other types of dancers need some type of ballet training.

The *interpretive* or *modern dancer* (sometimes referred to as a *classical dancer*) performs dances that interpret moods or characterizations. Facial expression and the body are used to express the theme of the dance.

The *tap dancer* performs a style of dancing that is distinguished by rhythm tapped by the feet in time with the music.

In all dancing, grace and execution are basic. Some dances require specific traditional movements and precise positions. Others provide for planned movement but permit sufficient variation in execution. The dancer thus is able to include a spin, a dip, a pause, or some other effect that provides a certain amount of individuality and flair to the performance.

Dancing is a profession that permits the performers to make the most of their physical features and personality. Part of the success of dancers depends on the ability to use their assets in ways that will permit their full expression.

Dancers may perform in classical ballet or modern dance, in dance adaptations for musical shows, in folk dances, or in tap and other types of popular dancing productions. Some dancers compete in contests for specific types of dancing such as ballroom dancing.

A few dancers have become choreographers, who create new ballets or dance routines. They must be knowledgeable about dancing, music, costume, lighting, and dramatics. Others are dance directors and train the dancers in productions. Many dancers combine teaching with their stage work or are full-time *dance instructors* in schools of the ballet or in colleges and universities. Some open their own dancing schools with specialties such as ballet for children or ballroom dancing.

Requirements

There are no formal educational requirements, but an early start (around eight for ballet) and years of practice are basic to a successful career. The preparation for a professional dancing career is as much a test of one's personal characteristics as it is of one's talent. The aspirant needs, first and foremost, to be enthusiastic about dancing, for the basic desire to achieve success is an ingredient that will help to overcome some of the disappointment and despair that seem to be hurdles normally encountered.

The physical demands of daily practice as well as the demands of the dance routine necessitate good health and a strong body. A dancer must also have a feeling for music, a sense of rhythm, and grace and agility. Good feet with normal arches are required. Persistence and sensitivity, as they apply to the day-to-day preparation of the dancer, are also important personal characteristics.

A good high school education is highly recommended for those interested in becoming dancers. Students should elect courses in speech, music, and dramatics, and engage in extracurricular activities that will enhance their knowledge of these areas. High school students may also continue their dance studies during the summer. Some summer camps feature dance training, and special summer classes are available in some large cities.

A number of avenues for advanced training are available. About 240 colleges and universities offer programs leading to a bachelor's or higher degree in dance, generally through the departments of physical education, music, theater, or fine arts. These programs provide an opportunity for a college education and advanced preparation and training. Other possibilities include study with professional dancing teachers or attendance at a professional dance school. There are a number of such schools in the country; most of them are located in large cities.

Experience as a performer is usually required for teaching in professional schools, and graduate degrees are generally required by colleges and conservatories.

As a dancer, director, and choreographer, Twyla Tharp, seen here with members of her troop, Twyla Tharp Dance, has been able to create and participate in her many original works.

Opportunities for experience and exploration

Dancing is a highly competitive profession, and interested students should take advantage of every opportunity to gain experience. It is not too difficult to find places to perform in one's own community, and it is wise to dance publicly early and often. Most dancers continue with classes in dance throughout their professional careers.

Methods of entering

The only way to get started in dancing is to dance, to take advantage of every performance opportunity possible. Local groups are usually in the market for entertainment at their meetings or social affairs. These appearances provide the opportunity to polish routines and develop the professional air that distinguishes the professional from the amateur performer. Breaking the professional barrier by achieving

one's first paid performance can be accomplished in several ways. Take advantage of every audition. Follow the announcements in the trade magazines. Circulate among other dancers. Attend shows and get to know everyone who may be in a position to help with a job. Another possibility that should be considered is to register with recognized booking agents.

Advancement

As in all performing arts, the star on the dressing room door is the dream of dancing aspirants. Yet top billing, the name in lights, the program headliner are positions of accomplishment reserved for a very small number. Most dancers will find that the opportunities for advancement are numerous and varied even though few will eventually achieve stardom. Many dancers start by earning a spot in the dancing chorus of an off-Broadway musical, in the line at a supper club, or in a dancing group

425

on a television variety show or spectacular. Such opportunities permit further study and lessons, yet enable one to work with experienced choreographers and producers. Earning a spot as a chorus dancer in television on a regular weekly show could provide as many as 13, 26, or 39 performances with the same group.

In recent years, a number of musical stock companies have originated throughout the United States, thus providing another avenue for employment. Although many of these operate only in summer, they provide experience of a Broadway nature. Outdoor spectaculars such as exhibitions, parades, fairs, and festivals often use dance acts.

Working on the road can be an exciting, yet tiring, opportunity. Chorus groups with traveling musicals and cafe shows provide regular employment for a season. The numbers are rehearsed before the tour and very little adaptation or change is possible. One does get a chance to perform in a variety of situations and with different bands or orchestras because accompaniments are different in each club or community performance.

Dancers may also advance to choreographing, one of the most creative and responsible jobs in dancing. Other dancers find positions as teachers and some eventually open their own schools.

Dancers join various unions depending on the type of dance they perform. The American Guild of Musical Artists is the union to which dancers belong who perform in opera ballets, classical ballet, and modern dance. Those on live or taped television join the American Federation of Television and Radio Artists. Dancers in films have the Screen Actors Guild or the Screen Extras Guild. Those who appear on stage in musical comedies join Actors' Equity Association. And those who dance in nightclubs and variety shows belong to the American Guild of Variety Artists.

Employment outlook

Employment of dancers is expected to increase faster than the national occupational average through the 1990s, but those seeking a career in dancing will find the field highly competitive and uncertain. For performers, there are limited opportunities since there are more trained dancers than job openings. Television has provided additional positions, but, the number of stage and screen productions is declining. The best opportunities may exist in regional ballet companies, opera companies, and dance groups affiliated with colleges and universities.

The turnover rate in dancing is rather high so there are always openings for the newcomer. Although generalization is difficult, the average chorus dancer can expect a career of five to ten years at best. Most ballet dancers stop dancing for an audience before they are 40 years of age.

The dancer who can move from performing to teaching will find other employment possibilities in colleges, universities, and schools of dance; with civic and community groups; and in the operation of dance studios.

Dancing as a performing career is characterized by irregular employment. There is often a long span of time between engagements. For that reason, it is difficult to calculate the exact number of people employed in this field. In the 1990s, it is estimated that professional dancers hold about 8,600 stage, screen, and TV jobs at any one time.

Dancers may find work throughout the United States, but most of the major dance companies are located in New York. Other cities that have full-time dance companies include San Francisco, Chicago, Boston, Philadelphia, Pittsburgh, Miami, and Washington, D.C.

Earnings

For the performing dancer, the conditions of employment, the hours of work, and salaries are established in agreements between the unions and the producers. Union contracts set only minimums, however, and a dancer's contract with the employer may contain more favorable terms.

The minimum salary for dancers in ballet and other stage productions is about $555 a week in the 1990s. The single performance rate for new first-year ballet dancers is $230. Dancers on tour are paid extra to cover room and board expenses. Minimum performance rates for dancers on television average $569 for a one-hour show. Dancers receive extra pay for any additional hours worked, including fees for rehearsal hours.

Many performing dancers must supplement their income with other work. Union contracts provide for various health and welfare benefits.

Conditions of work

The irregularity of employment is the most difficult aspect of the profession. Dancers are never certain where they will be employed or under what conditions. One may wait weeks for a contract. An offer may involve travel, night hours, or weekend rehearsals. Work on a Broadway stage show may last 20 weeks, 40 weeks, or three years, or possibly the show will fold after the third performance. With rehearsals and performances, a normal work week runs 30 hours (six hours a day maximum).

Dancing requires considerable sacrifices of both a personal and social nature. Dancing is the performing dancer's life. The demands of practice and the need to continue lessons and to learn new routines and variations leave little time for recreational or social activities. As a career, dancing necessitates greater emphasis on self than on others; the intensive competition and the need to project oneself to get ahead leave little time for other pursuits.

GOE: 01.05.01, 01.05.02; SIC: 7911, 7929; SOC: 327

American Dance Therapy Association
2000 Century Plaza, Suite 108
Columbia, MD 21044

American Guild of Musical Artists
1727 Broadway
New York, NY 10019

Dance Educators of America
85 Rockaway Avenue
Rockville Center, NY 11570

National Dance Association
1900 Association Drive
Reston, VA 22091

Canadian Dance Teachers Association
1123 McKeowan Avenue
North Bay ON P1B 7M4

◇ **SOURCES OF ADDITIONAL INFORMATION**

American Dance Guild
31 West 21st Street, 3rd Floor
New York, NY 10010

◇ **RELATED ARTICLES**

Volume 1: Performing Arts
Volumes 2–4: Actors; Circus performers; Recreation workers; Sports occupations

---

Data base managers

Definition

Data base managers are responsible for implementing and coordinating data processing systems that collect, analyze, store, and transmit computer information. They consult with other management officials to discuss computer equipment purchases, determine requirements for various computer programs, and allocate access to the computer system. They also direct training of data base personnel.

History

Computers play a large role in all aspects of our lives. Nowhere is this more apparent than in the private and government sectors where computers are being applied to a rapidly growing range of business, military, and educational situations. Recent developments in electronics have made it possible to build miniature digital computers, minicomputers, and microprocessors. Integrated circuits have made low-cost, high-speed computer systems available to many businesses and other organizations that previously could not afford them.

As more businesses acquire computer systems, other companies try to keep up, either to compete with these companies in information retrieval capabilities or cooperate with them in the rapidly developing area of linking up computers to exchange information. Exchanging computer information through telephone lines

DATA BASE MANAGERS

The responsibility of a data base manager includes verifying data over the phone with his clients.

develop a system for keeping track of merchandise in stock. In all cases, a data base manager must have a thorough knowledge and understanding of the company's computer operations.

A data base manager's responsibilities can be grouped into three main areas: planning what type of computer system a company needs, implementing and managing this system, and supervising computer room personnel.

To adequately plan a computer system, a data base manager must have extensive knowledge of the latest computer technology and the specific needs of a company. The data base manager meets with other high ranking company officials, such as the president or vice president, and together they decide on how to apply the available technology to their company's needs. Decisions include what type of hardware and software equipment to order and how the data should be stored, either in the computer's memory, on disk, or on tape. A data base manager must be aware of the cost of the proposed computer system as well as the budget within which the company is operating. Long-term planning is also important. The manager must ensure that the computer system can process the existing level of computer information the company receives as well as the anticipated load and type of information the company could receive five or ten years down the line. For large companies, this could mean purchasing several computers that have integrated systems with a large memory capability.

The data base manager must be familiar with accounting principles and mathematical formulas in developing proposals. It is not unusual for a manager to modify an existing computer system or develop a whole new system based on a company's needs and resources.

Implementing and managing a computer system entails a variety of administrative tasks. The manager must decide how to organize and store the information, or data, files so that the appropriate people get access to the right material. Program files must be coded for efficient retrieval. Scheduling access to the computer is another vital administrative function. The data base manager works with representatives from all the departments to create a schedule. The data base manager must prioritize needs and monitor usage so that each department can do its work. All computer usage must be documented and filed away for future reference.

Safeguarding the computer operations is another important responsibility of the data base manager. The manager must make plans in case a computer system fails or malfunctions so that the information stored in the computer

is going on at all levels of business and governmental activity. This explosion in growth in the computer field has led to increasingly large and complex data bases. (A data base is a collection of information stored in a computer.) Correspondingly, the need for trained professionals to manage these data bases has also grown.

Nature of the work

Data base managers are the professionals trained to develop, implement, and coordinate computer-driven information systems. They are responsible for the flow of computer information within an organization, so their tasks combine general management ability with a detailed knowledge of computer programming and systems analysis.

Specific responsibilities are determined by the size and type of organization. For example, a data base manager for a telephone company may develop a system for billing customers while a data base manager for a large store may

is not lost. A duplication of computer files may be a part of this emergency planning. A backup system must also be employed so that the company can continue to process information. Increasingly, a data base manager must also safeguard a system so that only authorized personnel have access to certain information. Computerized information may be of vital importance to a company, and the data base manager must ensure that it does not fall into the wrong hands.

Implementation of a computer operation often involves coordinating the integration of many complex computers into a single system. As an operation grows this may require the modification of the system.

A data base manager must be able to analyze a computer operation and decide if it is operating at top efficiency. The manager must be able to recognize equipment or personnel problems and adjust the system accordingly. The manager is often working with an operation that processes millions of bits of information at a huge cost. This demands accuracy and efficiency in decision-making and problem-solving abilities.

Like any type of manager, a data base manager must be able to supervise and motivate others. He or she must be able to train personnel and plan and coordinate all of their activities. Good communications skills are vital, as is the ability to solve touchy personnel issues.

Requirements

Prior experience with computers is vital. Students in high school should take computer programming courses and any electronics or other technical courses that provide understanding of how a computer operates. Mathematics and accounting courses are also desirable. Courses in English also are helpful.

A bachelor's degree in computer science or business administration is usually the minimum education needed for an entry position. Courses should include data processing, systems analysis methods, software and hardware concepts, management principles, and information systems planning. Many businesses, especially larger companies, want data base managers to have a master's degree in computer science or business administration. Experience as a computer programmer or systems analyst is also desirable.

Individuals interested in working for a particular type of company, for example an electronics firm, should acquire as much knowledge as possible about that specific field.

Some data base managers become certified for jobs in the computer field by passing an examination given by the Institute for Certification of Computer Professionals. The institute is sponsored by the Data Processing Management Association. The examination is offered in selected cities throughout the United States every year. For further information on certification, contact either of the above organizations at the addresses given at the end of this article.

Opportunities for experience and exploration

High school computer clubs offer a good forum for learning about computers and meeting others interested in the field. Some businesses offer part-time work or summer internships in their computer departments for students with some background in computers. In addition, there are training programs, such as those offered at summer camps, that use an intensive three-to six-week period to teach computer literacy.

Methods of entering

A bachelor's or master's degree in computer science or business administration is usually required for entry-level positions. Some applicants with extensive on-the-job computer training may be promoted to this position without a degree, but as the field gets more sophisticated a college degree will continue to be the most dependable means of entering the profession.

Advancement

Skilled data base managers have excellent advancement opportunities. As a manager gets experience in developing and integrating computer systems, advancement will take the form of more responsibilities and higher wages. A person at a small company may move to an upper-level position such as vice president of the firm or may move to a better-paying, more challenging data base manager position at a larger company. A skilled data base manager at a larger company may also be promoted to an executive position. Some successful data base managers become consultants or start their own businesses.

DATA BASE MANAGERS

Data base managers may work for investment companies, telecommunications firms, banks, insurance companies, publishing houses and a host of other large and middle-sized businesses. There are also many opportunities with the federal government and city and state governments. Teaching, either as a consultant or at a university or community college, is another option.

Employment outlook

The use of computers and data processing systems in almost all businesses creates tremendous opportunities for well qualified personnel. Employment is expected to increase faster than the average through the 1990s. Those with the best education and the most experience in computer systems and personnel management will find the best job prospects.

Employment opportunities should be best in large urban areas because of the multitudes of businesses that have computer systems. Smaller communities, however, are also rapidly developing significant job opportunities, so skilled workers should be able to pick from a wide range of jobs throughout the country.

Earnings

Earnings vary greatly according to the size and type of organization and an individual's experience, education, and job responsibilities. A person with a bachelor's degree at a medium-sized company can expect to earn between $22,000 and $28,000 per year to start. Those at a large company and those with a master's degree can expect to earn between $28,000 and $39,000 per year to start, perhaps more if the responsibilities are great.

Conditions of work

The work environment is a typical modern office, usually located next to the computer room. Most of the manager's planning and analysis activities are done in the office, with supervisory work and equipment monitoring taking place in the computer room. Occasionally, travel is required for conferences and visits to affiliated data base locations.

Data base managers average about 50 hours of work a week, but overtime is not unusual. Emergencies may require a manager to work long hours without a break, sometimes through the night.

GOE: 11.05; SIC: Any industry; SOC: 137

◇ SOURCES OF ADDITIONAL INFORMATION

Information of certification is available from:

Institute for Certification of Computer Professionals
2200 East Devon Avenue, Suite 268
Des Plaines, IL 60018

General information on career opportunities is available from:

Data Processing Management Association
505 Busse Highway
Park Ridge, IL 60068

For a list of publications and seminars for continued education in systems management, please write to:

Association for Systems Management
1433 West Bagley Road
Cleveland, OH 44138

◇ RELATED ARTICLES

Volume 1: Computer Hardware; Computer Software
Volumes 2–4: Computer programmers; Computer service technicians; Graphics designers; Graphics programmers; Systems analysts

Data entry clerks

Definition

Data entry clerks transfer information from paper documents to a computer system in a form that the computer can accept. They type data (information) on a typewriter-like keyboard. This converts the information into magnetic impulses or other forms of code that the computer can read and process electronically.

History

Following World War II, the electronic technology that had been used to solve scientific and communications problems during the war was transferred to peacetime government and business applications. This technology included early versions of what are now called computers. The first all-purpose electronic digital computer was named ENIAC. Developed at the University of Pennsylvania in 1946, it used thousands of vacuum tubes like the kind used in old televisions and radios. In 1951, UNIVAC became the first computer that could handle both numeric and alphabetic data easily.

In 1954, the first computer for commercial use was built. The invention of the transistor in the 1960s made it possible to build smaller, more powerful computers. By the 1970s a computer specifically for home use was introduced. Although none of these computers were as sophisticated as the ones used today, their efficiency and adaptability in processing, organizing, and storing data were quickly recognized. By the late 1970s computers were indispensable to private companies, schools, hospitals, and government agencies that handled large amounts of information.

As computer technology advanced and computers became faster, smaller, and less expensive, more and more businesses put them to use. Today, both large and small businesses use computers to process and organize all types of information. The boom in computer use has led to the need for qualified computer operating personnel, including data entry clerks.

Nature of the work

Data entry clerks are responsible for entering data into computer systems so that the infor-

mation can be processed later to produce such documents as sales reports, billing invoices, mailing lists, and other material. Specific job responsibilities vary according to the type of computer system being used and the type of company where the work takes place. For example, a data entry clerk may enter financial information for use at a bank, merchandising information for use at a store, or scientific information for use at a research laboratory.

From a source document such as a financial statement, data entry clerks type in information in either alphabetic, numeric, or symbolic code. The information from the source document is entered on a typewriter-like keyboard. The entry machine converts the coding information to either electronic impulses or a series of holes in a tape that the computer can read and process electronically. Newer, more sophisticated computers can have data input directly without having it recorded on a tape. Sometimes data entry clerks do not input actual information but rather type in special instructions that tell the computer what functions to perform.

In small companies data entry clerks may combine data entry responsibilities with general office work. Because of staff limitations, they may have to know and operate several types of computer systems. Larger companies tend to assign data entry clerks to one type of entry machinery.

Data entry clerks are responsible for adapting their entry machines for the type of data being input. For example, clerks that handle vast amounts of financial data can set their machines to record dollar amounts or transaction dates. Entry clerks are also responsible for loading their machines with the appropriate tape or other coding material and selecting the correct coding system (that is, the alphabetic, numeric, or symbolic representations).

Data entry clerks must always verify the accuracy of their work, either by checking the screen on which the work is displayed or by checking the data against the source document. Sometimes *verifier operators* are employed to check the accuracy of previously punched data cards and correct those that are inaccurate.

Data typists and *keypunch operators* prepare data for computer input by punching data into special coding cards or paper tapes. The cards may be punched on machines that resemble typewriters. If information is to be punched into tapes, the work is done on machines such as bookkeeping or adding machines that have

DATA ENTRY CLERKS

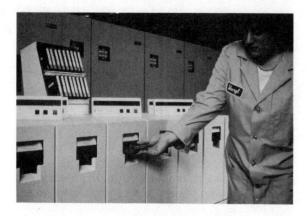

A data entry clerk inserts a cartridge of data in a computer system.

special attachments to perforate paper tape. Data typists and keypunch operators must be able to recognize any errors in the inputting process.

Data-coder operators examine the information in the source material to determine how it should be entered in codes and symbols into the computer. They may make up the operating instructions for the data entry staff and assist the system programmer in testing and revising computer programs. Data-coder operators also assist programmers in preparing detailed flow charts and in translating verbal ideas into coded instructions for the computer.

Terminal operators also use coding systems to input information from the source document into a series of alphabetic or numeric signals that can be read by the computer. After checking the entry to ensure its accuracy, they may send the data to the computer system via telephone lines or other remote-transmission methods.

Requirements

Although there are no specific educational requirements for data entry clerks, a high school diploma or its equivalent is usually required. In some cases, some college training is desirable. Some employees may receive on-the-job training. Data entry clerks should have the ability to scan and type source documents quickly before they begin their first job. High school students interested in becoming data entry clerks should take English, typing, and other business courses that focus on the operations of office machinery.

Many aspiring data entry clerks now complete data-processing courses that instruct students on proper inputting methods and other skills needed for the job. Technical schools, community colleges, business schools, and some adult education courses are among the avenues available to those who want to study data processing. Data-processing courses generally run anywhere from six months to two years. Secretarial or business schools may also offer data entry courses.

Many companies test new data entry clerks to determine their typing skills and their competency in data entry and mathematics. These companies often offer on-the-job training to instruct workers in the operation of specific data entry machinery. Data entry clerks must always be ready to learn new methods and techniques as the field of computers continues to evolve.

Opportunities for experience and exploration

High school students interested in pursuing a career in data entry are encouraged to talk with those already working as clerks. A visit to an office that uses data processing systems may be a good way of learning about the rewards and responsibilities of a career as a data entry clerk. Secretarial work or other similar office work may also be helpful in providing insight into this field. Students who are skilled typists may find part-time employment as keypunch operators.

Methods of entering

Many people entering the field have already completed an educational program at a technical school or other institution that provides data-processing training. Job placement counselors at these schools are often helpful in locating employment opportunities for qualified applicants. Local and state employment offices are also sources of employment information. Classified advertisements in newspapers may list job openings. Individuals may also contact those firms that they believe might have job openings.

Major employers of data entry clerks include insurance and utility companies, banks, and manufacturing firms. The federal government operates its own training program for data entry clerks. Applications for such positions may be made through the Office of Personnel Management.

Advancement

Skilled data entry clerks may be promoted to become computer programmers or peripheral equipment operators. Competition for these positions, however, may be intense, and advancement to them usually requires additional training and experience. In some instances, people may earn promotions to supervisory positions or jobs that combine a supervisory position with operating a computer. With the necessary education, training, and experience, data entry clerks can become computer center managers or programming managers.

Employment outlook

Because of improvements in data-processing technology that enable businesses to process greater volumes of information with fewer workers, employment opportunities for data entry clerks are expected to decline through the 1990s. Jobs are becoming limited, for example, because many computer systems can now send information directly to another computer system without the need for a data entry clerk to input the information a second time. In addition, the widespread use of personal computers, which permit numerous employees to enter data directly, will also lessen the need for skilled entry personnel.

Despite the slowdown in new job openings for data entry clerks, the computer industry as a whole will remain very strong, and continued employment opportunities should arise due to retirement or job promotions. Those with the most advanced skills and the ability to adapt to the changing needs of the computer processing field will stand the best chance for continued employment. Job opportunities will be greatest in and around large metropolitan areas where most banks, insurance and utility companies, and government agencies are located.

Knowledge of different computer languages enhances a data entry clerk's desirability among employers. The ability to work on different systems, particularly specialty systems like page layout programs and typesetting programs, offers the clerk greater job flexibility.

Earnings

Beginning data entry clerks can expect to earn anywhere between $13,000 and $15,000 a year, depending on their place of employment, the complexity of their jobs, and their training. Experienced clerks can expect to earn between $15,500 and $18,000, with those working for manufacturing and utility companies earning slightly more than their counterparts in banking and other service industries. Similarly, incomes tend to vary by region, with salaries in the West being the highest. Salaries for federal government employees are comparable to those earned in the private sector.

Conditions of work

Most data entry clerks work a standard 37- to 40-hour week. Full-time employees can expect to receive health insurance and other benefits, such as paid vacations and holidays. Their work spaces are usually located in comfortable, well-lighted areas. Data entry clerks must be able to work in tandem with other employees and, in most cases, under close supervision. Because the work may be tiresome and demands the constant use of the eyes and hands, data entry clerks must have patience and good concentration.

The continual need for accuracy may produce a strain on a person who does not easily adapt to such working conditions. Some duties may require lifting, reaching, and moving with boxes of cards, tapes, and other materials. Keypunch operators and other entry personnel may sit for long hours at a time. Exposure to video screens may produce eye strain, and continual use of the hands for typing may lead to nerve or muscle problems in the hands and arms such as carpal tunnel syndrome.

GOE: 07.06.02; SIC: Any industry; SOC: 4793

◇ **SOURCES OF ADDITIONAL INFORMATION**

Association for Computing Machinery
11 West 42nd Street, 3rd Floor
New York, NY 10036

Data Processing Management Association
505 Busse Highway
Park Ridge, IL 60068

Data Processing Institute
P.O. Box 2458, Stn. D
Ottawa ON K1P 5W8

Data-processing technicians

Definition

Data-processing technicians use computers to manage and store information. They provide complex and detailed information necessary to daily office operations in business and government. With the computers they can organize and analyze data, make complex mathematical calculations, and provide answers to complex scientific or engineering design problems. Data-processing technicians work with many different kinds of professionals including: information scientists; systems analysts; information processing engineers; and engineering, scientific, and business computer programmers.

History

The field of electronic data-processing is relatively new. Forerunners of today's modern computers were not developed until the 1930s, and the first all-electronic general-purpose computer was not completed until 1946. This computer was called ENIAC (Electronic Numerical Integrator and Calculator). It was built at the University of Pennsylvania and used 18,000 vacuum tubes. In 1951, the first U.S. census was processed by computer; in 1954, the first private business used a computer. Since then, public and private industries, universities, and other research centers have developed many new and different kinds of computers; through their new information processing discoveries, we are able to solve problems faster and more accurately than ever before.

The first computers were used to manage the huge quantities of data in business and government operations. Their use has now spread to almost all kinds of businesses, and typical uses now include payroll accounting, inventory control, customer billing, and market research.

Today, computers solve problems beyond human capability—even making thousands of complex mathematical calculations in minutes. They can store information for future use and display it instantly. Recent developments in electronics have made it possible to build miniature digital computers, minicomputers, and microprocessors. These have led to a flood of new uses in factory and office automation, scientific and medical research, robotics, aerospace engineering, and word and information processing. No other single technological innovation has had greater impact on the changing American scene than the computer.

Modern computer and information system advances have made it possible for large national and international systems to be put into operation. Examples include the Federal Bureau of Investigation's National Crime Information Center, the Federal Reserve's Money Transfer System, and the Department of Defense's Command and Control Systems. All these systems are computer based and managed. Computer systems have become so indispensable that corporations and governments now depend on them for daily operations, records, and reports.

Computer design improvements continue to decrease their cost. A computer that cost a million dollars in the 1960s costs less than a thousand dollars today. And although costs decrease, the technology improves. In the 1970s, the largest computers performed ten million operations per second. In 1982 they performed 100 million. Now processors are being designed to perform a billion operations per second. Lower costs and greater capacity explain why computers are used in more and more ways, and why so many data-processing technicians are needed today and in the future. The nation's computer labor force is well over 1.4 million, including about 565,000 personnel in various levels of programming jobs. Continued significant growth is expected in this area through the year 2005.

Two types of data-processing occupations are now generally recognized. The daily activities of business, such as payroll and accounting, are one type. This work requires a knowledge of business administration as well as specialized training in computer operations, programming concepts, and modern management accounting techniques. The second type is scientific data processing. It requires a knowledge of mathematics, physical science, or engineering, and specialized courses in analysis techniques, computer programming concepts, and statistical analysis.

Over the years, the *data-processing programmer* has become a key figure in computer usage; it is with this activity that data-processing technicians are most often linked. Since the early 1960s, two-year college programs in electronic data processing have been offered; the first ones were designed to train business data-processing technicians, and were soon followed by scientific data-processing programs. Now many schools offer two-year programs to prepare even more highly specialized technicians.

Nature of the work

To understand the work of scientific and business data-processing technicians, it is necessary to understand computers and how they are used to perform their thousands of complex tasks. There is one simple key, however: they cannot do anything without instructions. A computer needs to be told exactly how to do its assigned tasks. A human being has to tell the computer how to become a word processor, a gas gauge, a speedometer, an automatic dialer, a timer, or a welder. In fact, the only thing any computer can do by itself is accept instructions and carry them out. For this reason, most of the data-processing technician's specialized activities involve giving the computer its instructions, otherwise known as programming.

The central data processing computers in large systems are called mainframe computers —the first types of computers to be developed. Later, smaller computers called minicomputers were used to manage the program or list of instructions for the operation of complex programs for large mainframe computers. They also were used for relatively limited data-processing tasks.

Still more recently, the most modern and smallest computers called microcomputers or microprocessors were developed. They perform the same work as minicomputers did in large

Data-processing technicians spend much of their time debugging software that they have programmed. This work often requires the attention of several technicians.

systems, and in addition are used for many small, independent computer applications in small businesses, offices, schools, or as personal computers (PCs) in the home.

The personnel in large data-processing centers generally include *machine operators*, *data-processing technicians* (who may be called junior programmers or programmers), *senior programmers*, and *analysts*. Machine operators are not considered to be within the technician classification, although some operator positions are suitable entry-level positions for technicians. The analyst, who usually possesses a four-year college degree and sometimes a graduate degree, has overall responsibility for a project or system.

A computer program originates from the definition of a problem. The senior programmer and analyst define the problem in detail and identify the relationships between all factors to be considered. In this phase, education in a non-computer specialization is important. It makes the difference between business data processing and scientific data processing.

For example, if the problem deals with cost accounting or large inventory control, the analyst and senior programmer must know about accounting, operational procedures, file maintenance techniques, and related subjects.

If, however, the problems deal with genetics, engineering, or the design of a building, machine, or highway, the information analysts and senior programmers would need a strong background in engineering or science and the related mathematics. They must know about different types of computers, computer languages, and data-processing procedures.

Data-processing technicians receive the problem definition, the computer system and units to be used, and the required computer language as an assignment from the analyst and the senior programmer. The technicians then design the necessary flow charts and input-output forms. They collect necessary data and translate the problem definition into a set of instructions called a program.

Programs are written in systems of coding and organization called computer languages. There are many computer languages, and specific computers accept specific languages. Computers are designed to operate directly on a simple machine language, based on Boolean algebra and binary numbers (believe it or not, using only 0s and 1s). Beyond that, they process instructions and data entered by programmers in a computer language, which contains English letters and numbers.

One of the simplest languages is called BASIC—almost all new computer users learn programming with it. For business data processing, the most common language is COBOL, which means "Common Business Oriented Language." In the early 1990s more than half of all business programs used COBOL. Although other languages are gaining popularity, business data-processing technicians need to have a working knowledge of this language.

For scientific data processing, the technicians need to have a working knowledge of FORTRAN, whose name is derived from "Formula Translation." This language is most useful to solve mathematical equations found in engineering design analyses and other complex scientific applications.

Several other program languages are in use. RPG is used for simple business applications that do not require complex programs. It is most commonly run on minicomputers or small mainframes. PL/1 is a general purpose programming language and was designed to be an alternative to COBOL and FORTRAN. Other new languages that are gaining popularity include APL, which is a programming language developed by IBM for use on its PCs, and "C", which is a programming language developed by AT&T for use with its Unix operating system.

All of these languages, when used to program a problem for a computer, must be translated to the computer's basic machine language. This is done by a compiler, which is simply a separate program that accepts the program written in COBOL, FORTRAN, or whatever language is used to solve the problem. The compiler translates it or converts it step-by-step into the computer's own machine language.

It is the responsibility of the programmer to write the program in the language most suited to the problem definition and the computer involved. These are usually specified to the technician by the systems analyst or senior programmer. In addition to writing new programs, technicians constantly modify existing programs to meet new requirements or increase operating efficiency. A technician may share an office with as many as three or four other technicians or programmers. Technicians also spend considerable time in the computer room, checking on programs to be certain they have no errors and that the answers coming from the program are correct.

Under the technician's supervision, machine operators perform the actual tasks of computer operating required to produce the desired output. Both operator and technician must know the operating characteristics of the computer and be able to identify malfunctions. The greatest part of the operator's time is spent in the computer room with the technician or other responsible programmers.

When the program has been run for the first time, the programmer analyzes the results. Often some step in the program leads to a mistake and changes or corrections need to be made. This is called debugging. After all of the debugging is done, the program provides the answer or process it was planned to perform, and the technician moves to another problem.

Scientific or business data-processing technicians spend most of their time studying data and methods of defining problems and solutions to problems involving data in the field in which they are employed. Developing programs takes much more time and effort than the computer uses in the actual running time, which may be only a few minutes or at most a few hours.

The data-processing technician, in addition to programming for problem solutions, must maintain a current and effective program library. These programs may be stored on magnetic tape, storage disks, or other machine-readable mediums. They are subject to considerable revision and modification, which requires the maintenance of appropriate records.

In specialized jobs in the scientific data-processing field, the technician may spend time in other departments where the computer programs control the final work to be done. This adds variety to the data-processing technician's work.

Similarly, the business data-processing technician may work in the accounting department with the business methods planning, study, and control managers. Here they help gather data or plan the collection, storing, and the managing of the data to provide the most needed and useful information for managing the business.

The following paragraphs describe some of the specific entry-level positions that are available for data-processing technicians.

Junior programmers in business or science develop computer programs to solve specified problems. The problem specification is usually given to the technician in the form of a flow chart made by a senior programmer or an experienced programmer. The junior programmer must be able to read and interpret the flow chart in order to solve the problem.

Computer operators run the computers and load programs. They keep an eye on a program's progress and establish and maintain equipment usage records. Technicians or experienced programmers often direct the work of the operators. They also direct the work of the *peripheral equipment operators.*

Peripheral equipment operators process unit records and operate other equipment used to support the central processing unit. They may convert and prepare data for use in computer programs, or for activities completely independent of computers.

Requirements

The ability to think clearly and logically is the most important skill needed in the field of computer technology. Data-processing technicians need to communicate and work well with others. Because they often serve as communication channels between various people and the computer, they must be receptive to new ideas and diplomatic in resolving misunderstandings among workers. Prospective data-processing technicians should enjoy the challenge of solving problems.

High school students interested in becoming data-processing technicians should study accounting, business management, and computer technology. Most high schools across the nation offer at least an introductory course in computer programming. If students wish to be scientific data-processing technicians, they should take at least one year of algebra and at least a year of physics, chemistry, or biology. For students who plan to be business data-processing technicians, subjects such as accounting, inventory control, statistical methods, and similar business subjects are recommended.

Good language preparation is necessary, because technicians must be good readers and communicators. An elementary course in drafting or engineering drawing taken in high school will be very useful to data-processing technicians in the sciences. Drawing, diagramming, and sketching are also crucial to scientists and engineers. A course in graphic representation of business data will benefit business data-processing technicians. A course in engineering drawing is especially useful if the technician may seek employment in engineering or scientific research or design work.

Students who are seriously considering a career in this field should realize that their education will continue long after employment is secured. They need to keep up with advances in technology, which require changes in procedures, methods, equipment, and even computer language and programming concepts.

There are many excellent educational institutions, both private and public, that offer two year, post-high school programs designed to produce technicians who are employable upon graduation as junior programmers. The workload includes a number of specialized computer programming and system concepts courses. Laboratory work, using the most modern equipment, is a vital part of students' education. In addition, related courses in mathematics, statistics, accounting, business principles, economics, physics, engineering science, biology, or earth science are required for graduation. The selection of these courses depends on whether the student is interested in business or scientific data-processing. Many institutions offer an associate of science degree in both fields.

A two-year program in scientific data-processing technology might begin with an orientation seminar followed by an introductory course on data processing. Other courses might include communications skills, technical mathematics, a science course (physics, electronics, chemistry, or biology), techniques of real-time and remote computation, statistics, statistical programming, life sciences, graphical representation, and technical reporting.

The second year might include courses in fundamentals of scientific computation, Boolean algebra, linear programming, industrial organization and management, programming for engineering applications, scientific programming languages, introduction to operations research, a field project of the student's choosing, and general and industrial economics.

The two-year program in business data processing technology might begin with courses in communication skills, business machines, and technical mathematics. The first year would also include introduction to business, introduction to electronic data processing, business programming languages, business statistics, and principles of accounting.

In the second year of business data processing, courses typically include economics, technical reporting, business management, systems and procedures, applied business systems, computer peripheral equipment and data storage systems, introduction to operations research, and computer language survey.

Once employed, opportunities for further education include programs offered by company schools or equipment manufacturers. In some cases, technicians work with operations so new that formal training has yet to be developed. They may need to take supplementary courses scheduled for evenings or other time outside of the regular working week. Usually the employer pays tuition and other costs for job-related outside study.

Although not mandatory, special certification is available if the technician passes the examination to qualify for the Certificate in Computer Programming (CCP) conferred by the Institute for Certification of Computer Professionals. This institute is sponsored by the Data Processing Management Association, which started the program to encourage professional development within the field of data processing. The examination is offered in selected cities throughout the country each year. Even though the CCP certificate is not formally required by employers, it does provide favorable proof of accomplishment to employers when hiring or promoting technicians. The address of the Data Processing Management Association is given at the end of this article.

Most of the work takes place indoors in comfortable conditions. Because there are relatively few physical requirements, many people with physical limitations find this career to be very suitable.

Opportunities for experience and exploration

Interested high school students should ask their teachers and guidance counselors about suitable courses to acquaint them with the work of data-processing technicians. Any form of computer experience is helpful, even computer games. Science or business courses and hobbies can lead to activities involving the use of computers to solve problems in science or business activities.

Magazines and clubs are other ways for students to find out more about this career. Science magazines are available in the library; they can furnish interested students with ideas and opportunities. Similarly, joining a business or science club can open opportunities for high school students to become acquainted with and participate in activities that may lead to a technician career.

In addition to the traditional courses, high school students should read and study several professional journals and publications on computer technology. If it can be arranged, a visit to one or more computer installations would be most helpful. Several computer-user groups have formed professional organizations that offer opportunities for high school students to obtain information on educational and occupational requirements.

Students can gain valuable experience through part-time jobs, which may be found in school or in business computer centers. These jobs provide solid experience to prepare students for this demanding career.

Methods of entering

Many students in a data-processing technical program find jobs before they graduate. This can be accomplished in several ways. One is through the school's placement service, particularly those that maintain a current file on local and national job openings. Classified advertisements and employment agencies are also responsible for many placements.

Some industries and businesses send recruiters (usually personnel managers) to schools; they then set up on-campus interviews with qualified students.

Graduates of two-year technical programs seeking entry-level programming jobs may have to compete with many other job seekers. The great interest in the programming field in recent years has spurred the development of many training programs, including programs that provide four years of college preparation. In some circumstances employers are able to pick among a large pool of applicants with varying qualifications. As the field matures, technicians with only two years of formal training may have to look harder to find satisfactory jobs.

Training for the employer's specific data-processing system is often necessary. A period of orientation at the beginning of the job, sometimes several months or even a year in length, may be required before the beginning technician is expected to have mastered the details of the employer's needs and processes.

In recent years, the trend toward computer-controlled automation in industries such as computer manufacturing and radio and television products has increased the need for scientific data-processing technicians who know the industry. Many companies have met this need by sending their experienced electronic or electromechanical technicians to school to learn computer programming and data systems management. The same kind of program is also used to train other technical workers so that they can use the computer-controlled robots now being installed in some industries.

Advancement

Advancement opportunities for skilled data-processing technicians are good. In addition to the steps from junior programmer to senior programmer, there are parallel steps in supervision and management. Technicians who are considered extremely competent in the details of problem analysis and programming generally can progress to the analyst position. Advancement occurs faster for those whose education goes beyond a two-year technician program. Supervision and management positions are available to technicians who show promise in managing and supervising people and projects.

As more companies enter the computer age, experienced technicians are finding increased opportunities to work as consultants. There are many companies and businesses that need help in designing a custom system using a small computer, a storage and information processing system, and the programming know-how to apply computer technology to their work. Often such a system and the ability to use it will make the difference between failure and success of a business.

In a similar way, computer programming technicians and specialists in either numerical process control or computer graphics can often find excellent advancement opportunities working for consulting companies that specialize in these services.

Advancement often comes through activities and contacts in the many professional societies or organizations available to join. They range from organizations concerned with management of systems to special interest groups involved in research, statistical programming, and business programming.

The following professional occupations in the computer field are held by people who supervise data processing technicians and coordinate their supportive efforts. For each of the jobs described, technicians must obtain further education related to specific areas of computer

application, including physics, chemistry, genetics, statistics, the humanities, or one of the many other fields which rely on computer technology. For technicians in business data processing, continued study of both business and the developments in data-processing science and technology is a way of life.

Business or scientific programmers refine definitions of problems with the aid of library facilities and conferences. They determine the system and equipment that will be used in solving the problem. They also design flow charts and diagrams that express the problem and define objectives. After designing the flow chart, the programmers code the chart in an accepted computer language, compile the program, debug the program where necessary, and execute the compiled program.

Computer graphics technicians may work in an engineering research or design department. They use computer graphics to prepare design concepts and final engineering drawings.

Scientific data-system programmers evaluate, design, and implement computer based systems such as those used to process data from the movement of vehicles, from passenger cars to spacecraft.

Scientific programmers analyze, program, and debug computer solutions to problems in missile and space-vehicle engineering, guidance and mission planning, spacecraft dynamics, and other related areas.

Applications programmers in science and engineering solve problems in the design of computers, electronic components, and physical subsystems. Many of the problems involve the use of modern on-line graphics.

Numerical control programmers input the commands to program automatic tool-and-die machines.

Scientific information programmers and analysts work with problems that include all phases of scientific, engineering, and medical data processing and analysis. Current areas of interest include anti-submarine warfare, medical information retrieval, statistical analysis, and total information systems for industry and government. These positions require years of experience and further formal study.

Employment outlook

Employment in the data-processing field as a whole is expected to grow faster than the average for all occupations at least through the year 2005. Although demand for data-processing technicians has lessened a bit, the prospects for growth are still generally favorable. This is due to the great variety of computer applications constantly being devised.

As computers, software, and programming techniques are refined, many programming tasks become routine or are eliminated. This trend is slowing the growth in demand for personnel with two-year degrees in the data-processing field. In addition, competition for jobs among graduates of technical programs is increasing as more beginning programmers enter the job market with four-year degrees. As a result, technicians with only two years of formal training may find relatively fewer satisfactory jobs open to them in the future.

Earnings

The median annual income for junior peripheral equipment operators is $21,444; for senior computer operators, $24,161; for junior applications programmers, $25,577; for junior systems analysts, $28,501. Beginning technicians in scientific data processing usually earn more than beginning data-processing technicians in business. To provide an idea of the upper-level salaries (with advanced degrees and years of experience), applications programming managers can earn $60,709, and directors of the largest corporate data processing divisions can earn up to $175,000, including benefits.

The types of benefits available to data-processing technicians will vary from employer to employer. Generally, paid vacations, holidays, and some type of insurance program are provided. In addition, many companies have a tuition reimbursement policy for employees who wish to further their education in the evenings or on weekends.

Many employers provide liberal opportunities for technicians and other data-processing workers to study on the job or in school to keep the company up-to-date and competitive. Some employers also pay membership fees in scientific and technical societies.

Conditions of work

Both scientific and business data-processing technicians work in excellent environments. Their equipment usually requires minimum dust specifications and temperature control, especially if it is in a large, mainframe central computer operation. Thus, technicians will most likely be housed in a recently constructed or renovated building. However, the development of small computers makes it possible to have computer work stations wherever typewriters or business calculators would be used. These are normal office conditions and therefore are good in most cases.

The work week for the technicians usually does not exceed forty hours, although at times they may be required to work overtime. This is particularly true when the employer updates, modifies, or changes existing computer hardware. Some technicians work on a shift basis.

Technicians may work somewhat independently of others on specific assignments. Individual or group conferences with other programmers and information analysts are a regular part of the technician's work.

Advancement into duties and services often requires the technician to visit job sites where computer applications are in use. Working conditions may vary: if the job sites are at traditional offices in government, educational, or industrial operations, conditions will be good; occasionally, the technician may travel to remote locations, and should seek advice about safety, special clothing, or other matters.

To be successful, all programmers must possess the ability to accept problem definitions as presented by information analysts. They must be able to work in a logical, analytical way, with patience and care, sometimes under pressure, both independently and as team members. In advanced positions, technicians most likely supervise other technical workers. Even as beginning technicians or junior programmers, they will work closely with, and sometimes supervise, computer and peripheral equipment operators and other skilled workers or clerks.

Well-trained technicians who keep up with the field will find variety and challenge in this new and rapidly changing technological frontier.

GOE: 11.01.01; SIC: 7374; SOC: 397

◇ **SOURCES OF ADDITIONAL INFORMATION**

American Society for Information Science
8720 Georgia Avenue
Suite 501
Silver Spring, MD 20910-3602

Black Data Processing Association
PO Box 7466
Philadelphia, PA 19101

Data Processing Management Association
505 Busse Highway
Park Ridge, IL 60068

Institute for Certification of Computer Professionals
2200 East Devon Avenue
Suite 268
Des Plaines, IL 60018

Data Processing Management Association of Canada
4267 Moorpark Place
Victoria BC V8Z 6P1

◇ **RELATED ARTICLES**

Volume 1: Computer Hardware; Computer Software; Electronics; Engineering; Telecommunications
Volumes 2–4: Computer programmers; Computer-service technicians; Data base managers; Graphics programmers; Miscellaneous engineers; Numerical control tool programmers; Semiconductor-development technicians; Software technicians

Demographers

Definition

Demographers are population specialists who collect and analyze vital statistics related to human population changes, such as births, marriages, and deaths. They plan and conduct research surveys to study population trends and assess the effects of population movements.

History

Population studies of one kind or another have always been of interest for various reasons. As early as the mid-1600s, for example, the English were the first to systematically record and register all births and deaths. Over the years, recording techniques were refined and expanded to conduct more sophisticated population surveys, so that governments could collect information such as number of people and extent of property holdings, to measure wealth and levy taxes.

In recent years, census taking has become much more comprehensive, and the scientific methods of collecting and interpreting demographic information have also improved extensively. Demographers now have a leading role in developing detailed population studies that are designed to reveal the essential characteristics of a society, such as the availability of health care or the income level of constituents.

Nature of the work

Demography is a social science that organizes population facts into a statistical analysis. A demographer works to establish ways in which numbers may be organized to produce new and useful information. For example, demographers may study data collected on the frequency of disease in a certain area, develop graphs and charts to plot the spread of that disease, and then forecast the probability that the medical problem may spread.

Many demographers work on the basis of a "sampling" technique in which the characteristics of the whole population are judged by taking a sample of a part of it. For example, demographers may collect data on the educational level of residents living in various locations throughout a community. They can use this information to make a projection of the average educational level of the community as a whole. In this way, demographers conduct research and forecast trends on various social and economic patterns throughout an area.

Demographers not only conduct their own surveys but often work with statistics gathered from government sources, private surveys, and public opinion polls. They may compare different statistical information such as an area's average income level and its population and use it to forecast future educational and medical needs of the community. They may tabulate the average age, income, educational levels, crime rate, and poverty rate of a farming community

DEMOGRAPHERS

Demographers conduct extensive research. They transfer their work onto computers to calculate and organize vast amounts of data.

and compare it with the same statistics of an urban environment.

Computers have radically changed the role of the demographer. Now, much greater amounts of data can be collected and analyzed. In the Bureau of Census, for example, demographers work with material that has been compiled as a result of the nationwide census that is conducted every 10 years. Millions of pieces of demographic information, such as age, gender, occupation, educational level, and country of origin are collected from people around the country. A demographer may take this statistical information, analyze it, and then use it to forecast population growth or economic trends.

Government organizations of all types use the services of a demographer to investigate and analyze a variety of social science questions, such as rates of illness, availability of health and police services, and other issues that define a community. Private companies may use the information to make marketing decisions, such as where to open a new store and how to best reach possible customers.

Demographers may work on long-range planning for government or private agencies. Population trends are especially important in such areas as educational and economic planning, and a demographer's analysis is often used to help set policy on health care issues

and a host of other social science concerns. Local, state, and national governmental agencies all use the demographer's statistical forecasts in an attempt to accurately provide transportation, education, and other services.

Demographers may conduct research for colleges and universities. This may include teaching demographic research techniques to students. They may also work as consultants to private businesses. Much of their time is spent in library research, analyzing demographic information of various population groups.

An applied statistician, a specialized type of demographer, uses accepted theories and known statistical formulas to collect and analyze data in a specific area, such as the availability of health care in a specified location.

Requirements

A college degree in sociology with an emphasis in demography or a related field is usually required to work as a demographer. Potential demographers should enjoy employing logic to solve problems and have an aptitude for mathematics. They should enjoy detailed work and must like to study and to learn. Research experience is helpful.

A high school student interested in pursuing a career as a demographer should take college-preparatory courses, such as social studies, English, and mathematics (algebra and geometry). College course work should include classes in social research methods, public policy, statistics, and computer applications.

As the field gets more competitive, many demographers get a master's degree or a doctorate in sociology. Attaining a position with the federal government is especially competitive, and successful applicants usually require a master's degree or a doctorate in sociology.

Opportunities for experience and exploration

A part-time or summer job at a company with a statistical research department is a good way of gaining insight into the career of demographer. Discussions with professional demographers are another way of learning about the rewards and responsibilities in this field. Often, high school students may ask their mathematics teachers to give them some simple statistical problems related to population changes and then practice the kinds of statistical techniques that demographers use.

Methods of entering

The usual method of entering the profession is through completion of an undergraduate or graduate degree in sociology with an emphasis in demographic methods. Qualified applicants should apply directly to private research firms or other companies that do population studies. College placement offices may be helpful in supplying possible leads in this regard. For those interested in working for a government agency, jobs are listed with the Civil Service Commission. Most teaching jobs at the college level require a master's or other graduate degree.

Advancement

After having gained experience on the job, a demographer may become head of a research department, with an accompanying increase in salary and responsibility. Those with the most training and the highest degree of education are most likely to be promoted.

Employment outlook

The tremendous amount of social science research going on in the United States and elsewhere is expected to increase through the 1990s. Employment opportunities should be greatest in and around large metropolitan areas, where many colleges, universities, and other research facilities are located. Those with the most training and greatest amount of education, preferably a Ph.D., should find the best job prospects.

Earnings

Earnings vary widely according to education, training, and place of employment. A demographer with a bachelor's degree can expect to earn an average of $19,200 a year to start. Those beginning work with a graduate degree should earn about $25,000 per year. Experienced demographers should average between $35,000 and $40,000 per year, with very skilled workers earning even more.

Starting salaries may be somewhat higher in government agencies than private industry, although private industry may offer greater earning potential. Those in teaching should expect to earn somewhat less than other demographers.

Conditions of work

Most demographers work in offices or classrooms. Those engaged in research may work with other demographers assembling related information. Most of the work revolves around analyzing population data or interpreting computer information. A demographer is also usually responsible for writing a report detailing the findings.

There may be some travel to attend a conference or complete limited field research. A demographer should expect to work a 40-hour week and have an annual vacation and other benefits, such as sick leave and group insurance. Overtime may be required if a project is on deadline.

Demographers should be able to spend long hours working alone analyzing complex population statistics. They should be able to apply detailed mathematical formulas and draw conclusions from different types of data.

GOE: 11.03.02; SIC: 7392, 96; SOC: 1733, 1916

◇ SOURCES OF ADDITIONAL INFORMATION

American Sociological Association
1722 North Street, NW
Washington, DC 20036

American Statistical Association
1429 Duke Street
Alexandria, VA 22314

Population Association of America
1722 North Street, NW
Washington, D.C. 20036

Population Reference Bureau
777 14th Street, NW, Suite 800
Washington, DC 20005

Society for Industrial and Applied Mathematics
3600 University City Science Center
Philadelphia, PA 19104

For information on demographers for the U.S. government, contact regional offices of the Department of Commerce, or the national office at:

Census Bureau
Public Information Office
Department of Commerce
Jacob K. Javitz Federal Building, Room 37-130
New York, NY 10278

Federation of Canadian Demographers
c/o Department of Sociology
University of Western Ontario
London ON

◇ **RELATED ARTICLES**

Volume 1: Marketing; Mathematics; Social Services
Volumes 2–4: Actuaries; Marketing research personnel; Mathematicians; Sociologists; Statisticians

Dental assistants

Definition

Dental assistants work in dentists' offices, helping them treat and examine patients. They help by preparing the patient for the dental exam, handing the dentist the proper instruments, taking and processing X rays, preparing materials for making impressions and restorations, and instructing the patient in oral health care. They also perform administrative and clerical tasks that make the office run smoothly and free the dentist's time for working with patients.

History

The dentist's job has always required more than two hands. Drilling, pulling, cleaning, and operating on teeth requires one pair of hands to operate the instruments and another pair to hand the instruments to the dentist and to hold the patient's mouth open and keep it dry and clean. Since the 1800s dentists have had assistants to help them when they could not physically perform a dental operation or examination alone.

The job of the dental assistant as we know it is a creation of the 20th century. Techniques in dentistry and tooth care have undergone a revolution in the past 100 years, as discoveries in chemistry and the biomedical sciences made dental radiography, improved dental instruments and materials, and advanced dental treatment possible. In addition, the discovery that fluoride helps prevent tooth decay led to more work for dentists because fluoride treatments enabled many more people to keep their teeth throughout their lives. In recent decades, with the greater public awareness of the importance of dental care, more and more companies have begun providing dental insurance to employees.

These developments combined to result in a greater workload for dentists. As they took in more patients and performed more kinds of dental services, they had less time for performing routine tasks such as updating patients' files, instructing them on techniques of oral hygiene, and keeping the office sterile. With some training, other workers learned to take on these duties, and the dental assistant became indispensable to the modern, busy dental office.

Nature of the work

Dental assistants help dentists examine patients in the dentist's chair. They usually greet patients, escort them to the examining room, and prepare them by covering their clothing with paper or cloth bibs. They also adjust the head rest of the chair and raise the chair to the proper height. Many dental assistants take X rays of patients' teeth and process the film for the dentist to examine. They also obtain patients' dental records from the office files, so the dentist can review them before the examination.

During dental examinations and operations, dental assistants hand the dentist instruments as they are needed and use suction devices to keep the patient's mouth dry . When the examination or procedure is over, assistants may give the patient instructions for taking care of the mouth while it heals. They also provide instructions on preventing plaque build-up and keeping the mouth clean and healthy between office visits. Dental assistants are also responsible for infection-control procedures in the dentist's office.

Dental assistants also help with a variety of other clinical tasks. When a dentist needs a cast of a patient's mouth—used for diagnosing and planning the correction of dental problems—assistants may mix the materials necessary for this procedure. They may also pour, trim, and polish these study casts. Some assistants prepare materials for making dental restorations, and many polish and clean patients' dentures. Dental assistants may perform the laboratory work required to make temporary dental replacements. Some states allow dental assistants to apply medications to teeth and gums, isolate individual teeth for treatment using rubber dams, and remove excess cement after cavities have been filled. In some states dental assistants can actually put fillings in patients' mouths. Dental assistants may also check patients' vital signs, update and check medical histories, and help the dentist with any medical emergencies that arise during dental procedures.

Many dental assistants also perform clerical and administrative tasks. When they are not helping the dentist, they may sit at a desk and greet patients, type records, and answer the telephone. They often set up appointments for patients, prepare bills for services rendered, collect payment, and issue receipts. They may also keep the inventory of dental supplies and order new supplies when necessary.

State laws determine which clinical tasks a dental assistant is able to perform. Dental assistants are not the same as dental hygienists, who are licensed to perform a wider variety of clinical tasks such as scaling and polishing teeth.

Requirements

Most dental assistant positions are entry-level. Because many assistants learn their skills on the job, most positions usually require little or no experience and no education beyond high school. Many assistants, however, go on to receive training after high school at the many trade schools, technical institutes, and community and junior colleges that offer dental assisting programs. Armed Forces schools also train some dental assistants.

Students who attend two-year college programs receive associate's degrees, while those who attend trade and technical school programs finish after one year and earn a certifi-

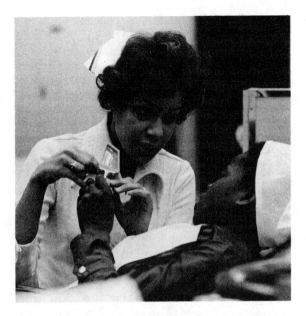

A dental assistant prepares a young patient for dental treatment.

cate or diploma. To enter these programs, a candidate must have a high school diploma. Some schools require that applicants have good grades in science, typing, and English on their high school transcripts; some require an interview or written examination; and some require that applicants pass physical and dental examinations. About 250 of these programs are accredited by the American Dental Association's Commission on Dental Accreditation. Some four- to six-month nonaccredited courses in dental assisting are also available from private vocational schools.

The University of Kentucky College of Dentistry offers a correspondence course for assistants who cannot participate full-time in an accredited, formal program. The course generally takes two years to complete, but is equivalent to one year of full-time formal study.

Accredited programs instruct students in dental assisting skills and theory through classes, lectures, and laboratory and preclinical experience. Students take courses in English, speech, and psychology as well as in the biomedical sciences, including anatomy, microbiology, and nutrition. Courses in dental science cover subjects such as oral anatomy, oral pathology, and dental radiography. Students also gain practical experience in chairside assisting and office management by working in dental schools and local dental clinics that are affiliated with their program.

Graduates of accredited programs may be allowed to perform a greater variety of tasks initially and may receive higher beginning salaries than assistants with high school diplomas alone. High school students who wish to work as dental assistants can prepare for this career by taking courses in general science, biology, health, chemistry, and office practices. Typing is also an important skill for dental assistants.

Dental assistants may wish to obtain certification from the Dental Assisting National Board, but this is usually not required for employment. Certified Dental Assistant (CDA) accreditation shows that an assistant meets certain standards of professional competence. To take the certification examination, assistants must be high school graduates who have taken a course in cardiopulmonary resuscitation and must have either a diploma from a formal training program accredited by the Commission on Dental Accreditation or two years of full-time work experience with a recommendation from the dentist for whom the work was done.

In 21 states dental assistants are allowed to take X rays (under a dentist's direction) only after completing a precise training program and passing a test. Completing the program for CDA certification fulfills this requirement. To keep their CDA credentials, however, assistants must either prove their skills through retesting or acquire further education.

Because they are primarily responsible for making patients comfortable in the dentist's office, dental assistants need a clean, well-groomed appearance and a pleasant personality. Manual dexterity and the ability to follow directions are also important in this field.

Opportunities for experience and exploration

Students in formal training programs receive dental assisting experience as part of their training. High school students can learn more about the field by talking with assistants in local dentists' offices. The American Dental Assistants Association, through the ADA SELECT program, can put students in contact with dental assistants in their areas. Part-time, summer, and temporary clerical work may be available in dentists' offices.

Methods of entering

High school guidance counselors, family dentists, dental schools, dental placement agencies, and dental associations may provide applicants with leads about job openings. Students in formal training programs often learn of jobs through school placement services.

Advancement

Dental assistants may advance in their field by moving to larger offices or clinics, where they can take on more responsibility and earn more money. In small offices they may receive higher pay by upgrading their skills through education.

Further schooling is required for advancing to positions in dental assisting education. Dental assistants who wish to become dental hygienists must enroll in a dental hygiene program. Because many of these programs do not allow students to apply dental assisting courses toward graduation, assistants who think they would like to move into hygienist positions should plan their training carefully.

In some cases, dental assistants move into sales jobs with companies that sell dental industry supplies and materials. Other areas open to dental assistants include office management, dental specialties, placement services, and insurance companies.

Employment outlook

According to the U.S. Department of Labor, dental assistants hold more than 176,000 jobs in private dental offices, group practices, dental schools, hospitals, public health departments, private clinics, and U.S. Veterans and Public Health Service hospitals. Opportunities for dental assistants should grow faster than average into the next century. As dental practices grow, the population increases, and dental insurance becomes more widely available, assistants will find increased job opportunities. Many openings will occur as workers change careers or leave the work force to assume family responsibilities. The Department of Labor projects that 60,000 more jobs in this field will open up by the year 2005, an increase of 34 percent.

Because of recent improvements in preventive dentistry and a growing supply of practicing dentists, some individual dentist offices may experience a drop in patient loads. This can adversely affect the employment outlook for some dental assistants. Nevertheless, through the foreseeable future, qualified dental assistants should have little trouble finding jobs. A recent ADA survey revealed that 90 percent of all dentists employ dental assistants, and most employ more than one.

Earnings

Dental assistants' salaries depend to a great extent on their particular responsibilities, the policies of the office in which they work, and the geographic location of their employer. According to the National Association of Dental Assistants, the mean salary for chair-side dental assistants is $11.35 per hour. This translates into an annual salary of around $23,000 for full-time workers. Salaries are highest on the West Coast and lowest in the Southeast.

Federal starting salaries for dental assistants vary with the educational background of the employee. Beginning assistants with a high school diploma earn $13,100 a year to start, while graduates of a one-year accredited program with one year of experience start at around $13,900. The average federal salary for dental assistants is $16,400.

Conditions of work

Dental assistants work in offices that are generally clean, modern, quiet, and pleasant. They are also well lighted and well ventilated. In small offices, dental assistants may work solely with dentists, while in larger offices and clinics they may work with dentists, other dental assistants, dental hygienists, and laboratory technicians. Although dental assistants may sit at desks to do office work, they spend a large part of the day beside the dentist's chair where they can reach instruments and materials.

About one-third of all dental assistants work 40-hour weeks, sometimes including Saturday hours. About one-half work between 31 and 38 hours a week. The remainder work less, but some part-time workers work in more than one dental office. Some offices offer benefit packages such as paid vacations and insurance coverage.

Taking X rays poses some physical danger if handled incorrectly, because regular doses of radiation can be harmful to the body. However, all dental offices must have lead shielding and safety procedures that minimize the risk of exposure to radioactivity.

GOE: 10.03.02; SIC: 8021; SOC: 5232

◇ **SOURCES OF ADDITIONAL INFORMATION**

American Dental Assistants Association
919 North Michigan Avenue
Suite 3400
Chicago, IL 60611

American Dental Association SELECT Program
211 East Chicago Avenue, Suite 1804
Chicago, IL 60611

Dental Assisting National Board
216 East Ontario Street
Chicago, IL 60611

◇ **RELATED ARTICLES**

Volume 1: Health Care
Volumes 2–4: Dental hygienists; Dental laboratory technicians; Dentists; Laboratory technicians; Medical assistants; Medical laboratory technicians; Medical technologists; Physician assistants

Dental hygienists

Definition

A *dental hygienist* administers preventive dental treatment, gives instructions on teeth care, may take X rays, and in general, assists the dentist in routine tasks.

The most common routine for the dental hygienist is the administration of a semi-annual

DENTAL HYGIENISTS

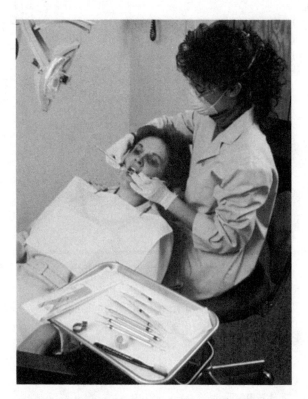

A dental hygienist cleans the teeth of a woman. In accordance with government regulations, hygienists must wear gloves, protective eyewear, and a mask during an examination.

cleaning. This involves removing tartar, stains, and plaque from teeth.

History

The work of the dental hygienist developed because dentists needed assistants to carry out routine tasks of dental care. The dental hygienist supplements the work of dentists, freeing them for more skilled work.

The first dental hygienists were trained by dentists themselves. The first school for dental hygiene was organized early in the 20th century, and in 1915 the first state legalized the practice of dental hygiene. Since then, the profession has expanded.

Nature of the work

The dental hygienist's task is to help clients prevent tooth decay and to maintain a healthy condition in the mouth. This is done mainly through cleaning teeth by removing stains and calcium deposits, polishing teeth, and massaging gums, a process called "oral prophylaxis."

The dental hygienist also instructs patients on the proper way to maintain dental health and to guard against oral disease. Other responsibilities depend on the employer.

Private dentists might require that the dental hygienist take and develop X rays, mix compounds for filling cavities, sterilize instruments, assist in surgical work, or even carry out clerical tasks such as making appointments and filling in insurance forms. Although some of these tasks might also be done by a dental assistant, only the dental hygienist is licensed by the state to clean teeth. Licensed hygienists submit charts of each patient's teeth, noting possible decay or disease. The dentist studies this in making further diagnoses. The hygienist might well fill the duties of receptionist or office manager, functioning in many ways to assist the dentist in carrying out the schedule.

The school hygienist has a busy program: that of cleaning and examining the teeth of students in a number of schools. The hygienist also gives classroom instruction on correct brushing and flossing of teeth, the importance of good dental care, and the effect of good nutrition. Dental records of the students are kept, and parents must be notified of any need for further treatment.

Dental hygienists may be employed by local, state, or federal public health agencies. These hygienists carry out an educational program for adults and children, as well as oral prophylaxis, in public health clinics, schools, and other public facilities. A few dental hygienists may assist in research projects. For those with further education, teaching in a dental hygiene school may be possible.

Requirements

Two types of training are available to the prospective dental hygienist. One is a four-year college program offering a bachelor's degree. More common is a two-year program leading to a dental hygiene certification. The bachelor's degree is often preferred by employers, and more schools are likely to require completion of such a degree program in the future. In the 1990s, there are more than 200 accredited schools in the United States that offer one or both of these courses.

The minimum requirement for admission to a dental hygiene school is graduation from high school. Aptitude tests sponsored by the American Dental Hygienists' Association are frequently required by dental hygiene schools to help the applicants determine whether they will succeed in this field. Skill in handling delicate instruments, a sensitive touch, and depth perception are important attributes. The hygienist should be personally clean and healthy.

Classroom work emphasizes basic and dental sciences and liberal arts. Lectures are usually combined with laboratory work and clinical experience.

Special requirements

Dental hygienists, after graduation from accredited schools, must pass state licensing examinations, both written and clinical. In the 1990s, candidates in 49 states and the District of Columbia could complete part of their state licensing requirements by passing the National Board of Dental Examiners' written examination. Upon passing the exam, a dental hygienist becomes an R.D.H., registered dental hygienist, but to practice in another state must pass that state's exam, though a temporary license may be given.

Opportunities for experience and exploration

Work as a dental assistant might be a stepping-stone to a dental hygienist's career. As a dental assistant, one could closely observe the work of a dental hygienist. The individual could then assess personal aptitude for this work, discuss any questions with other hygienists, and enroll in a dental hygiene school where experience as a dental assistant would certainly be helpful. A high school student might be able to find such work on a part-time or summer basis. A prospective dental hygiene student also might arrange to observe a dental hygienist working in a school or a dentist's office, or to visit an accredited dental hygiene school. The aptitude testing program required by most dental hygiene schools helps students assess their future abilities as dental hygienists.

Methods of entering

Once dental hygienists have passed the National Board exams and a licensing exam in a particular state, they must decide on an area of work, such as a private dentist's office, school system, or public health agency. Hospitals, industrial plants, and the armed forces employ a small number of dental hygienists. Most dental hygiene schools maintain placement services, and little difficulty arises in finding a satisfactory position.

Advancement

Opportunities for advancement, other than increases in salary and benefits that accompany experience in the field, usually require postgraduate study and training. Educational advancement may lead to a position as administrator, teacher, or director in a dental health program or to a more advanced field of practice.

Employment outlook

Dental hygienists hold about 97,000 jobs in the 1990s. About half of them work less than full-time.

The demand for dental care is expected to increase rapidly through the 1990s. Population growth, public awareness of the importance of oral health, and the availability of dental insurance should result in more jobs for dental hygienists. Job growth also depends on practice patterns in dentistry. The use of dental hygienists is more prevalent in some areas than in others. Young dentists are more inclined to hire hygienists because they have been taught in dental school how to make effective use of a support staff.

Earnings

The dental hygienist's income is influenced by such factors as education, experience, locale, and type of employer. Most dental hygienists who work in private dental offices are salaried employees, though some are paid a commission for work performed, or a combination of salary and commission. In the 1990s, the average earnings of full-time hygienists range between $24,500 and $31,500 a year. Beginning hygienists earn an average from $15,200 to $17,500. Salaries in large metropolitan areas are generally somewhat higher than in small cities and towns. In addition, dental hygienists in research, education, or administration may earn higher salaries.

Conditions of work

Work conditions for the dental hygienist in a private office, school, or government facility are pleasant, with well lighted, modern, and adequately equipped facilities. The hygienist usually sits while working. State and federal regulations require that hygienists wear masks, protective eyewear, and gloves as well as follow proper sterilizing techniques on equipment and instruments to guard against passing infection or disease. Full-time hygienists in a private office work a 35 to 40 hours per week; some work part-time at two jobs. Many private offices are open on Saturday. Government employees work hours regulated by the particular agency. For a salaried dental hygienist in a private office, a paid two- or three-week vacation is common. Part-time or commissioned dental hygienists in private offices usually have no paid vacation. Benefits will vary, however, according to the hygienist's agreement with the employer.

GOE: 10.02.02; SIC: 8021; SOC: 363

◇ SOURCES OF ADDITIONAL INFORMATION

American Association of Dental Examiners
211 East Chicago Avenue, Suite 844
Chicago, IL 60611

American Dental Hygienists' Association
444 North Michigan Avenue, Suite 3400
Chicago, IL 60611

American Dental Association
211 East Chicago Avenue
Chicago, IL 60611

Canadian Dental Hygienists Association
#201, 1018 Merivale Road
Ottawa ON K1Z 6A5

◇ RELATED ARTICLES

Volume 1: Health Care
Volumes 2–4: Dental assistants; Dental laboratory technicians; Dentists; Medical assistants

Dental laboratory technicians

Definition

Dental laboratory technicians are skilled craft workers who make and repair dental appliances such as dentures, inlays, bridges, crowns, and braces according to dentists' and orthodontists' written prescriptions. Dental laboratory technicians work with plastics, ceramics, and metals, using models made from impressions taken by the dentist of a patient's mouth or teeth.

Some dental laboratory technicians, especially those who work for smaller dental laboratories, perform the whole range of laboratory activities, while many others specialize in only one area. Some specialties include: making orthodontic appliances such as braces for straightening teeth; applying layers of porcelain paste or acrylic resin over a metal framework to form crowns, bridges, and tooth facings; making and repairing wire frames and retainers for teeth used in partial dentures; and making and repairing full and partial dentures.

History

Dental laboratory technicians are little known to most people who visit dentists, yet many dental patients today benefit from their skills. For centuries people have used many kinds of false teeth, with varying success. Thanks to sophisticated techniques and new materials such as acrylics and plastics, there are efficient, comfortable, and cosmetically acceptable aids available when natural teeth or tissue are missing or unsatisfactory.

Today nearly all dental practitioners utilize the services provided by commercial dental laboratories that handle tasks for a number of practitioners. This was not always the pattern, however.

Until the last years of the 19th century, dentists performed all their own lab work. The first successful commercial dental laboratory was established in 1887 by a partnership of a dentist and a machinist. The idea of delegating work to such laboratories was slow to catch on before World War II, when many dental technicians were trained to provide services at scattered military bases and on ships. In 1940, there were about 2,700 commercial dental laboratories in the United States; we have several times that number today. Their average size has remained small—only about half a dozen full-time workers per laboratory.

A growing number of technicians are employed directly by dentists, notably specialists in prosthodontics and orthodontics, to staff private dental laboratories. A recent estimate suggests that about one technician in five works in this type of private setting.

At first, dental laboratory technicians were trained on the job, but formal training programs are now the best way to prepare. In 1951, the American Dental Association began to accredit two-year post-secondary programs in dental technology. By the mid-1980s, 59 institutions offered such training.

A dental laboratory technician chips off the plastic impression of a mouth to reveal the positive plaster mold below. The plaster mold will then be sent to an orthodontist for analysis.

Nature of the work

Dental laboratory technicians often find that their talents and preferences lead them toward one phase of their field. The broad areas of specialization open to them include full and partial dentures, crowns and bridges, ceramics, and orthodontics.

Complete dentures, also called false teeth or plates, are worn by people who have had all their teeth removed on the upper or lower jaw, or both jaws. Applying their knowledge of oral anatomy and restoration, technicians who specialize in making dentures carefully position teeth in a wax model for the best occlusion (how the upper and lower teeth fit together when the mouth is closed), then build up wax over the denture setup. After the denture is cast in place, they clean and buff the product, using a bench lathe equipped with polishing wheels. When repairing dentures they may cast plaster models of replacement parts, and match the new tooth's color and shape to the natural or adjacent teeth. They cast reproductions of gums, fill cracks in dentures, and rebuild linings using acrylics and plastics. They may also bend and solder wire made of gold, platinum, and other metals and sometimes fabricate wire using a centrifugal casting machine.

Partial dentures, often called partials, restore missing teeth for patients who have some teeth remaining on the jaw. The materials and techniques in their manufacture are similar to those in full dentures. In addition, wire clasps are mounted to anchor the partial to the remaining teeth yet allow it to be removed for cleaning.

Crown and bridge specialists restore the missing parts of a natural tooth to recreate it in its original form. These appliances, made of plastics and metal, are sometimes called fixed bridgework because they are permanently cemented to the natural part of the tooth and are not removable. Technicians in this area are skilled at melting and casting metals. Waxing (building up wax around the setup before casting) and polishing the finished appliance are also usually among their responsibilities.

Some dental laboratory technicians are porcelain specialists known as *dental ceramists*. They fabricate natural-looking replacements to fit over natural teeth or to replace missing ones. Many patients concerned with personal appearance seek porcelain crowns, especially on front teeth. The ability to match color exactly and

451

delicately shape teeth is thus crucial for these technicians. To create crowns, bridges, and tooth facings, dental ceramists apply multiple layers of mineral powders or acrylic resins to a metal base and fuse the materials in an oven. The process is repeated until the result conforms exactly to specifications. Ceramists must know and understand all phases of dental technology and possess natural creative abilities. Because they require the highest level of knowledge and talent, ceramists are generally the best paid of dental technicians.

Orthodontics, the final area of specialization for dental laboratory technicians, involves bending wire into intricate shapes and soldering wires into complex positions. *Orthodontic technicians* shape, grind, polish, carve, and assemble metal and plastic appliances. Although tooth-straightening devices such as retainers, positioners, and tooth bands are not considered permanent, they may have to stay in place for long periods of time.

Dental laboratory technicians may work in a general or full-service laboratory, a category that includes nearly half of all dental laboratories. Or they may find employment with a laboratory that performs specialized services. Most specialized laboratories are concerned with the various uses of a particular material. For example, one specializing in acrylics is likely to make complete and partial dentures; another laboratory that does gold work will make gold inlays and bridges.

The lab's size may be related to the kinds of tasks its technical employees perform. Some large commercial laboratories may have staffs of 200 or more, allowing for a high degree of specialization. On the other hand, technicians working in a one- or two-person private laboratory may be called on to do a wide range of jobs.

Requirements

Successful dental laboratory technicians combine the precision, patience, and dexterity of a skilled craft worker with a generous amount of artistic talent. They must be able to carry out written and sometimes verbal instructions exactly, because each dental fixture has to be constructed according to very specific designs provided by the dentist. Good eyesight and color discrimination and the ability to do delicate work with one's fingers are very important. Although it is by no means a requirement, prospective technicians will profit from having had hobbies involving mixing and molding things

or from having built models of airplanes or cars.

The basic educational requirement is a high school diploma. Useful high school courses include chemistry, shop, mechanical drawing, art, and ceramics. Any other course or activity that allows the student to learn about metallurgy or the chemistry of plastics would be very helpful.

Inevitably, these technicians must learn much of their job by working under the supervision of experienced technicians. Three to four years of on-the-job training in a dental laboratory is the method of career entry used by some technicians. They start as trainees doing simple jobs such as mixing plaster and pouring it into molds. As they gradually gain experience, they are assigned more complex tasks.

Another way to prepare for the career is to enroll in a formal training program that leads to an associate degree in applied science. A typical two-year curriculum might include courses in denture construction, processing and repairing dentures, tooth construction, waxing and casting inlays, and crowns. In addition, the student may be expected to take courses such as biochemistry, English, business mathematics, and American government.

Although newly graduated technicians still need several years of further experience to refine their practical skills, these graduates benefit from a program combining academic courses with laboratory instruction. The broad exposure to the wide range of skills and materials pays off in the long run for most graduates; in fact, this approach is becoming the standard method of entry.

Special requirements

Technicians with appropriate training and experience can become Certified Dental Technicians, thus earning the right to place the initials C.D.T. after their names. Although certification is not mandatory for employment, many employers regard it as the best evidence of competence.

Certification is conducted by the National Board for Certification in Dental Laboratory Technology. For initial certification, candidates must pass a basic written and practical examination in at least one of the five laboratory specialties: complete dentures, partial dentures, crowns and bridges, ceramics, and orthodontics.

Certification requirements also include five years' experience in the field. Time spent in an approved dental laboratory technology training program may count towards the total.

Every year Certified Dental Technicians must meet specific continuing education requirements in order to maintain certification status.

Although membership is not required, dental laboratory technicians may choose to belong to various professional organizations. The most prominent among these are the National Association of Dental Laboratories and the American Dental Association. Local meetings bring together technicians and laboratory owners to share ideas of common interest and information about job opportunities.

Opportunities for experience and exploration

While in high school, students with an interest in this area can seek out courses and activities that allow exploration of ceramics, metal casting and soldering, molding, and the related skills practiced by dental laboratory technicians. A local dentist or school guidance counselor may be able to suggest a technician or laboratory in the area that the student might visit in order to get a first-hand idea of the work involved.

Part-time or summer jobs as laboratory helpers may be available. Such positions usually consist of picking up and delivering work to dentists' offices, but may also provide a chance to observe and assist practicing technicians. Students in dental laboratory technology training programs often have part-time jobs that develop into full-time technician positions after graduation.

Methods of entering

Newly graduated dental laboratory technicians seeking employment can apply directly to dentists' offices and laboratories as well as to private and state employment agencies. The best way for students to locate vacancies is through their school's placement office.

Local chapter of various professional associations are a good way to make contacts and keep up with new developments and employment openings. Sometimes more experienced dental technicians can get leads by inquiring at dental supply houses. Their sales workers are in constant contact with dentists and laboratories in the area and therefore know something about staffing needs.

In general, entry-level jobs are likely to include training and routine tasks that allow the technician to become familiar with the laboratory's operations. In a very large commercial laboratory, for instance, newcomers may be assigned to various departments. At the plaster bench they may make and trim models; some may do routine minor repairs of dentures and other appliances; others may polish dentures. As their skills become more evident, more complicated tasks may be added.

Advancement

The best way to advance is to develop individual skills. In general, technicians can expect advancement as they become expert in a specialized type of work. Depending on skill, experience, and education, some technicians become supervisors or managers in commercial laboratories. The prospect of such promotions is one reason why many technicians whose careers have begun with on-the-job training in a commercial laboratory later find it desirable to attend an accredited school program to obtain an associate degree.

Technicians interested in advancing can find out about new methods and update their skills in many ways: local, state, and national organizations provide a variety of learning opportunities; materials manufacturers also offer courses, often free, in the use of their products—outstanding technicians may be hired as instructors in these courses.

Some dental laboratory technicians, seeking variety and new outlets for their creativity, develop sideline activities that require similar skills and materials. Fine jewelry making, for example, is a natural career development for some technicians. Some technicians become teachers in training programs; others, sales representatives for dental products manufacturers.

Many technicians aspire to own and operate an independent laboratory. This requires a broad understanding of dental laboratory work, a well-developed business sense, and a considerable investment. Nonetheless, most of today's commercial laboratory owners have come up "from the bench."

Employment outlook

There are good reasons to expect that the demand for dental laboratory technicians will continue to grow fairly rapidly at least through the year 2000. Public awareness of dental health and appearance has increased substantially in recent years. At the same time, the number of people covered by dental insurance plans is rising. People in older age groups, who utilize a large share of dental appliances, are becoming an ever-greater segment of the population. The outlook is therefore optimistic for dental laboratory technicians, particularly those with exceptional ability and experience. In addition, the climate in future years should be good for entrepreneurial technicians setting out to establish new commercial laboratories, because more dentists will probably send work out instead of doing it themselves.

Earnings

There is limited information available relating to salaries of dental laboratory technicians. Recent graduates of a two-year program earn about $15,000 per year; with two to five years of experience, $18,200. The overall average salary for dental laboratory technicians is probably around $22,256 a year. Technicians with proven abilities and special skills earn more.

Generally technicians specializing in ceramics or gold make the most money, often over $33,000 a year. Managers and supervisors in large laboratories and self-employed technicians also exceed the average earnings.

Conditions of work

Most dental laboratory technicians work in well-lighted, calm, pleasant, and quiet surroundings. Usually technicians have their own workbenches and equipment.

The normal work week is 40 hours for technicians employed in commercial laboratories. Sometimes technicians face the deadline pressure, although dentists' requirements are usually flexible enough to allow for special problems or difficult jobs. Many laboratories must operate on weekends, and in areas where there is a shortage of technicians, it may be necessary to work overtime, with wages adjusted accordingly. Self-employed technicians or those in very small laboratories may have irregular or longer hours.

Technicians usually work by themselves, concentrating on details of the pieces they are making or repairing. While the work does not demand great physical strength, it does require deft handling of materials and tools. Technicians usually have little contact with people other than their immediate coworkers and the dentists whose instructions they follow. Work is often brought in and out by messenger or by mail.

Successful dental laboratory technicians enjoy detailed work, are good at following instructions, and take pride in perfection. They should be able to function independently but still be able to coordinate their activities with other workers in the same laboratory when necessary.

GOE: 05.05.11; SIC: 8072; SOC: 6865

◇ **SOURCES OF ADDITIONAL INFORMATION**

American Dental Association
211 East Chicago Avenue
Chicago, IL 60611

National Association of Dental Laboratories
3801 Mount Vernon Avenue
Alexandria, VA 22305

National Board for Certification of Dental Laboratories Technology
3801 Mount Vernon Avenue
Alexandria, VA 22305

Canadian Dental Association
1815 Alta Vista Drive
Ottawa ON K1G 3Y6

◇ **RELATED ARTICLES**

Volume 1: Health Care
Volumes 2–4: Biological technicians; Dental assistants; Dental hygienists; Dentists; Jewelers and jewelry repairers; Museum exhibit technicians; Optics technicians; Orthotic and prosthetic technicians

Dentists

Definition

Dentists attempt to maintain their clients' teeth through such preventive and reparative practices as extracting, filling, cleaning, or replacing teeth. They perform corrective work such as straightening teeth, and treat diseased tissue of the gums. They also perform surgical operations on jaw or mouth, and make and fit false teeth.

History

Dentistry was in earliest times a primitive yet necessary practice. For centuries, the practice of dentistry consisted largely of curing toothaches by extraction or the use of herbs and similar methods to alleviate pain, and was practiced not only by dentists but by barbers and blacksmiths as well. Dental care and correction have become a sophisticated branch of medicine, and dentists are professionals of great importance to the health of the public.

Nature of the work

A dentist may be a general practitioner or may specialize. Most dentists are general practitioners. Only 20 percent practice as specialists. The largest number of these specialists are orthodontists, followed by oral surgeons, pedodontists, periodontists, prosthodontists, endodontists, oral pathologists, and public health dentists.

General practitioners must be proficient in many areas of dentistry. They must not only be on the alert for any condition in the mouth requiring special treatment, such as crooked teeth, diseased gums, and oral cancer, but clean teeth, fill cavities, and extract teeth as well. General practitioners must be able to use and understand X rays and be well acquainted with laboratory work.

Specialists devote their time and skills to specific dental problems:

Orthodontists correct irregularities in the development of teeth and jaws by the use of braces and similar devices.

Oral surgeons perform difficult tooth extractions, remove tumors from the gums or jaw, and set jaw fractures.

Periodontists treat diseased gums and other tissues that support the teeth.

Prosthodontists specialize in making artificial teeth or dentures to precise specifications and measurements.

Pedodontists specialize in children's dental problems.

Oral pathologists examine and diagnose tumors and lesions of the mouth.

Endodontists treat diseased inner tooth structures, such as the nerve, pulp, and root canal.

Public health dentists deal with treatment and education of the public to the importance of dental health and care through public health agencies.

Dental service directors are in charge of dental programs in hospitals. These administrators help set policies and procedures, and establish training programs for students and interns. They supervise the hiring, promotion, duty assignments, and work schedules of staff members.

Requirements

The dental profession is selective, and standards are high. College grades and the amount of college education are carefully considered. All dental schools approved by the American Dental Association require applicants to pass the Dental Admissions Test, which tests a student's ability to succeed or fail in dental school. Information on tests and testing centers may be obtained from the Council on Dental Education of the American Dental Association.

A prospective dental student should plan an academic program of study in high school with an emphasis on science and math. Liberal arts courses are also significant for meeting college entrance requirements. Participation in extracurricular activities is also important. Experience in getting along with others is important in a profession so closely associated with people. The student should also note the importance of manual dexterity and scientific ability. Skilled, steady hands are necessary, as well as good space and shape judgment, and some artistic ability. Good vision is required because of the detailed work.

Dental schools require at least three to four years of college-level predental education. About 80 percent of students entering dental

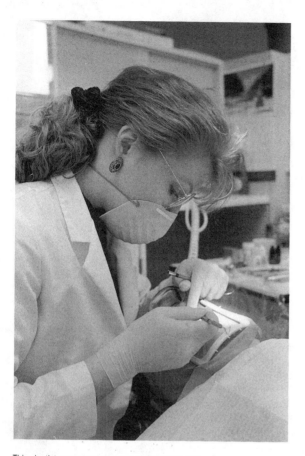

This dentist prepares to extract a diseased tooth.

schools have already earned a bachelor's or master's degree. Professional training in a dental school generally requires four academic years. Many dental schools have an interdisciplinary curriculum in which the dental student studies basic science with medical, pharmacy, and other health profession students. Clinical training is frequently begun in the second year. Most schools now feature a Department of Community Dentistry, which involves a study of communities, urban ghetto problems, sociology, and includes treatment of patients from the community. Generally the degree of doctor of dental surgery (D.D.S.) is granted upon graduation, although some schools give the degree of doctor of dental medicine (D.D.M. or D.M.D.).

Dental students who wish to enter a specialized field should plan on postgraduate study ranging from two to four years. A specialist can only become certified by passing specialty board exams. Further training may be obtained as a dental intern or resident in an approved hospital. Of course, a dentist must continually keep abreast of developments in the profession through reading professional magazines and journals, short-term graduate courses, and frequent seminars.

Special requirements

Dentists are required to qualify for a license in all states by graduating from an approved dental school and by passing a state board examination or, in some states, the National Board of Dental Examiner's exam. In 16 states and the District of Columbia, a specialist must pass a special state exam in order to be licensed. Generally, dentists licensed in one state are required to take another exam in order to practice in another state. However, 20 states grant licenses to dentists from other states based on their credentials.

Opportunities for experience and exploration

A high school student might be able to gain an awareness of the demands of dentistry by observing a dentist at work. Perhaps work as a dental hygienist, assistant, or laboratory technician might stimulate one to continue study in dentistry. Because of the nature of dentistry, however, actual practical experience would be impossible, although it might be helpful to develop a good manual dexterity through sculpting or metal working. A careful study of personal traits and aptitudes would be good preparation.

Methods of entering

Once a dentist has graduated from an approved dental school and passed a state licensing examination, there are three avenues of entry into private practice. A new dentist may open a new office, purchase an established practice, or join another dentist or group of dentists to gain further experience. There are, however, other choices for licensed dentists. They may enter the armed forces as a commissioned officer, or through civil service procedures may become eligible for work in the U.S. Public Health Service. They may choose to work in a hospital, clinic, or school. For some, the dental laboratory or teaching of dentistry will provide satisfying careers.

Advancement

Advancement for the newly licensed dentist in private practice depends on personal skill in handling patients as well as dental work. Through the years the successful dentist builds a reputation and thus advances with a growing clientele. The quality of the work depends in part on an ability to keep up with developments in the field. For salaried dentists in the various areas of employment, advancement will also depend on the quality and skill of their work. Advancement may take the form of a step from general practitioner to specialist, a step requiring further study and generally providing higher income. Teachers may look forward to administrative positions or to appointments as professors.

Advancement or success of dentists from a financial viewpoint may depend on the location of practice; people in higher income areas are more likely to request dental care. In small towns and sparsely populated areas a great need exists for dentists and competition is slight. In cities it may be more difficult to become known and competition is stiffer despite the larger pool of possible patients.

Employment outlook

Opportunities for dentists are anticipated to be very good through the 1990s. People are more concerned about dental health and can better afford dental care, especially because dental insurance is becoming more readily available.

Scientific advances in the field offer a promising future for specialists. The work, for example, of the oral pathologist or orthodontist increases as people become more aware of the need for such care. Public health programs, too, can be expected to expand. Dentistry today is becoming more a preventative than reparative practice.

Interestingly, the number of applicants to dental schools is decreasing, yet standards remain high and admission is competitive. High school students must be aware of the importance of maintaining high grades if they wish to meet this competition. Despite diminishing enrollments, the number of new graduates entering the field each year is larger than the number of openings. Dentists rarely leave the profession except to retire, and many continue to work beyond retirement age, simply reducing the number of hours they put in.

In the 1990s, there are about 174,000 dentists. Almost nine out of ten are in private prac-

tice. Of the remainder, about half work in research or teaching, or hold administrative positions in dental schools. Some practice in hospitals and clinics.

Earnings

Beginning dentists, faced with the expense of purchasing equipment and the problem of establishing a practice, generally earn enough to cover expenses and little more. But income rises rapidly as the dentist's practice becomes established. In the 1990s, the average income of the self-employed general practitioner after expenses is about $75,000 a year; specialists earn an average of $110,000.

The area in which a dentist practices also has an effect on income. In any high-income urban area, dental services are in great demand, but there is an advantage to setting up practice in a small town, where there is likely to be less competition and where the cost of living may be lower.

Dentists' earnings are lower during economic downturns when people tend to postpone dental treatment except for emergencies.

Conditions of work

Because most dentists are in private practice, they are free to set their own hours and establish offices and atmospheres suitable to their individual tastes. The beginning dentist must set aside expensive decorating plans in favor of suitable equipment, but most dentists' offices are designed to be pleasant and comfortable. Dentists may have a dental assistant, hygienist, or laboratory technician, or they may carry out the special duties of each themselves. The dentist in private practice sets individual hours and practices after office hours only in emergencies. Salaried dentists working for a clinic, hospital, or the Public Health Service are subject to conditions set by their employers.

Another qualification worth considering is the expense of education for a degree in dentistry as well as the initial expense of setting up a practice. The prospective dental student must be reasonably sure of meeting both of these financial demands.

GOE: 02.03.02; SIC: 8021; SOC: 262

◇ SOURCES OF ADDITIONAL INFORMATION

American Association of Dental Schools
1625 Massachusetts Avenue, NW
Washington, DC 20036

American Dental Association
211 East Chicago Avenue
Chicago, IL 60611

For a list of accredited schools for post-graduate and post-doctoral work, write to:

Accredited Dental School Educational Programs
American Dental Association
211 East Chicago Avenue
Chicago, IL 60611

Admission Requirements of US and Canadian Dental Schools
American Association of Dental Schools
1625 Massachusetts Avenue, NW
Washington, DC 20036

◇ **RELATED ARTICLES**

Volume 1: Health Care
Volumes 2–4: Dental assistants; Dental hygienists; Dental laboratory technicians

Deputy U.S. marshals

Definition

The United States Marshals Service forms a central part of the federal government's law enforcement efforts. As a bureau within the Department of Justice, the Marshals Service reports to the U.S. attorney general. Among the responsibilities of *deputy U.S. marshals* are providing court security, which includes personal protection of judges, judicial officials, and jurors; serving warrants and process documents; locating and apprehending fugitives; transporting prisoners; managing the Federal Witness Security Program; seizing assets used in or the result of criminal activity; and handling special assignments and operations.

History

The United States Marshals Service has its roots in the Judiciary Act, passed by Congress in 1789, which established not only the post of U.S. marshal but also the country's original federal court system. The act delegated two duties to the marshals: to enforce all precepts issued by the federal government and to protect and attend to the federal courts. They were also authorized to hire one or more deputies.

The first 13 U.S. marshals, appointed by President George Washington, were confirmed by the U.S. Senate on September 26, 1789. Over the next year two more marshals were chosen. Each of the 13 original states, as well as the districts of Kentucky and Maine, were assigned a marshal. The number of marshals and deputies increased as the United States expanded westward and, with a rise in the country's population, some states were assigned more than one marshal. By the early 1990s there were 95 U.S. marshals spread across the 50 states, the District of Columbia, Puerto Rico, Guam, the Virgin Islands, and the Northern Marianas.

The duties of the Marshals Service expanded soon after the appointment of the first marshals. Marshals and deputies were required, for example, to play a major role in taking the national census (a responsibility that lasted until 1870), to supervise federal penitentiaries in the western territories, to enforce precepts from the French consuls, to take custody of goods seized by customs officers, and to sell seized lands. Along with the increase in responsibilities came a corresponding growth in the number of superiors to which the Marshals Service was accountable. By the mid-19th century the federal courts, the Secretary of the Treasury, the Solicitor of the Treasury, and the Secretary of the Interior all had supervisory powers over some aspects of the work of the marshals and deputies. In 1861, however, the Marshals Service came under the exclusive power of the attorney general, and in 1870 the service became a part of the newly created Department of Justice.

U.S. marshals and their deputies have frequently faced potentially dangerous situations. The level of danger was especially great in the 19th century for those who were charged with keeping order in newly established western territories. During the Oklahoma land rush, for example, more than 60 marshals were killed in a span of just five years. It is the Marshals Service of the late 19th century—the time of legendary marshals Bat Masterson and Wyatt Earp, of posses and quick draws—that many people are most familiar with, as the role of marshals and deputies in the old west has been dramatized in numerous books and films. Some might also remember that marshals and deputies were charged with quelling civil disturbances, such as the Whiskey Rebellion of 1791, the Pullman Strike of 1894, and the antiwar protests of the late 1960s; enforcing school integration beginning in the 1960s; and confronting militant American Indians at Wounded Knee, South Dakota, in 1973. Today the men and women of the Marshals Service, trained in the latest techniques and equipment, continue to perform a wide variety of law enforcement duties under the attorney general and the U.S. Department of Justice.

Nature of the work

One of the oldest duties of the United States Marshals Service is court security. Originally this entailed the presence of a marshal or deputy in the courtroom to maintain order and to ensure the safety of the judge. In time, however, the job of protecting the courts has become much more complex. Now, depending on the trial, prosecutors, attorneys, jurors, witnesses, family members, and any other trial participant potentially in danger might be given security. The greater scope of responsibility has been aided by advanced equipment—high-tech alarm systems, for example—as well as by improved law enforcement techniques. The Marshals Service is sometimes alerted to dangers by threats mentioned in letters or phone calls or by informants, but deputies cannot rely on these explicit means of warning. Constant vigilance is required.

Escorting a prisoner to court, this U.S. marshal must make sure he doesn't escape.

A special area related to court security is the Witness Security Program. Witnesses who risk their lives to testify against organized crime figures or others involved in major criminal activity are given around-the-clock protection. After the trial, the witnesses are relocated to another part of the country and given a new identity. The Marshals Service provides support programs to help these witnesses adjust to their new identities and environments.

A significant part of the workload involves serving process documents and executing court orders. There are many kinds of process documents, including subpoenas, restraining orders, notices of condemnations, and summons. In the days of the old west, serving process documents used to be one of the most dangerous duties, sometimes entailing traveling on horseback for long distances, as well as face-to-face shootouts. Sophisticated equipment, allowing for better means of surveillance and coordination, has made this task less threatening. About one million process documents are now handled each year by the Marshals Service.

Even more dangerous has been the execution of arrest warrants and the apprehension of fugitives. Along with other federal agencies, such as the Federal Bureau of Investigation, the Marshals Service continues to perform these tasks, handling about 30,000 arrest warrants each year and apprehending more fugitives than all other federal law enforcement agencies combined. The Marshals Service is responsible for locating and apprehending many types of fugitives, including parole and probation violators and prisoners who have escaped from federal prison.

For most of its history, the Marshals Service has been charged with seizing, managing, and disposing property involved in criminal cases. Many of these cases now involve drug trafficking. Planes, cars, boats, houses and condominiums, ranches, businesses, and restaurants, as well as personal assets such as jewelry and cash, are some examples of the type of property seized. When seized property is forfeited under the law, it is sold off at public auctions or by other means or may be transferred to law enforcement agencies for official use.

The Marshals Service is also in charge of transporting federal prisoners. Using automobiles, buses, vans, and aircraft—some of which were acquired by the asset seizure program—more than 130,000 prisoner movements occur each year. After a trial, convicts awaiting a sentence are also the responsibility of the Marshals Service. The average number of prisoners held in custody each day by the Marshals Service exceeds 20,000.

Protecting the shipment of weapons systems is a more recent responsibility. Under an agreement with the United States Air Force, deputies help escort vehicles transporting weapons systems, deter or arrest anyone attempting to disrupt the shipment, and direct traffic.

Within the Marshals Service is a rapid deployment force called the Special Operations Group (SOG). The unit was formed in 1971 in order to handle national emergencies, such as civil disturbances, hostage cases, or terrorist attacks. Members of SOG are regular deputies, located in all parts of the country, who are given specialized training and who must always be on call for emergencies.

Requirements

Like those in other law enforcement positions, deputy U.S. marshals must be in excellent physical shape. Moreover, they must have no worse than 20/200 uncorrected vision in both eyes (corrected to at least 20/40 in one eye and 20/20 in the other); good hearing (equivalent to being able to hear a whispered voice at 15 feet); no disorders of speech, of the extremities and spine, or in the respiratory, cardiovascular, and gastrointestinal systems; or any other health condition that might interfere with job performance.

The Marshals Service requires that candidates have a minimum level of education or ex-

perience. A four-year bachelor's degree in any major is sufficient. Without an undergraduate degree, however, an applicant needs at least three years experience in a job demonstrating poise and self-confidence under stress, as well as the ability to reason soundly, make decisions quickly and find practical solutions, accept responsibility, interact tactfully with a wide range of people, and prepare reports. Although any number of occupations may fulfill these requirements, the following are examples of acceptable experience: (1) law enforcement; (2) correctional treatment and supervision of inmates; (3) classroom teaching; (4) volunteer work or counseling for a community action program; (5) sales work (but not over-the-counter sales positions); (6) interviewing; or (7) jobs such as a credit rating investigator, claims adjuster, or journalist that require public contact for the purpose of collecting information. For candidates who have been to college but do not have a degree, every year of study is accepted as nine months of experience.

All candidates are required to take a written test of 125 questions. A score of 78 or better is passing. The questions are intended to evaluate clerical skills, the ability to reason verbally, and proficiency in abstract reasoning (that is, using symbols and numbers). Candidates are also given a personal interview and must be willing to undergo an extensive background check.

Once hired, new deputy marshals are sent to a basic training program, lasting about three months, which includes courses in law enforcement, criminal investigation, forensics, and areas particular to the Marshals Service. There is also a rigorous physical fitness program, as well as 18 months of on-the-job training.

Opportunities for experience or exploration

For any law enforcement job, it is difficult to obtain practical experience prior to entering the field. Those who are interested in more information about working as a deputy U.S. marshal are encouraged to write directly to the Marshals Service at the address given below. A school guidance counselor, a college or university placement office, or a public library may also have additional information. For more background, an in-depth historical survey is found in the book The Lawmen: United States Marshals and their Deputies, 1789–1989 (Smithsonian Institution Press, 1990).

Methods of entering

The Marshals Service accepts only candidates who have fulfilled the necessary physical, educational, and experiential requirements listed above. Those interested in pursuing the field should contact the Marshals Service to find out when and where the written examination will take place.

In general, newly hired deputy U.S. marshals begin at job grade GS–5. After completing the training period, deputies are promoted to grade GS–7, which includes a substantial raise. Candidates with a graduate degree in law, police science, or in another field relating to law enforcement—as well as those who have a bachelor's degree and meet the service's requirements for superior academic achievement—may be hired at grade GS–7. With satisfactory work, promotions to grade GS–11 and above are possible.

Advancement

Advancement is made on the basis of merit and experience. Within a district office, the top position is that of U.S. marshal. U.S. marshals are appointed by the president of the United States and must be confirmed by the U.S. Senate. Directly under the U.S. marshal is the chief deputy U.S. marshal, who oversees the district's staff of supervisors, the deputy U.S. marshals, and the support staff. Each district also employs specialists in witness security, court security, and seized property.

Employment outlook

There are 2,200 deputy U.S. marshals in the early 1990s. Employment opportunities are expected to increase at an average rate throughout the 1990s and into the 21st century. Changes in the service's budget, as well as increases or decreases in the responsibilities assigned the service, could affect employment opportunities.

Earnings

The salaries for deputy U.S. marshals are comparable to those for many other law enforcement occupations. In the early 1990s the starting salary for deputies at the GS–5 job grade is about $19,000 (about $22,000 in New York City;

Los Angeles; Boston; San Francisco; Alexandria, Virginia; and Washington, DC).

Salaries for grades GS–7, GS–9, and GS–11 are, respectively, about $23,000, $27,000, and $32,000 (in the above cities, $27,000, $32,000, and $37,000). Chief deputy marshals earn about $55,000. All members of the Marshals Service are given a benefits package, including health and life insurance, paid vacation, and a pension program.

Conditions of work

In general, deputy U.S. marshals work 40 hours a week. These hours are usually during the daytime Monday through Friday, but overtime and other shifts are sometimes required. Travel—for example, to transport a prisoner from one state to another—may be necessary.

Deputies generally work out of well-maintained, clean offices, but their duties can take them to a wide variety of environments, such as a courtroom; an automobile, helicopter, or airplane; the streets of a major U.S. city; or, when trying to locate a fugitive, a foreign country.

Like all law enforcement jobs, personal safety is a concern. Those interested in working for the Marshals Service should be well aware of the potential for physical harm or even death. Because of the danger, deputies carry firearms and are well trained in self-defense. Strenuous physical exertion, emotional stress, and exposure to harsh conditions (such as poor weather) are often a part of the job.

For some deputies, an advantage of the job is the diversity of cases. Others find personal satisfaction in knowing that they are serving their country.

GOE: 04.01.02; SIC: none; SOC: 5134

◇ **SOURCES OF ADDITIONAL INFORMATION**

United States Marshals Service
Employment and Compensation Division
Field Staffing Branch
600 Army Navy Drive
Suite 890
Arlington, VA 22202-4210

Detectives

Definition

Detectives are usually plainclothes investigators who gather difficult-to-obtain information on criminal activity and other subjects. They conduct interviews and surveillances, locate missing persons and criminal suspects, examine records, and write detailed reports. Some make arrests and take part in raids. Most detectives work for government agencies, such as a police department or the U.S. Drug Enforcement Administration, but there are also a significant number of *private investigators*. Sometimes called *private detectives* or *private eyes*, private investigators may work for themselves, for a detective agency, or for a business.

History

The United States inherited much of its law enforcement tradition from England. During the early history of the United States, criminal investigation was often handled by bounty hunters, sometimes called stipendiary police or thieftakers. These early detectives were paid a reward or fee by governments, private individuals, or businesses (such as insurance companies) for apprehending suspected criminals or returning stolen property. Many were petty criminals themselves.

The early 19th century saw growing social unrest and criminal activity in the United States as the country moved from an agrarian to an industrialized urban economy. By the mid-1800s the upsurge in crime led to public calls for greater government action. The first police department in the United States was formed in New York City in 1844. Before long many cities and towns across the country also established organized police forces, including special investigative divisions. Investigation of crimes, however, was still commonly handled by stipendiary police and thieftakers. Although police departments were created with the hope of reducing crime, numerous scandals within their own ranks soon erupted. Corruption within local police departments was a continual problem and by the early 1900s became a motivating cause for police reforms and for the establishment of state police agencies, including state investigative divisions.

Also notable during the 19th century was the growth of private investigative firms. Probably the most famous was the Pinkerton National Detective Agency, formed by Allan Pinkerton in the early 1850s. The agency became famous for its ability to apprehend train robbers, kidnappers, thiefs, and forgers. Unlike stipendiary police and thieftakers, who were often viewed as criminals, agents of Pinkerton's firm had a reputation for honesty and integrity. The company's reputation, along with Pinkerton's rejection of rewards in favor of a set daily fee for his agents, helped establish professional standards for detective work.

The U.S. government began to increase its role in criminal investigation in the second half of the 19th century. In 1865 the United States Secret Service was formed. Although later associated with the protection of the president and other officials, the secret service was created to investigate counterfeit money. Another federal agency, the Bureau of Investigation (later the Federal Bureau of Investigation, or the FBI), was created in 1908 by executive order of Theodore Roosevelt. It began by investigating criminal activity on government property, crimes by government officials, antitrust cases, and numerous fraudulent schemes.

In the 20th century the federal government has established a number of other investigative agencies. During Prohibition thousands of detectives were employed by the Treasury Department to enforce the government's ban on alcoholic beverages, as well as to investigate the escalating crime surrounding the sale of liquor.

Narcotic squad detectives, employed by the U.S. Drug Enforcement Administration, are charged with a similar duty today.

The field of criminal investigation has been revolutionized by advances in technology. Of great impact was the use of fingerprinting for identification and detection of criminals. Fingerprinting began to be widely used by police departments in the early 1900s. Methods of analyzing bloodstains, saliva, and hair and skin traces, as well as precise ways to match up various inorganic substances, such as paint and cloth fibers, have also aided detectives. More recently, "voiceprinting" and the genetic technique of "DNA- printing" have shown promise for more sophisticated detection.

Nature of the work

The job of a police detective begins after a crime has been committed. Uniformed police officers are usually the first to be dispatched to the scene of a crime, however, and it is police officers who are generally required to make out the initial crime report. This report is often the material with which a detective begins an investigation.

Detectives may also receive help early on from other members of the police department. *Evidence technicians* are sometimes sent immediately to the scene of a crime to comb the area for physical evidence. This step is especially important because most crime scenes contain physical evidence that could link a suspect to the crime. Fingerprints are the most common physical piece of evidence, but other clues, such as broken locks, broken glass, and footprints, as well as blood, skin, or hair traces, are also useful. If there is a suspect on the scene, torn clothing or any scratches, cuts, and bruises are noted. Physical evidence may then be tested by specially trained *crime lab technicians*.

It is usually after this initial stage that the case is assigned to a police detective. Police detectives may be assigned as many as two or three cases a day, and having thirty cases to handle at one time is not unusual. Because there is only a limited amount of time, an important part of a detective's work is to determine which cases have the greatest chance of being solved. Only a few—serious offenses or those in which there is considerable evidence and obvious leads—are given high priority. All cases, however, are given at least a routine follow-up investigation.

Police detectives have numerous means of gathering additional information. For example, they contact and interview victims and wit-

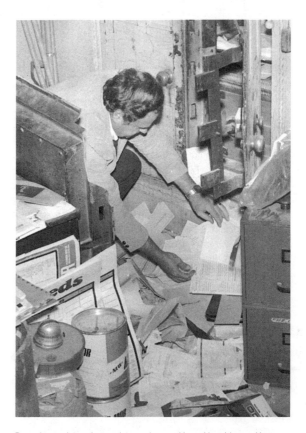

Detective work requires patience when working with evidence. Here, a detective sorts through piles of paper for clues.

nesses, familiarize themselves with the scene of the crime and places where a suspect may spend time, and conduct surveillance operations. Detectives sometimes have informers who are able to provide important leads. Because a detective must often work undercover, ordinary clothes, not a police uniform, are worn. Also helpful are existing police files on other crimes, on known criminals, and on people suspected of criminal activity. If sufficient evidence has been collected, the police detective will arrest the suspect, sometimes with the help of uniformed police officers.

Once the suspect is in custody, it is the job of the police detective to conduct an interrogation. Questioning the suspect may reveal new evidence and help determine whether the suspect was involved in other unsolved crimes. Before finishing the case, the detective must write a detailed written report. Detectives are sometimes required to present evidence at the trial of the suspect.

Narcotics squad detectives, officially called DEA (Drug Enforcement Administration) special agents, have similar duties as police detectives, but their focus is on one type of criminal—violators of the federal government's

463

Controlled Substance Act. Among the duties of a narcotics squad detective are investigating major drug cases, conducting surveillance, operating undercover in drug activities, and apprehending suspects. They also confiscate drug supplies and assets gained by drug trafficking, write detailed reports, and testify in court.

Criminal investigation is just one area in which private investigators are involved. Some specialize, for example, in finding missing persons, while others may investigate insurance fraud, gather information on the background of persons involved in divorce or child custody cases, provide lie detection tests, debug offices and telephones, or offer security services. Cameras, video equipment, tape recorders, and lock picks are used according to the law to obtain necessary information.

Some private investigators work for themselves, but many others work for detective agencies or businesses. Clients include private individuals, corporations concerned with theft, insurance companies suspicious of fraud, and lawyers who want information for a case. Whoever the client, the private investigator is usually expected to provide a detailed report.

Requirements

Because detectives work on a wide variety of cases, high school students interested in the field are encouraged take a diverse course load. English, American history, business law, government, psychology, sociology, chemistry, and physics are suggested, as are courses in journalism and a foreign language. The ability to type is often needed.

To become a police detective, one must first have experience as a police officer. Hiring requirements for police officers vary, but most departments require at least a high school diploma. In some departments a college degree may be necessary for some or all police positions. Many colleges and universities offer courses or programs in police science, criminal justice, or law enforcement. Newly hired police officers are generally sent to a police academy for job training.

After gaining substantial experience in the department—usually about three to five years—and demonstrating the skills required for detective work, police officers may be promoted to a position as a detective. In some police departments, candidates must first take a qualifying exam. For new detectives there is usually a training program, which may last from a few weeks to several months.

In almost all large cities the hiring of police officers must follow local civil service regulations. In such cases a candidate generally must be 21 years old, a U.S. citizen, and within the locally prescribed height and weight limits. Other requirements include 20/20 corrected vision and good hearing. A background check is often done.

The civil service board usually gives both a written and physical examination. The written test is intended to measure a candidate's mental aptitude for police work, while the physical examination focuses on strength, dexterity, and agility.

Narcotics squad detectives are required to have a college degree, usually with at least a B average. Only U.S. citizens between the ages of 21 and 34 are considered. Candidates must be in excellent shape and have an uncorrected vision no worse than 20/200 in both eyes (corrected to at least 20/40 in one and 20/20 in the other). All candidates are required to undergo an extensive background check. Experience in the military, law enforcement, a foreign language, navigation and aviation, computers, electronics, or accounting is helpful.

Private detective agencies usually do not hire individuals without previous experience. A large number of private investigators are former police officers. Those with no law enforcement experience but who want to become private investigators can enroll in special private investigation schools, although they do not guarantee qualification for employment. These schools teach skills essential to detective work, such as how to lift and develop fingerprints, pick locks, test for human blood, investigate robberies, identify weapons, and take pictures. The length of these programs and their admissions requirements vary considerably. Some are correspondence programs, while others offer classroom instruction and an internship at a detective agency. A college degree is an admissions requirement at some private investigation schools. Experience can also be gained by taking classes in law enforcement, police science, or criminal justice at a college or university.

Licensing for private investigators varies from state to state, but in general applicants must pass a written examination and file a bond. Depending on the state, applicants may also need to have a minimum amount of experience, either as a police officer or as an apprentice under a licensed private investigator. An additional license is sometimes required for carrying a gun.

Certain personal characteristics are helpful for detectives. Among the most important are an inquisitive mind, good observation skills, a keen memory, and well-developed oral and written communication skills. The large amount of physical activity requires that detectives be in good shape. An excellent moral character is especially important.

Opportunities for experience and exploration

There are few means of exploring the field of detective work, and actual experience in the field prior to employment is unlikely. Some police departments, however, do hire teenagers for positions as police trainees. Students and others interested in becoming a detective are advised to talk with a school guidance counselor, their local police department, local private detective agencies, a private investigation school, or a college or university offering police science, criminal justice, or law enforcement courses. Additional information may be found at a public library or from one of the organizations listed at the end of this article.

Methods of entering

Those interested in becoming a detective should contact local police departments, the civil service office or examining board, or private detective agencies in their area to determine hiring practices and any special requirements. Newspapers may list available jobs. Those who earn a college degree in police science, criminal justice, or law enforcement may benefit from the institution's placement or guidance office. Some police academies accept candidates not sponsored by a police department, and for some people this may be the best way to enter police work. To apply for a position as a narcotics squad detective, contact the local office of the U.S. Drug Enforcement Administration or the national office in Washington, DC.

Advancement

Advancement within a police department may depend on several factors, such as job performance, length of service, formal education and training courses, and special examinations. Large city police departments, divided into separate divisions with their own administrations,

often provide greater advancement possibilities.

Because of the high dropout rate for private investigators, those who stay in the field for more than five years have an excellent chance for advancement. Supervisory and management positions exist, and some private investigators start their own agencies.

Employment outlook

There are more than 250,000 detectives in the United States in the early 1990s. A large percentage of these work for police departments or other government agencies, such as the U.S. Drug Enforcement Administration. The rest work as private investigators, employed either for themselves, for a private detective firm, or for a business.

The employment outlook for police detectives is expected to be average throughout the 1990s and into the 21st century, although the number of available jobs could be affected by changes in government spending. Most openings will likely result from police detectives retiring or leaving their department for other reasons. Job openings for narcotics squad detectives are expected to continue attracting a large number of applicants.

The outlook for private investigators is expected to be much better, although it is important to keep in mind that law enforcement or comparable experience is often required for employment. The use of private investigators by insurance firms, restaurants, hotels, and other businesses is on the rise. An area of particular growth is investigation of computer fraud.

Earnings

The average salary of a new police officer in the United States is about $22,000 a year in the early 1990s. Salaries of police detectives range from $18,900 to $37,300. Compensation generally increases considerably with experience. Police departments generally offer better than average benefits, including health insurance, paid vacation, sick days, and pension plans. Starting salaries of narcotics squad detectives are either about $21,000 or $26,000, depending on the candidate's previous experience.

The salary range for private investigators is much greater. New detectives commonly earn from $9.00 to $12.00 an hour, although other compensation, such as depreciation payments for automobile use and reimbursement for gasoline, may be offered. Private investigators who are self-employed have the potential for making much greater salaries. Hourly fees of $30 to $150 and even more, excluding expenses, are possible. Detectives who work for an agency may receive benefits, such as health insurance, but self-employed investigators must provide their own.

Conditions of work

The working conditions of a detective are often quite diverse. Almost all work out of an office, where they may consult with colleagues, interview witnesses, read documents, or contact people on the telephone.

The variety of assignments brings detectives to a wide range of environments. A detective may work undercover as a janitor at a business, spend hours sitting in a car while waiting for a suspect to leave a suburban hotel, or follow an individual through a crowded city street. Interviews at homes or businesses may be necessary. Traveling is also common. Rarely do jobs expose a detective to possible physical harm or death, but detectives are more likely than most people to place themselves in a dangerous situation.

Schedules for detectives are often irregular, and overtime, as well as working at night and on the weekend, may be necessary. At some police departments and detective agencies, overtime is compensated with additional pay or time-off.

Although the work of a detective is portrayed as exciting in popular culture, the job has its share of monotonous and discouraging moments. For example, detectives may need to sit in a car for many hours waiting for a suspect to leave a building entrance, only to find that the suspect is not there. Even so, the great variety of cases usually makes the work interesting.

GOE: 04.01.02; SIC: none; SOC: 5132

◇ **SOURCES OF ADDITIONAL INFORMATION**

International Association of Chiefs of Police
515 North Washington Street
4th Floor
Alexandria, VA 22314

American Federation of Police
3801 Biscayne Boulevard
Miami, Florida 33137

DEA Headquarters
1405 I Street N.W.
Room 2558
Washington, DC 20537

International Security and Detective Alliance
PO Box 6303
Corpus Christi, TX 78466

◇ **RELATED ARTICLES**

Volume 1: Civil Service; Politics and Public Service
Volumes 2–4: Deputy U.S. marshals; FBI agents; Lawyers and judges; Police officers

---

Dialysis technicians

Definition

Dialysis technicians, also called *renal dialysis technicians,* set up and operate artificial kidney machines for patients with chronic renal failure, that is, whose kidneys no longer function; thus these patients require hemodialysis to sustain life. In dialysis, the patient's blood is circulated through the dialysis machine, which takes over for the kidneys by filtering out impurities, wastes, and excess fluids. The blood is then returned to the body.

There is no standard definition of technicians' duties. They may initiate, monitor, and discontinue the dialysis treatment; troubleshoot certain medical and technical complications that occur during treatment; maintain and repair dialysis equipment; monitor the patient's vital signs during the dialysis; record patient data; and help educate the patient and family about dialysis.

History

Dialysis was first described in 1854 by a Scottish chemist, Thomas Graham. In his early experiments, Graham separated crystalloids from colloids. Crystalloids are chemical salts that dissolve, and colloids are jelly-like materials that remain uniformly suspended in a solvent and will not dissolve.

In the experiments, the crystalloids in the solution passed through a membrane into another solution. They were then recovered by evaporating the solution. Graham predicted possible medical uses for the discovery, but did not do any experiments involving animals or humans.

In 1913, John J. Abel and Leonard G. Rowntree utilized the principle of dialysis in laboratory experiments using animals. Because the dialysis technique involved removing chemicals from the blood of animals, researchers called the process "hemodialysis." *Hemo* comes from a Greek word *haima*, which means "blood."

In the process, blood is taken from the body and passed through membranous tubes. The surfaces of the membranes are bathed with solutions, and normal body waste chemicals that are usually removed by the kidneys pass through the membranes into the chemical solutions. The blood cells and other proteins act as colloids, which means that they do not pass through the membranes. They return to the body with the blood but without the harmful waste chemicals. The waste materials are soluble, so they act as crystalloids and are removed. The rate of the waste removal depends on the amount of the waste products in the blood and the nature and strength of the solutions used to bathe the membranes through which the blood is flowing.

Improvements in equipment and the development of heparin, a drug that prevents clotting, made hemodialysis practical in humans in the early 1940s. Since then, further advances have made the process more efficient. By the late 1950s dialysis was available in health care facilities throughout the United States. During

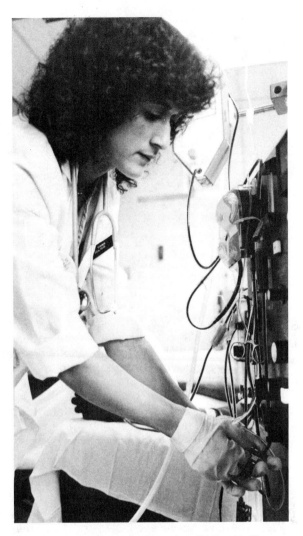

A dialysis technician prepares equipment that will be used to filter blood and remove excess fluid from a diabetic patient.

the 1960s it became apparent that self-care dialysis could be successfully carried out in the homes of patients much more economically than it could in hospitals. This was an important development because dialysis is a very expensive process.

Since 1973, Medicare funds have paid for dialysis carried out in health facilities. It now also pays for the equipment patients need for home dialysis.

While most dialysis is still carried out in hospitals or special dialysis facilities, special techniques and equipment have been devised that make home dialysis possible, and which some patients even administer to themselves. Even though they receive extensive education in the proper operation of the equipment, home dialysis patients must be monitored carefully by members of the dialysis team.

DIALYSIS TECHNICIANS

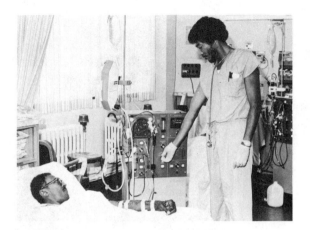

As a patient undergoes dialysis treatment, a dialysis technician monitors and adjusts the equipment.

Nature of the work

The technician's responsibilities and duties vary from one dialysis unit to another and sometimes even within the same unit. They may be limited to technical procedures and direct patient care, or may be expanded to include biochemical analyses, observations, and carrying out research studies to improve equipment. The dialysis technician's role is determined by a number of factors, including: the dialysis facility's management plan, the facility's leadership and staff, the technician's skills and background, the unit's equipment and facilities, other activities conducted by the unit's staff, the equipment available, and the long-term care plans for patients.

Renal dialysis is still evolving. For this reason, in most states, the technicians' duties are determined within the individual dialysis facilities; however, there are some aspects of the work of dialysis technicians that are common to all workplaces. For instance, dialysis technicians always work under the supervision of professional nurses and physicians. Some tasks that may be performed by dialysis technicians are described in the following paragraphs.

Prior to the actual dialysis treatment, technicians prepare the dialyzer by positioning the machine, attaching and installing all required tubing, preparing the fluid-delivery system, connecting the dialyzer and all its pumps, and assembling all necessary supplies and equipment at the patient's bedside. Dialysis technicians may also be called upon to calibrate and check alarms, set monitors, and test the dialyzer if necessary.

They prepare the patients for the dialysis first by weighing them and recording vital signs, including blood pressure, pulse, temperature, and rate of breathing. They also inspect and evaluate access sites (places to insert tubes to remove and return blood in the process), and obtain blood samples and culture specimens as ordered. Dialysis technicians begin the dialysis procedure using established access routes through veins or a catheter; they adjust the heparin dosage according to the procedure prescribed by the patient's supervising physician.

During dialysis, the technicians: measure and adjust blood-flow rates; measure, observe, and record this information, including other factors such as vital signs and weight changes; observe the fluid-delivery unit to be sure it is working properly; and respond to alarms and make appropriate adjustments.

Following the procedure, dialysis technicians clean and dress the access sites, clean and sterilize the equipment, properly dispose of used supplies, and perform routine maintenance tasks on the equipment. At any time during the procedure, they may be called upon to administer oxygen or to apply basic cardiopulmonary resuscitation measures in the event of a cardiac emergency.

The tasks performed by the dialysis technician may be carried out in a hospital, nursing home, dialysis center, or in a patient's home. To perform the tasks described, the technician must know and understand the equipment, its design characteristics, and the system's operating principles in order to obtain the best possible results safely and efficiently.

When performing dialysis treatment, technicians must understand all details of the standardized procedures and realize the importance of following them exactly. They must also master the standardized techniques that prevent potential dangers such as reaction to bacterial infections and to chemical substances.

In the self-care programs, the dialysis technician teaches patients about the principles of dialysis and the tasks that they must perform. Common problems are usually caused by poor technique, contamination of equipment or supplies, and failure of the equipment or supplies to work properly. Bacterial infections are of special concern. Patients must be able to reduce these risks to the very minimum, and must be able to recognize early symptoms if they occur.

Requirements

The career of dialysis technicians is still evolving. When dialysis was a new technique, health workers with little training but some aptitude and interest in the field learned the procedures on the job. Today, training in basic patient-care skills and in responding to emergency situations that can arise during dialysis have become additional requirements.

Interested high school students should study biology, chemistry, science, mathematics, communications, and health-related subjects. They should also learn to use a typewriter or word processor in order to prepare reports. The ability to talk easily with patients and other team members is essential; verbal information and descriptions of procedures and techniques must be clearly conveyed to patients and to their family members. In addition, technicians must be able to read scientific textbooks, technical manuals, and journals. Consequently, good language skills are crucial.

Formal preparation for this career generally takes place in programs conducted by renal units of hospitals or in free-standing dialysis centers. Only a few dialysis preparatory programs may be found in two-year colleges or in technical schools.

For dialysis technicians, the skills and knowledge are acquired through a systematic but loosely structured program of on-the-job supervised training in hospitals or health care units that provide dialysis services. Technicians are taught by the staff of the unit, according to an organized plan drawn up by the physicians, nurses, and experienced dialysis technicians. Classroom instruction, demonstrations, and independent study comprise the formal instruction of the program. Observation and supervised practice on the job provide the necessary clinical experience. As students acquire more knowledge and proficiency, they are given different tasks requiring more responsibility by the instructors. The rate of progress and the total content of the program depend upon the training facility's philosophy and staff, and on the trainee's ability and performance.

More complete preparatory programs are based on a general medicine core curriculum. It includes human anatomy, physiology, characteristics and nature of kidney disease, medical terminology, concepts of infectious diseases, microbiology, professional relationships, medications, medical record keeping, patient-care skills, vital signs, and emergency care procedures.

The specialized dialysis portion of the curriculum includes the history and principles of dialysis therapy, dialysis systems and components, technical dialysis procedures, equipment repair and maintenance, dietary considerations, drug therapy and potential complications in use of medicines, and basic biochemical principles and factors in dialysis treatments. It also may include a study of nephrology, the characteristics of normal and abnormal kidneys,

kidney transplantation, appropriate responses to behavior, ethical issues, and other studies.

In most states, dialysis technicians are not required to be registered, certified, or licensed; California presently requires certification. In some states dialysis technicians are required to pass a test before they can work with patients. A voluntary program for certification is offered by the Board of Nephrology Examiners (Nursing and Technology). The program is open to nurses and technicians. The purpose of the program is to identify safe and competent practitioners, to promote quality care of the nephrology patient, and to encourage the study of nursing and technological fields in nephrology. Once certified, technicians use the title CHT (Certified Hemodialysis Technician) after their names.

Technicians who apply for the certification examination must be high school graduates; have at least one year of experience in the care of nephrology patients who have serious renal disease requiring dialysis; be currently performing the functions described in the position paper published by the National Association of Renal Technologists, actively working in the care of nephrology patients on a regular and continuing basis in a federally recognized end-stage renal disease (ESRD) facility or Veterans Administration renal program.

The certification examination contains questions related to anatomy, normal and abnormal physiology, principles of dialysis, treatment and technology related to the care of patients with renal failure, and general medical knowledge. Certified technicians must be recertified every four years. To be recertified, technicians must continue working in the field and present evidence of having completed continuing education units related to the career.

Opportunities for experience and exploration

Students considering entry into this career may obtain information from both the Board of Nephrology Examiners—Nursing and Technology, and the National Association of Nephrology Technologists. Until there are organized and accredited dialysis technician programs, those who are interested in the career must obtain education information from local sources.

Sources of information include high school guidance centers, public libraries, and occupational counselors at technical or community colleges. Specific information is best obtained from dialysis centers, dialysis units of local hospitals, home-health-care agencies, medical societies, schools of nursing, and physicians who specialize in nephrology.

Opportunities for experience and exploration will be most likely available in hospitals, dialysis centers, or physician's offices. Most hospitals have volunteer programs open to high school students. Although these programs may not provide opportunities to participate directly in patient care, they do provide opportunities to observe various members of the health care team in action.

Training as a nursing assistant or as an emergency medical technician will provide the opportunity for students to learn some of the skills required of renal dialysis technicians. The skills will also be useful in various health care agencies.

Methods of entering

The best way to enter this field is through a formal training program in a hospital or other training facility. In the absence of formal training, a well-qualified high school graduate may contact the local hospital and dialysis center to determine the possibility of on-the-job training. Some hospitals provide training opportunities in work–study programs; the trainees are paid while they learn.

The Department of Veterans Affairs renal programs accept applications from employees of the Veterans Administration medical facility. Trainees in this program are paid and receive benefits while learning.

Other ways to enter are through schools of nurse assisting, practical nursing or nursing, and programs for emergency medical technicians. In these programs, students learn basic health care and elementary nursing. After that, they must gain the specific knowledge, skills, and experience required for the renal dialysis career. The length of time required for people to progress through the dialysis program and advance to higher levels of responsibility should be shorter if they first complete a nursing or related training program.

Advancement

Dialysis technicians who have gained knowledge, skills, and experience advance to positions of greater responsibility and can work more independently. Experienced technicians can advance to supervisory positions, where they manage the work of others. The necessary

skills can be acquired on the job, in the classroom, or through independent study. Technicians may also advance to positions in which they teach new techniques to student technicians and to patients and their families.

Further education opens other opportunities for career advancement. For the dialysis technician who wishes to become a nurse, both part-time and full-time training programs are available in public and private schools and in hospitals throughout the country. Program lengths range from one to two years. Nurses have more independence and advancement opportunities. They can administer drugs, perform additional procedures, and carry out other duties.

Dialysis technicians with a bachelor's degree in nursing have wider avenues for advancement. Completion of these programs increases the variety and importance of the duties the technician can assume, and therefore increases the certainty of an interesting and rewarding career. Opportunities to study nursing are widely available, and there is always a need for registered nurses. The health care industry is responding to this need with improved working conditions, salaries, and benefits.

A third area of advancement is counseling. The social and psychological services required by the patients and their families could provide an expanded role for technicians. The insights the technician/counselor brings to the dialysis team can be a valuable contribution.

Employment outlook

Because of dialysis, more patients are living longer. In 1988, there were nearly 90,000 people in the United States receiving dialysis treatment, more than double the number receiving the treatment in 1978. The survival of these patients depends on the continuation of dialysis programs. This means that dialysis technicians will continue to be needed to provide treatment and related services.

Although the staffing pattern for dialysis treatment facilities and units varies, technicians can make up a large percentage of the team that provides the treatments, up to 80 percent in some centers. These facts indicate the demand for technicians will remain strong through the year 2000.

A factor which may decrease employment demand is the advancement in procedures that may remove the need for dialysis treatments in health care facilities. For instance, if the percentage and number of individuals able to participate in home dialysis increases, the staffing requirements and numbers of dialysis facilities would be affected. Similarly, if more kidney transplants are done, the number of people needing dialysis will decrease and with it the demand for dialysis technicians. The number of kidney transplants increased nearly fourfold between 1978 and 1988, and this trend may continue, as it costs much less to treat a patient with a kidney transplant than with dialysis.

Earnings

Dialysis technicians earn salaries ranging from $15,000 to $30,000 per year, with entry-level personnel and trainees receiving the lowest rates of pay. Some employers pay more to technicians who are certified.

In addition to their salaries, technicians receive the customary benefits of sick leave, vacation, holiday leave, and health insurance. Also, as an incentive to further self-development, many hospitals or health-care centers pay for tuition and other education costs.

Conditions of work

Dialysis technicians customarily work 40 hours per week. Some evening and weekend shifts may be required if dialysis treatments are scheduled for these times. Flex-time is available in several units, offering four- and even three-day work weeks. Patients who work full-time or part-time often arrange to take their dialysis treatments at times that least interfere with their normal activities, and this may result in unusual working schedules for technicians. The work environment is usually a clean and comfortable patient-care setting.

The job may require some local travel. Patients who use machine dialysis at home need assistance while being dialyzed. Although family members or friends are taught to assist the patient, technicians may have to substitute for the partner during any absence.

Dialysis technicians have mastered a complex body of knowledge and have developed technical skills. The lives of the individuals they treat depend on their ability to practice these skills confidently and with a high degree of perfection. They must be able to keep up with a changing field and incorporate new technology as it becomes available.

Because of the nature of the treatment, technicians must make careful observations. Some observations require action; others re-

quire that the technician relate accurate and complete details to others on the dialysis team so they can take appropriate steps for the patient's care.

Dialysis technicians must be patient, attentive, systematic, and accurate in their work. The ability to work with patients, co-workers, and supervisors is an essential requirement for success in the career. It is important for technicians to remain calm under stressful situations, in order to ensure the patient's safety and well-being.

It can be upsetting to work with people who are ill; a cheerful disposition and pleasant manner will help ease the patient's anxiety. There is a great satisfaction in helping critically ill patients stay alive and active. Some patients are carried through a temporary crisis by dialysis treatments and return to normal after a period of time. Other patients may be best treated by kidney transplants. But while they wait for a suitable donated kidney, their lives depend on dialysis treatments.

GOE: 10.02.02; SIC: 8092; SOC: 369

◇ **SOURCES OF ADDITIONAL INFORMATION**

Board of Nephrology Examiners—Nursing and Technology
PO Box 4085
Madison, WI 53719

National Association of Nephrology Technologists
PO Box 4488
Bryan, TX 77805-4488

Canadian Society of Nephrology
Université de Montréal
P.O. Box 6128, Stn. A
Dept. of Physiologie
Montreal PQ H3C 3J7

◇ **RELATED ARTICLES**

Diesel mechanics

Definition

Diesel mechanics repair and maintain diesel engines that power such varied machines as trucks, buses, locomotives, ships, automobiles, electric power generators, irrigation pumps, drilling equipment for oil wells, construction equipment such as cranes and bulldozers, and farm equipment such as combines and tractors.

History

Rudolf Diesel, a German engineer, first patented the basic engine design that bears his name in 1892. Diesel wanted to create a more efficient engine than other engines of his era. Within five years he refined his theories and developed a revolutionary new engine that was simple and that soon became commercially very successful. The outstanding efficiency, durability, and economy of today's diesel engines is the main reason why they are the most common type of engine used to power heavy equipment and large vehicles.

Diesel and gasoline-powered engines are both internal combustion engines that produce power by burning fuel inside a cylinder, but they are different in important ways. In a conventional gasoline engine, fuel and air are mixed in a carburetor before entering the engine. When this mixture enters the cylinder, it is compressed and an electric spark from a spark plug ignites it. In a diesel engine, the fuel is sprayed or injected directly into the cylinder where the air has been compressed until the fuel is hot enough to ignite. Thus a diesel engine doesn't need spark plugs or an ignition system. It is more economical to operate than a gasoline engine because it utilizes more of the energy available from the fuel, and diesels can run on comparatively low-grade fuel.

Because early diesel engines were very large and heavy, they were initially used in stationary power plants. By 1908, however, a diesel engine was used to power a Russian tanker. In World War I, diesels were regularly used in submarines. By 1922, diesel-powered automobiles were being developed, and in 1931, a diesel-powered airplane made its first flight. The first commercial trucks with diesel engines appeared in 1932. Railroads began to switch from steam to diesel engines in 1934, when a passenger train with a diesel locomotive made a record run between Chicago and Denver.

Design improvements have made modern diesel engines much lighter in comparison to their power output than the diesel engines of a generation or two ago. For some applications diesels are now unchallenged as the preferred source of machine power.

Nature of the work

Most diesel mechanics work on the engines of heavy trucks such as those are used in hauling freight over long distances or in heavy industries like construction and mining. Many are employed by companies that maintain their own vehicles. Mechanics often do both preventive maintenance and repair tasks, and often work on parts of diesel vehicles other than the engine.

Maintenance activities keep vehicles in good operating condition, assuring safe, dependable vehicles, reducing expensive breakdowns, and prolonging the useful life of the vehicles. Maintenance procedures include tasks such as checking lubricating oil levels, replacing filters, checking cooling systems, and inspecting brakes and wheel bearings for wear. Mechanics often work from a checklist that covers all the truck's major systems. They make repairs or adjustments as appropriate and replace parts that are too worn.

Inevitably, some parts wear out, so mechanics must regularly remove, recondition, or replace such items as fuel injection units, fuel pumps, pistons, crankshafts, bushings, and bearings. Another routine repair job that mechanics frequently do is reseating or regrinding intake and exhaust valves. In some shops, mechanics do whatever repairs the vehicle needs, but in large shops, mechanics may specialize in certain vehicle components or types of work, such as transmission or brake repairs. On some jobs, mechanics may work in teams or be assisted by a helper or apprentice.

Diesel mechanics sometimes need to take a whole engine apart for rebuilding. This is usually scheduled at regular intervals, such as every 18 months or 100,000 miles. Mechanics use various instruments to check each part. Accurate measurements are important in doing this task. For example, rod alignments must be accurate to within .001 of an inch. Parts that are not in good enough condition must be reconditioned or replaced. Rebuilding an engine may be done by a single mechanic, or a number of mechanics may work separately on different parts of the engine.

In doing their work, diesel mechanics use many kinds of equipment and tools. They use engine-testing equipment like tachometers and computerized engine analyzers. They use ordinary hand tools like screwdrivers and pliers; jacks and hoists for lifting and moving large parts; gauges and other measuring devices to check the degree of wear on parts; power tools like pneumatic wrenches; welding and flame-cutting equipment; and machine tools like lathes and boring machines, especially when rebuilding engines. Mechanics customarily buy most of their own hand tools. Experienced mechanics may have thousands of dollars invested in tools.

Although many diesel mechanics work on trucks, others service automobiles, railway locomotives, farm machinery, or other diesel equipment. The various kinds of diesel engines and machines are different enough from each other in terms of transmissions, gear systems, and many other parts that it may be difficult for diesel mechanics to transfer from one type of equipment to another without additional training.

Annual tune-ups and routine maintenance often comprise the bulk of a diesel mechanic's schedule.

Requirements

Diesel mechanics may learn their skills in a variety of ways. Many start in unskilled positions and learn mechanics' skills through informal on-the-job training. However, employers generally prefer to hire workers who have already acquired skills and a broad knowledge of the field through attending a formal training program for diesel mechanics or completing an apprenticeship.

Mechanics who learn on the job usually begin by doing the simplest and most routine tasks, like cleaning parts and fueling vehicles. After gaining some experience, or if they have a background that includes servicing automobiles, they may move into jobs as mechanics' helpers. Helpers are assigned to routine service tasks and minor repairs, and they gradually learn more complicated work as the opportunity arises. With three or four years of this kind of experience, they may become all-around generalist diesel mechanics. To learn about specialty work such as servicing hydraulic systems, it may be necessary to have additional training.

Applicants for these unskilled entry-level jobs are often required to be high school graduates. They usually need to be at least 18 years old and in good physical condition. They need to have mechanical aptitude, and an educational background that includes high school courses in automobile repair, electronics, mathematics, and physical science is very desirable. Good English reading skills are also important, because mechanics frequently need to read and interpret technical manuals and service bulletins that describe new repair procedures. Applicants with related experience have an advantage. That experience may be gained by working on their own vehicle, in a gasoline service station, at an auto repair shop, or in the Armed Forces in sections that are concerned with servicing diesels.

A better way of becoming a diesel mechanic is to complete a formal training course, such as those offered by many public and private vocational and technical schools and community and junior colleges. The training provided in these programs is more complete than what is acquired on the job. It includes instruction in newer areas that are becoming increasingly important for mechanics to understand, such as electronics. Diesel equipment today is being built with more and more electronic components, and a knowledge of the field is a necessity in many jobs. Diesel mechanic training programs vary in length from about one to two years, and depending on the school, they may lead to a certificate of completion or an associate degree. People who have completed a training program find that once on the job, they can often master new skills and techniques much more quickly and receive better promotions than workers without such training.

Apprenticeship programs provide another very good way of being a diesel mechanic. However, there are relatively few apprenticeships available, and often many applicants compete for just a few slots. Apprenticeships combine a planned program of practical on-the-job training with classroom instruction in related subjects. They typically last four years and include about 8,000 hours of supervised work experience plus at least 576 hours of formal classroom work in subjects like blueprint reading, engine theory, applied mathematics, and safety practices.

Even after they have become experienced, well-qualified workers, diesel mechanics still need to keep up with the changing technology in their field. They need to read service manuals and other information about new products, and they may attend special training classes given by equipment manufacturers.

Mechanics who do heavy-duty truck repair may be certified by the National Institute for Automotive Service Excellence. While certification is voluntary, not a requirement, it is a recognized standard of competence among mechanics and employers. Mechanics may be certified in one or more of six areas of truck repair, including diesel engines, gasoline engines, electrical systems, drive trains, brakes, and suspension. Mechanics who wish to be certified in an area must pass a test and have at least two years experience. Time spent in a suitable training program may be substituted for up to one of the two years. Mechanics who achieve certification in all six areas are certified Master Heavy-Duty Truck Technicians. To retain certification, mechanics need to be retested every five years.

Opportunities for experience and exploration

Although they are not quite the same as diesels, working with various gasoline-powered engines, from lawn mowers to motorcycles, can be a way to begin learning about this field. A job in a repair shop or filling station where minor repairs are done, or even tinkering with engines at home, can be valuable experience. Some high schools teach courses about internal combustion engines, including diesel engines.

Perhaps with the help of a guidance counselor or automotive shop class teacher, it may be possible to arrange to visit a facility where diesel mechanics work, such as a bus company barn or a trucking firm's maintenance shop. Many people first become interested in this field while serving in the military. Both the Navy's diesel mechanic school and the Army's heavy equipment school can provide a good foundation on which to build a civilian career.

Methods of entering

People seeking to start out in this field in entry-level unskilled jobs and then learn as they work can locate job openings through such sources as the offices of the state employment service and classified ads in newspapers. They may also apply directly to potential employers. Students in training programs often receive placement assistance through the school they attend. They may also get valuable job leads from their instructors or other people they meet during the training program. Mechanics who have completed apprenticeships very often continue working at the same workplace after they have completed their training and become fully qualified mechanics.

Some diesel mechanics start out as mechanics working on gasoline-powered engines and transfer to working on diesels for some reason. For example, their employer may switch from using gasoline-powered vehicles to diesels. Depending on the kind of equipment and their area of specialization, mechanics may need to learn new skills to make this kind of transition.

Advancement

Advancement possibilities for skilled and experienced diesel mechanics vary according to the industry in which they are employed. For example, people who work for a firm that owns and services many vehicles, like a large trucking company or bus line, may move up to be master mechanics, assistant service managers, and service managers. Mechanics who work on locomotives or stationary power plants may advance to be shop supervisors or plant superintendents. Employees of companies that manufacture diesel equipment may become field representatives, training specialists, or sales workers. A few mechanics open up their own independent repair businesses.

Employment outlook

There are well over a quarter million diesel mechanics employed in the U.S. today. They work for such employers as trucking and construction companies, shipping lines, bus lines, electric power plants, farm equipment dealers and distributors, and federal, state, and local government bodies.

In the next 10 to 15 years, the total number of diesel mechanics will probably increase at about the same rate as the average of all other occupations. Much of this increase will be related to a well-established trend toward using trucks to transport freight instead of railroads or other means. Job opportunities during this period should generally be more available in the trucking industry than in other industries that employ diesel mechanics. Overall, the greatest number of jobs openings will develop because older workers are retiring from the work force. Workers who are well trained in formal training programs will have the best job opportunities.

Earnings

The earnings of diesel mechanics vary with the region where they live, the number of hours they work, the industry they are employed in, and other factors. Mechanics who live in the West and Midwest tend to make a little more than those in other regions; mechanics in the South usually make less. Diesel mechanics often work long hours, with an average workweek lasting between 40 and 59 hours; those with the longest workweeks can make significantly more money. Mechanics who work for companies that must operate around the clock, such as bus lines, may work at night, on weekends, or on holidays and receive extra pay for this time. Some industries in which diesel mechanics are employed are subject to seasonal variations in employment levels.

Mechanics employed by firms that maintain their own fleets of vehicles, such as trucking companies, can have earnings that average over $31,000 per year, assuming they work a standard 40-hour week. Those who put in longer hours or work during periods when they are eligible for extra pay may make substantially more. Among mechanics who service company vehicles, the best paid are usually those employed in the transportation industry. Mechanics employed by companies in the manufacturing, wholesale and retail trade, and service industries have average hourly earnings that may be as much as 10 or 15 percent lower.

Many diesel mechanics are members of labor unions, and their wage rates are established by contracts between the union and their employer. In addition to wages, mechanics usually receive various fringe benefits, such as health and life insurance plans and paid vacation and sick time.

When apprentices begin their training, they are paid wages that equal about 50 to 75 percent of the wages of fully qualified mechanics. Apprentices receive raises every six months until their training is complete and their pay is up to the rate of skilled workers.

Conditions of work

Diesel mechanics usually do their work indoors in a garage or shop. Most workplaces are adequately lighted and comfortably heated and ventilated. Mechanics regularly handle greasy and dirty parts, and many tasks require that they stand or lie down in awkward or cramped positions. Mechanics sometimes need to move heavy weights, but usually equipment like cranes and hoists is used to move the heaviest objects.

From time to time, diesel mechanics may do work outdoors away from the shop, such as when they fix vehicle breakdowns on the road or do repairs on construction equipment at a job site. In doing such tasks, mechanics sometimes have to use their ingenuity, because they may find that the preferred equipment or parts for making the repair has been left back at the shop.

As with other kinds of shop jobs, minor cuts, scrapes, bruises, and burns are fairly common. Mechanics can avoid serious injury by using good safety practices and keeping their work area orderly and clean.

Some of the unions to which diesel mechanics belong are the International Association of Machinists and Aerospace Workers; the Amalgamated Transit Union; the International Union, United Automobile, Aerospace and Agricultural Implement Workers of America; the Sheet Metal Workers' International Association; and the International Brotherhood of Teamsters, Chauffeurs, Warehousemen and Helpers of America.

GOE: 05.05.09; SIC: 7699; SOC: 6112

Dietetic technicians

Definition

Dietetic technicians work in hospitals, nursing homes, and other institutional settings where they participate in food-service management and nutritional-care services. They normally work under the direction of a *dietitian*, as members of a health team. In food-service management, dietetic technicians help plan menus that meet established guidelines and supervise the food production operation on a day-to-day basis. They may act as administrative assistants to dietitians; as part of their job they might set up work schedules, help implement cost-control measures, develop job specifications and job descriptions for food-service workers, and prepare and present orientation and education programs for workers. In the area of nutritional-care services, dietetic technicians provide dietary counseling and instruction in the basics of nutrition to individual patients and their families. They talk to these people to obtain dietary histories, assess the information they receive, and suggest improvements in food selection, menu planning, and food preparation to best meet their nutritional needs. Technicians may set up referrals for patients who need continued nutritional counseling and care after leaving hospital or other institutional setting.

History

Dietetics is the study of food preparation, diet planning, and the impact on health and well-being. In one way or another, dietetics has been an important concern throughout history. Religious dietary laws, folk tradition, and medical lore have provided guidance about foods for thousands of years, although in an unscientific way. The Greek physician Hippocrates, recognized as the father of medicine, is one of the earliest proponents of the importance of diet in the body's well-being. Hippocrates' observations and experimentation in the fourth and fifth centuries b.c. led him to some rather sound conclusions. A Roman cookbook from a few centuries later suggests that its author knew something about the importance of proper food preparation to preserve its nutritional content.

Although scientific knowledge about food grew slowly until the 18th century, dietetics was always a central concern, as evidenced by medical writings from earliest times. Philosophy, superstition, social customs, and religion are among the many influences through the centuries. A few physicians in the late Middle Ages, notably Paracelsus, thought that properly chosen foods could help the body to heal itself. Although the theory was correct, their chosen treatments were often ineffective.

In 1780, perhaps the first scientific nutritional discovery that led to our modern understanding occurred. Antoine Lavoisier, sometimes called the father of nutrition, and Pierre-Simon LaPlace realized that metabolism, the physiological process in which food is broken down and used, is a form of combustion. This discovery, coupled with Lavoisier's other work in the field, opened the way to much fruitful research into how and why fats, carbohydrates, and proteins affect health.

By the late 19th century, there was a great deal of knowledge concerning the benefits of good nutrition and proper food handling. Public interest in these subjects was substantial. Cooking schools that emphasized a scientific approach to food and health prospered in several large cities.

Around the turn of the century, several hospitals began to teach dietetics to nurses, stressing cookery as a means of therapy for the sick. Other workers were hired as specialists to prepare food for hospital patients in accordance with the most advanced knowledge of the day. The modern field of dietetics grew out of such early hospital work.

The importance of various minerals in diet emerged during the 19th century, but it wasn't until 1911 that vitamins were recognized by Casimir Funk as substances needed in metabolic processes. Since then, our knowledge about food and the way our body uses it has increased tremendously. Those in the dietetics field have put this information to good use in health maintenance and restoration, and in disease prevention.

The American Dietetic Association was formed in 1917 with 39 charter members. It worked to promote and disseminate educational materials in order to improve the dietary habits of individuals and groups, and today it still serves as the principal professional organization for advancing the fields of dietetics and nutrition.

As the field of dietetics grew, it encompassed a wider range of activities; several separate categories of workers evolved, differentiated by the amount of their training and their type of activity. Two important levels of workers now are dietitians and dietetic technicians. The position of dietetic technician is a relatively recent innovation designed to allow the more highly-trained dietitians to concentrate on work that only they are prepared to do. The separate status of dietetic technicians was given a boost in 1972 by a report of the Study Commission on Dietetics, an affiliate of the American Dietetic Association, that urged various changes in the field and greater coordination of dietetics with other allied health professions.

Although the demand for dietetic technicians was uneven during the 1970s, they are now considered a great asset. There are presently about 115,000 people working as dietetic technicians in the 1990s. As employers realize even more clearly the advantages of hiring technicians, the field is expected to continue to expand, at least for the foreseeable future.

At a health fair, a dietetic technician introduces a nutritional food program to an elderly woman.

Nature of the work

Dietetic technicians serve in two basic areas: as service personnel in food-service administration and as assistants in the nutrition care of individuals. Some dietetic technicians are involved in both kinds of activities. Most work in health-care facilities such as hospitals and nursing homes, although some dietetic technicians are employed in health agencies such as public health departments, neighborhood health centers, or home health agencies. Their specific duties and responsibilities vary widely, depending on the place of employment and on which of the two basic areas of the field they are working in.

In a medical center, where the food service prepares thousands of meals daily for patients and staff, there may be a staff of dietetic technicians, as well as dietetic aides, assistants, and other food-service workers, all working under a staff of dietitians. In such cases, each of the dietetic technicians may specialize in a few activities out of the whole range of work. On the other hand, in a small organization, such as some nursing facilities, Head-Start programs, or geriatric care programs, there may be just one dietetic technician responsible for the overall management of the food-service staff and also for some nutrition counseling. The technician in a small facility may be supervised only by a consultant dietitian and probably reports directly to the administrator or director of the institution. Such a technician is apt to be involved in every phase of supervising and coordinating other workers.

Dietetic technicians are generally distinguished from dietetic assistants in a few ways. Dietetic technicians have more training, and are more management-oriented with broader re-

A dietetic technician discusses the week-long menu with the cook of a soup kitchen. The technician must ensure that the cook is complying with government nutritional standards.

needs and circumstances of their institution. They may write modified diet plans for patients, using an approved diet manual, incorporating the patients' preferences or physicians' orders. They may process meal orders received from patients or from medical staff members who choose patients' food, and they sometimes help patients select their menus. They may keep track of food items on hand, process routine orders to the suppliers, order miscellaneous supplies as needed, and supervise food storage. They may be involved with departmental budget-control measures, and may participate in dietary department conferences. They may regularly serve as administrative assistants for dietitians, or substitute for dietitians on an occasional basis, and thereby become somewhat involved with various other office activities normally left to dietitians, such as basic meal planning.

At other times, dietetic technicians work more directly in the kitchen, overseeing and coordinating actual food production activities, including the preparation of special therapeutic food items as well as more routine fare. They may even participate in the preparation of meals; more usually, however, they monitor the preparations. They may supervise dietetic aides, who distribute food in the cafeteria and assemble and serve meals to patients in their rooms. Depending on their employers, some dietetic technicians maintain and improve the overall standards of the food-service operation; others may supervise and uphold high standards in such areas as sanitation, housekeeping, safety in equipment operation, and security procedures.

In some large health care facilities, dietetic technicians may manage the cafeteria; although responsibilities generally overlap that of the patient food service, each requires separate attention in planning and many production activities.

Another of the dietetic technician's responsibilities may be to train other personnel. When first hired, food-service workers (usually those most directly involved with food production), dietetic aides and assistants, and other dietetic technicians must be instructed in methods, procedures, and equipment operation and maintenance. Dietetic technicians may present training sessions that introduce employees to such routine aspects of the operation.

Dietetic technicians who specialize in nutrition care and counseling work under the direction of a clinical or community dietitian. They may work in a health care facility, where their duties include observing and interviewing patients about their eating habits and food preferences. Dietetic technicians report these diet

sponsibilities; dietetic assistants are food-service staff who concentrate on supervising the daily operational details of the food service. Each worker's activities depend on the type of employer, however.

Dietetic technicians working in food-service administration may plan and prepare schedules and activities, perhaps spending a substantial part of their time on the phone or doing paperwork. They may set up the work and time schedules for other employees, based on their knowledge and experience of the time required for different production activities, and post updated schedules and other information at designated times during each day. Later they may follow up by helping to prepare evaluations of the food program and assessments of the efficiency of employees or particular production processes.

They may also help to develop standardized recipes, adapting them to the particular

histories to the dietitians, along with the progress that patients are making. They or the dietitians utilize the information to outline any changes needed in basic diet plans and menus. They may supervise the serving of food to be sure that meals are nutritionally adequate and are in conformance with the physician's prescription.

Dietetic technicians teach the basic principles of sound nutrition, food selection and preparation, and good eating habits to patients and their families, so that after leaving the health care facility the patients may continue to benefit. Later the technicians may contact those patients to see how well they are staying on the modified diets and to help them make any further adjustments in accordance with their preferences, habits at home, and the physician's prescription. Dietetic technicians may also instruct employees in the policies and procedures for nutritional care of patients.

Dietetic technicians specializing in nutrition care may work in community programs rather than inside a hospital or other inpatient health care facility. Employed by a public health department, clinic, youth center, visiting nurse association, home health agency, or similar organization, dietetic technicians have many of the same counseling duties as they would in an inpatient institutional setting. They may work with low-income families, especially in inner cities, teaching the economics of food purchasing, preparation, and nutrition. They may assist people who have recently arrived from other countries to adapt their accustomed menu patterns to available food items and to purchase and prepare nutritious foods. Or they may help the elderly, parents of small children, or other special groups who develop characteristic dietary questions and problems.

Dietetic technicians may make follow-up home visits to check on clients' menu plans, food buying, and cooking skills. In some cases technicians may help establish a permanent arrangement for continuing nutrition care and assistance for the needy, either in the home or at central locations, such as hot meals for the elderly or school lunch programs.

Dietetic technicians may help prepare brochures, visual aids, and other teaching materials as part of a broad educational effort in the community. Making healthy people aware of nutritional issues and of beneficial dietary changes is a particularly important kind of work, because it may prevent the future development of many major health problems, such as heart disease, hypertension, diabetes, obesity, and other chronic conditions. Technicians may also contact and work with other community groups to promote interest in nutrition.

Some dietetic technicians work in other settings—in schools, colleges, industrial food-service establishments, and other organizations where large quantities of food are regularly prepared. These positions require technicians with some of the same administrative skills but do not emphasize meeting special dietary needs of individuals or the educational and counseling aspect of nutrition-care work. Other dietetic technicians are employed in research kitchens, working under the supervision of a dietitian, taking care of support activities. As part of their duties they may: inventory and order stocks of ingredients; inspect equipment to be sure it is functioning properly; weigh and package food items; check for inaccuracies in precise procedures; and maintain records.

Requirements

The educational preparation required for this career includes a high school diploma or its equivalent, plus completion of a two-year, American Dietetic Association–approved program leading to an associate degree. This vocational preparation is available in junior and community colleges, and combines classroom studies with practical instruction and experience in the field under real working conditions. There are now about 72 approved dietetic technician training programs.

During high school, prospective technicians should take courses in biology, chemistry, business mathematics, typing, English, and other courses that improve communications skills.

In post-high school training programs, students can expect to take a mix of general education courses, such as English, biological sciences, humanities, social science, business mathematics, and technical courses. The technical instruction is likely to include such courses as: normal nutrition and menu planning; nutrition related to disease and modified diets; interviewing techniques; food science; food purchasing, storage, preparation, and service; quantity food production; organization and management of food-service systems; sanitation and safety; laboratory work; and introduction to the organization of patient-care facilities and community agencies.

The period of supervised clinical experience, sometimes called a practicum, may last anywhere from a few weeks to a whole semester, depending on the school. It is intended to provide a close look at the work of a dietetic technician, as well as provide experience that can be valuable during permanent employment.

Students may be assigned for the practicum to a patient-care facility, where they help with preparing schedules, ordering food, cooking, or instructing patients. If they are assigned to a health agency, they might accompany a nutritionist on home visits, help with teaching individuals, assist in demonstrating cooking techniques to groups, or observe and analyze information on the types of food people purchase at local grocery stores.

Although dietetic technicians are not required to be licensed or certified, those who have completed an approved education program may take an examination to determine their credentials. Such an exam is given by the Commission on Dietetic Registration; those who successfully complete the examination will be designated a Dietetic Technician, Registered (DTR). Continuing education requirements are maintained by the Commission on Dietetic Registration. More than 2,200 dietetic technicians are members of the American Dietetic Association.

On the personal side, anyone considering this line of work should appreciate good food and have a flair for making it attractive and tasty. Equally important are a genuine interest in people, a desire to perform services for them, and the ability to follow orders while developing basic management skills.

Dietetic technicians should have reserves of patience and understanding, since they may have to deal with people who are ill or uncooperative. Technicians must be able to communicate well, both orally and on paper, and have a knack for planning and good organization. They must be adaptable and ready to explore new ideas and methods, because there are always changes in food products, equipment, and administrative practices.

Opportunities for experience and exploration

High school students interested in dietetics should try to find a part-time, summer, or even volunteer job in the food-service department of a hospital or other health care organization. This kind of position allows them to observe the work of the dietary department and to ask questions of people involved in the field. If such a job isn't possible, students should consider a job in another area of the hospital, which could provide first-hand contact with the general environment that dietetic technicians

work in. A job in a nonhospital food service, even a restaurant kitchen, could also be of value. With the help of teachers or counselors, students may arrange to meet with and talk to a dietitian or dietetic technician. Extracurricular activities such as service clubs might help students to judge their organizational and administrative abilities and their interest in helping people as individuals.

Methods of entering

Contacts gained during the clinical experience part of their training program are usually the best sources of first jobs for dietetic technicians. Applying to the personnel offices of potential employers can be another productive approach. Other good places to check are their school's placement office, the job listings in health care journals, newspaper classified ads, and private and public employment agencies.

In some areas close to schools that have dietetic technician training programs, the local labor market is oversupplied, so that new graduates may have better results if they extend their job search to other areas where competition is less intense.

Advancement

Beginning jobs are usually closely supervised, because there is so much to learn about the operations of their new employer. After a time, however, the technicians are often able to take on greater responsibilities and earn higher pay while still staying with the same employer, either keeping the same title but expanding the range of activities, or officially changing positions—for example, from dietetic technician to the position of *kitchen manager*. Experience and proven ability allow such advancement inside many organizations.

Some dietetic technicians return to school on a full- or part-time basis to complete a bachelor's degree program in a related field such as dietetics, nutrition, food science, or food-service management. To become a dietitian, a year of internship is necessary after the baccalaureate degree is completed.

Employment outlook

The outlook for dietetic technicians, particularly those with certification, is generally very good for the foreseeable future. This is partly because of the strong emphasis on nutrition and health in this country and the fact that more health services will be used in future years. The population is growing, and the percentage of older people, who need the most health services, is increasing even faster.

Another reason for the positive outlook for dietetic technicians is that health care organizations now realize the advantages of utilizing them for many jobs. Many tasks dietitians used to perform can be done well by dietetic technicians, while dietitians continue to be in short supply and are more expensive to hire.

Earnings

Earnings vary widely depending on the employer, the education and experience of the dietetic technician, the region of the country, and the nature of the technician's responsibilities. Generally, entry-level technicians earn $15,000 to $20,000 per year; with a few years' experience, they earn between $20,000 to $25,000; and those at the top of the pay scale earn between $25,000 to $30,000. Fringe benefits usually include paid vacations and holidays, health insurance plans, and meals during working hours.

Conditions of work

Dietary departments in health care facilities are generally well-lighted, clean, well-ventilated, and near to the kitchen area. Kitchens and serving areas may be intensely active at peak hours, often very hot, steamy, and noisy. Modern equipment, when correctly used, has eliminated most of the accident hazards previously associated with a food-service operation.

Most dietetic technicians in food-service administration jobs work 40-hour weeks, in 8-hour shifts, and may be required to work some nights, weekends, or on an irregular schedule, depending on the type of employer. Shifts usually are divided into three eight-hour periods, with each shift responsible for preparing one major meal.

Dietetic technicians may be on their feet most of the time. Periodically there may be intense pressure to work quickly and accurately. At such times, technicians must be able to give full attention to the details of their own job while coordinating the work of other employees.

Dietetic technicians employed in health agencies or research organizations are likely to have more normal hours and a smoother work pace. Jobs in nutrition care may involve local traveling to visit patients.

For someone who enjoys food, helping people, and the rewards of seeing a planned and organized effort worked out to its conclusion at every meal, this field can be very satisfying. Sometimes, however, technicians confront failure in the kitchen; the work may seem to be endless and very routine; and it is necessary to face the fact that good nutrition cannot solve all health problems. Nonetheless, many dietetic technicians find that the sense of achievement outweighs such negatives.

Dietetic technicians working in nutrition care may have a more personal sense of reward because they often have more personal contact with those who need their services.

Dietetic technicians should be able to work well in groups and to tolerate the stress of responding to emergency situations. Because technicians are a middle link connecting the dietitians with dietetic assistants and other food-service workers, technicians may feel the pressure from both sides. A stable personality and a sense of perspective will make it easier to do the job well on such occasions.

GOE: 05.05.17; SIC: 8049; SOC: 302

◇ **SOURCES OF ADDITIONAL INFORMATION**

American Dietetic Association
216 West Jackson Boulevard, Suite 800
Chicago, IL 60606

National Health Council
350 Fifth Avenue, Suite 1118
New York, NY 10118

◇ **RELATED ARTICLES**

Volume 1: Food Service; Health Care
Volumes 2–4: Cooks, chefs, and bakers; Dietitians; Food service workers; Food technologists; Health services administrators; Homemaker-home health aides; Restaurant and food service managers

Dietitians

Definition

A *dietitian* assures the proper feeding of individuals and groups by planning meals with proper nutritional value for hospitals, institutions, schools, restaurants, or hotels. They provide individuals with diet instructions, and purchase food, equipment, and supplies. They may also be responsible for food preparation directly, which requires supervising chefs and other food service employees and preparing various kinds of educational nutrition materials.

History

Until quite recently, little information has been available on how to prepare nutritionally sound meals. Families planned their meals on the basis of what they could afford and the need to introduce some variety in the diet occasionally. In the late 19th century, hospital workers were employed to teach ways of preparing food for patients, and the field of dietetics actually came into existence as an outgrowth of this early hospital work. Although the medical profession had been aware of the value of nutrition in developing and maintaining good health, the dietitian's profession was slow to develop.

In the last 50 years, however, scientists have learned more about nutrition and its influence on health. Nutritional information has been disseminated widely, and food planning has become important in the home and in institutional life. Hospitals, schools, industrial plants, and other institutions turned to the new dietetics profession for aid.

The modern dietitian is trained to function in a number of specialized areas, like hospital dietetics, research, teaching, writing, commercial food service, and school and college food service. In many ways the dietitian helps to promote health through nutrition.

Nature of the work

The dietitian's work may vary according to the chosen area of specialization. In general, the dietitian is trained in the science of foods and nutrition and in food service management. Various careers branch out from this basic foundation. One of the best known is the field of hospital dietetics. Dietitians work as part of the hospital's professional staff, dedicated to promoting the health of patients. In large hospitals there are opportunities for further specialization: food administration, therapeutics, outpatient clinic work, teaching, and research.

Administrative dietitians, also known as *chief dietitians*, are specifically trained in food administration or management. They are responsible for the training and work of food service supervisors and other assistants who prepare meals. They help formulate policies of the department, enforce sanitary and safety regulations, and prepare departmental budgets. They are in charge of buying food, equipment, and other supplies. This requires a sound understanding of purchasing techniques; menus must be planned on a large scale with a view toward economy. The administrative dietitian tries to coordinate the work of the dietetic department with that of other departments in the hospital so that they may function effectively for the patient's welfare.

The *clinical dietitian*, sometimes called a *therapeutic dietitian*, plans and supervises the preparation of diets to meet the individual needs of patients for whom physicians have prescribed dietary requirements. This dietitian discusses each patient's needs not only with the physician and other members of the health care team, but also with the patient and other family members. He or she explains the purpose of a diet, discusses likes and dislikes, and prepares the patient for carrying on the diet at home. The therapeutic dietitian also works with the hospital administration concerning policies in planning diets.

The *community dietitian* is usually associated with a community health program sponsored by a public or private health or social service agency. The dietitian counsels individuals and groups on proper nutrition to maintain health and prevent diseases. Special diets are planned for expectant mothers, diabetics, people who are overweight or recovering from an illness, the elderly, and others with special nutritional problems. Families are taught how to plan and prepare meals and how to shop for food wisely and economically.

Most dietitians do some teaching to explain their particular area of work to dietetic interns, nurses, and medical and dental students. Others teach on a full-time basis, usually in hospitals affiliated with medical centers. The *teaching dietitian* plans and teaches courses for the department of dietetics and supervises dietetic interns.

The *research dietitian* studies the nutritional needs of healthy and sick people. Research dietitians may specialize in how the body uses food, nutritional education, or food management. These specialists usually work in a hospital or university, and they need advanced training or education.

In a college with a home economics department, the dietitian may be a teacher as well as a food service manager. In public schools, dietitians plan and supervise the preparation of food that is attractive to young people yet economical and nutritious. These school and college dietitians may also be asked to perform catering services for school functions.

Many dietitians work as *consultant dietitians* to food companies, schools, hospitals, restaurants, and other public and private establishments. Some business organizations may conduct research in nutrition; a dietitian may work in the home economics division of food, equipment, and utility companies. This work may consist of promoting a product by developing recipes, giving information on nutrition that is related to the company's product, maintaining experimental kitchens, and presenting radio and television programs. Administrative dietitians also work in commercial food service, restaurant management, and in industrial food service where plants maintain cafeterias for their employees.

As a college or university teacher, the dietitian with advanced degrees may conduct research in foods and nutrition. Some dietitians specialize in foods and nutrition, and they often work for public health services or participate in nutrition research, which is considered increasingly important in new public health programs.

The armed forces and the U.S. Public Health Service offer many career opportunities for trained dietitians in administrative, therapeutic, teaching, and research areas.

Requirements

For those interested in dietetics as a career, a bachelor's degree, with a major in foods and nutrition or food service management, is necessary. Certain required courses have been recommended by the American Dietetic Association. Usually undergraduate courses include foods and nutrition, food service management, chemistry, bacteriology, physiology, mathematics, psychology, sociology, and economics.

The American Dietetic Association also recommends satisfactory completion of one year of dietetic internship in a program approved by the Association. A dietetic internship is required for active membership in the organization and for registration with the Commission on Dietetic Registration. Students may enter hospital food service administration or a clinical internship and gain practical experience based on what has been learned during college. Many employers prefer to hire dietitians who have had this particular kind of internship experience.

Graduate work is necessary to teach in colleges and universities. There are about 270 colleges or universities offering master's degrees in nutrition. Some junior colleges and vocational schools offer training in dietetics, but this does not qualify one professionally. Usually such graduates can find positions as food service supervisors or other jobs requiring a certain amount of training.

Dietitians must be able to get along with all types of people—physicians, administrators, patients, and kitchen employees. They must have a good sense of business and an ability to work with details. The administrative dietitian must supervise employees and will need teaching ability and patience in instructing interns and informing patients of their dietetic needs. A person in this career should have an interest in science because all aspects of dietetics and nutrition are related to science.

Opportunities for experience and exploration

High school students interested in dietetics should find part-time or summer employment in hospital kitchens, restaurants, or other food-related institutions. These are good places to see dietitians in action, talk with them and learn as much as possible about the demands of the profession. High school home economics courses or even practice in running a kitchen at home are other good opportunities.

Methods of entering

Generally, the dietitian completes all educational requirements before looking for a job. This educational program includes a nine- to 12-month dietetic internship where one can gain valuable on-the-job experience.

Dietitians often inspect institutional food to ensure that the nutritional value meets government standards.

Most colleges and universities offer placement services for graduate dietitians. In some cases, the dietitian in charge of the internship may be able to assist in finding positions. A graduate dietitian might apply to the personnel departments of business organizations that hire dietitians.

Advancement

Once dietitians have gained experience they may be promoted to assistant or chief director of a dietary department, or manager of a restaurant. Dietitians employed through the government's civil service program advance on the basis of seniority and performance.

Dietitians interested in teaching or research generally must have graduate education to get high-level positions. A master's degree or doctorate will also hold more weight with employers in business, as will previous hospital or institutional experience.

Most dietitians seeking success in the profession will gain greater professional status by meeting all requirements for membership in the American Dietetic Association and earning the credential Registered Dietitian (R.D.).

Employment outlook

In the 1990s, there are about 45,000 registered dietitians working in the United States. About half of those employed work in hospitals and other health care institutions, including the Department of Veterans Affairs and the U.S. Pub-

lic Health Service. Other employers of dietitians include local government programs and school systems, colleges, and universities, prison systems, hotels and restaurants, and companies that provide food service for their employees. Many dietitians work as consultants, either full- or part-time.

A career in dietetics is expected to offer excellent employment opportunities throughout the 1990s. Hospitals, nursing homes, retirement communities, and social service programs have an expanding need for qualified dietitians. Research programs in food and nutrition will need more experienced, qualified dietitians. Also, a number of dietitians are moving into management positions in private industry. Opportunities are expected to increase in colleges and universities, restaurant chains, catering companies, medical supply houses, and other businesses and industries.

Earnings

In the 1990s, hospitals start recent graduates of approved internship programs at an annual salary of about $20,600. Graduates without internship training generally receive lower starting salaries. Dietitians with experience working in hospitals are paid an average of $27,300 per year.

In the federal government, dietitians with a bachelor's degree who completed an internship start at $16,900. Experienced dietitians working for the federal government in the 1990s make an average of $36,200.

In addition to salary, dietitians usually receive the customary benefits, such as paid vacations and holidays, sick leave, health insurance, and retirement plans.

Conditions of work

Dieticians work in offices or kitchens, depending on they type of work they do. Some hospitals offer room, board, and laundry service for a small fee. Such living conditions are optional. Most college dietitians no longer live in; however, those in charge of a residence hall food service are usually provided with an apartment.

Dietitians commonly work a 40-hour week, although some hospital and restaurant dietitians have to work weekends and irregular hours. Staff dietitians usually take turns supervising on weekends and holidays. Dietitians usually have from two to four weeks of vacation each year after one year of service.

GOE: 05.05.17, 02.02.04, 11.02.02, 11.05.02; SIC: 5812, 8049; SOC: 302

◇ **SOURCES OF ADDITIONAL INFORMATION**

American Dietetic Association
216 West Jackson Boulevard, Suite 800
Chicago, IL 60606

American Institute of Nutrition
9650 Rockville Pike
Bethesda, Md 20814

Canadian Dietetic Association
#601, 480 University Avenue
Toronto ON M5G 1V2

◇ **RELATED ARTICLES**

Volume 1: Baking; Food Processing; Food Service; Health Care
Volumes 2–4: Caterers; Dietetic technicians; Food technologists; Home economists; Restaurant and food service managers

Dispensing opticians

Definition

Dispensing opticians measure and fit clients with prescription eyeglasses and contact lenses. They help clients with the selection of appropriate frames and order all necessary ophthalmic laboratory work.

History

The Chinese are thought to have invented glasses as a means of improving vision as early as 500 B.C. Glasses were used widely in Europe for reading during the 1500s, when printed matter first became widely available. The craft of grinding lenses to correct visual problems continued to spread throughout Europe over the next several hundred years.

Further development of eyeglasses was made by Benjamin Franklin, who invented the bifocal lens in the 18th century. Bifocals have a two-part lens: one part is used to aid reading and the other part is used to aid distance vision. By the late 19th century, a Swiss physician, A. E. Frick, had made the first contact lens. These first contact lenses were made of heavy glass and were rather uncomfortable to wear. By using lighter, more flexible material, later developers were able to create contact lenses that today only cover the cornea (a portion of the eyeball).

With more than 50 percent of people in the United States now wearing prescription glasses or contact lenses, dispensing opticians and others involved with eye care continue to develop ways of making corrective lenses more comfortable and easier to wear.

Nature of the work

Dispensing opticians must be familiar with methods, materials, and operations employed in the optical industry. Their tasks include making certain that the eyeglasses are made according to the optometrist's prescription specifications, determining exactly where the lenses should be placed in relation to the pupils of the eyes, assisting the customer in selecting appropriate frames, preparing work orders for the optical laboratory mechanic, and sometimes selling optical goods.

The dispensing optician should be good both at dealing with people and with administrative tasks. Dispensing opticians work with the customer in determining which type frames are best suited to the person's needs. Considerations include the customer's habits, facial characteristics, and the thickness of the corrective lenses.

The dispensing optician offers a variety of eye wear to her customer.

The dispensing optician prepares work orders for the ophthalmic laboratory so that the factory can grind the lenses and insert them in the frames. Opticians are responsible for recording lens prescriptions, the lens size, and the style and color of the frames.

After the lenses return from the lab, the dispensing optician ensures that the glasses fit the customer's face. The optician will use small hand tools and precision instruments to make minor adjustments to the frames. This requires steady hands and good hand-eye coordination.

Most dispensing opticians work with prescription eyeglasses, but some work with contact lenses. Dispensing opticians must exercise great precision, skill, and patience in fitting contact lenses. They measure the curvature of the cornea, and, following the optometrist's prescription, prepare complete specifications for the optical mechanic that manufactures the lens. They must teach the customer how to remove, adjust to, and care for the lenses, a process that can take several weeks.

Requirements

Although many dispensing opticians learn their skills on the job, in recent years there has been a trend toward a technical training program to provide the background necessary to be successful in this field. Employers prefer to hire graduates of two-year college programs in opticianry. These associated degree holders are able to advance more rapidly than those who simply complete an apprenticeship program. Two-year optician programs are offered at community colleges and trade schools, and include courses on mechanical optics, geometric optics, ophthalmic dispensing procedures, contact lens practice, and business concepts. The two-year program also includes courses in communications, mathematics, and laboratory work in grinding and polishing procedures.

Some dispensing opticians complete an apprenticeship program offered by optical dispensing companies. The program may be formal, such as in a large company, or informal, as is usually the case in smaller operations. These on-the-job programs include some of the same subjects as those covered in the two-year associate degree program, and may take two to four years to complete. Some specialized training programs may be offered by contact lens manufacturers and professional societies. These are generally shorter and usually cover a particular area of technical training, such as contact lens fitting.

A high school diploma is generally necessary to enter an apprenticeship or other training program. High school courses should include algebra, geometry, and physics. Mechanical drawing course work is also helpful.

Special requirements

More than 20 states currently require licensing of dispensing opticians. Licensing sometimes requires meeting certain educational standards and the ability to pass a written examination, and, in some states, a practical examination. For more specific information on the licensing procedure, the licensing boards of the individual states should be consulted.

Professional credentials may also include voluntary certification. Certification is offered by the American Board of Opticianry and the National Contact Lens Examiners. Addresses for these two organizations can be found at the end of this article.

Some states may permit dispensing opticians to fit contact lenses, providing they have additional training.

Opportunities for experience and exploration

Part-time or summer employment in an optical shop is an excellent method of gaining an insight into the skills and temperament needed to excel in this field. A high school student can also explore opportunities in the field through discussions with professionals already working as dispensing opticians.

Methods of entering

The usual ways of entering the field are either through completion of a two-year associate degree or though completion of an apprenticeship program.

Advancement

As dispensing opticians become more skilled, they usually advance to supervisory or managerial positions in a retail optical store or become sales representatives for manufacturers of eyeglasses or lenses. Some open their own stores. A few dispensing opticians, with additional college training, become optometrists. The amount of additional training a dispensing optician needs to become an optometrist depends on the individual's educational background.

Employment outlook

The demand for dispensing opticians is expected to grow much faster than the average through the 1990s. The reasons for this increased demand include an increase in the number of people who need corrective eyeglasses. The fact that good vision is being emphasized in home, school, and work environments has led to greater use of corrective lenses. Educational programs such as those for vision screening also have expanded awareness of eye problems. Insurance programs cover more optical needs, which means more clients can afford optical care.

Employment opportunities should be especially good in larger urban areas because of the greater number of retail optical stores. Those with an associate degree in opticianry should be most successful in their job search.

Earnings

Beginning salaries average between $15,000 and $20,000 per year for dispensing opticians just entering the field. Experienced workers can expect to make between $18,000 and $35,000; the average is about $25,000 per year. Supervisors earn about 20 percent more than skilled workers, depending on experience, skill, and responsibility. Dispensing opticians who own their own stores can make much more.

Conditions of work

The majority of dispensing opticians work in retail shops or department showrooms. The work requires little physical exertion and is usually performed in a well lighted, quiet environment. Customer contact is a big portion of the job. Some laboratory work may be required, especially if a dispensing optician works with a larger outfit that makes eyeglasses on the premises. The wearing of safety goggles and other precautions are necessary in a laboratory environment. Dispensing opticians should expect to work 40 hours a week, although overtime is not unusual. They should be prepare to work evenings and weekends, especially if employed by a large retail establishment.

Because the majority of the work entails customer service, a dispensing optician should be able to interact with a variety of people. Patience is important, as is the ability to advise people on decisions concerning eye wear. Dispensing opticians should be careful and accurate when adjusting frames and filling out work orders. They should be able to follow instructions and also display leadership abilities if they are left to manage the store, as sometimes occurs.

GOE: 05.05.11, 05.10.01; SIC: 5995; SOC: 449, 6864

◇ **SOURCES OF ADDITIONAL INFORMATION**

General information about career opportunities is available from:

National Academy of Opticianry
10111 Martin Luther King, Jr., Highway
Suite 112
Bowie, MD 20720

National Association of Optometrists and Opticians
18903 South Miles Road
Cleveland, OH 44128

Opticians Association of America
10341 Democracy Lane
Fairfax, VA 22030

Information on certification training programs is available from:

Commission on Opticianry Accreditation
10111 Martin Luther King, Jr., Highway #100
Bowie, MD 20720

◇ **RELATED ARTICLES**

Volume 1: Health Care
Volumes 2–4: Ophthalmic laboratory technicians; Opticians and optical mechanics; Optics technicians; Optometric technicians; Optometrists

Display workers

Definition

Merchandise displayers design and install displays of clothing, accessories, furniture, and other products in windows, in showcases, and on the sales floors of retail stores to attract potential customers. Display workers who specialize in dressing mannequins are known as model dressers. These workers use their artistic flair and imagination to create excitement and customer interest for the store. They are also beginning to use their talents in other types of merchandising to develop exciting images, product campaigns, and shopping concepts.

History

Eye-catching displays of merchandise attract customers and encourage them to buy. This effective form of advertising has been used throughout history by anyone with something to sell. As happens even today, farmers in the past who displayed their produce at market were careful to place their largest, most unblemished, most tempting fruits and vegetables at the top of the baskets. Peddlers opened their bags and cases and arranged their wares in attractive patterns. Store owners decorated their windows with collections of articles they hoped to sell. Their business success was often a matter of chance, however, and depended heavily on their own persuasiveness and sales ability.

As glass windows became less expensive, store fronts were able to accommodate larger window frames. This exposed more of the store to passersby, and stores soon found that the more decorative window displays were effective in drawing customers in. In many stores today, a customer can see practically the entire store and the displays of the products it sells just by looking in the front window.

The advent of self-service stores has minimized the importance of the salesperson's personal touch. The merchandise now has to sell itself. Displays have become a very important inducement for the customers to buy. Advertising will bring people into the stores, but an appealing product display can make the difference between a customer who merely browses and one who buys.

Small retail stores generally depend on the owner or manager to create the merchandise displays, or they may hire a freelance window dresser on a part-time basis. Large retail operations, such as department stores, retain a permanent staff of display and visual merchandising specialists. Competition among these stores is intense, and whether they are successful or not depends on capturing a significant portion of the market. Therefore, they allot a large share of their publicity budget to creating unique, captivating displays.

Nature of the work

Using their imagination and creative ability, as well as their knowledge of color harmony, composition, and other fundamentals of art and interior design, merchandise displayers in retail establishments create an idea for a setting designed to show off merchandise and attract customers' attention. Often the display is planned around a theme. After the approval of the *display manager*, the display workers construct backdrops, using hammers, saws, spray guns, and other hand tools; install background settings, such as carpeting, wallpaper, and lighting; gather props and other accessories; arrange the mannequins and the merchandise; and place price tags and descriptive signs where they are needed.

They may be assisted in some of these tasks by carpenters, painters, or store maintenance workers. They may use merchandise from various departments of the store or props from previous displays. Sometimes they borrow special items that their store may not carry—toys or sports equipment, for example—from other stores. The displays are dismantled and new ones installed every few weeks. In very large stores that employ many display workers, each may specialize, for example, in carpentry, painting, making signs, or setting up interior or window displays. A *display director* usually supervises and coordinates their activities and confers with other managers to select the merchandise to be featured.

Ambitious and talented display workers have many avenues to pursue in their careers. The importance of visual merchandising is being recognized more and more, as retail establishments fight for consumer dollars. Some display workers may move up to display director or even a position in store planning.

In addition to traditional stores, the skills of visual marketing workers are now in demand among many other types of establishments. Restaurants often try to capture a distinct image to enhance the dining experience. Outlet stores, discount malls, and entertainment centers also use visual marketing to establish their identities among the public. Chain stores often need to make changes in or redesign all their stores and turn to display professionals for their ideas. Even the makers of goods sold in stores are now heavily involved in visual marketing. They hire display and design workers to come up with exciting concepts such as "in-store shops," which present a unified image for the manufacturer's products and are sold complete to retail stores.

There are also opportunities for employment for visual talent in manufacturing store fixtures. Many companies build and sell specialized props, banners, signs, displays, and mannequins. Some people work as sales representatives for these companies. Their understanding of retail needs and insight into the visual merchandising industry make them valuable as consultants.

Display workers are needed year-round, but during the Christmas season, they often execute their most elaborate work.

Commercial decorators prepare and install displays and decorations for trade and industrial shows, exhibitions, festivals, and other special events. Working from blueprints, drawings, and floor plans, they use woodworking power tools to construct installations—usually referred to as a booth, no matter what its size—at exhibition halls and convention centers. They install carpeting, drapes, and other decorations, such as flags, banners, and lights. They also arrange furniture and accessories to attract the people attending the exhibition. Special event producers, coordinators, and party planners may also seek out the skills of display professionals.

This occupation appeals to imaginative, artistic persons who find it rewarding to use their creative ability to visualize a design concept and then apply their mechanical aptitude to transform it into reality. Original, creative displays grow out of an awareness of current design trends and popular themes. Although display workers use inanimate objects such as props and materials, an understanding of human motivations helps them create displays with strong customer appeal.

Requirements

Display workers at a minimum must have graduated high school, preferably with applicable courses such as art, woodworking, mechanical drawing, and merchandising. Some employers require college courses in art, interior decorating, fashion design, advertising, or related subjects.

High schools and community and junior colleges that offer distributive education and marketing programs often include display work in the curriculum. Courses useful to display workers are also offered by fashion merchandising schools and fine arts institutes.

Much of the training for display workers is received on the job. They generally start as helpers for routine tasks such as carrying props and dismantling sets. Gradually they are permitted to build simple props and work up to constructing more difficult displays. As they become more experienced, display workers who show artistic talent may be assigned to plan simple designs. The total training time varies depending on the beginner's ability and the variety and complexity of the displays.

Among the personal qualifications needed by display workers are creative ability, imagination, manual dexterity, and mechanical aptitude. Display workers should be in good physical condition to be able to carry equipment and climb ladders. They also need agility to work in close quarters without upsetting the props.

Opportunities for experience and exploration

Display work is included in many of the marketing programs taught in high schools and in community and junior colleges. Fashion merchandising schools and fine arts institutes offer courses that would be useful for this occupation. These courses usually combine hands-on work in class with the study of fashion and merchandising.

Part-time and summer jobs in department stores and other retail stores or at exhibition centers will provide interested students with an overview of the display operations in these establishments. Photographers and theater groups need helpers to work with props and sets, although they may require some experience or knowledge related to their work. Students may become active in school drama and photo clubs and be able to help with design.

Methods of entering

School placement offices may have listings of jobs in this and related fields. Persons wishing to become display workers may apply directly to retail stores, decorating firms, or exhibition centers. Openings may also be listed in the classified ads of the newspaper.

A number of experienced display workers choose to work as freelance designers. Competition in this area, however, is intense, and it will take time to establish a reputation, build a list of clients, and earn an adequate income. Freelancing part-time while holding down another job would be more feasible for most display workers. It would also give beginners a chance to develop a portfolio of photographs of their best designs, which they can then use to sell their services to other stores.

Advancement

Display workers with supervisory ability may become regional managers, then display directors of a large store, then heads of store planning.

Another way to advance is to start a freelance business in the design field. This can be done with very little financial investment. However, as described above, freelance design workers must spend many long hours generating new business and establishing their names in the field.

The skills developed in this occupation may lead to other jobs in art-related fields, such as interior design or photography, although these will require additional formal training.

Employment outlook

About 30,000 display workers are currently employed across the nation. Most of them work in department and clothing stores, but many are employed in other retail stores such as variety, drug, and shoe stores. Some have their own design businesses, and some are employed by design firms that handle interior and professional window dressing for small stores. Employment of display workers is distributed throughout the country along the lines of the population, with most of the jobs concentrated in large towns and cities.

The employment of display workers throughout the 1990s is expected to keep pace with the average for all occupations. Any growth in this profession will be the result of an expanding retail sector and the increasing popularity of visual merchandising. Most openings will occur as older, experienced workers retire, die, or leave the occupation.

The fluctuation of the economy affects the volume of sales in retailing, because people watch their money carefully and buy less in hard times. For display workers, this may result in lay-offs or a freeze on hiring. Opportunities for display workers are better in large stores, particularly in metropolitan areas.

Earnings

In the 1990s, large employers pay beginning display workers about $5.25 an hour, while those who have completed some college courses earn more. Experienced workers earn about $450 per week. Display managers receive around $30,000 per year, with some directors in large metropolitan stores earning more. It is possible for freelancers to earn upwards of $30,000 a year, but their income depends entirely on their talent, reputation, the number of their clients, and the amount of time they work.

Conditions of work

Display workers generally put in 35 to 40 hours a week, except during busy seasons such as Christmas and Easter. Large selling efforts at these and other times may force the display staff to work extra hours in the evening and on weekends.

The work of constructing and installing displays requires prolonged standing, bending, stooping, and working in awkward positions. There is some risk of falling off ladders or being injured from handling sharp materials or power tools, but serious injuries are uncommon.

GOE: 01.02.03; SIC: 7319; SOC: 322

◇ SOURCES OF ADDITIONAL INFORMATION

For more information, contact local retailers and the local offices of the state employment service.

The following associations may be of some assistance.

National Association of Display Industries
470 Park Avenue South, 17th Floor
New York, NY 10016

National Retail Federation
100 West 31st Street
New York, NY 10001

Retail Merchants Association of Canada
1780 Birchmont Road
Scarborough ON M1P 2H8

◇ RELATED ARTICLES

Volume 1: Advertising; Apparel; Design; Marketing; Packaging; Sales
Volumes 2–4: Advertising workers; Art directors; Commercial artists; Graphics designers; Light technicians; Photographers; Retail managers; Stage production workers; Stage technicians

Diving technicians

Definition

Diving technicians perform a wide variety of underwater jobs (both in oceans and in fresh water) using special underwater breathing equipment. Examples of these jobs include: off-shore oil well piping; building and repair of foundations and other underwater construction; salvage work; and ship repair and service.

491

DIVING TECHNICIANS

A diving technician fastens a sunken item onto a pulley system while his colleagues observe from the boat above.

Diving technicians may also serve as "tenders," (attendants or support workers) for divers. They often act as intermediaries between administrative, scientific, or engineering staff and other skilled workers in a wide range of marine activities. They are expected to be familiar with the many aspects of diving and its related equipment, and must also be able to perform numerous skilled-worker jobs while underwater.

History

Since earliest times, people have sought to go underwater to retrieve food or valuable items or to build and repair ships. Unfortunately, without equipment, a diver can stay under the surface only as long as a single breath allows. Other factors that limit the unaided diver's activities include cold water temperatures, the water pressure at great depths, and strong currents.

The first efforts to overcome these limitations with special equipment were primitive. To bring an air supply down, early divers used sections of hollow reeds as breathing tubes. As long ago as the time of ancient Greeks, crude diving bells were in use. But it was not until the late 18th century that a practical diving bell was invented. It allowed one person to descend into shallow water in an open-bottomed container supplied with air pumped by hand from above. In the 19th century, the first diving suit was devised, connected to the surface by a tube. Even with various improvements, however, diving suits were always rather clumsy. In 1943, the invention of scuba diving equipment (which stands for self-contained underwater breathing apparatus), allowed divers much more freedom of movement, opening up many new activities for divers. Since then, diving techniques and equipment have become increasingly sophisticated.

The records of salvage from the Spanish galleon *Santa Margarita*, which sank in about twenty feet of water on the lower Florida Keys in 1622, tell something about the development of diving technology.

In 1644, an effort was made to salvage the galleon's cargo of gold and silver. Diving crews, using a bronze bell as an air source, salvaged much of the silver coins and other items of value—but not the gold, which sank into the sand and could not be found. Some divers lost their lives, swept away by dangerous currents even in the shallow water.

In 1980, 336 years later, the wreck was found again. This time, diving teams used scuba equipment, electronic metal detectors, and special hydraulic jets that washed away the sand covering more than $20 million worth of gold and silver coins, ingots, gold chains, and other valuables. Modern equipment and techniques made all the difference.

One major problem with deep-water diving is caused by the additional pressure from the water's weight. This pressure causes the nitrogen in the air breathed by the diver to dissolve in the bloodstream. Normally, the nitrogen remains in the lungs and is simply exhaled in the breathing process. When a diver returns too rapidly from deep water to the surface, bubbles of nitrogen form in the blood vessels. These bubbles can cause serious sickness and even death. This condition is called "the bends" and is an ever-present hazard of deep-water diving. It can be prevented by making sure the diver returns slowly enough to the surface so the nitrogen in the blood can be freed in the lungs and breathed out normally, rather than forming bubbles in the blood vessels.

The U.S. Navy, which had a great amount of ship salvage and repair work to do during World War II, began to use new approaches to preventing the bends. A helium breathing mixture, instead of air, was shown to be safer and more efficient for deep-water divers. Divers who ascended too quickly were put in special decompression chambers.

In the late 1950s and 1960s, underwater exploration increased. The depths of the oceans, which cover three-fifths of the world's surface, were still the most uncharted part of the planet, presenting a challenge that, to many people, was comparable to the exploration of space. The growing offshore petroleum-drilling industry was another incentive to further develop diving technology. New kinds of diving bells, saturation diving systems, and a host of submersible devices now allow deeper and more effective underwater work, such as the 1985–86 exploration of the *Titanic* wreck several miles under the North Atlantic.

As diving and related activities came to involve more people and more complicated equipment, the need arose for workers who could handle many different kinds of technical tasks. Today diving technicians are employed mainly in commercial diving; a few also work in marine science and research activities. Commercial diving relies on numerous mechanical, engineering, and construction skills transferred to an underwater setting. These jobs can be physically demanding and hazardous, but they can also offer adventure and excitement.

Nature of the work

The largest number of job opportunities for the diving technician is with commercial diving contractors. The work is frequently dirty, exhausting, and dangerous; the duties broad and varying. To be successful, diving technicians must be skilled not only in current diving methods, but also in the many jobs they may be required to perform underwater. Some common underwater jobs include: inspection of structures or equipment by visual, photographic, or videotape methods; mechanical construction or servicing using hand or power tools; cleaning marine growth from structures; welding or cutting in salvage, repair, or construction; and geological or biological surveying.

Diving technicians do not always work below the water; sometimes they work on the surface, as experts in the life-support system for divers and in the management of the equipment. These technicians work with the controls

This diving technician prepares a deep-sea vehicle for launching. The vehicle will explore the ocean floor down to 20,000 feet (6,000 meters).

that supply the proper mixture of gases for the diver to breathe. They maintain the correct pressures in the hoses leading to the underwater worker and act as the communicator and life-support partner of the diver. They monitor water depth, conditions inside diving bells and chambers, and decompression schedules for divers. This is a highly skilled position involving many responsibilities, and is vital to the success of all deep-water diving operations.

It is possible that in the future, the scientific and technological demands made on the life-support team may cause the development of a group of specialists who do not dive. However, the usual practice now is for divers to work both underwater and on deck.

Other important areas of employment for diving technicians are oceanographic research and underwater military engineering. While the total number of technicians engaged in these activities is relatively small, it may increase as it becomes more desirable to extract minerals from the ocean floor. Even during peacetime, military diving crews are needed in rescue and reclamation.

Newly hired technicians are normally assigned work involving organizing the shop and caring for and maintaining all types of company equipment. Soon, they will be assigned a similar job on a diving boat or platform. When on a diving operation, technicians provide topside or surface support for the divers by assisting them with equipment, supply hoses, communications, necessary tools, and lines. They help maintain a safe and efficient operation. As a diver's tender, technicians may monitor and control diving descent and ascent rates, breathing gas supplies, and decompression schedules. They must also be able to assist in an emergency and help treat a diver injured in an accident or suffering from the bends.

As technicians gain experience in company procedures and jobs, they are given more responsibility. Technicians usually can start underwater work within a few months to two years after being hired. This depends on the technician's skills and desires, as well as the company's needs.

Technicians' first dives are shallow and relatively easy; subsequent dives match their ability and competence. With time and experience, they may advance to work deep-dive bell and saturation diving systems. Saturation divers are gradually compressed in an on-deck chamber, as they would be when diving, then transferred to and from the work site inside a pressurized bell. These divers stay in a pressure-controlled environment for extended periods.

All of the personnel on a diving crew should know how to care for and use a wide variety of equipment. Some of the commonly used diving equipment includes air compressors, decompression chambers, high-pressure breathing-gas storage tanks, pressure regulators and gas regulating systems, hoses and fittings for handling air and gas, and communications equipment.

A diver's personal equipment ranges from simple scuba, now seldom used, to full face masks; lightweight and heavy helmets for both air and helium/oxygen use; diving bells; and diving suits, from wet suits to the heavy dry suits that can be bolted to a breastplate to which the heavy helmet is attached. For cold water and deep or long-duration dives, a hot-water suit may be used. This allows a flow of warm water supplied from the surface to be passed through a loose-fitting wet suit on the diver's body, protecting the diver from body heat loss.

The diving crew uses simple hand tools, including hammers, crescent wrenches, screwdrivers, and pliers. Items such as wire cutters and volt/ohm meters are often needed. Divers should be versatile and may also be expected to use many types of power tools, as well as sophisticated and often delicate instruments, such as video and camera equipment, measuring instruments, ultrasonic probes, and metal detection devices. Knowledge of arc welding equipment and underwater arc or other metal-cutting equipment is very important for many kinds of work, such as salvage, construction, or repair and modification of underwater structures. These needs are often associated with underwater petroleum explorations, well-drilling, or management of piping systems.

Requirements

For persons who want to become diving technicians, it is not enough to have excellent diving ability; they must have diverse skills and abilities, since diving is only the process by which the technicians get to the job site.

Well-rounded diving technicians should be mechanically inclined, able to operate and maintain a wide variety of equipment; must understand drawings and simple blueprints; be familiar with piping and valves; know how to handle high-pressure gases, bottles, and gauges; and be able to write accurate reports, keep records, and do paperwork; must understand the physical and biological elements of the marine environment; and recognize the importance of teamwork, capable of working as an integral part of a team.

The best way to train for this career is to attend one of the post-secondary schools and colleges that offer an organized program, usually two years in length, to prepare such technicians. Typical basic requirements for enrollment are a high school diploma or its equivalent, ability to read and understand what is read, demonstrated capability to study college-level scientific subjects, completion of three to four years of language and communication subjects, at least one year of algebra, and one year of physics or chemistry with laboratory work.

Diving technicians are specialized engineering technicians. Therefore they need a basic theoretical and practical scientific background. In addition, they need to have mastered several construction-type work skills.

A typical post-secondary program consists of three types of courses. The first will develop the skills and knowledge required of a diving technician; the second gives students an understanding of the environment in which they will be working; the last consists of general education courses designed to broaden the student's knowledge and sharpen communication skills.

The first year's study includes such courses as seamanship and small-boat handling, basic diving, drafting, basic welding, technical writing, advanced diving, fundamentals of marine engines and compressors, marine welding, physical oceanography, and marine biology. Often students participate in a summer cooperative work–study program of supervised ocean dives before the second year of courses begins.

Second-year courses typically include underwater construction, biological oceanography, physics, fundamentals of electronics, machine shop operations, underwater operations, advanced diving systems, basic emergency medical technology, and speech and communications. The second year also may include fundamentals of photography, or a special project that relates specifically to diving or life-support technology. Additional studies such as economics, American institutions, or other general studies must usually be completed.

Physical requirements for the career include general good health, at least normal physical strength, sound respiratory functions, normal or better eyesight, and good hand-eye coordination and manual dexterity.

Special requirements

Schools that provide programs for these technicians often have special admission requirements relating to swimming ability and skills. As an example, one school's special requirements include: the completion of application, release, medical history, and waiver of liability forms for the diving technology program; an annual physical examination; and the successful performance of several tests in the presence of the school's diving officer. These tests include swimming without fins underwater for a distance of seventy-five feet without surfacing; swimming without fins underwater for a distance of 150 feet, surfacing four times; swimming without fins 1,000 feet in less than ten minutes, demonstrating swimming with snorkel and fins with and without face mask; skin diving to a depth of ten feet and recovering a ten-pound object; demonstrating the ability to rescue a swimmer and carry him or her seventy-five feet on the surface; and demonstrating the ability to tread water for ten minutes without swim aids.

When students seek employment, they usually find that many employers require completion of a recognized training program or documentation of comparable experience. A thorough physical examination may also be required. The hiring company will usually arrange for the physical with a physician of their choice. An emergency medical technician certificate is valuable and may be required by some companies.

There are no special requirements for licenses at the entry level in the United States. The United Kingdom and some of the North Sea countries do have specific requirements for divers, however, which can be met only by training in their countries.

For specific work beyond entry level, a welding certificate may be required. Also, a certification in nondestructive testing (NDT) may enhance the technicians's opportunities. Both

of these certificates are specific and beyond entry level. The employer will be able to specify the method of obtaining the special certificates desired.

Employment in areas other than commercial diving may impose more specific requirements. A specialty in photography, electronics, oceanography, biology, marine culture, or construction engineering may open other doors of opportunity for the diving technician.

Opportunities for experience and exploration

Information about training schools can be found in trade journals and sports publications. Libraries are a good place to look for program listings and descriptions. People interested in this career would be well advised to contact several training programs and compare the offerings to their own individual needs. It would also be good to ask about employment prospects for future graduates of each program.

A visit to one or more potential employers would certainly benefit the person considering diving technician training. While observations of an offshore job would be difficult, a tour of the company shop, a look at its equipment, and a chance to talk to technicians should be informative and worthwhile.

Anyone interested in this career should become proficient in scuba diving and outdoor swimming and diving. The experience of learning to feel at home in water and underwater not only can help the person to pass entry tests for a formal preparatory program, but also can allow students to find out if they really are suited for the career.

Methods of entering

Commercial diving contractors, where the majority of diving technicians seek employment, have in the past recruited personnel in one of three ways: those with Navy experience, those who had learned skills through informal apprenticeships or by themselves, or who were friends or relatives of employees, and even people right off the street. These employees had to learn on the job.

As diving technology advanced and diving equipment and techniques became more sophisticated, contractors looked more and more to schools to provide qualified entry-level help. Schools upgraded their programs to meet the industry's changing requirements. Today, most contractors primarily rely on approved schools to meet their entry-level personnel needs. Some contractors will hire only graduates of diving training programs.

Schools with diving technician programs usually have three or more staff members with professional commercial diving experience. These instructors keep abreast of the diving industry through occasional summer work, consultation, and professional and personal contacts. These contacts enable them to assess industry needs and the job market, and to offer job placement help.

Major offshore contractors and other potential employers may visit schools with diving programs each year before graduation to interview prospective employees. Some employers offer summer work to students who have completed one year of a two-year program.

Some employers contact schools whenever they need additional diving technicians. The school staff then directs them to interested job seekers. While many graduates find jobs in oil-drilling operations or other large industries, a few graduates find positions as diving school instructors, marine culture technicians, photographer/writers, marine research technicians, and submersible pilots.

One can enter the diving technician career by joining the U.S. Navy or specialized units of the Marines, Army Corps of Engineers, or Merchant Marine Corps. Some U.S. Military operations for salvage, recovery of sunken ships, or rescue require deep-water divers and life-support skills. Usually Navy and other experienced diving personnel can obtain civilian employment, but often need to learn a wider range of skills for underwater construction or other work.

Advancement

A well-trained, highly motivated diving technician can expect to advance steadily, depending on personal competence and the employer's needs. Over a three- to five-year period a technician may be a shop hand, a tender (tending equipment and maintaining gear), a combination diver/tender, a diver, lead diver, and possibly supervisor of a diving crew. Or a technician may advance from surface support duties to supervisor of surface support or supervisor of a diving crew, possibly within three to five years. This nondiving life-support career, however, is much more limited in terms of employment opportunities than the combined diving and support career. Management opportunities

within the company are also a possibility for a qualified technician. Those who want greater opportunities for earnings, independence, and growth may start their own business as a contractor or consultant.

Employment outlook

The world is increasingly turning to the sea to supply mineral resources, new and additional sources of food and medicine, transportation, and national defense. This growth of marine activity has resulted in a continuing demand for qualified diving technicians. In fact, there are approximately two to three jobs for every qualified graduate of technical diving programs.

In the past few decades, the greatest demand for skilled diving technicians has been related to the search for more petroleum and natural gas from undersea oil fields. With the production of oil and gas from the oceans, there was a virtual explosion in the amount of work and the numbers of people employed. Whether this activity will be a source of new jobs in the future is uncertain. Employment will depend on levels of drilling activity, which, in turn, depends on the levels of world oil prices. The recent history of these prices makes it impossible to predict with any confidence what will happen to employment in this field.

Hydroelectric power generating plants, dams, heavy industry, and sanitation plants that have cooling water lines or water discharges are also a source of work for divers and surface crews. Certain ship repairs (usually of an emergency nature), require divers who can repair the trouble at sea or in dock, without placing the ship in dry dock to correct the problem.

While some work is being done in aquaculture, marine culture, and ocean mining, these areas are currently relatively undeveloped. While the potential for these fields is great and the possibilities for technicians exciting, the total employment in these areas is presently small.

Earnings

Earnings in this career vary widely and depend on factors such as location, nature of the job, and the technician's skills or experience. A technician working in commercial diving might work almost anyplace in the oceans, rivers, and lakes of the world. Some types of work (e.g., most union jobs) pay the employee on an hourly or daily basis.

Recent graduates of diving technician programs often start as tenders (nondiving positions) and earn about $700 to $725 per week. With experience, the average pay for divers is $50,000 to $60,000 or more per year (working 180—220 days per year). A few highly experienced specialists may make up to about $110,000 a year.

Some contract jobs call for time on and time off, such as a thirty days on/thirty days off rotation, and the pay will reflect at least a certain amount of the off-time as full-time pay. An example of a rotational job would be service work on an exploratory oil-drilling vessel where diving crew members live aboard for their on-shift period and perform any work required during that time. Pay for this work includes both on and off time. Wages earned under an organized union contract are typically at higher rates, but the employee receives pay only for days worked.

Employees of diving contractors typically receive life and health insurance benefits. Some companies also provide paid vacation time.

Conditions of work

As previously stressed, diving technicians must possess numerous technical job skills. Working conditions may vary tremendously depending upon the nature of the work, the duration of the job, and the geographic location.

Some offshore sites could include boats ranging from under 100 feet long to much longer ocean-going ships. Also, oil drilling vessels and many types of barges provide working and living bases for diving technicians.

Working hours or shifts offshore may only require the diving crew to be available if needed, as is common on drilling vessels. More often, however, as in construction work or jobs that are continuous and predictable in nature, the dive crew will work up to twelve hours a day, seven days a week. As might be expected, the more rigorous work provides greater pay.

Living conditions aboard ship or barge are usually reasonably comfortable. Rooms may accommodate from two to as many as eight people, depending on vessel size, but they are at least adequate. Food, of course, is furnished on all rigs where crews must live aboard. Quite often it is unusually good.

Diving technicians are taught to be conscious of appropriate clothing and safety practices, and to follow these guidelines as they work in the potentially dangerous conditions encountered in deep-water diving.

Offshore work, especially construction diving, is rigorous and often physically demanding. Persons entering this field must be physically fit. Companies commonly place a maximum age limit, usually 30 to 32 years, for entry-level employees seeking to become divers. Although many divers work well into their forties or fifties and occasionally beyond, deep long-duration diving is considered a young person's work.

Travel, excitement, and some amount of risk are a part of the diving technician's life. On the job, technicians should be self-starters, showing initiative and ability to work independently as well as on a team.

People who choose a career in diving technology should be ready to adapt to a lifestyle that seldom offers stable home and family life. Technicians must be able to follow the work, and can expect occasional changes in job locations. There is also the reality of an uncertain work schedule where a job might last for months or where the only available work may be on a short-term basis. Offshore work tends to run in a "feast or famine" pattern.

These technicians must be confident of their own ability to cope with the uncertainties and risks of deep-water diving. They must be able to analyze and solve problems without panic or confusion. There is a real satisfaction in confidently and successfully performing tasks in an unconventional setting.

GOE: 05.10.01; SIC: 7389; SOC: 6179

◇ **SOURCES OF ADDITIONAL INFORMATION**

Association of Commercial Diving Educators
c/o Marine Technology Program
Santa Barbara City College
721 Cliff Drive
Santa Barbara, CA 93109

Association of Diving Contractors
4240 Highway 22, No. 3
Mandeville, LA 70448

College of Oceaneering
272 South Fries Avenue
Wilmington, CA 90744-6399

National Association of Underwater Instructors
Training Department
PO Box 14650
Montclair, CA 91763

The Ocean Corporation
10840 Rockley
Houston, TX 77099

Dog groomers

Definition

Dog groomers comb, cut, trim, and shape the fur of all types of dogs and cats. They comb out the animal's fur and trim the hair to the proper style for the size and breed. They also trim the animal's nails, bathe it, and dry its hair. In the process, they can check for flea or tick infestation and any health problems that are visible. In order to perform these grooming tasks, however, the dog groomer must be able to calm the animal down and gain its confidence.

History

The dog is one of the world's most beloved animals. It is likely that the dog was the first animal that people ever domesticated. More than 10,000 years ago, wild dogs resembling dingoes were captured, tamed, and put to work hunting other animals and protecting human settlements.

Today, dogs are still used for the types of work they performed centuries ago, such as herding sheep, retrieving game, and guarding property. However, most people keep dogs for the companionship and love they provide. In the United States, dogs are kept as pets in more than 40 million homes. Over 200 different breeds of dog can be identified, and many dog shows hold competitions for the best pedigree—or best family history—within each breed. However, whether a dog is a first-class pedigree or a mutt, it enjoys being bathed and groomed.

Nature of the work

Although all dogs and cats benefit from regular grooming, it is the shaggy, long-haired breeds that give dog groomers the bulk of their business. Some types of dogs need regular grooming for their standard appearance; among this group are poodles, schnauzers, cocker spaniels, and many types of terriers. Show dogs are also groomed very frequently. Before beginning grooming, the dog groomer will talk with the dog's owner to find out the style of cut the dog is to have. The dog groomer will also rely on experience to determine how the particular breed of dog is supposed to look.

The dog groomer first places the animal up on a grooming table. To keep the dog steady during the clipping, a nylon collar or noose, which hangs from an adjustable pole attached to the grooming table, is slipped around its neck. The dog groomer talks to the dog or uses other techniques to keep the animal calm and gain its trust. If the dog doesn't calm down but snaps and bites instead, the groomer may have to muzzle it. If a dog is completely unmanageable, the dog groomer may ask the owner to have the dog tranquilized by a veterinarian before grooming.

After calming the dog down, the groomer brushes it and tries to unmat its hair. If the dog's hair is very overgrown or is very shaggy like an English sheepdog's, the groomer may have to cut away part of its coat with scissors before beginning any real grooming. Brushing the coat is good for both long- and short-haired dogs because it removes shedding hair and dead skin. It also neatens the coat so the groomer can tell from the shape and proportions of the dog how to cut its hair in the most attractive way.

Once the dog is brushed, the groomer will cut and shape the dog's coat with electric clippers. Next, the dog's ears are cleaned and its nails are trimmed. The groomer must take care not to cut the nails too short because they may bleed and the dog will be in pain. If the nails do bleed, a special powder is applied to stop the bleeding. The comfort of the dog or cat is a very important concern for the groomer.

The dog is then given a bath, sometimes by a worker known as a *dog bather*. The dog is lowered into a stainless steel tub, sprayed with warm water, scrubbed with a tearless shampoo, and rinsed. This may be repeated several times if the dog is very dirty. The dog groomer has special chemicals that can be used to deodorize a dog that has had an encounter with a skunk or has gone for a swim in foul water. If a dog has fleas or ticks, the dog groomer treats them at this stage by soaking the wet coat with a solution to kill the insects. This toxic solution must be kept out of the dog's eyes, ears, and nose, which may be cleaned more carefully with a sponge or wash cloth. A hot oil treatment may also be applied to condition the dog's coat.

The groomer dries the dog after bathing, either with a towel, with a hand-held electric blower, or in a drier cage with electric blow driers. Poodles and some other types of dogs have their coats fluff-dried, then scissored for the final pattern or style. Poodles, which at one time were the mainstay of the dog grooming business, generally take the longest to groom because of their intricate clipping pattern. Most dogs can be groomed in about 90 minutes, although grooming may take several hours for shaggier breeds whose coats are badly matted and overgrown.

More and more cats, especially long-haired breeds, are now being taken to pet groomers. The procedure for cats is the same as for dogs, although cats are not dipped when bathed. As the dog or cat is groomed, the groomer will check to be sure there are no signs of disease in the animal's eyes, ears, skin, or coat. If there are any abnormalities, such as bald patches or skin lesions, the dog groomer will tell the owner and may recommend that the animal be checked by a veterinarian. The dog groomer may also give the owner some tips on hygiene for the animal.

Pet owners and other people in pet care generally have respect for dog groomers who do a good job and treat animals well. Many people, especially those who raise show dogs, grow to rely on particular dog groomers to do a perfect job each time. Dog groomers can earn

Dog groomers must develop a friendly rapport with animals so that the dogs will remain calm while getting their hair trimmed and nails cut.

a great deal of satisfaction from taking a shaggy, unkempt animal and transforming it into a beautiful creature. On the other hand, some owners may unfairly blame the groomer if the animal becomes ill while in the groomer's care or for some malady or condition that is not the groomer's fault. Because they must deal with both the pets and their owners, dog groomers can find their work both challenging and rewarding.

Requirements

A person interested in dog grooming can be trained for the field in one of three ways: enrolling in a dog grooming school; working in a pet shop or kennel and learning on the job; or reading one of the many books on dog grooming and practicing on his or her own.

Probably the best way to gain a thorough knowledge of dog grooming is to take an accredited dog grooming course or enroll in dog grooming school. The National Dog Groomers Association of America provides a referral listing of approximately 40 dog grooming schools throughout the United States. Five schools of dog grooming are recognized by the National Association of Trade and Technical Schools: the Pedigree Professional School of Dog Grooming, the New York School of Dog Grooming (three branches), and the Nash Academy of Animal Arts. Many other dog grooming schools advertise in dog and pet magazines. It is important for students to choose an accredited, licensed school, for the enhancement of both their employment opportunities and their own professional knowledge.

To enroll in most dog grooming schools, a person must be at least 17 years old and must be fond of dogs. Previous experience in dog grooming can sometimes be applied for course credits. Students study a wide range of topics, including the basics of bathing, brushing, and clipping; the care of ears and nails; coat and skin conditions; dog anatomy; terminology; and sanitation. They also study customer relations, which can be very important for those who operate their own shops. During training, students practice their techniques on live dogs, which people bring in for grooming at a discount.

Students can also learn dog grooming while working for a grooming shop, kennel, animal hospital, or veterinarian's office. They usually begin with tasks such as shampooing the dogs and trimming their nails, then gradually work their way up to brushing and basic cuts. With experience, they may learn more difficult cuts and use these skills to earn more pay or start their own business.

The essentials of dog grooming can also be learned from one of the several good books available on grooming. These books contain all the information a person needs to know to start his or her own dog grooming business, including the basic cuts, bathing and handling techniques, and the type of equipment needed. Still, many of the finer points of grooming, such as the more complicated cuts and various safety precautions, are best learned while working under an experienced groomer.

A high school diploma generally is not required for people working as dog groomers. A diploma or GED certificate, however, can be a great help to people who would like to advance within their present company or move to other careers in animal care that require more training, such as veterinary technicians. Courses that are useful in this career include English, business mathematics, general science, zoology, psychology, bookkeeping, office management, typing, art, and first aid.

State licensing or certification is not required of dog groomers at this time. To start a grooming salon or other business, a person may need to get a license from the city or town in which he or she plans to start a business.

The National Dog Groomers Association of America is an organization that promotes professional identification through membership and certification testing throughout the United States and Canada. The NDGAA offers continuing education, accredited workshops, certification testing, seminars, insurance programs, a job placement program, membership directory, and many other services and products. Dog groomers will find many benefits from membership in this and other groups, such as the Humane Society of the United States and the United Kennel Club. Because dog groomers should be concerned with the health and safety of the animals they service, membership in groups that promote and protect animal welfare is very common.

The primary qualification for a person who wants to work with pets is a love of animals. Animals can sense when someone does not like them or is afraid of them. A person needs certain skills in order to work with nervous, aggressive, or fidgety animals. They must be patient with the animals, be able to gain their respect, and like to give the animals a lot of love and attention. Persistence and endurance are also good traits for dog groomers, because grooming one dog can take three or more hours of strenuous work. Groomers should enjoy working with their hands and have good eyesight and manual dexterity to cut a clipping pattern accurately.

Opportunities for experience and exploration

To find out if they are suited for a job in dog grooming, students should know or try to find out how well they work with animals. This can be done in many ways, starting with the proper care of the family pet. Youth organizations such as the Boy Scouts, Girl Scouts, and 4-H Clubs sponsor projects that give members the chance to raise and care for animals. Students might also try to get a part-time or volunteer job working with and caring for animals at an animal hospital, kennel, pet shop, animal shelter, nature center, or zoo.

Methods of entering

Graduates from dog grooming schools can take advantage of the job placement services that most schools offer. Generally there are more job openings than qualified groomers to fill them, so new graduates may have several job offers to consider. These schools can find out about job openings in all parts of the country, and are usually happy to contact prospective employers and write letters of introduction for graduates.

Other sources of job information include the want ads of the daily newspaper and listings in dog and pet magazines. Job leads may also be available from private or state employment agencies, or from referrals of salon or kennel owners. People looking for work should phone or send letters to prospective employers, inform them of their qualifications, and, if invited, visit their establishments.

Advancement

Dog groomers who work for other people may advance to a more responsible position such as office manager or dog trainer. If a dog groomer starts his or her own shop, it might become successful enough to expand or to open branch offices or franchises around the area. Skilled groomers may want to work for a dog grooming school as an instructor, possibly advancing to a job as a school director, placement officer, or other type of administrator.

The pet industry is booming, so there are many avenues of advancement for groomers who like to work with dogs. With more education, a groomer may get a job as a veterinary technician or assistant at a shelter or animal hospital. Those who like to train dogs may open obedience schools, train guide dogs, work with field and hunting dogs, or even train stunt and movie dogs. People can also open their own kennels, breeder and pedigree services, gaming dog businesses, or pet supply distribution firms.

Employment outlook

The demand for skilled dog groomers has grown in recent years, and this trend is expected to continue. The National Dog Groomers Association estimates that more than 30,000 dog groomers are currently employed, and expects that more than 3,000 new groomers will be needed every year over the next decade.

Every year more people are keeping dogs and cats as pets. They are spending more money to pamper their animals, but often don't have enough free time or the inclination to groom their pets themselves. Grooming is not just a luxury for pets, however, because regular attention makes it more likely that any injury or illness they may have will be noticed and treated.

Earnings

Groomers can charge either by the job or by the hour. Generally they earn around $7.50 an hour. If they are on the staff of a salon or work for another groomer, they get to keep 50 to 60 percent of the fees they charge. For this reason, many groomers branch off to start their own businesses. Those who own and operate their own pet grooming service can earn anywhere from $20,000 to $50,000 annually, depending on how hard they work and the type of clientele they attract.

Groomers generally buy their own clipping equipment, including barber's shears, brushes, and clippers. A new set of equipment costs around $275, while used sets cost less. Groomers who work at salons, grooming schools, pet shops, animal hospitals, and kennels often get a full range of benefits, including paid vacations and holidays, medical and dental insurance, and retirement pensions.

Conditions of work

Working conditions can vary greatly, depending on the location and type of employment. Many salons and pet shops are clean and well lighted, with modern equipment and clean surroundings. Others may be cramped, dark, and smelly. Groomers need to be careful while on the job, especially when handling flea and tick killers, which are toxic to humans. When working with any sort of animal, a person may encounter bites, scratches, strong odors, and fleas and other insects. They may also have to deal with sick or bad-tempered animals. The groomer must regard every dog and cat as a unique individual and treat it with respect.

Groomers who are self-employed can work out of their homes. Some groomers buy vans and convert them into grooming shops. They can then drive to the homes of the pets they work on, which many owners find very convenient. Those who operate these "groomobiles" can work on 30 or 40 dogs a week, and factor their driving time and expenses into their fees.

Groomers usually work a 35-hour week, and may have to work evenings or weekends. If they work any overtime, they are compensated for it. Those who own their own shops or work out of their homes, like other self-employed people, work very long hours and can have irregular schedules. Other groomers may work only part-time. Groomers are on their feet much of the day, and their work can get very tiring when they have to lift and restrain large animals.

GOE: 03.03.02; SIC: 0752; SOC: 5624

Nash Academy of Animal Arts
595 Anderson Avenue
Cliffside Park, NJ 07010

◇ **SOURCES OF ADDITIONAL INFORMATION**

For a list of dog grooming schools across the country, send a self-addressed, stamped #10 envelope to:

National Dog Groomers Association of America
PO Box 101
Clark, PA 16113

Additional information is available from:

New York School of Dog Grooming
248 East 34th Street
New York, NY 10016

◇ **RELATED ARTICLES**

Volume 1: Agriculture; Personal and Consulting Services
Volumes 2–4: Animal production technicians; Animal trainers; Equestrian management workers; Farmers; Veterinarians; Veterinary technicians

Door-to-door sales workers

Definition

Door-to-door selling is a means of marketing goods and services by direct, personal contact with the consumer—usually, but not always, in the consumer's home. The distinguishing characteristic of this method of marketing is that the *door-to-door sales worker* arranges to contact the consumer to create a sale, instead of waiting for a buyer to come into a store or other permanent place of business. This kind of selling is also known as direct-to-consumer selling. Included in this type of sales are *peddlers* and *vendors*, who make their products available in public places.

History

Direct selling in North America goes back to the famous "Yankee Peddler" of colonial times who traveled by wagon, on horseback, and sometimes on foot, bringing to isolated settlers many products that were not easily available otherwise. As a forerunner of the modern door-to-door sales worker, this peddler anticipated the settlers' demands, satisfied their needs, and was always a welcome visitor.

In contrast to the popular image of door-to-door sales workers taken from cartoons and movies, these salespeople have useful, important products to sell. Over the years, direct selling has launched many now-familiar products for which there was little or no demand when they were first introduced. This type of commerce has created mass markets that support many important industries.

Today direct selling is one of four principal distribution channels for consumer goods and services, along with the retail store, direct-mail solicitation, and the mail order catalog. It is a multibillion dollar industry, and the thousands of companies engaged in direct selling market a wide variety of merchandise, including appliances and housewares, cookware, china, tableware and linens, foods, drugs, cosmetics and toiletries, costume jewelry, clothing, and greeting cards. The door-to-door sales worker usually represents only one company, and so becomes an expert about the features of just one or a few products. Direct selling is also an important method of securing subscriptions to many newspapers and magazines.

Direct selling can contribute to the educational efforts in a household because it is a basic marketing method for encyclopedias and other educational publications and materials. It is often said that encyclopedia sets cannot be successfully demonstrated by a retail clerk in a bookstore. The customer wants to know more about the product and needs a specialist to demonstrate it and answer questions.

Nature of the work

Direct selling requires the salesperson to go into an available sales territory; find prospective buyers; and introduce, explain, demonstrate, and take orders for the product or product line that he or she represents. Although there is a wide variety of types of direct selling plans, most fall into one or more of the major categories described below.

The Direct Company Plan. Under this plan a sales representative, who may be an employee or an independent contractor, is authorized by a company to take orders for a product and is compensated by a commission paid for each order. The direct company representative who is an independent contractor has the advantage of deciding when and how much time to devote to selling the company's product. Direct company representatives are usually very well trained in presenting their product. Most encyclopedias are sold by salespeople in this category. Workers who sell magazine subscriptions as direct company representatives may be hired, trained, and supervised by a *subscription crew leader,* who assigns crew members to a specific area, reviews the orders they take, and compiles sales records.

The Exhibit Plan. Sometimes the direct salesperson, with approval and cooperation of the company, will set up an exhibit booth at a place where large numbers of people are expected to pass, such as a state fair, trade show, or product exposition. Here the salesperson can sell to interested prospects and take down names and addresses for later demonstrations at home.

The Dealer Plan. This plan allows the direct salesperson to function as the proprietor of a small business. The dealer purchases the product wholesale and then resells it to consumers at the retail price, mainly through door-to-door sales efforts.

The Group Plan. Under this arrangement, an individual purchaser is contacted by the salesperson and given the opportunity to spon-

A door-to-door salesman offers a variety of aluminum sidings to a homeowner. Many door-to-door salespeople call ahead for appointments.

sor further sales. For example, under a "Party Plan," the sales representative arranges with an interested sales prospect to invite a group of friends to his or her home for a demonstration of the products for sale. The host or hostess receives free or discounted merchandise in return for the use of the home and for assembling other potential customers for the salesperson.

The C.O.D. Plan. In this method the direct seller carries sample merchandise or a sample book and sells for a direct-selling company at established list prices. The salesperson takes the order, perhaps collects an advance deposit, and sends the order to the company. The company in turn ships the merchandise directly to the customer on a cash-on-delivery (C.O.D.) basis, or to the salesperson who delivers the product and collects the balance owed.

Whatever the sales plan, door-to-door sales workers have some unique advantages over their counterparts in retail stores. Direct sellers do not have to wait passively for the customer to come to them; they can go out and aggressively find the buyers for their product. The direct seller often carries only one product or a limited line of products, and thus is much more familiar with the features and benefits of the merchandise. As a rule, the direct seller gets the chance to demonstrate the product where it will most likely be used—in the home.

On the other hand, there are drawbacks to this type of selling as well. Many customers grow impatient or hostile when salespeople come to their house unannounced. It may take several visits to convince someone to buy the product. To be highly successful, the door-to-door sales worker must develop strong selling skills and a persuasive sales pitch. In a brief visit, the direct seller must gain acceptance and win the confidence of the prospect, develop the prospect's interest in the product or service for sale, create the desire to buy, and close the sale.

To help those selling their products, merchandising companies provide training programs for the sales workers. In addition, companies sometimes supply appropriate gifts and premiums that salespeople can offer to prospects, and invest in advertising to make the selling job easier.

Requirements

There are very few requirements or prerequisites for entering this field. Most door-to-door sales workers have high school diplomas, and approximately 3 out of 10 have attended college. There seems to be little correlation, however, between courses taken in school and direct selling success, although English, public speaking, and psychology are undoubtedly helpful.

The basic requirement for success as a door-to-door sales worker is a desire to earn money while enjoying the freedom and independence of organizing one's own time and effort. Most successful direct salespeople share a few common personal traits. These include personal ambition and drive, self-confidence, strong persuasive skills, a responsible attitude, and self-discipline. Direct sales workers are usually independent and cannot rely on the boss for motivation. It takes a tremendous amount of self-discipline to organize one's own work every day and persevere in the face of repeated customer rejections.

Finally, it helps if the door-to-door sales worker has a genuine affection for people and a friendly personality. Officials in the direct sales trade emphasize, however, that a person need not be a hearty extrovert to succeed. Shyer, more introverted persons often possess a sensitivity that can be a decided advantage in winning customer confidence. Direct selling can be a satisfying occupation for the person who likes to meet people and face new challenges every day.

Opportunities for experience and exploration

Few careers offer so many opportunities for acquiring experience and background that can be helpful both in this particular field and in other occupations. Students can explore direct selling on a part-time basis during vacations or after school. Other interested people can sell door to door in the evening or on weekends while holding another job before deciding on it as a career. The only real investment is time and effort. Young people in Junior Achievement or in the Junior Sales Clubs of America, as well as those who take part in sales drives for their school or community group, all develop some experience in direct selling.

Methods of entering

Direct selling is an easy field to enter. As the general population and family incomes increase, direct selling companies are continually on the lookout for new salespeople to meet the requirements of this expanding market. These companies advertise for sales representatives in daily and community newspapers, in sales workers' specialty magazines, and on television and radio. Many people enter direct selling through contacts they have had with other direct sales representatives. Interested people can also contact the company of their choice by mail, phone, or personal visit. Most firms have district or area representatives who interview applicants and arrange the necessary training for those who show promise. A worker or student who starts on a part-time basis may be asked to take on a full-time position.

Advancement

All major companies in the direct-selling field present advancement opportunities to motivated, successful workers. Because direct selling offers people the chance to earn extra money for special purchases or emergencies, many temporary and part-time people are added to the ranks each year. This increases the number of career direct sellers needed to recruit, train, and manage new members of the sales force.

Sales representatives who demonstrate administrative and business skills, as well as the ability to train others in sound selling techniques, can be promoted to the position of area, branch, or district manager. A high percentage of the men and women now responsible for the management and direction of the most successful firms in this field got their start selling door to door.

Advancement opportunities are not limited to the sales end alone. Successful direct sales workers can move into non-sales executive positions with their companies—in marketing, merchandising, advertising, promotions, or purchasing. Their understanding of selling and the problems faced by the sales force can make them valuable decision-makers in the home office.

Employment outlook

Almost 5 million people currently work as door-to-door sales workers in the United States and Canada. Of these salespeople, 88 percent are women. Thoughtful men and women connected with direct selling look on their industry as a stable one with excellent growth possibilities. As new consumer products are developed, the need increases for direct salespeople to introduce, demonstrate, and create a demand for these products.

The number of direct selling companies has remained fairly constant over the past few years, and the growth in their sales volume has generally followed the statistical upswing seen in other types of retailing. One limiting factor in direct selling has been the lack of enough good salespeople to tap the potential of the market. This industry has also been an important source of jobs for people displaced during periods of economic decline or by changing technology.

Earnings

Direct salespeople usually earn a straight commission on their sales, ranging from 10 to 40 percent of an item's suggested retail price. Therefore, a typical or average income for this occupation is hard to estimate. Earnings are a product of each individual's desire to succeed, time and effort put into the job, training and ability, and ability to learn from failed sales efforts.

In the 1990s a realistic, average annual income figure for good, full-time direct sales workers is between $11,000 and $16,000. It can be more and it can, of course, be less. It is safe to say that incomes of door-to-door sales workers compare favorably with those in the selling profession overall. Sales workers frequently work more than a 40-hour week to earn more money or to maintain sales levels during slow periods.

Conditions of work

The door-to-door sales worker has been called the world's smallest independent business person. Some direct sellers work in their own or nearby communities. Some travel more widely to cover additional territory with the cooperation of their companies.

When selling items that represent a considerable financial investment for the customer, it is usually necessary to visit when both the husband and wife are at home and can make the buying decision together. For most items sold door to door, regular business hours are suitable.

Some direct salespeople set a certain minimum weekly income goal and put in just enough hours each week to achieve it. While there is nothing wrong with this, it is obviously not the best way for an ambitious person to advance in a direct selling career. This work involves being outdoors in all kinds of weather, and may also involve carrying heavy sample cases.

Direct selling requires the fortitude to endure periods of discouragement and the resilience that turns each rejection into a learning experience to be used at the next opportunity. The good salesperson must learn to expect a certain amount of rudeness from customers and still maintain tact and patience.

Direct selling may not appeal to the person who seeks the security of a weekly paycheck. Those who go into business for themselves must be willing to risk their livelihood on their ability to perform and forego the safety of a regular job in favor of greater monetary and personal rewards. While the incomes of direct sellers may fluctuate from week to week, the successful ones generally wind up with annual incomes that are far above average.

GOE: 08.02.05; SIC: Any industry; SOC: 4366

◇ **SOURCES OF ADDITIONAL INFORMATION**

Direct Selling Association
1776 K Street, NW
Suite 600
Washington, DC 20006

National Association for Professional Saleswomen
5520 Cherokee Drive, Suite 200
Alexandria, VA 22312

Canadian Direct Marketing Association
#607, 1 Concorde Gate
Don Mills ON M3C 3N6

◇ **RELATED ARTICLES**

Volume 1: Advertising; Marketing; Sales
Volumes 2–4: Advertising workers; Automobile sales workers; Buyers, wholesale and retail; Manufacturers' sales workers; Purchasing agents; Retail managers; Retail sales workers; Route drivers; Service sales representatives; Wholesale trade sales workers

Drafters

Definition

The *drafter* prepares working plans and detail drawings from the rough sketches, specifications, and calculations of engineers, architects, and designers, to be used for engineering or manufacturing purposes according to the specified dimensions. The drafter uses knowledge of various machines, engineering practices, mathematics, building materials, and other physical sciences to complete the drawings.

History

In industry, drafting is the conversion of ideas from people's minds to precise working specifications from which products can be made. Many people find it much easier to give directions by drawing than by telling or writing, and to assemble new equipment if the instructions include diagrams and drawings. Industry has come to rely on drafters to develop the working specifications from the new ideas and findings of those in the laboratories, shops, and factories.

Nature of the work

The drafter prepares detailed plans and specification drawings from the ideas, notes, or rough sketches of scientists, engineers, architects, and designers. Sometimes drawings are developed after a visit to a project in the field or as the result of a discussion with one or more people involved in the job. The drawings, which usually provide a number of different views of the object, must be exact and accurate. They vary greatly in size depending on the type of drawing. Some assembly drawings, often called "layouts", are 25 to 30 feet long, while others are very small. They must contain enough detail, whatever their size, so that the part, object, or building can be constructed from them. Such drawings usually include information concerning the quality of materials to be used, their cost, and the processes to be followed in carrying out the job. In developing their drawings made to scale of the object to be built, drafters use a variety of instruments, such as protractors, compasses, triangles, squares, drawing pens, and pencils.

Drafters are often classified according to the type of work they do or the level of responsibility. *Senior drafters* use the preliminary information and ideas provided by engineers and architects to make design layouts. They may have the title of *chief drafter* and assign work to other drafters and supervise their activities. *Detailers* make complete drawings, giving dimensions, material, and any other necessary information of each part shown on the layout. *Checkers* carefully examine drawings to check for errors in computing or in recording dimensions and specifications. *Tracers*, who are usually assistant drafters, make corrections and prepare drawings for reproduction by tracing them on transparent cloth, paper, or plastic film.

Drafters may also specialize in a particular field of work, such as mechanical, electrical, electronic, aeronautical, structural, or architectural drafting.

Although the nature of the work of drafters is not too different from one specialization to another, there is a considerable variation in the type of object with which they deal.

Commercial drafters do all-around drafting, such as plans for building sites, layouts of offices and factories, and drawings of charts, forms, and records. *Computer-assisted drafters* use computers to make drawings and layouts for such fields as aeronautics, architecture, or electronics.

Civil drafters make construction drawings for roads and highways, river and harbor improvements, flood control, drainage, and other civil engineering projects. *Structural drafters* draw plans for bridge trusses, plate girders, roof trusses, trestle bridges, and other structures that use structural reinforcing steel, concrete, masonry, and other structural materials.

Cartographic drafters prepare maps of geographical areas to show natural and constructed features, political boundaries, and other features. *Topographical drafters* draft and correct maps from original sources, such as other maps, surveying notes, and aerial photographs.

Architectural drafters draw plans of buildings, including artistic and structural features. *Landscape drafters* make detailed drawings from sketches furnished by landscape architects.

Heating and ventilating drafters draft plans for heating, air-conditioning, ventilating, and sometimes refrigeration equipment. *Plumbing drafters* draw diagrams for the installation of plumbing equipment.

Mechanical drafters make working drawings of machinery, automobiles, power plants, or any mechanical device. *Castings drafters* prepare detailed drawings of castings, which are objects formed in a mold. *Tool design drafters* draft manufacturing plans for all kinds of tools. *Patent drafters* make drawings of mechanical devices for use by lawyers to obtain patent rights for their clients.

Electrical drafters make schematics and wiring diagrams to be used by construction crews working on equipment and wiring in power plants, communications centers, buildings, or electrical distribution systems.

Electronics drafters draw schematics and wiring diagrams for television cameras and TV sets, radio transmitters and receivers, computers, radiation detectors, and other electronic equipment.

Electromechanisms design drafters draft designs of electromechanical equipment such as aircraft engines, data processing systems, gyroscopes, automatic materials handling and processing machinery, or biomedical equipment. *Electromechanical drafters* draw wiring diagrams, layouts, and mechanical details for the electrical

A drafter translates an engineer's rough sketches into working blueprints. The task requires concentration and precision.

components and systems of a mechanical process or device.

Aeronautical drafters prepare engineering drawings for planes, missiles, and spacecraft. *Automotive design drafters* and *automotive design layout drafters* both turn out working layouts and master drawings of components, assemblies, and systems of automobiles and other vehicles. Automotive design drafters make original designs from specifications, and automotive design layout drafters make drawings based on prior layouts or sketches.

Marine drafters draft the structural and mechanical features of ships, docks, and marine buildings and equipment. Projects range from petroleum drilling platforms to nuclear submarines.

Geological drafters make diagrams and maps of geological formations and locations of mineral, oil, gas deposits. *Geophysical drafters* draw maps and diagrams based on data from petroleum prospecting instruments such as seismographs, gravity meters, and magnetometers. *Directional survey drafters* plot boreholes for oil and gas wells. *Oil and gas drafters* draft plans for the construction and operation of oil fields, refineries, and pipeline systems.

A design team working on electrical or gas power plants and substations may be headed by a *chief design drafter*, who oversees architectural, electrical, mechanical, and structural drafters. Estimators and drafters draw specifications and instructions for installing voltage transformers, cables, and other electrical equipment that delivers electric power to consumers.

Requirements

Proper training is required for drafters. Interested high school students should take science and mathematics courses, mechanical drawing (minimum of one to two years) and wood, metal, or electric shop. They also should take English and social studies.

Training beyond high school is possible through apprenticeship, junior college, or technical institute programs. Apprenticeship programs usually run three to four years. During this period, the apprentice works on the job and is required to take related classroom work in theory and practice. Information about apprenticeship programs can be obtained from a school counselor, a mechanical drawing or shop instructor, a local union, or from the local, state, or national apprenticeship training representatives.

A number of two-year colleges and technical institutes offer drafting programs. Preparation beyond high school in the physical sciences, mathematics, drawing, sketching and drafting techniques, and in other technical or applied subject areas, is essential for certain types of beginning positions, and for advancement to positions of greater salary and more responsibility.

Students interested in drafting should have a good sense of space perception (ability to visualize objects in two or three dimensions); form perception (ability to compare and to discriminate between shapes, lines, and forms and shadings); and coordinated eye-finger-hand movements.

Opportunities for experience and exploration

High school programs provide several opportunities for gaining experience in drafting. Mechanical drawing is a good course to elect. There are many hobbies and leisure time activities that require the preparation of drawings or use of blueprints, like woodworking, building models, repairing or remodeling projects. After the completion of some courses in mechanical drawing it may be possible to locate a part-time or summer job in drafting.

Methods of entering

Beginning drafters should have graduated from a post-high school program in a technical institute or a junior college. Applicants for government positions may need to take a civil service examination. One also can enter the field of drafting first by attending an apprenticeship program.

Beginning or inexperienced drafters often start as tracers. Students with some formal post-high school technical training often qualify for positions as junior drafters who revise detail drawings and gradually assume assignments of a more complex drawing nature.

Advancement

With additional experience and skill, beginning drafters become checkers, detailers, design drafters, or senior drafters. Movement from one to another of these job classifications is not restricted; each business must modify work assignments based on its own needs.

Drafters often move into related positions. Some typical positions include those of technical report writers, sales engineers, engineering assistants, production foremen, and installation technicians.

Employment outlook

In the 1990s, more than 326,000 drafters are employed in business, industry, and government positions. About one-third work for engineering and architectural companies, and another third work for manufacturers of machinery, electrical equipment, fabricated metals, and other durable goods. Other industries that employ drafters include construction, communications, transportation, and utilities. More than 14,000 drafters work for government agencies, most of them at the state and local level. The majority of the federal government drafters work for the Department of Defense.

Employment of drafters is expected to grow more slowly than other occupations through the end of the 1990s, despite the anticipated expansion of technological and scientific processes. New products and processes of more complex design will call for more drafting services, as will the general growth of industry. However, the increased use of computer-aided design (CAD) systems is expected to offset some of the demand, particularly for lower-level drafters who do routine work. CAD equipment can produce more and better variations of a design, which could stimulate additional activity in the field and create opportunities for drafters who are willing to switch to the new techniques.

Employment trends for drafters fluctuate with the economy. In the event of a recession, fewer buildings and manufactured products are designed, which could reduce the need for drafters in architectural, engineering, and manufacturing firms.

Earnings

In private industry, the general salary average for beginning drafters is about $18,000 a year in the 1990s. Experienced drafters earn between $19,300 and $33,500 per year, depending upon the nature of their position and the responsibility involved. Those whose preparation qualifies them for positions as senior drafters have salaries averaging $36,200.

Conditions of work

The drafter usually works in a well lighted, air-conditioned, quiet room. This may be a central drafting room where drafters work side by side at large, tilted drawing tables. Some drafters work in an individual department, like engineering, research, or development, where they work alone or with one or two other drafters and with engineers, designers or scientists. Occasionally, drafters may need to visit other departments or construction sites to consult with engineers or to gain first-hand information. Most drafters work a 40-hour week with little overtime. Drafters work at drawing tables for long periods of time at arrangements that require undivided concentration, close eyework, and very precise and accurate computations and drawings. There is generally little pressure, but occasionally last-minute design changes, or a rush order, may necessitate a deadline.

GOE: 05.03.02; SIC: 871; SOC: 372

◇ SOURCES OF ADDITIONAL INFORMATION

American Design Drafting
966 Hungerford Drive, Suite 10-B
Rockville, MD 20854

International Federation of Professional and Technical Engineers
8701 Georgia Avenue, Suite 701
Silver Spring, MD 20910

National Association of Trade and Technical Schools
PO Box 2006, Department BL
Annapolis Junction, MD 20701

Manitoba Society of Certified Engineering Technicians and Technologists
#5, 1767 Portage Avenue
Winnipeg MB R3J 0E7

◇ RELATED ARTICLES

Volume 1: Automotives; Aviation and Aerospace; Construction; Design; Electronics; Engineering; Plastics; Rubber
Volumes 2–4: Architects; Architectural and building construction technicians; CAD/CAM technicians; Cartographers; Drafting and design technicians; Industrial designers; Miscellaneous engineers

Drafting and design technicians

Definition

Drafting and design technicians transform ideas into detailed drawings and specifications in order to make products. They assist architects and mechanical, electrical, civil, and other engineers to design and draw up plans for machines, electrical circuits, buildings, and many other structures and manufactured devices. They work either on paper or with computers to prepare layouts, detailed drawings, charts, graphs, diagrams, and models.

DRAFTING AND DESIGN TECHNICIANS

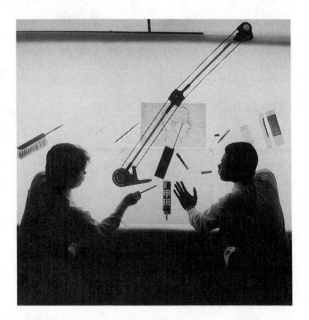

Two drafting and design technicians discuss the rough draft of a project. Often, technicians must make several revisions of a design before the final version is approved.

History

Drawings were the earliest method used to describe forms and objects. They are usually much easier to use than written or spoken language to describe complicated shapes and structures. Drafting, also called engineering drawing, has long allowed architects to develop and record their design ideas and to transmit those ideas to the people who construct their buildings. Certainly as early as Babylonian times, engineering drawings were used to plan buildings. A surviving example is a stone engraving of a fortress plan done by a Babylonian engineer about 4,000 years ago. Almost 2,000 years later the Romans designed and built excellent structures, many of which survive today. The Romans well understood the importance of drafting; in fact, the earliest known textbook on engineering drawing was done by the Roman architect Vitruvius around 27 b.c. Another important figure in the history of drafting was Leonardo da Vinci, who made many technical drawings and also wrote the first book explaining projection drawing.

The principles of modern engineering drawing were first organized around 1800 by the French mathematician Gaspard Monge. He developed ways to use geometry to solve construction problems, thus revolutionizing engineering design. His contributions formed the basis of orthographic projection, the most common form of engineering drawing today. In orthographic projection, any object, no matter how complex, can be seen from any direction. Objects are drawn as if projected onto three perpendicular planes, such as the front, side, and top of a box, then revolved into the positions of the other planes. This approach provided engineers and architects with a much more effective way to organize design ideas.

Leonardo da Vinci wrote, "All of our knowledge has its origin in our perceptions." Perception is the key to the work of modern drafting and design technicians. They have cultivated their perceptions as well as their ability to think in three dimensions and draw in two; to visualize objects and then present them so that others readily understand.

Drafting is being revolutionized by computer-aided drafting (CAD) systems. By the end of the 1990s, most drafters will sit, not at traditional drawing boards, but at computer work stations, drawing on video screens. Drafters will still need the same knowledge as before, along with some additional skills, but they will be much more productive, allowing instantaneous changes in a design without having to re-draw the whole design.

Today drafting work in many workplaces is still done using the traditional drawing board and tools like compasses, protractors, dividers, and triangles to make drawings on paper. Although CAD technology has been available for some years, it takes time to shift procedures in many offices, and the cost of new computer systems is not insignificant. The cost is dropping, however, and within a decade the transition to CAD as the main method of drafting should be largely complete.

Nature of the work

Drafting and design technicians illustrate designers' ideas in graphic form. They produce detailed drawings from notes, rough sketches, verbal instructions, and specifications, then they assemble the drawings into working plans. The final drawings will: show the product or structure from all sides, specify materials needed to make the product, procedures for making it, and other information needed to carry out the process. Technicians work as members of a team, primarily as intermediaries between architects, engineers, and scientists (who design products), and craft workers (who make products). In some settings, their drawings are entered into computers that control machines that make products.

Regardless of whether the technicians work on paper or on computer, they use technical handbooks, tables, and calculators to help them in their work. A finished drawing consists of lines that represent contours, edges, and surfaces together with symbols, dimensions, and notes. The drawings may be of machinery, buildings, consumer products, vehicles, or electrical systems—just about anything that is manufactured or constructed. Drafting technicians usually specialize in a particular field, such as architectural, mechanical, electrical, civil, or aeronautical drafting, and get to know the particular problems and methods of their field.

Beginning drafting and design technicians spend most of their time at the drawing board or computer work station. At this stage, their work may involve drawing detailed minor parts of a project based on engineering design sketches, design directives, and preliminary data; working with designers and engineers in the design and operation of production systems; making preliminary drawings and sketches of a proposed design in sufficient detail to resolve project problems; and investigating pertinent design factors such as ease of manufacture, interchangeability, replaceability, and efficiency of machine and tool designs.

Most of the jobs held by these workers are usually designated as particular kinds of drafters rather than as technicians.

On their first job, drafting and design technicians frequently hold the position of *detail drafter*. Detailers start with layout drawings and make complete detailed drawings in preparation for manufacturing. These show exact dimensions, tolerances, finish, material, number and all other information necessary for production. They may make simple decisions but they generally receive explicit instructions from an engineer or designer. Detailers must know about dimensioning practices and the basics of depicting designs to their best advantage.

The following short paragraphs describe other typical positions held by drafting and design technicians.

Aeronautical drafters specialize in drawing developmental and production airplanes, missiles, and supplementary equipment.

Architects' assistants help architects or structural engineers assemble specifications, perform routine calculations for quantity estimates, and complete drawings.

Architectural drafters carry out drafting tasks on architectural drawings, sketches, and presentations, as assigned by the chief drafter or architect. They complete drawings by detailing, "heavying up" or correcting existing prints, and preparing materials lists for architectural drawings. This position is a common starting position for architectural or building construction technicians.

Cartographic drafters draw maps of geographical areas showing natural and constructed features, political boundaries, and other features.

Civil drafters detail construction drawings and maps for use in planning and building highways, river and harbor improvements, flood control, drainage, and other civil engineering projects.

Electrical drafters draw up plans for electrical systems such as those in electrical power generation plants, large industrial plants, and municipal lighting systems.

Electromechanisms design drafters sketch designs of equipment such as rocket engine control systems, biomedical equipment, and automatic materials-handling machinery.

Engineering specifications technicians analyze plans and drawings to determine material specifications. They prepare lists of materials specifying quality, size and strength, and compare requirements to company, government, or other contract requirements.

Heating and ventilating drafters draw plans for installing heating, air conditioning, and ventilating equipment in buildings.

Landscape drafters prepare drawings and tracings of landscape site plans, including grading and drainage, irrigation, plantings, and garden structures.

Marine drafters draw the structural and mechanical features of ships, docks, and other marine structures and equipment.

Mechanical drafters work from engineering sketches to develop mechanical drawings for manufacturing equipment such as tools and machinery.

Patent drafting technicians prepare mechanical drawings of various devices for use by patent attorneys in obtaining and recording patents.

Quality-control technicians test and inspect components at various stages of manufacture, ensuring final quality of products as specified by engineering drawings.

Structural drafters draw plans and details for structures that employ reinforcing steel, concrete, masonry, wood, and other building materials. They develop plans for foundations, framing, and other major structural elements.

Technical illustrators draw pictures and diagrams for sales literature and owner's handbooks. They illustrate equipment to help purchasers assemble, install, operate, and repair the equipment on their own.

About a third of all drafters work for engineering and architectural firms. Another third work in industries that manufacture durable goods such as machinery, fabricated metals, and electrical equipment.

DRAFTING AND DESIGN TECHNICIANS

Requirements

Artistic ability is helpful in many fields. In addition, successful drafting and design technicians are: able to think in three dimensions; comfortable with construction projects, laboratories, and scientific instruments; good team members and listeners who can take as well as give directions; able to do very detailed work accurately and neatly.

The best way to become a drafting and design technician is to attend a two-year postsecondary training program, offered at many community and junior colleges, technical schools, divisions of universities, and vocational institutes. Some technical training programs are shorter than two years. Programs that are a year or even less in length can enable graduates to find jobs performing basic drafting functions. Employers increasingly prefer applicants, however, who have the more complete preparation that a two-year program provides. Depending on the program length, graduates receive a certificate or associate degree in their major field.

In high school, students interested in drafting and design should consult their guidance counselor to find out about the specific admission requirements of schools that they might attend later. Requirements are likely to include two years of mathematics, including algebra, geometry, and trigonometry; one year of physical science, preferably physics with laboratory work; four years of English and related courses that teach communications skills; and a year of mechanical or architectural drawing.

People who have not obtained a solid preparation in high school and develop an interest later should not be discouraged. Many technical training programs provide extra courses to help students fill gaps in their background.

In a two-year program, the first year may include courses in mathematics, mechanics, engineering design and drawing, production processes, introduction to CAD, and English composition. Second-year classes may cover engineering materials, tool and machine design, machining or other manufacturing practice, architectural drawing, advanced CAD, and technical report writing.

These programs involve demanding college-level study and are designed to provide students with a strong science and mathematics base. They also provide experience and practice in using modern drafting methods and equipment.

Some people enter the drafting field through an apprenticeship program. These programs usually take three to four years to complete and combine job training with classroom work on a part-time basis.

Training in specific industrial specialties can also be obtained through cooperative programs. In these, people who are already familiar with the fundamentals of drafting receive training in the practical and theoretical aspects of a particular field, enabling them to perform the specialized drafting duties associated with the craft.

Specialized training in the use of one manufacturer's CAD equipment may not be easily transferred to other types of CAD equipment. Because the various systems now in use are so different from each other, new employees may have to undergo a period of on-the-job training to acquaint them with the employer's system.

There are no requirements for licenses or certificates for this career. However, employers are favorably impressed by technicians who earn voluntary certification from the National Institute for Certification in Engineering Technologies. Certification is generally regarded as evidence that the technician is competent on the job and is interested in advancement.

Opportunities for experience and exploration

High school students should seek as much information about the field as they can, through their school's guidance counselor. Students should take a vocational education or drafting and design program if either is offered in the high school; if not, a visit to a nearby school that offers drafting courses could be very informative. Field trips to workplaces where drafting and design work is done are also helpful; students could see drafters at work and perhaps get them to talk about what they do and how they see the career field.

Part-time work can also be helpful. Prospective technicians may be able to get jobs as beginning clerks or assistants in an engineering and design department of a manufacturing company, architect's office, or other employer of drafters. Such part-time work or summer work provides a good understanding of what the work is all about.

Methods of entering

Technical schools and colleges help graduates find employment through their own student placement services and in cooperation with public and private employment agencies. Sometimes corporate recruiters visit schools to interview and hire students who are close to graduating. Job offers like this are usually the best, because this means that jobs will be waiting for students when they graduate from the program.

Newspaper classified advertisements and direct inquiries to employers of drafting and design technicians are other important ways of finding employment in the field.

Advancement

After several years of experience, technicians who start as detailers may advance to the position of layout drafter. Layout drafters transform sketches, models, or verbal instructions into assembly drawings that will be filled in by the detailer. Layout drafters must have a two-year technical school education with a good background in tolerances, algebra, geometry, and trigonometry. Previous experience as a detailer is almost always needed so the technician can work more closely with detailers as members of the engineering team.

Several years of experience in layout drafting can allow advancement to senior drafter. Senior drafters are sometimes referred to as designers, because they contribute to the initial development of the product rather than being concerned solely with the expression of an idea in graphic form. This job requires a combination of experience in the drafting and design area and specific technical know-how.

With further education, experienced technicians may advance to technical jobs in research, quality control, sales, management, product development, manufacturing, and perhaps ownership. The following paragraphs list some of the advancement possibilities, along with descriptions of job duties.

Assistant production managers manage production through involvement with receiving, manufacturing, and shipping operations. They also supervise other employees.

Customer relations engineers travel as company representatives to service equipment wherever it may be installed. They make necessary repairs and provide the technical know-how to do repair jobs.

Process engineers or *work simplification engineers* study engineering drawings and convert them to simpler process schedules showing a number of operations to be performed by semi-skilled machine operators.

Quality-control engineers help ensure precision in manufacturing through constant surveillance of the quality of finished products and of incoming raw materials and parts received from suppliers or subcontractors. Technicians in this position may supervise other workers.

Research designers develop new and better products through research and development procedures in laboratories.

Technical sales representatives show and demonstrate the company's products to possible consumers and provide any necessary advisory services.

Tool designers create tools such as milling machine cutters, fixtures, or jigs that are used to assemble manufactured products. They modify tool designs for new models, making changes necessary to improve the product.

Tool engineers or *machine designers* design special machines and equipment used in manufacturing and supervise other drafters and detailers.

Time-and-motion study engineers are responsible for a time-and-motion study department, which promotes more efficient work rates and use of time and materials in manufacturing.

Experienced drafters may also become teachers in schools and colleges that offer technical training.

Employment outlook

Through the year 2000, employment in the drafting and design field is expected to grow more slowly than average for other occupations. While growth in the manufacturing sector and the expanding use of sophisticated computer technology will probably create more demand for drafting services, CAD systems will increase each worker's productivity, which counteracts some of this increased demand. Many openings that do occur will be related to the need to replace workers who have retired or moved to other areas of the labor force. Increasingly, employers will seek workers who have solid training that prepares them to do more than basic routine tasks.

Because most drafters work in the building and manufacturing industries, which experience setbacks if the national economy is in a recession, they could have more difficulty finding jobs or staying employed during an economic downturn.

Earnings

Salaries vary according to area of the country, the type of work, and other factors. Graduates of technical training programs who become junior drafters in the 1990s can expect to start around $18,356 a year. After becoming senior drafters, they earn around $25,896. Drafters with considerable experience, especially in a specialized field, can earn $43,000 or more a year. Benefits depend on the employer and may include paid vacation days, holidays, insurance, pension plans, profit-sharing, and tuition refund plans.

Conditions of work

Most drafting duties confine technicians to indoor work, usually in an engineering department. Usually the work station is in a modern, adequately lighted, temperature-controlled office building. Safety and comfort are probably among the highest of any industrial job.

Some related tasks, however, may take technicians to a research laboratory, machine shop, or some manufacturing department. These tasks might be inspection or simple liaison duties between the engineering and design department and the producing or developing department. While on these assignments, technicians need to be aware of safety considerations and may need to wear protective clothing or other gear.

Drafting and design technicians usually work individually, yet each project represents a group effort. They must work well as part of a team; this means they be good at understanding and communicating in writing, sketching, and speaking. They must be analytical, careful, neat, and accurate in all they do because mistakes cause wasted time, material, and effort.

Often drafting and design technicians supervise other workers in drafting or in the production of the products. In this role they need to get along well with others, encouraging those whom they supervise to work efficiently.

GOE: 05.03.02; SIC: 7389; SOC: 372

◇ **SOURCES OF ADDITIONAL INFORMATION**

National Architectural Accrediting Board
1735 New York Avenue, NW
Washington, DC 20006

Industrial Designers Society of America
1142-E Walker Road
Great Falls, VA 22066

Accreditation Board for Engineering and Technology
345 East 47th Street
New York, NY 10017

◇ **RELATED ARTICLES**

Volume 1: Construction; Design; Engineering; Machining and Machinery
Volumes 2–4: Architects; Architectural and building construction technicians; CAD/CAM technicians; Cartographers; Drafters; Graphics programmers; Miscellaneous engineers; Surveying and mapping technicians

---

Dry cleaning and laundry workers

Definition

Dry cleaning and laundry workers dry clean, wash, dry and press all types of clothing, fabrics, and other materials. Using machines and special cleaning solvents, they work at removing dirt and stains from clothes, linens, curtains, rugs, and other articles. They may do this for customers at dry cleaning stores or work for linen and uniform supply companies, hospitals, schools, or other institutions.

History

As early as the Stone Age, people learned to weave fibers into cloth. The four natural fibers—cotton, linen, wool, and silk—were the world's only sources of fabric for many centuries. As soon as people learned to use fabric for clothing and other articles, they began to devise ways of cleaning it. Ancient peoples scrubbed their clothing in streams and rivers, using rocks and sticks to loosen and remove stains and dirt. In later centuries they learned to use soaps and other cleaning agents derived from natural sources.

People washed their clothing and other fabric items by hand until the 19th century, when machines to agitate and wring out clothes were invented. With the Industrial Revolution came automatic washing and drying machines. As the population grew, the number of hospitals, schools, factories, and other businesses increased, along with the need for a huge supply of textile items that had to be cleaned continually. Institutional laundries sprang up to fulfill these institutions' needs for fresh sheets, towels, uniforms, and other articles.

Also in the late 19th century, the first synthetic fabric—nitrocellulose rayon—was invented. Eventually hundreds of different synthetic fabrics were invented, derived from such sources as coal, wood, ammonia, and petroleum. These new fabrics called for new cleaning techniques. Items that would lose their shape or color in water needed to be cleaned with chemical solvents. Even some natural fibers were found to last longer and retain their appearance better when cleaned with chemicals. Dry cleaning stores were established to clean articles that could not be washed by normal methods at home.

Nature of the work

All regions of the country have laundries and dry cleaners. Some institutions such as hotels, schools, and prisons have their own laundries. Many schools, hospitals, and other institutions use linen suppliers, which launder linens, uniforms, and other articles and rent these items to their customers. Customers who own their washable articles may take them to commercial laundries. Other laundries may supply and launder work uniforms, gloves, rugs, mats, and other items to businesses and industries.

Dry cleaners clean, repair, and press items that cannot be laundered with water, although some large dry-cleaning plants also wash and press shirts and other clothing. Dry-cleaning operations are set up in various ways. One large plant may receive business through several of its own retail stores. A wholesale plant does cleaning for several independent stores.

A launderer steam presses a cotton shirt for a customer.

In addition, a single retail store may have its own plant.

In smaller laundries and dry cleaning plants, an individual worker may perform several different cleaning tasks. In larger plants, workers tend to be more specialized. *Dry-cleaning branch store managers* and sales clerks receive items from customers, add up the cost of cleaning them, write the customer a slip stating the charges and the day the items may be picked up, bundle and mark the clothing to identify the owner, and inspect the items for rips and stains. They also retrieve the cleaned items for the customer and receive payment. Some businesses have *curb attendants* who retrieve and deliver cleaned articles to customers who remain in their cars outside the store or plant.

Sales route drivers drive trucks to pick up and deliver garments and other laundry. They turn in bundles of soiled items to other workers at the dry cleaning plant. They also stop in at businesses and homes along the route to drum up business for the firm. *Laundry pricing clerks* work in commercial laundries where they compute the cost of a customer's laundry, keep inventory of customers' articles, and prepare statements and invoices.

Businesses that use industrial laundries may employ *laundry workers* to assemble bundles of soiled items for delivery to the laundry and to check and verify the contents of laundered bundles that are returned. At linen-supply establishments, *linen-supply load-builders* assemble bundles of laundered linens and uniforms to give to sales route drivers for delivery. *Linen-room supervisors, linen controllers,* and *linen graders* are responsible for keeping track of the number, type, and condition of items in a linen supplier and making sure customers receive and properly care for linens they order.

Once soiled items reach a laundry or dry cleaner, *markers* put tags on articles so they will not be lost and send the articles to rooms where they will be cleaned. There, *classifiers* sort articles into lots according to the treatment they need: different colors, fabrics, and types of garments go into different lots. *Sorters* in laundries may weigh laundry and put individual customers' items into net bags to keep them together, or sort items using machines.

Laundry spotters identify spots on articles and brush them with chemicals or other cleaners until the stain dissolves. In dry cleaning plants, spotters may be designated according to the type of material spotted, because different fabrics require different chemicals for safe spot removal. Establishments that wash or clean rugs may employ *rug measurers* to record the sizes of rugs so that the rugs can be restored to their original measurements after washing.

When articles are ready to be cleaned, *laundry laborers and loaders* take laundry to the washing machines. Some machines can hold more than 1,000 pounds. *Washing machine operators* load articles into washing machines and start them. They pull levers or throw switches to add water, bleach, soap, or starch. When the washing cycle is complete, they remove the articles and load them into extractors—machines that can remove about 50 percent of the water from the laundry. Machines in modern laundries may both wash and extract water from the articles. One worker may tend several machines. Workers then remove the damp laundry and put it on conveyor belts that take it to driers, conditioners, or other machines for further processing. In other laundries, workers may wash delicate articles in small machines or by hand.

Dry cleaners operate machines that clean garments, drapes, and other materials using solvents. Dry cleaners must know how different fabrics react to different chemicals and temperatures and select treatments for articles accordingly. They or their *assistants* place articles into the drum of a dry-cleaning machine, fasten its cover, and start the drum rotating. They then add cleaning solution to the drum. When the cleaning cycle is complete, they extract the solvent from the articles and later follow procedures to drain, filter, and reclaim the solvent for reuse. They put cleaned items into tumblers, which dry and deodorize them. *Hand dry cleaners* clean delicate items or those needing individual attention by hand.

Some workers specialize by cleaning rugs, furs, leather, pillows, or gloves using special processes. Fur cleaners put furs into special machines that use sawdust to clean. They then remove the sawdust with forced air or a tumbler drum. *Fur-lining scrubbers* clean linings with chemicals using sponges or pads. Some furs are cleaned by hand.

Conditioner-tumbler operators put damp laundry into a machine that semi-dries and untangles flatwork. *Tumbler operators* operate drying machines. *Operators of continuous towel rollers* put dry towels onto a machine that winds them into rolls before they are ironed or packaged. *Assemblers in wet-wash laundries* put customers' clothes together after washing and before finishing by comparing pinned-on tag numbers with numbers on customers' orders. *Dry-cleaning assemblers* assemble customers' orders after garments are finished.

When items are dry or partially dry, they are ready for pressing or finishing. *Pressers* or *finishers* use heat and steam to press items with machines that look like two padded ironing boards hinged together. A presser places a garment on the bottom board and activates a mechanism that lowers the top board and applies heat and steam. Finishers are often designated by the type of garment or fabric they work on, and those who press delicates by hand are called *hand ironers*. *Silk finishers* work on delicate items, pleats, velvet, and so on. *Flatwork finishers* feed linens into automatic pressing machines. *Puff ironers* pull portions of garments, such as sleeves, ruffles, or trim, over heated ball-shaped metal forms to press places that cannot be ironed with a flat press. Other types of finishers include *fur ironers, handkerchief pressers,* and *shirt pressers.*

Items that lose their shape during cleaning or laundering need to be blocked. *Blockers* measure knitted garments before and after cleaning. They then shrink or stretch the garment to its original shape and size, pin it to a machine, and apply steam to make it retain its shape. *Form pressers* operate pressing-blocking machines. *Hatters* and *hat blockers* use steam and special forms to clean, reshape, and stiffen hats. *Glove formers* and *sock ironers* use heated forms to reshape and dry articles.

If items are damaged during cleaning, they may need to be repaired. Table cloths, sheets, and uniforms are patched by *patching machine operators.* Menders repair rips and tears in garments. *Hat trimmers* replace and repair trim on cleaned hats by hand or machine. In dry-cleaning plants, *rug repairers* repair damaged rugs.

Other kinds of finishers include *shavers,* who brush cleaned suede to raise the nap, and *fur glazers* and *polishers,* who operate machines that restore luster and shine to cleaned furs. Some workers operate machines that fold items such as linens and shirts; some fold items by hand. *Flatwork tiers* tie finished linens into bundles and package them for delivery.

Laundries and dry cleaners also employ *checkers,* who verify the number and type of cleaned articles by checking against customer lists, and *inspectors,* who check to make sure items have been cleaned and finished in keeping with company standards. They return articles to be redone if they find wrinkles, spots, tears, and so on.

Management personnel in the field include *laundry superintendents* and *supervisors,* and *dry cleaning and rug cleaning supervisors.* These workers oversee the operations of plants and the activities of employees. *Sales managers* manage the sales functions of dry cleaning establishments. Some laundries also employ *laundry-machine mechanics* to maintain and repair machines.

Requirements

In most shops, laundry and dry-cleaning workers learn their skills on the job. The only requirement is usually a high school diploma or its equivalent. Large plants may offer more formal training programs. Spotters, because they must learn how different chemicals react with different fabrics and dyes, may take as long as two years to learn their trade completely. Finishers can learn to do their jobs skillfully in under a year, as can dry cleaners.

Depending on the job, high school courses that might be helpful to these workers include chemistry, textiles, and machine shop. Courses in sewing, clothing construction, and textiles would be especially useful for inspectors, repairers, and finishers.

Another way to learn dry cleaning and laundry skills is through various trade associations, which provide newsletters and seminars. The International Fabricare Institute, the Textile Rental Services Association of America, and the Neighborhood Cleaners Association, which operates the New York School of Drycleaning, offer many courses and seminars and also publish journals, newsletters, and bulletins to help workers learn new skills and techniques.

Workers need to be in good health. They should enjoy working with their hands and machines, and should have good eyesight and manual dexterity. They are on their feet most of the day and sometimes need to lift heavy bundles. They must be dependable, fast workers who can follow orders and handle repetitive tasks.

Opportunities for experience and exploration

To find out more about laundry and dry cleaning work, students may arrange to visit a plant and talk with workers. Students may try obtaining part-time or summer employment in the field to further explore these types of jobs.

Methods of entering

Persons interested in laundry or dry cleaning positions may contact state or local employment offices or read newspaper want ads to find job leads. The best way to find work, however, is to apply directly to dry cleaning or laundry plants.

Advancement

Workers in dry cleaning and laundry jobs generally advance by learning basic assignments and moving to more skilled tasks. Employers may send promising employees to programs offered by trade associations. Advancement in these jobs is generally limited, however.

Motivated workers may become plant managers after several years of experience. Many businesses, however, prefer to hire college graduates with degrees in management for these positions.

Employment outlook

More than 340,000 dry cleaning laundry workers are employed in the 1990s, most in institutional, industrial, and commercial plants in large cities. Many work in hotel and hospital laundries and in small family laundries.

The employment outlook for these positions is generally favorable, because the growth in the country's population and in the number of working people promises a continuing demand for laundry and cleaning services. Employment in this field is expected to grow about as fast as the average for all fields. In the next 10 years, however, automation advances will cut the number of unskilled and semiskilled workers needed, and most openings will be for skilled workers, drivers, and managers. In the dry cleaning industry, many opportunities exist for workers to learn pressing and spotting. Job prospects look best for workers who are versatile, who can do many of the jobs in the industry, and who have a good knowledge of textiles.

Earnings

The geographic location of the plant and the type of jobs individuals perform greatly affect their wages. Skilled employees earned more than unskilled. Skilled spotters and dry cleaners may earn $20,500 a year or more. Finishers can often earn more than $18,000 a year, working for a piecework rate with a guaranteed minimum wage. However, the average for all dry cleaning and laundry employees is about $13,000 a year.

Working 35 hours a week, beginning laundry workers earn between $7,800 and $8,600 a year. The more skilled a worker becomes, the higher the pay. General laundry workers can earn as much as $11,830. Workers receive time-and-a-half for working overtime and may receive slightly higher regular wages for working night shifts. Some plants award bonuses to fast workers, and many route sales workers earn a commission.

Conditions of work

Dry cleaning and laundry workers work in clean, well lighted plants that are ventilated to remove fumes. Most workers stand for long hours near machines whose noise and heat may be annoying. Workers occasionally suffer burns from hot equipment. Working with toxic chemical solvents requires caution, and other chemicals may cause allergic reactions in some people.

These workers generally work 35 to 40 hours a week, although the number of hours available may fluctuate with the amount of work. Many plants are open Saturdays. Dry cleaners often arrive at work early to ready garments for other workers to begin on. Many workers work overtime during spring and fall rush periods. Those who own their owns shops can work long hours six or seven days a week.

GOE: 06.02.16; SIC: 7216; SOC: 7659

◇ **SOURCES OF ADDITIONAL INFORMATION**

International Fabricare Institute
12251 Tech Road
Silver Spring, MD 20904

Institute of Industrial Launderers
1730 M Street, NW, Suite 610
Washington, DC 20036

Dry Cleaners and Launderer's Institute
#301, 5925 Airport Road
Mississauga ON L4V 1W1

◇ **RELATED ARTICLES**

Volume 1: Hospitality; Textiles
Volumes 2–4: Hotel and motel industry workers; Hotel and motel managers; Household workers; Janitors and cleaners; Tailors and dressmakers

---

Drywall installers and finishers

Definition

Drywall installers and *drywall finishers* plan and carry out the installation of drywall panels on interior wall and ceiling surfaces of residential, commercial, and industrial buildings. Drywall panels, also known as plasterboard, gypsum board, or wallboard, are large rigid sheets used in place of traditional plaster. Drywall install-ers, or *drywall applicators*, plan the installation of drywall panels; erect the metal framework to which the panels are fastened; and measure, cut, and install the drywall. Drywall finishers, or *tapers*, seal the joints between sections of drywall panel using a paste sealing compound and paper tape. Next, they sand the surfaces of the paste to make the wall smooth. This step prepares the surface for paint or wallpaper.

History

Well before people invented writing, they were using trowel-like tools to plaster wet clay over the walls of crude shelters in an attempt to keep out the wind and the rain. When the Great Pyramid of Cheops was built nearly 4,500 years ago, the Egyptians used a gypsum plaster in decorating the surfaces of its interior passages and rooms. But gypsum plaster is difficult to work with, because it may harden before it can be properly applied. It was not until around 1900 that additives began to be used to control the setting time of gypsum, thus opening the door for modern plastering techniques and products.

Drywall panels consist of a thin layer of gypsum plaster between two sheets of heavy paper. Different thicknesses and kinds of covering on the drywall offer different levels of moisture resistance, fire resistance, and other characteristics. Today, drywall construction is used in most new and renovated buildings because drywall can be installed cheaply and quickly. The panels are easier to work with than traditional plaster, which must be applied wet and allowed to dry before work can proceed. The widespread use of drywall has created a need for workers who are skilled in its installation.

Nature of the work

Drywall panels are manufactured in standard sizes, such as 4 feet by 12 feet or 4 feet by 8 feet. With such large sizes, the panels are heavy and awkward to handle. To be used, many panels must be cut into pieces. The pieces must be fitted together and applied over the entire surface of walls, ceilings, soffits, shafts, and partitions, including any odd-shaped and small areas, like those above or below windows.

Drywall installers begin by carefully measuring the wall or ceiling areas with tape measures and marking the drywall panels with chalk lines and markers. Using a straight edge and utility knife, they score the board along the cutting lines and break off the excess. With a keyhole saw, they cut openings for electric outlets, vents, air-conditioning units, and plumbing fixtures. Then they fit the pieces into place. They may fasten the pieces directly to the building's inside frame with adhesives, and they secure the drywall permanently with screws or nails.

Often the drywall is attached to a metal framework or a furring grid that the drywall installers put up to support the drywall. Fur-

A drywall finisher patches up marks and dents on newly installed drywall. Afterwards the wall will be covered with paint.

ring is thin strips of wood or metal nailed to the joists, studs, and other elements of the frame so that a level drywall surface can be installed and air can circulate freely behind the wall. When such a framework is to be used, installers must first study blueprints and other specifications to plan the work procedures and determine what materials, tools, and assistance they will require. They measure, mark, and cut metal runners and studs and bolt them together to make floor-to-ceiling frames. Furring is anchored in the ceiling to form rectangular spaces for ceiling drywall panels. Then the drywall, which has been cut to size, is fitted into place and screwed to the framework.

Because of the weight of drywall, installers are often assisted by helpers. Large ceiling panels may have to be raised with a special lift. After the drywall is in place, drywall installers may measure, cut, assemble, and install prefabricated metal pieces around windows and doors and in other vulnerable places to protect drywall edges. They may also fit and hang doors and install door hardware such as locks, as well as decorative trim around windows, doorways, and vents.

Drywall finishers seal and conceal the joints where drywall panels come together and prepare the walls for painting or papering. Either by hand or with an electric mixer, they prepare a quick-drying sealing material called joint compound, then spread the paste into and over the joints with a special trowel or spatula. While the paste is still wet, the finishers press perforated paper tape over the joint and smooth it to imbed it in the joint compound and cover the joint line. On large commercial projects, this pasting-and-taping operation is accomplished in one step with an automatic applicator. When the sealer is dry, the finishers spread another two coats of cementing material over the tape and blend it into the wall to completely conceal

519

the joint. Any cracks, holes, or imperfections in the walls or ceiling are also filled with joint compound, and nail and screw heads are covered. After a final sanding of the patched areas, the surfaces are ready to be painted or papered. Drywall finishers may apply textured surfaces to walls and ceilings with trowels, brushes, rollers, or spray guns.

There are presently around 85,000 drywall installers and finishers in the U.S. Most work for drywall contractors, while others are employed by general contractors.

Requirements

Most employers prefer applicants who have completed high school, although many hire workers who are not graduates. High school or trade school courses in carpentry provide a good background for drywall work. Installers also need to be skilled in arithmetic so that they can easily calculate the number of panels a job requires and efficiently plan the cutting and fitting of pieces so as to minimize waste of materials. Drywall workers should be in good physical condition, able to move their arms about freely and lift the heavy panels.

Most drywall installers and finishers are trained on the job, beginning as helpers aiding experienced workers. Installer helpers start out carrying materials, holding panels, and cleaning up. In a few weeks, they are taught to measure, cut, and install panels. Finisher helpers start out taping joints and sealing nail holes and scratches. In a short time, they learn to install corner guards and to conceal openings around pipes. After they have become skilled workers, both kinds of helpers complete their training by learning how to estimate the costs of installing and finishing drywall.

Some drywall workers learn the trade through apprenticeship programs, which combine classroom study with on-the-job training. A major union in this field, the United Brotherhood of Carpenters and Joiners of America, cooperates with local contractors in offering four-year apprenticeships in carpentry that include instruction in drywall installation. A similar four-year program for nonunion workers is conducted by local affiliates of the Associated Builders and Contractors and the National Association of Home Builders. A two-year apprenticeship program for finishers is run by the International Brotherhood of Painters and Allied Trades.

While union membership is not a requirement for all drywall workers, some installers belong to the United Brotherhood of Carpenters and Joiners of America, and some finishers are members of the International Brotherhood of Painters and Allied Trades.

Opportunities for experience and exploration

High school shop courses that teach basic carpentry and metal-working skills can provide students with an introduction to some of the activities of drywall workers. Perhaps with the help of a teacher or guidance counselor, it may be possible for students to visit a job site and observe installers and finishers at work. Part-time or summer employment as a helper to drywall workers, carpenters, or painters, or even as a laborer on a construction job, is a good way to get some practical experience in this field or related activities.

Methods of entering

People who want to work in this field can start out as on-the-job trainees or as apprentices. Those who plan to learn the trade as they work may apply directly to contracting companies for entry-level jobs as helpers. Good places to look for leads about job openings include the offices of the state employment service, the classified ads section in local newspapers, and the local offices of the major unions in the field. Information about apprenticeship possibilities may be obtained from local contractors or local union offices.

Advancement

Opportunities for advancement are rather limited for people who stay within the trade. Experienced workers who show leadership abilities and good judgment may be promoted to be supervisors of work crews. Sometimes they become cost estimators for contractors. Another option for some people in this field is to open their own drywall contracting business.

Employment outlook

Over the next 10 to 15 years, employment of drywall installers and finishers will probably increase at about the same rate as the average rate for all other occupations. Certainly drywall will continue to be used in many kinds of building construction, and it is expected that the level of construction activity will generally remain strong. Thus future opportunities for drywall workers will reflect a moderate increase in demand for drywall workers, as well as the need to replace workers who leave the occupation.

Jobs will be located throughout the country, although they will be more plentiful in metropolitan areas, where contractors have enough business to hire full-time drywall workers. In small towns, carpenters often handle drywall installation, and painters may do finishing work. Like other construction trades workers, drywall installers and finishers may go through periods of unemployment or part-time employment when the local economy is in a downturn and construction activity slows.

Earnings

The annual earnings of drywall workers vary widely. The majority of workers have earnings that fall roughly between $16,000 and $32,000, with some making significantly more. Installer and finisher trainees generally receive about half the rate earned by experienced workers.

Some drywall workers are paid according to the hours they work; the pay of others is based on how much work they complete. For example, a contractor might pay installers and finishers five to six cents for every square foot of panel installed. The average worker is capable of installing 35 to 40 panels a day, with each panel measuring 4 feet by 12 feet.

Drywall workers normally work a standard workweek of 35 to 40 hours. Construction schedules sometimes require installers and finishers to work longer hours or during evenings or on weekends. Workers who are paid by the hour receive extra pay at these times.

Conditions of work

Drywall installation and finishing can be strenuous work. The large panels are difficult to

handle and frequently require more than one person to maneuver them into position. Workers must spend long hours on their feet, often bending and kneeling. To work high up on walls or on ceilings, workers must stand on stilts, ladders, or scaffolding, risking falls unless they use caution. Another possible hazard is injury from power tools, such as saws and nailers. Because sanding creates a lot of dust, finishers sometimes wear protective masks and safety glasses.

Drywall installation and finishing is indoor work that can be done in any season of the year. Unlike workers in some construction occupations, drywall workers seldom lose time because of adverse weather conditions. However, they may face periods of unemployment between construction projects.

GOE: 05.05.04, 05.10.01; SIC: 15; SOC: 6424

◇ SOURCES OF ADDITIONAL INFORMATION

ABC/Merit Shop Foundation
729 15th Street, NW
Washington, DC 20005

National Joint Painting, Decorating, and Drywall Apprenticeship and Training Committee
1750 New York Avenue, NW, 8th floor
Washington, DC 20006

Canadian Paint and Coatings Association
#103, 9900 Cavendish Boulevard
Ville St. Laurent PQ H4M 2V2

◇ RELATED ARTICLES

Volume 1: Construction
Volumes 2–4: Architectural and building construction technicians; Bricklayers and stonemasons; Carpenters; Cement masons; Lathers; Painters and paperhangers; Plasterers

Ecologists

Definition

Ecologists study relationships between organisms and their environment and how factors such as population size, pollutants, rainfall, and temperature influence them. They seek to understand the implications of environmental problems and prescribe solutions.

History

Ancient Greeks recorded some of the earliest natural history observations, but the term "ecology" was first defined in 1866 by Ernst Haeckel, a German biologist.

Heightened public awareness over humankind's negative effect on the environment has brought ecology out of obscurity over the past 30 years. Although technological advances have improved the quality of life for humans, they also have upset nature's balance by producing air, soil, and water pollution, solid waste and depleted sources of raw materials such as iron and oil.

With technological advancements and an ever-increasing world population, ecological concerns must be tended in order to preserve the environment.

Ecology is just part of a wide scope of careers in the *biological sciences*. All bioscientists deal with living things that grow, develop and respond to the environment in predictable ways.

Nature of the work

Ecologists work to prevent environmental destruction by teaching, research and consulting with private companies and government agencies.

Their work involves preserving cultural, historical, and environmental heritage while determining ecological function and social value. While some ecosystems—functional ecological units such as a forest or a pond—need to be preserved, sometimes artificial ones are developed.

Ecologists use scientific and mathematic models to combine field and laboratory work to develop ecological concepts. They study specific organisms and groups of organisms within their habitats.

In addition to the technical aspects of ecology, ecologists communicate with professionals in other fields such as lawyers, urban planners, and political scientists. They present lectures and programs and write grant proposals.

An ecologists' work has many practical implications for the earth's environment. For example, ecologists prepare environmental impact studies that government agencies often request before building on a particular site. Ecologists may consult with economists and urban planners to develop cost-effective construction projects while raising questions on roadways and dams and how they may affect an environment.

Their duties also may include restoring water quality and purifying waste in a treatment system. An ecologist would attempt to design a natural waste treatment system by creating an ecosystem that restores water quality instead of just treating it.

Ecologists also help tree farmers manage forests so they are healthier, productive, and become less likely to catch fire. They also work to increase farm productivity by studying fertilizers, pesticides, and seed varieties and how they affect crop yield and other living things.

Ecologists help industry comply with government regulations. For example, fishermen may need help increasing their tuna catch without endangering the lives of dolphins. An ecologist would devise ways to do both.

Other careers in bioscience include positions as *biologists*, *geologists*, and *environmental engineers*.

Requirements

A bachelor of science degree is the minimum degree required for nonresearch jobs which include testing and inspection. A master's degree is necessary in applied research or management and for many jobs in inspection, sales and service. A Ph.D. is required to teach at the college level, do independent research, or advance into administrative positions.

Ecologists need a solid background in the sciences including biology, animal physiology, morphology, chemistry and geology.

Opportunities for experience and exploration

High school students should take advantage of science and math courses and seek more information about ecology from guidance counselors and professional ecologists who work at nearby colleges, universities, and government agencies.

Students should also seek volunteer opportunities by contacting groups like The Student Conservation Association of Charlestown, NH, which matches students and volunteer opportunities with government and private agencies.

Methods of entering

A bachelor's degree is sufficient for non-research jobs and positions in testing, inspection or sales and service. Others become medical laboratory technologists and high school biology teachers.

Entry-level ecologists also may take advantage of temporary or seasonal jobs. Such positions allow ecologists to prove themselves and make contact with more experienced scientists who can write recommendations.

Like other biological scientists, ecologists with advanced degrees often begin in research and teaching and advance into managerial positions in biology.

While earning a master's degree or a Ph.D., many ecology majors rely on teaching and research assistantships as their primary source of employment.

Advancement

Mid-level biological scientists may move to advanced managerial positions within biology or nontechnical administrative, sales or managerial jobs.

Ecologists with a Ph.D. may conduct independent research, advance into administrative positions, or teach on the college level, advancing in a university's hierarchy from assistant professor to associate and tenured professorships.

Employment outlook

Environmentally oriented jobs are expected to increase at a faster rate than the average for all occupations through 2005. Most growth will be

Cleaning up after an oil spill makes for dirty work for this ecologist. He will also investigate the effect it has on the environment.

in private industry. As past environmental mistakes are remedied, ecologists studying environmental problems will be in more demand than university-based ecologists. Those with advanced degrees will fare better than ecologists with only a bachelor's degree.

Earnings

Ecologists with a bachelor of science degree can expect to earn between $15,000 to $40,000 a year. Those with a master of science degree can earn between $22,000-$25,000 in entry-level positions up to $60,000 in advanced positions. Ph.D. holders may earn from $45,000 to more than $100,000 a year, depending on duties and level of experience.

Conditions of work

Ecologists work regular hours in offices and laboratories. Some may work with dangerous or toxic substances, and many take field trips involving strenuous physical activity in unusual climates and primitive living conditions. Ecologists should be able to work independently or on a team.

ECONOMISTS

GOE: 02.01.02; SIC: 9511; SOC: 1849

Student Conservation Association
PO Box 550
Charlestown, NH 03603

CEIP Fund
68 Harrison Avenue
Boston, MA 02111-1907

◇ **SOURCES OF ADDITIONAL INFORMATION**

American Institute of Biological Sciences
Office of Career Service
730 11th Street, NW
Washington, DC 20001-4584

Ecological Society of America
Center for Environmental Studies
Arizona State University
Tempe, Arizona 85287-3211

◇ **RELATED ARTICLES**

Economists

Definition

An *economist* is concerned with the solution of economic problems arising from the production and distribution of goods and services in such areas as the use of natural resources and manufactured products. The economist compiles, processes, and interprets economic and statistical data.

History

Economics as a career field is primarily a development of the 20th century, although people have always been concerned with the economic aspects of goods and resources. Economics specialists are needed in business, industry, and government to study problems of the nation's economy. The United States government relies on economists, for example, to provide advice on achieving a healthy economy by adjusting the money supply or manipulating taxes.

Nature of the work

The economist is concerned with a variety of problems, most of which are related to the sup-

ply and demand for goods and services and the means by which these goods are produced, traded, and consumed.

The majority of economists are engaged in college and university teaching and research or as researchers in government agencies. Some economists are employed in nonprofit research organizations.

Economics professors teach courses such as principles of economics, business cycles, history of economic thought, and labor economics. They also write reports, research, lecture, and offer consulting services. They contribute to the formulation of new ideas and economic theory and research the theoretical and practical economic problems of the times.

Government economists develop and conduct studies that collect information on various problem areas. Their data is used to study possible changes in government policies to encourage investments and to assess economic conditions of the country. This data is generally published in government bulletins and reports.

Economists are also employed by business and industrial firms. In such positions they concentrate on studying company policy in relation to general business conditions, national and international trade policies, and government regulations and policies. The results of their studies are used by company management in making financial decisions and for planning the future activities of the business.

Economists tend to specialize in one specific area. Examples of such specialization are noted below.

Agricultural economists study agricultural problems pertaining to use of rural resources and production and marketing of farm products. These studies improve efficiency of farm management, increase farm income, and encourage favorable agricultural legislation. Agricultural economists forecast production and consumption of agricultural products, locate optimum markets, and recommend improvements in agricultural financing.

Financial economists study the nature of and the relationships between the quantity of money, credit, and purchasing power to develop monetary policies and to forecast financial activity. They investigate credit structures and collection methods to improve them. They examine banking methods and procedures to devise techniques for regulation of lending and fixing interest and discount rates. They may recommend or establish domestic and international monetary policies.

International economists collect and analyze statistical data and other information on foreign trade to affect favorable trade balances and to establish acceptable international trade policies. They are concerned with the underlying reasons for trade controls and barriers such as tariffs and cartels. They also study exchange controls and the operation of foreign exchanges to formulate policies on investments and transfer of capital.

Labor economists attempt to forecast labor trends and recommend or establish labor policies on such subjects as labor legislation, social insurance, industrial accident provisions, and similar regulations. They study the operation of labor unions and industrial policies of management and may be called upon to devise techniques for settling labor disputes. They may act as an adviser or consultant to government agencies, business, or industrial organizations.

Industrial economists study the organizational structures of business concerns in relation to production and marketing of goods and services to make maximum use of assets and to develop desirable markets. They investigate methods of financing, production costs and techniques, and marketing policies to discover possible improvements. They analyze market trends to relate production to future consumption and interpret effects of government regulations and legal restrictions on industrial policies.

Many economists teach at universities on the graduate and undergraduate level. In addition to teaching, they often work as consultants on a freelance basis.

Requirements

A bachelor's degree with a major in economics is the minimum preparation for an entry job as an economist. Such positions usually involve research activity with an emphasis on the collection and treatment of study data. In beginning government positions, the candidate must have completed at least 21 semester hours in economics (economic theory, history, methods, and analysis) and three hours of statistics, accounting, or calculus. A master's degree or doctorate in economics is required for teaching positions in colleges and universities. Those who wish to advance to positions in government or industry involving more research opportunity and greater responsibility should plan additional graduate study beyond the bachelor's degree.

Interested high school students should plan to take a college preparatory program, with courses in mathematics and social sciences. A potential economist must be able to analyze and interpret data, reason abstractly and solve problems, and express ideas in speech and in writing.

Opportunities for experience and exploration

High school students can explore their interests and abilities in economics by studying topics in social studies related to economics and mathematics. The college student will find a number of extracurricular activities available that might be useful for exploratory purposes. Actual work opportunities in economics are limited; however, students should be alert to summer and part-time employment opportunities with business or industrial firms and in the field of agriculture.

Methods of entering

The bulletins of the various professional associations in economics are good sources of job opportunities for beginning economists. Each year the federal government has a number of beginning positions for economists. Applicants who can meet the stated qualifications, such as age, training, and experience, can arrange to take the civil service examination that is usually required. People seeking a job should watch for federal and state government announcements concerning open positions.

Advancement

An economist's advancement is dependent on such factors as amount and type of training, experience, personal interest, and drive. Promotion to jobs requiring more skill and competency is available in all specialized areas. Such jobs are characterized by more administrative, research, or advisory responsibilities. consequently, promotions are governed to a great extent by personal evaluation of job performance in the beginning or primary fields of work.

Employment outlook

In the 1990s, about 37,000 economists are employed in private industry and government, and another 22,000 hold faculty positions in economics or marketing at colleges and universities. Most of those in private industry work in economic and market research, management consulting, banking, securities and investments, advertising, and insurance. Most of the economists in government are employed at the federal level, primarily in the Departments of Agriculture, Labor, and State. About 20 percent of all economists own their own consulting firms.

The overall demand for economists is expected to increase rapidly through the end of the 1990s. The greatest growth will be evident in business, with little or no change in federal, state and local government and a decline in the employment of economists in colleges and universities.

Private industry will employ more economists as businesses become more accustomed to relying on scientific methods of analyzing business trends, forecasting sales, and planning purchases and production schedules. The best opportunities appear to be in manufacturing, financial services, advertising, research, and consulting. A number of jobs will be created to satisfy the continued need for economic analyses by lawyers, accountants, engineers, health service administrators, urban and regional planners, environmental scientists, and others.

Because of declining college enrollments, economists with master's degrees and doctorates will face strong competition in the academic field but may find good jobs in business, especially if they are skilled in quantitative techniques and their application to economic modeling and forecasting and market research, including the use of computers. People having only a bachelor's degree will experience great difficulty in finding employment as economists, but they may obtain jobs in related fields as management or sales trainees, or as research or administrative assistants.

The largest concentration of jobs for economists can be found in large cities, especially in New York and Washington, D.C. American economists are also employed in foreign countries by international companies and organizations and by U.S. government agencies.

Earnings

In the 1990s, the average starting salary for economists with a bachelor's degree is about $25,200 a year. The median annual earnings for all full-time economists is $36,800. Salaries are highest for economists in general administration and international economics, and lowest for those in market research and econometrics.

Business economists earn an average salary of $60,000 a year. The highest-paying businesses are securities and investment, retail and wholesale trade, and insurance; the lowest-paying are education, nonprofit research, and real estate.

Federal government positions for beginning economists with a bachelor's degree start at approximately $17,000 to $20,000, depending upon their academic records. Candidates with a master's degree start at approximately $25,700;

with a doctorate, from $31,000 to $37,300, depending on their qualifications. The average salary of experienced economists in federal government positions is about $50,100.

Conditions of work

In general, economists work in offices or classrooms. The average work week of most economists is 40 hours, particularly for those employed in governmental or business positions. The number of hours per day, holiday and vacation leave, and health and pension benefits are similar to those of workers in other organizations.

GOE: 11.03.05; SIC: 8732, 8733, 8748; SOC: 1912

◇ SOURCES OF ADDITIONAL INFORMATION

American Economic Association
2014 Broadway, Suite 305
Nashville, TN 37203

Joint Council on Economic Education
432 Park Avenue, South
New York, NY 10016

National Association of Business Economists
28790 Chagrin Boulevard, Suite 300
Cleveland, OH 44122

Canadian Economics Association
Stephen Leacoch Building
Department of Economics
McGill University
855 Sherbrooke Street, West
Montreal PQ H3A 2T7

◇ RELATED ARTICLES

Volume 1: Accounting; Banking and Financial Services; Civil Service; Education; Foreign Service; Foreign Trade; Law; Marketing
Volumes 2–4: Accountants and auditors; College and university faculty; Marketing research personnel

---

Education directors

Definition

Museums, zoos, and botanical gardens are visited by people who come to learn and observe. *Education directors* are responsible for helping these people enrich their visits. Education directors plan, develop, and administer educational programs at museums and other similar institutions. They plan tours, lectures, and classes for individuals, school groups, and special interest groups. The tours and classes may focus on a specific area of the museum or zoo, or may simply be an introduction or overview.

History

In early times, churches displayed art and furnishings for worshipers to view. The early equivalents of education directors were the priests or lay people who developed expertise in the collections. As public museums grew, so did their need for education directors. When Europeans began to encourage the idea of universal education, museums began to draw in uneducated visitors who needed to be taught about their collections.

Similarly, zoos and arboreta, which were originally organized to exhibit their animals and plants to experts, began to teach others about their collections. Education directors were hired to plan programs and tours for visitors.

In the United States, early museums displayed objects relating to colonial history. Some were in former homes of wealthy colonists and others were established at the first U.S. universities and colleges. In these early museums *curators* or *archivists* maintained the collections and also explained the collections to visitors. As the collections grew and more visitors and

An education director for a zoo demonstrates the techniques for handling an owl to zoo volunteers.

groups of visitors came, education directors were hired by the curators to coordinate educational programs.

Nature of the work

Education directors carry out the educational goals of a museum, zoo, botanical garden, or other similar institution. The educational goals of most of these institutions include nurturing curiosity and answering questions of visitors, regardless of age or background. Education directors work with administrators and museum or zoo boards to determine the scope of their educational programs. Large museums may offer full schedules of classes and tours, while smaller ones may only provide tours or lectures at the request of a school or other group.

Educational resource coordinators work with education directors. They are responsible for the collection of educational materials used in the educational programs. These may include slides, posters, videotapes, books, or materials for special projects.

Education directors plan schedules of courses to be offered through the zoo or mu-

seum. They may hire lecturers from local colleges or universities as well as regular educational staff members to lead tours or discussion groups. Education directors are usually responsible for training the staff members and may also work with professionals or university faculty to determine the content of a particular lecture, class, or series of lectures. They prepare course outlines and establish the credentials necessary for those who will teach the courses.

In smaller institutions the education director may do much of the teaching, lecturing, or tour leading. In zoos, the education director can arrange for small children to watch cows being milked or for the children to pet or feed such smaller animals as goats. In museums, the education director's job often depends on the museum's collection. In art museums, visitors are often older than in natural history museums, and the education director may plan programs that allow older children to explore parts of the collection at their own pace.

Education directors often promote their programs on local radio, television, or in newspapers. They may speak to community or school groups about the museum's education department and encourage the groups to attend. Sometimes education directors deliver lectures or offer classes away from the museum or zoo. Educational resource directors may then prepare slide shows or video presentations for follow-up.

The education director is responsible for the budget for all educational programs. Directors prepare budgets and supervise the records of income and spending. Often, schools or other groups are charged lower rates for tours or classes at museums or zoos. Education directors work with resource coordinators to establish budgets for resource materials. These need to be updated regularly in most institutions. Even in natural history museums, where the collections may change less than in other museums, slide collections may need to be updated or presentations altered if new research has led to different interpretations of the objects. The education director may also prepare grant proposals or help with fund-raising efforts for the museum's educational program. Once a grant has been received, or a large gift has been offered to the education department, the education director plans for the best use of the funds within the department.

Education directors train their staff members as well as volunteers to work with individual visitors and groups. Some volunteers may be trained to assist in presentations or to help large groups on tours. It is the responsibility of the educational director to see that the educational program is helpful and interesting to all of the various people who visit the museum or zoo. Education directors also evaluate the performance of their staff members and volunteers. They often arrange for vacations, leaves, or raises for the education department personnel. They also may advise staff members on the best educational path to follow in order to become education directors themselves. At a botanical garden, for instance, the education director may suggest certain courses in botany or biology to a volunteer who is starting college.

Special activities planned by educational directors vary widely depending on the institution. Film programs, field trips, lectures, and full-day school programs may be offered weekly, monthly, or annually. Some zoos and arboreta have ongoing tours offered daily, while others may only give tours for prearranged groups.

Educational resource coordinators prepare, buy, catalog, and maintain all of the materials used by the education department. They sometimes have a lending library of films, videos, books, or slides that people may borrow. Resource coordinators keep track of circulation of materials. They may also lead tours or workshops for educators or school personnel to teach them about the collection of the museum or zoo and to keep them apprised of new materials the educators may use in their tours or in their own classrooms. Resource coordinators and directors both attend conventions and teachers' meetings to promote their institution's educational program and to encourage participation in their classes or tours.

Education directors often work with exhibit designers to help create displays that are most effective for visitors. They may also work with illustrators to produce illustrations or signs that enhance exhibits. Zoos, for example, often display maps near the animals to show their countries of origin.

Requirements

Education directors must have a bachelor's degree. Many museums, zoos, and botanical gardens also require a master's degree. The largest zoos and museums prefer to hire education directors who have doctorate degrees. Most education directors work in museums that specialize in art, history, or science. These directors often have degrees in fields related to the museum's specialty. Those who work in zoos usually have studied biology or zoology or have worked closely with animals. Education directors who work in more specialized museums often have studied such specialized fields as early American art, woodcarvings, or the history of circuses. All education directors must have a good working knowledge of the animals, plants, or artifacts in their collection.

Opportunities for experience and exploration

Volunteer experience for students interested in becoming education directors is easy to obtain. Most zoos and museums have student volunteers. High school students can request a position in the education department. They may help with grade school tours, organize files or audio-visual materials, or assist a lecturer in a class.

College-preparatory courses are important for students interested in the field. They should apply to colleges or universities with strong liberal arts programs. Courses in art, history, science, and education are recommended for those who want to work at museums, and courses in biology, zoology, botany, and education for those who wish to work at zoos or botanical gardens. Some larger zoos and museums offer internships to college students who are interested in the field.

The American Association of Museums publishes an annual museum directory, a monthly magazine, and a bimonthly magazine. It also published *Museum Careers: A Variety of Vocations, Resource Report 2, Part 1*, in 1988. This report is helpful for anyone considering a career in the museum field. There is also an *Introduction to Museum Work* by George Ellis Burcaw, published in 1983 by the American Association for State and Local History, which discusses the educational programs at various museums.

Methods of entering

Students who wish to become education directors must first go to college and get a bachelor's degree. Their first job in a museum or zoo is usually as a teacher or resource coordinator working in the education department. With a few years of experience and improved understanding of the institution's collection, they may enter competition for promotion to education director. Many people in the field transfer from one museum to another, or from one zoo to another, in order to be promoted to the position of education director.

Advancement

Once in the education department most people learn much of their work on the job. Experience in working with different people and groups becomes very important. Education directors must continually improve their understanding of their own institution's collection so that they can present it to school and other groups in the best way possible. Some education directors work for the federal government in specific subject areas such as aeronautics, philately, or science and technology. They must be proficient in these fields as well as in education.

After two to four years in the education department, depending on the institution, most museums and zoos allow people to apply for education director positions. Some require advanced degrees first. Others only require proficiency in the collection and proven ability to coordinate educational programs.

Employment outlook

The employment outlook for education directors is expected to increase more slowly than average through the year 2000. Budget cutbacks have affected many museums and other cultural institutions, which have in turn reduced the size of their education departments. Many educators with specialties in sciences, the arts, or zoology, are interested in becoming education directors at museums and zoos. Competition is especially keen for positions in large cities and those with more prestigious reputations. Some smaller museums and botanical gardens may cut out their education director position altogether until the economic climate improves, or they may get by with part-time education directors.

Earnings

Salaries for education directors vary widely depending on the size and type of the institution and on the education and experience of the director. The average beginning salary for educational directors with bachelor's degrees is $15,700. Those with master's degrees earn starting salaries of $23,000. In general, the average salaries for education directors are from $20,000 to $53,000 annually. Some larger or better-funded zoos and museums pay significantly more, and some hire part-time education directors who may earn as little as $6,000 annually.

Conditions of work

Most people who choose to be education directors like to be in museums, botanical gardens, or zoos. They also enjoy teaching and working with students. Those in zoos usually enjoy animals and like being outdoors. Those in museums probably like the fascinating surroundings —the quiet of a natural history museum or the energy and life of a science museum aimed at children.

Vacation time and hours vary widely depending on the museum or zoo. Larger institutions often have stricter policies about hours than do smaller museums or zoos, but they may be more flexible with sick days or other holidays since they have larger staffs to work with. The salary and prestige level of an education director makes it an attractive career, and many people who enjoy academic environments thrive in the position of education director.

GOE: 11.07.03; SIC: none; SOC: 1283

Association of American Archivists
600 South Federal Street, Suite 504
Chicago, IL 60605

◇ **Sources of additional information**

**American Association of Botanical
Gardens and Arboreta**
786 Church Road
Wayne, PA 19087

American Association of Museums
1225 I Street, NW, Suite 200
Washington, DC 20005

**American Association of Zoological Parks
and Aquariums**
Route 88, Oglebay Park
Wheeling, WV 26003

◇ **Related Articles**

Volume 1: Education; Museums and Cultural
Centers
Volumes 2–4: Archivists; College and University faculty; Librarians; Museum curators; Museum directors; Museum teachers; Naturalists; Teachers, secondary school; Zoo and aquarium curators and directors

Electric-sign repairers

Definition

Electric-sign repairers inspect, maintain, and repair neon and other illuminated signs. They do both minor repairs at the site and major repairs in a shop. Repairers test the signs' operation, replace defective parts, repair transformers and structural damage, and sometimes install new signs.

History

Electric signs have long been used by businesses as an attention-getting device to advertise products and services. Early illuminated signs were often merely painted wooden panels topped or surrounded by light bulbs. Today's signs are much more sophisticated and colorful and come in a wide variety of styles and designs. Simpler signs may be made from plastic and lit from within, while other signs are complex animated displays made of glass tubing bent into shapes and filled with gases that can be made to glow. The most familiar of these gases is neon, which produces a reddish-orange light when an electric current is passed through it. Other colors can be produced by adding small quantities of other gases, such as argon, krypton, xenon, helium, and mercury vapor. The term "neon lights" is used to refer to signs of this general type, regardless of color.

Because the purpose of electric signs is to attract favorable attention, it is important that they be kept in good condition. Malfunctioning signs create a poor impression and must be repaired promptly. This work is the responsibility of electric-sign repairers.

Nature of the work

Many shops, restaurants, and other businesses depend on electric signs to advertise their products or services. If a sign doesn't function properly, it doesn't appeal to customers and may even cause the business to lose revenue. Whether the problem is a simple burned-out bulb or a major breakdown, the sign's owner requests a service call from an electric-sign repair shop and expects prompt attention.

Repairers drive to the location in trucks equipped with ladders and boom cranes so that they can reach signs high above the ground.

An electric sign repairer replaces the burned-out bulbs on a clock.

They carry a supply of replacement parts; a variety of hand and power tools, such as screwdrivers, pliers, saws, and drills; and electric testing devices, including ammeters and voltmeters. The repairers inspect and test the sign to determine the cause of the malfunction. Easy repairs, such as replacing burned-out bulbs and transformers and installing new wiring, can be made at the site. Major repairs, such as replacing broken glass tubing, may require that the repairers remove the entire sign and take it to the shop. To replace some burned-out parts, such as flashers in illuminated plastic signs, repairers may have to refer to wiring diagrams and charts.

When the job is completed, repairers usually have to fill out a report that includes the date, location, and nature of the service call. They sometimes estimate the cost of service calls and may sell maintenance contracts to sign owners.

Electric signs are often covered by service contracts. To prevent breakdowns and to keep the signs operating at peak efficiency, repairers inspect them on a regular schedule. They clear away any debris or water that may have accumulated on or inside the sign; tighten or weld parts that the wind may have loosened; and check, adjust, and lubricate motors, gears, bearings, and other parts of revolving signs. They also repaint beams, columns, other framework, and sometimes segments of the neon tubing so that distinct letters appear clearly to people reading the sign.

In some large cities, *night-patrol inspectors* drive a scheduled route in a company car, checking on the appearance and operation of illuminated and animated signs that their company has under service contract. They may do minor repairs, such as changing light bulbs, but generally they report faults to the service department so repairers may be sent out the next day to correct the problems.

Most sign repairers work for small shops that custom-build, install, and service electric signs and advertising displays. A smaller number of repairers work for firms that specialize either in manufacturing signs or in installation and maintenance. Some repairers who work for sign manufacturers help assemble new signs during periods when there are few service calls to make. Employees of large sign companies may specialize in one type of sign work and be designated *sign electricians, neon-tube benders, sign sheet-metal workers,* or *plastic-sign fabricators.*

Neon-tube pumpers charge illuminated-sign tubing with gases. They attach the glass tubing to a vacuum pump unit to remove air, then bombard the tubing with high-voltage electric current to eliminate any gaseous impurities. After the tubing has been properly prepared, the pumpers connect it to gas bottles and fill it with various amounts of neon, argon, helium, krypton, xenon, and mercury vapor, depending on the color desired. Finally, they test the sign and seal the tubing. Pumpers may also paint or tape out parts of the tubing to separate the letters, words, or symbols that make up the sign.

Requirements

Employers generally prefer to hire high school or vocational school graduates, although some may hire applicants who are not graduates. Among the courses that high school students who are considering this occupation should take are applied mathematics, electronics, electrical shop, and blueprint reading.

Electric-sign repairers may learn their skills in one of two ways: through informal on-the-job training or through apprenticeship programs. Most repairers start as trainees, performing basic tasks under the guidance of experienced workers. Beginners work in the shop learning to cut and assemble metal and plastic signs, mount neon tubing, wire signs, and install electric parts. After they master sign construction, they can accompany skilled repairers on service calls and learn repair and maintenance techniques. To become a fully qualified repairer may take at least four years of training and experience.

Apprenticeship programs also usually last four years. Sign repairer or electrician apprenticeships are conducted cooperatively by union locals and sign manufacturing shops. The programs combine on-the-job training with formal classroom instruction in such subjects as electricity theory and blueprint reading. To be eligible for apprenticeships, applicants must be at least 18 years old and have a high school diploma. Through the joint efforts of unions and the National Electric Sign Association, more apprenticeship programs should become available in the future for young people interested in this type of training.

Good color vision is important for sign repairers, because electric wires are frequently identified by color. Handling tools requires manual dexterity, and lifting transformers and other heavy equipment calls for physical strength. Repairers should not be afraid of heights, because they do much of their work while standing on ladders or from the baskets of boom trucks.

Many electric-sign repairers are union members. Unions that may represent workers in this occupation include the International Brotherhood of Electrical Workers, the Sheet Metal Workers' International Association, and the International Brotherhood of Painters and Allied Trades.

Special requirements

All electric-sign repairers must have a knowledge of the National Electric Code. In addition, many states require that repairers be licensed. To obtain a license, they must pass an examination testing their knowledge of local electric codes and electrical theory.

Opportunities for experience and exploration

High school students can begin to learn about some of the activities of workers in this field by taking such courses as electrical shop. Perhaps with the help of a teacher or guidance counselor, they may be able to arrange to visit a local sign manufacturing shop and observe repairers on the job.

Assembling electronic kits can be a good way for people to gauge their interest in and aptitude for this work. A part-time or summer job in a shop or business that handles electrical work could also be a useful experience.

Methods of entering

Recent graduates may be able to find job leads through their school's placement office. The classified advertising sections in newspapers may provide further ideas. Other information about employment opportunities and apprenticeship programs can be found through the local office of the state employment service or locals of the appropriate unions. It is also possible to apply directly to area sign manufacturing companies that seem likely to be potential employers.

Advancement

Opportunities for promotion are limited for electric-sign repairers who stay within the occupation. Skilled repairers with leadership abilities may become supervisors. Those who are experienced in dealing with customers may become sales representatives for sign manufacturers. Some repairers establish their own sign manufacturing or repair shops.

Employment outlook

There are presently around 18,000 persons employed as sign repairers in the United States. Over the next 10 to 15 years, employment in this field is expected to rise about as fast as the average for all occupations. The demand for electric signs will probably increase somewhat as more new businesses open and existing businesses modernize in order to try to keep up with the competition. In any case, the new signs and all the signs already in use will need regular maintenance if they are to remain functional and attractive.

Many of the new job openings that occur each year will be because experienced workers are changing occupations or leaving the labor force. Overall, opportunities will be best in large metropolitan areas, where electric signs are more plentiful.

Although this occupational field is sensitive to changes in the economy, sign repairers rarely suffer major layoffs. Occasionally, a downswing in the economy reduces the demand for new signs. When this occurs, sign companies usually shift their emphasis to maintenance work and thus are able to keep most workers employed.

Earnings

A survey of union wages and fringe benefits indicates that electric-sign repairers have earnings that compare favorably with those of other skilled workers. In the 1990s, experienced repairers are paid around $27,000 annually, on average.

Repairers generally work a five-day, 40-hour week and are paid extra for overtime. In addition, they may receive premium pay if they work at heights above 30 feet.

Conditions of work

Because most signs are situated outdoors, repairers are exposed to all kinds of weather in the course of doing their job. Emergency repairs may have to be made at night or on weekends or holidays. Repairers spend a lot of time traveling to the various locations of the signs they service.

Anyone who works with electricity, including electric-sign repairers, needs to use caution in order to avoid shocks and burns. Another possible hazard is falling, because many signs are installed in high places. Such accidents do not happen frequently, however, because employers have instituted training programs to make their repairers aware of the need to follow good safety practices. Special equipment, such as baskets on boom trucks, has been developed to allow easier, safer access to signs.

GOE: 05.05.10; SIC: 3993; SOC: 6159

◇ **SOURCES OF ADDITIONAL INFORMATION**

International Brotherhood of Electrical Workers
1125 15th Street, NW
Washington, DC 20005

National Electric Sign Association
801 North Fairfax Street, Suite 205
Alexandria, VA 22314

◇ **RELATED ARTICLES**

Volume 1: Construction; Electronics
Volumes 2–4: Appliance repairers; Electrical repairers; Electrical technicians; Electricians

Electrical and electronics engineers

Definition

Electrical and electronics engineering are branches of science centered around the study of the elementary particles, tinier than the atom, that make up all common matter—electrons. This field is enormously diverse, involving all aspects of the production, transmission, and utilization of electric power. *Electrical engineers* apply their knowledge of the sciences toward working with high-power electric generation, such as for lighting and heating homes and powering factories. *Electronics engineers* are more concerned with low-power engineering involved with communications. Some low-power engineering applications include computers, telephones, and radios.

History

Although many endeavors roughly considered as general engineering can be traced back thousands of years, electrical and electronics engineering weren't really born until the 19th century. Previous to that time, experiments and ideas in magnetism and static electricity were considered more as curiosities than as serious scientific endeavors.

In 1800, Alexander Volta made a discovery that opened a door to the science of electricity—he found that electric current could be harnessed and made to flow. By the mid-1800s the basic rules of electricity were established, and the first practical applications appeared. At that time, Michael Faraday discovered the phenomenon of electromagnetic induction. Further discoveries followed one after the other. In 1837 Samuel Morse invented the telegraph; in 1876 Alexander Graham Bell invented the telephone; the incandescent lamp (the light bulb) was invented by Thomas Edison in 1878; and the first electric motor was invented by Nicholas Tesla in 1888 (Faraday had built a primitive model of one in 1821). These inventions required the further generation and harnessing of electricity, and so efforts were concentrated on developing ways to produce more and more power and to create better equipment such as motors and transformers.

Edison's invention led to a dependence on electricity for lighting our homes, work areas, and streets. He later created the phonograph and other electrical instruments, which led to the establishment of his General Electric Company. One of today's major telephone companies also had its beginnings during this time— Alexander Bell's invention led to the establishment of the Bell Telephone Company, which eventually became American Telephone and Telegraph (AT&T).

Electronics engineering can be considered a branch of electrical engineering. The roots of electronics, which is distinguished from the science of electricity by its focus on lower power generation, can also be found in the 19th century. In the late 1800s, current moving through space was observed for the first time; this was the "Edison effect." In the early 20th century, devices (such as vacuum tubes, which are pieces of metal inside a glass bulb) were invented that could transmit weak electrical signals, leading to the potential transmission of electromagnetic waves for communication— radio broadcast.

Electronics today is dominated by applications for such devices as transistors, semiconductor diodes, and integrated circuits (microchips). The unreliability of vacuum tubes led to the invention of equipment that was more solid; hence transistors came to be known as "solid-state" devices. In the 1960s, transistors were being built on tiny bits of silicon and became known as microchips. The computer industry is a major beneficiary of the creation of these circuits, because vast amounts of information can be stored on just one tiny chip smaller than a dime.

Nature of the work

Because electrical and electronics engineering is such a diverse field, there are numerous divisions and departments within which engineers work. The discipline reaches nearly every other

This systems engineer operates a software program in search of design flaws.

field of applied science and technology. In general, electrical and electronics engineers use their knowledge of the sciences in the practical applications of electrical energy. They concern themselves with things as large as atom smashers and as small as microchips. They are involved in the invention, design, construction, and operation of electrical and electronic systems and devices of all kinds.

The work of electrical/electronics engineers touches almost every niche of our lives. Think of the things that have been designed, manufactured, maintained, or in any other way affected by electrical energy: the lights in a room; cars on the road; televisions, stereo systems, telephones; your doctor's blood-pressure reader; computers. Look around you and discover that the electrical engineer has in some way had a hand in science, industry, commerce, entertainment, even art.

The list of specialties that engineers are associated with reads like an alphabet of scientific titles—from Acoustics, Speech, and Signal Processing; to Electromagnetic Compatibility; Geoscience and Remote Sensing; Microwave Theory and Techniques; Quantum Electronics; Ultrasonics, Ferroelectrics, and Frequency Control; to Vehicular Technology. As evident in this selected list, engineers are apt to specialize in what interests them, such as communications, quantum mechanics, or automobiles.

As mentioned earlier, electrical engineers focus on high-power generation of electricity— how it is transmitted for use in lighting homes and powering factories. They are also concerned with how equipment is designed and maintained and how communications are transmitted over wire. Some are involved in the design and construction of power plants and the manufacture and maintenance of industrial machinery.

Electronics engineers work with smaller-scale applications—for example, how computers are wired, how appliances work, how electrical circuits are used in an endless number of applications. They may specialize in computers, industrial equipment and controls, and medical equipment.

In both divisions of the field, there are a number of categories in which workers find their niche: research, development and design, production, field service, sales and marketing, and teaching. In addition, even within each category there are divisions of labor.

Researchers concern themselves mainly with issues that pertain to potential applications. They conduct tests and perform studies to evaluate fundamental problems involving such things as new materials and chemical interactions. Those who work in design and development adapt the researchers' findings to actual practical applications. They devise functioning devices and draw up plans for their efficient production, using computer-aided design and engineering (CAD/CAE) tools. For a typical product such as a television, this phase usually takes up to 18 months to accomplish.

Production engineers have perhaps the most hands-on tasks in the field. They are responsible for the organization of the actual manufacture of whatever electric product is being made. They take care of materials and machinery, schedule assembly workers, and make sure that standards are met and products are quality-controlled. These engineers must have access to the best tools for measurement, materials handling, and processing.

After electrical systems are put in place, field service engineers must act as the liaison between the manufacturer or distributor and the client. They ensure the correct installation, operation, and maintenance of systems and products for both industry and individuals. In the sales and marketing divisions, engineers stay abreast of customer needs in order to evaluate potential applications, and they advise their companies of orders and effective marketing. A sales engineer would contact a client interested in, say, a certain type of microchip for its automobile electrical system controls. He would learn about the client's needs and report back to the various engineering teams at his company. During the manufacture and distribution of the product, the sales engineer would continue to provide information back and forth

between company and client until all objectives were met.

All engineers must be taught to be engineers, and so it is important that some remain involved in academia. Professors usually teach a portion of the basic engineering courses as well as classes in the subjects that they are specialized in. Conducting personal research is generally an ongoing task for professors in addition to the supervision of student work and student research. A part of the teacher's time is also devoted to providing career and academic guidance to students.

Requirements

Electrical and electronics engineers must have a solid educational background. The discipline is based on much in the applied sciences but requires a clear understanding of practical applications. To prepare for college, high school students should focus on mathematics, the physical sciences, computer science, and English and the humanities. It is recommended that students aim for honors-level courses.

A bachelor's degree in electrical engineering or another related science is generally required for professional positions. Many go on to receive a master's degree in a specialization of their choice; often these graduate-level courses are taken on a part-time basis while the student is employed. A doctorate is usually required in order to teach as a member of an engineering faculty; it is increasingly being required for research jobs as well.

By the time one reaches college, it is wise to be considering what specialty and position one might want to work in. In addition to the core engineering curriculum (mathematics, sciences, mechanical drawing, computer applications), students will begin to choose from the following types of courses: circuits and electronics; signals and systems; digital electronics and computer architecture; electromagnetic waves, systems, and machinery; communications; and statistical mechanics.

Opportunities for experience and exploration

Those who are interested in the excitement of electricity should tackle experiments such as building a radio or central processing unit of a computer. Special assignments can also be researched and supervised by teachers. It is a good idea to join a science club, such as the Junior Engineering Technical Society. Student members can join competitions and design structures that exhibit scientific know-how. The *JETS Report* is one type of journal that students should read; it includes articles on engineering-related careers and club activities.

One ideal way for high school students to learn more about electrical and electronics engineering is to attend a summer camp or academic program that focuses on scientific projects as well as recreational activities. For instance, the Delphi School in Oregon holds summer sessions where like-minded students are involved in leadership activities and special interests such as computers and electronics. Sports and wilderness activities are also offered. Summer programs such as the one offered by the Michigan Technological University focus on career exploration in computers, electronics, and robotics. This academic program for high school students also offers arts guidance, wilderness events, and other recreational activities. Often there are jobs available during these sessions for college students who are at least 19 years old. (For further information on clubs and programs, write to the addresses listed at the end of this article.)

Methods of entering

Most electrical/electronics engineers work in industry, such as with design and manufacturing firms or consulting agencies. Others work for the federal government; as teachers in engineering schools and programs; and in research. Some work as private consultants.

In each division of engineering—research, design and development, production, field service, sales and marketing, and teaching—there tends to be a hierarchy of workers. In an entry-level job, one is considered basically an engineer. After experience is gained, one can move on to become a project engineer and then a managing engineer; these positions involve supervising teams of engineers and making sure that they are working together efficiently. At the top of the hierarchy one is called a chief engineer; this position involves authority over project and managing engineers.

There is a change in the type of responsibility that engineers have as they move up the career ladder. As an engineer, one is concerned with technical matters and scientific problem solving; as a chief, one is responsible for matters such as management, scheduling, cost analysis, and client relations.

Advancement

As in any engineering field, people working in electricity and electronics must keep pace with technological changes, which occur rapidly in our society. Those who specialize in defense-related projects, for example, should be skilled in additional areas because of the expected cutbacks in the defense industry. Those who do not continue to learn what's new in the engineering field are more likely not to receive promotions.

Many professional electrical/electronics engineers, after having worked many years in the field, leave the electric industry to seek top-level management positions with other types of firms. Many leave to set up their own firms in design or consulting. Others change their focus and become teachers at high schools or universities.

Employment outlook

More engineers work in the electrical and electronics field than in any other division of engineering. In the United States, there were 426,000 such engineers holding jobs in the industry in 1990. Most work in manufacturing companies that produce electrical and electronic equipment, business machines, scientific equipment, and aircraft parts. Others work for computer and data processing companies, consulting firms, public utilities, and government agencies.

Although general unemployment is relatively high in 1992, growth in the computer and communications industries is expected to create a continual demand for electrical and electronics engineers. Further demand for household electrical goods will also create jobs, as will increased research and development on robots and other types of automation. Opportunities are expected to increase through the year 2005.

Moreover, as our country continues to compete on a global level, awareness has been focused on the continued advancement of technological change. For especially astute engineers with creative and effective ideas, the end of the 20th century may prove a ripe time for new applications to be discovered and put to use, such as high-speed electric commuter trains and artificial intelligence circuitry. However, engineers working in the defense industry should expect to face layoffs and decreasing opportunities because of anticipated cutbacks in government defense spending.

Earnings

Starting salaries for all engineers are generally much higher than for workers in any other field. Electrical and electronics engineers earn salaries about halfway between those of petroleum engineers and civil engineers. Entry-level electrical engineers with a bachelor's degree earn an average of $31,700 in private industry. After several years in the field, an engineer earns about $39,000. Those with doctorates earn about $51,000 about five years after receiving their Ph.D.

Conditions of work

Five-day, 40-hour weeks are the norm for electrical/electronics engineers. As in any occupation, however, there are often situations that require overtime.

Researchers often work in labs that are equipped with the instruments they need to conduct experiments. Designers are generally found at drawing tables and computer workstations. Production engineers usually work at the manufacturing facilities, unless they are involved in management, in which case they would be found at their desks in office environments. Engineers involved in field service and sales, in contrast, are often on the road, traveling to and meeting with clients.

Those who are professors have a range of working environments; they spend part of their time teaching in classrooms, part of it doing research either in labs or libraries, and some of the time still connected with industry.

GOE: 05.01.08; SIC: 8711; SOC: 1633

◇ **SOURCES OF ADDITIONAL INFORMATION**

The Delphi School
20950 SW Rock Creek Road
Sheridan, OR 97378

Institute of Electrical and Electronics Engineers (IEEE)
345 East 47th Street
New York, NY 10017

Junior Engineering Technical Society
1420 King Street, Suite 405
Alexandria, VA 22314

Michigan Technological University Summer Youth Program
Youth Programs Office, 1400 Townsend Drive
Houghton, MI 49931

◇ **RELATED ARTICLES**

Volume 1: Computer Hardware; Electronics **Volumes 2–4:** Appliance repairers; College and university faculty; Electrical repairers; Electrical technicians; Electricians; Electronics sales and service technicians; Electronics technicians; Instrumentation technicians; Line installers and cable splicers; Microelectronics technicians; Power plant occupations; Robotics technicians; Telecommunications technicians

◤ Electrical repairers

Definition

Electrical repairers, often called *maintenance electricians*, keep many different types of electrical equipment, machines, and circuits in good working order, principally by carrying out routine service procedures and finding and correcting problems in electrical systems before costly breakdowns occur.

History

The most important workhorse in the modern world is the electron, the lightest known subatomic particle and the most basic unit of electricity. When pushed and pulled through coils of wire, electrons can interact with magnetic fields to do work. The electric current that we use every day is essentially the result of the buildup in one place or the movement from one place to another of vast numbers of electrons.

When we push a button to turn on a light bulb or a complex piece of machinery, we are controlling a phenomenon that was first observed more than 2,500 years ago. Around that time, the ancient Greeks discovered that when a certain naturally occurring substance, amber, is rubbed with fur, it picks up bits of light materials like feathers. They assumed that the amber possessed an unknown force. (The Greek word for amber is "elektron".) For many hundreds of years, little was understood about that force, which we know today as electricity.

By the 18th century, people were seriously studying various forms of electricity. Their experiments led to some practical progress. Among the era's most important work was that done by Alessandro Volta, an Italian physicist who in 1800 created the first electric battery that could provide a continuous source of electric current.

Many other experimenters also contributed to the knowledge that has made possible the electrical devices and machines in our lives. A few of their names are Benjamin Franklin, Andre-Marie Ampere, Michael Faraday, James Clerk Maxwell, Nikola Tesla, and Thomas Edison.

By the end of the 19th century, enough was understood that modern uses of electricity began to be possible. Electric motors that resembled modern motors were developed and put in commercially successful machines. As more and more practical applications for electricity were developed, it became clear that electrical equipment needed regular servicing to continue operating properly. Electrical repairers, or maintenance electricians, are the workers who perform this vital function today.

Nature of the work

Maintenance electricians are responsible for maintaining safe, reliable, uninterrupted service of existing electrical equipment. They do tasks like routine cleaning of equipment, making minor adjustments, troubleshooting, and carrying out emergency repairs. They replace fuses, switches, circuit breakers, wiring, electronic components, and other elements that are worn or burned out. Like electricians involved in construction, they may also plan circuit layouts and wire new installations, particularly when a major overhaul, replacement, or addition to existing equipment is necessary.

Maintenance electricians often work for one organization, and their activities vary some-

A maintenance electrician rewires a prefabricated locomotive electrical cabinet for Santa Fe Railways.

what with the kind of organization. For example, electrical repairers who are employed in a large factory may repair motors, transformers, generators, and controllers on machine tools. In some settings, they may specialize in one particular kind of equipment, such as industrial robots. If they are employed in a smaller organization, such as an office building or a small manufacturing plant, they may work on a wide variety of electrical equipment, from lighting to security systems and time clocks. Sometimes maintenance electricians repair mechanical, hydraulic, or pneumatic parts of electrical equipment, in addition to the electrical components.

A major focus of the work of maintenance electricians is preventing trouble in electrical systems before it happens, so as to prevent inconvenience and expense to their employer. For this reason, maintenance electricians often inspect and service equipment according to a predetermined schedule. If something malfunctions anyway, they are supposed to diagnose and repair the problem quickly and efficiently in order to minimize the impact of the malfunction. In more serious emergency situations, they must be able to provide good estimates of how much time and resources will be needed to complete repairs, how dangerous the problem is, and whether other operations in the building need to be shut down.

In doing their work, maintenance electricians use instruments and test equipment such as test lamps, ammeters, volt meters, ohm meters, and oscilloscopes. They use hand and power tools like pliers, wrenches, screwdrivers, and drills. They need to read blueprints and wiring diagrams, make mathematical calculations, and splice, solder, cut, bend, measure, and install wire and conduit.

Requirements

Although the best way of becoming a maintenance electrician is to complete a formal apprenticeship for electricians, some people learn this trade informally on the job. They often start with only a little knowledge of the field and work as helpers to experienced electricians. Gradually they pick up skills as opportunities for learning arise during their work. Some helpers receive a variety of assignments and thus develop a range of skills, but others learn how to do relatively few kinds of tasks. People in such jobs may want to round out their training with courses at trade schools or correspondence courses in order to become qualified as maintenance electricians.

Apprenticeship programs usually provide much more comprehensive training. The programs are planned to cover a broad range of topics that well qualified electricians need to know. Because of the completeness of their training, maintenance electricians who have learned their skills in an apprenticeship are more likely to get the better jobs available in the field.

Apprenticeships are operated by joint union-management groups and by local chapters of contractor associations. They last four to five years and provide a combination of supervised practical job experience and formal classroom instruction in related subjects. During their on-the-job training, apprentices begin with easy tasks, then progress to activities that draw on their growing understanding of electrical systems. In the classroom, apprentices study such subjects as blueprint reading, electronics, job safety practices, first aid, and national and local electrical codes (the statements of basic standards that electrical installations are required to meet).

Many maintenance electricians are members of unions, including the International Brotherhood of Electrical Workers; the International Union of Electronic, Electrical, Salaried, Machine, and Furniture Workers; the International Association of Machinists and Aerospace Workers; and other unions.

A good background for anyone interested in entering this field includes high school courses such as electronics, electrical shop, applied mathematics, and mechanical drawing. Electronics is especially important for maintenance electricians, and students should try to take any available courses that introduce this field. Training in a technical school or in the Armed Forces can be very helpful. Applicants for apprenticeships usually need to be high school graduates and at least 18 years old.

Maintenance electricians need to have good color vision, because they must be able to identify wires of different colors. They should be in good health, agile, and have at least average strength. They also need manual dexterity and mechanical aptitude.

Maintenance electricians must be familiar with the National Electric Code and local electric and building codes. From time to time they need to take courses that update them on code changes or on new methods and materials that they will be using on the job. Courses that improve skills are often arranged by employers or sponsored by labor unions.

Special requirements

In many areas, these workers may need to meet some local licensure requirement. Obtaining a license usually involves passing an examination that covers electrical theory and national and local codes.

Opportunities for experience and exploration

A good way to learn first-hand about the work that maintenance electricians do is to obtain summer or part-time employment as a helper to an electrician. Even if the job seems menial and the pay is low, the experience is valuable. If a job is not available, it may be possible to visit a workplace where maintenance electricians are employed and talk with them about their work. Another way of testing aptitude and interest in this field is to take electrical shop or other high school courses that provide a hands-on experience of some of the work activities. Tinkering with or repairing electric motors, assembling ham radio kits, or working on similar equipment can also be a way of learning some of the skills electricians need.

Methods of entering

Most electrical repairers apply for apprenticeships through a union or through a local firm that employs maintenance electricians. The state employment service office is also a good resource to contact for information about training opportunities.

People who plan to learn the trade informally as they work may be able to locate openings for electrician's helpers through standard sources for job listings, such as newspaper classified ads and the state employment service. Graduates of vocational or technical schools can usually get help in finding jobs through their school's placement office.

Advancement

Experienced electrical repairers have several possible routes of advancement. They can become supervisors, overseeing the work of other electrical repairers, and eventually some can be promoted to plant maintenance superintendent. Or they may become expert in certain specialty maintenance and repair tasks, such as servicing the intricate control mechanisms on complex industrial machinery. With a good training background, such as that gained in an apprenticeship, they may have the option of moving into related fields that also employ electricians. For example, they may work as construction electricians, as sales or service representatives for electric utility companies, or as electrical inspectors for municipalities, determining whether electrical work conforms to code requirements. With appropriate additional training, they may become estimators for electrical contracting firms, charged with figuring the costs for doing work before it is done. Some maintenance electricians decide to go into business for themselves as independent electrical contractors.

Employment outlook

Electrical repairers are employed in every part of the country, with concentrations in the heavily industrialized states of California, New York, Pennsylvania, Illinois, and Ohio. Many work in manufacturing plants, especially where metal products, transportation equipment, chemical and allied products, and electrical and nonelectrical machinery are made. Others work in the transportation industry, communications and public utilities, mines, and wholesale and retail trade establishments.

Over the next 10 to 15 years, employment in this field is expected to increase at a faster rate than the average for all occupations. Much of this demand will be related to the need to maintain the growing amount of electrical equipment used in American business and industry. In addition, openings will always be developing as workers transfer to other positions or leave the labor force altogether.

Employment in some industries, such as automobile manufacturing, is expected to vary with economic conditions. Some maintenance electricians will probably be laid off during periods when production levels are low. However, maintenance electricians are generally less affected by ups and downs in the economy than electricians who work in construction.

Some companies will seek to reduce their costs by obtaining maintenance services from outside contractors instead of employing their own electrical repairers. Under these circumstances, more workers should be able to find employment with contracting firms that take care of maintenance tasks.

Earnings

The earnings of maintenance electricians vary depending on their geographical location, the industry in which they are employed, and other factors. Overall, those in metropolitan areas who work on a full-time basis have annual earnings that average around $34,000 or more. Maintenance electricians in the West and Midwest tend to make more than those in the South and Northeast.

Apprentices usually start at less than half of the wages of skilled workers. They receive periodic raises, so that by the end of their training their earnings approach that of fully qualified maintenance electricians.

In addition to their regular earnings, many maintenance electricians receive fringe benefits, such as employer contributions to health and life insurance plans, pension plans, and paid vacation days and holidays.

Conditions of work

Maintenance electricians usually work indoors, but their work environment may be anything from a comfortable, quiet office to the floor of a noisy industrial plant. Depending on the job, they may have to climb ladders, work in hot places and in cramped or awkward positions, and spend long periods of time on their feet.

The normal workweek is about 40 hours long, but this total may include regular night or weekend hours. Sometimes maintenance electricians must work overtime or must be available to be called to go to work should they be needed for a job.

All well trained maintenance electricians are very safety-conscious. Among the hazards in this occupation are electrical shocks, falls from ladders, and injury from industrial machinery. Following good safety practices can reduce these risks to a minimum.

GOE: 05.05.05; SIC: Any industry; SOC: 6153

◇ **SOURCES OF ADDITIONAL INFORMATION**

ABC/Merit Shop
729 15th Street, NW
Washington, DC 20005

Independent Electrical Contractors
PO Box 10379
Alexandria, VA 22310-0379

International Brotherhood of Electrical Workers
1125 15th Street, NW
Washington, DC 20005

National Electrical Contractors Association
7315 Wisconsin Avenue
Bethesda, MD 20814

◇ **RELATED ARTICLES**

Volume 1: Construction
Volumes 2–4: Appliance repairers; Communications equipment mechanics; Electric-sign repairers; Electrical technicians; Electricians; Electromechanical technicians; Electronics sales and service technicians; Elevator installers and repairers; Telephone and PBX installers and repairers

Electrical technicians

Definition

Electrical technicians work in nearly all phases and areas of the electric power industry, in support of and under the direction of electrical engineers. In general, they help design, assemble, test, and modify electrical circuits, devices, machines, and systems, both operational and experimental, in laboratories and industrial plants. Examples of equipment that electrical technicians might work on include motor-control devices, switch panels, transformers, generator windings, and solenoids (coils of wire which carry current).

As part of their work, electrical technicians may diagnose the causes of electrical or mechanical malfunctions and then correct them. They develop wiring diagrams, layout drawings, and engineering specifications to modify electrical systems or equipment. When periodic testing of electrical equipment is required, electrical technicians plan, direct, and record the test results. They will then modify or replace equipment that fails to meet acceptable operat-

ing standards, or will make recommendations to others for their repair. Electrical technicians also direct personnel performing routine installation and maintenance duties.

In their work, electrical technicians use precise electrical measuring devices as well as a variety of hand tools, such as screwdrivers, pliers, and soldering irons. They also read blueprints and consult electrical and engineering handbooks.

History

The modern electrical utility industry was born on September 4, 1882, in Thomas Edison's central generating station, a small brick building on Pearl Street near New York City's business district. On that day, a switch was thrown and immediately incandescent lamps began to glow in homes and offices in the surrounding neighborhood.

Edison first became interested in the possibilities of electrical lighting in 1878. The very next year he demonstrated the first practical incandescent lamp designed to give a soft, even glow instead of the hard, flickering light of gas jets. Then he turned his attention to developing the machinery and equipment necessary to distribute electrical power—including generators, sockets, fuses, and devices to measure and regulate the flow of current.

No special training was needed by workers in the early days of the electrical power business. Workers needed only to be handy with tools and have good common sense. The growing complexity of the industry, however, called for educated scientists and engineers and for trained assistants, now known as electrical technicians, to work with them. Today automation and advanced technology, including developments in microcircuitry and the laser, have made their work much more sophisticated than it was in the days of the first incandescent bulb.

Nature of the work

Electrical technicians are employed in many different settings: power plants, manufacturing facilities, research laboratories; and in many different capacities: research, maintenance, repair, sales, and employee supervision. One of the most frequently held positions is the *power system technician*. These technicians operate and maintain power generation and distribution equipment, and are usually employed by public utility companies and other institutions such as hospitals, colleges, military bases, and large industries that generate their own electricity. These technicians monitor control panels, diagnose equipment problems, carry out inspections, order repairs, and supervise crews of electrical workers performing routine work in the plant.

Another widely held position at electric power companies is that of *relay technician*. Relay technicians test and repair equipment and circuits used in the transmission and distribution of electric power. They also perform tests to locate defects such as poor insulation or malfunctioning relays.

Electrical research technicians, electrical laboratory technicians, and *engineering aides* are other positions for electrical technicians. These technicians often work with electrical engineers in commercial manufacturing companies or in engineering consulting firms. They design electrical equipment—from small household appliances to huge power generating stations; they prepare layout drawings, wiring diagrams, and

An electrical technician installs a switch near the doorway of a house that is being renovated.

engineering specifications for new equipment; and they also assemble, test, modify, and supervise the installation of new circuits, devices, and equipment.

Commercial manufacturing plants employ electrical technicians to repair, modify, and maintain manufacturing equipment powered or controlled by electricity. Automation and the growing number of computer-controlled machine tools have made the electrical technician an increasingly important member of the production team: an electrical technician on the scene can solve production bottlenecks and devise miniaturized backup power sources. A technician's skills may help with managerial decisions, such as in determining the position of electrically-powered machinery on the assembly line.

Possibly the most exciting opportunities for electrical technicians are in communications field. Telephone lines, for example, are used for more than spoken messages; pictures, video signals, and computer data are all capable of being converted into digital form and transmitted through a cable system alongside thousands of ordinary telephone calls traveling on the same cable. Satellites, cable television, and low-power television are all offer opportunities for the electrical technician eager for the challenge of developing new technologies.

Requirements

Successful electrical technicians possess good manual dexterity, the ability to learn new concepts and adapt to changing demands, well-developed communication skills, both spoken and written, and the ability to get along with others.

Preparation for this career should begin early in high school—the more thorough the preparation in mathematics and the physical sciences, the easier future training (and the resulting career) will be.

Students should investigate the entrance requirements of likely post-secondary schools as early in their high school programs as possible. This will ensure that they meet all the entrance requirements. The high school guidance counselor can direct students in their career preparation.

Students planning careers as electrical technicians should consider attending a two-year electrical technology program offered at a technical institute. Typical programs include such courses as basic electricity, electrical machinery, electrical power and control systems, and electronics.

Students may also take technical courses in mathematics, physics, and drafting; courses in written and spoken communications; and the humanities.

Licenses and certification are usually not required for most electrical technician positions. They are, however, a recognition of education, experience, and ability. Because of this, many employers and technicians feel that a license or certificate is well worth earning.

Some electrical technicians are required to belong to unions.

Opportunities for experience and exploration

Visits to electrical power plants, industrial laboratories, or manufacturing facilities can provide a vivid means of career exploration. In these facilities students can watch technicians actually involved in their work. It may also be possible to have the opportunity to speak with technicians about what they do on the job or talk with their employers about possibilities for future employment.

Electrical shop courses in high school offer a chance to work with electrical appliances and devices, and to learn some of their basic principles of operation.

Another way in which students can acquire more information about this career and its training requirements is by requesting program literature from the schools that provide this training.

Methods of entering

Private companies often post lists of job openings at schools which offer electrical technology. Companies may also send recruiters to interview students on campus. Most graduating students have their choice of a number of offers.

Some students may seek other employment opportunities; state employment agencies, school placement directors, and newspaper want ads may provide information on job openings. Students may also write directly to utility companies and other companies that hire technicians.

Advancement

As electrical technicians gain experience, they are generally given more responsibilities and need less supervision. Some technicians acquire advanced, specialized training and move into research activities or other areas that require more sophisticated skills. Other technicians move into supervisory positions, and those with exceptional ability can sometimes qualify for professional positions after receiving additional training.

The following is a list of some of the positions that electrical technicians commonly advance to:

Electrical construction supervisors arrange production scheduling, estimating, and coordinating.

Product-development technicians develop and research new products, including their market possibilities.

Electrical-laboratory associates handle complex testing and measuring on laboratory equipment and systems.

Field-service technicians handle technical sales, maintenance, service, and product adaptations to meet customer needs.

Senior technical writers develop complex instruction manuals involving operation, maintenance, and repair of electrical equipment and systems.

Electrical-instrumentation supervisors calibrate and design instruments such as measuring and control devices, and supervise their maintenance and repair procedures.

Electrical-research associates research electrical current phenomena, such as the behavior of electrical current at low temperatures or other specialized circumstances.

Employment outlook

The field of electrical technology is one of continuing growth; new electrical products and services are constantly being developed for military, industrial, and consumer markets. It appears that the employment levels in this area will grow faster than the average of all other occupations through the year 2000. Technicians who graduate from a two-year technical school will probably be able to find work most easily.

Recently created jobs for technicians include overseeing the operation of cable television networks that use their own cable system or share a cable with another transmission company. Many newspapers and magazines now require technicians to work with equipment for electronically transmitting typeset material from typesetting plants, via microwave frequencies, to presses hundreds of miles away.

As advanced forms of microcircuitry become more indispensable, so will the electrical technician. Technicians interested in research and development may find themselves devising miniature power systems for space capsules, and communications systems for orbiting satellites. An understanding of microcircuitry may even take them into such medical fields as heart transplant surgery.

Employment levels for electrical technicians working in defense-related industries could fall somewhat if the government decreases its rate of military spending.

Although electrical current can be dangerous, standard safety practices reduce problems to a level where they need not be a serious factor in considering employment in this field. Some electrical technicians working in generating plants or on production lines will be exposed to a high noise level. Hours may vary, and some technicians may be required to perform overtime work, especially in situations involving equipment failure.

Electrical technicians must be adaptable and willing to learn. The rapidly changing nature of electrical technology requires individuals who can remain current with advances in the field.

The days of inventors working alone in attics are gone. Technicians must be able to get along well with others, including skilled trade workers under their supervision, and the professionally trained scientists and engineers who hold final responsibility for a project or installation.

Electrical technicians are asked to handle a wide range of duties, from the uncomplicated and routine to the highly complex and challenging. Technicians need to have the flexibility to handle all of these duties with attention and precision.

GOE: 05.01.01; SIC: Any industry; SOC: 3711

Earnings

Most electrical technicians receive salaries that range from $20,000 to $37,000 a year, with the average roughly $28,500. Some electrical technicians, especially those at the beginning of their careers, earn as little as $15,000 a year. However, some senior technicians earn as much as $42,000 to $60,000 a year or more.

Other benefits that a company may offer will vary. Tuition refunds, paid holidays and vacations, health and life insurance, and profit-sharing may be included.

Conditions of work

The field of electrical technology is generally considered to have highly desirable working conditions. Facilities are usually quite new, and every attempt is made to keep the equipment and working areas in excellent condition.

◇ **SOURCES OF ADDITIONAL INFORMATION**

Institute of Electrical and Electronic Engineers
345 East 47th Street
New York, NY 10017

Junior Engineering Technical Society (JETS)
1420 King Street
Suite 405
Alexandria, VA 22314

National Action Council for Minorities in Engineering
3 West 35th Street
New York, NY 10001

British Columbia Electrical Association
#313, 13988 Cambie Road
Richmond BC V6V 2K4

Electricians

Definition

Electricians design, lay out, assemble, install, test, and repair electrical fixtures, apparatus, and wiring used in a wide range of electrical systems that provide light, heat, refrigeration, air conditioning, and power.

History

Perhaps more than any other single factor, the harnessing of electricity has pushed the modern world toward its future. Electrically powered devices and equipment have fundamentally altered our experience of work, communication, and a multitude of other aspects of daily life. We have so completely adapted to using electrical power that in many ways life without it is hard to imagine. Our dependence on electricity is likely to increase in the future, as new and different machines are perfected to serve human needs. And as long as electric power runs these machines, electricians, the skilled workers who know how to put together and maintain electrical systems, will be in demand nearly everywhere.

It was during the latter part of the 19th century that electric power entered everyday life. Before then, electricity was the subject of experimentation and theorizing, but few practical applications. The widespread use of electricity was spurred by a combination of innovations, especially the discovery of a way to transmit power efficiently via overhead lines and the invention of the incandescent lamp, the telephone, and the electric telegraph. In the 1880s, commercial supplies of electricity began to be available in some cities, and within a few years electric power was transforming many homes and factories.

Early electrical workers were mainly concerned with setting up the lines and supporting poles for distributing power around cities. The work of these pioneers, who were often called linemen, was difficult and dangerous, and serious accidents were common. As electrical distribution systems grew larger and more complicated and wiring was extended into many buildings, linemen developed new tools and techniques for safely installing circuits and equipment. Wiremen, specialists in wiring buildings, emerged as distinct group of essential craftworkers in the building and construction trades.

Today, electricians are the workers who perform such tasks. Along with the electricians who install and repair electrical systems for buildings, the field includes people who work on a wide array of telecommunications equipment, industrial machine-tool controls, marine facilities like ships and off-shore drilling rigs, and many other kinds of sophisticated equipment that have been developed using 20th-century technology. In all of these applications, electricians are responsible for establishing and maintaining vital links between power-generating plants and the many electrical and electronic systems that shape our lives.

Nature of the work

Many electricians specialize in either construction or maintenance work, although some work in both fields. Electricians in construction are usually employed by electrical contractors. Other construction electricians work for building contractors or for industrial plants, public utilities, state highway commissions, or other large organizations that employ workers directly to build or remodel their property. A few are self-employed.

Maintenance electricians may work in large factories, office buildings, small plants, or wherever existing electrical facilities and machinery need regular servicing to keep them in good working order. Many maintenance electricians work in manufacturing industries, such as those that produce automobiles, aircraft, ships, steel, chemicals, and industrial machinery. Some are employed by hospitals, municipalities, housing complexes, or shopping centers to do maintenance, repair, and sometimes installation work. Some work for or operate businesses that contract to repair and update wiring in residences and commercial buildings.

When installing electrical systems, electricians may follow blueprints and specifications, or they may be told verbally what is needed. They may prepare sketches showing the intended location of wiring and equipment. Once the plan is clear, they measure, cut, assemble, and install plastic-covered wire or electrical conduit, which is a tube or channel through which heavier grades of electrical wire or cable are run. They strip insulation from wires, splice and solder wires together, and tape or cap the ends. They attach cables and wiring to the incoming electrical service and to various fixtures and machines that use electricity. They install switches, circuit breakers, relays, transformers, grounding leads, signal devices, and other electrical components. After the installation is complete, they test circuits for continuity and safety, adjusting the setup as needed.

Electricians must work according to the National Electric Code and state and local building and electrical codes (electrical codes are standards that electrical systems must meet to ensure safe, reliable functioning). In doing their work, electricians should always try to use materials efficiently, plan for future access to the area for service and maintenance on the system, and avoid hazardous and unsightly wiring arrangements, making their work as neat and orderly as possible.

Electricians use a variety of equipment ranging from simple hand tools such as screwdrivers, pliers, wrenches, and hacksaws to power tools such as drills, hydraulic benders for metal conduit, and electric soldering guns, and also testing devices such as oscilloscopes, ammeters, and test lamps. Construction electricians often supply their own hand tools. Experienced workers may have hundreds of dollars invested in tools.

Maintenance electricians do many of the same kinds of tasks, but their activities are usu-

A worker connects hundreds of electrical wires, creating a "harness" that will be installed in a rebuilt train car.

ally aimed at preventing trouble before it occurs. They periodically inspect equipment and carry out routine service procedures, often according to a predetermined schedule. They repair or replace worn or defective parts and keep management informed about the reliability of the electrical systems. If any breakdowns occur, maintenance electricians must return the equipment to full functioning as soon as possible so that the expense and inconvenience are minimal.

A growing number of electricians are involved in activities other than constructing and maintaining electrical systems in buildings. Many are employed to install computer wiring and equipment, telephone wiring, or the coaxial and fiber optics cables used in telecommunications and computer equipment. Electricians also work in power plants, where electric power is generated; in machine shops where electric motors are repaired and rebuilt; aboard ships, fixing communications and navigation systems; at locations that need large lighting and power installations, such as airports and mines; and in numerous other settings.

Requirements

Some electricians still learn their trade the same way electrical workers did many years ago—informally on the job, while employed as helpers to skilled workers. Especially if that experience is supplemented with vocational or technical school courses, correspondence courses, or training received in the military, electrical helpers may in time become well qualified craft workers in some area of the field.

However, it is generally accepted that apprenticeship programs provide the best all-around training in this trade. Apprenticeships combine a series of planned, structured, supervised job experiences with classroom instruction in related subjects. Many programs are designed to give apprentices a variety of experiences by having them work for several electrical contractors doing different kinds of jobs. Typically, apprenticeships last four to five years. Completion of an apprenticeship is usually a significant advantage in getting the better jobs in the field.

Applicants for apprenticeships generally need to be high school graduates, at least 18 years of age, in good health, with at least average physical strength. Although local requirements vary, many applicants are required to take tests to determine their aptitude for the work.

All prospective electricians, whether they intend to enter an apprenticeship or learn informally on the job, ought to have a high school background that includes such courses as applied mathematics and science, shop classes that teach the use of various tools, and mechanical drawing. Electronics courses are especially important for those who plan to become maintenance electricians. Good color vision is necessary, because electricians need to be able to distinguish color-coded wires. Agility and manual dexterity are also desirable characteristics.

Most apprenticeship programs are developed and run jointly by contractor groups and union locals of the International Brotherhood of Electrical Workers. Some apprenticeships are sponsored by electrical contracting companies in cooperation with contractor organizations. A joint union-management apprenticeship committee establishes standards and pay levels for apprentices. Training is based on a written agreement between the apprentice and the committee.

Usually apprenticeships involve at least 144 hours of classroom work each year, covering such subjects as electrical theory, electronics, blueprint reading, mathematics, electrical code requirements, and first aid. On the job, apprentices learn how to use safely and to care for tools, equipment, and materials commonly encountered in the trade. Over the years of the program, they spend about 8,000 hours working under the supervision of experienced electricians. They begin with simple tasks, such as drilling holes and setting up conduit. As they acquire skills and knowledge, they progress to more difficult tasks, like diagramming electrical systems and connecting and testing wiring and electrical components.

Many electricians find that after they are working in the field, they still need to take courses to keep abreast of new developments. Unions and employers may sponsor classes introducing new methods and materials or explaining changes in electrical code requirements. By taking skill-improvement courses electricians may also improve their chances for advancement to better-paying positions.

Many electricians are union members. The unions that represent them include the International Brotherhood of Electrical Workers; the International Union of Electronic, Electrical, Salaried, Machine, and Furniture Workers; the International Association of Machinists and Aerospace Workers; and other unions.

Special requirements

Some states and municipalities require that electricians be licensed. To obtain a license, electricians usually must pass a written examination on electrical theory, National Electrical Code requirements, and local building and electrical codes.

Opportunities for experience and exploration

High school students can get an idea about their aptitude for and interest in tasks that come up regularly in the work of electricians by taking such courses as metal and electrical shop, drafting, electronics, and mathematics. Hobbies like repairing radios, building electronics kits, or working with model electric trains involve skills similar to those needed by electricians. In addition to sampling related activities like these, prospective electricians may benefit by arranging to talk with an electrician about their job. Perhaps with the help of a teacher or guidance counselor, it may be possible to contact a local electrical contracting firm and locate someone willing to give an insider's description of the occupation.

Methods of entering

People seeking to enter this field may either begin working as helpers with little background in the field, or they may enter an apprenticeship program. Leads for helper jobs may be located by contacting electrical contractors directly and by checking the usual sources for jobs listings, like the local offices of the state employment service and newspaper classified advertising sections. Students in trade and vocational school courses may be able to find job openings through the placement office of their school.

People who want to become apprentices may start by contacting the union local of the International Brotherhood of Electrical Workers or the local joint union-management apprenticeship committee. In some areas, it is possible to become an apprentice to a local electrical contractor by applying directly to the company. Information on apprenticeship possibilities can also be obtained through the state employment service.

Advancement

The advancement possibilities for skilled, experienced electricians depend partly on their field of activity. Those who work in construction may become supervisors, job site superintendents, or estimators for electrical contractors. Some electricians are able to establish their own contracting businesses, although in many areas contractors must obtain a special license. Another possibility for some electricians is to move, for example, from construction to maintenance work, or into jobs in the shipbuilding, automobile, or aircraft industry.

Employment outlook

During the next 10 to 15 years, employment of electricians is expected to grow at a faster rate than the average for all occupations. The growth in this field will be principally related to overall increased levels in construction of buildings for residential and commercial purposes. In addition, growth will be driven by our ever-increasing use of electrical and electronic devices and equipment. Electricians will be called on to upgrade old wiring and to install and maintain more extensive wiring systems than has been necessary in the past. In particular, the increased use of sophisticated telecommunications and data-processing equipment and automated manufacturing systems is expected to lead to many job opportunities for electricians.

While the overall outlook for this occupational field is good, the availability of jobs will vary over time and from place to place. In construction, the amount of activity goes up and down depending on the state of the local and national economy. Thus, during economic slowdowns, opportunities for construction electricians may not be plentiful. People working in this field need to be prepared for periods of unemployment between construction projects. Openings for apprentices also decline during economic downturns. Maintenance electricians are usually less vulnerable to periodic unemployment because they are more likely to work for one employer that needs electrical services on a steady basis. But if they work in an industry where the economy causes big fluctuations in the level of activity, like automobile manufacturing, they may be laid off during recessions.

Not many electricians switch completely out of their job field, because of the time that must be invested in training and the relatively good pay for skilled workers. Nonetheless, many of the job openings that occur each year develop as electricians move into other occupations or leave the labor force altogether. During the coming years, enough electricians are expected to retire that a national shortage of well-qualified workers could develop if training programs don't attract more applicants who can eventually take the place of the retirees.

Earnings

The earnings of electricians vary widely depending on such factors as the industry in which they are employed, their geographical location, union membership, and other factors. In general, the majority of electricians who are employed full-time have annual earnings in the range of $21,000 to $37,000 or more. One national survey has showed that the average wages for electricians who are union members are at least $33,700 a year. Another study has showed that maintenance electricians in metropolitan areas have earnings that average at least around $34,000 a year. Electricians in the West and Midwest tend to make more than those in the Northeast and South.

Wages rates for many electricians are set by agreements between unions and employers. In addition to their regular earnings, electricians may receive fringe benefits such as employer contributions to health insurance and pension plans, paid vacation and sick days, and supplemental unemployment compensation plans.

Wage of apprentices often start at about 40 to 50 percent of the skilled worker's rate and increase every six months until the last period of the apprenticeship, when the pay approaches that of fully qualified electricians.

Conditions of work

Electricians usually work indoors, although some must do some tasks outdoors or in buildings that are still under construction. The standard workweek is about 40 hours. In many jobs overtime may be required. Maintenance electricians often have to work some weekend, holiday, or night hours, because they must service equipment that operates all the time.

Electricians often spend long periods on their feet, sometimes on ladders or scaffolds or in awkward or uncomfortable places. The work is sometimes strenuous. Electricians may have to put up with noise and dirt on the job. They may risk injuries such as falls off ladders, electrical shocks, and cuts and bruises. By following established safety practices, most of these hazards can be avoided.

GOE: 05.05.05; SIC: Any industry; SOC: 6153, 6432

◇ **SOURCES OF ADDITIONAL INFORMATION**

ABC/Merit Shop
729 15th Street, NW
Washington, DC 20005

Independent Electrical Contractors
PO Box 10379
Alexandria, VA 22310-0379

International Brotherhood of Electrical Workers
1125 15th Street, NW
Washington, DC 20005

National Electrical Contractors Association
7315 Wisconsin Avenue
Bethesda, MD 20814

Canadian Electrical Contractors Association
#605, 161 Eglinton Avenue East
Toronto ON M4P 1J5

◇ **RELATED ARTICLES**

Volume 1: Construction
Volumes 2–4: Appliance repairers; Communications equipment mechanics; Electric-sign repairers; Electrical repairers; Electrical technicians; Electromechical technicians; Electronics sales and service technicians; Elevator installers and repairers; Telephone and PBX installers and repairers

Electrocardiograph technicians

Definition

Electrocardiograph technicians, sometimes called *EKG technicians*, operate electronic instruments called electrocardiograph machines. These machines detect the electronic impulses that come from a patient's heart during a heartbeat and record that information in the form of a paper graph called an electrocardiogram. By recording these impulses, the machines can provide physicians with information about the action of the heart during individual heartbeats. This helps the physicians diagnose heart disease, and to monitor progress during treatment.

To operate EKG machines, technicians attach electrodes to the arms, legs and chest, and operate controls on the machine, or enter commands into a computer. After the test, they prepare the electrocardiogram and forward it to the physician (usually a cardiologist) for interpretation and analysis. Electrocardiograph technicians sometimes conduct other tests, such as vectorcardiographs and phonocardiographs.

History

Electrocardiography can be traced back 300 years to the work of the Dutch anatomist and physiologist Jan Swammerdam who demonstrated in 1678 that a frog's leg will contract when stimulated with an electrical current. It was not until 1856, however, that two German anatomists, Albert von Kolliker and Heinrich M. Mueller, showed that when the frog's heart contracted, it produced a small electric current. In succeeding years the electrical behavior of beating hearts was extensively studied, but always with the chest open and the heart exposed.

In 1887, Augustus Desire Waller discovered that the electrical current of the human heart could be measured with the chest closed. He was able to do this by placing one electrode on a person's chest and another on the person's back and connecting them to a monitoring device. In 1903, a professor of physiology in Germany, Willem Einthoven, perfected the monitoring device so that even the faintest currents from the heart could be detected and recorded graphically.

Throughout the rest of this century, medical researchers have made further advancements and refinements on this machine. By the 1940s, for instance, portable electrocardiographs were in use, allowing electrocardiograms to be made in a physician's office or at a patient's bedside. During the 1960s, computerized electrocardiographs were developed to aid physicians in the interpretation of test results. Today, electrocardiographs are widely used in routine physicals, in presurgical physicals, in diagnosing disease, and in monitoring the effects of drug therapy. The continued wide use of these devices ensures a continuing need for trained personnel to operate them.

Nature of the work

Electrocardiograph technicians prepare the patient and the machine before the procedure begins, monitor both patient and machine during the procedure, and perform various other duties related to the machine's operation.

When preparing patients for the electrocardiography, technicians first explain the procedure to the patient. They then attach the electrodes, anywhere from 3 to 12 in number, to the chest, arms, and legs of the patient. In many cases, they apply a special cream or gel between the electrodes and the skin to help the monitor pick up the signals more easily.

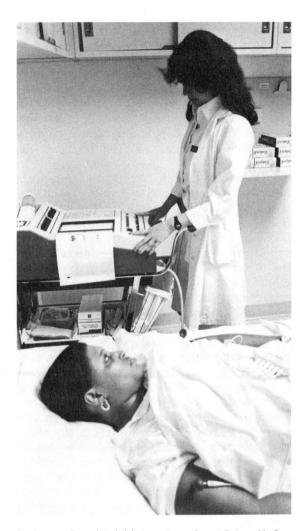

An electrocardiograph technician operates equipment that graphically records the electrical currents generated by a patient's heart.

During the test, technicians move the chest electrodes to different positions on the chest to get multiple tracings of the electrical activity occurring in various parts of the heart muscle. Meanwhile a stylus records the tracings on a long roll of graph paper. The test may be given while the patient is resting or while doing exercise.

While the machine is in operation, technicians must be sure that the machine is not recording stray electrical impulses, such as those coming from tremors in other muscles or from electrical vibrations of nearby equipment. They should also be able to detect other kinds of false readings and to take necessary corrective actions.

To do this work correctly, technicians must know about the anatomy and the function of the heart and chest. They need this knowledge to avoid placing the electrodes incorrectly. They must also know all about the machine so that they can spot malfunctions or other machine-related problems quickly.

After the electrocardiogram has been made, technicians remove the paper, edit or annotate the tracing as necessary, and forward it to the physician. Technicians must keep the machine supplied with paper and know generally how well the machine is operating; however, they are usually not responsible for repairing the machine.

Electrocardiograph technicians sometimes help to conduct other tests, such as vectorcardiographs, which produce multiple tracings of different aspects of the heart's electrical activity; phonocardiographs, which are sound recordings of the heart's valves and of the blood passing through them; stress tests, which record the heart's activity during physical activity; and echocardiographs, which use ultrasound to produce images of the heart's chambers and valves.

Another kind of test performed by more highly skilled electrocardiograph technicians is Holter monitoring. This procedure requires the patient to wear a small monitor device strapped to his or her body, often for 24 hours, while going about normal daily activities. Technicians who do this kind of testing are often called *Holter scanning technicians*. Their duties include attaching and strapping the test equipment to the patient, checking to be sure that the equipment is operating correctly, and reviewing and analyzing the information that comes from the monitor.

In addition to these duties, electrocardiograph technicians may also schedule appointments, write and type reports, and maintain patients' files.

By far the majority of electrocardiograph technicians work in hospitals, but other possible job sites include clinics, physicians' offices, or medical schools.

Cardiac monitor technicians are similar to and sometimes perform some of the same duties as electrocardiograph technicians. They usually work in hospitals in intensive-care units or cardiac-care units. It is their job to keep watch over all the screens that are monitoring the patients to detect any sign that a patient's heart is not beating as it should. To do this correctly, cardiac monitor technicians review each patient's records to determine what that patient's normal heart-rhythms are like, what the current pattern is, and what types of pattern deviations have been observed. The technician will then know which heart rhythms require prompt medical attention, and can immediately notify a nurse or doctor so that appropriate care can be given.

Requirements

Electrocardiograph technicians need to have good mechanical aptitude and the ability to follow directions. They should also have personalities that allow them to perform well under pressure, including medical emergencies, and to treat sick or nervous patients in a pleasant and reassuring manner.

Most electrocardiograph technicians are trained on the job in hospitals or in companies that manufacture the electrocardiograph equipment. These training programs, lasting from one month for basic electrocardiograph tests to up to one year for more advanced tests, teach the technicians how to operate the machines and read the tracings.

The basic requirement for receiving this kind of on-the-job training is a high school diploma or its equivalent. During high school, students should take courses in English, health, biology, and typing. In addition, students might consider courses in the social sciences, if they are available, to help them understand their patients' social and psychological needs.

In recent years, some vocational, technical, and junior colleges have begun to offer one- and two-year training programs in electrocardiography. These programs give technicians more extensive preparation in the subject and allow them to earn certificates for the one-year program and associate degrees for the two-year program. These programs are still rather new, and only a few have received full accreditation.

At the present time, electrocardiograph technicians are not required to be licensed; it is available, however, on a voluntary basis from the National Board of Cardiovascular Testing. These credentials may help technicians advance and obtain better salaries. In some cases, hospitals may require that their technicians be certified.

Opportunities for experience and exploration

Prospective electrocardiograph technicians will find it difficult to gain any direct experience on a part-time basis in electrocardiography. Their first direct experience with the work generally comes during their on-the-job training sessions. They may, however, be able to gain some exposure to patient-care activities in general by signing up for volunteer work at a local hospital. In addition, they could arrange to visit a hospital, clinic, or physician's office where electrocardiographs are taken. In this way they might be able to watch a technician at work or at least talk to a technician about what the work is like.

Methods of entering

Because most electrocardiograph technicians receive their initial training on their first job, great care should be taken in finding this first employer. Students should pay close attention not only to the pay and working conditions but also to the kind of on-the-job training that is provided in each prospective position. In many cases, hospitals earn reputations for their training programs, and high school guidance counselors may be the best source of information about those reputations. Additional information can be gained from classified ads in the newspaper, from friends and relatives who may work in hospitals, and from contacting hospitals directly.

For students who graduate from one- to two-year training programs, finding a first job should be easier. First, employers are always eager to hire people who are already trained. Second, these graduates can be less concerned about the training programs offered by their employers. Third, they should find that their teachers and guidance counselors can be excellent sources of information about job possibilities in the area. If the training program includes any practical experience, graduates may find that the hospital in which they trained or worked before graduation would be willing to hire them after graduation.

Advancement

Opportunities for advancement are best for electrocardiograph technicians who learn to do or assist with more complex procedures, such as stress testing, Holter monitoring, echocardiography, and cardiac catheterization. With proper training and experience, these technicians may eventually become *cardiovascular technicians, cardiopulmonary technicians, cardiology technologists,* or other specialty technicians or technologists.

In addition to these kinds of specialty positions, experienced technicians may also be able to advance to various supervisory and training posts.

Employment outlook

Openings for EKG technicians are expected to decline through the year 2000. The reason is that although there is an increased demand for the EKGs, the equipment and procedures are now much more efficient than they used to be. One technician can perform many more tests each day than was previously possible, and, because of this, fewer technicians are required. In addition, the newer equipment is easier to use, allowing employers to train other personnel, such as respiratory therapists or registered nurses, in its operation.

Most job openings will be to replace those technicians who are promoted, transferred, or retired.

Earnings

Beginning electrocardiograph technicians can expect to receive starting salaries of approximately $14,400 a year. Average pay for all EKG technicians is $18,020 per year, and experienced technicians can earn considerably more, in some settings more than $25,000 a year, not including overtime.

Those with formal training earn more money than those who trained on the job, and those who are able to perform more sophisticated tests are paid more than those who perform only the basic ones.

Electrocardiograph technicians working in hospitals receive the same fringe benefits as other hospital workers. These benefits usually include hospitalization insurance, paid vacations, and sick leave. In some cases they also include educational assistance, pension benefits, and uniform allowances.

Conditions of work

Electrocardiograph technicians should be able to adapt well to changing situations, as each patient presents a different personality and requires a different medical task. Technicians should also be able to work under pressure and remain calm in emergencies which may arise when providing care to patients.

Electrocardiograph technicians usually work in clean, quiet, well-lighted surroundings. They generally work 5-day, 40-hour weeks, although technicians working in small hospitals may be on 24-hour call for emergencies, and all technicians in hospitals, large or small, can expect to do occasional evening or weekend work. With the growing emphasis in health care on cost containment, more jobs are likely to develop in various outpatient settings, so that in the future it is likely that electrocardiograph technicians will work more often in clinics, cardiologists' offices, HMOs, and other non-hospital locations.

Electrocardiograph technicians generally work with patients who either are ill or who have reason to fear they might be ill. As such, there are opportunities for the technicians to do these people some good, but there is also a chance of causing some harm: a well-conducted test can reduce anxieties or make a physician's job easier; a misplaced electrode or an error in record keeping could cause an incorrect diagnosis. Technicians need to be able to cope with that responsibility and consistently conduct their work in the best interests of their patients.

Part of the technician's job includes putting patients at ease about the procedure they are to undergo. Towards that end, technicians should be pleasant, patient, alert, and able to understand and sympathize with the feelings of others. In explaining the nature of the procedure to patients, they should be able to do so in a calm, reassuring, and confident manner.

Inevitably, some patients will try to get information about their medical situation from the technician. In cases like this, technicians need to be both tactful and firm in explaining that they are only making the electrocardiogram; the interpretation is for the physician to make.

Another large part of a technician's job involves getting along well with other members of the hospital staff. This task is sometimes made more difficult by the fact that in most hospitals there is a formal, often rigid, status structure, and electrocardiograph technicians may find themselves in a relatively low position in that structure. In emergency situations or at other moments of frustration, electrocardiograph technicians may find themselves dealt with brusquely or angrily. Technicians should not take outbursts or rude treatment personally, but instead should respond with stability and maturity.

GOE: 10.03.01; SIC: 801, 806; SOC: 369

◇ RELATED ARTICLES

Volume 1: Health Care
Volumes 2–4: Biomedical equipment technicians; Electroencephalographic technicians; Medical assistants; Medical laboratory technicians; Medical technologists; Nurses; Nursing and psychiatric aides; Physician assistants

Electroencephalographic technicians

Definition

Electroencephalographic technicians, sometimes called *EEG technicians*, operate electronic instruments called electroencephalographs. These instruments measure and record the brain's electrical activity. The information gathered is used by physicians (usually neurologists) to diagnose and determine the effects of certain diseases and injuries, including brain tumors, cerebral vascular strokes, Alzheimer's Disease, epilepsy, some metabolic disorders, and brain injuries caused by accidents or infectious diseases. With this information, physicians are able to prescribe medications or perform surgery to correct the diagnosed problems.

First, EEG technicians prepare patients for this procedure: they take the patient's medical history, explain the procedure, and then fasten electrodes to the head. They attach the electrodes' terminals to monitoring devices and then carefully watch both the patient and the machine. Electroencephalographic technicians observe the patient's behavior, make notes on the graph for later reference by the physician, and perform minor adjustments and repairs to the machine as necessary.

Electroencephalographic technicians may also monitor other kinds of tracings of the patient's electrical activity, such as electromyograms (recordings of the electrical activity associated with the skeletal muscles), electrocardiograms (recordings of the activity associated with the heart), and electrooculograms (recordings of the electrical activity associated with the eye).

Those interested in this career should realize that the terms "electroencephalographic technician" and "electroencephalographic technologist" are sometimes used interchangeably and do not necessarily indicate any different level of skills or training.

In this article, the term "technician" is used, except to refer to those people who have received certification as Certified/Registered Electroencephalographic Technologists or as Registered Electroencephalographic Technologists; however, it is possible that in coming years the term "technologist" will come to replace "technician" as the job designation for this career.

History

The brain constantly discharges small electrical impulses that can be picked up from the surface of the head, amplified, and then recorded on paper. These currents were first detected in England in 1875 by Richard Caton. He reported having placed electrodes on the exposed brains of rabbits and monkeys. The picture, usually called a tracing, of this electrical brain activity is known as an electroencephalogram (EEG).

Other researchers independently discovered this phenomenon of brain activity in the late 1800s and early 1900s. In 1929, the first practical electroencephalograph for use on human beings was developed in Germany by Hans Berger. Berger's work also included extensive testing of both diseased and healthy brains.

In the mid-1930s, the use of electroencephalograms to diagnose epilepsy was developed. Shortly afterward, they were used to locate brain tumors. Thus, by the end of the 1930s, a new field had opened up through which doctors and technicians could improve the diagnosis and treatment of neurological diseases.

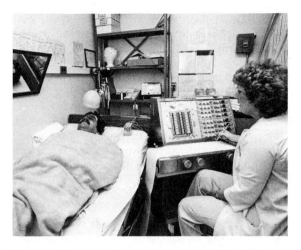

Before conducting any tests, an electroencephalographic technician asks the patient a few questions concerning his medical history and discusses the testing procedure.

Nature of the work

The basic principle behind electroencephalography is that the electrical impulses given off by the brain, often called brain waves, vary according to the brain's age, activity, and condition. Specifically, we know that certain brain conditions are accompanied by distinctive brain waves. Therefore, the EEG can aid the neurologist (a physician specially trained in the study of the brain) in making a diagnosis of a person's illness or injury. In some complex medical cases, electroencephalograms are also used to determine whether death has occurred in a patient.

The first step with a new patient is always to take a simplified medical history of the patient. This entails asking questions and recording answers about the person's family and personal history and specifically about his or her past health and present illness. This provides the technician with needed information about the patient's condition. It also provides an opportunity to help the patient relax before the test.

The technician then applies electrodes, held in place by adhesive, to the patient's head according to a prearranged plan. Often, technicians must choose the best combination of instrument controls and placement of electrodes to produce the kind of tracing that has been requested. In some cases, they will be given special instructions regarding the placement of electrodes.

Once in place, the electrodes are connected to the recording equipment, which includes a bank of extremely sensitive electronic amplifiers. Tracings from each electrode are made on a moving strip of paper in response to the amplified impulses coming from the brain. The resulting graph is a recording of the patient's brain waves during the test.

Electroencephalographic technicians are not responsible for interpreting the tracings (that is the job of the neurologist); however, they must be able to recognize any readings on the tracing that are coming from somewhere other than from the brain, such as from eye movement or from nearby electrical equipment. These stray readings are known as artifacts, and technicians must be able to determine which kinds of artifacts should be expected for an individual patient on the basis of his or her medical history or present illness. They should also be able to conduct their procedures so that any of these artifacts can be readily identified if they occur.

Faulty recordings may also be caused by technician error or by machine malfunctions. Technicians must be able to detect false readings of these sorts also. When mechanical problems occur, technicians notify their supervisors so that the machine can be repaired by trained equipment repairers.

Throughout the procedure, electroencephalographic technicians observe the patient's behavior and make detailed notes about any aspect of the behavior that might be of use to the physician later in interpreting the tracing. They also keep watch on the patient's brain, heart, and breathing functions for any signs that the patient is in danger.

During the testing, the patient may be either asleep or awake and alert. In some cases, the physician may want recordings taken in both states. Sometimes drugs or special procedures are prescribed by the physician to create in the patient a specific kind of condition. Administering the drugs or procedures is frequently the technician's responsibility.

Electroencephalographic technicians need a basic understanding of the kinds of medical emergencies that can occur during this procedure. By being prepared in this way, they can react properly if one of these emergencies should arise. For instance, if a patient suffers an epileptic seizure, technicians must know what to do.

Electroencephalographic technicians may also handle other specialized electroencephalograms. For example, in a procedure called ambulatory monitoring, both heart and brain activity is tracked over a 24-hour period by a small recording device on the patient's side. In evoked potential testing, a special machine is used to measure the brain's response to specific types of stimulus. And, electroencephalograms are increasingly used on a routine basis in the operating room to monitor patients during major surgery.

Besides conducting various kind of electroencephalograms, electroencephalographic technicians also keep the machine in good working order, perform minor repairs to the machine (major repairs require specially trained repairers), schedule appointments, and order supplies. In some cases they may have some supervisory responsibilities; however, most supervision is done by registered electroencephalographic technologists.

Requirements

Electroencephalographic technicians need good vision and manual dexterity, an aptitude for working with mechanical and electronic equipment, and the ability to get along well with patients, their families, and with members of the hospital staff.

Prospective electroencephalographic technicians should plan on getting a high school diploma, as it is usually a requirement for entry into any kind of EEG technician training program, whether in school or on the job. Specific course requirements will vary from program to program; students should investigate entrance requirements of programs they might be interested in to make sure that they can meet all of the requirements. In general, students will find it helpful to have three years of mathematics, including algebra; and three years of science, including biology, chemistry, and physics. In addition, students should take courses in English, especially those that help improve their communication skills; and in social sciences so that they can better understand the social and psychological needs of their patients.

There are two main types of post-high school training available for electroencephalographic technicians: on-the-job training and formal classroom training. Many technicians who are currently working received on-the-job training; however, EEG equipment is becoming so sophisticated that many employers prefer to hire technicians with prior formal training.

On-the-job training generally lasts from a few months to one year, depending on the employer's special requirements. Trainees learn how to handle the equipment and carry out procedures by observing and receiving instruction from senior electroencephalographic technicians or technologists.

Formal training consists of both practice in the clinical laboratory and instruction in the classroom. The classroom instruction usually focuses on basic subjects such as human anatomy, physiology, neuroanatomy, clinical neurology, neuropsychiatry, clinical and internal medicine, psychology, and electronics and instrumentation. The post-secondary programs usually last from one to two years and are offered by hospitals, medical centers, and community or technical colleges.

Students who have completed one year of on-the-job training or who have graduated from a formal training program may apply for certification and/or registration. There are two separate boards of certification and registration for electroencephalographic technicians in the United States: the American Board of Certified and Registered Electroencephalographic Technicians and Technologists (ABCRETT) and the American Board of Registration of Electroencephalographic Technologists (ABRET).

The American Board of Certified and Registered Electroencephalographic Technicians and Technologists offers the opportunity for certification at three levels: Certified Medical Electroencephalographic Technician (C.M.E.T.); Certified/Registered Electroencephalographic Technologist (C.R.E.T.); and Certified/Registered Neurodiagnostic Technologist (C.R.N.T.).

The American Board of Registration of Electroencephalographic Technologists registers technologists at one level of experience and education, that is, as a Registered Electroencephalographic Technologist (R/EEGT). Technicians who have been in the field for at least one year and who have completed a required number of electroencephalographic recordings can earn this registration by passing an examination.

Those certified/registered technologists on the job for five years or more and who have taken on more responsibilities and other electrophysiological testing should consider advanced levels of certification and registration.

Although none of these forms of registration or certification are requirements for employment, they are acknowledgments of the technician's training and do make advancement easier. They may also provide increases in salary ranges.

Opportunities for experience and exploration

Prospective electroencephalographic technicians will find it difficult to gain any direct experience on a part-time basis in electroencephalography. Their first direct experience with the work will generally come during their on-the-job training sessions or in the practical

experience portion of their formal training. They may, however, be able to gain some exposure to patient-care activities in general by signing up for volunteer work at a local hospital. In addition, they could arrange to visit a hospital, clinic, or doctor's office where electroencephalograms are taken. In this way, they might be able to watch technicians at work or at least talk to them about what the work is like.

Methods of entering

Technicians often obtain permanent employment in the hospital where they receive their on-the-job or work–study training.

Prospective technicians can also find employment through classified ads in newspapers and by contacting the personnel offices of hospitals, medical centers, clinics, and government agencies which employ electroencephalographic technicians.

Advancement

Opportunities for advancement for electroencephalographic technicians are good if they become certified/registered electroencephalographic technologists. Electroencephalographic technicians who do not take this step will find their opportunities for advancement severely limited.

Technologists are usually assigned to conducting more difficult or specialized electroencephalograms. They also supervise other electroencephalographic technicians, arrange work schedules, and teach techniques to new trainees. They may also establish procedures, manage a laboratory, keep records, schedule appointments, and order supplies.

Electroencephalographic technologists may advance to *chief electroencephalographic technologist* and thus take on even more responsibilities in laboratory management and in teaching new personnel and students from electroencephalographic training programs. Chief electroencephalographic technologists generally work under the direction of an electroencephalographer, neurologist, or neurosurgeon.

Employment outlook

The total number of people employed as electroencephalographic technicians is expected to grow much faster than the average for all occupations at least through the year 2000. This growth will be caused by a number of factors, most notable among them being the increased use of electroencephalographs in surgery, in diagnosing and monitoring patients, and in research on the human brain. The fastest growth will occur in neurologists' offices and clinics as more physicians purchase their own equipment. EEG technicians will be used to conduct new forms of electrophysiological examinations that are being developed by researchers in clinical neurophysiology.

Another factor contributing to this increased demand is the growth in the population in general, of which a high percentage are older people, the most frequent users of healthcare services.

Earnings

Starting salaries are approximately $16,000 a year. Experienced electroencephalographic technicians earn salaries that average approximately $26,499 a year, and range as high as $35,000 to $40,000 a year. Salaries for certified/ registered electroencephalographic technologists tend to be $2,000 to $4,000 a year higher for equivalent experience.

The highest salaries for electroencephalographic technicians tend to go to those who work as laboratory supervisors, teachers in training programs, and program directors in schools of electroencephalographic technology.

Electroencephalographic technicians working in hospitals receive the same fringe benefits as other hospital workers. These benefits usually include hospitalization insurance, paid vacations, and sick leave. In some cases the benefits also include educational assistance, pension plans, and uniform allowances.

Conditions of work

Electroencephalographic technicians usually work five-day, 40-hour work weeks, with only occasional overtime required. Some hospitals require them to be on call for emergencies during weekends, evenings, and holidays. Technicians doing sleep studies may work most of their hours at night.

Electroencephalographic technicians work in clean, well-lighted surroundings.

Electroencephalographic technicians generally work with people who are ill and may be frightened or perhaps emotionally disturbed. Successful technicians are the ones who like people, can quickly recognize what others may be feeling, and have a pleasing and reassuring manner. At the same time, they need to be realize that some patients will be very ill; others may be in the process of dying. Technicians need to be able to carry out their responsibilities accurately and efficiently even in the face of case histories that may be quite tragic.

Most electroencephalographic technicians work in hospitals, where it is very important that they get along well with other staff members. This task is sometimes made more difficult by the fact that in most hospitals there is a formal, often rigid, status structure, and electroencephalographic technicians often find themselves in a relatively low position in that structure. In emergency situations or at other moments of frustration, electroencephalographic technicians may find themselves dealt with brusquely or angrily. Technicians should not take these outbursts or rude treatment personally, but instead should respond with stability and maturity.

GOE: 10.03.01; SIC: 801, 806; SOC: 369

◇ **SOURCES OF ADDITIONAL INFORMATION**

American Electroencephalographic Society
1 Regency Drive
PO Box 30
Bloomfield, CT 06002

American Board of Registration of Electroencephalographic Technologists
PO Box 11434
Norfolk, VA 23417

◇ **RELATED ARTICLES**

Volume 1: Health Care
Volumes 2–4: Biomedical equipment technicians; Electrocardiograph technicians; Licensed practical nurses; Medical assistants; Medical laboratory technicians; Medical technologists; Nurses; Nursing and psychiatric aides; Physician assistants; Registered nurses

Electrologists

Definition

Electrologists are trained technicians who remove unwanted hair from the skin of patients. To remove the hair and prevent further hair growth in an area of the body, electrologists insert sterilized needles that conduct electricity into the hair follicle and deaden the hair root using small charges of electricity. They then use tiny forceps to remove the loosened hair.

History

Different cultures dictate the concepts of beauty that the members of the general population follow and imitate. In various places, beauty treatments are used for ritual purposes, ornamentation, or to simply make a person feel better about his or her appearance. In modern societies many people find excess facial hair unappealing and unattractive. This is particularly a problem among young girls and women. Chemicals are sometimes used to dissolve the hair, but they have the potential to irritate the skin. Shaving, waxing, or tweezing have also been used to provide temporary relief from the problem.

Technological advances and research in skin treatment have made it possible for people to remove unwanted hair permanently through the use of electrolysis. Electrolysis can be used by both women and men to remove unwanted hair from almost any area of their bodies. It is also safer than many chemical products and treatments when performed by a professional electrologist.

Nature of the work

Electrologists, who usually conduct business in a beauty salon or medical clinic, work with only one patron at a time. This enables them to give patients their complete attention and concentrate exclusively on the delicate treatment they are performing. Since electrolysis can sometimes be painful or uncomfortable, it reassures patrons to know that the practitioner's complete focus is on them and their needs.

The first step in the treatment is the sterilization of the patch of skin that will be worked on. Rubbing alcohol or an antiseptic is often used for this purpose. Once everything is germ-free, the hair removal can begin. Electrologists use a round-tipped needle to enter the opening of the skin fold, also known as the hair follicle. The needle also probes the papilla, which is the organ beneath the hair root. The electrologist sets the proper amount and duration of the electrical current in advance and presses gently on a floor pedal to distribute that current through the needle. The electrical current helps deaden the tissue, after which the hair can be lifted out gently with a pair of tweezers or forceps.

Electrologists can remove hair from almost any area of the body. The most common areas they treat are the arms, legs, chest, and portions of the face such as upper or lower lip, chin, or cheek. Electrologists are not permitted to remove hair from inside the ears or nose or from the eyelids. They must also have the written consent of a physician, as well as legitimate malpractice insurance coverage, to remove hair from a mole or birthmark.

Electrologists determine the extent of a patron's treatments that will be necessary for complete removal of the unwanted hair. They may schedule weekly appointments that last 15, 30, 45, or even 60 minutes. The length of the individual appointments depends on both the amount of hair to be removed and the thickness and depth of the hair. If a patient is very sensitive to the treatments, the electrologist may set up shorter appointments so as not to put the patron through undue discomfort.

Electrolysis is mainly performed for aesthetic reasons. As is the case with cosmetic surgery, the procedure can be fairly expensive. The electrologist should first consult with a client to determine what is desired and why and then discuss the cost of the procedure.

Electrologists help people feel good about themselves by improving aspects of their physical appearance. They feel a sense of accomplishment for helping patients through the various stages of their treatment. They may sometimes feel the pressure of a patient who is impatient or unrealistic about the results, or is nervous about the process. Because electrologists perform personal and sometimes painful treatments for their clients, it is impor-

ELECTROLOGISTS

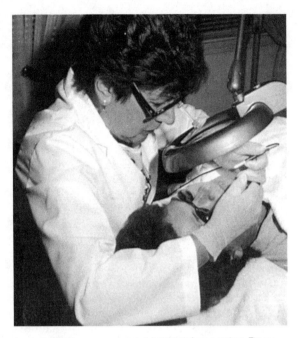

An electrologist removes unwanted facial hair from a patient. The patient must wear eye protection to shield herself from the intense light.

tant that the they be patient and caring and develop a good bedside manner.

Requirements

Students with high school diplomas or equivalency certificates may enroll in trade schools or professional schools that offer electrolysis training. In these programs students study microbiology, dermatology, neurology, and electricity. They also learn about proper sterilization and sanitation procedures to avoid infections or injury. Cell composition, the endocrine system, the vascular-pulmonary system, and basic anatomy may also be covered.

Though the training offered is designed to educate students about the theory of electrolysis and its relation to the skin and tissue, the greater part of the training is of a practical nature. Many hours of the student's training is spent learning the purpose and function of the different types of equipment. In addition, hands-on experience with patrons needing different treatments gives the student confidence in running the equipment and working with patients.

Programs may be offered on a full-time or part-time basis. Though tuition varies, some schools offer financial assistance or payment plans to make their programs more affordable. Sometimes lab and materials fees are charged.

Applicants should determine whether the school is accredited or associated with any professional organizations. Licensing requirements of the various states may also affect the length and depth of training that the schools offer.

States that require licensing offer examinations through the state health department. The examination usually covers various topics in the areas of health and cosmetology. Students should become familiar with their state's licensing requirements prior to beginning their training so they can be sure their education provides them with everything necessary to practice.

Electrologists have many professional organizations that provide information on new equipment, special seminars, and networking and employment opportunities. The American Electrolysis Association, the International Guild of Professional Electrologists, and the Society of Clinical and Medical Electrologists offer useful information for beginning practitioners and guidelines for certification and advanced study.

Opportunities for experience and exploration

Students interested in finding out more about the field of electrologists may wish to write for information from local trade schools. Also, some two-year colleges that offer course work in medical-technician careers may be able to supply literature on programs and training in that field.

Cosmetology schools, which are located in many different areas of the country, may also prove helpful for investigating this profession. Some schools and training programs allow interested students to speak with faculty and guidance counselors for additional information.

Methods of entering

Many newly licensed electrologists begin as assistants to a technician who is already practicing. They may handle extra patrons when the office is overbooked or have new patrons referred to them. In this way, beginning electrologists can build a clientele without having to cover the costs of equipment and supplies themselves.

Some electrologists may open their own business in a medical office complex and receive referrals from their neighboring health care professionals. Others may be employed by clinics or hospitals before deciding to get their own office space.

Advancement

Electrologists usually advance through building up the various aspects of their practices. As an electrologist becomes more experienced and gains a reputation, he or she often attracts more new patients and repeat customers. Some electrologists who work as part of a clinic staff may open their own shop or move to a more visible and accessible location or office complex.

Employment outlook

A moderate increase in employment opportunities is expected to continue for electrologists. Many hospitals and clinics strive to develop new services and technologies, which can result in more jobs for electrologists. In addition, there is a trend among medical professionals toward large group practices to pool resources and offset joint costs, such as common supplies, support staff, and so on. This may make it more feasible for beginning electrologists to open their own practices right out of school.

Earnings

Because electrologists schedule patient treatments that vary in length, their fees are often based on quarter-hour appointments. Rates for a 15-minute treatment may begin at $10 in some cities, while electrologists in large urban regions may begin at $20. Treatments lasting 30 minutes or 60 minutes in large cities may begin at $50 and $100, respectively. Though rates in smaller towns are often less, electrologists still earn a competitive wage for their work. Electrologists who are employed by a medical practice or clinic may have to charge more if a portion of their fee must help cover office space, utilities, and support staff like receptionists and bookkeepers.

Conditions of work

Whether the electrologist works in a beauty salon, a medical center, or a private shop, the nature of the work requires the environment to be clean, comfortable, and professional. Because electrologists perform delicate work, they may operate in spaces that are quiet to allow for greater concentration. Sometimes music is played in the background to help put patients at ease.

A neat appearance is important, so often electrologists wear uniforms or lab coats. As well as being comfortable and practical for the electrologist, a regular medical uniform may also reassure and comfort the patient.

GOE: 09.05.01; SIC: 7299; SOC: 5253

◇ **SOURCES OF ADDITIONAL INFORMATION**

American Electrology Association
106 Oak Ridge Road
Trumbull, CT 06611

National Commission for Electrologist Certification
96 Westminster Road
West Hempstead, NY 11552

Society of Clinical and Medical Electrologists
6 Abbott Road
Wellesley Hills, MA 02181

International Guild of Professional Electrologists
202 Boulevard, Suite B
High Point, NC 27262

Canadian Cosmetics Careers Association, Inc.
26 Ferrah Street
Unionville ON L3R 1N5

◇ **RELATED ARTICLES**

Volume 1: Health Care; Personal and Consulting Services
Volumes 2–4: Barbers; Cosmetologists; Electrocardiograph technicians; Electroencephalographic technicians; Medical laboratory technicians

Electromechanical technicians

Definition

Electromechanical technicians work with automated mechanical equipment that is controlled by electronic sensing devices. They assist mechanical engineers in the design and development of such equipment, analyze test results, and write reports. The technician follows blueprints, operates metalworking machines, and uses hand tools and precision measuring and testing devices to build instrument housings, install electrical equipment, and calibrate instruments and machinery. Technicians who specialize in the assembly of prototype instruments are known as *development technicians.* Those who specialize in the assembly of production instruments are known as *fabrication technicians.*

History

Electromechanical technology is a relatively new field dealing with the interaction of electrical, electronic, and mechanical devices. Its roots lie in the late 18th and early 19th centuries, when countless machines were designed to do work previously done by people. Many of these mechanical devices, however, could not be considered fully automated, for they still required alert and sharp-eyed people to operate, monitor, and control all of their activities.

During the first half of the 20th century, electronic devices were invented that could sense various aspects of their environment. These devices included photocells that sense the presence or absence of an object between itself and a light source; thermocouples and resistance thermometers that electronically measure and reveal changes in temperature; stress and strain sensors that convert mechanical stresses into measurable electrical currents; and proximity sensors that can measure the distance between two electrical conductors or any two objects to which the conductors are attached. It was the coupling of electrical or electronic devices with various kinds of automated machinery that gave birth to the field of electromechanical technology.

Today, many electromechanical technicians work in the field of computer and office equipment; in addition, electromechanical devices are employed in many other industries, including: automatic guidance systems in rockets, missiles, and satellites; quality control systems in manufacturing; and in oil and gas exploration.

Nature of the work

Electromechanical technicians build, test, install, and repair electromechanical devices and systems, including plant automation equipment, automated environmental control systems, elevator controls, missile controls, computer tape drives, and other auxiliary computer equipment.

Computer industry technicians often work in manufacturing and product-development divisions; they develop and test precision mechanical devices such as magnetic tape drives and readers as well as high-speed printing machines.

In the continuing quest to increase speed and reliability, these technicians research assembly and manufacturing problems, conducting lab studies in: experimental applied physics, vibration analysis, and environmental testing.

Computer industry technicians are also required to handle preventive maintenance and to repair existing equipment, both in-factory and on-site.

In addition to direct computer work, electromechanical technicians also work in manufacturing, research, and repair occupations. In the course of their work, they may: operate electronic control systems in factories; ensure proper quality control during manufacturing; work in the new-product field; or provide maintenance services for electromechanical devices, including factory returns and products still on the customer's premises.

Technicians who operate electronic manufacturing-control systems are usually experts in the calibration, maintenance, and repair of specialized control devices. These devices electronically sense a material's temperature, thickness, or color, and will automatically carry on the manufacture within accepted guidelines. In paper manufacturing, for example, certain devices determine the fiber's texture and the finished product's overall thickness. Each field has controls similar to these, but designed to meet its own specific needs. For example, these controls can be adapted to steel-rolling mills, ball-bearings manufacturers, and plastics manufacturers.

Electromechanical devices may vary greatly, depending on which manufacturing processes they are used for. Sometimes, manufacturing processes require especially sophisticated control, which calls for specially trained *operations technicians*, to work in conjunction with those technicians performing repairs and recalibration. These operations technicians control the day-to-day functioning of complex manufacturing equipment whose workings are much too complicated for ordinary operating personnel to handle.

Quality control technicians are usually required to adjust, interpret, and calibrate complex equipment. After learning more about the products, such technicians may test completed assemblies that interact with each other to form a larger system; for example, a radar station, a computer network, or a communications system.

Electromechanical technicians working in maintenance may take on a variety of roles, depending on their knowledge and experience. For example, the knowledge needed to maintain a dictating machine is not as extensive as that required for a missile guidance system. Maintenance opportunities are wide ranging and, for those technicians so inclined, include the opportunity for travel. Some especially complex products, once installed, need the technician to travel to them for maintenance. Some examples include the probes used in oil and gas exploration and drilling, and the electrical control or detection devices used in military and industrial security. These may be installed anywhere in the world.

Electromechanical technicians working in maintenance may also be employed at the manufacturing plant or branch facilities, where they maintain electromechanical equipment that has been removed from the installation site and returned for overhaul, recalibration, or repair. These technicians need special skills to maintain the product, but do not require the same customer relations skills needed by the traveling technician.

Technicians employed in product development need the ability to conceive new ideas and to imagine the results of design modifications, or innovations. Because new products are meant to be better than the ones they replace, technicians should be able to analyze how new or modified techniques will work in place of the old. These technicians operate under the supervision of development engineers; thus, they need to understand engineering terminology in order to translate the ideas and principles into functioning products.

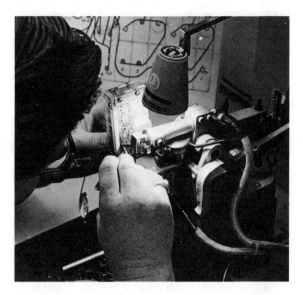

An electromechanical technician repairs a control device that maintains the quality of a product during its manufacture. Such work requires patience and manual skill.

Research technicians frequently work with no direct supervision. They may work on their own or as part of a team doing research and design of an entirely new product. Successful research technicians frequently advance to engineering work or are classified as engineers for the work they do.

Requirements

Successful electromechanical technicians have an aptitude for mathematics and science, and the patience to methodically pursue complex questions. A tolerance for following prescribed procedures is essential, especially when undertaking assignments requiring a very precise, unchanging system of problem-solving, such as in troubleshooting a complex computer. They need the kind of motivation for their work that will help sustain interest, patience, and steady habits even when faced repetitive tasks.

For those involved in on-site repair of customer equipment need to maintain good customer relations. Those who repair electronic manufacturing/control systems need the ability to remain calm under pressure: the equipment they repair is essential to continuing production, so delays can cost tens of thousands of dollars. Successful technicians are able to provide solutions quickly and accurately even in stressful situations.

Technicians in operations and manufacturing control need to have a strong background

ELECTROMECHANICAL TECHNICIANS

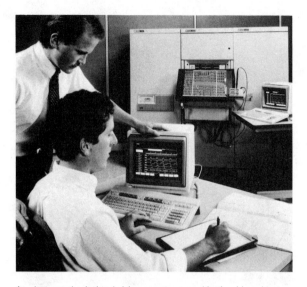

An electromechanical technician operates a combinational board-test system that performs both in-circuit component tests and functional tests.

in basic electrical, electronic, and mechanical principles. They also need a broad understanding of the system, machinery, or equipment to which the electromechanical controls are being applied. In addition, operations technicians should thoroughly understand all of the functions of the equipment they handle, including its purpose and finished product.

Although technicians should possess accuracy and be willing to follow strict procedures, their jobs are not limited to a rigid performance of duties. Electromechanical technicians are something like physicians: they must diagnose the "ailment" before treating it. Also like physicians, they must be ready and able to find new and original answers when a prescribed treatment does not work. Many improvements result when technicians discover that a theory does not always work and that a practical approach sometimes can solve problems that were not anticipated by the original designers.

There are excellent advancement possibilities in this field; thus a technician's ability to accept change and remain up-to-date on new products and scientific discoveries is important.

For those involved only in the assembly of electromechanical devices, the personal qualifications are not as varied as those mentioned above. In such capacities, the manufacturer is likely to place more emphasis on the study of related subject matter than on the ability to improvise solutions or work with other team members or customers.

High school students interested in a career in electromechanical technology should learn all of the mathematics and science possible.

Courses designed to prepare students for engineering education are also appropriate for the technician. Minimum requirements for most post-secondary programs usually include one year of geometry and one year of algebra (or two years of algebra), a year of physics, and another year of a laboratory science. English courses are a basic requirement in all high school programs, and potential technicians should look especially for English courses that stress speech and composition skills.

Students who lack this background should not be discouraged, however; most schools of higher education provide courses or intensive-study programs designed to overcome a lack of preparation in various subjects.

For those who expect to make electromechanical technology a lifetime career, education beyond high school is essential. Many colleges and technical training institutes offer training programs in electromechanical technology. Others offer programs in related areas such as electronics or electrical or mechanical engineering technology. Such programs usually take two years to complete. Typical courses during the first year include electricity and electronics, principles of physics, mathematics, technical graphics, English composition, introduction to data processing, and mechanisms. Typical courses for the second year include digital computer fundamentals, electromechanical components, control systems, digital computing systems, input-output devices, storage principles and devices, psychology and human relations, and hydraulics and pneumatics.

Companies which employ technicians in the business equipment field usually provide supplementary training programs for employees recruited from technical institutes and colleges.Introductory new-employee training may extend from 8 to 15 weeks. Upon graduation from this basic program, those selected for technical training are then sent to a special school where all the techniques required by the company are taught. The time spent in both schools may last nearly one year, during which the technician receives a weekly salary and living expenses.

Electromechanical technicians still in school may become members of the Institute of Electrical and Electronic Engineers or the American Society of Certified Engineering Technicians, provided they are in an engineering technology program. Membership in either of these associations is voluntary.

Some of the organizations listed at the end of this article offer certification programs for electromechanical technicians. Although seldom a requirement for employment, it is a way to demonstrate interest and accomplishment in the field.

Some technicians are required to belong to a union.

Opportunities for experience and exploration

There are a number of ways to explore the various fields in which electromechanical technicians are employed. In towns with equipment manufacturing facilities, repair shops, or industrial laboratories, school counselors may plan field trips. It may be possible for a student to get a summer or weekend job at such a facility or to arrange to accompany a technician on service rounds. Even in their own school, students may observe the repair and installation of data-processing or other office machines. Visits to major industrial installations, such as steel mills, automobile factories, or petroleum refineries, offer an excellent opportunity to see electronic manufacturing-control devices in operation.

Methods of entering

The most reliable and accepted way to enter into this field is through the student's technical training school. Most of these institutions have a student placement service and are in constant touch with those industries in need of technicians.

People not enrolled in a technical institute or college should visit companies where they hope eventually to find employment. In the course of such a visit they should inquire about employment opportunities and about what courses of study will be most helpful.

Advancement

Advancement in this field is quite regular for those who continue studying during employment. Technicians usually begin work under the direct supervision of an experienced technician, scientist, or engineer, and then, as they gain experience, are given more responsible assignments, often carrying out particular work programs under only very general supervision.

From there, technicians may move into supervisory positions; those with exceptional ability can sometimes qualify for professional po-

sitions after receiving additional training. Some technicians advance by becoming technical writers, sales representatives, or instructors.

Employment outlook

The long term outlook for the computer and business equipment industries—major employers of electromechanical technicians—is favorable. In addition, the ongoing movement towards more automation in manufacturing industries will call for more technicians with a combined knowledge of electronic, electrical, and mechanical principles. Because of these factors, the demand for electromechanical technicians should remain strong through the year 2000. However, all of these industries are vulnerable to downturns in the economy. During these periods, the demand for electromechanical technicians slackens and competition for good jobs increases. In periods like this, technicians with less training and motivation may find good jobs hard to find.

Earnings

Salaries for electromechanical technicians vary considerably depending on the extent of the individual's education, experience, area of specialization, the type of firm in which the technician is employed, and the geographical location of the job.

In general, however, starting salaries for those who are graduates of post-high school technical programs average about $19,000 per year in industry. Those with less formal training earn somewhat less. Most experienced electromechanical technicians earn between $20,000 and $40,000 a year, and some successful technicians earn between $30,000 and $45,000 a year or more.

Conditions of work

Because the work of electromechanical technicians is connected with and serves other industries, the conditions vary greatly from place to place. In general, however, electromechanical equipment will only work well in temperature- and humidity-controlled environments. Therefore most electromechanical technicians can be assured of a safe and comfortable working environment. Most technicians work regular 35- to 40-hour weeks, although some service technicians may be required to work overtime on short notice or to be away from home for several days in a row traveling on a service call. Some technicians do elect to work for extended periods of time on equipment in rugged or out-of-doors environments; however, such technicians are compensated financially for the hardships involved.

The technician's work rarely requires great strength or strenuous exertion, although it may require the technician to spend hours in an awkward position, standing, sitting, or crouched beside a machine.

Electromechanical technicians may work alone, in pairs, or as part of a small team. Almost all technicians need the ability to get along well with and work cooperatively with other people—both customers and coworkers. In some cases, electromechanical technicians need to be able to work well under pressure. Most will also need a healthy tolerance for routine, uncomplicated, and sometimes repetitive tasks.

The electromechanical technology field is constantly changing. These changes bring both an opportunity for advancement and a risk of being left behind by advancing technology. The successful technician makes it a priority to remain knowledgeable in order to take advantage of the available opportunities.

GOE: 05.05.11; SIC: Any industry; SOC: 6171

◇ **SOURCES OF ADDITIONAL INFORMATION**

International Society of Certified Electronics Technicians
2708 West Berry Street, Suite 8
Fort Worth, TX 76109

Institute of Electrical and Electronic Engineers
345 East 47th Street
New York, NY 10017

American Society of Mechanical Engineers
345 East 47th Street
New York, NY 10017

Computer and Business Equipment Manufacturers Association
311 First Street, NW
Suite 500
Washington, DC 20001

American Society for Engineering Education
11 Dupont Circle
Suite 200
Washington, DC 20036

Electrical and Electronic Manufacturers Association of Canada
#500, 10 Carlson Court
Rexdale ON M9W 6L2

◇ **RELATED ARTICLES**

Volume 1: Engineering; Machining and Machinery
Volumes 2–4: CAD/CAM technicians; Computer programmers; Computer-service technicians; Electronics sales and service technicians; Electronics technicians; Industrial engineering technicians; Industrial machinery mechanics; Instrumentation technicians; Mechanical technicians; Miscellaneous engineers; Robotics technicians

Electronics sales and service technicians

Definition

Electronics sales and service technicians assist consumers in their purchase of electronics equipment, for use in either their homes or businesses. This equipment typically includes televisions, audio and video equipment, microwave ovens, and other kinds of home electronic devices. Technicians meet with potential customers to discuss their requirements, then discuss the various kinds of equipment available to meet those requirements. In order to meet special needs, technicians may show the customer how to modify existing equipment, or else a new way to combine it with other equipment to provide what the customer wants. Once equipment has been selected, the technician supervises its installation and maintains the equipment in good working order. Technicians also make repairs when necessary and advise customers on the equipment's replacement when it is no longer practical to maintain. Some electronics sales and service technicians may work with electronic office equipment, such as photocopy machines, dictating machines, and fax (facsimile) machines.

History

Most electronics products in use today were developed during the 20th century; however, most of these products are based on electronics principles discovered in the 19th century. Modern television, for instance, is based on principles first demonstrated in the 1850s by Heinrich Geissler, whose experiments showed that electricity discharged in a vacuum tube causes small amounts of rare gases in the tube to glow. Later investigations showed that the glow is caused by the freeing of electrons. Experimenters in the late 1800s and early 1900s worked further with vacuum tubes until Karl Braun, in 1898, made the first cathode ray tube that could control the electron flow. In 1907 Lee De Forest developed the first amplifying tube, used to strengthen electronic signals.

At this point, the basic elements of modern television transmission existed, but they had not yet been combined into a workable system. In 1922, a sixteen-year-old named Philo Farnsworth developed a practical electronic scanning system. Shortly afterwards, in 1923, Vladimir Zworykin developed the iconoscope and the kinescope, which were, respectively, the basic elements of the television camera and the television receiver. Zworykin's first practical all-electronic television system was demonstrated for the first time publicly in 1929.

Radio followed a similar path of development. But, although the roots of television and radio lie in the 1800s, neither medium had developed to the point of needing a sales and service industry until regular commercial broadcasting began and people began to purchase receivers. For radio, commercial broadcasting began in 1920, when KDKA, Pittsburgh, and WWJ, Detroit, went on the air. For television, regular broadcasting began in 1946, when six stations went on the air. By 1950 there were 6 million television sets in the United States; by 1989 there were more than 100 million. Almost every household now has at least one television, and almost two-thirds of U.S. households have two or more.

Owners of the early radios handled most of their own repairs; sets were simple, and the range of possible solutions to problems was small. As the broadcasting industry grew and new improvements resulted in more complicated sets, trade and technical institutes were established to train technicians. Correspondence schools started and became popular during the Great Depression of the 1930s, when many people were seeking new careers or ways to supplement their incomes.

The explosive growth of television broadcasting after World War II created an almost instant demand for trained television service technicians. Trade and technical schools again boomed, aided this time by the GI Bill's educational benefits, which enabled many veterans to study television servicing. The field was especially attractive to those ex-servicemen who had been communications or electronics technicians in the U.S. Armed Forces. The subsequent development of the transistor, stereophonic sound, and color television resulted in television sets, radios, and other home electronics equipment that could only be serviced by trained technicians with adequate testing equipment and repair tools.

The 1970s and 1980s saw a tremendous growth in the number and variety of electronic devices introduced into homes and businesses. Miniature and super screen projection televisions, video cameras and videocassette recorders (VCRs), microcomputers and printers, microwave ovens, telephone answering machines—

An electronics sales and service technician must know how to install and repair electronic business equipment.

all became common household items, and fax machines, desktop photocopiers, and electronic securities systems became common in offices. The growth in this field has led to a continuing and expanding need for trained technicians to assist in the sales, installation, maintenance, and repairing of home and office electronics equipment.

Nature of the work

The primary work of technicians involved with service and repair is to diagnose and repair malfunctions in electronic home-entertainment equipment, including television sets and video recording equipment, radios and audio recording equipment, personal computer peripheral equipment, and such related electronic equipment as garage door openers, microwave ovens, electronic organs, and amplifying equipment for other electrified musical instruments. They usually begin by gathering information from customers about the problems they are having with their equipment. A preliminary inspection may reveal a loose connection or other simple problem, and the technician may be able to complete repairs quickly. In other cases a problem may be more complicated and may require that the equipment be taken to a shop for more thorough testing and the installation of new components.

Electronics sales and service technicians are classified as inside or outside technicians. The outside technicians make service calls on customers, gather information, and make preliminary examinations of malfunctioning equipment. Inside, or bench, technicians work in shops where they make more thorough examinations of problems using testing equipment and hand tools such as pliers and socket wrenches to dismantle sets and make repairs. The testing equipment used includes voltmeters, oscilloscopes, and signal generators.

The servicing of other kinds of electronic equipment, such as audio and videocassette recorders, requires special knowledge of their components. Electronics technicians gain knowledge about such special areas and keep up with new developments in electronics by attending short courses given by manufacturers at their factory or by a factory technician at local shops.

Technicians involved with the sale of electronics equipment meet with potential customers to discuss and explain the kinds of equipment available to meet the specific needs of the customer. They describe the equipment's features, explain the manufacturer's specifications, and demonstrate how to use the equipment. For customers with special needs, they may recommend ways to either modify existing equipment or combine it with other equipment to provide what the customer wants. Once equipment has been selected, the technician may also be involved, often in a supervisory capacity, with the installation and maintenance of the equipment. These technicians also make repairs when necessary, and advise customers regarding replacement of equipment that is no longer practical to maintain.

Requirements

Students interested in careers as electronics sales and service technicians should take mathematics courses at least through algebra and plane geometry in high school, and should have a good working knowledge of shop math. They should develop their language skills so they can read electronics texts and manuals comfortably and express themselves well when making spoken and written proposals. People interested in electronics should have at least two years of training beyond high school in a technical institute or community college, studying electronics theory and repair of televisions, radios, and other electronic equipment.

To be successful, technicians need to possess mechanical aptitude and a solid knowledge of practical electronics. They should be familiar with and able to use electrician's hand tools and basic electronic and electrical testing equipment. Precision and accuracy are often required in adjusting electronic equipment. The physical requirements of their work are moderate, sometimes involving lifting and carrying television sets and other equipment. Technicians are often required to stand and bend for extended periods while working.

Technicians often work in customer's homes; therefore, they should be able to meet and communicate clearly with strangers. The ability to extract useful information from customers about their equipment can be a great time-saver.

Some states require some electronics sales and service technicians to be licensed. Such licenses are obtained by passing tests in electronics and demonstrating proficiency with testing equipment. Prospective technicians should check with a training institution in their state to determine whether licensing is required.

Only a few technicians belong to labor unions. Most of those who belong are members of the International Brotherhood of Electrical Workers.

Opportunities for experience and exploration

Local electronics sales and service technicians are usually willing to share their experience and knowledge with interested young people. Owners of stores or repair shops may be especially helpful with the business aspects of a career in the field. Summer employment as a helper or a delivery person can provide an opportunity to observe the day-to-day activities of technicians.

Schools that offer training in radio, television, and other related technology fields are usually happy to supply program information to prospective students. Local chapters of the International Brotherhood of Electrical Workers and local offices of the state employment service can also supply information about training opportunities as well as the employment outlook in your area.

Methods of entering

Entry into this field may be through: graduation from a technical school; an apprenticeship program; or on-the-job training.

By far the majority of people entering the television and radio service technician field graduate from an accredited technical training

program and begin work as a trained technician. These technicians either apply directly to a prospective employer for a position or receive help from their school placement officer. Most of them require a further year of shop supervision before they are able to work independently without the direction of a more experienced electronics technician.

Apprenticeship programs stress practical experience over theory. In a typical four-year post-secondary school program comprising about 8,000 hours, approximately 550 of them are devoted to classroom work; the remainder consist of supervised shop work.

On-the-job training is becoming much less common. Where shops formerly provided complete on-the-job instruction for untrained employees, they are now usually limiting such training to current employees—delivery drivers, antenna installers, and so forth—who show a basic understanding of electronics, an aptitude for careful work, and an interest in learning. Such opportunities usually occur in shops that place a higher value on practical experience than on theory. Even so, individuals in such programs will have to supplement their practical training with evening school or home–study courses.

Advancement

Advancement in this field depends to a large extent on the size and character of the technician's place of employment. Early advancement usually comes in the form of increased salary and less supervision as a recognition of the technician's increasing skill. In a small shop, the only other advancement possibility may be for the technician to go into business alone, if the community can support another retail store or repair shop.

In a larger store or shop, the electronics technician usually advances to a supervisory position, as a *crew chief, sales supervisor, senior technician,* or *service or sales manager.* This may involve not only scheduling and assigning work, but also training new employees and arranging refresher courses and factory training in new products for experienced electronics technicians.

Technicians with strong theoretical training in electronics may go on to become technical school instructors. They may also become service representatives for manufacturers. Those employed in stores or shops that handle a wide variety of electronics sales and service work may become involved in working on the more complicated equipment, from radio-frequency heating equipment to electron microscopes.

This work may also lead to working with engineers in designing and testing new electronic equipment.

Employment outlook

Employment of electronics sales and service technicians is expected to increase about as fast as the average of other occupations through the year 2000. The increased demand will stem from an increased number of television and radio receivers in service, and from the rapid growth of other home electronics equipment such as VCRs and computer video games operated through television sets. On the other hand, continuing improvements in electronics technology and the increasing use of modular components will limit somewhat the demand for service technicians and will keep employment levels from rising as fast as might otherwise be expected.

Earnings

As trainees, electronics sales and service technicians earn around $16,068 a year. More experienced technicians earn between $24,500 and $50,000 a year, with the average being about $36,000 a year. Self-employed technicians earn higher than average salaries, generally, but they also work longer hours. For employed technicians, 40-hour weeks are normal, with time-and-a-half for overtime and an increment for night work.

Conditions of work

The work of electronics technicians is performed indoors, in homes and shops, under generally comfortable conditions. Outside technicians may spend considerable time driving from call to call. All technicians risk occasional electrical shock, but this risk is minimized greatly by following proper safety precautions.

Once they have completed their training, electronics sales and service technicians work with a minimum of supervision. They must be able to work carefully and accurately. Because the result of their work is often immediately evident to the owner of the equipment, service technicians especially must be able to handle criticism when they are not completely successful.

Because of the constantly changing technology of electronic devices, electronics sales and service technicians must be willing to keep growing and learning in their trade skills if they are to be successful.

GOE: 05.05.05, 05.10.03; SIC: 367; SOC: 6153, 6155

◇ **SOURCES OF ADDITIONAL INFORMATION**

American Electronics Association
5201 Great America Parkway
Suite 520
Santa Clara, CA 95054

Electronics Industries Association
2001 Pennsylvania Avenue NW
Washington, DC 20006-1813

Electronic Industries Foundation
1901 Pennsylvania Avenue, NW
Suite 700
Washington, DC 20006

Electronics Technicians Association
602 North Jackson
Greencastle, IN 46135

International Society of Certified Electronics Technicians
2708 West Berry Street
Suite 3
Fort Worth, TX 76109

Semiconductor Industry Association
4300 Stevens Creek Boulevard
Number 271
San Jose, CA 95129

American Society of Certified Engineering Technicians
PO Box 371474
El Paso, TX 79937

Canadian Electronic and Appliance Service Association
#115, 10 Wynford Heights Cres.
Don Mills ON M3C 1K3

◇ **RELATED ARTICLES**

Volume 1: Electronics
Volumes 2–4: Audiovisual technicians; Electromechanical technicians; Electronics technicians; Office machine servicers; Retail business owners; Retail managers; Retail sales workers

Electronics technicians

Definition

Electronics technicians work with electronics engineers to develop, manufacture and service industrial and consumer electronic equipment, including sonar, radar, navigational equipment, computers, radios, televisions, stereos, and calculators. Those involved in the development of new electronic equipment help make changes or modifications in circuitry or other design elements.

Other electronics technicians inspect newly-installed equipment or instruct and supervise lower-grade technicians' installation, assembly, or repair activities.

As part of their normal duties, all electronics technicians set up testing equipment, conduct tests, and analyze the results; they also prepare reports, sketches, graphs, and schematic drawings to describe electronics systems and their characteristics. Their work involves the use of a variety of hand and machine tools, including such equipments as bench lathes and drills.

Depending on their area of specialization, electronics technicians may be designated *computer-laboratory technicians, development-instrumentation technicians, electronic-communications technicians, nuclear-reactor electronics technicians, engineering-development technicians,* or *systems-testing laboratory technicians.*

History

Strictly speaking, electronics technology deals with the behavior of electrons as they pass through gases, liquids, solids, and vacuums. Originally this field was an outgrowth of electrical engineering, an area concerned with the movement of electrons along conductors. As the field of electronics has expanded in scope, however, so has its definition, and today the term encompasses all areas of technology concerned with the behavior of electrons in electronic devices and equipment, including electrical engineering.

Although the field of electronics has had its most spectacular growth and development during the 20th century, it is actually the product of more than 200 years of study and experiment. One of the important early experimenters in this field was Benjamin Franklin. His experiments with lightning and his theory that electrical charges are present in all matter influenced the thinking and established much of the vocabulary of the researchers who came after him.

The invention of the electric battery, or voltaic pile, by the Italian scientist Alessandro Volta in 1800, ushered in a century of significant discoveries in the field of electricity and magnetism. Researchers working throughout Europe and the United States made important breakthroughs in how to strengthen, control, and measure the flow of electrons moving through vacuums. Around the turn of the century these experiments culminated in the description and measurement by Sir Joseph John Thomson of the particle we call the electron.

During the early years of the 20th century, further discoveries along these lines were made by experimenters such as Lee De Forest and Vladimir Zworykin. These discoveries led the way to developing equipment and techniques for long-distance broadcasting of radio and television signals. It was the outbreak of World War II, however, with its needs for long-distance communications equipment, and ultimately missile-guidance systems, that brought about the rapid expansion of electronics technology and the creation of the electronics industry.

As the field of electronics technology turned to the creation of consumer and industrial products following the end of the war, its growth was spurred by two new technological developments. The first was the completion in 1946 of the first all-purpose, all-electronic digital computer. This machine, crude as it was, could handle mathematical calculations a thousand times faster than the electromechanical calculating machines of its day. Since 1946, there has been a steady growth in the speed, sophistication, and versatility of computers.

The second important development was the invention of the transistor in 1948. The transistor provided an inexpensive and compact replacement for the vacuum tubes used in nearly all electronic equipment up until then. Transistors allowed for the miniaturization of electronic circuits and were especially crucial in the development of the computer and in opening new possibilities in industrial automation.

Discoveries during the 1960s in the fields of microcircuitry and integrated circuitry led to the development of microminiaturized and more sophisticated electronic equipment, from pocket calculators, digital watches, and micro-

When assembling circuit boards, electronics technicians must have steady hands, keen eyesight, and patience.

wave ovens to high-speed computers and the long-range guidance systems used in space flights.

By the 1970s, electronics had become one of the largest industries and most important areas of technology in the industrialized world, which, in turn, has come to rely on instantaneous worldwide communications, computer-controlled or computer-assisted industrial operations, and the wide-ranging forms of electronic data processing made possible by electronics technology.

Throughout the growth and development of the electronics field, there has been a need for skilled assistants in the laboratory, on the factory floor, and in the wide variety of settings where electronic equipment is used. As the technology has become more sophisticated, the need has increased for these assistants to be specially trained and educated. Working in partnership with scientists and engineers, today's electronics technicians belong to one of the fastest-growing occupational groups in the United States.

Nature of the work

Most electronics technicians work in one of three broad areas of electronics: product development; manufacturing and production; and service and maintenance. Technicians involved with service and maintenance are known as *electronics sales and service technicians*, featured in a separate entry of the same name.

In the product-development area, electronics technicians work directly with engineers and scientists. They build, test, and modify prototype or experimental models of new electronics products. As part of their work they use hand tools and small machine tools; make complex parts, components, and subassemblies; conduct physical and electrical tests using complicated instruments and test equipment; and make complete reports of their observations.

Electronics technicians in the product-development field may make suggestions for improvements in the design of a device. They may also have to construct, install, modify, or repair laboratory test equipment.

Electronics drafting is a field of electronics technology closely related to product development. *Electronics drafters* convert rough sketches and written or verbal information provided by the engineers and scientists into easily understandable schematic, layout, or wiring diagrams to be used in manufacturing the product. These drafters may also prepare a list of components and equipment needed for producing the final product, as well as bills for materials.

Another closely-related field is cost estimating. Those technicians working in this area prepare estimates of the costs of manufacturing a new product with sufficient accuracy to allow the sales department to determine in advance the price at which a product can be sold. After the engineers have prepared drawings, engineering specifications, and other information on the new product, cost estimators will use this engineering data to estimate all labor and material costs involved in assembling the product, lay out the assembly processes, plan the type of tools required and the cost of such tools, and determine whether the component parts should be manufactured or purchased. They may even find it advisable to review the design with the engineering department and suggest changes to lower costs or facilitate manufacture.

In the manufacturing and production phase, electronics technicians work in a wide variety of capacities, generally with the day-to-day handling of production problems, schedules, and costs. Some supervise and train production teams in testing or building methods as they proceed from the development to the production phase. Others maintain the complex automated machines used to build the electronics product.

Those involved in quality-control inspect and test the products at various stages of completion. They also maintain and calibrate test equipment used in all phases of the manufacturing. They determine the causes for rejection of parts or equipment by assembly-line inspectors, and then analyze field and manufacturing reports of product failures.

These technicians may make specific recommendations to their supervisor to eliminate the causes of rejects, and may even suggest design, manufacturing, and process changes, and establish quality-acceptance levels. They may interpret quality-control standards to the manufacturing supervisors. And they may establish and maintain quality limits on items purchased from other manufacturers, thus insuring the quality of parts used in the equipment being assembled.

One other area of electronics technology worth mentioning is that of technical writing and editing. Technicians in this area compile, write, and edit a wide variety of technical information. This includes instructional leaflets, operating manuals, books, and installation and service manuals having to do with the products of the company. To do this, they must confer with design and development engineers, production personnel, salespeople, drafters, and others to obtain the necessary information to prepare the text, drawings, diagrams, parts, lists, and illustrations. They must understand thoroughly how and why the equipment works to be able to tell the customer how to use it and the service technician how to install and service it.

At times, they may help prepare technical reports and proposals and write technical articles for engineering societies, management, and other publications. Their job is to produce the means (through printed word and pictures) by which the customer can get the most value out of the purchased equipment.

Requirements

Prospective electronics technicians should have an interest in and an aptitude for mathematics and science, and should enjoy using tools and scientific equipment; on the personal side, they should be patient, methodical, persistent, and able to get along with a variety of different kinds of people.

While still in high school, interested students should take two years of mathematics including algebra and geometry, and one year of physical science, preferably physics, or an introductory electricity or electronics course. Four years of English and/or communications skills courses are usually required for graduation. Shop courses and courses in mechanical drawing are also desirable.

Most employers prefer to hire graduates of two-year, post-high school training programs. These programs are designed to develop proficiency in electronics and to supply enough general background in science as well as other career-related fields such as business and economics to aid the student in advancing to positions of greater responsibility.

Typical first-year courses include physics for electronics, technical mathematics, electronic devices, communications, circuit analysis—AC and DC, electronic amplifiers, and instruments and measurements.

Typical second-year courses include communications circuits; introduction to digital electronics; technical reporting; drawing, sketching, and diagramming; control circuits and systems; communications systems; electronic design and fabrication; introduction to new electronic devices; and industrial organizations and institutions.

Students unable to attend a post-high school technical training program, but still desire technical training, should not overlook the training programs offered to active-duty members of the U.S. Armed Forces and reserves.

Most jobs involving radio and television transmission equipment require certification from the International Society of Certified Electronics Technicians (ISCET). Usually the certification may be earned before graduation in a post-high school program or through home–study.

Although the majority of jobs available to electronics technicians require neither licenses nor certification, some employers do require certification, either by ISCET, or by the Institute for the Certification of Engineering Technicians.

Opportunities for experience and exploration

Anyone considering a career as an electronics technician should take every opportunity to discuss the field with people working in it. It is advisable to visit a variety of different kinds of electronics facilities—service shops, manufacturing plants, and research laboratories—either through individual visits or through field trips organized by teachers or guidance counselors. These visits will provide a realistic idea of the opportunities in the different areas of the electronics industry. It is also suggested that students take an introductory course in basic electricity or electronics to test their aptitude, skills, and interest.

Students can also gain relevant experience by taking shop courses, by belonging to electronics or radio clubs in school, and by assembling electronic equipment with commercial kits.

Methods of entering

Before completing their technical training, students may be hired through on-campus interviews by a company representative. Most schools have excellent placement programs with high student placement rates by the time they graduate.

Another way to obtain employment is through direct contact with a particular company. It is best to write to the personnel department and to include a resume summarizing one's education and experience. If the company has an appropriate opening, a company representative will schedule an interview for the prospective employee. There are also many excellent public and commercial employment organizations that can help graduates obtain a job appropriate to their training and experience. In addition, the classified ads in most metropolitan Sunday newspapers list a number of job openings with companies in the area.

Advancement

Advancement possibilities in the field of electronics can be almost unlimited. Technicians usually begin work under the direct and constant supervision of an experienced technician, scientist, or engineer. As they gain experience or additional education, they are given more responsible assignments, often carrying out particular work programs under only very general supervision.

From there technicians may move into supervisory positions; those with exceptional ability can sometimes qualify for professional positions after receiving additional academic training.

The following short paragraphs describe some of the positions to which electronics technicians can advance.

Engineering technicians are senior technicians or engineering assistants who work as part of a team of engineers and technicians developing new products.

Production-test supervisors determine what tests should be performed on equipment as it progresses down an assembly line. They may be responsible for designing the equipment set-up used in production testing.

Quality-assurance supervisors determine the scope of a product-sampling and the kinds of tests to be run on production units. They translate specifications into testing procedures.

Employment outlook

There is good reason to believe that the electronics industry will be one of the most important industries—if not the most important—in the United States through the year 2000. Computers, in general, are the biggest growth area for electronics. New and exciting consumer products such as videocassette recorders, compact-disc players, home computers, and home appliances with solid-state controls are very popular and in high-demand. Increasing automation and computer-assisted manufacturing processes rely on advanced electronic technology.

All of these new uses for electronics should continue to stimulate growth in the electronics industry. Hence, the job outlook for electronics technicians is favorable through at least the year 2000. Foreign competition, general economic conditions, and levels of government spending may impact certain areas of the field to some degree. This is an industry, however, that is becoming so central to all our lives and for which there is still such growth potential that it seems unlikely that any single factor could substantially curb its growth and its need for specially trained personnel.

Earnings

Electronics technicians who have completed a two-year post-high school training program and are working in private industry earn starting salaries of about $18,000 to $19,000 a year. Average yearly earnings of all electronics technicians range from approximately $33,000 to $49,000. At the very top pay levels, technicians earn between $60,000 to $66,000.

Electronics technicians generally receive premium pay for overtime work on Sundays and holidays and for evening and night-shift work. Many workers in electronics manufacturing plants receive two to four weeks vacation with pay, depending on their length of service. In almost all cases, electronics technicians are covered by pension plans and other fringe benefits, including financial aid and released time to obtain more education.

Conditions of work

Because electronics equipment usually must be manufactured in a dust-free, climate-controlled environment, electronics technicians can expect to work in modern, comfortable, well-lighted surroundings. Many electronics plants have been built in industrial parks with ample parking and little traffic congestion. Frequency of injuries in the electronics industry is far less than in most other industries, and injuries that do occur are usually not serious.

Many workers in electronics manufacturing are covered by union agreements. The principal unions involved are the International Union of Electrical, Radio and Machine Workers; International Brotherhood of Electrical Workers; International Association of Machinists and Aerospace Workers; and the United Electrical, Radio and Machine Workers of America.

Being able to work as a team member and the ability to get along well with others are important qualities for electronics technicians. They may also be called upon to supervise or direct other personnel, thereby becoming intermediaries between the scientists and engineers who design the projects, and the craft workers who carry them out.

For other electronics technicians, the work may be more monotonous and repetitious. Some technicians resent this aspect of the work; others find it a welcome relief.

Electronics technicians who wish to advance in their careers should be willing and able to continue their education, either formally or informally, in order to keep up with new developments in the field.

GOE: 05.01.01; SIC: 36; SOC: 3711

◇ RELATED ARTICLES

Volume 1: Electronics; Engineering
Volumes 2–4: Computer-service technicians; Electromechanical technicians; Electronics sales and service technicians; Instrumentation technicians; Microelectronics technicians; Semiconductor-development technicians; Telecommunications technicians

Electroplating workers

Definition

Electroplating is the process of plating, or coating an article with a thin layer of metal, by using a liquid solution of the metal and an electric current that causes the metal to deposit on the article's surface. The various workers who carry out this process are known as *electroplaters* or *platers*.

History

Alessandro Volta's discovery in 1800 of how to make a dry cell battery marked the beginning of modern electroplating. Early experimental uses of the process involved a simple battery as a source of direct current electricity. Electroplating did not become possible on a commercial basis until around 1840. Initially it was used in

ELECTROPLATING WORKERS

Electroplaters immerse jewelry in a solution, electroclean the jewelry, and then plate it with a protective metal.

applying a coating of gold and silver to cheap base metals like copper and brass. Plated objects found an immediate market in the rising middle classes, who wanted to be seen as possessing expensive luxury goods like gold and silver tableware. In 1925, chromium plating was introduced. Chromium produced a long-lasting, good-looking bright finish that was soon widely used, especially on the trim of automobiles and appliances.

Many other applications of electroplating have been developed, including numerous industrial uses. Not only can plating make surfaces more attractive, but it can also protect them. The plating process also helps to build up worn areas, and change the characteristics of surfaces of objects so that the objects can be used in ways that would otherwise not be possible. As examples, silver is sometimes used to plate electrical contacts and engine bearings; zinc is applied to steel to prevent corrosion; nickel is used as a decorative plating; copper plating can prevent steel from hardening at the surface and is used in fabricating many steel parts; gold is commonly used to plate jewelry.

If properly treated, even nonmetals like plastic, wood, or leather can be electroplated. Today, electroplating treatments are applied to many ordinary articles. These applications can be as diverse as electronic components and bronzed baby shoes, which are all produced using this essential process.

Nature of the work

To achieve a good result, electroplating workers often must closely control the composition and temperature of the liquid solution containing the plating metal and the amount of electric current that is run through the plating bath. Platers begin by checking a work order that specifies what parts of the product are to be plated, the type of plating is to be used, how thick the metal is to be applied, and the time and amount of electric current that will be required for the plate to reach the desired thickness. Sometimes they are responsible for mixing and testing the strength of the plating bath.

The platers must prepare the object for the plating process. They put it through various cleaning and rinsing baths. They may have to measure, mark, and mask off with lacquer, rubber, or tape parts of the object that are to be left unplated. Then they put the article into the plating tank, suspending it in the plating solution from what amounts to the negative terminal of a battery. Sometimes they have to put together special racks to hold the product in position. A piece of the plating metal is suspended from the positive terminal.

Once the apparatus is ready, the platers operate the controls on a rectifier, which is a device that converts electricity supply from the usual alternating current to direct current. This makes electricity (that is, a stream of electrons) flow continuously from the negative terminal. Positively charged ions of the plating metal are drawn to the negative terminal, where they combine with some of the negatively charged electrons and deposit out as a thin metal layer on the object. In some plating operations, platers must pull the object out of the solution from time to time to monitor the development of the metal layer and then adjust the flow of current based on their observations.

When the desired result has been achieved, the article is removed from the tank, rinsed, and dried. The platers examine it for any defects and recheck the thickness of the plating with micrometers, calipers, or electronic devices. This examination may be done by *plating inspectors*.

Sometimes workers are designated according to a specific activity or the electroplating equipment they operate. *Barrel platers* operate machines that hold objects to be plated in perforated or mesh barrels that are immersed in plating tanks. *Electrogalvanizing-machine operators* and *zinc-plating-machine operators* run and maintain machines that coat steel strips and wire with zinc. *Production platers* operate and maintain automatic plating equipment. To prepare objects for plating that do not conduct electricity, such as plastic items, *electroformers* coat the items with a conductive substance. Platers may be designated according to the metal they work with, such as *tin platers, cadmium platers,* and *gold platers. Anodizers* control equipment that provides a corrosion-resistant surface on aluminum objects. *Plating strippers* operate equipment with the positive and negative terminals reversed so that old plating is removed from objects.

The duties of platers also vary according to the size of the shop in which they work. In some large shops, all major decisions are made by chemists and chemical engineers, and the platers do only routine plating work. In other shops, platers are responsible for the whole process, including ordering chemicals and other supplies, preparing and maintaining solutions, plating the products, and polishing finished objects. If they have helpers, platers may be called *plater supervisors,* while the assistants may be called *electroplating laborers.*

Today, a majority of electroplating workers are employed in independent shops that specialize in plating and polishing metals for other businesses and individuals. Other electroplaters work for large manufacturing firms that utilize plated parts in their products, such as the makers of plumbing fixtures, electric appliances, automobiles, kitchen utensils, wire products, and hardware items.

Many electroplating workers are members of unions, notably the Metal Polishers, Buffers, Platers and Allied Workers International Union. Other unions in this field are the International Union, United Automobile, Aerospace and Agricultural Implement Workers of America and the International Association of Machinists and Aerospace Workers.

Requirements

Many electroplaters start out as helpers with little or no prior training and learn the trade by working with skilled platers. Using this approach, it often takes at least four years to become a skilled plater. Platers may work with just one or two metals, because it takes too much time to learn the necessary techniques for more than that. Workers who know only one or two metals may have trouble transferring to other shops where different metals are used.

The trend in this industry has been for plating processes to involve increasing complexity and engineering precision. This suggests that in the future, electroplating workers may need more specialized training and technical education. Some community colleges and vocational schools presently offer courses in electroplating that are one to two years in length. In addition, some branches of the American Electroplaters and Surface Finishers Society conduct courses in electroplating.

Apprenticeship programs are another method of getting a better all-around preparation for this occupation than is provided by ordinary on-the-job training. However, relatively few people have taken advantage of apprenticeship opportunities. Apprenticeships combine supervised job experience with classroom instruction in related subjects, such as the properties of metals, chemistry, and electrical theory as applied to plating. Apprentices learn each phase of the plating process, step by step, in a planned program. By the end of three or so years of training, apprentices are qualified to carry out the entire process and perhaps to supervise other workers.

Opportunities for experience and exploration

A good background for people interested in this field would include high school courses in applied mathematics, science subjects like chemistry and physics, electrical shop, metal shop, and blueprint reading. Classes like these introduce some of the basic concepts underlying the industrial applications of electroplating, as well as give students a hands-on sense of related technical fields. To get more direct experience of this occupation, it may be possible to arrange a part-time or summer job in a plant where electroplating is done, or at least to speak with workers in such a plant about their activities.

Methods of entering

People who are seeking to enter this trade often begin in helper positions and learn as they work. Listings of local job openings are available through the state employment service and in the classified advertising section of newspapers. Students in vocational programs may be able to get job leads through their school's placement service. Information on apprenticeship possibilities may be obtained from the state employment service and sometimes from local companies that have electroplating operations.

ELECTROPLATING WORKERS

Advancement

Electroplating workers who are skilled and experienced may be promoted to supervisory positions in which they coordinate and direct the activities of other workers. Platers who know how to work with a variety of metals may have the opportunity to transfer to other shops that offer higher pay. Some platers may be able to increase their pay levels by getting training in additional metal finishing methods.

Employment outlook

In the coming years, an increasing amount of electroplated items will probably be produced. This increase will be related to continuing growth in various manufacturing industries that utilize electroplated parts and to the development of new or improved ways of applying electroplating technology. However, the trend is for the processes related to electroplating to be mechanized wherever possible. For this reason, employment levels in this field will not grow at rates that match the growth in output of electroplated products.

Nonetheless, every year new job openings will occur, both for new positions and to replace workers who are transferring to other occupations or leaving the labor force altogether.

Earnings

Limited information available about this field indicates that the earnings of electroplaters vary widely depending on skills and experience, the type of work being done, geographical location, and other factors. On average, platers appear to make around $18,500 a year or more. Experienced workers may make up to $30,000 a year or more. Many electroplaters are paid according to wage scales that are established by agreements between unions and company management.

Apprentices start at comparatively low wages and receive raises at regular intervals throughout their training until their earnings approach those of skilled electroplaters.

Working conditions

Job conditions are generally good for platers today. In most plants, improved ventilating systems have reduced the odor and humidity problems that used to be common. Many plants are completely modernized, with automated electroplating equipment. Although there are some hazards associated with using strong chemicals, good safety practices and protective clothing minimize the risk of injury. Electroplaters may have to lift and carry moderately heavy objects, but in most cases, mechanical devices are used for the heavy work.

GOE: 06.02.21; SIC: 3471; SOC: 7343

◇ SOURCES OF ADDITIONAL INFORMATION

National Association of Metal Finishers
402 North Michigan Avenue
Chicago, IL 60611-4267

American Electroplaters and Surface Finishers Society
12644 Research Parkway
Orlando, FL 32826

Metal Industries Association
#507, 4190 Laughud Highway
Burnaby BC V5C 6A8

◇ RELATED ARTICLES

Volume 1: Machining and Machinery; Metals
Volumes 2–4: Electrotypers and stereotypers; Forge shop occupations; Heat treaters; Iron and steel industry workers; Metallurgical technicians; Silverware industry workers

Electrotypers and stereotypers

Definition

Electrotypers and *stereotypers* are skilled craftworkers who reproduce the printing surfaces used in certain letterpress and other printing processes. The duplicate printing surfaces they make are more long-lasting than the original pages of set type and illustrations.

History

The German printer Johannes Gutenberg is generally regarded as the inventor of printing with movable pieces of metal type. His invention made it possible for books to become a great tool of learning and preserver of knowledge for ordinary people. Before his era, books were rare, hand-made treasures, and very few people knew how to read them.

Around 1455, Gutenberg published his famous edition of the Bible, the first complete book known to have been produced in the western world using movable type. In this process, the printer could compose any page of text by assembling the words, letter by letter, from many separate pieces of metal type, each with a raised letter on its surface. Then many identical copies of the page could be run off by putting ink on the type and pressing sheets of paper against it. Later, when the printing job was done, the type pieces could be disassembled, saved, and used again. Thanks to Gutenberg's invention, books soon became relatively cheap and available everywhere. Many more people learned to read than ever before, making books much in demand. By around 1500, printing was an established industry in Europe.

As the demand for printed matter grew, so did the need for more durable type and faster printing methods. Stereotyping was one response to this problem. About 1727, William Ged, a Scottish goldsmith, invented a process for making a mold of composed type out of plaster of paris or clay so that a duplicate printing plate could be made. For decades, his method was rejected by printers. But by the late 18th century, stereotyping gained acceptance. Not only was it a way of saving wear on the original type, but also it allowed printers to set the type for a whole book before beginning to print pages and then to reprint the book any time. Stereotyping later become widely used in printing newspapers. The New York *Herald* had the first stereotyped plates made to fit the curve of a cylinder press.

Electrotyping represented another improvement in making duplicate printing plates. It could be used for reproducing pictorial illustrations like linoleum cuts, as well as composed type. Electrotyping was perfected about 1837 by a German physicist, M. H. von Jacobi. His process involved a wax mold on which a copper deposit was formed in a chemical bath. Because the result was especially durable and high in quality, it could be used in long press runs. Electrotyping is still employed in some book and magazine printing.

Until well into the 20th century, electrotyping and stereotyping were used extensively in printing great quantities of books, newspapers, magazines, and other publications. Until recent times, these processes were common ways of duplicating printing plates, allowing printers to operate many presses simultaneously. But the technology of printing continues to change, and today electrotyping and stereotyping are much less used. Text is now more often set using computers than metal pieces of type.

Nature of the work

Electrotyping and stereotyping are two different processes. Electrotyping is more complicated and expensive and produces a finer quality, more durable printing plate.

The first step in the electrotyping process is making a wax or plastic mold of a typeform that has already been composed. To do this, electrotypers use sheet-molding fiber and a hydraulic press. They spray the mold they have produced with a silver nitrate solution or graphite and suspended it in a tank of a chemical solution containing a metal. Through a process called electrolysis, a shell of that metal is deposited on the coated mold when electric current is passed through the tank. The shell, which duplicates the original typeform, is then stripped from the mold and backed with lead or plastic to give it body. The electrotypers examine the newly duplicated plate for defects and correct any problems with engravers' hand tools.

In the stereotyping process, stereotypers operate machines to create molds from which printing plates are cast. In this case, the molds are mats made of wood fibers. The stereotypers

ELECTROTYPERS AND STEREOTYPERS

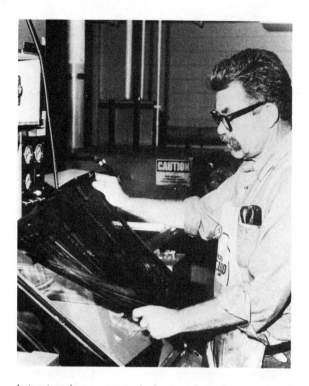

A stereotyper for a newspaper checks a negative produced by a laser machine. All errors must be caught before the negative is placed into the platemaking machine.

place a moist mat—or a dry mat for newspaper printing—on the type form; adjust gauges that control time, heat, and pressure; and then run the form under heavy steel rollers to impress the type and photoengravings onto the mat. The impressed mat is placed in a casting box, and molten metal is poured in, producing a stereotype that duplicates the typeform and illustrations. Some plants use automatic machines to cast stereotypes.

Requirements

Nearly all electrotypers and stereotypers learn their trades through apprenticeship programs that are four to six years in length. During this training period, apprentices learn all phases of the work. In most plants, however, a particular phase of the work is emphasized and apprentices have the opportunity to develop specialist skills. Applicants for apprenticeships must be at least 18 years old and have a high school education or the equivalent. A good high school background would include shop classes, chemistry, and courses in applied science and graphic arts.

Applicants are likely to be given aptitude tests and a physical examination to make sure

they are in good health. Good eyesight, good eye-hand coordination, and full use of arms and hands are important.

While it is not necessarily a requirement for employment, almost all electrotypers and stereotypers are union members.

Opportunities for experience and exploration

High school courses including chemistry, print making, electrical and metal shop, and mechanical drawing provide an introduction to some of the concepts and activities that are part of this field. Experience on the staff of a printed school newspaper is also valuable. Perhaps with the help of a teacher or guidance counselor, it may be possible to arrange to visit a printing plant and see workers in these occupations on the job.

Methods of entering

Information on apprenticeship opportunities can be obtained from local union offices and from the state employment service. High school vocational counselors may also be able to provide interested students with information on apprenticeships.

Advancement

Apprentices who complete their training advance to become fully qualified electrotypers or stereotypers. Because these are separate crafts with separate training, there is little transferring between them. In both fields, experienced workers may be promoted to supervisory positions, but further training or experience in another field may be necessary for other kinds of advancement.

Employment outlook

In both these fields, the number of workers is low and has been declining for years. This trend is expected to continue in the future, because technological changes in the printing industry have significantly reduced the need for people in these occupations. Except for specialized applications, electrotyping and stereotyping have been largely replaced by other techniques such as offset printing, automatic plate composition, and nonmetallic plates.

Earnings

The average minimum union annual wage rate is about $24,450 for electrotypers and $25,880 for stereotypers in book and job plants in the 1990s.

Conditions of work

Electrotypers and stereotypers usually do their jobs in busy, well lighted, well equipped indoor work areas. Although machines do much of the physical work, workers in both groups may still need to lift moderately heavy weights. Electrotypers may be exposed to wet conditions and fumes. They must use caution and follow good safety practices when working around chemicals and sources of electric current.

GOE: 05.05.13; SIC: 2796; SOC: 6849

◇ **SOURCES OF ADDITIONAL INFORMATION**

Graphic Communications International Union
1900 L Street, NW
Washington, DC 20036

Printing Industries of America
100 Daingerfield Road
Alexandria, VA 22314-2888

Printing and Graphics Industries Association of Alberta
PO Box 4091, Stn C
Calgary AB T2T 5M9

◇ **RELATED ARTICLES**

Volume 1: Book Publishing; Magazine Publishing; Metals; Newspaper Publishing; Printing
Volumes 2–4: Compositors and typesetters; Electroplating workers; Lithographic occupations; Photoengravers; Printing press operators and assistants

Elevator installers and repairers

Definition

Elevator installers, also called *elevator constructors* or *elevator mechanics*, and *elevator repairers*, also known as *elevator mechanics*, are skilled craft workers who assemble, install, and repair elevators, escalators, dumbwaiters, and similar equipment.

History

The use of mechanical devices for lifting loads dates back at least to the time of the ancient Romans, who utilized platforms attached to pulleys in constructing buildings. In the 17th century, a crude passenger elevator known as the "flying chair" was invented. These early elevators were operated by human, animal, or water power.

By the early 19th century, steam was used to power machines that raised elevators. For about the first half of the century, elevators were almost always used for lifting freight. This was because the hemp ropes that hauled the elevators were not strong enough to be safe for passenger use. In 1852, Elisha G. Otis designed and installed the first elevator with a safety device that prevented it from falling if the rope broke. Five years later, Otis' first safety elevator for carrying passengers was put into use in a store in New York City, and it was immediately declared a success.

Steam-powered elevators were used until the 1880s, when elevators powered by electricity were introduced. Subsequent design changes brought a series of improvements such as push-button operation; taller shafts and

ELEVATOR INSTALLERS AND REPAIRERS

An elevator constructor installs guide rails in a new elevator shaft.

faster speeds, so that the elevators could be used even in skyscrapers; and power doors and automatic operation, which made elevators more economical than they had been when human operators were necessary. Today's elevators are often electronically controlled and may be capable of moving up and down at 2,000 feet per minute.

The escalator, or moving stairway, was invented in 1891 by Jesse W. Reno. Early escalators, like modern ones, were electrically powered and resemble an inclined endless belt held in position by two tracks. Moving sidewalks and ramps are based on the same principle, but they are level or inclined at much lower angles than escalators. Today it is rare to find a newer commercial, industrial, or apartment building that is not equipped with elevators for passengers or freight, and perhaps escalators as well.

Almost as long as these machines have been in use in buildings to move people and their belongings, there has been a need for workers who specialize in assembling, installing, and maintaining them. Elevator installers and repairers are the people who do these

tasks. There are presently over 19,000 workers in this field in the United States, and the majority are employed by contractors specializing in the elevator field.

Nature of the work

Elevator installers and repairers may service and update old equipment that has been in operation for many years, or they may work on new systems, which may be equipped with state-of-the-art microprocessors capable of monitoring a whole elevator system and automatically operating it with maximum possible efficiency. Installing and repairing modern elevators requires a good understanding of electricity, electronics, and hydraulics.

Installers begin their work by examining plans and blueprints that describe the equipment to be installed. They need to determine the layout of the components, including the framework, guide rails, motors, pumps, cylinders, plunger foundations, and electrical connections. Once the layout is clear, they install the guide rails (for guiding the elevator as it moves up and down) on the walls of the shaft. Then they run electrical wiring in the shaft between floors and install controls and other devices on each floor and at a central control panel. They assemble the parts of the car at the bottom of the shaft. They bolt or weld together the steel frame and attach walls, doors, and parts that keep the car from moving from side to side as it travels up and down the shaft. They also install the entrance doors and door frames on each floor.

Installers also set up and connect the equipment that moves the cars. In cable elevator systems, steel cables are attached to each car and, at their other end, to a large counterweight. Hoisting machinery, often located at the top of the shaft, moves the cables around a pulley, thus moving the elevator car up or down and the counterweight in the opposite direction. In hydraulic systems, the car rests on a hydraulic cylinder that is raised and lowered by a pump, thus moving the elevator car up and down like a automobile on a lift. After the various parts of the elevator system are in place, the elevator installers test the operation of the system and make any necessary adjustments so that the installation meets building and safety code requirements.

In hotels, restaurants, hospitals, and other institutions where food is prepared, elevator installers may work on dumbwaiters, which are small elevators for transporting food and dishes from one part of a building to another. They may also work on escalators, installing wiring, motors, controls, the stairs, the framework for the stairs, and the tracks that keep the stairs in position.

After elevator and escalator equipment is installed, it needs regular adjustment and maintenance services to assure that the system continues to function in a safe, reliable manner. Elevator repairers routinely inspect the equipment, perform safety tests using meters and gauges, clean parts that are prone to getting dirty, make adjustments, replace worn components, and lubricate bearings and other moving parts.

Repairers also do minor emergency repairs, such as replacing defective parts. Finding the cause of malfunctions often involves troubleshooting. For this reason, repairers need a sound working knowledge of electricity, electronics, and computerized controls. In addition, repairers may work as part of crews that do major repair and modernization work on older equipment.

Elevator installers and repairers use a variety of hand tools, power tools, welding equipment, and electrical testing devices like test lamps, ammeters, and voltmeters.

Requirements

Employers prefer to hire high school graduates who are at least 18 years of age and in good physical condition. Mechanical aptitude, an interest in machines, and some technical training related to the field are other important qualifications. High school or vocational school courses that would be good background for this field include mathematics, machine shop, applied physics, electronics, and blueprint reading.

Most elevator installers and repairers learn their skills in training programs operated by committees composed of local employers and representatives of local branches of the International Union of Elevator Constructors. The programs consist of on-the-job training under the supervision of experienced workers, together with classroom instruction in related subjects. In the work portion of the program, trainees begin by doing the simplest tasks and gradually progress to more difficult activities. In the classroom they learn about electrical theory, electronics, job safety, and other topics.

Trainees spend their first six months in a program in a probationary status. Those who complete the period successfully can go on to become fully qualified workers in about four years. They may be able to advance more

quickly if they already have a good technical background, especially in electronics, acquired by taking courses at a post-secondary technical school or junior college.

Because the technology used in elevator systems is constantly changing, even well trained and experienced elevator installers and repairers may periodically have to upgrade their skills by attending courses that introduce new equipment and techniques or by taking correspondence courses.

While union membership is not necessarily a requirement for employment, most elevator installers and repairers are members of the International Union of Elevator Constructors.

Special requirements

Most states and municipalities require that elevator installers and repairers pass a licensing examination.

Opportunities for experience and exploration

High school courses such as electrical shop, machine shop, and blueprint reading can give students a hands-on sense of tasks that are similar to everyday activities of elevator installers and repairers. A part-time or summer job as a helper at a commercial building site may provide an opportunity to observe the conditions that these workers encounter on the job. If it can be arranged, a visit to an elevator manufacturing firm can be informative. It also may be possible to learn about working in this field by talking to someone recommended by local representatives of the International Union of Elevator Constructors.

Methods of entering

People seeking information about trainee positions in this field should try contacting contractors who specialize in elevator maintenance and repair work, the local office of the International Union of Elevator Constructors, or elevator manufacturers. The local office of the state employment service may also be a source of information and job leads.

ELEVATOR INSTALLERS AND REPAIRERS

Advancement

When they have completed their approximately four-year training program and met any local licensure requirements, workers in this field are considered fully qualified. With further experience, those who work for elevator contracting firms may become eligible for promotion to positions such as mechanics-in-charge or supervisors, coordinating the work done by other installers. Or they may become estimators, figuring the costs for supplies and labor for work before it is done. Working for an elevator manufacturer, they may move into sales positions, jobs related to product design, and management. Other experienced workers become inspectors employed by government bodies to check over elevators and escalators to make sure that they comply with specifications and safety codes.

Employment outlook

Over the next 10 to 15 years, employment of elevator installers and repairers is likely to increase at about the same rate as the average for other occupations. The demand for these workers will be related to the level of building construction activity and to the need to modernize old elevator installations. Because the amount of construction work undertaken varies with economic conditions, the need for these workers will vary from time to time and place to place. But even during economic downturns, installers and repairers will be needed to do maintenance work and to put in replacement equipment from minor components to large portions of elevator systems.

Most new job openings that develop will occur when workers change to new occupations or leave the labor force altogether. As the technology in the industry becomes more complex, employers will increasingly seek workers who are technically well trained, especially in electronics.

Earnings

Earnings depend on a variety of factors such as experience and geographical location. Overall, the average annual earnings of elevator installers and repairers are in the range of $37,000 or more. Mechanics-in-charge may have earnings over $56,000 a year. Probationary beginners start at about 50 percent of the wages of experienced workers; after the initial period, trainees earn about 70 percent of the full wage. In addition to regular wages, elevator installers and repairers receive other benefits including health insurance, pension plans, and some tuition-free courses in subjects related to their work.

Conditions of work

The standard workweek for elevator installers and repairers is 40 hours in length. However, some workers put in overtime hours (for which they are paid extra), and some repairers are on call for responding to emergencies for 24-hour periods.

Most of the work is done indoors, so little time is lost because of bad weather. Not infrequently it is necessary to lift heavy equipment and parts and to work in cramped or awkward places.

GOE: 05.05.05; SIC: 1796; SOC: 6176

◇ **SOURCES OF ADDITIONAL INFORMATION**

International Union of Elevator Constructors
3530 Clark Building, Suite 530
5565 Sterrett Place
Columbia, MD 21044

National Elevator and Escalator Association
#403, 6299 Auport Road
Mississauga ON L4V 1N3

◇ **RELATED ARTICLES**

Volume 1: Construction
Volumes 2–4: Electrical repairers; Electrical technicians; Electricians; Electronics technicians; Industrial machinery mechanics

Emergency medical technicians

Definition

Emergency medical technicians, often called *EMTs*, respond to medical emergencies to provide immediate treatment for ill or injured persons both on the scene and during transport to a medical facility. They function as part of an emergency medical team, and the range of medical services they perform varies according to their level of training.

EMTs drive specially equipped emergency vehicles, respond to instructions of an *emergency medical dispatcher* and maintain constant two-way radio contact with the dispatcher. At the site of the emergency, EMTs respond to the most urgent needs first: they free trapped victims from the accident or catastrophe if necessary, and determine the nature and extent of the illness or injury. Relying on their knowledge and their examination of the victims, the EMTs perform certain pre-hospital emergency care procedures, and determine the need for additional assistance. Using the communications equipment in the vehicle, EMTs obtain instructions for any further on-site treatment, and arrange to bring the victims to the facility. After transferring victims to the facility, they help the admitting staff to obtain and record necessary information about the victims and the circumstances of the emergency.

EMTs must also see that the emergency vehicles and communications equipment are maintained in good operating condition and that the vehicles are adequately stocked with the required medical supplies.

History

The systems for providing emergency medical services and transport to hospitals for the American public did not receive much attention until the 1960s. Prior to that time, ambulance drivers and attendants were often volunteers who had undergone some first-aid training, but the quality and quantity of their instruction and experience varied widely, as did the equipment they had available in their vehicles. By current-day standards, much of the nation's ambulance service was deplorable.

Changes in emergency services came about because of medical advances; very sick and badly injured victims could be saved, provided they were reached by skilled care providers within a very short time. In particular, during the 1950s and 1960s, Americans began to drive more and more, and they became involved in more and more automobile accidents. Growing public awareness that better emergency medical services would save victims of these accidents sparked the effort to upgrade public emergency services.

A major milestone in this movement was the federal Highway Safety Act of 1966 which included, for the first time, uniform standards for emergency medical services. Another important piece of federal legislation was the Emergency Medical Services System Act of 1973, which authorized funds for research and training. In addition this act also made money available for organizing regional emergency medical systems.

In the late 1960s the emergency medical technician's fledgling vocation was finally beginning to receive careful study and consideration. Beginning in 1968, the Committee on Emergency Medical Services of the National Academy of Sciences, and the National Research Council published a series of recommendations and guidelines on the training of ambulance personnel. Working with the Committee on Highway Safety, which was established by President Lyndon Johnson, the American Medical Association's Commission on Emergency Medical Services studied the feasibility of a national certification organization for EMTs.

In response, the National Registry of Emergency Medical Technicians (NREMT) was formed in 1970. Today NREMT is an independent agency that establishes qualification levels for EMTs, determines the competency of working EMTs (through examination), and promotes the improved delivery of emergency medical services through educational and training programs. NREMT provides uniform national certification for qualified EMTs who wish to be included in the National Registry.

In 1971 the U.S. Department of Transportation published a national standard basic training course to increase the competence of ambulance personnel. By 1977 all the states had adopted the Department of Transportation course or a close equivalent as the basis for state certification. By the 1990s, more than 600,000 persons have taken this basic training course.

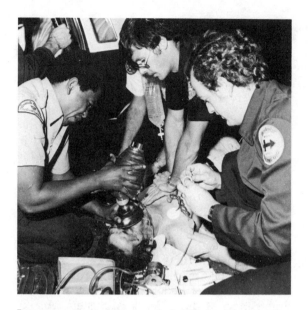

Emergency medical technicians are the first to arrive at the scene of an accident. Their assessment of treatment is crucial to the life of an accident victim.

Nature of the work

EMTs work in fire departments, private ambulance services, police departments, volunteer community Emergency Medical Services (EMS) squads, hospitals, industrial plants, or other local organizations that provide pre-hospital emergency care. This care aims to rapidly identify the nature of the emergency, stabilize the patient's condition, and initiate proper procedures at the scene and en route to a hospital. Unfortunately, even well-intentioned emergency help from persons who are not trained can be disastrous, especially for automobile accident victims. Communities often take great pride in their emergency medical services, knowing that they are as well-prepared as possible and that they can minimize the tragic consequences of mishandling emergencies.

EMTs are sent out in an ambulance to the scene of an emergency by the dispatcher who acts as a communication channel for all aspects of emergency medical services. The dispatcher may also be trained as an EMT. It is normally the dispatcher who receives the call for help, sends out the appropriate medical resource, serves as the continuing link between the emergency vehicle and the medical facility throughout the situation, and relays any requests for special assistance at the scene.

EMTs, who often work in two-person teams, must be able to proceed safely yet quickly to an emergency scene in any part of their geographical area. For the protection of the public and themselves, they must obey the traffic laws that apply to emergency vehicles. They must be familiar with the roads and any special conditions affecting the choice of route, such as traffic, weather-related problems, and road construction.

Once at the scene, they must cope immediately and effectively with whatever awaits them. They may find victims who appear to have had heart attacks, are burned, trapped under fallen objects, lacerated, in childbirth, poisoned, or emotionally disturbed—in short, people with any urgent problem for which medical assistance is needed. If no police are available, the EMTs may have to get bystanders to help with the rescue effort by directing traffic, moving debris, or providing other assistance. Because people who have been involved with an emergency directly or indirectly are sometimes very upset, EMTs often have to exercise skill in calming both victims and bystanders. They must do their work efficiently and in a reassuring manner.

EMTs are often the first qualified personnel to arrive on the scene, so they must make the initial evaluation of the nature and extent of the medical problem. The accuracy of this early assessment can be crucial. EMTs must be on the lookout for any clues, such as medical identification emblems, indicating the victim has significant allergies, diabetes, epilepsy, or other conditions that may affect the choice of emergency treatment. The EMTs must know what questions to ask bystanders or family members if there is a chance they need more information before proceeding.

On the basis of such information and their own observations, EMTs establish the priorities of required care and administer specified procedures and emergency treatment under standing orders or in accordance with specific instructions received over the radio from a physician. For example, they may have to control bleeding, open breathing passages, perform cardiac resuscitation, immobilize fractures, treat shock, or restrain emotionally disturbed patients.

The particular procedures and treatments that EMTs may carry out depend partly on the level of certification they have achieved. A majority of EMTs have only basic certification. A growing number of EMTs have attained the highest level of certification as *Registered EMT-Paramedics*—there are over 60,000 in the United States. EMT-Paramedics are authorized to administer drugs intravenously or to operate complicated life-support equipment in an advanced life-support ambulance—for example, an electric device (defibrillator) to shock a stopped heart into action.

When victims are trapped, EMTs must first assess the medical problem; only after administering suitable medical care and protection do the EMTs remove the victims, using special equipment and techniques. The EMTs may have to radio requests for special assistance in order to free victims. During a longer extrication process, it may be necessary for EMTs to help police with crowd control and protecting valuables. Sometimes freeing victims involves lifting and carrying them, climbing to high places, or dealing with other difficult or physically demanding situations.

Victims who must be transported to the hospital are put on stretchers, lifted into the ambulance, and secured in place for the ride. The choice of facilities is not always up to the EMTs, but when it is they must base the decision on their knowledge of the equipment and staffing needed by the patients. The receiving hospital's emergency department must be informed by radio, either directly or through the dispatcher, of details such as the number of persons being transported and the nature of their medical problems, to prepare them for the arrival. Meanwhile the EMTs must continue to monitor the patients and administer care as directed by the medical professional with whom they are maintaining radio contact. When necessary the EMTs also try to be sure that contact has been initiated with any utility companies, municipal repair crews, or other services that should be called to correct dangerous problems at the emergency scene, such as fallen power lines or tree limbs.

Once at the hospital, EMTs help the staff bring the victims into the emergency department, and they may assist with the first steps of in-hospital care. They supply whatever information they can, verbally and in writing, for the hospital's records on the patients. In the case of a victim's death, they complete the necessary procedures to ensure that the deceased's property is safeguarded.

After the patient has been delivered to the hospital, the EMTs must check in with their dispatchers and then prepare the vehicle for another emergency call. This includes replacing used linens and blankets; replenishing supplies of drugs, oxygen, and so forth; sending out some equipment to be sterilized; and inventorying the contents of the vehicle to assure completeness. In the case of any special kind of contamination, such as certain contagious diseases or radioactivity, the EMTs report the situation to the proper authorities and follow procedures for decontamination.

In addition, EMTs must see to it that the ambulance is clean and in good running condition. At least once during the shift, they must

After an immediate examination, two emergency medical technicians prepare to take an accident victim to the hospital for further tests.

check the gas, oil, battery, siren, brakes, radio, and other systems.

Requirements

Anyone contemplating a career as an EMT should possess a combination of personal characteristics including a desire to serve people, a strong interest in the health field, a stable and adaptable personality, and good physical health. Other requirements include good manual dexterity and motor coordination; the ability to lift and carry up to one hundred pounds; good visual acuity, with lenses for correction permitted; accurate color vision, enabling safe driving and immediate detection of diagnostic signs; and competence in giving and receiving verbal and written communication.

While still in high school, interested students should take courses in health and science, driver education, and English. To be admitted to a basic training program, applicants usually must be at least 18 years old, have a high school diploma and a valid driver's license. Exact requirements vary slightly in different states and in different training courses. Many EMTs first become interested in the field while in the U.S. Armed Forces, where they received training as medics.

The standard basic training program for EMTs was designed by the U.S. Department of Transportation. It is taught in many hospitals, community colleges, and police, fire, and health departments across the country. It is approximately 110 hours in length and constitutes the minimum mandatory requirement to become an EMT. In this course, students learn to manage common emergencies such as bleeding, cardiac arrest, fractures, and airway obstruction; and how to handle equipment such as stretchers, backboards, fracture kits, and oxygen delivery systems.

Successful completion of the basic course opens several training opportunities for EMTs. Among these are a two-day course on removing trapped victims, and a five-day course on driving emergency vehicles. Another several-day course trains dispatchers. Completion of these recognized training courses may be required for EMTs to be eligible for certain jobs in some areas. In addition, EMTs who have graduated from the basic program may work toward meeting further requirements to become registered at one of several levels recognized by the National Registry of Emergency Medical Technicians.

All fifty states have some certification requirement. Certification is only open to those who have completed the standard basic training course. In some states, EMTs meet the certification requirement by meeting the requirements for basic registration with the National Registry of Emergency Medical Technicians. Some states offer new EMTs the choice of the National Registry examination or the state's own certification examination. A majority of states accept national registration in place of their own examination for EMTs who relocate there.

At present, the National Registry of Emergency Medical Technicians (NREMT) recognizes three levels of competency. While it is not always essential for EMTs to become registered with one of these three ratings, EMTs can expect better prospects for good jobs as they attain higher levels of registration. As time passes, requirements for registration may increase, and a larger proportion of EMTs are expected to become registered voluntarily.

Candidates for the basic level of registration, known as Registered EMT, must have completed the standard Department of Transportation training program (or their state's equivalent), have six months' experience, and pass both a state-approved practical examination and a written examination.

Since 1980, the National Registry has recognized the EMT-Intermediate level of competency. This registration requires all candidates to have current registration at the basic EMT level. They must also have experience and pass a written and a practical examination that together demonstrate knowledge and skills above

those of basic registered EMTs, but below those of the highest-rated registrants.

EMT-Paramedics (or EMT-Ps), the EMTs with the highest of the levels of registration, must be already registered at least at the basic level. They must have completed a special EMT-Paramedic training program, have six months' experience as an EMT-Paramedic, and must pass both a written and a practical examination. Because their training is much more comprehensive and specialized than other EMTs, EMT-Ps are prepared to make more physician-like observations and judgments.

The training programs for EMT-Paramedics are now accredited by the Committee on Allied Health Education and Accreditation of the American Medical Association. In 1991 there were 92 such accredited programs, and 450 state-approved programs. They are roughly nine months in duration. Course length depends largely on the availability of actual emergency care incidents in which students can gain supervised practical experience. The course is very broad in scope, and includes classroom instruction and in-hospital clinical practice in addition to the field internship.

Once they have attained registration, EMTs must re-register every two years. To re-register, they must meet certain experience and continuing education requirements. Refresher courses that help EMTs keep current on new techniques and equipment are available.

Opportunities for experience and exploration

Students in high school have little opportunity for direct experience with the emergency medical field. However, they can probably arrange to talk with local EMTs who work for the fire or police department, or for a voluntary agency which provides emergency ambulance service to the community. It may be possible to learn a great deal about the health-services field through a part-time, summer, or volunteer job in a hospital or clinic. Service jobs can provide students a chance to observe and to talk to staff members concerned with emergency medical services.

Health courses in high school are a useful introduction to some of the concepts and terminology that EMTs use. Students may be able to take a first-aid course or training in cardiopulmonary resuscitation. Local organizations such as the Red Cross can provide details on training available in the area.

Methods of entering

A good source of employment leads for a recent EMT graduate of the basic training program is the school or agency that provided the training. EMTs can also apply directly to local ambulance services, hospitals, other potential employers, and to private and public employment agencies.

New EMT graduates can face stiff competition in many areas if they are seeking full-time paid employment. Although these EMTs may sometimes qualify to apply for positions with fire and police departments, they are generally much more likely to be successful in pursuing positions with private companies. Volunteer work is another option for EMTs. Volunteer EMTs, who are likely to average 8 to 12 hours of work per week, do not face the same competition. Beginning EMTs without prior work experience in the health field may therefore find it advantageous to start their careers as part-time volunteers. As they gain training and experience, these EMTs can work toward registration, thus opening for themselves many new job opportunities.

Flexibility about location of work may help new EMTs gain a foothold on the career ladder. In some areas, salaried positions are hard to find because of a strong tradition of volunteer ambulance services. In other areas the demand for EMTs is much greater, although the greatest demand is likely to be for EMT-Paramedics.

Advancement

With experience, EMTs can gain more responsibility while holding the same essential job. But more significant advancement becomes possible with moving up through the progression of ratings recognized by the NREMT. These ratings acknowledge increasing qualifications, making higher paying jobs and more responsibility easier to obtain. In general, public EMT jobs, such as those with public hospitals, police, and fire departments, offer the best salaries and fringe benefits and are thus the most sought-after by EMTs with good experience and training.

Another avenue of advancement for some EMTs leads to becoming an *EMT administrator*. For others, experience as an EMT prompts further training in another area of the health care field.

Employment outlook

The employment outlook for paid EMTs will depend on the community in which they are seeking employment. In many communities, especially those in which the public and the health-care planners perceive the advantages of high-quality emergency medical services and are willing to raise tax dollars to support them, the employment outlook should remain favorable. Volunteer services are being phased out in these areas, and well-equipped emergency services operated by salaried EMTs are replacing them. In a growing number of municipalities, private ambulance companies contract to provide emergency medical services to the community. If this trend continues, job opportunities with these private companies should be good.

Another important factor affecting the outlook for EMTs is that the proportion of older people, who use most emergency medical services, is growing in many communities, placing more demands on the emergency medical services delivery system and increasing the need for EMTs.

In some communities, however, the employment outlook is not so favorable. Maintaining a high-quality emergency medical services delivery system can be expensive, and financial strains on some local governments could inhibit the growth of these services. In addition, cutbacks in federal aid to local communities and an overall national effort to contain medical expenditures may lead health-care planners to look for ways that growth in community-based health-related costs may be controlled or reduced. Under economic conditions such as these, communities may not be able to support the level of emergency medical services that they would otherwise like to, and the employment prospects for EMTs may remain limited.

Earnings

Earnings of EMTs are dependent on the type of employer, geographic location, and individual level of training and experience. Those working for police and fire departments usually receive the same salaries and benefits as other department members.

The average starting salary is $19,220 for those classified as EMT-Basic; $20,637 for EMT-I (Intermediate); and $23,385 for EMT-Paramedic. To show the wide disparity in pay between employers, the average pay for an experienced EMT-I at a private ambulance service is $19,097; at a fire department, it would be $32,176.

Benefits vary widely depending on the employer, but generally include paid holidays and vacations, health insurance, and pension plans.

Conditions of work

EMTs must work under all kinds of conditions, both indoors and outdoors, sometimes in very trying circumstances. They must do their work regardless of the weather and are often called on to do fairly strenuous physical tasks such as lifting, climbing, and kneeling while dealing with life and death matters. Usually they must work irregular hours including some nights, weekends, and holidays. Those working for fire departments often put in 56-hour weeks, while EMTs employed in hospitals, private firms, and police departments often work 40 hours a week. Volunteer EMTs work much shorter hours. Because the working conditions are so trying, many EMTs find that they must have a high degree of commitment to the job.

It is important that EMTs project an impression of confidence and efficiency to both victims and bystanders. They have to exhibit leadership qualities, acting firm but pleasant and courteous. Their appearance should be neat and clean.

Moreover, EMTs must back up the impression of competence with genuine levelheadedness and sufficient calmness to let them consistently exercise good judgment in times of stress. They must be efficient, neither wasting time nor working too fast to do a good job. EMTs should have stable personalities, yet remain flexible in their approach to problems. A strong desire to help people, even when that involves difficult work, is essential.

An additional stress factor faced by EMTs is concern over contracting AIDS or other infectious diseases from bleeding patients. The actual risk of exposure is quite small, and emergency medical programs have procedures in place to protect EMTs from exposure to the greatest possible degree; however, some risk of exposure does exist, and prospective EMTs should be aware of this factor as they consider the career.

In spite of the intensity of their often-demanding job, EMTs can derive enormous satisfaction from knowing that they are able to render such a vital service to the victims of sudden illness or injury.

GOE: 10.03.02; SIC: 8049; SOC: 369

◇ SOURCES OF ADDITIONAL INFORMATION

National Registry of Emergency Medical Technicians
PO Box 29233
Columbus, OH 43229

National Association of Emergency Medical Technicians
9140 Ward Parkway
Kansas City, MO 64114

American Ambulance Association
3814 Auburn Boulevard, Suite 70
Sacramento, CA 95821

Emergency Paramedic Association of Calgary
#256, 1207 11 Avenue SW
Calgary AB T3C 0M5

◇ RELATED ARTICLES

Volume 1: Health Care
Volumes 2–4: Fire fighters; Homemaker-home health aides; Medical assistants; Nurses; Nursing and psychiatric aides; Physicians; Physician assistants; Police officers; Surgical technicians

Employment counselors

Definition

Employment counselors, which are also known as *vocational counselors*, provide educational and vocational guidance services to individuals and to groups. They assess their clients' interests and skills and help them obtain suitable employment.

History

Around the turn of the 20th century, public interest in improving educational conditions began to develop. The Civic Service House in Boston began the United States' first program of vocational guidance, and the Vocational Bureau, advocated by Frank Parsons, was established in 1908 to help young people choose, train, and enter appropriate careers.

The idea of vocational counseling became so appealing that by 1910 a national conference on vocational guidance was held in Boston. The federal government gave support to vocational counseling by initiating a program to assist veterans of World War I in readjusting to civilian life. During the Depression years, agencies such as the Civilian Conservation Corps and the National Youth Administration made attempts at vocational counseling.

On June 6, 1933, the Wagner-Pyser Act established the United States Employment Service. Adequate provisions were made for training and staffing the program. States came into the Service one by one, with each state developing its own plan under the prescribed limits of the Act. By the end of World War II, the Veterans Administration was counseling more than 50,000 veterans each month. Other state and federal government agencies involved with vocational guidance services include the Bureau of Indian Affairs, the Bureau of Apprenticeship and Training, the Office of Manpower Development, and the Department of Education.

The profession of employment counseling has become important to the welfare of society as well as to the individuals within it. Each year thousands of people need help in acquiring the kinds of information that make it possible for them to take advantage of today's career opportunities.

Nature of the work

Employment counselors work with people of all ages and of all educational backgrounds. *Vocational-rehabilitation counselors* work with disabled individuals.

In their work, educational counselors perform many services. They establish a friendly relationship with their clients. The counselor tries to discover the right positions for them by evaluating their skills and administering tests, like standardized achievement and aptitude tests.

Vocational counselors help the counselees understand what skills they have to offer to an employer. A good counselor knows the working world and how to obtain detailed information about specific jobs. To assist with career decisions, counselors must know about the availability of jobs, the probable future of certain jobs, the education or training necessary to enter them, the kinds of salary or other benefits that certain jobs offer, the conditions that certain jobs impose on employees (night work, travel, work outdoors), and the satisfactions that certain jobs provide their employees.

An important part of employment counseling and placement is meticulous record keeping. The follow-up of successfully placed applicants and satisfied employers is another aspect of the job.

Requirements

Entry requirements for employment and placement counselors are not uniform. Some states require a master's degree in counseling or a related field. The majority of counselors in state agencies, however, have a bachelor's degree and additional courses in guidance and counseling. Experience in counseling, interviewing, and job placement also may be required, particularly in the case of those without advanced degrees.

Most private agencies prefer, or require, a master's degree in vocational counseling or in a related field such as psychology, personnel administration, counseling, guidance education, or public administration. Many private agencies hire at least one staff member with a doctorate in counseling psychology or another advanced degree. Experience in related work, such as rehabilitation counseling, employment interview-

591

Personnel workers spend much of their time interviewing prospective employees.

Opportunities for experience and exploration

Summer employment in an employment agency is a good way to explore the field of employment counseling. Interviewing the director of a public or private agency might offer an understanding of what the work involves and the qualifications such an organization requires of its counselors.

Interested high school students who enjoy working with others will find helpful experiences in working in the dean's or counselor's office. A student's own experience in seeking summer and part-time work is also valuable in learning what the job seeker must confront in business or industry.

Methods of entering

Qualified college graduates who wish to become vocational counselors should seek information about the necessary examinations by contacting one of the addresses listed at the end of this article. To enter a public vocational or employment service, one should write to the director of that service to learn what sort of qualifying examination is given, and when and where it is administered. If the position requires the civil service examination, local postmasters can provide the name and address of the nearest civil service examiner

If prospective vocational counselors wish to be employed in a private agency, industry, or labor union, they should get in touch with the personnel officer in the concern in which they hope to work. The American Association for Counseling and Development regularly issues a Placement Service Bulletin for its members.

Advancement

New employees in federal or state employment services, or other vocational counseling agencies, are usually considered trainees for the first six months of employment. During this time, they learn the specific skills that will be expected of them during their career with the agency. The first year of employment is probationary.

Positions of further responsibility include supervisory or administrative work, which may be attained by counselors after several years of experience on the job. Advancement to administrative positions often means giving up the

ing, school or college counseling, teaching, social work, or psychology, is an added advantage.

As in any profession, there is usually an initial period of training for newly hired counselors or counselor trainees. Some skills of employment counselors such as testing procedures and interviewing skills can only be acquired through training.

High school students interested in becoming employment counselors should take college preparatory courses. Computer science classes also are valuable. Course work in college should emphasize psychology and sociology. Graduate level courses include techniques of counseling, psychology of careers, assessment and appraisal, cultures and environment, and occupational information. Counselor education programs at the graduate level are available in nearly 500 colleges and universities, mainly in departments of education and psychology. In order to obtain a master's degree, students must complete one to two years of graduate study, including actual supervised experience in counseling.

actual counseling work, which may not be an advantage to those who enjoy working with counselees.

Experienced counselors may advance to directors of agencies or supervisors of guidance counselors. Some move into research, consulting work, or college teaching. Others go into private practice and set up their own counseling agencies.

Employment outlook

There should be faster than average growth in employment in this field through the 1990s. Although only moderate opportunities are anticipated for employment and rehabilitation counselors in state and local governments, rapid growth is expected in the development of human resource and employment assistance programs in private business and industry, which should produce more jobs.

In the 1990s, some 4,000 people hold positions in public employment offices as employment counselors or counseling supervisors. Several hundred other workers, although not classified as employment counselors, are engaged in counseling activities in these offices. In addition, several thousand placement and employment counselors work for various private or community agencies, primarily in large cities. Some work in institutions such as prisons, training schools for delinquent youths, and mental hospitals.

Earnings

Salaries of employment counselors in state employment offices vary considerably from state to state. The average minimum salary in the 1990s is about $15,700 and the average maximum salary is about $21,400 a year. Earnings in private industry are generally much higher. Counselors generally receive benefits such as vacations, sick leave, pension plans, and insurance coverage.

Conditions of work

Employment counselors usually work about 40 hours a week, but in some agencies there is a more flexible schedule for clients who work during the day.

Counseling is done in offices designed to be free from noise and distractions to allow confidential discussions with clients.

Employment counselors help people evaluate their interests, abilities, and attitudes toward work and assist them in finding the job that best suits them. A person's work occupies the greatest part of his or her waking life and counselors need to be respectfully aware of the importance of their work in the life of other people. The counselor must also have fair judgment of the potential of clients to guide them realistically.

GOE: 10.01.02; SIC: 8299; SOC: 24

◇ SOURCES OF ADDITIONAL INFORMATION

American Association for Counseling and Development
5999 Stevenson Avenue
Alexandria, VA 22304

Council on Rehabilitation Education
PO Box 1680
Champaign, IL 61824

Employability Resource Network, Inc.
#1200, 55 Metcalfe Street
Ottawa ON K1P 6L5

◇ RELATED ARTICLES

Volume 1: Education; Human Resources; Social Services
Volumes 2–4: Career counselors; Career guidance technicians; Correction officers; Employment firm workers; Guidance counselors; Human services workers

Employment firm workers

Definition

Employment firm workers act as intermediaries in the employment process by helping people find jobs and employers fill vacancies. They assist job seekers by assessing their interests and skills and helping them obtain suitable employment. They assist employers by recruiting qualified personnel for available positions.

History

The success of any business depends on the quality of its employees, which in part depends on successfully matching job seekers with appropriate jobs. This matchmaking process is used in both government agencies and private firms to place qualified people in jobs that match their interests and abilities.

The first employment firms in the United States were private establishments, but state governments in the mid-1800s created agencies in New York, Massachusetts, and several other states. The federal government became involved in helping job seekers find work in the early 1900s. These efforts increased dramatically in the 1930s as a result of the millions of workers left jobless because of the Great Depression. The U.S. Employment Service was established in 1933, and agencies like the Civilian Conservation Corps and the National Youth Administration also made an effort in job placement and vocational counseling.

Each year, thousands of workers turn to employment firms to help them find appropriate jobs. Large and small businesses both use employment firms for assistance in finding qualified applicants. This has led to a demand for skilled employment firm workers.

Nature of the work

Specific job responsibilities depend on the several types of positions within the employment firm worker field.

Personnel recruiters seek out and recruit qualified applicants for existing job openings with companies. They maintain contacts within the local business community and may travel extensively to find qualified applicants. After interviewing applicants, recruiters recommend those most qualified to fill positions within a company. To aid in the analysis of the applicants, recruiters may arrange skills tests, evaluate the applicant's work history, and check personal references. Much of this work is done by phone or through computer matching services.

Recruiters must be able to present applicants with an accurate picture of companies seeking employees. They need to know about the company's personnel policy in regard to wages and promotional possibilities. They must also be familiar with equal employment opportunity and affirmative action guidelines.

Employment interviewers often have many of the same responsibilities as personnel recruiters, but may also have administrative tasks such as giving skills tests or completing a background check on the applicant.

Employment consultants help job seekers find employment and help businesses find workers for existing positions. They interview job seekers and use tests to evaluate the skills and abilities of applicants. They discuss such issues as job responsibilities and benefits. The employment consultant then attempts to find job openings that match the skills and interests of individual applicants. They often put an applicant directly in touch with a potential employer. If a specific opening does not exist, they may contact various firms to see if they need an applicant or suggest that the applicant take additional skills training to qualify for existing positions.

Consultants may also offer suggestions on resume writing, interviewing techniques, and personal appearance to help applicants secure a position. Often, a consultant will have expertise in a particular area, such as accounting or law, and work with applicants interested in jobs in that field.

Employment clerks function as intake workers and interview job seekers to get pertinent information, such as work history, education, and occupational interests. They refer the applicant to an employment consultant or counselor. Employment clerks also have administrative duties such as checking applicant references, filing applications, and compiling personnel records.

Employment agency managers supervise the business operations of an employment agency. They establish agency rules and regulations, prepare agency budgets, purchase appropriate equipment and supplies, resolve client complaints. In general they are responsible for the day-to-day operations of the agency. They are also responsible for hiring and evaluating staff workers, and overseeing their training.

Government personnel specialists do essentially the same work as their counterparts in private companies, except they deal with openings that are subject to civil service regulations. Much of government personnel work concentrates on job analysis because civil service jobs are strictly classified according to entry requirements, duties, and wages.

Requirements

Although there are no specific educational requirements for work in this field, most employers require a college education for all employment firm workers. High school graduates occasionally may start as employment clerks and advance with experience to the position of employment consultants. Some employers favor college graduates who have majored in personnel administration while others prefer individuals with a general business background. People interested in personnel work with a government agency may find it an asset to have a degree in personnel administration or public administration.

High school students interested in pursuing a career in the employment firm field should take college-preparatory courses, such as social studies, English, mathematics, and speech arts. Business courses are also valuable. In college, a combination of courses in the social sciences, behavioral sciences, business, and economics is recommended. Other relevant courses might include principles of management, business administration, psychology, and statistics.

Although most employment firms must be licensed, the workers themselves do not normally need any special license or certificate. Those individuals who plan to work for the government usually must pass a civil service examination.

As a way of attaining increased professional standing, employment workers may become certified by the National Association of Personnel Consultants (NAPC). Employment workers who have at least two years of work experience may receive the title of Certified Personnel Consultant after passing an examination. Further information on the certification process is available from the NAPC at the address given at the end of this article.

Employment firm workers evaluate a person's credentials, provide advice concerning future employment, and match a person's abilities with current jobs that are available.

Opportunities for experience and exploration

Part-time work as a clerk or a personnel assistant are good ways of exploring this field. Large department stores and other large firms usually have personnel departments and are good places to begin looking for part-time or temporary work. High school students may also find part-time work in their school's counseling department. Discussions with employment firm workers are another good way of learning about the rewards and responsibilities in this field.

Methods of entering

Those with a bachelor's degree in personnel administration or related fields should apply directly to employment firms for a job opening. Colleges and universities have placement offices that can be helpful in supplying possible leads. Those interested in working for a government agency must pass a civil service test. Openings in the government are usually listed with the Office of Personnel Management. High school graduates may apply for entry-level jobs as an employment clerk or personnel assistant, but these positions increasingly require a college degree.

Entry-level workers are usually trained on the job or in formal training programs, where

595

they learn how to classify jobs and interview applicants.

Advancement

After trainees have mastered the basic personnel tasks, they are assigned to specific areas, such as personnel recruitment. In time, skilled workers may become department heads or office managers. A few highly skilled employees may become top executives with employment firms. Advancement may also be achieved by moving into a higher position in another firm.

Employment outlook

Employment opportunities are expected to grow as fast as the average for all occupations through the 1990s. The demand will be greatest in private industry as employers become more aware of the benefits of using employment firms to find part-time and temporary help. Opportunities in government work will result primarily from the need to replace workers rather than to fill new positions.

Jobs in the employment field are protected somewhat against changes in the economy. If the economy is growing and businesses are expanding, companies will use employment firms to fill existing positions. If there is a downturn in the economy, more job seekers will use these firms in an attempt to improve their job prospects. Job opportunities will be greatest in large urban areas, where there are more jobs, and a higher degree of job turnover.

Although opportunities in this field will continue to grow, the competition for each job will be keen. There is expected to be an abundance of college graduates and experienced workers for each opening.

Earnings

Employment firm fees are usually paid by the company that hires an applicant, but occasionally the applicant will pay the fee. Earnings vary widely and depend on job responsibilities and the size of the firm. Employment clerks usually start at between $13,500 and $15,000 per year, and experienced clerks earn between $18,000 and $21,000 per year. Beginning employment consultants earn between $19,000 and $23,000 per year. Experienced consultants earn $25,000 or more, depending on success in placing workers. In most private companies, employment consultants are paid a basic salary and they earn a commission for each job opening that they fill. Federal employees are usually paid according to civil service grade level, with merit increases. Employment agency managers usually start at between $29,000 and $32,000 per year, with experienced managers earning $50,000 and up depending on specific job responsibilities and the size of the firm. Some managers are also paid a commission on each job opening they help fill. Full-time employment firm workers receive health insurance, vacation, and other benefits.

Conditions of work

Employment firm workers work in pleasant conditions. Their offices are designed to make a good impression on outside visitors and prospective employees and most are modern, attractive, and nicely furnished. Employees work a 40-hour week, unless they are working on a special project. There may be some clerical work, such as typing and filing. Many agencies are small, but some can be quite large, employing over 50 employees.

Some personnel recruiters travel extensively. Recruiters attend professional conferences and visit college campuses to interview prospective employees.

Workers in this field should have a pleasant outgoing personality and enjoy working with people of different levels of education and experience. Much of the day is spent talking to job seekers or prospective employers, either on the phone or in person. Employment firm workers must exercise sensitivity and tact when interviewing potential customers or clients. Good writing and speaking skills are vital. Attention to detail is another valued characteristic.

GOE: 11.03.04; SIC: 7361; SOC: 143

◇ **SOURCES OF ADDITIONAL INFORMATION**

Information on certification is available from:

National Association of Personnel Consultants
3133 Mount Vernon Avenue
Alexandria, VA 22305

General career information is available from:

Society for Human Resource Management
606 North Washington Street
Alexandria, VA 22314

International Personnel Management Association
1617 Duke Street
Alexandria, VA 22314

National Employment Counselors Association
Education Office
5999 Stevenson Avenue
Alexandria, VA 22304

◇ **RELATED ARTICLES**

Volume 1: Business Administration; Human Resources; Social Services
Volumes 2–4: Career counselors; Career guidance technicians; Clerical supervisors and managers; Employment counselors; Human services workers; Personnel and labor relations specialists

Energy-conservation technicians

Definition

Energy-conservation technicians identify and measure the amount of energy used to heat and cool or operate a facility or industrial process. They assess efficient use of energy and determine the amount of energy lost through wasteful processes or lack of insulation. They also prescribe corrective steps to conserve energy. These technicians are trained in the use and conversion of energy, techniques for improving or preventing loss of energy, and the determination of the optimum energy required in a given system or process.

History

At the start of the 20th century, energy costs were only a small part of the expense of operating homes, offices, and factories, and of providing lighting, communication, and transportation. Coal and petroleum were abundant and relatively inexpensive. These low energy prices contributed to the United States' emergence as not only the leading industrialized nation in the world, but also its largest energy user.

Because petroleum was inexpensive and easily produced heat, steam, electricity, and fuel, it displaced coal for many purposes. This caused the nation's coal-mining industry to de-

cline, and the United States to become dependent on foreign oil for half its energy supply.

In 1973, many foreign oil-producing nations stopped shipments of oil to the United States and other Western nations; fuel costs suddenly became a large expense. Although oil prices have become more moderate since then, the prices are still very volatile, subject to the whims of the Arab countries which supply most of the world's oil. The threat of oil-price increases or a cutoff of supplies in the future never quite disappears.

These events spawned energy conservation as a new technology in the United States, one which works to discover new sources of energy, find more efficient methods and equipment to use energy, and seek and eliminate sources of wasted energy. This has created a large need for energy conservation technicians.

Nature of the work

Thanks to the energy crisis of 1974, energy efficiency and conservation are major concerns in nearly all homes and workplaces today. This means that job settings and work assignments for energy-conservation technicians vary greatly, ranging from power plant operation to research laboratory assisting, energy audits, and equipment sales and service. The jobs

This energy-conservation technician is inspecting a home for places where heating and air conditioning can escape outdoors. He will then suggest affordable ways to make the home energy-efficient.

els or other resources into useful energy. Systems may be plants that produce hot water, steam, mechanical motion, or electrical power. Typical systems include furnaces, electrical power plants, and solar heating systems. They may be controlled manually, by semi-automated control panels, or by computers. Technicians in this area frequently supervise other workers.

In the field of energy use, technicians might work to improve efficiency in industrial engineering and production line equipment, and in equipment and building maintenance (particularly in such places as hospitals, schools, apartments, etc.)

In energy conservation, typical employers include manufacturing companies, consulting engineers, energy-audit firms, and energy-audit departments of public utility companies. Technicians are also hired by municipal governments, hotels, architects, private builders, and heating, ventilating and air-conditioning equipment manufacturers.

Technicians working in energy conservation typically work on a team led by an engineer. They determine building specifications, modify equipment and structures, audit energy use and efficiency of machines and systems, then recommend modifications or changes to save energy.

Requirements

Energy-conservation technicians must be broadly trained and systems-oriented. They must be able to work with many types of devices and mechanisms with a knowledge of how the various components and devices relate to one another. Technicians can apply this knowledge in a variety of ways to develop, construct, test, sell, install, operate, modify, and maintain today's equipment in energy-related fields.

The equipment needed to produce, control, use, and conserve energy is typical of most technologically complex machinery. It may contain electric motors, heaters, lamps, electronic controls, mechanical drives and linkages, thermal systems, lubricants, optical systems, microwave systems, pneumatic and hydraulic drives, pneumatic controls, and, in some instances, even radioactive samples and counters. In order to work effectively with equipment of this kind, technicians must have a thorough understanding of the many underlying technical disciplines and their interrelationships.

Successful energy-conservation technicians are interested in machines and how they oper-

these technicians perform can be divided into four major areas of energy activity: research and development, production, use, and conservation.

In research and development, typical employers include organizations in institutions, private industry, government, and the military. Working under the direction of an engineer, physicist, chemist, or metallurgist, technicians use specialized equipment and materials to perform laboratory experiments involving mechanical, electrical, chemical, pneumatic, hydraulic, thermal, or optical scientific principles. Technicians also perform tests to measure system performance, then document the results in reports or laboratory notebooks, and also perform periodic maintenance and repair of equipment. Test data frequently are developed and analyzed using complex measuring instruments and laboratory microcomputers. Technicians also supervise other skilled research workers.

In energy production, typical employers include solar energy equipment manufacturers, installers, and users; power plants; and process plants that use high-temperature heat, steam, or hot water. Technicians in this field work with engineers and managers to develop, install, operate, maintain, modify, and repair systems and devices used for the conversion of fu-

ate. They not only know how machines are made, how the parts fit and work together, but they can also figure out what is wrong if parts are not working properly. Once technicians identify the problem, they know how to correct it.

Students entering this field must have a practical understanding of the physical sciences, a good aptitude for math, and the ability to communicate in writing and in speaking with technical specialists and also with persons not trained in the field. Their work requires a clear and precise understanding of operational and maintenance manuals, schematic drawings, blueprints, and computational formulas; thus the ability to communicate clearly in scientific and engineering terms is a basic requirement.

At least two years of formal technical education beyond high school is the best preparation for this career. While still in high school, however, students who are interested in this field should study both algebra and geometry for at least one year. Courses in physics, chemistry, and ecology, including laboratory work, would also form a base for the post-secondary program that follows. High school courses in computer science and drafting (either mechanical or architectural) would also be very helpful.

Post-secondary programs in energy conservation focus on the principles and applications of physics, energy conservation, energy economics, instrumentation, electronics, electromechanical systems, computers, heating systems, and air conditioning. A typical curriculum in a technical institute, community college, or other specialized two-year program would offer a first year of study in physics, chemistry, mathematics, the fundamentals of energy technology, energy production systems, the fundamentals of electricity and electromechanical devices, and microcomputer operations.

The second year of study would include courses in mechanical and fluid systems; electrical power and illumination systems; electronic devices; blueprint reading; energy conservation; codes and regulations; heating, ventilation, and air conditioning; technical communications; instrumentation and controls; and energy economics and audits. Considerable time is spent in laboratories, where students gain hands-on experience by assembling, disassembling, adjusting, and operating devices, mechanisms, and integrated systems of machines and controls.

Students should note that many technical colleges, community colleges, and technical institutes provide two-year programs under the specific title of energy conservation and use

technology or energy management technology. In addition, many other schools offer related programs in solar power, electric power, building maintenance, equipment maintenance, and general engineering technology.

A certificate from the National Institute for Certification in Engineering Technologies and a degree or certificate of graduation from an accredited technical program, while not required, are valuable credentials and proof of recognized preparation for work as energy-conservation technicians.

Some positions in electrical power plants require energy-conservation technicians to pass certain psychological tests to predict their behavior during crises. Security clearances, arranged by the employer, are required for employment in nuclear power plants or other workplaces designated by the government as high-security facilities.

Opportunities for experience and exploration

Students who are considering entry into the field of energy conservation should obtain all the information they can from high school or post-secondary school guidance counselors and occupational information centers. School guidance programs often can arrange field trips to industrial, commercial, and business workplaces to discuss careers in the energy efficiency field.

The electric utility company in nearly every city will have an energy analyst or a team of energy auditors in its customer service department. Consulting engineering offices are also located in major cities. Interested students may be able to talk with these energy specialists about the field, and to find out about opportunities for part-time or summer work. Energy conservation specialists may also be found working in large hospitals, major office buildings, and hotel chains. Frequently, universities and large manufacturing plants will employ energy specialists in their plant engineering departments.

A partial understanding of the field can be gained by enrolling in seminars sometimes offered by community colleges or equipment and material suppliers on topics such as building insulation, storm windows, heat pumps, solar heaters, and the like. Useful experience can also be obtained by undertaking student projects in solar equipment, energy audits, or energy efficient equipment.

ENERGY-CONSERVATION TECHNICIANS

Methods of entering

Most graduates of technical programs are able to secure jobs in energy conservation before graduation with assistance from their school's placement office. The placement staff works closely with potential employers, especially those that have hired graduates in recent years. Many large companies schedule regular recruiting visits to schools before graduation. Students may also write or visit potential employers.

It is possible to enter the field of energy conservation on the basis of work experience. Industrial technicians, experienced industrial equipment mechanics, and people with extensive training in military instrumentation and systems control and maintenance may enter the field with the help of intensive study to supplement the knowledge and skills they bring to the job from previous experience.

Some jobs in energy production, such as in electrical power plants, can be obtained with only a high school diploma. New employees, however, are expected to successfully complete company-sponsored training courses to keep their jobs and advance to positions with more responsibility.

Many positions in building or equipment maintenance are available to persons who were trained and employed in the military, particularly in the U.S. Navy. Former Navy technicians are particularly sought in the field of energy production.

Many of the jobs offered to high school graduates in electrical power production are represented by employee unions such as the International Brotherhood of Electrical Workers or the International Association of Machinists and Aerospace Workers. Workers often start as apprentices with a planned program of work and study for three to four years.

Graduates with associate degrees in energy conservation and use, instrumentation, electronics, or electromechanical technology will normally enter employment at a higher level, with more responsibility and correspondingly higher pay, than those with less preparation. Jobs in energy research and development almost always require an associate degree.

Because these technicians are prepared to function in all of the energy conversion fields, their adaptability to many kinds of highly technical work at the technician level makes them attractive to a variety of employers. Some employers, such as power companies, need technicians to perform energy audits. Such a job could involve assisting energy-use auditors and energy-application analysts while they make audits or analyses in businesses or homes of their customers. This provides new technicians with a period of orientation to learn about specific duties, after which they perform regular audits and analyses on their own. The resulting data forms a base for making specific recommendations to reduce energy consumption and costs for the company or customer.

Some employers seek graduate energy technicians because of their flexibility and versatility as members of research teams. Their broad understanding enables them to function as researchers who can quickly comprehend problems and propose solutions. Their ability to make many different kinds of measurements and to gather, analyze, and interpret data makes them ideal for research and development assignments.

Other employers seek energy technicians to work in engineering departments. Their broad technical base and versatility make them promising workers in the design or modification of products. Some technicians prefer to work in engineering production activities such as process control, planning for energy-efficient production systems, and related engineering activities. Their broad technical training prepares them to be more productive at entry-level than persons who have only mechanical or electrical technician preparation.

Another major area that energy-conservation technicians are especially prepared to enter is the management of machinery and equipment, including its planning, selection, installation, modification, and maintenance. Energy-conservation technicians are thoroughly trained to understand all the aspects of energy as it relates to modern machinery. Therefore, they can quickly find out what is wrong if the machines or devices are not working as they should and direct the work needed to correct them.

For the energy technician who is especially interested in machines and mechanical systems, there are a number of attractive career opportunities in machinery engineering and management. Modern machines and machinery systems are rapidly becoming more technologically complex and expensive. This means that keeping the equipment in efficient working order is increasingly important. Here again, post-secondary energy conservation programs provide the training necessary for success in this field.

Finally, there are sales opportunities for trained energy-conservation technicians with this talent. Many manufacturers of energy-efficient or energy-conservation equipment use energy-conservation technicians to help customers determine their needs for certain kinds of equipment and systems.

Advancement

Because the career is relatively new, well-established patterns of advancement have not yet emerged. Nevertheless, technicians in any of the four areas of energy conservation can advance to higher positions, such as senior technicians and supervisory positions. These advanced positions require a combination of formal education, diligent on-the-job study, and special seminars or classes (usually sponsored or paid for by the employer).

Technicians can also advance by progressing to new, more challenging assignments. For example, hotels, restaurants, and stores hire experienced energy technicians to manage energy consumption. This often involves visits to each location to audit and examine its facilities or procedures to see where energy use can be cut back. The technician then provides training in energy-saving practices. Other experienced energy technicians may be employed as special sales and customer service representatives for producers of power, energy, special control systems, or equipment designed to improve energy efficiency.

Technicians with experience and money to invest may start their own businesses, selling energy-saving products or providing audits, weatherizations, or energy-efficient renovations. Private companies already serve government, industry, and homeowners' needs for energy audits.

Employment outlook

A slow economy increases financial pressures on businesses to reduce costs, and so energy costs may well be an area they will look to. This could lead to a greater need for trained energy-conservation technicians.

Future employment in this career is somewhat uncertain and depends in large part on what happens to the price of oil and other energy sources. If energy costs decline, some of the economic motivation may lessen, which could cause the demand for energy-conservation technicians to decrease. On the other hand, if costs increase, energy use will continue to constitute a major expense to industry, commerce, government, institutions, and private citizens, and the demand for technicians trained in energy conservation will remain strong.

In addition, the United States is still far from independent of foreign fuel supplies. The possibility of an interruption in foreign supplies of petroleum or an increase in its cost continues

to require all energy consumers to conserve energy as a matter of economic efficiency and competitiveness.

Earnings

Earnings of energy-conservation technicians vary significantly with the amount of their formal training and experience. High school graduates with little or no experience who begin as trainees will earn $15,400 to $19,800 per year. Technicians with military experience and three to six years of technical experience earn from $19,500 to $33,000 annually. Graduates of postsecondary technician programs earn the same.

Energy-conservation technicians with five to ten years of experience in research, engineering design, or in machinery engineering and maintenance can earn up to $39,000 annually.

Technicians typically receive paid vacations, group insurance benefits, employee retirement plans, and the like. In addition, they often have the benefit of company support for all or a part of their educational programs. These are important benefits because technicians must continually study to keep up to date with technological changes that occur in this developing field.

Conditions of work

Work assignments for energy-conservation technicians will vary from day to day and change as new innovations and equipment are introduced.

Energy conservation technicians employed in research and development and also in engineering design and product planning generally work in laboratories or engineering departments with normal daytime work schedules. Although technicians must often travel to customer locations or work in their employer's plant, they usually work normal schedules.

Energy production and energy-use work frequently involves around-the-clock operations that require shifts. In these two areas technicians work either indoors or outdoors at the employer's site. Such assignments require little or no travel, but the work environments may be dirty, noisy, and sometimes hot or cold.

Appropriate work clothing must be worn in shop or factory settings and safety awareness and safe working habits must be practiced at all times.

Jobs in energy production and energy management are in-plant jobs where the energy-conservation technician interacts with only a small group of people. Energy research and development jobs involve laboratory activities and require social interaction with engineers, scientists, and other technicians.

Energy-conservation jobs require technicians to provide special technical services to customers, and rely on them to successfully communicate and interact with the public. In some cases, they may be considered public relations representatives, which calls for careful attention to the way they present themselves: their personality, dress, attitude, and special communication skills are a reflection on the company, and should help create a favorable impression.

Nearly all jobs in this field require energy-conservation technicians to communicate in a clear, concise manner, whether orally or in the form of laboratory notebooks, reports, or letters.

Job stress in this field varies. At times the pace is relaxed but businesslike, typically in engineering, planning, and design departments or in research and development. At other times, technicians respond to urgent calls and crisis situations involving unexpected breakdowns of equipment that must be diagnosed and corrected as soon as possible.

Energy technicians must be able to maintain an orderly, systematic, and objective approach to solving problems suing logic and judgment.

Energy-conservation technicians gain a sense of satisfaction in helping their clients. When technicians complete an analysis of a problem in energy use and effectiveness, they can state the results in tangible dollar costs, losses, or savings. This is a highly valuable service because it provides a basis for important decisions on using and conserving energy.

GOE: 05.03.06; SIC: Any industry; SOC: 371

◇ SOURCES OF ADDITIONAL INFORMATION

American Petroleum Institute
1220 L Street, NW
Washington, DC 20005

Association of Energy Engineers
4025 Pleasantdale Road, Suite 420
Atlanta, GA 30340

Energy Conservation Coalition
6930 Carroll Avenue, 6th Floor
Takoma Park, MD 20912

Center for Energy Policy and Research
c/o New York Institute of Technology
Old Westbury, NY 11568

Alliance to Save Energy
1925 K Street, NW
Suite 206
Washington, DC 20006

Energy Action Council of Toronto
11 Audley Avenue
Toronto ON M4M 1P5

◇ RELATED ARTICLES

Volume 1: Energy; Physical Sciences; Public Utilities
Volumes 2–4: Air-conditioning, refrigeration, and heating mechanics; Air-conditioning, heating, and refrigeration technicians; Chemical technicians; Electromechanical technicians; General maintenance mechanics; Industrial engineering technicians; Industrial machinery mechanics; Instrumentation technicians; Miscellaneous engineers; Nuclear reactor operator technicians; Petroleum technicians; Power plant occupations; Service sales representatives; Solar collector technicians; Stationary engineers; Stationary firers, boiler tenders

Enologists (wine makers)

Definition

Enologists direct and manage most activities of a winery, including planting grapes and producing, storing, and shipping wine. They select the type of grapes grown and supervise workers in the production process from harvesting to fermenting, aging, and bottling. Enologists work with different varieties of grapes in a type or species to develop the strongest and most flavorful wines.

History

Wine making has been practiced for more than 5,000 years. Ancient Egyptians had hieroglyphics (picture writings) representing wine making, and it was an important commodity in Palestine during the time of Jesus. The Chinese made wine more than 4,000 years ago and the Greeks and Romans also used wine.

Throughout history, wine has been used as a drink to accompany meals or as part of religious practices. In fact, the use of wine spread throughout Europe because of its use in religious services. Wine also was used as a medicine or curative.

Grapes have been cultivated in the United States since the late 1700s. Enology or viticulture, the cultivation of grapes, is a major industry now, primarily in California and the eastern part of the country. More than 80 percent of the domestic wine is cultivated in California. Enologists have played an instrumental role in the growth of the wine industry, experimenting with different types of grapes and growing conditions, and improving the quality of wines made.

Nature of the work

Enologists are involved in all aspects of wine production and therefore must have a thorough knowledge of the wine making business. They should be able to analyze the quality of grapes, decide what vines are best to grow, determine when vines are ripe enough to be picked, and coordinate the production of the wine making process. Production decisions include which yeast or bacteria to use, at what temperature

fermentation should occur, and how the wine is to be aged.

Selection of the proper grapes is a vital part of an enologist's planning responsibilities. This selection process includes analyzing the various varieties of European grapes to determine which are best suited to grow in a specific area, given existing soil and climate conditions. For example, an enologist in California must ensure that grapes chosen to grow in that climate can withstand the heat of the summers, while an enologist in New York must ensure that grapes chosen to grow in that climate can withstand the lower temperatures present there. Other factors determining which type of grapes to grow include the desired flavor and aroma of wines and the species' ability to withstand disease.

Grapes producing red wine are processed in a different fashion than grapes producing white wine. Production methods also vary according to the size of the winery and the type of containers and stainless steel tanks used in the crushing and fermentation processes. Enologists have the final word in all production decisions. They consult with other winery staff and then decide issues involving the testing and crushing of grapes, the cooling, filtering, and bottling of the wine, and the type of storage casks in which to place the wine. The enologist is also responsible for researching and implementing appropriate modifications in the growing and production techniques to ensure the best quality product at the lowest possible cost. This involves keeping up with technological improvements in production methods and an ability to read and analyze a profit-and-loss statement and other parts of a balance sheet.

As a manager, the enologist is responsible for overseeing personnel matters. Enologists may hire and train employees—like the workers in the vineyard—coordinate work schedules, and develop a salary structure. Good communications skills are needed to present written and oral reports.

Although bookkeeping, reporting to government agencies, and other administrative tasks are often delegated to an assistant, enologists must have an understanding of industry regulations, accounting, and mathematics. Production costs and other expenses must be carefully recorded. Because of the increased use of computers for recording composition and grape details, blending and production alternatives, and analyzing information,

603

ENOLOGISTS (WINE MAKERS)

The staff members of a wine-making company gather at a laboratory to sample wine. They must ensure a consistent taste and quality in the wine they produce.

As competition in the field increases, many enologists are choosing to pursue a master's degree and to gain experience in related scientific research.

Although no licenses or certificates are necessary to work in the field, many enologists chose to continue professional enrichment through continuing education classes and affiliation with organizations such as the American Society for Enology and Viticulture. The address for professional organizations can be found at the end of this article.

enologists should have some training in computer science.

An enologist is sometimes involved with decisions regarding the marketing of the finished product. Transportation and other distribution costs, the potential markets on the national and international level, and other production costs must be calculated, to determine the price of the finished wine and where the wine will be sold.

Opportunities for experience and exploration

Part-time or summer employment at a winery is an excellent method of gaining an insight into the skills and temperament needed for this profession. A high school student can also explore opportunities in the field through discussions with professionals already working as enologists. Because many technical colleges offer evening courses, it may be possible for a high school student to audit a course or take a course for future college credit.

Requirements

Although some wineries offer on-the-job training in the form of apprenticeships to high school graduates, the majority of entry-level positions go to college graduates, so a college degree is the recommended first step on the career path for those looking to enter the field. High school students should take courses in mathematics, biology, chemistry, and physics. English and other courses that enhance communications skills should also be taken. Foreign languages, particularly French and German, may enhance opportunities for study or research abroad.

A college degree in enology or viticulture is preferred, but a degree in food or fermentation science, or related subject, like microbiology or biochemistry, is acceptable. Specific courses related to winery management should include wine analysis and wine microbiology. Business, economics, marketing, and computer science should also be part of the degree program. There are three universities in the United States that offer enology programs: University of California at Davis, California State University at Fresno, and Cornell University.

Methods of entering

The usual method of entry is to be hired by a winery after completing an undergraduate or graduate degree in enology, fermentation, or food science. Sometimes, summer or part-time employment can lead to an offer of a permanent job and an apprenticeship program at the winery provides the necessary training.

Advancement

Advancement depends on performance, experience, and education. Enologists at small wineries may become managers at larger facilities. Those at larger facilities may move on to direct a number of wineries as part of a nationwide organization. A small number of enologists may start their own wineries.

Because of the relatively small number of wineries in the country, and the fact that enologists have high-level management positions from the start, advancement opportunities are somewhat limited.

Employment outlook

Job growth is tied somewhat to the acceptance of, and demand for, American wines. Technological advances in wine production may create more job opportunities. Employment is expected to grow a little faster than average in the 1990s. Obviously, job opportunities will be best in California, where most of the U.S. wineries are located. Most of the California wine is cultivated in the San Joaquin, Napa, and Sonoma valleys, the central coast, and the Sierra foothills.

Earnings

Beginning salaries average between $20,000 to $30,000 per year, depending on experience, education, and the size of the winery. Larger wineries tend to pay more than smaller operations. Experienced enologists can make anywhere from $30,000 to $85,000 per year, with some highly skilled enologists making even more.

Conditions of work

An enologist can expect to work primarily indoors in a winery, with some outdoors activities in a vineyard. Indoor work will be divided between planning and administrative tasks that may take place in an office setting and supervisory tasks that take place in the fermentation and aging cellars, the laboratory, and the bottling area.

Enologists have a good deal of variety in their jobs as they constantly alternate between analyzing the grapes in the field, assessing the development of wines, studying current production techniques, planning marketing strategies for the upcoming harvest, and other responsibilities. Physical labor, such as lifting a 40-pound wine case or pruning a vineyard may be required, but as a rule the job is not that physically demanding.

During most of the year an enologist works 40 hours a week, but during the late summer and early fall when the grape harvest occurs, an enologist should expect to work long hours six or seven days a week for a four- to six-week period.

As a manager, an enologist should be able to communicate and work well with people. The ability to interpret data is vital as much of the enologist's planning responsibilities involve working with crop and market forecasts. Attention to detail is critical. An enologist should be able to spend long hours analyzing information, and also be able to make and implement decisions concerning this information. Some travel may be necessary for conferences or other professional obligations such as tastings and public presentations.

GOE: 05.02.03; SIC: 2084; SOC: 132

◇ SOURCES OF ADDITIONAL INFORMATION

American Society for Enology and Viticulture
PO Box 1855
Davis, CA 95617

General information about career opportunities is available from:

American Wine Society
3006 Latta Road
Rochester, NY 14612

Association of American Vintners
Box 307
East Rochester, NY 14445

Canadian Wine Institute
#215, 89 The Queensway West
Mississauga ON L5B 2V2

◇ RELATED ARTICLES

Volume 1: Agriculture; Biological Sciences; Chemistry
Volumes 2–4: Agribusiness technicians; Agricultural equipment technicians; Agricultural scientists; Biological scientists; Biological technicians; Chemists; Farmers

Environmental engineers

Definition

Environmental engineers research and discover methods to prevent, control, and eventually eliminate environmental problems. They are employed by government agencies, manufacturing companies, consulting firms, and attorneys to handle pollution problems. Locally, this work might involve cleaning a pond. Globally, it could involve researching the earth's ozone layer and determining causes of damage.

History

Environmental engineering is considered a special branch of civil engineering. Historically, *civil engineers* have been involved in public works like road building and developing water works and waste disposal systems. In the past 20 years, more specialized areas of civil engineering have evolved to deal with problems such as pollution, industrial hygiene, and toxic waste.

Nature of Work

Since environmental engineers spend a lot of time cleaning polluted sites, they may spend much of their time outdoors. Basic research would dictate visiting a work site and gathering soil and water samples.

Environmental engineers study radioactive waste disposal and whether such waste should be dumped, burned, or buried. It is important to determine the danger of potential problems after disposing of radioactive waste. Environmental engineers may seek input from other engineers handling similar situations. Environmental engineers need to know government regulations dictating proper disposal and clean-up requirements.

Environmental engineers inspect public buildings, food processing plants, and transportation systems for cleanliness. They test animals used for food, such as fish, pigs and cattle, for diseases.

Some environmental engineers install equipment within an industry to control and monitor output of contaminants. For example, a company may need to have pollution control devices installed in a smokestack to comply with clean air regulations. Environmental engi-

neers constantly search for and invent methods of monitoring pollution.

Environmental engineers also have traveled into space with the National Aeronautics and Space Administration to explore new life support systems, such as a closed-loop life support system in which water, oxygen, and food can be recycled and used. This would let astronauts spend more time in space with limited resources and live comfortably in a space station for an extended period of time.

Government agencies need personnel who can untangle volumes of regulations, and companies look to environmental engineers to environmentally audit them to ensure they comply with government regulations. An environmental engineer also may help devise a plan to fix problems within a realistic time frame and cost. Environmental engineers help companies choose the right sites to develop. For example, they may study the effects a new plant would have on the environment and assess options for waste disposal, drainage, noise levels and sustaining wildlife reproduction in the area. They also give expert testimony in environmental litigation, and their opinions carry much weight when determining who pays for cleaning up a polluted site. The time span for a project returning to normal could be as short as a month, depending on the problem's simplicity, or it may never be realized in an environmental engineer's lifetime.

Requirements

A bachelor's degree is mandatory. Within the engineering curriculum other studies such as chemical, civil, electrical or mechanical engineering are acceptable. Those hoping to get into research or teaching need a master's degree or a Ph.D. Licensing is required for most engineers working within the public health and safety fields.

Opportunities for experience and exploration

Students should take as many science and math courses as possible; chemistry, biology, and ecology courses are recommended. Most employers provide on-the-job training. Many seminars, clinics, and organizations give up-to-date information on issues, methods, and procedures. Local environmental organizations and watchdog groups can provide insight.

Methods of entering

After earning a degree, an environmental engineer typically will start working in the field with opportunities to move into technical or nontechnical management. In technical management, engineers oversee groups of people working on projects.

Advancement

Nontechnical management jobs include administrative positions leading to executive officer positions in companies. In such upper echelon positions, environmental engineers can earn up to $100,000 a year.

Employment Outlook

An environmental engineering career is in high demand because of new regulations and a shortage of people trained to enforce them. Public awareness of a range of environmental issues is causing industry and government to do more to protect the environment by encouraging legislation.

According to the Association of Environmental Engineering Professors, universities produce only one third of the graduates needed to fill 5,000 openings a year, and schools likely won't meet the demand until around 2000.

Earnings

Entry-level environmental engineers with bachelor's degrees can expect to earn between $27,000 and $35,000 per year. After gaining experience, the average yearly salary increases to about $45,000. New engineers with master's degrees will earn about $40,000 to $45,000 to start. Mid-level salaries range from between $55,000 to $70,000. Supervisors and experts within the field can earn as much as $75,000 to $100,000 per year.

Conditions of work

The majority of environmental engineers work in an office setting. However, some do extensive work managing field sites and taking samples.

Many environmental engineers specialize in one area. Here, a hydrologist is testing the water.

GOE: 05.01.02; SIC:8711, 9511; SOC: 1628

◇ **SOURCES OF ADDITIONAL INFORMATION**

American Society of Sanitary Engineering
PO Box 40362
Bay Village, OH 44140

Inter-American Association of Sanitary Engineering and Environmental Sciences
18729 Considine Drive
Brookville, MD 20833

Association of Environmental Engineering Professors
Civil and Environmental Engineering Department
University of Cincinnati
Cincinnati, OH 45221-0071

◇ **RELATED ARTICLES**

Volume 1: Biological Sciences; Chemistry; Environmental Sciences; Physical Sciences
Volumes 2–4: Health and regulatory inspectors

Equestrian management worker

Definition

Equestrian management jobs include positions such as farriers, horse breeders, horse trainers, judges, jockeys, stable managers, and riding instructors.

History

Historically used for work and transportation, horses have been in use since 2000 B.C. when they were introduced in Babylonia and in Egypt 300 years later. Chariots with mounted soldiers were popular in parades, and equestrian displays were featured in early Olympic Games in Greece and at ancient Roman celebrations. In the 16th century, Spanish conquistadors brought the first horses to America. Interest in horses changed from functional to recreational in the late 1800s and early 1900s, when it began to decline until about 1960. In the later quarter of the 20th century, however, horse events have come to rival other sports as a recreational pursuit, although fewer gambling dollars are available since horse racing now has to compete with other forms of legalized gambling such as lotteries, casino gambling, sports betting, and river boat gambling.

Nature of Work

Equine management positions include "contact" and "noncontact" positions. Contact jobs are hands-on positions actually working with horses, at a track, on a farm or breeding association. Noncontact jobs may involve working in the marketing department of a race track or selling equipment, feed or pharmaceuticals.

Equine-related careers all require long hours whether a person is working directly with horses or in an office setting. Regardless of the position, employers look for people with a knowledge of horses, flexibility, and a willingness to start small and work their way up.

For example, a *riding instructor* may work from 8 A.M. to 10 P.M. if a schedule mandates such lesson times. There may be long breaks, but during show season, days can be long. An instructor may take two or 20 pupils to a horse show and be responsible for coaching them before, during, and after classes.

A *stable management worker* is similar to a store manager. Responsibilities include ensuring feed and bedding is well stocked and ordered. He or she may be required to give medicine to sick or injured horses, which usually requires constant monitoring. A *stable manager's* duties include hiring personnel to clean stalls, feed, and groom horses. In a small operation, the manager may do such tasks himself. He may organize clinics or horse shows at a stable for large groups of riders and work with judges, stewards, food vendors, and various horse organizations. Turning a horse into a paddock or pasture daily is usually necessary for a horse's health. In a large stable, a manager must know which horses get along and which must be left alone in its own paddock. New horses have to be introduced to the herd, a process of increasing interaction spent with a new horse and its pasture mates.

Horse breeders must match mates and monitor offspring. A breeder must research and be familiar with varying bloodlines and breeds to select the right mate for a race horse. For example, a breeder may know the bloodline of the sire (father), such as his physical conformation and speed. The breeder may know the dam's (mother) bloodline to contain many previous winners, but smaller sized horses with big strides.

Care is also necessary for a mare during her 11 months of pregnancy. Breeders will attempt to have a mare deliver her foal in the spring because it is easier to care for both mare and foal and develop a proper training schedule if the horse will race. This may require monitoring a mare's estrous cycle and coordinating veterinary visits. In today's breeding world, artificial insemination is very popular for breeding purposes. A stallion's sperm can be shipped all over the country to impregnate mares and increase the strength of a bloodline.

Horse trainers work with young, old, troubled, or well trained horses. A trainer matches a rider's capabilities with a horse's training level. Many trainers ride young horses around the age of 3. Care is given to the length of workout so as to not stress the bones of a young horse or to make it frustrated or sour. The length of workout and training is increased as a horse gets older and its discipline is decided. For example, a jumper may be required to put years of training on the flat (on ground), learning to bend, lengthen and shorten its strides so its bones can reach full strength and

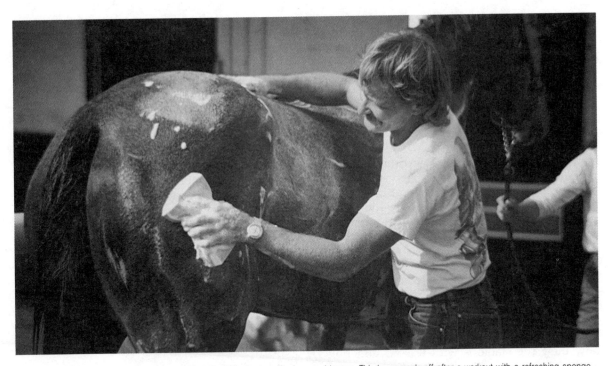

One of the many duties of an equestrian worker is keeping the horses clean and happy. This horse cools off after a workout with a refreshing sponge bath.

size. Around 5 years old, a horse may begin jumping small fences, and by the age of 6 or 7, continue jumping regular course. This takes patience and time, and many hours of hard work, as horses can be unpredictable and strong. A good trainer knows when to quit for the day and when to push for more.

Jockeys ride racehorses. A harness jockey sits in a sulky and guides trotters around the track; a steeplechase jockey rides a horse cross-country on a course with large brush jumps; and a flat racing jockey rides horses on a flat track at varying distances. Many jockeys work as independent contractors who ride for different barns, trainers, and owners. A good jockey may be hired by a specific barn for a whole season because he may work particularly well with a certain horse. Generally, jockeys have fairly stable working hours during racing season but usually begin early in the morning and finish in early evening after a day of racing.

Judges are used at all levels and disciplines with the horse industry. Horse showing is popular from the 4-H club level to the international show circuit. Judges grade and place riders in order of excellence. Some judges travel internationally, and others may officiate each summer at a local show.

Riding discipline forms include breed, English or Western, jumping, dressage, and rodeo. Judges grade riders and horses on various fac-

tors including performance, riding capability, and strength of breed classification.

Farriers maintain a horse's hooves. Their work involves visiting a horse every 6 to 8 weeks for trimming hooves, resetting shoes, installing pads, or putting on new shoes. Experienced farriers have an in-depth command of anatomy and physiology, and they can make horse shoes.

A horse's gait affects the angle at which each hoof hits the ground. Since every hoof is different, a farrier must determine which areas of a hoof to trim and which work best for a particular type of riding.

Veterinarian technicians are the equivalent of nurses in the veterinary field. They tend to general animal care and do tests, administer medicine, radiology, ultrasound therapy, and wound care.

The equine industry is a business like any other, so capable *administrators* with a knowledge of horses and office management are necessary. One administrative position is that of a *marketing representative* whose duties include promoting and organizing horse shows and races. Marketing representatives also develop brochures and video tapes of horses and their offspring to promote various breed associations. Such promotional materials are sent to schools, colleges, and clubs to develop a following for a particular breed association.

Sales representatives sell everything from feed to trailers, trucks, and pharmaceuticals. They must know what's going on in the equine industry to keep up with competitors and what makes one product different from another.

Requirements

Instructing requires patience and the ability to calm nervous students. Many universities offer certification for riding instruction at beginning, intermediate, and advanced levels. Riding instructors or trainers must have an extensive background in riding or teaching and possibly certification from an accredited school.

Stable management positions may also require a degree from an accredited two-year program. Students learn everything from feeding rations and veterinary maintenance to handling troublesome horses and managing a show. Long hours may be required depending upon how busy the stable is with lessons and how many horses are in the facility.

Jockeys must be small. The majority of jockeys do not weigh more than 125 pounds with their height proportionate to their weight. Jockeys may begin by riding whenever they can, such as working as an exerciser for early morning workouts. They must be in very good physical shape and have a feel for a horse and its capabilities. Being a jockey may require a fair amount of travel to gain enough experience to work in one place for a season.

Being a farrier requires great physical strength, especially in the arms and back. Certification is required from an accredited school (usually a six-week full-time course) and an apprenticeship with an experienced farrier is recommended. It is not absolutely necessary to have a background with horses; however a good and respected farrier will have an excellent eye in spotting problems with a horse's gait and the ability to know what is right or wrong with its movements.

Aspiring breeders must live around horses for several years, working on farms while getting to know various horse bloodlines. Research and study also helps breeders know how to pick horses for breeding.

To become a trainer, a person must know how to groom and care for horses and build a reputation as a competent trainer who is sensitive to a horse's needs and abilities.

Veterinarian technicians should have experience working on a farm, including knowing how to lead horses in and out of a pasture, how to bandage and monitor sick animals and how to act quickly in an emergency. They also need a two-year degree from an accredited vet-tech program.

Being a judge requires good horsemanship, a good eye, and several years' experience in the horse industry. Depending on the show and riding discipline, some judges may need accreditation, training experience, or must attend certain courses and clinics.

Anyone expecting to advance through management ranks should have a college degree. Some colleges and universities offer equine management or science programs, and students often take business administration courses.

A college degree is not mandatory for sales positions but it is preferable. More importantly, knowledge of the horse industry and enthusiasm is required to be a successful sales representative.

Opportunities for experience and exploration

Anyone interested in a career with horses should take riding lessons. Equestrian management is a hands-on field with much learned from time spent with an animal and instructor. Some stables need part-time and full-time help depending on the season and location. Many larger facilities offer positions where a person may clean stalls, feed and groom horses, and maintain stables.

Advancement

It is possible go from lower level grooming jobs to higher level positions such as a barn or farm manager. A farrier or veterinarian-technician may become self-employed after building a reputation and customer base.

With proper certification and a college degree, it's possible to start work in entry-level management and progress to top management positions.

Employment Outlook

Fewer jobs will be available in the horse industry in coming years since the industry has been on the decline since the mid-1980s. A recession, revised tax laws, and competition with other sports and forms of gambling has taken dollars away from the industry that had been on a steady incline since the 1960s.

There is an oversupply of farm managers since many farms have gone out of business, but opportunities for farriers and veterinarian-technicians are plentiful. A lot of farm work is seasonal, and most people who work with horses have another form of income they use to support their horse business.

Earnings

Stable management workers earn minimum wage. Sometimes they get free housing on the farm where they work.

Horse breeders may earn from $15,000 to $25,000 a year.

Horse trainers earn from $15,000 a year to $50,000 depending on years of experience, reputation, and commissions on horses they have sold and the breeds. If a trainer can rent out all of his stalls, instead of putting his own horses in them, he can earn more money to pay for expenses.

Jockeys get a percentage of the purse or overall winnings of a race. For example, if a purse if $3,000, a jockey may get 10 percent or $300. Purses depend on the track where a race is being held. A few purses are as much as $1 million, although these are exceptions, according to the Jockeys Guild of Lexington, Kentucky. The best-paying races are in Kentucky, California, and New York.

Most judges have other jobs and get paid for each show they judge. Their pay ranges from $300 to $500 per show.

Farriers may earn $15,000 a year to start, and their earning ceiling is about $30,000 a year.

Veterinarian-technicians earn between $16,000 and $27,000 a year.

Marketing representatives start at $16,000 in entry-level positions, but over several years, their earning potential is unlimited.

Sales representatives start low at $12,000 a year and usually also receive a commission.

Conditions of work

All positions in the horse industry require long hours, especially during show season. Many contact, or farm, positions are seasonal, which requires employees to have some other form of employment to support their equine career.

◇ **SOURCES OF ADDITIONAL INFORMATION**

University of Louisville
Equine Administration
School of Business
Louisville, KY 40292

United States Dressage Association
PO Box 80668
Lincoln, NE 68501

American Horse Council
1700 K Street, NW
Washington, DC 20006

◇ **RELATED ARTICLES**

Volume 1: Agriculture; Personal and Consulting Services; Sports
Volumes 2–4: Farmers; Veterinarians; Zookeepers

Ergonomists

Definition

Ergonomists study the workplace to determine effects of the work environment on the activities of individuals and groups. They focus on activities such as conducting research and analyzing data concerning the physical factors of the workplace, like noise and temperature, and they evaluate the design of machines to see that they are safe, usable, and conducive to productive work. Ergonomists are frequently the specialists who advise factory owners, managers, or other top business officials on how to best plan and implement design proposals that integrate human factors into the work environment.

History

"Ergonomics" comes from the Greek word *ergon*, meaning work. The study of people at work began about one hundred years ago as employers and employees began to realize that job productivity was tied to job satisfaction and the nature of the work environment. The concerns of many of the early ergonomists centered around increasing industrial production while maintaining safety on the job. They began to design machines and other equipment that improved production but also reduced the number of job-related accidents. As it became clear that improved working conditions increased productivity and safety and improved workers' morale, ergonomists began investigating other physical and psychological factors that influenced people at work.

Today, with the world of work constantly changing and workplaces using computers and other forms of automation, there is a need for professionals to help adapt the workplace to reflect these changes. The ergonomist can help businesses develop methods that will more humanely adapt the workplace to technological changes and also prepare the workplace for the different types of jobs and other changes that are sure to follow.

Nature of the work

Ergonomists are concerned with the relationship between people and work. They deal with organizational structure, worker productivity, and job satisfaction. A major portion of their work concerns designing machines and other equipment that is both usable and comfortable to the user. For example, ergonomists may study assembly line procedures and suggest changes to reduce monotony and make it easier to unload, thereby obtaining optimum efficiency in terms of human capabilities. They may also investigate environmental factors such as lighting and room temperature, which might influence workers' behavior and productivity.

Ergonomists usually work as part of a team, with different specialists focusing on a particular aspect of the work environment. For example, one ergonomist may focus on the safety aspects of machinery, and another may specialize in environmental issues such as the volume of noise and the layout of the surroundings.

After analyzing relevant data and observing how workers interact in the work environment, ergonomists submit a written report of their findings and make recommendations to company executives for changes or adaptations in the workplace. They may make proposals for new machinery or suggest a revised design for machinery already in place. They may also suggest environmental changes, like painting walls, so that employees can better enjoy the work environment.

Ergonomists design or redesign workplaces that are productive yet comfortable. They may focus on something as large as redesigning the computer terminals for a large multinational corporation, or they may focus on designing more comfortable chairs or easier-to-use telephones at a local family-owned business. Ergonomists may work as consultants for governmental agencies and manufacturing companies, or engage in research at colleges or universities. Often, an ergonomist will specialize in one particular area of work analysis.

Ergonomists are concerned with both the social and physical work environments. They are involved with personnel training and development, and with the interaction between people and machines. Ergonomists may, for example, plan various kinds of tests that will help screen applicants for employment with the firms. They assist engineers and technicians in designing systems that require people and machines to interact. Ergonomists may also develop aids for training people to use those systems.

Requirements

The ergonomist must possess a variety of business administration and interpersonal relationship skills. Most ergonomists have their undergraduate degrees in either psychology or industrial engineering. These undergraduate degrees are usually not enough, however, to prepare a person for an entry-level position. Instead they most often serve as the best preparation for graduate work in the same areas. College courses should include industrial engineering, psychology, statistics, computer applications, and health sciences. Research techniques should also be studied as part of the degree program. In general, a master's degree is required for most positions, and a doctorate is an advantage, especially for those who want to work as an instructor or in upper management.

Interested high school students should take college-preparatory courses, such as mathematics, physical sciences, English, psychology, and statistics. Students should also take science courses in order to prepare for later work with scientific methods, as well as modern foreign languages, especially French or German. Mathematics is valuable for graduate work in statistics.

Ergonomists who decide to work for the federal government may need to pass a civil service test. The American Board of Examiners in Professional Psychology offers diplomas in industrial-organizational psychology to those people with a doctorate and experience who can pass the required psychology examinations. Because ergonomics is a new and growing field, it is especially important for people in the field to keep up-to-date on the latest developments. Belonging to a professional organization, such as the American Psychological Association or the Human Factors Society, is a good way of doing this. Addresses for several such organizations are listed at the end of this article.

An ergonomist conducts a test to measure human static strength. He is applying the concept of fitting a task to a worker.

Opportunities for experience and exploration

Only those with the required educational credentials can get hands-on experience, so the most practical way to explore career opportunities is to talk with those already working in the field. A great deal of career information can also be found in professional journals or other similar publications.

Methods of entering

Those with the proper credentials should contact large industrial companies or manufacturing firms to apply for a position. Governmental agencies, consulting firms, and college and university research departments also hire qualified ergonomists. College placement offices may be helpful in providing job leads in this regard. Public and private employment services may also refer qualified applicants to suitable entry positions.

People with a post-graduate degree in psychology or industrial engineering should have the best employment opportunities.

Advancement

Because ergonomics is still a relatively new field, advancement opportunities are consid-

613

ered good for the foreseeable future. There are not that many people involved in the field, and therefore there are many opportunities for qualified individuals, especially those who have a special area of expertise. Many ergonomists develop skills at a first job and then either use that experience to find higher paid work at a different company or use it to get increased responsibility at their initial firm.

Qualified ergonomists often are promoted to management positions, with an accompanying increase in earnings and responsibility. They can also start their own consulting firms or branch off into teaching or research. Those in government work may choose to move to the private sector, where salaries are higher. But others may opt for the security and job responsibilities of a government position.

Employment outlook

As the work environment has become more complex and workers expect more from their jobs, the opportunities for ergonomists continue to grow. This trend is expected to continue through the 1990s. The occupation should be somewhat insulated from changes in the economy. If the economy grows, more companies will need to adapt workplaces to increase production capabilities. If the economy slows down, many companies will need to cut costs and improve productivity. The skilled ergonomist can facilitate both situations.

The majority of ergonomists now work for large manufacturing firms and this should continue into the future. Smaller firms will also continue to use ergonomists. Computer companies and others that use automated systems will need ergonomists to help them develop effective and stimulating work environments. The government also hires experts who can design safe and productive work environments. Colleges, universities, and other research facilities also need ergonomists to interpret data and supply new ideas for productive work environments. Some ergonomists will specialize in being freelance consultants and witnesses in legal proceedings.

Earnings

Earnings depend on the individual's education and experience and the type of work sought. Beginning ergonomists may earn anywhere from $26,000 to $55,000 per year; those with a doctorate earn more. Experienced ergonomists

often earn over $60,000 a year, especially those who work in private industry. Those with a doctorate tend to earn more than those with a master's degree. Full-time employees usually receive health insurance, vacation, and other benefits.

Ergonomists who work as consultants usually get paid a negotiated fee, with rates ranging from $60 to $180 per hour, depending on the individual's skill and reputation. These consultants have more control over their working hours, but usually do not receive health insurance or other benefits. Many ergonomists may hold a full-time positions and then consult or teach part-time.

Conditions of work

Ergonomists encounter various working conditions, depending on specific duties and responsibilities. An ergonomist may work in a typical office environment, with computer and data processing equipment close at hand, or the ergonomist may work in a factory, investigating production problems. Usually, ergonomists do both, working in an office setting and making frequent visits to a factory or other location to work out particular production issues. Although the majority of work is not strenuous, ergonomists may occasionally assemble or revamp machines.

Ergonomists often work as part of a team, but they may also work on an individual research project, spending much time alone. They usually work a 40-hour week, although overtime is not uncommon, especially if a particular project is on deadline. There may be occasional weekend and evening work. Those involved with research or teaching may only work 10 months a year, although many of these ergonomists work as consultants when not working full-time.

GOE: 11.03.01; SIC: Any industry; SOC: 1915

◇ **SOURCES OF ADDITIONAL INFORMATION**

Career information is available from:

American Psychological Association
750 First Street, NE
Washington, DC 20002

Human Factors Society
PO Box 1369
Santa Monica, CA 90406

Industrial Designers Society of America
1142-E Walker Road
Great Falls, VA 22066

◇ **RELATED ARTICLES**

Volume 1: Human Resources; Personnel and Consulting Services; Social Services
Volumes 2–4: Career counselors; Psychologists; Sociologists

Export-import specialists

Definition

Export-import specialists plan and coordinate business transactions involving importing or exporting goods from one or more foreign countries. They may work for the government, an international company, or as a representative of an individual client. Export-import specialists may be involved in various aspects of foreign trade, from negotiating trade agreements to planning and supervising the actual delivery of goods.

History

International trade has historically been tied to the conquering of one nation by another. During the expansion of the Roman Empire, for example, there was much trade between the Far East and Europe. In the 15th and 16th centuries, explorers such as Christopher Columbus, Vasco da Gama, and Ferdinand Magellan undertook long voyages to open new trade routes. The early North American colonists traded products or raw materials from this country, such as tobacco and furs, and received clothes and other manufactured goods from England in return.

Today, the importing and exporting of goods in the United States accounts for almost $900 billion in sales each year; familiar terms such as "trade deficit" or "balance of trade" are reported daily in the news. The growth of foreign business and its importance to the national economy has created a need for specialists who can handle the complex problems of international business.

Nature of the work

There are a variety of professionals involved in the export-import industry. Some may be involved only with the importing of raw materials or finished goods, while others may only be involved with exporting. Many specialists, however, are involved in both the importing and exporting of foreign trade. All specialists must understand international law and be aware of export-import regulations, such as duty fees, but specific responsibilities vary according to the area of specialization.

Export managers direct foreign sales activities, including negotiating sales and distribution contracts and arranging payment for exported goods. They handle details involved in the transportation of goods, including licensing agreements, customs declarations, and packing and shipping. Export managers work with foreign buyers, federal agents, and company executives to coordinate shipping, air freight, and other transportation methods. They also supervise clerical staff in preparing foreign correspondence and in the preparation of foreign language material, such as sales literature and bid requests, meant to expedite foreign trade.

Customs-house brokers act as intermediaries between importers and the customs service through the preparation of entry papers for goods arriving from abroad. They file appropriate documents to allow delivery of foreign goods and assess import duties and taxes. Custom-house brokers act as trouble-shooters between importers and the federal government, counseling importers on relevant rules and regulations, working out any last minute problems, and arranging for storage of goods in warehouses, if necessary.

EXPORT-IMPORT SPECIALISTS

An export-import specialist leads a group of retailers through an overseas production facility. He can advise them on legal means of importing the goods.

Wholesalers buy imported goods for sale on domestic markets or buy domestic products for sale abroad. Some may buy both imported and exported material for later sale. Often, wholesalers specialize in buying or selling a specific good or raw material from a foreign country, such as clothes or jewelry. Wholesalers often arrange for the packing and shipping of goods, and work with U.S. and foreign customs officials to ensure timely and accurate delivery.

Import-export agents manage activities of import-export firms, coordinating settlements between foreign and domestic buyers and sellers. They plan delivery of goods and supervise workers in the shipping and receiving departments. Import-export agents act as trade representatives throughout the freight handling process. They oversee the assessment of import and export taxes and the granting of entry permits. They also resolve any questions or concerns on the part of customs officials or foreign or domestic business people.

Requirements

A college degree is becoming more important in the export-import field. Specific degree programs depend on the type of job desired, but in general undergraduate degrees in business management, political science, or economics are helpful. Course work should include classes in international trade, marketing, business administration, communications, computer applications, and statistics. Many people who want management positions in the export-import field are now deciding to get a master's in business administration (MBA), with an emphasis in international trade.

High school students interested in a career as an export-import specialist should take college-preparatory classes, such as English, social studies, geography, and mathematics. Developing a fluency in a foreign language, especially one that is widely used in international trade, such as Japanese, Russian, or German, is very important.

Customs-house brokers must be licensed by the U.S. Customs Service. The licensing process requires passing a written examination that covers export-import rules and regulations. Specifics on the licensing procedures are available from the U.S. Customs Service at the address given at the end of this article.

In some areas of wholesaling, such as the buying or selling of technical equipment, wholesalers may need to have technical training and belong to appropriate professional groups. Companies that export sensitive material, such as military hardware, must get an export license from the U.S. Department of Commerce.

Opportunities for experience and exploration

High school students can seek part-time or summer employment in a large store or other retail establishment, which may provide helpful insight into a merchandising career. After graduation from high school, an internship with an international company would be very valuable in ascertaining the rewards and responsibilities of a career as a export-import specialist. In addition, discussions with professionals already working in the field are an excellent way of learning about career opportunities.

Methods of entering

Those without a college degree may begin as a clerk or assistant in a warehouse and work their way up by learning shipping and receiving procedures. The vast majority of entry-level positions, however, are now reserved for college graduates. Most college graduates secure their first position by applying directly to the U.S. Customs Service, individual seaports and airports, international trading companies, and other organizations that hire export-import specialists. Public and private employment services may also refer qualified applicants to suitable entry positions.

People with a master's in business administration, and a fluency in one or more foreign languages, will have the best opportunities in this field.

Advancement

Those in the export-import field usually have constant contact with other international firms, and therefore have frequent opportunities to switch employers. Specific advancement opportunities depend to some extent on the specialty within the field, and vary greatly depending on the skill and drive of the individual.

Experienced export managers may become the marketing manager or vice president in charge of coordinating overseas distribution. Customs-house brokers may become export managers or may be promoted to another position within the export-import department of a company. After developing contacts and sales expertise, wholesalers may also become management consultants or start their own export-import firm. Import-export agents may also become sales representatives for other export-import firms, or go into business for themselves.

Employment outlook

Opportunities in the export-import field should grow at an average rate through the 1990s. Employment stability in this field is largely dependent on the general economic conditions, and job prospects will vary from industry to industry and firm to firm. For example, it may be harder to find work as a textile wholesaler representing a U.S. firm than as a computer wholesaler.

Job prospects should be best in major trade cities, such as New York, Chicago, Los Angeles, and New Orleans. Other large metropolitan areas should also offer good employment opportunities. Major employers will include the U.S. government, airlines, shipping firms, international manufacturing companies, and oil companies. Many people will find work overseas, either with a foreign company, or as a representative of a U.S. company.

Those with the most experience and education will have the best job possibilities, particularly in a competitive or desirable job market.

Earnings

Earnings vary widely depending on specific job responsibilities and the size of the export-import firm. In the 1990s, beginning export managers earn from $20,000 to $25,000 a year. Experienced managers earn more than $37,000 per year.

Custom-house brokers are paid according to the amount of foreign trade they handle. Beginning brokers can expect to earn $19,000 to 24,000 per year, and experienced brokers earn over $35,000 per year.

The salaries of wholesalers are directly related to the amount of goods they buy and sell. Earnings range from $23,000 to $90,000 per year; highly skilled wholesalers earn over $150,000 annually. Some companies adjust salaries to reflect total volume of sales. Other companies pay straight commission (usually about 10 percent of total sales), while others pay a combination of salary, commission, and benefits. While wholesalers can make huge amounts of money, a slow period could adversely effect their earning potential.

Import-export agents may also earn a bonus if they buy or sell merchandise. Beginning agents earn between $16,000 and $20,000 per year, with experienced agents earning between $23,000 and $35,000 per year.

Conditions of work

Export-import specialists usually work in comfortable offices or customs buildings. They usually work a 40-hour week, although long hours may be required to negotiate a trade agreement or plan and coordinate delivery of goods. Evening and weekend work may be necessary at times.

There may be a lot of travel, especially for wholesalers and those stationed overseas. These employees must adapt to the living and working conditions of the host country, and should be aware of, and sensitive to, cultural differences in these countries.

Export-import professionals should have a variety of personal characteristics, such as the ability to quickly analyze purchasing decisions and evaluate products being shipped in. They should have good verbal and written communication skills and be able to work well with other people. Those who speak one or more foreign languages will be able to communicate far more effectively with trading partners and other foreign representatives.

617

Export-import specialists should be able to write trade agreements and deal with customs rules and regulations.

GOE: 11.05; SIC: 2371; SOC: 125, 1342

National Customs Brokers & Forwarders Association of America
One World Trade Center
Suite 1153
New York, NY 10048

◇ **SOURCES OF ADDITIONAL INFORMATION**

American Association of Exporters and Importers
11 West 42nd Street
New York, NY 10036

National Association of Export Companies
PO Box 1330, Murray Hill Station
New York, NY 10156

◇ **RELATED ARTICLES**

Volume 1: Foreign Trade; Sales
Volumes 2–4: Buyers, wholesale and retail; Customs officials; Economists; Marketing research personnel; Retail business owners; Retail sales workers; Shipping and receiving clerks; Traffic agents and clerks; Wholesale trade sales workers

Farm crop production technicians

Definition

Farm crop production technicians help farmers and agricultural businesses with all aspects of planting, growing, and marketing of the crops they produce. Those who specialize in orchard and vineyard crops are often referred to as *orchard and vineyard technicians;* those technicians who perform tests and experiments to improve the crops' yield, quality, or resistance to disease, and other hazards, are referred to as *plant technicians.*

Farm crop production technicians work in a variety of places, including laboratories and farms; some work for farm-product or service vendors as researchers in new-product development, *production technicians* in manufacturing, or as *sales representatives;* others are employed as *farm workers* supervising unskilled workers, or *field representatives* assisting in the sale of crops to customers. Some farm crop production technicians work for food-processing and packaging firms as *purchasing agents* or *assistants to purchasing agents.* Although not specifically discussed in this article, some technicians might also find employment in enterprises such as mushroom or mustard farming.

History

Food is one of the most basic human needs, consumed by everyone every day. One of the most important food-related discoveries was that plants could be grown from seeds. Once humans realized that food supplies could be controlled, our early ancestors gave up their nomadic existence and established permanent fields and orchards to raise their own food. Through experimentation, early farmers slowly learned when and where to produce certain crops.

With every increase in the world's population comes an increased need for greater and more efficient food production. To spur this production, imaginative research programs are being carried on in the scientific laboratories of public and private firms. As a result, new crops and production methods are continually being developed. For example, farmers now make many difficult decisions with the aid of computers and delicate recording instruments, which were not available in the past.

Modern farming requires that scientific knowledge, both natural and physical, be applied directly to production. Farm crop production has become increasingly complex, creating a vital role for technicians involved in the production, processing, or marketing of farm products.

Nature of the work

Farm crop production technicians either service and supply the farmer, increase farm product production, or process and distribute the farm products.

Nearly everything used in a farm is now purchased from outside suppliers: seed, fertilizer, pesticides, machinery, fuels, and general supplies. Companies selling these products need farm-trained and farm-oriented technicians who can understand buyers' farming problems and needs.

Farm supply companies also need technicians to assist in research. They work under the supervision of feed or chemical company scientists, carrying out the details of the testing program. The *farm-machinery technician* tests and recommends improvements or adaptations in machinery designed by company engineers.

Farm crop production technicians who specialize in sales and services to orchards and vineyards usually work with the suppliers of nursery stock, fertilizer, pesticides, herbicides, and machinery. These well-trained technicians help fruit growers with research information, seek solutions for production problems, or produce new products for those seeking the latest and best rootstocks or pest controls.

In the production phase of crop technology, some technicians make soil or tissue tests to determine the efficiency of fertilizer programs; others may be responsible for certain kinds of farm machinery; and more experienced farm crop production technicians may oversee the complete management of a farm, including personnel, machinery, and finances.

In the fruit industry, some of the larger production firms hire technicians to run soil and tissue tests for fertilizer programs, and to handle machinery and labor management. Orchard management for resident or absentee owners is a common occupation in the industry; those technicians who take on management responsibilities need to be able to make decisions regarding new equipment, production techniques, and weed and frost control.

Practically all agricultural products need some processing before they reach the consumer. Processing involves testing, grading, packaging, and transporting. Some of the technicians in this area work closely with farmers and need to know a great deal about crop production. For example, *field-contact technicians*

Two farm crop production technicians take samples of wheat to study the DNA structure of the plants. Such research will help develop methods to prevent diseases, increase crop yield, and enhance seed quality.

employed by food-processing companies monitor crop production on the farms they buy products from. In some processing companies, they supervise the whole crop operation; in others, they act as buyers, or determine when crops will be harvested for processing and shipping. They often do public relations with farmers for the food-processing company.

Some technicians may work in a laboratory doing quality-control work or nutrition research; others work as inspectors, or in any of a number of phases of processing.

Processing and distributing technicians in the fruit industry may find jobs with canneries, freezing and packing plants, cooperatives, distributors, or with public or private agencies. They may work either in the laboratory, or out in the field with the grower. The laboratory technician works with a scientist to process, maintain quality control, test, grade, measure,

A farm crop production technician adjusts the track mechanism on a mobile canopy that measures the effect of acid rain on soil quality and crop yield.

and keep records; the field technician supervises seed selection and planting, weed and pest control, irrigation, harvesting, and on-the-spot testing to make sure crops are harvested at precisely the right state of maturity; some technicians inspect the products to ensure that quality and grade standards are maintained; others are involved in product sales and distribution.

Within these three broad areas are a number of specific occupations which employ farm crop production technicians. The following short paragraphs describe some of these positions, each of them appropriate for entry-level technicians.

Farm-and-orchard supply sales workers sell their company's products to farmers. They must understand farmers' production problems in order to show how their products will be most useful.

Seed production field supervisors help coordinate the activities of farmers who produce seed for commercial seed companies. They inspect and analyze soil and water supplies of farms, and study other growing conditions in order to plan production of planted crops. They distribute seed stock to farmers, specify areas and numbers of acres to be planted, and give instructions to workers engaged in cultivation procedures, such as fertilization, tilling, and detasseling. They may also determine dates

and methods for harvesting, storing, and shipping of seed crops.

Biological aides assist research workers in biology, bacteriology, plant pathology, mycology, and related agricultural sciences. They set up laboratory and field equipment, perform routine tests, and clean up and maintain field and laboratory equipment. They also keep records of plant growth, experimental plots, greenhouse activity, insecticide use, and other agricultural experimentation.

Soil conservation aides work with professional soil scientists to collect information by examining and recording data in field notes and soil maps. They also help prepare conservation plans, present the information to farmers, and help them select the appropriate plans. This occupation is described in more detail in the entry entitled *soil conservation technicians*.

Farm technicians have various duties depending on the needs of the farm. They may take soil samples to gauge fertilizer needs, read tensiometers to determine irrigation schedules, or run maturity tests to plan harvesting schedules.

Rodent-control assistants usually work for state departments of agriculture. They estimate rodent damage, determine the rodent count, and help inspectors perform various rodent-control measures.

Agricultural inspectors work for state, county, and federal departments of agriculture. In order to inspect grain, vegetables, or seed, they must know grades and standards, and be able to recognize common pests and disease damage. They may work in the field, at a packing shed or shipping station, or at a terminal market.

Disease and insect control field inspectors, work under the supervision of insect and disease inspection supervisors. They inspect fields to detect the presence of harmful insects and plant diseases. They walk through fields and examine plants at periodic intervals. They count numbers of insects on examined plants or numbers of diseased plants within a sample area. They record the results of their counts on field work sheets. They also collect samples of unidentifiable insects or diseased plants for identification by a supervisor.

Picking-crew or *packing-house supervisors* schedule jobs, supervise crews, and keep records. They must know grades and standards used for maturity tests on crops ready for picking.

Plant propagators work for nurseries. They cultivate new plants by various methods to produce new rootstocks of trees and vines. They select the best hybrid seeds or cuttings to start young plants and bud them over to other trees.

Spray equipment operators work for pest-control companies. They select and apply the proper herbicides or pesticides for particular jobs, formulate mixtures, and operate various types of spraying and dusting equipment. A specialized technician within this occupation is the *aircraft crop duster* or *sprayer*. The person who enters this career must have a current license to operate a plane or helicopter.

Requirements

Farm crop production technicians need manual skills and mechanical ability to operate various kinds of equipment and machinery. They must also have the knowledge to apply scientific principles to the processing procedures, materials, and measuring and control devices found at the modern laboratory or farm. They must be able to communicate what needs to be done and interpret orders given to them.

A career as a farm crop production technician requires training in a rigorous, two-year technical or agricultural college program in order to understand fully the principles of crop production. To prepare for this, students should have a good high school background in mathematics and science. They should complete as much vocational agriculture work as possible, including agricultural mechanics. In addition, English is very important, because much of the work requires good communication skills.

Once enrolled in a two-year post-high school training program, prospective farm crop production technicians can expect to take a broad range of courses relating to agriculture in general and farm crop production in particular, as well as some general education courses. Typical first-year courses include the following: introduction to agricultural machinery, introduction to animal husbandry, introduction to soil science, entomology, English, physical education, science, and mathematics.

Typical second-year courses include agricultural economics, soil fertility, plant pathology, forage and seed crops, and social science.

Technicians who wish to specialize in vegetable or fruit production can sometimes modify their programs to place concentration in these areas. They may add courses such as vegetable and fruit production in the first year and fruit and vegetable marketing in the second.

The majority of technicians in the field are not required to have a license or certification. However, those technicians involved in grading or inspecting for local, state, or federal government units must pass examinations to be qualified. Some other government jobs, such as that of research assistant, may also require taking a competitive examination.

Opportunities for experience and exploration

Traditionally, those students who have grown up on farms will have the best opportunity to decide whether to specialize in this area. But a farm background is no longer essential; 4-H Clubs and the National FFA Organization are open to anyone with a genuine interest. It is also relatively easy to obtain work experience on farms during the summer when extra labor is always required for planting and harvesting. During post-high school training, heavy emphasis is placed on supervised occupational experience, so that students become familiar with job requirements.

Methods of entering

Students should decide as early as possible in their school programs which phase of crop technology they prefer to enter, because contacts made while in school can be helpful in obtaining a job after the program's completion. One of the common ways to find employment is for students to be hired by the same firm they worked for during a work–study program. If that firm does not have a position open, a recommendation from the employer will help with other firms.

Most faculty members in a technical program have contact with prospective employers and can help place qualified students. Many schools also maintain a placement service and arrange interviews between students and prospective employers. For those students who complete the technical program and are willing to work to advance on the job, employment possibilities are very good.

Advancement

Technicians in the field of farm crop production have many opportunities for advancement. Early advancement will be easier for those who combine a formal technical education with work experience. Those who have had several jobs in the industry will probably advance to managerial levels more rapidly than those who have not. As more post-secondary schools are established in local communities, it becomes easier for employed persons to continue their education through evening classes while they work.

The following short paragraphs describe some employment possibilities that are appropriate for experienced technicians.

Farm managers and *farm owners* perform or supervise all farm activities, including buying and selling, keeping records and accounts, and hiring and supervising employees.

Managers of cooperatives supervise and schedule crop planting and harvesting, handle buying and selling, and supervise employees.

Sales managers supervise company sales forces. They help train new salespeople, set up sales territories, and make studies of product demand and selling techniques.

Secretary-managers of growers' or dealers' associations do public relations work. They keep the membership informed of important legal and other matters affecting their business; they collect dues and maintain membership lists; and they represent the group at various meetings and on legislative matters.

Employment outlook

The student exploring a career in crop production technology should not be misled by the fact that the number of farms is decreasing. Although the part of the population living on farms has decreased over the last century from 85 percent to just a few percent, farming has not decreased in importance. There may be fewer farmers today, but they farm more acres, are more mechanized, and are outproducing the farmers of 100 years ago. As the number of farmers decreases, there is a proportionately greater gain in the number of workers in service and supply or processing and distribution. In addition to jobs within the United States, such agencies as the Peace Corps and other organizations can use greater numbers of agricultural technicians in the underdeveloped nations of the world.

Because of all of these factors, food production in all of its facets should continue to provide good employment opportunities throughout the coming years.

For technicians interested specifically in orchard and vineyard production, the future is also good. Those technicians looking forward to owning or operating their own orchards or vineyards should remember, of course, that not all crops are necessarily good investments at all times. Local conditions, business cycles, and supply and demand must be considered when making decisions on the planting of a certain kind of orchard, grove, or vineyard. However, a person who can obtain good land in the right location and who can grow efficiently will find fruit-growing offers great rewards.

Employment opportunities for those who do not wish to own their own orchard, but to specialize in one of the many aspects of this profession, should find an increasing demand for their services. The orchard and vineyard industry needs technicians both in the United States and abroad. Technical help is in demand in many foreign fruit-growing and processing industries. Such careers offer a chance to travel and see the world, as well as to help other people.

Earnings

Salaries of farm crop production technicians vary widely. For instance, technicians employed in off-farm jobs often receive higher salaries than technicians working on a farm; those working on a farm, however, often receive food and housing benefits that can be the equivalent of several thousand dollars a year. Salaries also vary according to the geographical area in which the technician is working, with jobs in the northeast region being at the lower end of the scale and jobs in California, Minnesota, and Iowa being at the upper end of the scale.

Salaries also depend on the technician's educational background, agricultural experience, and the type of crop involved.

In general, most farm crop production technicians receive starting salaries in the range of $14,000 to $18,000 a year; however, some technicians may receive salaries that are significantly above or below this range.

Conditions of work

Many technicians in this field work outdoors a great deal of the time. They should like outdoor work and be able to adapt to extreme weather conditions. There may be certain seasons of the year when they are required to work long hours under considerable pressure to get a crop harvested or processed at the right time.

The work of laboratory technicians in this field involves exacting systematic procedures in facilities that are generally clean and well lighted. Inspection technicians may work long hours during harvest season. Those involved in sales may spend considerable time traveling.

Work in the processing phase is usually indoors, except for the field-service or field-contact personnel who spend much of their time outdoors.

Planting a new field, orchard, or vineyard, then watching it grow and develop, can be extremely satisfying work. But the continual uncertainties of weather conditions: possible blight, premature frost, and the wiping out of one's labor and investment call for a stable temperament and the ability to withstand setbacks.

For technicians who feel they may lack some of these characteristics, employment in the sales, services, or other off-farm area may be better. Here too there is the satisfaction of knowing that one is playing a vital role in producing humanity's most basic need.

GOE: 02.04.02, 03.02.01, 03.02.04; SIC: 01; SOC: 382, 5611

◇ SOURCES OF ADDITIONAL INFORMATION

American Society of Agronomy
677 South Segoe Road
Madison, WI 53711

National FFA Organization
PO Box 15160
Alexandria, VA 22309

U.S. Department of Agriculture
Washington, DC 20250

Canadian Society of Agronomy
Crop Development Center
University of Saskatchewan
Saskatoon SK S7N 0W0

◇ RELATED ARTICLES

Volume 1: Agriculture
Volumes 2–4: Agribusiness technicians; Agricultural scientists; Agricultural extension service workers; Biological scientists; Biological technicians; Buyers, wholesale and retail; Farmers; Food technologists; Grain merchants; Pest control workers; Purchasing agents; Soil conservation technicians; Soil scientists

Farm-equipment mechanics

Definition

Farm-equipment mechanics maintain, adjust, repair, and overhaul equipment and vehicles used in planting, cultivating, harvesting, moving, processing, and storing plant and animal farm products. Among the specialized machines they may work on are tractors, harvesters, combines, pumps, tilling equipment, silo fillers, hay balers, and sprinkler irrigation systems.

History

The purpose of the mechanical devices used in farming has always been essentially to save human labor. In the most distant prehistoric times, people had only simple wood and stone implements to help turn soil, plant seeds, and harvest crops more efficiently than they could with their bare hands. With the introduction of metal tools and the domestication of animals that could pull plows and vehicles, people were able to produce much more. Until the 19th century, farmers around the globe relied on human labor, animal power, and relatively simple equipment to accomplish all the tasks involved in agriculture.

Modern mechanized agriculture got started in the early 1800s with the experimental application of steam power to a few kinds of farm equipment. More practical innovations became familiar on farms in the early part of this century. Gasoline-powered tractors began to be

623

A farmer discusses the maintenance of his harvesting equipment with a mechanic who specializes in farm equipment repairs.

common just after World War I. Not long after that, diesel engines were used in various kinds of farm machinery. The use of motor-driven machines on farms caused far-reaching effects. Machines improved agricultural productivity while lessening the need for human labor. A consequence of the increasing use of farm machines in the 20th century has been that in many countries around the world, the number of people working on farms has steadily decreased.

Today, a few people with sophisticated modern machines can accomplish many different specialized activities that once would have meant back-breaking labor for many workers. Farm machines are useful in preparing soil for planting, applying fertilizers and pesticides, irrigating crops, handling animal feed and bedding, milking dairy cows, and many other vital tasks.

Especially in recent decades, many farm machines have become large and complex, with electronic and hydraulic systems. Farms today are likely to be big, and agriculture is often a business operation that requires a variety of extremely expensive equipment capable of doing specialized tasks quickly and efficiently. Farmers cannot afford for their equipment to be sidelined by breakdowns for long. More and more, they are depending on the dealers who sell equipment to be their source for the emergency repairs and routine maintenance services that keep the machines functioning well. Farm-equipment mechanics are the skilled specialists who carry out these tasks, usually as employees of equipment dealers or of independent repair shops.

Nature of the work

The success of today's large-scale farming operations depends on the reliability of many complex machines. It is the responsibility of farm-equipment mechanics to keep the machines in good working order and to repair or overhaul them when they break down.

When farm equipment is not working properly, farm-equipment mechanics must begin by making a diagnosis of the trouble. Although the equipment owner may be able to describe the symptoms well enough to pinpoint the problem, mechanics may use testing devices to help in the diagnosis. A compression tester, for example, can determine whether cylinder valves leak or piston rings are worn, and a dynamometer can measure engine performance. Mechanics also examine the machine, observing and listening to it in operation and looking for clues like leaks, loose parts, and irregular steering, braking, and gear-shifting. It may be necessary to dismantle whole systems in the machine to diagnose and correct malfunctions.

When the problem is located, the broken, worn-out, or faulty components are repaired or replaced, depending on the extent of their defect. The machine or piece of equipment is reassembled, adjusted, lubricated, and tested to be sure it is again operating as it should.

Farm-equipment mechanics use many tools in their work. Besides hand tools such as wrenches, pliers, and screwdrivers, and precision instruments such as micrometers and torque wrenches, they may use welding equipment, power grinders and saws, and other power tools. In addition, they sometimes do major repairs using machine tools such as drill presses, lathes, and milling and woodworking machines. Much of the time, farmers can bring their equipment into the shop, where mechanics have all these tools available. But during planting or harvesting seasons, when timing may be critical for the farmers, the mechanics may have to travel to farms for emergency repairs in order to return the equipment to service as soon as possible.

Farmers usually bring movable equipment in on a regular schedule for preventive maintenance services such as adjusting and cleaning parts and tuning engines. Routine servicing not only makes the job easier for the mechanics, but it also assures the farmers that the equipment will be ready when it is needed. Shops in the rural outskirts of metropolitan areas often handle maintenance and repairs on a variety of lawn and garden equipment, especially lawn mowers.

In large shops, mechanics may specialize in certain systems in farm equipment. For example, some mechanics overhaul gasoline or diesel engines; others repair clutches and transmissions; still others concentrate on the air-conditioning units in the cabs of combines and large tractors. Some mechanics, called *farm-machinery set-up mechanics* uncrate, assemble, adjust, and often deliver machinery to farm locations. Mechanics sometimes also do body work on tractors and other machines, repairing damaged sheet metal body parts.

Mechanics may work exclusively on certain types of equipment, such as hay balers or harvesters. Some mechanics work on equipment that is installed on farms. For example, *sprinkler-irrigation-equipment mechanics* install and maintain self-propelled circle-irrigation systems, which are like giant motorized lawn sprinklers. *Dairy-equipment repairers* inspect and repair dairy machinery and equipment such as milking machines, cream separators, and churns.

Most farm-equipment mechanics work in the service departments of equipment dealerships. Others are employed by independent repair shops. A smaller number work on large farms that have their own shops.

Requirements

Most farm-equipment mechanics learn their trade on the job. They are hired as helpers and receive training from experienced mechanics. Trainees begin by helping with simple tasks and gradually take on more difficult ones. The speed of their progress is related to their previous education and experience. It usually takes at least two years of on-the-job training before a mechanic is qualified to handle almost any type of repair work that comes into the shop. Some specialized skills take longer to learn.

Employers almost always prefer to hire high school graduates, and increasingly they seek people who have also completed training programs for mechanics, such as those offered at vocational and technical schools and community and junior colleges. These programs may last one to two years and cover such fields as the maintenance and repair of diesel and gasoline engines, hydraulic systems, welding, and electronics. Some high schools also offer courses that introduce these fields.

Employers also look for applicants with mechanical aptitude. A farm background is considered desirable, because people who have grown up on a farm usually are familiar with farm equipment and may have had some experience with its repair. The ability to understand circuit diagrams and read blueprints is important, because farm-equipment mechanics must develop these skills to make repairs on electrical and electronic systems.

Some mechanics learn their trade through apprenticeship programs. Apprenticeships combine three to four years of on-the-job training with classroom study related to farm-equipment repair and maintenance. The few farm-equipment mechanics who enter the occupation as apprentices are usually selected from among shop helpers.

Many people who become trainees in this field have already worked in related occupations. They may have been farmers, farm laborers, heavy-equipment mechanics, automobile mechanics, or air-conditioning mechanics. Although people with this kind of related experience are likely to begin as helpers, their training period may be considerably shorter than the training for beginners with no such background.

To stay up-to-date on technological changes that affect their work, mechanics and trainees may take special short-term courses conducted by equipment manufacturers. In these programs, which may last a few days, company service representatives explain the design and function of new models of equipment and teach the mechanics how to maintain and repair them. Some employers help broaden their mechanics' skills by sending them to local vocational schools for special intensive courses in subjects such as air-conditioning repair or hydraulics.

Farm machinery is usually large and heavy. Mechanics need the strength to lift heavy machine parts like transmissions. They also need manual dexterity to be able to handle tools and small components.

Farm-equipment mechanics are usually expected to supply their own hand tools. After years of accumulating favorite tools, experienced mechanics may have collections that represent an investment of thousands of dollars.

625

Employers generally provide all the large power tools and test equipment needed in the shop.

Relatively few farm-equipment mechanics are members of labor unions. Those who join unions belong to the International Association of Machinists and Aerospace Workers; the International Union, United Automobile, Aerospace and Agricultural Implement Workers of America; or the International Brotherhood of Teamsters, Chauffeurs, Warehousemen and Helpers of America.

Opportunities for experience and exploration

High school students can test their aptitude for this work by taking courses such as electrical shop, welding, mechanical drawing, and automobile mechanics. Prospective farm-equipment mechanics may also want to try vocational school courses related to farm equipment to get a better idea of whether they want to continue with the field.

A practical knowledge of how farm machines work is very helpful for farm-equipment mechanics. Living on a farm or working on a farm after school hours, on weekends, or during the summer would provide valuable experience. If working on a farm is not feasible, a part-time or summer job in a gasoline service station, automobile repair shop, or automotive supply house can at least introduce the basic tools, skills, and vocabulary used by mechanics.

Methods of entering

People who are interested in becoming farm-equipment mechanics usually apply directly to local farm-equipment dealers or independent repair shops. Graduates of vocational schools can often get help in locating jobs through their school's placement service. The local office of the state employment service is another source of job leads, as well as a source of information on any apprenticeships that may be available in the region.

Advancement

After they have gained some experience, farm-equipment mechanics employed by equipment dealers may be promoted to such positions as shop supervisor, service manager, and eventually manager of the dealership. Some mechanics eventually decide to open their own repair shops (about one mechanic in seven is self-employed). Others become service representatives for farm-equipment manufacturers. Additional formal education, such as completion of a two-year associate degree program in agricultural mechanics or a related field, may be required of service representatives.

Employment outlook

Over the next 10 to 15 years, broad trends that are already affecting farming in the United States are expected to continue. The result for farm-equipment mechanics is expected to be that their occupational field will grow more slowly than the average rate for other fields. As farmland is consolidated into larger farms, farming operations will be run more efficiently, with less duplication of equipment and greater use of technologically sophisticated equipment. During coming years, farmers are expected to be getting rid of much of their oldest, most worn machinery and buying more new equipment than they have during the last decade or so. This is because farming is now emerging from a period of economic troubles, and many farmers are once again financially able to replace aging machines.

Because new farm machines are increasingly complex, farmers will find it more difficult to do their own repairs, and they will need the services of highly trained mechanics more than ever before. For example, many large tractors manufactured today have transmissions with as many as 24 speeds, electronically controlled engines, monitors for nearly every system of the vehicle, and also climate controls and even sound systems that keep the rider comfortable for long hours inside the cab. Skilled mechanics are needed to keep all the parts of such complex equipment in good working order.

Future prospects will be best for mechanics who have completed formal training programs in diesel or farm-equipment mechanics, especially if they also have some training in electronics. People without formal training will probably find that their job opportunities are limited. Most job openings that develop will occur when experienced mechanics retire.

Other changes will affect the range of available jobs in coming years. As the average size of farms grows larger, more of the biggest farms will employ their own mechanics. In suburban areas, the home use of small tractors and other machines for lawns and gardens has increased tremendously in recent years. The trend is expected to continue, and dealerships and small shops will need more mechanics to service this equipment.

Earnings

The earnings of farm-equipment mechanics vary considerably. Average annual earnings are around $18,200, although some mechanics make closer to $14,000 a year, while others make over $26,000. During the busy planting and harvest seasons, mechanics may substantially increase their pay by working overtime hours, for which they are usually paid time-and-a-half rates. On the other hand, during the winter months some mechanics may work short hours or they may be temporarily laid off, reducing their total earnings.

Workers with the most experience and technical skills may have earnings in the $35,000 to $40,000 range. Wages are highest in heavily agricultural areas, where there is keen competition for highly skilled mechanics.

Conditions of work

Farm-equipment mechanics are employed throughout the country, with the greatest concentration in small cities and towns. Most independent repair shops employ fewer than 5 mechanics, while in dealers' service departments there may be 10 or more mechanics on the payroll.

Farm-equipment mechanics generally work indoors on equipment that has been brought into the shop. Most modern shops are properly ventilated, heated, and lighted. Some older shops may be less comfortable. Especially during busy seasons, mechanics may leave the shop frequently and travel many miles to farms, where they perform emergency repairs outdoors in any kind of weather.

In such situations, mechanics often work independently, with little supervision. They need to be self-reliant and able to solve problems under pressure. When a farm machine breaks down, the lost time can be very expensive for the farmer. Mechanics must be able to diagnose problems quickly and do repairs without delay.

Mechanics have to contend with grease, gasoline, rust, and dirt as they work on farm machinery. They must take care when lifting heavy equipment and parts with jacks or hoists, because there is always the chance the equipment may slip and fall. Other hazards they must routinely guard against include burns from hot engines, cuts from sharp pieces of metal, and toxic farm chemicals. Following good safety practices can reduce the risks of injury to a minimum.

GOE: 05.05.09; SIC: 7699; SOC: 6118

◇ **SOURCES OF ADDITIONAL INFORMATION**

Equipment Manufacturers Institute
10 South Riverside Plaza
Chicago, IL 60606-3710

North American Equipment Dealers Association
10877 Watson Road
St. Louis, MO 63127-1081

Canadian Farm and Industrial Equipment Institute
#307 720 Guelph Line
Burlington ON L7R 4E2

◇ **RELATED ARTICLES**

Volume 1: Agriculture; Automotives
Volumes 2–4: Air-conditioning, refrigeration, and heating mechanics; Agricultural equipment technicians; Animal production technicians; Automobile mechanics; Diesel mechanics; Electrical repairers; Farm crop production technicians; General maintenance mechanics

Farmers

Definition

Farmers raise crops such as corn, wheat, tobacco, cotton, vegetables, and fruits; specialize in some phase of raising animals or poultry, mainly for food; or maintain herds of dairy cattle for the production of milk. While some farmers may combine several of these activities, most specialize in one specific area. They are helped by farm laborers, who are either hired workers or members of farm families and who perform all types of tasks. Farm supervisors work on large farms where they coordinate the work of laborers and hire additional crews as needed. Farm operatives and managers bring a knowledge of business and farm management to either their own farms or to those of others.

Farmers own or lease the property they work, although many farm owners also lease extra land. The economics of farming is accelerating a trend toward larger and larger farms. Most farms are now thousands of acres in size and are the site of substantial—even massive—animal and plant production operations. Subsistence farms that produce only enough to support the farmer's family are growing more rare.

History

Farming is an ancient occupation that has its origins before the beginnings of recorded history. Before farming began, people were hunters. Tribes roamed from area to area, killing animals for food, clothing, and shelter, and picking whatever wild berries, nuts, and fruits they could find. As the population grew, rudimentary efforts to tame wild animals and cultivate wild plants for food began to provide a more constant diet.

The big breakthrough in farming came when people realized that seeds saved through the winter could be planted in the spring. People could now plan which crops to raise and harvest. There is evidence that wheat was cultivated in Mesopotamia (now Iraq) as early as 4700 B.C. Ancient people also planted cotton for use in producing cloth, as well as food crops such as peas, beans, rice, and barley.

Early farming methods and implements were crude. Oxen dragged forked sticks through the ground to break up the soil. Scattered seeds were pressed into the earth by the feet of sheep driven over the land. Family members often sat in the fields guarding the newly planted seeds from scavenging birds.

In colonial America almost 95 percent of the people were farmers, planting such crops as corn, wheat, flax, and, further South, tobacco. With the exception of turkeys, all of the livestock raised in America was brought over from the Old World. Chickens, which were introduced by the Spaniards in the 16th century, were brought over by the English colonists to Virginia and Massachusetts. Hogs, cattle, sheep, and goats were also imported from Europe. Farmers raised hay to feed livestock and just enough other crops to supply their families with a balanced diet throughout the year.

The invention of farm machines in the 1800s, such as the reaper, the threshing machine, the steel plow, and the two-horse cultivator, enabled farmers to put a great deal of land under cultivation, and the widespread sale of farm products began. In the early 20th century, the tractor was developed, and soybeans—a new and important crop imported from the Orient—was widely planted and processed.

Along with the introduction of many labor-saving farm machines came new and improved methods of soil conservation. The use of fertilizers, contour farming, strip cropping, and crop rotation greatly increased the productivity of the land and at the same time preserved it. The Department of Agriculture, which was created in 1862, and the state agricultural colleges, with their various extension services, combined to make the farmer more knowledgeable, productive, and efficient in the use of land and livestock.

As a result of massive technological changes and an enormous increase of productivity, a relatively small number of farms are today producing greater amounts of America's farm products.

Nature of the work

There are probably as many different types of farmers as there are different types of economically important plants and animals. In addition to *diversified crops farmers*, who grow different combinations of fruits, grains, and vegetables, and *general farmers*, who raise livestock as well as crops, there are *cash grain farmers*, who grow barley, corn, rice, soybeans, and wheat; *vegetable farmers*; *tree-fruit-and-nut crops farmers*; *field crops farmers*, who raise alfalfa, cotton, hops, peanuts, mint, sugarcane, and tobacco; *animal breeders*; *fur farmers*; *livestock ranchers*; *dairy farmers*; *poultry farmers*; *beekeepers*; *reptile farmers*; *fish farmers*; and even *worm growers*.

Corn and wheat farmers begin the growing season by breaking up the soil with plows, then harrowing, pulverizing, and leveling it. Some of these tasks may be done after the harvest the previous year, and others just before planting. Corn is usually planted around the middle of May with machines that place the corn seeds into "hills" a few inches apart, making weed control easier. On the average a crop is cultivated three times during the season. Corn is also used in the making of silage, a type of animal feed made by cutting the corn and allowing it to ferment in storage silos.

Wheat may be sown in the fall or spring, depending on the severity of winter and the variety of wheat. It is planted with a drill, close together, thus allowing greater cultivation and easier harvesting. The harvest for winter wheat occurs in early summer, as farmers use combines to gather and thresh the wheat in one operation. The wheat is then stored in large grain storage elevators, which are owned by private individuals, companies, or farming cooperatives.

Cotton planting is begun in March in the Southwest, and somewhat later in the southern states. Tobacco plants must be carefully tended and protected from harsh weather conditions. The soil in which they are grown must also be thoroughly broken up, smoothed, and fertilized before planting, as tobacco is very hard on the soil. The peanut crop can be managed more like other types of farm crops. It is not nearly so sensitive to weather and disease, nor does it require the great care of tobacco and cotton.

Specialty crops such as fruits and vegetables are the most subject to seasonal variations, so the farmer must rely heavily on hired seasonal labor. Also, this type of farmer employs more specialized equipment than do general farmers.

The mechanization of farming has not eliminated all the problems of raising crops. Judgment and experience are always important in making decisions. The hay farmer, for example, must be able to judge the exact time for mowing that will yield the best crop in terms of stem toughness, leaf loss, and the growing season left for subsequent cuttings. All of this must be weighed in terms of weather conditions. To harvest this crop, the farmer must use specialized equipment such as mowing machines and hay rakes that are usually drawn by tractors.

Farmers try to offset the high cost of machinery by either increasing their yields or sharing equipment with other farmers.

The hay is pressed into bales by another machine for easier storage and then transported to storage facilities or to market.

Decisions about planting are just as crucial as those about harvesting. Such crops as potatoes need to be planted during a relatively short span of days in the spring. The fields must be tilled and ready for planting, and the farmer must estimate weather conditions so the seedlings will not freeze from late winter weather.

The crop specialty farmer often uses elaborate irrigation systems to water the crops during those seasons of inadequate rainfall. Often these systems are portable, since it is necessary to move large sections of piping from field to field.

Farmers must make many managerial decisions. Their farm output is strongly influenced by the weather, disease, fluctuations in prices of domestic and foreign farm products, and, in some cases, federal farm programs. Farmers must carefully plan the combination of crops they will grow so that, if the price of one crop drops, they will have sufficient income from another to make up for it. Since prices change from month to month, farmers who plan ahead may be able to store their crops or keep their livestock to take advantage of better prices later in the year.

Livestock farmers generally buy calves from ranchers who breed and raise them. They feed and fatten young cattle and generally raise their own corn and hay to lower feeding costs. They must know a little about the diseases of cattle and the proper methods of feeding. In addition to their crop acreage, they must also provide their cattle with fenced pasturage and adequate shelter from rough weather. Some livestock farmers may specialize in breeding stock for sale to ranchers and dairy farmers. These specialists are interested in maintaining and improving purebred animals of a particular breed. Bulls and cows are then sold to ranchers and dairy farmers who want to improve their herds.

Sheep ranchers raise sheep primarily for their wool. Large herds are maintained on rangeland in the western states. Since large areas of land are needed, the sheep rancher must usually buy grazing rights on government-owned lands.

Although dairy farmers' first concern is with the production of high-grade milk, they also will raise corn and grain to provide feed for their animals. The dairy farmer must be able to repair the many kinds of equipment essential to their business and know about diseases, sanitation, and methods of improving the quantity and quality of the milk.

Milking must be done every day, once in the morning and once at night. Records are kept of each cow's production of milk to discover which cows are profitable and which should be traded or sold for meat. After milking, when the cows are at pasture, the farmer cleans the stalls and the barn by washing, sweeping, and sterilizing it with boiling water. This is extremely important because dairy cows contract diseases from unsanitary conditions easily, and this in turn may contaminate the milk. Dairy farmers must have their herds certified to be free of disease by the Department of Health.

The great majority of poultry farmers do not hatch their own chicks but buy them from commercial hatcheries. The chicks are kept in brooder houses until they are seven or eight weeks old and are then transferred to open pens or shelters. After six months the hens begin to lay eggs, and roosters are culled from the flock to be sold for meat.

The basic job of poultry farmers is to keep their flocks healthy. They must provide shelter from the chickens' natural enemies and from extreme weather conditions. The shelters must be kept extremely clean, because diseases can spread through a flock rapidly. The poultry farmer must choose the food that will allow each chicken to grow or produce to its greatest potential, while at the same time keep costs down.

Raising chickens to be sold as broilers or fryers requires equipment to house them until they are 6 to 13 weeks old. Those farmers specializing in the production of eggs must gather eggs at least twice a day, and more often in very warm weather. The eggs must then be stored in a cool place, inspected, graded, and packed for market. The poultry farmer who specializes in producing broilers is usually not an independent producer but is under a contract with a backer, who is often the operator of a slaughterhouse or the manufacturer of poultry feeds.

Farmers and farm managers make a wide range of administrative decisions. In addition to their knowledge of crop production and animal science, they have to determine how to market the foods they produce. They keep an eye on the commodities markets to see which crops will provide the greatest return. They take out loans to buy farm equipment or extra land for cultivation. They keep up with new methods of production and new markets. Farms today are actually large businesses, with all the attendant worries about cash flow, competition, markets, and production.

Requirements

While there are no specific educational requirements for this field, every successful farmer, whether working with crops or animals, must have a knowledge of the principles of soil preparation and cultivation, disease control, and machinery maintenance, as well as a knowledge of business practices and bookkeeping. Farmers must know their crops well enough to be able to choose the proper seeds for their particular soil and climate. They also need experience in evaluating crop growth and weather cycles. Those working with animals should have a basic affection for them and a thorough knowledge of their special requirements.

High school courses that will help in farming include algebra, geometry, biology, chemistry, carpentry, accounting, and English. Extension courses should also be taken to keep abreast of all the new developments in farm technology.

The state land-grant universities across the country were established to encourage agricultural research and to educate young people in the latest advancements in farming. They offer agricultural programs that lead to bachelor's degrees, as well as shorter programs in specific areas. Some universities offer advanced studies in horticulture, animal science, agronomy, and agricultural economics. Motivated students can pursue studies leading to master's degrees or doctorates. Most students in agricultural colleges are also required to take courses in farm management and in business, finance, and economics.

Technical schools often have home-study courses, and evening courses are available in many areas for adult farmers. Two-year colleges often have programs leading to associate degrees in agriculture.

Opportunities for experience and exploration

Few people enter farming as a career unless they grew up on or around a farm, but the opportunities for experience are plentiful from childhood on for those who want to make this their business. For young people whose families do not own farms, there are many opportunities for part-time farm work as a hired hand, especially during seasonal operations.

In addition, organizations such as the 4-H Club and Future Farmers of America offer especially good opportunities for learning about, visiting, and participating in farms and farming activities. Agricultural colleges often have their own farms where students can gain actual experience in farm operations as well as classroom work.

Methods of entering

In general, it is becoming increasingly difficult for a person to purchase land for farming. The capital investment in a farm today is so great that it is almost impossible for anyone to start from scratch. However, those who lack a family connection to farming or considerable financial support from some source can lease land for cultivation from other farmers. Money for leasing land and equipment may be available from local banks or from the Farmers Home Administration.

Because the capital outlay is so high, many wheat, corn, and specialty crop farmers start by being tenant farmers and renting land and equipment, or by sharing the cash profits with the owner of the land. In this way, these tenants hope to gain both the experience and cash to purchase and manage their own farms.

Generally, livestock farmers also start by renting property and sometimes animals, on a share-of-the-profits basis with the owner. Government lands, such as national parks, can be

rented for pasture as well. Later, when the livestock farmer wants to own property, it is possible to borrow based on the estimated value of the leased land, buildings, and animals. Dairy farmers can begin in much the same way. Loans are becoming more difficult to obtain, however. After several years of lenient loan policies, financial institutions in farm regions have tightened their requirements.

The best way to get into the poultry industry is to work part time on a poultry farm during time off from school. Another possibility is to seek a job with a firm closely related to poultry farming, such as a feed or equipment dealer. This may lead to full-time work and ultimately a position as manager of the farm. Most poultry farms are actually owned by large firms such as feed producers.

Advancement

Farmers advance by buying their own farms or additional acreage to increase production and, thus, income. The same holds true for livestock, dairy, or poultry farmers. In farming as in other fields, a person's success depends greatly on formal education and keeping up with the latest developments.

Employment outlook

About 1,313,000 people are employed as farm owners or managers, and another 1,079,000 are employed as farm workers of all kinds. The long-range forecast is for a decrease in the number of people working in agriculture as farmers and farm laborers, although it will decrease at a slower rate than in the recent past. Increases in automation and crop productivity mean that fewer people and less land is required to produce the same amount of food. The surpluses that exist for many farm products make it even harder to earn a living by farming.

Large corporate farms are fast replacing the small farmer, who is being forced out of the industry by the spiralling costs of feed, grain, land, and equipment. The late 1970s and early 1980s were an especially hard time. Many small farmers were forced to give up farming; some lost farms that had been in their families for generations.

FARMERS

Earnings

Farmers' incomes vary greatly from year to year, since the prices of farm products fluctuate according to weather conditions and the amount and quality of what all farmers were able to produce. A farm that shows a large profit one year may show a loss for the following year. Many farmers, especially small ones, earn incomes in nonfarm activities that are several times larger than their farm incomes.

Farm income also varies greatly depending on the size and type of farm. According to the Department of Agriculture, vegetable and melon, cotton, horticultural specialty, and rice farms generated an average income of over $100,000 in 1990. On the other hand, cattle, general crop, corn, tobacco, and other livestock farms generated an average income of less than $15,000. In general, large farms generate more income than small farms. Exceptions include some specialty farms that produce low-volume but high-quality horticultural and fruit products.

Farm managers' incomes also vary substantially. According to limited information, most farm managers earn between $25,000 and $27,000, although they can earn up to $65,000.

Conditions of work

Farming can be a difficult and frustrating career, but it can be very satisfying as a way of life. The hours are long and the work is physically strenuous, but working outdoors and watching things grow can be very rewarding. The changing seasons bring variety to the day-to-day work. Farmers seldom work five eight-hour days a week. When harvesting time comes or the weather is right for planting or spraying, farmers work long hours to see that everything gets done. Even during the cold winter months they stay busy repairing machinery and buildings. Dairy farmers and other livestock farmers work seven days a week all year round.

Dangers to farmers include machine-related injuries, exposure to the weather, and illnesses caused by allergies or animal-related diseases. Fires and falls can cause accidents on farms, but by being careful, farmers can avoid these dangers. In addition, many farms are often isolated, away from many conveniences and at times from some necessities such as immediate medical attention.

GOE: 03.01.01; SIC: 019, 029; SOC: 56

◇ SOURCES FOR ADDITIONAL INFORMATION

American Farm Bureau Federation
225 Touhy Avenue
Park Ridge, IL 60068

Farmers' Educational and Cooperative Union of America
10065 East Harvard Avenue
Denver, CO 80251

National Council of Farmer Cooperatives
50 F Street, NW
Suite 900
Washington, DC 20001

National Grange
1616 H Street, NW
Washington, DC 20006

National Young Farmer Educational Association
5632 Mt. Vernon Memorial Highway
PO Box 15160
Alexandria, VA 22309

U.S. Department of Agriculture
Higher Education Program
Washington, DC 20250

National Farmers Union
250-C 2 Avenue South
Saskatoon SK S7K 2M1

◇ RELATED ARTICLES

Volume 1: Agriculture
Volumes 2–4: Agribusiness technicians; Agricultural extension service workers; Agricultural scientists; Animal production technicians; Equestrian management workers; Farm crop production technicians; Fish production technicians; Grain merchants; Range managers; Soil conservation technicians; Soil scientists; Veterinarians; Veterinary technicians

Fashion designers

Definition

Fashion designers create original designs for clothing.

History

Before the invention of the sewing machine by Elias Howe, in 1846, all garments were made by hand—thread was spun by hand and material was woven by hand from the spun thread. Often, people wore the same kinds of garments all their lives. Their concern was not so much for unusual styles as it was for garments that would help them maintain body temperature.

The wealthy, who had leisure time, were greatly concerned with fashion and had complex garments designed and made by individual dressmakers and tailors. The French fashion designers were particularly well known for their display of lavish styles, a tradition carried into the 20th century. French designers still dominate the field, even though the U.S. garment industry has assumed a position of leadership in clothing production.

Nature of the work

Fashion designers create designs for almost anything that is a part of the costume of men, women, or children. They may design both outer and inner garments, or hats, purses, shoes, gloves, costume jewelry, scarves, or beachwear.

The designer's original idea for a garment is usually sketched. After a first rough sketch has been prepared, the designer begins to shape the pattern pieces that make the garment. The pieces are then drawn to actual size on paper, and cut out on a rough material, often muslin. The muslin pieces are sewn together and fitted on a model.

The designer makes modifications in the pattern pieces or other features of the rough mock-up to complete the design. From the rough model, sample garments are made in the fabric that the designer intended to use. Sample garments are displayed at a "showing," to which press representatives and buyers are invited and which designers supervise.

In some companies, designers are involved in every step of the production of the line, from the original idea to the completed garments. Many designers prefer to supervise their own workrooms. Others work with supervisors to solve problems that arise in the production of the garments.

Most manufacturers produce new styles four times each year: spring and summer; fall and winter; "cruise," for people on vacations; and, "holiday," or special styles, for the winter holiday season. Designers may be expected to create between 50 to 150 styles for each showing. Their calendar of work differs from that of the rest of the world. They must be working on spring and summer designs during fall and winter months, on fall and winter clothing during the warm seasons of the year.

Designers work cooperatively with the head of their manufacturing firm. They design a "line" that is consistent with the ideas of their employers. They also must work cooperatively with those who do the actual production of the garments and must be able to estimate the cost of a garment.

Designers must spend time in exploration and research, visiting textile manufacturing and sales establishments to learn of the latest fabrics and their uses and capabilities. They must know about fabric, weave, draping qualities, and strength of materials. A good understanding of textiles and their potentialities underlies much of designers' work. They browse through stores to see what things are being bought by the public and which are passed by. They visit museums and art galleries to get ideas about color and design. They go to places where people congregate—to the theater, sports events, business and professional meetings, and resorts—to discover what people are wearing.

Designers must keep abreast of changing styles. If the styles are too far ahead of public taste, they will find that purchasers reject the designs. If, however, they cling to styles that have been successful in the past, they may find that the taste of buyers has surged ahead. Either way it may be equally disastrous for their employers.

There are many opportunities for specialization in fashion designing. The most common of the specialties is that of a particular type of garment such as resort wear or sports fashionwear.

One of the interesting specialties in fashion designing is theatrical design, a relatively lim-

FASHION DESIGNERS

This fashion designer examines photo spreads of clothing that she and her colleagues designed.

ited field but challenging to those who are interested in combining a liking for the theater with a talent for clothing design.

Requirements

Fashion designing is a highly competitive business. The better an aspiring designer is prepared, the broader the opportunities will be. A college degree is recommended, though not required. Graduation from a special school for fashion design is highly desirable. Employers seek designers who have had courses in mathematics, business, design, sketching, art history, costume history, literature, pattern-making, clothing construction, and textiles.

Some colleges offer a four-year degree in fine arts with a major in fashion design. Many reputable schools of fashion design in the United States offer a two- or three-year program that does not lead to a degree but instead offers a diploma or certificate.

High school students who are interested in fashion designing should take as many courses as possible in art, clothing construction, and textiles.

Prospective fashion designers must be artistically creative, with an unusual ability in garment construction. They should also be imaginative and able to work well with their hands.

Opportunities for experience and exploration

The young person who enjoys sewing and who sews well may have taken the first step toward exploring a career in the fashion world. If the skills in garment construction are adequate, the next step may be an attempt at designing and making clothing. Courses in art and design will help assess any talent and ability as a creative artist.

Students who are able to obtain a summer job in a department or specialty store can observe retailing practices and gain some practical insights into the merchandising aspects of the fashion world. They should visit a garment manufacturer to see fashion employees at work.

Those who are interested in fashion design should take every opportunity to attend style shows, visit art galleries, observe clothing worn by fashion leaders, and browse through all kinds of stores in which garments are sold. They should read widely in the many books and magazines that are published about fashion, particularly *Women's Wear Daily*, which is the best known periodical of the garment industry.

Methods of entering

Few people ever begin their careers as fashion designers. Frequently, well trained college graduates begin in positions as assistant designers and must prove that they have ability before they are entrusted with the responsible job of the designer. Many young people find that assistant designer jobs are difficult to locate, so they accept beginning jobs in the workroom where they spend time cutting or constructing garments.

Advancement

Advancement in fashion designing varies a great deal. There is much moving around from firm to firm, and vacancies occur rather regularly. Aspiring designers should continue to create their own designs and should look for opportunities to show their work to employers. They should collect a portfolio of work as fast as possible.

Employment outlook

The designer is the key person in the garment industry, yet relatively few of them are needed to make employment possible for thousands of people. It is estimated that there are more than 30,000 designers and assistant designers in the United States and that they represent less than 1 percent of the garment industry employees. Some designers work only for the high-priced custom trade, some for the mass market, some work on exclusive designs, which will be made for only one person. Many designers are employed by manufacturers of paper patterns.

Good designers will always be needed. They will not, however, be needed in great numbers. Fashion designers enjoy high pay and prestige, and those at the top of their profession rarely leave their positions. Therefore, opportunities for newcomers are limited. There are always more people hoping to break into the field than there are jobs available. It takes a great deal of talent and perseverance to achieve success as a high-fashion designer. The employment outlook may be better in other fields, such as children's clothing. Openings are more readily available for assistant designers.

Earnings

Fashion designers are to be found in almost every income bracket. Income depends in part upon the size of the firm for which the designer works and the volume of business that it does. Income also depends upon the kind of fashion designing in which the designer is engaged.

In the 1990s salaries for entry positions average from $12,000 to $14,000 per year. For experienced designers, salaries may range between $19,000 and $40,000 a year. A few highly skilled and well known designers have annual incomes of better than $62,000. As designers become well known, they are usually offered a share of the ownership of the company for which they design. Their percentage of ownership increases with their reputation.

Theatrical designers usually work on a contract basis. Although the remuneration for the total contract is usually good, there may be long periods of idleness between contracts. The annual income for theatrical designers may not exceed that of designers on regular salary, though while they are working they may be making more than $1,000 per week.

Conditions of work

Many designers work in cluttered and noisy surroundings. Their work space may consist of a large room that has long tables for cutting out patterns or garments. There may be only one or two other people working in the room, or there may be many others. The designer may have a small office adjacent to the working space.

Some designers have spacious, well lighted, and well ventilated work spaces that are arranged neatly and are free from undue disturbance.

Many designers travel a great deal, either to other cities or to other locations in the same city for showings or conferences. They may spend time in stores or shops looking at clothing that has been manufactured by competitors.

Although some designers may observe traditional work hours during many weeks of the year, they may have to work many more than 40 hours each week during rush periods. Styles previewed in spring and fall require a great amount of work during the weeks and months before a show.

GOE: 01.02.03; SIC: 513; SOC: 6859

◇ **SOURCES OF ADDITIONAL INFORMATION**

International Association of Clothing Designers
240 Madison Avenue
12th Floor
New York, NY 10016

National Association of Schools of Art and Design
11250 Roger Bacon Drive, Suite 21
Reston, VA 22090

Ontario Fashion Exhibitors Inc.
#244, 370 King Street West
Box 1
Toronto ON M5V 1J9

◇ **RELATED ARTICLES**

Volume 1: Apparel; Design; Performing Arts; Textiles
Volumes 2–4: Buyers, wholesale and retail; Costume designers; Jewelers and jewelry repairers; Models; Textile technicians

Fast food workers

Definition

Whether the restaurant's menu lists pizza, tacos, hamburgers, or fried chicken, a *fast food worker* is responsible for serving each customer the correct order in an efficient, professional, and courteous manner. Fast food workers may be employed by large chain restaurants or privately owned shops. Though most of these places serve only one kind of food, some establishments have a wide selection of dishes. In either type of restaurant, fast food workers should be familiar with the menu, including price, size of the portion, any side dish or condiments included, and how the food is prepared.

History

The continual development and improvement of transportation methods throughout history has made it easier for people to travel. While away from their homes and kitchens, these travelers needed other places to eat. As a result, concepts in alternative dining facilities have multiplied. Early travel routes often took people through the centers of towns, where they would pay for meals at hotels, inns, and taverns. When train layovers began to allow for meal breaks, food carts offering stews and quick dinners soon appeared near train depots. Many scheduled stops were longer and provided passengers with the opportunity to enjoy a more leisurely meal at local inns and diners.

After the turn of the century train travel in the U.S. became more popular and efficient. Passengers commonly took much longer trips from state to state. At the same time, trains offered travelers good, reasonably priced meals in dining cars. When automobile travel became popular, small independent stands were built along roadsides, offering the hurried traveller meals and sandwiches that were prepared and served quickly. With the development of highways and freeways, restaurants were built near exits and feeder roads.

Today, strings of well known fast food franchises can be found both in metropolitan areas and dotted along highways throughout the United States. Many American restaurant chains can be found in other countries around the world. The most famous is probably McDonald's, though historically it is only third oldest.

In 1930 fried chicken was the specialty in a small Kentucky restaurant opened by a man named Colonel Sanders. By 1956 Sanders was promoting his own recipe throughout the area, and eventually his one-restaurant business became the famous Kentucky Fried Chicken now known throughout the world. The second-oldest fast food chain is Burger King, which was opened by the Burger King Corporation of Miami, Florida, in 1954.

Fast food has become increasingly popular because it fits the busy schedules of most working families. In addition, the restaurants are conveniently located, offer moderately priced meals, and serve a consistent, dependable food product. In addition, many fast food restaurants offer certain price specials or discounts, such as "two-for-one" deals. Others offer prizes or hold contests that encourage repeat business. Responding to the widespread interest in more healthy lifestyles, some restaurants are supplementing their menus with food such as salads and soups.

Nature of the work

Fast food workers may have a variety of duties. Some fast food establishments require employees to be familiar with all aspects of the restaurant: greeting and serving customers, cleanup and maintenance, and preparation of some of the simpler food items. Smaller restaurants, not having enough staff to allow specialization, may follow this pattern out of necessity. Larger chain restaurants may institute this practice as a way of familiarizing the fast food worker with the restaurant's needs as a whole, with the possibility of specialization later.

Fast food workers who are part of the kitchen staff may begin as assistants to the trained cooks. These assistants may help setting up supplies, refilling condiment containers, or doing prep work such as slicing meats or vegetables. For the sake of sanitation as well as a safety, these assistants may be responsible for general clean-up duties in the kitchen area.

Kitchen staff employees who cook the food are responsible for preparing everything to meet the company's standards. In this regard, the meal must be made consistently and neatly.

Cooks must be agile and quick in their handling of food.

The cashier in a fast food restaurant may be responsible for taking the customer's order, entering the order into the computer or cash register, taking payment, and returning proper change. In some fast food establishments the cashier may act as counter worker and have additional tasks. These added duties can include filling the customer's order; selecting the various sandwiches, side orders, or beverages from those stations; and serving it to the customer on a tray or in a carry-out container. It is often the cashier's duty to greet customers, welcoming them to the restaurant in a friendly and courteous way. Since these employees are responsible for interacting with customers, they are required to keep their immediate work stations clean and neat.

In addition to interacting with the customers, the counter worker must also be able to communicate effectively with the kitchen and managerial staff. The counter worker may have to tell the kitchen staff about a special order for a sandwich or shortages of certain food items. The counter worker may need to notify the manager about a problem with the register or a disgruntled customer. Since delays can take away from customer satisfaction and hurt the restaurant's business, the counter worker must be able to identify, communicate, and solve problems quickly.

Fast food employees develop professional attitudes and marketable work skills. They learn to work under pressure and to meet the work standards that their managers expect. A fast food worker also learns tangible skills like working a cash register, cooking, and effective communication. In the different areas of fast food work, employees must be able to keep up the pace, show personal motivation, and be willing to work as part of the team.

Unlike some other types of work, however, the fast food business is a no-nonsense job. A cashier or counter worker may handle hundreds of dollars a day. Cooks work over fryers and grills and handle knives and meat slicers. The work requires concentration and a professional attitude.

Requirements

For an entry-level position at a fast food restaurant, a worker should be motivated, cheerful, and cooperative. The fast food business requires a quick pace during the breakfast and lunch rush periods. A motivated employee is willing to work extra hard and offer help to a

Fast food workers must work quickly and efficiently and cooperate well with their coworkers.

fellow employee during these times. When the restaurant is busy, attention and quick thinking are as necessary in accepting money and counting back change as they are for the handling of food.

Fast food workers should be neat in appearance as well as in work habits. Some fast food restaurants require that their employees wear uniforms or follow a dress code. They also may have rules of behavior. Because such guidelines are important for both safety reasons and the atmosphere of the restaurant, employees must respect and follow them. Failure to do so may result in the employee being sent home or having his or her pay reduced. The good qualities and work habits that are found in reliable fast food workers reflect the professional attitude that managers and franchise owners strive for in their restaurants.

As fast food workers make their way up the ranks of the restaurant, they may decide to pursue special training or education. If they are working at a part-time job and are still in high school, courses such as home economics, advanced cooking, or health and sanitation may be helpful.

If a fast food employee is already working full time at a large franchise and is interested in pursuing management training, there are many outlets for career preparation. Many franchises have their own training programs for future managers and franchise owners. McDonald's, Dunkin' Donuts, and Burger King all offer serious course work in such areas as maintaining restaurant equipment; hiring, training, and motivating employees; and purchasing supplies. Most other chain franchises offer employee instruction as well, so that the product and image of their restaurants are kept consistent and so that they may offer new franchise owners assistance in getting started in the business.

FAST FOOD WORKERS

Opportunities for experience and exploration

Course work in home economics courses and other classes that develop cooking skills can provide good preparation for the job of a fast food worker. In addition, general business or management courses provide a solid basis for entry-level workers. Students should also look into opportunities for working in the school cafeteria or other food service area. Neighborhood restaurants and local hot dog or hamburger stands may also hire summer help.

Certain high schools offer cooperative work-study programs to students to assist them in gaining job experience. Such programs may offer concentrations in the food service industry or host lectures from community members already involved in the field.

Methods of entering

At some fast food restaurants, more than 50 percent of the positions are for part-time employees. These restaurants rely heavily on their part-timers and are accustomed to planning their work schedules accordingly. Applying at restaurants that hire part-time or student help is a good way to enter this field. Even at smaller, privately owned establishments, the fast food worker will be introduced to some of the common factors of the industry: working with and for a variety of people, keeping up a quick pace, cooking, and packaging and serving food in a friendly way.

Local papers often advertise for help in neighborhood restaurants, and some establishments contact school counseling departments to post job openings. However, the majority of positions are available to those who walk in and fill out an application. Since entry-level positions open up and are filled quickly, applicants are advised to contact restaurants regularly if no openings are immediately available.

Advancement

Because of the diversity in the restaurant business, there is ample opportunity for workers to find an area of interest or specialization. Fast food workers may take advantage of manager-trainee opportunities or tuition assistance to move higher up within the company. Some fast food workers use their experience to go on to other areas of food service, such as waiting ta-

bles or working as a restaurant hostess or manager. Others may decide to go to a vocational cooking school or pursue hotel and restaurant management.

Employment outlook

Because of the quality of training and preparation that parent companies offer to franchise owners, more than 95 percent of fast food restaurant businesses stay in business after they open. More than 550,000 people are employed at fast food restaurants in the 1990s. A 31 percent increase in employment is projected through the year 2000, which would bring the total number of workers to more than 775,000. Job opportunities for all types of food and beverage workers are expected to be plentiful for the next decade or more.

Entry-level jobs are not difficult to come by. Submitting an application and keeping in touch with managers for openings can lead to the beginning of a successful career in the fast food industry. Owning a franchise is a popular business venture, but one that demands the recruitment and promotion of reliable, capable staff. Knowledge of the business from the bottom up is a definite advantage for franchise owners.

Earnings

Like other entry-level workers with part-time jobs, fast food workers can expect to begin at the minimum hourly wage. Larger restaurant franchises often offer annual and bonus raises. Restaurants that have late evening or all-night hours may compensate employees working those shifts with higher hourly wages. Sometimes employees earn additional compensation or time-and-a-half for working overtime or on holidays. Some restaurants and individually owned franchises offer bonuses for tuition assistance, as well as periodic bonuses.

Conditions of work

Fast food restaurants need to meet the safety and sanitary standards enforced by local and state health departments. These agencies require an establishment to have proper lighting and adequate heating, cooling, and ventilation systems so employees can work in a comfortable environment.

Large fast food franchises are often decorated pleasantly, incorporating the logo, color schemes, or trademark characters of their parent companies. They supply adequate and comfortable seating facilities, as well as rest rooms and water fountains. These all are maintained according to corporate standards.

Fast food employees may work shifts of five to nine hours and receive appropriate coffee and lunch breaks. Often these establishments have private rooms, separated from the main dining rooms, for employees to eat lunches and relax.

Fast food workers may have regular work hours (mornings only, for example) or floating schedules that require them to work a combination of evenings, afternoons, and weekends. Fast food workers may be called in by their managers to work an extra shift or work overtime if another employee is ill or if the restaurant is very busy. Fast food workers should be fairly flexible because their managers have no way to determine in advance how busy or understaffed the restaurant will be.

GOE: None; SIC: 5812; SOC: None

◇ **SOURCES OF ADDITIONAL INFORMATION**

National Soft Serve and Fast Food Association
7321 Anthony Highway
Waynesboro, PA 17268-9736

Educational Foundation of the National Restaurant Association
250 South Wacker Drive, 14th Floor
Chicago, IL 60606

Restaurant and Foodservices Association
#204, 4190 Lougheed Highway
Burnaby BC V5C 6A8

◇ **RELATED ARTICLES**

Volume 1: Food Service; Hospitality
Volumes 2–4: Cashiers; Caterers; Cooks, chefs and bakers; Counter and retail clerks; Dietetic technicians; Dietitians; Food service workers; Restaurant and food service managers

FBI Agents

Definition

Special Agents of the Federal Bureau of Investigation are employees of the federal government. The FBI, a part of the U.S. Department of Justice, investigates violations of many different federal laws. The agency's jurisdiction covers over 270 violations of federal law in the areas of criminal and civil law and government intelligence.

History

The Federal Bureau of Investigation began in 1908, when it was founded as the investigative branch of the U.S. Department of Justice. The FBI experienced a rather slow development until 1924, when J. Edgar Hoover was appointed its director. As it gained increased responsibilities for enforcing a number of federal laws, the FBI under Hoover began its progress towards becoming the internationally famous crime detection laboratory it is today.

As a part of its growth, the FBI was given the general authority to handle federal crime investigation in 1934. Through its work in this area, within three years, more than 11,000 criminals were convicted. In 1939, the FBI was further established as the clearinghouse for all matters pertaining to the internal security of the United States. During World War II, the FBI rendered many security services for plants involved in war production and worked to gather evidence on espionage activities within the plants.

Today the FBI is involved in a wide variety of law-enforcement activities using the latest scientific methods. The FBI laboratory is one of the largest and most comprehensive crime laboratories in the world. Since its inception in 1932, it has provided leadership and service in the scientific solution and prosecution of

This FBI employee analyses specimens of suspected narcotics. Her experiments render evidence that helps solve crimes.

crimes. It is the only full-service federal forensic laboratory in the United States.

The FBI's Identification Division serves as the nation's repository and clearinghouse for fingerprint records. In this capacity, the division provides the following services: identifying and maintaining fingerprint records for arrested criminal suspects and for applicants to certain sensitive jobs; posting notices for people wanted for crimes and for parole or probation violations; examining physical evidence for fingerprints and providing occasional court testimony on the results of examinations; training in fingerprint science; maintaining fingerprint records of people currently reported missing; and identifying amnesia victims and unknown deceased people. The fingerprint section of the FBI laboratory is the largest in the world, containing millions of sets of fingerprints.

Nature of the work

The headquarters of the FBI is located in Washington, D.C., and from this location the work of some 56 field divisions is supervised. FBI Agents can be assigned to investigate any case, irrespective of its nature, unless they have specialized skills in some particular field. In such situations they are most likely assigned to work on those cases that demand their specialized talents.

For any case, the responsibility of the FBI Agent is to investigate violations of federal laws. Violations may include such crimes as bank robbery, extortion, kidnapping, fraud and theft against the federal government, espionage, interstate transportation of stolen property, mail fraud, sabotage, and infractions of the Atomic Energy Act. FBI Special Agents are responsible for protecting the security of the United States and for investigating any subversive acts that might threaten that security. In performing investigative work, Agents have at their disposal a vast network of communication systems and the crime detection laboratory in Washington. When cases are completed, they submit full reports to the Bureau's headquarters.

FBI Agents usually carry special identification to identify themselves as employees of the Bureau. They wear ordinary business suits almost all the time, not special uniforms such as police wear. Agents are required to carry firearms while on duty.

FBI Agents usually work on their own unless there is potential danger or the nature of the case demands two or more people. An Agent's work is always confidential and may not be discussed except among other authorized Bureau members. This prevents any discussion of work assignments even with immediate family or friends. The Bureau and its Agents work in close cooperation with law enforcement agencies from all over the country and around the world, although the FBI does not function as a law enforcement agency. FBI Agents function strictly as investigators.

Agents perform their work in various ways, depending upon the nature of the case. They may need to travel for periods of time or live in various cities. Agents may interview people to gather information, spend time searching various types of records, and observe people, especially those who are suspected of criminal intentions or acts. FBI Agents take part in arrests and may participate in or lead raids of various kinds. On occasion, they are summoned to testify in court cases regarding their investigative work and findings. It is not the Agent's role, however, to express judgments or opinions regarding the innocence or guilt of those people being tried in court. The Agent's work is to gather facts and report them.

Requirements

To carry out its mission, the FBI needs men and women who can fill a variety of demanding positions. To qualify for training as an FBI Agent, a candidate must be a U.S. citizen between the ages of 23 and 37 when entering duty and must meet certain physical requirements.

All Special Agent candidates must hold a degree from a four-year resident program at a college or university that is accredited by one of the six regional accrediting bodies of the Commission on Institutions of Higher Education.

Candidates must fulfill the requirements of one of five entry programs: Law, Accounting, Engineering/Science, Language, and Diversified. Other degree titles may also qualify for the Special Agent position. Entry through the Law program requires a JD degree from an accredited resident law school; through Accounting, a BS degree with a major in accounting and eligibility to take the Certified Public Accountant examination; through Engineering/Science, a BS degree in engineering, computer science, or one of the physical sciences, with other additional experience possibly required; through Language, a BA or BS degree in any discipline and proficiency in Spanish, Russian, Arabic, Chinese, or other language that meets the needs of the FBI; and through Diversified, a BS or BA degree in any discipline plus three years of full-time work experience, or an advanced degree accompanied by two years of full-time work experience.

All candidates must complete a rigorous application process. For those who successfully complete the written tests and interview, the Bureau conducts a thorough background investigation that includes credit and criminal record checks; interviews with associates; contact with personal and business references; interviews with past employers and neighbors; and verification of educational achievements. Drug testing and a physical examination are required. A polygraph examination may also be required. The completed background investigation is then considered when the final hiring decision is made.

All newly appointed Special Agents must complete 16 weeks of intensive training at the FBI Academy in Quantico, Va. Classroom hours are spent studying a variety of academic and investigative subjects, accompanied by training in physical fitness, defensive tactics, and the proper use of firearms.

After graduation from the FBI Academy, new Agents are assigned to an FBI field office. This assignment is determined by the individual's special skills and the current needs of the FBI. During the first months of employment, the novice Agent is guided by a veteran Special Agent who will help show how the lessons learned at the Academy can be applied on the job. As a part of their duties, Special Agents are required to relocate during their careers.

The education and training of the FBI Agent is virtually never-ending. New techniques and better methods in criminal investigation are continually taught throughout a Special Agent's career, either through experience on the job, advanced study courses, in-service training, or special conferences.

Potential candidates must be in excellent physical health to pass the rigid physical examination. They must have very good eyesight and unimpaired hearing so that they are capable of hearing a normal conversation from at least 15 feet away with each ear. Applicants cannot have any physical defects that would interfere with their job performance, which may demand participation in raids, climbing, running, using firearms, and using defensive tactics to protect themselves or others. All applicants must be able to stand rigorous physical strain and exertion.

FBI Agents assume grave responsibilities as a normal part of their jobs. Their reputation and character must be above reproach, as must their dependability, integrity, and courage. Agents must be able to accept continual challenges in their jobs, realizing that no two days of work assignments may be exactly alike. A stable and personally secure person who can work daily with challenge, change, and danger may find an FBI career satisfying.

Opportunities for experience and exploration

Practically no opportunity exists for summer or part-time work experience in this occupation because of the education and training required and because of the nature of the work. Those people who are interested in the FBI, however, may explore the occupation by reading about the Bureau and its operations, or by visiting and taking a guided tour of the FBI headquarters in Washington, D.C., which is open to the public.

Methods of entering

Persons interested in the occupation of FBI Special Agent should write directly to the Director of the Federal Bureau of Investigation. The Bureau will send information on existing vacancies, requirements for the positions, how to file applications, and locations where examinations will be given.

Applicants may be interviewed and tested in FBI field offices. Although the FBI has its own methods of selecting employees, the examinations it gives are similar to those administered by the Office of Personnel Management. Periodically, the FBI sends out announcements concerning examination dates and possible vacancies to be filled.

Advancement

Although FBI Special Agents are not appointed under the Federal Civil Service Regulations like other federal workers, they are eligible to receive salary raises periodically within the grade set for their positions. These within-grade increases depend, of course, upon a satisfactory job performance. Grade advancements may be earned as the Agent gains experience through satisfactory job performance.

Higher-grade administrative and supervisory positions in the FBI are filled by those advancing within the ranks. Positions open to advancement may include Special Agent in charge of a field office, inspector, and field supervisor.

Employment outlook

The FBI has traditionally enjoyed a low employee turnover rate. As a lifetime service-career field, the FBI makes most job appointments to fill vacancies occurring because of retirement, death, or promotions from within the ranks. Some appointments are made to fill new positions created through the expansion of the Bureau. During World War II, there were approximately 5,000 FBI Agents. As of September 30, 1991, 10,314 Special Agents worked in the FBI's 56 field offices.

In spite of the somewhat limited number of new positions available, the FBI encourages qualified and interested people to submit applications. While competition is keen for openings that come available, openings for candidates do arise on a regular basis.

Earnings

Beginning FBI Agents earn a salary of $28,300. This wage is slightly above the beginning salary of recent college graduates hired by other federal agencies. Experienced field Agents earn around $44,300 a year, while annual salaries for supervisory Agents start at around $52,400. Under certain circumstances, Agents may work overtime and receive overtime pay up to approximately $6,120 a year.

Conditions of work

Depending on their case assignments, FBI Agents may work a very strenuous and variable schedule, frequently more than the customary 40-hour week. They are on call for possible assignment 24 hours a day. Assignments may be given for any location at any time. Agents may work under potentially dangerous circumstances in carrying out their assignments. Every aspect of the Agent's work is of a confidential nature. Agents must retire at age 55 if they have served 20 years.

FBI Agents receive fringe benefits of paid vacations, annuities on retirement, and sick leave. Although conditions of work for some case assignments may possibly be hazardous, the career of an FBI Special Agent offers responsibility and adventure.

GOE: 04.02; SIC: 9221; SOC: None

◇ **SOURCES OF ADDITIONAL INFORMATION**

The Federal Bureau of Investigation
U.S. Department of Justice
Washington, DC 20535

Friends of the FBI
1001 Connecticut Avenue, NW, Room 1135
Washington, DC 20036

◇ **RELATED ARTICLES**

Volume 1: Civil Service; Law; Politics and Public Service
Volumes 2–4: Border patrol officers; Customs officials; Deputy U.S. marshals; Detectives; Forensic experts; Intelligence officers; Lawyers and judges; Police officers

Field technicians

Definition

Field technicians set up and operate portable radio and television transmitting equipment in locations remote from the main station. In order to obtain a link with the station, they locate telephone wires that can carry transmissions, then connect microphones, amplifiers, and a source of power supply to the lines. Where no wires are available, technicians set up, test, and operate microwave transmitters to broadcast to the station control center.

During remote broadcasts they monitor sound and video transmissions, control volume and picture quality, and maintain the link with the station. Field technicians may occasionally be called on to perform announcing duties in the field. Technicians who are restricted to working with microwave transmitting equipment are usually called *microwave technicians.*

History

The field of broadcasting, which has its roots in the late 1800s, began when scientists discovered methods by which they could use electromagnetic waves to send wireless messages. At first these transmissions covered short distances, but in 1901 Guglielmo Marconi received in Newfoundland a radio message transmitted from England, thus marking the birth of the broadcast industry.

Modern television is based on electronic theory that grew out of the experiments of Heinrich Geissler in 1857, in which he discharged electricity in a vacuum tube, causing rare gases in it to glow. Other scientists immediately began to experiment with vacuum tubes, and in 1898 Karl Braun made the first cathode-ray tube in which he could control the flow of electrons being released. These developments, along with the discovery of radio tubes that could detect and amplify electromagnetic radio waves, set the stage for the development of modern television. The only element missing by 1907 was a device for scanning and transmitting a picture—a camera.

It was not until 1927 that the first workable cathode-ray-tube camera was invented by a 16-year-old boy named Philo T. Farnsworth. Improvements by Vladimir Zworykin made the system practical. It was demonstrated in 1929, and regular television programming began at the World's Fair of 1939, although it was later interrupted by World War II.

Meanwhile, radio had been used for communications between ships at sea and from ships to shore receivers. In 1920, however, two commercial radio stations went on the air: KDKA in Pittsburgh and WWJ in Detroit. They were followed by stations in all parts of the United States. The first network broadcast (more than one station sharing a broadcast) was of the 1922 World Series. The period from these early years through the early 1950s has been called the Golden Age of radio, because radio programming dominated home entertainment and information. With the rapid growth of television in the 1950s, radio lost its place as prime home entertainer, but it remained a vital source of entertainment, news, sports, and other information in American life.

In 1946, with World War II over, the interest and energy that had been diverted from television returned. The first commercial broadcasts were beamed along the East Coast (all early broadcasts originated in New York City) and gradually made their way to cities farther west, until by 1951 broadcasts were reaching coast-to-coast. In 1950 there were 6 million television sets in the United States; by 1960 there were 60 million.

Color programs began to be broadcast regularly in 1953, and the use of video recording tape was introduced in the 1950s as a major production technique. *Early Bird*, the first commercial communications satellite, was launched in 1965 and was followed by many more in the ensuing years.

By the end of the 1940s engineers were able to record light as well as sound waves as electromagnetic impulses. By the mid-1950s, it had become a regular practice of the television networks to videotape programs for presentation at a later time. Today, news, sports, and special events are the only live broadcasts on television, and even these include inserted videotaped material and instant replays.

The history of cable television can be traced to the development of coaxial cable (copper wire inside a copper tube, both with the same axis), which was invented in the 1930s in the Bell Telephone Laboratories, primarily to improve telephone transmission. It was soon found that a coaxial cable could also carry television transmissions very efficiently.

Today radio and television continue to be major forces in American life, in entertainment,

Before broadcasting a live interview outdoors, field technicians adjust their equipment to ensure adequate lighting and sound.

education, public affairs, and advertising. Virtually every American home has at least one radio, and 98 percent have at least one television set. Surveys show the average American views more than thirty hours of television per week and that 85 percent of all Americans listen to a radio at least once every day.

Nature of the work

Technicians usually travel to the site of a remote broadcast in a truck or van which also carries their equipment and any tools and parts needed to make emergency repairs. The van is usually also equipped with a microwave transmitter. At the remote site, technicians set up and test their equipment, locate and test telephone links for transmission to the main station control room, and make any other arrangements required for the successful transmission of the broadcast.

As the only technician in the crew, the field technician must test, replace, or repair microphones, amplifiers, auxiliary power supply, and wire connections. Technicians must be able to make emergency repairs using electricians' hand tools such as screwdrivers, pliers, and soldering irons, and be able to test for malfunctions using electrical test meters. The mobile units of larger stations are usually equipped with spare microphones, cameras, and parts, but the technicians of smaller stations have to rely on quick repair, rather than replacement, of malfunctioning equipment.

When the transmitting equipment is ready, the technicians switch cameras and microphones on and off and direct transmissions to

the main station control room where they are broadcast live or recorded for use in a later broadcast.

Requirements

Students interested in careers as field technicians should take high school mathematics courses at least through solid geometry, as well as physics, electrical shop, and electronics, if possible. Because field technicians also act as announcers on occasion, speech courses and experience in a school radio station as an announcer can be helpful. The ability to read and understand technical information is useful, since technicians must face technical repair problems on location with only their technical manuals to assist them.

Like other technicians in the broadcast industry, field technicians should expect to follow at least a two-year program of training beyond high school, concentrating on courses in electronics and radio and television theory. They should also continue to gain experience as announcers.

Potential field technicians should have a sincere interest in electronic devices, be of above average intelligence, and capable of learning radio repairing and radio communication. More important, they need to be able to work independently without much support and to solve problems involving both equipment and people quickly and effectively without becoming confused or distracted by what is going on around them.

According to federal law, anyone who generates microwave or certain other radio communications equipment must have a general radio telephone operator license issued by the FCC after the applicant has passed a series of written tests. Counselors can provide more information about agencies to contact regarding current licensing requirements and procedures.

Opportunities for experience and exploration

There are numerous ways for interested students to gain some experience and learn more about the work of field technicians or the broadcasting industry in general. Many high schools, community colleges, and technical institutes have radio and television stations of their own where students can experience the actual production of a broadcast program.

Many schools also have clubs for persons interested in broadcasting that sponsor trips to broadcasting facilities, schedule lectures, and provide a place where students can meet others with an interest in broadcasting.

Local radio and television station technicians are usually willing to share their experience with interested young people. They can be a helpful source of informal career guidance. Summer employment may also be available to students.

Methods of entering

Field technicians need to gain experience before they are sent out to the field. For their first job they should apply directly to the chief engineer or the personnel manager of the station where they wish to work. Help in arranging interviews or career counseling in general can be obtained from the placement office of the applicant's school.

New technicians at a station, even those with formal training and experience, normally begin employment with a period of instruction from the chief engineer or a senior engineer. Each station has its own procedures that technicians must learn and follow carefully.

The number of noncommercial, educational radio and television stations is increasing. They offer another opportunity for entry into the field.

Work–study programs offer another excellent method of getting started in a career field. These programs are run by schools in cooperation with local employers and offer students the opportunity to have part-time or summer employment in jobs related to the student's studies. Very often, the part-time or summer employer becomes the student's full-time employer after graduation.

Advancement

Advancement in the broadcast industry is usually from a trainee position to one of independent responsibility and then to a supervisory position. The path of the successful technician often leads from a small station, where the opportunity to perform a wide variety of duties provides excellent experience, to larger stations, where there are more supervisory positions to aim for and where the financial rewards are potentially greater.

The broadcast engineering field in general is highly competitive. Some technicians turn to teaching (in technical schools or in high schools that have radio stations) as a means of advancement. High school teaching requires a college degree and certification.

Employment outlook

The employment outlook for field technicians is influenced by the fact that competition is always extremely keen for positions in large metropolitan stations. Those technicians who are best prepared in electronics will have an advantage. However, there are usually good prospects for entry-level positions in smaller stations and in smaller cities.

Overall, the need for field technicians is expected to grow about as fast as the average for all other occupations through the year 2000. New openings will appear as new stations open and as currently employed technicians retire or advance to higher positions. The growth of cable television systems is expected to create openings in various related fields. This increased need may be offset by the increasing use of computerized automatic switching devices and other new labor-saving technology. These new kinds of equipment, however, do require maintenance work, which is often performed by qualified field technicians.

Earnings

Technicians entering their first job can expect a starting salary of about $17,000 to $19,000 a year. These averages are based on a regular 40-hour week which is standard in the industry. Overtime is fairly common, especially in smaller stations, and is usually paid at time-and-a-half. The average is $27,000, with a high of about $37,000 per year.

Technicians in the largest urban stations earn, as a rule, two-thirds more than those in the smallest rural stations. Technicians employed by educational broadcasting stations generally earn less than those employed by commercial stations.

Conditions of work

The work of field technicians is not strenuous, although it does involve carrying or moving equipment from the truck to the remote site and setting it up. Persons in this career must be able to meet and deal with the public easily, since they will be working in many different settings and must secure the cooperation of the people who live or work on the location to be able to function.

When working in remote setups, technicians are required to work in all kinds of weather and sometimes in uncomfortable locations. They must be able to set up and adjust their equipment on the spot to carry out their part of a broadcast.

Most radio and television stations operate 24 hours a day, 7 days a week. Shift work may be necessary, especially for new employees.

Constant close attention to detail and to making split-second decisions can cause tension. In emergency situations, especially in small stations, long hours and high pressures may result. When equipment fails, pressure to return it to service is great. Persons who enjoy meeting challenges will find satisfaction in coping with these emergencies.

On the positive side, technicians can take pride in their ability to master the complex, and sometimes hectic, operations necessary to maintain a radio or television broadcast. Their work also offers constantly varying subject matter and opportunities for meeting new challenges.

GOE: 05.03.05; SIC: 483; SOC: 393

◇ **RELATED ARTICLES**

Volume 1: Broadcasting; Electronics; Telecommunications
Volumes 2–4: Audio control technicians; Electronics technicians; Photographers and camera operators; Radio and television announcers and newscasters; Sound-recording technicians; Studio technicians; Video technicians

---

File clerks

Definition

File clerks review and classify letters, documents, articles, and other types of business information and then file this material so it can be retrieved quickly at a later time. File clerks may file the information by subject matter or by an alphabetical or numerical system. They usually file the material in a folder and put it in a filing cabinet or other appropriate location. File clerks retrieve this material as needed and then ensure that it is returned to its place after use.

History

When people in business make decisions, they want to be sure they are taking all the relevant information into account. For this and other reasons, swift and reliable access to letters, sales reports, newspaper articles, and other documents is very important. Over time, businesses and government agencies have established filing systems for these documents, and these systems are maintained by file clerks.

File clerks and other office workers have become increasingly important as computers, word processors, and other technological advances have increased both the volume of business information available and the speed in which administrative decisions are made. File clerks play a vital role in the efficient organization and rapid retrieval of information and thus are important components of a company's organizational structure. Today, businesses and government agencies depend on file clerks to file and sort business communications properly and cooperate with other office workers in maintaining a system that can distribute information accurately and swiftly.

Nature of the work

File clerks carefully arrange all office information so that it can be located and retrieved quickly. One of their primary job responsibilities is to examine incoming material, determine its important features, and file it according to a numerical system, by letter of the alphabet, or by subject matter. For example, if a company thinks a certain magazine article on advances in farming is important, the file clerk would probably place the article in the "F" file folder. This information would then be available to anyone interested in the subject at a later date.

File clerks must be sure that the information in the files is kept up-to-date. They add new information to existing files as it becomes available and periodically discard outdated material or transfer it to an inactive file. File clerks regularly check the files to make sure that all the material is in order. If a piece of information cannot be found, file clerks search for the missing record.

When someone requests information, file clerks locate the appropriate file or files. This is usually done by locating the item in an index and then finding it in the specified location. File clerks must make sure that all borrowed files are returned in a timely manner. In some cases, the file clerk will make copies of the file information so that the borrower can use the material at his or her own convenience.

Although a growing number of computerized filing and retrieval systems are being used, most file clerks still place paper files in file cabinets. Some clerks operate mechanized files that rotate to bring the needed records to them. Other storage methods include using microfilm, microfiche, or optical disks. In most cases, file clerks working with computerized or otherwise automated filing systems are responsible for coding and inputting the material into the system.

When they are not busy with filing responsibilities, file clerks may be asked to perform other clerical duties, such as operating photocopy machines or sorting mail. While performing their duties, file clerks and other office personnel may find opportunities to learn more about the business world in general, and this experience may open doors for advancement to higher positions in related fields.

Certain industries have specialized names for their file clerks. *Morgue librarians* maintain and update files of news articles, encyclopedia entries, or other information for reference use by news reporters or other staff when preparing material for publication. In the fabric industry, *record clerks* file sample pads of yarn and other textiles for color comparison and stock reference. *Record custodians* classify and store a bank's financial records and retrieve the information as requested by bank officials. *Tape librarians* classify and store magnetic tapes that have computer programs embedded in them.

File clerks must be well organized so that they can retrieve records quickly.

These magnetic tapes are used to compute company payrolls and other purposes and can be reused for different sets of computations each time the same information is needed.

Requirements

A high school diploma is usually sufficient for beginning file clerk positions, although typing skills and knowledge of office practices are also helpful. Prospective file clerks should have some mechanical ability for operating business machines, as well as mathematical skills and the ability to concentrate for long periods of time on repetitious tasks. Legible handwriting is an absolute necessity. To prepare for this field, high school students should take courses in English, mathematics, and as many business-related courses (such as typing and bookkeeping) as possible.

Community colleges and vocational schools often offer business education courses that provide training for file clerks. Skills in library and documentation cataloguing may be acquired through classroom or work-study opportunities.

File clerks should have an even temperament and the ability to work well with others. They should find systematic and orderly work appealing and like to work on detailed tasks. Other personal qualifications include dependability, trustworthiness, and a neat personal appearance.

Opportunities for experience and exploration

Interested students may get experience in this field by taking on clerical responsibilities for a school club, student government, or some other organization. In addition, some school work-study programs may be able to arrange part-time, on-the-job training with local businesses. It may also be possible to get a part-time or summer job in a business office by contacting companies on your own. Training in typing and office practices and procedures is available through evening courses offered by business schools.

Methods of entering

Those interested in securing an entry-level position should contact private companies or governmental agencies directly. Major employers of file clerks include banks, insurance agencies, real estate companies and other large businesses. Smaller companies often hire file clerks as well. Jobs may also be located through the classified advertising sections of newspapers.

Because each company has its own filing system, most companies provide entry-level file clerks with several weeks of on-the-job training, during which company policy and procedures are explained. File clerks work with experienced personnel during this period.

Advancement

With experience, file workers may advance to more complicated filing assignments and assume supervisory responsibilities over other clerks. Those who show the desire and aptitude may be trained as a secretary, receptionist, or office machine operator. To be promoted to a professional position such as accountant, it is

necessary to earn a college degree or have other specialized training.

The high turnover rate in the file clerk position increases the opportunities for promotion. The number and kind of opportunities, however, may depend on the place of employment and the ability, training, and experience of the employee.

Employment outlook

About 271,000 people hold jobs as file clerks. While file clerks are found in nearly every sector of the economy, about four out of five are employed in service companies; finance, insurance, and real estate firms; and government agencies. More than 10 percent are employed by temporary agencies and about one out of three works part time.

As more and more companies automate their record-keeping systems, employment opportunities for file clerks are expected to diminish. The spread of personal computers and other forms of automated filing and retrieval systems will eliminate many opportunities for file clerks. Nevertheless, numerous job opportunities will be available as people leave the field. Employment opportunities should be especially good for those who are skilled typists and are trained to operate computers and other types of automated equipment.

Opportunities should be good in the health, legal, and computer services industries and in the federal government. There should also be an increase in the number of opportunities for temporary or part-time work, especially during busy business periods.

Earnings

Beginning file clerks earn an average salary of between $9,000 and $13,000 a year, depending on the size and geographic location of the company and the skills of the worker. Experienced clerks should average around $14,700 per year; higher wages will be paid to those with the greatest number of job responsibilities. The highest wages are usually found with utility companies, while those file clerks in real estate, insurance, and construction can expect to receive somewhat lower salaries. The federal government generally offers salaries competitive with those in the private sector.

Conditions of work

Like most office workers, file clerks usually work a 37- to 40-hour week. Full-time workers can expect to receive paid vacations, health insurance, and other benefits.

The working environment in an office is usually well ventilated and well lighted, but the job itself can be fairly routine and repetitive. Clerks often interact with other office personnel and may work under close supervision. They may do a lot of bending and reaching, although heavy lifting is a rarity.

GOE: 07.05.03, 07.07.01; SIC: Any industry; SOC: 4696

◇ SOURCES OF ADDITIONAL INFORMATION

Career information is available from local business schools and from:

Office and Professional Employees International Union
265 West 14th Street, Suite 610
New York, NY 10011

◇ RELATED ARTICLES

Volume 1: See Table of Contents for areas of specific interest
Volumes 2–4: Archivists; Billing clerks; Bookkeeping and accounting clerks; Clerical supervisors and managers; Data base managers; Data entry clerks; Financial institution clerks and related workers; General office clerks; Indexers; Insurance policy processing occupations; Librarians; Medical record technicians; Postal clerks; Shipping and receiving clerks; Statistical clerks; Stock clerks

Film editors

Definition

Film editors edit motion-picture film, videotape for television, or soundtracks. Their work is essential in the television and motion-picture industries. They take the unedited draft of the film and use editing equipment to improve the draft until it is ready for viewing. It is the responsibility of the film editor to make the most of the material in order to create the most effective film possible.

History

The motion-picture and television industries have mushroomed in the last few years in the United States. As more people have had access to cable television, that industry has grown too. The effects of this growth have been very positive for film editors. More editors are now needed to work with film producers and direc-

tors, and more are needed in television work as well. Where one film editor might have been responsible for editing an entire motion picture 15 years ago, many are now needed, and their work has become more specialized. In many studios an editor is now responsible for work on only one type of editing, such as sound editing or visuals.

Early film editing was sometimes done by directors, studio technicians, or others for whom this was not their specialty. Now every film, including the most brief television advertisement, has a film editor who is responsible for the continuity and clarity of the film.

Nature of the work

Film editors work with producers and directors from the earliest phases of filming and production. In meetings with producers, the film ed-

While listening to a soundtrack, this film editor will break the film into smaller segments.

itor learns about the objectives of the film. If it is an advertisement, for example, the film editor must be familiar with the product it is aiming to sell. If it is a feature-length film, the editor must understand the story line. The producer may explain the larger scope of the project so that the film editor knows the best way to handle the work. In consultation with the director, the film editor may discuss the best way to accurately present the screenplay or script. He or she may discuss different settings, scenes, or camera angles even before filming begins. With this kind of preparation, once film reels begin coming to the film editor, the editor is ready to proceed. This way, the producer and director may continue their work while the editor is editing.

Feature-length films, of course, take much more time to prepare than television commercials. Therefore, some film editors may spend months on one project, while others may be working on several shorter films simultaneously.

Film editors assess all of the film segments as they arrive from the camera operators. The editors are usually the final decision-makers when it comes to choosing which segments will stay in the film, which segments will be cut, or which may need to be redone. The film editor looks at the quality of the film segment, its dramatic value, and its relationship to other segments. The editor then arranges the segments in an order that creates the most effective finished product. In commercials and other short films there are very strict time limitations. The film editor must time the segments to comply with these limitations.

Editing equipment varies from one studio to another. Some studios still have their film editors cutting and splicing the film with razor blades and special tape. Others have much of the work computerized. Most studios require their film editors to review assembled film segments on video monitors. At that point the director usually returns to go over the film and participate in decisions about timing, placement, or order, with the editor.

Some editors specialize in certain areas of television or film. *Sound editors* work on the soundtracks of television programs or motion pictures. They often keep libraries of sounds that they reuse for various projects. These include natural sounds such as thunder or raindrops, animal noises, motor sounds, or musical interludes. Some sound editors specialize in music and may have training in music theory or performance. Others work with sound effects. They may use unusual objects, machines, or computer-generated noisemakers to create a desired sound for a film.

Some film editors work primarily with news programs, documentaries, or with special features. They may develop ongoing working relationships with directors or producers who hire them from one project to another.

Requirements

Some studios require a bachelor's degree for those seeking positions as film editors. Degrees in liberal-arts fields are preferred, but courses in cinematography and audio-visual techniques help film editors get started in their work. Liberal-arts educations are available at four-year colleges, universities, and some two-year colleges.

Training as a film editor takes from four to 10 years. Many editors learn much of their work on the job. Some two-year colleges offer film-editing courses. Training in film editing is also available in the military, including the air force, marine corps, coast guard, and navy.

Opportunities for experience and exploration

Many high schools have film clubs and some have cable television stations affiliated with the school district. These are good places for young people to get experience. Often school-run channels allow students to do actual creation and editing of short programs.

The best way to prepare for a career as a film editor is to read widely. High school English classes, as well as later college literature classes, help future film editors learn to think critically. In reading literature, students get a sense of the different ways in which stories can be presented. Some high schools offer film classes. Community and two-year colleges often offer courses in film as literature. Some of these colleges also teach film editing. Universities with departments of broadcast journalism offer courses in film editing and also may have contacts at local television stations. They may offer seminars for students or present lectures by broadcasters that are open to the public.

Film editors should be familiar with all different kinds of films, including documentary and nonfictional films, educational films, and dramatic or fictional films. Each kind of film requires a different type of editing. Transitions in most fictional films, for example, are very smooth and subtle, while those in documentaries or news films are often sharp and fast-paced.

Large television stations and film companies occasionally have volunteers or student interns. It is possible to get a position helping in a film studio—even doing menial tasks—so that one may later get an apprenticeship with a film editor. Most people in the film industry start out dong minor tasks helping with production. They have a chance to see all of the different people necessary to put a film together. They may see the work of the film editor and what an essential role the editor plays in the process of creating a film. By working closely with an editor, young people learn television or film operations as well as specific film editing techniques.

Methods of entering

With a minimum of a high school diploma or a degree from a two-year college, a young person can apply for entry-level jobs in film or television studios. Most, however, will not consider people for film editor positions without a bachelor's degree. Larger studios may have apprenticeships for film editors. In the apprenticeship, an editor has the opportunity to see the work of the film editor up close. The film editor may eventually have the apprentice perform the manual editing, while the editor makes the decisions. After a few years the apprentice may be promoted to film editor, or may apply to other studios.

Some sound or sound-effects editors may wish to broaden their skills by working as general film editors. Some film editors may, on the other hand, choose to specialize in sound effects, music, or some other editorial area. Some film editors who work in television may move to motion pictures, or may move from working on commercials or television series to television movies.

Advancement

Once film editors have work in their field their advancement comes with experience and reputation. Some film editors develop good working relationships with directors or producers. The editors may be willing to leave the security of a studio job for the possibility of working one-on-one with the director or producer on a project. These opportunities often provide film editors with the autonomy they may not get in their regular jobs. Some are willing to take a pay cut to work on a project they feel is important.

Some film editors choose to stay at their studios and advance through seniority to editing positions with higher salaries. They may be able to negotiate better benefits packages or to choose the films they will work on. They may also choose which directors they wish to work with. In larger studios they may train and supervise staffs of newer editors.

Employment outlook

The outlook for film editors is good. Opportunities in cable television and in independent film studios are increasing. They are also forcing the studios to be more competitive to get the best film editors. Therefore, salaries may rise. More jobs should be opening in the field and film editors should be able to find positions despite the high level of competition.

Earnings

Film editors are not as highly paid as others in the film or television industries. They have less clout than directors or producers, although they have a bit more say in their films than other film technicians. In the 1990s the minimum weekly salary for a film editor is about $1,400. The minimum weekly salary for an assistant film editor is about $1,000, and the minimum for a sound-effects or music editor is about $960. A film or tape editor working in television broadcasting earns about $20,000 annually. Some rare well-known editors command higher salaries.

Conditions of work

Most of the work done by film editors is done in film studios with editing equipment. The studios are usually small and not particularly glamorous. Working hours vary widely depending on the film. During the filming of a commercial, for instance, film editors may be required to work overtime, at night, or on weekends to finish the project by a certain date. Many feature-length films are kept on tight production schedules that allow for steady work unless filming gets behind.

During filming, film editors may be asked to be on hand at the filming location. Locations may be outdoors or in other cities, and travel is occasionally required. More often, however, the film editor edits in the studio, and that is where the bulk of the editor' time is spent.

Disadvantages of the film editor's job involve the editor's low rank on the totem pole of film or television industry jobs. However, most editors feel that this is outweighed by the advantages. Editors can look at films on which they have worked and be proud of the role they had in creating them.

GOE: 01.01.01; SIC: 7929 ;SOC: 324

◇ **SOURCES OF ADDITIONAL INFORMATION**

American Cinema Editors
4416 Finley Avenue
Los Angeles, CA 90027

American Film Institute
John F. Kennedy Center for the Performing Arts
Washington, DC 20566

Association of Independent Video and Filmmakers
625 Broadway, 9th Floor
New York, NY 10012

◇ **RELATED ARTICLES**

Volume 1: Broadcasting; Motion Pictures
Volumes 2–4: Art directors; Book editors; Broadcast technicians; Cable television technicians; CAD/CAM technicians; Layout workers; Magazine editors; Motion picture cameramen; Motion picture directors; Motion picture producers; Radio and television program directors; Screenwriters; Sound mixers; Sound technicians; Sound-effects technicians; Sound-recording technicians; Studio technicians; Video technicians

Financial institution clerks and related workers

Definition

Financial institution clerks and related workers perform many tasks in banks and other savings institutions. Job duties usually vary with the size of the bank. In small banks, a clerk or related worker may perform a combination of tasks, while in larger banks an employee may be assigned to one specialized duty. All banking activities are concerned with the safekeeping, exchange, record keeping, and credit use of money.

History

The profession of banking is nearly as old as civilization itself. Early literature makes reference to "money-lenders" and "money-changers" as ancient writers and travellers describe how they bought money in other countries by trading coins from their own homelands.

The term "banking" is derived from the Italian *banco*, meaning bench. Since the times of the Roman Empire, Italy has been an important trading and shipping nation. In medieval times, bankers set up benches on the streets and from these conducted their business of trading currencies and accepting precious metals and jewels for safekeeping. They also lent money at interest to finance the new ventures of shipping merchants and other businesses. Italian cities eventually established permanent banks, and this practice gradually spread north throughout Europe. During the 17th century important banking developments took place in England, which by the time had become a major trading nation. In 1694, the Bank of England was founded in London.

In the United States in 1782, the Continental Congress chartered the Bank of North America, which was opened in Philadelphia. The first state bank was chartered in Boston in 1784 as the Bank of Massachusetts. Although the development of banking in the United States has experienced periods of slow growth and numerous failures throughout history, Congress and the federal government have done a great deal to make the nation's banking system safer and more effective.

Today, banking, like many other professions, has turned to the use of automation, mechanization, computers, telecommunications, and many modern methods of bookkeeping and record systems. For all the modern banking conveniences that Americans enjoy today, banks and savings institutions employ thousands of workers so that they can offer these services.

Nature of the work

In the back offices of banks and other institutions, financial institution clerks and related workers perform the work that keeps depositors' money safe, the bank's investments healthy, and government regulations satisfied. All such workers assist in processing the vast amounts of paper work that a bank generates. This paperwork may consist of deposit slips, checks, financial statements to customers, correspondence, record transactions, or reports for internal and external use. Depending on their job responsibilities, clerks may prepare, collect, send, index, or file these documents. In addition, they may talk with customers and other banks, take telephone calls, and perform other general office duties.

The range of tasks an employee performs depends on the size of the financial institution. Duties may be more generalized in smaller facilities and very specialized at larger institutions. The nature of the bank's business and the array of services it offers may also determine a clerk's duties. Services may differ somewhat in a commercial bank from those in a savings bank, trust company, credit union, or savings and loan. In the past banks generally lent money to businesses while savings and loans and credit unions lent to individuals, but these differences are slowly disappearing.

New accounts clerks and *loan interviewers* interview and compile information about customers who wish to open new savings or checking accounts or apply for loans. Workers called *account analysts* and *fee clerks* compute and supply data about the fees that banks charge for services.

Many banks offer trust services that manage investments for customers. *Trust clerks*

Much of the work performed by financial institution clerks involves organizing and filing bank slips. In this case, a woman is compiling canceled checks.

Collection clerks process checks, coupons, and drafts that customers present to the financial institution for special handling. *Commodity-loan clerks* keep track of commodities (usually farm products) used as collateral by the foreign departments of large banks.

Banks employ *bookkeepers* to keep track of countless types of financial and administrative information. *Bookkeeping clerks* file checks, alphabetize paper work to assist senior bookkeepers, and sort and list various other kinds of material.

Mortgage clerks type the legal papers necessary to transfer real estate titles, record the transactions, and maintain records of mortgage and tax payments. Many of these clerks work for savings and loan associations. Other clerks called *mortgage-loan-computation clerks* and *mortgage-processing clerks* keep track of how much people have paid and owe on their mortgages, or prepare paper work when customers apply for loans. *Loan closers* perform essential duties when developers apply for loans to finance new construction projects.

Proof machine operators handle a machine which, in one single operation, can sort checks and other papers, add their amounts, and record totals. *Transit clerks* sort and list checks and drafts on other banks and prepare them for mailing back to those banks. *Statement clerks* send customers their account statements listing the withdrawals and deposits they have made. *Bookkeeping machine operators* maintain records of the various deposits, checks, and other items that are credited to or charged against customer accounts. Often they cancel checks and file them, provide customers with information about account balances, and prepare customers' statements for mailing.

Messengers deliver checks, drafts, letters, and other business papers to other financial institutions, business firms, and local and federal government agencies. Messengers who work only within the bank are often known as pages. *Trust-mail clerks* keep track of mail in trust departments.

Other clerks—*collateral-and-safekeeping clerks, reserves clerks,* and *interest clerks,*—collect and record information about collateral, reserves, and interest rates and payments. *Letter-of-credit clerks* keep track of letters of credit for export and import purposes. *Wire-transfer clerks* operate machines that direct the transfer of funds from one account to another.

Many banks now use computers to perform the routine tasks that workers formerly did by hand. To operate these new machines, banks employ *computer operators, tabulating machine operators, microfilming machine operators,* and *electronic reader-sorter operators. Encoder operators* run

work in trust departments, where they compile, record, and disseminate information about estates, stock transfers, trust department savings accounts, and the transactions and values of trust accounts. *Trust-securities clerks* keep records of investments made on behalf of customers by the bank's trust officers.

Clerks involved with safeguarding money, securities, and other valuables include *securities vault supervisors, trust-vault clerks,* and *vault attendants.* Some clerks called *reconcilement clerks, clearing-house clerks,* and *routing clerks* process information and items received from other banks. *Foreign-exchange-position clerks* and *exchange clerks* deal with information about the monetary systems and economies of other countries, including data about the bank's foreign investments and the value of foreign currencies it holds.

Head stock-transfer clerks, bond clerks, advice clerks, margin clerks, trust-evaluation supervisors, securities clerks, brokerage clerks, coupon clerks, and *credit-card-control clerks* keep track of transactions and information about the bonds, securities, and credit cards in which a bank invests or deals. Employees called *currency sorters* and *coin-machine operators* sort and count currency using special machines. Other clerks include *insurance clerks, check-processing clerks* and *return-item clerks,* all of whom process checks. *Statement-request clerks* and *telephone-quotation clerks* provide information about the status of loan applications or stock prices.

machines that print information on checks and other papers in magnetic ink so that machines can read them. *Control clerks* keep track of all the data and paper work transacted through the electronic data-processing divisions.

Almost all businesses and industries use banking services of one form or another. People employed in banking are usually exposed to a great deal of knowledge of how the general world of business operates, and how the stock market operates and influences banking. Banks are usually pleasant, low-stress places to work and have very up-to-date equipment and business machines. People who work in banking are usually people of good character and reputation who enjoy detailed work.

Requirements

Most banks today prefer to hire individuals who have completed high school. Applicants who have taken courses in bookkeeping, shorthand, typing, business arithmetic, and business machines while in high school may have an advantage. Some banks are interested in hiring college graduates (or those who have completed at least two years of college training) who can eventually move into managerial positions. Exchange clerks may be expected to know foreign languages.

Because the work involves so many details, one of the prime requirements for all bank employees is accuracy. Even the slightest error can cause untold extra hours of work and inconvenience, or even monetary loss. A pleasing and congenial personality and the ability to get along well with fellow workers are also necessary in this employment. Often an employee will be required to work closely with other employees or with the public.

The physical requirements of the work are not very demanding. Applicants for jobs are expected to be neat, clean, and appropriately dressed for business.

Banks occasionally require lie detector tests of applicants, as well as fingerprint and background investigations if the job requires handling currency and finances. Those employees handling money may have to qualify for a personal bond. Some banks now require pre-employment drug testing, and random testing for drugs while under employment is becoming more acceptable.

Although integrity and honesty are important traits for an employee in any type of work, they are absolutely necessary for those persons employed in banks and other financial institutions where large sums of money are handled

every day. Workers must also exhibit sound judgment and intelligence in their job performance.

Opportunities for experience and exploration

Individuals interested in these positions may explore them further by visiting local financial institutions and talking with the directors of personnel or with people who work in these jobs. Sometimes banks offer part-time employment to young people who feel they have a definite interest in pursuing a career in banking or those with business and clerical skills. Other types of part-time employment where employees learn basic business skills may also be valuable training for those planning to enter these occupations.

Methods of entering

Private and state employment agencies frequently list available positions for financial institution clerks and related workers. Newspaper help wanted advertisements sometimes carry listings for such employees. Some large financial institutions visit schools and colleges to recruit qualified applicants to fill positions on their staff.

People who are interested in jobs as financial institution clerks should contact the director of personnel at a bank or other institution to see if any positions are available. If any jobs are open, the applicant may be asked to come in and fill out an application. It is very important, however, to arrange the appointment first by telephone or mail because drop-in visits are disruptive and never welcome.

Applicants who know someone who is willing to give them a personal introduction to the director of personnel or to the officers of a bank may find that this will help them secure employment. Personal and business references can be important to bank employers when they hire new personnel.

Many financial institution clerks begin their employment as trainees in certain types of work such as business machine operation or general or specialized clerical duties. Employees may start out as file clerks, transit clerks, or bookkeeping clerks, and in some cases as pages or messengers. In general, beginning jobs are determined by the size of the institution and the nature of its operations. In banking work, employees are sometimes trained in related job tasks so that they might be promoted later.

Advancement

Financial institution clerks who perform their jobs well may receive promotions to low-level supervisory positions or advance to positions as tellers or credit analysts. After proving themselves in these positions, they may be promoted to senior supervisory positions. Advancement to an officer position at a bank, however, is usually open only to those employees with college degrees.

Financial institution clerks may receive promotions as they gain job experience and pursue specialized educational training. The Bank Administration Institute, the American Institute of Banking, and the Institute of Financial Education both offer courses in various banking topics that can help employees show their initiative, learn new skills, and prepare for promotions.

In some cases, financial institution clerks may change jobs or move to larger or different types of banks. Increases in salary or job status may be gained in this way. Other factors that influence promotional opportunities are length of service, extent of educational or specialized training, and job performance.

Employment outlook

In the 1990s, about 41,000 statement clerks and 80,000 new-account clerks are employed nationwide. The U.S. Department of Labor predicts average growth for these positions through the year 2005, so thousands of job opportunities for bank clerks and related workers can be anticipated during the coming years. Many of these opportunities will result from the high turnover rate that exists for these occupations.

As urban areas continue to expand, many banks, trust companies, and savings and loan associations are opening branch operations to bring their services to new customers. This may increase the demand for clerks and related workers. This trend is being countered, however, by recent troubles in the financial business. Overexpansion by some banks and competition from non-bank financial services companies has led to many closings, mergers, and consolidations. This has made job opportunities harder to predict in some areas of the country.

It seems likely that the increasing use of computers and electronic data-processing methods will decrease the need for some employees such as check sorters, index filers, and bookkeeping machine operators. Financial institutions now face the problem of moving their displaced workers into other jobs through on-the-job training or educating employees in the operation of electronic data processing and computers.

Earnings

Bank clerical workers earn from $8,550 to $12,040 per year. Safe deposit clerks earn somewhat higher salaries, ranging from $9,960 to $12,700 per year. In general, salaries for all bank workers tend to be lower in smaller cities than in larger metropolitan areas.

Conditions of work

Most financial institution workers work a 40-hour week. Bank clerks and accounting department employees may have to work overtime at least once a week and often at the close of each month's banking operations to process important paperwork. Check processing workers who are employed in large financial institutions may work late evening or night shifts. Those employees engaged in computer operations may also work evening or night shifts because this equipment is usually run around the clock using two or three shifts of workers. Pay for overtime work is usually straight compensation.

Financial institution clerks and related workers may receive up to 12 paid holidays a year, depending on their locale. A two-week paid vacation is common after one year of service, and can increase to three weeks after 10 or 15 years of service. Fringe benefits usually include group life and health insurance, hospitalization, and jointly financed retirement plans.

Banks and other depository institutions are usually air-conditioned, pleasantly decorated, and comfortably furnished. Financial institutions have excellent alarm systems and many built-in features that offer protection to workers and facilities. The job duties are not strenuous and can often be adapted for disabled people. In many tasks, very little physical movement is required. The work performed is usually of a very repetitive nature and the duties are very similar from day to day. Most of the work is paperwork, computer entry, data processing, and other mechanical processes and does not frequently involve customer or client contact. Individuals must be able to work closely with each other, sometimes on joint tasks, as well as under supervision.

GOE: 07.02.01; SIC: 60; SOC: 471

Institute of Financial Education
111 East Wacker Drive
Chicago, IL 60601

Canadian Institute of Credit and Financial Management
#501, 5090 Explorer Drive
Mississauga ON L4W 3T9

◇ **SOURCES OF ADDITIONAL INFORMATION**

American Bankers Association
1120 Connecticut Avenue, NW
Washington, DC 20036

Bank Administration Institute
One North Franklin
Chicago, IL 60606

◇ **RELATED ARTICLES**

Volume 1: Accounting; Banking and Financial Services
Volumes 2–4: Accountants and auditors; Billing clerks; Bookkeeping and accounting clerks; Collection workers; Data entry clerks; Financial institution tellers; General office clerks; Insurance policy processing occupations; Postal clerks; Statistical clerks; Statisticians; Typists and word processors

Financial institution officers and managers

Definition

Financial institution officers and managers oversee the activities of banks and personal credit institutions such as credit unions and finance companies. These establishments serve business, government, and individuals. They lend money, keep savings, enable people and businesses to write checks for goods and services, rent safe-deposit boxes for storing valuables, manage trust funds, advise clients on investments and business affairs, issue credit cards and traveler's checks, and take payments for gas and electric bills.

History

The modern concept of bank notes, or currency, developed in the 17th century. Goldsmiths in London began to issue paper receipts for gold and other valuables that were deposited in their warehouses. The paper money we use today is a modern version of these 17th-century receipts.

The first bank in the United States opened during the term of George Washington. By the early 1900s, banks had become so numerous that federal control of banks was needed. The Federal Deposit System, as we know it today, is the result of the efforts to coordinate the activities of the many banks throughout the nation. As banks have grown in numbers, so have their services. They have even changed some of our ideas about money. For example, banks have simplified the problem of carrying around and exchanging large sums of money. Today we use checks. More than 90 percent of all business today is conducted by the use of checks. The number of banks and other financial institutions has grown extensively within the past 25 years, creating many positions for people to conduct their services.

Nature of the work

Financial institutions include commercial banks, which provide full banking service for business, government, and individuals; investment banks, which offer their clients financial

657

FINANCIAL INSTITUTION OFFICERS AND MANAGERS

The officers of financial institutions often gather to discuss analyses and reports executed by the younger members of the firm.

counseling and brokering; Federal Reserve Banks, whose customers are affiliated banks in their districts; or other organizations such as credit unions and finance companies.

These institutions employ many officers and managers whose duties vary depending on the type and size of the firm as well as on their own area of responsibility within it. All financial institutions operate under the direction of a president, who is guided by policies set by the board of directors. Vice presidents are department heads who are sometimes also responsible for certain key clients. Controllers handle bank funds, properties, and equipment. Large institutions may also have treasurers, loan officers, and officers in charge of departments such as trust, credit, and investment. A number of these positions are described in more detail below.

The *financial institution president* directs the overall activities of the bank or consumer credit organization, making sure that its objectives are achieved without violating government regulations or overlooking any legal requirements. The officers are responsible for earning as much of a return as possible on the institution's investments within the restrictions demanded by government and sound business practices. They help set policies pertaining to investments, loans, interest, and reserves. They coordinate the activities of the various divisions, and delegate authority to subordinate officers, who administer the operation of their own areas of responsibility. Financial institution presidents study financial reports and other data to keep up with changes in the economy that may affect their firm's policies.

The *vice president* coordinates many of the operations of the institution. This person is responsible for the activities of a regional bank office, branch bank, and often an administrative bank division or department. As desig-

nated by the board of directors, the vice president supervises programs such as installment loan, foreign trade, customer service, trust, and investment. They also prepare studies for management and planning, like workload and budget estimates and activity and analysis reports.

The *administrative secretary* usually writes directions for supervisory workers that outline and explain policy. The administrative secretary acts, in effect, as an intermediary between minor supervisory workers and the executive officers.

The *financial institution treasurer* directs the bank's monetary programs, transactions, and security measures in accordance with banking principles and legislation. Treasurers coordinate program activity and evaluate operating practices to ensure efficient operations. They oversee receipt, disbursement, and expenditure of money, and sign documents approving or affecting monetary transactions. They direct the safekeeping and control of assets and securities and maintain specified legal cash reserve. They review financial and operating statements and present reports and recommendations to bank officials or board committees.

Controllers authorize and control the use of funds kept by the treasurer. They also supervise the maintenance of accounts and records. They also analyze these records so that the directors or other bank officials will know how much the bank is spending for salaries, operating expenses, and other expenses. Controllers often formulate financial policies.

The *financial institution manager* establishes and maintains relationships with the community. This person's responsibility is to supervise accounting and reporting functions and establish operating policies and procedures. The manager directs several activities within the bank. The assets, records, collateral, and securities held by the financial institution are in the manager's custody. Managers approve credit and commercial, real estate, and consumer loans and direct personnel in trust activities.

The *loan officer* and the credit and collection manager both deal with customers who are seeking or have obtained loans or credit. The loan officer specializes in examining and evaluating applications for lines of credit, installment credit, or commercial, real estate, and consumer loans, and has the authority to approve them within a specified limit or recommend their approval to the loan committee. To determine the feasibility of granting a loan request, the officer analyzes the applicant's financial status, credit, and property evaluation. The job may also include handling foreclosure proceedings. Depending on training and experience, officers may analyze potential loan markets to develop prospects for loans. They negotiate the terms of transaction and draw up the requisite documents to buy and sell contracts, loans, or real estate. Credit and collection managers make up collection notices for customers who already have credit. When the bank has difficulty collecting accounts or receives a worthless check, credit and collection managers take steps to correct the situation. Managers must keep records of all credit and collection transactions.

Loan counselors study the records of the account when payments on a loan are overdue and contact the borrower to discuss payment of the loan. They may analyze the borrower's financial problems and make new arrangements for repayment of the loan. If a loan account is uncollectible, they prepare a report for the bank or thrift institution's files.

Credit card operations managers are responsible for the overall credit card policies and operations of a bank, commercial establishment, or credit card company. They establish procedures for verifying the information on application forms, determine applicants' creditworthiness, approve the issuance of credit cards, and set a credit limit on each account. These managers coordinate activities involved with reviewing unpaid balances, collecting delinquent accounts, investigating and preventing fraud, voiding lost or stolen credit cards, keeping records, and exchanging information with the company's branches and other credit card companies.

The *letter of credit negotiator* works with clients who hold letters of credit used in international banking. This person contacts foreign banks, suppliers, and other sources to obtain documents needed to authorize the requested loan, then checks the documents to see if they have been completed correctly so that the conditions set forth in the letter of credit meet with policy and code requirements. Before authorizing payment, the negotiator verifies the client's credit rating and may request increasing the collateral or reducing the amount of purchases, amending the contract accordingly. The letter of credit negotiator specifies the method of payment and informs the foreign bank when a loan has gone unpaid for a certain length of time.

The *trust officer* directs operations concerning the administration of private, corporate, and probate trusts. Officers examine or draft trust agreements to ensure compliance with legal requirements and terms creating trusts. They locate, inventory, and evaluate assets of probated accounts. They also direct realization of assets, liquidation of liabilities, payment of bills, preparation of federal and state tax returns on trust income, and collection of earn-

ings. They represent the institution in trust fund negotiations.

Reserve officers maintain the institution's reserve funds according to policy and as required by law. They regulate the flow of money through branches, correspondent banks, and the Federal Reserve Bank. They also consolidate financial statements calculate the legal reserve, and compile statistical and analytical reports of the reserves.

Foreign-exchange traders maintain the balance that the institution has on deposit in foreign banks to ensure its foreign exchange position and determine the prices at which that exchange will be purchased and sold. Their conclusions are based on an analysis of demand, supply, and the stability of the currency. They establish local rates of exchange based upon money market quotations or the customer's financial standing. They also buy and sell foreign exchange drafts and compute the proceeds.

The *securities trader* performs securities investment and counseling service for the bank and its customers. They study financial background and future trends and advise financial institution officers and customers regarding investments in stocks and bonds. They transmit buy-and-sell orders to a trading desk or broker as directed, and recommend purchase, retention, or sale of issues, then notify the customer or the bank of the execution of trading orders. They compute extensions, commissions, and other charges for billing customers and making payments for securities.

The *operations officer* is in charge of the internal operations in a department or branch office of a financial institution. This person is responsible for the smooth and efficient operation of a particular area. Duties include interviewing, hiring, and directing the training of employees, as well as supervising their activities, evaluating their performance, and making certain that they comply with established procedures. Operations officers audit accounts, records, and certifications and verify the count of incoming cash. They prepare reports on the activities of the department or branch, control the supply of money for its needs, and perform other managerial tasks of a general nature.

The *credit union manager* directs the operations of credit unions, which are chartered by the state or federal government to provide savings and loan services to their members. This manager reviews loan applications, arranges automatic payroll deductions for credit union members wishing to make regular savings deposits or loan payments, and assists in collecting delinquent accounts. Managers prepare financial statements, help the government audit credit union records, and supervise bookkeeping and clerical activities. Acting as management representative of the credit union, credit union managers have the power to sign legal documents and checks on behalf of the board of directors. They also oversee control of the credit union's assets and advise the board on how to invest its funds.

Requirements

People interested in becoming a financial institution officer should have a college education. Many bank officials have followed a liberal arts or general course of study; others have obtained a business administration background with a major in banking. The variety of services offered by bank and thrift institutions gives the student flexibility in choosing a major.

In some cases high school graduates who exhibit executive ability in clerical, supervisory, and administrative work are considered for officer positions as they occur. Many organizations have their own educational programs in which employees, on a voluntary basis, may participate. Most costs are usually borne by the bank.

In the banking business the ability to get along well with others is essential. Financial institution officers should show tact and should convey a feeling of understanding and confidence in their employees and customers. Honesty is perhaps the most important qualification in financial institution officers. They handle large sums of money. They have access to confidential financial information about the individuals and business concerns associated with their institutions. They, therefore, must have a high degree of personal integrity.

Opportunities for experience and exploration

Except for high school courses that are business oriented, the average high school student will find few opportunities for experience and exploration during the school year. Teachers may be able to arrange for a class tour through a financial institution so that some knowledge about banking services can be gained. The most valuable experience will be gained through a part-time or a summer job in banks or other institutions that sometimes hire qualified high school students.

Methods of entering

One way to enter banking as a regular employee is through part-time or summer employment. Anyone can apply for a position by writing to a financial institution officer in charge of personnel or by arranging for an interview appointment. Many institutions advertise in the classified section of local newspapers. The larger banks recruit on college campuses. An officer will visit a campus and conduct interviews at that time. Student placement offices can also arrange for interviews.

Advancement

There is no one method for advancement among financial institution officers. Advancement depends on the size of the institution, the services it offers, and qualifications of the employee. Usually, the smaller the employer the slower the advancements. Financial institutions often offer special training programs that take place at night, during the summer, and in some special instances, during scheduled working hours. People who take advantage of these opportunities usually find that advancement comes more quickly. The American Banking Institute, for example, offers training in every phase of banking through its own facilities or the facilities of the local universities and banking organizations. The length of this training may vary from six months to two years. Years of service and experience are required for a top-level financial institution officer to become acquainted with policy, operations, customers, and the community. Similarly, the National Institute of Credit offers training and instruction through its parent entity, the National Association of Credit Management.

Employment outlook

Approximately 200,000 officers and managers are employed in banks and other financial institutions in the 1990s. The number of job openings is expected to increase at a faster than average rate during the 1990s. New jobs will be created by a general expansion of financial services, and the more extensive use of electronic computer equipment will make financial managers more productive. The need for skilled professionals will increase primarily as a result of greater domestic and foreign competition, changing laws affecting taxes and other financial matters, and a growing emphasis on accurate reporting of financial data for both financial institutions and other corporations.

Competition for these jobs will be strong, however, for several reasons. Financial institution officers and managers are often promoted from within the ranks of the organization, and, once established in their jobs, they tend to stay for many years. Also, more qualified applicants are becoming available each year to fill the vacancies that do arise. Chances for employment will be best for people familiar with a range of financial services, such as banking, insurance, real estate, and securities, and for those experienced in computers and data processing systems.

Financial institution officers and managers enjoy job security even during economic downswings, which seem to have little immediate effect on banking activities.

Earnings

Those who enter banking in the next few years will find the earnings to be dependent on their experience, the size of the institution, and its location. In general, starting salaries in financial institutions are not usually the highest, although among larger financial institutions in big cities, starting salaries often compare favorably with salaries in large corporations. After 5 to 10 years' experience, the salaries of officers usually are slightly higher than those in large corporations for people of comparable experience.

In the 1990s, financial managers earn a median annual salary of $35,800. The lowest 10 percent, which included those in entry-level and trainee positions, are paid $18,300 or less, while the top 10 percent receive more than $68,000 a year. Group life insurance, paid vacations, profit sharing plans, and hospitalization and retirement plans are some of the benefits offered.

Conditions of work

Working conditions in financial institutions are very pleasant. They are usually clean, well maintained, well lighted, and often air-conditioned. They are generally located throughout cities for convenience of their customers and thus for employees also. For financial institution officers, hours may be somewhat irregular as many organizations have expanded their hours.

GOE: 11.05.02; SIC: 602, 603; SOC: 122

◇ SOURCES OF ADDITIONAL INFORMATION

American Bankers Association
1120 Connecticut Avenue, NW
Washington, DC 20036

American Financial Services Association
919 18th Street, NW
Washington, DC 20006

Federal Reserve System
Human Resources Management Division
Washington, DC 20551

Financial Women International
500 North Michigan Avenue, Suite 1400
Chicago, IL 60611

Institute of Financial Education
Financial Managers Society
111 East Wacker Drive
Chicago, IL 60601

National Association of Credit Management
8815 Centre Park Drive
Columbia, MD 21045

Canadian Institute of Credit and Financial Management
#501, 5090 Explorer Drive
Mississauga ON L4W 3T9

◇ RELATED ARTICLES

Volume 1: Banking and Financial Services
Volumes 2–4: Accountants and auditors; Business managers; Credit analysts, banking; Economists; Financial institution clerks and related workers; Financial institution tellers; Financial services brokers

Financial institution tellers

Definition

Tellers are employees of banks and other financial institutions who handle certain types of customer account transactions. At the teller window, they may receive and pay out money, record customer transactions, cash checks, sell traveler's checks, and perform other banking duties. Most people are familiar with commercial tellers who cash checks and handle deposits and withdrawals from customers. Many specialized tellers are employed, too, especially in large financial institutions.

History

Throughout the centuries various methods of banking have been used. Although history does not record with certainty when banking first started in the world, Babylonian records reflect that their people had a rather complex system of lending, borrowing, and depositing money even before 2500 B.C.

In ancient times men would sit at low benches or tables in public squares to transact financial business and exchange money with customers. In fact, the word "bank" comes from the Italian word *banco,* meaning bench. Today, the work of the teller is in essence quite similar to that performed in ancient times: they receive money for safekeeping and pay out money on checks and drafts. The teller remains the initial contact between bank and customer, working from behind a service counter even as bankers through history worked from behind their benches in the ancient public squares.

Nature of the work

Tellers may perform a variety of duties in their jobs, but all of these duties involve accepting and disbursing funds to customers and keeping careful records of these transactions. *Commercial* or *paying and receiving tellers* serve the public directly by accepting customers' deposits and providing them with receipts; paying out withdrawals and recording the transactions; cashing checks; exchanging money for customers to provide them with certain kinds of change or currency; and accepting savings account deposits. When cashing checks, tellers are responsi-

ble for checking the signatures to make sure they are valid, getting a reliable identification of the person cashing the check, and sometimes verifying that the account against which the check is drawn has enough money to cover the amount.

Tellers must be careful that deposit slips, deposit receipts, and the amount entered in passbooks are correctly recorded. They must be very cautious when counting amounts of money that they pay out or accept for deposit. Machines are often used to add and subtract, make change, print records and receipts for customers' records, and post transactions on ledgers. Almost all banks today are computerized. In some large institutions with many branches, the teller uses a computer linked to the records in the main office to conduct transactions and verify balances.

At the beginning of every day, tellers are given cash drawers from the vault, containing a certain amount of cash. During the day, they use this money to pay customers and also add deposited money to the cash drawer. After their shift, tellers must count the money in their cash drawers, add up the transactions they have conducted, and balance the day's accounts. If their calculations show that they may have made mistakes, they double check their math and their account sheets. A conscientious teller should be able to balance the day's accounts to the penny (or almost) every day.

Tellers may be responsible for sorting checks and deposit slips, counting and wrapping money by hand or machine, filing new-account cards, and removing closed-account cards from the files. They give customers written information about the types of services and accounts available at the bank and answer any questions. They are supervised by *head tellers* and *teller supervisors,* who train them, arrange their schedules, and monitor their records of the day's transactions, helping to reconcile any discrepancies in balancing.

In large financial institutions, tellers may be identified by the specialized types of transactions that they handle. *Note tellers* are responsible for receiving and issuing receipts or payments on promissory notes and recording these transactions correctly. *Discount tellers* are responsible for issuing and collecting customers' notes. *Foreign banknote tellers* work in the exchange department, where they buy and sell foreign currency. When customers need to trade their foreign currency for U.S. currency, these tellers determine the current value of the foreign currency in dollars, count out the bills requested by the customer, and make change. These tellers may also sell foreign currency and traveler's checks for people travelling out of the country. *Collection and exchange tellers* accept payments in forms other than cash—contracts, mortgages, and bonds, for example.

Tellers may be employed by financial institutions other than banks. These institutions might include savings and loan associations, personal finance companies, credit unions, government agencies, and large businesses operating credit offices. While the particular duties may differ among institutions, the responsibilities and need for accuracy are the same. Tellers make up the largest specialized occupational group among bank employees.

With the increasing use of automatic banking machines, bank tellers tend to perform complex tasks that the machine cannot handle.

Requirements

Most banks and financial institutions require that applicants have at least a high school education. Many bank employees today have college educations or have taken specialized training courses offered by the banking industry. Many individuals who have earned a college education work as tellers to gain experience in this aspect of banking, anticipating promotions to higher positions within the bank.

Training opportunities for this occupational group are numerous. Many business schools, junior colleges, and universities offer programs in business administration or special programs in banking. Many people apply for jobs in banking immediately after graduating from high school. They then continue to prepare for better jobs through their bank's specific training programs or by taking night courses offered by colleges or professional training associations.

The educational division of the American Banking Association—the American Institute of Banking—has a vast program of adult education in business fields and offers training courses in numerous parts of the country that enable people to earn standard or graduate certificates in bank training. Individuals may also enroll for correspondence study courses. Other educational institutions, such as the New York Institute of Finance and the Stonier Graduate School of Banking, offer opportunities for experienced bankers to study specialized areas of banking.

Desirable aptitudes for a bank teller are accuracy, speed, a good memory, the ability to work with figures, manual dexterity to handle money quickly, and neatness and orderliness.

An essential prerequisite for tellers is that their honesty be above reproach, reflecting absolute trustworthiness. The work of the teller involves handling large sums of money. Therefore, bank tellers must be able to meet the standards set up by bonding companies to be personally bonded as employees.

A prospective teller must be able to present a list of references that will attest to the person's good character and high standards of moral conduct. The teller must be able to work cooperatively with others and have a pleasant personality and friendly manner when working with the public. The nature of the teller's work and the bank's responsibility to its customers demand that all banking business be treated as confidential and not be discussed with anyone outside the workplace.

Tellers must always take the responsibilities of their work seriously. Carelessness is not tolerated in this occupation. A temperament for calmness, emotional stability, and patience for routine tasks are positive assets for the teller, who sometimes must work under pressure at busy periods.

Opportunities for experience and exploration

Individuals may explore their interest in this occupation in numerous ways. Summer or part-time work is frequently available, depending on the locality. Students can work in clerical jobs, as messengers, or in other duties to observe the work of the tellers. Interested people may also visit banks and other financial institutions to talk with the people employed there.

For those interested in working for a bank or financial institution, participating in school clubs and community activities such as Junior Achievement will give them experience in working with people, handling money, and functioning as part of a team. Employers view these types of activities favorably when they consider applicants for teller positions. Commercial courses in high school may also be helpful, such as business arithmetic, business law, typing, and business machines.

Methods of entering

Most tellers are promoted to these positions from beginning jobs as bookkeeping or other general clerks. The skills and aptitudes people show in these beginning jobs, in addition to seniority, usually determine who is promoted to a teller position. On the other hand, some applicants may be able to obtain beginning jobs as tellers, especially in banks in large cities that offer on-the-job training programs.

Job opportunities can be found by applying in person to the institution for which a person would like to work or which the person has heard is hiring. Openings can also be found through newspaper help wanted ads, private or state employment agencies, or school placement services.

Advancement

Many banks and financial institutions follow a "promote-from-within" policy. Promotions are usually given on the basis of past job performance considering the employee's seniority, ability, and general personal qualities. Tellers may be promoted to head teller or to other supervisory positions such as department head. Some head tellers may be transferred from the main branch bank to a smaller branch, and through experience and seniority be promoted to assistant branch manager or even branch manager.

Employees who have shown initiative in their job responsibilities, pursued additional formal education and job training, and shown their ability to assume leadership may in time be promoted to junior bank officer positions. These positions include such jobs as assistant cashier, assistant trust officer, or assistant departmental vice president. Such advancements reflect a recognition of the individual's potential for even greater future job responsibilities.

Advancement to the higher echelons of the bank usually require formal college degrees or advanced degrees.

Employment outlook

Of the more than 1.5 million people working in banks today, 517,000 are tellers. The employment outlook for tellers is predicted to be slower than average through the next decade. In recent years, overexpansion by banks and competition from companies that offer bank-like services have resulted in closings, mergers, and consolidations in the banking industry. Furthermore, the rate of employment for tellers is not expected to keep pace with overall employment growth in other banking occupations because of the increasing use of automatic teller machines and other technology that increases teller efficiency or removes the need for tellers altogether.

Most employment opportunities will arise from the need to replace those workers who have retired, moved into other job fields, or died. This occupation provides a relatively large number of job openings due to its large size and high turnover rate. Demand for part-time tellers, especially during peak periods, is expected to be particularly strong. The field of banking offers a greater degree of job stability than some other fields because it is less likely to be affected by dips in the general economy.

Earnings

Yearly salaries and hourly wages paid to tellers vary across the country and may depend on the bank's size and geographic location, and the employee's experience, responsibilities, formal education, specialized training, and ability. In the 1990s tellers earn an average of about $14,200 a year. The highest paid tellers earn about $21,500 a year, while those with fewer responsibilities in lower-paying areas of the country may earn as little as $10,000.

In most cases, fringe benefits for these workers are very good. Paid holidays may range from 5 to 12 days, depending on the bank's geographic location. Paid vacation periods vary, but many employees receive a two-week paid vacation after one year of service, three weeks after 10 to 15 years, and four weeks after 25 years. Group life, hospitalization, and surgical insurance plans are usually available, and employees frequently participate in shared employer–employee retirement plans. In some banks profit-sharing plans are open to employee enrollment.

Conditions of work

Most bank employees work a 40-hour week; however, in some areas of the Northeast the workweek may average 35 to 37 hours. Tellers may sometimes be required to work irregular hours or overtime. Many banks today stay open until 8:00 on Friday nights to accommodate workers who receive paychecks on that day but cannot get to the bank until after normal business hours. Part-time work for tellers is increasingly available.

Banks and financial institutions are usually pleasant and attractive places in which to work. Office equipment and furnishings are usually very modern, and efforts are made to create a relaxed but efficient work atmosphere. While tellers usually do not perform any physically strenuous work, they may have to stand at their stations for long periods of time. Dealing with customers may be tiring, especially during busy periods or when customers are difficult or demanding.

GOE: 07.02.02, 07.03.01; SIC: 60; SOC: 4364, 4791

Financial services brokers

Definition

Financial services brokers, sometimes called *registered representatives*, *account executives*, or *securities sales representatives*, work to represent both individuals and organizations who wish to invest in and sell stocks, bonds, or other financial products. Financial services brokers analyze companies offering stocks to see if investing in them is worth the risk. They also advise clients on proper investment strategies for their own investment goals.

Broker's floor representatives are responsible for buying and selling securities on the floor of a stock exchange. *Securities traders* also buy and sell securities but usually as a representative of a private firm. *Financial services sales agents* assist clients in developing sound financial plans for their businesses.

History

When a government wants to build a new sewer system or a company wants to build a new factory, it rarely has the money—or capital—required to do it readily at hand. It must first raise the capital from among people interested in investing. Historically, raising capital to finance the needs of government and commerce was—and often still is—an arduous task. European monarchies, particularly during the 18th and 19th centuries, relied heavily upon

FINANCIAL SERVICES BROKERS

The computer and the telephone are vital tools to the busy stockbroker.

bankers to meet the costs of the interminable wars that devastated the Continent and to help in the industrial expansion that was beginning. This system had been outgrown, however, and governments, banks, and industry turned to the burgeoning middle class for funds. They offered middle class investors securities and stocks—a fractional ownership in a company or enterprise—in exchange for their money. Soon, dealers emerged that linked government and industry with the smaller investor. In London, dealers in these shares first organized in 1773. In the United States the New York Stock Exchange was first incarnated in 1790 and was officially established in 1817.

The stock exchange functions as a marketplace where stockbrokers buy and sell securities for individuals or institutions. Stock prices can fluctuate from minute to minute, with the price of a stock at any given time determined by the demand for it. As a direct result of the disastrous stock market crash of 1929, the Federal Securities Act of 1934 set up a federal commission to control the handling of securities and made illegal any manipulation of prices on stock exchanges. Today the public is protected by regulations that set standards for stock listings, require public disclosure of the financial condition of companies offering stock, and prohibit stock manipulation and trading on inside information.

Nature of the work

The duties of financial services brokers are varied and interesting. They open accounts for new customers, after getting all the personal information that is required to allow the customers to trade securities through the brokerage firm. They execute buy and sell orders for customers by relaying the information to the floor of the stock exchange, where the order is actually put into effect. Depending on a customer's knowledge of the market, the broker may explain the meaning of stock market terms and trading practices; offer financial counseling; and devise an individual financial portfolio for the customer, including securities, life insurance, corporate and municipal bonds, mutual funds, certificates of deposit, annuities, and other investments. The broker must determine the customer's investment goals— whether the customer wants long-term, steady growth or a quick turnaround of stocks for short-term gains—and then offers advice on investments accordingly.

From the research department of the brokerage firm, brokers obtain information on the activities and projected growth of any company that is offering or will offer stock. The actual or perceived strength of a company is a major factor in a stock-purchase decision. Brokers must be prepared to answer all questions on the technical aspects of stock market operations and also be informed on current economic conditions. They are expected to have the market knowledge to anticipate certain trends and to counsel customers accordingly in terms of their particular stock holdings.

Some financial services brokers specialize in specific areas such as handling only institutional accounts, bond issues, or mutual funds. Whatever their areas of specialization, financial services brokers must keep abreast of all significant political and economic conditions, maintain very accurate records for all transactions, and continually solicit new customers.

Requirements

Because of the specialized knowledge necessary to perform this job properly, a college education is increasingly important, especially in the larger brokerage houses. To make intelligent and insightful judgments, a broker must be able to read and understand financial reports and evaluate statistics. For this reason, although employers seldom require specialized academic training, degrees in business administration, economics, and finance are helpful.

Because of the continual public contact, interested individuals should be well groomed, have a pleasant manner, and large reserves of tact and patience. Employers look for individuals with sales ability and a strong desire to succeed. Brokers also need self-confidence and the ability to handle frequent rejections. Above all, they must have a highly developed sense of responsibility, because in many instances they will be handling funds that represent a client's life savings.

Almost all states require financial services brokers to be licensed. Some states administer written examinations and some require brokers to post a personal bond.

Financial services brokers must also register as representatives of their firm in accordance with the regulations set forth by the securities exchange where they do business or the National Association of Securities Dealers. In addition, a beginning broker must pass an examination in order to qualify as a registered representative.

Opportunities for experience and exploration

Interested high school students should try to acquire selling experience of any kind because this provides a good background for the financial services broker. Occasionally, young people can find summer employment in a brokerage house. A visit to a local investment office, the New York Stock Exchange, or one of the commodities exchanges located in other major cities will provide a valuable opportunity to observe how transactions are handled and what is required of people in the field.

Methods of entering

Many brokerage firms hire beginning workers in financial services sales, provide them with a training program, and then retain them for a probationary period to determine their talents and ability to succeed in the business. The training period usually lasts about six months and includes both intensive classroom instruction and on-the-job training. Applications for these beginning jobs may be made directly to the personnel offices of the various securities firms.

The most important part of a broker's job is finding customers and building a client base. Beginning brokers spend much of their time searching for customers, relying heavily on telephone solicitation. They may also find customers through business and social contacts or be given a list of likely prospects from their brokerage firm.

Advancement

Depending upon their skills and ambitions, financial services brokers may advance rapidly in this field. Accomplished brokers may find that the size and number of accounts they service will increase to the point where they no longer need to solicit new customers. Others become branch managers, research analysts, or partners in their own firms.

Employment outlook

About 97,000 people are employed as financial services brokers in the 1990s. Job opportunities are expected to grow much faster than the average for all occupations through the next decade because of the continual interest in investing in the stock market. Economic growth, rising personal incomes, and greater inherited wealth are increasing the amount of funds available for investment. People with limited means can also invest small amounts of money through a variety of methods such as investment clubs, mutual funds, and monthly payment plans. In addition, the expansion of business activities together with new technological breakthroughs will create increased demand for the sale of stock to meet capital requirements for companies around the world.

Demand for financial services brokers fluctuates with the economy. Turnover among beginners is high because they have a hard time soliciting enough clients. Because of potentially high earnings, competition in this business is very intense.

Earnings

The salaries of trainees and beginners range from $1,200 to $1,500 per month, although larger firms pay a somewhat higher starting wage. Once the financial services broker has acquired a sufficient number of accounts, he or she works solely on a commission basis, with fees resulting from the size and type of security bought or sold. Some firms pay annual bonuses to their brokers when business warrants it. Since earnings can fluctuate greatly depending on the condition of the market, some financial services brokers may find it necessary to supplement their income through other means during times of slow market activity.

According to the Securities Industry Association, average annual earnings for beginning financial services brokers are about $28,000.

The median earnings are about $36,800 a year, with the middle 50 percent earning between $25,500 and $53,200.

Experienced financial services brokers dealing with individual investors make an average of about $76,000 annually. Those who handle institutional accounts make an average of about $187,000 a year.

Conditions of work

Financial services brokers have offices that are generally clean and well lighted. The work week is somewhat more flexible than in other fields, with brokers working overtime dealing with paper work during busy periods. They may work comparably fewer hours during dull trading periods. It is sedentary work, requiring little physical effort.

The atmosphere of a brokerage firm is frequently highly charged, and the peaks and drops of market activity can produce a great deal of tension. Watching fortunes being made is exciting, but the reverse occurs frequently, too, and it requires much responsibility and maturity to weather the setbacks that one inevitably encounters. It is, however, one of the more interesting, challenging, and rewarding fields in which to work.

GOE: 11.06.03; SIC: 6211; SOC: 4124

◇ **SOURCES OF ADDITIONAL INFORMATION**

National Association of Securities Dealers
1735 K Street, NW
Washington, DC 20006

New York Stock Exchange
11 Wall Street
New York, NY 10005

American Stock Exchange
86 Trinity Place
New York, NY 10006

◇ **RELATED ARTICLES**

Volume 1: Banking and Financial Services; Personal and Consulting Services; Sales
Volumes 2–4: Credit analysts, banking; Economists; Financial institution clerks and related workers; Financial institution officers and managers; Insurance agents and brokers, life; Insurance agents and brokers, property and casualty; Real estate agents and brokers; Service sales representative

Fire fighters

Definition

Fire fighters are responsible for protecting people's lives and property from the hazards of fire. They provide this protection by fighting fires to prevent property damage, by rescuing people trapped or injured by fires, and through inspections and safety education to prevent fires.

Fire fighters also assist in other types of emergencies and disasters in community life. Although fire fighters in many rural areas serve on a volunteer basis, this article is mainly concerned with describing full-time career fire fighters.

History

Civilization would not be possible without fire, but this essential tool can often turn destructive and deadly. For centuries people have fought to protect their lives and property from fire. In biblical times, people would group themselves into brigades to form firefighting lines. Even in early colonial days in America, settlers used the bucket brigade to pass water buckets from person to person in combating fires.

Many U.S. museums today house some of the old-time firefighting equipment that was invented in this country, such as hand-pulled vehicles with water tanks that could be pumped to direct a stream of water through a hose onto a fire. In those days, the tanks were still filled and refilled by bucket brigades. Many of these vehicles were themselves destroyed by fire, since the hand-pumped force of the water was weak, the hoses were short and stiff, and the vehicles, of necessity, had to be drawn close to the fires.

As automobiles, trucks, and industrial machinery were invented and improved, new and better firefighting equipment also appeared. Other scientific advancements have also made contributions, such as the invention of the fire extinguisher. Today, huge fire trucks roll with great speed and blasting sirens, carrying terrifically powerful mechanized pumps, scientifically designed rescue equipment, and workers who are well trained in protecting the public from the many perils of fire.

Nature of the work

The range of duties of career fire fighters varies with the size of the fire department and the population of the city in which they are employed. However, each fire fighter's individual responsibilities are well defined and clear-cut. In every fire department there are divisions of labor among fire fighters. For example, when their department goes into action, fire fighters know whether they are to rescue people caught in fires; raise ladders; connect hoses to water hydrants; or attempt to break down doors, windows, or walls with fire axes so that other fire fighters can enter the area with water hoses. Fire fighters are often known by the job duties they perform. They may be referred to as hose handlers, ladder handlers, truck drivers, engineers, inspectors, or tiller handlers, who steer the rear wheels on very long fire trucks that carry aerial ladders.

Fire fighters may fight a fire in a massive building giving off intense heat, or they may be called to extinguish nothing more than a small brush fire or a blazing garbage can. Fire fighters on duty at fire stations must be prepared and able to go on alarm call at any moment. Time wasted may result in more damage or even loss of life. Fire fighters wear protective suits in some situations to prevent their hands and bodies from being burned. At other times, instead of suits, they may wear protective gloves, helmets, boots, coats, and self-contained breathing apparatuses. Because of the mass confusion that occurs at the scene of the fire and the dangerous nature of the work, the fire fighters are well organized into details and units. They work under the supervision of com-

Fire fighters aim high-pressure water hoses on a flaming warehouse. It takes two strong people to control the hose.

manding officers, such as *fire captains, battalion chiefs*, or the *fire chief*. These officers may reassign the fire fighters' duties at any time, depending on the needs of a particular situation.

Once fire fighters have extinguished a fire, they often remain at the site for a certain length of time to make sure that the fire is completely out. *Fire investigators* or *fire marshals* may examine the causes of the fire, especially if it resulted in injury or death or may have been set intentionally. These officials may determine the cause and origin of the fire, testify in court, or arrest suspected arsonists.

Sometimes fire fighters answer calls requesting emergency medical care, help in giving artificial respiration to drowning victims, or emergency aid for heart attack victims on public streets. They may also administer emergency medical care in other types of situations.

Some fire fighters are assigned as *fire inspectors*. Their work is to prevent fires. They inspect buildings for trash, chemicals, and other materials that could easily ignite; for poor, worn-out, or exposed wiring; for inadequate alarm systems, blocked hallways, or impassable exits;

and for other conditions that pose fire hazards. These conditions are usually reported to the owners of the property for correction; if not corrected, the owners could be fined and held criminally liable if any fires occur. Fire inspectors also check to see that public buildings are operated in accordance with fire codes and city ordinances and that the building management complies with safety regulations and fire precautions. Often fire fighters are called on to give speeches on fire prevention before school and civic groups. A *fire prevention bureau captain* is sometimes in charge of these and other fire-prevention efforts.

While fire fighters are on station duty and between alarm calls, they perform various duties on a regular basis. They must keep all firefighting equipment in first-class condition for immediate use. This includes polishing and lubricating mechanical equipment, keeping water hoses dry and stretched into shape, and keeping their own personal protective gear in good repair. They hold practice drills for timing and procedure, verify and record fire alarms, and stand watch at the fire alarm instrument stations.

Many fire fighters study while on duty to improve their skills and knowledge of firefighting and emergency medical techniques. They also prepare themselves for examinations given regularly that may determine to some extent their opportunities for promotion. They are often required to participate in training programs to hone their skills and learn new techniques.

Since many fire fighters must live at the fire station for duty periods of 24 hours at a time, housekeeping duties and cleaning chores are performed by the on-duty fire fighters on a rotation basis. In some small towns, fire fighters are only employed on a part-time basis. They are on alarm call from their homes, except perhaps for practice drills. Usually in such situations, only a fire chief and assistant live at the station and are employed full time.

Fire fighters work in other settings as well. Many industrial plants employ *fire marshals* who are in charge of fire-prevention and firefighting efforts and personnel. At airports, potential or actual airplane crashes bring out crash, fire, and *rescue workers* who prevent or put out fires and save passengers and crew members.

The job of fire fighters has become more complicated in recent years due to the use of increasingly sophisticated equipment. In addition, many fire fighters have assumed additional responsibilities—for example, working with ambulance services that provide emergency medical treatment, assisting in the recovery from natural disasters such as earthquakes and tornadoes, and getting involved with the control and cleanup of oil spills and other hazardous chemical incidents. The work of fire fighters is very dangerous. The nature of the work demands training, practice, courage, and teamwork. However, fire fighting is more than a physical activity that requires strength and alertness. It is also a science that demands continual study and learning.

Requirements

Most job opportunities open to fire fighters today require applicants to have a high school education, although this prerequisite is sometimes waived in smaller communities. In most cases, applicants are required to pass written intelligence tests. Some municipalities may require a civil service examination. Formal education is an asset to potential fire fighters because part of their training involves a continuous education program, and a person's educational progress may affect future opportunities for advancement.

Many junior and community colleges offer two-year fire technology programs. Courses involve the study of physics and hydraulics as they apply to pump and nozzle pressures. Fundamentals of chemistry are taught to provide an understanding of chemical methods of extinguishing fires. Skill in communications—both written and spoken—is also emphasized.

Very rigid physical examinations are usually required for the job of fire fighter. Applicants must also pass physical performance tests, which may include running, climbing, and jumping. These examinations are clearly defined by local civil service regulations.

In most cases, fire fighters must be at least 21 but not more than 31 years of age. Candidates must also meet height and weight requirements. Applicants are required to have good vision (20/20 vision is required in some departments), no physical impairments that could keep them from doing their jobs, and great physical stamina. Most fire fighters join the International Association of Fire Fighters (AFL-CIO) when they are hired.

Usually the individuals who score the highest on these tests have the best chances of getting jobs as fire fighters. Those who gained firefighting experience in the military or who have served as volunteer community fire fighters may receive preferential consideration on their job applications.

Beginning fire fighters may receive several weeks of intensive training, either as on-the-job training or through formal fire department training schools. In these training periods, they are taught the fundamentals of city laws and ordinances, fire prevention, ventilation, first aid, the use and care of equipment, and general job duties. After this period, the fire fighter usually starts out on the job as a ladder handler or hose handler and is given additional responsibilities with training and experience.

A mechanical aptitude is an asset to a person in this career. Also important are a congenial temperament and the ability to adapt to uncertain situations that call for teamwork. Fire fighters must be willing to follow the orders of their superiors. Fire fighters need sound judgment, mental alertness, and the ability to reason and think logically in situations demanding courage and bravery.

Opportunities for experience and exploration

Individuals interested in becoming fire fighters may explore the occupation by talking with local people who are employed as fire fighters. They may also be able to get permission to sit in on some of the formal training classes for fire fighters offered by city fire departments. In some cases, depending on the size and regulations of the town or city department, young people may be able to gain experience by working as volunteer fire fighters.

Courses in lifesaving and first aid offer students experience in these aspects of the fire fighter's job. Students can explore these areas through community training courses and the training offered by the Boy Scouts or the American Red Cross. Those interested individuals who are serving in the military may request training and assignment to firefighting units to gain experience.

Methods of entering

Applicants may enter this occupation by applying to take the local civil service examinations. This usually requires passing the physical health, physical performance, and written general intelligence examinations.

Applicants who successfully pass all of the required tests and receive a job appointment may serve a probationary period during which they receive intensive training. After the completion of this training, they may be assigned to a fire department or engine company for spe-

cific duties. The probationary period may extend beyond the basic training period in some situations.

In some small towns and communities, applicants may enter this occupation through on-the-job training as volunteer fire fighters or by applying directly to the local government for the position.

Advancement

Fire fighters are generally promoted from within the department, first to the position of "fire fighter, first grade." After they demonstrate successful job performance and gain experience, fire fighters may be promoted to lieutenants, captains, deputies, battalion chiefs, assistant chiefs, and finally fire chief. Fire fighters may sometimes work three to five years or more to receive a promotion to lieutenant. Promotions usually depend upon the fire fighter's position rating, which is determined by scores made on the periodic written examinations, seniority, and job performance.

Employment outlook

More than 280,000 fire fighters are currently employed, mostly by municipal fire departments. The outlook for job opportunities as fire fighters through the 1990s is relatively good, with several thousand openings anticipated yearly. The majority of job opportunities are likely to occur to replace those fire fighters who have died, retired, or resigned from the occupation. A larger number of replacements is required in this occupation than in some others because most fire fighters have the opportunity to retire at an early age.

Most new jobs will be created as small communities grow and augment their volunteer staffs with career fire fighters. Little growth is expected in large, urban fire departments. A small number of local governments are expected to contract for firefighting services with private companies. In some fire departments, the hours of each work shift have been shortened, and two persons may be employed to cover a shift normally worked by one person.

Competition for firefighting jobs is keen in most cities. This occupation attracts many people because a high school education is usually sufficient, earnings are relatively high, and a pension is guaranteed upon retirement. In addition, the work is frequently exciting and challenging and affords an opportunity to perform a valuable public service. The number of qualified applicants in most areas generally exceeds the number of job openings, even though the written examination and physical requirements eliminate many applicants. However, layoffs of fire fighters are uncommon. Fire protection is an essential service, and citizens are likely to exert considerable pressure on city officials to maintain or expand their level of fire-protection coverage. Even when budget cuts do occur, local fire departments usually cut expenses by postponing equipment purchases rather than laying off staff.

Earnings

Average beginning salaries for full-time fire fighters are about $20,000 a year. Experienced fire fighters earn an average of about $25,000 a year, but their earnings vary considerably depending on city size and region of the country. Average annual earnings range from about $23,000 in the smaller cities to $31,400 in the largest cities, and from $21,500 in the South to $29,300 in the West. Fire lieutenants, captains, and fire chiefs earn considerably more.

Volunteer fire fighters are not paid, but they earn the satisfaction of serving their communities. Experience as a volunteer fire fighter is also valuable to a person applying to a city department.

Conditions of work

The work of the fire fighter can often be exciting; the job, however, is one of grave responsibilities, and life or death often hangs in the balance. The working conditions are frequently dangerous and involve risking one's life in many situations. Floors, walls, or even entire buildings can cave in on fire fighters as they work to save lives and property in raging fires. Exposure to smoke, fumes, chemicals, and gases can end a fire fighter's life or cause permanent injury.

In many fire departments, fire fighters may be on duty and live at fire stations for long periods of time. They may· work 24-hour shifts and then have an equal amount of time off; they periodically receive 72 hours off after a certain number of days on duty. In large cities and metropolitan areas, fire fighters usually work shorter hours. Shifts may vary between 8 and 14 hours, depending on whether they are day or night shifts and the shift rotation. Work weeks may range from 40 to almost 96 hours,

though they usually average between 50 and 60 hours. While on duty, fire fighters generally have some time to follow leisure interests if such interests do not interfere with their alertness to the call of duty.

This occupation requires a great deal of physical strength and stamina, so fire fighters must work to keep themselves physically fit and in condition. They must be mentally alert at all times. Fire fighters may be called into action at any time of the day or night and be required to work in all types of weather conditions, sometimes for long hours. Fire fighters must do their work in highly organized team efforts to be effective, since a great deal of excitement and public confusion is usually present at the site of a fire.

Fringe benefits for these employees usually include free protective firefighting clothing or a salary allowance to cover the cost of the clothing. They also receive compensatory time off or overtime pay (usually straight pay or time-and-a-half) for additional hours worked beyond the regular work schedule. Fire fighters enjoy liberal pension plans that provide for disability benefits and early retirement options; paid vacations; paid sick leave; and in some cases, paid holidays or compensatory time off for holidays worked.

GOE: 04.02.04; SIC: 9224; SOC: 5123

◇ SOURCES OF ADDITIONAL INFORMATION

International Association of Fire Chiefs
1329 18th Street, NW
Washington, DC 20036

International Association of Fire Fighters
1750 New York Avenue, NW
Washington, DC 20006

National Fire Protection Association
Batterymarch Park
Quincy, MA 02269

◇ RELATED ARTICLES

Fire safety technicians

Definition

The work of *fire safety technicians* emphasizes the prevention of fires. Typical services they perform include conducting safety inspections and planning fire protection systems. In the course of their job, fire safety technicians recognize fire hazards, apply technical knowledge, and perform services to control and prevent fires.

History

Fires in homes and at workplaces are the greatest destroyers of human life and property. Every year thousands of people in the United States die due to fires. Property destroyed by fire costs billions of dollars each year. In some states, grass or brush fires periodically rage uncontrolled and advance at the speed of the wind; buildings are destroyed and livestock is lost. Forest fires consume millions of feet of lumber every year. Some fires increase the problems of wildlife conservation and flood control, requiring that considerable sums be spent on reforestation programs.

In the early days of the United States, fire protection was usually left to a few volunteers in a community. This group formed a fire brigade and had simple firefighting devices. Later, fire departments were established and firefighting equipment became more sophisticated. Even so, fire protection was still mostly left to a small group. As cities grew and large industrial plants were built, it became apparent that fire prevention was possibly even more important than firefighting skills and techniques.

Today, business and industrial firms realize that fire protection is one of the most important considerations in the construction and operation of their plants. Fire insurance rates are determined by fire probability factors, such as the type of construction, ease of transporting personnel, and the quality and quantity of fire protection equipment available. Managers realize that payments from fire insurance claims will not cover the total loss caused by fire. Lost production or sales during a shutdown can cause serious financial hardship.

In addition, all property owners demand adequate protection for their homes and property; employees expect their employers to have warning and fire extinguishing devices. The public expects fire departments to be well staffed with competent specialists and fire fighters who can minimize property damage and save lives. Their jobs involve: rescuing people from fire, giving safety education courses, and conducting inspections, which may include a thorough examination of exits, corridors, and stairways designed to carry traffic in an emergency.

The need for carefully planned, well-organized fire protection has created a demand for highly trained personnel. Specialists are needed who are skilled in the newest methods of fire prevention and firefighting. Such specialists are also familiar with new synthetic materials used in building construction, decorative drapes, floor coverings, furnishings, and even clothing. These materials have made fire protection more complicated because of the dangerously toxic fumes they produce when burned.

Because of all of these factors, an increasing number of well-trained fire safety technicians are being hired by business, industry, and other employers to prevent loss of life and property from fires while people are on the job, in school, in recreational or entertainment places, or traveling.

Nature of the work

Fire safety technicians are employed by local fire departments, fire insurance companies, industrial organizations, government agencies, and businesses dealing with fire protection equipment and consulting services.

The range of duties performed by fire fighters varies with the size of the city's fire department and the general population. Within the fire department, however, each worker's responsibilities are clearly defined. For example, when their department goes into action, fire fighters each know their exact duties, which may be to: rescue people caught in fires; raise ladders; connect hoses to hydrants; or break down doors, windows, or walls with fire axes where necessary.

Between alarm calls, fire fighters are on station duty, where they perform varied but regular duties. They must: keep all firefighting equipment in top condition; hold practice drills for timing and procedure; verify and record fire

FIRE SAFETY TECHNICIANS

A fire safety technician inspects an automatics fire and explosion system that detects fires and suppresses them. Such equipment must be tested periodically.

alarms; and stand watch at fire alarm instrument stations.

Workers in fire departments are mostly highly skilled workers. In the 1990s there were more than 280,000 fire department workers. However, only a small percentage of these were technically prepared inspectors, supervisors, or technical workers.

In large public fire departments, experience gained on the job plus further study can lead to good technician-level jobs in inspection, public information services, or supervision.

Fire science specialists employed by insurance companies make recommendations for fire protection and safety measures in specific buildings. As part of their duties they help set insurance rates, examine water supply and sprinkler facilities, and make suggestions to correct hazardous conditions. They may be part of an arson investigation squad, or work with adjusters to determine the amount of personal injury or property loss caused by fire.

In industry, fire safety technicians are often part of an industrial safety team. They inspect areas for possible fire hazards and formulate company procedures in case of fire. They make periodic inspections of firefighting equipment such as extinguishers, hoses and hydrants, fire doors, automatic alarms, and sprinkler systems. An important part of their duties is to hold fire prevention seminars to keep department heads and key workers aware and alert to potential fire hazards in their particular areas. Technicians also teach these employees what to do in case of fire or other emergencies.

Because of the large number of people occupying their facilities, many restaurants, large hotels, and entertainment or recreational centers employ fire safety technicians. There is a great hazard of fire from food cooking in kitchens, lint in laundries, and sparks that fall on draperies and bedding. The possible loss of life from fire makes it necessary to have the best possible fire protection program.

Many government agencies employ fire safety technicians. They are largely responsible for inspecting government buildings, property and storage, or handling systems for reducing fire hazards. They arrange for installation of adequate alarm systems and fire protection devices. They may be required to organize a firefighting unit in a government agency or assist with designing sprinkler systems in buildings.

Many technicians are employed by companies that manufacture fire protection devices and alarm systems. Their training enables them to explain technical functions to customers and to give advice on installation and use. They also help to place smoke detectors and other fire prevention or extinguishing devices in the correct locations to give the greatest protection from fire.

Public education is also an important area of activity for fire control and safety technicians. By working with the public through schools, businesses, and service clubs and organizations, they can expand the level of understanding about the dangers of fire and teach people about methods of fire protection and fire prevention.

Newly hired technicians generally receive on-the-job orientation before they are given full responsibility in an entry-level position. Examples of entry-level positions are described in the following paragraphs.

Fire insurance inspectors inspect buildings and offices and make recommendations for fire protection and general safety conditions.

Fire insurance underwriters help set rates to conform with company policies and building codes.

Fire insurance adjusters determine losses due to fire and compute rates for adjustment and settling claims.

Fire protection engineering technicians draft plans for the installation of fire protection systems for buildings and structures. Using their knowledge of drafting and fire protection codes, they analyze architectural blueprints and specifications to determine which type and size of fire-protection system is required to meet fire protection codes, and then estimate its cost. During building construction, they work with the superintendent to ensure proper installation of the system. They may specialize in one kind of fire protection system, such as foam, water, dry chemicals, or gas. After a fire they may inspect fire-damaged buildings to check for malfunctioning systems.

Fire inspectors check firefighting equipment and report any potential fire hazards. They recommend changes in equipment, practice, materials, or methods to reduce fire hazards.

Plant protection inspectors inspect industrial plants for fire hazards, report findings, and recommend action. *Fire alarm superintendents* inspect alarm systems in government buildings and institutions.

Fire service field instructors hold training sessions throughout a state to keep fire fighters up to date on firefighting methods and techniques. They may also inspect small fire departments and report on personnel and equipment.

Requirements

The educational requirements for becoming a fire safety technician are similar to those for industrial engineering technicians. Both are scientific technicians, and need to learn the science and mathematics fundamentals that support their field. For example, they need to master the chemistry and related science of how things burn, and what makes some things more likely to catch fire and generate fumes, heat, and smoke.

These technicians must also learn about materials, combustion, structures, and devices and equipment that prevent or extinguish fires. They must be able to read and write with ease and to communicate well in order to study technical information and give good written or oral reports.

Technicians do not have to qualify in all areas to enter fire departments because an increasing number of these technicians are being employed by industries. Those who seek technician jobs in fire departments, however, usually must meet rigorous physical requirements. They frequently start as fire fighters and are promoted to such positions as supervisors or fire inspectors.

High school students who plan to attend a two-year, post-secondary program in fire technology should study the physical sciences. They should take either physics or chemistry courses that include laboratory work. Fire science demands some knowledge of hydraulics, physics, and chemistry. For example, laying out sprinkler systems requires skills that are introduced in high school mechanical drawing courses. Algebra and geometry are also recommended, as well as English and writing courses.

Two-year, post-secondary fire technology programs are now available at more than 100 technical institutes and community colleges. These programs provide an in-depth education in the fire science specialization for people seeking to work for industries, institutions, or government as fire safety technicians. These programs are also available to members of fire departments or related fire science specialists.

Courses in these programs include physics and hydraulics as they apply to pump and nozzle pressures. Fundamentals of chemistry are taught to help students understand chemical methods of extinguishing fires and the chemistry of materials and combustion. Communications skills are also emphasized.

Typical courses in the first year of a two-year program include firefighting tactics and strategy, fire protection equipment and alarm systems, fundamentals of fire suppression, introductory fire technology, chemistry (especially combustion and chemistry of materials), college mathematics, and communications skills.

Second-year courses may include building construction for fire protection, hazardous materials, fire administration, industrial fire protection, applied physics, introduction to fire prevention, and applied economics.

Like most professional workers in high-technology careers, fire safety technicians must continue to study during their careers in order to keep up with new developments in their field. Improved fire detection and prevention instruments, equipment, and methods for making materials fireproof or fire-suppressing are being developed all the time.

Those who wish to work in fire science technology in fire departments may train as technicians and apply for specialist jobs in large fire departments. Others may choose to enter the fire department as untrained fire fighters. For the latter group, very rigid physical examinations are usually required. Fire fighters must keep themselves physically fit and conditioned since they may be required to do hard work in all types of weather and sometimes for long hours.

Fire fighters must be able to follow orders and to accept the discipline that is necessary for effective teamwork. While on active call, fire fighters usually work under the close supervision of commanding officers such as battalion chiefs or assistant fire chiefs. Their work requires highly organized team efforts to be effective, since there is usually a great deal of excitement and confusion at fires.

FIRE SAFETY TECHNICIANS

For fire safety technicians in industry or government, no licenses are usually required. Good records of study in educational programs and an appropriate two-year degree or certificate are given special consideration by most employers. Becoming a member of the Society of Fire Protection Engineers is a valuable mark of achievement of which employers take note.

For those who want to enter fire departments as fire fighters and work toward technician-level tasks, civil service examinations are required in most cases.

Fire fighters are a highly organized occupational group; many fire fighters belong to the International Association of Fire Fighters.

Special requirements

Because of the physical demands of the profession, physical performance tests are required, and may include running, climbing, and jumping. These examinations are clearly defined by local civil service regulations, but may vary from one community to another.

In most cases, prospective fire fighters must be at least 21 but not over 31 years of age. They must also meet height and weight requirements. Applicants must have good vision (20/20 vision is required in some departments), no hindering physical impairments, and strong stamina. Some fire departments require that applicants be nonsmokers.

Fire science technicians who do not work as fire fighters but as industrial or government inspectors, consultants, or fire preventers do not need unusual physical strength.

Opportunities for experience and exploration

High school students and graduates who are interested in fire science can obtain valuable information from their school guidance departments. Science teachers can also provide information about the various careers in fire protection, safety, and prevention. Students can visit their fire department, look at the equipment, and talk with the fire fighters and their commanding officers. In some departments, students may be able to gain experience by working as volunteer fire fighters. Courses in lifesaving and first aid also offer helpful experience. Summer jobs as aides with the government park and forest service are available as well. In these jobs, students may learn about

fire prevention, control, and detection in forest and grassland conservation work.

It is usually possible for students to arrange a visit with an insurance company to learn about the huge economic losses caused by fire. Large insurance offices often have agents or officers who can describe fire technician jobs or services in inspection, fire insurance, rate setting or claim settlement, and fire prevention services.

Methods of entering

Graduates of two-year programs in technical colleges, community colleges, or technical institutes usually secure jobs before they graduate. They are hired by company recruiters sent to the school placement offices, which arrange interviews for graduating students. The placement officers or fire science instructors usually keep contacts open to help place their current graduates, and are usually aware of job openings.

Some schools have cooperative work–study programs where students study part-time and work part-time for pay. Employers who participate in cooperative programs provide experience in different tasks so the student learns about various aspects of the job. Often students in such programs are hired permanently by the cooperating employer.

Some students may find jobs in fire departments that are large enough to need special technicians outside the ranks of regular fire fighters. Others may choose to become fire fighters and advance to technical positions.

Some fire departments place new employees on probation, a period during which they are intensively trained. After training is completed, they may be assigned to specific duties.

Students with a high school diploma or its equivalent can enter a fire department apprenticeship program. These programs run from three to four years, combining intensive on-the-job training with active firefighting service, and include related study in the science and theory of firefighting. These apprenticeship programs may or may not be union-sponsored.

Even after completing an apprenticeship program, fire fighters seeking to advance to the level of supervisor or inspector must continue to study. Part-time courses are available in community colleges or technical institutes.

In some small communities, applicants may enter through on-the-job training as volunteer fire fighters or by direct application for such an appointment.

Advancement

Examples of advanced positions are described below.

Fire prevention analysts analyze overall fire prevention systems in an organization and confer with fire inspectors to obtain detailed information and recommend policies and programs for fire prevention. Safety directors are responsible for general safety throughout a plant as well as fire safety.

Deputy fire marshals inspect possible fire hazards and analyze the amount of loss resulting from a fire. If necessary, they have the authority to condemn buildings. They report cases of arson and work with district attorneys to prosecute arsonists. This is an appointed position, although those holding the position usually have considerable fire experience.

Fire captains work under the supervision of a fire chief on a military base or in a municipal area. They are responsible for fire protection in a specific location. *Fire chiefs* are responsible for all firefighting units in a municipal area. Several fire captains may report to and support the activities of this administrator.

Owners of fire equipment or consulting businesses employ *fire prevention and control technicians and specialists*. Their employees contract for, deliver, and install equipment and provide training and other services in fire prevention.

Employment outlook

Technical careers in fire prevention and control are predicted to grow more rapidly than the average for all other occupations. In coming years, these technicians will probably be needed in more places and industries than ever before.

The greatest increase in employment will be in industry. More and more industries are finding that the cost of replacing buildings and property destroyed by fire is greater than the yearly cost of fire protection and control expertise and equipment.

New products are being developed and used in almost all areas of modern living. Many have different characteristics that relate to fire hazards. As new products appear, new fire prevention and control techniques must be developed. The ever-changing techniques of fire prevention and protection make this a most challenging field with unlimited opportunities for the person with ambition and imagination.

For fire fighters, there is considerable competition for available job openings, and this should continue through the year 2000.

Earnings

Beginning salaries for fire safety technicians who qualify for technical jobs tend to be higher than those of other technicians. This is partly due to the shortage of qualified personnel in the field.

Starting salaries are approximately $18,000 to $20,000. Experienced technicians earn salaries that average between $33,000 to $42,890 per year. Those who advance to positions of great responsibility in the various industrial or fire department careers may earn up to $60,000 per year or more.

Benefits for these employees usually include compensatory time off or overtime pay for hours worked beyond the regular work schedule. Other benefits include liberal pension plans, disability benefits, and early retirement options. Also included are paid vacations, paid sick leave, and in some cases, paid holidays or compensatory time off for holidays worked.

Conditions of work

Working conditions for fire safety technicians may involve danger when assisting or observing firefighting, or when inspecting and analyzing structures damaged or destroyed by fire. Floors, walls, or entire buildings can collapse on fire fighters as they work to save lives and property. Exposure to smoke, fumes, chemicals, and gases can injure or kill them. Most of the duties of technicians, however, are performed in offices where the surroundings are typically well-lighted, clean, and comfortable.

When performing routine building inspections, these workers must follow safety regulations and wear protective clothing when appropriate. They must be confident and comfortable in the environments they visit, inspect, and analyze.

Fire safety technicians must have a natural curiosity about everything that relates to fire and the property for which they are responsible.

They must be patient and willing to study the physics and chemistry of fire as well as fire prevention and control. They must also be able to think systematically and objectively as they analyze fire hazards, damages, and prevention.

FIRE SAFETY TECHNICIANS

Technicians must be observant and understand how human factors of carelessness, thoughtlessness, fatigue, or haste may cause fires. One of the great challenges of the career is to learn how to teach people to avoid the mistakes that cause fires and to establish safety procedures and controls that prevent fires.

Fire is one of the most feared and most destructive hazards. Fire science technicians can find continuing satisfaction and challenge in saving lives and property by preventing fires.

GOE: 05.01.02, 05.03.06, 11.10.03; SIC: 6411; SOC: 1472, 1473, 1634, 5122

American Society of Safety Engineers
1800 East Oakton Street
Des Plaines, IL 60016

National Fire Protection Association
Batterymarch Park
Quincy, MA 02269

Board of Certified Safety Professionals
208 Burwash Avenue
Savory, IL 61874

Fire Prevention Canada Association
#1590, 7 Liverpool Court
Ottawa ON K1B 4L2

◇ **SOURCES OF ADDITIONAL INFORMATION**

Society of Fire Protection Technicians
c/o John Fannin
2106 Silverside Road
Wilmington, DE 19810

Society of Fire Protection Engineers
One Liberty Square
Boston, MA 02110

◇ **RELATED ARTICLES**

Volume 1: Civil Service; Engineering
Volumes 2–4: Fire fighters; Health and regulatory inspectors; Industrial engineering technicians; Industrial safety-and-health technicians; Miscellaneous engineers; Nuclear power plant quality control technicians; Nuclear power plant radiation control technicians; Occupational safety and health workers

Photographic Credits

Index

681

688

690